SOCIOLOGY NOW

Third Edition

Michael Kimmel,
Stony Brook University

Amy Aronson,
Fordham University

Tristan Bridges,
University of California–Santa Barbara

 **Pearson**

330 Hudson Street, NY NY 10013

VP, Product Development: Dickson Musslewhite
Portfolio Manager: Jeff Marshall
Editorial Assistant: Christina Winterburn
Program Team Lead: Amber Mackey
Content Producer: Mary Donovan
Development Editor: Renee Eckhoff and Megan Vertucci, Ohlinger Publishing Services
Field Marketing Manager: Brittany Pogue-Mohammed
Product Marketing Manager: Candice Madden
Operations Manager: Mary Fischer
Senior Operations Specialist: Mary Ann Gloriande
Director of Design: Blair Brown
Interior Designer: Kathryn Foot
Cover Design: Lumina
Digital Studio Project Manager: Rich Barnes
Full-Service Project Management: Integra Software Services Pvt. Ltd.
Cover Printer: Phoenix Color/Hagerstown
Printer/Binder: LSC Communications, Inc.
Text Font: Palatino LT Pro 9.5/13

Credits and acknowledgments borrowed from other sources and reproduced with permission in this textbook appear on the appropriate page within text or on page 789.

Copyright © 2019, by Michael Kimmel, Amy Aronson, and Tristan Bridges. All Rights Reserved. Printed in the United States of America. This publication is protected by copyright, and permission should be obtained from the publisher prior to any prohibited reproduction, storage in a retrieval system, or transmission in any form or by any means, electronic, mechanical, photocopying, recording, or otherwise. For information regarding permissions, request forms and the appropriate contacts within the Pearson Education Global Rights & Permissions Department, please visit www.pearsoned.com/permissions/.

Library of Congress Cataloging-in-Publication Data
Kimmel, Michael S., author. | Aronson, Amy, author. | Bridges, Tristan, author.
Sociology Now/Michael Kimmel, Amy Aronson, Tristan Bridges
Description: Third Edition. | Hoboken: Pearson Higher Education, [2017] |
    Revised edition of Sociology now, c2011.
Identifiers: LCCN 2017024779 | ISBN 9780134531847 (pbk.) | ISBN 0134531841
Subjects: LCSH: Sociology. | Sociology—Study and teaching.
    Classification: LCC HM585 .K57 2017 | DDC 301—dc23
p. cm.
Includes bibliographical references and index.
ALC: 9780134631578, 0134631579
IRC: 9780134629117, 0134629116
1. Sociology. 2. Sociology–Study and teaching. I. Aronson, Amy.
II. Dennis, Jeffery P. III. Title.
HM585.K57 2011
301–dc22

2009050884

1 18

Rental Edition

ISBN 10:   0-134-53184-1
ISBN 13: 978-0-134-53184-7

Revel Access Card

ISBN 10:   0-134-63157-9
ISBN 13: 978-0-134-63157-8

Brief Contents

Part 1 Foundations of the Field

1   What Is Sociology?   1

2   Culture and Media   44

3   Society: Interactions, Groups, and Organizations   73

4   How Do We Know What We Know?
    The Methods of the Sociologist   110

5   Socialization   158

6   Crime and Deviance   191

Part 2 Identities and Inequalities

7   Social Class and Stratification: Identity and Inequality   234

8   Race and Ethnicity   279

9   Sex and Gender   335

10 Age: From Young to Old   388

11 The Body: Health and Sexuality   428

Part 3 Social Institutions

12 Families   479

13 Education   528

14 Economy and Work   567

15 Politics and Religion   609

16 Sociology of Environments: The Natural,
    Physical, and Human World   660

Contents

Features   xi
Preface   xiii
About the Authors   xxxv
About the Supplements   xxxvii

Part 1   Foundations of the Field

1   What Is Sociology?   1

Introduction   2
1.1 Sociology as a Way of Seeing   2
         Beyond Either–Or: Seeing Sociologically   3
         Making Connections: Sociological Dynamics   4
         Sociological Understanding   5
         Getting beyond "Common Sense"   7
1.2 iSoc: Sociological Frames of Analysis   9
         Identity, Intersectionality, and Inequality 9
         Interactions and Institutions   10
         iSoc in Action: What's in a Name?   12
         Names and the Sociological Imagination   16
1.3 Where Did Sociology Come From?   19
         Before Sociology   19
         The Invention of Sociology   21
         Classical Sociological Thinkers   22
            AUGUSTE COMTE   22 • ALEXIS DE TOCQUEVILLE   23 •
            KARL MARX   23 • ÉMILE DURKHEIM   24 •
            MAX WEBER   25 • GEORG SIMMEL   27 • SOCIOLOGY
            COMES TO THE UNITED STATES   27 • MARGARET
            FULLER   27 • FREDERICK DOUGLASS   28 • LESTER
            WARD   28 • CHARLOTTE PERKINS GILMAN   28 •
            THORSTEIN VEBLEN   28 • W. E. B. DU BOIS   29 •
            GEORGE HERBERT MEAD   29
         Contemporary Sociology   30
            SYMBOLIC INTERACTIONISM AND THE SOCIOLOGY
            OF THE SELF   30 • STRUCTURAL FUNCTIONALISM
            AND SOCIAL ORDER   31 • CONFLICT THEORIES: AN
            ALTERNATIVE PARADIGM   32
1.4 Sociology NOW: New Issues, New Lenses   34
         Globalization and Multiculturalism   34
            GLOBALIZATION AND MULTICULTURALISM:
            INTERRELATED FORCES   35
Global Tensions   36
Conclusion: Sociology NOW: Sociology and You   37
         Chapter Review What Is Sociology?   39 • Self-Test:
         Check Your Understanding   42

2   Culture and Media   44

Introduction   45
2.1 Thinking about Culture and Media Sociologically   45
         Culture and Media   46
         iSoc: Culture and Media   48
         Culture and Identity: Diversity and Universality   50
         Identity and Inequality: Subcultures
         and Countercultures   51
2.2 Culture in Interactions   53
         Material Culture and Symbols   53
         Language   54
         Rituals, Norms, and Values   55
         Types of Norms and Values   56
2.3 Cultural Institutions and the Institutionalization
         of Culture   58
         Cultural Institutions: The Mass Media   59
            PRINT MEDIA   60 • RADIO, MOVIES,
            AND TELEVISION   61 • THE INTERNET   62
         High Culture and Popular Culture   62
         The Politics of Popular Culture   64
            TYPES OF POPULAR CULTURE   64
         The Globalization of Popular Culture   66
2.4 Continuity and Change in Culture and Media   67
         Cultural Change   67
Conclusion: Culture and Media NOW   69
         Chapter Review Culture and Media   70 • Self-Test:
         Check Your Understanding   72

**3   Society: Interactions, Groups,
      and Organizations   73**

Introduction   74
3.1 Thinking about Interactions, Groups,
         and Organizations Sociologically   74
         Society: Putting Things in Context   75
         iSoc: The Social Construction of Identity   76
         Thinking "Dramaturgically": Toward a
         Sociology of the Self   77
3.2 Understanding Society and Social Life
         as Socially Structured   79
         Nonverbal and Verbal Communication   79
         Patterns of Social Interaction   80
         Elements of Social Structure   82

Social Status   82
Social Roles   84

3.3 Groups, Networks, and Social Life   85
Social Groups and Identity   86
Types of Groups   87
Group Dynamics   89
Social Networks   91
Networks, Experience, and Opportunity   93
Networks and Globalization   94

3.4 Organizations, Power, and Inequality   96
What Are Organizations and Why Do
Sociologists Care?   96
Are We a Nation of Joiners?   98
Examining Organizations and Inequality
Intersectionally   100
Bureaucracy: Organizations and Power   100
Organizations and Globalization   104

Conclusion: Groups 'R' Us: Interactions,
Groups, and Organizations NOW   105
Chapter Review Society: Interactions, Groups,
and Organizations 105 • Self-Test: Check
Your Understanding 109

**4 How Do We Know What We Know?
The Methods of the Sociologist**   110

Introduction   111

4.1 How Do We Know What We Know?   112
Why Sociological Research Methods Matter   113
Sociology and the Scientific Method   115
iSoc: Research Methods   117
The Qualitative/Quantitative Divide   118
WHEN IS A FACT A FACT? 121
What Do Sociologists Consider as "Data"?   122

4.2 Types of Sociological Research Methods   124
Categorizing Sociological Research Methods   124
Observational Methods   127
EXPERIMENTS 127 • FIELD STUDIES 129 •
INTERVIEW STUDIES 132
Quantitative Analysis   133
SURVEYS 134 • SURVEY QUESTIONS 135
Secondary Analysis and Other Types of Data   137
CONTENT ANALYSIS 137 • NETWORK ANALYSIS 140
Making the Right Comparisons   142

4.3 Research Methods NOW   143
Social Science and the Problem of "Truth"   144
Predictability and Probability   145
Why Claiming Causality Is Tricky Business   146
Doing Sociological Research   147
Issues in Conducting Research   150
THE INSTITUTIONAL REVIEW BOARD 151

Conclusion: Social Science NOW: Emergent
Methodologies   153
Chapter Review How Do We Know What We Know?
The Methods of the Sociologist 154 • Self-Test: Check
Your Understanding 157

5 Socialization   158

Introduction   159

**5.1 Understanding What Socialization Is
and How It Works**   160
Where Does Identity Come From?   160
iSoc: Socialization   162
How Socialization Works   163

5.2 Models of Socialization   165
Taking the Role of Others   166
Stage Theories of Development   168
Problems with Stage Theories   169

5.3 Socialization and Inequality   171
Socialization and Racial Inequality   171
Socialization and Social Class   171
Socialization and Gender
and Sexual Inequality   173

5.4 Institutions of Socialization   176
Socialization in the Family   176
Socialization in Education   177
Socialization in Religion   178
Peer Socialization   180
Socialization from the Media   181
Socialization in the Workplace   183

5.5 Socialization and Ongoing and Unending   185
Socialization across the Life Course   185
iSoc in Action: Socialization in a Global Society   186

Conclusion: Socialization NOW   187
Chapter Review Socialization 188 • Self-Test: Check
Your Understanding 190

6 Crime and Deviance   191

Introduction   192

**6.1 Thinking Sociologically about Crime
and Deviance**   192
Distinguishing Deviance from Crime   193
iSoc: The Sociology of Crime and Deviance   194
Deviance, Conformity, and Identity   195

6.2 Theorizing Crime and Deviance   196
Rational Actor and Social Control Theories of Crime
and Deviance   197
Subculture Theories of Deviance   199
Youth Gangs as Deviant Subcultures   200
Labeling Theory and Inequality   203
Social Stigma   204
Deviance, Crime, and Inequality   206

6.3 The Social Organization of Crime   208
Understanding the Crime Rate Sociologically   208
Types of Crime   209
Intersections with Gender and Age   213
Intersections with Race and Class   215
Guns and Crime   217
Global Inequality and Crime   218

GLOBALIZATION: NETWORKS OF PRODUCTION, DISTRIBUTION, AND PROTECTION 219 • DRUGS AND THE CRIMINAL JUSTICE SYSTEM 219 • DRUGS AND PUBLIC POLICY 219

6.4 Understanding Crime and Deviance Institutionally 219
Police and Policing 220
Courtrooms and Court Proceedings 221
Punishment, Corrections, and Incarceration 223
Does Incarceration Work? 225
The Death Penalty 226
Conclusion: Deviance and Crime NOW 228
Chapter Review Crime and Deviance 229 • Self-Test: Check Your Understanding 232

Part 2 Identities and Inequalities

7 Social Class and Stratification: Identity and Inequality 234

Introduction 235
7.1 Thinking Sociologically about Social Class and Stratification 236
What Is Social Stratification? 236
iSoc: The Sociology of Social Class and Stratification 237
Systems of Stratification 240
CASTES 240 • FEUDALISM 240 • CLASS SYSTEM 241
Social Mobility 242
7.2 Class Identity and Inequality 245
Social Class and Identity 246
Theories of Social Class—Marx 247
Theories of Social Class—Weber 248
CLASS POSITION 248 • STATUS 248 • POWER 248 • MEASURING SOCIAL STATUS 249
Class and Culture 250
Class, Culture, and Musical Taste 252
7.3 Class Inequality in the United States 253
The American Class System 253
The Myth of the Middle Class 256
Class Inequality in Perspective 257
Intersections with Class, Race, and Gender 259
Who Is Poor in America? 261
Explaining Poverty: Interactions and Institutions 263
7.4 Resistance and Change in Class Inequality 265
Global Class Inequality 265
Classifying Global Class Systems 267
HIGH-INCOME COUNTRIES 267 • MIDDLE-INCOME COUNTRIES 267 • LOW-INCOME COUNTRIES 267
Explaining Global Inequality 268
Reducing Poverty 270
Political Resistance to Class Inequality 271
Conclusion: Social Class and Stratification NOW 273
Chapter Review Social Class and Stratification: Identity and Inequality 274 • Self-Test: Check Your Understanding 277

8 Race and Ethnicity 279

Introduction 280
8.1 Thinking Sociologically about Race and Ethnicity 281
What Is Race? 282
What is Ethnicity? 283
iSoc: The Sociology of Race and Ethnicity 286
Biracial and Multiracial Identities 287
Minority Groups and "Majority" Groups 289
8.2 Racial and Ethnic Inequalities: Interactions and Institutions 291
Prejudice and Stereotypes 292
Understanding Racism Sociologically 294
Racial Discrimination 295
Institutional Racism 296
Color-Blind Racism 299
Racial Segregation 301
Thinking Historically about Racial Inequality 303
Understanding Racial and Ethnic Inequality Intersectionally 304
8.3 Ethnic Identities in the United States 305
People from Europe 306
People from North America 308
People from Latin America 311
People from sub-Saharan Africa 313
People from East and South Asia 314
People from the Middle East 316
A Profile of Ethnicity in the United States 318
8.4 Resistance and Mobilization to Racial and Ethnic Inequality 319
Identities and Interactions: Can Prejudice Be Overcome? 319
Ethnicity: Identity and Conflict 320
Challenging Institutional Inequalities 321
Multiculturalism 324
Movements for (and Against) Racial and Ethnic Equality 326
Resistance to Racial and Ethnic Equality 328
Conclusion: Race and Ethnicity NOW 330
Chapter Review Race and Ethnicity 331 • Self-Test: Check Your Understanding 334

9 Sex and Gender 335

Introduction 336
9.1 Thinking Sociologically about Sex and Gender 337
What Are Sex and Gender? 338
iSoc: The Sociology of Sex and Gender 340
The Biology of Sex and Gender 341
The Medicalization of Sex and Gender 343
Transgender Identities: Blurring the Boundaries of Gender 346
FROM SEEING IS BELIEVING TO BELIEVING IS SEEING 349
9.2 The Social Organization of Gendered Interactions and Inequality 350

The Bathroom Problem: Organizing Our
World Around Gender   351

Gender Socialization: Learning about
Gender Difference   352

Gender Socialization: Learning about
Gender Inequality   354

Gendered Interactions   356

"Gender Policing" and Gender Accountability   358

Gender, Friendship, and Love   360

**9.3 Studying Gender Inequality Institutionally and
Intersectionally**   362

Gender Bias in Orchestras and
Student Evaluations   363

Gender and Education   366

The Gendered World of Work   367

Balancing Work and Family   369

Gender and Marriage   370

Gender and Politics   372

Gender and Violence   374

9.4 Gender Inequality at the Global and Local Level   375

Understanding Gender Inequality Globally   376

Resistance to Gender Inequality   378

Fighting Inequality: Movements for Gender
Equality   379

Challenges to Gender Inequality
and the Endurance of Gender Gaps   381

Conclusion: Sex and Gender NOW   383

Chapter Review Sex and Gender   384 • Self-Test:
Check Your Understanding   386

10 Age: From Young to Old   388

Introduction   389

10.1 Age, Identity, and the Stages of Life   389

Age and Identity   390

iSoc: The Sociology of Aging   391

Thinking about Age Sociologically   393

The Stages of Life   394

Childhood   395

Adolescence   396

Young Adulthood   398

Middle Age   400

Old Age   401

**10.2 Boomers, Busters, and Boomlets: The Generations
of Youth**   403

Baby Boomers   403

Generation X   405

Millennials—Generation Y   406

Global Youth—A Dying Breed?   408

10.3 Age and Inequality   410

Age and Poverty   411

Age Inequalities in Interactions   412

Retirement   413

Elder Care   415

Aging and Dying   416

**10.4 Institutional Age Inequalities in Global
and Local Perspectives**   417

Aging, Health, and the Life Course   418

Child Labor in the United States   418

Child Labor Around the World   420

THE NEW SLAVERY   421 • THE WORST FORMS
OF CHILD LABOR   422

Opposition and Mobilization: The Politics
of Age   423

Conclusion: Youth and Aging NOW   424

Chapter Review Age: From Young to Old   425 •
Self-Test: Check Your Understanding   427

11 The Body: Health and Sexuality   428

Introduction   429

11.1 Embodying Identities and Inequality   430

Thinking Sociologically about Beauty   430

iSoc: The Sociology of Bodies and Embodiment   431

Embodying Identity—Tattoos and
Cosmetic Surgery   432

Gender and Body Dissatisfaction   435

Changing Identity by Changing the Gendered Body:
Embodying Transgender Identities   436

Obesity and Fatness   438

The "Disabled" Body   439

Embodied Inequality   441

**11.2 Understanding Health and
Illness Sociologically**   443

Health and Inequality   444

Thinking Intersectionally about
Health Inequality   445

The Global Distribution of Health and Illness   447

Sickness and Stigma   449

Mental Illness   451

Health as a Social Institution   454

**11.3 The Social Organization of Sexuality and Sexual
Inequality**   456

Researching Sexuality   456

What Is Sexuality?—The Social Ingredients
of Sexuality   458

Studying Sexual Interactions: Sexual Scripts   460

Desires and Behaviors   461

The Sexual Identity Binary   462

SEXUAL IDENTITIES OUTSIDE THE BINARY: BISEXUALITY
AND ASEXUALITY   463

The Gendered Construction of Sexual Interactions   465

Convergence on Campus: Hooking Up and Sexual
Consent   467

Sexual Inequality: Attitudes, Prejudice,
and Discrimination   470

Resistance to Inequality: The LGBT Movement   472

Conclusion: Bodies, Health, and Sexualities NOW   475

Chapter Review The Body: Health and Sexuality   475 •
Self-Test: Check Your Understanding   477

Part 3   Social Institutions

12   Families   479

Introduction   480
12.1   The Family as a Social Institution   481
Families as Kinship Systems   481
Sex, Marriage, and Family   483
iSoc: The Sociology of Families   484
A Brief History of "The Family"   485
The Origins of the Nuclear Family   486
Family Diversity   489
12.2   Forming Families   491
Courtship and Dating   491
Shifting Contexts for Family Formation   493
Same-Sex Marriage and LGBT Family Forms   494
Interracial Marriage   496
Delayed Marriage   498
Cohabitation   500
Living Alone   502
Thinking Sociologically about Nonmarital Choices   503
12.3   Children, Parents, and Parenting   505
Gender, Sexuality, and Parenting   505
Single Parents and Grandparents   507
Adoptive Parents   508
Childfree versus Childless   510
12.4   Family Transitions, Inequality, and Violence   512
Separation and Divorce   513
After Divorce   515
Remarriage and Blended Families   517
Intimate Partner Violence   519
Family Violence between Generations   521
Conclusion: Families NOW   524
Chapter Review Families   524 • Self-Test: Check
Your Understanding   527

13   Education   528

Introduction   529
13.1   Education and Society   529
Education in Social Context   530
iSoc: The Sociology of Education   531
A Brief History of Education   532
The Sociology of Education   534
13.2   Education as a Mechanism of Social Inequality   536
Education and Inequality   537
Education Inequality on a Global Scale   539
A REPORT CARD ON EDUCATION IN THE
UNITED STATES   542
Understanding Educational Improvement   542
13.3   Institutional Differences, Interactions,
and Inequality   544
How Much Does Your School Matter?   544
Social Inequality and Institutional Differences   546
Tracking   547

Understanding Educational Inequality Intersectionally   548
THE RACIAL ACHIEVEMENT GAP   550
Gender Inequality in Education   552
13.4   Higher Education   554
A Brief History of Changes in Higher Education   555
Preparing for College   555
Higher Education and Inequality   558
GENDER SEGREGATION IN HIGHER EDUCATION   558
The Transformation of Higher Education   561
Conclusion: Education NOW   563
Chapter Review Education   563 • Self-Test: Check
Your Understanding   566

14   Economy and Work   567

Introduction   568
14.1   Economy and Society   569
What Is an Economy?   569
iSoc: The Sociology of Work   570
The Changing Economy   572
THE AGRICULTURAL ECONOMY   572 • THE INDUSTRIAL
ECONOMY   572 • THE MODERN CONSUMER
ECONOMY   573 • THE POSTINDUSTRIAL ECONOMY   573
Knowledge Work   574
Globalization and Rootlessness   575
Economic Systems—Capitalism   577
Economic Systems—Socialism and Communism   580
Economies and Politics: Protest and Change   582
14.2   Institutionalizing Inequality at Work   583
Studying the Way We Work   584
Types of Jobs   586
Wages: High, Minimum, and Living   587
Part-Time and Contingent Work   589
Unpaid Work   590
The Informal Economy   591
Unemployment   592
14.3   Workplace Identities, Interactions, and
Inequalities   594
Workplace Diversity   594
Racial Diversity   595
Gender Diversity: Wage Inequality   596
Gender Diversity: Occupational Segregation   598
Gender and Work–Family Dynamics   599
Emotional and Aesthetic Labor and Inequality   601
Sexual Diversity   602
Conclusion: Work and Economy NOW   604
Chapter Review Economy and Work   604 • Self-Test:
Check Your Understanding   608

15   Politics and Religion   609

Introduction   610
15.1   Politics, Religion, and Social Life   611
Comparing Politics and Religion   611
iSoc: The Sociology of Politics and Religion   612
Just How Separate Are Church and State?   614

15.2 Politics 616

Politics: Class, Status, and Power 617

Authoritarian Political Systems 618

Democratic Political Systems 619

Problems with Political Systems I: Corruption and Bureaucracy 621

Problems with Political Systems II: Reproducing Intersectional Forms of Inequality 622

The Political System of the United States 623

American Political Parties: Examining Intersections 625

Political Participation versus Political Apathy 627

Political Change 630

15.3 Religion 635

Classical Theories of Religion 635

Religious Groups 637

Religions of the World 639

Thinking about Religion Sociologically: Secularization or Resurgence? 642

Religion in the United States 644

Thinking Intersectionally: Religious Diversity in the United States 646

On the Religiously Unaffiliated 647

15.4 Politics and Religion in Everyday Life 650

Religion as Politics 650

Everyday Religion 651

Everyday Politics 653

Conclusion: Politics and Religion NOW 655

Chapter Review Politics and Religion 655 • Self-Test: Check Your Understanding 659

16 Sociology of Environments: The Natural, Physical, and Human World 660

Introduction 661

16.1 The Human Environment 662

iSoc: The Environment 663

Population and Its Institutions 664

Populations on the Move 666

Studying Immigration 668

Population Composition 671

Explaining Populations Sociologically 673

Population Bombs and Booms 674

The Politics of Human Environments 677

16.2 The Urban Environment 677

The City and the Countryside 678

THE COUNTRYSIDE 680

Suburbs: Identity and Inequality 682

REVITALIZING DOWNTOWN 683

Understanding Urban Life Sociologically 684

GLOBAL URBANIZATION 686

16.3 The Natural Environment 688

Understanding the Natural World Sociologically 688

Energy and Other Resources 689

Environments, High-Risk Technology, and "Normal Accidents" 690

Vanishing Resources 691

Environmental Threats 692

POLLUTION 693 • GARBAGE 693 • CLIMATE CHANGE 694

The Sociology of Environmental Disasters 696

Environmental Inequalities 698

The Politics of Environments 699

Conclusion: Environments NOW 700

Chapter Review Sociology of Environments: The Natural, Physical, and Human World 701 • Self-Test: Check Your Understanding 704

Glossary 705

References 723

Name Index 764

Subject Index 772

Credits 789

Features

Sociology and Our World

The Sociological Imagination (Chapter 1) 3

Why Popular Boy Names Are More Popular than Popular Girl Names (Chapter 1) 14

Why Names that Regain Popularity Wait a Century (Chapter 1) 18

Two Alternative Views of the World (Chapter 1) 38

Using Media Use to Detect Rhythms in Our Lives (Chapter 2) 47

U.S. Race Relations and the Confederate Flag (Chapter 2) 54

The High Culture–Low Culture Divide (Chapter 2) 64

Using Selfies to Understand My "I" and My "Me" (Chapter 3) 78

Elevator Behavior, Norms, and Social Inequality (Chapter 3) 81

Why Liberals Drink Lattes (Chapter 3) 93

Organizing Without Organizations? (Chapter 3) 99

Are People Lying on Surveys? … Sometimes. (Chapter 4) 119

Hidden Facts: On the Power of Ethnography (Chapter 4) 131

Shifts in Men's Facial Hair Styles Are Patterned (Chapter 4) 138

What Can We Learn about Socialization from Family Trips to the Zoo? (Chapter 5) 167

Can Gay and Lesbian Schoolteachers Be "Out" at Work? (Chapter 5) 184

Stereotype Threat and Stereotype Promise (Chapter 6) 204

Abortion and the Crime Rate (Chapter 6) 209

Driving While … Black? (Chapter 6) 221

Apartheid—A Caste System (Chapter 7) 241

Prestige Means Not Having to Deal with People (Chapter 7) 249

The Hidden Injuries of Class (Chapter 7) 262

Prostitution and the World System (Chapter 7) 270

Why Filipino Americans Don't Identify as Asian (Chapter 8) 285

Perceptions of Prejudice Vary by … Race! (Chapter 8) 296

Is Living on the "Wrong Side of the Tracks" a Social Reality? (Chapter 8) 303

Why Hispanic Went from Being a Race to an Ethnicity (Chapter 8) 312

Learning the Language (Chapter 8) 325

Monogamous Masculinity, Promiscuous Femininity (Chapter 9) 342

Pink for Boys and Blue for Girls (Chapter 9) 353

Will Young People Today Produce a Gender Revolution in Marriage Tomorrow? (Chapter 9) 371

Men and Feminism (Chapter 9) 380

Education as Age Graded (Chapter 10) 391

Sons Are More Likely to Live with Parents than Daughters (Chapter 10) 408

Retiring and Gay? Where? (Chapter 10) 414

How Women with Ink Illustrate Gender Policing (Chapter 11) 433

Criminalizing Sickness? (Chapter 11) 450

What Happens to Men Who Wait? (Chapter 11) 469

Gay Men and Lesbians Congregate, But Not Always Together (Chapter 11) 474

Why Separate Spheres Meant "More Work for Mother" (Chapter 12) 488

Dating in Japan (Chapter 12) 493

Is There a Shortage of "Marriageable" Men Today? (Chapter 12) 504

Home Economics, Adoption, and Cornell's "Practice Babies" (Chapter 12) 509

Instant Divorce (Chapter 12) 516

Single-Sex Schooling and Student Success (Chapter 13) 546

Random School Shootings (Chapter 13) 553

The Chosen (Chapter 13) 559

Cardboard: A Goldmine in a Globalized World (Chapter 14) 576

The Sociology of the Recent Global Recession (Chapter 14) 593

Are Some Emotions Off Limits for Non-white Employees? (Chapter 14) 602

Do You Have a "Gay" Resume? (Chapter 14) 603

Social Movements and the Media (Chapter 15) 632

Is Religious Pluralism Responsible for Americans' Enduring Religious Beliefs? (Chapter 15) 644

People Espouse Political Opinions Even When They Don't Have an Opinion (Chapter 15) 654

"Missing Women" and "Surplus Men" (Chapter 16) 672

The Urban Village (Chapter 16) 685

How Do We Know What We Know?

Suicide Is *Not* an Individual Act (Chapter 1) 26

Christmas Gift Giving as a Method of Norm Enforcement (Chapter 2) 56

Our Values—and Others' Values (Chapter 2) 59

Group Conformity (Chapter 3) 88

Do Formal or Informal Procedures Result in Greater Productivity? (Chapter 3) 103

Thinking Methodologically about the Heritability of Intelligence (Chapter 4) 114

Interviewing People about How They Answer Survey Questions about Ethnicity (Chapter 4) 133

We Can't Predict Almost Anything as Well as the Weather (Chapter 4) 145

Twin Studies (Chapter 5) 162

How Do We Know We're Socialized to Believe in Racial Inequality? (Chapter 5) 172

Just How Violent Is the United States? (Chapter 6) 210

Racial Bias in the Courtroom (Chapter 6) 222

Does the Death Penalty Act as a Deterrent to Crime? (Chapter 6) 227

Mobility Studies (Chapter 7) 243

Race and Intelligence (Chapter 8) 294

Do Employers Discriminate Based on Race? (Chapter 8) 300

Do Mascots Depicting Racial Stereotypes Really Matter? (Chapter 8) 309

Just How Many Transgender People Are There? (Chapter 9) 347

Women and Men Are Far More Similar Than They Are Different (Chapter 9) 354

Why Middle Age Can Be So Challenging (Chapter 10) 400

How Many Sex Partners Do People Have? (Chapter 11) 466

Why Hooking Up Might Be Less Empowering than You Think (Chapter 11) 468

Measuring Time Spent (Chapter 12) 506

Gender Symmetry in IPV (Chapter 12) 521

How Universities Reproduce Class Inequality (Chapter 13) 560

The Poor Work Harder than the Rich (Chapter 14) 589

Workplace Discrimination (Chapter 14) 600

Measuring Democracy (Chapter 15) 620

Life Expectancy and Intersectionality (Chapter 16) 676

Why Facts about Climate Change Do Not Change People's Opinions about Climate Change (Chapter 16) 695

What Do You Think? What Does America Think?

How Scientific Is Sociology? (Chapter 1) 8

Confidence in the Press (Chapter 2) 61

Group Membership (Chapter 3) 90

How Happy Are We? (Chapter 4) 120

Being Christian, Being American (Chapter 5) 180

Following the Law (Chapter 6) 202

Conflict Between Poor and Rich in the United States (Chapter 7) 256

The Melting Pot (Chapter 8) 322

Women and Politics (Chapter 9) 373

Teen Sex (Chapter 10) 397

MacArthur Mental Health Module (Chapter 11) 452

Attitudes Toward Abortion (Chapter 12) 511

Confidence in Education (Chapter 13) 562

The Rich and Taxes (Chapter 14) 581

Voting and Citizenship (Chapter 15) 627

Environmental Threats and Science (Chapter 16) 694

U.S./World

How Globalized Are We? (Chapter 1) 6

Print Newspaper Reach, 2014/2015 (Chapter 2) 60

Social Networking (Chapter 3) 95

How Important Is Sociology? (Chapter 4) 149

How Important Is Religion as a Socializing Force? (Chapter 5) 179

U.S. Cybercrime in International Perspective (Chapter 6) 212

U.S. Mobility in International Context (Chapter 7) 245

Who's Foreign Born? (Chapter 8) 322

The Global Gender Gap (Chapter 9) 377

Youth Unemployment Around the World (Chapter 10) 419

Divorce Rates in International Comparison (Chapter 12) 514

The Prosperity of Nations: Nations with the Highest Per Capita Income, 2016 (Chapter 14) 579

Women in Parliament (Chapter 15) 624

Religious Tradition and Variation Around the World (Chapter 15) 640

Life Expectancy Changes in the United States and Select Countries since 1813 (Chapter 16) 666

Sociology is a social science and a profession. But it is also a temperament—a way of experiencing, observing, and understanding the world around you. I'm Michael Kimmel, one of the coauthors of this book. (This is the only part of the book I am writing myself.) I am a sociologist—both by profession and by temperament. It's what I do for a living and how I see the world. I consider myself enormously lucky to have the kind of job I have, teaching and writing about the world in which we live.

I love sociology. I love that it provides a way of seeing the world that is different from any other way of seeing the world. It's a lens, and when we hold that lens up to the world, we see shapes and patterns that help us understand it, colors and movement that enable us to perceive depth and shading. I love sociology because when we see those shapes, patterns, and shades of gray, we feel hopeful that we can, as citizens and sociologists, contribute to making that world a better place for all of us.

Teachers in general are a pretty optimistic bunch. When we work with you to develop your own critical engagement with the world—developing ideas, using evidence to back up assertions, deepening and broadening your command of information—we believe that your life will be better for it. You will get a better job, be a more engaged and active citizen, maybe even be a better parent, friend, or partner than you might otherwise have been. We believe that education is a way to improve your life on so many different levels. Pretty optimistic, no?

In this book, we have tried to communicate that way of seeing and that optimism about how you can use a sociological lens whether you go on to study sociology in depth or take this lens with you wherever else you may go.

WHY STUDY SOCIOLOGY? A MESSAGE TO STUDENTS.   So, what did people say when you told them you were taking sociology?

They probably looked at you blankly, "Like, what is sociology?" They might say, "And what can you do with it?" Sociology is often misunderstood. Some think it's nothing more than what my roommate told me when I said I was going to go to graduate school in sociology. (He was pre-med.) "Sociology makes a science out of common sense," he said dismissively.

It turns out he was wrong: What we think of as common sense turns out to be wrong a lot of the time. The good news is that sociologists are often the ones who point out that what "everybody knows" isn't necessarily true. In a culture saturated by self-help books, pop psychology, and TV talk shows promising instant and complete physical makeovers and utter psychological transformation, sociology says, "Wait a minute, not so fast."

Our culture tells us that all social problems are really individual problems. Poor people are poor because they don't work hard enough, and racial discrimination is simply the result of prejudiced individuals.

And the "solutions" offered by TV talk shows and self-help books also center around individual changes. If you work hard, you can make it. If you want to change, you can change. Social problems, they counsel, are really a set of individual problems all added together. Racism, sexism, or homophobia is really the result of unenlightened people holding bad attitudes. If they changed their attitudes, those enormous problems would dissolve like sugar in your coffee.

Sociology has a different take. Sociologists see society as a dynamic interaction between individuals and institutions, like education, economy, and government. Changing yourself might be necessary for you to live a happier life, but it has little impact on the effects of those institutions. And changing attitudes would make social life far more pleasant, but problems like racial or gender inequality are embedded in the ways those institutions are organized. It will take more than attitudinal shifts to fix that.

One of sociology's greatest strengths is also what makes it so elusive or discomfiting. We often are in a position in which we contrast U.S. mythologies with sociological realities.

I remember a song as I was growing up called "Only in America" by Jay and the Americans, which held that only in this country could "a guy from anywhere," "without a cent" maybe grow up to be a millionaire or president. Pretty optimistic, right? And it takes a sociologist, often, to burst that bubble, to explain that it's really not true—that the likelihood of a poor boy or girl making it in the United States is minuscule and that virtually everyone ends up in the same class position as his or her parents. It sounds almost unpatriotic to say that the best predictors of your eventual position in society are the education and occupation of your parents.

Sociology offers some answers to questions that may therefore be unpopular—because they emphasize the social and the structural over the individual and psychological, because they reveal the relationship between individual experience and social reality, and because structural barriers impede our ability to realize our dreams.

This often leads introductory students to feel initially depressed. Because these problems are so deeply embedded in our society, and because all the educational enlightenment in the world might not budge these powerful institutional forces—well, what's the use? Might as well just try and get yours, and the heck with everyone else.

But then, as we understand the real mission of sociology, students often feel invigorated and inspired. Sociology's posture is exactly the opposite—and that's what makes it so compelling. Understanding those larger forces means, as rock band The Who put it, "we won't get fooled again!"

What also makes sociology compelling is that it connects those two dimensions. It is because we believe that all social problems are really the result of individual weaknesses and laziness that those social problems remain in place. It is because we believe that poverty can be eliminated by hard work that poverty doesn't get eliminated. If social problems are social, then reducing poverty, or eliminating racial or gender discrimination, will require more than individual enlightenment; it will require large-scale political mobilization to change social institutions. And the good news is that sociologists have also documented the ways that those institutions themselves are always changing and are always being changed.

WHY STUDY SOCIOLOGY RIGHT NOW? A MESSAGE TO STUDENTS AND INSTRUCTORS. Understanding our society has never been more important. Sociology offers perhaps the best perspective on what are arguably the two dominant trends of our time, globalization and multiculturalism.

Globalization refers to the increasingly interlocked processes and institutions that span the entire world rather than one country. Goods and services are produced and distributed globally. Information moves instantly. You want to know how much things have changed? More than 2,000 soldiers in both the Union and Confederate armies were killed in the summer of 1865—that is, after the Civil War had ended. Why? Because no one had told them the war was over.

Globalization makes the world feel smaller, leaves us all far more intimately connected. And because people all over the world are wearing the same sneakers, eating the same fast food, and connecting by the Internet and texting each other, we are becoming more and more similar.

On the other hand, multiculturalism makes us keenly aware of how we are different. Globalization may make the world smaller, but we remain divided by religious-inspired wars, racial and ethnic identities, blood feuds, tribal rivalries, and what is generally called "sectarian violence."

Multiculturalism describes the ways in which we create identities that at once make us "global citizens" and also, at the same time, local and familial, based on our membership in racial, ethnic, or gender categories. Here in the United States, we have not become one big happy family, as some predicted a century ago. Instead of the "melting pot" in which each group would become part of the same "stew," we are, at our best, a "beautiful mosaic" of small groups that, when seen from afar, creates a beautiful pattern while each tile retains its distinct shape and beauty.

Globalization and multiculturalism make the world feel closer and also more divided, and they make the distances between us as people seem both tiny and unbridgeably large.

Globalization and multiculturalism are not only about the world—they are about us, individually. We draw our sense of who we are, our identities, from our membership in those diverse groups into which we are born or that we choose. Our identities—who we think we are—come from our gender, race, ethnicity, class, sexuality, age, religion, region, nation, and tribe. From these diverse locations, we piece together an identity, a sense of self. Sometimes one or another feels more important than others, but at other times other elements emerge as equally important.

And these elements of our identities also turn out to be the bases on which social hierarchies are built. Social inequality is organized from the same elements as identity; resources and opportunities are distributed in our society on the basis of race, class, ethnicity, age, sexuality, gender, and so forth.

A sociological perspective has never been more important to enabling us to understand these problems because sociology has become the field that has most fully embraced globalization and multiculturalism as the central analytic lenses through which we view social life.

WHY USE *SOCIOLOGY NOW,* THIRD EDITION? A MESSAGE TO INSTRUCTORS.
As all three authors have seen, the field of sociology has changed enormously since Michael first went to graduate school in the mid-1970s. At that time, two paradigms, functionalism and conflict theory, battled for dominance in the field, each claiming to explain social processes better than the other. And symbolic interactionism was the premier paradigm used to consider micro-level processes. That was an era of great conflict in our society: the Civil Rights, women's, and gay and lesbian movements; protests against the Vietnam War; hippies. On campuses these groups vied with far more traditional, conservative, and career-oriented students whose collegiate identity came more from the orderly 1950s than the tumultuous 1960s.

Just as the world has changed since then, so, too, has sociology—both substantively and demographically. New perspectives have emerged from older models, and terms like *rational choice, poststructuralism, collective mobilization, cultural toolkit*—not to mention *multiculturalism* and *globalization*—have become part of our daily lexicon.

Demographically, sociology is the field that has been most transformed by the social movements of the last decades of the twentieth century. Because sociology interrogates the connections between identities and inequalities, it has become a home to those groups who were historically marginalized in U.S. society: women, people of color, and gays and lesbians. The newest sections in the American Sociological Association are those on the body, sexualities, and race, class, and gender; the largest sections are no longer medical sociology and organizational sociology, but now sex and gender, culture, and race.

It turned out that symbolic interactionism was resilient enough to remain a theoretical lens through which social interactions and processes can still be understood.

That's largely because the old textbook model of "three paradigms" placed the three in a somewhat stilted competition: Conflict and functionalism were the macro theories; interactionism stood alone as a micro theory.

But *Sociology NOW* bypasses these tired and outdated debates, offering an exciting perspective new to the third edition—something we call "**iSoc**." Rather than offering competing theories that no longer vie for dominance in the field, we examine the ways that sociological research and theory share a focus on five "I's": identities, interactions, institutions, inequalities, and intersections. This framework offers a more useful collection of lenses that contemporary sociology makes use of to analyze the social world. We introduce this framework in the introductory chapter, but you'll also find it throughout the book as a way of connecting the diverse topics, methods, discoveries, and theories that sociologists rely on to study the social world today.

Content Highlights

THE "ISOC" MODEL: IDENTITY, INEQUALITY, INTERACTIONS, INSTITUTIONS, AND INTERSECTIONS. One of the biggest differences you'll see immediately in *Sociology NOW* is that we have replaced the older functionalism–conflict theory–interactionism models with a contemporary approach, "iSoc". We no longer believe these paradigms are battling for dominance; students don't have to choose between competing models. Sociology is a synthetic discipline—for us the question is almost never "either–or," but rather almost always "both–and." And understanding how different theories, methods, and research illuminates different aspects of society is an integral piece of what we refer to as the "iSoc model."

And using globalization and multiculturalism as the organizing themes of the book helps to illustrate exactly how "both–and" actually works. The world isn't smaller or bigger—it's both. We're not more united or more diverse—we're both. We're not more orderly or more in conflict—we're both. And sociology is the field that explains the way that "both" sides exist in a dynamic tension with each other. What's more, sociology explains why, how, and in what ways they exist in that tension. And by learning about the iSoc perspective, students will come to appreciate how the world often looks different when we stress or examine it relying on different "i's" or combinations.

The general sections of the book, and the individual chapter topics, are not especially different from the chapter organization of other textbooks. There are, however, some important differences.

First, globalization is not the same as cross-national comparisons. Globalization is often imagined as being about "them"—other cultures and other societies. And although examples drawn from other cultures are often extremely valuable to a sociologist (especially in challenging ethnocentrism), globalization is about processes that link "us" and "them." Thus, many of our examples, especially our cultural references, are about the United States—*in relation to* the rest of the world. This enables students both to relate to the topic and also to see how it connects with the larger global forces at work. Globalization is woven into every chapter—and, perhaps more important, every U.S. example is connected to a global process or issue.

Second, multiculturalism is not the same as social stratification. Every sociology textbook has separate chapters on class, race, age, and gender. (We have added a few, which we will discuss in more depth.) But in some books, that's about as far as it goes; chapters on "other topics" do not give adequate sociological treatment to the ways in which our different positions affect our experience of other sociological institutions and processes. How, in other words, do these various *identities intersect* with one another to shape our experience and opportunities in patterned ways and shape social *inequality* (to use a bit of iSoc language). Multiculturalism is used as a framing device in every chapter. Every chapter describes the different ways in which race, class, age, ethnicity, sexuality, and gender organize people's experiences within social institutions.

Within Part Two, on "Identities and Inequalities," we deal with each of these facets of identity—age, class, race, ethnicity, gender, sexuality—separately, of course. But we also address the ways in which they intersect with each other, providing new and cutting-edge research as illustrations of the processes and patterns we describe. When, after all, do you start being middle class and stop being black? Contemporary sociological inquiry requires that we examine the intersections among these various elements of identity and inequality, understanding how they interact, amplify, and contradict each other, as well as how they become embedded within social institutions.

These aspects of identity both unite us (as elements of identity) and divide us—into groups that compete for scarce resources. These are the dimensions of social life that organize inequality. Thus, we explore both—identity and inequality. Multiculturalism requires not just that we "add women (or any other group) and stir"—the ways that some courses and textbooks tried to revamp themselves in the last few decades of the twentieth century to embrace diversity. Multiculturalism requires that we begin from questions of diversity and identity, not end there. This book attempts to do that.

Distinctive Features

Sociology NOW offers these features that are unique applications of sociological concepts to illustrate chapter concepts:

SOCIOLOGY AND OUR WORLD. Among the most exciting and rewarding parts of teaching introductory sociology is revealing to students how what we study is so immediately applicable to the world in which we all live. Thus, each chapter has "Sociology and Our World" boxes that make this connection explicit. They're there to help the student see the connections between their lives—which they usually think are pretty interesting—and sociology, which they might, at first, fear as dry and irrelevant. And these boxes also are there to facilitate classroom discussions, providing exciting examples of how sociological concepts, theories, and ideas are applied in sociological research. Classic sociological research is sometimes discussed here. But we also provide a collection of new and exciting examples of recent and ongoing research to help students consider how the ideas and discoveries they are reading about are being put to use today.

U.S./WORLD. To better grasp globalization, a graphic feature in each chapter frames a sociological issue comparatively, comparing U.S. data with data from the rest of the world. We try to set the United States in a global context, comparing it both to countries similar to the United States (other G7 countries, for example) as well as to countries very different from ours in the developing world. Learning to understand the organization of our own society as only one possible option is a challenge best offered by examining some of the diverse ways societies are organized around the world. And U.S./World boxes help to illustrate these cross-cultural comparisons and offer opportunities to reflect on this.

HOW DO WE KNOW WHAT WE KNOW? This feature enables us to show students how methods actually work in the exploration of sociological problems. In the third edition, we've made more use of these boxes and provide exciting examples of research that relies on sociological methods to answer questions in ways that challenge students to think creatively

SOCIOLOGY AND OUR WORLD

MONOGAMOUS MASCULINITY, PROMISCUOUS FEMININITY

Are we cherry-picking biological evidence to suggest men are naturally more promiscuous?

One group of evolutionists—evolutionary psychologists—argue that the size and number of reproductive cells lead inevitably to different levels of parental "investment" in children. (Males produce millions of tiny sperm; females produce only a few dozen comparatively huge eggs.) Sarah Blaffer Hrdy (1981) adds a few more biological facts to the mix. Unlike other mammals, she notes, human females conceal estrus; that is, they are potentially sexually receptive throughout their entire menstrual cycle, unlike other female mammals that go "into heat" when ovulating and who are otherwise utterly uninterested in sex. What is the evolutionary reason for this? Hrdy asks. (*Hint:* The female knows that the baby is hers, but the male can never be exactly sure.)

Could it be, she asks, that females might want to mate with as many males as possible, to ensure that all of them (or as many as possible) will provide food and protection to the helpless and dependent infant, thereby increasing its chances of survival? (Remember that infant mortality in those preindustrial cultures of origin was extraordinarily high.) Could it be that females have a natural propensity toward promiscuity to

ensure the offspring's survival and that males have a natural propensity toward monogamy, lest they run themselves ragged providing food and protection to babies who may—or may not—be theirs? Wouldn't it be more likely for males to devise a system that ensured women's faithfulness—monogamy—and institutionalize it in marriage and then develop a cultural plan that would keep women in the home (because they might be ovulating and thus get pregnant)? And because it often takes a couple more than one "try" to get pregnant, wouldn't regular couplings with one partner be a more successful strategy for a male than a one-night stand?

Of course, no one would suggest that this interpretation is any more "true" than the one proposed by evolutionary psychologists. What Hrdy revealed is that one can use different (sometimes better) biological evidence and construct the exact opposite explanation. What Hrdy illustrates is that we should be *extremely* cautious in accepting evolutionary arguments about gender. But she also illustrates how readily we often accept arguments that support existing beliefs about gender.

U.S./WORLD

THE GLOBAL GENDER GAP

Each year, the World Economic Forum (WEF), a European-based nonpartisan policy institute, ranks 130 countries on their level of gender inequality. The WEF uses four criteria: level of economic participation, educational attainment, health, and political empowerment.

Overall Index Rank
- N/A
- 1–20
- 20–40
- 40–60
- 60–80
- 80–100
- 100–120
- 120–140
- > 140

Explore the map to see where different countries rank on the most recent report. The United States ranked only 45, well behind Iceland (1), Finland (2), Norway (3), Sweden (4), Rwanda (5), Switzerland (11), South Africa (15), France (17), Canada (35) and others.

SOURCE: Data from World Economic Forum, Global Gender Gap Report 2016, The Global Gender Gap Index 2016 Ratings. Available at: http://reports.weforum.org/global-gender-gap-report-2016/rankings/.

INVESTIGATE FURTHER

1. Why do you think the top-ranked countries are all in Scandinavia? And why do you think the countries ranked lowest are in the Middle East and South Asia?

2. If you were a policy maker, how would you mix cultural ideology and social policy to reduce the gender gap?

about social problems and inequality. Instead of confining methods to a single chapter and then ignoring them for the remainder of the book, we ask, for example, how sociologists measure social mobility (Chapter 7), or how we use statistics to examine the relationship between race and intelligence (Chapter 8), or how demographers attempted to rely on publicly available data to try to discover how many people might be transgender in the United States (Chapter 9). In this way, students can see method-in-action as a tool that sociologists use to discover the patterns of the social world. It helps students recognize the "work" of sociology and highlights the nuts and bolts of sociological discoveries.

HOW DO WE KNOW WHAT WE KNOW?

JUST HOW MANY TRANSGENDER PEOPLE ARE THERE?

Estimating the size of the transgender population is more difficult than you might think. Currently, there are no nationally representative surveys that ask questions that would enable transgender people to anonymously identify themselves. This is part of the reason that estimates of the size of the population vary so widely. *The Williams Institute*—an independent research think tank conducting rigorous research on issues of gender and sexuality—suggests that the transgender population in the United States is approximately 700,000 people (Gates 2011). This is a higher estimate than other scholars suggest, but a more accurate estimate is challenging to achieve for two separate reasons. First, we lack questions on nationally representative surveys that might help us better enumerate transgender people (Westbrook and Saperstein 2015). Second, existing research suggests that, even if we were able to add a question, the changes necessary are much more complex than simply adding "transgender" as a third option when asking questions about gender (Schilt and Bratter 2015). This means that estimating the size of this population is challenging.

More recently, the U.S. Bureau of the Census published a report attempting to identify people who are likely to be transgender persons based on how they answer other questions that relate to sex and gender *identity* (Harris 2015). As we mentioned in Chapter 1, research on names can tell us more than you might think. In a 2015 report, Benjamin Harris attempted to identify the number of what he refers to as "likely transgender individuals" in the United States by combining Census data with data collected by the Social Security Administration, the latter of which collects three important pieces of data on every citizen with a Social Security Number: first and middle name, sex-coding (male or female), and date of birth. Harris combines these data sets to identify how many adults in the U.S. changed information in their accounts in ways that are consistent with a gender transition. Thus, by linking these data with the Census, Harris was also able to provide some basic demographic characteristics of "likely transgender people" as well as residential patterns.

To identify whether people are likely transgender, Harris first identified people who changed their names from a traditionally male name to a traditionally female name (or vice versa), and then asked whether those people also changed their sex coding (from male to female, or vice versa) in the same direction. Whether a name is "male" or "female" is determined by the proportion of people with that name who have a sex coding of "male" of "female." Some names (like John) are virtually only given to boys, whereas others (like Val) are given to boys and girls in roughly equal numbers. So, he had to think carefully about whether a name change might likely indicate transgender *identity* or not. Although the number of people who qualified as "likely transgender" in Harris's (2015) study was smaller,

he was able to produce new knowledge about who transgender Americans are, where they live, and whether they are more likely to pursue legal transitions (measured by name and sex code changes with the Social Security Administration).

Likely Transgender Individuals in the United States
Here you can also see that the people Harris was able to identify as "likely transgender individuals" are not evenly distributed around the United States. That in and of itself is an interesting finding. And it could mean more than one thing. A larger proportion of the population in Washington, Oregon, and Vermont is transgender, for instance, than in Utah, Iowa, and Louisiana.

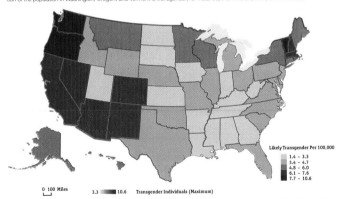

0 100 Miles   3.3 ▬▬ 10.6   Transgender Individuals (Maximum)

Likely Transgender Per 100,000
1.4 – 3.3
3.4 – 4.7
4.8 – 6.0
6.1 – 7.6
7.7 – 10.6

SOURCE: Data from U.S. Census Bureau, as of 2010. Refreshed July 13, 2015. Available at https://www.census.gov/content/dam/Census/library/working-papers/2015/adrm/carra-wp-2015-03.pdf.

WHAT DO YOU THINK? WHAT DOES AMERICA THINK?   Part of an introductory course requires students to marshal evidence to engage with and often reevaluate their opinions. Often our job is to unsettle their fallback position of "This is just my own personal opinion," which floats unhinged from social contexts. We ask that they contextualize, that they refer to how they formed their opinions and to what sorts of evidence they might use to demonstrate the empirical veracity of their positions. How they came to think what they think is often as important as what they think. But students often benefit enormously from knowing what other people think as well. What percentage of Americans agrees with you? In each chapter, we've included a boxed feature that asks students questions taken directly from the General Social Survey (with data from the recent 2016 update). We include information about what a representative sample of Americans thinks about the same topic, to give students a sense of

WHAT DO YOU THINK? WHAT DOES AMERICA THINK?

Women and Politics

The gender distribution in U.S. politics is still unequal, with local and state governments tending to have more female representatives than the national government.

What do you think?

Most men are better suited emotionally for politics than are most women.

○ Agree
○ Disagree

What does America think?

	Less than High School		High School		College +		Bachelor's Degree		Graduate School	
	Men	**Women**	**Men**	**Women**	**Men**	**Women**	**Men**	**Women**	**Men**	**Women**
Agree	51.28%	46.9%	27.7%	20.6%	25.6%	19.13%	19.6%	11%	17.36%	11.63%
Disagree	48.72%	53.1%	72.3%	79.4%	74.4%	80.87%	80.4%	89%	82.64%	88.37%

SOURCE: Data from General Social Survey 2016.

As you might notice, there appears to be a strong correlation between gender and how people feel about women's and men's emotional suitability for politics. In general, men are more likely than women to agree with the statement. But when we examine how this trend intersects with education, it is also true that those with more education are less likely to agree with the statement. So more men than women agree with the statement in each educational group. But similar proportions of women with only a high school degree disagree with this statement compared with men with a bachelor's degree. Many of these beliefs were put on dramatic display in the 2016 presidential election between Hillary Clinton and Donald Trump.

And when asked directly whether they would vote for a qualified candidate for president who happened to be a woman, there are also differences.

What do you think?

If your party nominated a woman for president, you would vote for her if she was qualified for the job.

○ Agree
○ Disagree

What does America think?

	Less than High School		High School		Some College		Bachelor's Degree		Graduate School	
	Men	**Women**	**Men**	**Women**	**Men**	**Woman**	**Men**	**Women**	**Men**	**Women**
Agree	80.8%	76.48%	90.7%	93.4%	92.83%	93.8%	95.4%	95.9%	96.13%	95.3%
Disagree	19.2%	23.52%	9.3%	6.6%	7.17%	6.2%	4.6%	4.1%	3.87%	4.7%

SOURCE: Data from General Social Survey 2016.

Although it is true that both women and men are much more likely to vote for a woman nominated in their political party than not solely because she is a woman, it is also true that women show a stronger commitment here than men—at least until they receive graduate degrees.

THINKING CRITICALLY ABOUT SURVEY DATA

More respondents said they would vote for a female president than said that women were as emotionally suited for politics as men are. What do you think explains that difference?

where their opinions fit with the rest of the country and to allow students the opportunity to examine some of their own biases as well. Critical-thinking questions based on the data encourage students to think about how factors like race, gender, class, and age might influence our perceptions and attitudes.

CHAPTER REVIEW. To help students master the material in each chapter, we have a review section at the end of each chapter, which includes section summaries and key terms with definitions

AN ENGAGING WRITING STYLE. All textbook writers strive for clarity; a few even reach for elegance. This book is no exception. We've tried to write the book in a way that conveys a lot of information but also in a way that engages the students where they live. Not only are concepts always followed by examples, but we frequently use examples drawn from pop culture—from TV, movies, and music—and even from videos, video games, social media, and Internet memes.

This will not only make the students' reading experience more enjoyable, but it should also enable the instructor to illustrate the relevance of sociological concepts to the students' lives.

Organization

In this third edition, we have organized the book slightly differently than in the first two editions. In between the second and third editions, we collected a new author as a part of the *Sociology NOW* team—Tristan Bridges. And the field also changed in the intervening years as well. In light of these changes, we elected to provide more of a substitution for the old "three frameworks" model (functionalism, conflict theory, and symbolic interactionism) that we never used to frame the book. Though it became increasingly obsolete in the field, it was still used in textbooks because of what it provides students—a touchstone to which they can regularly return as an introduction to sociology. So, the largest element of our reorganization involved the insertion of a new perspective that offers a similar touchstone—the "iSoc model." Introduced in the first chapter, this model helps students understand what sociologists are actually looking at as they investigate the world around them.

Although not all sociological research examines society by looking at the same set of "i's," iSoc helps students to learn to understand how the diverse collection of research, theory, concepts, and ideas are connected in one field. Sociologists all share a common set of methods, and something we sometimes call the "sociological perspective." Once you have it (the sociological perspective, that is), it's sometimes hard to explain exactly what *it* is. The iSoc perspective offers an answer to this that is intuitive and simple, but also enables us to get students to understand the perspective in greater depth. The iSoc model is incorporated throughout the textbook. The introductory chapter explains the model in depth, and each chapter after that begins with a section on "iSoc" inviting students to consider how the perspective can be applied in the chapter they are reading.

In addition to this, this edition has a greater focus on application, summarizing many more examples from actual sociological research so that students can learn not only the concepts and language sociologists use to write about the world around them, but also how these concepts are being put to use, and the projects out of which they emerged. This also means that there is a bit more "data" in this edition—new graphs, maps, and figures that help to illustrate content in new ways and to provide students with more data literacy. Learning to "read" graphs and maps is a sociological skill as well. We provide captions and interesting visualizations of data to help students learn to identify what graphs, maps, and charts are intending to illustrate. In the Revel edition of the book, many of these visualizations are also interactive.

Finally, we have also reorganized the chapters a bit. The biggest change within Part II is Chapter 11, which now combines sociological research on bodies, sexualities, and health. Part III is reorganized as well. In this section, we now attempt to move out from families into wider and wider social institutions. So, the chapter on education (Chapter 13) now follows the chapter on families (Chapter 12) and is no longer combined with religion. This also means that we have a more complete treatment of the sociology of education as well. We found a greater elective affinity between research on politics and religion and now combine these topics for an exciting chapter with an incredibly global focus (Chapter 15). The book still concludes with both demographic and environmental sociological perspectives and concerns (Chapter 16).

All of the chapters in the book are fully updated, framed with the iSoc perspective (new to the third edition), and they each provide new and exciting applications of ideas and research.

NEW to This Edition

Every publication is a conversation—between authors and readers. A new edition provides an opportunity to continue that conversation. We have tried to listen to the concerns and questions from students, faculty, reviewers, and sales people (who are often a marvelous conduit of informal reviews and concerns). Many of the revisions in this third edition are responses to concerns raised by you.

One thing you'll notice is that the book looks different. Not only does it include a vibrant new layout and design, but it also contains more sophisticated graphics within multiple new figures, as well as new photos and feature content.

Of course, we've updated the data in each chapter, and we've tried to present the most current and relevant information to you. But more than that, we have tried to bring forward a distinctly sociological understanding of the statistics and studies that we cite, all relying on the iSoc perspective to ground this summary investigation of the field. With a journalistic commitment to currency and a sociological commitment to context, we've brought in discussions of the 2016 presidential vote (in Chapter 15, Politics and Religion, and also to some extent in Chapter 7, Stratification and Social Class); and we've also added new chapters devoted to age (Chapter 10) and education (Chapter 13), just to name a few.

NEW to the Structure of the Third Edition

- **Learning objectives** tied to the major subheadings in every chapter identify the key concepts students should know and understand with respect to introductory sociology.

- A running **marginal glossary** that clearly defines bold key terms for students at the points in the chapters where the terms are discussed.

- **iSoc Framework:** Every academic field uses a framework or a lens through which to view the phenomena it observes, a "story" that is the field's master narrative. For sociologists, it's how to locate biographies in history—that is, sociology is about who you are—but in context. Sociologists see the link between identity and larger structures of inequality. And we, as authors, see identity and inequality in constant operation, in every interaction with others and in every institution in which we find ourselves. In this book, we refer to this sociological perspective as "iSoc."
  - **iSoc levels of analysis:** Because the sociological lens examines the "both–and" and not the "either–or," we can explain the sociological framework with two sets of "i's": (1) *Identity, Intersectionality*, and *Inequality*, and (2) *Interaction* and *Institution*. Understanding these five "i's" is what we mean by the sociological perspective—or, as we like to call it, "iSoc."
  - **iSoc major sections** appear early in every chapter to define the iSoc framework in relation to that chapter's main themes. The two sets of "i's": (1) Identity, Intersectionality, and Inequality, and (2) Interaction and Institution are individually addressed within the context of the chapter, as well as interrelated, with contemporary examples. Learning to see the world around you from the perspective of iSoc is what it means to understand the sociological perspective. Many sections also offer new iSoc introductions to frame chapter discussions.
  - **"iSoc and You" summaries** appear at the end of every major section to reinforce these five levels of analysis and provide students with both a theoretical lens through which to view social life and the analytic method to situate any particular phenomenon.
  - **Chapter Conclusion** sections are more clearly defined to align with major *Sociology NOW* themes, as well as iSoc levels of analysis.

Finally, this third edition is now available through Pearson's digital platform: Revel.

Revel™

Revel is an interactive learning environment that deeply engages students and prepares them for class. Media and assessment integrated directly within the authors' narrative lets students read, explore interactive content, and practice in one continuous learning path. Thanks to the dynamic reading experience in Revel, students come to class prepared to discuss, apply, and learn from instructors and from each other.

Learn more about Revel
www.pearson.com/revel

Revel for *Sociology NOW*, Third Edition

Sociology NOW, Third Edition, features many of the dynamic interactive elements that make Revel unique. In addition to the rich narrative content, *Sociology NOW* includes the following Revel-specific elements (Please note that for ease of use in your course, links to videos, Social Explorer visualizations, and currency window content are all available in the instructor Resources folder *within* Revel.):

- New Video Program:
  - **Chapter-Opening Videos.** Lead author Michael Kimmel provides a contemporary vignette that illustrates key themes and content in the chapter.
  - **Topic-Based Animation Videos.** These videos, one per chapter, focus on a wide range of contemporary subjects that illuminate sociological concepts by providing Revel-only coverage of such wide-ranging issues as "fads," friendship networks, the feminization of poverty, historical research on transgender classification, the gender wage gap, and more.
  - **Pearson Originals.** The Pearson Original docuseries videos highlight stories that exemplify and humanize the concepts covered in Sociology courses. These videos illustrate a variety of social issues and current events, bringing key topics to life for students while creating opportunities to further develop their understanding of sociology. Therefore, students not only connect with the people and stories on a personal level, but also view these stories and individuals with greater empathy all while contextualizing core course concepts. With accessible video links located in the instructor's manual, authors will offer a brief introduction and suggestions for incorporating these videos into your introductory sociology course. Video topics for this title include:
    - Fakenews: Can the Press Fight Back?; Gender Identity: Meant to be Maddie; The Inequality Conversation; Fighting for Racial Equality: A Conversation Between Generations; Sex and Gender; Transgender Bathrooms: The Debate in Washington State; America's Opioid Crisis: Portraits of an Epidemic; Population and Family Size; Education Inequality; School Districting and the Achievement Gap: A Tale of Two Communities; Shifting Social Structures; What Jobs Disappeared: A Coal Miner's Story; The American Working Class: Voices from Harrisburg, IL; Interpreting the First Amendment: Regulating Protest in Minnesota; A Nation of Immigrants; Seeking Refuge from the Syrian War: The Abdi Family; Taking a Stand Against Environmental Injustice
- **New interactive maps, figures, and tables** in all chapters feature Social Explorer technology that allows updates to the latest data, increases student engagement, and reinforces data literacy.
- **Currency windows** in each chapter's conclusion section feature author-written articles, updated or replaced twice each year, that put breaking news and current events into the context of sociology. Examples include "Sociology NOW: Sociology and Common Sense" (Chapter 1); "Social Science NOW: When Experiments Happen Organically" in Chapter 4; and "Sex and Gender NOW: Just How Many Genders Are There?" in Chapter 9.

- **Key Terms** appear in bold with pop-up definitions that allow students to see the meaning of a word or phrase while reading the text, providing context. They are in flashcard form at the end of each chapter as well as in a comprehensive glossary.

- **Did You Know?** Each chapter is punctuated by several "Did You Know?" boxes, many new to this edition and available only through Revel. These are generally short sociological factoids, tidbits of information that are funny, strange, and a little offbeat, but illustrate the sociological ideas being discussed. For example, did you know that Georgia was founded in 1732 as a penal colony for British criminals, or that Eskimos really do have about 50 words for snow? You won't draw their attention to all of these factoids, but the students are going to enjoy reading them. And we guarantee that there are at least a few that you didn't know!

- **Assessments** include multiple-choice end-of-module and end-of-chapter quizzes that test students' knowledge of the chapter content.

- **The Chapter Review** contains module summaries and key term flashcards that allow students to review and test their knowledge about concepts covered in each chapter.

- **Integrated Writing Assessments:** Revel is rich in opportunities for writing about chapter topics and concepts.

  - ○ **Journal Prompts** allow students to explore themes presented in the chapter through "teaser" questions linked to each Sociology and Our World feature that require students to apply chapter concepts and the iSoc levels of analysis to contemporary social questions. The ungraded Journal Prompts are included in line with content and can be shared with instructors.

  - ○ **Shared Writing Prompts** provide peer-to-peer feedback in a discussion board, developing critical thinking skills and fostering collaboration among a specific class. These prompts appear once per chapter, and are linked to each What Do You Think? What Does American Think? Social Explorer survey.

  - ○ **Writing Space** is the best way to develop and assess concept mastery and critical thinking through writing. Writing Space provides a single place within Revel to create, track, and grade writing assignments; access writing resources; and exchange meaningful, personalized feedback quickly and easily to improve results. For students, Writing Space provides everything they need to keep up with writing assignments, access assignment guides and checklists, write or upload completed assignments, and receive grades and feedback—all in one convenient place. For educators, Writing Space makes assigning, receiving, and evaluating writing assignments easier. It's simple to create new assignments and upload relevant materials, see student progress, and receive alerts when students submit work. Writing Space makes students' work more focused and effective, with customized grading rubrics they can see and personalized feedback. Writing Space can also check students' work for improper citation or plagiarism by comparing it against the world's most accurate text comparison database available from Turnitin.

Chapter-by-Chapter Changes

CHAPTER 1: WHAT IS SOCIOLOGY?

Content Changes:

- NEW sections "iSoc: Sociological Frames of Analysis" and "Sociology Now: New Issues, New Lenses"
- NEW SOCIOLOGY AND OUR WORLD features include:
  - ○ Why Popular Boy Names Are More Popular Than Popular Girl Names
  - ○ Why Names that Regain Popularity Wait a Century, and Two Alternative Views of the World

- NEW figures and tables include:
  - TABLE 1.1 Top 10 Names for Boys and Girls in the United States
  - FIGURE 1.1 Rank of Mary, Emma, and Jessica among Most Popular U.S. Girls' Names at Birth, 1900–2016
  - FIGURE 1.2 Name Popularity for Ellen, Monica, and Forrest, 1950–2015

CHAPTER 2: CULTURE AND MEDIA

Content Changes:

- NEW discussion of media now combined with culture chapter
- NEW sections "Thinking about Culture and Media Sociologically," "Culture and Media," and "iSoc: Culture and Media"
- NEW SOCIOLOGY AND OUR WORLD features include:
  - Using Media Use to Detect Rhythms in Our Lives
  - U.S. Race Relations and the Confederate Flag
- NEW figures and other features include:
  - FIGURE 2.1 How Fast Can a Society Change Its Values?
  - U.S./WORLD Print Newspaper Reach, 2014/2015
  - WHAT DO YOU THINK? WHAT DOES AMERICA THINK? Confidence in the Press
  - HOW DO WE KNOW WHAT WE KNOW? Christmas Gift Giving as a Method of Norm Enforcement

CHAPTER 3: SOCIETY: INTERACTIONS, GROUPS, AND ORGANIZATIONS

Content Changes:

- NEW sections "Thinking about Interactions, Groups, and Organizations Sociologically," "iSoc: The Social Construction of Identity," and "Understanding Society and Social Life as Socially Structured"
- NEW coverage of the "small world problem" to social networks
- NEW discussion of organizations now emphasizes power and inequality, using the iSoc framework
- NEW Conclusion "Groups 'R' Us: Interactions, Groups, and Organizations NOW"
- NEW SOCIOLOGY AND OUR WORLD features include:
  - Using Selfies to Understand My "I" and My "Me"
  - Elevator Behavior, Norms, and Social Inequality
  - Why Liberals Drink Lattes
  - Organizing Without Organizations?
- NEW figures and other features include:
  - MAP 3.1 SMALL WORLD PROBLEM: Internet Connectivity
  - FIGURE 3.2 Even in Nursing, Men Earn More

CHAPTER 4: HOW DO WE KNOW WHAT WE KNOW? THE METHODS OF THE SOCIOLOGIST

Content Changes:

- NEW introductory vignette
- NEW sections "iSoc: Research Methods," "When Is a Fact a Fact?—Why Operationalization Is So Important," and "What Do Sociologists Consider as 'Data'?"
- NEW discussion of network analysis, social networks, and social ties
- NEW SOCIOLOGY AND OUR WORLD features include:
  - Are People Lying on Surveys? … Sometimes.
  - Hidden Facts: On the Power of Ethnography
  - Shifts in Men's Facial Hair Styles Are Patterned

- NEW figures and tables include:
  - FIGURE 4.3 Spurious Correlations
  - FIGURE 4.4 The General Social Survey (GSS)
  - FIGURE 4.5 Main Broadcast Network Coverage of Women's Sports (1989–2014) and SportsCenter Coverage of Women's Sports (1999–2014)
  - FIGURE 4.6 Research in the Social Sciences
  - TABLE 4.3 The Institutional Review Board

- NEW HOW DO WE KNOW WHAT WE KNOW? features include:
  - Thinking Methodologically about the Heritability of Intelligence
  - Interviewing People about How They Answer Survey Questions about Ethnicity
  - We Can't Predict Almost Anything as Well as the Weather

CHAPTER 5: SOCIALIZATION

Content Changes:

- NEW introductory vignette

- NEW sections "Understanding What Socialization Is and How It Works," "iSoc: Socialization," "Socialization and Inequality," "Socialization and Racial Inequality," "Socialization and Gender and Sexual Inequality," "Institutions of Socialization," "Socialization and Ongoing and Unending," "iSoc in Action: Socialization in a Global Society," and "Conclusion: Socialization NOW"

- NEW SOCIOLOGY AND OUR WORLD features include:
  - What Can We Learn about Socialization from Family Trips to the Zoo?
  - Can Gay and Lesbian Schoolteachers Be "Out" at Work?

- NEW HOW DO WE KNOW WHAT WE KNOW? features include:
  - Twin Studies
  - How Do We Know We're Socialized to Believe in Racial Inequality?

- NEW figures and other features include:
  - FIGURE 5.2 Importance of Children Learning Obedience vs. Learning to Think for Themselves
  - FIGURE 5.3 Gender Balance of Dialogue for Characters in Disney Movies
  - FIGURE 5.4 Gender Balance of Dialogue for Characters in Movies on IMDB.com
  - MAP 5.1 Proportion of Americans with Bachelor's Degrees and with Household Incomes Among the Top 40 Percent
  - FIGURE 5.5 Proportion of Time Spent with Friends at Different Locations among U.S. Teens
  - FIGURE 5.6 Media Use by Age, Race, and Ethnicity
  - FIGURE 5.7 Percentage of 25- to 34-Year-Olds Living in Multigenerational Households by Gender, 2010–2012

CHAPTER 6: CRIME AND DEVIANCE

Content Changes:

- NEW sections "Thinking Sociologically about Crime and Deviance," "iSoc: The Sociology of Crime and Deviance," and "Understanding Crime and Deviance Institutionally"

- NEW SOCIOLOGY AND OUR WORLD features include:
  - Stereotype Threat and Stereotype Promise

- NEW HOW DO WE KNOW WHAT WE KNOW? features include:
  - Just How Violent Is the United States?
  - Racial Bias in the Courtroom

- NEW figures and other features include:
  - ○ U.S./WORLD U.S. Cybercrime in International Perspective
  - ○ FIGURE 6.2 Crime Rates by Age and Gender in Nineteenth-Century Great Britain and Late-Twentieth-Century Chicago
  - ○ FIGURE 6.3 U.S. Men in Prison or Jail, 2015
  - ○ FIGURE 6.4 Trust in the Police, by Race
  - ○ FIGURE 6.5 Prisoners under the Jurisdiction of State or Federal Correctional Authorities, 1978–2015
  - ○ FIGURE 6.6 The Death Penalty in the United States, 1937–2016

CHAPTER 7: SOCIAL CLASS AND STRATIFICATION: IDENTITY AND INEQUALITY

Content Changes:

- NEW sections "Thinking Sociologically about Social Class and Stratification," "iSoc: The Sociology of Social Class and Stratification," "Class Identity and Inequality," "Class, Culture, and Musical Taste," "Resistance and Change in Class Inequality," "Political Resistance to Class Inequality," and "Conclusion: Social Class and Stratification NOW"

- NEW SOCIOLOGY AND OUR WORLD features include:
  - ○ Apartheid—A Caste System
  - ○ Prestige Means Not Having to Deal with People

- NEW figures, tables, and other features include:
  - ○ FIGURE 7.1 How Americans Stand Out in Understanding Social Class
  - ○ TABLE 7.1 Top 10 Prestigious Occupations
  - ○ MAP 7.1 The Intersections Between Poverty and Race in the United States
  - ○ FIGURE 7.2 Income Distribution by Class in the United States
  - ○ FIGURE 7.3 Subjective Class Identification among Americans, 1975–2016
  - ○ FIGURE 7.5 Median Household Income by Race and Ethnicity, 1967–2015
  - ○ FIGURE 7.6 A Profile of Poverty in the United States, 1959–2015
  - ○ MAP 7.2 Income Inequality on a Global Scale

CHAPTER 8: RACE AND ETHNICITY

Content Changes:

- NEW sections "Thinking Sociologically about Race and Ethnicity," "What Is Ethnicity,?, "iSoc: The Sociology of Race and Ethnicity," "Racial and Ethnic Inequalities: Interactions and Institutions," "Color-Blind Racism," "Ethnic Identities in the United States," "Resistance and Mobilization to Racial and Ethnic Inequality," "Movements for (and Against) Racial and Ethnic Equality," and "Conclusion: Race and Ethnicity NOW"

- NEW SOCIOLOGY AND OUR WORLD features include:
  - ○ Why Filipino Americans Don't Identify as Asian
  - ○ Perceptions of Prejudice Vary by … Race!
  - ○ Is Living on the "Wrong Side of the Tracks" a Social Reality?
  - ○ Why Hispanic Went from Being a Race to an Ethnicity
  - ○ Learning the Language

- NEW HOW DO WE KNOW WHAT WE KNOW? features include:
  - ○ Do Employers Discriminate Based on Race?
  - ○ Do Mascots Depicting Racial Stereotypes Really Matter?

- NEW figures, tables, and other features include:
  - ○ TABLE 8.1 Distinctions Between Race and Ethnicity
  - ○ FIGURE 8.1 Approval of Marriages Between Black and White Americans by Race, 1958–2013

- ○ FIGURE 8.2 Percentage of Racial/Ethnic Groups Reporting Multiple Racial Identities, 2010
- ○ FIGURE 8.3 The Racial and Ethnic Composition of the United States, 1970–2060
- ○ FIGURE 8.4 Racial Wealth Gap Between Black and White Americans, 1983–2013
- ○ FIGURE 8.5 Median Household Income by Race/Ethnicity, 1967–2015
- ○ MAP 8.1 Native American Reservations in the Continental United States
- ○ FIGURE 8.7 Who Make Up "Asians" in the United States?
- ○ MAP 8.2 U.S. Ethnicities by County

CHAPTER 9: SEX AND GENDER

Content Changes:

- NEW sections "Thinking Sociologically about Sex and Gender," "iSoc: The Sociology of Sex and Gender," "The Medicalization of Sex and Gender," "Transgender Identities: Blurring the Boundaries of Gender," "The Bathroom Problem: Organizing Our World Around Gender," "Gender Socialization: Learning about Gender Inequality," "Gender Policing" and Gender Accountability," "Studying Gender Inequality Institutionally and Intersectionally," "Gender Bias in Orchestras and Student Evaluations," "Challenges to Gender Inequality and the Endurance of Gender Gaps," and "Conclusion: Sex and Gender NOW"

- NEW SOCIOLOGY AND OUR WORLD features include:
  - ○ Pink for Boys and Blue for Girls
  - ○ Will Young People Today Produce a Gender Revolution in Marriage Tomorrow?
  - ○ Men and Feminism

- NEW HOW DO WE KNOW WHAT WE KNOW? features include:
  - ○ Just How Many Transgender People Are There?
  - ○ Women and Men Are Far More Similar Than They Are Different

- NEW figures and other features include:
  - ○ MAP 9.1 Mapping Gender-Diverse Cultures Around the World
  - ○ FIGURE 9.1 Movies Assessed by the "Bechdel Test," 1970–2015
  - ○ FIGURE 9.2 Changes in the Proportion of Women in U.S. Symphony Orchestras, 1940–1996
  - ○ FIGURE 9.3 Frequency of Terms Used in Student Evaluations of Women and Men Professors on RateMyProfessor.com
  - ○ FIGURE 9.5 Politics and Business: Public Perceptions of Men and Women as Political Leaders, 2014
  - ○ FIGURE 9.6 World Record Times in 1500-Meter Running for Women and Men, 1912–2015
  - ○ FIGURE 9.7 Shifts in the Gender Wage Gap, 1940–2014

CHAPTER 10: AGE: FROM YOUNG TO OLD

Content Changes:

- NEW expanded coverage, with entire chapter devoted to age

- NEW introductory vignette

- NEW sections "iSoc: The Sociology of Aging," "Childhood," "Boomers, Busters, and Boomlets: The Generations of Youth," "Baby Boomers," "Generation X," "Millennials—Generation Y," "Global Youth—A Dying Breed?", "Age Inequalities in Interactions," "Retirement," "Elder Care," "Aging and Dying," "Institutional Age Inequalities in Global and Local Perspectives," "Aging, Health, and the Life Course," "Child Labor in the United States," "Child Labor Around the World," "The New Slavery," "Opposition and Mobilization: The Politics of Age," and "Conclusion: Youth and Aging NOW"

- NEW SOCIOLOGY AND OUR WORLD features include:
  - Education as Age Graded
  - Sons Are More Likely to Live with Parents than Daughters
  - Retiring and Gay? Where?
- NEW figures, tables, and other features include:
  - MAP 10.1 Life Expectancy Around the World
  - FIGURE 10.1 Proportions of Young Adults (18–34) Living with Their Parents, 1880–2014
  - HOW DO WE KNOW WHAT WE KNOW? Why Middle Age Can Be So Challenging
  - FIGURE 10.2 U.S. Birth Rate, 1940–2015
  - FIGURE 10.3 Racial and Ethnic Diversity Among Age Cohorts, 2014
  - FIGURE 10.4 Global Population Distribution Projections by Age Group, 2014 to 2050
  - FIGURE 10.5 Population Pyramids—Mexico, Italy, and Iraq, 2015
  - FIGURE 10.6 Child Poverty Rate by Race, 1976–2013
  - FIGURE 10.7 Life Expectancy and Retirement Years
  - FIGURE 10.8 Life Expectancy Around the World
  - U.S./WORLD Youth Unemployment Around the World
  - FIGURE 10.9 Global Trends in the Number of Employed Children—2008, 2012
  - MAP 10.2 Global Flow of Child Slavery

CHAPTER 11: THE BODY: HEALTH AND SEXUALITY

Content Changes:

- NEW sections "iSoc: The Sociology of Bodies and Embodiment," "Changing Identity by Changing the Gendered Body: Embodying Transgender Identities," "The "Disabled" Body," "Embodied Inequality," "Understanding Health and Illness Sociologically," "Health and Inequality," "Sickness and Stigma," "Mental Illness," "Researching Sexuality," "Resistance to Inequality: The LGBT Movement," and "Conclusion: Bodies, Health, and Sexualities NOW"
- NEW SOCIOLOGY AND OUR WORLD features include:
  - How Women with Ink Illustrate Gender Policing
  - Criminalizing Sickness?
  - What Happens to Men Who Wait?
  - Gay Men and Lesbians Congregate, But Not Always Together
- NEW figures and other features include:
  - FIGURE 11.1 Number of News Articles Containing "Obesity," "Overweight," "Anorexia," and "Eating Disorder," 1950–2016
  - FIGURE 11.2 Prevalence of Any and Severe Disabilities and Needs for Assistance by Age, 2010
  - MAP 11.1 Food Scarcity in the United States, 2015
  - FIGURE 11.3 Leading Causes of Death in the United States, by Sex and Race, 2013
  - MAP 11.2 Under-Five Mortality Rate Around the World, 2015
  - WHAT DO YOU THINK? WHAT DOES AMERICA THINK? MacArthur Mental Health Module
  - FIGURE 11.4 Percentage of U.S. Adults without Health Insurance
  - FIGURE 11.5 U.S. Adults Identifying as LGBT, 2012–2016
  - FIGURE 11.6 Proportions of LGBT Persons by Relationship Type and the Importance of Sexual Orientation to Their Identity
  - FIGURE 11.7 Proportion of Youth Who Have Had Sex by Age and Gender
  - HOW DO WE KNOW WHAT WE KNOW? Why Hooking Up Might Be Less Empowering Than You Think
  - FIGURE 11.8 Proportion of Americans Defining Premarital Sex, Extramarital Sex, and Same-Sex as "Always Wrong" or "Almost Always Wrong"

CHAPTER 12: FAMILIES

Content Changes:

- NEW sections "iSoc: The Sociology of Families" and "Family Transitions, Inequality, and Violence"

- NEW SOCIOLOGY AND OUR WORLD features include:
  - Why Separate Spheres Meant "More Work for Mother"
  - Is There a Shortage of "Marriageable" Men Today?
  - Home Economics, Adoption, and Cornell's "Practice Babies"

- NEW figures, tables, and other features include:
  - FIGURE 12.1 Proportion of U.S. Households, by Type (1940–2016)
  - FIGURE 12.2 Polls of Americans' Attitudes Toward Same-Sex Marriage, 1988–2017
  - MAP 12.1 Same-Sex Marriage Law Around the World
  - TABLE 12.1 Interracial Marriage in U.S. States, 1913
  - FIGURE 12.3 Child Marriage Rates Around the World
  - FIGURE 12.4 Household Earnings by Couple Employment Status and Marital Status among Heterosexual Couples, 2016
  - FIGURE 12.5 Proportions of Men and Women Living Alone by Age Group, 2016
  - FIGURE 12.6 Shifts in the Timing and Sequence of Sex, Marriage, and Reproduction in the United States
  - HOW DO WE KNOW WHAT WE KNOW? Measuring Time Spent
  - FIGURE 12.7 Percent of Childless Women Ages 40–44, 1976–2014
  - FIGURE 12.9 Living Arrangements for U.S. Children, 1960–2014
  - FIGURE 12.10 Intimate Partner Violence Against Women, by Age Group, Race, and Marital Status, 1993–2010
  - FIGURE 12.11 Percentage of Americans who "Agree" or "Strongly Agree" with Spanking as an Important Form of Discipline for Children, 1986–2016

CHAPTER 13: EDUCATION

Content Changes:

- NEW expanded coverage, with entire chapter devoted to education

- NEW sections "Education and Society," "iSoc: The Sociology of Education," "Education as a Mechanism of Social Inequality," "Education Inequality on a Global Scale," "A Report Card on Education in the United States," "Institutional Differences, Interactions, and Inequality," "How Much Does Your School Matter?", "Social Inequality and Institutional Differences," "Tracking," "Understanding Educational Inequality Intersectionally," "Preparing for College," "Gender Segregation in Higher Education," and "Conclusion: Education NOW"

- NEW SOCIOLOGY AND OUR WORLD features include:
  - Single-Sex Schooling and Student Success

- NEW figures, tables, and other features include:
  - FIGURE 13.1 Proportion of Americans 25 and Older with High School or College Degrees, 1940–2016
  - FIGURE 13.2 A Brief Summary of Americans' Understandings of Basic Scientific Knowledge
  - FIGURE 13.3 How Is Education Related to Economic Growth Around the World?
  - FIGURE 13.4 High School Graduation Rates by Gender and Race/Ethnicity, 1972–2014
  - TABLE 13.1 Average Performance on International Student Achievement Tests
  - MAP 13.2 Literacy Rates around the World, by Age Group, 2015
  - FIGURE 13.5 Educational Attainment by Race among Adults Age 25 and Older, 2013

○ FIGURE 13.6 Educational Attainment among Hispanic/Latino People Age 25 and Older, by Ethnicity, 2013

○ MAP 13.3 Rates of College Preparedness, by State

○ FIGURE 13.8 Average SAT Scores of High School Seniors in the United States, 1976–2014

○ FIGURE 13.9 Growth in the Cost of Higher Education, 1976–2017

CHAPTER 14: ECONOMY AND WORK

Content Changes:

- NEW sections "iSoc: The Sociology of Work," "Economies and Politics: Protest and Change," "Workplace Identities, Interactions, and Inequalities," "Gender Diversity: Occupational Segregation," "Emotional and Aesthetic Labor and Inequality"

- NEW SOCIOLOGY AND OUR WORLD features include:
  ○ Cardboard: A Goldmine in a Globalized World
  ○ Are Some Emotions Off Limits for Non-White Employees?
  ○ Do You Have a "Gay" Résumé?

- NEW figures and other features include:
  ○ MAP 14.1 Global Gross Domestic Product (GDP)
  ○ U.S./WORLD The Prosperity of Nations: Nations with the Highest Per Capita Income, 2016
  ○ FIGURE 14.4 Proportion of *Standard & Poor*'s 500 Board Seats Held by Women, by Race, 2014
  ○ FIGURE 14.5 Number of U.S. Workers and Proportions of Men and Women, 1948–2016
  ○ FIGURE 14.6 Median Annual Earnings by Gender, 1960–2014
  ○ FIGURE 14.7 Women as a Proportion of Different Economic Sectors, 1972–2017

CHAPTER 15: POLITICS AND RELIGION

Content Changes:

- NEW combination of politics and religion content provides a global focus

- NEW introductory vignette

- NEW sections "Politics, Religion, and Social Life," "Comparing Politics and Religion," "iSoc: The Sociology of Politics and Religion," "Just How Separate Are Church and State?" "Politics: Class, Status, and Power," "Problems with Political Systems II: Reproducing Intersectional Forms of Inequality," "Political Participation versus Political Apathy," "Thinking about Religion Sociologically: Secularization or Resurgence?" "Thinking Intersectionally: Religious Diversity in the United States," "On the Religiously Unaffiliated," "Politics and Religion in Everyday Life," and "Conclusion: Politics and Religion NOW"

- NEW SOCIOLOGY AND OUR WORLD features include:
  ○ Social Movements and the Media
  ○ Is Religious Pluralism Responsible for Americans' Enduring Religious Beliefs?
  ○ People Espouse Political Opinions Even When They Don't Have an Opinion

- NEW figures and other features include:
  ○ MAP 15.1 The Geography of Apostasy and Blasphemy
  ○ FIGURE 15.1 Numbers of Democracies and Autocracies Around the World, 1915–2015
  ○ HOW DO WE KNOW WHAT WE KNOW? Measuring Democracy
  ○ FIGURE 15.2 Proportion of U.S. Women in Positions of Political Leadership, 1965–2017

- ○ WHAT DO YOU THINK? WHAT DOES AMERICA THINK? Voting and Citizenship
- ○ FIGURE 15.4 Voting Behavior in National Elections in OECD Countries
- ○ MAP 15.2 Felony Disenfranchisement Laws in the United States by State, 2016
- ○ FIGURE 15.5 The Effects of Terrorism in the United States, 1995–2014
- ○ U.S./WORLD Religious Tradition and Variation Around the World
- ○ FIGURE 15.6 Projected Shifts in Religious Populations Around the World, 2010–2050
- ○ FIGURE 15.8 Shifts in Religious Identity in the United States, 2007–2014
- ○ MAP 15.3 The Global Distribution of the Religiously Unaffiliated
- ○ FIGURE 15.9 Growth Among the Religiously Unaffiliated in the United States, 2007–2014
- ○ FIGURE 15.10 Distribution of Race and Ethnicity by U.S. Religious Groups, 2014

CHAPTER 16: SOCIOLOGY OF ENVIRONMENTS: THE NATURAL, PHYSICAL, AND HUMAN WORLD

Content Changes:

- NEW introductory vignette
- NEW sections "iSoc: The Environment," "Environments, High-Risk Technology, and "Normal Accidents," "Environmental Inequalities," and "The Politics of Environments"
- NEW SOCIOLOGY AND OUR WORLD features include:
  - ○ "Missing Women" and "Surplus Men"
  - ○ The Urban Village
- NEW figures, tables, and other features include:
  - ○ FIGURE 16.1 Where Refugees Around the World Found Asylum, 2015
  - ○ TABLE 16.1 Tracking Migration in the United States: How "Magnetic" or "Sticky" Is Your State?
  - ○ FIGURE 16.2 Global Population Pyramid, 2016
  - ○ FIGURE 16.3 Population Growth Around the World: 1960 to 2015
  - ○ MAP 16.1 Percent of Population Living in Urban Areas, by Nation, 2016
  - ○ HOW DO WE KNOW WHAT WE KNOW? Why Facts about Climate Change Do Not Change People's Opinions about Climate Change
  - ○ FIGURE 16.5 Global Death Rate from Natural Disasters, 1900–2013

We hope as you use the book—as a reader or as an instructor—that you will continue to tell us what works and what doesn't, how you respond to different features, and what we might do in the future to improve it. The conversation continues!

Acknowledgments

To say that every book is a conversation is true, but insufficient. Every book is many conversations at once. To be sure, it's a conversation between authors and readers, and it's designed to stimulate conversations among readers themselves. But writing a book is itself saturated with other conversations, and though we cannot possibly do justice to them all, it is important to acknowledge their presence in this process.

First, there are our conversations, as authors, with this field of research and our profession. How have we understood what others have written, their research, and their way of seeing the world? And how can we best communicate that to a new generation of students encountering sociology for the very first time?

We've had conversations with dozens of other sociologists who have read these chapters and provided enormously helpful feedback. Their candor has helped us revise, rethink, and reimagine entire sections of the book, and we are grateful.

Manuscript Reviewers for *Sociology NOW*, Third Edition. Johnie Daniel, Howard University; Joanna Dennis, Florida International University; Mary Gallagher, Kent State University at Stark; William Hale, Belmont University; Arman Mgeryan, Moorpark College; Sandra Nelson, University of Houston, Clear Lake; JoAnn Rogers, Clarkson University; Christina Partin, University of South Florida; Carrie Summers-Nomura, Clackamas Community College; Ruth Thompson-Miller, University of Dayton; Nishanth Sanjithkumar, Southern Illinois University, Carbondale; Gina Petonito, Miami University, Middletown

Manuscript Reviewers for *Sociology NOW: The Essentials*, Second Edition. Andre Arceneaux, St. Louis University; Sheli Bernstein-Goff, West Liberty University; Shannon Carter, University of Central Florida; Ruth A. Chananie-Hill, University of Northern Iowa; Erica Chito Childs, Hunter College; Susan Ciriello, Naugatuck Valley Community College; Theodore Cohen, Ohio Wesleyan University; Laura Colmenero-Chilberg, Black Hills State University; Jason Cummings, Indiana University; Louwanda Evans, Texas A&M University/Blinn College; Siddig Fageir, Tougaloo College; Paul Farcus, Mt. Aloysius College; Carol Fealey, Farmingdale State College; Kathleen Fitzgerald, Columbia College; Pamela J. Forman, University of Wisconsin—Eau Claire; Anita Gardner, Cleveland Community College; Heather Griffiths, Fayetteville State University; Kellie Hagewen, University of Nebraska—Lincoln; Lisa Handler, Community College of Philadelphia; Laura Hansen, University of Massachusetts—Boston; Jennifer Hartsfield, University of Oklahoma; Theresa Hibbert, University of Texas at El Paso; Xuemei Hu, Union County College; A. J. Jacobs, East Carolina University; Tiffany Jenson, University of Oklahoma; Kimberly M. Johanek, Boise State University; Irwin Kantor, Middlesex County College; Mara Kent-Skruch, Anne Arundel Community College; Brian Klocke, SUNY Plattsburgh; Caroline Kozojed, Bismarck State College; Jamee Kristen, University of Nebraska; Todd Krohn, University of Georgia; Amy Lane, University of Missouri; Jynette Larshus, Georgia Southern University; Dwayne Lee, Midlands Technical College; Shelby Longard, Belmont University; Cheryl Maes, University of Nevada, Rio; Fortunata Songora Makene, Worcester State College; Harry Mersmann, San Joaquin Delta College; Melinda Miceli, University of Hartford; Amanda Miller, Ohio State University; Jane Morgan, Cuesta College; David Nicholson, University of Oklahoma; Amy Palder, Georgia State University; Harriet H. Perry, University of Texas at El Paso; Joleen L. Pietrzak, University of South Dakota; Pam Rosenberg, Shippensburg University; Michael Ryan, Dodge City Community College; Teresa Sobieszczyk, University of Montana; Richard Steinhaus, New Mexico Junior College; LaRoyce Sublett, Georgia Perimeter College; Laura Toussaint, Green River Community College; Rollin Watson, Somerset Community College; Joann Watts Sietas, Palomar College; Michael Wehrman, Ohio University; Michael Weissbuch, Xavier University; Shonda Whetstone, Blinn College; Elena Windsong, University of New Mexico; Susan Wortmann, University of Nebraska—Lincoln

Manuscript Reviewers for *Sociology NOW*, First Edition. Boyd Bergeson, Oregon Health and Sciences University; Susan Blackwell, Delgado Community College; Ralph Brown, Brigham Young University; Philip J. Crawford, San Jose Community College; Kris de Welde, University of Colorado at Boulder; Brenda Donelan, Northern State University; Catherine Felton, Central Piedmont Community College; Dian Fitzpatrick, East Stroudsburg University; Risa L. Garelick, Coconino Community College; Ann Marie Hickey, University of Kansas; Candace L. Hinson, Tallahassee City College; Michael L. Hirsch, Huston-Tillotson University; Amitra Hodge, Buffalo State College; Lynette F. Hoelter, University of Michigan; Amy Holzgang, Cerritos College; William Housel, Northwestern Louisiana State University; H. David Hunt, University of Southern Mississippi; Judi Kessler, Monmouth College; Amy Manning Kirk, Sam Houston State University; Jennifer Lerner, Northern Virginia Community College;

Ami Lynch, George Washington University; Karen E. B. McCue, University of New Mexico; Shelley A. McGrath, Southern Illinois University; Abigail McNeely, Austin Community College; Stephanie R. Medley-Rath, University of West Georgia; Sharon Methvin, Clark College; Barbara J. Miller, Pasadena City College; Beth Mintz, University of Vermont; Monique Moleon-Mathews, Indian River Community College; Adam Moskowitz, Columbus State Community College; Elizabeth Pare, Wayne State University; Joseph Keith Price, West Texas A&M University; Cynthia K. S. Reed, Tarrant Community College; Susan Smith-Cunnien, University of St. Thomas; Ryan Spohn, Kansas State University; Marybeth C. Stalp, University of Northern Iowa; Kell J. A. Stone, El Camino College; Richard Valencia, Fresno City College; Dean Wagstaffe, Indian River Community College; Georgie Ann Weatherby, Gonzaga University; Pamela Williams-Paez, Canyons College; S. Rowan Wolf, Portland Community College

Each chapter includes a box called "What Do You Think? What Does America Think?"—a feature that started with contributions from Kathleen Dolan of North Georgia College and State University. These help the students gauge their own opinions next to the results of data from the General Social Survey and other surveys of Americans' opinions. Such a gauge is pedagogically vital. Often our students begin a response to a question with a minimizing feint: "This is just my own personal opinion, but …" What a relief and revelation to see their opinions as socially shared (or not) with others. We continue to be grateful to Kathleen for her efforts to contextualize those "personal opinions."

At the end of each chapter, the "Chapter Review" provides students with a quick, effective recap of the chapter's material—all of which were initially contributed by Lisa Jane Thomassen of Indiana University. I'm grateful to Lisa for her efforts to create precise summaries and interesting review questions for each chapter.

Michael also carried on a conversation with colleagues at Stony Brook University for more than two decades in a department that strongly values high-quality teaching. In particular, he is grateful to his chair, Daniel Levy, for managing such a diverse and collegial department where he has felt so comfortable. Every single one of his colleagues—both past and present—has assisted him in some way in the work on this book, guiding his encounter with areas of his or her expertise, providing an example he or she has used in class, or commenting on specific text. And we are grateful to them all.

There has also been an ongoing conversation with our students, both graduate and undergraduate, throughout our careers. They've kept us attentive to the shifts in the field and committed to working constantly on our own pedagogical strategies to communicate them. Michael's teaching assistants over the years have been especially perceptive—and unafraid to communicate their thoughts and opinions!

Michael has spent his entire career teaching in large public universities—UC Berkeley, UC Santa Cruz, Rutgers, and now Stony Brook—and teaching undergraduate students who are, overwhelmingly, first-generation college students, many of whom are immigrants and members of minority groups. They represent the next generation of Americans, born not to privilege but to hope and ambition. More than any other single group, they have changed how he sees the world.

Many other sociologists have influenced Michael's thinking over the years as well. Were he to list them all, the list would go on for pages! So we only thank some recent friends and colleagues here who have contributed their advice, comments, or criticisms on specific items in this book, and those old friends who have shared their passion for sociology for decades: Elizabeth Armstrong, Troy Duster, Paula England, Cynthia and Howard Epstein, Abby Ferber, John Gagnon, Josh Gamson, Erich Goode, Cathy Greenblat, Michael Kaufman, Mike Messner, Rebecca Plante, Lillian Rubin, Don Sabo, Wendy Simonds, Arlene and Jerry Skolnick, and Suzanna Walters.

For the rest of Michael's far-flung friends and colleagues, we hope that you will find the fruits of those conversations somewhere in these pages.

Tristan also relied on colleagues, friends, and family in an attempt to make the book more useful, engaging, and often, just to mentally unload and unwind. Tristan is particularly grateful to Tara Leigh Tober who discussed this revision at length and provided so many ideas to use as illustrations. Tara's enthusiasm for this project and support helped us every time we came up blank in considering how to best explain complex social phenomena in an engaging way. Additionally, Tristan would like to thank Rosemary Eichas and Jim Tober who helped care for Tara and his children during the years he was working on this project. Sarah Diefendorf provided fact-checking help and assistance with updates to facts and figures in the third edition—but she also was a useful colleague to bounce ideas off of and to ask how material read and flowed in the book. C.J. Pascoe and D'Lane Compton were friends and colleagues throughout this project, helping provide support, suggestions and ideas, many of which are reflected in the revisions for this new edition. Additionally, Tristan would like to acknowledge conversations, help, and assistance from: Melody Boyd, Matthew Hughey, Sharon Preves, Elliot Weininger, Denise Copelton, Amy Guptill, Julie Ford, Lisa Wade, and Philip Cohen. Finally, Tristan wants to thank his family (John, Kathy, Kevin, Grainne, Joe, Jim, Livy, Jarrod, Portia, Rob, Ryann, Alana, and Joey) for putting up with a lot of sociology talk over the past couple years as this project came together. He couldn't have done it without their support.

One person stands out as deserving of special thanks. Jeffery Dennis began his career as Michael's graduate student—an enormously gifted one at that. We engaged Jeff as a colleague to work with us to develop the first edition of this book—to help us develop chapters, explore arguments, clarify examples, track down obscure factoids, organize thematic presentations—and with everything we asked of him, he delivered far more than we hoped. He helped to launch this project.

A textbook of this size and scale is also the result of a conversation between author and publisher—and there we have been enormously lucky to work with such a talented and dedicated team as we have at Pearson. We've had a series of editors and production teams, and we've been so lucky that Pearson continues to hire such talented people. Billy Greico inherited us, and guided this project through for several years before handing it off, at the one-yard line, to Jeff Marshall, who pushed us over the goal line. Our development and production team, especially Renee Eckhoff, Megan Vertucci, and Brooke Wilson, have been superb in shepherding the project through its various production stages.

At the beginning of this preface, I said I was really lucky because my job is so amazingly rewarding and because I get to do something that is in harmony with my values, with how I see the world.

But I'm also really lucky because I get to do virtually everything—including the writing of this book—with my wife, Amy Aronson. Amy is a professor of journalism and media studies at Fordham University; she comes to her sociological imagination through her background in the humanities and her experiences as a magazine editor (*Working Woman*). In the writing of this book, we have been completely equal partners—this is the only part I have written myself. (Don't worry—she edited it!)

Amy thanks her colleagues at Fordham University, Lincoln Center, for their support and various helpful comments. She's grateful always to Robert Ferguson for his unwavering encouragement over the years.

And we both thank our respective families—Winnie Aronson, Barbara Diamond, Sandi Kimmel, and Patrick Murphy, for believing in us and cheering us on.

And we thank Zachary, our son. Now 18, and about to enter college himself—maybe he'll use this book! He's been a lively critic of some of our ideas, a curious listener, and a patient family member. (He helped pick some of the pictures!) Every single day, when he recounts the day's events at school, or is at soccer practice, or observes something in the neighborhood, or asks a question about the news, he reminds us of the importance of a sociological perspective in making sense of the world.

And finally I thank Amy. As partners in our lives, as parents to our son, and in our collaboration on this and other books, we work toward a marriage of equals, in which the idea of gender equality is a lived reality, not some utopian dream.

Michael Kimmel, Distinguished Professor of Sociology at Stony Brook University, is one of the pioneers in the sociology of gender and one of the world's leading experts on men and masculinities. He was the first man to deliver the International Women's Day lecture at the European Parliament; he was the first man to be named the annual lecturer by the Sociologists for Women in Society; and he has been called as an expert witness in several high-profile gender discrimination cases. Among his many books are *Men's Lives, The Gendered Society, Manhood in America*, and *Revolution: A Sociological Perspective*. He is also known for his ability to explain sociological ideas to a general audience. His articles have appeared in dozens of magazines and newspapers, including *The New York Times, The Nation, The Village Voice, The Washington Post*, and *Psychology Today*.

Amy Aronson is Associate Professor of Journalism and Media Studies at Fordham University. She is the author of *Taking Liberties: Early American Women's Magazines and Their Readers* and an editor of the international quarterly, *Media History*. She has coedited several books, including a centennial edition of Charlotte Perkins Gilman's *Women and Economics* and the two-volume *Encyclopedia of Men and Masculinities*, which was honored by the New York Public Library with a Best of Reference Award in 2004. A former editor at *Working Woman* and *Ms. Magazine*, she has also written for publications including *BusinessWeek, Global Journalist*, and the Sunday supplement of *The Boston Globe*.

Tristan Bridges is Assistant Professor of Sociology at the University of California, Santa Barbara. He is the coeditor of *Exploring Masculinities: Identity, Inequality, Continuity, and Change* and book review editor at *Men and Masculinities*. Tristan has also published extensively on issues to do with transformations in masculinity and gender and sexual inequality and is an avid public sociologist.

About the Supplements

Instructor Supplements

Unless otherwise noted, instructor's supplements are available at no charge to adopters and available in printed or duplicated formats, as well as electronically through the Pearson Higher Education Instructor Resource Center (www.pearsonhighered.com/irc) *as well as in the* instructor Resources folder within the Revel product.

Instructor's Manual

For each chapter in the text, the Instructor's Manual provides chapter summaries and outlines, teaching suggestions (which include film suggestions, projects, and homework exercises), discussion questions, and references for further research and reading.

Test Bank

The Test Bank contains approximately 50 questions per chapter in multiple-choice and essay formats. All questions are tagged with a Learning Objective, Topic, Difficulty Level, and Skill Level.

MyTest Computerized Test Bank

The printed Test Bank is also available online through Pearson's computerized testing system, MyTest. This fully networkable test-generating program is available online. The user-friendly interface allows you to view, edit, and add questions; transfer questions to tests; and print tests in a variety of fonts. Search and sort features allow you to locate questions quickly and to arrange them in whatever order you prefer. The Test Bank can be accessed anywhere with a free MyTest user account. There is no need to download a program or a file to your computer.

PowerPoint™ Presentation

Completely new PowerPoint™ slides in three formats, lecture, art only, and LiveSlides, bring the powerful Kimmel content and design right into the classroom, drawing students into the lecture and providing wonderful visuals. The LiveSlides include every Social Explorer data visualization and interactive map within the Revel product. Visit the Resources folder within Revel for *Sociology NOW*, Third Edition or the Pearson Higher Education Resource Center (www.pearsonhighered.com/irc) for these and other invaluable teaching tools.

CHAPTER 1

WHAT IS SOCIOLOGY?

Most people reading this book are likely not homeless, though some of you may have been at some point in your life. When we see images like this, they put the poles of possibility in a society into relief: money and status alongside poverty and hardship. Sociologists are interested in understanding how differences like these are defined by societies. The ways societies are organized shape our life possibilities. While many grow up in the U.S. believing that anyone can be the president or famous or a millionaire, sociologists want to understand—among other things—whether these kinds of aspirations are as plausible for different groups. To sociologists, it is axiomatic that our lives are often subject to forces far beyond our control. And learning to look at the world this way is part of the process of learning to see sociologically.

→ LEARNING OBJECTIVES

In this chapter, using the iSoc framework, you should be able to:

1.1.1 Understand the sociological imagination as both a set of skills and as a way of seeing.

1.1.2 Summarize why sociologists study the order and organization of societies.

1.1.3 Explain why sociologists study both social order and social disorder.

1.1.4 Using the nature–nurture debate as an example, explain why what passes as "common sense" is often more complicated than it first appears.

1.2.1 Define the first three components of the iSoc perspective (identity, intersectionality, and inequality), as well as how they are interrelated.

1.2.2 Define the final two components of the iSoc perspective (interactions and institutions) as well as how they are interrelated.

1.2.3 Explain how sociologists look at changes in popular baby names to describe changes in other parts of society.

1.2.4 Summarize the ways that trends in baby names illustrate each element of the iSoc perspective.

1.3.1 Understand how "The Enlightenment" is connected with challenges to the social order that created a new way of understanding society and inequalities between different groups.

1.3.2 Understand how the Industrial Revolution changed almost everything about the societies it affected and how this created new fears about whether and how society could persist.

1.3.3 Describe the issues that motivated classical sociological thinkers to create a science of society—consider the types of questions they were asking and why they sought answers.

1.3.4 Explain how contemporary sociologists build on classical sociological thinkers and what

kinds of new and different questions they are asking.

1.4.1 Understand how and why globalization and multiculturalism are central issues for sociologists to study today.

1.4.2 Explain the ways that globalization and multiculturalism are interrelated forces in the world today.

Introduction

It was the best of times, it was the worst of times, it was the age of wisdom, it was the age of foolishness, it was the epoch of belief, it was the epoch of incredulity, it was the season of Light, it was the season of Darkness, it was the spring of hope, it was the winter of despair, we had everything before us, we had nothing before us, we were all going direct to Heaven, we were all going direct the other way—in short, the period was so far like the present period.

Charles Dickens (1859)

These are the first lines of one of Western literature's greatest novels, *A Tale of Two Cities* by Charles Dickens. In it, Dickens recounts the saga of the French Revolution, a period of unparalleled optimism about the possibilities of human freedom and some of the most barbaric and repressive measures ever taken in the name of that freedom.

Well, which is it: best or worst? Dickens insisted that it was both—and there lies the essence of sociological thinking. Most of the time, it's difficult to hold both ideas in our heads at the same time. More often, we take a position—usually at one extreme or the other—and then try to hold it in the face of any evidence that suggests otherwise. Logic and common sense insist that it can't possibly be both.

That's what makes sociology so fascinating. Sociology is constantly wrestling with two immense and seemingly contradictory questions, social order and social disorder—how it often feels that everything fits together perfectly, like a smoothly functioning machine, and how it often feels as if society is coming apart at the seams. If every single individual is simply doing what is best for himself or herself, why is there any social order at all? Why are we not constantly at war with each other? And how is order maintained? How is society possible in the first place?

On the other hand, why does it often seem that society is falling apart? Why do so many people in society disobey its laws, disagree about its values, and differ about the political and social goals of the society? Why is there so much crime and delinquency? Why is there so much inequality? Why does society keep changing?

These sorts of giant questions are what sociology sets out to answer. Sociologists analyze the ways that social institutions like family, marketplace, military, and government serve to sustain social order and how problems like inequality, poverty, and racial, gender, or sexual discrimination make it feel as if it is falling apart. And it turns out that most of the answers aren't so obvious or commonsensical after all.

1.1 Sociology as a Way of Seeing

sociology
The study of human behavior in society.

If you're like most people, you know that **sociology** is the study of human behavior in society. But we don't typically ask much more than that. What is society? And how do we study it?

Unlike other social sciences, the field of sociology is not immediately evident from just its name, like economics or political science. Nor are there many TV or movie characters who are sociologists, as there are psychologists (like Dr. Phil) or anthropologists (Indiana Jones). In the classic movie *Animal House*, the protagonist encounters two sorority girls at a party. The writers wanted to portray these girls as gum-chomping, air-headed idiots. So what are they majoring in? Right—sociology.

Sociology sets for itself the task of trying to answer certain basic questions about our lives: the nature of identity, why some people seem to have more than others, and our relationships with others. Sociologists try to explain the paradoxes that we daily observe in the world around us: for example, how economic changes bring us closer and closer, and, at the same time, we fragment into smaller religious, tribal, or ethnic enclaves. Or how we observe that society is divided into different unequal groups based on class, race, ethnicity, sexuality, and gender, despite the fact that, at the same time, everyone's values are remarkably similar.

Every field that ends in "–ology" is a science of something. Sociology is the science of society. And like every other science, it is simultaneously a field of study and an orientation to the world. Sociology is both a field of study and a way of seeing—it is both a science and a perspective. Learning to understand sociology, thus, involves two tasks: You will become familiar with the types of things that sociologists study as well as how it is that sociologists go about studying them. But, you must also learn to think about the world and look at it as a sociologist. This latter skill is sometimes just as challenging to achieve as the former.

Beyond Either–Or: Seeing Sociologically

1.1.1 Understand the sociological imagination as both a set of skills and as a way of seeing.

As a field, perhaps the pithiest definition was written 50 years ago, by C. Wright Mills (1959), a professor at Columbia University. Sociology, he wrote, is an "imagination," a way of seeing, a way of "connecting biography to history." What Mills means is that the **sociological imagination** sees our lives as *contextual* lives—our individual identities are understandable only in the social contexts in which we find ourselves. So, our race, gender, class, or sexual identities can only be understood within the social and historical contexts in which they are made meaningful. A sociological perspective is a perspective that examines connections and contexts. Sociology connects you to the worlds in which you live.

sociological imagination

The ability to see the connection between our individual identities and the social contexts (family, friends, and institutions) in which we find ourselves.

SOCIOLOGY AND OUR WORLD

THE SOCIOLOGICAL IMAGINATION

Part of learning to think sociologically involves learning to understand yourself and the various identities you have as a lot less unique than you might imagine them to be. What does this mean?

In his famous essay, C. Wright Mills (1959) argued that the sociological imagination "enables us to grasp history and biography and the relations between the two within society. That is its task and its promise." This means connecting our individual lives to the large-scale events in the world, seeing the impact of such things as climate change, economic shifts, or immigration on our sense of ourselves and on our day-to-day interactions with others. This sometimes comes as a great relief, to know that we don't create our lives in some vacuum but rather in relationship to others, in a specific time and place. We're not alone. On the other hand, it does mean that we are less "special" than we might like to think: that the unique people we feel ourselves to be are in constant relationship to the world around us. We may choose our own direction, but we choose from a rather limited set of options. And it's sociology's task to explore what those options are by examining the forces that limit our choices. Thus, sociology is not only about how we create our identity, but also about what sorts of resources we use to construct it.

To help orient you to the field of sociology, read again the quote that begins this chapter. Now, take a look at your local daily newspaper or watch your local TV news. Notice how often they're telling you how things are getting worse, much worse than they've ever been. Crime threatens our safety, teenage drinking and drug use are epidemic, fundamentalist fanatics make the entire world unsafe. The media fret about the spiraling divorce rate, teen pregnancies, and the collapse of marriage; or we worry about new strains of diseases, like Zika virus or about old diseases like smallpox being unleashed as weapons, and about the microbial dangers lurking in our food. We fret about the collapse of morality and the decline in religion. Is the country falling apart?

Perhaps the opposite is true. We're also bombarded with stories about the enormous social changes that have made the world a smaller and smaller place, where millions of people can communicate with one another in an instant. Dramatic technological breakthroughs expand the possibilities for trade, cultural exchange, and economic development. Scientific advances make it possible to live longer, healthier lives than any people who have ever lived. The mapping of the human genome may enable scientists to eliminate many of the diseases that have plagued human beings for millennia while the rise of the Internet will enable us to communicate that knowledge in a heartbeat. Americans are going to college in greater numbers, and today we have women, African American, Asian American, Hispanic, and gay CEOs, corporate board members, and business owners. Freedom and democracy have spread throughout the world. Is society getting better and better?

To the sociologist, neither of these polar positions is completely true—nor completely false. The sociologist is as concerned about the collapse of traditional social institutions and values as he or she is about the extraordinary ways society is improving. Sociologists see *both* sides at once. They don't think in "either–or"; they usually think in "both–and." And what's more, sociologists don't see the glass half-full or half-empty, as the classic formulation of optimist or pessimist goes. Sociologists see the glass half full—and want to know where the other half went and if anyone is getting more than anyone else. They see the glass half-empty and want to know about the quality of the water as well.

For example, as you'll see in this book, most sociologists believe our identities come from *both* nature and nurture; that people are getting *both* richer and poorer (it depends on which people in what places); that our racial and ethnic identities *both* draw us closer together and further fragment us.

Making Connections: Sociological Dynamics

1.1.2 Summarize why sociologists study the order and organization of societies.

The sociologist is interested in the connections between things getting better and things getting worse. In our globalizing world, where daily the farthest reaches of the world are ever more tightly connected to every other part, where changes in one remote corner of Earth ripple through the rest of society, affecting every other institution—in such a world, the sociologist attempts to see both integration and disintegration and the ways in which the one is related to the other.

Take one example. In New York City, we are occasionally aghast that some innocent person, calmly waiting on a subway platform, is pushed in front of an oncoming train and killed—all for apparently no reason at all. On the freeway, we daily hear of cases of "road rage" that got a little out of control. Instead of being content with giving each other the finger and cursing at the tops of our lungs, occasionally someone gets really carried away and pulls a gun out of the glove compartment and opens fire on a stranger, whose only "crime" might have been to have cut that person off. Immediately, the headlines blare that society is falling apart, that violence is on

Half-full or half-empty? We often think we have to choose, but sociologists see the glass as both half-full and half-empty—and explore the relationship between the two halves. Context also matters: When are we seeing the picture? If the water's just been poured, the glass is half full. If you've just been drinking from it, it's half empty. Besides, how big is the glass? A champagne glass or a shot glass?

the rise. Psychologists offer therapeutic salve and warn of the increasing dangers of urban or suburban life. "It's a jungle out there," we'll say to ourselves. "These people are nuts."

But sociologists also ask another sort of question: How can so many people drive on clogged freeways, on too-little sleep, inching along for hours, surrounded by maniacs who are gabbing on their cell phones, ignoring speed limits and basic traffic safety—many also going either toward or away from stressful jobs or unbalanced home lives? How can we stuff nearly 2 million human beings, who neither know one another nor care very much for any of them, into large metal containers, packed like sardines, hurtling through dark tunnels at more than 60 miles an hour? How is it possible that these same people don't get so murderously angry at their conditions that people aren't pushed in front of subway trains at every single subway stop every single day of the year? How come more people aren't driving armed and dangerous, ready to shoot anyone who worsens an already difficult morning commute?

Is it simply the threat of coercion—that we'd all be wreaking murder and mayhem if we weren't afraid of getting caught? We think it's something more, and that's what sociology—and this book—is about.

Sociological Understanding

1.1.3 Explain why sociologists study both social order and social disorder.

Our interest is not entirely in social order, nor is it entirely social disintegration and disorder. Let's return for a moment to that person who pushed someone in front of a subway train. Sure, that person probably needs to have his or her head examined. But a sociologist might also ask about governmental policies that deinstitutionalized millions of mentally ill people, forcing them onto ever-shrinking welfare rolls and often into dramatically overcrowded prisons. And perhaps we need also to examine the income disparities that collide in our major cities—disparities that make the United States perhaps the most unequal industrial country and the modern city as the most heterogeneous collection of people from different countries, of different races, speaking different languages, in the entire world.

And what about that person who opened fire on a passing motorist? Can we discuss this frightening event without also discussing the availability of guns in America and the

Chaos or order? Cars, buses, rickshaws, bicycles, and pedestrians crowd the street in Dhaka, Bangladesh, in what appears to be a jumble. Yet everyone manages to get where they are going, without much violence or many accidents.

paucity of effective gun control laws? Shouldn't we also discuss suburban and urban sprawl, overwork, the number and size of cars traveling on decaying roads built for one-tenth that many? Or maybe it's just those shock jocks that everyone is listening to in their cars—the guys who keep telling us not to just get mad but to get even?

A comparison with other countries is usually helpful (see U.S./WORLD How Globalized Are We?). No other industrial country has this sort of road rage deaths; they are far more common in countries ruled by warlords, in which a motorist might unknowingly drive on "their" piece of the highway. And though many other industrial nations have intricate and elaborate subway systems, people being pushed in front of trains is exceedingly rare. And are those same countries far more homogeneous than the United States with well-financed institutions for the mentally ill or with a more balanced income structure? Or maybe it's that people who live in those countries are just more content with their lives than we are.

U.S./WORLD

HOW GLOBALIZED ARE WE?

The forces of globalization are evident in our daily lives, from the 3.6 billion people worldwide who watched the Rio Olympics in 2016, to the financial crisis that began with mortgage lenders in the United States and quickly sapped markets around the world. Four components have been used to measure the level of globalization: trade and investment flows, the migration of people across borders, use of communication technologies, and participation in international organizations. The KOF Globalization index relies on information about economic, social, and political globalization to come up with a globalization score for each country. Which countries are the most globalized in the world—and which are the least?

Top 10 Most Globalized Countries	Top 10 Least Globalized Countries
1. Netherlands	1. Virgin Islands (U.S.)
2. Ireland	2. Somalia
3. Belgium	3. San Marino
4. Austria	4. Democratic Republic of Korea
5. Switzerland	5. Northern Mariana Islands
6. Singapore	6. Marshall Islands
7. Denmark	7. Monaco
8. Sweden	8. Liechtenstein
9. Hungary	9. Isle of Man
10. Canada	10. Guam

SOURCE: Data from KOF Index of Globalization (2016). Available at http://globalization.kof.ethz.ch/.

INVESTIGATE FURTHER

1. What factors do you think might explain the discrepancies between the most and the least globalized countries?

2. What social effects do you think the size of the globalization gap might have?

Getting beyond "Common Sense"

1.1.4 Using the nature–nurture debate as an example, explain why what passes as "common sense" is often more complicated than it first appears.

Sociology is not just "common sense," not simply what everybody knows. In fact, very often what "everybody knows" turns out, after sociological examination and study, not to be true. Commonsense explanations trade in stereotypes—"women are more nurturing"; "men are more aggressive"—that are almost never true of everyone. What's more, common sense assumes that such patterns are universal and timeless—that, for example, men and women are from different planets (Mars and Venus) and that we're programmed somehow to be completely alien creatures. But what if you actually decide you want to be different—that you want to be an aggressive woman or a nurturing man? Can you? Commonsense explanations have no room for variation, and they have no history. And they leave no room for freedom of choice.

Take, for example, that tired argument between "nature" and "nurture." It describes a debate about whether we behave the ways we do because our biology, our "nature," determines our actions—as they say, because we are "hard-wired" to do so—or because our ancestors millions of years ago found it to their evolutionary advantage to behave in such a way to ensure their survival? Or, in contrast, do we do the things we do because we have been taught to do them, socialized virtually from the moment we are born by institutions that are bigger and more powerful than we are?

Nature and nurture: LeBron James may have been born with prodigious athletic ability, but if he didn't have lots of help along the way, and practice extraordinarily hard, he would never have become the one of the greatest basketball players in the history of the NBA.

To the sociologist, the answer is clear but complex. Our behavior does not result from *either* nature *or* nurture; our behavior results from *both* nature *and* nature. Looking through a sociological lens reveals that it's not a question of either–or. It's all about seeing both–and as well as investigating how that relationship is playing out. Of course the things we do are the result of millennia of evolutionary adaptation to our environments, and of course we are biologically organized to do some things and not others. But that environment also includes the social environment. We adapt to the demands and needs of the social contexts in which we find ourselves, too. And we frequently override our biological drives to do things that we are *also* biologically programmed to do. Just as we are hardwired to preserve ourselves at all costs, we are also biologically programmed to sacrifice our own lives for the survival of the group or for our offspring.

But to the sociologist, the two sides of the nature–nurture debate share one thing in common: Each considers the individual person a passive object of larger forces, with no real ability to act for himself or herself and therefore no role in history. According to the either–or perspective, nature or nurture, we can't help doing what we do: We're either biologically destined or socially programmed to act as we do. "Sorry, it's in my genes!" is pretty much the same thing as "Sorry, I was socialized to do it!" Neither of these positions sees the *interaction* of those forces as decisive. That is the domain of sociology.

What makes a more thorough analysis of social life possible and makes the sociological perspective possible is the way we have crafted the lens through which we view social problems and processes. It is a lens that requires that we see events in their contexts and yet remain aware of how we, as individuals, shape both the contexts and the events in which we participate.

A sociological perspective helps you to see how the events and problems that preoccupy us today are timeless; they do not come from nowhere. They have a history. They are the result of the actions of large-scale forces—forces that are familial, communal, regional, national, or global. And they enable you to see the connections between those larger-scale forces and your own experience, your own participation in them. Sociologists understand that this history is not written beforehand; it is changeable, so that you can exert some influence on how it turns out.

That's why Mills's definition of the sociological imagination, the connection between biography and history, is as compelling today as when it was written half a century ago. Sociology connects you, as an individual, to the larger processes of both stability and change that comprise history. Sociologists see the link between your identity and larger structures of inequality. And we see identity and inequality in constant operation, in every interaction with others and in every institution in which we find ourselves. We call it "iSoc."

WHAT DO YOU THINK? WHAT DOES AMERICA THINK?

How Scientific Is Sociology?

Some people perceive great differences between what are sometimes referred to as the "hard" and "soft" sciences—with the former being more "scientific" than the latter.

What do you think?

- ○ Sociology is very scientific.
- ○ Sociology is pretty scientific.
- ○ Sociology is not too scientific.
- ○ Sociology is not scientific at all
- ○ I haven't heard of it.

What does America think?

The question "How scientific is sociology?" has been asked on the General Social Survey to a random sample of Americans in 2006 and again in 2012. Although Americans in general appear uncertain of the status of sociology, they rated sociology as more scientific in 2012 than they did in 2016. See how Americans' opinions changed over these 2 years:

	2006	2012
very scientific	8.6%	10.2%
pretty scientific	43.8%	40.7%
not too scientific	30.3%	32.9%
not scientific at all	9.1%	7.7%
haven't heard of it	8.2%	8.5%

SOURCE: Data from General Social Survey, 2006 and 2012.

Today, around 1 in 10 Americans suggests that sociology is a "very scientific" field. Interestingly, this belief is highly correlated with education. Those with graduate degrees rate sociology as "very scientific" at a rate of about 1 in 6 as of 2012.

THINKING CRITICALLY ABOUT SURVEY DATA

In 2012, more than 50 percent of Americans ranked sociology as a field as either "pretty" or "very" scientific. Perhaps you'll reconsider your assessment of the field over the course of your reading this text and taking the associated class. What do you think? Just how scientific is sociology?

---

iSOC AND YOU Sociology as a Way of Seeing

Sociology is about you—not as some free-floating individual, who somehow magically plopped down where you are right now, but someone with a story, a history, a background, a context. You are socially located in all the locations that make you a unique person because of larger historical and social circumstances. Sociology understands your roots, but also measures the conditions of the soil and light and nutrients. But it doesn't tell the branches exactly which way they should bend toward the sun, though it provides lots of clues for where you might end up or will likely end up. But, sociologists also know that you're still you.

1.2 iSoc: Sociological Frames of Analysis

Every academic field uses a framework or a lens through which to view the phenomena it observes, a "story" that is the field's master narrative. For example, for economists, it's how individual rational actors interact to maximize their individual interests in a self-regulating market. For psychologists, it's that what makes us human is our minds—whether we try and understand it through dreams, cognition, developmentally, or by brain chemistry. For anthropologists, it's how people form and sustain lasting communities, whether by symbolic or material means.

For sociologists, as C. Wright Mills said, it's how to locate your biography in history—that is, sociology is about who you are—but in context. Because the sociological lens examines the "both–and" and not the "either–or," we can explain the sociological framework with two sets of "I's": (1) *Identity, Intersectionality*, and *Inequality*, and (2) *Interaction* and *Institution*. Understanding these five "I's" is what we mean by the sociological perspective—or, as we like to call it, "iSoc."

Sociology is about your identity but in the context of social dynamics, and particularly the unequal distribution of rewards, or what we'll call inequality. And it's about the processes by which we experience identity and inequality, both in our daily interactions with others and in every institution in which we find ourselves. More than that, it's about the connections *between* identity and inequality, and *between* interactions and institutions, and also about the connections between identity and inequality on the one hand, and interaction and institutions on the other. Sociologists examining these connections are looking at intersections. Learning to see the world around you from the perspective of iSoc is what it means to understand the sociological perspective.

Identity, Intersectionality, and Inequality

1.2.1 Define the first three components of the iSoc perspective (identity, intersectionality, and inequality) as well as how they are interrelated.

Sociology is concerned with identity: what makes you *you*. Who are you? How do you know? How do you become who you are? Really, you have a collection of identities that all overlap to shape what you come to think of as a singular identity. Your age, race, ethnicity, social class, gender, sexuality, religion, height, musical interests, talents, and abilities all help to construct your **identity**. And each element of your identity affects each of the others, producing a unique individual—the sum of all those overlapping identities—and a distinct way in which each of those affects where you will end up in society. So, somewhat paradoxically, what makes you unique is your connections with other people and groups. It turns out that some of the very factors that you use to construct your social identity are those factors that express the unequal distribution of rewards in society. The combination of all these factors is what sociologists mean when they use the term **intersectionality**. Sociologists are interested in the ways that

identity

The unique combination of group affiliations and social characteristics that each individual develops.

intersectionality

Sociological term for the ways that different identities "intersect" with one another to shape our social identity and our experience of inequality.

social inequality

The social process by which valued goods, opportunities, and experiences are unequally distributed throughout a population.

social groups

A collection of individuals bound by a common social identity or by some shared goal and purpose.

different identities "intersect" with one another to shape our social identity and our experience of **social inequality**).

Take, for example, an exercise I often do in my introductory sociology class. Write down five social groups to which you belong, that define who you are, from which you derive your identity. I don't mean five adjectives that describe you, like "tall" or "pretty." I mean **social groups**. Here is what happens in my classes. Very few men write down "male" or "man" but almost all the women write down "female" or "woman." Virtually no white students write down "white" but virtually all the students of color write down their race. No one has ever written down "English" or "Scottish" but lots of students with Italian, Turkish, Korean, and with other racial or ethnic heritage write that down. Almost no one writes down "Protestant," but I get a lot of Jewish, Catholic, evangelical, and Muslim responses that note religion. Most wealthy students don't say anything about class—indeed, few middle-class students do. But poor students often say something about being poor or working class. I have rarely seen anyone write down "heterosexual" or "straight," but virtually every single out LGBT student makes note of their sexual orientation or transgender identity. Able-bodied students rarely think of this as a central element of their identity, but students with disabilities always write it down.

What do you make of this? It's not that young men with English ancestry, who are straight, white, and Methodists don't use gender ethnicity, sexuality, race, and religion to construct their identities. Of course they do! But what a sociologist makes of this is that the aspects of our identity that are the most visible to us are often those in which we feel we do not fit into the mainstream, by which we are discriminated against.

Consider another example. You probably use Google to search the Web all the time; most of you reading this probably rely on Google in one capacity or another every day. But when you go to the website www.Google.com, you may not be aware that you are actually searching the Web as an American. Have you ever thought about why it's uncommon to have Japanese websites suggested to you after you search for something on Google? Or Irish websites or Mexican websites? If you are from a country outside of the United States or if you have visited a website from another country, you may have noticed an important difference in the Web address—it ends with a "country code." So, for example, if you were searching google in Ireland, you'd have to visit www.Google.co.ie (the ".ie" is the country code). You'd finish the Web address to search Google in South Africa with ".za," or ".jp" for Japan, or ".uk" for England (United Kingdom), or ".mx" for Mexico.

But when you search Google in the United States, you simply use ".com" (which is digital shorthand used for "commercial"—a designation for websites). ".com" is not the country code for the United States. We simply don't have one. Why is it that the United States doesn't have a country code? The aspects of our identity that are most visible to us are those in which we experience inequality. As a powerful nation, one privilege Americans receive is that their national identity is often invisible to them on a daily basis. Even on the Internet!

Identity and inequality are not separate features of social life. They are linked. And, identities intersect with one another to shape different and unequal opportunities and experiences for different groups. The most visible elements of our identities are often those aspects that are based on social inequality.

Google websites are a powerful illustration of an invisible privilege Americans receive. In other countries, Google websites remind users where they are geographically located (as in "Google France" for instance). Here, Google France changed the home page in January of 2015, reading "Je Suis Charlie" (I Am Charlie) following an Islamic terrorist attack on the main offices of the satirical magazine, *Charlie Hedbo*.

Interactions and Institutions

1.2.2 Define the final two components of the iSoc perspective (interactions and institutions) as well as how they are interrelated.

How are identity and inequality linked? That's the other both–and pairing: Sociologists look at different levels of social life, different patterns of behavior. Identity isn't something that is done *to* you. You construct your identity actively, through your interactions. But you undertake this process in circumstances not entirely of your choosing—you construct it in social arenas, what sociologists call **social institutions**. Institutions are patterned sets of interactions that work to meet collective needs that are not easily met by individuals working alone. They include such social arenas as markets, families, schools, corporations, factories, and prisons.

Often we think of these as two separate levels of analysis—micro and macro, for example. And, yes, sociologists often study society and social life from one level or the other. But we are also interested in the relationships *between* the two, between our day-to-day interactions with our friends, for example, and the social institutions in which those interactions take place. After all, you don't exactly interact with your friends the same way in church as you might on a sports field. Your interactions aren't the same in front of your parents or your teachers as they are when you are by yourselves.

Perhaps you've had that uncomfortable experience when a professor walked into a bar where you were hanging out with your friends. Or imagine the way you might interact with your instructor if you were to invite him or her over for dinner with your family. What would happen if your instructor turned to you, in the course of the conversations, and said "You might want to take notes on what I'm going to say next. It's important." You'd think he or she was truly strange, right? And what if he or she turned to your parents and said that? You'd think he or she was crazy.

Why? Because the way we interact with others often depends on the context of that interaction. Those patterns of interaction are how we express and achieve our identity, but we shape it differently depending on where we are.

Looking at the world from a sociological perspective can be a little disorienting. One sociological truism is that we are a lot less in control of our lives than we often like to believe. It doesn't mean that we exert no control over our lives, but various social forces push us around and encourage us to take some paths over others. Learning to understand how this works and what the consequences of it are requires learning to look at the world around you like a sociologist. And the trouble with learning to *see* like a sociologist is that sociologists don't actually see in just one way. They have a variety of ways of looking at and analyzing the world around them. It depends on what questions they are asking, where they are, what they hope to highlight, and more.

Think about it this way: Have you ever been to the eye doctor to be fitted for a pair of glasses? Even if you haven't, you'll probably recognize the device I'm talking about. Eye doctors refer to it as a refractor and it's a common device used by eye-care professionals in an eye examination. It's the device the eye care professional asks you to sit up and look through when they determine whether you need glasses and, if you do, what prescription. It looks like a pair of high tech binoculars with lots of knobs on them for adjustment. Typically, patients sit down looking through the refractor at an eye chart placed on the wall. As a patient, your job is simply to tell your eye-care professional when an adjustment makes your vision clearer, or less focused. The lens you look through is changing; the idea is to find the lens that works best for you, the lens that helps you see the world as clearly as possible. Sometimes, the eye chart is then moved closer to you and you do the exercise again because some people require a separate lens for reading. Pairs of glasses with two prescriptions built in are called bifocals. They allow people to look through their glasses one way throughout much of their life, but read through a separate lens.

Learning to see the world around you from the perspective of the iSoc model requires five separate lenses—one for each component: *identity, interaction, intersections, institutions,* and *inequality.* Sometimes, sociologists are looking through just one of those lenses, such as when they look for patterns in social interactions. More commonly, sociologists use overlapping lenses or examine the same phenomenon from various different perspectives.

Think about the example of identity formation. How do we come to understand who *we* are? Sociologists have long been interested in the question of social identity. So, they will

social institutions
Patterned sets of interactions that work to meet collective needs that are not easily met by individuals working alone. They include such social arenas as markets, families, schools, corporations, factories, and prisons.

be looking through the *identity* lens. But, understanding how people come to understand who they are requires examining the social interactions that help shape their sense of self. So, we need to include the *interaction* lens as well. But, really appreciating why social interactions look and feel the way they do means that we need to consider how various social institutions shape and give meaning to interactions. So, we need our *institutional* lens as well. And, if identity formation processes are different for different groups, we need to be able to think about what aspects of social identity produce these differences. We need to examine the ways that the collection of different identities each of us has intersect with each other to produce different kinds of outcomes and experiences. And to fully appreciate this, we need to examine the world through our *intersectional* lens. Finally, if people in different groups end up with not only different identities, but also different experiences and opportunities, sociologists want to examine how this social inequality is produced. Add in the *inequality* lens.

So, what started out as a simple question turns out to be more complex. What started out as a question about individuals turns into an examination of the relationship between the individual and society. And this is how sociologists learn to see the world around them. They are constantly switching lenses, overlapping lenses, and looking through all five in an attempt to examine social issues and phenomena from different perspectives. Learning to see like a sociologist means getting comfortable with this process. And throughout this book, you'll see how different research and ideas highlight the distinct components of the iSoc model. By the end of the book, you'll see the world through sociological lenses too.

That's what we mean when we talk about "iSoc." iSoc consists of these five levels of sociological analysis. Using these five levels of analysis provides you with both a theoretical lens through which to view social life *and* the analytic method to situate any particular phenomenon. It is the sociological lens, our framework. It is how sociologists *do* sociology now. Next, we provide an example of thinking sociologically with iSoc by looking at a practice that often feels intensely personal but is actually guided by social forces: selecting a name for a child.

iSoc in Action: What's in a Name?

1.2.3 Explain how sociologists look at changes in popular baby names to describe changes in other parts of society.

IDENTITY—What could be more "you" than your name? Your name is the first signpost of your *identity*, a reference point throughout your life. Yet to a sociologist, nothing could be more individual and more social at the same time. Your name itself is a good example of what C. Wright Mills said was the core imperative of sociology: to connect biography to history. In fact, we can learn a great deal both about you as well as about the society in which you live by looking at the ways parents choose to name their children. Consider the following example. A list of the Top 10 names for boys and girls in the United States in 2016 follows along with the frequency of each name (the percentage of babies born in the United States given each name). This means that, for example, 1.01 percent of all baby girls born in the United States were given the name Emma—or, about 1 in 100 baby girls born in 2016 was named Emma (see TABLE 1.1)

What do you notice? Some of you might see some similar names. William and James, for example, appear on both lists. But not a single girl's name appears on both lists. And you're probably thinking that a lot of the names from 1916 (perhaps for girls especially) seem rather, well, "older," more "traditional." Do you think that people will think that Emma and Liam and Mia and Mason are going to sound "older" and "traditional" a hundred years from now? It's also true that the boys' names seem more familiar than the girls' names.

INEQUALITY—Popular names change over time. And we can learn a lot about a group from understanding which names are popular among which groups, how popular, and when and why they change. We learn about the power of distinct social *institutions* in a

TABLE 1.1 Top 10 Names for Boys and Girls in the United States

Top-Ranked Boys' Names and Frequencies (1916)	Top-Ranked Boys' Names and Frequencies (2016)	Top-Ranked Girls' Names and Frequencies (1916)	Top-Ranked Girls' Names and Frequencies (2016)
1. John 5.42%	1. Noah 0.95%	1. Mary 5.66%	1. Emma 1.01%
2. William 4.38%	2. Liam 0.90%	2. Helen 3.01%	2. Olivia 1.00%
3. James 3.85%	3. William 0.78%	3. Dorothy 2.53%	3. Ava 0.85%
4. Robert 3.44%	4. Mason 0.77%	4. Margaret 2.30%	4. Sophia 0.84%
5. Joseph 2.59%	5. James 0.74%	5. Ruth 2.14%	5. Isabella 0.77%
6. Charles 2.56%	6. Benjamin 0.73%	6. Mildred 1.44%	6. Mia 0.75%
7. George 2.53%	7. Jacob 0.72%	7. Anna 1.40%	7. Charlotte 0.68%
8. Edward 1.84%	8. Michael 0.70%	8. Elizabeth 1.38%	8. Abigail 0.61%
9. Frank 1.66%	9. Elijah 0.69%	9. Frances 1.27%	9. Emily 0.57%
10. Thomas 1.30%	10. Ethan 0.68%	10. Virginia 1.15%	10. Harper 0.56%

SOURCE: Data from U.S. Social Security Administration (2017). Available at: https://www.ssa.gov/oact/babynames/index.html#&ht=1.

society. We can learn about *inequality* by examining which names become popular and unpopular and when. And we learn about how these things change over time. Name popularity appears to move through a population in a manner similar to an infectious disease. It catches on, and spreads. Sometimes they spread slowly or only appear to spread to some states and not others. But other times, they spread quickly.

The name given to you feels intensely personal, and it's an intimate part of your *identity*. Indeed, part of the reason parents labor over the decision of what name to give a child is because they understand this on some level. But when parents choose names for their children, they do so in a particular historical moment in a particular social context. And these particularities of history and social context help shape the names parents select, whether they are aware of this fact or not. It's a powerful illustration of Mills's sociological imagination—your biography is connected to history. Consider trends in the popularity of three names given to girls in the United States: Mary, Emma, and Jessica (see FIGURE 1.1).

Mary was the most popular name between 1880 and 1961—after that, Mary has declined in popularity quite a bit. In 1900, Emma was a top 20 name given to girls. Emma gradually became much less popular, hitting a low point of the 461st most

FIGURE 1.1 Rank of Mary, Emma, and Jessica among Most Popular U.S. Girls' Names at Birth, 1900–2016
What can we learn about the types of institutions that shape our lives and how that might have changed by examining shifts in the popularity of the different kinds of names we select for children? Choosing a name feels like an intensely personal decision. But like so many things sociologists study, it's a decision that is powerfully influenced by the world around us.

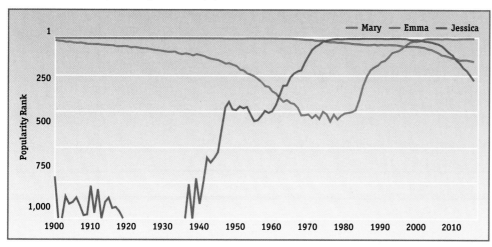

NOTE: Name ranking stops at 1000.

SOURCE: Data from U.S. Social Security Administration.

SOCIOLOGY AND OUR WORLD

WHY POPULAR BOY NAMES ARE MORE POPULAR THAN POPULAR GIRL NAMES

What can we learn about society by examining just how common popular baby names actually are?

In 1880, the top 10 names given to baby boys accounted for more than 40 percent of all baby boys born that year; almost 23 percent of girls born in 1880 received a name from the top 10. Having a popular name was the norm. But having a popular name has become less common. In 2016, the top 10 names given to babies born that year accounted for fewer than 8 percent of them. Using one of the lists of names we just examined, we saw that 5.66 percent of all baby girls born in 1916 were given the name Mary. That means that more than 1 in 20 girls born that year were named Mary. The same is true of John. The most popular boy and girl names weren't just trendy; they were incredibly popular and widespread. Giving a child the most popular boy or girl name was extraordinarily common by today's standards. If you had a baby girl and named her Mary and so did your friend down the street and your cousin, it might not have been so strange. The most popular names today are simply much less common than the most popular names a century ago (see Proportion of Boys and Girls Receiving Top 10 Name by Birth Year, 1880–2016).

But what does this mean? Sociologist Stanley Lieberson wrote a book examining all we can learn about a society by looking at the names people select for their babies—*A Matter of Taste: How Names, Fashion, and Culture Change* (Lieberson 2000). And he was interested in this trend in particular—why is it that the most popular names aren't as popular as they used to be? It's a great example of iSoc analysis. His theory is that as institutional pressures associated with names decline, we see the proliferation of more diverse names. By "institutional pressures," Lieberson is referring to pressures associated with social *institutions* like extended family rituals or religious rituals associated with the naming of children. Lieberson refers to this

as the "modernization theory" of name trends. And it's been documented in other societies as well.

But you might notice that this is an incomplete explanation if you examine the graph. It's true for both boys and girls that the most popular names have become less popular over time. But, in the United States, the most popular boys' names have always been more popular than the most popular girls' names, though the gap in popularity has decreased over time. In 1880, the top 10 boys' names accounted for almost 20 percent more of the boys born that year than the top 10 girls' names did for girls. That's a big gap! And you can see that it's narrowed over time. But, even in 2016, the top 10 boys' names accounted for more than did the girls, by just a fraction of a percent. Why?

Sociologist Alice Rossi (Rossi 1965) suggested that gender inequality accounts for this discrepancy. Because men are often seen as symbolic carriers of the family from one generation to the next (think of how heterosexual couples often both take *his* last name, for instance), they are more likely to be given names ensuring the family's continuity over time. Many boys have the first name of their fathers or grandfathers—like Robert Smith IV. This is really rare among women.

It's an interesting example of how much we can learn about a society from looking at something as simple as data on how we name our children. From this chart, we can see how certain institutional pressures on individuals have loosened over the last century. We can also see one small way that gender inequality has been challenged, in a way you might not have noticed.

SOURCE: Tristan Bridges (2016). "Why Popular Boy Names are More Popular than Popular Girl Names." *Feminist Reflections*, blog. Available at: https://thesocietypages.org/feminist/2016/02/25/why-popular-boy-names-are-more-popular-than-popular-girl-names/

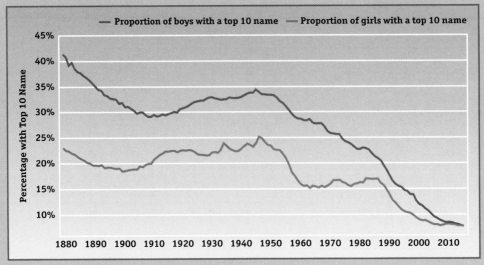

Proportion of Boys and Girls Receiving Top 10 Name by Birth Year, 1880–2016

— Proportion of boys with a top 10 name   — Proportion of girls with a top 10 name

SOURCE: Data from U.S. Social Security Administration.

popular name in 1976. But by 2015 and 2016, Emma was the top name given to baby girls born in the United States. The name Jessica follows a different trend entirely. Not until 1947 is Jessica among the top 500 names given to baby girls in the United States. Starting in the 1960s, the name Jessica saw a dramatic increase in popularity. For 20 years, between 1977 and 1997, Jessica was a top 5 name given to girls at birth. But as of 2015, Jessica is not even among the top 200. Why? What happened? And what can we learn about our society from these cultural trends?

Names fall in and out of fashion. And some fall out of favor and then climb back up. For example, what happened to Emma? (Here are a few hints: the revival of interest in Jane Austen, the fact that Ross and Rachel named their baby "Emma" on television sitcom *Friends*, and the proto-feminist witch Hermione in the *Harry Potter* movies was played by Emma Watson.) Names can often be celebrity driven, but they need to be common enough that it might appear you thought of it yourself. So there aren't a lot of 70 year-old Elvises or Ringos running around these days, nor are there a lot of tiny LeBrons or Gagas. But "Isabella" and "Jacob" increased dramatically following the publication of the *Twilight* novel series in 2005 and movies starting in 2008.

On closer examination, you might notice if you look at the differences in the popular names from 1916 versus 2016 (see FIGURE 1.1) reflect changes in institutional pressures. Family names and Biblical names are high on the list (this is what accounts for the incredible popularity of Mary for such a long period of time). Over the course of the twentieth century, religion appears to exert less pressure on naming practices in the United States. This is consistent with the **"modernization theory" of name trends**. By 2016, media and popular culture appear to have started to play the role that religion and family tradition once did in helping many parents select names for their children. Though Biblical names are not entirely absent either.

But, pressure to name children works in two ways: Social forces help us consider some names and steer clear of others. In the 1990s, three popular names in the United States took a nose dive in popularity because of their association with particular historical events. Forrest, Monica, and Ellen had held steady as reasonably popular names—in the top 200–300 until Ellen DeGeneres came out as gay (Ellen falls in the rankings from 245 to 655); the President Clinton/Monica Lewinsky scandal hits news headlines (Monica went from 79 to 589); and the movie *Forrest Gump* was released in theaters (Forrest fell from 217 to outside the top 1,000 from 2004 to 2012—climbing back to 633 in 2016) (see FIGURE 1.2).

"modernization theory" of name trends

Stanley Lieberson's explanation for the reduction in pressures associated with social institutions like extended family rituals or religious rituals associated with the naming of children—trends that led to more name diversity.

FIGURE 1.2 Name Popularity for Ellen, Monica, and Forrest, 1950–2016
Just as we can learn a lot about a society by looking at the names that become popular, so too can we learn about a society by looking at the baby names that lose popularity. Often, this is a powerful way to learn something about systems of inequality that shape a society.

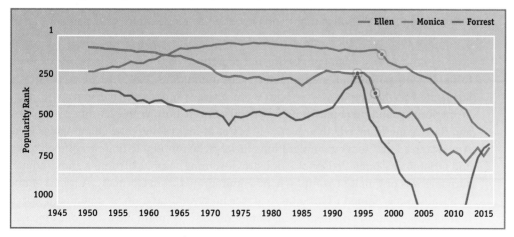

NOTE: Name ranking stops at 1000. Read more about name contamination at Cohen, Philip. 2012. "Big Name Drops in the News." Family Inequality (blog). December 12. Available at https://familyinequality.wordpress.com/2012/12/10/big-name-drops-in-the-news/.

SOURCE: Data from U.S. Social Security Administration.

When names become less popular, it often tells us something about society. In this case, we can see how certain groups are viewed unfavorably and subject to social inequality, just by watching name trends. Names are one indicator of social inequality in our society—of the ways that different groups receive systematically different treatment (like individuals identifying as gay or lesbian, for instance, or disabled persons, or women with sexual desires).

Names therefore not only provide us with a primary identity, but they reveal patterns of inequality as well. For example, in a classic study, students at Harvard were given a story about Heidi Roizen, a successful venture capitalist in the Silicon Valley, who had become successful partly because of her outgoing personality and networking skills. Half of the students, however, read a story about "Howard" Roizen. Same exact story, but the names were different. The students were then asked a series of questions about Howard and Heidi. Students found them both equally "competent," but Howard was rated as far more "likeable" than Heidi, who was seen as "selfish" and "not the type of person you would want to hire or work for." In her book *Lean In* (2013), Facebook COO Sheryl Sandberg argues that this shows that for men, success and likeability are linked, but for women, they are seen as a trade-off. All this, remember, from a name!

Not only Heidi and Howard, but also Jamal and Lakisha. People who have distinctly "black" sounding names on their resumes get 50 percent fewer callbacks for interviews than those with white-sounding names like Emily or Greg—even when they have equivalent credentials. The phenomenon also affects other minority groups (Bertrand and Mullainathan 2003; Yoshino 2006). We will learn more about this in Chapter 14.

And yet, it's also true that a politician named Barack Hussein Obama from an interracial family was elected president of the United States in 2008 and reelected in 2012. In 2004, when Obama was a Senate candidate for the state of Illinois, he delivered a keynote address at the Democratic National Convention in Boston. In his speech, he mentioned his name. He said: "My parents shared not only an improbable love; they shared an abiding faith in the possibilities of this nation. They would give me an African name, Barack, or 'blessed,' believing that in a tolerant America, your name is no barrier to success." Of course, sociologists know that names are barriers to success for many people. But, as President Obama illustrates so well, just what qualifies as a "barrier" and for whom is something that will change over time and by social context.

Names and the Sociological Imagination

1.2.4 Summarize the ways that trends in baby names illustrate each element of the iSoc perspective.

That names carry elements of *identity* and reproduce *inequality* has long been known to us. If your parents or grandparents were immigrants, ask them if your current last name was the one they were born with. A large number of Americans, with very "American" sounding names, both first and last, were born with very different names, and they "Americanized" their names to better fit in. In some cases, their names were Americanized for them by immigration officials who found it tedious or difficult to try and pronounce Donatelli (Donald) or Estrovic (Strong). Donald Trump's grandfather's surname was originally Drumpf when he immigrated from Germany. A friend of one of the authors is named Charlie Lee. He was born Xiou-Su Li in Shanghai, but feared that if people couldn't pronounce his name correctly he might have a harder time getting ahead in the United States.

INTERACTIONS—This leads to the third and fourth components of the iSoc model—interactions and institutions—the how and the where of social life. Names may express both *identity* and reveal *inequality*. But they do not do so in a social vacuum. You become, to take our cases, Michael or Amy or Tristan through your *interactions* with others. You are often assumed to share characteristics with others who share your name. People will have expectations of you based on your name, especially when you look at your given name and your surname (or "last name"). Our surnames reveal ethnicity and nationality, and frequently religion, and thus carry expectations and stereotypes about who we are and how we will behave.

Consider how many Jewish immigrants changed their names when they started their careers in the entertainment industry to become more "acceptable": Joan Perske (Lauren Bacall), Charles Buchinsky (Charles Bronson), Allen Konigsberg (Woody Allen), Isadore Demsky (Kirk Douglas), Larry Leach (Cary Grant), Esther Friedman (Ann Landers), Robert Zimmerman (Bob Dylan). And it wasn't just Jewish immigrants either, as fears of discrimination led many others to change their names to more comfortably "American" names: Michael Gubitosi (Robert Blake), Anna Maria Louisa Italiano (Anne Bancroft), Dino Crocetti (Dean Martin), Ann Von Kappelhoff (Doris Day), Ramon Antonio Gerardo Estevez and his son Carlos (Martin and Charlie Sheen). Marion Michael Morrison was afraid his name sounded too feminine, so he changed it to John Wayne and became one of the most heroically masculine actors ever.

Similarly, the Oscar-winning actor Cary Grant, considered a heartthrob in the 1930s and 1940s was born Archibald Leach. It's because of him that the name Cary took off among boys for a while, until 1960 when the name became one we associate with girls. We'll explain how and why this happens with androgynous names (names given to both boys and girls) in more detail in Chapter 9.

INSTITUTIONS—Social *institutions* play an enormous role in naming as well. Many of you are named after family members. Some traditions prohibit naming children after living family members, but other traditions require it. Do any of the guys reading this carry a "Jr." or "III" after their name? Every one of John F. Kennedy's brothers either was a Jr. or had a son who was a Jr. Martin Luther King Jr., was simultaneously named after his father and for the leader of the Protestant Reformation in sixteenth-century Germany. Political life often inspires names; for example, for many years, certain presidents were popular as boys' names in the African American community: Lincoln, Jefferson, and Washington. In the first half of the twentieth century, it was not uncommon to see a jump in the rankings among boys' names for U.S. presidents.

First ladies influence names as well. Consider "Franklin" and "Eleanor" following the Roosevelt presidential election in 1932. Although Franklin didn't generate any sustained interest in that name for boys after Franklin Deleano Roosevelt's presidency, his wife, Eleanor Roosevelt, may have inspired people to select "Eleanor" as a name for girls. Many of the issues she stood for are issues young people care deeply about today as well. Indeed, Eleanor was a very popular girl's name in the 1930s, and started gaining popularity again in the 1980s. As of 2016, "Eleanor" ranked 41st among girls' names in the United States. Conversely, Franklin enjoyed a very brief spike following Roosevelt's election, but has fallen in popularity ever since. In 2016, "Franklin" ranked 423rd among boys' names in the United States.

The media exerts a powerful influence on your name, too. How many of you were named after celebrities? You might not even realize it if you were. Take one of our names as an example—"Tristan." Tristan was not even among the top 1,000 names given to boys in 1970. But, in 2016, Tristan ranked 108th. When your author, Tristan, was born, the name had just cracked the top 500 in the United States for the first time. But it started falling again through the mid-1990s. Then, between 1994 and 1995, Tristan jumped from the 452nd to the 121st most popular boys' name in the United States in a single year. In 1996, it ranked 68th. What happened? The media. In 1994, the film *Legends of the Fall* was released starring Brad Pitt as a character named "Tristan." The film won an Oscar that year and was nominated for several others. Brad Pitt won a Golden Globe award for "best actor" in 1995 for his performance. It's just one small way of illustrating how sociologists use the "sociological imagination." Our biographies are connected to

SOCIOLOGY AND OUR WORLD

WHY NAMES THAT REGAIN POPULARITY WAIT A CENTURY

Why is it that some common names from the past gain popularity again while others may never be common again, and why does it usually take a while?

Some names that sound "old-fashioned" today have become common again. Emma and Eleanor are good examples. So are Frances and Evelyn. Mildred, on the other hand, was a top 10 girl's name 100 years ago, but never became popular again.

Just like fashions in anything, fashions in names sometimes recycle. But they don't just recycle at random. Sociologists have discovered that fashions recycle in patterned ways. Think about how music or clothing fashions recycle. Who'd have thought the garish colors and fashions of the 1980s would have ever seen a come-back? But they did. In fact, dressing "'80s" today is sometimes thought of as "fashion *forward*"! After 20 years, many of the features of 1980s' fashion reappeared in popular culture (from the shape of "stylish" sun glasses, to a return to neon and "loud" colored clothing). Fashions in clothing and music tend to recycle over shorter periods of time, while fashions in names take a bit longer. Sociologist Stanley Lieberson (2000) refers to this as the "ratchet effect"—tastes do not bounce around unpredictably; they tend to move consistently in one direction for a defined period of time and then reverse themselves.

Not every name on the list of the top 10 in the early twentieth century has become popular again, but those that have follow a strikingly similar pattern. If a name loses popularity and becomes popular again, it takes about one century to do so. Eleanor, Emma, and Evelyn all follow this pattern. As you can see from the figure below, Frances started to lose popularity a bit later than these three, starting to see a big loss in popularity between 1950 and 1960. And if the trend continues, Frances may rise to her former popularity again in another three or four decades.

The ratchet effect is at work in all kinds of different fashions. From the length of skirts to the whether or not men wear facial hair (and if so, what type), what is considered "fashionable" changes over time. And fashions tend to move in the same direction over time (toward *less* facial hair, for instance, or *shorter* skirt length) until they "ratchet" back and change direction (toward *more* facial hair, or *longer* skirts). But, for an "old" fashion to become fashionable again requires waiting for a sufficient period of time that it will not be confused as simply being "out of date." And while we may change the style of clothing or facial hair we wear over the course of our lives, most people live their entire lives with the same first name. As a result, it takes a longer period of time for the fashion to recycle. Lieberson discovered that for first names to recycle, it almost always happens in about 100-year increments—just long enough for a name like "Emma" to not sound like the name of someone's grandmother anymore.

Rankings of U.S. Girls' Names: Eleanor, Emma, Frances, Mildred, Evelyn, 1900–2016

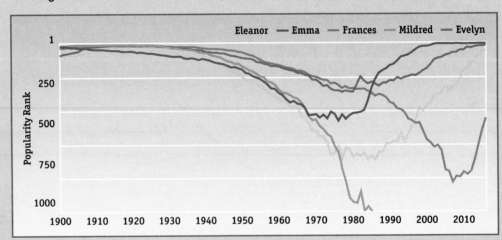

NOTE: Name ranking stops at 1000.
SOURCE: Data from U.S. Social Security Administration.

history. Our names are one small example of this. And family, politics, and media are just three social institutions that shape our individual names.

INTERSECTIONS—Finally, there is a fifth "i" in iSoc: intersections. Intersections are the place where all the other components meet. Identities are shaped and formed in a context of inequality, through interaction, and within institutions. And, in turn, your individual identity can exert influence on those institutions, can perpetuate or challenge inequality, and can transform and be transformed through interaction. All of our different *identities* connect and collide in different ways—by race, gender, ethnicity, age, religion, etc. Sociologists try to understand these *intersections* when they speak of the context for any *interaction*, the ways in which some identities and inequalities are foregrounded and which are pushed to the background in any given interaction.

The iSoc model reveals how even the most intimate and personal aspects of our identity are also shaped by intersecting systems of social inequality, created through interactions, and formalized in social institutions.

---

iSOC AND YOU

As you've seen with the discussion of names, each element of iSoc illuminates another aspect of your social lives. The very elements of *identity* that feel most personal and individual, like your name, embeds you in a web of social relationships, whether with family history, religious tradition, or media cultures of celebrity. Names can reflect—or, as you've seen, even cause—some aspects of inequality. These aspects of *inequality*—class, race, sexuality, gender, etc. *intersect* in specific ways that sociologists also examine. You interact with others, forming patterns of *interaction* that become formalized within *institutions* like the workplace or education.

1.3 Where Did Sociology Come From?

The issues that animate sociology today—identity, inequality, interaction, institutions, intersections—were the founding ideas of the field. Sociology emerged in Europe in the early nineteenth century. At that time, European society had just passed through a calamitous period in which the Enlightenment, the French Revolution, and the beginnings of the Industrial Revolution collectively transformed the landscape of European society. Society was transforming at a rapid pace and many people wondered how and even whether or not society could persist.

In fact, understanding the emergence of the field of sociology is best done with the sociological imagination. The field of study is connected with the historical moment and context in which it emerged. Scholars started asking questions about how society works and when it breaks down, not surprisingly, in a historical context in which almost everything people knew about the world was changing at an incredible pace. New identities were emerging causing people to interact in new ways. Social institutions were transforming and the relationship between the "haves" and the "have nots" was being perpetuated in a new way, giving rise to new forms of social inequality. At the time, scholars were concerned with more than just understanding how society works. They were worried about how and whether society could survive the changes they were witnessing.

Before Sociology

1.3.1 Understand how "The Enlightenment" is connected with challenges to the social order that created a new way of understanding society and inequalities between different groups.

Even in the seventeenth and eighteenth centuries, philosophers were attempting to understand the relationship between the individual and society. Political revolutions and intellectual breakthroughs led to this period being called the "Age of Reason" or "**The Enlightenment**." Theorists challenged the established social order, like the rule of the monarchy and hereditary aristocracy, and the ideas that justified it, like the "divine right of kings." It was during the Enlightenment of the seventeenth and eighteenth centuries that the idea of the "individual" took shape.

The Enlightenment
Also called "The Age of Reason," theorists challenged the established social order, like the rule of the monarchy and hereditary aristocracy, and the ideas that justified it, like the "divine right of kings." It was during the Enlightenment of the seventeenth and eighteenth centuries that the idea of the "individual" took shape.

John Locke (1632–1704) believed that society was formed through the rational decisions of free individuals, who join together through a "social contract" to form society.

Jean-Jacques Rousseau (1712–1788) believed that people were basically good and innocent but that private property creates inequality and with it unhappiness and immorality.

John Locke (1632–1704), for example, believed that society was formed through the rational decisions of free individuals, who join together through a "social contract" to form society. Society permits and even facilitates the free movement of goods, making life easier and more predictable. The purpose of government, Locke argued (1689/1988), was to resolve disagreements between individuals and ensure people's rights—but that's all. If the government goes too far, Locke believed, and becomes a sort of omnipotent state, the people have a right to revolution and to institute a new government.

In France, meanwhile, Jean-Jacques Rousseau (1712–1788) had a rather different perspective. Rousseau (1754/2007) believed that people were basically good and innocent but that private property creates inequality and with it unhappiness and immorality. Rousseau believed that a collective spirit, what he called the "general will," would replace individual greed and that through social life people could be free—but only if they were equal.

These two themes—Locke's emphasis on individual liberty and Rousseau's idea that society enhanced freedom—came together in the work of Thomas Jefferson, when he penned the Declaration of Independence in 1776, the founding document of the United States. That document asserted that all men are equal in rights and that government is the servant, not the master, of human beings. Jefferson fused Rousseau's vision of a community with Locke's ideal of limited government into a document that continues to inspire people the world over.

Mary Wollstonecraft (1759–1797), a passionate advocate of the equality of the sexes, has been called the first major feminist. She argued that society couldn't progress if half its members are kept backward, and she proposed broad educational changes for both boys and girls. But she also suggested the problems are cultural. Women accept their powerlessness in society because they can use their informal interpersonal power to seduce men. Men who value women only as objects of pleasure and amusement allow themselves to be manipulated, and so the prison of self-indulgence corrupts both sexes. Wollstonecraft was the first classical theorist to apply the ideas of the Enlightenment to the position of women—and find the Enlightenment, not women, to be the problem!

These ideas—"discovery" of the individual, the relationship of the individual to society, the position of women (and minorities), and the regulation of individual

Both Locke's emphasis on individual liberty and Rousseau's idea that society enhanced freedom influenced Thomas Jefferson when he penned the Declaration of Independence in 1776, the founding document of the United States.

Mary Wollstonecraft (1759–1797), a passionate advocate of the equality of the sexes, has been called the first major feminist. She argued, among other things, that society couldn't progress if half its members are systematically held back.

freedom by governments—were the critical ideas circulating in Europe on the eve of the nineteenth century. And these were among the fundamental questions addressed by the new field of sociology.

The Invention of Sociology

1.3.2 Understand how the Industrial Revolution changed almost everything about the societies it affected and how this created new fears about whether and how society could persist.

The economic and political changes heralded by the **American Revolution** of 1776 and the **French Revolution** of 1789 were in part inspired by the work of those Enlightenment thinkers. Between 1776 and 1838, European society underwent a dramatic change—politically, economically, and intellectually. The American and French revolutions replaced absolutist monarchs with republics, where power rested not on the divine right of kings and queens but on the consent of the people. The **Industrial Revolution** reorganized the production and distribution of goods from the quaint system of craft production, in which apprentices learned trades and entered craft guilds, to large-scale factory production in which only the very few owned the factories and many workers had only their ability to work to sell to the highest bidder.

The foundation of society, one's identity, the nature of politics, the justifications for inequality, and economic systems changed fundamentally between the collapse of the "old regime" in the late eighteenth century, and the rise of the new "modern" system in the middle of the nineteenth century (see TABLE 1.2).

These changes also changed the way we saw the world. Even the language that we used to describe that world was transformed. It was during this era that the following words were first used with the meaning they have today: *industry, factory, middle class, democracy, class, intellectual, masses, commercialism, bureaucracy, capitalism, socialism, liberal, conservative, nationality, engineer, scientist, journalism, ideology*—and, of course, *sociology*

American Revolution and **French Revolution**

Between 1776 and 1838, European society underwent a dramatic change—politically, economically, and intellectually—in part inspired by the work of Enlightenment thinkers. These revolutions replaced absolutist monarchs with republics, where power rested not on the divine right of kings and queens but on the consent of the people.

Industrial Revolution

The rapid development of industry that occurred in numerous countries in the eighteenth and nineteenth centuries reorganized the production and distribution of goods from the quaint system of craft production, in which apprentices learned trades and entered craft guilds, to large-scale factory production in which only the very few owned the factories and many workers had only their ability to work to sell to the highest bidder.

TABLE 1.2 Contrasting the "Old Regime" and the New Social Order

	Old Regime	New Order
Basis of economy	Land	Property
Location of economic activity	Rural manors	Urban factories
Source of identity	Kinship	Work
	Status/caste	Class
Ideology	Religion	Science
Type of government	Monarchy	Republic
Basis of government	Divine right	Popular consent

(Hobsbawm 1962). Politically, some revolutionaries thought we should continue those great movements; conservatives thought we'd gone too far, and it was time to retreat to more familiar social landscapes. Sociologists both praised and criticized these new developments.

Classical Sociological Thinkers

1.3.3 Describe the issues that motivated classical sociological thinkers to create a science of society—consider the types of questions they were asking and why they sought answers.

The word *sociology* itself was introduced in 1838 by a French theorist, Auguste Comte. To him, it meant "the scientific study of society." Most of the earliest sociologists embraced a notion of progress—that society passed through various stages from less developed to more developed and that this progress was positive, both materially and morally. This notion of progress is central to the larger intellectual project of "modernism" of which sociology was a part. *Modernism*—the belief in evolutionary progress, through the application of science—challenged tradition, religion, and aristocracies as remnants of the past and saw industry, democracy, and science as the wave of the future.

AUGUSTE COMTE Auguste Comte (1798–1857) believed that each society passed through three stages of development based on the form of knowledge that provided its foundation: religious, metaphysical, and scientific. In the religious or theological stage, supernatural forces are understood to control the world. In the metaphysical stage, abstract forces and what Comte called "destiny" or "fate" are perceived to be the prime movers of history. Religious and metaphysical knowledge thus rely on superstition and speculation, not science. In the scientific, or "positive," stage (the origin of the word *positivism*) events are explained through the scientific method of observation, experimentation, and analytic comparison.

Comte believed that, like the physical sciences, which explain physical facts, sociology must rely on science to explain social facts. Comte saw two basic facts to be explained: "statics," the study of order, persistence, and organization; and "dynamics," the study of the processes of social change. Comte believed that sociology would become "the queen of the sciences," shedding light on earlier sciences and synthesizing all previous knowledge about the natural world with a science of the social world. Sociology, he believed, would reveal the principles and laws that affected the functioning of all societies. Comte hoped that the scientific study of society would enable sociologists to guide society toward peace, order, and reform.

Comte's preoccupation with sociology as a science did not lead him to shy away from moral concerns; indeed, Comte believed that a concern for moral progress should be the central focus of all human sciences. Sociology's task was to help society become better. In fact, sociology was a sort of "secular religion," a religion of humanity, Comte argued. And he, himself, was its highest minister. Toward the end of his life, he fancied himself a secular prophet and signed his letters "the Founder of Universal Religion, Great Priest of Humanity." After Comte, the classical era of sociological thought began. Sociologists

Auguste Comte coined the term *sociology* as the scientific study of society.

have never abandoned his questions: The questions of order and disorder, persistence and change, remain foundations of contemporary and classical sociological thought.

ALEXIS DE TOCQUEVILLE   Alexis de Tocqueville (1805–1859), a French social theorist and historian, is known for studies of American democracy and the French Revolution. Tocqueville saw the United States as the embodiment of democracy. Without a feudal past that tied us to outdated ideas of monarchy or aristocracy and with nearly limitless land on which the country could grow prosperous, democracy flourished. But democracy contains tensions and creates anxieties that European societies did not face.

Tocqueville's greatest insight is that democracy can either enhance or erode individual liberty. On the one hand, democracy promises increasing equality of conditions and increasingly uniform standards of living. On the other hand, it also concentrates power at the top and weakens traditional sources of liberty, like religion or the aristocracy (which he believed were strong enough to protect individuals from encroachments by the state). Democracies can lead to mass society, in which individuals feel powerless and are easily manipulated by the media. As a result, democratic societies are faced with two possible outcomes, free institutions or despotism. When he tried to predict the direction America was heading, he thought it depended on Americans' ability to prevent the concentration of wealth and power and on the free spirit of individuals. And the solution, he believed, lay in "intermediate institutions"—the way that Americans, as a nation of "joiners," developed small civic groups for every conceivable issue or project.

During a period of dramatic social change, thinkers around the world began to ask questions about the form and function of society and in this moment, sociology was born. We turn now to some of the founders and a discussion of the various social problems and issues that caused them to theorize about and study societies and the people who make them up.

KARL MARX   Karl Marx (1818–1883) was the most important of all socialist thinkers. Marx's greatest sociological insight was that all societies were characterized by inequality, and that inequality based on class was the organizing principle of society; all other divisions would eventually become class divisions.

Marx's great intellectual and political breakthrough came in 1848 (Marx and Engels 1848/1998). Before that, he had urged philosophers to get their heads out of the clouds and return to the real world—that is, he urged them toward "materialism," a focus on the way people organize their society to solve basic "material" needs such as food, shelter, and clothing as the basis for philosophy, not "idealism," with its focus on society as the manifestation of either sacred or secular ideas. As revolutions were erupting all across Europe, he saw his chance to make that philosophy into a political movement. With Engels, he wrote *The Communist Manifesto*. Asserting that all history had "hitherto been the history of class struggles," the *Manifesto* linked the victory of the proletariat (the working class) to the development of capitalism itself, which dissolved traditional bonds, like family and community, and replaced them with the naked ties of self-interest.

Initially, Marx believed, capitalism was a revolutionary system itself, destroying all the older, more traditional forms of social life and replacing them with what he called "the cash nexus"—one's position depended only on wealth, property, and class. But eventually, capitalism suppresses all humanity, drowning it in "the icy waters of egotistical calculation." We are not born greedy or materialistic; we become so under capitalism.

His central work was *Capital* (Marx 1867/1998), a three-volume work that laid out a theory of how capitalism worked as a system. His central insight was that the exchange of money and services between capitalists (those who own the means of production) and labor (those who sell their "labor power" to capitalists for wages) is unequal. Workers must work longer than necessary to pay for the costs of their upkeep, producing what Marx called "surplus value." And because of competition, capitalists must try to increase the rate of surplus value. They do this by replacing human labor with machines,

Karl Marx argued that, as capitalism progressed, the rich would get richer and the poor would get poorer—until it exploded in revolution.

social solidarity
Émile Durkheim's term for the moral bonds that connect us to the social collectivity.

mechanical solidarity
Émile Durkheim's term for a traditional society where life is uniform and people are similar. They share a common culture and sense of morality that bonds them.

organic solidarity
Émile Durkheim's term for a modern society where people are interdependent because of the high division of labor; they disagree on what is right and wrong but share solidarity because the division of labor makes them dependent on each other.

lowering wages (and cutting any benefits) until workers can't afford even to consume the very products they are producing, and by centralizing their production until the system reaches a crisis. Thus, capitalists are not only fighting against labor, but they are also competing against each other. Eventually, Marx believed, it would all come tumbling down.

This work inspired socialists all over the world who saw the growing gap between rich and poor as both a cause for despair about the conditions of the poor and an occasion for political organizing. Marx believed that the "laws of motion" of capitalism would bring about its own destruction as the rich got so rich and the poor got so poor that they would revolt against the obvious inequity of the system. Then workers would rise up and overthrow the unequal capitalist system and institute communism—the collective ownership of all property.

Marx believed this would take place first in the industrial countries like Britain and Germany, but the socialist revolutions of the twentieth century that used Marx as inspiration were in largely peasant societies, like Russia and China, for example. Nowhere in the world has Marx's political vision been implemented. His economic theory that the development of capitalism tends to concentrate wealth and power, however, has never been more true than today, when the gap between rich and poor is greater than ever in U.S. history. Currently, the richest 1 percent of people in the world receives as much income as the bottom 99 percent. Globally, the United States has the most unequal distribution of income of all high-income nations (UC Atlas of Global Inequality 2016).

ÉMILE DURKHEIM Émile Durkheim (1858–1917) was a master of sociological inquiry. He searched for distinctly social origins of even the most individual and personal of issues. His greatest work, *Suicide* (1897/2007), is a classic example of his sociological imagination. On the surface, suicide appears to be the ultimate individual act. Yet Durkheim argued that suicide is profoundly social, an illustration of how connected an individual feels to others. Durkheim tried to measure the amount of integration (how connected we feel to social life) and regulation (the amount that our individual freedoms are constrained) by empirically examining what happens when those processes fail.

In a sense, Durkheim turned the tables on economists who made a simple linear case that freedom was an unmitigated good and that the more you have the happier you will be. Durkheim argued that too much freedom might reduce the ties that one feels to society and therefore make one *more* likely to commit suicide, not less! Durkheim's study of suicide illustrated his central insight: that society is held together by **"social solidarity,"** moral bonds that connect us to the social collectivity. "Every society is a moral society," he wrote. Social order, he claimed, cannot be accounted for by the pursuit of individual self-interest; solidarity is emotional, moral, and non-rational. Rousseau had called this "the general will," Comte called it "consensus," but neither had attempted to actually measure it (see also Durkheim 1893/1997).

In traditional society, solidarity is relatively obvious: Life is uniform and people are similar; they share a common culture and sense of morality that Durkheim characterizes as **mechanical solidarity**. He called it mechanical solidarity because Durkheim believed it was automatic; we felt a connection with others because our lives were all so similar to one another. It's easy to feel a connection with people whose life is similar to your own. In modern society, with its division of labor and diverse and conflicting interests, common values are present but less obvious. And Durkheim was interested in how social solidarity was possible in societies in which people's lives were dramatically different from one another—how is it that people still feel connected to each other? In modern societies, he suggested that people become interdependent, and Durkheim calls this mutual dependence on each other **organic solidarity**. Organic solidarity is based on the interactions of dissimilar individuals, who must somehow work together within social institutions. Think of it like organs in a body—they don't all do the same thing, but each of them is necessary for the health and functioning of the body. Durkheim thought modern societies worked in a similar way.

Durkheim's influence has been immense, not only in sociology, where he ranks with Marx and Weber as one of the founders of the discipline, but also in anthropology, social psychology, and history. Durkheim's use of statistics was pioneering for his time, and his concept of the "**social fact**," his rigorous comparative method, and his "functional" style of analysis have been widely adopted (Durkheim 1895/1997). His emphasis on society as a moral entity has served as a powerful critique of abstract individualism and rationality and of a definition of freedom that places human liberty in opposition to society.

MAX WEBER   Max Weber (1864–1920) was an encyclopedic scholar whose expertise left hardly a field untouched. But his chief interest in all his studies was the extraordinary importance of "**rationality**" in the modern world. His major insights were that rationality was the foundation of modern society and that while rationality organized society in more formal, legal, and predictable ways, it also trapped us in an "iron cage" of bureaucracy and meaninglessness.

To understand society, Weber developed a sociology that was both "interpretive" and "value free." Weber's interpretive sociology understands social relationships by showing the sense they make to those who are involved in them. Weber also insisted that experts separate their personal evaluations from their scientific pronouncements because such value judgments cannot be logically deduced from facts. By protecting science from the taint of ideology, Weber hoped also to protect political debate from unwarranted claims by experts. "Value freedom" does not mean sociologists should not take political positions but that we must use value judgments to select subjects deemed worthy of research and must engage with the minds and feelings of the people being studied.

Weber's most famous work, *The Protestant Ethic and the Spirit of Capitalism* (1904, 1905/2004), was a study of the relationship of religious ideas to economic activity. What made European capitalism unique, he argued, was its connection to the ideas embodied in the Protestant Reformation, ideas that enabled individuals to act in this world. Essentially, Weber argued that the Puritan ethic of predestination led to a deep-seated need for clues about whether one is saved or not. Seeking some indication, Protestants (particularly Calvinists) began to value material success and worldly profit as signs of God's favor. And this need, Weber argued, supported capitalism as a new economic system.

At the end, however, Weber was pessimistic. Rationality can free us from the theocratic past but also imprison us in an "**iron cage**"—an utterly dehumanized and mechanized world. Like Marx, Weber believed that the modern capitalist order brought out the worst in us: "In the field of its highest development, in the United States, the pursuit of wealth, stripped of its religious and ethical meaning, tends to become associated with purely mundane passions, which often actually give it the character of sport." And, like Marx, Weber believed that, in the long run, class was the most significant division among people. But Weber had a more complicated understanding. At any one moment, he wrote, there are other less economic factors that divide people from each other, as well as unite them into groups. To class, Weber added the idea of "status" and "party." "Party" referred to voluntary organizations that people would enter together to make their voices heard collectively because individually we would be unable to affect real change.

While one's class position was objective, based on the position in the labor market, status groups were based, Weber believed, on social factors—what other people thought about one's lifestyle. Class is based on one's relationship to production; status is based on one's relationship to consumption. Although people really couldn't do much about class, they can definitely try to transform their status because it depends on how others see them. The desire to have others see one as belonging to a higher status group than one actually belongs to leads to extraordinary patterns of consumption—buying very expensive cars and homes to "show off" or "keep up with the Joneses," for example.

In later writings, Weber argued that the characteristic form of modern organization— whether in the state, the corporation, the military, university, or church—is bureaucratic. Whereas Marx predicted a revolution that would shatter capitalism, and Durkheim foresaw new social movements that would reunify people, Weber saw a bleak future

Émile Durkheim was fascinated with the question of how we come to feel connected with those with whom we share a society.

social fact
Émile Durkheim's term for the values, norms, and structures that transcend individuals, exercising social control over them, and amenable to scientific study.

rationality
A chief interest of Max Weber, who argued that rationality was the foundation of modern society—an escalating process of order and organization with dire consequences.

iron cage
While Weber contended that rationality can free us from the theocratic past, he also argued that rationality can imprison us in an utterly dehumanized and mechanized world he termed "the iron cage."

Max Weber introduced purely social processes, like charisma and status, as sources of identity and inequality.

HOW DO WE KNOW WHAT WE KNOW?

SUICIDE IS *NOT* AN INDIVIDUAL ACT

On the surface, there is no act more personal or individual than suicide. Taking your own life is almost always explained by individual psychopathology because a person must be crazy to kill himself or herself. If that's true, Durkheim reasoned, suicide would be distributed randomly among the population; there would be no variation by age, religion, region, or marital status, for example. Yet that is exactly what he found; suicide varies by:

1. *Religion*. Protestants commit suicide far more often than Catholics, and both commit suicide more often than Jews (he did not measure Muslims).
2. *Age*. Young people and old people commit suicide more often than middle-aged people.
3. *Marital status*. Single people commit suicide more often than married people.
4. *Gender*. Men commit suicide more often than women.
5. *Employment*. Unemployed people commit suicide more often than the employed.

Because we can assume that unemployed, unmarried young male Protestants are probably no more likely to be mentally ill than any other group, Durkheim asked what each of these statuses might contribute to keeping a person from suicide. And he determined that the "function" of each status is to embed a person in a community, to provide a sense of belonging, of "integrating" the person into society. What's more, these statuses also provided rules to live by, solid norms that constrain us from spinning wildly out of control, that "regulate" us. The higher the level of integration and regulation, Durkheim reasoned, the lower the level of suicide. Too little integration leads to what Durkheim called "egoistic" suicide, in which the individual kills himself or herself because he or she doesn't feel the connection to the group. Too little regulation led to what Durkheim called "anomic" suicide, in which the person floats in a sense of normlessness and doesn't know the rules that govern social life or when those rules change dramatically.

But sometimes there can be too much integration, where the individual completely loses himself or herself in the group and therefore would be willing to kill himself or herself to benefit the group. A suicide that resulted from too much integration is one Durkheim called "altruistic"—think of suicide bombers, for example. And sometimes people feel overregulated, trapped by rules that are not of their own making, that lead to what Durkheim called "fatalistic" suicide. Durkheim saw this type of suicide among slaves, for example, or, as he also hypothesized, "very young husbands." Why do you think he thought that?

Types of Suicide and Integration and Regulation

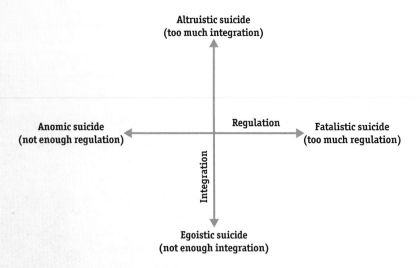

Durkheim's methodological innovation was to find a way to measure something as elusive as integration or regulation—the glue that holds society together and connects us to each other. Ironically, he found the way to "see" integration and regulation at those moments it wasn't there!

in which individual freedom is increasingly compressed by corporations and the state. Weber's often dense and difficult prose was matched by the enormous range of his writings and the extraordinary depth of his analysis. He remains the most deft thinker of the first generation of classical theorists, both appreciating the distinctiveness of Western society's promotion of individual freedom and deploring its excesses, celebrating rational society, and fearing the "iron cage" of an overly rational world.

GEORG SIMMEL   Georg Simmel (1858–1918) is among the most original and far-ranging members of the founding generation of modern sociology. Never happy within the academic division of labor, he contributed to all of the social sciences but remained primarily a philosopher.

Simmel was on a quest for a subject matter for sociology that would distinguish it from the other social sciences and the humanistic disciplines. He found this not in a new set of topics but in a method, or rather, in a special point of view. The special task of sociology is to study the *forms* of social interaction apart from their content. Simmel assumes that the same **social forms**—competition, exchange, secrecy, domination—could contain quite different content and that the same social content could be embodied in different forms. It mattered less to Simmel what a person was competing about, or whether domination was based on sheer force, monetary power, or some other basis; what mattered to him were the ways that these forms of domination or competition had specific, distinctive properties.

Social forms arise as people interact with one another for the sake of certain purposes or to satisfy certain needs. They are the processes by which individuals combine into groups, institutions, nations, or societies. Forms may gain autonomy from the demands of the moment, becoming larger, more solid structures that stand detached from, even opposed to, the continuity of life. Some forms may be historical, like "forms of development"—stages that societies might pass through. Unlike Marx, Durkheim, or Weber, then, Simmel never integrated his work into an overarching scheme. Instead he gathered a rich variety of content under each abstract form, allowing for new and startling comparisons to emerge among social phenomena.

Although this all sounds somewhat "formal" and abstract, Simmel's major concern was really about individualism. His work is always animated by the question of what the social conditions are that make it easier for persons to discover and express their individuality. In modern society, with its many cultural and social groups, individuals are caught in crosscutting interests and expectations. We belong to so many groups, and each demands different things of us. Always aware of the double-edged sword that characterizes sociology, Simmel saw both sides of the issue. For example, in his major philosophical work on money, he argued that money tends to trivialize human relationships, making them more instrumental and calculable, but it also enlarges the possibilities of freedom of expression and expands the possibilities for action. Like a good sociologist, Simmel argued that money is neither the root of all evil nor the means to our emancipation: It's both.

SOCIOLOGY COMES TO THE UNITED STATES   Sociology arrived in the United States toward the end of the nineteenth century. These U.S. sociologists took the pivotal ideas of European sociology and translated them for the American experience. They have each, since, joined the classical **canon** as the officially recognized set of foundational sociologists.

MARGARET FULLER   Margaret Fuller (1810–1850) was the first female foreign correspondent in the United States. Her book *Woman in the Nineteenth Century* (1845/1994) became the intellectual foundation of the U.S. women's movement. The book is a bracing call for complete freedom and equality, a call that "every path be open to woman as freely as to man." Fuller calls on women to become self-reliant and not expect help from men and introduces the concept of sisterhood—women must help one another, no matter whether they are scholars, servants, or prostitutes. Her research documents women's capabilities from an immense catalogue of mythology, folklore, the Bible, classical antiquity, fiction, and history. She explores the image of woman, in all its ambiguity, within literature and myth, and asserts "no age was left entirely without a

Georg Simmel wanted to distill the basic properties associated with different forms of social interaction.

social forms

A special task of sociology is to study the forms of social interaction apart from their content. Georg Simmel assumed that the same social forms—competition, exchange, secrecy, domination—could contain quite different content and that the same social content could be embodied in different forms. Each social form, according to Simmel, would have distinctive properties.

canon

The officially recognized set of foundational sociologists.

Margaret Fuller had been editor of the important Transcendentalist journal, *The Dial*, for 2 years and was literary critic for Horace Greeley's famous paper, *The New York Tribune*, when she published *Women in the Nineteenth Century* (1845/1994), a variegated argument for women's independence and critique of gender inequality in nineteenth-century U.S. society.

Social Darwinism

A model of social change that saw each succeeding society as developing through evolution and the "survival of the fittest."

conspicuous consumption

Thorstein Veblen's term to describe a new form of prestige based on accumulating and displaying possessions.

Charlotte Perkins Gilman argued that defining women solely by their reproductive role is harmful to women—as well as to men, children, and society.

witness of the equality of the sexes in function, duty, and hope." She also calls for an end to sexual stereotyping and the sexual double standard.

FREDERICK DOUGLASS   Frederick Douglass (1817–1895) was the most important African American intellectual of the nineteenth century. He lived 20 years as a slave and nearly nine as a fugitive slave and then achieved international fame as an abolitionist, editor, orator, and the author of three autobiographies. These gave a look into the world of oppression, resistance, and subterfuge within which the slaves lived. Sociologically, Douglass's work stands as an impassioned testament to the cruelty and illogic of slavery, claiming that *all* human beings were equally capable of being full individuals. His work also reveals much about the psychological world of slaves: its sheer terror but also its complexities. Its portraits of slave owners range from parody to denunciation and, in one case, even respect, and all serve Douglass's principal theme: that slaveholding, no less than the slave's own condition, is learned behavior and presumably can be unlearned.

LESTER WARD   Lester Ward (1841–1913) was one of the founders of U.S. sociology and the first to free it from the biological fetters of the Darwinian model of social change. Ward rebelled against **Social Darwinism**, which saw each succeeding society as improving on the one before it. Instead, Ward stressed the need for social planning and reform, for a "sociocratic" society that later generations would call a welfare state. Ward argued that, unlike Darwinist predictions, natural evolution proceeded in an aimless manner, based on adaptive reactions to accidents of nature. In nature, evolution was more random, chaotic, and haphazard than Social Darwinists imagined. But in society, evolution was informed by purposeful action. Ward welcomed the many popular reform movements because he saw enlightened government as the key to social evolution. Education would enable the common man and woman to participate as democratic citizens. The bottom layers of society, the proletariat, women, even the underclass of the slums, are by nature the equals of the "aristocracy of brains," he wrote. They lack only proper instruction.

CHARLOTTE PERKINS GILMAN   Most readers who know Charlotte Perkins Gilman (1860–1935) at all know her for her short story "The Yellow Wallpaper" (1899) or for her novel *Herland* (1915/1998). But sociologists know her for her groundbreaking *Women and Economics* (1898/1998), a book in which she explores the origin of women's subordination and its function in evolution. She argued that woman makes a living by marriage, not by the work she does, and so man becomes her economic environment. As a consequence, her qualities as a *woman* dominate her *human* qualities because it is through those traits that she earns her living. Women are raised to market their feebleness, their docility, and so on, and these qualities are then called "feminine." Gilman was one of the first to see the need for innovations in child rearing and home maintenance that would ease the burdens of working women. She envisaged housework as being like any other kind of work—as a public, social activity no different from shoemaking or shipbuilding. In her fiction, she imagines a range of institutions that overcome the isolation of women and children, such as communal kitchens, daycare centers, and city plans that foster camaraderie rather than withdrawal.

THORSTEIN VEBLEN   Thorstein Veblen (1857–1929) is best known for his bitingly satirical work, *The Theory of the Leisure Class* (1899/1994). Here, he argued that America was split in two, between the "productive class"—those who work—and the "pecuniary class"—those who have the money. That is, he divided Americans into workers and owners, respectively (similar to Marx). The wealthy, he argued, weren't productive; they lived off the labor of others, like parasites. They spent their time engaged in competitive displays of wealth and prestige, which he called "**conspicuous consumption**"—consumption that is done because it is visible and because it invites a certain social evaluation of "worth." One comes to advertise wealth through wasteful consumption. Veblen also saw a tension between the benevolent forces of technology and the profit system that distorts them. Modern society was neither a simple Marxian class struggle between the malevolent wealthy owners of technology and their naïve and innocent workers, nor was technology inevitably leading to either social uplift or social decay. It was not a matter of the technology but of its ownership and control and the uses to which it was put.

W. E. B. DU BOIS   W. E. B. Du Bois (1868–1963) was the most original, and widely read advocate for the civil rights of Black people for a period of over 30 years. A social scientist, political militant, essayist, and poet, he wrote 19 books and hundreds of articles, edited four periodicals, and was a founder of the NAACP and the Pan-African movement. His work forms a bridge between the nineteenth century and the Civil Rights movement of the 1960s. Today he is recognized as one of the greatest sociologists in our history.

W. E. B. Du Bois identified racism as the most pressing social problem in the United States—and the world.

Du Bois believed that race was the defining feature of U.S. society, that, as he put it, "the problem of the twentieth century was the problem of the color line," and that, therefore, the most significant contribution he could make toward achieving racial justice would be a series of scientific studies of the Negro. In 1899, he published *The Philadelphia Negro*, the first study ever of black people in the United States; he planned an ambitious set of volumes that would together finally understand the experiences of the American Negro (DuBois 1899/1996). In his most famous work, *The Souls of Black Folk* (1903/1999), Du Bois explored the psychological effects of racism, a lingering inner conflict resulting in what Du Bois referred to as a **double consciousness** among black Americans. "One feels ever his two-ness—an American, a Negro, two souls, two thoughts, two unreconciled strivings; two warring ideals in one dark body, whose dogged strength alone keeps it from being torn asunder." His work defines a "moment in history when the American Negro began to reject the idea of the world belonging to white people" (DuBois 1903/1961). Gradually disillusioned with white people's resistance to integration, Du Bois eventually called for an increase in power and especially economic autonomy, the building of separate black businesses and institutions.

double consciousness

W. E. B. Du Bois term for the social experience of black Americans as divided, often against oneself, as "two unreconciled strivings; two warring ideals in one dark body, whose dogged strength alone keeps it from being torn asunder."

GEORGE HERBERT MEAD   George Herbert Mead (1863–1931) studied the development of individual identity through social processes. He argued that identity is the product of our interactions with ourselves and with others, which is based on the distinctly human capacity for self-reflection. He distinguished between the "I," the part of us that is inherent and biological, from the "me," the part of us that is self-conscious and created by observing ourselves in interaction. The "me" is created, he said, by managing the **generalized other**, by which he meant a person's notion of the common values, norms, and expectations of other people in a society. Thus, Mead developed a distinctly *social* theory of the self (the "me")—one that doesn't bubble up from one's biology alone but a self that takes shape only through interaction with society (Mead 1967). This "pragmatic" approach—in which one examines social phenomena as they occur—actually made Mead optimistic. Mead believed that each of us develops through play, first by making up the rules as we go along, then later by being able to follow formal rules, and still later by learning to "take the role of the other"—to put ourselves in others' shoes. The ability to step outside of ourselves turns out to be the crucial step in developing a "self" that is fully able to interact with others. Mead's work is the foundation for much of the sociological research in interactionism.

generalized other

The organized rules, judgments, and attitudes of an entire group. If you try to imagine what is expected of you, you are taking on the perspective of the generalized other.

Because several of these founders of sociological thought were minorities or women, they were constantly defiled and denounced because of their views. Indeed, sociology's historical difficulty to establish itself as a credible social science may have been because so many of its pioneers were women or minorities. Du Bois and Gilman were denounced because each gave such weight to economic independence for blacks and for women; they were accused of reducing social issues to simple economic autonomy. And Douglass was consistently denounced because he extended his cry for black freedom to women as well. It was Douglass who provided the oratorical support for the suffrage plank at the first convention for women's rights in Seneca Falls, New York, in 1848—for which he was denounced the next day as an "Aunt Nancy man," the nineteenth-century equivalent of a wimp.

Doing sociology is not always comfortable, nor is sociology done only by those whose material lives are already comfortable. Sometimes sociology challenges common sense and the status quo. And good sociologists never shy away from either.

Contemporary Sociology

1.3.4 Explain how contemporary sociologists build on classical sociological thinkers and what kinds of new and different questions they are asking.

Contemporary sociologists return constantly to the ideas of its founders for inspiration and guidance as they develop their own questions about how society works—and doesn't work. Classical theories provide orientation for the development of sociological thinking.

In the United States, sociology developed as an academic field in the period between 1930 and 1960. It promised to be a social science that could explain the historical origins and dynamics of modern society. Two questions dominated the field: What could sociology contribute to the study of identity? And what social dynamics ensure social order? Stated differently, the first question was about the distinction of sociology from psychology: What is the self, our sense of "identity," and how is it different from what psychologists call "personality"? And the second question was really about why there had been such dramatic political upheavals in Europe (Nazism, Fascism, Communism) and how, despite the terrible ravages of the Great Depression and the instability of World War II, the United States was able to remain relatively stable and orderly.

Questions of *identity, interactions, institutions, inequality*, and *intersections* are embedded in this discussion from the start. Though, at different points throughout its history as a field, sociology has stressed different elements of the iSoc model to different degrees (occasionally disregarding some almost entirely). When understood as sociological lenses, however, understanding different forms and ideas that developed in contemporary sociology means understanding them as one way sociologists can understand the world—one method of study and examination, that is, among many.

symbolic interactionism

Sociological perspective that examines how individuals and groups interact, focusing on the creation of personal identity through interaction with others. Of particular interest is the relationship between individual action and group pressures.

SYMBOLIC INTERACTIONISM AND THE SOCIOLOGY OF THE SELF Where does our identity come from? The creation of a stable social "self" rested on interest in micro-level interactions, interactions among individuals, and the interactions of those individuals within the various social institutions that constitute society. Sociologists who studied these micro-level interactions called themselves "symbolic interactionists." **Symbolic interactionism** examines how an individual's interactions with his or her environment—other people, institutions, ideas—help people develop a sense of "self." The "symbolic" part was the way we use symbol systems—like language, religion, art, or body language and decoration—to navigate the social world. Symbolic interactionists follow in the sociological tradition of George Herbert Mead.

Herbert Blumer, who studied with Mead at the University of Chicago, coined the term "symbolic interactionism" in 1937. According to Blumer, people were active agents in the construction of their identities and the meanings they give to their experiences. According to Blumer, the way people view the objects in their environment depends on the meanings that these things have for them. Meanings are, in other words, the result of social interaction, and they change over time. Here Blumer echoes one of the most famous sociological axioms, written by W. I. and Dorothy Swain Thomas: "Those things which men believe to be true, are true in their consequences." That is, if we perceive something to be true, we ordinarily will act on those perceptions, and that therefore, the "consequences"—namely, our actions—confirm that perception.

Erving Goffman, an influential symbolic interactionist, used what he called a **dramaturgical model** to understand social interaction. Like an actor preparing to perform a part in a play, a social *actor* practices a part "backstage," accumulating *props* and testing out different ways to deliver his or her *script*. The actual "frontstage" performance, in front of the intended audience, helps us refine our presentation of self: If the people we want to like us do, in fact, like us, we realize that our performance is successful, and we will continue it. But if they reject us or don't like us, we might try a different strategy, rehearse that "backstage," and then try again. If that fails, our identity might get "spoiled," and we would have to either change the venue of our performance, alter our part significantly, or accept society's critical reviews.

In one of Goffman's most important works, he looked at what happens to individuals' identities when all their props are removed and they are forced to conform to an absolutely rigid regime. In a **total institution** such as a prison, mental hospital, and concentration camp, Goffman discerned that individuals are routinely stripped of anything that identifies them as individuals. And yet, still, they try to assert something that is theirs alone, something that enables them to hold on to their individual senses of themselves. In his conclusion to his book *Asylums* (1961), Goffman describes this dynamic, an eloquent expression of "iSoc"—the connections between identity and inequality, and interaction and institutions. He writes that

> without something to belong to, we have no stable self, and yet total commitment and attachment to any social unit implies a kind of selflessness. Our sense of being a person can come from being drawn into a wider social unit; our sense of selfhood can arise through the little ways in which we resist the pull. Our status is backed by the solid buildings of the world, while our sense of personal identity often resides in the cracks. (Goffman 1961, p. 320)

In other words, identity comes from our interactions with others in the institutions of the social world.

STRUCTURAL FUNCTIONALISM AND SOCIAL ORDER   At the larger, structural, or "macro" level, sociologists were preoccupied with political and social stability and order. Talcott Parsons (1902–1979), the leading exponent of what he called **structural functionalism**, looked to Durkheim's idea of organic solidarity—the idea that society is held together as an organic whole through shared values and norms and the division of labor—as the inspiration for his theory. According to Parsons, social life consisted of several distinct integrated levels that enable the world—and individuals who are within it—to find stability, order, and meaning. Functionalism offers a **paradigm**, a coherent model of how society works and how individuals are socialized into their roles within it (Parsons 1937, 1951).

Parsons believed that like most natural phenomena, societies tend toward balance—balance within all their component parts and balance within each individual member of society. The functionalist model stresses balance and equilibrium among the values of the society, its norms, and the various institutions that develop to express and sustain those values over time. According to this perspective, every institution, every interaction has a "function"—the reproduction of social life. Thus, for example, educational institutions function to ensure

dramaturgical model
Erving Goffman's conception of social interaction as like an actor preparing to perform a part in a play.

total institution
An institution that completely circumscribes your everyday life, cutting you off from life before you entered and seeking to regulate every part of your behavior.

structural functionalism
A sociological paradigm that contends that all social life consists of several distinct, integrated levels that enable society—and individuals who are within it—to find stability, order, and meaning.

paradigm
An example, pattern, or model, especially an outstandingly clear or typical example or archetype.

The British say the king (or queen) "reigns but does not rule." To the sociologist, the monarchy symbolically represents the nation, providing a sense of unity and shared purpose.

the steady transmission of social values to the young and to filter their entry into the labor force until the labor force can accommodate them. (If every 18-year-old simply went off to work, more than half wouldn't find jobs!) Families "function" to regulate sexual relationships and to ensure the socialization of the young into society.

It was left to Robert K. Merton (1910–2003), Parsons's former student and colleague, to clarify functionalism and also extend its analysis. Like Parsons, he argued that society tends toward equilibrium and balance. Those processes, events, and institutions that facilitate equilibrium he called "functional," and those that undermine it he called "dysfunctional." In this way, Merton understood both the forces that maintain social order and that threaten to undermine it (Merton 1949/1976)

Merton argued that the functions of any institution or interaction can be either "manifest" or "latent." **Manifest functions** are overt and obvious, the intended functions, while **latent functions** are hidden and unintended but nonetheless important. For example, the manifest function of going to college used to be that a person educated in the liberal arts would be a better, more productive citizen. The latent function was that going to college would also enable the graduate to get a better job. However, that's changed significantly, and the manifest function for most college students today is that a college education is a prerequisite for getting a good job. Latent functions today might include escape from parental control or access to a new set of potential dating partners, because many people meet their future spouses in college.

Functionalists believed that every social institution helped to integrate individuals into social life. What *was*, they argued, "was" for a reason—it worked. When there was a problem, such as, for example, juvenile delinquency, it was not because delinquents were bad people but because the system was not socializing young boys adequately or properly. Poverty was not the result of the moral failings of the poor but a systemic incapacity to adequately provide jobs and welfare to all. Although functionalism was criticized for its implicit conservatism—if it exists it serves a purpose and shouldn't be changed—the theory also expressed a liberal faith in the ability of American institutions to eventually respond to social problems. From an iSoc perspective, functionalism has been subsequently understood as paying too little attention to intersections and inequality.

Functionalism was, itself, "functional" in explaining society during a period of stability and conformity like the 1950s. But by the end of the decade there were rumblings of change—from individuals and groups who came to believe that what functioned for some groups wasn't so functional for other groups. These shifts and the social inequality and intersections they revealed helped push sociologists to see the world differently.

CONFLICT THEORIES: AN ALTERNATIVE PARADIGM   In the 1960s, many sociologists, inspired more by Marx and Weber than by Durkheim and Parsons, argued that this celebrated ability of American institutions to respond to social problems was itself the problem. American institutions did not solve problems; they caused them by allocating resources unequally. The United States was a society based on structural inequality, on the unequal distribution of rewards. The rich got richer, and the poor got poorer—and the institutions of the economy, the political process, and social reforms often perpetuated that inequality.

Generally, these sociologists adopted a theoretical paradigm that was called **conflict theory**—a theory that suggested that the dynamics of society, both of social order and social resistance, were the result of the conflict among different groups. Like Marx and Weber before them, conflict theorists believed that those who had power sought to maintain it; those who did not have power sought to change the system to get it. The constant struggles between the haves and the have-nots were the organizing principle of society, and the dynamic tension between these groups gave society

manifest functions
The intended consequences of an action or event.

latent functions
The unintended consequences of an action or event.

conflict theory
Theoretical approach that stresses the competition for scarce resources and unequal distribution of those resources based on social status (such as class, race, gender).

Rich or poor? No, rich *and* poor. Conflict theorists argue that society is held together by the tensions of inequality and conflict. Globally, relations between countries often mirror relations within a country.

its motion and its coherence. Conflict theories included those that stressed gender inequality (feminist theory), racial inequality (critical race theory), or class-based inequality (Marxist theory or socialist theory).

For two decades, the 1970s and 1980s, these two theories, functionalism and conflict theory, were themselves in conflict as the dominant theoretical perspectives in sociology. Were you to pick up an introductory sociology textbook originally written in the last two decades of the twentieth century, between 1980 and 2000, it would likely describe these two theoretical perspectives (as well as symbolic interactionism to describe micro-level social interactions) as the dominant and competing perspectives of the field (see TABLE 1.3).

Today the dramatic global economic and political shifts of the past decades, the rise of new transnational institutions like the European Union (EU) and trade agreements like the North American Free Trade Act (NAFTA), and the rise of new social movements based on ethnicity or religion to challenge them require that sociologists shift the lenses through which they view the social world. iSoc helps sociologists do just this.

Today we no longer see a struggle between an emphasis on order or conflict, or between identity of the individual and larger social inequalities. Sociology understands that identity and inequality are linked, that the very mechanisms by which we create

TABLE 1.3 Major Sociological Schools of Thought, 1950–2000

Theory	Level of Analysis	Order: What Holds Society Together?	Individual to Society	Change	Direction of Change
Structural-functionalism	Macro	Society is a stable system of interrelated elements—shared values, institutions—and there is general agreement (consensus) about how society should work.	Individuals are integrated into society by socialization.	Incomplete integration leads to deviance. Change is progressive.	Positive: Society is evolving to more and more equality.
Conflict theory	Macro	Society is a dynamic tension among unequal groups marked by an unequal distribution of rewards and goods.	Individuals belong to different groups that compete for resources.	Groups mobilize to get greater goods.	Short term: conflict. Longer term: greater equality.
Symbolic interactionism	Micro	Society is a set of processes among individuals and groups, using symbolic forms (language, gestures, performance) to create identity and meaning.	Individuals connect to others symbolically.	Tension between institutions and individual identity.	No direction specified.

our own identity are related to those social mechanisms by which social inequality is created and sustained. We don't see our interest in the micro-level interactions of individuals to be at odds with a focus on social institutions like the workplace or education anymore. Today, we see interactions embedded within institutions—and those institutions founded on regular, routine, and patterned interactions that shape not only our identities as members of a society, but also forms of inequality best understood by attending to the various intersecting identities we each possess.

---

iSOC AND YOU

The great theorists and founders of the field of sociology were each concerned with aspects of iSoc. Some, like Marx and Weber, stressed larger-scale *inequalities* based on class or status, and suggested that *identities* were derived almost entirely from your position in society. Others, like Mead and Simmel, stressed how patterns of *interaction* could both reproduce those *inequalities* and also enable individuals to develop a sense of *identity*. And many, like Fuller, Gilman, and Du Bois suggested that sociology should be concerned with doing more than simply documenting *inequalities* in society, but working to uncover solutions and programs for social change. These are all issues sociologists still care deeply about today, and perspectives that continue to shape sociological research.

1.4 Sociology NOW: New Issues, New Lenses

Sociologists are interested in the forces that pull societies together as well as those that push them apart. And often, different forces are at work at the same time such that we are all being tugged and pulled in all sort of directions. Sociologists rely on iSoc thinking to attempt to better understand what is pulling or pushing us and where we are being pulled or pushed. But they are equally interested today in examining the ways that different groups in society are pushed and pulled in different directions. Societies today are among the most diverse they have ever been. And the cultural diversity that exists around the world is something sociologists find awe-inspiring. And yet, we also know that some of that cultural diversity is changing—societies are becoming *less* different and distinct than they once were at the same time as societies are becoming *more* diverse than ever before.

How is that possible? Sociologists today not only examine interaction within societies, but between societies as well. We are all "global citizens" today more so than ever before in our history. You might have eaten a banana from Costa Rica for breakfast while reading news about economic changes in Europe on your smart phone assembled in China, wearing clothes from around the world, from South America to Southeast Asia. We're not always aware of all of the global connections necessary to pull all of this off—and most of the time, we simply don't need to be aware of it. But, that does not mean it is without consequence. To understand why we are both more diverse than ever at the same time as societies around the world are becoming less distinct, we need to ask new questions and combine our iSoc lenses in new ways.

Globalization and Multiculturalism

1.4.1 Understand how and why globalization and multiculturalism are central issues for sociologists to study today.

The events of the past few decades have seen these older divisions among sociologists subsiding and the incorporation of new lenses through which to view sociological issues.

The concepts that most epitomize these new lenses are *globalization* and *multiculturalism*. By **globalization**, we are referring to the interconnections—economic, political, cultural, social—among different groups of people all over the world, the dynamic webs that connect us to one another, and the ways these connections also create cleavages among different groups of people. Within the iSoc framework, globalization expresses the large scale inequalities and their institutional arrangements. Globalization is the new social context for interactions, identity, and institutions. It is the complex connectedness and patterned inequalities in which people interact.

By **multiculturalism**, literally the understanding of many different cultures, we come to understand the very different ways that different groups of people approach issues, construct identities, and create institutions that express their needs. Within the iSoc framework, multiculturalism describes how we develop identities in and through those structures of inequality, and how our interactions express those identities.

Globalization focuses on larger, **macro-level analysis**, which examines large-scale institutional processes such as the global marketplace, corporations, and transnational institutions such as the United Nations or World Bank. Multiculturalism stresses both the macro-level unequal distribution of rewards based on class, race, region, gender, and the like and also the **micro-level analysis**, which focuses on the ways in which different groups of people and even individuals construct their identities based on their membership in those groups. For example, the globalization of the media industries allows books, magazines, movies, television programs, and music from almost every country to be consumed all over the world. A macro-level analysis of globalization might point to ways global information exchange promotes interconnection and mutual understanding. A micro-level, multiculturalist analysis might point out, however, that the flow of information is mostly one way, from the West and particularly the United States into other countries, dominating other cultures, reinforcing global economic inequalities, and promoting a homogeneous, Westernized global society. Or a multiculturalist might argue that global media, particularly the Internet, are playing a role in reinvigorating local cultures and identities by promoting mixing and fusion and by allowing a diversity of voices—including "alternative" and "radical" ones—to be heard (Williams 2003).

GLOBALIZATION AND MULTICULTURALISM: INTERRELATED FORCES Today the world often seems to alternate between feeling like a centrifuge, in which everything at the center is scattered into millions of individual, local particles, and a great gravitational vacuum that collects all these local, individual particles into a congealing center.

There are numerous, formerly unimaginable changes that go under the heading of "globalization"—scientific advances, technological breakthroughs that connect people all over the globe, the speed and integration of commercial and economic decisions, the coherence of multinational political organizations and institutions—like the recently "invented" European Union and G8 organizations, not to mention the older and venerable organizations like the United Nations (founded in 1945) and NATO (the North Atlantic Treaty Organization, founded in 1950). The increased globalization of production of the world's goods—companies doing business in every other country—is coupled with increasingly similar patterns of consumption as teenagers all over the world are listening to Coldplay or Lady Gaga on portable stereo equipment made in Japan, talking on cell phones made in Finland, wearing clothing from the Gap that is manufactured in Thailand, walking in Nikes or Reeboks, shopping at malls that feature the same boutiques, which they drive to in cars made in Germany or Japan, using gasoline refined by American or British companies from oil extracted from the Arabian peninsula.

Just as our societies are changing dramatically, bringing the world closer and closer together, so too are those societies changing, becoming multiracial and multicultural. Increasingly, in **industrial societies**, the old divisions between women and

globalization
A set of processes leading to the development of patterns of economic, political, cultural, and social relationships that transcend geographical boundaries; a widening, deepening, and speeding up of worldwide interconnectedness in all aspects of contemporary life.

multiculturalism
The doctrine that several different cultures (rather than one national culture) can coexist peacefully and equitably in a single country.

macro-level analysis
Analysis of the large-scale patterns or social structures of society, such as economies or political systems.

micro-level analysis
Analysis of small-scale social patterns, such as individual interactions or small group dynamics.

industrial societies
Those societies driven by the use of technology to enable mass production, supporting a large population with the capacity for a high division of labor.

men and among various races and ethnicities are breaking down. Women and men are increasingly similar: both work, and both care for children, and the traits that were formerly associated with one sex or the other are increasingly blurred. Most of us know that we possess both the capacities for aggression, ambition, and technical competence as well as the abilities to be compassionate and caring. Industrial countries like the United States or the nations of Europe are increasingly multicultural. Gone are the days when to be American meant being able to trace your lineage to the Mayflower or when to be Swedish meant uniformly blond hair and blue eyes. Today, even the U.S. Census cannot keep up with how much we're changing—among the fastest-growing racial categories in the United States in recent history has been "multiracial." Just who are "we" anyway?

At the same time that we've never been closer or more similar to each other, the boundaries between us have never been more sharply drawn. The collapse of the Soviet Union led to the establishment of dozens of new nations, based entirely on ethnic identity. The terrifying explosion of a murderous strain of Islamic fundamentalism vows to purify the world of all nonbelievers. Virtually all the wars of the past two decades have been interethnic conflicts, in which one ethnic group has attempted to eradicate another from within the nation's borders—not necessarily because of some primitive bloodlust on the part of those neighboring cultures, but because the political entities in which they were forced to live, **nation-states**, were themselves the artificial creations of powerful nations at the end of the past century. The Serbian aggression against Bosnia, Croatia, and Kosovo; the Hutu and Tutsi in Rwanda; the past or current tribal civil wars in Somalia or Congo; plus dozens of smaller-scale interethnic wars have given the world a new term for the types of wars we witness now—**ethnic cleansing**.

The drive for uniformity as the sole basis for unity, for sameness as the sole basis for security, leads to internal efforts at perpetual self-purification—as if by completely excluding "them," we get to know what "us" means. Such efforts are accompanied by a dramatic (and often violent) restoration of traditional roles for women and men. Women are "refeminized" by being forced back into the home, under lock and key as well as under layers of physical concealment; men are "remasculinized" by being required to adopt certain physical traits and return to traditional clothing and the imposition of complete control over women.

nation-states
A sovereign state whose citizens or subjects are relatively homogenous in factors such as language or common descent.

ethnic cleansing
The mass expulsion or killing of members of an unwanted ethnic or religious group in a society.

Global Tensions

1.4.2 Explain the ways that globalization and multiculturalism are interrelated forces in the world today.

In the world, there are some master trends—such as globalization and multiculturalism; technological and marketplace advances; religious fundamentalism and local tribalisms—which do not simply conflict with one another. They are not simply competing worldviews,

Religion can bring us together in joy and song …

… or drive us apart in anger and hatred.

a "clash of civilizations." Such a view imagines these as two completely separate entities, now on a collision course for global conflagration, and ignores the ways in which each of these trends is a reaction to the other, is organized in response to the other, is, in the end, *produced* by the other. And such a view also misses the ways in which these master trends are contained within any society—indeed, within all of us.

Globalization is often viewed as increasing homogeneity around the world. The sociologist George Ritzer calls it **McDonaldization**—the homogenizing spread of consumerism around the globe (1996). *New York Times* columnist Thomas Friedman (2000) once predicted that "no two countries which both have a McDonald's will go to war with each other."

McDonaldization
The homogenizing spread of consumerism around the globe.

Friedman's prediction turned out to be wrong—in part because he saw only that part of globalization that flattens the world and minimizes cultural and national differences. But globalization is also accompanied by multiculturalism, an increased awareness of the particular aspects of our specific identities, and a resistance to losing them to some global identity, which most people find both grander and blander. In the words of political scientist Benjamin Barber (1996), our world is characterized by *both* "McWorld" and "Jihad"—the integration into "one commercially homogeneous network" and also increased tribalization and separation.

Globalization and multiculturalism express *both* the forces that hold us together—whether the repression of armies, police forces, and governments, or the shared values of nationalism or ethnic pride—*and* the forces that drive us apart. These are, actually, the same forces.

For example, religion both maintains cohesiveness among members and serves as one of the principal axes of division among people in the world today. Ethnicity provides a sense of stable identity and a way of distinguishing ourselves from others, as well as a way that society unequally allocates resources. Gender, race, youth/age, and social class also contribute to stable identity and can help us feel connected to groups, but they similarly serve as major contributors to social inequality, thus pulling society apart.

One impetus for the recognition of globalization and multiculturalism as among the central organizing principles of society is the continued importance of race, class, and gender in social life. In the past half-century, we've become increasingly aware of the centrality of these three categories of experience. Race, class, and gender are among the most important axes around which social life revolves, the organizing mechanisms of institutions, the foundations of our identities. Along with other forms of identity and mechanisms of inequality—ethnicity, sexuality, age, and religion—they form a matrix through which we understand ourselves and our world. This is the **matrix of inequality**—those various and overlapping and intersecting levels of inequality based on age, race, ethnicity, class, gender, sexuality, religion, and the like. Its connection to the way we develop our identities and interact in and with social institutions is integral to sociological thinking today.

matrix of inequality
The various and overlapping intersections of inequality an individual might experience based on age, race, ethnicity, class, gender, sexuality, religion, and the like.

Conclusion

Sociology NOW: Sociology and You

Sociologists are part of a larger network of social scientists. Sociologists work in colleges and universities, teaching and doing research, but they also work in government organizations, doing research and policy analysis; in social movements, developing strategies; and in large and small organizations, public and private.

Sociologists reflect and embody the processes we study, and changes in the field of sociology are, in a way, a microcosm of the changes we observe in the society in which we live. Over the past few decades, the field has undergone more dramatic changes than many other academic fields of study. Sociology's mission

SOCIOLOGY AND OUR WORLD

TWO ALTERNATIVE VIEWS OF THE WORLD

How does the way we visualize the globe affect the ways we think about different societies and groups of people?

These two maps of the world are altered in ways that are meant to convey different kinds of information. People and wealth are not evenly distributed around the world. Some societies have enormous populations; others are dwarfed by comparison. The top image here alters the size of the physical land spaces of different countries by population. The map below depicts the world based on the side of the gross domestic product per capita, rather than by land mass. Here, nations that appear larger have higher levels of gross domestic product (GDP) per capita; those that appear smaller have lower levels of GDP. It's a powerful way of illustrating economic inequality around the world. On the bottom map, Africa is barely visible at all, most of Asia is dramatically smaller when compared to the map above. Indeed, a small collection of nations appear to be most of the world when looked at from this perspective. This is one small way you can learn to *see* like a sociologist.

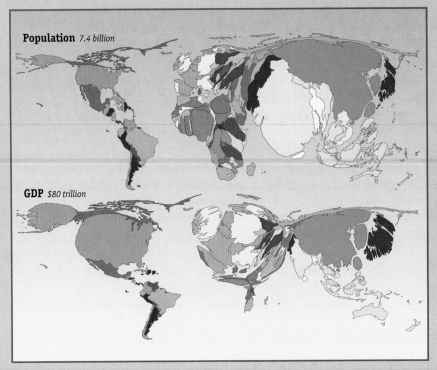

SOURCE: Cartogram image from Benjamin J. Hening (May 11, 2016). "The World in 2016." Available at http://www.viewsoftheworld.net/?p=4822.

is to understand what differentiates different groups in society (what causes "us" to feel different from "them") and what kinds of consequences are associated with this process. We endeavor to understand the dynamics of both identity and inequality that belonging to these groups brings and our various identities intersect in ways that cause us to feel pushed and pulled in multiple directions sometimes. Sociologists also want to understand the role of different social institutions—the family, education, workplace, media, religious institution, and the like—in shaping the experiences and opportunities of diverse groups of people throughout social life. It makes a certain logical sense, therefore, that many members of marginalized groups, such as racial, sexual, and ethnic minorities and women, would find a home in sociology. It is a field dedicated to valuing diverse perspectives and identities.

Once, of course, all academic fields of study were once the dominion of white men. Today, however, women and racial, ethnic, and sexual minorities have transformed collegiate life. Not that long ago, women were excluded from many of the most prestigious colleges and universities; now, women outnumber men on virtually every college campus. Not that long ago, racial minorities were excluded from many U.S. universities and colleges; today, universities have special recruiting task forces to ensure a substantial minority applicant pool. Not that long ago, gays and lesbians, bisexuals, and transgender people were expelled from colleges and universities for violating ethics or morals codes; today, there are lesbian, gay, bisexual, transgender (LGBT) organizations on most college campuses. Sociology has been one of the fields that has pioneered this inclusion. It is a source of pride to most sociologists that today sociology is among the most diverse fields on any campus.

In the past 50 years (since 1966), the percentage of BA degrees in sociology awarded to women has increased 116 percent, and the percentage of MA degrees has more than doubled, from 30.7 percent to 67.7 percent, and the percentage of PhD degrees rose a whopping 414 percent (American Sociological Association 2014). At the same time, the percentage of African American PhDs in sociology has almost doubled, while the percentage of Hispanic PhDs increased by ten times in the same period, and Asian American degrees almost quadrupled—all of these are among the highest percentages in any social science (American Sociological Association 2012).

We live in a society composed of many different groups and many different cultures, subcultures, and countercultures, speaking different languages, with different kinship networks and different values and norms. It's noisy, and we rarely agree on anything. And yet we also live in a society where the overwhelming majority of people obey the same laws and are civil to one another and in which we respect the differences among those different groups. We live in a society characterized by a fixed hierarchy and in a society in which people believe firmly in the idea of mobility, a society in which one's fixed, ascribed characteristics (race, class, and sex) are the single best determinants of where one will end up, and a society in which we also believe anyone can make it if he or she works hard enough.

This is the world sociologists find so endlessly fascinating. This is the world about which sociologists develop their theories, test their hypotheses, and conduct their research. Sociology is the lens through which we look at this dizzying array of social life—and begin to try and make sense of it. Welcome to it—and welcome to sociology and iSoc as a new way of seeing that world.

CHAPTER REVIEW What Is Sociology?

1.1 Sociology as a Way of Seeing

Sociologists use their "sociological imagination" as a lens to see beyond individual behavior to the larger social forces and regularities that affect society and the people who comprise it. This allows us to consider social behavior from numerous perspectives, across a wide variety of social phenomena, at many levels of analysis. We can focus on regularities, or on divergences from the usual; on social order or on disorder. As sociologists recognize, what appear to be contradictions are part of the whole fabric of society. The discipline of sociology considers the context

for human behavior and looks beyond the individual experience. When seen through the lens of the sociological imagination, the invisible and dynamic connections at play in the social order are revealed. Sociological understanding goes beyond either–or.

1.1 Key Terms

sociology The study of human behavior in society

sociological imagination The ability to see the connection between our individual identities and the social contexts (family, friends, and institutions) in which we find ourselves

1.2 iSoc: Sociological Frames of Analysis

Social behavior is complex. It can be studied at many levels; for example, we can consider small groups, countries, cultures, or even a global economy. For a sociologist, seemingly private or personal problems are seen as public, or societal, issues. For sociologists, as Mills said, sociology is how to locate your biography in history—that is, sociology is about who you are—but in context. Because the sociological lens examines the "both–and" and not the "either–or," we can explain the sociological framework with five "I's": *Identity; Inequality; Interaction; Institution; Intersectionality.* Sociology is about your *identity* but in the context of social dynamics, and particularly the unequal distribution of rewards, or *inequality.* And it's about the processes by which we experience identity and inequality, both in our daily *interactions* with others and in every *institution* in which we find ourselves. More than that, it's about the connections *between* identity and inequality, and *between* interactions and institutions, and also about the connections between identity and inequality on the one hand, and interaction and institutions on the other. Sociologists examining these connections are looking at *intersections.* Learning to see the world around you from the perspective of iSoc is what it means to understand the sociological perspective.

1.2 Key Terms

identity The unique combination of group affiliations and social characteristics that each individual develops.

intersectionality Sociological term for the ways that different identities "intersect" with one another to shape our social identity and our experience of inequality.

social inequality The social process by which valued goods, opportunities, and experiences are unequally distributed throughout a population.

social groups A collection of individuals bound by a common social identity or by some shared goal and purpose.

social institutions Patterned sets of interactions that work to meet collective needs that are not easily met by individuals working alone. They include such social arenas as markets, families, schools, corporations, factories, and prisons.

"modernization theory" of name trends Stanley Lieberson's explanation for the reduction in pressures associated with social *institutions* like extended family rituals or religious rituals associated with the naming of children—trends that led to more name diversity.

1.3 Where Did Sociology Come From?

Historical changes in governments, economies, and beliefs raised questions about the nature of society. During the Enlightenment, as science gained credence, secularism advanced, religion receded from civic life, and monarchy

subjects became citizens, philosophers explored the relationship of the individual to society. Ideas formative for new republics, including France and United States, were important in the emergence of sociology, the name Comte gave the science that studied the changes and challenges facing society to help it progress. Durkheim, one of sociology's founders, explored changes in the individual's relationship to others as societies moved toward modernization in his discussion of mechanical solidarity and organic solidarity. Ward, a U.S. sociologist, like Comte believed that sociology could improve society through planning and reform, instead of allowing social Darwinism to prevail, to the detriment of society. Mead's work in identity developed the idea of the self as social, internalizing the generalized other. White males traditionally dominated sociology, but more recently, black and female theorists who explored inequality, long ignored, are now recognized for their contributions. Since the modern era, sociology has emphasized the self in society and social stability amid change. Three main paradigms emerged in the twentieth century. Symbolic interactionism emphasized the role of micro-level interaction in the construction of self and society, while structural functionalism developed a paradigm of societal equilibrium and order through institutions, which serve both manifest functions and latent functions. In the turbulent 1960s, as many societies grappled with issues of inequality, conflict theory held great relevance. Based on the writings of Marx and Weber, it emphasized social conflict, identifying structural inequities in power and resources as the source of social inequality. Today, the twin lenses of globalization, emphasizing cross-cultural interaction and integration, and multiculturalism, awareness of cross-cultural differences, are used to view social issues, and a matrix of inequality, in which various overlapping and intersecting levels of inequality based on difference—race, class, gender, sexuality, religion, ethnicity, age, and the like—is integral to sociological thinking.

1.3 Key Terms

The Enlightenment Also called "The Age of Reason," theorists challenged the established social order, like the rule of the monarchy and hereditary aristocracy, and the ideas that justified it, like the "divine right of kings." It was during the Enlightenment of the seventeenth and eighteenth centuries that the idea of the "individual" took shape.

American Revolution and French Revolution Between 1776 and 1838, European society underwent a dramatic change—politically, economically, and intellectually—in part inspired by the work of Enlightenment thinkers. These revolutions replaced absolutist monarchs with republics, where power rested not on the divine right of kings and queens but on the consent of the people.

Industrial Revolution The rapid development of industry that occurred in numerous countries in the eighteenth and nineteenth centuries reorganized the production and distribution of goods from the quaint system of craft production, in which apprentices learned trades and entered craft guilds, to large-scale factory production in which only the very few owned the factories and many workers had only their ability to work to sell to the highest bidder.

social solidarity Émile Durkheim's term for the moral bonds that connect us to the social collectivity.

mechanical solidarity Émile Durkheim's term for a traditional society where life is uniform and people are similar. They share a common culture and sense of morality that bonds them.

organic solidarity Émile Durkheim's term for a modern society where people are interdependent because of the high division of labor; they disagree on what is right and wrong but share solidarity because the division of labor makes them dependent on each other.

social fact Émile Durkheim's term for the values, norms, and structures that transcend individuals, exercising social control over them, and amenable to scientific study.

rationality A chief interest of Max Weber, who argued that rationality was the foundation of modern society—an escalating process of order and organization with dire consequences.

iron cage While Weber contended that rationality can free us from the theocratic past, he also argued that rationality can imprison us in an utterly dehumanized and mechanized world he termed "the iron cage."

social forms A special task of sociology is to study the forms of social interaction apart from their content. Georg Simmel assumed that the same social forms—competition, exchange, secrecy, domination—could contain quite different content and that the same social content could be embodied in different forms. Each social form, according to Simmel, would have distinctive properties.

canon The officially recognized set of foundational sociologists.

Social Darwinism A model of social change that saw each succeeding society as developing through evolution and the "survival of the fittest."

conspicuous consumption Thorstein Veblen's term to describe a new form of prestige based on accumulating and displaying possessions.

double consciousness W. E. B. Du Bois term for the social experience of black Americans as divided, often against oneself, as "two unreconciled strivings; two warring ideals in one dark body, whose dogged strength alone keeps it from being torn asunder."

generalized other The organized rules, judgments, and attitudes of an entire group. If you try to imagine what is expected of you, you are taking on the perspective of the generalized other.

symbolic interactionism Sociological perspective that examines how individuals and groups interact, focusing on the creation of personal identity through interaction with others. Of particular interest is the relationship between individual action and group pressures.

dramaturgical model Erving Goffman's conception of social interaction as like an actor preparing to perform a part in a play.

total institution An institution that completely circumscribes your everyday life, cutting you off from life before you entered and seeking to regulate every part of your behavior.

structural functionalism A sociological paradigm that contends that all social life consists of several distinct, integrated levels that enable society—and individuals who are within it—to find stability, order, and meaning.

paradigm An example, pattern, or model, especially an outstandingly clear or typical example or archetype.

manifest functions The intended consequences of an action or event.

latent functions The unintended consequences of an action or event.

conflict theory Theoretical approach that stresses the competition for scarce resources and unequal distribution of those resources based on social status (such as class, race, gender).

1.4 Sociology NOW: New Issues, New Lenses

The events of the past several decades have seen the older divisions among sociologists subsiding and the incorporation of new lenses through which to view sociological issues. The concepts that most epitomize these new lenses are globalization and multiculturalism. By globalization, we are referring to the interconnections—economic, political, cultural, social—among different groups of people all over the world, the dynamic webs that connect us to one another, and the ways these connections also create cleavages among different groups of people. Globalization is the new social context for interactions, identity, and institutions. It is the complex connectedness and patterned inequalities in which people interact. By multiculturalism, literally the understanding of many different cultures, we come to understand the very different ways that different groups of people approach issues, construct identities, and create institutions that express their needs. Globalization is often viewed as increasing homogeneity around the world, what one social scientist called "McDonaldization"—the homogenizing spread of consumerism around the globe. Another characterized its outcome as "McWorld." But globalization is also accompanied by multiculturalism, an increased awareness of the particular aspects of our specific identities, and a resistance to losing them to some global identity. In the world, there are some master trends—such as globalization and multiculturalism; technological and marketplace advances; religious fundamentalism and local tribalisms—which do not simply conflict with one another. They are not simply competing worldviews, a "clash of civilizations." Such a view imagines these as completely separate entities, now on a collision course, and misses the ways in which these master trends are contained within any society—indeed, within all of us. Globalization and multiculturalism express *both* the forces that hold us together—whether the repression of armies, police forces, and governments, or the shared values of nationalism or ethnic pride—*and* the forces that drive us apart. These are, actually, the same forces. This is the world sociologists find so endlessly fascinating. This is the world about which sociologists develop their theories, test their hypotheses, and conduct their research. Sociology is the lens through which we look at this dizzying array of social life—and begin to try and make sense of it.

1.4 Key Terms

globalization A set of processes leading to the development of patterns of economic, political, cultural, and social relationships that transcend geographical boundaries; a widening, deepening, and speeding up of worldwide interconnectedness in all aspects of contemporary life.

multiculturalism The doctrine that several different cultures (rather than one national culture) can coexist peacefully and equitably in a single country.

macro-level analysis Analysis of the large-scale patterns or social structures of society, such as economies or political systems.

micro-level analysis Analysis of small-scale social patterns, such as individual interactions or small group dynamics.

industrial societies Those societies driven by the use of technology to enable mass production, supporting a large population with the capacity for a high division of labor.

nation-states A sovereign state whose citizens or subjects are relatively homogenous in factors such as language or common descent.

ethnic cleansing The mass expulsion or killing of members of an unwanted ethnic or religious group in a society.

McDonaldization The homogenizing spread of consumerism around the globe.

matrix of inequality The various and overlapping intersections of inequality an individual might experience based on age, race, ethnicity, class, gender, sexuality, religion, and the like.

SELF-TEST

〉 CHECK YOUR UNDERSTANDING

1. The term *sociological imagination* refers to
   a. a personality trait shared by all sociologists.
   b. an analytic perspective that considers the context for individual behavior.
   c. the ability to come up with creative explanations for unusual human behavior.
   d. the fact that sociologists find people fascinating, which fuels their curiosity.

2. Which of the following best typifies the approach a sociologist might take toward understanding the situation faced by a father who is depressed because he lost his job?
   a. Figuring out which sort of psychiatric treatment would be most appropriate as an intervention to restore individual functioning
   b. Prescribing a medication that alleviates the symptoms of depression
   c. Exploring factors of the global economy that result in job loss or studying gender identities related to wage-earning.

   d. Developing an essay that compares representations of despair in postmodern societies found in paintings and literature

3. Sociologists approach social issues by
   a. focusing solely on stability and the social order.
   b. focusing primarily on disorder and chaos.
   c. concentrating on what is unique in an individual's experience.
   d. recognizing both stability and disorder.

4. Which of the following was not identified in the text examples of societal changes influenced by ideas important in the development of sociology?
   a. The American Revolution
   b. The Industrial Revolution
   c. The Cognitive Revolution
   d. The French Revolution

5. Durkheim found that suicides varied by age, religion, marital status, and employment status because of differences in

   a. integration and regulation.
   b. intelligence and mental illness.
   c. spirituality and morals.
   d. locus of control and education.

6. Du Bois coined which of the following terms to describe the experience of black Americans?

   a. the Iron Cage
   b. Social Darwinism
   c. double consciousness
   d. the irony of slavery

7. Goffman's dramaturgical model emphasizing people as social actors in roles is based on which paradigm?

   a. Symbolic interactionism
   b. Structural functionalism
   c. Conflict theory
   d. Globalization

Self-Test Answers: 1. b, 2. c, 3. d, 4. c, 5. a, 6. c, 7. a

CHAPTER 2

CULTURE AND MEDIA

The Squire's Nephews introduced to Miss Forester.

Culture and media both impact each other. The media we consume is, in part, a reflection of the culture of the society in which we live. But, so too does media influence culture. So, although etiquette manuals provide cultural templates for behavior and interactions, new technologies and media create the need for new forms of interactions and new norms and roles associated with them.

→ LEARNING OBJECTIVES

In this chapter, using the iSoc framework, you should be able to:

2.1.1 Illustrate culture and cultural elements using media as an example.

2.1.2 Recognize how each of the five elements of the iSoc model can be used to examine culture and media sociologically.

2.1.3 Explain how ethnocentrism and cultural relativism lead to different understandings of cultural diversity.

2.1.4 Differentiate between subcultures and countercultures.

2.2.1 Explain what symbols are and how sociologists understand them as pieces of culture that simultaneously unite and divide.

2.2.2 Describe the ways that language shapes the ways we understand ourselves and the societies in which we live.

2.2.3 Differentiate among rituals, norms, and values, and identify the ways they are socially enforced.

2.2.4 Distinguish among folkways, mores, and laws, and recognize societal values as subject to change and disagreement.

2.3.1 Describe the primary components of contemporary mass media and how they have been subject to cultural change.

2.3.2 Differentiate between high and popular culture and how they relate to cultural capital.

2.3.3 Understand fads and fashions, how they emerge, and how they are a part of our cultural tool kits.

2.3.4 Explain the movement of culture around the world and the process by which some cultures are situated as more dominant than others as a result of this movement.

2.4.1 Summarize the ways that cultural change occurs and is resisted.

Introduction

Look around your class. Odds are that some students are wearing a team logo on a T-shirt or jersey. Someone will be wearing something that proclaims the name of the school or perhaps a popular band or television show. Some will have the name of local professional sports teams. Some will wear easily identifiable athletic logos, like swooshes or stripes, and others will have large or discrete insignias that denote the designer of the clothing.

An enormous number of people are "branded"—wearing an article of clothing that indicates membership in a group. We often signal our membership by what we wear, what sorts of things we buy, or the kind of music we listen to. Wearing a logo or decal is a way of connecting, a way of feeling a part of some group or interest greater than ourselves.

Americans may be branded, but at the same time, we don't really like to be "labeled." We resist the stereotypes that might be associated with someone who is a loyal adherent to a particular brand or band. We're more than that, different from that. We're unique individuals and are not reducible to what we wear and what media we like and choose to consume. Yet culture and media have a complex reciprocal relationship whereby media can be understood as both shaping and reflecting our identities and the culture in which they emerge.

We are constantly constructing our identities—that sense of who we are that feels both internally authentic and that we present to others. And the way we construct that identity is through culture. Culture provides the arena in which we interact, the various symbols we use to signal our identities to others, and the means by which we do it. If societies are defined as bounded collections of individuals, then culture can be understood as all that "stuff" that bonds us together and pushes us apart. The "stuff" from which culture is composed is more diverse than you might think. That Green Day T-shirt and those Nike shoes, that butterfly tattoo and that earring all signal to others who we think we are. They are pieces of culture. But culture isn't limited to material objects and images. Sets of values, ideas, and ideals are also aspects of culture that help us to distinguish "me" from "you" and "us" from "them."

It's even more than that. While you are choosing what you will wear to signal your identity, those choices are based on tremendous social inequality. Who made that Green Day T-shirt? Who made those Nike shoes? How much were they paid? Were they made in sweatshops, by impoverished workers in parts of the world you may never visit? Who can afford to don those designer items to signal belonging to those particular groups? Does your expression of identity come at the expense of others—even if you are unaware of this? Global, economic, cultural, and political inequalities are part of the larger context that structure our identities.

It is this connection—between the personal and the structural—that defines the sociological perspective. Culture gives us the means by which we create that connection. It gives us the tools and materials to forge our identities and the perspective that tells us how and why to put things together that way. Culture helps us shape our destinies while simultaneously conditioning the course our destinies can take. In all its various formats, our media rank high among our culture's most powerful institutional forces today, providing so many of the tools we use to make and mark our identities as well as the stories we tell ourselves about what they mean.

2.1 Thinking about Culture and Media Sociologically

Sociology uses specific terms and concepts that enable us to see those linkages discussed in the preceding introduction and to make sense of both ourselves and the world in which we live. Every academic field uses certain concepts as the lenses through which it sees and therefore understands the world. The lenses through which sociologists see the world are broad terms like *society* and *culture*; structural terms like *institutions*; and cultural terms like *values* and *norms*. (We will discuss and define all these terms in the coming chapters.) Larger structures—institutions or organizations like the economy, government, family, education, or mass media—offer general patterns that shape and give meaning to virtually every aspect of our lives. Agency stresses the individual decisions that we make to shape our own destiny, enabled and constrained by social structures. In this sense, we can understand culture as something by which we are simultaneously empowered and dominated.

In this section, you will come to understand culture as the glue that binds societies together as well as that "stuff" that threatens to tear them apart. Culture is a broad term for all of that social "stuff" that helps us feel like an "us"—like cohesive units with a sense of solidarity. The media is quite possibly the fastest-growing, and one of the most all-encompassing elements of our culture today. So, we examine this to illustrate both transformations in our culture as well as the extent to which we rely on culture every day. To understand how culture both unites and divides us, sociologists consider culture by relying on what we refer to in this text as the "iSoc model" (introduced in Chapter 1). You'll become more familiar with this model because we will be relying on it in each chapter to help you understand the ways that sociological knowledge and inquiry are connected. In this chapter, we will be learning about why sociologists argue that we form identities from culture and our identities are also embedded in large-scale institutions that further shape and mold them. Alongside this, and often less visibly, when we consider culture intersectionally, we begin to understand that culture also shapes social inequalities as well.

Culture and Media

2.1.1 Illustrate culture and cultural elements using media as an example.

culture

Both the material basis for social life and the sets of values and ideals that we understand to define morality, good and evil, appropriate and inappropriate.

material culture

The physical objects and spaces that people use to define their culture, including homes, cities, mosques, factories, works of art, clothes and fashions, books and movies, as well as the tools they use to make them.

nonmaterial culture

Often just called "culture," the ideas and beliefs that people develop about their lives and their world.

media

The plural form of "medium," it is the term for the ways that we communicate with each other, from voice to gestures to methods of mass communication like publishing, broadcasting and the internet.

mass media

Any of the means of communication, such as books, newspapers, magazines, comic books, films and DVDs, radio, television, CDs and MP3s, and a range of digital and social media platforms, that reach large numbers of people.

Culture refers to the sets of values and ideals that we understand to define morality, good and evil, appropriate and inappropriate. Culture defines larger structural forces and also how we perceive them. Culture is what distinguishes humans from other animals; we transmit our culture from one generation to the next. What makes human life different is that we alone have a conscious "history," a continuity of generations and a purposive direction of change. Humans have culture. Culture is the foundation of society—both the material basis for social life and the ideas, beliefs, and values that people have. **Material culture** consists of the physical objects and space people use to define their culture and what they use to make them—the tools they use, the physical environment they inhabit, the clothes they wear, the books they read, the movies they see, and more. **Nonmaterial culture** consists of the ideas, values, and beliefs that people develop and share.

The cultural elements that make up media consist of both material and nonmaterial culture. **Media** refer to the ways that we communicate with each other. If I am talking, I am using the medium of speech. I could also sing, gesture, and make smoke signals. In the Canary Islands, people used to communicate through the medium of whistling. Right now, I am writing, or more precisely typing, using alphabetic symbols instead of sounds. Technological innovations like the printing press, the radio, the television, and the Internet have created **mass media**—ways to communicate with vast numbers of people at the same time, usually over a great distance. Mass media have developed in countless directions: There are books, newspapers, magazines, motion pictures, CDs and DVDs, radio and television programs, comic strips and comic books, and a whole range of new digital and social media. New forms of media are constantly emerging, and old forms are constantly falling into disuse.

Sometimes the new forms of mass media can revive or regenerate the old. Teenagers used to keep their diaries hidden in their rooms, with little locks to deter nosy family members. Today they are likely to publish them on the Internet as blogs, and post photos of themselves in the middle of all manner of silly, mundane, dangerous, and odd activities on social media platforms. Sociologists are interested in the access to media by different groups with different resources and also in the effects of media—how they affect our behaviors and attitudes, how they bring some of us together while driving some of us apart, how they shape the very rhythm of our days and lives.

Our culture shapes more than what we know, more than our beliefs and our attitudes; culture actually shapes our human nature. Some societies, like the Yanomamo in Brazil, "know" that people are, by nature, violent and aggressive, and so they

SOCIOLOGY AND OUR WORLD

USING MEDIA USE TO DETECT RHYTHMS IN OUR LIVES

How does technology use intersect with our lives in ways that might enable us to learn more about our daily rhythms?

Dr. Stephen Wolfram is a particle physicist, mathematician, and software entrepreneur. Unlike many of us, Dr. Wolfram documents his own media use in incredible detail. For instance, Dr. Wolfram knows that, since 1989, he has sent slightly more than 300,000 e-mails. He knows how many words he has typed, how many times he hits the "backspace" button, his sleep schedule, how much time he has spent on the phone, walking, eating, and more. He's collected an incredible amount of data on his own life. Examine the chart that plots individual e-mails sent by time of day from 1989 through 2012. The bottom of the chart is midnight. So, as you raise your eyes from the bottom, you are getting a glimpse of Dr. Wolfram's day. And as you move your eyes from left to right on the chart, you are seeing how Dr. Wolfram's days have (and haven't) changed over that period of time. What do you see?

It's hard not to notice the sheer volume of his e-mail activity. He's constantly e-mailing people. And from the density of the dots, we can see that he's started sending more e-mails over time. We also see that he's a bit of a night owl. The white band in the chart is when Dr. Wolfram is sleeping (and not e-mailing)—typically from about 3:00 A.M. until noon. And we can see another faint white band right around 7:00 P.M. every day (it's a bit less pronounced)—that's dinner. Dr. Wolfram's media use is part of the structure and rhythm of his life. And although he is probably an outlier in terms of media use and time spent, we can probably tell a great deal about our own lives by looking at how and when we leave digital footprints like Dr. Wolfram.

SOURCE: Wolfram, Dr. Stephen. "The Personal Analytics of My Life," March 8, 2012, *Stephan Wolfram blog*. Available at: http://blog.stephenwolfram.com/2012/03/the-personal-analytics-of-my-life/.

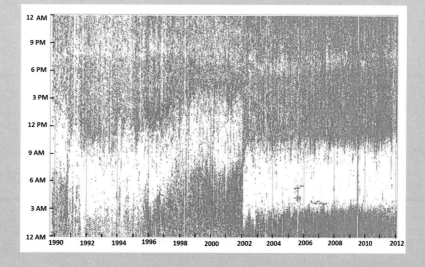

raise everyone to be violent and aggressive. But others, like the Tasaday tribe in the Philippines, "know" that people are kind and generous, and so everyone is raised to be kind and generous. In the United States, our culture is diverse enough that we can believe both sides, and more.

Sociological analyses of culture help us learn to see the ordinary as *extra*ordinary, and in so doing, to uncover the ways that identities, interactions, institutions, and inequalities are socially organized in ways that often make them appear to be natural and inevitable when they are anything but.

iSoc: Culture and Media

2.1.2 Recognize how each of the five elements of the iSoc model can be used to examine culture and media sociologically.

Culture is the foundation of society, the basis on which social institutions like the family, religion, and education are built and maintained over time. And media are one of the most pervasive and powerful elements and institutions of culture. As such, culture and media are central to the five elements of the iSoc model.

IDENTITY—Culture provides you with the tools and the arena to experience yourself as a "self"—a sense of group membership, a sense of belonging, which is the basic way that you anchor yourself. Indeed, it is only through culture that you can feel yourself to actually be a "self." Culture is what makes you feel like you—both how you fit in, and how you stand out. As an important aspect of culture, it is also through media that people actively create their *identities*. You use media to express yourself—from your Facebook page to your Instagram account, your texts, tweets, and e-mails, your family photos and videos. And media are also *how* you create that identity in the first place, providing a set of ideas, references, styles and products with which to mark yourself and a range of possible communities in which to situate yourself.

INEQUALITY—Cultures are not necessarily equal. Cultures provide a justification for *inequalities*, both among members of the culture itself and between your culture and others. For example, some cultures teach us that there are natural or theological reasons why women are not equal to men and are therefore not to be treated as equal. Some cultures teach that homosexuality is a cultural abomination, and others think it's just another way for people to love each other. These cultural ideas then become the basis for unequal treatment in society. What's more, many cultures also believe that their ways are superior to the ways of other cultures. This can serve to justify anything from wars and conquest to simply avoiding them and staying out of their way. Although a focus on identity helps us understand culture as the "stuff" that binds us together, focusing of inequality helps sociologists simultaneously consider the ways culture drives us apart.

Because media provide both the tools of identity creation, and some arenas in which identity is performed and evaluated, social inequality shapes the abilities of different groups to create and express their identities. Some media images of success or sexiness are simply out of reach for some people and groups; because of systems of inequality, media representations and voices privilege some characters and stories, skin colors, sexualities and body types, over others. If you don't have access, you may not be included, or you may not be credited as being a success or as sexy or attractive. Media inequality leads to some people having a harder time than others in creating their *identities*.

INTERACTION—Culture not only provides us with a sense of belonging, but it also provides a set of practices that remind you of this feeling and reinforce it. Traditions and rituals are handed down from generation to generation as "this is how our culture works," which enable you to feel more firmly rooted in place. Sometimes families develop their own traditions, such as who sits where at the dinner table or secret whistles or signals—all to remind you that you are "one of us" and that "we" are different from "them."

People also use the media as a means to facilitate social *interactions*—from telephones to Twitter to Instagram. But increasingly media *are* the interactions themselves. You might play "Words with Friends" or XBox games with people you don't know in other countries, or with your best friend. You "like" their posts on their Facebook page, comment on articles read online, and text friends and family. In fact, Americans spend so much time interacting *through* media that it might be hard for us to live without it. All of our interactions can be "mediated" in this way—from shopping to having sex, from paying bills to interacting with professors and students in online classes. And as mass and social media make new kinds of interactions possible, we are constantly developing new traditions and rituals to help structure mediated interactions. We are evolving and playing with culture.

INSTITUTIONS—These rituals and traditions can also become codified into organized, coherent *institutions*, with formal rules and procedures governing how you will interact with members of your group, and with members of other groups. One of the chief functions of many social institutions such as the family, education, or religion, is to transmit the values and rules of a society to the next generation, to give you a sort of map to guide you through your life according to the values of your culture.

Mass media have become so large and extensive that they saturate our lives. And the various institutions that develop media, present it, and regulate it, compose an increasingly large amount of social life. Every other social institution—the economy, education, religion, family life—all rely on various media to function effectively. Just as the media institutions have become much larger and more powerful; however, the purview of institutions charged with overseeing their content and accuracy have shrunk. Thus, mass media have become a social institution in their own right, and one that exerts enormous influence over our lives and our culture.

INTERSECTIONS—Many cultures also draw boundaries between different groups within a society by age, sex, race, nationality, religion, and more. For instance, some groups in society are simply much more likely to be reflected in the media than other groups. White, heterosexual men and women are disproportionately more likely to see people "like them" when they turn on the television, are bombarded with advertisements, flip through magazines, and more. Examining *intersections* help sociologists understand how culture works to differently position groups relative to one another in society.

Ask yourself: who, exactly are you? You're likely to describe yourself first by your membership in a cultural group. "I'm Irish," or "I'm a Midwesterner," or "I'm a Christian" (*identity*). And because of that, you have certain assumptions, which you could explain to others, about why you feel the way you do about, say, gay people, or the proper relationships between women and men, or about religious toleration (*inequality*). And you'll assume that because you are who you are, you can perform certain activities with other members of your group to reinforce your feelings of belonging (*interactions*). And, finally, you'll know that you can always find people who think and believe as you do in your school church, family, or community center (*institutions*).

Membership in one group doesn't prohibit membership in another. Sometimes our membership in one group is more visible to us than at other times, when that other group becomes more visible. For example, most Americans, most of the time, don't feel themselves to be very "American," which is to say that they look to other cultural groups first as the foundations of their identity (*intersections*). Your race, your ethnicity, your sexuality, your religious affiliation—these are often more important to you.

For the rest of this chapter—indeed, for the remainder of this book—we'll explore the five elements of the iSoc model (*identity, inequality, interaction, institutions,* and *intersections*) as the guiding principles of *Sociology NOW*.

Culture and Identity: Diversity and Universality

2.1.3 Explain how ethnocentrism and cultural relativism lead to different understandings of cultural diversity.

cultural diversity

The vast differences between the cultures of the world as well as the differences in belief and behavior that exist within cultures.

Cultural diversity means that cultures around the world are vastly different from each other. Their rich diversity sometimes appears exotic, sometimes tantalizing, and sometimes even disgusting. Even within American culture, there are subcultures that exhibit beliefs or behaviors that are vastly different from those of other groups. And, of course, culture is constantly changing, as beliefs and habits change. For example, in the early nineteenth century, it was a common prescribed cultural practice among middle-class New Englanders for a dating couple to be expected to share a bed together with a board placed down the middle, so that they could become accustomed to each other's sleeping behavior but without having sex. Parents would welcome their teenage children's "bundling" in a way they might not feel particularly comfortable doing today.

culture shock

A feeling of disorientation when the cultural markers that we rely on to help us know where we are and how to act have suddenly changed.

Often, when we encounter a different culture, we experience **culture shock**, a feeling of cultural disorientation brought on when the cultural markers we rely on to help us know where we are and how to act have suddenly changed. Sometimes, the sense of disorientation leads us to retreat to something more comfortable and reassert the values of our own cultures. We find other cultures weird, or funny, or sometimes we think they're immoral. In the 2003 movie *Lost in Translation*, Bill Murray and Scarlett Johansson experience the strange limbo of living in a foreign culture during an extended stay at a Tokyo hotel. They develop an unlikely bond of friendship, finding each other as a source of familiarity and comfort as so much around them feels unfamiliar and uncomfortable.

ethnocentrism

The use of one's own culture as the reference point by which to evaluate other cultures; it often depends on or leads to the belief that one's own culture is superior to others.

The condemnation of other cultures because they are different is called **ethnocentrism**, a belief that one's culture is superior to others. We often use our own culture as the reference point by which we evaluate others. William Graham Sumner, the sociologist who first coined the term, described ethnocentrism as seeing "one's own group [as] the center of everything, and all others … scaled and rated with reference to it" (Sumner 1906/2002, p. 12). Ethnocentrism can be relatively benign, as a quiet sense of superiority or even cultural disapproval of the other culture, or it can be aggressive, as when people try to impose their values on others by force.

cultural relativism

A position that all cultures are equally valid in the experience of their own members.

Sociologists must constantly guard against ethnocentrism because it can bias our understandings of other cultures. It's helpful to remember that each culture justifies its beliefs by reference to the same guiding principles. So when Yanomamo people act aggressively, they say, "Well, that's just human nature," which is exactly what the Tasaday say when they act kindly toward each other. Because each culture justifies its activities and organization by reference to these universals—God's will, human nature, and the like—it is difficult for any one of us to stand in judgment of another's organization and activities. Therefore, to a large extent, sociologists take a position of **cultural relativism**, a standpoint that considers all cultures as equally valid from the perspective of their own members.

In this cartoon we see ethnocentrism as a two-way street. People from different cultures often see elements of culture from other societies through the lens of their own culture. To many Westerners, the hijab is a symbol of women's subordinate status. But this Muslim woman thinks otherwise.

At the same time, many sociologists also believe that we should not shy away from claiming that some values are, or should be, universal values to which all cultures should subscribe. For example, the ideals of human rights that all people share—these are values that might be seen as condemning slavery, female genital mutilation, the killing of civilians

during wartime, the physical or sexual abuse of children, the exclusion of married men from prosecution for rape of their wives. Some have suggested that these universal human rights are themselves the ethnocentric imposition of Western values on other cultures, and they may be. But they also express values that virtually every culture claims to hold. Cultural relativism makes us sensitive to the ways other people organize their lives, but it should not absolve us from taking moral positions ourselves.

Cultures vary dramatically in the ways they go about the most basic activities of life: eating, sleeping, producing goods, raising children, educating them, making friends, making love, forming families. This diversity is sometimes startling; and yet, every culture shares some central elements. Every culture has history, a myth of origin, a set of guiding principles that dictates right and wrong, with justifications for those principles. Every culture has a language, kinship and education systems (formal and informal), systems of social control and punishment. Every culture has music, dance, art, and more. Sociologists refer to these elements that appear in virtually every society as **cultural universals**.

cultural universal
One of the rituals, customs, and symbols that are evident in all societies.

Cultural universals are broad and basic categories, allowing for significant variation as well. Not every society speaks the same language. And even among those that do, there are regional dialects, words, sayings and more that distinguish "our" culture from "their" culture. Focusing on cultural diversity and universality can help us recognize the ways that different cultures are often more alike than they sometimes appear. Cultural universals are expressed locally, experienced at the level of families, communities, and regions in ways that connect us not only to large and anonymous groups like our country but also to smaller, more immediate groups.

Identity and Inequality: Subcultures and Countercultures

2.1.4 Differentiate between subcultures and countercultures.

Because cultures can be large and diverse, we often find ourselves drawing on smaller parts of the larger culture for our identity, our sense of ourselves as rooted in some groups larger than ourselves. Even within a particular culture there are often different subgroups. Subcultures and countercultures are two kinds of subgroups that often develop within a culture.

A **subculture** is a group of people within a culture who share some distinguishing characteristics, beliefs, values, or attributes that set them apart from the dominant culture. Because ethnic and sexual minorities are often subjected to negative stereotyping, for instance, they often produce their own organizations, media, and even travel agencies. Subcultures are communities that constitute themselves through a relationship of *difference* to the dominant culture. So, for example, generation Y is a youth subculture, a group for which membership is limited to those of a certain age who believe they have characteristics that are different from the dominant culture. Members of a subculture are part of the larger culture, but they may draw more on their subcultural position for their identity.

subculture
Group within a society that creates its own norms and values distinct from the mainstream and usually its own separate social institutions as well.

Subcultures that identify themselves through their difference and opposition to the dominant culture are called **countercultures**. Countercultures offer an important grounding for identity, but they do so in *opposition* to the dominant culture. As a result, countercultures demand a lot of conformity from members. One can imagine, for example, belonging to several different subcultures, while also maintaining membership in the dominant culture. But countercultural membership often requires a sign of separation from dominant culture. Countercultures may exist parallel to the dominant culture, or they may be outlawed and strictly policed. For example, lots of contemporary music has associated subcultures, like hip-hop, punk, and alternative. But, some musical subcultures are more totalizing and border on countercultures—like goth and hard core—requiring clothing, hairstyles, tattoos, and makeup that are dramatically

counterculture
Subculture that identifies itself through its difference and opposition to the dominant culture.

Sometimes a countercultural movement can change a society. And sometimes, society can co-opt elements of a countercultural movement and make it mainstream. Consider the ways we have sold the identity of the "hippie" in the United States. Companies like Ben and Jerry's ice cream or Magic Hat Brewing Company continue to use many of the symbols made famous by young people fighting for peace, equality, and "free love" in the 1960s. This illustrates how countercultures can sometimes be assimilated into the official culture—a process that can be a sign of change, but is often a sign that the movement goals were not actually met. Today, for instance, "hippy" often feels like it is more about peace signs and tie-dye than radical politics and social revolution.

different from dominant culture and sometimes containing beliefs and values at odds with dominant culture as well.

Like subcultures, countercultures create their own cultural forms—music, literature, news media, art. Sometimes these may be incorporated into the official culture as signs of rebellion. For example, blue jeans, tattoos, rock and rap music, leather jackets, and wearing black pants and shirts together all have their origins as signs of countercultural rebellion from the hippie, ghetto, or fringe sexual cultures. But they were all incorporated into consumerism and have now achieved mainstream respectability.

The term *counterculture* came into widespread use during the 1960s to describe an emerging subculture based on age (youth), behaviors (marijuana and psychedelic drug use, "free" sexual practices), and political sensibilities (liberal to radical). Gradually, this subculture became well-defined in opposition to the official culture, and membership required wearing certain androgynous fashions (tie-dyed shirts, peace symbols, sandals, bell-bottom blue jeans, "peasant" blouses), bodily practices (everyone wearing their hair long, holding up two fingers), musical preferences, drug use, and anti-Vietnam War politics.

Countercultures are not necessarily on the left or the right politically—what they *are* is oppositional. In the contemporary United States, there are groups such as White supremacist survivalists as well as back-to-the-land hippies on communes: Both represent countercultures (and, given that they tend to be rural and isolated, they may also be neighbors).

---

iSOC AND YOU Thinking about Culture and Media Sociologically
Culture is a foundation for *identity*. Our *identities* are formed within culture, through culture, and we use cultural methods to express them. But that doesn't mean that all culture is equal to all other culture. You may think that all culture is equal in an ideal sense, in some religious or ideological scheme, but dominant cultures often use those differences to justify economic or social *inequalities*. Cultural *inequalities* may even be more painful than economic ones, because you may believe you can improve your economic situation, but your cultural situation is so deep that it defines who you "really" are. Within any large and complex cultural system, smaller groups—subcultures, countercultures—serve to further anchor our *identities* and as foundations for social conformity, resistance, or escape from the dominant and unequal cultural landscape.

2.2 Culture in Interactions

Interaction, without culture, is not possible. We rely on shared values, beliefs, understandings and more when we interact with anyone, anywhere, and any time. Our interactions require shared symbols, gestures, and language to make them possible and social rituals and norms to make those interactions patterned and, for the most part, predictable. You engage in all manner of activities to communicate with other people all of the time, even when you're not necessarily aware of the fact that you're doing this. Inside of the tools we use to interact with each other are the values and beliefs that shape the societies in which we live. And those values and beliefs become embedded in shared norms we all rely on to interact with one another. These values and beliefs are some of the basic building blocks out of which our identities, interactions, and institutions are produced and maintained over time. But values and beliefs are also used to justify inequality, and when we learn to examine them intersectionally, we can learn a lot about lines of authority, power, difference, and discrimination from the very same materials we rely on to identify ourselves and others.

From making decisions about whether and where to sit on public transportation, to navigating the intricacies of interacting with strangers on elevators, to talking with family members and friends, we all rely on culture to provide a blueprint for our interactions—a blueprint we both internalize and are constantly editing. In this section, we will focus primarily on six important elements of culture in interactions: material culture, symbols, language, norms, rituals, and values. You will come to understand just how much we need each one and how much of our lives and societies is organized around these basic building blocks.

symbol

Anything—an idea, a marking, a thing—that carries additional meanings beyond itself to others who share in the culture. Symbols come to mean what they do only in a culture; they would have no meaning to someone outside.

Material Culture and Symbols

2.2.1   Explain what symbols are and how sociologists understand them as pieces of culture that simultaneously unite and divide.

All cultures share six basic elements: material culture, symbols, language, rituals, norms, and values. We'll discuss the first three here, and the second three next. As we mentioned previously, material culture consists of both what people make and what they make it with. Material culture includes the environment we inhabit and the tools we develop to survive in it. But it's equally important for human societies to solve a need that is different from basic subsistence or survival: the basic human need for meaning. As humans wrestle with the meanings of their material environment, we attempt to represent our ideas to others. We translate what we see and think into symbols.

A **symbol** is anything—an idea, a marking, an image, an object—that carries additional meanings beyond itself to others who share in the culture. Symbols come to mean what they do only within a cultural context. Symbols can be created at any time. Witness the recent various ribbons—red for AIDS awareness, pink for breast cancer awareness. But many symbols developed over centuries and in relative isolation from one another. In the case of older symbols, the same ones may have completely different meanings in different cultures. For example, the color red means passion, aggression, or danger in the United States, while it signifies purity in India and is a symbol of celebration and luck in China. That's what we mean when we say that symbols take on their meaning only inside culture. Symbols are representations of ideas or

Flags can be powerful cultural symbols, eliciting strong emotions. To some, the "Stars and Bars" (a battle flag of the Confederate states during the Civil War) is a symbol of Southern heritage; to the majority of Americans (and people around the world), it is a symbol of racism and a reminder of slavery.

SOCIOLOGY AND OUR WORLD

U.S. RACE RELATIONS AND THE CONFEDERATE FLAG

How can we better understand the political upheaval in South Carolina to remove the Confederate flag at the Statehouse by understanding the meaning and power of cultural symbols?

On the evening of June 17, 2015, a 21-year-old white man entered a historic African Methodist Episcopal Church in Charleston, South Carolina. He sat briefly at a prayer service with ten Black Americans and then opened fire on them, killing all but one. The shooter's hope was to ignite a race war in the United States, a fact that became clearer when his racist manifesto surfaced after the act of domestic terrorism occurred. Pictures surfaced of the shooter holding a Confederate flag and wearing symbols associated with white supremacist organizations. National attention was quick to focus on the Confederate flag, a symbol that the shooter was depicted holding in an image that went viral after the attack.

Many South Carolinians recognized the symbol immediately, because the Confederate flag had been flying above the South Carolina Statehouse since 1962, when an all-white legislature voted to place it there. After the shooting in 2015, the Confederate flag became a symbol around which Americans discussed the issue of race and inequality in the United States. People began to protest the flag flying on state buildings. Ten days following the massacre, activist and filmmaker Bree Newsome climbed the flagpole and removed the Confederate flag at the South Carolina Statehouse. Newsome was promptly arrested. The flag was raised again less than an hour after she removed it. But Newsome's act, too, was symbolic.

By July 9, 2015, Then-Governor Nikki R. Haley of South Carolina signed a bill into law that ordered the removal of the Confederate flag from the Capitol grounds. Her decision illustrates a tension in U.S. culture concerning issues related to race. Consider the data that shows, although the majority of Americans supported Governor Haley's decision, different groups were more and less in favor of the decision. A Pew Survey (2015) conducted very quickly after the bill signing discovered that the majority of Americans (57 percent) agree with the decision to remove the flag. But 34 percent felt that it was the wrong decision. White people surveyed were consistent with Americans' feelings more generally—56 percent agreed and 34 percent disagreed. Among black Americans, however, only 12 percent disagreed with removing the flag, while 76 percent agreed. Similarly, Republicans were more likely to disagree than were Democrats. Agreement and disagreement surrounding this cultural symbol intersected with race and political party in ways that illustrate enduring forms of social inequality. It's a powerful illustration of just how much a cultural symbol can unite and divide.

feelings. Symbols stand in for something more complex. This is why symbols can also elicit powerful emotions: They express the emotional foundations of our culture.

Language

2.2.2 Describe the ways that language shapes the ways we understand ourselves and the societies in which we live.

language
An organized set of symbols by which we are able to think and communicate with others; the chief vehicle by which human beings create a sense of self.

Language is an organized set of symbols by which we are able to think and communicate with others. Language is also the chief vehicle by which human beings create a sense of self. It is through language that we pose questions of identity—"Who am I?"—and through our linguistic interactions with others that we constitute a sense of ourselves. We need language to know what we think as well as who we are. What makes the human use of language different from that of animals is that we use language to transmit culture, to connect us to both the past and the future, to build on the experiences of previous generations. And language does not merely reflect the world as we know it; language actually shapes our perceptions as well.

In 1929, two anthropologists, Edward Sapir and Benjamin Whorf, noticed that the Hopi Indians of the Southwest seemed to have no verb tenses, no ways for them to state a word in the past, present, or future tense. Imagine speaking to your friends without being able to put your ideas in their proper tense. Although common sense held that the function of language was to express the world we already perceived, Sapir and Whorf concluded that language, itself, provides a cultural lens through which people perceive the world. What became known as the **Sapir-Whorf hypothesis** states that language shapes our perception (Sapir 1921; Whorf 1956). We often say that we'll "believe it when we see it"—that empirical proof is required for us to believe something. But it's equally true that we "see it when we believe it"—we cannot "see" what we don't have the conceptual framework (language) to understand.

Sapir-Whorf hypothesis
A theory that language shapes our reality because it gives us a way to talk about the categories of life that we experience.

Because language not only reflects the world in which we live but also shapes our perception of it, language is also political. Consider, for example, the battles over the implicit gender bias of using the word *man* to include both women and men, and the use of the masculine pronoun *he* as the "inclusive" generic term. Some words, such as *chairman* or *policeman*, make it clear that the position carries a gender—whether the occupant of the position is male or female. Even the appellation for women and men was made the object of political struggle. Although referring to a man as "Mr." indicates nothing about his marital status, appellations for women referred only to their status as married (Mrs.) or unmarried (Miss). To create a neutral, parallel term for women, Ms., took several years before it became commonplace.

Rituals, Norms, and Values

2.2.3 Differentiate among rituals, norms, and values, and identify the ways they are socially enforced.

Another element enabling culture to persist over time is ritual. **Rituals** refer to practices by which members of a culture engage in routine behaviors to express their sense of belonging to the culture. Rituals both symbolize the culture's coherence by expressing our unity and also create that coherence by enabling each member to feel connected to the culture. Rituals are typically ceremonial; they are performed at significant times and often in exactly the same way each time. In this way, rituals not only bind people to the specific group of which they are a member but also bind them across generations to past and future members. Think of the way Americans sing the national anthem at the beginning of every professional sports game. No other country in the world does that. Participation in the ritual cements one's sense of belonging to the community and its shared cultural history. Most cultures have specific rituals to mark the specific transitions in a person's life: birth, coming of age, marriage, children, and death. It's often through our participation in these rituals that we know how to feel about our stage of life and our place in the community.

ritual
Enactment by which members of a culture engage in a routine behavior to express their sense of belonging to the culture.

Norms refer to the rules a culture develops that define how people should act and the consequences of failure to act in the specified ways. Cultural "norms" and cultural "values" are often discussed together. **Values** are the ethical foundations of a culture, its ideas about right and wrong, good and bad. Values are the ideas that justify norms; norms are behavioral reflections of values. Norms prescribe behavior within the culture; values explain to us what the culture has determined is right and wrong. Norms tell us how to behave; values tell us why. Like the other components of culture, norms and values vary from place to place. What might be appropriate behavior in one culture, based on its values, might be inappropriate or even illegal in another.

norm
One of the rules a culture develops that defines how people should act and the consequences of failure to act in the specified ways.

value
If norms tell us how to behave, values tell us why. Values constitute what a society thinks about itself and so are among the most basic lessons that a culture can transmit to its young.

HOW DO WE KNOW WHAT WE KNOW?

CHRISTMAS GIFT GIVING AS A METHOD OF NORM ENFORCEMENT

In the 1920s and again in the 1930s, a sociologist couple—Helen Merrell Lynd and Robert Staughton Lynd—conducted a famous collection of case studies on a small city they referred to as "Middletown" and considered a typical small American city (it was actually the city of Muncie, Indiana). The study was so famous that Muncie, Indiana, has retained a reputation of being an "average" small American city ever since. Another sociologist, Theodore Caplow, built on the Middletown Study by interviewing a random sample of Muncie residents about their Christmas gift-giving practices (1984). Caplow discovered that residents of Middletown (who were and still are almost entirely

Christian) followed incredibly nuanced rules surrounding Christmas. Caplow was not fascinated by the mere existence of the rules; rather he wanted to explain why and how gift-giving norms elicited more conformity than most laws—almost everyone followed them in exactly the same ways. People break rules all the time; yet virtually no one broke *these* rules. But nowhere were these rules written down, no institution or group of people was established to enforce them, and there was little indignation against or punishment for people who failed to follow them. Consider the following rules he discovered:

- *The "Wrapping Rule":* Christmas gifts must be wrapped before they are presented.
- *The "Gathering Rule":* Christmas gifts should be distributed at gatherings where every person gives and receives gifts.
- *The "Money Rule":* Money may only be given as a gift from someone of higher status (a parent or grandparent) to someone of lower status (a child). Gift certificates allow children to "cheat" on this rule—but actual cash or a check always follows this rule.

So, why did residents of Middletown all give gifts and celebrate Christmas in identical and patterned ways even though no one made them do it? As Caplow wrote, "Gift exchange, in effect, is a language that employs objects instead of words" (1984: 1320). People all celebrate Christmas in so many of the same ways in Middletown for many of the same reasons you say "Fine" when someone asks how you are even if you're having a tough day. We are all working together to produce patterned and predictable interactions—and we rely on both verbal and nonverbal communication to enable this process to take hold.

SOURCE: Caplow, Theodore. Rule Enforcement without Visible Means: Christmas Gift Giving in Middletown. *American Journal of Sociology* 89, 6 (1984): 1306-1323.

Types of Norms and Values

2.2.4 Distinguish among folkways, mores, and laws, and recognize societal values as subject to change and disagreement.

Norms and values also vary within cultures. For example, although images of wealth and success may be inspiring to some Americans, Hispanic Americans tend not to approve of overt materialistic displays of success. While Americans older than age 40 might find it inappropriate for you to text message in a social situation, younger people often feel virtual relationships are just as important and "present" as interpersonal ones right in the same room (Twenge 2006). Enforcement varies, too. Teenagers, for example, may care deeply about norms and standards of their peers but not about the judgment of others. Norms also change over time. Not that long ago, norms surrounding the use of telephones included not calling someone or talking on the phone during the dinner hour unless it was an emergency. Now people check voice mail and Facebook and text message each other during college classes (!) and during business meetings, when it used to be considered highly inappropriate to initiate or allow interruptions in these settings, again, except in an emergency. New media and technology have been a major catalyst of new norms and values over the past several decades. After all, technological inventions have created some entirely new social situations, new kinds of encounters and relationships, which have spawned new social rituals, norms, and even language to organize them.

Norms consist of folkways, mores, and laws, depending on their degree of formality in society. **Folkways** are relatively weak and informal norms that are the result of patterns of action. Many of the behaviors we call "manners" or etiquette are folkways. Other people may notice when we break them, but infractions are seldom punished. For example, there are no formal laws that prohibit women guests from wearing white to a wedding, which is informally reserved for the bride alone. But people might think you have bad taste or bad manners, and their informal evaluation is often enough to enforce those unwritten rules. **Mores** are informal norms about moral behavior that members of a society feel are especially important. These are perceived as more than simple violations of etiquette; they are moral attitudes that are seen as serious even if there are no actual laws that prohibit them. Today, some would argue that showing up for a college interview wearing flip-flops or with hair still wet from a shower violates mores; it doesn't break any laws, but it would probably sink your application. **Laws** are norms that have been organized and written down. Breaking these norms involves the disapproval not only of immediate community members but also the agents of the state, who are charged with publishing such norm-breaking behavior. Folkways, mores, and laws all reflect the values of a society. And as values shift and change, norms respond in kind (and vice versa).

When members of a culture decide that something is right or wrong, they often enact a law to prescribe or proscribe it (see FIGURE 2.1). Less than 100 years ago, women were not permitted to vote, because they were not considered rational enough to make an informed decision or because, as married women, they were the property of their husbands. Less than 40 years ago, women were prohibited from service alongside men in the nation's military, police forces, and fire departments. Today, our values have changed about women's abilities, and discriminatory laws (norms) have been defeated. Similarly, when our values about racial equality or sexual equality began to change, laws were enacted to prohibit discrimination. These laws were not completely popular when they were first enacted, but over time our values shift to better conform to the laws. Seat belt and helmet laws were incredibly unpopular when they were first passed, over significant resistance from both individuals and the automobile manufacturers. But now most Americans conform to these laws, even when there are no police around to watch them.

Even the values we hold are more fluid than we often think. Values are both consistent abstract ethical precepts and convenient, fluid, and internally contradictory rationalizations of our actions. Sometimes we consider them before we act; other times we apply them after the fact. How can we hold contradictory values at the same time? For one thing, we don't apply them all to every situation: We apply values situationally. And we often hold those values more fervently with others than we do with ourselves—"it's true for thee but not for me." That is, we employ those values strategically, depending on the person and the situation. One of the wonderful aspects of human beings is that we are able to hold contradictory views: We can believe that "he who hesitates is lost" and caution others to "look before you leap."

folkway
One of the relatively weak and informal norms that is the result of patterns of action. Many of the behaviors we call "manners" are folkways.

mores
Informally enforced norms based on strong moral values, which are viewed as essential to the proper functioning of a group.

law
One of the norms that has been organized and written down. Breaking these norms involves the disapproval not only of immediate community members but also of the agents of the state, who are charged with punishing such norm-breaking behavior.

Showing up for an interview in professionally appropriate attire is a small indication that you understand social norms. And conveying that understanding in how you dress and comport yourself during the interview is an interactional accomplishment on your part; it helps to demonstrate that you share some of the same values as your potential future colleagues.

FIGURE 2.1 How Fast Can a Society Change Its Values?
It's a challenging question to ask. But one measure of social change is law. And often, the kind of change involving challenges to moral beliefs is taken in small steps. One way to consider the pace of change is to consider how our values have changed over time. Here, you can see a graphic representation of several issues that involved reshaping U.S. values over time by the number of states enacting laws that removed bans on the following: interracial marriage, prohibition, women's right to vote, abortion, same-sex marriage, and recreational marijuana use. Circles denote the years in which federal laws were passed.

What we see here is that some changes happen slowly, and others take place relatively quickly. This does not mean our values cannot or will not shift again. It also does not mean everyone in the society agrees with these values. But changing laws are one way we can visualize transformations in the value structure of our society.

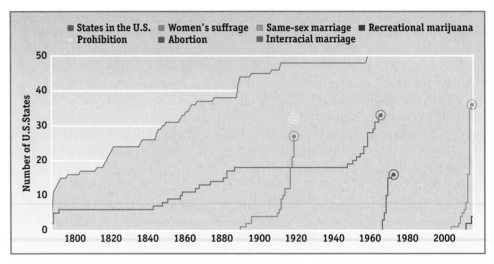

SOURCE: Data from Tribou, Alex and Keith Collins. "This is How Fast America Changes Its Mind." Bloomberg.com, June 26, 2015. Available at: https://www.bloomberg.com/graphics/2015-pace-of-social-change/.

---

iSOC AND YOU Culture in Interactions

The elements of culture—values, rituals, norms, language—are the means by which we build our *identities* within our society. They enable us to participate in social life, and play an integral role in how we come to understand whether social *inequality* is legitimate or not. These elements of culture are also how we "do" culture; they are the tools we rely on to interact with each other in socially meaningful ways. In society, they become institutionalized, such that social *institutions* (like the family, education, or law) are organized in ways that transmit cultural values, regulate our *interactions*, and ensure we are all playing by the same rules regardless of whether or not we are aware of that fact.

2.3 Cultural Institutions and the Institutionalization of Culture

Talking about culture for most people is the equivalent of fish talking about water. It is all around us and it has a taken-for-granted quality precisely because it is everywhere. This is why identifying culture is often easier when we travel to different societies. We are often quick to recognize social interactions, norms, and rituals that seem odd to us elsewhere. But within our own societies, it is more challenging to look at all of the shared norms, values, beliefs, rituals, norms, and mores that we learn to casually ignore over the course of our lives. Although they shape out beliefs, identities, and interactions, culture does not require us to actively acknowledge it each time we interact for its continued existence. Rather, culture provides the frameworks within which interactions take place. And culture is able to accomplish this because it becomes embedded within the various social institutions that make up our society.

In this section, we will consider the mass media as a key social institution to understand what it means to talk about cultural institutions and to study the institutionalization of culture. We will consider the ways that different types of culture are afforded different statuses in society, statuses that work in ways that subtly perpetuate inequality between groups.

HOW DO WE KNOW WHAT WE KNOW?

OUR VALUES—AND OTHERS' VALUES

We often think of our values as a consistent set of ethical principles that guide all our actions, but the reality is more complex. Anyone who has ever made, but not kept, a New Year's resolution knows that there are often big gaps between our values and our actions. It turns out we are quite forgiving of our own failures to live up those ideal values, although we are often less forgiving of others' failures. We hold others to higher standards than we hold ourselves. And we also believe that we live closer to our values than others do. Americans are also more individualistic than other nations. Americans are, for instance, much more likely to agree with the idea that if you work hard, you'll be able to get ahead in life, no matter who you are. See the graph of Americans' opinions and values relative to those of other countries. Why do you think that Americans stand out internationally on questions about how much control we have over our lives?

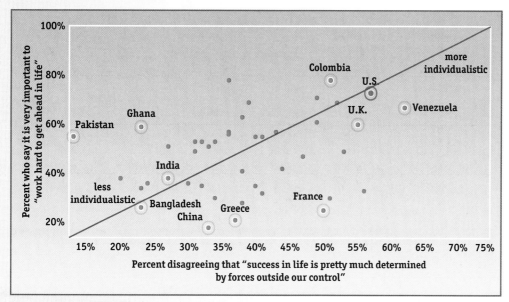

SOURCE: Data from Pew Research Center, Spring 2014 Global Attitudes survey. Q13b & Q66b. http://www.pewglobal.org/files/2014/10/Pew-Research-Center-Inequality-Report-FINAL-October-17-2014.pdf.

Cultural Institutions: The Mass Media

2.3.1 Describe the primary components of contemporary mass media and how they have been subject to cultural change.

Cultural institutions are elements within a culture (or a subculture) that are important to its members for their identity. Our mass media are among the most powerful and pervasive cultural institutions in our society today. They create and circulate representations—images, words, characters and stories—that help us understand who we are, how we fit in (or don't), and ways of seeing the world. Media representations are not neutral or objective; they convey information, but also norms and values. As a result, mass media can purvey and perpetuate dominant social and cultural ideas or be sites of contestation and change. There are many types of mass media. All have experienced enormous growth since the nineteenth century, and today media animate—some would say dominate—our everyday lives. Consider some of their forms. (see U.S./WORLD Print Newspaper Reach, 2014/2015).

U.S./WORLD

PRINT NEWSPAPER REACH, 2014/2015

Globally, one can discern the difference between rich and poor nations by the proportions of their populations newspapers reach. Japanese and Austrian newspapers reach an incredible proportion of their populations, with 77.1 percent and 68.4 percent, respectively. That figure is only 41.6 percent in the United States. And look at the poorer nations: 14 percent in Uganda, 10.5 percent in Syria, and only 4.3 percent in Iraq. Some of this is exacerbated by a change from print to digital news media. Some countries have made this switch more completely than others.

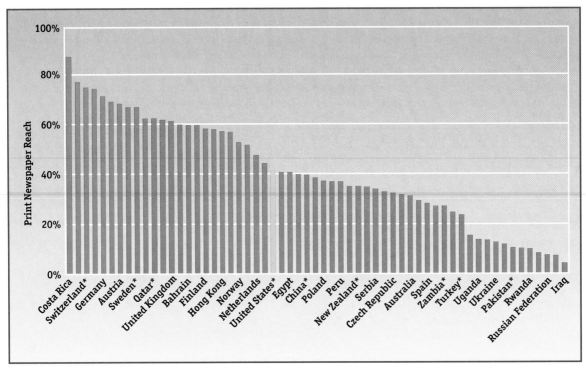

NOTE: * Indicates 2014 data where 2015 data were not available.

SOURCE: Data from WAN-IFRA. "World Press Trends 2016." WAN-IFRA, 2016. Available at: http://www.wan-ifra.org/microsites/world-press-trends.

INVESTIGATE FURTHER

1. How might newspaper circulation offer us one way of thinking about inequality in a global world?

2. Interacting with a common set of cultural symbols is one way societies establish solidarity. How might newspapers play one small role in this process?

PRINT MEDIA The printing press, which appeared in China in the eighth century and Europe in the fifteenth, changed the way we record and transmit information (Eisenstein 1993). The new technology allowed media to be produced more quickly, more cheaply, and in larger numbers. Reading shifted from a privilege of upper-class males to a much wider population, and the literacy rate in Europe jumped from less than 1 percent to between 10 and 15 percent. In the first decades of the twentieth century, reading became a mass middle-class activity (Radway 1999). People read cheap paperbacks, newspapers, and magazines. The newspaper and the magazine were originally vehicles for general interest. Today, the more than 7,200 magazines published in the United States are increasingly specialized publications, targeted to a selected "niche" audience (Magazine Publishers of America 2017).

RADIO, MOVIES, AND TELEVISION   Before 1880, if you wanted music, you had to make it yourself or hire someone. That all changed when Thomas Edison recorded his voice at the end of the nineteenth century. Within a few decades, the gramophone (a machine that enabled you to listen to recorded music) was a staple of American life. And, at the same time, entrepreneurs sought to harness the power of transmitting sound via invisible "radio waves" and make them profitable. Movies were born with a 12-minute clip of *The Great Train Robbery* in 1903—and the media world changed forever.

By the mid-1930s, more than half of the U.S. population went to the movies—every single week. And such an outing would include, typically, two full-length features, newsreels, serial dramas, cartoon shorts—and commercials. And television, introduced in the late 1940s, was geared to commercial sponsorship of shows. With variety shows and commercial spots every few minutes, the connection between selling products and consuming media was indelibly tightened. European television and radio are state sponsored and, until the 1980s, had no commercials at all. Today, the average American home has more television sets than people—2.5 people versus 2.6 TVs (Nielsen 2010), although the number of television sets her household has been declining (Nielsen 2010; U.S. Energy Information Administration 2017). Although fewer Americans today consider television to be a necessity in their lives, we continue to buy television sets for our homes. And it is still true today that Americans report a similar average numbers of hours of television watching per day that they reported forty years ago, and ever since—around 3 (General Social Survey 1972–2016).

WHAT DO YOU THINK? WHAT DOES AMERICA THINK?

Confidence in the Press

In an age of globalization and media conglomerates, many sources of news are controlled by a small number of large corporations and powerful individuals.

What do you think?

As far as the people running the press are concerned, would you say you have a great deal of confidence, only some confidence, or hardly any confidence at all in them?

- ○ A great deal of confidence
- ○ Only some confidence
- ○ Hardly any confidence

What does America think?

The General Social Survey results for 2016 indicate that 50 percent of the population has "hardly any" confidence in the press. Almost half of respondents had only some confidence in the press. Only 8 percent of respondents reported having "a great deal" of confidence in the press. But these responses are different depending on other factors as well, like age. The youngest Americans have the least confidence in the press—57 percent of 18- to 34-year-olds report having "hardly any." Compare that with only 41 percent of adults 65 years and older who report the same level of confidence. The percentage of respondents reporting "hardly any" confidence in the press has steadily increased since 1972 among all age groups, but the change is most pronounced among the youngest.

SOURCE: Data from General Social Survey, 2016.

THINKING CRITICALLY ABOUT SURVEY DATA

Why do you think older Americans might be more likely to be confident in the press when compared with younger Americans? What might that mean?

Personal computers, now nearly universal in the industrialized world, are the centerpiece of our interface with media—they store information, give access to the Web, and thanks to wifi, can provide access to the Internet in more and more places. They also store music, video, movies, TV, and old love letters. The first general-purpose computer, called the Electronic Numerical Integrator and Computer (ENIAC), was built by the U.S. Army in the 1940s. It weighed 30 tons, was 8 feet high, 3 feet deep, 100 feet long, and contained more than 18,000 vacuum tubes that were cooled by 80 air blowers. And it mainly stored information.

Globally, television is similar to the newspaper, saturating rich countries, rare in poor countries. As of 2003, there were 803 television sets per 1,000 people in the United States; there were fewer than half that in Portugal (328) or Turkey (326), but that's more than enough to immerse the population in the latest game shows and reality series. Among poorer countries though—with 65 TVs per 1,000 people in India, 16 in Somalia, and 4 in Haiti, for example—there is no unifying national television culture (Nationmaster 2003).

THE INTERNET   With development of the World Wide Web in the 1980s, online usage grew 3,000 percent per year: There were 10,000 network hosts in 1987 and 1,000,000 in 1992. By 2017, every country in the world, with very few exceptions is online (Abbate 2000; Campbell-Kelly 2004; Internet World Stats 2017). As of 2017, the Internet is accessed by 94.6 percent of the population of Sweden, 88.6 percent in the United States, and 94 percent in Japan. Beyond the core countries, penetration is considerably smaller: 58.6 percent in Colombia, 61.5 percent in Venezuela, 63.6 percent in Saudi Arabia, 18.2 percent in Pakistan, and 11.1 percent in Ethiopia. In poor countries, Internet access remains an overwhelmingly elite activity, available to a small fraction of the population. But even there, change is coming. In 2000, Somalia had 200 users; by 2017 it had more than 660,000 (Internet World Stats 2017).

The Internet has not only transformed mass media but is a new form of mass media in its own right. A website is its own medium, like nothing that has ever come before, with text, graphics, and sounds combined in a way that no previous medium could do. The Internet has been accused of facilitating increased isolation—all those millions of teenagers who spend the time they should be doing their homework in chat rooms, playing online poker, blowing up the galaxy on online games, or downloading songs and pornography. But at the same time, it's also a new form of community, a new social arena within which interactions take place. As an element of culture, mass media are not a cultural universal—but they're getting close.

High Culture and Popular Culture

2.3.2 Differentiate between high and popular culture and how they relate to cultural capital.

When we hear the word culture, we often think of an adjective describing someone (a "cultured" person) or a possession, as in a line in a song by Paul Simon, "The man ain't got no culture." In the common usage, culture refers to having refined aesthetic sensibilities: knowing fine wines, classical music, opera, and great works of literature. That is, the word *culture* is often synonymous with what sociologists call "high culture." High culture attracts audiences drawn from more affluent and largely white groups, as any visit to a major art museum will attest.

High culture is often contrasted with "popular culture," the culture of the masses, the middle and working class. **Popular culture** includes a wide variety of popular music, non-highbrow forms of literature (from dime novels to comic books), any forms of spectator sports, and other popular forms of entertainment, like television, movies, and video games. Sociologists are interested less in what sorts of cultural activities are classified as high or low and more interested in the relationships between those levels. And we are interested in the ways that certain cultural forms shift their position, from low to high or high to low. Notice, for example, how comic books have been the subject of major museum shows in recent years, and they are now being seen both as high culture and popular culture. "I get so tired of people saying 'this is classical' and 'this is jazz,'" said noted pianist Jean-Yves Thibaudet. "At the time of Chopin, everything was pop."

popular culture

The culture of the masses, the middle and working classes, that includes a wide variety of popular music, non-highbrow forms of literature, any forms of spectator sports, and other popular forms of entertainment, like television, movies, and video games.

The actress Lily Tomlin used to delight her audiences with a clever critique of this distinction. Portraying a homeless "bag lady" she professed confusion about modern culture. She held up a picture of a big Campbell's soup can (on right). "Soup," she said. Then she held up a poster of the Andy Warhol painting of that same soup can—a poster from the Museum of Modern Art. "Art," she said. Back and forth she went. "Soup." "Art." "Soup." "Art." Confusing, huh? The soup can sells for $0.89 at the supermarket; the painting of the soup can (at left) sold for $11.7 million at auction.

Sociologists approach this divide between high culture and popular culture as, itself, a sociological issue. French sociologist Pierre Bourdieu (1984) argued that different groups possess what he called "cultural capital," a resource that those in the dominant class can use to justify their dominance. **Cultural capital** is any "piece" of culture—an idea, an artistic expression, a form of music or literature, etc.—that a group can use as a symbolic resource to exchange with others. Cultural capital is not something that some groups have and others lack. Rather, different groups have different kinds of cultural capital and different cultural capital is differently valuable in different settings. So, knowing how to play golf and having knowledge of fine wine might help you achieve status among the wealthy and elite, but those same pieces of cultural capital might work very differently at a college party. Despite these differences, not all cultural capital is equally powerful. If I have access to this form of culture, and you want to have access to it, then I can "exchange" my access to access those forms of capital that you have. The key is that not everyone desires access to all kinds of cultural capital—some forms are more powerful than others.

If there is a divide between high culture and popular culture, Bourdieu argues, then the dominant class can set the terms of training so that high culture can be properly appreciated. That is, the proper appreciation of high culture requires the acceptance of certain rules, certain sets of criteria for evaluation. And this establishes certain cultural elites with privileged knowledge—cultural "gatekeepers" who permit entry into high culture circles. Actually, both high and popular culture consumption have rules for appreciation. Imagine someone who doesn't know these rules attending the opera in the way he or she might attend a U2 concert: singing along loudly with each aria, holding up a cell phone to take pictures, standing on his or her chair, and swaying to the music. Now, imagine an opera buff attending a U2 concert, sitting politely, applauding only at the end of the concert, and calling out "Bravo!" to the band. Both concertgoers failed to express the appropriate ways to show they like something.

The sociologist tries to make no value judgment about which form of culture one appreciates—actually, virtually all of us combine an appreciation of both popular and high culture in different contexts. To the sociologist, what is interesting is how certain cultural forms become established as high or popular and how they change, which groups promote which forms of culture, and how different forms of culture work in ways that perpetuate—and often justify—inequalities between groups.

cultural capital
French sociologist Pierre Bourdieu's term for the cultural articles—ideas, artistic expressions, forms of music or literature—that function as resources that people in the dominant class can use to justify their dominance.

SOCIOLOGY AND OUR WORLD

THE HIGH CULTURE–LOW CULTURE DIVIDE

Why is it that what qualifies as "high" vs. "popular" culture is much more about identities and inequality than it is about any intrinsic quality distinguishing the two?

The divide between popular culture and high culture is blurry; many of those cultural products that are now enshrined in "high culture" were originally popular forms of entertainment. Did you know that originally, Shakespeare's plays were performed for mass audiences, who would shout out for the performers to do encores of their favorite scenes? In fact, Shakespeare himself added a little blood and gore to his tragedies to appeal to the mass audience. Opera also was originally a mass entertainment, which was appropriated by music critics in the nineteenth century, when they developed rules for appreciating it that excluded all but the elite (see Levine 1988). Equally, some elements of high culture can become part of popular culture. For example, various fashion styles of upper-class life—collared "polo" shirts, even those decorated with little polo players—are worn by large numbers of people who would never set foot in the upper-class arena of the polo field.

The Politics of Popular Culture

2.3.3 Understand fads and fashions, how they emerge, and how they are a part of our cultural tool kits.

Most cultural elites are culturally conservative (regardless of how they vote or what sorts of policies they favor). That is, they wish to *conserve* the cultural forms that are currently in place and the hierarchies of value that are currently given to them. The status quo, as the French sociologist Bourdieu argued, reproduces their cultural dominance. As a result, changes in popular culture typically come from the margins, not the center—from those groups who have been excluded from the cultural elites and thus develop cultural expressions that are, at least in part, forms of cultural resistance.

TYPES OF POPULAR CULTURE   Popular culture refers not only to the forms of high culture (like art, music, or literature) that are enjoyed by the middle and working classes. Popular culture also refers to those objects, ideas, and values that people may hold at a specific moment. While we have seen that high culture changes, one of popular culture's defining qualities is its fluidity; it is constantly changing, constantly establishing new trends and discarding old ones. We can differentiate between two types of popular culture trends: **fads** and **fashions**.

fad
Short-lived, highly popular, and widespread behavior, style, or mode of thought.

fashion
A behavior, style, or idea that is more permanent and often begins as a fad.

Fads are defined by being short-lived, highly popular, and widespread behaviors, styles, or modes of thought. Often they are associated with other cultural forms. They are often created and marketed to generate "buzz" because if they catch on they can be enormously profitable. Sociologist John Lofland (1993) identified four types of fads:

1. *Objects.* These are objects people buy because they are suddenly popular, whether or not they have any use or intrinsic value. Hula hoops, yo-yos, poodle skirts, Pet Rocks, Beanie Babies, Cabbage Patch Kids, Furbies, Pokemon or Yu-Gi-Oh! trading cards, and various children's confections are often good examples of object fads. As are Crocs, the colored plastic clog-style shoes.
2. *Activities.* These are behaviors that suddenly everybody seems to be doing, and you decide to do it also, or else you'll feel left out. These can include various risk-taking behaviors—car surfing—or sports like rock climbing, or leisure activities like Sudoku. Dances like the moonwalk or the twist and the watusi are activity fads. Diets are top examples of activity fads today.
3. *Ideas.* Sometimes an idea will spread like wildfire, and then, just as suddenly, slip out of view. The Celestine Prophesy, beliefs in UFOs, various New Age ideas, and "everything you needed to know you learned in kindergarten" are examples of idea fads.
4. *Personalities.* Some celebrities burst on the scene for their accomplishments, for example, athletes (Tiger Woods, LeBron James) or rock stars (Lil' Wayne, Bono,

Eminem). Yet others are simply "famous for being famous"—everyone knows about them and seems to care about them, but few actually know what they've done to merit the attention. "Celebutantes" like Paris Hilton, Kim Kardashian, and Jessica Simpson are examples of the latter.

5. *Internet Memes.* Today there are also Internet fads, which suddenly circulate wildly or draw millions of hits through the World Wide Web. Internet memes, defined as "self-propagating units of culture," include people (like Mr. T, the A-Team actor who is considered one of the earliest Internet fads), audio clips, animation segments, or video clips such as "Ken Lee," a short clip from the auditions of the Bulgarian version of American Idol, which drew more than 10 million views in its first 6 months in 2008, or "Rick Roll," a homemade karaoke music video that drew more than 15 million hits that year. "The Double Rainbow guy" is one of the most famous people in the world today. More generally, various websites and blogs can be Internet fads, when they quite suddenly become "in" places to read and post.

Fashion is a bit different. A fashion is a behavior, style, or idea that is more permanent than a fad. It may originate as a fad and become more widespread and more acceptable over time. For example, the practice of tattooing, once associated with lower-class and even dangerous groups, became a fad in the 1990s but is today an accepted part of fashion, with one out of five American adults and four in ten 18- to 29-year-olds having at least one tattoo (Pew Research Center 2010).

Fashions involve widespread acceptance of the activity, whether it is music, art, literature, clothing, or sports. Because fashions are less fleeting than fads, they involve the cultural institutions that mediate our relationships with culture. Fashions may become institutionalized and aggressively marketed to ensure that people know that unless you subscribe to a particular fashion, you will be seen as an outsider. Although fads may appear to bubble up from below, fashions are often deliberately created. (In reality, fads are also likely to have been created.)

Take clothing, for example. Blue jeans were once a workingman's attire. In fact, Levi Strauss invented blue jeans to assist gold miners in California in their muddy work. Appropriated by the youth culture in the 1960s as a form of clothing rebellion against the bland conformity of 1950s campus fashion, blue jeans were considered a fad—until kids' parents started to wear them. Then fashion designers got into the act, and the fad became a fashion. Today these symbols of a youthful rejection of materialism can cost up to $500 a pair.

Trends in clothing, music, and other tastes in popular culture often originate today among three marginalized groups: African Americans, young people, and the LGBT community. As we've seen, blue jeans were once a youthful fashion statement of rebellion. Many men's fashions in clothing or accessories often have their origins among gay men (clothing styles, pierced ears) or black inner-city youth (hoodie sweatshirts, skater shoes and pants). White suburban embrace of hip-hop and rap echoes the same embrace of soul and R&B in the 1960s, or even the same white embrace of jazz and bebop in successive generations. Clever marketers are constantly on the lookout for trends among socially marginalized groups that can be transformed into luxury items. If you want to know what white suburban boys will be wearing and what music they'll be listening to in 5 years, take a look at what black teenagers or gay men are wearing and listening to today.

The social movement of popular culture from margin to center reveals a final element in the sociological approach to culture. Culture is not a thing one does or does not have, nor is it a level of refinement of taste and sensibility. It is not a constant throughout our lives, and it doesn't simply evolve and grow as we mature and develop. Culture is a complex set of behaviors, attitudes, and symbols that individuals use in their daily relationships with others. It is, as sociologist Ann Swidler (1986) calls it, a **"cultural tool kit"**—a sort of repertoire of habits, skills, and styles from which people construct their identities. Culture is diverse, and one uses different parts of it in different circumstances with different groups for different reasons.

cultural tool kit
A repertoire of habits, skills, and styles from which people construct their identities.

The Globalization of Popular Culture

2.3.4 Explain the movement of culture around the world and the process by which some cultures are situated as more dominant than others as a result of this movement.

A note on symbols: The New York Yankees hat has become a universal symbol of urban style—likely because of the fact that international hip hop superstar, Jay-Z is most often seen sporting a Yankees cap. As Jay-Z sang in "Empire State of Mind" (2009): "I made the Yankee hat more famous than a Yankee can." He might just be right.

cultural imperialism

The deliberate imposition of one country's culture on another country.

The Harlem shake emerged as a very particular configuration of bodily movements. But, what people think of today when they think of the dance might have changed because of how it became more popular in 2012. It's a good example of how culture can change as it moves within and between societies.

It's not just American teenagers who are dressing in the latest fashions. Tourists visiting in other countries are often surprised at how closely the fashion styles resemble those in the United States. Interestingly, this occurs both through the deliberate export of specific cultural items and also through the ways in which cultural forms of resistance are expressed by young people and minorities. For example, hip-hop culture, which originated among blacks in American inner cities, has gone global. Spread by the global music and television industries and the Internet, it is taking hold among youths seeking expressions of resistance and authenticity around the world (Chang 2007; Pennycock 2007). The music, dance, and clothing styles have been adopted and adapted by young people in countries across Northern and Western Europe; in Asia, including South Korea and Japan; as well as in African countries such as Senegal, Middle Eastern countries like Lebanon, and in Latin American countries including Brazil, Chile, and Argentina.

Sometimes culture is exported deliberately. Popular culture—movies, music, books, television programs—is the second largest category of American export to the rest of the world (the first is aircraft). Large corporations like Nike, Disney, Coca-Cola, and Warner Brothers work very hard to ensure that people in other countries associate American products with hip and trendy fashions in the States.

Some see this trend as a form of **cultural imperialism**—the deliberate imposition of one country's culture on another country. The global spread of U.S. fashion, media, and language (English as the world's lingua franca in culture, arts, business, and technology) is often seen as an imposition of U.S. values and ideas as well as products. Cultural imperialism is not usually imposed by governments that require citizens to consume some products and not others. It is "cultural" in that these products become associated with a lifestyle to which citizens of many countries aspire. But it is criticized as "imperialist" in that the profits from those sales are returned to the U.S. corporation, not the home country. And the U.S. ideas, ideals, identities, and more get framed globally as those to which all should aspire.

On the other hand, cultural transfer is not nearly as one directional as many critics contend. There are many cultural trends among Americans that originated in other countries. Imported luxury cars, soccer, reggae, wine, beer, and food fads all originate in other countries and become associated with exotic life-styles elsewhere.

And sometimes, global cultural trends emerge from below. In 1981, Al B, a resident of Harlem, New York, became known around Harlem for his dancing. The dance was originally referred to as the "albee," but later became known as the "Harlem shake" as it gained in popularity. In 2001, G. Dep, a hip-hop artist from Harlem, put the dance in the music video for his hit single, "Let's Get It," and it has received attention from hip-hop artists since. But, it is probably best known today because of a song titled "Harlem Shake" (2012) recorded by American DJ, Baauer. The song was catapulted to international popularity in 2013 when it was promoted by an associated Internet meme in which groups of people danced in a characteristic (and odd) style to a portion of the song and uploaded their videos on YouTube. Look up "Harlem Shake" and the name of your college or university on YouTube.com—chances are, some students uploaded videos in 2013. And although the Harlem shake might have been new to many in 2012, it is far from new. In fact, the Internet video meme—which, at the height of its popularity involved more than 4,000 uploaded videos around the world every day—is not actually an accurate portrayal of the dance. In February of 2013, the *New York Times* wrote a story about this interesting fact—"It's a Worldwide Dance Craze, but It's Not the Real Harlem Shake" (Gregory 2013). Al B may have invented a dance whose popularity is now known around the world—but it may not be the Harlem shake Al B created. As this example illustrates, when culture is shared, it can change in both meaning and form.

---

iSOC AND YOU

Culture is not some timeless monolithic bubble that surrounds you, but rather culture is a kind of "tool kit" from which you build your *identity*. Nor is it equal; cultural values emphasize some cultural expressions over others. That means it's always evolving as new trends vie for entry into the dominant culture: Fads, trends, fashions are all efforts to influence cultural inequalities and to upset cultural hierarchies that help to differentiate groups and, often, work to justify *inequality*. Nor does culture simply float in the atmosphere; it is institutionalized in cultural *institutions*, like museums that tell you what is—and by default, what is *not*—"art," or global commercial institutions like record companies.

2.4 Continuity and Change in Culture and Media

Societies are always changing; but they are able to shift and transform because of what remains the same. This means that our values and beliefs about specific issues will change over time and we are capable, as a society, of moving forward and adapting to these shifts (sometimes less willingly for some individuals and group than others) because of our continued investments in elements of culture that remain the same. This means that our society can tolerate shifts in laws and policies surrounding highly contentious social issues like abortion, same-sex marriage, what kinds of assistance we offer the poor, disabled, or elderly. Even as we do so with fierce debate, we know that we will all continue to be members of the same society after the dust of debate settles. Sociologists study continuity and change in culture because we are interested in those moments when ideas, beliefs, and values come into conflict with each other and how societies put themselves back together. But we are equally interested in the ways that culture resists change, when continuity reigns even when change might have seemed imminent.

In this final section of the chapter, you will develop a set of sociological tools for understanding and studying continuity and change in culture and the media. We will explore the ways that cultural transformations are often precipitated by technological shifts. We will come to understand that changes in culture often happen either faster or slower than you might have imagined possible. And you will come to understand that culture is sometimes resistant to change when change threatens to challenge systems of power and inequality deeply embedded in social institutions and the fabric of society.

Cultural Change

2.4.1 Summarize the ways that cultural change occurs and is resisted.

Cultures are dynamic, constantly changing. Sometimes that rate of change may seem faster or slower than at other times. And sometimes change feels sudden

We're constantly creating new norms to respond to technological and other cultural changes—like laws regarding cell phone use while driving or policies on text messaging in class.

culture wars

Often symbolic clashes of ideas, symbols, or values between groups who support certain changes and those who want to resist change.

culture lag

The relatively gradual process by which nonmaterial elements of culture catch up with changes in material culture and technology.

cultural diffusion

The spreading of new ideas through a society, independent of population movement.

and dramatic, producing conflict between those who support change and those who resist it. **Culture wars** often are symbolic clashes—of ideas, symbols, values—between groups who support certain changes and those who want to resist change. And although some change is inevitable, not every change is necessarily beneficial.

Although cultures are constantly changing, all the elements of culture do not change at the same time or in the same ways. In some cases, as we saw, changes among some marginalized groups become fashions for the mainstream after a period of time. It is often the case that changes in material culture (the level of technology, material resources) change more rapidly than changes in cultural institutions like the family or religion. At those moments, societies experience what sociologist William Ogburn (1922/1966) called **culture lag**—the gap between technology and material culture and its social beliefs and institutions. For example, changes in communication technology have dramatically transformed social life, but our values have failed to keep pace. Cell phones, text messaging, and instant messaging, combined with e-mail and other Internet-based modes of communication, have dramatically altered the ways in which people interact. Yet the cultural mores that govern such interaction (etiquette, manners, norms governing appropriate behavior) have not yet caught up to the technology. Occasionally, this results in confusion, discomfort, or conflict.

Culture lag is a relatively gradual process by which nonmaterial elements of culture catch up with material culture. In this instance, we can also speak of **cultural diffusion**—the spreading of new ideas through a society, independent of population movement. As the impact of the technological innovation ripples through the rest of society, eventually a new equilibrium will be reached. Then all goes smoothly until the next technological breakthrough. If you can, ask your own grandparents what they think of Twitter, Instagram, and iPhone apps, and you'll get the idea.

But sometimes, technological breakthroughs enable groups within a society, or an entire society, to impose its values on others. Cultures can change dramatically and suddenly by conquest as well as by diffusion. The impact is often stark, sudden, and potentially lethal. Sometimes conquest can deliberately transform the culture of the colonized, as when missionaries force conquered groups to convert to the religion of the conqueror or be put to death. In those instances, the entire belief system of the culture, its foundation, is dismantled and replaced by a foreign one.

In other cases, it is less immediate or direct but no less profound. The first European colonists who came to the New World in the sixteenth century were able to subdue the indigenous peoples of North America by superior technology (like muskets and artillery), by the manipulation of religious beliefs about the potential benevolent foreigners, and by the coincidental importation of diseases, like syphilis, which killed millions more Native Americans than the colonists' bullets. It is possible that other food-borne diseases, like avian flu and mad cow disease, could have an almost equally devastating impact on local cultures today.

Intercultural contact need not be accomplished through force. Today, global cultural forms are emerging that diffuse across national boundaries and are incorporated, unevenly and incompletely, into different national and local cultures. These often result in odd juxtapositions—a consultant in rural Africa talking on a cell phone or downloading information from a laptop standing next to a woman carrying a pail of water on her head. But these are no odder than a scene you might well have witnessed in many parts of the United States just 70 years ago—cars speeding past homes with outhouses and outdoor water pumps. Culture spreads unevenly and unequally and often is accompanied by significant opposition and conflict.

iSOC AND YOU Continuity and Change in Culture and Media

In this chapter, you've seen how your *identity* is grounded in culture and how many of the elements of culture, such as norms and values, are used to justify *inequality*. You've seen how access to different cultural tools—like language, media, and mores—express and reproduce that inequality and how your everyday *interactions* depend on access to those cultural media. Cultural *institutions*—everything from media like movies and newspapers and TV shows, to music concerts and art museums—become the places where each society tells their story about themselves to one another. It is a ritual of solidarity that simultaneously brings us closer together and highlights the differences that mark inequality and tear us apart. All these levels of culture *intersect* in a multicultural society. Culture is how you find yourself and how you tell others where to find you.

Conclusion

Culture and Media NOW

Concepts such as culture, values, and norms help orient the sociologist, providing a way to understand the world he or she is trying to study. They provide the context, the "field," in which myriad individual experiences, motivations, and behaviors take place. And the media are one of the most-powerful and pervasive forms of culture. They are necessary to situate our individual experiences; they are the concepts by which sociologists connect individual biography and history. They are the concepts that we'll use to understand the forces that hold society together and those that threaten to drive it apart.

Cultures are constantly changing—from within and through their contact with other cultures. And the media are a dominant means of intercultural contact and cultural transmission and diffusion. A global culture is emerging of shared values and norms, shared technologies and media enabling common behaviors and attitudes. Increasingly, we share habits, fashions, language, and technology with a wider range of people than ever in human history. We are in that sense all becoming "one." And, at the same time, in our daily lives, we often resist the pull of these global forces and remain steadfastly loyal to those ties that bind us to local cultural forms—kinship and family, our ethnic group, religion, or community. And elements of culture that get imported from one culture into another do not always retain the meanings and values they had in their culture of origin.

The cultural diversity that defines most industrialized societies also defines American society, and that diversity will continue to provide moments of both combination and collision, of separation and synthesis. Most people are rarely "all-American" or feel completely like members of one ethnic or racial subculture. We're both. To be a hyphenated American—an Asian-American or Italian-American, for example—is a way of expressing the fact that we don't have to choose. Sometimes you may feel more "Italian" than American, and other times you

As U2's hit song One suggests, cultural diversity has come to describe many societies around the world, including the United States. Many societies, like the United States, are becoming more culturally diverse every day. As cultural diversity becomes more of a norm, sociologists will continue to ask questions about how societies navigate cultural difference.

may feel more "American" than Italian. And then, finally, there are times when you feel specifically Italian-American, poised somewhere between, distinct and unique, and yet not completely fitting into either. As Bono sings in the U2 song "One": "We're one but we're not the same."

CHAPTER REVIEW Culture and Media

2.1 Thinking about Culture and Media Sociologically

Culture is the glue that binds societies together as well as that "stuff" that threatens to tear them apart. It is a broad term for all of that social "stuff" that helps us feel like an "us"—like cohesive units with a sense of solidarity. And the media is quite possibly the fastest-growing, and one of the most all-encompassing elements of our culture today.

Cultures differ from one another and even change over time, which may be unsettling. When confronted with cultural diversity we may experience culture shock. Ethnocentrism is a common response to different cultures, but sociologists strive for cultural relativism. There are subgroups within cultures, and these subcultures often provide an important source of identity for members. Developing in instances when members are different from the mainstream culture and consequently experience prejudice, yet also possess social power, a subculture is embedded within, yet distinct from, the larger, dominant culture. A counterculture is a subculture that is in opposition to the larger culture and hence often threatening to the dominant culture. The mass media are among the most pervasive and powerful cultural institutions in our society, and so they both shape and reflect many of the elements and dynamics of the wider culture in which they participate.

2.1 Key Terms

culture Both the material basis for social life and the sets of values and ideals that we understand to define morality, good and evil, appropriate and inappropriate.

material culture The physical objects and spaces that people use to define their culture, including homes, cities, mosques, factories, works of art, clothes and fashions, books and movies, as well as the tools they use to make them.

nonmaterial culture Often just called "culture," the ideas and beliefs that people develop about their lives and their world.

media The plural form of "medium," it is the term for the ways that we communicate with each other, from voice to gestures to methods of mass communication like publishing, broadcasting and the internet.

mass media Any of the means of communication, such as books, newspapers, magazines, comic books, films and DVDs, radio, television, CDs and MP3s, and a range of digital and social media platforms, that reach large numbers of people.

cultural diversity The vast differences between the cultures of the world as well as the differences in belief and behavior that exist within cultures.

culture shock A feeling of disorientation when the cultural markers that we rely on to help us know where we are and how to act have suddenly changed.

ethnocentrism The use of one's own culture as the reference point by which to evaluate other cultures; it often depends on or leads to the belief that one's own culture is superior to others.

cultural relativism A position that all cultures are equally valid in the experience of their own members.

cultural universal One of the rituals, customs, and symbols that are evident in all societies.

subculture Group within a society that creates its own norms and values distinct from the mainstream and usually its own separate social institutions as well.

counterculture Subculture that identifies itself through its difference and opposition to the dominant culture.

2.2 Culture in Interactions

All cultures share six basic elements: material culture, symbols, language, rituals, norms, and values. The content and nature of each of these vary widely, change over time, and are often unique to the culture, providing great diversity across cultures. Material culture arises as a result of solving the basic problem of survival and includes everything created and used for meeting needs, including the environment itself. Nonmaterial culture also varies widely. A symbol conveys meaning within a culture, while language transmits culture, and, according to the Sapir-Whorf hypothesis, shapes perception. Ritual binds members of a culture together, often transcending time. A norm sets the standards or expectations for situation-specific behavior. Norms are of varying types, depending on the formality, and sanctions for violating them. A folkway is informal, mores are stronger and informally enforced, and laws are codified and formally enforced. A value captures what a culture finds desirable and may be in contradiction with other aspects of the culture, including other values.

2.2 Key Terms

symbol Anything—an idea, a marking, a thing—that carries additional meanings beyond itself to others who share in the culture. Symbols come to mean what they do only in a culture; they would have no meaning to someone outside.

language An organized set of symbols by which we are able to think and communicate with others; the chief vehicle by which human beings create a sense of self.

Sapir-Whorf hypothesis A theory that language shapes our reality because it gives us a way to talk about the categories of life that we experience.

ritual Enactment by which members of a culture engage in a routine behavior to express their sense of belonging to the culture.

norm One of the rules a culture develops that defines how people should act and the consequences of failure to act in the specified ways.

value If norms tell us how to behave, values tell us why. Values constitute what a society thinks about itself and so are among the most basic lessons that a culture can transmit to its young.

folkway One of the relatively weak and informal norms that is the result of patterns of action. Many of the behaviors we call "manners" are folkways.

mores Informally enforced norms based on strong moral values, which are viewed as essential to the proper functioning of a group.

law One of the norms that has been organized and written down. Breaking these norms involves the disapproval not only of immediate community members but also of the agents of the state, who are charged with punishing such norm-breaking behavior.

2.3 Cultural Institutions and the Institutionalization of Culture

Our mass media are among the most powerful and pervasive cultural institutions in our society today. They create and circulate representations—images, words, characters and stories—that help us understand who we are, how we fit in (or don't) and ways of seeing the world. Media representations are not neutral or objective; they convey information, but also norms and values. As a result, mass media can purvey and perpetuate dominant social and cultural ideas or be sites of contestation and change. Sociologists explore the construction of meaning within the mass media and also surrounding them; for example, how popular culture has less cultural capital than high culture, with elites investing high culture with status and controlling access and consumption. Popular culture is more dynamic than high culture, with passing fads and fashions. The global distribution of popular culture and media products has been seen as cultural imperialism, in which ideas, norms, and cultural values flow into a country while money flows out to add to the wealth of a foreign corporation. Cultural transfer flows both ways, however, and both cultural fusions and cultural resistance

may occur. People can therefore use culture as a "tool kit" to construct their selves.

2.3 Key Terms

popular culture The culture of the masses, the middle and working classes, that includes a wide variety of popular music, nonhighbrow forms of literature, any forms of spectator sports, and other popular forms of entertainment, like television, movies, and video games.

cultural capital French sociologist Pierre Bourdieu's term for the cultural articles—ideas, artistic expressions, forms of music or literature—that function as resources that people in the dominant class can use to justify their dominance.

fad Short-lived, highly popular, and widespread behavior, style, or mode of thought.

fashion A behavior, style, or idea that is more permanent and often begins as a fad.

cultural tool kit A repertoire of habits, skills, and styles from which people construct their identities.

cultural imperialism The deliberate imposition of one country's culture on another country.

2.4 Continuity and Change in Culture and Media

Societies are always changing, but they are able to shift and transform because of what remains the same. This means that our values and beliefs about specific issues will change over time and we are capable, as a society, of moving forward and adapting to these shifts (sometimes less willingly for some individuals and group than others) because of our continued investments in elements of culture that remain the same. While culture is dynamic, always changing, different aspects change at different rates, so that conflict, discontent, or dissatisfaction with cultural changes is not unusual. With cultural diffusion, there is often culture lag. Technological advancements in particular result in fast cultural changes, as do contacts with outside cultures, which have historically often been the result of technological advances leading to subsequent conquest or colonization. Even as technology pulls us into a global culture, our identities remain bound up with local forms of culture in multicultural societies. This dichotomy of cultural membership is not either–or; we are both locally diverse and globally unified.

2.4 Key Terms

culture wars Often symbolic clashes of ideas, symbols, or values between groups who support certain changes and those who want to resist change.

culture lag The relatively gradual process by which nonmaterial elements of culture catch up with changes in material culture and technology.

cultural diffusion The spreading of new ideas through a society, independent of population movement.

SELF-TEST

〉 CHECK YOUR UNDERSTANDING

1. Identify which of the following is true, according to the text.
   a. Members of a subculture have no power.
   b. Members of a counterculture are in opposition to the dominant culture.
   c. Members of a subculture appear indistinguishable from the larger culture.
   d. Members of a counterculture wish to be members of the dominant culture.

2. Which of the following is the most dynamic, fluid, quickest to change, and of shortest duration?
   a. Fad
   b. Fashion
   c. High culture
   d. All of these are equally dynamic and of equal duration.

3. Of the following, which did the text identify as an agent of great change and cultural diffusion?
   a. Religion
   b. Art
   c. Language
   d. Media

4. The relatively gradual process by which nonmaterial elements of culture catch up with changes in material culture is known as _____
   a. cultural diffusion.
   b. culture lag.
   c. cultural relativism.
   d. culture shock.

5. A nation's flag is an example of a _____
   a. value.
   b. norm.
   c. folkway.
   d. symbol.

6. Coca-Cola is available worldwide, although the company's home is in Atlanta, Georgia. Critics of this brand's popularity overseas, which results in the transfer of cultural ideas and values to other countries and revenue from local economies to America, accuse Coca-Cola of _____
   a. multiculturalism.
   b. cultural diffusion.
   c. cultural imperialism.
   d. ethnocentrism.

7. The unsettled or disoriented feeling experienced by a traveler to another land, where all the habits are unfamiliar, is known as _____
   a. ethnocentrism.
   b. culture shock.
   c. cultural imperialism.
   d. cultural diffusion.

8. Many cultures have a traditional ceremony in the days or months following the birth of a baby, recognizing and welcoming the child into the group. These events are examples of _____
   a. norms.
   b. folkways.
   c. rituals.
   d. laws.

Self-Test Answers: 1. b, 2. a, 3. d, 4. b, 5. d, 6. c, 7. b, 8. c

CHAPTER 3

SOCIETY: INTERACTIONS, GROUPS, AND ORGANIZATIONS

Our social behavior is dramatically shaped by the contexts within which we interact and the types of people with whom we are interacting. Crowded elevators are an interesting example. We interact in astoundingly patterned ways when we ride elevators. Our interactions have also been shaped by the rise of new forms of technology. It's not uncommon to see people "hanging out" together while on their phones and mobile devices interacting with people that may be very far away.

→ LEARNING OBJECTIVES

In this chapter, using the iSoc framework, you should be able to:

3.1.1 Distinguish among society, social institutions, and social structure.

3.1.2 Recognize how each of the five elements of the iSoc model can be used to examine interactions, groups, and organizations sociologically.

3.1.3 Describe the role that social interaction plays in shaping our understandings of our self from the dramaturgical perspective.

3.2.1 Summarize the role of verbal and nonverbal communication in research using an ethnomethodological approach to studying interaction.

3.2.2 Differentiate between the five basic patterns of social interaction.

3.2.3 Explain the ways in which role performances are shaped by social structure.

3.2.4 Understand the distinction between ascribed and achieved statuses and the role each plays in social reproduction.

3.2.5 Understand the ongoing work required to negotiate between role expectations and role performances.

3.3.1 Explain how groups differ from crowds.

3.3.2 Delineate the differences between primary and secondary groups and explain how groups promote conformity.

3.3.3 Understand the predictable characteristics and dynamics exhibited by groups.

3.3.4 Describe the small world problem and how it helps us understand social networks.

3.3.5 Explain the difference between weak and strong ties in terms of what they provide.

3.3.6 Understand the ways that the rise of global social networks simultaneously bring us all closer together while also exacerbating existing forms of social inequality.

3.4.1 Define organizations, and understand how they vary and exert power over our lives.

3.4.2 Describe the ways that Americans can be understood as simultaneously individualistic and collectively minded.

3.4.3 Explain the ways that organizations participate in structuring social inequality.

3.4.4 Define bureaucracy, and explain how the emergence of this organizational form shaped identities, interactions, and inequality.

3.4.5 Summarize the ways that organizations are increasingly globalized.

Introduction

In 2001, the first year of the new century, Harvard political scientist Robert Putnam proclaimed the end of U.S. community. We were estranged from our neighbors, geographically separate from our families, and maintained little civic sense of connectedness. Where once the United States was a nation of joiners—clubs, fraternal lodges, community organizations—we were now, as he put it in the title of his book, "bowling alone" (Putnam 2001).

And yet nearly every day, we receive a request from someone we barely know to be our friend on Facebook—or any of the dozens of new networking sites. It's become so common that the word "friend" has become a verb, as in "Do you want to friend me?" Many of you have more than 500 "friends." But you probably don't go bowling with them.

So which is it? Are we a nation of disconnected atoms, drifting aimlessly without the traditional anchors of community and family, or are we completely connected into new communities via our educational communities, athletic allegiances, or fashion tastes? Sociologists think it's both. It's true that the traditional ties of civic engagement have waned, but our sense of allegiances and identification with groups outside of ourselves has not diminished. It's been transferred from those traditional anchors of community and family to our consumer tastes and leisure activities.

In the 1960s, sociologist David Riesman (1961) called our society a "lonely crowd." Perhaps the flip side is also true and we are also "intimate strangers" (see Rubin 1983). Sociology's chief concern is to understand the constituent elements of society—the immediate interactions, the groups we belong to, the networks that connect us, and the organizations in which we work and live. These are the core units of society.

"So which is it? Are we a nation of disconnected atoms, drifting aimlessly without the traditional anchors of community and family, or are we completely connected into new communities via our educational communities, athletic allegiances, or fashion tastes? Sociologists think it's both. We're a "lonely crowd" and "intimate strangers."

3.1 Thinking about Interactions, Groups, and Organizations Sociologically

Sociological research is conducted from a particular vantage point. Although sociologists are not alone in studying interactions, groups, and organizations (indeed, these are topics studied by psychologists, political scientists, anthropologists, economists, and others), the ways that sociologists examine these social phenomena is unique. Sociologists examine patterns in interactions and groups and the processes through which organizations emerge as well as the impact each have on our lives. We are interested in patterns in experiences and opportunities and how those patterns both emerge out of the complex interplay between structure and agency.

It is axiomatic in sociology that we are less in control over our lives than we often believe. Our interactions are structured to a level you might find surprising. The groups we understand ourselves to be a part of shape our identities, inform our interactions, and play a critical role in shaping the identities and interactions we may experience in the future. It is helpful to compare societies to theatrical performances. And in this section, we will examine this metaphor (something sociologists refer to as "dramaturgy"). There are directors, actors, scripts, audiences, and more. People can be understood as back stage helping to organize things so that the action going on front stage can be pulled off. Learning to view society and social interactions in this way is a useful exercise. Applying the iSoc model, we can then learn how identities and interactions are given shape and meaning within social institutions. We will learn to examine interactions and group intersectionally to help us understand how interactions also play an important role in the reproduction of social inequality.

Society: Putting Things in Context

3.1.1 Distinguish among society, social institutions, and social structure.

Sociology is a way of seeing that can be described as "contextualizing." Sociologists seek to understand the social *contexts* in which our individual activity takes place, the other people with whom we interact, the dynamics of interaction, and the institutions that shape and give meaning to that activity. Sociologists are less concerned with the psychological motivations for actions and more concerned with patterns in social action, the social forces that shape motivation, and the meanings we derive from the action. Understanding social behavior is a constant process of "contextualizing"—placing behavior in different frameworks to better understand its complexity. The chief context in which we try to place individuals, locate their identity, and chart their experiences is generally called *society*. But what is this thing called "society" that we study? Is society simply a collection of individuals, or is it something more?

Sociologists understand society as much more than a collection of individuals—as greater than the sum of its parts. This basic insight instructs the ways that sociologists see and study the world around us. **Society** refers to *an organized collection of individuals and institutions bounded by space in a coherent territory, subject to the same political authority, and organized by a shared set of cultural expectations, beliefs, and values.* Societies shape the identities, interactions, and systems of power and authority of the members. And society is composed not only of individuals but also the various **social institutions** in which we find ourselves. A social institution is an organized and established set of social relationships and networks, bounded by relatively fixed boundaries that meet specific social needs (for example, the family, the economy, schools). In this way, sociologists understand our behaviors as not only governed by what others expect of us but also as motivated by shared beliefs and values.

This definition of society, however, rests on large-scale structures and institutions, territorial arrangements, and uniform political authority (a "macro-level perspective"). But societies are built from the bottom up as well. In this chapter, we will look at the basic building blocks of society from the smallest elements (interactions) to ordered sets of interactions with particular members (groups) and within particular contexts (organizations). From the ground up—from what sociologists refer to as a "micro-level perspective"—societies are composed of *structured social interactions*, bound by norms and motivated by shared values and beliefs. Even when we are just sitting around in

society

An organized collection of individuals and institutions, bounded by space in a coherent territory, subject to the same political authority, and organized through a shared set of cultural expectations and values.

social institutions

Patterned sets of interactions that work to meet collective needs that are not easily met by individuals working alone. They include such social arenas as markets, families, schools, corporations, factories, and prisons.

our homes or dorm rooms with a bunch of friends, "doing nothing," we are interacting in structured, patterned ways.

Sociologists have discovered that even a small group of friends makes different decisions than the individual members would alone (think of "peer pressure"). And it doesn't end there. Groups are embedded in other groups, in social institutions, in identities, in cultures, in nation-states, all the way up to that enormous edifice, society. Societies take shape as a result of something sociologists call **social structure**—a complex framework, composed of both patterned social interactions and institutions that collectively organize social life. It consists of different positions, resources, groups, and relationships. Social structure is both formal and informal, fixed and fluid. It is both a web of affiliations that supports and sustains us and a solid walled building from which we cannot escape. In other words, we are simultaneously enabled and constrained by social structures.

Sociologists use a set of concepts and tools to understand the ways we construct our identities. Some—like *socialization*, discussed in detail in Chapter 5—refer to processes by which society incorporates individuals, shaping them to be part of the collectivity. Other terms—like *roles, statuses, groups,* and *networks*, discussed later in this chapter—help us understand the ways individuals negotiate with others to create identities that feel stable, consistent, and permanent. Finally, other terms—like *organizations*, discussed below, and *institutions*, discussed throughout this book as part of the iSoc model—describe the more formal and stable patterns of interaction among larger groups of individuals. And *society* refers to the sum of all these other elements, and more.

social structure

A complex framework composed of both patterned social interactions and institutions that together organize social life and provide the context for individual action.

iSoc: The Social Construction of Identity

3.1.2 Recognize how each of the five elements of the iSoc model can be used to examine interactions, groups, and organizations sociologically.

Although culture is the foundation of society, interactions, groups, and organizations help societies persist over time. The five dimensions of the iSoc model are integral to understanding interactions, groups, and organizations as "social" and "structured," but also to making sense of the fact that they are often structured in ways that work to the collective advantage of some identities or others. In other words, while social structures both enable and constrain us, they do not enable and constrain us all in the same ways. Some groups are more enabled than others, while others are more constrained. The iSoc model provides a lens through which we can understand how this process works.

IDENTITY—Our identities are formed through our interactions with others in formal or informal groups. Think about who you are: Our identity is likely to begin your membership in groups—your ethnicity, your national origin. Or your membership in an organization: a soldier, a veteran, a lawyer. Thus, while our identity is what makes us feel special and unique, we are only able to have identities because we are a part of groups within which those identities make sense. Being a "class clown" makes little sense without a formal system of education, a classroom, and a patterned hierarchy of social relationships (teachers, students, etc.), and social norms governing how students are supposed to act in class.

INEQUALITY—Interactions, groups, and organizations can often appear unbiased—as though they are not working in any one groups interest. But sociologists are not only interested in how interactions, groups, and organizations shape our behavior and identities; they are also interested in how these social forms and processes work in ways that systematically advantage some groups and identities over others. For example, being socialized as, say "Irish" means that your family will teach you a host of things about how badly the Irish have been treated over the centuries. We become members of the group and embrace our identity in a context of inequality.

INTERACTION—Groups and organizations take shape through organized patterns of interaction. Interactions help to shape our understanding of ourselves as well as how we see various others in society. Groups and organizations are both produced by and help to shape interactions as well. Think back to that first day at this school, when you first interacted with a group of students. Whether you were nervous or not, you probably quickly recognized that most of these early interactions have elaborate **social scripts**. For instance, you might have formed a circle and someone might have prompted each of you to share some basic information (names, where you traveled from to get here, hobbies, interests, etc.). These sorts of icebreakers are common at the beginning of each semester and work to help new groups (classes, clubs, sports teams, fraternities or sororities, etc.) feel connected by sharing a focused interaction.

INSTITUTIONS—As we defined social institutions previously (organized and established sets of social relationships and networks, bounded by relatively fixed boundaries that meet specific social needs), they are integral to understanding interactions, groups, and organizations. Institutions work in ways that spread norms, values, and beliefs and patterned interactions; groups and organizations are, in some ways, what those norms, values, and beliefs look like when they take shape in societies.

INTERSECTIONS—Boundaries are key components of every society—between right and wrong, rich and poor, ugly and beautiful, children and adults, and much more. Examining intersections helps sociologists not only identify that these boundaries exist in societies, but also how they work. Paying close attention to intersections helps us understand how social interactions, group dynamics, and organizations may not be experienced by every member of a society in quite the same way. And these different experiences form boundaries that shape both our identities and inequalities.

Simply put, society is not simply something "out there" but something that gets inside of us. It shapes who we understand ourselves to be and both how and where we feel like we "fit in" in the society in which we live. But this makes it sound like we have little power or control over this process. And although that might be a basic sociological insight, it is also true that societies take shape in two directions—from the top down and from the bottom up. Our interactions help shape large-scale institutions and organizations just as those institutions and organization promote certain kinds of interactions among certain kinds of people and inhibit others. Through this dynamic process, societies emerge, reproduce themselves over time, and transform.

Thinking "Dramaturgically": Toward a Sociology of the Self

3.1.3 Describe the role that social interaction plays in shaping our understandings of our self from the dramaturgical perspective.

Social life is essentially patterns of **social interaction**—behaviors that are oriented toward other people. Other people are also interacting as well, and these near-infinite interactions cohere into patterns. But because everyone has different ideas, goals, beliefs, and expectations, how does it all fit together with any semblance of order? According to Peter Berger and Thomas Luckmann (1966), we "construct" social reality through social interaction. We follow conventions that everyone (or almost everyone) in the group learns to accept: that grandmothers and buddies are to be treated differently, for instance, or that teachers like students who express their own opinions. These social conventions become social reality, "the way things are."

One of the first sociologists to argue that the identity is formed through social interaction was Charles Horton Cooley, who coined the term **looking-glass self** to describe the process by which our identity develops (Cooley [1902] 1983). Cooley argued that we develop our looking-glass self in three stages: (1) We imagine how we appear to others around us; (2) we draw general conclusions based on the reactions of others;

social scripts

Term for a sequence of expected behaviors in a given situation.

social interaction

The foundation for societal groups and relationships and the process of how people behave and interact with each other.

looking-glass self

Cooley's term for the process of how identity is formed through social interaction. We imagine how we appear to others and thus develop our sense of self based on the others' reactions, imagined or otherwise.

(3) based on our evaluations of others' reactions, we develop our sense of personal identity. Our conclusions do not need to be accurate. Misinterpretations, mistakes, and misunderstandings can be just as powerful as truthful evaluations. If I imagine that many people think I am stupid, or even just one important person (like a teacher or a parent), then I will be more likely to conclude that I am stupid. This is never a finished process. We are constantly meeting new people, receiving new reactions, and revising our looking-glass self.

Similarly, George Herbert Mead believed that our self arises through taking on the role of others. Mead understood interaction as the foundation for this theory of the construction of identity: We create a "self" through our interactions with others. (We will discuss Mead further in Chapter 5.) Mead said that there were two parts of the self: the "I" and the "me." The "I" is the self as subject—the self that thinks and acts. The "me" is self as object—the attitudes we internalize from interactions with others, the social self. We achieve our sense of self-awareness when we learn to distinguish between the two. In doing so, Mead argued that we are internalizing the **generalized other**.

Erving Goffman went beyond the concept of the looking-glass self and the generalized other. Goffman believed that our selves change not only because of other people's reactions but also because we actively manage our presentations of ourselves. We modify our behavior in accordance with what particular people expect of us. This forms the foundation for Goffman's theory of **dramaturgy**. Social life is like a theatrical performance, with our performances changing according to the characters on stage, direction, the script, and more. Everyone tries to give the best performance possible; Goffman call this **face work**, because when we make a mistake or do something wrong, we feel embarrassed and "lose face." We are always in danger of losing face because no performance is perfect, but we learn to avoid losing face through observation and

generalized other

The organized rules, judgments, and attitudes of an entire group. If you try to imagine what is expected of you, you are taking on the perspective of the generalized other.

dramaturgy

Erving Goffman's conception of social life as being like a stage play wherein we all work hard to convincingly play ourselves as "characters," such as grandchild, buddy, student, employee, or other roles.

face work

A dramaturgical theory, the possible performance of ourselves, because when we make a mistake or do something wrong, we feel embarrassed, or "lose face."

SOCIOLOGY AND OUR WORLD

USING SELFIES TO UNDERSTAND MY "I" AND MY "ME"

How do "selfies" provide a simple example of the ways that sociologists think about identities?

Taking pictures of ourselves has become so common that we have a name for them: "selfies." It's not that selfies didn't always exist, but people didn't always take so many and have so many different places to post and share them. Taking a selfie and posting to Twitter or Instagram is a way of telling your network where you are, how you feel, what you're doing, and more. But, inside a selfie, we can see Mead's distinction between "I" and "me." Try it out. Take out a device with a camera and snap a picture of yourself. Look at the picture and answer the following questions: *Who is in that picture?* ("Me.") *Who took that picture?* ("I did.")

Selfies are a good example of how we learn to internalize and respond to "see" ourselves through Mead's "generalized other."

Here, just as Mead understood, the "me" is that piece of yourself the "I" endeavors to interpret on which the "I" acts. The "I" is the active doer, the piece of the self that actively creates the self (the part of you that actually took the picture). The "me," on the other hand, is not so much the subject as the object being constructed; it is that version of yourself that the "I" is interpreting and on which the "I" is acting. When we look at these images of ourselves, we are looking at a snapshot of an ongoing process through which we create and manage our selves. The way we regard and interpret our selfies is the result of internalizing the ways we imagine others see us—something Mead called the *generalized other*.

experimentation. Perhaps when I am with my buddies, I tell vulgar jokes and playfully insult them because they approve of this sort of behavior as a form of male bonding. However, I would never consider such behavior when I am visiting my grandmother. Goffman (1959) calls this **impression management**. I am not merely responding to the reactions of others. According to Goffman, I am actively trying to control how others perceive me by changing my behavior in response to perceived expectations and in an attempt to shape others opinions of me.

impression management
Erving Goffman's term for our attempts to control how others perceive us by changing our behavior to correspond to an ideal of what they will find most appealing.

---

iSOC AND YOU Thinking about Interactions, Groups, and Organizations Sociologically
You're not born "you." You become "you" in a context—a specific place at a specific moment in historical time. Society is that context: It is through your *interactions* with others, in groups and within social *institutions* like religion or education, that you become who you are—and know yourself.

3.2 Understanding Society and Social Life as Socially Structured

Social interactions are structured to an incredible degree. Consider for a moment just how predictable social interactions are for the most part. When you walk into a busy shopping mall, you are aware of an incredible array of social cues, scripts, and more that help you navigate the seemingly endless potential interactions you might have. Part of how we navigate this is understanding that most of these interactions need not take place. We understand that we can ignore most of the people around us. When we enter a store and an employee comes up to us to ask how we are and whether we would like any assistance, we understand this script and know approximately how long we will be interacting with this person depending on how we answer and what we ask for. We know when we are allowed to simply walk by and ignore people on the street (sometimes even people asking for our help or trying to invite us to interact). We know to casually ignore people having intimate conversations on cell phones in public. And we know much more than this.

Coming to understand how we know all of this and communicate that knowledge to other people is part of what it means to understand social interactions and identities as socially constructed. Interaction and communication is patterned. This makes a great deal of social life much more predictable than it would be otherwise. But it also shapes our understandings of who we are and where we "fit" into the societies in various hierarchies throughout the societies in which we live. Coming to understand these processes sociologically by relying on the iSoc model means appreciating the ways that our interactions help us construct a sense of ourselves (our identity). But more than this, interactions are structured by social institutions and powerful systems of inequality. When we examine social interaction and communication intersectionally, we also learn more about how inequality affects different groups in our society in different ways.

Nonverbal and Verbal Communication

3.2.1 Summarize the role of verbal and nonverbal communication in research using an ethnomethodological approach to studying interaction.

One of the most important ways of constructing our social identities and social reality is through **nonverbal communication**: our bodily movements, gestures, facial expressions, and even our placement in relation to others. There is evidence that some basic nonverbal gestures are universal—happiness, sadness, anger, disgust, fear, and surprise (Ekman and Friesen 1978).

nonverbal communication
The communication with others that occurs without words, including apparent behaviors such as facial expressions and less obvious messaging including posture and the spatial distance between two or more people.

Most facial expressions, however, must be interpreted depending on social situations that vary from culture to culture, era to era and must be learned. Thus, even if some nonverbal gestures exist almost everywhere in the world, someone who grew up in New Guinea and someone who grew up in Los Angeles, California, would certainly disagree over what sort of smile people use when they are pretending to be unhappy over something about which they are actually thrilled.

Through socialization, by observing and experimenting in a wide variety of situations, we learn the conventions of nonverbal communication. Consider one example: laughter. Theorists have often misunderstood laughter, assuming that it was a cognitive reaction: You hear a joke, you get the joke, you laugh at it—*because* the joke is funny. But research has shown that laughter is not principally about getting the joke. It's about getting along. Laughter is a powerful bonding tool used to signal readiness for friendship and to reinforce group solidarity by mocking outsiders. It also helps establish status hierarchies; it is a tool used to make us learn to be comfortable with inequality. Women tend to laugh more than men, and everyone laughs at jokes by the boss—even if the jokes he or she tells aren't funny (Tierney 2007). You might do the same for your college professors who tell jokes when teaching—sometimes students laugh even if our jokes are stale and our delivery is poor.

Nonverbal communication is so subtle that it requires a great deal of socialization, but *verbal communication*—talking—is not as straightforward as you might think either. Consider how many times someone has said the right words but his or her tone of voice or posture hinted at something else entirely. Even the most inconsequential statements, a "Hello" or "How are you?," can be full of subtle meanings. Sociologists often study these verbal and nonverbal interactions, trying to understand how we communicate information and validate our sense of belonging.

Sociologist Harold Garfinkel (1967) asked his students to engage in conversations with family and friends that violated social norms. People frequently ask each other "How are you?" as a polite greeting, and they expect to hear "Fine!" even if we are not fine. But Garfinkel asked his students to conduct an experiment and report back; he asked them to take the question at face value and ask for clarification: "How am I in regard to what? My health, my finances, my peace of mind …?" The typical reactions students received were anger and annoyance. But often, people were unable to explain exactly why they were angry or annoyed. The students had violated a norm of social interaction that we depend on to maintain a coherent society.

ethnomethodology

The study of the social knowledge, codes, and conventions that underlie everyday interactions and allow people to make sense of what others say and do.

Garfinkel called this form of research **ethnomethodology**, in which the researcher tries to expose the common unstated assumptions that enable such conversational and social shortcuts to work. Ethnomethodologists do not break social norms frivolously; they break norms to expose the unstated, nonverbal agreements necessary for those norms to work in the first place. For example, try getting on an elevator and singing, staring at other people instead of the elevator floors, or striking up a serious conversation with a stranger. Nowhere has anyone written "the norms of elevator riding," but you know you've broken the norm when you do it, and you know when someone else does as well.

Patterns of Social Interaction

3.2.2 Differentiate between the five basic patterns of social interaction.

Interactions with others are the social glue that enables us to express our identity and orient ourselves to our social environments. There are five basic patterns of social interaction, what sociologist Robert Nisbet (1970) calls the "molecular cement" that links individuals in groups from the smallest to the largest:

1. *Exchange.* According to sociologist Peter Blau (1964), exchange is the most basic form of social interaction—we give things to people after they give things to us or in expectation of receiving things in the future. Individuals, groups, organizations, and nations keep an informal running count of the kindnesses and slights

SOCIOLOGY AND OUR WORLD

ELEVATOR BEHAVIOR, NORMS, AND SOCIAL INEQUALITY

Can we see social inequality just by looking at how people ride elevators?

Elevator behavior is incredibly scripted. For the most part, we all follow an elaborate set of norms when we ride elevators and so do all of the people who ride them with us. We get on, stand facing the doors, position ourselves at the back and to the sides when strangers ride with us, and talk about precious few topics, if we talk at all. Some of this is the result of socialization that was accomplished in other ways when passenger elevators began to be in widespread use. During the latter half of the nineteenth century, passenger elevators were generally equipped with benches along the back wall. Perhaps people just got used to sitting there and when the benches were taken away, they just continued and the rest of us are following norms created by benches that haven't existed in elevators in over 100 years.

But these aren't the only scripts we follow on elevators. Research suggests that our elevator behavior might also uphold social hierarchies between groups of people. Rebekah Rousi—a cognitive scientist by training—ethnographically studied elevator behavior in Adelaide, Australia. She wanted to know whether people move about and segregate themselves within the limited space of an elevator in patterned ways. To study this, Rousi rode two elevators in two office towers in downtown Adelaide for a series of days. Each ride, she recorded where people stood and how they behaved to search for patterns in behavior, collecting an enviable quantity of data on fairly mundane behavior. What she discovered is that people tend to ride elevators in ways that might reproduce inequalities between men and women.

The most senior men riding the elevator (in terms of age) rode at the back of the elevators. Younger men tended to ride in the middle. And at the front, facing the doors with their backs to all the men, were the women. The other thing she noticed related to looking around. Men were much more likely to use the reflective spaces in the elevator to look at themselves and other passengers. Women watched the floors, elevator monitors, and generally avoided eye contact with others (unless in conversation). Men stand in places where they can look (at themselves and others); women stand in places where they will be looked at. Could it be that the way we situate ourselves in elevators is one small way we uphold unequal relationships between men and women? Does the pattern hold for elevator behavior in the United States? We need new research to tell us more.

SOURCES: Gray, Lee. 2002. *From Ascending Rooms to Express Elevators: A History of the Passenger Elevator in the 19th Century*. Mobile, AL: Elevator World, Inc. Rousi, Rebekah. April 2, 2013. "An Uplifting Experience: Adopting Ethnography to Study Elevator User Behavior." *Ethnography Matters*—blog. http://ethnographymatters.net/blog/2013/04/02/an-uplifting-experience-adopting-ethnography-to-study-elevator-user-experience/

they have received and act according to the **norm of reciprocity**—the social expectation that people will respond to us favorably, or with hostility or indifference depending on how we interact with them.

norm of reciprocity
The social expectation that people will respond to us favorably, or with hostility or indifference depending upon how we interact with them.

2. *Cooperation.* Running counts of good and bad exchanges are overlooked when we must work together toward a common goal: growing food, raising children, and protecting our group from enemies. Without cooperation, any social organization more complex than a small group of family and friends would be impossible. Large-scale social institutions like the economy or education could not exist.

3. *Competition.* Sometimes some form of inequality is inherent in the outcome of an interaction because of limited resources. Several candidates may be interested in the same job. Interested parties must compete for the scarce resource. In modern societies, competition is especially important in economies built around capitalism, but it affects every aspect of social life. Colleges compete for the best students, workplaces for the best applicants, religious groups for new members.

4. *Conflict.* In a situation of conflict, the competition becomes more intense and hostile; competitors may actively hate one another and perhaps break social norms to acquire the prized goal. In its basic form, conflict can lead to violence. However, sociologist Lewis Coser (1956) argued that conflict can also be a source of solidarity. And sometimes conflict can also lead to positive social change, as groups struggle to overcome oppression.

5. *Coercion.* The final form of social interaction is coercion, in which individuals or groups with social power (**superordinates**) use the threat of violence, deprivation, or some other punishment to control the actions of those with less power (**subordinates**) (Simmel [1908] 1956). Coercion is often combined with other forms of social interaction. For instance, we may obey the speed limit on the highway

superordinate
Individual or group that possesses social power.

subordinate
Individual or group that possesses little or comparatively less social power.

through coercion (the threat of getting a traffic ticket) as well as through cooperation (the belief that the speed limit has been set for the public good). A great deal of our interactions are coercive, though very often the threat is not violence but being laughed at, stared at, or otherwise embarrassed.

Exchange, cooperation, competition, conflict, and coercion govern our interactions with one another. These patterns of social interaction are what make social life predictable (usually). But we have to be socialized to understand how each of these patterns is flexible enough to be applicable to an infinite number of possible interactions.

Elements of Social Structure

3.2.3 Explain the ways in which role performances are shaped by social structure.

Just because we are constantly creating our identities doesn't mean we make it up as we go along. We are simultaneously *enabled* and *constrained* by social structure. Using metaphors from the theater, the dramaturgical perspective suggests that we do so using props and sets available to us and appropriate to our situations. We follow cultural "scripts." This is what helps us know we ought to answer "Fine" when asked "How are you?" by a stranger. Indeed, our interactions are "rehearsed" and may feel "choreographed" and "scripted" by someone else entirely. And we often act a bit differently "front stage" than we do when we are "backstage." Social life requires us to adopt many different roles, appropriate to different situations. As William Shakespeare wrote, "All the world's a stage, and all the men and women merely players; they have their exits and their entrances, and one man in his time plays many parts."

We must behave according to the role of "parent" around our children, "student" while in class, and "employee" at work. We know the basic rules of each role: that "students" sit in chairs facing a central podium or desk, keep quiet unless we raise our hands, and so on, but we also have a great deal of freedom and, as we become more experienced in playing the role, we can become quite creative. The particular emphasis or interpretation we give a role, our "style," is called **role performance**.

Sociologists use two terms, *status* and *role*, to describe the elementary forms of interaction in society. By **status**, sociologists mean the social identities that are understood as meaningful by a group or society. **Roles** refer to the behaviors expected of individuals who are understood to occupy a given status in a given context. So, there are various roles associated with different social statuses. Beyond this, as noted previously, social structure creates the framework within which we interact with one another. Institutions emerge and are sustained that promote that structure. And we learn to identify ourselves within social structures by understanding the roles we can play and the status we have while occupying each role. Yet, it is also true that our various identities also intersect with each other and, sometimes, create conflict and inequality.

Social Status

3.2.4 Understand the distinction between ascribed and achieved statuses and the role each plays in social reproduction.

In everyday life we use the term *status* to refer to people who have a lot of money, power, and influence. But sociologists use status to refer to any social identity recognized as meaningful by the group or society. A "social status" is a position that carries with it certain expectations, rights, and responsibilities. Being a Presbyterian, an English major, a teenager, or a "redhead" is a status in contemporary American society, but liking pizza is not. Many statuses are identities fixed at birth, (like race, sex, or ethnicity); others we enter and exit (like different age statuses, or levels of education).

role performance

The particular emphasis or interpretation each of us gives a social role.

status

One's socially defined position in a group; it is often characterized by certain expectations and rights.

role

Behavior expected of people who have a particular status.

Statuses change from culture to culture and over time. Having red hair was once a negative status, associated with being quick tempered, cruel, and possibly demonic. In fact, redheads still receive attention for their hair color—redheaded women are often perceived to be "wild," but redheaded men are stereotyped as "wimpy." And research on redheads suggests that they manage this status over the course of their lives, changing it from something that might hurt their status into a social status in its own rite (Heckert and Best 1997).

When pizza was first introduced into the United States in the early 1900s, only a few people knew what it was, and "liking pizza" was a status. But today, liking pizza is more of a taste than a status; it is no longer all that meaningful among Americans because it has become ubiquitous in the United States to eat pizza. Many statuses are identical to roles—son or daughter, student, teacher—but others (like resident of Missouri or cyberathlete) are more complex, based on a vast set of interlocking and sometimes contradictory roles (Merton 1968). Sociologists distinguish between two types of social status: "ascribed" and "achieved."

An **ascribed status** is a status that we receive involuntarily, without regard to our unique talents, skills, or accomplishments: for instance, our place of birth, parents, first language, racial and ethnic background, gender, sexual identity, and age (Figure 3.1). Many ascribed characteristics are based on genetics or physiology; so we can do little or nothing to change them. We have the ascribed status as "male" or "female," whether we want it or not. Sociologists study the effects of ascribed statuses because they are often used to confer privilege and power and to reproduce marginalization and disadvantage. In this way, inequality gets institutionalized. Yet, which statuses are presented as superior and inferior differs from culture to culture and across eras.

ascribed status
Status that is assigned to a person and over which he or she has no control.

An **achieved status** is a status that we attain through talent, ability, effort, or other unique personal characteristics. Some of the more common achieved statuses are being a high school or college graduate; being rich or poor; having a certain occupation; being married or in a romantic relationship; belonging to a church or club; being good at a sport, hobby, or leisure pursuit; or having a specific point of view on a social issue. Achieved statuses are often dependent on ascribed statuses. People who excel at playing polo, for instance, tend to be wealthy, and white. In this way, ascribed statuses can make it easier or more challenging to achieve other statuses. Race, gender, and ethnicity all affect our ability to achieve certain statuses. The status of "male" vastly increases your likelihood of being hired as an airline pilot or dentist, and the status of "female" increases your potential of being hired for a job involving child care.

achieved status
Status or social position based on one's accomplishments or activities.

We are able to change achieved statuses. We can change jobs, religions, or political affiliations. We can learn new skills, develop new interests, meet new people, and change our minds about issues. In fact, we usually do. We all have most of the same ascribed statuses now that we did when we were 16 years old (except for age), but our achieved statuses are dramatically different: We have changed jobs, political views, tastes in music, and favorite television programs. In traditional societies, most statuses are ascribed. People are born rich or poor and expect to die rich or poor. They eventually hold the same jobs their parents had and cannot even think of changing their religion because only one religion is practiced throughout the society. They dress the

FIGURE 3.1 Ascribed, Achieved, and Master Statuses: Justin Bieber
Consider how the different components of Justin Bieber's identity can be made sense of sociologically by delineating between his achieved, ascribed, and master statuses.

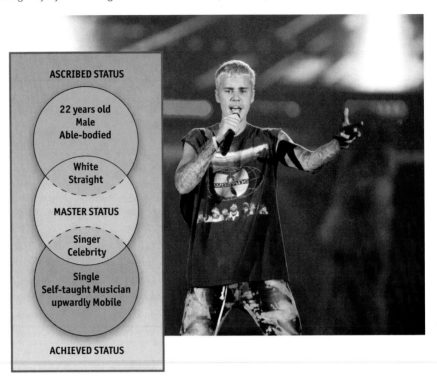

social reproduction

The structures and activities that transmit social inequality from one generation to the next.

master status

An ascribed or achieved status presumed so important that it overshadows all of the others, dominating our lives and controlling our position in society.

same and listen to the same songs and stories, so they can't even change their status based on artistic taste. This is what sociologists mean when they use the concept **social reproduction**. However, in modern societies, we have many more choices, and more and more statuses are attained. This does not mean social reproduction no longer takes place; rather, it means that social reproduction is open to challenge and may be perpetuated in new ways.

When ascribed or achieved status is presumed so important that it overshadows all of the others, it becomes a **master status** (Hughes 1945). Being poor or rich tends to be a master status because it dramatically influences other areas of life, such as education, health, and family stability. People with disabilities often find that many people ignore all their other statuses, seeing only "disabled." Other common master statuses are race, ethnicity, religion, and sexual identity (see FIGURE 3.1). Members of ethnic, religious, and sexual minorities often complain that their associates treat them as representatives of their status rather than as individuals, asking "What do gay people think about this?" or "Why do Muslims do that?" but never about last night's ball game. Occupation may also be a master status; this is why we so often ask and answer, "What do you do for a living?" at social gatherings.

Social Roles

3.2.5 Understand the ongoing work required to negotiate between role expectations and role performances.

social role

Sets of behaviors expected of a person who occupies a certain social status.

Social roles are sets of behaviors expected of a person who occupies a certain social status. A social role is like the "role" an actor plays in a drama: It includes the physical presentation, props, and costume; the actor's motivation and perspective; and all the actor's lines, as well as the physical gestures, accent, and timing (the "script"). As in the theatrical world, our experience of roles is a negotiation between role *expectations* and role *performances*. We learn what sorts of behaviors are expected from specific roles, and then we perform those roles in conformity with those expectations to varying degrees. Our roles are constantly being evaluated. And if we begin to dislike the expectations that accompany a role, we may try to modify it to suit our needs, convince others that our performance is better than they seemed to think, or even reject the role altogether.

Because roles contain many different behaviors for use with different people in different situations, they can sometimes contradict each other. We experience **role strain** when the same role has demands and expectations that contradict each other, so we cannot possibly meet them all at once. For instance, the role of "student" might ask us to submit to the professor's authority *and* exercise independent thought. How can a single behavior fulfill both demands? We are so proficient at navigating the internal contradictions within a given role that we are often able to compartmentalize without even noticing the contradiction existed in the first place (Goode 1960).

A related problem, **role conflict**, happens when we try to play different roles with extremely different or contradictory rules at the same time. If I am out with my buddies, playing the cool, irreverent role of "friend," and I see my teacher, who expects the quiet, obedient "student," I may experience role conflict. If I suddenly become polite, I may lose face with my friends; but if I remain irreverent, I may lose face with my teacher. Because everyone is playing multiple roles all the time, role conflict is a common problem.

What happens when we must leave a role that is central to our identity? **Role exit** describes the process of adjustment that takes place when we move out of such a role. Sometimes we leave roles voluntarily: We may change jobs or religions, get divorced or widowed, finish our schooling, and so on. Sometimes we leave roles involuntarily: we change age groups (suddenly our parents say, "You're not a kid anymore"), get arrested, or get fired. Whether we leave voluntarily or involuntarily, we are likely to feel lost, confused, and sad.

Roles and statuses give us, as individuals, the tools we need to enter the social world. We feel grounded in our statuses; they give us roots. And our roles provide us with a playbook, a script, for any situation. We are ready to join others.

Tennis Superstar or Seductress and Royalty? Women who enter traditionally male domains—from the operating room to the boardroom to the sports stadium—must constantly negotiate between different sets of role expectations. Serena Williams may be one of the greatest tennis players ever to hit the court, but she still has to look like a cover girl to reaffirm traditional gender expectations.

role strain
The experience of difficulty in performing a role.

role conflict
What happens when we try to play different roles with extremely different or contradictory rules at the same time.

role exit
The process we go through to adjust when leaving a role that is central to our identity.

---

iSOC AND YOU Understanding Society and Social Life as Socially Structured
Like actors in a play, you learn specific roles that are appropriate to a specific situation. You don't behave in every situation like the same person: Sometimes you're deferential and sometimes you might expect, or even demand, deference from others. That is, your roles teach you the proper mechanics of *interacting* in *unequal* situations.

3.3 Groups, Networks, and Social Life

The groups and networks to which we belong shape much more of our lives than you may realize. Groups help us to make sense of our own identities and consider them against the identities of people who belong to other groups. They shape what kinds of people we understand ourselves to be, our likes and dislikes, our experience of the world around us, and the opportunities we may encounter. Social networks are, quite literally, the fabric of social life. And sociologists who study groups and networks want to know both what they provide and how they work. Social networks provide us access to status, power, and money (or not). But they also help us when we are most in need.

Examining groups and networks allow sociologists to look at interactions and how connections between people shape their experiences and opportunities in society.

It allows us to ask questions like, "Are you more likely to get a job from a close friend, or someone at a firm who is close friends with one of your best friend's uncles?" We can learn more about whether teens accurately understand their level of risk of contracting sexually transmitted infections from their sexual behavior and their beliefs about how it connects them with others. We can ask why and how affirmative action policies might help to challenge biases in many institutions and organizations and work to straight, white, men's advantage. From the iSoc perspective, groups and networks shape our sense of identity and inform our interactions with each other. These interactions create intricate webs of relationships that cause some of them to take the form of "groups" and institutions emerge and help provide groups with form and meaning when different groups are systematically treated in different ways. This also means that when we examine groups and networks intersectionally, we come to understand the role that groups and networks play in challenging and reproducing forms of social inequality in society.

Social Groups and Identity

3.3.1 Explain how groups differ from crowds.

group
Collection of individuals who are aware that they share something in common and who interact with one another on the basis of their interrelated roles and statuses.

dyad
A group of two people, the smallest configuration defined by sociologists as a group.

triad
A group of three people.

tetrad
A group of four people.

crowd
An aggregate of individuals who happen to be together but experience themselves as essentially independent.

Apart from individuals, then, the smallest unit of society is a **group**—any assortment of people who share (or believe that they share) the same norms, values, and expectations. And the smallest group is a **dyad**, a group of two (groups of three are called **triads**, four—**tetrads**). Anytime you meet with another person, you are in a group. And every time the configuration of people meeting changes, the group changes. Groups can be *formal* organizations with well-defined rules and procedures or they may be *informal*, like friends, coworkers, or whoever happens to be hanging around. A group can be very small (your family and friends), or very large (your religion or nation). But the most significant groups in our lives are the ones large enough that we do not know everyone, but small enough that we feel we play an important role.

Passengers on an airplane or the customers in a restaurant are not a group. Sociologically speaking, they are a **crowd**—an aggregate of individuals who happen to be together but experience themselves as essentially independent. But the moment something goes wrong (the flight is cancelled or the service is inexplicably slow), they begin to take on group-like qualities. They may start looking to each other for validation and emotional support. On the TV series *Lost* (2004–2010), an airplane crashes on a mysterious island in the South Pacific, and the survivors band together to fight a

Passengers on an airplane are a crowd—individuals who happen to be in the same place, but do not experience group cohesion. During and after a crisis, they may become a group. The passengers on USAir 1549 shared an experience that drew them together into a group—surviving a crash landing in the Hudson River. Here they stand on the wings of the plane awaiting rescue crews. In 2013, the pilot, Chesley "Sully" Sullenberger had a reunion with several of the surviving passengers (and some of their children born since the crash landing on Katie Couric's talk show, "Katie"). The reunion is a powerful illustration of how a crisis can make a group out of a crowd.

series of weird supernatural threats. On the airplane, they had been reading, napping, or staring into space, basically ignoring each other. But tragedy unites them and they become a group, establish roles for different members, leaders, and people begin to take on different group roles.

Groups differ from crowds in their **group cohesion**, or the degree to which the individual members identify with each other and the group. In groups with high cohesion, individual members will be more likely to follow the rules and less likely to drop out or defect. Because every group wants to decrease deviance and keep the members from leaving, studies about how to increase cohesion have proliferated. It's not hard to do: shift the group importance from second place to first place, transform the office or cult into "a family," force members to spend time together and make emotional connections. Wilderness retreats and "trust exercises" jump-start this connection. And it helps to find a common enemy.

Everyone belongs to many different groups: families, friends, co-workers, classmates, churches, clubs, organizations, plus less tangible groups. Are you a fan of country blues music? Justin Bieber? Lady Gaga? Do you oppose gun control legislation? Even if you never seek out an organized club, identify as a "Belieber" (fan of Justin Bieber) or "Little Monster" (Gaga fans), or find others who share your beliefs about the right to bear arms, you are still part of a group. Your gender, sexual orientation, race, ethnicity, age, class, nationality, and even your hair color place you in groups and form part of your identity. Often our membership in a group is a core element of our identity but not always. Imagine an Asian American gay man who is an avid mountain biker who joins every mountain biking club in his community and is a central person in all club activities. Mountain biker is the core of his identity, he believes. But without his bicycle, other people may assume that his core identity is his membership in a racial and sexual group.

What is visible and invisible to us as a facet of our identity is often related to the organization of society, institutions, intersecting identities, and powerful systems of inequality. Social inequality works the most seamlessly when we fail to recognize it is inequality. Think about which pieces of your identity are important to you. When we ask students to list the five most important elements of their identities, it is not uncommon for African American, Latino, and Asian American students to list their race. But white students do not generally think to list "white." Women are more likely to list their gender than men. And although many students list "gay" or "lesbian," almost no one ever writes "heterosexual." *Why does this happen?* Generally, people are more aware of the ways they are marginalized than the ways they are privileged.

Types of Groups

3.3.2 Delineate the differences between primary and secondary groups and explain how groups promote conformity.

There are many different types of groups, depending on their composition, permanence, fluidity of boundaries, and membership criteria. You are born into some groups (family, race). In other groups, you may be born into the group, but membership also depends on your own activities and commitments, like ethnic or religious groups. Some are based entirely on expression of interest (clubs, fans), and others are based on formal application for membership.

Small groups (small enough so that you know almost everybody) are divided into two types, primary and secondary. According to the sociologist Charles Horton Cooley (1909/1990), **primary groups**, such as friends and family, come together for *expressive reasons*: they provide emotional support, love, companionship, and security. **Secondary groups**, such as coworkers or club members, come together for *instrumental reasons*: they want to work together to meet common goals. Secondary groups are generally larger and make less of an emotional claim on your identity. In real life, most

group cohesion
The degree to which individual members of a group identify with each other and with the group as a whole.

primary group
One such as friends and family, which comes together for expressive reasons, providing emotional support, love, companionship, and security.

secondary group
Coworkers, club members, or another group that comes together for instrumental reasons, such as wanting to work together to meet common goals. Secondary groups make less of an emotional claim on one's identity than do primary groups.

HOW DO WE KNOW WHAT WE KNOW?

GROUP CONFORMITY

How can we observe these processes of conformity to group norms? In a classic experiment in social psychology, a group of strangers was gathered together under the pretense of testing their visual acuity. They were shown two cards, one with one line and one with three lines of different lengths. (In the group, however, only one person was really the subject of the experiment; all the rest were research assistants!) The group was then asked which of the lines on the second card matched the line on the first. When the subject was asked first, he or she answered correctly. (It didn't matter what others said.) But when the first group members to respond were the research assistants, they gave wrong answers, picking an obviously incorrect line and insisting it was the match (Asch 1955).

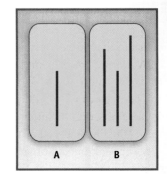

Surprisingly, the test subjects would then most often give the wrong answers as well, preferring to follow the group norm rather than trust their own perceptions. When asked about it, some claimed that they felt uncomfortable but that they actually came to see the line they chose as the correct one. Psychologist Solomon Asch concluded that our desire to "fit in" is very powerful, even in a group that we don't belong to.

in-group
A group with which you identify and that you feel positively toward, producing a "we" feeling.

out-group
One to which you do not belong and toward which you feel either neutral or hostile; the "they" who are perceived as different from and of lower stature than ourselves.

in-group heterogeneity
The social tendency to be keenly aware of the subtle differences among the individual members of your group.

out-group homogeneity
The social tendency to believe that all members of an out-group are exactly the same.

groups have elements of both. You may join the local chapter of the Green Party because you want to support its political agenda, but you are unlikely to stay involved unless you form some emotional connections with the other members.

William Graham Sumner (1906/2002) identified two different types of groups that depend on membership and affinity: in-groups and out-groups. An **in-group** is a group I feel positively toward and to which I actually belong. An **out-group** is one to which I do not belong and do not feel very positively toward. We may feel competitive or hostile toward members of an out-group. Often we think of members of out-groups as bad, wrong, inferior, or just weird. But, in-groups and out-groups do not have to be built around any sort of socially meaningful characteristic. In the 1960s, an Iowa grade school teacher named Jane Elliot performed an experiment in her class: She created an out-group from the students with blue eyes, telling the class that the lack of melanin in blue eyes made them inferior (Elliot 1970; Verhaag 1996). She did not instruct the brown-eyed students to treat the blue-eyed students differently, but was horrified by how quickly the out-group was ostracized and attacked. Elliot also found that she could not call off the experiment: Blue-eyed children remained a detested out-group for the rest of the year! Gerald Suttles (1972), studying juvenile groups in Chicago housing projects, found that boys formed in-groups and out-groups based on whether the brick walls of their buildings were lighter or darker in color.

Membership in a group changes your perception. You become keenly aware of the subtle differences among the individual members of your group, which we call **in-group heterogeneity**, but tend to believe that all members of the out-group are exactly the same, which we call **out-group homogeneity** (Meissner, Brigham, and Butz 2005; Voci 2000). Researchers at Stony Brook University asked some members of fraternities and sororities, as well as some dormitory residents, about the people in their own living group (house or dorm) and the people in others. What were they like? Consistently, people said of their in-group that they were "too different"—each member being "unique" to generalize (in-group heterogeneity). When asked about the other groups, however, they were quick to respond, "Oh, they're all jocks," or "That's the egghead nerd house" (out-group homogeneity). The finding that we tend to perceive individual differences in our in-group and not perceive them in out-groups holds mainly in Western societies. It doesn't hold, or it holds only weakly, for China, Korea, and Japan (Quattrone 1986).

Our membership in groups not only provides us with a source of identity, but it also orients us in the world, like a compass. We *refer* to our group memberships as a way of navigating every interaction we have every day. We orient our behavior toward group norms and consider what group members would say before (or after) we act. A **reference group** is a group toward which we are so strongly committed or one that commands so much prestige that we orient our actions around what we perceive that group's perceptions would be. In some cases the reference group is the in-group, and the rest are "wannabes." In other cases, your reference group can be one to which you aspire; reference groups do not just guide your actions as a member of a group but guide your actions as a *future* member of a different group. If you want to join a particular sorority or fraternity, for instance, you might begin to dress and act like members and cultivate some shared interests in anticipation of joining later. Thus, your reference group and your membership groups are not always the same. Both reference groups and membership groups will change over the course of your life, as your circumstances change as well.

In the classic movie series, *Harry Potter*, children are depicted in cliques in a variety of ways. Collections of friends are most often found within (not between) the different houses the children are sorted into at the outset (Slytherin, Gryffindor, Hufflepuff, Ravenclaw). But there are also cliques within each house. They sit together in classes, tease a common group of "other" kids, or simply hang out together and think of themselves as different from other groups at school in an important way.

One of the best illustrations of group dynamics is the high school clique. A **clique** is a group of people who share some important quality and interact with each other more frequently and intensely than others in the same setting. All across the United States, middle and high school students seem to form the same groups: jocks, nerds, preps, skaters, posers, gang-bangers, wannabes, princesses, stoners, brainiacs (Milner 2006). Cliques are organized around inclusion and exclusion. Ranked hierarchically, those at the bottom are supposed to aspire to be in the cliques at the top. Cliques provide protection, elevate one's status, and teach outsiders a lesson. Many high schools are large enough to accommodate several cliques. In smaller schools, though, exclusion from the most popular group may be a source of significant pain.

Group Dynamics

3.3.3 Understand the predictable characteristics and dynamics exhibited by groups.

Groups exhibit certain predictable dynamics and have certain characteristics. Often these dynamics are simply a function of formal characteristics—size or composition—and other times they are due more to their purpose. Often groups promote thinking and consequences that are beneficial to themselves and outsiders. But, just as often, groups promote inequality and sometimes even disastrous effects.

When it comes to groups, size matters. Small groups, in which all members know each other and are able to interact simultaneously, exhibit different features than larger groups, in which other members of the group do not always observe our behavior. Large groups may be able to tolerate more diversity than small groups, although the bonds among small groups may be more intense than those in larger groups. Small groups may engage us the most, but larger groups are better able to influence others.

Every group, even the smallest, has a structure that sociologists can analyze and study. There is always a **leader**, someone in charge, whether that person was elected, appointed, or just informally took control, and a small number of **hardcore members**, those with a great deal of power to make policy decisions. Leaders and hardcore members spend an enormous amount of time and energy on the group; it forms an important part of their identity. As a consequence, they have a vested interest in promoting the norms and values of the group. They are most likely to punish deviance

reference group
A group toward which one is so strongly committed, or one that commands so much prestige, that we orient our actions around what we perceive that group's perceptions would be.

clique
A small group of people with shared interests or other features in common who spend time together and do not readily allow others to join them.

leader
People in charge, whether they were elected, appointed, or just informally took control, of a group.

hardcore members
The small number of group members, the "inner circle," who wield a great deal of power to make policy decisions.

WHAT DO YOU THINK? WHAT DOES AMERICA THINK?

Group Membership

Research shows that those with stronger social ties and networks lead happier, healthier lives.

What do you think?

Are there any activities that you do with the same group of people on a regular basis, even if the group doesn't have a formal name, such as a bridge group, exercise group, or a group that meets to discuss individual or community problems?

- ○ Yes
- ○ No

What does America think?

This was most recently asked on the 2004 General Social Survey. At that point, almost three-quarters of respondents reported not being part of a regular informal group. However, white respondents (29.3 percent) were more likely than black respondents (19.1 percent) to be part of such a group. Those who were of another racial classification were least likely to report being part of a group (14.1 percent). There was no difference in group membership by gender.

SOURCE: Data from General Social Survey, 2004.

THINKING CRITICALLY ABOUT SURVEY DATA

Were you surprised that so few respondents report being members of informal groups? These data are older now. Do you think that more people might be involved in informal group activities more recently, or less? Why do you think so few people belong to groups? And how might this intersect with race in ways that make people of color less likely to be a part of regular informal groups than white people?

among group members and to think negatively about other groups. Ordinary members split their time and energies among several groups, so they are not as likely to be strongly emotionally invested. They are more likely to commit minor acts of deviance, sometimes because they confuse the norms of the various groups they belong to and sometimes because they are not invested enough to obey every rule.

The groups we belong to hold a powerful influence over our norms, values, and expectations. When we belong to a group, we prize conformity over "rocking the boat," even in minor decisions and even if the group is not very important to us. Conformity may be formally required by the norms of the group. For example, cadets at military schools often have their heads shaved on their enrollment, and members of some groups wear specific clothing or get identical tattoos. Membership requires conformity to these group norms. Other times, however, we volunteer our conformity. We will often imitate the members of our reference group and evaluate ourselves and our attitudes based on group norms—even among groups to which we do not formally belong (Deux and Wrightsman 1988; Merton 1968). For instance, you may have paid special attention to the popular clique in high school and modeled your dress, talk, and other behaviors on them. Marketing makes use of this dynamic, aiming to get the "opinion leaders" in selected reference groups to use, wear, or tout a product, in the hopes that others will imitate them (Katz and Lazarsfeld 1955; Gladwell 1997; PBS/Frontline 2001).

Psychologist Irving Janis called the process by which group members try to preserve harmony and unity despite their individual judgments **groupthink** (Janis 1972). Sometimes groupthink can have negative or tragic consequences. For example, on January 28, 1986, the Space Shuttle *Challenger* exploded shortly after takeoff, killing the seven astronauts aboard. A study afterward revealed that some of the NASA scientists involved with the project believed that the O-ring seal on the booster rocket was unstable due to abnormally cold temperatures the day of the launch, but they invariably deferred their judgments to the group.

groupthink

Irving Janis's term for social process in which members of a group attempt to conform their opinions to what they believe to be the consensus of the group, even if, as individuals, they may consider that opinion wrong or unwise.

Group conformity and large bureaucratic organizations can often lead to a diffusion of responsibility. Who was really responsible for the oil spill in the Gulf Coast in the summer of 2010? Was it the company doing the drilling (BP), the company who owned the rig BP was leasing to do the drilling (Transocean), the company that built the rig that Transocean owned (Hyundai Heavy Industries), the company in charge of the material pumped into the drilling hole prior to the explosion (Halliburton), or some combination? Or was it the federal government's failure to regulate the drilling that led to such irresponsibility or the Interior Department's Mineral Management Service inspectors fault for failing to ensure that federal regulations were upheld?

One of the characteristics of large groups is that responsibility is diffused. The chain of command can be long enough or authority can seem dispersed enough that any one individual, even the one who actually executes an order, may avoid taking responsibility for his or her actions. If you are alone somewhere and see a person in distress, you are far more likely to help that person than if you are in a big city with many other people streaming past. This dynamic leads to the problem of **bystanders**: those who witness something wrong, harmful, dangerous, or illegal, yet do nothing to intervene. In cases where there is one bystander, he or she is more likely to intervene than when there are more bystanders. In some cases, bystanders simply assume that as long as others are observing the problem, they are no more responsible than anyone else to intervene. Sociologists refer to this dynamic as the **bystander effect**.

Stereotyping is another dynamic of group life. **Stereotypes** are assumptions about what people are like or how they will behave based on their membership in a group. Often our stereotypes revolve around ascribed or attained statuses, but any group can be stereotyped. Think of the stereotypes we have of cheerleaders, jocks, and nerds. In the hit movie series *High School Musical* (2006, 2007, 2008), members of each group try to downplay the stereotypes and be seen as full human beings: The jock/basketball star wants to be lead in the school play; his black teammate is a wonderful chef who can make a fabulous crème brûlée. Sometimes you don't even need a single case to have a stereotype; you can get your associations from the media, from things people around you say, or from the simple tendency to think of out-groups as somehow bad or wrong. Stereotypes are so strong that we tend to ignore behaviors that don't fit. If we have a stereotype of teenagers as lazy and irresponsible, we will ignore hardworking, responsible teenagers, maybe thinking of them as exceptions to the rule. Stereotypes are a foundation of *prejudice*, where we "prejudge" people based on their membership in a specific group. (We will discuss this more fully in Chapter 8.)

Social Networks

3.3.4 Describe the small world problem and how it helps us understand social networks.

A **social network** is a type of group that is both looser and denser than a formal group. Sociologist Georg Simmel used the term *web* to describe the way our collective membership in different groups constitutes our sense of identity. Sociologists often use this metaphor to describe a network as a web of social relationships that connect people to one another, and, through those connections, with other people. A network is both denser than a group, with many more connecting nodes (individuals within the network), and

bystander

Someone who witnesses something wrong, harmful, dangerous, or illegal, yet does nothing to intervene.

bystander effect

The diffusion of responsibility among groups of bystanders, in which they assume that as long as others are observing the problem, they are no more responsible than anyone else to intervene.

stereotype

Generalization about a group that is oversimplified and exaggerated and that fails to acknowledge individual differences in the group.

social network

Often conceived as a web of social relationships, a type of group that is both looser and denser than a formal group but connects people to each other, and, through those connections, with other people.

looser, in that people may be less connected in their daily lives and you may experience little influence on your behavior. The interconnectedness of these webs—how they connect, overlap, intermingle—has become a major way we understand our world.

Have you ever met someone new only to realize that you both know someone or a collection of people in common? Sometimes it can feel as though it is a very small world after all. A social psychologist, Stanly Milgram, wondered precisely this and wanted to know just how "small" the world actually is in terms of how interconnected we all are. Have you ever heard of the term "six degrees of separation"? It refers to the idea that we are all connected to everyone else on earth by our social connections and that it takes no fewer than six social connections to reach anyone else on earth; social scientists refer to this as the **small world problem**.

Milgram (1967) studied this issue to assess just how interconnected we are by asking a group of people in Lincoln, Nebraska, to try to send a letter to a stock broker living in Boston, Massachusetts. They were told to mail the letter to someone who might know the stock broker or someone who might be able to mail it to someone else who knows him. The idea was to see how many mailings it took to get there. In the end, only around one in five of the original letters made it to the stock broker in Boston and it took an average of just over five people to get the letter there…. hence "six degrees of separation." Subsequent research on the small world problem has discovered that we are less connected than Milgram thought (Watts 2003)—but more than you might have initially thought (see MAP 3.1).

Sociologists studying social networks seek to ask questions that can be answered by looking at **network effects** that we might not otherwise be able to answer. Consider the small world problem. If most of us were asked how many connections it would take us to connect with the Prime Minister of Germany, we have a guess. But we would have to analyze our social network to get an answer in which we were confident. Social networks shape our identities, interactions, and social institutions. But, they also give rise to inequality.

small world problem

The name for sociological research conducted by Milgram and others that suggests human society is a small network characterized by short paths between strangers. The research is often associated with the phrase "six degrees of separation" (although Milgram himself did not use that phrase).

network effects

The sociological idea that we end up sharing a lot in common with people with whom we share a social network.

MAP 3.1 SMALL WORLD PROBLEM: Internet Connectivity

Duncan Watts used e-mails to work on the small world problem in the twenty-first century and challenged some of Milgram's suggestions about connectivity. But, here we can see that context matters as well. Some places in the United States are much more connected than others. It might have been very important that Milgram started his letters in Lincoln, Nebraska (which he probably perceived as fairly remote in the 1960s). More letters might have made their way to Boston and with fewer connections if he started the chains in Los Angeles, New York City, or somewhere else. Some places are just more connected than others. For instance, as of 2013, roughly 84 percent of U.S. households had a computer (smartphones and tablets included), and approximately 74 percent of households had Internet access at home. But, as you can see here, Internet access is not equitably distributed in the United States.

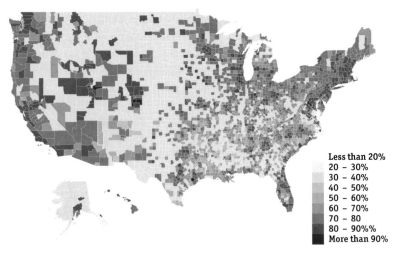

Less than 20%
20 – 30%
30 – 40%
40 – 50%
50 – 60%
60 – 70%
70 – 80
80 – 90%%
More than 90%

NOTE: Data are only collected from counties with a population of 20,000 or more.

SOURCE: Data from U.S. Census Bureau, American Community Survey.

SOCIOLOGY AND OUR WORLD

WHY LIBERALS DRINK LATTES

What is the relationship among your tastes in things like music, clothes, cars, and beverages and your political views and beliefs?

It is a stereotype that liberals like things like lattes, organic food, and are more likely to see independent films while conservatives are more likely to drive trucks, hunt, and listen to country music. Sociological research, however, suggests that there is some truth to these beliefs, but not for the reason you might think. Sociologists Daniel Dellaposta, Yongren Shi, and Michael Macy (2015) discovered that political ideology (whether you are liberal or conservative) is correlated with cultural preferences (for certain brands and styles of clothing, and things like lattes or country music) fairly consistently. That is, there are fewer country music-loving liberals and latte-sipping conservatives than you might imagine. But does a love of lattes or country music actually persuade someone to take on a particular political ideology? Or does being liberal or conservative somehow shape the cultural preferences and tastes we come to have?

Dellaposta, Shi, and Macy found that neither of these things are happening. The real reason cultural preferences are tied to political beliefs and ideologies has to do with something sociologists who study social networks call "network effects"—the notion that we end up sharing a lot in common with people with whom we share a social network. As Dellaposta, Shi, and Macy write, lifestyle preferences and political views correlate with one another as a result of interactions between people. Groups of people develop ideas about politics and tastes together. The connections might start off as arbitrary. But over time, and as result of network effects, some of them will become pervasive enough to give rise to stereotypes. And although network effects are studied here to look at the relationship between politics and tastes, they are more commonly studied in terms of how inequalities are transmitted (DiMaggio and Garip 2011).

Networks, Experience, and Opportunity

3.3.5 Explain the difference between weak and strong ties in terms of what they provide.

The social connectedness of certain groups in the society can produce interaction patterns that have a lasting influence on the lives of people both within and outside of the network. For example, prep schools not only offer excellent educations but also produce social networks among wealthy children who acquire "cultural capital" (those mannerisms, behaviors, affectations that mark one as a member of the elite, as we discussed in Chapter 2) that prepares them for life among the elite (Cookson and Persell 1985; Khan 2011). Sociologist G. William Domhoff found that many of the boards of directors of the largest corporations in the world are composed of people who went to prep school together or at least who went to the same Ivy League college (Domhoff 2002).

Social networks provide support in times of stress or illness; however, some research finds that social networks are dependent on people's ability to offer something in exchange, such as fun, excitement, or a sparkling personality. Therefore, they tend to shrink precisely during the periods of stress and illness when they are needed the most. If you are sick for a few days, you may be mobbed by friends armed with soup and get-well cards. But if your sickness lingers, you may gradually find yourself more alone.

Networks exert a powerful influence on the most crucial aspects of our lives; our membership in certain networks is often the vehicle by which we get established in a new country or city, meet the person with whom we fall in love, or get a job. Examine

strong ties
Term used by Mark Granovetter to characterize those people in your interpersonal network who actually know you.

weak ties
Granovetter's term for people in your interpersonal network whom you may not know personally, but perhaps you know *of* them, or they know *of* you.

your own networks. There are your friends and relatives, your primary ties. Then there are those people whom you actually know, but who are a little less close—classmates and coworkers. These are your secondary ties. Together they form what sociologist Mark Granovetter (1973, 1974) calls your "**strong ties**"—people who actually know you. But your networks also include "**weak ties**"—people whom you may not know personally, but perhaps you know *of* them, or they know *of* you. They may have strong ties to one of your strong ties.

Interestingly, it is not only your strong ties that most influence your life, but possibly, centrally, your weak ties. Granovetter (1995) calls this "the strength of weak ties." Although one might think strong interpersonal ties are more significant than weak ones because close friends are more interested than acquaintances in helping us, this may not be so, especially when what people need is information. Because our close friends tend to move in the same circles that we do, the information they receive overlaps considerably with what we already know. Acquaintances, by contrast, know people whom we do not and thus receive more novel information. This is in part because acquaintances are typically less similar to one another than close friends and in part because they spend less time together. Moving in different circles from ours, they connect us to a wider world and to new social networks—connections that bring with them new information and resources we may lack in our primary network.

Some new social-networking sites, such as LinkedIn, seek to expand the range of our networks. Friendster, Facebook, Instagram, Twitter, and others use the ever-expanding web of the Internet to create new network configurations with people whom you will never meet but rather get to know because they are a friend of a friend of a friend of a friend of—your friend (see Kirkpatrick 2010).

Of course, social networks not only bring people together, but also reproduce inequalities. Prep school networks, for instance, connect groups with a great deal of economic and social status to one another. One thing prep schools do is help ensure that those social advantages are reproduced for the next generation. Colleges and universities provide many of the same benefits. And the more elite the college and university, the more powerful the social network to which you may be connected.

Networks and Globalization

3.3.6 Understand the ways that the rise of global social networks simultaneously bring us all closer together while also exacerbating existing forms of social inequality.

New technology, such as text messaging, satellite television, and especially the Internet, has allowed us to break the bounds of geography and form groups made up of people from all over the world. The Internet is especially important for people with very specialized interests or very uncommon beliefs. You are unlikely to find many people in your hometown who collect antique soda bottles or who believe that Earth is flat, but you can go online and meet hundreds, maybe thousands. People who are afraid or embarrassed to discuss their interests at home, such as practitioners of witchcraft or S&M, also find that they can feel safe in Internet message boards and chat rooms. And there are also thousands of Internet groups formed around more conventional interests, such as sports or movie thrillers.

Social networking brings us closer together—our far-flung friends, and "friends," are only a mouse-click away. But new technology has also given rise to social networks that exaggerate existing social inequalities between countries and among different groups within countries. Networking means that those who are connected become more connected, globally and locally, while those who are not connected slip ever further behind (see U.S./WORLD Social Networking).

U.S./WORLD

SOCIAL NETWORKING

More and more people are using social-networking sites, but you may be surprised at just where in the world this growth is occurring. Although the number of new users of social-networking sites is starting to level off in North America (only 6 percent growth in the last year) the world audience of social networks has grown by 10 percent in the past year, with 25 percent growth in Africa, 14 percent growth in the Asia-Pacific region, 13 percent growth in the Middle East, and 3 percent growth in Europe.

Top 10 Social-Networking Countries	Average Hours Per Person
Philippines	3.7
Brazil	3.3
Mexico	3.2
Argentina	3.2
United Arab Emirates	3
Malaysia	3
Saudi Arabia	2.9
Thailand	2.9
Indonesia	2.9
South Africa	2.7

For comparison: The United States ranks 16th, with social media users averaging 1.7 hours of access per day

SOURCE: Data from Statistica.com (2016). "Average numbers of hours per day spent by social media users on all social media channels as of 4th quarter 2015, by country." Available at: http://www.statista.com/statistics/270229/usage-duration-of-social-networks-by-country/.

INVESTIGATE FURTHER

1. What have been the benefits of the increased density of our social networks? What are the problems with it?

2. How can a sociologist study social-networking sites as a research site? What might they be interested in finding out?

Social networks sustain us; they are what communities are made of. At the same time our networks are expanding across the globe at the speed of light, there is also some evidence that these networks are shrinking. For instance, sociologists found that Americans are far more socially isolated than we were even in the 1980s. Between 1985 and 2004 the size of the average network of confidants (someone with whom you discuss important issues) fell from just under three other people (2.94) to just over two people (2.08). And the number of people who said that there is no one with whom they discuss important issues nearly tripled. In 1985, the most frequent response was three; in 2004, the popular response was zero—no confidants. Both kin (family) and non-kin (friendship) confidants were lost (McPherson, Smith-Lovin, and Brashears 2006).

On the other hand, in some ways, young people today are far *less* isolated than their parents might be. The Internet has provided users with a dizzying array of possible communities and potential confidants, friends, and acquaintances. People who have never met find love, romance, sex, and friendship in cyberspace. Numerous increasingly-specific apps, like eharmony.com, okcupid.com, tinder, or match.com, have been created to assist us—from finding potential cybersex partners to marriage-minded others. In fact, 5 percent of Americans who are married or in a committed relationship claim to have met their spouse or partner online (Smith and Anderson 2016). This is a growing trend, though the recent numbers discovered a smaller proportion of American couples who first met online than websites like match.com claim. Beyond marriage, however, the data indicate that 15 percent of adults in the U.S. have used online dating sites/mobile dating apps—among 18- to 24-year olds, the numbers have tripled, and usage among 55- to 64-year olds has doubled (Smith and Anderson 2016). So, although companies interest in courting new users might have exaggerated how many marriages have come out of online meetings so far, it is clear that it is a growing trend.

---

iSOC AND YOU Groups, Networks, and Social Life
Identity depends on *interaction* within social *institutions* in an *intersectional* field of *inequality*. That's as simple as it comes. Today, you're both more connected through more networks than any generation of human beings in world history, and yet many of you have never felt more alone and isolated. Networks will continue to bring you closer to others like yourselves and also, possibly, leave you stranded when those interactions are not regularized in institutions.

3.4 Organizations, Power, and Inequality

Organizations are extremely large groups that structure our experience more than you may realize. There are a variety of types of organizations in society, but they all exist to accomplish goals and improve efficiency. This stress on efficiency, however, reverberates throughout the societies in which organizations exist. Sociologists who study organizations are interested in how they shape our lives. Organizations dominate a great deal of our time and energy. Deciding to join some organizations virtually requires having others take care of much of the rest of your life so that you can participate meaningfully and achieve success. And what the rest of your life looks like also shapes the roles you can play within organizations. Simply put, your identity shapes the ways in which you receive status and rewards within organizations in patterned ways.

Thus, although organizations appear to be primarily about efficiency, they are also about social inequality. Using the iSoc model to examine organizations and people's experiences with and of them allows us to examine them intersectionally and to begin to understand the ways in which social inequality is often institutionalized within organizations in ways that can make it hard to place the blame on any single person or group when others experience systematically different types of treatment. The iSoc model helps us to sociologically examine this process.

What Are Organizations and Why Do Sociologists Care?

3.4.1 Define organizations, and understand how they vary and exert power over our lives.

organization
A formal group of people with one or more shared goals.

organizational culture
The system of norms and values, routines and rituals, symbols and practices that governs an organization.

Organizations are large secondary groups designed to accomplish specific tasks in an efficient manner. They are thus defined by their (1) *size*—they are larger, more formal secondary groups; (2) *purpose*—they are purposive, intent to accomplish something; and (3) *efficiency*—they determine their strategies by how best to accomplish their goals. We typically belong to several organizations—corporations, schools and universities, churches and religious organizations, political parties. Organizations tend to endure over time, and they are independent of the individuals who compose them. They develop their own formal and informal **organizational culture**—consisting of norms and values, routines and rituals, symbols and practices. Yet, as a result of their longevity and their often hierarchical structures, organizations also tend to reproduce social inequality. And because organizations appear to be merely acting rationally, the inequalities they reproduce can sometimes be challenging to see. Sociologists categorize organizations in different ways. One of the most common is by the nature of membership. Sociologist Amitai Etzioni (1975) identified three types of organizations: normative, coercive, and utilitarian.

People join a normative organization to pursue some interest or to obtain some form of satisfaction that they consider worthwhile. **Normative organizations** are typically voluntary organizations; members receive no monetary rewards and often have to pay to join. Members are not paid, but participate because they believe in the goals of the organization. They can be service organizations (like Kiwanis), charitable organizations (like the Red Cross), or political parties or lobbying groups. Many political organizations, such as the Sierra Club, AARP, or the National Rifle Association are normative organizations; they seek to influence policies and people's lives. Because these organizations make no formal claims on one's time or energy, people tend to remain active members only as long as they feel the organization is serving their interests. With no formal controls, they may lose members as quickly as they gain them.

There are some organizations that you do not volunteer, but are forced, to join. **Coercive organizations** are organizations in which membership is not voluntary. Prisons, reform schools, and mental institutions are examples of coercive institutions. Coercive organizations tend to have very elaborate formal rules and severe sanctions for those seeking to exit voluntarily. They also tend to have elaborate informal cultures, as individuals try to create something that makes their experience a little bit more palatable.

Coercive institutions are sometimes what sociologist Erving Goffman (1961) called total institutions. A **total institution** is one that completely formally circumscribes your everyday life. Total institutions cut you off from life before you enter and seek to regulate every part of your behavior. They scrutinize everything you do, from what you wear, to what you eat, to how you talk and when. Goffman argued that total institutions tend to follow certain methods to incorporate a new inmate. First, there is a ceremonial stripping of the "old self" to separate you from your former life: your head may be shaved, your personal clothes may be replaced with a uniform, you may be given a number instead of your name. Then the total institution begins to rebuild an identity through conformity with the institutional definition of what you *should* be like. Goffman suggested, however, that even in total institutions individuals tend to find some clandestine way to hold onto a small part of their prior existence, to remind

normative organization

A voluntary organization wherein members serve because they believe in the goals of the organization.

coercive organization

One in which membership is not voluntary, with elaborate formal rules and sanctions.

total institution

An institution that completely circumscribes your everyday life, cutting you off from life before you entered and seeking to regulate every part of your behavior.

Total institutions use regimentation and uniformity to minimize individuality and replace it with a social, organizational self.

them that they are not only inmates but also individuals. Small reminders of your former life (a tattoo, a cross, a family photo) enable inmates to retain a sense of individuality and dignity.

Utilitarian organizations are those to which we belong for a specific, instrumental purpose. To earn a living or to get an advanced degree, we enter a corporation or university. We may exercise some choice about which university or which corporation, but the material rewards (a paycheck, a degree) are the primary motivation. A large business organization is designed to generate revenues for the companies, profits for shareholders, and wages and salaries for employees. We remain in the organization as long as the material rewards we seek are available. If, suddenly, businesses ceased requiring college degrees for employment, and the only reason to stay in school was the sheer joy of learning, would you continue reading this book?

This typology distinguishes between three different types of organizations. But there is considerable overlap. For example, some coercive organizations also have elements of being utilitarian organizations. The recent trend to privatize mental hospitals and prisons, turning them into for-profit enterprises, has meant that the organizational goals are changed to earning a profit, and guards' motivations may become more pecuniary.

utilitarian organization
An organization, like the college we attend or the company we work for, whose members belong for a specific, instrumental purpose or tangible material reward.

Are We a Nation of Joiners?

3.4.2 Describe the ways that Americans can be understood as simultaneously individualistic and collectively minded.

In his nineteenth-century study of America, *Democracy in America*, the French sociologist Alexis de Tocqueville called America "a nation of joiners." It was the breadth and scale of our organizations—everything from local civic organizations to large formal institutions—that gave American democracy its vitality. A century later, the celebrated historian Arthur Schlesinger (1944, p. 1) pointed out that it seems paradoxical "that a country famed for being individualistic should provide the world's greatest example of joiners." That is another sociological paradox: How can we be so individualistic *and* so collectively minded—at the same time?

But recently it appears this has been changing. As we saw at the beginning of the chapter, Robert Putnam argued that the organizations that once composed daily life—clubs, churches, fraternal organizations, civic organizations—had been evaporating in American life. In the 1950s, two-thirds of Americans belonged to some civic organization, but today that percentage is less than one-third. This decline is particularly pronounced among normative organizations that membership has decreased most dramatically—that is, among those organizations in which people are not paid, but join and participate because they believe in the goals of the organization.

For example, if your parents were born and raised in the United States, it is very likely that *their* parents (your grandparents) were members of the PTA and regularly went to functions at school. It is very likely that your grandparents were members of local civic organizations, like Kiwanis, or a fraternal organization (like Elks or Masons). But it is far less likely that your parents are members, and even less likely that you will join them.

On the other hand, as we also have seen, we join more forums, Internet groups, chat groups, and the like than any people in history—and it is pretty unlikely that our parents or grandparents are going to join them. It isn't so much that we are, or are not, a nation of joiners. Rather, it is what organizations and networks we choose to join, the impact they have, and how they integrate with the rest of our lives. Here, Putnam may have a point: We still may join groups, but the groups we choose to join may also exert far less influence over our daily lives than they once did.

SOCIOLOGY AND OUR WORLD

ORGANIZING WITHOUT ORGANIZATIONS?

How has the Internet changed the ways we connect and collaborate with other like-minded people?

These days, digital media have become recognized tools for group formation and social action. Many of us see digital petitions and Facebook protests on a fairly regular basis, and might "Like" then repost those positions we endorse and want to advance. From grass-roots community organizing, to campus-based protests, to national and international political campaigns, groups around the world are employing the Internet

and social media platforms to try to engage with others, build consensus, garner attention, and develop agendas for action. Digital scholar Clay Shirky (2008) has called these new group dynamics "organizing without organizations," and celebrates the lowered barriers to collective participation. Consider some of the top-trending hashtags used on social media around the world in 2016. Many are attempts to garner attention and support for political issues, protests, and campaigns. Others address the ways that we are increasingly globally connected with one another, highlight global events (like the Olympics) or global-level phenomena (like the release of the massively multiplayer online role playing game released by Nintendo in 2016—Pokemon Go).

At the same time, other thinkers are less sanguine about the turn toward "clicktivism" or "slactivism"—the simple, low-risk group affiliation and online participation that they see as pseudo-activism. Such commentators have seen digital activism as inferior to the old-fashioned way, when people would join together into physical groups to work and protest together; they question the ability of social media to build the powerful bonds and long-term investments in a cause that groups to bring about social change. Real political activism, they would argue, requires us to step up and live our Likes.

To social scientists, the question is not either–or, effective or not, but what kinds of digital actions, in what context, and with which individuals, may succeed with particular groups and goals. Sara Vissers and Dietlind Stolle (2014), for example, examined which concrete digital activities might mobilize people best for political participation offline. One finding: that posting and reading political messages and comments on Facebook, whether on other people's walls or your own, tends to inspire political actions in other venues in the future, but mainly certain kinds of actions as compared to others. They found Facebook posts are especially good at getting people to sign a political petition, make a donation to a political cause, or contact a politician. Other researchers remind us that when we consider this finding

intersectionally, not all people respond in the same ways to activist posts and appeals; due to race, class gender and other differences in social position and cultural perspective, few messages about collective action will meet with universal success, but rather will reach some people while repelling others. (Hamedani, Markus and Fu 2013)

Lindsey Kingston and Kathryn Stam (2013) studied digital organizing in a larger context, examining the use of websites and social networking by human rights organizations and nongovernmental organizations. They found that many such organizations use new digital tools to build on existing strategy rather than using "theory 2.0" organizing. That is, these organizations deploy digital technologies to enhance existing activities and programs, and rarely embrace the potential of new technologies to develop novel approaches. These choices, they suggest, influence the efficacy of the organizations' outreach as well as its advocacy.

"Despite the prominence of 'Twitter revolutions,' 'color revolutions,' and the like in public debate," argue Sean Aday et al. (2010), we need to know more "about whether and how new media affect contentious politics." Studying Iran for the United States Institute for Peace, they emphasize that digital and social media carry multiple capabilities and possibilities. These tools have the potential to change how people act and how they think, and can generate attention to a particular cause or country. Going further, they can also both mitigate and exacerbate group conflict, and both promote and undermine collective action by facilitating group in-fighting or government repression. To understand the dynamics of new media and political action, they argue, we must examine multiple goals and impacts, and they offer these five: individual transformation, intergroup relations, collection action, regime policies and external attention.

Digital activism itself can mean many things. It can be thought about "along a spectrum: from online 'mobs' that form spontaneously around particular issues, to the longer-term social movements that employ digital tools to further their goals, and finally to the established civil society organizations, which are more permanent and may have 'offline' infrastructure in addition to online elements." Researchers in the social sciences as well as communication remind us that digital organizing offers a range of new opportunities for group formation and political action, but they also require us to think sociologically about it—about what works, what doesn't, when, where, why, and with whom (See Zuckerman 2013)

Examining Organizations and Inequality Intersectionally

3.4.3 Explain the ways that organizations participate in structuring social inequality.

We often think that organizations and bureaucracies are formal structures that are neutral. They have formal criteria for membership, promotion, and various rewards, and to the extent that any member meets these criteria, the rules are followed without prejudice. Everyone, we believe, plays by the same rules. What that ignores, however, is that the rules themselves may favor some groups over other groups. They may have been developed by some groups to make sure that they remain in power. What appear to be neutral criteria are also socially weighted in favor of some and against others. To give one example, membership in a political party was once restricted to those who could read and write, who paid a tax, and whose fathers were members of the party. This effectively excluded poor people, women, and black people in the pre–Civil Rights South.

Sociologists of gender have identified many of the ways in which organizations reproduce gender inequality. In her now-classic work, *Men and Women of the Corporation,* Rosabeth Moss Kanter (1977) demonstrated that the differences in men's and women's behaviors in organizations had far less to do with their characteristics as individuals than they had to do with the structure of the organization. **Organizational positions** "carry characteristic images of the kinds of people that should occupy them," she argued, and those who do occupy them, whether women or men, exhibited those necessary behaviors. Though the criteria for evaluation of job performance, promotion, and effectiveness seem to be gender neutral, they are, in fact, deeply gendered (see FIGURE 3.2). Many organizations are structured in ways that work to men's collective advantage and to women's collective disadvantage (we will return to this in Chapter 14).

Here's an example. Many doctors complete college by age 21 or 22 and medical school by age 25 to 27 and then face three more years of internship and residency, during which time they are occasionally on call for long stretches of time, sometimes even two or three days straight. They thus complete their residencies by their late 20s or early 30s. Such a program is designed not for a doctor, but for a *male* doctor—one who is not pressured by the ticking of a biological clock, for whom the birth of children will not disrupt these time demands, and who may even have someone at home taking care of the children while he sleeps at the hospital. No wonder women in medical school—who number nearly one-half of all medical students today—often complain that they were not able to balance pregnancy and motherhood with their medical training. The entire structure is not set up to accommodate pregnant people.

organizational positions

Rosabeth Moss Kanter's term to describe the gendered expectations for behavior within organizations. The differences in men's and women's behaviors have far less to do with their characteristics as individuals than with the "characteristic images of the kinds of people that should occupy" particular positions. People who do occupy them, whether women or men, exhibited those necessary behaviors.

Bureaucracy: Organizations and Power

3.4.4 Define bureaucracy, and explain how the emergence of this organizational form shaped identities, interactions, and inequality.

When we hear the word *bureaucracy,* we often think it means a series of increasingly complex and seemingly arbitrary hoops through which you have to jump to realize our goals—"red tape." We often experience bureaucracies as impeding the purpose of the organization. Sociologists define a **bureaucracy** as a formal organization, characterized by a division of labor, a hierarchy of authority, formal rules governing behavior, a logic of rationality, and an impersonality of criteria. It is also a form of domination, by which those at the top stay at the top and those

bureaucracy

Originally derived from the French word *bureau,* or office, a formal organization characterized by a division of labor, a hierarchy of authority, formal rules governing behavior, a logic of rationality, and an impersonality of criteria.

FIGURE 3.2 Even in Nursing, Men Earn More

Although you might not be surprised to learn that occupations we think of as "masculine" and that are dominated by men, as a group, tend to be paid higher than occupations we consider "feminine" and that are dominated by women. Yet, it is also true that men out-earn women even when they participate in feminine occupations. Consider this graph. It shows the average wage gap throughout nursing professions and specialties. Whether you work with newborns and obstetricians or cardiothoracic surgeons, men in nursing earn more than women with only one exception: senior academics. As this example illustrates, even in occupations for which women occupy what we think of as the characteristic image of the person who ought to hold such a job, inequality still works to men's collective advantage.

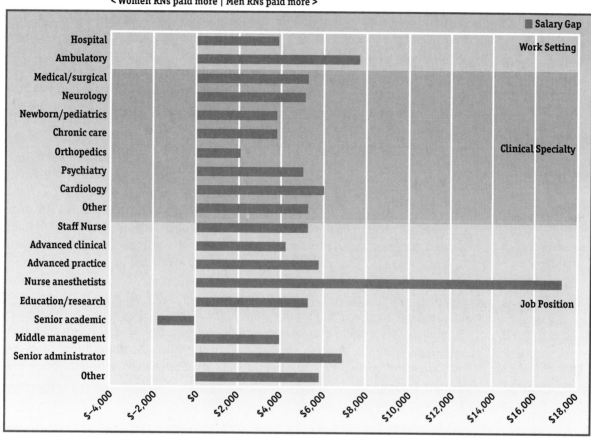

SOURCE: Data from Muench, Ulrike, Jody Sindelar, Susan H. Busch, Salary Differences Between Male and Female Nurses in the United States, Journal of the American Medical Association 313(12) (2015).

at the bottom believe in the legitimacy of the hierarchy. We accept the legitimacy of the power of those at the top because bureaucracy appears to be simply a form of organization. But, as Max Weber understood, it is by embedding power in formal rules and procedures that it is most efficiently exercised. Bureaucracies are thus the most efficient organizations in getting things done *and* for maintaining inequality.

Weber (1978) is credited with first describing the essential characteristics of bureaucracies. Although these characteristics are not found in every single bureaucratic organization, they represent the **ideal type** of bureaucracy—an abstract mental concept of what a pure version of the phenomenon (in this case, a bureaucracy) would look like. (1) *Division of labor.* Each person in a bureaucratic organization has a specific role. (2) *Hierarchy of authority.* Positions in a bureaucracy are arranged vertically (often resembling a pyramid) into an impersonal chain of command. (3) *Rules and regulations.* Those in the hierarchy follow formalized rules and regulations defining appropriate procedures for the function of each unit within the organization. (4) *Impersonality.* Members of bureaucratic organizations are detached

ideal type

The abstract mental concept of what a pure version of a social phenomenon, such as a bureaucracy, would look like.

and impersonal. (5) *Career ladders*. There are clearly marked paths and formal requirements for advancement. (6) *Efficiency*. The formality of the rules, the overarching logic of rationality, the clear chain of command, and the impersonal networks enable bureaucracies to be extremely efficient and to coordinate the activities of a large number of people.

Bureaucracies exhibit many of the other problems of groups—groupthink, stereotypes, and pressure to conform. But as much as they make life more predictable and efficient, bureaucracies also exaggerate certain problems of all groups. (1) *Overspecialization*. Individuals may become so specialized in their tasks that they lose sight of the broader consequences of their actions. (2) *Rigidity and inertia*. Rigid adherence to rules makes the organization resistant to change, which can make bureaucracies inefficient. (3) *Ritualism*. Formality and impersonality can lead individuals to lack strong commitment to the organization. (4) *Suppression of dissent*. There is little room for individual initiative, alternate strategies, or even disagreement. (5) *The bureaucratic "catch-22."* This phenomenon, named after a famous novel by Joseph Heller, refers to a process by which the bureaucracy creates more and more rules and regulations, resulting in greater complexity and overspecialization, and ultimately reducing coordination and eventually creating contradictory rules.

As a result of these problems, individual members of the bureaucratic organization may feel alienated and confused. Sociologist Robert Merton (1968) identified a specific personality type that he called the **bureaucratic personality** to describe those people who become more committed to following the correct procedures than to getting the job done. In the classic comedy movie *Ferris Bueller's Day Off* (1986), school Vice Principal Rooney is so focused on catching Ferris Bueller skipping class that he abandons his work for the day, embarrasses himself in front of his secretary, breaks into the family's home, and is mauled by their dog—and still fails to catch Ferris breaking the rules. At times, these problems may drag the bureaucracy toward the very dynamics that the organization was supposed to combat.

bureaucratic personality

Robert Merton's term to describe those people who become more committed to following the correct procedures than they are to getting the job done.

Bureaucracies depend on the impersonal application of rules. They structure people's choices and actions and it is also the case that it is individual people who enact and enforce bureaucratic rules, often in circumstances the rules could never have conceivably been designed to address.

HOW DO WE KNOW WHAT WE KNOW?

DO FORMAL OR INFORMAL PROCEDURES RESULT IN GREATER PRODUCTIVITY?

Does the informal culture of bureaucracy enhance or detract from worker productivity? In a classic study of a Western Electric factory in Hawthorne, Illinois, in the 1930s, Elton Mayo and W. Lloyd Warner found that the informal worker culture ran parallel to the official factory norms. In the experiment, a group of 14 men were paid according to their individual productivity. Productivity did not increase; the men feared that the company would simply raise the expectations for everyone (Mayo 1933). In another classic study, though, Peter Blau (1964) found informal culture increased both productivity and effectiveness. Blau studied a government office charged with investigating possible tax violations. The formal rules stated that when agents had questions about how to handle a particular case they should consult their supervisors. However, agents feared this would make them look incompetent. So, they violated the official rules and asked coworkers. They ended up getting concrete advice about solving problems and produced a collection of informal procedures that permitted more initiative and productivity than the formal rules allowed.

Formal procedures, according to Meyer and Rowan (1977), are often quite distant from the actual ways people work in bureaucratic organizations. People will often make a show of conforming to them and then proceed with their work using more informal methods. They may use "the rules" to justify the way a task was carried out, then depart considerably when actually performing the tasks at hand.

Weber was deeply ambivalent about bureaucracy. On the one hand, bureaucracies are the most efficient, predictable organizations, and officials within them all approach their work rationally and according to formal rules and regulations. But on the other hand, the very mechanisms that make bureaucracies predictable and efficient often lead those organizations to work against their stated goals. Sometimes, for example, students feel trapped in an avalanche of requirements and large classes, and the purpose of their education slips away. At such times, they may go through the motions—sitting in class, taking exams—but they don't feel *meaningful*. When that happens on a large scale, the organization becomes unwieldy and unequal. The very things we thought would give meaning to our lives end up trapping us in what Weber called the "iron cage." The **iron cage** describes the increasing rationalization of social life that traps people in the rules, regulations, and hierarchies that they developed to make life sensible, predictable, and efficient. Ironically, while bureaucracies promised to streamline our lives and enable us all to live more rationally, Weber feared they had

iron cage

While Weber contended that rationality can free us from the theocratic past, he also argued that rationality can imprison us in an utterly dehumanized and mechanized world he termed "the iron cage."

Bureaucracies are large-scale organizational attempts to achieve increasing levels of efficiencies. But, as bureaucracies grow, they become increasingly complex. And that complexity, ironically, leads them to become less efficient.

the potential to crush innovation and imagination and destroy the human spirit (Weber 1958, p. 128).

Organizations and Globalization

3.4.5 Summarize the ways that organizations are increasingly globalized.

In large complex societies, bureaucracies are the dominant form of organization. We deal with bureaucracies every day—when we pay our phone bill, register for classes on our campus, go to work in an office or factory, see a doctor, or have some interaction with a local, state, or federal government. And when we do, we act as *social actors*—we adopt roles, interact in groups, and collectively organize into organizations.

Groups and organizations are increasingly globalized. Global institutions like the World Bank, or International Monetary Fund, or even private commercial banks like UBS or Bank of America are increasingly the institutional form in which people all over the world do their business. It is likely that if you have a checking account, it is at a major bank with branches in dozens of countries. Fifty years ago, if you had a checking account at all, it would have been at the "Community Savings and Loan," and your banker would have known you by name. Today, most of your bank transactions will be done online, and if you call your bank, you'll probably be speaking to someone in another city—probably in another country. Political institutions like the United Nations, or regional organizations like the European Union, attempt to bring different countries together under one bureaucratic organization.

And, of course, even the reactions *against* globalization use the forms and institutions of globalization to resist it. Religious fundamentalists or political extremists who want to return to a more traditional society all use the Internet to recruit members. Global media organizations like Al Jazeera (a global Arabic Muslim media source, with TV and online outlets) spread a specific form of Islam as if it were the only form of Islam—and Muslims in Indonesia begin to act more like Muslims in Saudi Arabia. Every anti-globalization political group—from patriot groups on the far right to radical environmentalists on the far left—uses websites, bloggers, and Internet chat rooms to recruit and spread its message. Globalization may change some of the dynamics of groups and organizations, but the importance of groups and organizations in our daily lives cannot be overstated.

---

iSOC AND YOU Organizations, Power, and Inequality

Humans live in groups. We form our identities in and through groups. Social life is just that: social. But sociologists understand that social life is far from randomly organized. It's not chaotic; it's organized and patterned. You are embedded in networks, and these crisscross and *intersect* through all the various pieces of your life and *identity* that make you a unique member of the society in which you life. But group life is unequal. These constant *interactions* among groups, these networks of interaction, are the webs of social life. They are the social safety nets that keep you knowing who you are and where you belong—and where you're likely to feel "out of place." And these networks and groups, these large patterns of interaction, cohere into *institutions* that provide the organizational framework or structure for all those interactions. But the *interactions* and groups they produce are the building blocks of social life.

Conclusion

Groups 'R' Us: Interactions, Groups, and Organizations NOW

Although we belong to fewer groups than our parents might have, these groups may also be increasingly important in our lives, composing more and more the people with whom we interact and the issues with which we concern ourselves. We're lonelier than ever, and yet we continue to be a nation of joiners, and we locate ourselves still within the comfortable boundaries of our primary groups. Our interactions with groups still are a fundamental part of how we form our identities. And groups play a major role in both reproducing and challenging social inequality.

We live in a society composed of many different groups and many different cultures, subcultures, and countercultures, speaking different languages, with different kinship networks and different values and norms. It's noisy, and we rarely agree on anything. And yet we also live in a society where the overwhelming majority of people obey the same laws and are civil to one another and in which we respect the differences among those different groups. We live in a society characterized by a fixed, seemingly intransigent hierarchy and a society in which people believe firmly in the idea of mobility; a society in which your fixed, ascribed characteristics (race, class, sex) are the single best determinants of where you will end up and a society in which we also believe anyone can make it if he or she works hard enough. This means we must learn to understand how social institutions shape society in ways that perpetuate existing inequalities between groups. We need to think intersectionally to think about how social interactions often reiterate organizational rules and roles that systematically advantage certain groups over others. Sociologists want to understand how this process occurs.

It is a noisy and seemingly chaotic world and also one that is predictable and relatively calm. The terms we have introduced in these two chapters—*culture, society, roles, status, groups, interaction,* and *organizations*—are the conceptual tools that sociologists use to make sense of this teeming tumult of disparate parts and this orderly coherence of interlocking pieces. And the iSoc model can help us understand how they are connected.

CHAPTER REVIEW Society: Interactions, Groups, and Organizations

3.1 Thinking about Interactions, Groups, and Organizations Sociologically

It is axiomatic in sociology that we are less in control over our lives than we often believe. Our interactions are structured to a level many might find surprising. Sociologists view society from a macro-level perspective, in terms of institutions and other large, more stable social structures, while also recognizing that social structure is created in the face-to-face micro-level emergent interactions between people. After all, institutions are made up of the people in them.

Social life is essentially patterns of social interaction—behaviors that are oriented toward other people. Other people are also interacting as well, and these near-infinite interactions cohere into patterns. This is how we "construct"

social reality through social interaction. We form a "self" through our interactions with others, by imagining how we are seen, and we follow conventions that everyone (or almost everyone) in the group learns to accept. Our selves change in different contexts. This is the case not only because of other people's reactions to us, but also because we actively manage our presentations of ourselves, we construct how we *want* to be seen. We modify our behavior in accordance with what particular people expect of us. Thus, you're not born "you." You become "you" in a context—a specific place at a specific moment in historical time. Society is that context: It is through your interactions with others, in groups and within social institutions, that you become who you are—and know yourself.

3.1 Key Terms

society An organized collection of individuals and institutions, bounded by space in a coherent territory, subject to the same political authority, and organized through a shared set of cultural expectations and values.

social institutions Patterned sets of interactions that work to meet collective needs that are not easily met by individuals working alone. They include such social arenas as markets, families, schools, corporations, factories, and prisons.

social structure A complex framework composed of both patterned social interactions and institutions that together organize social life and provide the context for individual action.

social scripts Term for a sequence of expected behaviors in a given situation.

social interaction The foundation for societal groups and relationships and the process of how people behave and interact with each other.

looking-glass self Cooley's term for the process of how identity is formed through social interaction. We imagine how we appear to others and thus develop our sense of self based on the others' reactions, imagined or otherwise.

generalized other The organized rules, judgments, and attitudes of an entire group. If you try to imagine what is expected of you, you are taking on the perspective of the generalized other.

dramaturgy Erving Goffman's conception of social life as being like a stage play wherein we all work hard to convincingly play ourselves as "characters," such as grandchild, buddy, student, employee, or other roles.

face work A dramaturgical theory, the possible performance of ourselves, because when we make a mistake or do something wrong, we feel embarrassed, or "lose face."

impression management Erving Goffman's term for our attempts to control how others perceive us by changing our behavior to correspond to an ideal of what they will find most appealing.

3.2 Understanding Society and Social Life as Socially Structured

Social interactions are structured, and coming to understand how we know all of this and communicate that knowledge to other people is part of what it means to understand social interactions and identities as socially constructed. One of the most important ways of constructing our social identities and social reality is through nonverbal communication: our bodily movements, gestures, facial expressions, and even our placement in relation to others. Through socialization, by observing, and experimenting in a wide variety of situations, we learn the conventions of nonverbal communication. Although nonverbal communication is subtle, and requires a great deal of socialization, verbal communication—talking—is not as straightforward as it might appear. Common, unstated assumptions enable many conversational and social shortcuts to work. And just because we are constantly creating our identities doesn't mean we make it up as we go along. We are simultaneously *enabled* and also *constrained* by social structure, by statuses—some we are born into and others we achieve—which vary by culture and over time, and by roles. Roles teach us when to be deferential and when to expect deference from others, what vocabulary to use appropriate and what to avoid, and other rules of the road for successful social interaction; roles teach us the proper mechanics of interacting in unequal situations. Our interaction and communication is patterned. This makes a great deal of social life much more predictable than it would be otherwise. But it also shapes our understandings of who we are and where we "fit" into the societies in various hierarchies throughout the societies in which we live.

3.2 Key Terms

nonverbal communication The communication with others that occurs without words, including apparent behaviors such as facial expressions and less obvious messaging including posture and the spatial distance between two or more people.

ethnomethodology The study of the social knowledge, codes, and conventions that underlie everyday interactions and allow people to make sense of what others say and do.

norm of reciprocity The social expectation that people will respond to us favorably, or with hostility or indifference depending upon how we interact with them.

superordinate Individual or group that possesses social power.

subordinate Individual or group that possesses little or comparatively less social power.

role performance The particular emphasis or interpretation each of us gives a social role.

status One's socially defined position in a group; it is often characterized by certain expectations and rights.

role Behavior expected of people who have a particular status.

ascribed status Status that is assigned to a person and over which he or she has no control.

achieved status Status or social position based on one's accomplishments or activities.

social reproduction The structures and activities that transmit social inequality from one generation to the next.

master status An ascribed or achieved status presumed so important that it overshadows all of the others, dominating our lives and controlling our position in society.

social role Sets of behaviors expected of a person who occupies a certain social status.

role strain The experience of difficulty in performing a role.

role conflict What happens when we try to play different roles with extremely different or contradictory rules at the same time.

role exit The process we go through to adjust when leaving a role that is central to our identity.

3.3 Groups, Networks, and Social Life

The groups and networks to which we belong shape much more of our lives than we may realize. Groups help us to make sense of our own identities and consider them against the identities of people who belong to other groups. They shape what kinds of people we understand ourselves to be, our likes and dislikes, our experience of the world around us, and the opportunities we may encounter. Social networks are, quite literally, the fabric of social life. And sociologists who study groups and networks want to know both what they provide and how they work. Social networks provide us access to status, power, and money (or not). But they also help us when we are most in need.

The smallest unit sociologists study is the group. Groups may be any size, from a dyad up, but crowds are not groups, as they lack group cohesion. Primary group members are bound by expressive ties, and secondary group members are together for instrumental reasons. We identify with an in-group and are in opposition to an out-group. Even our perceptions are influenced by our small group memberships, such that we perceive in-group heterogeneity but out-group homogeneity. A reference group can influence us even if we aren't members. Groups have predictable dynamics. In large groups, responsibility is diffused. In small groups, the leader and hardcore members have greater investment in the group, conformity is an aspect of group membership, and members work to preserve group cohesion and harmony at the expense of autonomy, even at times exhibiting groupthink. We often stereotype group members, rather than perceiving distinctions between them. We are also connected to others through social networks. Members of our primary and secondary groups are obvious members of our networks, but we are also connected less directly to others, including acquaintances, and people we know of, or who know of us. These weaker ties can be an important resource. Social-networking websites are

an example of how people can connect locally, nationally and globally today.

3.3 Key Terms

group Collection of individuals who are aware that they share something in common and who interact with one another on the basis of their interrelated roles and statuses.

dyad A group of two people, the smallest configuration defined by sociologists as a group.

triad A group of three people.

tetrad A group of four people.

crowd An aggregate of individuals who happen to be together but experience themselves as essentially independent.

group cohesion The degree to which individual members of a group identify with each other and with the group as a whole.

primary group One such as friends and family, which comes together for expressive reasons, providing emotional support, love, companionship, and security.

secondary group Coworkers, club members, or another group that comes together for instrumental reasons, such as wanting to work together to meet common goals. Secondary groups make less of an emotional claim on one's identity than do primary groups.

in-group A group with which you identify and that you feel positively toward, producing a "we" feeling.

out-group One to which you do not belong and toward which you feel either neutral or hostile; the "they" who are perceived as different from and of lower stature than ourselves.

in-group heterogeneity The social tendency to be keenly aware of the subtle differences among the individual members of your group.

out-group homogeneity The social tendency to believe that all members of an out-group are exactly the same.

reference group A group toward which one is so strongly committed, or one that commands so much prestige, that we orient our actions around what we perceive that group's perceptions would be.

clique A small group of people with shared interests or other features in common who spend time together and do not readily allow others to join them.

leader People in charge, whether they were elected, appointed, or just informally took control, of a group.

hardcore members The small number of group members, the "inner circle," who wield a great deal of power to make policy decisions.

groupthink Irving Janis's term for social process in which members of a group attempt to conform their opinions to what they believe to be the consensus of the group, even if, as individuals, they may consider that opinion wrong or unwise.

bystander Someone who witnesses something wrong, harmful, dangerous, or illegal, yet does nothing to intervene.

bystander effect The diffusion of responsibility among groups of bystanders, in which they assume that as long as others are observing the problem, they are no more responsible than anyone else to intervene.

stereotype Generalization about a group that is oversimplified and exaggerated and that fails to acknowledge individual differences in the group.

social network Often conceived as a web of social relationships, a type of group that is both looser and denser than a formal group but connects people to each other, and, through those connections, with other people.

small world problem The name for sociological research conducted by Milgram and others that suggests human society is a small network characterized by short paths between strangers. The research is often associated with the phrase "six degrees of separation" (although Milgram himself did not use that phrase).

network effects The sociological idea that we end up sharing a lot in common with people with whom we share a social network.

strong ties Term used by Mark Granovetter to characterize those people in your interpersonal network who actually know you.

weak ties Granovetter's term for people in your interpersonal network whom you may not know personally, but perhaps you know *of* them, or they know *of* you.

3.4   Organizations, Power, and Inequality

Sociologists who study organizations are interested in how they shape our lives. Although organizations appear to be primarily about efficiency, they are also about social inequality.

An organization is a large, stable, secondary group, independent of its members. A normative organization is composed of volunteers who come together for personal satisfaction, while membership in a coercive organization, which Goffman identified as a total institution, is mandatory and exerts total control. A utilitarian organization fulfills specific instrumental purposes for its members. Americans used to be a nation of joiners, belonging to numerous civic organizations, but this has changed. While the formal structures of organizations make them appear neutral, they may actually institutionalize inequality. A bureaucracy is an efficient hierarchical formal organization with clear rules and regulations and division of labor, which tends to concentrate power at the top, where the rules often don't seem to apply, and often rigidity and ritualism at the lower levels, which gives rise to the bureaucratic personality. Today, compared with the past, organizations we encounter are often global bureaucracies.

3.4 Key Terms

organization A formal group of people with one or more shared goals.

organizational culture The system of norms and values, routines and rituals, symbols and practices that governs an organization.

normative organization A voluntary organization wherein members serve because they believe in the goals of the organization.

coercive organization One in which membership is not voluntary, with elaborate formal rules and sanctions.

total institution An institution that completely circumscribes your everyday life, cutting you off from life before you entered and seeking to regulate every part of your behavior.

utilitarian organization An organization, like the college we attend or the company we work for, whose members belong for a specific, instrumental purpose or tangible material reward.

organizational positions Rosabeth Moss Kanter's term to describe the gendered expectations for behavior within organizations. The differences in men's and women's behaviors have far less to do with their characteristics as individuals than with the "characteristic images of the kinds of people that should occupy" particular positions. People who do occupy them, whether women or men, exhibited those necessary behaviors.

bureaucracy Originally derived from the French word *bureau*, or office, a formal organization characterized by a division of labor, a hierarchy of authority, formal rules governing behavior, a logic of rationality, and an impersonality of criteria.

ideal type The abstract mental concept of what a pure version of a social phenomenon, such as a bureaucracy, would look like.

bureaucratic personality Robert Merton's term to describe those people who become more committed to following the correct procedures than they are to getting the job done.

iron cage While Weber contended that rationality can free us from the theocratic past, he also argued that rationality can imprison us in an utterly dehumanized and mechanized world he termed "the iron cage."

SELF-TEST

〉 CHECK YOUR UNDERSTANDING

1. Cooley used the term _____ for the process by which we construct our identities from the imagined response of others.
   a. looking-glass self
   b. impression management
   c. ethnomethodology
   d. dramaturgy

2. As the text points out, race and ethnicity are both examples of a(n)
   a. role performance.
   b. achieved status.
   c. master status.
   d. group.

3. Goffman's view of social interaction as the performance of roles is known as
   a. ethnomethodology.
   b. dramaturgy.
   c. groupthink.
   d. looking-glass self.

4. The Los Angeles Lakers basketball team is an example of a
   a. primary group.
   b. secondary group.
   c. dyad.
   d. crowd.

5. A workgroup maintained cohesion and consensus to the extent that members kept their concerns about the project to themselves, instead of voicing them. This is an example of
   a. impression management.
   b. diffusion of responsibility.
   c. in-group heterogeneity.
   d. groupthink.

6. Identify which of the following is not a characteristic of bureaucracies identified by Max Weber:
   a. efficiency
   b. division of labor
   c. hierarchy of authority
   d. bureaucratic personality

7. Compared with the last century, for Americans in the twenty-first century, participation in organizations overall has
   a. increased.
   b. declined.
   c. remained constant.
   d. failed to follow a consistent pattern.

8. According to the text, the dominant form of organizations we encounter in large complex societies like the United States are
   a. normative organizations.
   b. total institutions.
   c. bureaucracies.
   d. primary groups.

Self-Test Answers: 1. a, 2. c, 3. b, 4. b, 5. d, 6. d, 7. b, 8. c

CHAPTER 4

HOW DO WE KNOW WHAT WE KNOW? THE METHODS OF THE SOCIOLOGIST

Good sociological research involves making difficult decisions about how to think about the social world around us, what sorts of phenomena to compare to what. Sometimes, it's as simple as asking whether we're comparing apples to oranges or not.

→ LEARNING OBJECTIVES

In this chapter, using the iSoc framework, you should be able to:

4.1.1 Understand why predicting human behavior is so challenging and what sets sociology apart from other sciences.

4.1.2 Summarize the scientific method and how deductive and inductive approaches to sociological research enter this process at different points.

4.1.3 Recognize how each of the five elements of the iSoc model are important in helping sociologists decide which research methods might best suit their research questions.

4.1.4 Explain the role of operationalization in helping to make decisions about whether quantitative or qualitative methods are more appropriate for sociological research.

4.1.5 Describe what it means that sociologists consider just about anything as a potential source of data to study the social world.

4.2.1 Identify the key differences between the three different "types" of sociological research methods.

4.2.2 Describe the primary components of observational research, considering what kinds of questions it is well-suited to answer.

4.2.3 Explain the elements that distinguish quantitative analyses from observational research, considering what kinds of questions these methods are designed to answer.

4.2.4 Summarize the kinds of questions and sources of data that qualify as secondary analyses.

4.2.5 Understand the ways sociologists select among and between research methods to provide comparisons that enable them to scientifically examine social life and behavior.

4.3.1 Explain what it means to suggest that sociology might be better thought of as an explanatory science than a predictive science.

4.3.2 Understand the difference between probability and predictability and some of the popular misunderstandings of probabilistic statements.

4.3.3 Enumerate the necessary conditions to make a causal argument, and understand how and why this is a challenging standard to achieve in sociological research.

4.3.4 Understand and describe the various steps involved in doing sociological research and how and why different types of research requires beginning at different steps.

4.3.5 Summarize the three primary concerns sociologists must all navigate in conducting and reporting their research.

Introduction

Seventeen-year-old Gaby Rodriguez wanted to know whether and how people treat unwed pregnant teenagers differently, whether they hold stereotypes about their behavior, their morals, and their choices. So this high school senior in Yakima, Washington, an honor student, designed a little experiment: She pretended she was pregnant. She told only her mother, her boyfriend, and the high school principal and school superintendent. She didn't even tell six of her seven siblings, or her boyfriend's parents.

Her boyfriend was a little worried, fearing that her brothers might come after him. Her mom was nervous, and the school administrators said they were in awe of her courage and were a bit apprehensive as well. But for more than 6 months, Gaby carefully padded her stomach every day, and grew bigger in the eyes of the world. Lots of people touched her "bump," but no one suspected a thing.

Then, in April, 2011, she gave a presentation called "Stereotypes, Rumors and Statistics" to the assembled students and teachers. She had people read statements they had made about her—about how irresponsible she was, how immoral. Students were dismissive, saying that they "knew she was going to get pregnant" and that "she just ruined her life." (No one commented on the responsibility or morality of her boyfriend.) "Her attitude is changing," said one student, "and it might be because of the baby or she was always this annoying and I never realized it." One teacher confessed that he was concerned when he heard Gaby was pregnant. He wanted to make sure that it did not "define who she is and let it be a roadblock to what she wants to accomplish."

After listing all the stereotypes of teen moms that she had heard over the previous 6 months, she confessed, "I'm fighting against those stereotypes and rumors because the reality is I'm not pregnant." The audience was silent, stunned. And then they did something that had never happened in the school's history, according to the principal. They gave Gaby a standing ovation! "She sacrificed her senior year to find out what it would be like to be a potential teen mom," said the principal. "I admire her courage. I admire her preparation."

Gaby is now in college, majoring in, you guessed it, sociology. "I'm not planning to have a child until I graduate," she says now. ("Toppenish Teen Fakes Pregnancy as School Project," *Seattle Times*, April 21, 2011; *Daily Mail*, April 22, 2011).

Gaby had engaged in a scientific social experiment: She was curious about how people would treat her if they thought

Gaby Rodriguez reveals her fake pregnancy at the school assembly, May 2011.

she was pregnant. Her research design was inventive, but also raises several concerns for sociologists. For one thing, the information she gleaned was at the expense of fooling others. One teacher, who supported her, also felt manipulated, "lied to." She tricked people. Her research design might not have been granted approval from a university research oversight board, because all research must involve the "informed consent" of the subjects of the experiment (in this case, the entire school). Sometimes, sociologists deliberately deceive people they are studying in conducting experimental research, but this is only done when we feel confident that we are treating people ethically, with respect and dignity, and ensuring that our research could not cause any kind of harm.

Sociologists have developed a wide variety of methods to investigate such questions. Sociology enables us to use scientific thinking to see and endeavor to understand the complexity of our social world. In this chapter, we'll discuss these methods, what we can find out and what we cannot. Just remember: If you can develop a compelling research question, generate a careful research design, determine the appropriate methods, are ethical in your data collection, and are brave enough to carry it out, you too, might receive a standing ovation when you present it!

4.1 How Do We Know What We Know?

In 1998, Istvan Banyai published an illustrated book for children entitled, *Zoom* (Banyai 1998). It's a provocative book of illustrations without words. It begins with an image of a strange design with triangular red shapes. You turn the page and realize that what you were looking at was a rooster's comb up close, now seeing a rooster standing on a fence. Turn the page, and children appear looking through a window at the rooster standing on the fence. Turn another page, and we see that the children are looking out of a window at the back of a house on a farm with pigs, cats, geese, and chickens out front. Turn the page again, and you realize that the farm is a set of toys on a children's table and another child is playing with them. And then you see that that child is actually on the cover of a magazine being held by a young boy on a boat. Another page shows you that that boat is simply a decal on the side of a bus on a crowded city street. And so on. It keeps zooming out, widening the aperture, providing new and surprising information about what you're seeing. It ends zoomed so far out that you can barely make out the planet earth.

Sociological research methods help you achieve a similar outlook on the world. If you think about research methods as different kinds of cameras, telescopes, binoculars, microscopes, and more, that focus on different elements of society, this is similar to what sociological research methods are designed to accomplish. Although some research methods are designed to help you get a really good picture of what is going on "on the ground" in society, sociologists zoom in and out to see how the picture changes when we compare our data with data collected with different methods, in different locations, and via different means. We zoom out a bit to get a better sense of how representative what we're looking at on the ground is of larger structures and institutions in society. And we zoom back in to try to figure out what these patterns mean, how they feel, and to examine precisely how they might be produced and reproduced in social life.

Sometimes, we zoom way out and compare entire societies to one another. And with each zoom, methodological considerations are at stake. When we zoom far out, we lose the ability to focus on some of the minute behaviors that shape social interactions and that are used to craft social identities in everyday life. But if we only take this level of zoom into account, we can sometimes forget what we're looking at relates to a large group of people who represent those we're looking at up close. Zooming out helps us refocus on institutions, and allows us to paint a more general picture of the forms of inequality that affect whole categories of people in societies.

This ability to zoom in and out is a fundamental tool sociologists use when they look at the world around them. Throughout the textbook, you'll see us zooming in and out to help you get a better picture of both the structure of society and the nitty gritty of everyday interactions.

In this section, you will read an overview of some of the important considerations sociologists consider when selecting from the diverse research methods that make up the field. Although sociologists are a diverse collection of scholars who study the social world in an incredibly variety of ways, we are united by the sociological perspective outlined in Chapter 1, alongside an agreed-upon set of methods we rely on to answer the questions we ask. These two things are what classify sociologists as a "group" compared with other fields. Read on to learn more about why research methods matter and why sociologists use so many—a fact that results from the diverse kinds of information we collect and use as data to study the world around us.

Why Sociological Research Methods Matter

4.1.1 Understand why predicting human behavior is so challenging and what sets sociology apart from other sciences.

Sociology is a "social science," a phrase that requires some consideration. As a social *science*, sociology, like economics or political science, uses methods derived from the natural sciences to study social phenomena. For instance, when some new element (some kind of social catalyst) is introduced to a given situation, we can attempt to isolate and measure its impact. But, unlike the way we might try to isolate the effect of a single element in a laboratory experiment, this is often more challenging (and not always ethical) when dealing with actual people.

But sociology is also a *social* science, like anthropology or history, attempting to study human behavior as it is lived by conscious human beings. Unlike electrons, for instance, human behavior does not follow physical laws by which *all* humans behave. Because sociologists study collections of sentient beings capable of rational and irrational thoughts and behavior, we also acknowledge that we are studying something difficult to isolate in a lab or test tube. As a result of their consciousness, human beings don't behave in exactly the same ways all the time, the ways that natural phenomena like gravity, or planetary orbits, might. People possess **subjectivity**—a complex of individual perceptions, motivations, ideas, and really messy things like emotions.

"Imagine how hard physics would be if particles could think" is how the Nobel Prize–winning physicist Murray Gell-Mann once put it (cited by Angle 2007). Think of it this way: We often compare challenging topics of study to "rocket science." "It's not rocket science!" is something we declare when we want to explain how (relatively) easy something is; we compare it to a field we seem to have collectively agreed is challenging. Physicist-turned-sociology professor Duncan Watts discusses the issue this way:

> "I'm no rocket scientist, and I have immense respect for the people who can land a machine the size of a small car on another planet. But the sad fact is that we're actually much better at planning the flight path of an interplanetary rocket than we are at managing the economy, merging two corporations, or even predicting how many copies of a book will sell. So why is it that rocket science *seems* hard, whereas problems having to do with people—which arguably are much harder—*seem* like they ought to be just a matter of common sense?"

The reason people are so much less predictable than particles or rocket flight plans is that people can do something that particles can't and that rockets are designed not to do. People have free will. Often, people act "rationally" (as economists put it); that is to say, they act in their own interest. But the fact of the matter is, they don't all act in their own interest and even those who appear to do so, do not do so all of the time. People's lives are dramatically shaped by the societies and social contexts in which

subjectivity
The complex of individual perceptions, motivations, ideas, and emotions that give each of us a point of view.

research methods
The processes used to systematically collect and analyze information from the social world for the purposes of sociological study and understanding.

they live. But people, unlike particles, sometimes behave in ways we might not expect. This makes them simultaneously fascinating and challenging to study.

To deal with this, sociology uses a wide variety of **research methods**—perhaps a greater variety than any other academic field. The range of different methods sociologists use extends from complex statistical models, carefully controlled experiments, and enormous surveys to such methods as the literary analysis of texts, linguistic analysis of conversations, ethnographic and field research, "participant observation," and historical research in archives. The reason we rely on such a diverse collection of research methods is because the range of questions that sociologists pose for research is similarly enormous. Almost nothing is "off limits" to sociologists. And just about anything you can imagine is something sociologists might consider "data." Students of sociology should be exposed to a wide variety of methodologies. The method we use should depend less on some preexisting prejudice and more on what we want to study.

HOW DO WE KNOW WHAT WE KNOW?

THINKING METHODOLOGICALLY ABOUT THE HERITABILITY OF INTELLIGENCE

Here's a recent example. For centuries people have argued about "nature" versus "nurture." Which is more important in determining your life course, heredity or environment? In recent years, the argument has been tilting increasingly toward nature. These days, "everybody knows" intelligence is largely innate, genetically transmitted. The most famous—or, to schoolchildren, infamous—test of all is the IQ test, a test designed to measure your "innate" intelligence, or aptitude, the natural genetically based ability you have to understand things. Sure, good schools and good environments can help, but most studies have found that about 75 percent of intelligence is hereditary. That, in other words, is a fact. Typically, these sorts of studies are used by opponents of affirmative action to argue that no amount of intervention is going to help those at the bottom; they're at the bottom for a reason.

It turns out, though, that this "fact" was the result of the methods being used to discover it. Most of the data for the genetic basis for intelligence are based on studies of twins. Identical twins share exactly the same DNA; fraternal twins, or other siblings, share only half. Researchers have thus taken the finding that the IQs of identical twins were more similar than for nonidentical twins and other siblings as a demonstration that heredity determines intelligence.

Eric Turkheimer (Turkheimer et al. 2003, 2005) and his colleagues reexamined those studies and found something curious. Almost all the studies of twins were of *middle-class* twins (poor people tend not to volunteer for research studies). When he examined the results from a massive study of more than 50,000 children and factored in class background, a startling picture emerged. For the children from wealthy families, virtually all the differences in IQ could be attributed to heredity. But among poor children, the IQs of identical twins varied a lot—as much as the IQs of fraternal twins. The impact of growing up in poverty (an environmental effect) completely offset the effects of heredity. For the poor, home life and environment are absolutely critical. "If you have a chaotic environment, kids' genetic potential doesn't have a chance to be expressed," Turkheimer told a journalist. "Well-off families can provide the mental stimulation needed for genes to build the brain circuitry for intelligence" (Turkheimer, cited in Kirp 2006).

It turns out that a certain environmental threshold has to be reached before heredity can kick in and "determine" anything. Only under some environmental conditions can the genetic ability emerge. It is a clear indication that it's rarely either–or—nature *or* nurture. It's almost always both. But it took careful research to see the shortcomings in those previous studies and help to correct the misunderstanding that resulted. And think, then, of the potential geniuses whose environments have never enabled their ability to emerge!

Is intelligence the result of nature or nurture? Both. Class matters also. Poor twins show greater differences in IQ than do middle class twins, whose IQs are very similar.

You might think that the choice of method and the type of data that you use are of little importance. After all, if you are trying to find out the truth, won't every method basically get you to the same results? In fact, though, the methods we use and the kinds of questions we ask are often so important that they actually lead to some answers and away from others. And such answers have enormous implications.

Sociology and the Scientific Method

4.1.2 Summarize the scientific method and how deductive and inductive approaches to sociological research enter this process at different points.

As social scientists, sociologists follow the rules of the scientific method. As in any argument or debate, science requires the use of evidence, or data, to demonstrate a position. The word *data* (the plural of datum) refers to formal and systematic information, organized and coherent. Data are not simply a collection of anecdotes; they are systematically collected and organized.

To gather data, sociologists use a variety of methods. Sociologists share many of these methods with other social sciences. To the sociologist, the choice of method is determined by two things: (1) the sorts of questions we want to answer and (2) the type of data we're able to collect to answer the questions we ask. Some sociologists perform experiments just as natural scientists do. Other times they rely on large-scale surveys to provide a general pattern of behaviors or attitudes. They may use historical materials found in archives or other historical sources, much as any historian would. Sociologists will reexamine data from other sources. They might analyze systematically the content of a cultural product, such as a novel, a magazine, a film, or a conversation. Some sociologists rely on interviews or focus groups with particular kinds of people to understand how they see things. Another sociologist might go into the field and live in another society or among a particular group of subculture, participating in its customs and rituals much as an anthropologist might do. Different kinds of data are analyzed by sociologists by using different research methods.

Additionally, although all sociologists participate in research that is broadly connected by being part of the research cycle (see FIGURE 4.1), not all sociological research enters the cycle at precisely the same point. Some of these research methods use **deductive reasoning**; that is, they logically proceed from one demonstrable fact or existing theory to deduce plausible hypotheses that can support or refute the theory. Then they collect data that can test those hypotheses and analyze the data to assess whether their hypothesis was supported or not and what that means about an existing theory or set of facts we had previously held to be true—was the theory/were the facts we'd previously held to be true supported, challenged, amended? Deductive research is the method used in much of the natural sciences, and the results we obtain are independent of any feelings that the researchers or their subjects may have. It's often impossible to then reason from the general to the specific: If you were to find out that a majority of U.S. teachers supported the use of corporal punishment in the schools, you wouldn't be able to predict what your own teacher will do if you misbehave. (Don't worry, it's not true. Most teachers oppose it.)

In other situations, the feelings of our research subjects are exactly what we are trying to study or we may be examining something in social life without a ready-formed hypothesis, and we will need to rely on **inductive reasoning**. In this case, the research leads the researcher to a conclusion about all or many members of a class based on an in-depth examination of only a few members of that class. For example, if you want to understand *why* teachers support corporal punishment, you might interview a few of them in depth, go observe their classrooms for a period of time, or analyze a set of texts that attempt to explain it from the inside. This research begins with observations and analysis rather than an existing theory or initial hypothesis. But it will return to

deductive reasoning
Research that logically proceeds from one demonstrable fact to the next. It often moves from the general to the more specific.

inductive reasoning
Research in which one reasons to a conclusion about all or many members of a collectivity based on examination of only a few members of that class. Loosely, it is reasoning from the specific to the general.

FIGURE 4.1 Inductive and Deductive Research Models
The distinction between *inductive* and *deductive* sociological research is less about a different set of steps and more about where sociologists are entering the research cycle. Deductive research begins with theories and hypotheses, and inductive research often begins with observations and analysis.

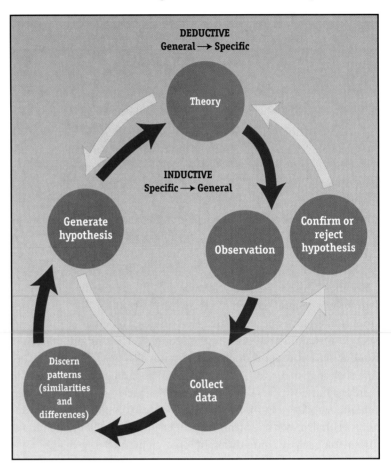

theories that may generate hypotheses at the end. It is simply entering the research process at a different stage in the cycle.

Sociologists study an enormous range of issues. Virtually every area of human behavior is studied, from the large-scale activities of governments, corporations, and international organizations like the European Union or the United Nations, to the most minute and intimate decision making about sexual practices or conversations or self-presentation. As a result, the methods that we use to study sociological problems depend more on the kind of issue or problem we want to study than whether one method is better than any other. Each method provides different types of data, and each type of data can be enormously useful and illuminate a different part of the problem.

Research methods are like the different ways we use glass to see objects. Some of us will want a magnifying glass, to bring the object so close that we can see every single little feature of the particular object. Others will prefer a prism, by which the object is fragmented into hundreds of tiny parts. A telescope is useful if the object is really far away but pretty useless if you need to see what's happening next door. Bifocals are best if you want to view both close and distant objects through the same lens. Just like iSoc, each of these ways of seeing is valuable. A specific method may be inappropriate to adequately study a specific problem, but no research method should be dismissed as inadequate or inappropriate in all situations. It depends on what you want to know.

iSoc: Research Methods

4.1.3 Recognize how each of the five elements of the iSoc model are important in helping sociologists decide which research methods might best suit their research questions.

Although the iSoc model is most suited to summarize the substantive areas of sociology, each of the different elements of the model can be explored using different methods. In general, large-scale quantitative data are useful to get the big picture, while qualitative methods like participant observation or ethnography, provide a more fine-grained and nuanced picture. Think of methods as a camera lens: Sometimes you'll want a wide-angle lens to get a panoramic frame; at other times, a telephoto lens can give you a close-up that shows intricate detail. We need both, of course. Sometimes, like satellites from outer space, we use methods that capture an entirely different perspective. So, as we learned to think about iSoc as a pair of sociology spectacles with multiple lenses through which sociologists look at the world, research methods might best be understood as the different kinds of equipment we use to focus on the world around us in different ways and at different scales. And if we think about research methods as a series of cameras that provide different kinds of pictures about the social world, learning about research methods has two parts: (1) you need to know which cameras to use to provide you with the information you are interested in discovering, and (2) you need to learn how to operate the cameras to understand the uses and capabilities of each. No matter the lens, you still have to learn how to focus.

IDENTITY—Although quantitative methods can be used to describe how various aspects of our *identities* are shared with others of our own groups, or of different groups, qualitative methods, such as ethnographies and interviews can explore the meanings that we make of our membership in certain groups.

INEQUALITY—Large-scale quantitative surveys can show us the rough parameters of various levels of *inequality:* different rates of incarceration or different prison sentences by race or class or gender, for example, or large-scale differences in income. But to understand how inequalities feel, or how they are actually experienced in people's lives, how inequalities shape the ways we interact (and fail to interact) with others around us requires methods that get up close and personal. We need methods capable of capturing those lived moments to make sense of these questions.

INTERACTIONS—To see how large structures and *institutions* are experienced in everyday micro-level settings—and to see the ways that those micro-level *interactions* create the very structures we can see from afar, sociologists typically use close-up methods such as ethnography and interviews, as well as methods that parse pieces of speech or nonverbal communication. Experiments also allow us to examine interactions in settings designed to focus intently on social behavior.

INSTITUTIONS—Although we can use survey methods or large-scale data to understand the ways in which large scale *institutions* operate in society, we can also look closely at how those institutions operate "on the ground." Ethnographies of schools or participant observation studies of corporations, for example, often color in the broad outlines we can see from the large-scale methods. A survey might tell you that certain schools are struggling with behavioral issues and are less able to prepare students academically for their next transition in life. You might look at teacher-to-student ratios, amounts of money spent on each student, grade differences, etc. But interview and ethnographic research often helps us to make meaning out of those numbers and shape the ways we make sense of the data from afar. Conversely, methods better suited to examining large representative swaths of society (like survey methods) provide more information for us to consider just how typical or atypical our findings are from research examining social life up close.

INTERSECTIONS—New perspectives require both revamping old methods and inventing new ones. Just as *intersectional* analysis requires that you see different aspects of your experiences operating at the same time—like, for example, the way that age and race and gender and class and religion all collide and intersect in shaping your political party affiliation—we need methods that are also able to see the big picture as well.

Sociological methods are like the old story of the blind men and the elephant. All aspects of society and your experience in it and of it require a full arsenal of methods. We shouldn't exclude any; each one illuminates a different aspect.

The Qualitative/Quantitative Divide

4.1.4 Explain the role of operationalization in helping to make decisions about whether quantitative or qualitative methods are more appropriate for sociological research.

quantitative methods

Numerical means to drawing sociological conclusions using powerful statistical tools to help understand patterns in which the behaviors, attitudes, or traits under study can be translated into numerical values.

survey

Research method in which one asks a sample of people closed-ended questions and tabulates the results.

qualitative methods

Inductive and inferential means to drawing sociological understanding, usually about less tangible aspects of social life, such as the actual felt experience of social interaction.

bias

A systematic prejudice in favor of or against one thing, person, or group compared with another.

operationalization

The process of attempting to define the topic of your study into measurable factors.

social desirability bias

The term social scientists use to describe a form of response bias wherein people being studied tend to present themselves in a manner they believe will be perceived favorably.

Most often we think that the real divide among social science methods is between quantitative and qualitative methods. Using **quantitative methods**, one uses powerful statistical tools to help understand patterns in which the behaviors, attitudes, or traits under study can be translated into numerical values. Typically, though not always, quantitative methods rely on deductive reasoning. So, for example, checking a box on a **survey** that gives your gender as "man" or "woman" might enable the researcher to examine the relative percentages of men and women who subscribe to certain ideas, vote for a particular political party, or avoid certain behaviors. Let's consider we're interested in knowing how men and women feel about gender equality in the United States. Is there a meaningful divide, or is gender unrelated to how people feel about gender equality? This is a *quantitative* question. We're not asking *why* men and women might feel the way they do. We're simply interested in knowing *what* they feel and whether women have different or similar opinions on this issue when compared with men.

And it turns out that there are meaningful differences between how women and men feel about this particular question. Slightly more than half of Americans (53 percent) believe that "significant obstacles still make it harder for women to get ahead than men"; 63 percent of women agree with that statement, compared with only 41 percent of men (Fingerhut 2016).

Qualitative methods often rely on more inductive and inferential reasoning to understand the texture of social life than the actual felt experience of social interaction. Sometimes, the questions that we ask about the social world do not involve answers that can easily be enumerated in numerical form. Qualitative methods are sometimes derided as "less scientific," as quantitative researchers often assume that their own methods eliminate **bias** and that therefore only quantitative methods are "scientific." These are convenient myths, but they are incorrect; they are, themselves, the result of bias. Both quantitative and qualitative methods are capable of understanding social reality—although each type of method illuminates a different aspect of that reality. Both types of methodologies have biases, but qualitative methodologists endeavor to make their biases explicit (and thus better control them), while quantitative scholarship sometimes fails to examine their own biases.

After all, most great scientific discoveries initially relied on simple and close observation of some phenomenon—like the apple falling on the head of Sir Isaac Newton leading to his "discovery" of gravity. Gradually, from such observations, other scientists are able to expand the reach of explanation to include a wider variety of phenomena, and these are then subject to more statistical analysis. This is a dilemma facing every scientist attempting to study anything—the problem of operationalization. **Operationalization** refers to the process of attempting to define the topic of your study into measurable factors. Sometimes, we have a very clear idea of what we want to study and operationalizing it into something we can measure and assess is very easy. But often, sociologists are interested in examining aspects of social life that are notoriously tricky to operationalize. And we always have to be aware of the possibility of **social desirability bias**.

SOCIOLOGY AND OUR WORLD

ARE PEOPLE LYING ON SURVEYS? ... SOMETIMES.

Why might people lie on surveys, and what can we learn by looking at how people tend to lie when they do?

Church attendance is one of those funny survey questions that's likely to elicit lies from respondents. Sociologists are interested in that fact, but also interested in why people are not only more likely to lie on this question; they also all lie in the same way. Why?

Much of what we know quantitatively about the social world is the result of large-scale surveys that attempt to gather information from representative samples from the population. Social surveys are often anonymous—that is, we don't ask people to write down their names. The idea is not to be able to link information back to actual individuals. Rather, we're interested in what kinds of identity categories checks off on a survey and whether they share experiences, opinions, and more with other people who share some of those same categories (like members of the same racial or ethnic category, or people of similar ages, for instance).

Often, surveys ask people to report on their actual behavior. For instance, sociologists who study religion are often interested in religious behavior, like praying or attending church or synagogue. In fact, church attendance is a behavior that sociologists studying religion use as a good *quantitative* measure of just *how* religious someone is. So, people are regularly asked to report how often they attend church on surveys to provide some sort of numerical value to their religious convictions. Church attendance, however, is also a sort of infamous survey question among sociologists. It's a question that is very likely to succumb to what social scientists refer to as social desirability bias. This is a term social scientists use to describe a form of response bias wherein people being surveyed tend to answer questions

in a manner that they believe will be perceived favorably by others. This means that people are likely to over-report behavior socially understood as "good" and possibly under-report behavior socially understood as "bad."

Church attendance is something many people understood as a social responsibility; it's a demonstration of faith that involves us giving something up: time. It's not social desirability bias simply because people are more likely to lie on this question than others. This example qualifies as social desirability bias because when people lie about church attendance, they all lie in the same direction: They say they attend more often than they actually do. One study that sought to measure just how much people lie did so by collecting two representative samples of Americans and surveying both of them about church attendance, but varying one important element. One group took the survey over the phone with someone on the line asking them questions and recording their responses. The other group took the survey online, reading and responding to questions without speaking to someone else. What happened? When they had to respond to an actual person to tell them how often they attended church, they said they attended more often than when they replied to online surveys—a lot more often.

These data show us two things. One is that sociologists are interested in what they can learn from large-scale surveys from representative samples of a population. But we should also continue to consider that surveys are, in the end, a collection of responses from actual people who are influenced to answer and behave in all sorts of different ways.

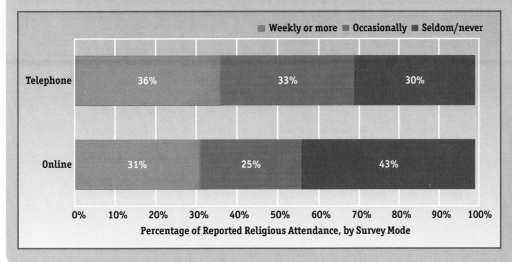

Weekly or more ■ **Occasionally** ■ **Seldom/never**

Telephone	36%	33%	30%
Online	31%	25%	43%

0% 10% 20% 30% 40% 50% 60% 70% 80% 90% 100%

Percentage of Reported Religious Attendance, by Survey Mode

SOURCE: Data from Cox, Daniel, Robert P. Jones, Juhen Navarro-Rivera, (2014). "I Know What You Did Last Sunday: Measuring Social Desirability Bias in Self-Reported Religious Behavior, Belief, and Identity." Paper presented at the Public Religion Research Institute, May 17, 2014. Available at: https://www.prri.org/academic/study-know-last-sunday-finds-americans-significantly-inflate-religious-participation/.

In this case, sociologists are, as a group, a creative collection of scientists who often find interesting sources of data that provide clues to answer the questions that interest them and new insights on how the world around you actually works.

Debates among sociologists and other social scientists often focus on which method leads to the "truth." But the correct answer is *both* methods lead us to the

WHAT DO YOU THINK? WHAT DOES AMERICA THINK?

How Happy Are We?

Large-scale representative surveys can tell us a lot about our population, about social trends, and about attitudes, behaviors, and beliefs. National survey data tell us that, when asked about their level of happiness in life, most Americans say they are happy. So where do you fit in that survey?

What do you think?

Would you say that you are very happy, pretty happy, or not too happy?
- ○ Very happy
- ○ Pretty happy
- ○ Not too happy

What does America think?

In 1972, 30 percent of respondents identified themselves as "very happy"; in 2016 the proportion of Americans identifying as "very happy" was exactly the same—30 percent again. But, when we examine these data over time, it's clear that trends in Americans' self-assessed levels of happiness have been far from static. If we only considered the years 1972 and 2016, we might assume nothing happened in the intervening years. But levels of happiness have actually fluctuated quite a bit.

Like many valued resources, happiness is not evenly distributed throughout the population. The various identities we each occupy shape different amounts and possibly levels of access to even something as intangible as "happiness" (at least as happiness is measured here). Consider how men and women of two separate racial groups answered this question differently. While the proportions of respondents classifying themselves as "very happy" move around from year to year, the general trend remains the same: White men are the happiest group shown here, and black women are the least happy. When we compare each group to everyone sampled as well, we see that white men consistently identify as happier than the average person in the population, while white women and black men and women are more likely below this line. Interestingly, we also see that what we might call the "happiness gap" (the gap in happiness between white men and the rest) appears here to be closing. In 1972, 29.5 percent of white men identified themselves as "very happy"; that same year, only 22.9 percent of black women, 34.8 percent of white women, and 15.6 percent of black men claimed the same. By 2016, 29.9 percent of white men identified as "very happy"—whereas 30.0 percent of black men, 31.4 percent of white women, and 18.6 percent of black women identified themselves at the same rate.

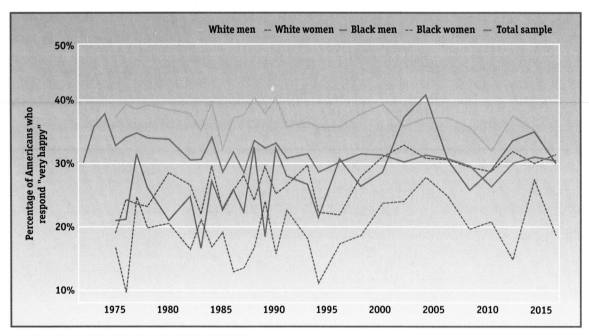

SOURCE: Data from the General Social Survey, 1972–2016.

THINKING CRITICALLY ABOUT SURVEY DATA

Is happiness inequitably distributed throughout the population? Does your level of happiness depend on your gender, race, and other social identities? Do you think this survey question is a good measure of how happy people feel? Or is there a better way to operationalize how happy people are?

"truth"—that is, each method is adept at revealing a different part of the entire social experience. And sociologists use the term **triangulation** as it pertains to research methods when they use more than one research method to reach a conclusion. Often we "triangulate" our findings by putting them into conversation with research on our topic of interest that might have operationalized the topic of study a bit differently or collected a different kind of data or analyzed that data with a different research method. Each of these decisions sometimes leads to different kinds of findings. And sociologists understand that each of these different findings is best understood as partially true; it is true from a particular perspective. Putting all of these perspectives together can help us all obtain the best answers to the questions we want to ask about how the social world is organized.

WHEN IS A FACT A FACT?   Why Operationalization Is So Important. Consider a really important topic of sociological research: sexual violence. How much rape is there in the United States? It's an important question. And it's something that, on the face of it, seems like we ought to be able to enumerate. But different credible sources of information provide wildly different information. For instance, in 2014, the FBI's Uniform Crime Report found that there were 84,041 rapes reported to law enforcement that year. This number was just a bit higher than their estimate in 2013. But it was 10.9 percent lower than the same estimate they generated for the year 2005. Rape, according to the FBI Uniform Crime Report has been declining in recent history in the United States. But, the Bureau of Justice reports a much higher rate of rape than the FBI. In 2010, for instance, the Bureau of Justice claimed approximately 287,100 rapes occurred that year; the vast majority of victims were women. And the Center for Disease Control and Prevention survey has shown that roughly one in five women has experienced a rape in her lifetime.

All of these findings are facts. They have been discovered by carefully conducting research on the population of the United States. Some of these facts make rape appear to be a relatively common crime, and others might make it seem less common. So, which is it? Is rape common, rare, or something in between? And why is it that different sources seem to disagree?

Lots of different issues are at stake here. But, thinking about this issue sociologically will lead you to a logical conclusion related to operationalization. The rate of rape and sexual assault in the United States depends, in large part, on how we measure rape and sexual assault. How we define what qualifies as "rape," in other words, will shape what we are able to discover about this pressing social issue. For example, the Uniform Crime Report produced by the FBI counts cases of "rape" that are reported to them by local police. So, to meet their criteria, a sexual assault must have occurred, been reported to local police, and they have to assess whether or not the case is well-founded enough to pass on to the federal level. So, unreported rapes will not be counted here, nor will cases that were not assessed as "well-founded" by local police. Conversely, the Bureau of Justice relies on a different instrument to measure rape; they rely on a representative survey of U.S. households, a questionnaire that includes questions about, among many other things, rapes that may have never been reported to the police. And both of these reports document the number of rapes per year, not per person. The Center for Disease Control and Prevention survey asks questions that include rapes committed at any point in the life course.

And to make matters even more complicated, answering the question of whether these numbers are higher or lower than they were in even recent history is challenging because our understandings of rape and sexual assault have undergone tremendous shifts. Consider this: Even in the twenty-first century, some police departments in the United States had a policy of regularly considering rape complaints as "unfounded" when made by drug users and sex workers (cited from Luker 2008: 116). And during the past two to three decades, what is now often referred to as "date rape," has gone

triangulation

A research technique that uses cross-verification to ensure the validity of conclusions. When several research methods are used to study the same phenomenon, researchers can be more confident with a result.

from being not recognized as a form of sexual violence and assault to one that is. And even this is still ongoing and a work in progress.

Although this is an extreme example, it highlights the issue of operationalization as an important one to consider in sociological research. All of these "facts" are true about rape. But how we define what qualifies as "rape" will shape how we study it, what we discover, and more. Sociologists are, as a group, a skeptical bunch. When we encounter facts, we think about them sociologically, too. We want to know how the facts were produced. We will ask what methods were used to produce the facts. We consider how the issues were operationalized within that method. And beyond that, we are interested in examining how something that is given the status of "fact" about the social world compares to other related facts we know. We ask about what the purpose of making a fact known might be. Sociological research methods help us to discover facts about the social world. But sociologists also know that facts require research to uncover, our task is not done once facts are found; facts then require critical reflection, critique, and reconsideration as we endeavor to better understand our social world.

Sociological research on sexual violence and assault is incredibly important because it has helped to identify not only who is most at risk, at what points in their lives, and why. But it has also helped us better understand the experiences of those affected by sexual violence and how the rest of us can do more to prevent sexual violence and to better support those most affected.

What Do Sociologists Consider as "Data"?

4.1.5 Describe what it means that sociologists consider just about anything as a potential source of data to study the social world.

Sociologists are interested in studying the social world in its entirety. As a result, you might be hard pressed to find something that a sociologist hasn't at one point considered to be data that might tell us something about society or allows us to systematically examine some part of society. To the sociologist, **data** refers to the information we can collect from the social world to study, analyze, or calculate something in a systematic way. But there is a wide variety of sources of information about the social world. And sociologists used different types of methods to help us study different types of data in systematic ways.

Lots of data about the world around us can be easily transformed into numerical form (*quantitative data*). We might want to know, for instance, what proportion of the U.S. population have bachelor's degrees. We might want to know how much income an average single-mother household lives on in the United States and how we compare with other societies around the world on that measure. We might be interested in examining people's opinions on any number of issues we can convert to numerical form—like same-sex marriage, abortion reform, rights to racially segregated neighborhoods, the minimum wage, and more. Much of this kind of information can be assessed on surveys, converted into numbers, and sociologists use an array of statistical methods to analyze the opinions, attitudes, experiences, and opportunities of different groups.

A good deal of data, however, is less amenable to being easily converted into numbers (we call this *qualitative data*). Consider the following fact. It is a fact that in the United States poor mothers are more likely to have children outside of marriage than are women in other social classes. This is a fact discovered *quantitatively*. That is, we can look at the proportions of out-of-wedlock births to women in different socioeconomic classes.

Because income is often measured by households rather than at the individual level, education is often used as a proxy for class identity (because we know that education and income are correlated to a strong degree). Despite a signficant decline recently in births to women with a high school diploma or less, women with less

data

The plural of datum. Data are systematically collected and systematically organized bits of information.

education remain more likely to have children outside of marriage and to have more of them (Pew Research Center 2013). That is a *quantitative* fact, one we can measure by looking at the actual proportions of women with different educational backgrounds, what proportion of each educational grouping had children outside of marriage, and the average number of births each group has by the end of their childbearing years. But let's say we have a different question. What if we want to know *why* poor women are more likely to have their children outside of marriage? That's a question that is less easy to answer with quantitative evidence.

Sociologists Kathryn Edin and Maria Kefalas (2005) set out to answer precisely this question in their research on poor women. You might have an idea about why poor women have children outside of marriage at higher rates than women in other social classes. Whether or not you are correct, however, is not a matter of opinion. It is something else that can be studied. The "Why?" associated with this fact involves a different type of data. Edin and Kefalas (2005) collected a huge number of interviews from poor women living in Philadelphia to answer the question. It wasn't a representative sample of all Americans. But it's a large sample of poor women, and they were able to collect information that would be difficult to collect from a larger survey.

What did they discover? They found that the reason poor women have children outside of marriage had nothing to do with poor women valuing the institution of marriage less than middle- and upper-class women. In fact, they hold marriage in at least as high of regard as do women (and men) in other social classes. They perceived the likelihood of finding someone who would be able to fulfill their idea of what they wanted out of a marriage to be low. But this did not mean that they felt compelled to give up on having children as well. Although the *quantitative* data leads some to suggest that poor women simply don't value marriage in the same ways as women and men in other social classes, Edin and Kefalas collected a different kind of data that allowed them to argue that that interpretation was false. The real reason, they discovered, was that these women felt that men suitable for marriage were in short supply (something we discuss in more depth in Chapter 12). It's just one small example, but a powerful illustration of what different kinds of data can tell us. Often, looking at different types of data to assess the same social issue or phenomenon will yield information that requires new and different types of interpretation as well. (As referenced previously, this process is what sociologists refer to as triangulation.) And, while not every sociological project relies on several sources of data, it is well worth considering whether a different kind of data might yield different answers to the questions that interest us and why.

iSOC AND YOU How Do We Know What We Know?

Part of what makes sociology so exciting is that almost nothing is beyond the bounds of sociological inquiry and analysis. And because of this, we have an eclectic set of research methods—cohesive enough that it allows us to qualify as a "field," but diverse enough that it enables us to answer the different types of questions we ask. Questions about each element of the iSoc model are amenable to being studied in a variety of ways. If we are interested in the *identities* people form in different contexts and with different kinds of resources at their disposal, we might rely on quantitative data from surveys, but we may decide that we need to know more about how people make meaning out of those distinctions with a more in-depth qualitative analysis of the topic. Similarly, *interactions*, *institutions*, *inequality*, and *intersections* are all open to being studied via multiple different types of methods. But in deciding which elements of iSoc sociological research is interested in considering, sociologists make choices about precisely *how* to use those methods in addition to assessing *which* methods are best used for the research questions we consider. And learning how and when to rely on distinct methods and which methods best answer which types of questions is among the best uses of a properly tuned sociological imagination.

4.2 Types of Sociological Research Methods

As we said previously, research methods are like the different kinds of optical devices; some give you close-ups that are rich with detail but make it hard to discern large patterns. Others pull way back and give a panoramic view, but can miss subtle differences. In Chapter 1, we described the various components of iSoc as analogous to different "lenses" through which different elements of society and social life can be more readily seen. Taking that analogy one step further, research methods are the various apparatuses into which we put these lenses to look at the world. As we learned previously, each element of the iSoc perspective can be analyzed with each research method. But precisely *what* kinds of data we are examining and what we learn as a result differs by what sort of research method we rely on.

Like all photographs, a single representation is not the "real thing"; rather, they are a *representation* of the real thing. The "real thing"—society and social interaction—remains so complex and multifaceted that you can often feel that you can't really fathom it in its totality. Different research methods are designed to help simplify elements of this complexity so that we can identify patterns and attempt to explain how they emerge, what they accomplish, whether they have changed, and why they persist (if, indeed, they do).

In this section, you'll read about the three broad categories of sociological research and consider, in a bit of depth, a selection of the most common methods used by sociologists today.

Categorizing Sociological Research Methods

4.2.1 Identify the key differences between the three different "types" of sociological research methods.

Sociologists typically use one of three basic types of research methods. One type of method relies on the observation of behavior, either in a controlled setting, like a lab, or more often in sociology, in its natural setting, where people are actually enacting the behavior you're studying (what we call the "field"). Another type of sociological research relies on quantitative analysis of accumulated data (typically from surveys). And a third type relies on data that can be accumulated from other sources (methods that are sometimes referred to as *secondary analysis* of existing data). And each of these basic types is composed of several subtypes.

What social scientists call *variables* help us measure whether, how, and in what ways something changes (varies) in the social world. There are different kinds of variables. An **independent variable** is the event or item in your research that is considered to be the cause or influence of the other, *dependent*, variables. Sociologists are able to manipulate the independent variable to see if that difference has an impact. If it does, it will affect what's called the *dependent variable*. So, if you wanted to know whether and in what ways education affects income, we're interested in asking how an independent variable (in this case, education) affects a dependent variable (here, income). The **dependent variable** gets its name because it depends on, or is caused or influenced by, the independent variable. The dependent variable is the variable that the researcher thinks might *depend on* the independent variable. It is what gets measured in the research. It is the change in the dependent variable that constitutes your results.

So, consider our example again between education and income. Most of you are in college because you believe that these two variables are related to one another—at least, you sure hope they are. And you're correct—statistically speaking, education and income are **correlated** with one another. A change in one (education, the *independent variable*) is associated with a change in the other (income, the *dependent variable*)

independent variable

In an experimental study, the agent of change, the ingredient that is added to set things in motion.

dependent variable

The variable whose change depends on the introduction of the independent variable.

correlation

The term for the fact of some relationship between two phenomena.

FIGURE 4.2 Work/Life Earnings

Education is correlated with income for everyone, on average. These two variables exhibit a positive relationship with one another in which higher levels on the independent variable are associated with higher values on the dependent variable. As you acquire more and higher educational degrees and credentials, your income also rises. But, sociologists are also interested in inequality and intersections. So, although this relationship is true for all groups, it is more true for some groups than others. See how the relationship between education and income differs by gender and race here.

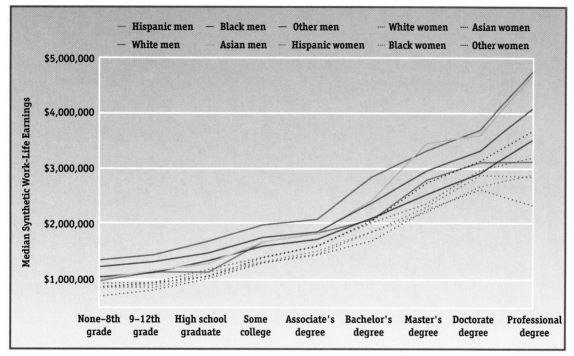

SOURCE: Data from U.S. Census Bureau, American Community Survey, 2010. Available at http://www.census.gov/content/dam/Census/library/publications/2011/acs/acs-14.pdf

(see FIGURE 4.2). Just because two variables are *correlated* with each other, however, does not necessarily indicate a **causal relationship**, that is, the discovery that an independent variable actually *causes* a change in a dependent variable in reliable ways that are due only or primarily to shifts in the independent variable.

Sociologists refer to a correlation as "spurious" when it is not actually causal. This is sometimes difficult because when we see two trends that seem like they are related to one another, the data almost begs us to attempt to assign a reason to explain that relationship. Consider the following spurious relationship drawn from *Spurious Correlations*, a website set up by a JD student at Harvard Law that allows you to chart nonsensical correlations (http://www.tylervigen.com/spurious-correlations): The relationship between the number of iPhones sold alongside the number of people who died as a result of falling down the stairs (see FIGURE 4.3). Looking at the two lines alongside one another, it might seem like the relationship is causal; that is, it might seem like changes in one of these variables is *causing* changes in the other. For instance, you might think that people are often looking at their smartphones while they ought to be paying attention to something else. If people are walking down stairs while looking at their phones and enough people have phones, then deaths due to falling down the stairs will likely increase. Sociologists refer to this as **confirmation bias**, that is, the tendency to interpret new evidence as confirmation of our existing beliefs. Sociologists must beware of confirmation bias because *correlations do not always imply causation*.

In fact, *causal relationships* are notoriously challenging to establish in the social sciences. This is because people's lives are a lot less predictable than are electron orbits or chemical reactions. But it is also because of the incredible complexity of social life. To establish a causal relationship between two variables in sociology requires three

causal relationship

A relationship between two or more variables in which one (independent) variable can be shown to actually *cause* a change in a dependent variable or variables in reliable ways.

confirmation bias

The tendency to interpret new evidence as confirmation of our existing beliefs.

FIGURE 4.3 Spurious Correlations

The two separate *y* axes here illustrate that, although the two lines have similar slopes, there are dramatically fewer deaths as a result of falling down stairs than there are iPhones sold. While the two social indicators might seem to be related to one another when presented alongside each other in this way, this is insufficient evidence to claim that one of these things is actually *causing* the other. And in fact, this is a good example of a spurious correlation. It might look like these two variables are related, almost begging for an explanation. But in truth, iPhone purchases and deaths as a result of falling down stairs are unrelated social phenomena.

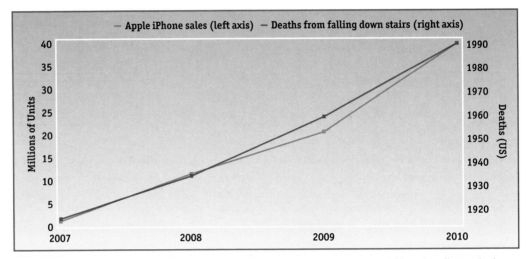

SOURCE: Data from Tyler Vigen, (2017). *Spurious Correlations*. Accessed April 28, 2017. Available at: http://www.tylervigen.com/spurious-correlations.

separate steps. *First*, you need to establish a correlation—demonstrating concurrent changes in two variables. *Second*, you need to be able to establish time order. Consider the relationship above between education and income. If we're suggesting that our independent variable (education) *causes* changes in a dependent variable (income), we need to be able to demonstrate that changes in education happen *before* changes in income. It might be the case, for instance, that increases in income lead people to get more education (a situation sociologists refer to as **reverse causality**). *Third* and finally, we have to be able to rule out all of the alternative explanations that might explain that relationship. Might it be, for instance, that a third variable (like age) is causing changes in both education and income?

Independent and dependent variables are the key types of variables. But there are others. For instance, let's say you want to actually test whether increases in education cause increases in income. Although this might seem like a simple example, there are **confounding variables** that may be affecting the results of the study but for which you haven't adequately accounted. Again, in the preceding example, both education and income are related to age. Accruing years of education and new educational degrees and credentials requires having lived long enough to accrue them. Similarly, acquiring higher levels of income often necessitates working long enough to be promoted, gain expertise, etc.—something that also takes years. Thus, age is a variable that affects the relationship between education and income. It's an effect we can control for, but an effect nonetheless. Finally, an **intervening variable** is a variable that intervenes—that is, gets in between—the two variables and thus makes accurate measurement difficult. Both gender and race might be considered intervening variables here (as may be the case in FIGURE 4.2). Although education and income are correlated, the relationship they have with one another differs between men and women of different racial backgrounds.

Sociologists first consider a research question. And then they ask what kinds of variables they are interested in studying to answer it and whether it will require them to learn more about identity, inequality, a specific institution, the meanings associated with a particular interaction, the intersections between groups, or some combination.

reverse causality

Refers either to a direction of cause-and-effect contrary to the presumed relationship between variables or to a two-way causal relationship in, as it were, a loop (a relationship sociologists refer to as "reciprocal").

confounding variables

The elements that impede accurate measurements of the impact of one variable on another.

intervening variable

A variable that may not have been measured, but is responsible for the presumed relationship between independent and dependent variables in research.

Sociologists have different methods that help us answer different kinds of questions about the social world, or questions that are likely to result in different types of information (data) that sociologists analyze in search of patterns. In general, sociologists are likely to use one or more of these five research methods:

- *Observation.*   Observing people in their natural habitat, joining their clubs, going to their churches, getting jobs in their offices.
- *Interviews.*   Asking a small group of people open-ended questions, such as "Can you describe your last road rage experience?"
- *Surveys.*   Asking a lot of people closed-ended questions, such as "How many times have you gotten angry in traffic in the last month?"
- *Content analysis.*   Analyzing artifacts (books, movies, TV programs, magazine articles, and so on) instead of people.
- *Network analysis.*   Studying what we can learn from the webs of social relationships people form with their relationships with others.

Let's examine each of these methods in more detail.

Observational Methods

4.2.2 Describe the primary components of observational research, considering what kinds of questions it is well-suited to answer.

In all observational studies, we directly observe the behavior we are studying. We can do this in a laboratory, conducting an experiment, or we can conduct this type of sociological research in the settings in which it more "naturally" occurs. The latter is much more common today. For one thing, in lab experiments it is often too difficult to change the independent variable. Say you want to know if children of divorced parents are more likely to become juvenile delinquents. You can hardly divide children into two groups and force the parents of the first to divorce and the second to stay together. But in either case, when we observe phenomena, we do more than just watch; we watch *scientifically*, testing hypotheses against evidence (deductive research) or considering how evidence might connect with existing theories in the field (inductive research). In this section, we summarize a collection of forms of observational research: experiments, field research, and interviews.

All the methods included in this section involve actually interacting with real people—either in a controlled environment or in their natural habitat. These methods give us an up-close and personal feel to the research, an intimate knowledge with fine nuance and detail.

You know the old expression of being unable to see the forest through the trees. Observational methods such as ethnographies, experiments, and interviews are often so focused on the minute patterns of leaves and bark on individual trees that they are less well attuned to providing scholars with an overall sense of the shape and size of the forest. Because scholars are also interested in understanding broad patterns of behaviors and attitudes, sociologists also use different sorts of research methods involving our interaction not with people but with large pools of evidence they leave behind (sociological data). We address those methods in the following section. And there, of course, it is important to remember that although those methods might reveal the larger patterns, we have to remember that they too have some weaknesses in terms of an inability to make out the nuances and subtleties of the individual trees. It's for this reason that the best sociologists understand how to use the iSoc perspective to shift our focus, and examining the same phenomena with different methods is one of the ways we accomplish that systematically.

EXPERIMENTS.   An **experiment** is a controlled form of observation in which the researcher manipulates independent variables to observe their effects on a dependent

experiment
A research process that is performed under controlled conditions to examine the validity of a hypothesis by carefully varying conditions between groups.

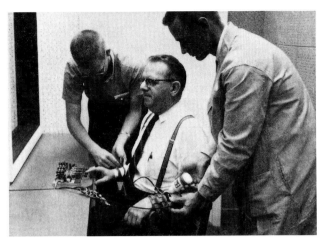

In the "Obedience to Authority" studies, social psychologist Stanley Milgram pretended to attach electrodes to his associate to administer increasingly painful electric shocks when he answered questions incorrectly. Two out of every three test subjects (65 percent) administered shocks all the way up to the maximum level.

experimental group

In an experiment, the group that will experience the experimental condition being measured to examine what happens. *See control group.*

control group

In an experiment, the comparison group that will not experience the manipulation of the independent variable (the experimental group). Having a control group enables sociologists to compare the outcomes of the experiment to determine if the changes in the independent variable had any effects on the dependent variable.

variable. To make an experiment valid, one typically uses two groups of people. One is the **experimental group**, and they are the group that will have the change introduced to see what happens. The other is the **control group**, and they will not experience the manipulation of the variable. A control group enables us to compare the outcomes of the experiment to determine if the changes in the independent variable had any effects on the dependent variable. It is therefore important that the experimental group and the control group be as similar as possible (by factors such as age, race, religion, class, gender, and so on), so that we can reduce any possibility that one of these other factors may have caused the effects we are examining.

In one of the most famous, or infamous, experiments in social psychology, Stanley Milgram (1963, 1974) wanted to test the limits of people's obedience to authority. During the trials that followed the end of World War II, many Nazis defended themselves by claiming that they were "only following orders." Milgram decided to test whether this might be true. He designed an experiment in which a subject was asked to participate in an experiment ostensibly about the effects of negative reinforcement on learning. The "learner" (a colleague of the experimenter) was seated at a table and hooked up to a machine that would supposedly administer an electric shock of increasing voltage every time the learner answered the question wrong. The "teacher" (the actual subject of the experiment) sat in another room, asked the questions to the learner, and had to administer the electric shock when the learner gave the wrong answer.

The machine that administered the shocks had a dial that ranged from "Minor" at one end of the dial to a section marked in red that said "Danger—Severe Shock." And when the teacher reached that section, the "learner" would scream in apparent agony. (Remember, no shocks were administered; the experiment was done to see how far the teacher would go simply by being told to do so by the experimenter. The researcher would only say, "Please continue," or "The experiment requires that you continue.") Milgram's experiment did not use the two groups—experimental and control—but it did include the essential element of experiments: an intervention or manipulation by the researcher. The independent variables included the orders given by the researcher and the distance between the "teacher" and the "learner"; the dependent variable was the amount of "shock" the participant was willing to give when instructed to do so.

The results were startling. Most people, when asked, say they would be very unlikely to do such a thing. But in the experiment, over two-thirds of the "teachers" administered shocks that would have been lethal to the learners. They simply did what they were told to do, despite the fact that they could hear the learners screaming in pain and the shocks were clearly labeled as potentially fatal. (After the experiment was over, the teacher and learner met, and the teachers were relieved to realize that they did not actually kill the learners.) And virtually no one refused to administer any shocks to another person. From this, Milgram concluded that people obey authority figures without much less protest than you might have thought.

Consider an equally startling but less controversial experiment. In the late 1960s and early 1970s, sociologists Robert Rosenthal and Lenore Jacobson decided to test the *self-fulfilling prophecy*—the idea that you get what you expect (Rosenthal and Jacobson 1968/1992). They hypothesized that teachers had expectations of student performance and that students performed to those expectations. That is, they wanted to test whether teachers' expectations were actually *causing* student performance outcomes, not the other way around. If the teacher thinks a student is smart, the student will do well in the class. If the teacher expects the student to do poorly, the student will do poorly.

Rosenthal and Jacobson administered an IQ test to all the children in an elementary school. Then, without looking at the results, they randomly chose a small group of students and told their teachers that the students had extremely high IQs. This, Rosenthal and Jacobson hypothesized, would raise the teachers' expectations for these randomly chosen students (the experimental group), and these expectations would be reflected in better performance by these students compared with other students (the control group). At the end of the school year, Rosenthal and Jacobson returned to the school and administered another IQ test to all the students. The "chosen few" performed better on the test than their classmates, yet the only difference between the two groups was the teachers' expectations. It turned out that teacher expectations were the independent variable, and student performance was the dependent variable—not the other way around.

Neither of these experiments could be conducted in this way today because of changes in the laws surrounding experiments with human subjects. This is another reason sociologists are doing fewer experiments now than they once did.

FIELD STUDIES.   Many of the issues sociologists are concerned with are not readily accessible in controlled laboratory experiments. Instead, sociologists go "into the field" to conduct research among the people they want to study. (The **field** is any site where the interactions or processes you want to study are taking place, such as an institution like a school or a specific community.) In observational studies, we rely on ourselves to interpret what is happening, and so we test our sociological ways of seeing. It involves wearing our iSoc lenses to systematically collect information about social interactions and behavior as they occur. As you'll learn, sometimes field studies enable us to collect information about the social world that we might have missed with other research methods.

Some observational studies require **detached observation**, a perspective that constrains the researcher from becoming in any way involved in the event he or she is observing. This posture of detachment is less about some notion of **objectivity**— after all, we are relying on our subjective abilities as an observer—and more because being detached and away from the action reduces the amount that our observation will change the dynamic we're watching. (Being in the field, even as an observer, can change the very things we are trying to study.) For example, let's say you want to see if there is a gender difference in children's play. If you observe boys and girls unobtrusively from behind a one-way mirror or screen, they'll play as if no one was watching. But if they know there are grownups watching, they might behave differently. Detached observation is useful, but it doesn't enable you as a researcher to get inside the experience. For that sociologists sometimes engage in research methods that require them to participate in the activities of the people you are studying. **Participant observation** requires that the researcher do both, participate and observe. Many participant observers conceal their identity to blend in better with the group they're studying.

Juggling these two and identities is often difficult. In one famous case, Laud Humphreys (1970) was interested in the negotiation of anonymous sex between men in public restrooms. He volunteered to act as a lookout for the men who waited at a rest stop along the New Jersey Turnpike because it was against the law to have sex in public restrooms. As the lookout, he was able to observe the men who stopped there to have sex and jotted down their license plate numbers. Later, he was able to trace the men's addresses through their license plate numbers and went to their homes posing as a researcher doing a general sociological study. (This allowed him to ask many questions about their backgrounds.) His findings were as astonishing as they were controversial. Most of the men who stopped at public restrooms to have sex with other men were married and considered themselves heterosexual. Most were working class and politically conservative and saw their behavior simply as sexual release, not

field

Any site where the interactions or processes you want to study are taking place, such as an institution like a school or a specific community.

detached observation

A perspective that constrains the researcher from becoming in any way involved in the event he or she is observing. This reduces the amount that the researchers' observations will change the dynamic that they are watching.

objectivity

A posited ideal for social science researchers, it is a perspective that is free of bias, judgment, or prejudice.

participant observation

Sociological research method in which one observes people in their natural habitat.

institutional review boards (IRBs)

A committee established to review and approve research involving human subjects, it works to ensure that researchers comply with standards and ethics in conducting their research.

ethnography

A type of field method in which the researcher inserts himself or herself into the daily world of the people he or she is trying to study to understand the events from the point of view of the actors themselves.

as an expression of "who they really were." Humphreys's research has been severely criticized because he deceived the men he was studying. As a result, universities developed **institutional review boards (IRBs)** to ensure that researchers comply with standards and ethics in conducting their research (more detail on IRBs to come later). But Humphreys was also able to identify a population of men who had sex with other men who did not identify as gay, and this was later thought to be one of the possible avenues of transmission for HIV from the urban gay population into heterosexual suburban homes.

Increasingly, field researchers use the ethnographic methods of cultural anthropology to undertake sociological research. **Ethnography** is a field method used most often by anthropologists when they study other cultures. Although you don't pretend to be a participant (and you identify yourself as a researcher), you try to understand the world from the point of view of the people whose lives you are interested in and attempt, as much as possible, to put your own values and assumptions about their activities "on hold." This avoids two extreme outcomes: (1) If you try to forget your own cultural assumptions and immerse yourself, you risk "going native"—which means you uncritically embrace the group's way of seeing things. (2) If you see the other group only through the filter of your own values, you impose your way of seeing things and can't really understand how they see the world. At its most extreme, this is a form of cultural imperialism—imposing your values on others. Ethnographers attempt to steer a middle path between these extremes.

Ethnographers live and work with the group they're studying to try to see the world from the others' point of view. Two of the most famous of such studies are William F. Whyte's *Street Corner Society* (1993) and Elliot Liebow's *Tally's Corner* (1968). Both studies examined the world of working-class and poor men. Whyte's subjects were white, Italian men in Boston; Liebow's were black men in Washington, D.C. In both cases, readers learned more about the complexity in these men's lives

Anthropologists traditionally use ethnography to study cultures and societies that differ from their own. As a methodology, however, ethnography can be used to study any group. Sociologists often deploy the method to study particular groups in society in depth or to examine a particular environment or social issue in close detail: like urban street vendors, street gangs, or the close-knit community of Italian Americans in Little Italy to name a few.

SOCIOLOGY AND OUR WORLD

HIDDEN FACTS: ON THE POWER OF ETHNOGRAPHY

Why does ethnography and in-depth qualitative research sometimes help us answer questions about sensitive topics, like inequality in sexual and domestic violence?

Sensitive topics, like cheating on one's spouse or issues related to gender or sexual violence, are challenging to study sociologically for many reasons. And sometimes, when we only study them one way, we miss something important that ethnography can help to illustrate.

Ethnographic research collects information about individuals and their behaviors over time and often in extremely close detail. As a result, ethnographers amass data not only about how people describe themselves and their behavior—ethnographers record detailed information about what people *do* as well. Ethnographers engage with the people they are studying, participating in and observing many different realms of their lives and asking questions all along the way to help them better understand what they are recording. Alongside all of this observation, however, something else happens. Ethnographers often establish trusting relationships with those they are studying. As a result of this, ethnographies sometimes are able to discover information less accessible by other research methods. By the extensive engagement in their lives required of this research method, ethnographers are simply more likely to be present when those they are studying are ready to disclose information they might have previously concealed from researchers. And when those moments arise, good ethnographers have often earned the trust of their research participants (by showing up, keeping their promises, listening without judgment, and keeping their information confidential).

Consider one such discovery made from an ethnographic study of economically disadvantaged families in three separate cities (Boston, Chicago, and San Antonio). Rarely are ethnographic projects this large scale. A collection of sociologists collaborated to make this possible. The project was designed to gain more information about the impacts of welfare reform on low-income families (you can learn more about the project and data at www.jhu.edu/~welfare if you're interested). But the study revealed information about domestic abuse and sexual violence in the lives of low-income women than previous research had recognized.

In total, there were 256 separate families who participated in this study. More than one-third of the mothers in their sample (36 percent) reported sexual and physical abuse; another 6 percent reported that they had been abused sexually, but not physically; and an additional 26 percent revealed they had been abused physically, but not sexually. In total, more than two-thirds of the women in their study revealed that they had experienced domestic violence in some form (Burton, Purvin, and Garrett-Peters 2009). Domestic abuse, they discovered, was far more prevalent in low-income women's lives than previous research had suggested. Why?

Of all of the low-income women in their sample who reported domestic violence, only 10 percent of them reported that violence when they were directly asked about their past and current experiences with sexual and domestic violence. Nine in 10 women who had experienced domestic violence simply did not share that information when asked; 71 percent of the women revealed this during discussions of other topics that triggered information about domestic violence. For instance, one woman in the study was asked about her work history during a routine visit from the researchers, their 21st visit to her home, and she shared that she'd had to quit her job because her former husband had given her a black eye and she was embarrassed to go to work with it. This information was shared in trust. Also, because ethnography requires repeated and sustained visits and observation, the additional 19 percent of women who experienced domestic violence in their study revealed that information unintentionally—either as a result of a crisis situation or when confronted with contradictory information. Sometimes, for instance, the researchers showed up during a crisis and abuse these women were unable to conceal was brought to the attention of the researchers because of the crisis situation. Finally, it took more than 7 months to learn this information about more than half of these women.

People are rarely *completely* open and honest about their lives (about the things they say, do, and have experienced) when they are in the presence of other people. This is because people know that sharing information often comes with consequences—some desirable, others undesirable. As a method, ethnography can sometimes help people share information they might not have otherwise revealed and can provide us with important information about their lives that might not be possible to gather using another research method.

than anyone had ever imagined. Recent field work among urban minorities has echoed these themes. Martin Sanchez-Jankowski (1991) lived with Latino gangs in Los Angeles. Contrary to popular assumptions that might hold that gangs are composed of children from broken homes, adrift and delinquent because they are psychologically maladjusted, Sanchez-Jankowski found that most came from intact families, were psychologically better adjusted than non–gang members, and saw gang membership as a reasonable economic alternative to unemployment and poverty. Gangs provided good steady jobs, high wages (with high risks), and the rich social relationships that come from community. Similarly, Elijah Anderson's (1992,

2000) research on young black men in inner city Philadelphia and Victor Rios's (2011) research on young black and Latino men in Oakland, California demonstrate that lower-class Latino and black men's lives are much more complex than our one-dimensional stereotypes might reveal.

Ethnography taxes our powers of observation and stretches our sociological muscles to try to see the world from the point of view of other people. Philippe Bourgois (1995) lived for 3 years in New York City's Spanish Harlem, studying the culture of crack dealers. Loic Wacquant (2003) trained for more than 3 years right alongside local boxers in a training gym on Chicago's South Side. Mitchell Duneier (1999) hung out with unlicensed and often homeless street vendors in New York. And Sudhir Venkatesh (2008) was "gang leader for a day" in a gang on Chicago's South Side. Ethnographic methods enable us to see people's worlds up close, in intimate detail, bringing out both subtle patterns and structural forces that shape social realities.

INTERVIEW STUDIES. The most typical type of qualitative study uses **interviews** with a small sample. These studies use a **purposive sample**, which means that respondents are not selected randomly and are not representative of the larger population but selected *purposively*—that is, each subject is selected precisely because he or she possesses certain characteristics that are of interest to the researcher. As with every method, there are strengths and weaknesses—things we can learn and things we will be unable to learn. One problem with interview studies is not the size of the sample but the fact that the sample is not a probability sample—that is, it is not a random sample, but rather the sample is selectively drawn to make sure that specific characteristics are included or excluded. Purposive samples do not allow sociologists to generalize about their results as reliably as they can with random samples. However, they do enable researchers to identify common themes in the data and can sensitize us to trends in attitudes or behaviors among specifically targeted groups of people.

For example, let's say you wanted to study feelings of guilt among new mothers, to see how much these feelings were influenced by television shows and magazine articles that instruct women on how to be good mothers. It wouldn't make much sense to conduct a random sample, because you wouldn't get enough new mothers in the sample. You could use a "snowball" technique—asking one new mother to refer you to others. Or you could draw a random sample from a nonrandom population—if, for example, the manufacturers of baby foods could be persuaded to give you their mailing lists of new mothers and you selected every hundredth name on the list. (We discuss sampling later.)

Interviews allow us to gather a different quality of information than we might from something like a survey. Consider asking someone to, on a survey, categorize their level of support for (or opposition to) easy access to abortion for women in the United States on a scale from 1 to 5 (1 being completely opposed, 3 being neither opposed nor supportive, and 5 being completely supportive). Now consider asking someone in person to explain their views about abortion, having the opportunity to stop them to ask them to explain something in more detail along the way. The first might enable us to state the average level of support among Americans for abortion. But the latter helps us interpret what that level of support might actually mean to those people who checked off "2" as a shorthand for their opinions about a complex social issue. Although some scholars differ as to the utility of different methods, it is probably most accurate to say that different research methods and kinds of data provide different kinds of information about the social world. And depending on what kind of information you want to gather, you might need to select a different research method to help you access it.

---

interview
Research method in which a researcher asks a small group of people open-ended questions.

purposive sample
Sample in which respondents are not selected randomly and are not representative of the larger population but are selected precisely because they possess certain characteristics of interest to the researcher.

HOW DO WE KNOW WHAT WE KNOW?

INTERVIEWING PEOPLE ABOUT HOW THEY ANSWER SURVEY QUESTIONS ABOUT ETHNICITY

We've been collecting data about race for a long time. It's a standard question on surveys. Today, when you fill out the U.S. Census for your household, you are asked "What is Person 1's race?" (you're person 1 if you're filling out the survey for the whole household). It used to be that you could only check one box, but today you are told to "Mark one or more boxes"—more of a "check all that apply" sort of approach to collecting data on race. You're also asked to provide information about your ethnicity. And in the 1980s, sociologist Mary Waters (1990) noticed that people were becoming more likely to add an ethnicity as well (like Irish, German, Italian, etc.). Ethnic identity appeared to be in flux for a portion of the U.S. population: white people. She was fascinated and wondered what it meant. How were white people deciding what to select, and why might some people have been making different decisions about this question than they had in the past?

To figure this out, Waters conducted interviews. She sat down with a purposive sample of people from different racial and ethnic backgrounds and asked them a predetermined list of questions. It started with her showing the interviewee the ancestry question from the Census form. They were asked "How would you answer this question?" and "Why?" Waters discovered that a number of factors shaped how white people decided to answer this question: knowledge about one's own ancestors, surname, and the relative rankings of groups.

Some of these make more sense than others on the face of them. For instance, if you know your parents or grandparents immigrated to the United States from Ireland, identifying as "Irish" seems natural. If you're last name is among the most popular Irish surnames (e.g., Murphy, Kelly, or O'Sullivan), you might identify as "Irish" even if you have a relatively mixed ethnic background. But she also discovered that many white people identify with an ancestry not because of their actual ancestry, genealogy or surname, but based off of stereotypes they have about the relative desirability or undesirability of particular ancestries. Consider one interviewee Waters calls Sean O'Brien. He has mixed ancestry, but identifies as Irish. Here's an excerpt from his interview:

O'Brien: I always say I am Irish. Because I am proud to be Irish. On my father's side, my grandmother was born in Ireland and my grandfather was born here in the United States. On my mother's side, her mother was born in Ireland and her father was born in Scotland.

Waters: Do you ever say you are Scottish?

O'Brien: No, I never say I am Scottish.

Waters: Why?

O'Brien: We used to tease my mother about being part Scottish…. we said, "I am not telling anyone I am part Scottish because they are so cheap," and all that. We teased my mother, it got to be a habit, a family joke.

Sean O'Brien would have only filled out "Irish" on a survey. But that's not actually his ethnicity, not in a genealogical sense anyway. And Waters had participants with far less of an ancestral claim to a particular ethnicity than Sean's claim to be Irish or Italian, for instance, because they felt they shared a lot in common with some cultural stereotype of Irish or Italian people. It doesn't mean that the information we gathered on surveys about ethnicity is false. But through interviews, Waters was able to show that the ways we had been interpreting some of that information was incorrect. But we needed the interviews to recognize this issue. (We'll read more about this example in Chapter 8 on race and ethnicity.)

Quantitative Analysis

4.2.3 Explain the elements that distinguish quantitative analyses from observational research, considering what kinds of questions these methods are designed to answer.

Lots of sociologists find sources of data that make it harder to see the individual trees that make up the forest that is society, but give us a much more accurate picture of things that are missed when we are examining social life up close and personal. This collection of methods involves quantitative data analysis, the use of surveys and other instruments and methodologies to understand those larger patterns that give structure and shape to our social world. So, although these methods are sometimes less attuned to analyzing social interactions, for instance, they provide access to information about social institutions that are difficult to surmise from interviews and observations alone. They allow us to draw larger conclusions and to examine how different people's opinions, experiences, and opportunities fit with others who are "like" them (in terms of occupying similar identities and locations in society).

Here, we'll explore why surveys are such a powerful tool used by sociologists. And although surveys are a tool that is used to attempt to collect massive amounts of data from large samples and populations in efficient ways, sociologists also have a set of methods that attempts to collect data from large groups, issues, and ideas, without asking anything from people at all. We'll explore some of those methods as well. As people live in and engage with the world, they sometimes leave traces of their behavior, beliefs, and experiences, bits of data we can collect systematically to examine something in closer detail. This will involve understanding how to take a meaningful sample from a population of people you're interested in studying, what kinds of samples provide the most accurate information, and what it means to gauge the accuracy of information from a sample in the first place.

SURVEYS. Surveys are among the most common methods that sociologists use to collect information about attitudes and behaviors. For example, you might be interested in how religion influences sexual behavior. A survey might be able to tell you whether an adolescent's religious beliefs influence whether he or she has had sex (it does) or whether a married person has committed adultery (it doesn't). Alternatively, you might also be able to assess whether people's sexual behavior influences their religious beliefs (this too, is true). Or a survey might address whether being a registered Republican or Democrat has any relationship to the types of sports one likes to watch on television (it does). To construct a survey, we first decide the sorts of questions we want to ask and how best to ask them. Although the simplest question would be a dichotomous question, in which "yes" and "no" were the only choices, this form of question provides limited information. For example, if you asked, "Do you believe that sex before marriage is always wrong?," you might find out some distribution of moral beliefs, but such answers would tell you little about how people *use* that moral position, whether they apply it to themselves or to others, and how they might deal with those who transgress.

Usually, we ask questions that can be graded on a scale. The most common form is a **Likert scale** that arranges possible responses from lowest to highest. Instead of a simple "yes" or "no" answer, survey respondents are asked to place themselves on a continuum at one of (typically) five or seven points. When respondents answer a question on a survey by saying whether we "strongly agree," "agree," "neither agree nor disagree," "disagree," or "disagree strongly," the researchers are using a Likert scale. We do this to create *quantitative measures* from issues that might resist quantification. Here, we're attempting to convert data about the social world into numerical form so that we can study it using statistical methods. This is valuable because we can study large samples drawn from even larger populations. But it's important to remember that sometimes, information can get lost in translation.

Once we've decided what questions to ask, we have to decide to whom to ask them. But you can't ask everyone: It would cost too much, take too long, be impractical, and in some cases, be impossible to analyze. Sociologists take a **sample** (or a subset) of the population they want to study. (We've already discussed the purposive sampling of interview studies; sampling is part of almost all research; sociologists always have to decide who to study.) Surveys are often done by telephone or by mail. A **random sample** is a sample in which every member has an equal (non-zero) chance of being selected, sort of like tossing pieces of paper with one person's name on each piece into a hat. Another good type of sample, the **systematic sample**, is done

---

Likert scale

The most common form of survey coding, it arranges possible responses from lowest to highest.

sample

A limited group of research subjects whose responses are statistically developed into a general theme or trend that can be applied to the larger whole.

random sample

A sample chosen by an abstract and arbitrary method, that gives each person an equal chance of being selected, such as tossing a piece of paper with each person's name on it into a hat.

systematic sample

A type of sample that starts at a random position on a list and selects every *n*th unit (skip interval) of a population until the desired sample size is reached.

by choosing every tenth name in a telephone book or every thousandth name on the voter registration list. Technically, this sample is not random, because the researcher is following a system, but it is still a good method because it is not biased.

When you take a random sample, you assume that those not in the population from which you are choosing your sample are themselves or are representative of the entire population from whom you're interested in collecting data. For example, choosing from the phone book would exclude those people who don't have telephones (who tend to be rural and conservative) as well as those who use only their cell phones and are not listed (who tend to be urban and liberal). Often the differences between different groups of people are what you actually want to study. In that case, you'd take a **stratified sample**, in which you divide people into different groups before you construct your sample and ensure that you get an adequate number of members of each of the groups. A stratified sample divides the sample into proportions equal to the proportions found in the population at large and then randomly samples from the various groups.

Let's say you wanted to study racial attitudes in Chicago Heights, Illinois. (Chicago Heights is 41.5 percent African American, 23.3 percent white, 33.9 percent Hispanic, 2.9 percent multiracial, and 0.6 percent Native American [U.S. Census Bureau 2015].) A random sample might actually give you an inaccurate portrait because you might, inadvertently, have an unrepresentative sample, with too few or too many of a particular group. What if your random sample was gathered through voter records, (a common method)? You'd lose all those residents who are not registered to vote, who tend to be concentrated among minorities and the poor, as well as the young (and the median age in Chicago Heights is 31.2 years old [U.S. Census Bureau 2015]). What if you called every one-hundredth number in the phone book? You'd lose all those who were unlisted or who don't have landline phones and over-represent statistically those who have several numbers (and would therefore stand a higher chance of being called). So your random sample could turn out to be not very **representative**. A stratified sample would enable you to match, in the sample, the percentages in the actual population. This means that the data have greater **generalizability**.

Surveys are extremely common in the contemporary United States. There are dozens of organizations devoted to polling Americans on every possible attitude or behavior on a daily basis. Some surveys are created by websites or popular magazines, and these sometimes get attention for their results even though most fail to use valid methods of sampling and questioning. Still, numerous surveys that we see, hear, or read about are developed and privately administered by bona-fide research organizations like Roper or Gallup; other sound surveys are publicly financed and available to all researchers for low or no cost, such as the General Social Survey at the National Opinion Research Center out of the University of Chicago. The General Social Survey has been surveying U.S. attitudes since 1972, and so one can easily track changes in those attitudes over time (see FIGURE 4.4).

SURVEY QUESTIONS.   Surveys are the mainstay of sociological research, but coming up with good survey questions is difficult. The wording of the question, the possible answers, even the location of the question in the survey questionnaire can change the responses. For one thing, we have to construct questions that everyone we want to survey will understand. But beyond that, we need everyone reading the questions to understand them in the same way. Take a classic example (Rugg 1941). In a national survey, respondents were asked two slightly different questions about freedom of speech:

- Do you think the United States should forbid public speeches against democracy?
- Do you think the United States should allow public speeches against democracy?

When the results came in, 75 percent of respondents would *not allow* the speeches, but only 54 percent would *forbid* them. Surely "forbid" and "not allow" mean the same thing in practice, but the wording changed the way people thought about the issue. In many cases asking both questions helps us test the validity of our methods—whether

stratified sample
Sample in which research subjects are divided into proportions equal to the proportions found in the population at large.

representative sample
A sample that is scientifically designed to accurately reflect a larger population.

generalizability
Also called external validity or applicability; the extent to which the results of a study can be generalized to the larger population.

FIGURE 4.4 The General Social Survey (GSS)

This figure tracks Americans' opinions surrounding social inequalities along the lines of race, class, gender, and sexuality. The lines chart shifts in Americans' opinions about specific issues to do with inequality. Here, you can see the proportion of Americans who: (1) disagree with the statement, "most men are better suited emotionally for politics than are most women"; (2) say we are spending "too little" when asked, "Are we spending too much, too little, or about the right amount on assistance to the poor?"; (3) who claim that "sexual relations between two adults of the same sex" are "not wrong at all"; and (4) who say "yes" when told that "African-Americans have worse jobs income and housing than white people" and asked whether this is due to discrimination. As you can see here, there has been less progress on Americans' opinions about racial inequality measured this way than there has on Americans' opinions about these other types of social inequality.

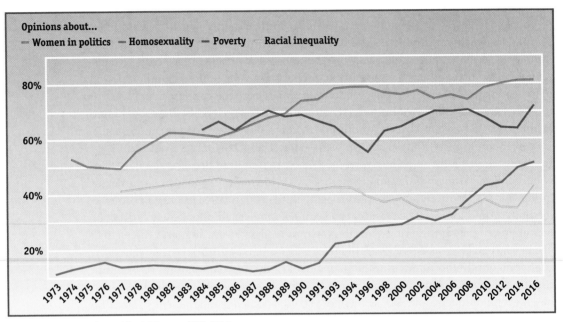

SOURCE: Data from General Social Survey, 1972–2016.

the question is measuring what we think it is measuring. But researchers are still trying to figure out how to avoid this problem. The same issue occurs on issues related to sexuality. A great deal of survey questions that have been asked for many years word the question negatively. Consider the GSS variable in Figure 4.4, "What about sexual relations between two adults of the same sex—do you think it is always wrong, almost always wrong, wrong only sometimes, or not wrong at all?" We could equally ask whether people think sexual relations between two adults of the same sex are "always right, almost always right…" etc. And when questions about sexuality are worded that way, people tend to, on average, express more sexually liberal positions on surveys.

Have you ever shoplifted? No? Well, then, have you ever taken an object from a store without paying for it? Respondents are much more likely to answer "yes" to the second version because it somehow doesn't seem as bad, even though it's really the same thing. Do you think women should have the right to have an *abortion*? How about the right to *end their pregnancy*? You guessed it—far more respondents favor the right to end a pregnancy than to have an abortion. Should gays and lesbians be allowed to serve in the military? What about "homosexuals"? In a recent survey, half the respondents got a survey with the words "gay and lesbian" and the other half got "homosexuals." Those who got "gay and lesbian" scored 11 percent higher than those who got "homosexual." Maybe it's the word *sex* contained in "homosexual" (Blow 2010)?

How about the placement of the question in the survey? Respondents are much more likely to respond honestly to the shoplifting question if it's near the end of the survey. When sensitive or embarrassing questions come early, respondents are put off, wondering how intimate the questions are going to get. After they get a little practice by answering questions about their gender, race, age, and occupation, then they are able to handle the tough questions more readily.

Secondary Analysis and Other Types of Data

4.2.4 Summarize the kinds of questions and sources of data that qualify as secondary analyses.

Given the enormous amount of time and money it takes to conduct a survey from scratch, many sociologists rely on the survey data previously collected by others (like the U.S. Census, or the General Social Survey, for instance). **Secondary analysis** involves reanalyzing data that have already been collected. Research on baby names that we discussed in Chapter 1 often involves secondary analysis and creating data sets that include names as meaningful variables. Often this new analysis looks at the data in a different way or compares different variables. Others may need to use existing historical data. After all, if you're interested in political debates in seventeenth-century France, you can't very well conduct a survey or interview the participants.

For example, let's say you were interested in the effect of political persuasions on moral attitudes and behavior. Perhaps your hypothesis was that the more conservative someone is politically, the more conservative one might be morally. You've operationalized your variables on political persuasion by assuming conservatives are registered Republican and liberals are registered Democratic and that morally conservative people will disapprove of divorce and be less likely to get a divorce. You decide to test the hypothesis that because Republicans are less likely to approve of divorce than Democrats are, then Republicans are less likely to get divorced (a basic "attitudes ought to lead to behavior" hypothesis). Importantly, these research methods can be either quantitative or qualitative and often combine elements of both.

You find that a reputable social scientific researcher had done a survey of a sample of Americans, but this researcher was interested only in gender and racial differences in moral attitudes and behavior. It's possible that the research contains other background variables, such as age, political persuasion, educational background, or occupation. Secondary analysis of the existing data will enable you to answer your questions. In addition, you might be able to find data on statewide divorce rates and statewide political attitudes; although these will not answer the question at the more individual level, they can point to broad patterns about whether conservatives are true to their beliefs and so less likely to divorce. (The answer is apparently no; states that voted Republican in the last few presidential elections have higher divorce rates than states that voted Democratic).

Also, there may be different forms of data you can use. Sometimes, for example, researchers will conduct an interview and use only a numeric scale to register responses. But then certain answers to certain questions might prompt the interviewer to ask for more information. These responses may be written down as notes or sentences on the initial interview forms. Going back to these forms might require you to do content analysis of the narrative responses people gave to the questions. Although field studies do not permit exact **replication**—the cultural group you study is indelibly changed by the fact that *you* have studied it—one can reasonably "replicate" (reproduce) a field study by careful research. For example, if you are in the field, doing an ethnography, and you keep a running record of both your observations and the research strategies and decisions you made while in the field, other researchers can follow your decision making and attempt to understand a similar phenomenon.

CONTENT ANALYSIS. **Content analysis** can be done either *quantitatively* or *qualitatively* and is often undertaken in both ways. The method involves an intensive reading of certain "texts"—perhaps books, or pieces of conversation, or a set of articles from a newspaper or magazine, advertisements, or even snippets from television shows. Some content analysis involves taking a random, systematic, or other type of sample of such pieces of conversation or media representations and then develop intricate coding procedures for analyzing them. These answers can then be

secondary analysis
Analysis conducted using data previously collected by others for other reasons.

replication
One of the main principles of the scientific method, replication is the ability of an entire experiment or study to be duplicated by others.

content analysis
Research method in which one analyzes artifacts and cultural "texts" (books, movies, TV programs, magazine articles, advertisements, and so on) instead of people.

analyzed quantitatively, and one can generate observable variations in the presentations of those texts.

If you want to know if the media images of girls or boys have changed much over the past 10 years, then content analysis might enable you to do this. You might choose ten magazines, the five most popular among boys and girls of a certain age. Then

SOCIOLOGY AND OUR WORLD

SHIFTS IN MEN'S FACIAL HAIR STYLES ARE PATTERNED

What can we learn from patterns in men's facial hair?

Just like baby names, all sorts of elements of our identities are associated with tastes. What kind of haircut you get, what style of clothing you wear, what sorts of music you like (and dislike), and more are issues that feel deeply personal. They are elements of our identity that we might feel are part of what makes each of us unique. Ironically, crafting an identity requires you to do things that are not unique, to connect yourself with different groups through decisions about what you wear, what you believe, how you act, what you like, and more. And although these things can feel like deeply private decisions, expressions of our unique selves, sociologists understand that how we make all sorts of decisions related to identity expression are dramatically influenced by the world around us. And for this reason, tastes in fashion (just like baby names) follow patterns that we can study to learn more about the world around us.

Take fashions in men's facial hair. Lots of things shape whether and what kind of facial hair men wear. In the 1970s, sociologist Dwight Robinson (1976), interested in patterns in fashions and trends, sought to answer this question—and he did so using a content analysis methodology. Robinson wanted to figure out something that would allow him to collect some kind of meaningful sample from a single society over a prolonged period of time. Men rarely record their shaving preferences. So, a survey is unlikely to have this information. But magazines include pictures. And pictures can be coded for different configurations of facial hair, like beards, mustaches, side burns, clean shaven faces, or some combination. Certainly magazines don't represent everyone in a society, but magazines with wide circulation might represent cultural ideals associated with shaving. Robinson was intrigued.

What publication did he choose? He went through approximately 130 years of the *Illustrated London News*. And he counted all of the beards, sideburns, mustaches, and clean shaven faces he saw. Take a look at what he discovered.

As you can see, at the start of Robinson's study, clean-shaven faces were a bit more popular in the magazine than they were between 1884 and 1888 (the least popular time for clean shaven faces depicted here). Being clean shaven became much more popular over time and you can also see trends in the popularity sideburns, beards, and mustaches as well. By the 1970s, facial hair was going out of style. Whether that trend continued forward is an open question. You might have opinions about whether beards are "in" again. Certainly, there are some limitations to Robinson's study. But he used content analysis to answer a question we might not have been able to meaningfully answer without it. It's only one answer; but it's an interesting one.

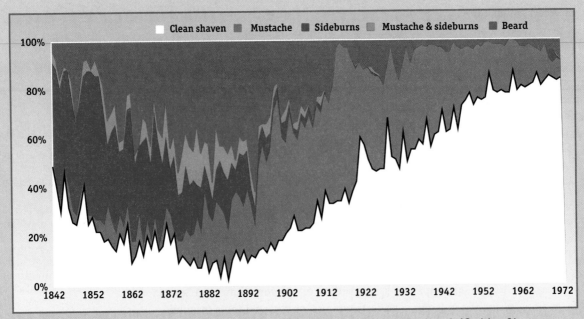

SOURCE: Data from Robinson, Dwight E. "Fashions in Shaving and Trimming of the Beard." *American Journal of Sociology* 81, 5 (1976): 1133–1141.

Content analysis of media (such as movies and magazines) can be used to chart the differences in gender ideals. Women today are less likely to be defined only as mothers, or in relation to their husbands' occupations, and more likely to be seen as independent and complex individuals. But these displays of women are still among the dominant ways women are depicted in media and popular culture.

you might look at all the issues of those magazines in the month of August of every year for the past 10 years and look at the sections called "Back-to-School Fashions." You could devise a coding scheme for these fashions, to judge whether they are more or less gender conforming in terms of style, color, and the like. Then you could see if and how the race or class of the models who are wearing those clothes changes. Each of the factors you are measuring is a variable: The independent variable is type of magazine (whether it is intended for boys or intended for girls); and the dependent variables are the details of the way fashions are shown: the models' race, the color and style of the clothes.

Strictly speaking, content analysis often involves a type of quantification—counting various elements associated with something in which you are interested in from a sample (like the number of beards in a magazine, for instance). But as we mentioned, research like this often does a bit more than counting alone. And when that is the case, the research is engaging in a method referred to as **discourse analysis**, which is slightly different. Discourse analysis is more interested in patterns of portrayal evident in a collection of "texts" that might be difficult to quantify.

For instance, sociologists Cheryl Cooky, Michael Messner, and Michela Musto (2015) updated a longitudinal content and discourse analysis study of women's representation in sports media over a 25-year period. Separate studies collected data on women's representation in sports media in 1989, 1993, 1999, 2004, 2009, and 2014. This allows them to discuss women's representation today, but also to talk about how women's representation has changed over time. It's probably not a surprise to hear that sports media is gender-biased, with an inequitable amount of time and attention spent on men's sports.

Cooky, Messner, and Musto's (2015) research is of interest here because it's a wonderful example of research using both methods: It is both a content and discourse analysis of sports media. They're interested in questions that require counting things. For instance, they calculate the precise amount of time men's and women's sports receive coverage. But they are also interested in questions that involve analyzing the quality of the time dedicated to reporting on men's and women's sports and men and women athletes. Are women's sports, for instance, more likely to be covered in ways that highlight athletic prowess and competence? Are women's sports trivialized? Are women more likely to be sexualized in the time dedicated to reporting on their accomplishments? And if so, how? These questions involve analyzing quantities and qualities associated with sports media. They recorded 3 week blocks of sports media news on three major networks (CBS, ABC, and NBC) in addition to ESPN. Their sample was stratified by sport season so that they would be sure to collect data from periods of time when different sports are played. And they code all of those hours of broadcasting for each of the questions they asked.

discourse analysis

Is more interested in patterns of portrayal evident in a collection of "texts" that might be difficult to quantify.

FIGURE 4.5 Main Broadcast Network Coverage of Women's Sports (1989–2014) and SportsCenter Coverage of Women's Sports (1999–2014)

Time dedicated to women's sports and women athletes has not changed much in recent history, but the changes that have occurred are toward less representation of women's sports and women athletes (not more).

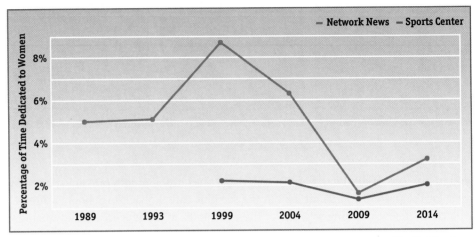

SOURCE: Data from Cooky, Cheryl, Michael A. Messner, and Michela Musto, (2015). "It's Dude Time!": A Quarter Century of Excluding Women's Sports in Televised News and Highlight Shows. *Communication & Sport*, 1-27.

What's more, they used the same sampling method and coding measures across each year they ran the study. So, it's a great comparison of shifts over 25 years. The study has discovered a great deal. One of the most striking discoveries, however, is that women's representation has shrunk over this period (see FIGURE 4.5), not grown. Women's sports and women athletes are dedicated *less* coverage (as a proportion of all sports coverage) today than they were 25 years ago!

Studies using content and discourse analysis are important illustrations of the sociological axiom that virtually nothing is off limits to sociologists. We are interested in just about every element, cultural product, form of behavior, and more that exists in society. Content analysis studies have considered how different races are depicted in high school textbooks, proportions of protagonists who are men in children's stories, online descriptions people leave when looking for love, sex, and relationships in the digital world, and much, much more.

NETWORK ANALYSIS. Sometimes, we're less interested in information that can be gathered from texts that represent larger issues and patterns we are interested in studying. Sometimes, we want to know something about relationships between people and groups, but that information might not be information that any individual member of the group could tell us. Rather, to gather this information might require examining the social networks that are the building blocks of relationships and groups. A **social network** refers to webs of relationships held together by what sociologists refer to as "ties." **Social ties** refer to the connections between individuals and groups. And ties are measured not just in their existence (i.e., Do you know Sally or not?), but also in their strength (i.e., Would you trust Sally to watch your dog while you're on vacation? How often do you two eat meals together?).

Ties vary a great deal in terms of content and strength. And the simplest way to think about what social ties is that they are stories about our relationships with each other. Simple stories are often associated with *weak* ties, as in the following example: Sean is the barista who makes my latte whenever I visit the campus café. More complex stories are often associated with *strong* ties: Samantha and I met in high school, play intramural sports together, dated in high school, but now just play laser tag on weekends and co-host horror movie viewing parties at my house every

social network

Often conceived as a web of social relationships, a type of group that is both looser and denser than a formal group but connects people to each other, and, through those connections, with other people.

social ties

Refer to the social connections or relationships between individuals and groups.

other Thursday evening. Sociologists who study social networks know that everyone has strong and weak ties. Strong ties provide love, support, and assistance at the times we need it most. But strong ties are also "strong" because they are reinforced by lots of other ties in a social network. If you need someone to babysit your kid, or you need to borrow a couple hundred bucks to make rent one month, strong ties are your best bet.

But weak ties are valuable for different reasons. Weak ties often bring with them new information. So, if you're looking for work and none of your strong ties have any leads, you might be better off exploiting one of your weak ties—someone who has knowledge of a social network to which you are only loosely connected. Sociologist Mark Granovetter (1973) refers to this quality as **the strength of weak ties**—the notion that weak ties are valuable because they provide new information that is often less available from strong ties. Weak ties allow people to bridge what sociologists refer to as **structural holes**. We can learn a lot about people from both what the social networks look like that they belong to as well as where they are positioned within those social networks.

Consider an example. Lots of research on college students has shown that peer groups play an important role in student life—they're a good predictor of whether and how students drink, how often they attend class, how caught up they are in their courses, and much more. And here's the hitch, not all college student friend networks look the same—you form different kinds of social networks. Sociologist Janice McCabe (2016) wanted to know both what sorts of advantages and disadvantages different friendship networks might produce. In a close examination of the friendship networks of 67 students at a university in the Midwest, McCabe discovered that college student friendship networks could be classified into three separate types. And different kinds of students pursued different types of friendship networks: "tight-knitter" (single group of friends who almost all know each other), "compartmentalizer" (students who are part of a couple different clusters of close friends), and "samplers" (friendships with individuals who do not know each other).

What your friendship network in college looks like might tell sociologists more about you than you realize. We might, for instance, be able to guess whether you are white or not. We also have a bit of information about how susceptible you might be to forms of peer pressure likely to get in the way of you completing college on time or receiving the best grades you are capable of earning. Tight-knitters, for instance, certainly benefit from the social support they receive from their friendship networks. But they have to be more on the lookout for friends who might drag them down academically than do compartmentalizers.

Interestingly, McCabe also studied this same group of students years later, after they'd left college. Again, she asked them about their friendship networks and who they remained in contact with from their college friendship networks. What did she find? The friendship network "types" that her sample pursued remained fairly stable, with one exception. Tight-knitters and compartmentalizers were very likely to have the same kinds of friendship networks after they left college. Samplers, however, mostly turned into tight-knitters themselves. The content of those networks shifted a lot. Only about one in four friends from college were still part of their networks after college. But, when they made new friends and forged new friendship networks, tight-knitters and compartmentalizers found the same "types" of networks even though they were full of new groups of people. Examining friendship networks helps us learn something about friendship and what it does for people (how it can help, and sometimes hurt, us). But people themselves might be unaware of what their networks look like or how they compare. By examining the social network, we can sometimes learn things about people and groups that the individuals themselves are not capable of telling us.

"the strength of weak ties"
Mark Granovetter's discovery that weak ties are valuable precisely because they provide new information that is often less available from strong ties.

structural holes
A concept from social network research, the term refers to a gap between two networks of individuals who have complementary sources to information.

Making the Right Comparisons

4.2.5 Understand the ways sociologists select among and between research methods to provide comparisons that enable them to scientifically examine social life and behavior.

No matter what research method we choose, it is always important to make sure we are comparing things that are, in fact, comparable (see TABLE 4.1). Otherwise, one risks making claims that turn out not to be true. Consider an example of how researchers compared the wrong groups. You've probably heard the idea that homosexuality is often the result of a certain family dynamic. Specifically, psychiatrists found that the gay men they saw in therapy often had over-dominant mothers and absent fathers (which, the theory goes, *caused* their homosexuality by preventing the men from making the healthy gender transition away from mother and identifying with father [Bieber et al. 1962]). Such a dynamic would, the researchers believed, keep them "identified" with their mothers and therefore "feminine" in their psychological predisposition. For decades, this family dynamic was the foundation of the psychological treatment of gay men. The problem was in the comparative group. The gay men in therapy were compared with the family arrangements of heterosexual men who were not in therapy.

It turned out, though, that the gay men who were not in therapy did not have over-dominant mothers and absent fathers. And it also turned out that heterosexual men in therapy *did* have over-dominant mothers and absent fathers. In other words, having an over-dominant mother and an absent father didn't seem to be the cause of homosexuality but was probably a good predictor of whether a man, gay or straight, decided to go into therapy.

TABLE 4.1 Research Methodologies

Method	Key Strengths	Problems/Weaknesses
Experiments	Variables can be carefully controlled and monitored to help isolate the effects of a single element under consideration. Replication is relatively easy.	It is difficult to control independent variables. Ethical considerations prevent experiments on many issues that might interest us. Whether people behave differently "in the lab" than outside cannot be meaningfully assessed.
Field Studies	Sociologists can conduct research directly with people they want to study. Populations can be identified that are of interest to the research before a specific hypothesis has been formed. The information gathered is some of the most in depth data we have about social behavior. What people say can be confirmed by examining (over time) what they do.	Research findings are difficult to generalize to other populations.
Interview Studies	A carefully selected sample makes it easy to identify common themes and can highlight trends in experiences, strategies of explanation, opportunities, behavior, and talk within a very specific group.	Generalizing about results is not reliable because the sample group (even when extremely large) is often very targeted.
Surveys	It is easy and convenient to collect large amounts of data about equally large numbers of people. Representative samples can be drawn from populations of interest (sometimes, entire populations can be studied).	Much of what we might want to know about the world is difficult to distill into survey questions. Data corruption can occur in survey research as well, often due to poorly worded questions and the order in which answers are provided.
Secondary Analysis	It is often easier and cheaper to rely on information collected by others. Sometimes, this is the only way to replicate a field study. This method can also enable us to attempt to more quickly answer research questions.	Researchers are completely dependent upon the original data and sources. So, any problems with those data are passed on to subsequent secondary analysis as well.
Content Analysis	Researchers can often answer questions that people would not be able to answer meaningfully. If samples are drawn well, this research can also be generalizable and replicable.	Constructing a sample that is free of bias can be challenging. Subjectivity and bias may also present in the coding of texts (which is why many scholars using this method will have more than one coder and present data on how reliably they each coded the same texts in the same ways).
Network Analysis	Researchers can make discoveries about groups and relationships that are unknown to members of those groups. Often, by examining social networks, we can learn information that would be difficult to acquire in any other way.	Network analysis attempts to quantify the types of connections we have with people ("strong" and "weak" ties) and sometimes treats all connections as though they are equal. Whether it is possible to quantify relationships in this way and whether this assumption is warranted is subject to some disagreement.

The same problems exist in a wide variety of issues and phenomena sociologists study. Consider another example: It is often assumed that divorce has negative consequences for children, both in terms of their school achievement and in terms of their psychological health and well-being. But such studies were based on comparisons of children from divorced and married parents and never examined the quality of the marriage. Children from intact *but unhappy* marriages actually do worse (have lower grades and more psychological problems) than children from divorced families! Perhaps the *right* comparison is to consider how much better off children from divorced families are than they were before their parents divorced (research we discuss more in Chapter 12).

Making the right comparisons is a challenging element of sociological research. And because social life is organic and constantly changing, the research methods sociologists use to study this process as it takes place offer valuable insights and are subject to a range of problems that can affect the outcome of our research. Consider TABLE 4.1, which summarizes some of the primary contributions and problems of each research method we have described so far.

---

iSOC AND YOU Types of Sociological Research Methods

All of the methods we have discussed can all be used to address the elements of iSoc. For example, network analysis may help locate you in your social worlds, identifying the matrix that enables you to create your *identity*. Or they may be used to plot your *interactions* with others. Similarly, large scale surveys can identify patterns of *inequality* and help delineate the ways that the various aspects of your *identity intersect* to produce sets of experiences and opportunities that you might share with others who are similarly positioned in society. And other methods help us to better understand how and why these patterns exist and what they might mean.

4.3 Research Methods NOW

Sociological research today is as innovative and exciting as it has ever been. Consider this: The composition of families changed more in your parents' lifetimes than it had throughout all of U.S. history. Schools, workplaces, religious life, and more have all seen similar seismic shifts. The sociologist Jürgen Habermas once wrote, "It takes an earthquake to make us aware that we had regarded the ground on which we stand everyday as unshakable" (1989: 100). These shifts illustrate a more general truism in sociology; social life could be organized dramatically differently than it is. Understanding social change and when social change fails to happen is a primary concern for sociological research. And contemporary sociological scholarship is well aware that social life is "on the move." Things are changing at a rapid pace. And our research methods have evolved and are continuously applied in innovative ways to keep up.

As the previous sections have addressed a consideration of research methods as different types of optical devices, this section addresses some of the ethical concerns inherent in this project. What kinds of images and data should sociologists be allowed to collect? What sorts of obligations should they have in ensuring that their research is not harming those from whom they are attempting to collect data? These are complex questions without easy answers. And the answers are changing all of the time as new sources of data produce new kinds of concerns.

In this section, we examine why sociology is better understood as an *explanatory* rather than *predictive* science. Part of this has to do with the kinds of "truths" sociologists are attempting to uncover and our firm belief that a single capital "T" Truth about the questions that interest us often does not exist. Looking at social phenomena from different perspective enables us to understand that most social phenomena are just much more complex than that. We'll reexamine some of the basics of conducting sociological research, including information about how sociologists endeavor to be ethical while conducting their research. And we conclude with a discussion of some of the new methods sociologists are exploring today.

Social Science and the Problem of "Truth"

4.3.1 Explain what it means to suggest that sociology might be better thought of as an explanatory science than a predictive science.

One thing that is certain about social life is that nothing is certain about social life. Sociology is both a social *science*, sharing basic strategies and perspectives with the natural sciences, and a *social* science, attempting to study living creatures who often behave unpredictably and irrationally, for complex rational, emotional, or psychological reasons. Because a single "truth" is neither knowable nor even possible, social scientists approach their research with the humility of the curious but armed with a vast array of techniques that can help them approach "truths."

Even if truth is impossible, we can approach it. Like all other sciences, we approach it through addressing two central concerns, predictability and causality. **Predictability** refers to the ability to generate testable hypotheses from data and to "predict" the outcomes of some phenomenon or event. **Causality** refers to the relationship of some variable to the effects it produces. According to scientific requirements, a cause is termed "necessary" when it always precedes an effect and "sufficient" when it initiates or produces the effect. This is why, as you learned previously in this chapter *correlation* is a necessary, but insufficient, condition to establish a causal relationship. Put simply, all relationships between variables that are causal exhibit correlations, but not all correlations are causal.

To make matters more complex, sociologists study phenomena that are moving targets. For example, consider how this differs from another field. As a field of research, a great deal of what we have learned in Astronomy comes from what we know about the properties of a single phenomenon: light. Much of the "data" that we can collect about our solar system, galaxies, and outer space more broadly comes to us from a single source of information: light that we can gather on earth. It's not the only source of data astronomers use in their research, but it's the primary source of a great deal of data. And light always behaves the same way. Different elements, for instance, produce different characteristic colors when they burn. This is why fireworks are different colors. Copper, for instance, burns blue or green depending upon its chemical makeup. Magnesium burns white. And different combinations emit varying colors. Heat *causes* chemical compounds to produce visually distinct patterns. It's one of the ways we can gather information about the composition of stars—the "stuff" different stars are made of.

But here's the difference between a field like Astronomy and a field like Sociology—heat *always* produces the same effects under the same conditions. The effect of heat is measureable and predictable, because that effect is subject to laws that heat always obeys. The "stuff" that sociologists study is unlikely to exhibit these same qualities for a few different reasons. The effects that we measure are sometimes causal; though figuring out just what *causes* what is more difficult to ascertain when studying social life. But beyond that, even when we discover that one variable can be shown to *cause* a predictable change in another, the relationship is one that can change over time—it can decrease, intensify, disappear, reverse. And because of that, sociologists understand that we are often not seeking a single truth. Prediction is tricky business and terribly imperfect when it comes to social behavior. What sociology does well is to *explain* social phenomena.

predictability
The degree to which a correct prediction of a research outcome can be made.

causality
The term used when one variable causes another to change.

Predictability and Probability

4.3.2 Understand the difference between probability and predictability and some of the popular misunderstandings of probabilistic statements.

Auguste Comte (1798–1857), often considered the founder of sociology, actually founded a field that he called "social physics." He believed that human society follows permanent, unchangeable laws, just as the natural world does. If they know just two variables, temperature and air pressure, chemists can predict with 100 percent certainty whether a vial of H2O will be solid, liquid, or gas. In the same way, according to Comte, social physicists would be able to predict with 100 percent certainty the

HOW DO WE KNOW WHAT WE KNOW?

WE CAN'T PREDICT ALMOST ANYTHING AS WELL AS THE WEATHER

Do you check with the weather station before deciding what to wear? Do you check an app on your phone or mobile device when you get up in the morning to make a decision about bringing a jacket with you, or an umbrella? If you do, you are making a decision based on a prediction. It's what meteorologists (weathermen and women) are in the business of providing: predictions about the weather. They amass huge amounts of data about specific geographic locations and make predictions. What's fascinating is that they are often correct. We can predict weather better than we can predict almost anything. But most people have a dismal understanding of statistics and probability; yet, this is the language of prediction. And figuring out how to convey just what a prediction means (and doesn't mean) is tricky business. And meteorologists understand this as much as anyone and more than most.

To better understand this we have to look at it in aggregate to understand. So, if there's a 10 percent chance that it will rain tomorrow, it *probably* won't rain. But, on average, on 10 percent of the days that weather forecasts predict a "10 percent chance of rain," it should actually rain if the predictions are accurate. But, here's the twist: Many local weather forecasters lie about how likely precipitation is when they present probabilities of rain, snow, sleet, etc. In other words, local weather stations are guilty of telling people that something like rain is *more* likely than it actually is. Why do they do that? They go to a great deal of work to create an extremely accurate prediction and then, when they present it to the public, they lie in a way that makes that prediction worse than the one they know to be true. Historically, for instance, when the Weather Channel has predicted a 20 percent chance of rain, it has only rained on roughly 5 percent of those days (Silver 2012). Otherwise the Weather Channel is pretty close. For instance, it rains on almost exactly 50 percent of the days they say have a "50 percent chance of rain." That's a perfect prediction. It can't tell you whether it will rain on any individual day they predict a 50 percent chance of rain, but they do know that on one out of every two days they have given that prediction, it has, in fact, rained.

Local weather stations are even worse. They overestimate rain and snow quite a bit. There's a "wet bias"—the local meteorologist is saying precipitation is more likely than it actually is. Why? Meteorologists do this because they know most people do not have a strong understanding of probability (it's also why casinos are such lucrative businesses).

If your local weather station tells you that there is a 5 percent chance of rain, would you bring an umbrella? Many people wouldn't, thinking (correctly) that it is unlikely to actually rain. Weather prediction is precise enough, however, that 5 percent of the days that have the same prediction will actually have rain. You'd probably remember if you were rained on and didn't bring an umbrella because a meteorologist told you there was a 5 percent chance. But if you were told there was a "20 percent chance" and it rained, you'd be less likely to blame the prediction. They tell you rain is more likely than it actually is because they know it will make you more likely to change your behavior and understand what they actually mean when they tell you that there is a "20 percent chance of rain."

behavior of any human population at any time. Will the crowd outside the football game get violent? What political party will win the election? The answer should be merely a matter of analyzing the right variables. Comte, it turns out, was overly optimistic in his suspicions.

For 50 years, sociologists analyzed variables. They made a lot of predictions. Some were accurate, many not particularly accurate at all. It turns out that human populations have many more variables than the natural world. Yet predictability is of central concern to sociologists because we hope that if we can understand the variations of enough variables—like race, ethnicity, age, religion, region, and the like—we can reasonably guess what you would be more likely to do in a particular situation. And that—being able to use these variables to predict future behavior—is the essence of predictability.

The number of predictive variables increases dramatically as the group gets bigger and the behavior more complex, until the sociologist has no chance of ever finding them all. But even if we could, predicting human behavior might still be inaccurate in many cases because of the **observer effect**: People *know* that they are being studied. People change their behavior, and even their beliefs and attitudes, based on the situation that they are in, so the variables that are predictive today may not be tomorrow.

observer effect

The direct effect that observation can be shown to have on the phenomenon being observed.

Why Claiming Causality Is Tricky Business

4.3.3 Enumerate the necessary conditions to make a causal argument, and understand how and why this is a challenging standard to achieve in sociological research.

Students who take a foreign language in high school tend to be less xenophobic (fearful or suspicious of people from foreign countries). Does taking a foreign language decrease their level of xenophobia, or are xenophobic people less likely to sign up for foreign language classes? Questions about causality attempt to disentangle sociological puzzles like this one. Causality attempts to answer the question we have asked each other since primary school: Which came first, the chicken or the egg? Which "caused" which to happen? Which is the independent variable (the cause), and which is the dependent variable (the effect)?

In quantitative research, variable *A* is supposed to have a causal impact on variable *B*, but it is not always easy to decide which is the cause and which is the effect. Scientists use a number of clues. Let's look at the old idea that watching violence on television and in the movies (variable *A*) makes children violent (variable *B*).

Imagine I place 50 children at random into two groups. One group of 25 children watches a video about bears learning to share, and the other watches a video about ninjas chopping each others' heads off. I then monitor the children at play. Sure enough, most of the children who watched the sharing video are playing nicely, and the ones who watched the ninjas are pretending to chop each others' heads off. Can I establish a causal link? In other words, would this enable me to claim that watching the more violent video *caused* the children to behave more violently? The answer is "maybe." There are several other questions that you have to answer:

1. Does variable *B* come after variable *A* in time? Were the children calm and docile until after they watched the ninja video?
2. Is there a high correlation between variable *A* and variable *B*? That is, are all or almost all of the children who watched the ninja video behaving aggressively and all those who watched the bear video behaving calmly?
3. Are there any extraneous variables that might have contaminated the data? Maybe the sharing bears were so boring that the children who watched them are falling asleep.

4. Is there an observer effect that might be contaminating the data? Maybe I'm more likely to classify the behaviors of the ninja video kids as aggressive because I already have an idea that this is the effect that will be produced.

Any or all of these questions might render your assertion that watching ninja videos "causes" violent behavior unreliable. Sociologists must constantly be aware of possible traps and biases in their research—even in a controlled experimental setting like this one (see TABLE 4.2).

TABLE 4.2   Potential Traps in Experimental Research

Issue	Question to Ask	Applied?
Sequence	Does *A* come before *B* in time?	Were the children calm and docile when they watched the ninja video?
Correlation	Is there a high correlation between *A* and *B*?	Are all or almost all the children who watched the ninja video behaving aggressively?
Variables	Are there other variables that might have contaminated the data?	Is it possible that the sharing bears video is so boring that everyone just fell asleep?
You (the Researcher)	Is there an observer effect?	Are you more likely to classify the behaviors of ninja video kids as aggressive?

One must also always be on guard against logical fallacies that can lead you in the wrong direction. One problem is what is called the "**compositional fallacy**" in logic: comparing two groups that are different, assuming they are the same, and drawing an inference between them. Even if all members of category *A* are also members of category *B* doesn't necessarily mean that all members of category *B* are members of category *A*. In its classic formulation: Just because all members of the Mafia *(A)* are Italian *(B)* doesn't mean that all Italians *(B)* are members of the Mafia *(A)*.

compositional fallacy

An error in logic that results when comparing two groups that are different, assuming they are the same, and drawing an inference based on that false assumption.

Doing Sociological Research

4.3.4 Understand and describe the various steps involved in doing sociological research and how and why different types of research requires beginning at different steps.

The research method you use depends on the question you want to address in your research. Once you have formulated your research question, you'll begin to think about the best method you can use to generate the sort of information you will need to address it. Often, you have more than one option depending on which elements of the iSoc model you are interested in examining and stressing in your discoveries. And once you've chosen the method that would be best to use, you are ready to undertake the sociological research project. Research in the social sciences follows eight basic steps (see FIGURE 4.6). But it's best understood as a research cycle, because not all research begins at the same spot. Deductive research typically starts this process at step #1 here. But, not all research proceeds from the first step. Inductive research, as we learned previously, starts at a different stage in this process (typically steps 4 and 5 here come first in inductive research).

1. *Choosing an issue.*   What sort of issue interests you? Sometimes sociologists follow their curiosity, and sometimes they are invited to study an issue by an agency that will give them a grant for the research. Sometimes sociologists select a problem for research in the hopes that better understanding of the problem can lead to the formulation of policies that can improve people's lives.
2. *Defining the problem.*   Once you've chosen the issue you want to understand, you'll need to refine your questions and shape them into a manageable research topic.

FIGURE 4.6 Research in the Social Sciences

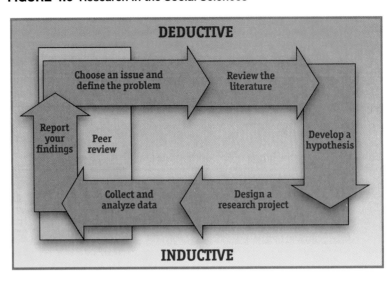

3. *Reviewing the literature.* Chances are that other social scientists have already done research on the issue you're interested in. You'll need to critically read and evaluate the previous research on the problem to help you refine your own thinking and to identify gaps in the research. Sometimes a review of the literature will find that previous research has actually yielded contradictory findings. Perhaps you can shed a clearer light on the issue—provide more evidence for one side or the other. Or perhaps you'll find the research has already been done conclusively, in which case you'll probably want to find another research question.

4. *Developing a hypothesis.* Having now reviewed the literature, you can state what you anticipate will be the result of your research. A **hypothesis** predicts a relationship between two variables, independent and dependent. As we learned previously, *deductive* research begins with this hypothesis before actually collecting and analyzing data; *inductive* research sometimes skips this step and returns to it later.

5. *Operationalize your variables.* Considering, for instance, the effects of divorce on children, you might develop a hypothesis that "children from divorced families are likely to have more psychological problems and lower school achievement than children in intact families." Now you have to figure out what sorts of variables will enable you to address this hypothesis. What kinds of outcomes would help you assess whether or not that prediction is true or not? In this case, you might use the marital status of the parents—whether or not they are divorced—as the independent variable. That's the aspect you would manipulate to see if it causes change in the dependent variable(s). The psychological and educational consequences are those dependent variables; changes in those areas are the things you would measure to get your results.

6. *Designing a project.* Now that you've developed a hypothesis, you are ready to design a research project to find out the answer. Choose the method best suited to the question or questions you want to ask. Would quantitative or qualitative methods be more appropriate to address this question? What sorts of data might enable you to test your hypotheses? For example, let's say the question you're interested in is the effect of divorce on children's educational achievement. You might consider a large survey project in which you compare students' test scores and measures of different types of behavior that might indicate psychological struggles and their parents' marital status. But if you wanted to know how divorce makes children *feel*, you might consider interviewing children from divorced and intact families to understand their emotional experiences in more depth.

hypothesis

A testable prediction for an event or phenomenon that assumes a relationship between two or more variables.

7. *Collecting data.* The next step of the research is to collect data that will help you answer your research question. The types of data that you collect will depend on the research method you identify and the questions you ask. But whatever research method you use, you must ensure that the data are valid and reliable. **Validity** means that your data must actually enable you to measure what you want to measure, and **reliability** means that another researcher can use the same data you used and would find similar results.

8. *Analyzing the data.* There are several different ways to analyze the data you have collected, and the technique you choose will depend on the type of method you have adopted. Large surveys need to be coded and analyzed statistically to discern whether there are relationships among the variables that you predicted in your hypotheses, and, if there are such relationships, how strong they are or whether they might have been produced by chance. If you've used qualitative techniques, interviews would need to be coded for their narrative content, and observational field notes would need to be organized and systematically coded and examined. Requiring care, precision, and patience, data analysis is often the most cumbersome

validity

The extent to which a concept, conclusion, or question is well-founded, and measures what a researcher thinks it is measuring.

reliability

Means that another researcher can use the same data you used and would find similar results.

U.S./WORLD

HOW IMPORTANT IS SOCIOLOGY?

Countries differ on the level of funding for social science research. Consider the ways the United States compares to other nations around the world.

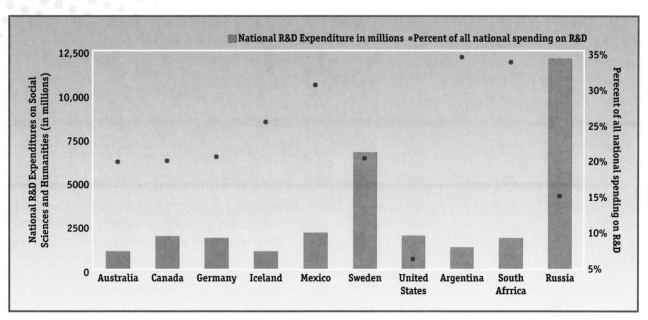

NOTE: Data recorded are for the most recent year of data available (as of September 2017).

SOURCE: Data from Organization for Economic Cooperation and Development (OECD). Available at https://stats.oecd.org/Index.aspx?DataSetCode=ONRD_COST.

INVESTIGATE FURTHER

1. What is the significance of government support for social science research? Why should the government fund it?

2. Where is social science research well-funded and where is funding lacking? How do you think the level of funding for social science research might impact a society?

and tedious element in the research process, whether you are "crunching the numbers" or transcribing, coding, and analyzing interviews or field notes.

9. *Reporting the findings.*   No research project is of much use unless you share it with others. Typically, one seeks to publish the results of research as an article in a peer-reviewed journal or in an academic book, which also passes peer review. **Peer review** is a process by which others in the field are asked to anonymously evaluate the article or book, to make sure the research meets the standards of adequate research. Peer review accomplishes two tasks: (1) It ensures that the research is evaluated by those who are competent to evaluate it and assess the adequacy of the research; and (2) it ensures that the editor's own particular biases do not prejudice her or him in the decision to accept or reject the article. Peer review is the standard model for all serious academic and scholarly journals. More than simple gatekeeping, peer review provides a valuable service to the author, enabling him or her to see how others read the work and providing suggestions for revision.

peer review
A process by which other scholars in the field are asked to anonymously evaluate one's research before it is published, to ensure it meets the standards of sociological research.

Issues in Conducting Research

4.3.5 Summarize the three primary concerns sociologists must all navigate in conducting and reporting their research.

No research project involving human beings is without controversy. Debates have always raged about the validity of studies, and we often come to believe that we can explain anything by statistics. That may be true—that you can prove even the most outrageously false things by the use of statistical manipulations—but not all "proof" will be considered equally valid or hold up in the court of review by other social scientists. Most sociological research is published in academic or scholarly journals—such as the *American Sociological Review, Social Problems, Social Forces,* or the *American Journal of Sociology.* The American Sociological Association sponsors several "flagship" journals and controls the selection of editors to ensure that the entire range of topics and perspectives is covered. Each subfield of sociology has its own journals, devoted to those specific areas of research. In all such reputable journals, articles are subject to peer review.

1. **Remain Objective and Avoid Bias.**   You must strive for objectivity, to make sure that your prejudices and assumptions do not contaminate the results you find. That is not to say that your political persuasion or your preconceived assumptions cannot guide your research: They can. The research methods you use and the questions you ask have to allow for the possibility that you're wrong. And you, as a researcher, have to be prepared to be surprised, because we often find things we didn't expect to find. Bias comes in many forms. For instance, it is not only the researcher who might have his or her own sets of assumptions coming into a research project. Additionally, it is possible for the research design itself to be biased in favor of certain findings (like the assumption that attitudes about sexual assault, violence, and rape espoused by male college students at larger research universities are a representative sample of American men more generally—they're not!).

2. **Avoid Overstating Results.**   Overstating one's findings is one of the biggest temptations to any sociological researcher. Findings are often not "newsworthy" unless you find something really significant; and funding sources, such as governmental research institutes and private foundations, often link continuing funding to such glamorous and newsworthy findings. Even when you do your first research project, you'll likely be tempted to overstate your results, if for no other reason than to impress your professor with some "big" finding and get a better grade.

But there are temptations to overstate within the research methodologies themselves. In ethnographic research, for example, one can say a lot about a little—that is, one's insights are very deep, but one has only examined a very small phenomenon or group of people. One cannot pretend that such insights can be generalized to larger populations without adequate comparisons. In survey research one can say a little about a whole lot: By writing a lot of questions and choosing a large sample, one can find out the attitudes or behaviors of Americans, but one cannot explain *why* they hold such beliefs or take such actions, nor can one explain *how* they "use" their beliefs. As a result of all these potential problems, researchers must be careful not to overstate their information and aware of a variety of possible explanations for the results they find. And when we read the results of others' research, we must also maintain a critical posture, and not be seduced by science.

3. **Maintain Professional Ethics.** The researcher must also be ethical. As scientists, sociologists are constantly confronted with ethical issues. For example, what if you were interested in studying the social impact of oil drilling in the Alaska wilderness on indigenous people who live near the oil wells? And suppose that the research would be funded by a generous grant from the oil companies who would profit significantly if you were to find that the impact would be either minimal or beneficial. Even if your research were completely free of corporate influence, people would still be suspicious of your results. Research must be free of influence by outside agencies, even those that might provide research grants to fund the research. The most important ethical issue is that your research should not actually hurt the people you are researching.

Recall the example of psychologist Stanley Milgram's experiment on obedience to authority in which one subject administered "shocks" to another. The psychological consequences of deceptive research led to significant changes in research ethics. An act of Congress in 1970 made **informed consent** a requirement of research. Only after all adult subjects of research (or the parents of minors) are clearly informed about its object and assured of confidentiality can they consent to participate. And only then can the experiment proceed. Today, all major research universities have a committee on research involving human subjects (CORIHS) or an IRB that oversees all research undertaken at the university.

"informed consent"
An act of Congress in 1970 made this a requirement of research. Only after all adult subjects of research (or the parents of minors) are clearly informed about its object and assured of confidentiality can they consent to participate. And only then can research proceed.

THE INSTITUTIONAL REVIEW BOARD. Every research project that goes through a university must pass the inspection of an institutional review board that has strict guidelines to protect test subjects (see TABLE 4.3).

TABLE 4.3 The Institutional Review Board

Guidelines	The researcher cannot even begin data collection unless he or she can guarantee: Test subject protections
Informed consent	Generally, research subjects must be informed, in advance, of the nature of the project, what it's about, what they will have to do in it, and any potential risks and benefits they will face. It's possible to waive informed consent but only under certain circumstances. If the subjects are not being harmed, and if full information would affect the results, then it's OK not to have informed consent. For example, you might not tell subjects that you were focusing specifically on racial or gender attitudes because then they might tend to answer "the right way." Instead, you might say you were asking "general" questions. So, sometimes a certain amount of deception is important to maintain.
Continuous consent	Research subjects must be informed that they can back out of the project at any time for any reason, no questions asked.
Confidentiality	Any information that would allow the subject to be identified must be stored separately from the other research data, and it must never be published.
Anonymity	Research subjects must be anonymous. Pseudonyms (fictitious names) must be used instead of real names; and, if there is any question, even the respondents' biographical data must be modified.
Freedom from deception	Research subjects must not be deceived unless it is absolutely necessary for the research, the deception is unlikely to cause major psychological trauma, and they undergo debriefing immediately afterward.
Freedom from harm	Research subjects must not be subjected to any risk of physical or psychological injury greater than they would experience in real life, unless it is absolutely necessary—and then they must be warned in advance. "Psychological injury" extends to embarrassing questions like "Have you ever been pregnant?"
Protected groups	Children and adolescents, college students, prisoners, and other groups have a protected status because they cannot really give consent (children are too young, and college students may believe that they must participate or their grade will suffer). The IRB requires special procedures for research involving these groups.

One of the most infamous research studies in U.S. history was the Tuskegee experiment, in which nearly 400 African American men with late-stage syphilis were deliberately left untreated to test what the disease would do to them. Here, then-President Bill Clinton apologizes on behalf of the country to survivors of the experiment.(We discuss this unethical research in more depth in Chapter 8.)

In recent years, IRBs have expanded the scope of their review to include any research that involves human subjects in any way whatever. Sometimes, this has resulted in oversight leading to "overreach." For example, one review board asked a linguist studying a preliterate culture to "have the subjects read and sign a consent form." Another IRB forbade a white student studying ethnicity from interviewing African American PhD students "because it might be traumatic for them" (Cohen 2007, p. 1).

But what if the questions you want to answer are answerable only by deception? Sociologist Erich Goode undertook several research projects that used deceptive research practices (Goode 1996a, 1996b, 2002). Refusing to submit his research proposals to his university's CORIHS guidelines, he listed fictional personal ads in a local magazine to see the sorts of responses he would receive. (Though the ads were fictitious, the people responding to them were real and honestly thought they were replying to real ads.) He took out four ads to determine the relative importance of physical attractiveness and financial success in the dating market. One was from a beautiful waitress (high attractiveness, low financial success); one was from an average-looking female lawyer (low attractiveness, high success). One was from a handsome male taxicab driver (high attractiveness, low success), and the final one was from an average-looking male lawyer (low attractiveness, high success). Although about 10 times more men than women replied to the ads at all, the two ads that received the most replies from their intended audience were for the beautiful waitress and the average-looking male lawyer. Goode concluded that in the dating marketplace, women and men often rank potential mates differently, with men seeking beauty and women seeking financial security.

Although these were interesting findings, many sociologists question Goode's research methods (e.g., Saguy 2002). Goode defended his behavior by saying that the potential daters didn't know that they were responding to fake ads and that therefore no harm was done because people often receive no reply when they respond to ads. But ask yourself: Did he have to deceive people to find this out? How else might he have obtained this information? Do you think he crossed a line?

In every research project, you must constantly balance the demands of the research (and your own curiosity) against the rights of the research subjects. This is a delicate balance, and different people may draw their lines in different places. To cause possible harm to a research subject is not only unethical, it is also illegal.

iSOC AND YOU Research Methods NOW
It is the sociological perspective along with the collection of research methods addressed in this chapter that distinguishes sociology as a unique "field" of study. Research methods are best understood as different types viewing instruments into which we place our iSoc lenses. They allow us to put different elements of social life into focus and to zoom in and out to better understand the societies in which we live. We need this diversity of research methods because there is very little beyond the boundaries of what sociologists consider suitable for study. And each element of the iSoc perspective can be addressed using different research methods, providing new information about how our lives are structured by *identity, interaction, institutions, inequality*, and *intersections* between them all. So too are sociologists attuned to maintaining an ethical stance toward their research and the people they study. This is not always easy and involves careful consideration.

As you consider the remainder of the book, keep in mind that the research you're learning about was discovered by relying on the methods outlined in this book. It's a powerful reminder that facts don't grow on trees. They're produced by people working diligently to solve what are often terribly complex puzzles about social life and inequality.

Conclusion

Social Science NOW: Emergent Methodologies

New technologies provide opportunities for new research methods. For example, a new methodology called "**field experiments**" combines some of the benefits of both field methods and experimental research. On the one hand, they are experiments, using matched pairs and random assignment, so that one can infer causality. On the other hand, they take place "in the field"—that is, in real-life situations. We'll read more about these experiments throughout the textbook. You've probably seen field experiments reported on television because they often reveal hidden biases in employment, housing markets, or consumer behavior.

Consider some examples of how field methods reveal biases and discrimination in employment, housing, and consumerism. Matched pairs of prospective "car buyers" go to an auto showroom, or prospective "tenants" walk into a real estate office, or "job seekers" answer a help wanted ad. In each case, the prospects consist of a white couple and a minority couple, or a man and a woman. They go to the same showroom, and look at the same cars, and get different price quotes. Or the white couple is shown several houses that are listed with the real estate broker, but the black couple is told they've been rented or sold. And while a male and female applicant answered the same job ad, the male job applicant is told about a managerial opening and the female applicant is given a typing test. Because the experiment was conducted in real time in real life, the discrimination is readily evident because the only variable that was different was race or gender. (When shown on TV, the news reporter will often go back to the car showroom or real estate office with videotape made by the participants and confront the dealer or agent with the evidence of the discrimination [Ayres and Siegelman, 1995 Cross et al. 1990; Yinger 1998].)

Just as social scientists are finding new methods, they are always trying to refine older survey techniques to obtain the most accurate data. For example, surveys of sexual behavior always find that people are somewhat self-conscious about revealing their sexual behaviors to strangers talking to them on the phone—let alone someone sitting

field experiments
The experimental examination of an intervention in a naturally occurring environment rather than in the laboratory.

Recently, field experiments have revealed what minorities had long suspected but could never prove: They are discriminated against by taxi drivers who do not stop for them.

across from them in a face-to-face survey interview. Researchers have developed a new survey technology—telephone audio computer-assisted self-interviewing—that greatly reduces the requirement of revealing your sexual behavior to a stranger. And some of the results indicate that a significantly higher percentage of Americans report same-sex sexual behavior than previously estimated (Villarroel et al. 2006).

Perhaps the most significant new technology is the proliferation of Internet chat rooms and listservs that has created virtual online communities of people who are drawn to particular issues and interests. If you want to study, for example, collectors of Ming dynasty pottery or buffalo head nickels, you would find several chat groups of such people online. Imagine how much time and energy you would save trying to track them down! They're all in one place, and they all are guaranteed to be exactly what you are looking for. It also enables the collection of data that might otherwise be difficult to collect.

Any new method should be embraced cautiously and only when accompanied by research using more traditional methodologies. In fact, it is often the combination of different methods—secondary analysis of already existing large-scale survey data coupled with in-depth interviews of a subsample—that provides some of the most exciting research findings in the social sciences today. You needn't choose one method over another; all methods allow you to approach social life in different ways. Combined in creative combinations, research methods can shed enough light on a topic that many of its characteristics and dynamics can become clear.

CHAPTER REVIEW How Do We Know What We Know? The Methods of the Sociologist

4.1 How Do We Know What We Know?

Sociology is a "social science." As a social *science,* sociology, like economics or political science, uses methods derived from the natural sciences to study social phenomena. But sociology is also a *social* science, like anthropology or history, attempting to study human behavior as it is lived by conscious human beings. Sociologists measure social phenomena in wide range of topics, from emergent social interaction and groups to large organizations, and it is all the more challenging because of subjectivity—people don't just react, they also plan, think, and act. Fortunately, sociologists have many different methods to draw on in collecting data, each of which may yield different insights. Some methods aid in deductive reasoning, others in inductive reasoning. Quantitative methods use statistical analysis of numerical data to deduce results, while qualitative methods gather rich detail to find regular patterns of behavior. Both methods have strengths and weaknesses, and good sociology can be done with both. They reveal different aspects of social phenomenon. The methods used depend on the research question.

4.1 Key Terms

subjectivity The complex of individual perceptions, motivations, ideas, and emotions that give each of us a point of view.

research methods The processes used to systematically collect and analyze information from the social world for the purposes of sociological study and understanding.

deductive reasoning Research that logically proceeds from one demonstrable fact to the next. It often moves from the general to the more specific.

inductive reasoning Research in which one reasons to a conclusion about all or many members of a collectivity based on examination of only a few members of that class. Loosely, it is reasoning from the specific to the general.

quantitative methods Numerical means to drawing sociological conclusions using powerful statistical tools to help understand patterns in which the behaviors, attitudes, or traits under study can be translated into numerical values.

survey Research method in which one asks a sample of people closed-ended questions and tabulates the results.

qualitative methods Inductive and inferential means to drawing sociological understanding, usually about less tangible aspects of social life, such as the actual felt experience of social interaction.

bias A systematic prejudice in favor of or against one thing, person, or group compared with another.

operationalization The process of attempting to define the topic of your study into measurable factors.

social desirability bias The term social scientists use to describe a form of response bias wherein people being studied tend to present themselves in a manner they believe will be perceived favorably.

triangulation A research technique that uses cross-verification to ensure the validity of conclusions. When several research methods are used to the study of the same phenomenon, researchers can be more confident with a result.

data The plural of datum. Data are systematically collected and systematically organized bits of information.

4.2 Types of Sociological Research Methods

Researchers explore how an independent variable affects the dependent variable, ensuring the results are not due to extraneous variables, confounding variables, or an intervening variable. Research goes beyond the literature review of a research paper for new insights. An experiment is a controlled observational method where something is manipulated for the experimental group, but not the control group, to see the manipulation's effect. Milgram's study of obedience is a famous experiment. Field studies are observational, gathering data where they occur naturally, using detached observation or participant observation. In an ethnography, the researcher gains deeper understanding from the participants' perspective, through immersion. Interviews with a purposive sample is a typical qualitative method. It is useful, although less generalizable. A survey is a common quantitative method, gathering data on attitudes and behavior, using tools such as a Likert scale. Sample types include random sample, systematic sample, stratified sample, or cluster sample. Secondary analysis uses existing data and data sets. Whichever method is used, generalizability is important to consider. Content analysis is a method that often involves both quantitative and qualitative methods. Whichever method is used, making the right comparisons matters. Researchers have ethical obligations, not only to conduct their work as free of bias or values as possible, honestly reporting only what is found, but to be beyond influence and avoid doing harm, too. Informed consent is required by law, and all institutional research is approved by an institutional review board (IRB), ensuring compliance with research ethics, including obtaining informed consent, protecting participant confidentiality and anonymity, protecting special populations, limiting deception, and ensuring that participants are not harmed.

4.2 Key Terms

independent variable In an experimental study, the agent of change, the ingredient that is added to set things in motion.

dependent variable The variable whose change depends on the introduction of the independent variable.

correlation The term for the fact of some relationship between two phenomena.

causal relationship A relationship between two or more variables in which one (independent) variable can be shown to actually *cause* a change in a dependent variable or variables in reliable ways.

confirmation bias The tendency to interpret new evidence as confirmation of our existing beliefs.

reverse causality Refers either to a direction of cause-and-effect contrary to the presumed relationship between variables or to a two-way causal relationship in, as it were, a loop (a relationship sociologists refer to as "reciprocal").

confounding variables The elements that impede accurate measurements of the impact of one variable on another.

intervening variable A variable that may not have been measured, but is responsible for the presumed relationship between independent and dependent variables in research.

experiment A research process that is performed under controlled conditions to examine the validity of a hypothesis by carefully varying conditions between groups.

experimental group In an experiment, the group that will experience the experimental condition being measured to examine what happens. *See control group.*

control group In an experiment, the comparison group that will not experience the manipulation of the independent variable (the experimental group). Having a control group enables sociologists to compare the outcomes of the experiment to determine if the changes in the independent variable had any effects on the dependent variable.

field Any site where the interactions or processes you want to study are taking place, such as an institution like a school or a specific community.

detached observation A perspective that constrains the researcher from becoming in any way involved in the event he or she is observing. This reduces the amount that the researchers' observations will change the dynamic that they are watching.

objectivity A posited ideal for social science researchers, it is a perspective that is free of bias, judgment or prejudice.

participant observation Sociological research method in which one observes people in their natural habitat.

institutional review boards (IRBs) A committee established to review and approve research involving human subjects, it works to ensure that researchers comply with standards and ethics in conducting their research.

ethnography A type of field method in which the researcher inserts himself or herself into the daily world of the people he or she is trying to study to understand the events from the point of view of the actors themselves.

interview Research method in which a researcher asks a small group of people open-ended questions.

purposive sample Sample in which respondents are not selected randomly and are not representative of the larger population but are selected precisely because they possess certain characteristics of interest to the researcher.

Likert scale The most common form of survey coding, it arranges possible responses from lowest to highest.

sample A limited group of research subjects whose responses are statistically developed into a general theme or trend that can be applied to the larger whole.

systematic sample A type of sample that starts at a random position on a list and selects every nth unit (skip interval) of a population until the desired sample size is reached.

random sample A sample chosen by an abstract and arbitrary method, that gives each person an equal chance of being selected, such as tossing a piece of paper with each person's name on it into a hat.

stratified sample Sample in which research subjects are divided into proportions equal to the proportions found in the population at large.

representative sample A sample that is scientifically designed to accurately reflect a larger population.

generalizability Also called external validity or applicability; the extent to which the results of a study can be generalized to the larger population.

secondary analysis Analysis conducted using data previously collected by others for other reasons.

replication One of the main principles of the scientific method, replication is the ability of an entire experiment or study to be duplicated by others.

content analysis Research method in which one analyzes artifacts and cultural "texts" (books, movies, TV programs, magazine articles, advertisements, and so on) instead of people.

discourse analysis Is more interested in patterns of portrayal evident in a collection of "texts" that might be difficult to quantify.

social network Often conceived as a web of social relationships, a type of group that is both looser and denser than a formal group but connects people to each other, and, through those connections, with other people.

social ties Refer to the social connections or relationships between individuals and groups.

"the strength of weak ties" Mark Granovetter's discovery that weak ties are valuable precisely because they provide new information that is often less available from strong ties.

structural holes A concept from social network research, the term refers to a gap between two networks of individuals who have complementary sources to information.

4.3 Research Methods NOW

Because human society is dynamic and changing, with so many variables, and values, there is no single unchanging truth sociologists can hope to find. But Comte understood that, as scientists, sociologists can conduct research *scientifically*. This allows us to, sometimes, gain predictability and discover relationships and causality in social life and behavior. Overall, there are eight steps in sociological research. After choosing an issue, defining the problem, and reviewing the literature, a hypothesis is developed, variables are operationalized, the project is designed, data are collected and analyzed, and findings are reported. Peer review by other scientists prior to journal publication is a check on bias, and on methodology—data, analysis, and conclusions. Researchers are innovative and find new ways of collecting data. Like society itself, sociology is dynamic, and responsive to changes, and new methods of research take advantage of technological advances and changes in how people connect.

4.3 Key Terms

predictability The degree to which a correct prediction of a research outcome can be made.

causality The term used when one variable causes another to change.

observer effect The direct effect that observation can be shown to have on the phenomenon being observed.

compositional fallacy An error in logic that results when comparing two groups that are different, assuming they are the same, and drawing an inference based on that false assumption.

hypothesis A testable prediction for an event or phenomenon that assumes a relationship between two or more variables.

validity The extent to which a concept, conclusion, or question is well-founded, and measures what a researcher thinks it is measuring.

reliability Means that another researcher can use the same data you used and would find similar results.

peer review A process by which other scholars in the field are asked to anonymously evaluate one's research before it is published, to ensure it meets the standards of sociological research.

"informed consent" An act of Congress in 1970 made this a requirement of research. Only after all adult subjects of research (or the parents of minors) are clearly informed about its object and assured of

confidentiality can they consent to participate. And only then can research proceed.

field experiments The experimental examination of an intervention in a naturally occurring environment rather than in the laboratory.

SELF-TEST

⟩ CHECK YOUR UNDERSTANDING

1. According to the text, which type of research primarily uses statistics to deduce findings?

   a. Qualitative methods
   b. Quantitative methods
   c. Both qualitative and quantitative methods
   d. Neither qualitative nor quantitative methods

2. Which method gathers data on attitudes and behaviors using numerically coded measurement instruments such as a Likert scale?

   a. Surveys
   b. Experiments
   c. Participant observation
   d. Interviews

3. Identify the correct order for the basic steps of deductive sociological research, according to the text:

   a. define problem, design project, review literature, choose issue, develop hypothesis, analyze data, operationalize variables, report findings;
   b. design project, review literature, choose issue, operationalize variables, develop hypothesis, analyze data, define problem, report findings;
   c. review literature, define problem, operationalize variables, design project, choose issue, develop hypothesis, analyze data, report findings;
   d. choose issue, define problem, review literature, develop hypothesis, operationalize variables, design project, analyze data, report findings

4. Which of the following methods is used for the General Social Survey (GSS)?

   a. Content analysis
   b. Survey
   c. Field experiment
   d. Ethnography

5. A sociologist interested in studying the impact of coal mining on Appalachian people cannot receive funding from a coal producer because of problems with

   a. research ethics.
   b. causality.
   c. predictability.
   d. generalizability.

6. A researcher studying alcoholism attends a meeting of Alcoholics Anonymous (AA) and interviews people there. This is an example of which type of sample?

   a. Random sample
   b. Cluster sample
   c. Purposive sample
   d. Stratified sample

7. An act of Congress mandated that all researchers must

   a. avoid deception.
   b. protect the anonymity of participants.
   c. obtain informed consent.
   d. All of the above

Self-Test Answers: 1. b, 2. a, 3. d, 4. b, 5. a, 6. c, 7. c

CHAPTER 5

SOCIALIZATION

Harry Potter offers a dramatic example of socialization. A young boy has to relearn much of what he knows about the world as he encounters a magical world that had, unbeknownst to him, been there the whole time. His experience, however, is far from fictional. Socialization is a process we endure throughout our lives as we encounter new contexts, institutions, and spaces. And just like Harry, we're better equipped to keep up than we often appreciate.

LEARNING OBJECTIVES

In this chapter, using the iSoc framework, you should be able to:

5.1.1 Differentiate between nature and nurture, and understand how socialization and identity fit into this interplay.

5.1.2 Recognize how each of the five elements of the iSoc model can be used to examine socialization sociologically.

5.1.3 Understand popular assumptions surrounding socialization and how sociologists challenge some of our deeply held beliefs about identity and behavior.

5.2.1 Explain Mead's conceptualization of the "generalized other" and how this ideal shapes our actions.

5.2.2 Describe the differences between Freud, Piaget, Kohlberg, and Gilligan in terms how they each

see our personalities as accomplished through a series of stages.

5.2.3 Understand the problems with stage theories of socialization and how anticipatory socialization and resocialization help to illustrate these issues.

5.3.1 Explain how the Clarks' experiments helped us to understand how socialization causes us to internalize systems of inequality.

5.3.2 Explain the role that social class plays in shaping how parents view their status as role models for their children.

5.3.3 Explain how children's movies play a role in socializing children to make sense of gender and sexual inequality.

5.4.1 Explain how socialization works to ensure that most children will belong to the same social classes as their parents.

5.4.2 Understand how tracking systems work in education in ways that help reproduce class inequality.

5.4.3 Describe the role of religion in the early socialization of U.S. children.

5.4.4 Understand the role that peer groups play in the socialization process alongside more formal agents of socialization.

5.4.5 Define the ongoing role that the media play in socializing us throughout our lives.

5.4.6 Explain the ways that the workplace socializes us and shapes our behavior and identities.

5.5.1 Describe the ways that our understanding of the life course in addition to the different stages we recognize as distinct is a product of socialization.

5.5.2 Understand how socialization helps us navigate the interplay between local and global identities and culture.

Introduction

One day you're a sad little boy, living with a cruel family that keeps you locked in a cupboard under the stairs on Privet Drive. The next day some enormous bearded man shows up, tells you that you are a famous wizard, that you have been accepted into a wizarding school you never knew existed, and whisks you off on a train to a magical school known as Hogwarts. Virtually overnight, you are given a new identity and interacting with a world you never knew existed. But you can't enact this identity, at least not meaningfully, until you learn what it means, how to cast spells, and how to interact with the magical world. This, Harry Potter, is your "true self" and it's your "destiny" to be a great wizard—so great, in fact, that seven volumes of epic storytelling later, you are in the final showdown with the Dark Lord Voldemort himself.

But even Harry Potter has to *learn* to be a wizard. And he needs to learn much more than that to exist in the magical world in which he comes to feel at home. Initially, Harry needs to know what supplies are necessary for wizarding school and where to buy them, how to select and use a wand, learn the right spells, how to mix the right potions, and even how to ride a broom. Much of this Harry learns through interactions, with peers, teachers, and various people he meets along the way. But Harry also learns what it means to be a wizard by interacting with the social institutions that make up the magical world: their banking system (Gringotts), educational institutions (like Hogwarts), the political system that governs the magical realm (the Ministry of Magic), and much more. Finally, Harry must learn to understand inequality in this new world. Not all wizards are equal, and wizards—just like non-magical folk—have hierarchies of status. And with that status comes rewards. You might think that wizards are simply born to their destiny, right? Not really. Nothing comes "naturally." Everyone, even the world's greatest wizard, experiences socialization.

It's a process we are vividly aware of when we experience something new and dramatically different from the world we know, as Harry did. But, socialization is no less present at other times. Sociologists see your identity less as a "thing" that you possess, like a car, but as a process—not a thing that you have but a collection of ideas, desires, beliefs, and behaviors that is constantly changing as we grow, experience new situations, operate in different contexts, and interact with other people. But we don't just learn who we are; we are also learning to understand and accept inequalities between different groups in our societies as well. Identity is social: You are different today than you were 10 years ago, or even last month, and you will be different tomorrow. You are different when you are at home than you are at school, when talking to your boss versus talking to your grandmother. Sociologists understand these differences not as simply different performances all enacted by one "true self," but as fundamentally different selves. Our identity is a process, in constant motion.

The sociological perspective may make us feel more creative because we are constantly revising our identity to meet new challenges, but it may also make us feel more insecure and unstable because it illustrates that there is nothing permanent or inevitable about the self. Change means creative potential, but it also means instability and the potential for chaos.

5.1 Understanding What Socialization Is and How It Works

Socialization is an elaborate process. The concept is so widely used that you may have already encountered the term. Although many people assume that the definition is simply "social learning," socialization is a much more complex process than you may realize. Every society confronts the same dilemma: how to ensure that the most people conform to most norms and identify with most social values in their societies most of the time. Why is it that so few people break the rules? Why don't more people steal? Why do so many of us remain stopped at red lights when driving alone at night even when no one else is around? How is it possible to move through crowds on densely populated streets? These things are all made possible because most of us conform to most of the rules in our societies most of the time. And we conform to a much more intricate set of rules than you might realize. We are not only following laws and attempting to be good citizens. We also follow rules when we line up to get coffee or food; we follow social norms surrounding how to interact with strangers on the street. We are constantly leaning on social norms to make decisions about how to behave in different contexts. And we are simultaneously continually learning about new norms or new ways of applying norms we know. It's a lifelong process.

Through this process, we come to know who we are—we form an identity within our society. Our understandings of ourselves are embedded in the world all around us and we are continually shaping and reshaping the ways we perceive ourselves and the ways in which we are perceived by others. In this section, we will consider what socialization is, how our identities are formed, and learn to look at the process of socialization from the iSoc perspective. As you'll see, socialization is not only about learning who we are, but it is also a process through which powerful inequalities between different groups are established and perpetuated.

Just ask Harry Potter. He also had to learn those inequalities—who was a "pureblood" and who was a "muggle," differences between rich and poor wizarding families (the Weasleys and the Malfoys), which houses were better than others (no one seemed to want to be in Hufflepuff), and that Hogwarts was known as one of the *best* schools (there were others). Socialization is about knowing yourself and finding your place.

Where Does Identity Come From?

5.1.1 Differentiate between nature and nurture, and understand how socialization and identity fit into this interplay.

Our identity is based on the interplay of nature and nurture. *Nature* means our physical makeup: our anatomy and physiology, our genes and chromosomes. *Nurture* means how we grow up: What we learn from our physical and social environments and our encounters with other people. Nature and nurture both play a role in who we are, but scientists and philosophers have debated for centuries over how much each contributes and how they interrelate.

Before the Enlightenment of the seventeenth and eighteenth centuries, nature reigned supreme. People understood identity as created by God and the natural world as, important, not something that could be changed by mere circumstances. Nurture was understood to play virtually no role at all; identities were understood as foregone conclusions. Theologian John Calvin taught that we were predestined to be good or evil, and there was nothing we could do about it. But in the seventeenth century, British philosophers like John Locke rejected the idea of nature as solely responsible for our identity, that biology or God placed strict limits on what we can become. They went in the other direction, arguing that each of us is born as *tabula rasa*—a blank slate—and that our environment in early childhood determined what we become. The French philosopher Jean-Jacques Rousseau proposed a compromise. He argued that human beings do inherit identities: All children, and adults in their natural state, are "noble savages," naturally warm, sociable, and peace loving. However, their environment can also change them. Industrial civilization teaches children to become competitive, belligerent, and warlike. Thomas Jefferson based his ideas for the American experiment on Locke and Rousseau: "All men are created equal," that is, they derive some basic qualities from nature.

In the nineteenth century, the nature side of the debate got a boost when Charles Darwin observed that animal species evolve, or change over time. He was not aware of genetic evolution, so he theorized that they develop new traits to adapt to changing food supplies, climates, or the presence of predators. Because human beings, too, are the result of millions of years of adaptation to the physical changes in their world, identity was discussed as a product of biological inheritance (unchangeable, at least during any one individual's lifetime). But growing up in different environments changes our ideas about who we are and where we belong without having to wait millions of years. Just consider how different would be the worldview of the daughter of a European aristocrat compared to a mother in an impoverished family living in sub-Saharan Africa. The type of environment doesn't determine what sort of "human nature" you will think you have; the environment plays a role in calculating it. Even identical twins, separated at birth and raised in these two different areas, think and act differently (Farber 1982; Loehlin and Nichols 1976).

The choice is not *either* nature *or* nurture, but both: Our biological inheritance, physical surroundings, history, civilization, culture, and personal life experiences all interact to create our identity. Sociologists tend to stress *nurture*, not because we think nature unimportant but because the ongoing interaction with people and objects in the real world throughout our life course has a profound impact on the creation of individual identity. Biology and the physical world give us the raw materials from which to create an identity, but it is only through human interactions that identities cohere and make sense to us.

Socialization is the process by which we become aware of ourselves as part of a group, learn how to communicate with others in the group, and learn the behavior expected of us: spoken and unspoken rules of social interaction, how to think, how to feel, how to act. Socialization imbues us with a set of norms, values, beliefs, desires, interests, and tastes to be used in specific social situations. Socialization can take place through formal instruction, but usually we are socialized informally by observing other people's behaviors, attitudes, and reactions around us. Socialization is at its busiest during childhood, but it also happens throughout our lives. Every time we join a new group, make new friends, change residences or jobs, we are being socialized, learning new expectations of the group and modifying our behavior, thoughts, and beliefs accordingly. And others are being socialized by watching us.

People, groups, and social institutions socialize new members, either formally (as in lessons about traffic safety in school) or informally (as in cartoon characters on television behaving according to social expectations). **Primary socialization**, which occurs

socialization

The process by which we become aware of ourselves as part of a group, learn to communicate with others, and learn how to behave as expected.

primary socialization

A culture's most basic values, which are passed on to children beginning in earliest infancy.

HOW DO WE KNOW WHAT WE KNOW?

TWIN STUDIES

In late December of 1988, two sets of identical twins were born in Bogotá, Colombia—Jorge & William and Carlos & Wilber. Through an accidental mix-up at the hospital, they were separated and Jorge was not raised with his identical twin brother William, but with Carlos instead. And William was raised with Carlos's identical twin brother, Wilber. Identical twins, mixed up in the hospital, went home as "fraternal twins" in two separate households. But in 2013, a young woman saw William behind a butcher counter in a grocery store and was certain that she was looking at Jorge, a colleague of hers from work. This happenstance meeting started a larger investigation and eventually the brothers found out about one another and met. They were all shocked to learn about the mix-up. And once they became more comfortable with learning what happened, they started quizzing each other to see what they shared in common with their identical twins. They'd been separated for 25 years. Did they share anything in common? And if so, what would that mean? They learned that Carlos and Wilber were each understood as the "crybabies" in their families and also as much more organized than Jorge and William. Jorge and William both had sweet temperaments and were understood as the strongest. Later, Yesika Montoya, a psychologist at Columbia University, found out about the twins and studied them. Research like this is sometimes used to try to assess where nature ends and socialization begins.

Twin studies refer to research done on sets of twins (who share a common biology and genetic structure) to assess the relative importance of genetic ("nature") versus environmental ("nurture") influences on individuals. Identical twins share nearly 100 percent of their genes at birth. This means that any differences between them (related to their bodies, interests, personalities, and more) are likely due to experiences that one twin has, but another has not. When research shows a patterned presence in a trait that only one member of a pair of identical twins possesses (something scholars refer to as *discordance*), this provides more evidence to look further into environmental effects. By comparing large samples of families with twins (sometimes around the world), we can understand more about the roles of genetic effects, shared environment, and unique environment in shaping behavior. Most twin research has shown that less is completely genetically ordained than you might think and that the relative heritability of most aspects of your identity and personality is much more complex than the nature versus nurture framework might lead you to suspect. Although the evidence did suggest that the brothers from Bogotá seemed to share interesting things in common with their identical twins, in the end, it is only a study of two. And we can't generalize from their experiences.

secondary socialization

Occurring throughout the life span, it is the adjustments we make to adapt to new situations.

during early childhood, gives us basic behavioral patterns but allows for adaptation and change later on. **Secondary socialization** occurs throughout life, every time we start a new class or a new job, move to a new neighborhood, make new friends, or change social roles. Secondary socialization is what allows us to abandon old, outdated, or unnecessary behavior patterns, giving us new behavioral patterns necessary for the new situation.

iSoc: Socialization

5.1.2 Recognize how each of the five elements of the iSoc model can be used to examine socialization sociologically.

Socialization is a process of incorporation, of inclusion. It is how we learn about society and it is the process through which we internalize social norms, roles, and expectations—how society gets inside of us. Through it, you learn the appropriate behaviors and attitudes that are prescribed for you. As you'll see in this chapter, socialization is a process by which you come to feel like you, how you come to have the identity you have, and the social forces that help shape what that identity looks like, and how it might be experienced.

IDENTITY—Most of us want to "stand out"—to be noticed—but we don't want to "stick out"—be noticed for the wrong things. Socialization teaches us what those rules are. We actively shape our *identities* as we grow and mature, and so too are our identities actively shaped by forces beyond our direct control.

INEQUALITY—You're not only socialized into a sense of identity, but through socialization you learn the reasons why other people, with other identities, experience discrimination, why the goods of any society are not distributed equally, why some get more and others less. You are socialized into *inequality*, and to see that inequality as somehow justified and natural.

INTERACTIONS—The processes of socialization involve your *interactions* with others. It is through these interactions that you come to know who you are and what your place is. For example, gender socialization means you come to understand and accept what is considered appropriate behavior for boys and for girls. If you do the opposite, or don't at least appear to make an effort to do what is considered appropriate, you will not be accepted by others.

INSTITUTIONS—Every society entrusts socialization to its most basic *institutions*—the family, religion, and school. It is within these social institutions that socialization begins. But it doesn't end there. Every workplace and every relationship you will ever experience contains instances of socialization—from job training to learning the quirks and styles of your partner.

INTERSECTIONS—Socialization is a process that varies by race, class, gender, sexuality, and more. Although we are all getting similar general instructions in both manifest and latent forms in terms of how to behave, which social norms to follow, what to pay attention to, and more, we receive these messages refracted through the various identity categories of which we have learned to understand ourselves as a part. All children are socialized; but not all children are socialized in exactly the same ways. And to completely appreciate these differences, we need to think about socialization *intersectionally*.

Socialization is an interactional process in which we are active participants. It helps us understand who we are and how and where we fit in the society in which we live. But we learn much more than this as well; we also learn about powerful systems of difference and inequality. And we often learn about social inequalities in ways that makes them feel inevitable. This is partly because our socialization is bolstered by social institutions in which these messages are embedded as well. It is a powerful example of society working together in remarkable ways with both astonishing and awful consequences.

How Socialization Works

5.1.3 Understand popular assumptions surrounding socialization and how sociologists challenge some of our deeply held beliefs about identity and behavior.

In Edgar Rice Burroughs's novel *Tarzan of the Apes* (1914), the infant Lord Greystoke is orphaned on the coast of Africa and raised by apes. A childhood without human contact does not affect him at all; the adult Tarzan is fluent in English, French, and many African languages and fully comfortable in human society. But real "feral children," who spend their toddler years in the wilderness, are not so lucky. The most famous feral child was the "Wild Boy of Aveyron," probably 12 years old when he was discovered in the woods of southern France in 1800. No one knew where he came from or how long he had been alone. He was unable to speak or communicate, except by growling like an animal. He refused to wear clothes. A long, systematic attempt at "civilizing" him was only partially successful. He was toilet trained, and he learned

The Wild Boy of Aveyron

to wear clothes. He exhibited some reasoning ability. But he never learned to speak more than a few words (Lane 1979; Shattuck 1980). Though feral children may be largely a myth, some children have been isolated from almost all human contact by abusive caregivers. They can also be studied to determine the impact of little or no early childhood socialization.

One of the best-documented cases of an isolated child was "Isabelle," who was born to an unmarried, deaf-mute teenager. The girl's parents were so afraid of scandal that they kept both mother and daughter locked away in a darkened room, where they had no contact with the outside world. In 1938, when she was 6 years old, Isabelle escaped. She was unable to speak except to make croaking sounds, extremely fearful of strangers, and reacted to stimuli with the instinct of a wild animal. Gradually she became accustomed to being around people, but she expressed no curiosity about them; it was as if she did not see herself as one of them. But doctors and social scientists began a long period of systematic training. Within a year she was able to speak in complete sentences, and soon she was able to attend school with other children. By the age of 14, she was in the sixth grade, happy and well adjusted. She managed to overcome her lack of early childhood socialization, but only through exceptional effort.

Studies of other isolated children reveal that some can recover, with effort and specialized care, but others suffer permanent damage. It is unclear exactly why, but no doubt some contributing factors are the duration of the isolation, the child's age when the isolation began, the presence of some human contacts (like Isabelle's mother), other abuse accompanying the isolation, and the child's intelligence (Birdsong 1999; Candland 1993; Newton 2003). But lack of socialization has serious consequences; it is socialization that makes human beings *human*.

Consider the case of "maternal instinct." When a mother sees her newborn baby for the first time, we expect her to feel a special bond of love and devotion: The maternal "instinct" has kicked in. But how instinctive is it? In *Mother Nature: A History of Mothers, Infants, and Natural Selection* (1999), Sarah Hrdy points out that little actual research has been done on mothers and children. Scientists assume that they have an instinctual bond based on millions of years of evolution. Yet, women raised by abusive parents tend to be abusive to their own children, and women raised by indifferent parents tend to be indifferent.

Children can't be deliberately raised in isolation for the sake of scientific research. But we can study primates, who require the longest period of socialization other than humans. Psychologists Harry Harlow and Margaret Harlow studied rhesus monkeys raised apart from others of their species and found severe physical and emotional problems. The monkeys' growth was stunted, even when they received adequate nutrition. They were fearful of others in their group and refused to mate or associate with them socially. Those returned after 3 months managed to reintegrate with the group, but after 6 months the damage was irreparable. The females who gave birth (through artificial insemination) neglected their offspring, suggesting that "maternal instincts" must be learned through the experience of being nurtured as a child (Griffin and Harlow 1966; Harlow, Dodsworth, and Harlow 1965; Harlow et al. 1966; Harlow and Suomi 1971).

Social expectations and socialization play an important role in how mothers respond to their children. In some human cultures, mothers are supposed to be cool and unfriendly to their children. In others, they are not supposed to know them at all. Children are raised by uncles and aunts, or by strangers, and the biological mother ignores them. Mothers are certainly capable of profound love and devotion to their children. But so are fathers, grandparents, uncles, aunts, brothers, sisters, and adults who have no biological connection to the child at all. And not every mother is capable of such

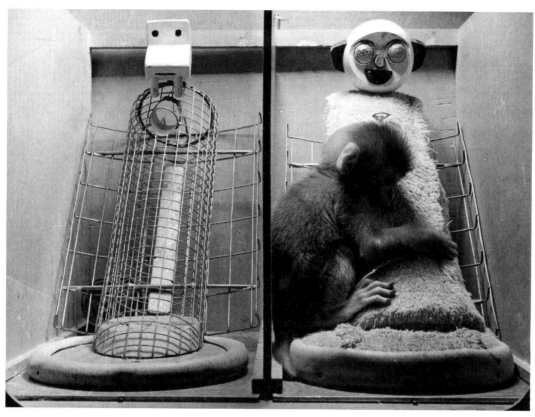

In an experiment, Harry Harlow offered baby monkeys a "choice" between two surrogate mothers. One was made entirely of cold wire, but offered a bottle with milk. The other had soft terrycloth, but no milk. The monkeys consistently chose the terrycloth mother, even though it did not provide food. Harlow hypothesized that monkeys—and all primates—crave emotional attachment, sometimes even more than they crave food.

devotion. Biological instinct may play a part in the bond between mother and child, but early training at home and social expectations later in life make all the difference.

> **iSOC AND YOU Understanding What Socialization Is and How It Works**
> "No man is an island," wrote the great British poet John Donne. You become who you are through your *interactions* with others, within social *institutions* that provide rules, values, and the reasons to do what you "naturally" do. It's through those interactions that you develop and perform and refine your *identity*—who you think you are. And the social context for that performance of identity is an unequal playing field, that is, social *inequalities* based on all the other identities that you could have.

5.2 Models of Socialization

Socialization doesn't happen all at once but proceeds in stages. Both psychologists and sociologists have proposed different stages, based on the accomplishment of specific tasks.

Both sociology and psychology address the issue of socialization. And although there are overlapping components—you will find courses in social psychology in both sociology and psychology departments—there are also some differences. Using iSoc language and speaking generally, psychologists tend to focus on the individual and sociology focuses on the various groups and institutions in which you are embedded, with which you interact, and the ways that your identity is interactively produced within these contexts. The psychological dynamic of socialization is that you move through various stages by accomplishing specific developmental "tasks," and in the end, you establish a stable, permanent "personality." Sociologists see socialization taking place at all of those pivotal moments, because you are embedded in different institutions, interacting with different people. But for sociologists, the process of socialization is never complete.

In a sense, then, psychology may see your biological makeup and your family dynamics as the formative element of your personality, whereas sociologists see your identity developing all through your life. Sociology sees your identity as more "contingent," depending at least as much on the circumstances in which you find yourself as on your family of origin. Beyond this, sociologists are centrally interested in the unequal relationships among different groups; racial or ethnic hierarchies, gender, or sexual inequalities become part of that process of socialization as well. Simply put, the identities into which each of us are socialized are not all equal.

It may seem ironic. The field (psychology) that stresses the individual's socialization into a personality ultimately understands your identity to be more fixed, the inevitable product of biological inheritance and early-childhood nurture. Meanwhile, the field (sociology) that stresses group memberships and unequal hierarchies actually sees more fluidity and flexibility in the development of your identity—that is, giving you more freedom through the course of your life to shape, and reshape, who you actually are.

Taking the Role of Others

5.2.1 Explain Mead's conceptualization of the "generalized other" and how this ideal shapes our actions.

George Herbert Mead, whose notions of the difference between the "I" and the "me" we discussed in Chapter 3, developed a stage theory of socialization, stages through which children pass as they become better integrated into society. Mead argued that there are three stages in the development of the perspective of the other:

Imitation is not only "the sincerest form of flattery," it is also a crucial element of socialization, according to George Herbert Mead. Children imitate the behaviors, and adopt the prejudices, of their parents.

1. *Imitation.* Children younger than age 3 can imitate others, but they cannot usually put themselves into the role of others.
2. *Play.* Children ages 3 to 6 pretend to be specific people or kinds of people that they think are important (their parents, doctors, firefighters, superheroes or princesses). They say and pretend to do things that these people might say and do. But they are learning more than a repertoire of behaviors and cultural scripts. Mead understood children's play as crucial to the development of their ability to take the perspective of others. They must anticipate how the people they are pretending to be would think, feel, and behave in various situations, often necessitating playing multiple roles simultaneously: As "parents," for instance, they may play at disciplining their "children," first playing a parent who believes that a misdeed was deliberate and then a child who insists that it was an accident.
3. *Games.* In early school years, children learn to play games and team sports. Now they must interpret and anticipate how other players will act, who will do what when the ball is hit, kicked, passed, or thrown.

Complex games like chess and checkers require strategy, the ability to anticipate the thoughts of others. And, perhaps most important, the children are learning to place value on actions, to locate behavior within a sense of generalized morality (M. Mead 1935).

Only in this last phase do children "internalize" the expectations of more and more people, until eventually they can take on the role of their group as a whole. Mead called this the **generalized other**—the collection of roles and attitudes that people use as a reference point as they figure out how to behave in any given situation. It is the generalized other that surrounds you in most contexts and provides a constant internalized orientation against which we consider our actions and shape our behavior. When we learn to understand how others expect us to behave, what others expect us to take note of and ignore, we are also learning an important social skill—shaping our behaviors according to the generalized other. Think about public activities parents do with their children; they are constantly suggesting ways of behaving and helping them pay attention to what children are supposed to understand as important.

generalized other

The organized rules, judgments, and attitudes of an entire group. If you try to imagine what is expected of you, you are taking on the perspective of the generalized other.

SOCIOLOGY AND OUR WORLD

WHAT CAN WE LEARN ABOUT SOCIALIZATION FROM FAMILY TRIPS TO THE ZOO?

When families with children visit zoos, what are children learning about besides animals?

Zoos are odd places. They have an aura of empire about them—bringing animals back to the capital from various exotic places around the world. Today, they are more likely to be frequented by families. Kids run around, learn about animals, and "oooh" and "aaah" at the collections of animals zoos create habitats to display. During all of this, it might be less apparent that within these moments fleeting

family frivolity is something of much larger significance: a process of socialization in which we teach children to see the world as "one of us."

Have you ever watched a young child run up to a zoo habitat and begin looking at the rocks, the cage, or be fascinated by what is inside a food bowl on the ground. These are mundane details. They are aspects of the zoo experience most of us casually ignore. Parents get down with their children, direct their gaze at the things they came at the zoo to see (the animals) and ask kids questions about them. They learn to go up to habitats in which the animals are not immediately apparent and look for them. And they learn that, if the animals are not visible, their time would be better spent elsewhere and that they should move along to the next exhibit.

We are not only socialized to understand who to talk to and when, to learn what proper manners are and when we are allowed to violate them, and the like. We are also socialized to see and interpret the world around us as members of our society do as well. When parents get down and point at the animals, they are helping to shape the ways that their children see the world around them, distinguish between *meaningful* information and things and stuff we can ignore. As sociologist Marjorie DeVault (2000) explains, zoo visits convey "relatively unnoticed but profound social messages. Though the zoo visit may be experienced by participants in myriad ways—with pleasure, boredom, or indifference; as simple fun, nature education, or a difficult ordeal; and so on—its core activities virtually always involve family members in practices that define and reinforce a series of significant boundaries: between humans and animals, between properly viewable and insignificant sights, and between family and others." We are learning to *see* the world as members of our society see the world—what to pay attention to, what to ignore, what to call other people's attention to, and more. And it is through interactions like this that we become a part of the *we*.

FIGURE 5.1 **The Human Psyche According to Freud**
Freud's theory of human psychology divides the mind into three interconnected parts: the id, ego, and superego.

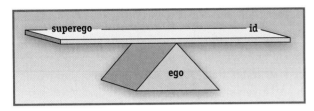

id
Sigmund Freud's label for that part of the human psyche that is pure impulse, without worrying about social rules, consequences, morality, or other people's reactions.

superego
Freud's term for the internalized norms, values, and "rules" of our social group that are learned from family, friends, and social institutions.

ego
Freud's term for the balancing force in the psyche between the id and the superego; it channels impulses into socially acceptable forms.

Stage Theories of Development

5.2.2 Describe the differences between Freud, Piaget, Kohlberg, and Gilligan in terms how they each see our personalities as accomplished through a series of stages.

Understanding the process of development has been an important part of other social sciences, such as psychology and anthropology. Psychologists have studied different aspects of socialization to explain the different stages through which we pass to become healthy, functioning adults.

Psychiatrist Sigmund Freud (1856–1939), the founder of psychoanalysis, believed that the self consisted of three interrelated elements. (1) The **id**, which is the inborn drive for self-gratification; the *id* is pure impulse, without worrying about social rules, consequences, morality, or other people's reactions. (2) The **superego** is internalized norms and values, the "rules" of our social group, learned from family, friends, and social institutions. It provokes feelings of shame or guilt when we break the "rules," pride and self-satisfaction when we follow them. (3) The **ego**, which is the balancing force between the id and the superego, or impulses and social rules; the *ego* channels impulses into socially acceptable forms (see FIGURE 5.1). Because the id can never have everything it wants, the task of socialization is twofold. First the ego must be strong enough to handle being rebuffed by reality and able to find acceptable substitutes for what the id originally wanted. (Psychoanalysis is supposed to strengthen the ego to handle this task.) And second, the superego must be strong enough to prevent the id from going after what it wants in the first place. Thus, the superego is the home of guilt, shame, and morality.

Swiss psychologist Jean Piaget (1896–1980) studied children of different ages to understand how they solve problems and make sense of the world (Piaget 1928, 1932, 1953, 1955). He argued that their reasoning ability develops in four stages, each building on the last (see TABLE 5.1). In the *sensorimotor stage* (birth to age 2), children experience the world only through their senses. In the *preoperational stage* (about ages 2 through 7), children can draw a square to symbolize a house or a stick with a blob at the end to signify a tree, but are not yet able to understand metrics like size, speed, or weight. In the *concrete operational stage* (about ages 7 through 12), children's reasoning is more developed: They can understand size, speed, and weight and can use numbers. They can perceive causal connections. But their reasoning is still concrete; they are not able to reach conclusions based on general principles. In the *formal operational stage* (after about age 12), children are capable of abstract and critical thinking. They can talk about general concepts like "truth." They can reach conclusions based on general principles, and solve abstract problems. Piaget believed, along with

TABLE 5.1 Piaget's Cognitive Stages of Development

Stage	Age Range	Characteristics
Sensorimotor stage	Birth–2 years	Still in the sensory phase; can understand only what they see, hear, or touch
Preoperational stage	2–7 years	Capable of understanding and articulating speech and symbols, but can't understand common concepts like weight
Concrete operational stage	7–12 years	Causal relationships are understood, and they understand common concepts, but they can't reach conclusions through general principles
Formal operational stage	12 years and up	Capable of abstract thought and reasoning

other social scientists, that social interaction is the key to cognitive development. Children learn critical and abstract thinking by paying careful attention to other people behaving in certain ways in specific situations.

According to Piaget, morality is an essential part of the development of cognitive reasoning. Children younger than 8 have a black-and-white view of morality: Something is either good or bad, right or wrong. They can't see "extenuating circumstances," acts that could be partially right, partially wrong, or right under some circumstances, wrong under others. As they mature, they begin to experience moral dilemmas of their own, and they develop more complex reasoning. Psychologist Lawrence Kohlberg (1927–1987) argued that our sense of morality developed from the concrete to the abstract, that is, from real-life situations to the ability to apply abstract principles. Kohlberg's famous question set up the ethical dilemma: Your wife is sick, and you cannot afford the necessary medication. Should you break into the pharmacy and steal it? Stealing is wrong, but does the situation merit it anyway (Kohlberg 1971)?

Kohlberg's graduate student Carol Gilligan wondered why women usually scored much lower than men on Kohlberg's morality scale. Were they really less moral? Instead, she hypothesized that Kohlberg's experiment assumed a male subject. (Notice the dilemma posed that "your wife" is sick.) He interviewed only men, made up a story about a man breaking into the pharmacy and assumed that moral reasoning was dictated by masculine-coded justice asking "What are the rules?" instead of a more feminine-coded emotion asking "Who will be hurt?" She argued that there is a different guide to moral reasoning, one more often exhibited by women, called "an ethic of care," based on people sacrificing their own needs and goals for the good of people around them (Gilligan 1982). Although all of us exhibit characteristics of both justice and care as ethical systems, women are socialized to gravitate toward care and men toward ethics. Gilligan's argument is that, by focusing only on justice, we will miss an equally important ethical system.

Most social scientists today do not believe that women and men have completely different forms of moral reasoning. Both women and men develop ethics of care and ethics of justice. These systems are not specific to gender; they are simply different ways of resolving moral dilemmas.

In his studies of the development of moral reasoning, psychologist Lawrence Kohlberg argued that an abstract "ethic of justice," as in this symbol of U.S. jurisprudence, was the highest form of ethical thought. His student, Carol Gilligan, disagreed, arguing that just as important, though not as recognized, was an "ethic of care," in which people's moral decision making is based on how it will actually affect people.

Problems with Stage Theories

5.2.3 Understand the problems with stage theories of socialization and how anticipatory socialization and resocialization help to illustrate these issues.

Stage theories are extremely popular. Many best-sellers describe the "seasons of our lives," "passages," or "the fountain of age." And we often use stage theory to describe a problem, preferring to believe that someone will "grow out of" a problematic behavior than to believe that such a behavior is part of who they "really are." It is interesting, and often amusing, to try to fit our own experiences into the various theorists' stages of human development, but the whole idea of stages has some problems in the real world:

- The stages are rigidly defined, but many of the challenges are lifelong. Erikson (1959) puts the conflict between being part of a group and having a unique identity in adolescence, but every time we join a new club, get a new job, move to a new town, or make new friends, we face the same conflict, even in old age.
- It is not clear that failure to meet the challenges of one stage means permanent failure. Maybe we can fix it during the next stage.
- Stage theorists usually maintain that the stages are universal, but do people in all cultures and all time periods really develop in the same way? In cultures where there are no schools, is there a preadolescence? In many parts of the world, the life expectancy is about 40; are middle adulthood and old age the same there

At Virginia Military Institute, upper-class cadets are in charge of the resocialization of first-year students (called "rats").

anticipatory socialization
The process of learning and adopting the beliefs, values, and behaviors of groups that one anticipates joining in the future.

resocialization
The process of learning a new set of beliefs, behaviors, and values that depart from those held in the past.

as in the United States, where we can expect to live to about 80? Even within the same culture, people do not develop in the same way. Piaget argued that the formal operational stage of abstract reasoning begins during adolescence, but Kohlberg and Gilligan (1971) found that 30 percent of the U.S. population never develop it at all.

Two other problems with stage theories result from the fact that we assume that one passes through a stage fully and never returns to that stage. But we are also constantly cross-cutting stages, moving back and forth. Socialization turns out to be a lifelong and fluid process.

Given this, sociologists are also interested in two other socialization processes left out of stage theories: anticipatory socialization and resocialization.

Even while you occupy one status, you may begin to anticipate moving to the next stage and begin a future-oriented project of acting *as if* you were already there. **Anticipatory socialization** is when you begin to enact the behaviors and traits of the status you expect to occupy. For example, young adolescents might decide to begin drinking coffee, in anticipation of the onset of adulthood, when they will drink coffee the same as grownups do. Often people begin to imitate those who occupy the statuses *to which we believe we will eventually belong*. You might begin to imitate a new group of people at college as you adapt to a new environment and decide where you want to try to fit in (changing your clothing, adopting a new hair style, developing interests you never had before because they are popular among a new group you hope to join).

Moving from one stage to another is not an easy process. Often, we have to relearn elementary components of our roles when we enter a new status. **Resocialization** involves learning new sets of values, behaviors, and attitudes different from those you previously held. Resocialization is also something that happens all through your life. Some resocialization is coerced: Let's say you are a happy-go-lucky sort of person, loud and rambunctious, and you are arrested for disturbing the peace and sent to jail. Failure to resocialize to a docile, obedient, and silent prisoner can result in serious injury. Indeed, a central mission of prison is supposed to be resocialization—this is why we call them "correctional" facilities. But, resocialization can also be voluntary, as when someone joins the military or enters a monastery or convent.

One of the more shocking moments in resocialization happens to college students during their first year in school. Expectations in college are often quite different from high school, and one must "resocialize" to these new institutional norms. When resocialization is successful, one moves easily into a new status. When it is unsuccessful, or only partially realized, you will continue to stick out uneasily.

---

iSOC AND YOU Models of Socialization
Socialization is complicated. It doesn't just happen once and "shazam" you are "socialized." It's an ongoing process through the course of your life. And you are not simply some blank slate onto which society "writes" its script for you to follow to the letter. Everyone shapes these ideas differently, uniquely. You are an active agent in the creation of your own *identity*. You receive signals about your place in the *unequal* social world, through your *interactions* in the larger society, through social *institutions*, and you bring these *intersecting* ideas into an identity that feels coherent and meaningful to you.

5.3 Socialization and Inequality

There's a line in a song in the classic Broadway musical *South Pacific* that begins, "You have to be taught, to hate and fear … you have to be carefully taught." Nelson Mandela, the former President of South Africa and former anti-apartheid revolutionary, said something similar: "People must learn to hate, and if they can learn to hate, they can be taught to love." But is that true? Aren't humans "naturally" suspicious of others, competitive and selfish? Or are we "naturally" communal and egalitarian? The answer is yes. We're both. The question isn't whether we are one or the other—it's *how* and *when* and *under what circumstances*. And yet, the sentiments expressed in the preceding quotes bring up an important issue: socialization is not only positive, helping the child adjust to life. Some of the norms we are socialized into are oppressive, shortsighted, and wrong. We can be socialized into believing stereotypes, into hating out-groups, into violence and abuse. Children of different cultures might be curious about differences they see, even somewhat uneasy, but they aren't biologically programmed to commit genocide as adults. That is a learned—and thus, taught—behavior.

Socialization can enable us to see problems that we might not have otherwise seen. For example, imagine two U.S. children, one raised in the pre-Civil Rights era south and the other in New York City. On a trip Michael's family took to visit a friend in Georgia, they passed through small towns with segregated restrooms, drinking fountains, and entrances to buildings. Michael had been socialized to "see" these as different, unusual, and, morally repugnant. But when he asked his friend's family about it, they replied with neither anger nor guilt. It was simply the way things were supposed to be, they explained. Socialization can also keep us blind to cruelties or inequalities that are presented to us as natural and inevitable.

Socialization and Racial Inequality

5.3.1 Explain how the Clarks' experiments helped us to understand how socialization causes us to internalize systems of inequality.

If socialization is the process by which individuals are incorporated into their society, then it is a question of the social norms that constitute life in that society that determine your socialization. Socialization can enable us to accept inequality as natural (even as morally unquestionable or good), or it can inspire us to fight against it.

Or both. Many of us feel that something is wrong when we read of people starving, homeless, or otherwise so physically or mentally helpless as to be unable to care for themselves. That's being socialized. And yet many of us can also accept an explanation for that suffering—they didn't work hard enough, they're alcoholic, it's their own fault—and not consider offering to help. That's socialization too. And what's more, the choices we make about how to act and why, these are the result of our own individual interaction with the legacy of that socialization. We're socialized, but we also make choices.

Socialization and Social Class

5.3.2 Explain the role that social class plays in shaping how parents view their status as role models for their children.

For decades, sociologists believed that parents socialized their children to grow up like them; that is, parents saw themselves as positive role models for their children. And that was true for middle-class parents. But this is not true for the working class. In a landmark study, *The Hidden Injuries of Class* (1972), sociologists Richard Sennett and Jonathan Cobb interviewed hundreds of working-class

HOW DO WE KNOW WE'RE SOCIALIZED TO BELIEVE IN RACIAL INEQUALITY?

Two psychologists active in the Civil Rights Movement—Kenneth Bancroft Clark and Mamie Phipps Clark—conducted a series of experiments in the 1940s using dolls to study African American children's self-perceptions related to race. The experiment involved a child being presented with two dolls identical in every way except for skin and hair color (one doll was white with yellow hair, the other was brown with black hair). The child was asked which doll looks nice, which doll looks bad, which doll they would like to play with, and more. The Clarks discovered that black children showed a patterned preference for the white doll—a fact which dramatically exposed internalized racism in African American children.

And although you might think that these racial preferences are the result of childish naïveté, research has since documented similar findings among adults as well. Research testing the implicit associations we have with words like black and white or man and woman has shown that we have all internalized stereotypes about different groups in society. When shown a series of words related to work and family and asked to associate the work-related words with men and the family-related words with women, implicit-association tests show that we all have an easier time doing this than when asked to associate family-related terms with men and work-related terms with women. Similarly, when shown a series of pleasant and unpleasant terms and asked to associate the pleasant terms (*kind, nice,* etc.) with "white" and the unpleasant terms (*mean, rude,* etc.) with "black," research has shown that we are all better and faster at doing this than we are at associating pleasant terms with "black" and unpleasant terms with "white." We have been socialized to internalize inequality so much so that being asked to change that perception is challenging; when we stumble, we illustrate just how powerful that initial process of internalization really is.

Try it yourself. Harvard University's Project Implicit posts a series of implicit-association tests online for anyone to take. Go to https://implicit.harvard.edu/implicit/takeatest.html to take one and see whether you hold any implicit associations of which you were unaware.

Dr. Kenneth B. Clark is depicted here watching as one of the children in his research with Mamie P. Clark encounters the dolls and grabs hold of one.

women and men, many of whom were immigrants or children of immigrants. They found that these people felt inadequate, sometimes like frauds or imposters, ambivalent about their success. They had worked hard but hadn't succeeded, and because they were fervent believers in the American Dream—where even a poor boy can grow up to be the president—they blamed themselves for their failure. Sennett and Cobb attributed this to "status incongruity"—living in two worlds at the same time.

And how did they manage to ward off despair when they were at fault for their own failures? They deferred success from their own lives to the lives of their children. They worked at difficult, dirty, and dangerous jobs not because they were failures but

FIGURE 5.2 Importance of Children Learning Obedience vs. Learning to Think for Themselves
Whether Sennett and Cobb's finding still holds is a question sociologists are still asking. What is clear from their finding, however, was that parents clearly thought it was possible for their children to attain a higher social class than they did—they believed social mobility was both desirable and possible. And yet, when we examine classed differences in the ways parents feel about obedience and independence, it is also true that parents with less education are likely to value obedience over independence in their children. If this is what they are rewarded for at work, it is not surprising to find that they hope to instill this skill in their children. Yet, it might also work to situate their children as more likely to find themselves in occupations that reward obedience over innovation. The General Social Survey has not asked this question since 1994. So, it will also be interesting to see how this has changed since then.

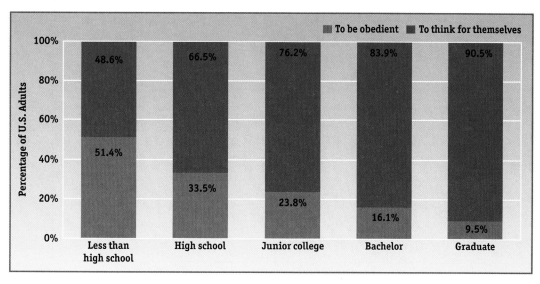

SOURCE: Data from General Social Survey, 1994.

because they were sacrificing to give their children a better life. They were noble and honorable. But they saw themselves not as role models to be emulated but as cautionary tales to be avoided. It turns out that whether your parents see themselves as positive or negative role models for you may depend, in part, on what social class you belong to (see FIGURE 5.2).

Socialization and Gender and Sexual Inequality

5.3.3 Explain how children's movies play a role in socializing children to make sense of gender and sexual inequality.

Gender and sexual inequality are separate systems of inequality that we are socialized to take for granted. The belief, for instance, that men are smarter, stronger, or somehow more naturally suited to be in positions of authority is a belief many have been socialized to accept. The process of how we take on and accept gender differences and roles in society is a topic we will return to later in Chapter 9. But one of the ways we are socialized to understand gender and sexual differences and (less explicitly) inequality at a young age is through the media. Research on media made primarily with children audiences in mind is one way we can examine patterns in some of the socialization young people receive on a massive scale. And a great deal of research has considered how patterns in depictions of men and women in children's movies might shape their understandings of gender and inequality.

There are a variety of different ways that we might consider studying portrayals of men and women in children's movies. Some recent data was published considering gender differences in Disney movies examining something that might initially seem superficial: the proportion of dialogue men and women have in different movies. Web developers and data analysts Hanah Anderson and Matt Daniels at Polygraph.com

FIGURE 5.3 Gender Balance of Dialogue for Characters in Disney Movies

Some movies have begun to give great voice to girls and women—quite literally—by giving them at least 50 percent of the spoken lines in the films. *The Incredibles*, for instance, achieves much more of a gender balance in dialogue than does *Toy Story*. And some films, like *Inside Out*, have girls and women speaking more than boys and men. But those films are still in the minority when we examine the Disney collection. And although you might be tempted to think that things are getting better, female characters received a significant proportion of the spoken lines in many of the previous movies Disney produced. Women then began to receive a smaller proportion of the lines over time, and today, there is more variation by movie. Even *Frozen*, a movie about two sisters, dedicates more spoken dialogue to men.

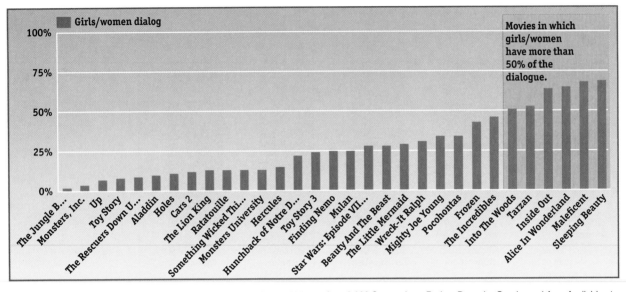

SOURCE: Data from Hannah Anderson and Matt Daniels (2016). Film Dialogue from 2,000 Screenplays, Broken Down by Gender and Age. Available at https://pudding.cool/2017/03/film-dialogue/index.html.

discovered that men have more dialogue in 27 of 33 Disney movies examined. A major reason for this in many Disney films is that there are simply more speaking roles for boys and men than there are for girls and women. But, even when that is less the case, boys and men are simply speaking more and for more time on screen than are girls and women in most Disney movies. The worst offender? *The Jungle Book* (see FIGURE 5.3).

And it's not just Disney movies. This trend exists throughout popular media. But movies are, perhaps, an easy way to measure this. Andrews and Daniels also examined 2,000 separate screenplays to assess the proportion of dialogue given to girls and women versus boys and men. In their analysis, boys and men were given at least 60 percent of the dialogue in more than 75 percent of the 2,000 films they analyzed. In slightly more than 15 percent of the movies, boys and men accounted for at least 90 percent of the dialogue! Perhaps not surprisingly, action movies were among the worst offenders. Horror movies had the highest proportions of films exhibiting gender parity in speaking roles. And women spoke most in comedies. (See FIGURE 5.4 to see where different films fell.)

And although you might have thought about the messages about gender portrayed in children's movies, sociologists have studied the portrayals of sexuality in children's movies as well. For instance, Karin Martin and Emily Kazyak (2009) investigated the ways that children also receive messages about sexuality in ways that support existing kinds of inequality. A great deal of scholarship suggests that by the time children enter elementary school, they have already learned to think of heterosexuality as normal and natural. Children learn this message from parents, peers, and various institutions that socialize them to understand heterosexual relationships as the dominant and most desirable form of intimate relationship—as an ideal at which everyone is assumed to be aiming. Martin and Kazyak examined all of the G-rated movies produced in the United States between 1990 and 2005 that grossed more than

FIGURE 5.4 Gender Balance of Dialogue for Characters in Movies on IMDB.com

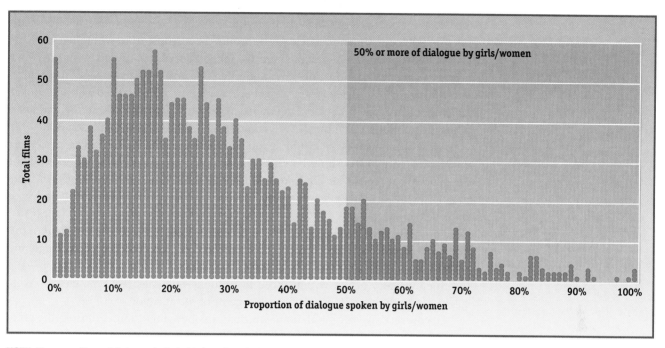

NOTE: The proportions of dialogue dedicated to boys/men is the inverse of girls/women's dialogue such that in films in which girls/women are afforded 15 percent of the dialogue, the remaining 85 percent is dedicated to boys/men.

SOURCE: Data from Hannah Anderson and Matt Daniels (2016). Film Dialogue from 2,000 Screenplays, Broken Down by Gender and Age. Available at: https://pudding.cool/2017/03/film-dialogue/index.html.

$100 million in profits. They were interested in examining any depictions of sexuality in each of the films to search for patterns in the major motion pictures reaching the largest audiences.

One discovery they made was that although G-rated films are assumed to be devoid of "sexual" content, Martin and Kazyak discovered sexual content in all but two of the films in their sample. A number of movies depict men sexually ogling women's bodies. But the larger finding from this research was that heterosexual love is most often depicted in these films as magical, exceptional, and transformative. Romantic heterosexual relationships are portrayed as a special, distinct, and exceptional form of relationship—different from all other relationship types. This is a powerful presentation of one type of relationship between characters. Friendships, for instance, were not portrayed in the same way at all.

All of this research uncovered patterns in the ways that children and adults are socialized by mass media to encounter messages about gender and sexuality at a young age. And these messages help shape what we understand as "normal" and "desirable." Indeed, one of the reasons that social inequality can be difficult to challenge is that we are socialized to accept and desire unequal relationships in many ways. Major motion pictures for children illustrate one way we receive these messages. And, as the data from Polygraph.com suggest, movies for adults are no different.

iSOC AND YOU Socialization and Inequality

Socialization is a form of accommodation, a way for you to feel like the social arrangements of society are "normal" or natural. That's how your *identity* becomes embedded in a social word that is characterized by *inequality*. The *intersecting inequalities* that we see around us are not inevitable, but through your *interactions* with others and in larger social *institutions*, you can come to believe in ideas, like "natural selection," that make inequality feel natural.

5.4 Institutions of Socialization

Socialization takes place in every institution in which we find ourselves. From the nursery to the nursing home, we are surrounded by people from whom we learn appropriate behaviors and emotions and we inhabit social institutions with their own norms for behaviors and values that underlie them. We actively engage in socialization throughout our lives. When we get a new job, we are socialized into the spoken and unspoken rules of the job: Do you eat your lunch at your desk, in the employee lounge, or out at a restaurant? Are you supposed to discuss your personal life with your coworkers or limit your interactions to polite greetings? Should you profess an interest in opera or the Super Bowl? Socialization is usually about what "should" be done, not what "must" be done. You will not be thrown out onto the street for mentioning the Super Bowl when the social norm is to like opera, but you will find your status lessened.

For a long time psychologists and sociologists argued that the major agent of primary socialization was the family, with school and religion becoming increasingly important as children grew up. These three institutions—family, school, religion—and the three primary actors within those institutions—parents, teachers, clergy—were celebrated as the central institutions and agents of socialization.

Of course, they *are* central; no institutions are more important. But from the point of view of the child, these three institutional agents—parents, teachers, clergy—are experienced as "grownups, grownups, and grownups." Asking children today about their socialization reveals that two other institutions—mass media and peer groups—are also vital in the socialization process. These two institutions become increasingly important later in childhood and especially in adolescence. Later, government, the workplace, and other social institutions become important, too. **Agents of socialization** tend to work together, promoting the same norms and values, and they socialize each other as well as the developing individual. It is often impossible to tell where the influence of one ends and the influence of another begins, and even a list seems arbitrary. Although there are many agents of socialization, in this chapter we will focus on six of the most important: family, education, media, peers, religion, and the workplace.

agents of socialization
The people, groups, and institutions that teach all of us how to be functioning members of society.

Children are socialized by their parents in all sorts of ways. This parent socializes his child into the science fiction universes and stories he enjoys as an adult.

Socialization in the Family

5.4.1 Explain how socialization works to ensure that most children will belong to the same social classes as their parents.

There are many different child-rearing systems in cultures around the world. In the United States, we are most familiar with nuclear families (father, mother, children) and extended families (parents, children, uncles, aunts, grandparents). But in some cultures, everyone in the tribe lives together in a longhouse; or men, women, and children occupy separate dormitories. Sometimes, biological parents have little responsibility for raising their children or are even forbidden from seeing them. But there is always a core of people—parents, brothers, sisters, and others—who interact with the children constantly as they are growing, giving them their first sense of self and setting down their first motivations, social norms, values, and beliefs. From our family we receive our first and most enduring ideas about who we are.

Our family also gives us our first statuses, our definitions of ourselves as belonging to a certain class, nationality, race, ethnicity, religion, and gender. In traditional societies, these remain permanent parts of our self-concept. We would live in the same village as our parents, work at their occupation, and never aspire to a status greater than they enjoyed. In modern societies, we are more likely to experience **social mobility**, occupying different jobs and residences from those of our parents, having different political and religious affiliations, changing our religions. But even so, the social statuses from our childhood often affect the rest of our lives.

Studies show that different sorts of families socialize their children in different ways. Melvin Kohn (Kohn 1959a,b, 1963, 1983, 1989; Kohn and Schoenback 1993; Kohn, Slomczynski, and Schoenbach 1986) found that working-class families are primarily interested in teaching the importance of outward conformity—of neatness, cleanliness, obedience to the rules, and staying out of trouble—and middle-class families focus on developing children's curiosity, creativity, and good judgment. Lower-class families are similar to working-class families in favoring conformity and obedience, and the affluent follow the middle class in favoring creativity and good judgment. Kohn (1977) found that these differences are determined by the pattern of the parents' jobs. Blue-collar workers are closely supervised in their jobs, so they tend to socialize their children into the obedience model, but skilled tradesmen, who have more freedom, tend to socialize their children into the creativity model (Lareau 2003).

African American parents may socialize their children to prepare for bias and in coping strategies to deal with discrimination (Hughes, et al. 2006). They may also socialize children to be wary of people of other racial backgrounds (Hughes, et al. 2006).

Socialization in the family is both the result of intentional training as well as through the kind of environment the adults create. The vast majority of socialization occurs unintentionally in so far as it has much more to do with the kinds of environments in which children grow up, the diverse people with whom they interact, and the cultural cues they learn to follow and avoid. Yet, whether children see themselves as smart or stupid, loved or simply tolerated, whether they see the world as safe or dangerous, depends largely on what happens at home during the first few years of their lives.

Socialization in Education

5.4.2 Understand how tracking systems work in education in ways that help reproduce class inequality.

In modern societies, we spend almost a third of our lives in school. Eighty-one percent of the U.S. population graduate from high school after 12 or 13 years of education, and 31 percent complete 4 to 6 years of college (U.S. Department of Education 2015). Graduate school or professional school can add another 5 to 10 years. During this time, we are learning facts, concepts, and skills that we will use throughout our lives. But education also has a *latent function*, a "hidden curriculum" that instills the social norms and values of a particular culture, such as the importance of competition or the value of gaining attention for one's ideas.

Education has an enormous impact on our sense of self, and it is nearly as important as family in instilling us with our first social statuses. To fully appreciate how education "works" as a social institution means looking at it intersectionally. For example, high school curricula are typically divided into "academic" and "practical" subjects. Most students are channeled into one or the other. And although it is not legal to explicitly separate students into the academic and practical tracks on the basis of their race or class, research has shown race and class to be good predictors of exactly where students are tracked in education. As an institution, education in the United States works in ways that ensure that white middle-class children prepare for college and middle-class careers, and many non-white and working-class children prepare for working-class jobs (see MAP 5.1).

social mobility
The process of moving between different positions in social hierarchies within society (e.g., from one social class to another).

MAP 5.1 Proportion of Americans with Bachelor's Degrees and with Household Incomes among the Top 40 Percent
Receiving a bachelor's degree is an individual accomplishment, and it's hard work. But some of us are much more likely to receive the degree than others. Consider this map of the United States illustrating the proportion of people who are among the wealthiest 40 percent of Americans in different counties and the proportions of the people in those counties who have a bachelor's degree. You are simply much more likely to get a degree if you grew up in a wealthy community than you are if you didn't.

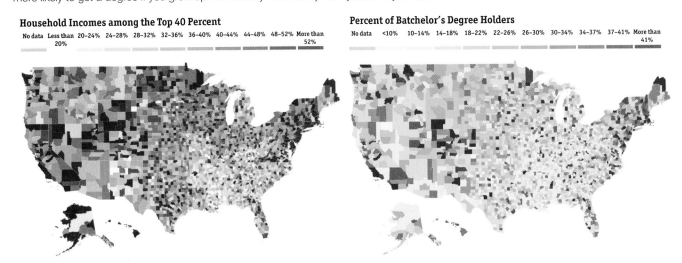

SOURCE: Data from Pell Institute (2015). Indicators of Higher Education Equity in the United States. Philadelphia, Pell Institute. Available at: http://www .pellinstitute.org/downloads/publications-Indicators_of_Higher_Education_Equity_in_the_US_45_Year_Trend_Report.pdf.

Education socializes us not only into social class, but also into race, gender, and sexual identity statuses. "Tracking" in schools is an important mechanism of institutional socialization because while it appears to simply sort students on the basis of individual talents and skills, it simultaneously works in ways that reproduce the social world in which some people are systemically (indeed, structurally) pushed ahead and others held back.

Socialization in Religion

5.4.3 Describe the role of religion in the early socialization of U.S. children.

The United States is the most religious nation in the Western world: 36 percent of the population attend religious services every week, and 53 percent of adults say that religion is "very important" in their lives (see U.S./WORLD How Important is Religion as a Socializing Force?). And 55 percent of Americans pray every day or several times a day—higher for blacks and Latinos (Pew Research Center 2015). But we are socialized into religious beliefs in many places besides churches, mosques, and temples. Often we pray or hear religious stories at home. Nearly two-thirds of Americans with Internet access have used it for religious purposes (Hoover, Clark, and Rainie 2004). In school, we recite the Pledge of Allegiance, which since the mid-twentieth century has included the phrase "one nation under God," and increasingly school boards are requiring that biblical creation be taught along with (or instead of) evolution in science class as an explanation for the origin of the world. Every political candidate is expected to profess publicly his or her religious faith; an atheist would have a very difficult time getting elected to any office. (In fact, a 2015 Gallup Poll found that 74 percent of Americans would vote for a lesbian or gay president, compared to 58 percent who would vote for an atheist for president. Roughly 24 percent of Americans said they would *not* vote for a lesbian or gay president, and approximately 40 percent said they would *not* vote for an atheist president [McCarthy 2015].) And other studies have found the prejudice against atheists has increased since then (e.g., Miller 2007).

Religion is an important agent of socialization because it provides a divine motivation for instilling social norms in children and adults. Why do we dress, talk, and behave in a certain way? Why do we refuse to eat pork when our neighbors seem to like it? Why are we not allowed to watch television or go to school dances? Why are men in charge of making money, and women in charge of child care? Why are most of the elite jobs occupied by white people? Religion may teach us that these social phenomena are not arbitrary, based on outdated tradition or on in-groups competing with out-groups.

In traditional societies, religious affiliation is an *ascribed status*. You are born into a religion, and you remain in it throughout your life, regardless of how enthusiastically you practice or how fervently you believe (or even whether you believe at all). Several of the religions practiced in modern societies continue to be ascribed. For instance, if you are born Roman Catholic and later decide that you don't believe in the Roman

U.S./WORLD

HOW IMPORTANT IS RELIGION AS A SOCIALIZING FORCE?

Religion is one of the major institutions of socialization, instilling community feeling and cultural values. We also know, however, that not all countries around the world are equally religious. And the level of wealth of different countries has been shown to be significantly related to how religious people say they are. Consider the graph, illustrating that wealthier nations (nations with a higher per capital gross domestic product) tend to be less religious. Interestingly, the United States is a major outlier here—something we will return to in Chapter 15.

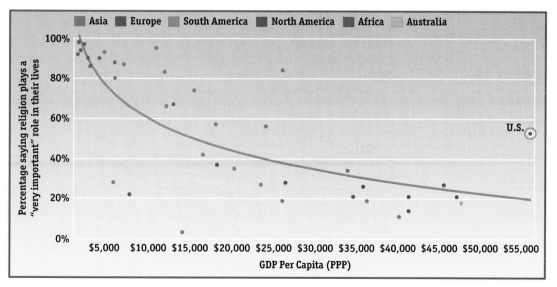

NOTE: The trendline represents a logarithmic relationship between GDP per capita (PPP) and the percentage of people saying that religion plays a "very important" role in their lives.

Data from Pew Research Center, Spring 2011, 2012, 2013 Global Attitudes survey. Data for GDP per capita (PPP) from IMF World Economic Outlook Database, April 2015.

INVESTIGATE FURTHER

1. What might explain the tremendous differences among countries in their rating of the importance of religion in socialization?

2. What other socializing forces might take the place of religion in more secular countries?

WHAT DO YOU THINK? WHAT DOES AMERICA THINK?

Being Christian, Being American

Some people believe the United States was founded on Christian values, and others see religious identity and nationality as unrelated.

What do you think?

How important is being Christian to being an American?

- ○ Very important
- ○ Fairly important
- ○ Not very important
- ○ Not important at all

What does America think?

Roughly one third of all respondents said being Christian is "very important" to being an American, and an additional third of respondents said it was "not important at all." It was much more important for black respondents (56.8 percent indicated "very important") than for white (28.7 percent).

SOURCE: Data from General Social Survey, 2014.

THINKING CRITICALLY ABOUT SURVEY DATA

Why do you think so many Americans believe being Christian is important to a U.S. identity? How do you explain the differences in response between black and white respondents?

Catholic Church anymore, you are simply a "lapsed Catholic." However, in many modern societies, religions operate in a "religious marketplace," with hundreds and even thousands of different groups competing for believers and the freedom to select the religious group that will best fit into our other social roles. Instead of religion being a more formal and comprehensive socializing institution, different religious groups now offer guidelines for socialization in a virtual spiritual shopping mall, in which we exercise far more individual choice in our religious socialization than any generation in history.

Peer Socialization

5.4.4 Understand the role that peer groups play in the socialization process alongside more formal agents of socialization.

At school, in the neighborhood, at our clubs, and eventually at work, we develop many groups of friends, wider groups of acquaintances, and a few enemies. In modern societies, our **peer groups** (the friends) are usually age specific—a third grader hardly deigns to associate with a second grade "baby" and might be ostracized by groups of fourth graders. As adults, we expand the boundaries of age a bit, but still, 50-year-olds rarely pal around with 30-year-olds. Peer groups also tend to be homogeneous, limited to a single neighborhood, race, religion, social class, gender, or other social status. The smart kids may sit at one table in the cafeteria, the jocks at another, and Hip-Hop fans at a third.

Peer groups have an enormous socializing influence, especially during middle and late childhood. Peer groups provide an enclave where we can learn the skills of social interaction and the importance of group loyalty, but those enclaves are not always safe and caring. Peers teach social interaction through coercion, humiliation, and bullying as well as through encouragement, and group loyalty often means being condescending, mean, or even violent to members of out-groups (see FIGURE 5.5).

peer group
Our group of friends and wider group of acquaintances who have an enormous socializing influence, especially during middle and late childhood.

FIGURE 5.5 Proportion of Time Spent with Friends at Different Locations among U.S. Teens
Consider how much time young people spend around each other. It should come as no surprise that they are socializing one another. Teens are so connected today that they are often together even when they're not in each other's presence; they "hang out" online together. Among teens, both boys and girls hang out digitally by texting, talking on the phone, and posting on various social media sites. But boys are much more likely to also do so using online video games.

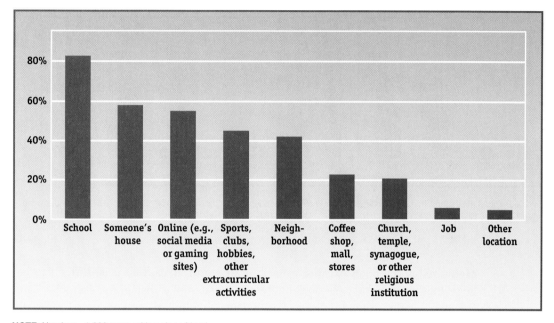

NOTE: Number = 1,009 teens with a close friend.

SOURCE: Data from Pew Research Center (2015). Teen Relationships Survey, Sept. 25-Oct. 9, 2014 and Feb. 10-March 16, 2015. Available at http://www.pewinternet.org/2015/08/06/teens-technology-and-friendships/.

Sometimes peer groups resist the socialization efforts of family and schools by requiring different, contradictory norms and values: rewarding smoking, drinking, and vandalism, for example, or punishing good grades and class participation. But more often they merely reinforce the socialization that children (and adults) receive elsewhere. Barrie Thorne (1993) looked at gender polarization (separating boys and girls) among elementary school students and found that peer groups and teachers worked together. The teachers rewarded boys for being "masculine"—aggressive, tough, and loud—and girls for being "feminine"—shy, quiet, and demure. Peer groups merely *reinforced* gender polarization. Boys' groups rewarded athletic ability, coolness, and toughness; and girls' groups rewarded physical appearance, including the ability to use makeup and select fashionable clothing.

We continue to have peer groups throughout adulthood. Often, we engage in anticipatory socialization, learning the norms and values of a group that we haven't joined yet. For example, we may mimic the clothing style and slang of a popular peer group with the hope that we will be accepted.

Socialization from the Media

5.4.5 Define the ongoing role that the media play in socializing us throughout our lives.

We spend all day, every day, immersed in mass media—popular books and magazines, radio, television, movies, video games, the Internet, and even sociology textbooks. Although media use varies somewhat by race and ethnicity, gender, education, and income, overall, young people in the United States spend more than 9 hours every day with one form or another of mass media (Common Sense Media 2015a) (as compared to about 6.5 hours for Americans overall (Rideout, et al. 2010).

FIGURE 5.6 Media Use by Age, Race, and Ethnicity

Young Americans (8–10 year olds) have less media use and exposure than Americans throughout their teenage years. And the forms of media each age group consumes vary as well. So, media use and exposure intersect with age.

Black, white, and Hispanic Americans also have different media exposure and use in a typical day. As a group, white Americans consume and are exposed to less media in an average day than are black and Hispanic Americans. Just as media use and exposure intersect with age, so too do they intersect with race and ethnicity.

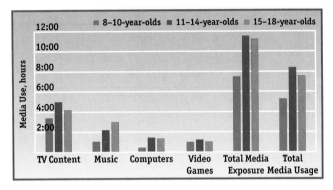 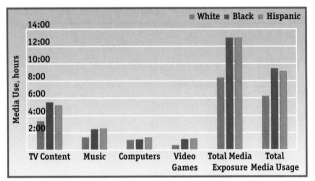

SOURCE: Data from Rideout, Victoria J., Ulla G. Foehr, and Donald F. Roberts, Kaiser Family Foundation Study, January (2010). "GENERATION M2: Media in the Lives of 8-to-18 Year-Olds: 9 (January 2010). Available at https://kaiserfamilyfoundation.files.wordpress.com/2013/01/8010.pdf.

Media today are such fixtures, especially in young lives, that it is difficult to believe that so many types—social-networking sites like Instagram, Snapchat, and Facebook, online games, video-sharing sites like Vine, and gadgets, especially mobile phones—barely existed less than a decade ago. Both mass media and social media are powerful agents of socialization today, from childhood through adulthood (see FIGURE 5.6).

Television is probably the dominant form of mass media across the developed world. And viewing is dependent on status: generally, the higher the socioeconomic class, the less television viewing. Women watch more than men, African Americans and Hispanics more than white Americans. But children of all classes, races, and genders watch the most. The Kaiser Family Foundation's representative survey of the United States in 2009 found that of the 7 hours and 38 minutes that children ages 2 through 18 spend consuming mass media every day, more than 3 hours and 15 minutes are spent watching television by white children, nearly 5.5 hours by Hispanics, and close to 6 hours by black children (the rest of the time is devoted to listening to social media, listening to music, reading, playing video games, and using the computer). And a more recent report from Common Sense Media found even higher results. They found that U.S. teens consume an average of 9 hours of media daily (not including for school or homework). They also discovered that black youth spend substantially more time with media than both white and Hispanic youth, reporting an average of 11 hours of media a day, compared with almost 9 hours among Hispanics and 8.5 hours among Whites (Common Sense Media 2015b).

Many scholars and parents are worried about the impact of heavy television watching, arguing that it makes children passive, less likely to use their imagination (Christakis 2009; Healy 1990), and more likely to have short attention spans. But other scholars disagree. Television has been around for more than 50 years. So, the worried parents watched themselves when they were children with no catastrophic loss of creativity or rise in mass murder; in previous generations, similar fears were voiced about radio, movies, comic books, and dime novels.

Video games, too, are a prevalent form of mass media. More than 80 percent of American teenagers have access to a game console today, including 85 percent of whites, 84 percent of African Americans, and 71 percent of Latinos (Pew Research Center 2015). The vast majority of players are children and teenagers, making video games nearly the equal of television in popularity. (The genres aren't strictly separate;

Video games play a role in socializing children and adults—in addition to learning logic, reasoning, and developing technological and motor skills, however, children are also being socialized by the content of the games and how different groups (like women or non-white characters) are portrayed.

the same characters and situations may appear in television, movies, comic books, and video games simultaneously.) Adult observers have the same sorts of concerns as they have with television: lack of creativity and decreased attention span, plus rampant sexism. Women are often portrayed as passive victims who must be rescued, or hypersexual babes who can be raped and murdered to score points or advance in the fame. But some studies show that video games develop logic, reasoning, and motor reflexes, skills useful in a technological future (Johnson 2005).

And "new media" may be playing the most important role of all. Contemporary social media today are becoming one of the primary institutions of peer culture for U.S. teenagers, joining the ranks of school, home, the street, or the mall as places of socialization and identity-building (Ito, et al. 2008; MacArthur Foundation 2008). About one-fourth of all teenagers (24 percent) go online "almost constantly"; some 13-year-olds check their favorite platforms 100 times a day (Lenhart 2015). Girls dominate social media sites, especially visually oriented ones like Instagram, Snapchat, and Pinterest, and boys are more likely to play video games, either on a console, a computer, or on their phones. (Lenhart 2015).

Media dominate our lives to such an extent that they are a principal institution of socialization in our society. This is why so many parents are worried about how to filter and monitor the online activities and interactions of their kids, while still carrying more traditional concerns about things like the ratings of different movies. Video games are now rated as well, again, in large part because we recognize the media as playing some role in socializing the people consuming it.

Socialization in the Workplace

5.4.6 Explain the ways that the workplace socializes us and shapes our behavior and identities.

We spend about one-third of our lives in the workplace, and we often define ourselves most essentially by our jobs: If you ask someone "What are you?" he or she will probably reply "I am an architect" or "I am a hair stylist" rather than "I am somebody's brother." In traditional societies, your job was less a marker of identity because there were only a few specialized jobs: a religious sage, a tribal chief, and perhaps a few skilled artisans. Everyone else in the community did everything else necessary for survival, from gathering crops to spinning cloth to caring for children.

SOCIOLOGY AND OUR WORLD

CAN GAY AND LESBIAN SCHOOLTEACHERS BE "OUT" AT WORK?

Think about the term *professional*. What comes to mind? What kind of person do you picture? Is it a man or a woman? Is the person a particular race? What kinds of clothes is he or she wearing? What about his or her sexual orientation?

Catherine Connell was interested in precisely these issues when she conducted interview research with 45 gay and lesbian schoolteachers for her book, *School's Out: Gay and Lesbian Teachers in the Classroom*. Connell (2014) discovered that the teachers she studied struggled with feeling that they needed to be "out" in the classroom to fulfill their responsibilities to gay pride while simultaneously feeling that coming out to their students meant they were failing their responsibilities as teaching professionals.

The teachers in Connell's research experienced a dynamic tension in the workplace between *pride* and *professionalism*. As one of her interviewee's put it, "I think, first and foremost, I see myself as a teacher. I don't mix my sexual orientation with my career. You know, it's my career first." Connell shows that not everyone experiences this tension and argues that heterosexuality is an obscured component of norms of professionalism in the workplace; it is a taken-for-granted feature of organizational policies, practices, and procedures. And Connell suggests that gay and lesbian teachers are in the best position to illustrate this.

In modern societies we receive specialized training, and we have jobs that usually require us to leave home and family and spend all day in a workplace (although staying home to take care of the household is often considered a job, too). In many ways, workplaces are similar to schools: Supervisors assign tasks like teachers, and there are peer groups (those we interact with all the time), acquaintances, and sometimes enemies. We are expected to behave in a "professional" and "business-like" fashion, but depending on the social class of the job, what that means varies tremendously.

iSOC AND YOU Institutions of Socialization

Nelson Mandela, the great South African leader, said his favorite poem was "Invictus" by William Ernest Henley. It gave him great comfort in prison to remember the words "I am the master of my fate/I am the captain of my soul." To a sociologist, that inspiring poem emphasizes that you are an active agent in your socialization, that you create your own *identity*, through your *interactions* with others and within the social *institutions* that comprise society. You can accept some parts, push back against others. Some *inequalities* feel acceptable, while others feel intolerable. You create this creature called "you" as all these *intersecting* ideas, rules, and values collide around you. You're neither a robot, passively accepting the same script as everyone else, nor do you operate in a vacuum, all by yourself. You become "you" through socialization.

5.5 Socialization and Ongoing and Unending

Stage theories of socialization often implicitly present socialization as a goal, an ultimate destination—as though, if things proceed as they should, we will all be completely "socialized" at some point in our lives. Sociologists understand socialization as an ongoing and unending process. We are never completely "socialized"; rather, we are continually socialized and resocialized throughout our lives as we encounter new life stages, institutions, and contexts that require us to reexamine ourselves and the roles we play in society. This means that sociologists study socialization across the life course. Although we are interested in the primary socialization that happens in early childhood, our interest in socialization does not stop there. We are equally interested in the ways the elderly in society come to understand what it means to be "old" and how to take on this new status as they enter that stage of their lives.

And sociologists are also interested in the ways that socialization is a phenomenon on a global scale. With the advent of an increasingly global economy, we are constantly interacting with goods, services, and ideas that are circulated around the world. Although we may put a unique local spin on this interaction, we need to acknowledge the fact that socialization occurs on a much larger scale than you may have previously thought possible. This also means that while we are socialized to understand inequalities between groups within our own societies, we are also being socialized to make sense of inequalities between societies. In this final section, we consider the scope and scale of socialization.

Socialization across the Life Course

5.5.1 Describe the ways that our understanding of the life course in addition to the different stages we recognize as distinct is a product of socialization.

Stages of life may be marked by distinct physiological changes, but the meanings associated with life stages are socially constructed, varying by culture and even by status within a culture (for example, by gender, race, or social class). Childhood is a relatively recent construct. In some parts of the world, children still work like adults. Similarly, the stage we know as "adolescence" has developed as separate from adulthood. During this time of extended education, we are shielded from all of the responsibilities and rights of adulthood. Adolescents do not have all of the responsibilities (and freedoms) of adults, but they are understood as meaningfully distinct from "children."

Cultures often mark passage into adulthood by rituals that scholars refer to as **rites of passage**. While getting a job, or getting married long served as a clearly defined rite of passage into adulthood, the boundaries between childhood and adulthood are less clear today. Sociologists have attempted to define who qualifies as an adult by using specific life stages as **markers of adulthood**—finishing school, getting a job, moving out, marrying, having a child. One thing we have learned is that Americans are delaying and foregoing some of these stages much longer than they used to (and sometimes foregoing them altogether).

As a result of this, it is probably the case that fewer Americans would be willing to call themselves "adults." In step, sociologists also study a group they refer to as young adults. **Young adulthood** refers to the period of your life when you are clearly no longer a child or adolescent, but have not yet reached adulthood either. If finishing school, becoming financially independent, entering into a lifelong partnership with someone, and having children have historically been relied on to identify "adulthood," we know that young people in the United States today are delaying these demographic milestones longer than they used to. Adulthood seems to have become a bit more elusive as 20-, 30-, and even 40-year olds in the United States might increasingly feel like they are not quite there (see FIGURE 5.7).

Similarly, as a result of people delaying becoming adults, other stages of the life course have been pushed off as well. Middle age and old age happen later than at any

rites of passage

A marker, often a ceremony, that denotes an important stage in someone's life, such as birth, puberty, marriage, death.

markers of adulthood

Specific life stages that define who qualifies as an "adult," such as finishing school, getting a job, moving out of the parental home, marrying, and having a child.

young adulthood

The life stage at which people are clearly no longer children or adolescents, but have not yet reached full adulthood either.

FIGURE 5.7 Percentage of 25- to 34-Year-Olds Living in Multigenerational Households by Gender, 2010–2012

The recent economic recession, coupled with a new economy and job market has forced many college graduates to move back home with their parents after graduating. News media have dubbed these young adults, "boomerang kids." Surveys suggest that men are more likely to move back home than are women, though the rates have increased for both men and women in recent history. This trend is higher among racial and ethnic minorities than it is among whites.

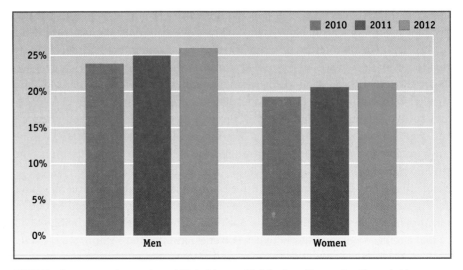

NOTE: Numbers represent percentage of 25- to 34-year-olds living in multigenerational households.

SOURCE: Data from Fry, Richard and Jeffrey Passel, (2014). In Post-Recession Era, Young Adults Drive Continuing Rise in Multi-Generational Living. *Pew Research Center*, July 17, 2014. Available at: http://www.pewsocialtrends.org/2014/07/17/in-post-recession-era-young-adults-drive-continuing-rise-in-multi-generational-living/.

time in the past, due to delay reaching adulthood, and longer life spans. Similarly, new stages of the life course emerge as a result of these transitions. For instance, in 1900, the life expectancy for someone growing up in the United States was slightly younger than 50 years old. By 2014, the average life expectancy for people born in the United States was almost 80 years. These averages, however, vary significantly by race and class, among other categories. For African Americans, for example, the average life expectancy is younger than 75. Nevertheless, the added years mean that new stages of the life course exist now that simply couldn't have existed in 1900—great grandparenthood for instance. But, things like "empty nest" syndrome also exist now in part due to a greater life expectancy. Increasingly, adults with children will live a good chunk of their lives without their children around. And this has given rise to a new stage in the life course adults are navigating today that their grandparents might not have been fully able to imagine.

iSoc in Action: Socialization in a Global Society

5.5.2 Understand how socialization helps us navigate the interplay between local and global identities and culture.

Although each culture—and each subculture—generates their own definition of what constitutes "normal" and "healthy" identity, and then proceeds to socialize children into those models, it is equally true that these models must also connect with larger global identities. After all, you increasingly interact with other people in other cultures, with very different understandings of what it means to be a person in that society. On Facebook or Twitter, for example, you may have friends or followers from all over the world. How can you communicate?

There are emerging global ideas of what it means to be a person, and these are transmitted through various media that transcend national boundaries. For example, an international businessman cannot only interact with another international businessman about some financial transaction, but they also have dinner together,

Globalization has meant more interactions between different societies around the world. And these new interactions bring with them new requirements to be socialized to norms, roles, and expectations from societies different from our own.

share an appreciation of the local gourmet meal, and discuss a movie they've both seen on Netflix. You are socialized into **local cultures**—your local understanding of gender, sexuality, race, ethnicity, and so on—but these identities cannot stray too far from these emerging global identities, or we couldn't communicate with each other.

This socialization process is not uniform: We are being socialized to accept inequalities as somehow normal or justified. Thus, some ideas of what it means to be, say, a woman in one culture, have to roughly correspond to some ideas in other cultures—that is, some versions are more "credited" than others. We learn that the ones that intersect with other global identities are better, more highly valued.

And the emergence of these globally intersecting types of socialization may not only reflect existing inequalities based on race or ethnicity or sexuality, but also expand them, as some notions of identity from the global South are discredited as "older" and "traditional" and thus pushed aside as new, global identities are produced. Parents socialize their children with one eye on the past—"how we have always done things"—and one eye toward the future—"what sort of person does my child have to be to participate in this world." The mix is rarely symmetrical, and those who cling most tenaciously to the past may be those whose identities are least likely to survive into the future.

local culture

The cultural norms, roles, values, expectations, and beliefs that shape distinct social contexts.

---

iSOC AND YOU Socialization and Ongoing and Unending

Socialization is a lifelong process by which you become aware of your own *identity* in *interaction* with others. As a social process, socialization is deceptively simple because the various identities that make up who you are *intersect* in unique enough ways that socialization takes different forms for different people and is enacted in distinct ways in different social *institutions*. Sociologists are both interested in how this process takes place, but also in how socialization works in ways that reinforce existing forms of social *inequality*, providing support for them. Increasingly, sociologists are interested in these inequalities not only within societies, but between them as well as socialization is something sociologists understand as occurring on a global scale.

Conclusion

Socialization NOW

We have selves, supported by social structures and our primary socialization, but we are also continually changing, responsive to our current social environments, in interaction with increasing numbers of agents of socialization. This is the dynamic tension of self in society, which the sociologist Erving Goffman understood so well. What this means is that sociologists understand socialization as a dynamic and lifelong process. You are never fully socialized. Across your life span, new and different agents of socialization come into play.

This also means that sociologists do not understand people as capable of achieving single, "true" identity; rather, our identities are best understood as always, inevitably shifting. This complex process offers us constant opportunities for self-creation and growth. But it is also a process rife with tensions between autonomy and belonging, between individuality and group identification. As Goffman captured it:

> "Without something to belong to, we have no stable self, and yet total commitment and attachment to any social unit implies a kind of selflessness. Our sense of being a person can come from being drawn into a wider social unit; our sense of selfhood can arise through the little ways in which we resist the pull. Our status is backed by the solid buildings of the world, while our sense of personal identity often resides in the cracks" (Goffman 1961: 320).

We learn about our own identity and the identities of others through our social interactions with other people and social institutions. And we also learn about systems of social inequality and to examine how the various intersections of our own identities and those of others position people differently in the society in which we live. It is through socialization that we find ways of standing out by fitting in. And socialization is not just something happening *to* you; it is also something in which you are actively engaged. You resist, go along, pave your own way, and more. And you are involved in socializing others as well—sometimes, and perhaps most effectively, when you are not even aware of the fact that you're doing it.

Socialization never ends.

CHAPTER REVIEW Socialization

5.1 Understanding What Socialization Is and How It Works

Humans have long pondered what makes us who we are—nature or nurture? Before the Enlightenment, the prevailing European view was that we are creatures of nature, made by God. This began to change as environment was recognized as a force shaping human nature; in Locke's view, we are born as blank slates, wholly shaped by environment. Rousseau tempered this view, recognizing nature and nurture, and Darwin's work supported the primacy of biology. We are products of both, but biology focuses on the nature and the basic physiological aspect of our being, and sociology focuses on socialization; how we develop, becoming who we are, and continually changing, through social interaction. Compared with other species, even other primates, humans are helpless and dependent the longest—up to a quarter of the normal life span. As we develop physically, we develop socially, not just through formal instruction but more often informally through social interaction. Experimental work with monkeys confirms the importance of early social interaction. Even things thought biologically innate, like the maternal instinct, are socialization dependent.

5.1 Key Terms
socialization The process by which we become aware of ourselves as part of a group, learn to communicate with others, and learn how to behave as expected.

primary socialization A culture's most basic values, which are passed on to children beginning in earliest infancy.

secondary socialization Occurring throughout the life span, it is the adjustments we make to adapt to new situations.

5.2 Models of Socialization

Stage theories dominate developmental models, in sociology and psychology, too. Mead discussed three stages in childhood—first imitation, then role play in the play stage, and finally, in the game stage, taking the role of the other, ultimately internalizing the generalized other. In Freud's theory of sexual development we go through three stages of developing gender identity, each oriented around how the ego meets the id's urges. Successfully socialized adults have egos that channel the id's impulses in socially acceptable ways and superegos that internalize society's rules. Piaget studied cognitive development, identifying four stages: sensorimotor, preoperational, concrete operational, and finally, formal operational, which is adult-like in reasoning ability. Kohlberg's view of moral development, from concrete to abstract principles, was challenged by Gilligan for neglecting other equally moral ethical systems. Stage theories are criticized because development may not be as invariant, discrete, or progressive as these theories propose, nor are they necessarily universal. For example, socialization continues throughout life, with anticipatory socialization and resocialization.

5.2 Key Terms

generalized other   The organized rules, judgments, and attitudes of an entire group. If you try to imagine what is expected of you, you are taking on the perspective of the generalized other.

id   Sigmund Freud's label for that part of the human psyche that is pure impulse, without worrying about social rules, consequences, morality, or other people's reactions.

superego   Freud's term for the internalized norms, values, and "rules" of our social group that are learned from family, friends, and social institutions.

ego   Freud's term for the balancing force in the psyche between the id and the superego; it channels impulses into socially acceptable forms.

anticipatory socialization   The process of learning and adopting the beliefs, values, and behaviors of groups that one anticipates joining in the future.

resocialization   The process of learning a new set of beliefs, behaviors, and values that depart from those held in the past.

5.3 Socialization and Inequality

The former President of South Africa and former anti-apartheid revolutionary said "People must learn to hate, and if they can learn to hate, they can be taught to love." But is that true? Aren't humans "naturally" suspicious of others, competitive and selfish? Or are we "naturally" communal and egalitarian? The answer is yes. We're both. The sociological question isn't whether we are one or the other—it's *how* and *when* and *under what circumstances*. Socialization can enable us to see problems that we might not have otherwise seen. Socialization can also keep us blind to inequalities that are presented to us as natural and inevitable. If socialization is the process by which individuals are incorporated into their society, then it is a question of the social norms that constitute life in that society that

determine your socialization. Socialization can enable us to accept inequality as natural (even as morally unquestionable or good) or it can inspire us to fight against it. Or both. The choices we make about how to act and why, these are the result of our own individual interaction with the legacy of our socialization. We're socialized, but we also make choices.

5.4 Institutions of Socialization

We encounter agents of socialization throughout our lives. Much of the socialization is unintentional. Primary socialization occurs during childhood, through family, school, and religion, with mass media and our peer group gaining considerable influence in middle and late childhood. Secondary socialization occurs during adulthood, through the workplace and other social institutions, like the government. Aspects of self developed during primary socialization may always influence us, in one form or another, particularly social statuses, such as religion, even though values, beliefs, and behaviors are not always explicitly taught. Education teaches but also sorts and socializes by gender and class; this is the "hidden curriculum." Religion is a source of community and culture but divides societies, too, sometimes demonizing out-groups. Peer groups informally reinforce the socialization of other institutions in interaction, through encouragement, bullying, and coercion. Mass media, from television, movies, and magazines, to more recent video games, web platforms, and social media, are extraordinarily influential and create global connections. For adults, the workplace is so important that we often identify ourselves by our job.

5.4 Key Terms

agents of socialization   The people, groups, and institutions that teach all of us how to be functioning members of society.

social mobility   The process of moving between different positions in social hierarchies within society (e.g., from one social class to another).

peer group   Our group of friends and wider group of acquaintances who have an enormous socializing influence, especially during middle and late childhood.

5.5 Socialization: Ongoing and Unending

Stages of life may be marked by distinct physiological changes, but meanings associated with life stages are socially constructed, varying by culture and even by status within a culture; for example, by gender, race, or social class. Childhood is a relatively recent construct. In some parts of the world, children still work like adults. Adolescence has developed as separate from adulthood. During this time of extended education, we are shielded from all of the responsibilities and rights of adulthood. Cultures often mark passage into adulthood by ritual. The sociological markers of adulthood—finishing school, getting a job, moving out, marrying, having a child—now occur later. Young adulthood refers to the period before adulthood. Middle age and old age happen later than at any time in the past, due to delay reaching adulthood, and longer life spans.

5.5 Key Terms

rites of passage A marker, often a ceremony, that denotes an important stage in someone's life, such as birth, puberty, marriage, death.

markers of adulthood Specific life stages that define who qualifies as an "adult," such as finishing school, getting a job, moving out of the parental home, marrying, and having a child.

young adulthood The life stage at which people are clearly no longer children or adolescents, but have not yet reached full adulthood either.

local culture The cultural norms, roles, values, expectations, and beliefs that shape distinct social contexts.

SELF-TEST

> CHECK YOUR UNDERSTANDING

1. Which of the following is an example of secondary socialization?
   a. A child develops the understandings that pink is for girls, blue is for boys, and she is supposed to be afraid of spiders instead of interested in them, from things other children say at preschool.
   b. Pointed remarks from coworkers help a college graduate realize that casual Friday means khaki pants and a sport shirt with a collar, instead of cut-off shorts and a T-shirt.
   c. Factory workers on the line are obedient and deferential to all authorities in their workplace, just as they were to their teachers in grade school.
   d. A young adult continues to give up candy and sweets for Lent.

2. According to the text, which of the following agents of socialization are especially influential during adolescence?
   a. The family and education
   b. Mass media and peers
   c. Education and the workplace
   d. The government

3. During which stage of Mead's theory are the expectations of society internalized as the generalized other?
   a. Imitation stage
   b. Play stage
   c. Games stage
   d. In Mead's theory, during all of the above stages, children have internalized the generalized other.

4. Kohn's research found that working-class families instill in their children the importance of _____, while middle-class and affluent families encourage the development of _____.
   a. discretion; industriousness.
   b. friendliness; courage.
   c. good judgment; self-control.
   d. conformity; creativity.

5. Martin and Kazyak's research on sexuality in children's movies found that
   a. G-rated movies are devoid of sexual content.
   b. children's movies depict men and women as equals.
   c. heterosexual love is portrayed as exceptional and transformative as compared with other types of relationships.
   d. friendships are portrayed as special and exceptional forms of relationships.

6. Anderson and Daniels' research on Disney movies found that
   a. none of the movies show girls and women with half or more of the speaking roles.
   b. none of the movies have more female characters with speaking roles than men.
   c. earlier movies gave girls and women a larger proportion of speaking lines than they do today.
   d. all of the choices were found by Anderson and Daniels.

7. Sociologists find that the transition to adulthood is marked by the completion of which of the following?
   a. Finishing school and getting a job
   b. Getting married and having a child
   c. Leaving their parents' home for one of their own
   d. All of the choices are markers of the transition to adulthood

8. The first year of college is often difficult as expectations are very different from high school. Successful adjustment to college the first year is an example of:
   a. primary socialization.
   b. secondary socialization.
   c. resocialization.
   d. anticipatory socialization.

Self-Test Answers: 1. b, 2. b, 3. c, 4. d, 5. c, 6. c, 7. d, 8. c

CHAPTER 6

CRIME AND DEVIANCE

Sometimes, people follow social norms—they lead their lives in culturally "normative" ways. But everyone violates some social norms at least some of the time. And some people transgress social norms all of the time. Sociologists are interested in what we can learn about a society from culturally normative and deviant identities and behaviors.

→ LEARNING OBJECTIVES

In this chapter, using the iSoc framework, you should be able to:

6.1.1 Explain the distinction between deviance and crime.

6.1.2 Recognize how each of the five elements of the iSoc model can be used to examine crime and deviance sociologically.

6.1.3 Distinguish among folkways, mores, and taboos.

6.2.1 Understand the differences among social control theories of deviance.

6.2.2 Explain the conditions that cause a subculture to qualify as "deviant."

6.2.3 Summarize how youth gangs went from being considered youthful mischief to deviant and criminal subcultures.

6.2.4 Understand how labeling theory explains deviance, and distinguish among primary, secondary, and tertiary deviance.

6.2.5 Summarize what sociologists mean by "stigma" and the strategies stigmatized individuals rely on to interact with others.

6.2.6 Explain why sociologists argue that deviance and crime work in ways that both produce and reproduce systems of inequality.

6.3.1 Understand the differences among three separate sociological explanations that tie crime rates to society.

6.3.2 Distinguish between types of crime, and provide examples to illustrate your understanding.

6.3.3 Identify social factors that cause young men and women to engage in different levels of types of criminal activity.

6.3.4 Identify social factors that put racial minorities and the poor at disproportionate risk of being arrested.

6.3.5 Understand what sociologists mean by "gun culture," and use this to explain why gun crime in the United States is so much higher than other industrialized countries around the world.

6.3.6 Using the example of drugs, explain the ways that local crimes are related to global trends.

6.4.1 Explain the split image of police in the United States and how that is related to different experiences of the police among different groups in society.

6.4.2 Summarize the social problem of bias in the courtroom including why and how mandatory sentencing legislation failed.

6.4.3 Explain shifts in the U.S. incarceration rate, and consider them in international perspective.

6.4.4 Summarize the four goals of incarceration and whether they are achieved in the United States or not.

6.4.5 Summarize why sociologists are confident that the death penalty does not actually deter people from committing the crimes associated with this sentence.

Introduction

There's a good chance that every person reading this book is a law-abiding citizen. We don't steal each other's cars; we don't open fire at the quarterback or point guard of opposing teams; we don't burn down dormitories or plunder the provost's office. We pay our taxes and drive under the speed limit, at least most of the time.

Yet there is an equally good chance that each person reading this book is a "criminal"—that is, has done something illegal. We may have run a red light, had a drink while underage, or gambled on a sporting event in an unauthorized setting or while underage. We may have stolen a library book or plagiarized a paper. (These last few might not land you in jail, but they could get you kicked out of school.)

Most of us probably break the rules a little bit. But we're also likely to get outraged, even to the point of violence, if someone cuts into a line for tickets at the movie theater. Is it just because it's OK for us and not OK for others? Or is it because we carry inside us a common moral standard, and we are willing to cheat a little to make things come out the way we think they are supposed to but resent it when others violate that same moral contract?

So, is the question whether you are a law-abiding citizen or a criminal? To the sociologist, you're both. The more interesting questions are when and where you are one or the other, under what circumstances you obey or disobey the law, and what the social and legal consequences of your behavior are. Do you get away with it or get sent to jail?

And how do we think about crime? What crimes should be punished, and how severe should those punishments be? In some respects, one might say that the United States is soft on crime: Most arrests are not prosecuted, most prosecutions do not result in jail time, and most prisoners are paroled before they serve their full terms. In other respects, the United States is hard on crime: It is the number-one jailer in the world and the only industrialized nation that still has the death penalty. It seems to be a matter of working very hard to achieve very limited results. In fact, we are both soft *and* hard on crime; to the sociologist what is most interesting is the how and why of that "softness" and "hardness" and measuring the effectiveness of the institutions that are designed to handle deviance and crime.

6.1 Thinking Sociologically about Crime and Deviance

Thinking sociologically about crime and deviance, like thinking sociologically more generally, often means that we take a step back and ask less about individuals and more about the contexts in which they find themselves. Studying crime and deviance sociologically entails examining both issues within the iSoc model. This means that we are critically interested in how individuals come to understand themselves and come to be understood by others as "deviant" or "criminal." These identities are imposed on us from outside of ourselves, but some endure this imposition more regularly and may more readily accept the label than others. Sociologists are interested in how and why that happens as well as in tracing the consequences of this process.

Distinguishing Deviance from Crime

6.1.1 Explain the distinction between deviance and crime.

Breaking a social rule, or refusing to follow one, is called **deviance**. Deviant acts may or may not be illegal; they can also violate a moral or a social rule that may or may not have legal consequences. This week, many of you will do something that could be considered deviant—from the illegal behaviors like shoplifting, underage drinking, or speeding, to arriving at a party or one of your college classes too late.

We can also be considered deviant without doing, saying, or believing anything bad or wrong but just by belonging to the "wrong" group in some circumstances (Hispanic, gay, Jewish, for example) or by having some status that goes against what's considered "normal" (e.g., mentally ill, disabled, atheist, being overweight at a fitness club). There is even deviance by association: If you have a friend or romantic partner who belongs to the minority group, you may be labeled as deviant just for being seen with them.

Most deviance is not illegal, and many illegal acts are only mildly deviant or not deviant at all. But when lawmakers consider a deviant act bad enough to warrant formal sanctions, it becomes a crime, and laws are enacted to regulate it. Some common sexual practices—like oral sex or masturbation—are illegal in a number of states because lawmakers at one time found them sufficiently deviant to be criminal. But, even if those laws are still "on the books" in some states, they are, for the most part, no longer understood as "deviant" in quite the same way. This illustrates an important point: Some crime is deviant and some deviance is criminal, but they are also distinct. Some criminal acts are actually not all that deviant at all. Consider jay walking, underage drinking, downloading music illegally. These are criminal acts (we have laws about each of them), but we also acknowledge that people are not transgressing social norms much if they violate them. And lots of deviance is not criminal. Think of showing up too early for a party you were invited to or reading a newspaper in the back of one of your college classes while the professor is lecturing. It's not illegal, but it certainly feels like a lapse in good judgment, and it would likely merit some type of comment or justification. And there are also acts that are understood as both deviant and criminal, like murder, domestic violence, or sexual assault.

Some sociologists study minor forms of deviance, but most are interested in the major forms of deviance. These are acts that can get you shunned or labeled an "outsider" (Becker 1966); or they are the sorts of crimes that get you thrown in prison. These are not matters of mere carelessness: The rules come from many important agents of socialization, and the penalties for breaking them are high. So why do people break them? And why don't most of us break them all the time? What makes a deviant or a criminal? Who decides? How does what is considered deviance vary from society to society? How does it change over time? What can we do about it? These are the central questions to a sociologist because they illustrate our concern for

deviance
Violating a social or moral rule, or refusing to follow one, whether or not that act is illegal.

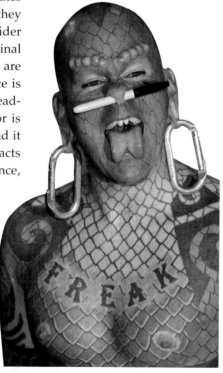

We can also be considered deviant without doing, saying, or believing anything bad or wrong but just by having some status that goes against what's considered "normal," like "Lizardman" who breaks social norms about appearance.

social order and control—both when they are present and people obey the rules and when they are absent and people feel unconstrained by those same rules.

iSoc: The Sociology of Crime and Deviance

6.1.2 Recognize how each of the five elements of the iSoc model can be used to examine crime and deviance sociologically.

As we'll see, just because you might do something that might be considered deviant, or even that might be labeled a crime, doesn't necessarily mean that "deviant" or "criminal" will become who you are, part of your identity. Yet, it is simultaneously the case that we live in societies structured by powerful systems of inequality. So, some people are assumed deviant or criminal even when that is not the case, and not all groups that commit deviant or criminal acts receive the same kinds of consequences or face the same punishments. The institutions associated with deviance and crime have been shown to treat different groups in patterned and distinct ways and this fact means that we need to also understand crime and deviance intersectionally so that we can appreciate the ways that the same issues take on distinct meanings and consequences for different groups in society.

IDENTITY—Deviance and crime are as much "processes" as they are singular acts. Becoming deviant or a criminal is not simply the result of your behavior, but also the result of a process of interactions. One *becomes* deviant or criminal through these interactions with others and institutions. This means that the identities of "deviant" and "criminal" are dramatically shaped by our social positioning and the ways in which we interact with the world around us. Not everyone we might identify as "deviant" or "criminal" thinks of themselves in this way (as a part of their *identity*). And sociologists are interested in how crime and deviance *become* identities for some and not others and what the consequences of these identities are.

INEQUALITY—Sometimes, the same behavior might be labeled deviant or criminal if one person does it, and a harmless prank if another person does it. (See the story about kiddie crime.) It's not simply that deviance and crime are in the eye of the beholder; it's that the beholder has to be able to impose opinions on everyone else, including you. Who gets labeled deviant and sometimes criminal often expresses the elements of *inequality* in a society: Those at the top are able to maintain their position by labeling the actions of those at the bottom as deviant. So, learning about what a society defines as deviant and criminal activity can also tell us a lot about social hierarchies and systems of inequality in those societies. The laws of a society are expressions of its values, and social values are often tied to powerful systems of status, power, and authority.

INTERACTION—Becoming deviant, or a criminal, obviously requires social interactions—and not only with those in power who can enforce their definition of the situation. One also becomes enmeshed in networks of people who are similar to you, people who might support your deviance, rationalize it, encourage it. Even criminals experience constant social *interaction*; even those lone gunslingers of the Wild West were connected to groups of comrades and fellow criminals.

INSTITUTIONS—Whether you are labeled deviant or not, whether you are accused of committing a crime or not, every one of us has to interact, on an almost daily basis, with the social *institutions* that every society has created to control crime and maintain social order. The police represent society's "thin blue line," a first defense against crime, but there are other institutions related to the police, such as courts and prisons. Indeed, the criminal justice system is a complex network of institutions whose mission it is to maintain social order, and administer justice when that order breaks down.

INTERSECTIONS—Some groups are more likely to be labeled deviant than others. Some groups are more likely to be punished, to have legal action taken against them, and once in the courtroom are also more likely to receive harsher punishments. This fact means that to fully understand crime and deviance, we need to look at them *intersectionally*. We need to consider the ways that different groups are subject to different types and degrees of social control. And sociologists who study this help you understand why and how this happens as well as more completely appreciating the full extent of the consequence of these distinctions.

At the conclusion of the chapter, you'll better appreciate why sociologists think of crime and deviance as processes rather than discrete states of being. The iSoc model helps to illustrate these facts and will help you to understand crime and deviance as negotiated and renegotiated on an ongoing basis in our identities and interactions and shaped by social institutions. It will help you to better understand how our understandings of crime and deviance are powerfully shaped by social inequalities. As you learn to think intersectionally, you will learn that our systems of social control are not controlling everyone in precisely the same ways. And these differences might seem small or inconsequential on a small scale. But they are part of a collection of cumulative advantages that shape the experiences and opportunities of different groups in our society in dramatically different ways.

Deviance, Conformity, and Identity

6.1.3 Distinguish among folkways, mores, and taboos.

Each culture develops different types of rules that prescribe what is considered appropriate behavior in that culture. We develop our identity, our sense of ourselves as individuals and our membership in different groups, by our relationship to these rules—which ones we obey, which ones we disobey, and the rationales we develop for our choices. Social rules vary by how formalized they are, how central to social life, the types of consequences associated with breaking them, and whether they are institutionalized.

As you will remember from Chapter 2, **folkways** refer to routine, usually unspoken conventions of behavior; our culture prescribes that we do some things in a certain way, although other ways might work just as well. For example, we face forward instead of backward in an elevator, and answer the question "How are you?" with "Fine." Breaking a folkway may make others in the group uncomfortable (although they sometimes don't understand why they're uncomfortable), and violators may be laughed at, frowned on, or scolded. **Mores**, on the other hand, are norms with a strong moral significance, viewed as essential to the proper functioning of the group: We absolutely *should* or *should not* behave this way. You might break a *mos* (the singular form of mores) by assaulting someone or speaking abusively to someone, or even flaming someone in a chat room or in a group e-mail. Breaking mores makes others in the group upset, angry, or afraid, and they are likely to consider violators bad or immoral. Mores are often made into laws.

Sociologists use the term **taboos** to address social prohibitions viewed as essential to the well-being of humanity. To break a *mos* is bad or immoral, but breaking a taboo is unthinkable, beyond comprehension. For example, Sigmund Freud considered the **incest taboo**—one should not have sex with one's own children—to be a foundation of all societies. If parents and children had sex, then lines of inheritance, family name, and orderly property transfer would be completely impossible. Taboos are so important that most cultures have only a few. In the United States, for instance,

folkways
One of the relatively weak and informal norms that is the result of patterns of action. Many of the behaviors we call "manners" are folkways.

mores
Informally enforced norms based on strong moral values, which are viewed as essential to the proper functioning of a group.

taboos
Address social prohibitions viewed as essential to the well-being of humanity. To break a *mos* is bad or immoral, but breaking a taboo is unthinkable, beyond comprehension.

incest taboo
Sigmund Freud identified the taboo that one should not have sex with one's own children as a foundation of all societies.

murder and assault violate mores, not taboos. Breaking taboos causes others to feel disgusted. The violators are considered sick, evil, and monstrous. Taboos are always made into laws, unless they are so unthinkable that lawmakers cannot believe that anyone would break them.

It is equally true, however, that our understandings of deviance change and shift over time. Behavior that might once have qualified as the norm may later qualify from emergent mores in a society. Remember the diagram from Chapter 2 (see FIGURE 2.1 How Fast Can a Society Change Its Values?) showing the passage of laws over time regarding issues that might have once been understood as "deviance"? There were laws in the United States against interracial marriage and abortion. Although both issues still provoke disagreement, it is also true that they are no longer written into law as "deviant" (even if people who marry someone of another race or elect to terminate a pregnancy experience social disapproval, stigma, and other social consequences).

> **iSOC AND YOU Thinking Sociologically about Crime and Deviance**
> Deviance and crime are defined through *interaction*. By this, sociologists mean that our actions can only be understood as "deviant" or "criminal" only in relation to a set of social norms or laws of which they are seen as in violation. These understandings become embedded in society when *institutions* systematically come to treat different groups in different ways. Over time, these patterned *interactions* may influence your *identity*—you may become a "deviant" or a "criminal," but only after the label is successfully applied to you. This different treatment creates boundaries and barriers between groups and perpetuates *inequality* in ways that come to feel inevitable, but are in fact socially structured.

6.2 Theorizing Crime and Deviance

There is no shortage of theories that sociologists have offered to explain deviance. Some rest on the characteristics of the deviant actor himself or herself, others on the social context in which they find themselves, and still others stress the interactions between the two. But all of these theories can be considered within the iSoc model. Deviance is something that comes into being in interaction, deviant identities are formed and challenged through this process as well. And theories of deviance are also often interested in the ways that structured forms of inequality shape the experiences of different groups such that some are more likely to be seen as deviant, whereas others might avoid being seen as deviant despite incredible transgressions from social norms.

Emile Durkheim suggested that deviance actually serves society: Having some number of rule breakers reminds everyone what the rules are in the first place, and affirms their identity as rule-followers. Without knowing what is wrong, we can't know what's right. Deviance heightens social solidarity among members of the group, and lets those groups or societies draw a clear distinction between right and wrong, good and bad. If we don't have that, Durkheim argued, we risk falling into what he called **"anomie"** or normlessness. Deviance is socially useful because it reminds "us" that we are "normal"—it's *they* who are different and deviant. Durkheim's theory explains how deviance serves to unite us all under common beliefs and moral codes, but it doesn't explain why or how it happens in the first place. Most sociological theories stress the interaction of the individual or group that breaks norms or contravenes values with the larger group or society of which they are a part. Why do they do it? What makes them think they can or should?

anomie
A term developed by Émile Durkheim to describe a state of disorientation and confusion that results from too little social regulation, in which institutional constraints fail to provide a coherent foundation for action.

Rational Actor and Social Control Theories of Crime and Deviance

6.2.1 Understand the differences among social control theories of deviance.

Edwin H. Sutherland's (1940) theory of **differential association** suggests that deviance is a matter of rewards and punishment. Deviance occurs when an individual receives more prestige and less punishment by violating norms rather than by following them. What is deviant to one group might be something that enhances our status in another group. For example, students who behave in an irreverent, disrespectful fashion in class may be seen as deviant by the teachers and even punished for it, but they might also receive a great deal of prestige from their peers. They may calculate that the benefit (increased prestige) is worth the minor punishment they might receive. Thus, Sutherland argued, individuals become deviant by associating with people or joining groups that are already deviant and therefore are in the position to reward deviant behavior (Sutherland 1940). Deviance is learned. Sutherland's theory helps to explain the way we sometimes have multiple moral voices in our heads—like the little devil and angel versions of ourselves often depicted on TV—and why sometimes we choose to be deviant. But the theory does not explain how the "carriers of criminality" became deviant in the first place. It also does not explain acts that occur without a community, when everyone around disapproves, or when no one is even aware of the deviance.

Robert K. Merton (1938) offered a more social element to the strict rational calculator model. Society itself is an actor in the interaction. Merton argued that excessive deviance is a by-product of inequality. When a society promotes certain goals but provides unequal means of acquiring them, there will always be deviance. This is called **structural strain theory**. For instance, in the United States, and to some degree in all industrialized societies, we promote the *goal* of financial success and claim that it can be achieved through the *means* of self-discipline and hard work. But these qualities will lead to financial success only when channeled through a prestigious education or network of prestigious social contacts, advantages many people do not have. They will therefore feel pressured to use alternative *means*, legitimate or illegitimate, to achieve

differential association

Edwin H. Sutherland's theory suggesting that deviance occurs when an individual receives more prestige and less punishment by violating norms than by following them.

structural strain theory

Robert K. Merton's concept that excessive deviance is a by-product of inequality within societies that promote certain norms and versions of social reality yet provide unequal means of meeting or attaining them.

Differential association means choosing which direction you're going to go, and which group you want to associate with. In the iSoc model, differential association is all about "interactions" and how they shape our understandings of deviance and decisions to engage in deviant behavior (or not).

that common goal (Merton 1968). According to Merton there are five potential reactions to the tension between widely endorsed values and limited means of achieving them.

1. *Conformists* accept both the means and the values, whether they achieve the goal or not. Conformists may not achieve financial success, but they will still believe that it is important and that self-discipline and hard work are appropriate means of achieving it. Most people are conformists.

2. *Innovators* accept the values but reject the means. Innovators believe that financial success is an important goal but not that self-discipline and hard work are effective means of achieving it. Instead, they seek out new means to financial success. They may try to win the lottery, or they may become con artists or thieves.

3. *Ritualists* accept the means but reject the values. Ritualists follow rules for their own sake, conforming to standards even though they have lost sight of the values behind them. They will work hard but have no aspirations to financial success.

4. *Rebels* reject both the means and the values and substitute new ones. Instead of financial success, for instance, rebels may value the goal of spiritual fulfillment, to be achieved not through hard work but through quiet contemplation.

5. *Retreatists* reject both the means and the values and replace them with nothing. Retreatists do not accept the value of working hard, and they have not devised any alternative means. They have no aspirations to financial success or any alternative goal, such as spiritual or artistic fulfillment.

Critics of strain theory point out that not everyone shares the same goals, even in the most homogeneous society. There are always many potential goals, conflicting and sometimes contradictory. And while strain theory may adequately explain some white-collar crime, such as juggling the books at work, and some property crimes, such as stealing a television set, it is less effective when explaining those crimes that lack an immediate financial motive.

Travis Hirschi (1969; Gottfredson and Hirschi 1995) argued that people do not obey lots of hidden forces: They are *rational*, so they decide whether to engage in an act by weighing the potential outcome. If you knew that there would be absolutely no punishment, no negative consequences of any sort, you would probably do a great many things that you would never dream of otherwise, like propositioning an attractive coworker or driving like a maniac or stealing something you couldn't afford to buy. Hirschi imagined that people perform a sort "cost-benefit analysis" during their decision-making process to determine how much punishment is worth a degree of satisfaction or prestige. People who have little to lose are therefore more likely to become rule-breakers because for them the costs will almost always be less. Hirschi assumed that most people have the same motivation to commit crime, so the differences are that people vary more in the way they control themselves and the way they weigh the costs versus the benefits of engaging in deviant behavior.

Walter Reckless (1973), on the other hand, suggests that such cost-benefit analysis really concerns our connections to others. **Social control theory** suggests that people are discouraged from deviance by the social ties within their immediate communities. These can be formal and coercive (like the police and prison system) or informal (like disapproval from family or peers). If you really think that you'll get caught, you are subject to *outer controls*: family, social institutions, and authority figures (like the police) who influence you into obeying social rules (Costello and Vowell 1999). But even when you know there is no one looking, you are subject to *inner controls*: internalized socialization, religious principles, your self-conception as a "good person" (Hirschi 1969; Rogers and Buffalo 1974). **Self-control theory** places the emphasis on inadequate socialization and thus a weakened internal monitor system.

social control theory

As Walter Reckless theorized, people don't commit crimes even if they could probably get away with them due to social controls. There are outer controls—family, friends, teachers, social institutions, and authority figures (like the police)—who influence (cajole, threaten, browbeat) us into obeying social rules; and inner controls—internalized socialization, consciousness, religious principles, ideas of right and wrong, and one's self-conception as a "good person."

self-control theory

In explaining deviance, places the emphasis on inadequate socialization and thus a weakened internal monitoring system.

We often fail to break rules even when the benefits would be great and the punishment minimal. Have you ever been driving alone late at night stopped at a red light and thought about running it, but waited for the green anyway. There would be a substantial benefit: You'd get home or wherever you're headed more quickly. And, with no one around, there would be no punishment. Nevertheless, despite that internal dialogue, despite the benefits and lack of punishment, it's probably not uncommon to wait for the light to change.

All of these theories consider deviance as determined by the social structures within which people exist. Deviance, according to each of these theories, is rational (sometimes). Similarly, sometimes we conform to social norms even when breaking the rules would be perfectly acceptable. It shows just how much we internalize those norms. They are institutionalized to such an extent that they become a part of our identities whether we're deviant or not.

Subculture Theories of Deviance

6.2.2 Explain the conditions that cause a subculture to qualify as "deviant."

A **subculture** is a group that evolves within a dominant culture, always more or less hidden and closed to outsiders. It may be a loose association of friends who share the same interests, or it may be well organized, with its own alternative language, costumes, and media. Although most subcultures are not deviant, the separation from the dominant culture allows deviant subcultures to develop their own norms and values. For a deviant subculture to develop, the activity, condition, identity, and so on must meet three characteristics:

1. It must be punished but not punished too much. If it is not punished enough, potential recruits have no motivation to seek out the subculture. If it is punished too much, the risks of membership are too great.
2. It must have enough participants but not too many. If it has too few participants, it will be hard to seek them out locally. If it has too many, it would be pointless.
3. It must be complex but not too complex. If it is not complex enough, you could engage in it by yourself. If it is too complex, it could exist only within a counterculture or dominant culture: You would need a college degree.

Notice that each of these criteria is not a simple either–or proposition but rather the achievement of a balance between heavy punishment and leniency and between size and complexity.

There are many different kinds of deviant subcultures. Many are based on lifestyle differences—sex, or drugs, or rock and roll. Deviant sexual subcultures, for example, might include people whose sexualities are organized around practices outside prescribed patterns, like S&M (sadomasochism) or B&D (bondage and discipline). Drug subcultures range from small groups of potheads to crack cocaine dens run by drug cartels. (Participants in drug cartels are typically not, themselves, users of the drugs;

subculture

Group within a society that creates its own norms and values distinct from the mainstream and often its own separate institutions as well.

they are simply traffickers whose motives are money and power.) And anyone who has ever been to a Grateful Dead or a Phish concert knows what a musical deviant subculture looks like. One thing is certain: Wherever there are deviant subcultures, there are sociologists studying them.

Richard Cloward and Lloyd Ohlin (1960) built on *differential opportunity* and *structural strain* theories by arguing that crime actually arises from opportunities to commit crime. **Opportunity theory** holds that those with more opportunities will be more likely to commit crimes than those with fewer opportunities. They agreed with Merton that people who lack access (or easy access) to acceptable means of achieving material success may experience "strain," but that doesn't explain why most poor people are *not* criminals. In fact, studies show that most qualify as "conformists," with the same values and goals as the dominant society. Like Sutherland, Cloward and Ohlin emphasized *learning*—people have to learn how to carry out particular forms of deviance, and they must have the opportunity to actually deviate. They revised differential association theory to propose several different types of deviant subcultures based on the opportunities to deviate.

opportunity theory

Cloward and Ohlin's 1960 theory of crime, which holds that those who have many opportunities—and good ones at that—will be more likely to commit crimes than those with few good opportunities.

1. In stable neighborhoods where most people know each other throughout their lives, *criminal subcultures* develop, devoted to such activities as burglary and theft. Young men can rely on social contacts with experienced older men to learn the roles of being a criminal.

2. In unstable neighborhoods where people are constantly moving in and out, there are few opportunities to learn about burglary and theft, and boys who are mostly strangers to each other must find some way to establish dominance. They develop *violence subcultures*, gaining tough reputations through fighting and assaults.

3. In neighborhoods too disorganized for either crime or violence, people withdraw from society altogether through the use of alcohol and drugs. They develop *retreatist subcultures*.

These are not necessarily exclusive groups. A gang that may start out as part of a violent subculture in an unstable neighborhood may become a criminal subculture as the members become involved in more stable criminal activities like protection rackets and drug trafficking and begin recruiting younger members.

Some aspects of opportunity theory have been confirmed by subsequent research (Allan and Steffensmeier 1989; Uggen 1999). Also, the theory defines deviance in a way that targets poor people—if we include white-collar crimes like stock fraud, neighborhood dynamics become much less significant.

Youth Gangs as Deviant Subcultures

6.2.3 Summarize how youth gangs went from being considered youthful mischiefs to deviant and criminal subculture.

Youth gangs are a good example of a deviant subculture. Before the 1950s, youth gangs were considered to be relatively innocent. Their "deviance" consisted of swiping apples from fruit stands and swimming in the East River despite the "no trespassing" signs. Meanwhile they helped out mothers and friends in distress and sometimes even cooperated with the police. They were juvenile delinquents with hearts of gold, mischievous but not bad. It was the adult gangsters who posed a threat, trying to seduce them into lives of adult, hard-core crime.

In 1955, juvenile delinquency was getting a lot of publicity in the United States. Sociologist Albert Cohen wondered why young people, mostly working-class and poor boys, were rejecting the values of the dominant society and committing so many crimes. As lower-class youths, they had the least opportunity to achieve economic success, but their crimes were usually not economically motivated. They were not trying to get rich. Cohen drew upon Sutherland's theory of differential association (see chapter section Rational Actor and Social Control Theories of Crime and Deviance) to propose that the gang members were not being socialized with the same norms and values as lower-class non–gang members or the middle class. Walter B. Miller (1958/1970) agreed, but argued that it is not just lower-class boys in gangs whose norms and values differ from those of the dominant society; he suggested that it was the entire lower class. In other words, behavior that mainstream society might consider deviant actually reflects the social norms of the lower-class *subculture*. Miller implied that lower-class culture was conducive to crime, despite the overwhelming number of lower-class people who are law-abiding, decent citizens and the many upper-class people who reverse Robin Hood's ethic and rob from the poor to give to themselves.

Today, though, our image of youth gangs is quite different, closer to the film *Straight Outta Compton* (2015). And they no longer swipe apples. There are some nearly 31,000 youth gangs in the United States (National Youth Gang Survey 2012), with more than 1 million active members ages 5 to 17 (Pyrooz and Sweeten 2015). These figures do not even include informal gang-like cliques, crews, and posses who may dress alike and share common customs and rituals but do not engage in organized criminal activity (National Gang Intelligence Center 2012). Almost 9 in 10 cities with populations of 50,000 or more now have a "gang problem." (National Gang Center 2012). Yet, although the media sometimes portray gang activity as on the rise, it has been relatively steady since the mid-1990s in the United States, even when we consider rates of gang activity in different types of locations, like larger cities versus rural counties. Larger cities have more gang activity than suburban counties, but the level of gang activity within each area type has not changed dramatically in recent history (National Gang Center 2012).

Most gangs are composed of poor or working-class adolescents, typically boys and young men (Sanchez-Jankowski 1991). Members are startlingly young, often preteen when they start, and they generally retire (or go to prison or die) by their mid-twenties. Racial and ethnic minorities are overrepresented, in part because, as numerical minorities, they often feel a stronger need to belong to a group that can provide identity and protection (see FIGURE 6.1). The National Youth Gang Survey found that 46 percent of gang members are Hispanic, 35 percent black, 11 percent white, 7 percent all others (National Gang Center 2012). The racial composition of gangs, however, reflects the

Youth gangs are seen as deviant subcultures, with their own norms, values, and rules of conduct. The number of female gang members has been increasing, but most gang members are male.

FIGURE 6.1 Race, Ethnicity, and Gender of Gang Members

Here, you can see that gangs are disproportionately composed of men, and that black and Hispanic men are over-represented in gang populations when compared with their proportions in the U.S. population more generally. This is important, as gang involvement intersects with other areas of social life. Sociologists are interested in examining what pushes some groups toward gang participation and seems to protect others from needing or wanting to join.

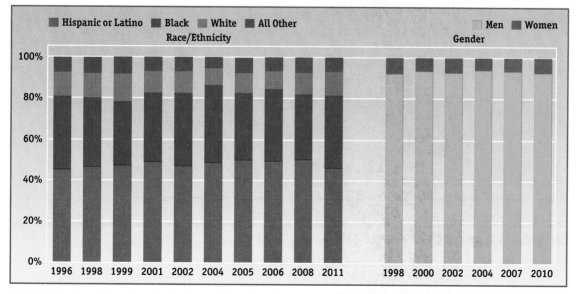

SOURCE: Data from National Gang Center, National Youth Gang Survey Analysis, 2012. Available at http://www.nationalgangcenter.gov/Survey-Analysis/Demographics#anchorgender.

characteristics of the larger community and so varies considerably by location (Howell, Egley, and Gleason 2002; see Egley and O'Donnell 2009).

As you can see, women represent a smaller proportion of youth gang members (Moore and Hagedorn 2001; National Gang Center 2012). As young teenagers, roughly one-third of all youth gang members are women (U.S. Department of Justice 2008); however, women tend to leave gangs at an earlier age than men (Gottfredson and Gottfredson 2001; Hunt, Joe-Laidler, and MacKenzie 2005; Thornberry et al. 2003). And some research suggests that the gender composition of a gang affects its delinquency rates. In one study, women in all- or majority-women gangs had the lowest delinquency rates, while both men and women in majority-men gangs had the highest—including higher rates than men in all-men gangs (Fleisher and Krienert 2004).

Sociologist Sudhir Venkatesh (2008) lived with a gang in Chicago. And despite their depiction in a great deal of media, he discovered a different image of gang life altogether. Venkatesh found that those at the top do well financially, but regular members averaged only about $3.30 an hour. Some even supplemented their gang income by working at McDonald's. But he also found that gangs are active in the local community, creating stability and providing resources that the city did not: paying the women who look after children and the elderly in the housing projects, for example. Venkatesh found that the gang he worked with prohibited members from using hard drugs (it would spoil the gang's image) and insisted that young members stay in school—that is, gangs may give young people a coherent structure to their lives. But most of all, they have good parties, provide easy access to alcohol and drugs, and "know how to have fun," as one gang member said. This helps us better understand gangs are responses to institutionalized forms of inequality. And as we've examined this intersectionally (see FIGURE 6.1), you can see how different groups are more and less likely to participate. Or, it might be more accurate to say that different groups are more and less likely to *need* to participate.

WHAT DO YOU THINK? WHAT DOES AMERICA THINK?

Following the Law

Some people feel the law is the bedrock of a civil society and without law anarchy would result. Others are socialized to conform and obey. Would you say that people should obey the law without exception, or are there exceptional occasions on which people should follow their consciences even if it means breaking the law? There are different opinions as to what it takes to be a good citizen. As far as you are concerned personally on a scale of 1 to 5, where 1 is not at all important and 5 is very important, how important is it to "always obey laws and regulations"?

What do you think?

1. Not at all important
2. Unimportant
3. Neutral
4. Important
5. Very Important

What does America think?

Eighty-six percent of respondents said that they thought always obeying laws and regulation was "very important." In fact, only 4 percent said it was neither important nor unimportant and only 3 percent said that it was unimportant at all.

SOURCE: Data from General Social Survey, 2014.

THINKING CRITICALLY ABOUT SURVEY DATA

Can you think of situations in which you might be doing something right by disobeying a law or regulation? Are there circumstances where laws or regulations might impede people from doing the "right" thing?

Labeling Theory and Inequality

6.2.4 Understand how labeling theory explains deviance, and distinguish among primary, secondary, and tertiary deviance.

We used to think that the wrongdoing in deviance resided somewhere in the wrongdoer: You break a social rule because you are "that kind of person," with faulty genes, a criminal personality, or a defective soul. But now we know that wrongdoing is not inherent in an act or an actor but in the social context that determines whether an act is considered deviant or not and how much punishment it warrants. Although some sociological theories of deviance and crime focus on the characteristics of the group or on the motivations of the deviant actor or group, others stress the power imbalances between the deviant and the majority—or *inequality*. After all, if most people do something, is it "deviant" in the strictest sense of the term? The ability to label something deviant, and to have that label stick to others, is an expression of one's relative power. You may decide, for example, that text messaging is deviant, but unless you have a lot of support, it probably won't make much of a difference.

Howard Becker (1966) used the term *labeling theory* to stress the relativity of deviance. Labeling describes a relationship between a dominant group and the actor. For something to be "deviant," it has to be labeled as deviant by a powerful group—a group powerful enough to make that label stick. (If you do something wrong and your little sister declares it deviant, it doesn't have the same sort of weight as if all your friends label it deviant, or, even more, if the police and the juvenile courts call it deviant.) **Labeling theory** understands deviance to be a *process*, not a categorical difference between the deviant and the non-deviant.

The same act might be deviant in some groups and not in others. It might be deviant when one person commits it but not when another person commits it. In fact, an action, belief, or condition is neutral in itself. It only becomes "deviant" when someone decides that it is wrong, bad, or immoral and labels it as deviant. For example, think of women who are sexually aggressive or enjoy pornography. Society might call them "sluts" and shun them. But if a man did any of those things, other men might call him a "stud" and perhaps hang out with him. But deviance does not only reside in whether other people apply the label "deviant" to your acts. To become a deviant actor, you also have to believe the deviant label; you have to agree with the labels other people ascribe to you. And labeling theory helps us understand when, how and why we accept labels and when we don't. Sociological research examining **stereotype threat** and **stereotype promise** provide examples of just how powerful social labels and identities can be.

Edwin Lemert (1972) theorized that most deviant acts, which he called **primary deviance**, provoke very little reaction and therefore have little effect on your self-concept. If I decide one day to run that red light on campus at 6:00 A.M., a passing police officer may label me as reckless and irresponsible, but I am unlikely to believe it. Only when I repeatedly break a norm, and people start making a big deal of it, does **secondary deviance** kick in. My rule breaking is no longer a momentary lapse in judgment, or justifiable under the circumstances, but an indication of a permanent personality trait: I have acquired a deviant identity. Finally, sociologists also have identified **tertiary deviance**, in which a group formerly labeled deviant attempts to redefine their acts, attributes, or identities as normal—even virtuous. John Kitsuse (1980) and others point to the ways some formerly deviant groups have begun to stand up for their rights, demanding equality with those considered "normals." Similar to "militant chauvinism" defined by Goffman when discussing stigma (which you'll read about next), examples might include the disability rights movement, which has attempted to redefine disabilities from deviant to "differently abled."

labeling theory

Howard Becker's theory stresses the relativity of deviance, naming the mechanism by which the same act is considered deviant in some groups but not in others. Labels are used to categorize and contain people.

stereotype threat

Term coined by Claude Steele to assess the extent to which labels about people "like us" have measurable impacts on their performances. It refers to the variation in performance measured when the belief that people who belong to an identity category you share are worse at a particular task than the comparison group.

stereotype promise

Term coined by Jennifer Lee and Min Zhou to address the "promise" of being viewed through the lens of a positive stereotype that leads one to perform in ways that confirms the positive stereotype (the counterpart to "stereotype threat").

primary deviance

Any minor, usually unnoticed, act of deviance committed irregularly that does not have an impact on one's self-identity or on how one is labeled by others.

secondary deviance

The moment when someone acquires a deviant identity, occurring when he or she repeatedly breaks a norm and people start making a big deal of it, so the rule-breaking can no longer be attributed to a momentary lapse in judgment or justifiable under the circumstances but is an indication of a permanent personality trait.

tertiary deviance

Occurs when members of a group formerly labeled deviant attempt to redefine their acts, attributes, or identities as normal—even virtuous.

SOCIOLOGY AND OUR WORLD

STEREOTYPE THREAT AND STEREOTYPE PROMISE

How can stereotypes get inside of us and affect our behavior?

To assess the extent that labels about people "like us" stick, psychology professor Claude Steele coined the term *stereotype threat*. Steele wanted to assess whether stereotypes about groups could have measurable impacts on their performances. Stereotype threat refers to the variation in performance measured when the belief that people who belong to an identity category you share are worse at a particular task than the comparison group is made salient. So, there is a tacit belief among many Americans,

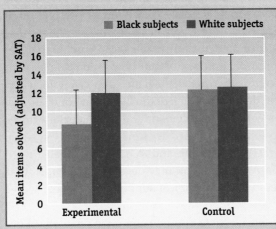

SOURCE: Steele, Claude M. and Aronson, Joshua. 1995. "Stereotype Threat and the Intellectual Test Performance of African Americans," *Journal of Personality and Social Psychology*, 69: 800.

when they were reminded of a stereotype about their group directly before engaging in a task on which they might confirm that stereotype. It's a powerful illustration of how labels have actual effects; they can become self-fulfilling prophecies. A great deal of research supports Steele's finding. And stereotype threat has been found to affect an incredible diversity of groups about which there are negative stereotypes when the stereotype is somehow made salient. Women perform worse on mathematics exams, for in-

for instance, that white people are smarter than black people or that women are somehow naturally inferior at mathematics when compared with men. Steele wanted to know whether activating these stereotypes (reminding people of the stereotype in some small way) could actually affect measureable outcomes. To test this, Claude Steele and Joshua Aronson performed an experiment. They created two groups of college students composed of both black and white students and they had both groups answer a series of challenging GRE questions. One of the two groups was told that the test would assess intellectual ability (potentially activating stereotypes for black students). The other group was told that the test was simply a problem-solving task that did not tell them anything about intellectual ability. But, both groups were actually given the same test.

What Steele and Aronson proved is that stereotype threat actually has measureable effects on objective tasks. Black students did not underperform compared with white students in the control group (the group told it was a problem-solving test that told the researchers nothing about their intellectual abilities). But black students dramatically underperformed

stance, when they are reminded of gender stereotypes about women and math. Black people are not inherently less intelligent than white people, and women do not possess inherent deficiencies in mathematics.

Sociologists Jennifer Lee and Min Zhou (2015) were interested in whether positive stereotypes have a similar effect and might work in ways that actually boost performance. They refer to this process as stereotype promise—the promise of being viewed through the lens of a positive stereotype that leads one to perform in ways that confirms the positive stereotype. Lee and Zhou use Asian American students as a prime example in their book, *The Asian American Achievement Paradox* (2015). And although not true of all Asian-Americans, Lee and Zhou discovered that many Asian American students are put on the advanced tracks in school under the assumption that they must belong there (regardless of prior performance), and many rise to meet the expectations. They are stereotyped as smart, hard-working, and high achieving. When stereotypes are pervasive enough, and those labels about our groups get inside of us, they have a sneaky way of coming true.

Social Stigma

6.2.5 Summarize what sociologists mean by "stigma" and the strategies stigmatized individuals rely on to interact with others.

Sometimes, you don't have to *do* anything to be considered deviant. You just have to *be* it—that is, you just have to be a member of a group that is considered deviant. If some part of you—your race or sexuality, for example—is considered deviant, you would be considered "stigmatized." The sociologist Erving Goffman (1963) used the term **stigma** to refer to an attribute that changes you "from a whole and usual person to a tainted and discounted one." Deviant behavior or a deviant master status creates stigma, although not in every case. Other people might ignore our deviance or "forgive" it as an anomaly. Goffman believed that people with stigmatized attributes are constantly practicing various strategies to attempt to mitigate the negative consequences of stigmatization. So, someone who identifies as gay or lesbian might choose not to be "out" at work for fear of negative consequences. Because being stigmatized will "spoil" your identity (as Goffman put it), you are likely to adopt one of three strategies to alleviate it.

Goffman identified three strategies to neutralize stigma and save yourself from having a spoiled identity. He listed them in order of increased social power—the more power you have, the more you can try and redefine the situation.

MINSTRELIZATION: If you're virtually alone and have very little power, you can over-conform to the stereotypes that others have about you. To act like a "minstrel," Goffman says, is to exaggerate the differences between the stigmatized and the dominant group. Thus, for example, did African Americans overact as happy-go-lucky entertainers when they had no other recourse? A contemporary example might be women who act ultra-feminine—helpless and dependent—in potentially harassing situations. Note that minstrels exaggerate difference in the face of those with more power; when they are with other stigmatized people, they may laugh about the fact that the powerful "actually think we're all like this!" That's often the only sort of power that they feel they have.

NORMIFICATION: If you have even a small amount of power, you might try to minimize the differences between the stigmatized groups. "Look," you'll say, "We're the same as you are, so there is no reason to discriminate against us." Normification is, for instance, the process that gays and lesbians refer to when they argue for same-sex marriage or that women use when they say they want to be engineers or physicists. Normification involves emphasizing similarities and downplaying differences.

MILITANT CHAUVINISM: When your group's level of power and organization is highest, you may decide to again *maximize* differences with the dominant group. But militant chauvinists don't just say "we're different," they say "we're also better." For example, there are groups of African Americans ("Afrocentrists" or even some of the Nation of Islam) who proclaim black superiority. Some feminist women proclaim that women's ways are better than the dominant "male" way. These trends try to turn the tables on the dominant group. (*Warning*: Do not attempt this if you are the only member of your group in a confrontation with members of the dominant group.)

stigma

An attribute that changes you "from a whole and usual person to a tainted and discounted one," as sociologist Erving Goffman defined it. A stigma discredits a person's claim to be normal.

Deviants or folk heroes? Jesse James and the Black Panthers were considered criminals by law enforcement agencies, but they were folk heroes in their communities, celebrated in folk songs and tributes.

These three responses to stigma depend on the size and strength of the stigmatized group. If you're all alone, minstrelizing may be a lifesaving technique. If there are many of you and you are strong, you might try to militantly turn the tables. Sociologists understand that deviance is not solely a product of "bad" people doing the "wrong" things but also of the bad, wrong, or unfair social conditions of people's lives. What is labeled as deviant is applied differently to different groups of people as well. The powerful and the privileged often escape the label and the punishment. Therefore, deviance—and crime as well—are themselves products of social inequality.

Deviance, Crime, and Inequality

6.2.6 Explain why sociologists argue that deviance and crime work in ways that both produce and reproduce systems of inequality.

In a groundbreaking article entitled "Nuts, Sluts, and Perverts: The Poverty of the Sociology of Deviance" (1972), Alexander Liazos noted that the people commonly labeled deviant are always powerless. Why? The answer is not simply that the rich and powerful make the rules to begin with or that they have the resources to avoid being labeled deviant. The answer lies in the fact that those who have the power can make us believe that the rules are "natural" and "good" to mask their political agenda. They can then label actors and acts "deviant" to justify inequalities in gender, sexual orientation, race, ethnicity, and social class (Daly 1989; Daly and Chesney-Lind 1988; Hagan and Peterson 1995). They need not be aware of the fact that the rules seem to be systematically working to their benefit for this to be happening. But a great deal of sociological research has illustrated that groups with less power are subjected to harsher punishments than those with more. In this section, we focus more on the relationship between deviance, crime, and inequality to better understand this process.

In a classic study of a suburban high school, there were two "gangs" of boys, what the researcher called the "Saints" and the "Roughnecks." The Roughnecks were working-class boys, who were on the vocational track in school, and not college bound. Teachers thought of them as deviant, and they wore clothing styles like those in the movie *Grease* (1978)—black leather jackets, jeans, and white T-shirts. They were known to commit petty crimes and were called "hooligans" by the school administrators. The "Saints," by contrast, were middle-class boys, and they dressed the part—crew cuts, button-down "preppy" shirts, and penny loafers. They played sports, were popular, and were college bound. They also spent their weekends breaking into people's homes and committing serious burglaries. Despite this, they were not considered deviant because they were "wholesome" and middle class (Chambliss 2000). Similarly, Sociologist Julie Bettie (2003) later studied different groups of girls in high school and discovered a similar set of findings that prevented middle- and upper-class white girls from having their behavior closely monitored and scrutinized when compared with their working-class, Mexican-American classmates. Bettie's research takes more of an intersectional approach than Chambliss did to discover the ways that gender, race, and class interact to produce very different school experiences for different groups.

Ironically, the relationship of inequality and crime and deviance often leads us to see and punish the behaviors of the less fortunate and forgive the behavior of the more fortunate. Sometimes, it is more appropriate to say that we are criminalizing groups of people rather than the acts they are committing. From this perspective, it is more likely that a poor person who stole a few dollars from a company would end up in jail than a CEO who steals millions of dollars from millions of shareholders. We may condemn the unequal application of the law, but some sociologists want us to go further than that, to give some thought to whether the laws themselves are inherently unfair. Richard Quinney (1977) argued that the dominant class produces deviance by making and enforcing laws that protect its own interests and oppress the subordinate class. Law becomes an instrument of oppression, designed to maintain the powerful in their privileged position (Chambliss and Zatz 1993).

Some media outlets exhibited clear racial bias in reports during coverage of the aftermath of Hurricane Katrina in 2005. Many stories referred to white victims of the disaster as "survivors" and "residents," whereas blacks were referred to as "looters" and "criminals."

It's not simply that basically neutral and equal laws are applied unequally, meaning that poor people get longer and harsher sentences when they commit the same crimes as upper-class people. That fact is true. But it's also that the laws themselves are designed in ways that make sure that the rich stay rich and the poor stay poor. And, as we will see later, laws and systems of punishment also reinforce inequality intersectionally. So, to understand how deviance and crime are simultaneously produced by inequality as well as playing a key role in the reproduction of inequality means paying close attention to the ways that different groups in our society are impacted by punishments for breaking norms and laws.

iSOC AND YOU Theorizing Crime and Deviance
Sociological theories of crime and deviance focus less on the inherent properties of the act itself, and more about the social dynamics that label some actions as deviant and others not. Some people are labeled as deviant, or criminal, so that deviance may become part of their *identity*. All deviance is based on *interaction*—some act and others label those actions as "deviant." Given that, deviance is always about *inequality*, such that some have more power to label others as deviant. And the *institutional* power that some people have can make their labeling of you stick. So, for example, you and a police officer might disagree. The policeman says you're the criminal, but you think the police officer is the criminal, doing something illegal by arresting you, an innocent person. Standoff? Hardly. The police possess the legitimate use of force, and all the institutions of the criminal justice system to make their perception of things the one that gets legitimated. All the different groups that might be seen as deviant *intersect* with each other, so that some groups are dramatically over-represented among those considered deviant or criminal.

6.3 The Social Organization of Crime

In 2014, there were more than 1.1 million violent crimes in the United States, a rate of 365.6 per 100,000 inhabitants. There were 8.2 million property crimes committed, at a rate of 2,596.1 per 100,000 inhabitants (U.S. Department of Justice 2015). While these statistics are considerably lower than they were 30 years ago, the United States still has higher crime rates than many other countries in the world: It ranks third in drug offenses per capita, fifth in assaults, eighth in murders with firearms, ninth in rape, eleventh in robberies, and sixteenth in burglaries. (And remember, half of all crime victims do not report their crimes to the police.)

When compared with most other advanced countries, the United States stands out for its very high homicide rates (Kurki 1997; Van Kesteren, Mayhew, and Nieuwbeerta 2000). With 5.2 murders for every 100,000 people, the rate of lethal violence in the United States is nearly five times higher than that of France, Germany, or England (U.S. Department of Justice 2015; Van Kesteren, et al. 2000; Wacquant 2006; Zimring and Hawkins 1997).

Sociologists study crime as *socially organized*. By this, they mean that different factors associated with society play a role in determining both the type and extent of criminal activity in a given society. So, when sociologists hear these facts about how the United States stands out internationally when discussing crime, we are interested in examining the types of social forces that play a role in producing these outcomes. In some ways, this ought to be a liberating way of looking at an examining crime. Sociologists do not understand a certain type or level of criminal activity to be inevitable.

Here, we'll consider how we can apply the iSoc model to understand which types of individuals are more likely to engage in criminal activity than others (or perhaps more accurately, which types of individuals are caught and punished at higher rates for their participation in criminal activity). We will examine the ways that crime is both a cause and consequence of inequality in a society. And when we examine crime intersectionally, we realize that certain groups in our society are likely to receive harsher penalties for crime when compared with others. And a variety of social institutions participate in producing this reality. From the level of violence in the United States, to the likelihood of interacting with the police, to the probability of being arrested, to differences in the average sentences afforded different groups, crime is socially organized. And we can learn a great deal about inequality in any society by examining who commits criminal acts and what types of consequences different groups encounter for participating.

Understanding the Crime Rate Sociologically

6.3.1 Understand the differences among three separate sociological explanations that tie crime rates to society.

What social factors explain our rates of crime? Sociologists have considered three explanations:

1. U.S. culture emphasizes individual economic success as *the* measure of self-worth, at the expense of family, neighborhood, artistic accomplishment, and spiritual well-being (Currie 1985).
2. Not everyone has a high standard of living. The United States has one of the largest income differentials in the world. When the gap begins to shrink, as it did during Clinton-era prosperity, the crime rate declines (Martens 2005).
3. Guns—that is, the easy availability of guns and the lax enforcement of loose gun control measures, coupled with a U.S. value system that places gun ownership as a sacred right—are a contributor to the crime rate.

SOCIOLOGY AND OUR WORLD

ABORTION AND THE CRIME RATE

Could the legalization of abortion really have caused crime rates to decline in the United States?

Did the legalization of abortion cause the decline of crime? In the book, *Freakonomics* (2005), economist Steven Levitt and journalist Stephen Dubner suggest the controversial idea that the legalization of abortion in 1973 meant that far fewer unwanted children were born, and that these children would have had fewer economic opportunities and lower levels of education and employment. They would have become adults in the mid-1990s—which is exactly when the crime rate began to decline. Thus, many would-be criminals—those with the demographic "profile" of criminals—were simply never born. Some disagree with their calculations (Foote and Goetz 2005).

This is a marvelous example of what sociologists call a "specious correlation." Sure, the two variables may be correlated, but there are so many intervening variables, not to mention 20 years of other factors that might have influenced things, that one cannot possibly say with any certainty that this one variable *caused* another. For one thing, how do we know that the fetuses that were aborted were more likely to be criminals? Or that the legalization of abortion was not also connected to a larger set of social and economic reforms that reduced the crime rate? Do you think, perhaps, that all the recent efforts to make abortions more difficult will result in a dramatic increase in crime 20 years from now? We doubt it.

Despite the fact that our overall crime rates are higher than some other advanced countries, such as Ireland and Austria, and our outsize homicide rate distinguishes the United States from all of Western Europe (Wacquant 2006), it is also true that crime rates in the United States have been falling. The National Crime Victimization Survey (2014), which addresses victims of crime (and therefore leaves out murder), reports that the violent crime rate has dropped by nearly 60 percent and the property crime rate has dropped by more than 50 percent since 1973. Violent crime dropped 14 percent in just *2 years*, between 2001 and 2003, and has dropped slightly every year since, with an overall 14.5 percent additional decrease since 2003 (FBI Uniform Crime Reports 2016; U.S. Department of Justice 2015).

Types of Crime

6.3.2 Distinguish between types of crime, and provide examples to illustrate your understanding.

Crime can be defined as any act that violates a formal normative code that has been enacted by a legally constituted body. Simple violation of mores or a folkway may not be a crime, unless you violate a formal code. Likewise, you can commit a crime (actually break a law) and not be seen as deviant if other people see your act as acceptable. Sometimes, people commit crimes and are seen as heroes. Other times, people have not committed crimes, but are suspected anyway. Some crimes are defined by being bad in and of themselves—bad because they violate formal group norms—like homicide, rape, or assault. Other crimes are not as obvious violations of group norms and are considered bad mostly because they have been prohibited.

The efforts to control and punish crime have become so extensive and the institutions that have developed—prisons, courts, police, to name a few—so large, that the study of crime, **criminology**, has developed into a subdiscipline separate from the sociology of deviance, with its own special theories about the causes and consequences of different kinds of crimes. There are many different types of crime. Some are crimes against other people; others are crimes against property. They are handled differently by the police, courts, and penal system, depending on how serious the society believes the crime to be. Sociologists study all types of crime. We explain four types in a bit of depth.

crime
A deviant act that lawmakers consider bad enough to warrant formal laws and sanctions.

criminology
The study of crime that has developed into a subdiscipline separate from the sociology of deviance, with its own special theories about the causes and consequences of different kinds of crimes.

HOW DO WE KNOW WHAT WE KNOW?

JUST HOW VIOLENT IS THE UNITED STATES?

The Organization for Economic Cooperation and Development (OECD) is composed of a group of 30 democratic countries that support free-market economies and discuss economic and social policies. Because of this cooperation, we are able to glean insights from some international comparisons when common data across many different national contexts can be challenging to produce. Sociologist Kieran Healy analyzed data on deaths due to assault in each of the participating countries as one measure of just how violent different societies are. To compare countries with wildly different sized populations, social scientists will often discuss the relative prevalence of something per 100,000 people in the population. So, rather than comparing the overall number of assaults in different countries, it makes more sense to compare the number of assaults relative to the size of their overall populations. This allows us to compare the level of one type of violence across many different societies and over time.

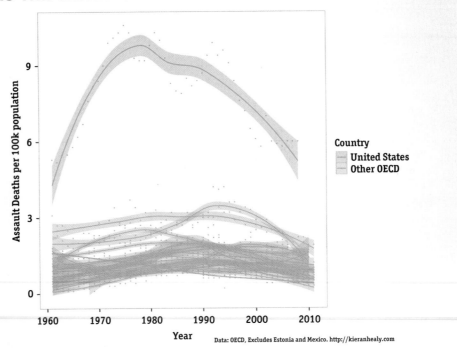

Data: OECD, Excludes Estonia and Mexico. http://kieranhealy.com

SOURCE: Data from Organization for Economic Cooperation and Development (OECD). Available at https://data.oecd.org/.

Healy's analysis illustrates that the level of violence has shifted over time as well. There was a spike in violence in the United States between 1960 and 1980. But deaths due to assault have been steadily declining ever since. Despite that, we are still well above the relative level of assault deaths when compared with these other countries.

SOURCE: Healy, Kieran. July 20, 2012. "America is a Violent Country." Available at https://kieranhealy.org/blog/archives/2012/07/20/america-is-a-violent-country/.

white-collar crime

Edward Sutherland's term for the illegal actions of a corporation or people acting on its behalf, by using the authority of their position to commit crime.

occupational crime

The use of one's professional position to illegally secure something of value for oneself or for the corporation.

Workplace crime is more common than you might think. Theft at work, whether simply pocketing office supplies or exercising the "100 percent employee discount" at the department store, costs U.S. employers increasing amounts each year. What is called "retail shrinkage," the combined loss from employee theft and shoplifting, amounted to more than $45 billion a year at last count (National Retail Federation 2016). But there are many other crimes that you can commit at work, using the authority of your position, with the direct or indirect consent of the boss. In 1940, Edwin Sutherland introduced the term **white-collar crime** for the illegal actions of a corporation or people acting on its behalf (Sutherland 1940). Today, white-collar crime is an increasing problem across the globe, with more than 82 percent of companies worldwide falling victim to employee fraud in 2016 alone (Kroll Global Fraud and Risk Report 2016). White-collar criminals might commit **occupational crime**, using their professional position to illegally secure something

Media entrepreneur Martha Stewart went to prison for 5 months between 2004 and 2005 for lying about her insider trading when she used her fame to find out that a company whose stock she owned was about to suffer a significant setback; she sold her stock the day before its price collapsed (she claimed it was a co-incidence). Although Stewart spent time in prison for her crime, 5 months struck many as a small sentence for a fairly serious crime.

organizational crime

Illegal actions committed in accordance with the operative goals of an organization, such as antitrust violations, false advertising, or price fixing.

cybercrime

The growing array of crimes committed via the Internet and World Wide Web, such as Internet fraud and identity theft.

organized crime

Like corporate or white-collar crime, it is a business operation whose purpose is to supply illegal goods and services to others.

of value for themselves or the corporation (crimes like income tax evasion, stock manipulation, bribery, and embezzlement). Or they might commit **organizational crime**, illegal actions committed in accordance with the operative goals of an organization (crimes like stock manipulation, anti-trust violations, false advertising, and price fixing). The cost of white-collar crime is substantial—between $300 and $660 billion a year in the United States alone, which is far more than the "paltry" $15 billion for "regular" street crime (National White Collar Crime Center 2010). Yet most cases of white-collar crime go unpunished or are settled outside of court. In rare cases, when white-collar criminals are charged and convicted, white-collar offenders are more likely to receive fines than prison sentences. Even if they do go to jail, white-collar criminals are typically sentenced to terms averaging 2 years (U.S. Sentencing Commission 2014).

The use of the Internet and World Wide Web to commit crime—**cybercrime**—is a relatively new form of crime. Some of these crimes involve fraudulent maneuvers to get victims to reveal personal information that can then be used to commit crimes; others involve theft of online identities. The rise of personal computers and the Internet have made some criminal activities, such as money laundering and fraud, easier. This situation has spawned a whole new field of crime. Internet-based crime is the fastest-growing category of crime in the United States. The year 2014 marked the fifteenth year in a row that identity theft topped the list of consumer complaints with the U.S. Federal Trade Commission, accounting for 13 percent of the total (Federal Trade Commission 2015). Nearly 12.7 million Americans have been victimized by identity theft and have experienced losses totaling $16 billion in 2014 alone (U.S. Department of Justice 2015; Federal Trade Commission).

Like corporate or white-collar crime, **organized crime** is a business operation, whose purpose is to supply illegal goods and services to others. Often these goods

Charles Ponzi

U.S./WORLD

U.S. CYBERCRIME IN INTERNATIONAL PERSPECTIVE

Cybercrime is the fastest-growing type of crime; but it's more costly in some countries than others. A recent cost of cybercrime study sampled organizations in advanced capitalist countries around the world. You can see that the United States ranks as an outlier in international comparison. The results indicate that the cost of cybercrime appears to be much higher, on average, in the United States when compared with some nations we might consider our peers.

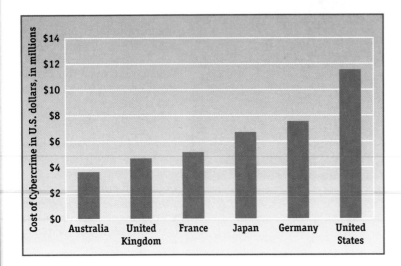

Although the average cost of cybercrime among the 60 sampled U.S. organizations at $11.56 million was high (26 percent higher than the average cost according to the 2012 survey), the survey has also helped us to identify which industries appear to be at the greatest risk. For instance, financial services (perhaps not surprisingly), defense, and energy and utilities have much higher average costs associated with cybercrime than do retail, hospitality, and consumer products. This helps to illustrate a sociological truism of many forms of crime: We are all at risk of cybercrime, but we're not all equally at risk. Some groups (like the elderly for instance) are more likely to be targeted than others, just as some industry sectors have been shown to pay a higher cost for cybercrime.

SOURCE: Data from Ponemon Institute, 2013 *Cost of Cyber Crime Study: United States*: 2. Available at: https://media.scmagazine.com/documents/54/2013_us_ccc_report_final_6-1_13455.pdf.

INVESTIGATE FURTHER

1. Why do you think cybercrime is so much more costly in the United States in comparison with other nations?

2. How can we think about intersecting identities to examine which groups are more and less at risk of cybercrime?

and services are widely desired but still illegal. During Prohibition, for example, organized crime syndicates provided alcohol to a thirsty public and gambling venues to circumvent prohibitions on gambling. Contemporary organized criminal activities include loan-sharking, prostitution, money laundering, drug trafficking, and warehouse or truck theft. Although glamorized by television shows such as *The Sopranos*, by movies such as *The Godfather* and *Scarface*, and by celebrity criminals such as "The Teflon Don," organized crime is often routine and boring work, making rounds to small businesses who pay "protection money," keeping track of the finances of a large-scale enterprise, and managing subordinates in a large-scale hierarchical organization. Organized crime has also found legitimate businesses to be quite lucrative. Criminal enterprises have infiltrated such legitimate organizations as unions, the construction industry, international banking, and transportation (trucking and shipping).

A separate category of crime, **hate crime**, is a criminal act committed by an offender motivated by bias against race, ethnicity, religion, sexual orientation, or disability status. Anyone can commit a hate crime, but perpetrators usually belong to dominant groups (white, Christian, straight) and victims to disenfranchised groups (black, Jewish, Muslim, or gay). The FBI records more than 5,000 hate crimes per year, but because state and local law enforcement agencies differ in their reporting procedures, and some do not report at all, this number is no doubt extremely low. Bias based on race/ethnicity or national origin is the largest motivating factor in hate crimes (59 percent of cases), followed by religion (19.7 percent), sexual orientation (17.7 percent), gender identity (1.7 percent) and disability (1.2 percent) (FBI Hate Crime Statistics 2016). Overall, hate crime in the U.S. swelled by 6 percent recently, driven by an increase in attacks against American Muslims (Lichtblau 2016). Hate crimes are distinguished because they affect not only the individual but the entire community as well. Lynchings in the American South were used to terrorize the entire black population, and contemporary anti-gay hate crimes demonstrate to all gay people that they are unwelcome and unsafe in the community. **Hate groups** are defined by groups with beliefs or practices that attack or malign a class of people often due to immutable characteristics associated with the group (like sexual orientation, skin color, ancestry, gender identity). Importantly, *hate crimes* are not only committed by members of *hate groups* (for a current geographic representation of hate groups across the United States, go to Southern Poverty Law Center Hate Map, available at https://www.splcenter.org/hate-map).

hate crime

A criminal act committed by an offender motivated by bias against race, religion, ethnicity, sexual orientation, or disability status. Anyone can commit a hate crime, but perpetrators usually belong to dominant groups (white, Christian, straight) and victims to disenfranchised groups (black, Jewish, Muslim, or gay).

hate groups

Groups with beliefs or practices that attack or malign a class of people often due to immutable characteristics associated with the group (like sexual orientation, skin color, ancestry, gender identity).

Intersections with Gender and Age

6.3.3 Identify social factors that cause young men and women to engage in different levels of types of criminal activity.

When looking at crime statistics, there is a significant gender gap. In the United States in 2014, only 26.9 percent of people arrested for all crimes were women. Women committed only 20.3 percent of violent crimes. The gender gap is relatively narrow in only two categories of crime—embezzlement and larceny—and women outranked men in embezzlement, prostitution, and runaways (Federal Bureau of Investigation 2015). Otherwise, women were significantly less likely to be arrested, less likely to be convicted, and less likely to serve sentences. And yet the United States has the largest arrest and conviction rate of women in the world: 8.54 per 1,000, nearly double the United Kingdom and four times higher than Canada (Schaffner 2006). (And the rate for women is increasing at a rate faster than that for men.) Nonetheless, when we say *crime*, we might as well say *men*.

The gender gap may be influenced by the "**chivalry effect**": police, judges, and juries are likely to perceive women as less dangerous and their criminal activities less consequential, so they are more often let go with a warning (Pollak 1950/1978). Women who belong to stigmatized groups—who are black, Hispanic, or lesbian, for instance—are more likely to be arrested and convicted, perhaps because they are not granted the same status as women in the mainstream. Feminists note that women receive harsher treatment when their behavior deviates from feminine stereotypes, that is, when they "act like a man" (Edwards 1986). But even when we take the chivalry effect into account, men still commit more violent crimes and property

the "chivalry effect"

The sociological thesis that women are treated more leniently for committing certain crimes by police, judges, and juries who are likely to perceive them as less dangerous and their criminal activities less consequential. Women who belong to stigmatized groups—who are black, Hispanic, or lesbian, for instance—are more likely to be arrested and convicted, perhaps because they are not granted the same status as more privileged women in the mainstream.

FIGURE 6.2 Crime Rates by Age and Gender in Nineteenth-Century Great Britain and Late-Twentieth-Century Chicago

These two charts look at crime rates and homicide rates by age and gender. Whether in Great Britain in the middle of the nineteenth century or in urban Chicago for the last decades of the twentieth century, the graphs look similar because age and gender are the two most consistent variables that predict becoming a violent felon.

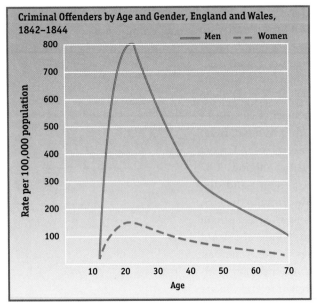

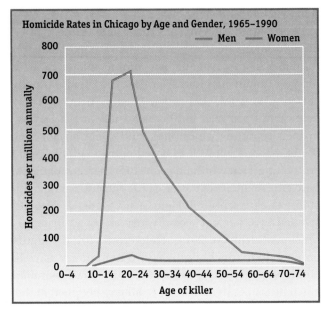

SOURCE: Great Britain data from F. G. P. Neison, *Contributions to Vital Statistics*, 3rd ed. (London 1857), pp. 303–304, as plotted by Travis Hirschi and Michael Gottfredson, "Age and the Explanation of Crime," *American Journal of Sociology*, 89, 1983, p. 556. Chicago data from "Darwinism and the Roots of Machismo," *Scientific American*, Special Issue, 2002.

"sneaky thrills"

Jack Katz's concept that crimes like shoplifting, burglary, joyriding, and vandalism are committed by amateurs, mostly adolescents, for the fun of it, not necessarily to acquire money or property. Katz theorized that sneaky thrills offer the adolescent perpetrators an experience similar to sexual experimentation.

crimes than women. Some criminologists argue that, biologically, males are a lot more aggressive and violent, and that explains the high levels of assaults and other violent crimes (see FIGURE 6.2). However, this biological theory does not explain why men's crime (or at least criminal arrests) occurs primarily in working-class and poor communities. Middle-class men have testosterone, too; shouldn't they be committing assault and murder? Nor can "male aggression" explain the gender gap in property crime.

A more sociological explanation is the model of working-class masculinity. In the working-class and poor subcultures where most crimes (or at least most criminal arrests) occur, men are socialized to believe that "defending" themselves, violently if necessary, is appropriate masculine behavior (see, for example, Willis 1977). Nonviolent crimes can also be gender coded. Men almost always commit stick-up burglary—crimes in which people are robbed face-to-face, usually by threatening them with a gun. Shoplifting, by contrast, is more predominantly associated with women. Sociologist Jack Katz (1988) studied what he called "**sneaky thrills**," crimes like shoplifting, burglary, joyriding, and vandalism committed by amateurs, mostly adolescents, for the fun of it, not necessarily to acquire money or property. He found that not only were most shoplifters young women, but they also steal artifacts that were notably "feminine"—a necklace, earrings, sexy underwear, lipstick. Katz theorized that sneaky thrills offer the adolescent perpetrators an experience similar to sexual experimentation. The stick-up artist enters the victim's world, demonstrates that he is in control, and forcibly leads the action to his desired conclusion. The shoplifters often tell tales of seduction, using metaphors of flirting and enticement, "a rush of excitement as contact is made with the item and inserted into a private place" (p. 71). These crimes are one of the ways we learn about gender and gender differences (more on this in Chapter 9).

When we say *crime*, we might also just as well also say *young* (as you saw). Since the rise of the first adolescent subcultures in the 1940s, minors have been committing far more than their share of crimes. In 2014, 15- to 24-year-olds constituted about 14 percent of the U.S. population but nearly 41 percent of arrests for property crime and 36.1 percent of arrests for violent crime. Young people under 25 were arrested for 44.6 percent of all murders, 55.9 percent of all robberies, and 49.6 percent of all vandalism (Federal Bureau of Investigation 2015). In search of explanations, many sociologists point to gang activity, which has infiltrated every aspect of community life. Also, because most of the youthful offenders are young men, the culture of masculinity may also be at fault—a 15-year-old boy can hardly demonstrate his "masculine" toughness, aggression, and control through academic, occupational, or artistic accomplishments. He can go out for sports; but, in the inner city, school sports have substandard facilities and underpaid staff, and there are few private after-school programs. He may attempt to prove his masculinity with violence and crime. Certainly, women are in gangs as well (as we learned previously in this chapter), and crimes by young women have increased in recent decades. But even the phrase "prove your femininity" is hard to translate into a provocation to crime. And the data make it clear that crime is largely an activity of young men—and has been for some time.

Just because other men are the most frequent victims of violent crimes doesn't mean that girls and women are not also vulnerable. They are. In 2014, according to the FBI, 2,564 boys younger than the age of 18 were arrested on charges of rape and sexual assault (15.5 percent of the total). Six percent (1,009) were younger than age 15. There are more than 1,000 treatment programs in the United States devoted solely to treating youthful sex offenders. Psychologists believe that these boys are still developing their notions of appropriate sexual behavior, so their preference for coercive and violent sexual activity is capable of change. But college students are old enough to have already developed their **sexual scripts**—their cognitive map about how to have sex and with whom—and they sometimes exhibit a similar interest in sexual coercion. According to a 2003 Bureau of Justice Statistics study, rape is the most common violent crime at colleges and universities in the United States. Nearly one in five college women are victims of rape or attempted rape during their freshman year (Carey, et al. 2015), and 2.8 percent of college women experience either a completed rape or an attempted rape every year, most often by a male peer, boyfriend, or classmate (80 percent of college women know their assailants) (Bureau of Justice Statistics 2014; Cole 2006).

sexual scripts
A cognitive map about how to have sex and with whom.

More recently, a new study surveying 27 universities across the United States found that 11.7 percent of the students reported nonconsensual sexual contact by physical force, threats of physical force, or as a result of being incapacitated since enrolled in college (Association of American Universities Campus Climate Survey on Sexual Assault and Sexual Misconduct 2015). But, these experiences intersect with gender in important ways, illustrating forms of power and inequality. Among undergraduates who are women, 23.1 percent reported experiences of reported sexual assault, including 10.8 percent of undergraduate women who reported penetration during the assault.

About 15.2 percent of women and 5.6 percent of men have experienced stalking victimization in their lifetimes, and slightly more than half of the women and just less than half of the male victims experienced it before age 25 (National Center for Victims of Crime 2015). The research shows that aggression and control seem socially connected to young men's understandings of masculinity. It does not mean men are biologically programmed to be physically and sexually violent. But we learn a lot about how different societies understand gender by looking at how those least able to approximate gender ideals behave.

Intersections with Race and Class

6.3.4 Identify social factors that put racial minorities and the poor at disproportionate risk of being arrested.

If we were to judge solely by arrest and conviction rates, we might conclude that if the gender of crime is masculine, the race of crime is black. When we examine crime and punishment intersectionally, minorities are dramatically overrepresented in the criminal justice system—both as offenders and as victims (Rosich 2007). African Americans are arrested at a rate two, three, or even five times greater than statistical probability: They comprise 12.5 percent of the population but almost 56 percent of arrests for robbery, 51.3 percent for murder, more than 29.1 percent of drug abuse violations for drug use (FBI Uniform Crime Reports 2014). And they are considerably more likely to become the victims of crime (Truman and Langton 2015). Blacks are also overrepresented among arrestees for offenses that involve considerable discretion at the scene, such as loitering (46.2 percent), disorderly conduct (33.9 percent), or suspicion (44.7 percent) (FBI Uniform Crime Reports 2014). Black men are incarcerated at 6 times the rate of white men (Drake 2013), more than 10 percent of all black men ages 25 to 39 are behind bars on any given day, and more than 30 percent of black men ages 25 to 34 without a high school diploma are incarcerated (Neal and Rick 2014). And black overrepresentation does not happen only in the United States. In the United Kingdom, blacks are seven times more likely than whites or Asians to be stopped or arrested. In Britain, however, blacks, whites, and Asians are equally likely to be crime victims, and it is those of mixed race who face a significantly higher risk (Ministry of Justice 2015).

But it isn't just black Americans; Latinos are overrepresented in the U.S. criminal justice system as well (see FIGURE 6.3). Although Latinos make up about 16 percent of the U.S. population, they make up almost twice that share of those incarcerated in the federal system (Bureau of Justice Statistics 2016). Latino defendants are imprisoned three times as often as whites and are detained before trial for first-time offenses almost twice as often as whites, despite the fact that they are the least likely of all ethnic groups to have a criminal history (Noguera, Hurtado and Fergus 2013; Walker et al. 2004). They are also disproportionately charged with nonviolent drug offenses (despite having the second-lowest rate of illicit drug use, next to Asians) (Substance Abuse and Mental Health Services Administration 2009) and represent the vast majority of those arrested for immigration violations (National Council of La Raza 2004; Weich and Angulo 2000).

What is the link between crime and race? Each of the theories we have discussed in this chapter offers a perspective on this issue. Scholars adopting *strain theory* suggest

FIGURE 6.3 U.S. Men in Prison or Jail, 2015
This chart illustrates a stark reality in the United States, particularly for black men. As you can see, the rates of incarceration for men in the United States vary by race, but also by age. Men in their 20s to 40s are the largest groups that are affected. But black men are affected much more than white or Latino men. Look at the 30- to 34-year-old men on the chart. Less than 2,000 out of every 100,000 white men is in prison or jail in this category (put another way, less than 2 percent of 30- to 34-year-old white men in the United States are in prison or jail). The number of black men in this category is roughly 5 times that rate. Approximately 6 percent of black men in the United States between the ages of 30 and 34 are in prison or jail. And this rate of incarceration affects more than just these men, but also the communities in which they lived prior to being locked up.

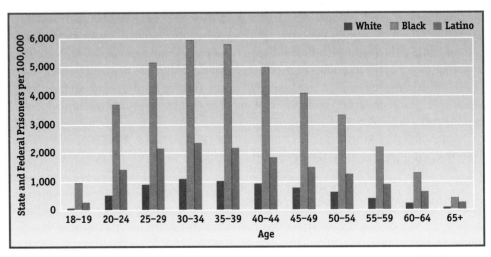

SOURCE: Data from Bureau of Justice Statistics, 2016. Available at https://www.bjs.gov/content/pub/pdf/p15.pdf.

that it's really a matter of social class, not race. Blacks are more likely to be poor, and poor people living amid affluence are more likely to perceive society as unjust and turn to crime (Anderson 1994; Blau and Blau 1982). Yet, even within the lower classes, blacks are significantly more likely to be arrested and sentenced than whites. Scholars relying on *differential opportunity* theory highlight that black children are much more likely to be raised by single mothers than are white children. They receive less supervision, and are more likely turn to crime. Yet, it is also true that the vast majority of children raised by single parents (mostly mothers) do not turn to crime. Scholars using *labeling theory* understand being black is a master status equated with violence and criminality in many societies. So, people (black or white) tend to view black behavior as more threatening and report on it more often, police officers (black or white) tend to arrest blacks more often, and juries (black or white) tend to give them stiffer sentences.

Sociologists agree that those with less power in society—women, minorities, young people—are more likely to be arrested. So, too, with class. The poorer you are, the more likely that you will be arrested for a crime. While the crime rate goes up as the person's socioeconomic status goes down, this may be caused less by economic deprivation—people stealing because they are hungry or don't have enough money to pay their rent—and more because their crimes are more visible and their "profile" is more likely to fit our understandings of which identities and which groups are likely to commit crimes in the first place.

Equally, the poorer you are, the more likely you are to be the victim of crime, both property crime and violent crime. The wealthy are more insulated in their neighborhoods, better served by the police, and more likely to press charges against offenders.

Guns and Crime

6.3.5 Understand what sociologists mean by "gun culture," and use this to explain why gun crime in the United States is so much higher than other industrialized countries around the world.

The United States has the weakest laws on handgun ownership in the industrialized world. As a result, there are as many guns as there are people, and it shows in crime statistics. Six million Americans carry a gun on a daily basis; about one-third of all U.S. households have a gun at home (National Public Radio 2016). Sixty eight percent of murders, 41 percent of robberies, and 21 percent of aggravated assaults are committed with guns (National Institute of Justice 2017). Globally, the United States ranks in the middle of all countries' rates of deaths by guns. But no other industrialized country comes close to the United States; indeed, our rate is nearly double that of our nearest "rival."

The United States has had difficulty passing minimal regulations to monitor the distribution of guns. Federal efforts to institute simple safeguards such as criminal background checks on prospective gun owners have met with fierce opposition from gun lobbyists. Many efforts—such as attempts to block convicted criminals from obtaining guns or to revoke the licenses of gun dealers who break the law—remain under attack by gun advocates. In fact, since approximately 2000, some of the scattered state laws that had been in effect for a decade or more have been weakened or repealed, particularly in the South (Hemenway 2005). For example, although criminologists have shown that limiting volume purchases of handguns is effective at stemming illegal gun trafficking, South Carolina abolished a one-per-month purchase rule in 2004 that had been in place for nearly 30 years. That same year, the state of Virginia weakened a similar law that had been on the books since 1993 (Wirzbicki 2005). Also, recently, joining Alaska and Vermont, Arizona's concealed weapons bill allows a person to carry concealed weapons without a permit (see http://www.rightpundits.com/?p=6063). Several states also allow students to carry concealed weapons on college campuses.

Global Inequality and Crime

6.3.6 Using the example of drugs, explain the ways that local crimes are related to global trends.

Although the Internet may have expanded the global networks of crime, crime as a global enterprise has a long history, from ancient slave traders (who kidnapped their "cargo") to criminal networks operating in many different countries. There were pirates on the seven seas, hoisting their proverbial black flags beyond territorial waters; and there are contemporary pirates who operate in countries where it is legal to steal and duplicate material from the Internet or to ransack corporate funds into offshore bank accounts. Today, global criminal networks operate in every arena, from the fake Gucci handbags for sale on street corners to the young girls who are daily kidnapped in Thailand and other countries to serve as sex slaves in brothels around the world; from street gangs and various ethnic and national organized crime networks (the "Russian Mafia," the Italian Mafia) to the equally well-organized and equally illegal offshore bankers and shady corporate entities that incorporate in countries that have no regulations on toxic dumping, environmental devastation, or fleecing stockholders.

And yet much crime also remains decidedly "local"—an individual is assaulted or robbed, raped, or murdered in his or her own neighborhood. Despite the massive networks of organized global crime, it is still true that the place where you are most likely to be the victim of a violent crime is your own home (U.S. Department of Justice 2014).

A good example of this connection between the local and the global is the subject of drugs. Examining the sociology of drug use provides a window into the various aspects of deviance and crime that sociologists study.

---

27 million Americans ages 12 and older used an illicit drug in the past 30 days. Almost 7.1 million Americans are dependent on drugs. And nearly 2.5 million Americans are in treatment for their addiction (Substance Abuse and Mental Health Services Administration 2014). The most commonly used drugs are marijuana, cocaine, and painkillers. Using some drugs is illegal, and abusing others (such as prescription medications) is illegal, but is it "deviant"? Some sociologists have examined drug use and its consequences intersectionally—looking at rates of use of different drugs by different groups and the consequences of those differences in arrests and prison sentences. Other sociologists examine the social processes by which someone "becomes" a marijuana user—a process that resembles the socialization into any other social group, deviant or not (e.g., Becker 1953).

GLOBALIZATION: NETWORKS OF PRODUCTION, DISTRIBUTION, AND PROTECTION.   Because drug use is illegal, different types of criminals produce and distribute them. Sociologists of organizations can examine how different networks may connect your local campus pot dealer with murderous organized drug cartels in other countries—from the local peasants who grow various drugs to large bureaucratic organizations that handle production, transportation, distribution, and protection. In some countries, illegal drugs are among that country's leading exports.

DRUGS AND THE CRIMINAL JUSTICE SYSTEM.   According to the Federal Bureau of Prisons, 46.3 percent of incarcerated adults are serving time for a drug offense (Federal Bureau of Prisons 2017). More than one-fourth are incarcerated for simple possession, and nearly 70 percent are there for trafficking (Mumola and Karberg 2006; Sabol and West 2008). The War on Drugs propelled the incarceration rate to a nearly 10-fold rate of convictions. But that war's casualties have been distributed unequally toward poor and minority young men, who compose the large majority of all drug-related arrests and convictions. Black people account for 13 percent of the U.S. population, but 31 percent of those are arrested for drug law violations and almost 40 percent of those are incarcerated in state and federal prisons for drug violations. Similarly, Latinos make up 17 percent of the U.S. population but account for a much larger share of those incarcerated for drug offenses, 20 percent in state prisons and 37 percent in federal ones. In 2014, Latinos were 22 percent of those arrested for drug violations. (The Drug Policy Alliance 2016). Research finds that people of color are no more likely than whites to sell or use drugs, but tend to face tougher charges when arrested; so, their higher rates of conviction also result in lengthier prison terms (Rothwell 2014).

DRUGS AND PUBLIC POLICY.   In 2009, New York State abolished the punitive "Rockefeller Drug Laws," which severely punished possession and use of drugs like marijuana with significant prison sentences. Defendants convicted of selling two ounces or possessing four ounces, for instance, faced a mandatory sentence of 15 years to life in prison. Sociologists study drug policies ranging from legalization of drugs, drug law reform, funding for rehabilitation and treatment, to medical use of marijuana. Yet, relatively little research suggests that harsher penalties for drug use will resolve this social problem. Sociological research shows that more punishment is not the answer.

---

iSOC AND YOU The Social Organization of Crime

There are many different types of crimes, and many different types of criminals. Yet somehow different groups are over- or underrepresented among different types of crimes. Unless you believe that some groups have some genetic disposition to steal apples, for example, you can't explain that except through the tools of the sociologist. Some groups are more likely to be seen as criminals (men members of minority groups, younger people) or live in neighborhoods that are seen as crime-infested. The *intersection* of several of these factors— young, African-American, men—for example, may be perceived as potentially criminal just for walking around in a hoodie. By examining crime, we can actually understand the social dynamics through which *inequality* is reproduced, how crime is based on *interactions* between an individual or group and other groups with greater power, and how these interactions become *institutionalized*.

6.4 Understanding Crime and Deviance Institutionally

"In the criminal justice system, there are two separate but equally important groups: the police who investigate crimes and the district attorneys who prosecute the offenders. These are their stories." So says the narrator at the beginning of each episode of *Law and Order*, the most successful crime franchise in television history, combining both police and legal drama. It's mostly right. The criminal justice system is a complex of institutions that includes the police and the courts, a wide range of prosecuting and defense lawyers, and also the prison system. And learning to think sociologically about crime necessitates an understanding of some of the primary institutions involved.

In this section, we investigate police and processes of policing, what happens in courtrooms, institutions of punishment and "correction" in our society, and we will learn to think about the social problem of incarceration from a much more sociological perspective. This means not only considering how different groups are more and less likely to be policed, punished, and incarcerated, but also examining the multidimensional consequences that stem from these differences. Relying on the iSoc model, we will examine the impacts of crime on identities and interactions, and we will examine the ways that intersectional forms of inequality become institutionalized in ways that work to reproduce the experiences and opportunities of members of different groups across time and space.

Police and Policing

6.4.1 Explain the split image of police in the United States and how that is related to different experiences of the police among different groups in society.

The number of police officers in the United States has increased 35 percent over the past 30 years (Reaves 2015). In 2014, there were 3.4 full-time law enforcement employees (this includes sworn officers and non-sworn civil employees) for every 1,000 people (Federal Bureau of Investigation 2014). This is more than most countries: France has 2.3, Japan 2.3, and Canada 1.95.

But police officers actually spend only about 20 percent of their time in "crime-fighting" activity. A surprising amount of their daily routine involves completing departmental paperwork: arrest and accident reports, patrol activity reports, and judicial statements. Their "on" time mostly involves routine public order activity and communicating information about risk control to other institutions in society (insurance companies, public health workers, social welfare agencies, and schools). Today the police have become "knowledge workers" as much as they are "crime fighters" (Ericson and Haggerty 1997): They offer tips and techniques, such as "stay in well-lighted areas," but in the end, you are responsible for your own safety.

The police have a split image. To some people, seeing a police officer on the street makes them feel safe and secure, as if no harm will come to them. To others, seeing that same police officer is a terrible threat, and they might feel that they are in danger of being arrested or killed simply for being there. Some people see the police as protection; others see them as an occupying army.

The police understand this dichotomy. In many cities, like Los Angeles, their motto is "to protect and to serve"—they want people to feel safe, and they want to be of service to those who feel threatened (see FIGURE 6.4). Some of this is the result of **racial profiling** by the police.

racial profiling

Stopping and searching minorities because members of minority groups are seen as "more likely" to be criminals. It's more a self-fulfilling prophecy: Believing is seeing.

The most important trends in police forces across the country have been to embed the police within the communities they serve; to encourage more minority police, especially in minority areas; and also, to train new groups of women officers, especially to respond to complaints about domestic violence. Since the 1990s, the number of women and minority police officers has increased. Minority representation among local police officers has almost doubled between 1987 and 2014, with an increase from 14.6 percent in 1987 to about 27 percent in 2013. About one in eight police officers are women, who made up about 58,000 local police officers in 2013 (Bureau of Justice Statistics 2014).

FIGURE 6.4 Trust in the Police, by Race

The Pew Research Center regularly polls representative samples of the U.S. public to ask their opinions on a variety of issues. Since 2007, they have been asking how much confidence Americans have in the police to treat black and white people equally. Respondents are asked to rank whether they have "very little," "just some," a "fair amount," or a "great deal" of confidence in the police to treat black and white people equally. You can see that the number of Americans who claim to have a "great deal" of confidence in the police has been declining. But, when we look at this *intersectionally* and examine the ways that black and white Americans respond to this question, the divide is put into sharper contrast. In 2014, 46 percent of black respondents said they have "very little" confidence in the police to treat black and white people equally (only 12 percent of white respondents answered that way). These data are one small illustration of different experiences with police for black and white people in the United States.

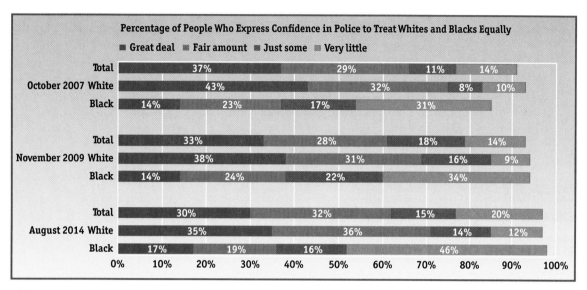

Percentage of People Who Express Confidence in Police to Treat Whites and Blacks Equally
■ Great deal   ■ Fair amount   ■ Just some   ■ Very little

		Great deal	Fair amount	Just some	Very little
October 2007	Total	37%	29%	11%	14%
	White	43%	32%	8%	10%
	Black	14%	23%	17%	31%
November 2009	Total	33%	28%	18%	14%
	White	38%	31%	16%	9%
	Black	14%	24%	22%	34%
August 2014	Total	30%	32%	15%	20%
	White	35%	36%	14%	12%
	Black	17%	19%	16%	46%

0%   10%   20%   30%   40%   50%   60%   70%   80%   90%   100%

NOTE: Figures do not add to 100% because of rounding and because 'don't know' responses are not shown.

SOURCE: Data from Pew Research Center, "Blacks Express Less Confidence than Whites in Local Police to Treat Blacks and Whites Equally." Available at http://www.pewresearch.org/fact-tank/2015/04/28/blacks-whites-police/.

Courtrooms and Court Proceedings

6.4.2 Summarize the social problem of bias in the courtroom including why and how mandatory sentencing legislation failed.

The court system is an important arena of the social institution of criminal justice. In criminal court, the district attorney's office prosecutes those arrested by the police for criminal offenses; the accused are defended in adversarial proceedings by a defense attorney. Thus, criminal proceedings pit the government (its agents, the police, lawyers,

SOCIOLOGY AND OUR WORLD

DRIVING WHILE ... BLACK?

How does inequality shape the likelihood that some groups will be more likely than others to interact with the police?

The perceived connection between race and crime is often painful to those who are targeted. African Americans sometimes refer to the phenomenon of being constantly stopped by the police as "DWB"—"driving while Black." Studies of traffic stops have found that while 5 percent of the drivers on Florida highways were black or Latino, nearly 70 percent of those stopped and 80 percent of those searched were black or Latino. A study in Maryland found that although blacks were 17 percent of the motorists on one freeway, they accounted for 73 percent of those stopped and searched. An Illinois study found that a black driver is roughly three times more likely to be the subject of a search when compared with white drivers (Hispanic drivers were 2.4 times as likely). A study in Philadelphia found that 75 percent of the motorists were white and 80 percent of those stopped were minorities (Cannon 1999; Cole 1999). Stopping and searching minorities is a form of "racial profiling" in which members of minority groups are seen as "more likely" to be criminals and therefore stopped more often. It's more a self-fulfilling prophecy: Believing is seeing.

and the like) against a defendant, unlike civil courts in which the court is an arbiter of arguments between two individuals or groups. Although the criminal courtroom drama is a staple of U.S. movies and television, more than 90 percent of criminal cases never go to trial. Instead, most are resolved by plea bargaining or pleading guilty to a lesser crime.

In the early 1990s, **mandatory sentencing rules** were enacted across the United States. These laws applied to about 64,000 defendants a year and required certain sentences for certain crimes, allowing little room for discretion. The laws were supposed to be tough on crime and eliminate bias in prosecutions and sentencing. The primary result, however, has been an explosion in the prison population. Bias related to race, class, gender and more remains in both arrests and prosecutions—yet under mandatory sentencing judges couldn't take dependent-specific circumstances—which could help the poor, minorities, mentally unstable, the sick, or addicted—into account. In early 2005, the Supreme Court ruled that federal judges no longer must abide by the guidelines, saying they violated a defendant's right to a fair trial.

mandatory sentencing rules
Rules enacted across the United States in the early 1990s that were supposed to be tough on crime and eliminate bias in prosecutions and sentencing. The primary result, however, has been an explosion in the prison population.

HOW DO WE KNOW WHAT WE KNOW?

RACIAL BIAS IN THE COURTROOM

Whether you have ever stood trial for committing a crime or not, you probably know that if you are convicted of committing the crime, there are a range of possible outcomes—various "sentences" you may be required to endure for the crime. In social science language, *sentences vary*. As a result of this, we can examine how sentences vary and for whom. In other words, we can ask questions about which groups are more and less likely to receive harsh and lenient penalties when compared with others committing similar crimes. Research has shown a great deal of bias in sentencing practices in the United States. What this means is that different races are given different sentences, on average, when they are tried for the same crimes.

And racial bias proceeds through a set of cumulative stages. Black and Hispanic men, for instance, are more likely to be arrested or cited for crimes than are white men for committing the same crimes. This means that they are more likely, on average, to enter a courtroom in the first place. But once they get there, they are encountering a new institution that has been shown to disproportionately punish non-white men with harsher sentences.

Part of this has to do with racial bias in the jury selection process (at least for cases tried by jury). Jury selection is intentionally random. We can all be called upon to serve on a jury, and we are legally obligated to show up when we are "summoned." But, once summoned, defense and prosecuting

attorneys select the jury based on the pool of people summoned. And this is when racial bias creeps in. A great deal of research has shown that black jurors are removed at a much higher rate than white jurors as the jury that will sit and hear the case constructed in the courtroom. Despite the fact that we know this problem exists, it's been challenging to eradicate in practice. The Supreme Court heard a case in November 2015—*Foster v. Chatman, 2015*—on racial discrimination in jury selection. The case is primarily about prosecutors using peremptory challenges to systematically remove black jurors while keeping white ones. (And this was the first time in 30 years that the Court has entertained a case about rules on racial discrimination in jury selection). As of writing this, there has been no decision.

But even once juries are selected, another form of racial bias occurs in the sentencing of defendants of different races. One recent study of 185,275 different criminal cases heard by the New York County District Attorney's office found black and Latino defendants more likely to be detained and to be incarcerated for their crimes when compared with white defendants committing the same crimes. They also discovered that black and Latino men in particular were likely to receive especially punitive outcomes for person offenses (or crimes in which they injured or attacked another person) when compared with white men (Kutateladze, et al. 2014).

Punishment, Corrections, and Incarceration

6.4.3 Explain shifts in the U.S. incarceration rate, and consider them in international perspective.

Today the United States has 2.3 million people in jail or prison, about 1 in 110 adults, many more than any other industrialized country in the world; see MAP 6.1 (Prison Policy Initiative 2017). Russia has the second-highest incarceration rate, incarcerating 474 per 100 thousand (APA 2014). The incarceration rate in the United States is three and a half times the European rate and four times the world average (National Council on Crime and Delinquency 2006). The United States has more total inmates

MAP 6.1 Incarceration Rates Around the World

The United States incarcerates a larger proportion of its population than any other country in the world. View incarceration rates in comparison to the United States to see just how far of an outlier we are on this issue.

SOURCE: Data from World Prison Brief. "Prison Population Rate." Available at http://www.prisonstudies.org/highest-to-lowest/prison_population_rate?field_region_taxonomy_tid=All.

Prison rate per 100,000 population
- N/A
- 1–20
- 20–40
- 40–80
- 80–120
- 120–180
- 180–250
- 250–350
- > 350

than the 26 European countries with the largest inmate populations put together—even though we have 500 million fewer people than the total population of those countries (Pew Center on the States 2008). We have more people in prison than the total number of U.S. military personnel—Army Navy, Air Force, Marines, Coast Guard, Reserves, and National Guard—combined. The United States also imprisoned at least three times more women than any other nation in the world. Although more men are incarcerated than women, 6.7 percent of those incarcerated in the United States are women (which accounts for slightly more than 200,000 inmates) (Federal Bureau of Prisons 2017).

And the high incarceration rate in the United States is not the result of higher rates of crime; with the single exception of incarceration rates in Russia for robbery, we lock up more people per incident than any other country in the world (National Council on Crime and Delinquency 2006). When we add the 4.8 million people on probation or parole, we come up with an amazing statistic: 3.2 percent of the adult U.S. population is currently immersed somewhere in the criminal justice system. And the numbers are increasing dramatically. Between 1980 and 2008, the national prison population nearly quadrupled (NAACP Fact Sheet 2016). Over the same time period, state spending on corrections increased 12 percent. Eleven states—Michigan, Oregon, Arizona, Vermont, Colorado, Pennsylvania, New Hampshire, Delaware, Rhode Island, Massachusetts and Connecticut—spend more on corrections than on higher education (American Academy of Arts and Sciences 2015). Recently, economic shifts have stemmed this tide (see FIGURE 6.5).

The Great Recession has made the high cost of so many incarcerations impossible to sustain. During 2008, 20 states reduced their prisoner counts by a total of about 10,000 inmates. As a result, the number of state and federal prisoners grew by less than 1 percent overall nationwide, the smallest increase in nearly a decade, and the number of African Americans behind bars has dropped nearly 10 percent from its peak (Von Drehle 2010).

FIGURE 6.5 Prisoners under the Jurisdiction of State or Federal Correctional Authorities, 1978–2015

While the population of prisoners in the United States has fallen slightly since 2009, the population has grown substantially over the past 30 to 40 years. The United States incarcerates an enormous number of people, far more than our peer nations around the world.

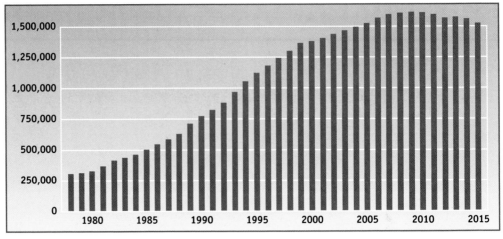

SOURCE: Data from Bureau of Justice Statistics, "National Prisoner Statistics, 1978–2015." Available at https://www.bjs.gov/content/pub/pdf/p15.pdf.

Does Incarceration Work?

6.4.4 Summarize the four goals of incarceration and whether they are achieved in the United States or not.

People convicted of crimes may be asked to pay fines and restitution to victims or to engage in community service. For most offenses, however, the main penalty is incarceration: jail or prison terms of up to 84 months for violent crimes, 48 months for drug crimes, and 41 months for property crimes (not including those rare instances when life in prison or the death penalty is imposed). But criminologists, lawgivers, and private individuals have often wondered *why*. What are the goals of incarceration? Are they actually being achieved? Four goals have been proposed (Goode 2004; Siegel 2000):

1. *Retribution.* People who break rules must be punished; they "owe a debt to society." Children who break their parents' rules are often grounded, temporarily losing their liberty and some of their privileges (the freedom to watch television or play video games, for instance). In the same way, adults who break laws can be effectively punished through the loss of their liberty and some of their citizenship privileges (the freedom to vote, sign contracts, take gainful employment, and so on). A problem with the retribution goal is that we believe that the punishment should fit the crime: The greater the degree of social harm, the worse the punishment. However, incarceration can only be extended, not worsened. Also, justice is not blind: Prison terms are longer for minorities than whites, and for men than for women, even when both have been convicted of the same offense (Mustard 2001). So, if retribution is a goal, it is one we are inequitably applying.

2. *Deterrence.* Children may not understand or agree with the reasoning behind their parents' rules, but the threat of grounding deters them from most rule-breaking in the first place, and the memory of punishment is sufficient to hinder future rule-breaking. In the same way, the threat of prison decreases the likelihood of a first offense, and the memory of prison is assumed to deter people from future crimes. But does it? Between 30 and 50 percent of people released from prison commit new crimes, often of the same sort that got them the prison sentence in the first place. Criminologists have found that fear of prison itself plays virtually no role in the decision-making process of either first-time or repeat offenders. Criminologists refer to this as **recidivism**—an individual's relapse into criminal behavior after having served time or endured some intervention aimed to affect their future behavior. Thus, the "recidivism rate" is the rate at which people who have served time will commit another crime after leaving. And that rate is higher than you might have thought if you understood prison sentences as something that would deter future criminal behavior.

3. *Protection.* When we "take criminals off the streets," they will not be able to commit further crimes (at least, not on the streets), and society is protected. However, only a few of the most violent criminals stay off the streets forever. Nationally, more than half of criminals released are back in prison within 3 years, either for breaking parole or for a new crime (Pew Center on the States 2008). Many social scientists argue that although serving time, offenders are in "crime school," with seasoned professionals teaching them how to commit more and better crimes (e.g., Califano 1998). Johnny Depp portrays a cocaine smuggler who got connected with a cartel while in prison in the film, *Blow* (2001). As Depp's character says of his prison experience, "Danbury wasn't a prison. It was a crime school. I went in with a Bachelor of Marijuana, came out with a Doctorate of Cocaine." Sociologists have also discovered that prison serves this purpose for many, helping them learn to commit more crimes, and to commit crime more effectively.

recidivism

An individual's relapse into criminal behavior after having served time or endured some intervention aimed to affect their future behavior. Thus, the "recidivism rate" is the rate at which people who have served time will commit another crime after leaving.

4. *Rehabilitation.* Criminals lack the skills necessary to succeed (or even survive) in mainstream society. The National Literacy Survey of 16,000 inmates found that 63 percent were at the lowest levels of functional illiteracy. Less than half have high school diplomas or GEDs. So prison time can be used for rehabilitation. They can get drug and alcohol therapy, learn a trade, get their GED, and even take college classes. A 4-year study conducted by the Department of Education found that inmates who participate in any education program are 23 percent less likely to be reincarcerated. A CUNY study at Bedford Hills Correctional Facility, New York's only maximum-security women's prison, found that prisoners who took college courses were more than 60 percent less likely to return than those who did not (Clark 1991). An extensive study of rearrests, reconvictions, and reincarcerations found that prison education reduces overall relapses into crime by nearly 30 percent (Coley and Barton 2006; Steurer and Smith 2003). But prisons offer few rehabilitation programs, and those available are seriously understaffed and underfunded. Most prisoners do not receive counseling or drug and alcohol therapy, and budget cuts terminated almost all of the prison education programs in 1994. Those prisoners who do take classes often find that they have not acquired the skills for real-world jobs, nor have they received any training on how to find work.

Sociologists understand that we sent people to prison and jail for four reasons: as punishment, protection, deterrence, and rehabilitation. Because the vast majority of those incarcerated will rejoin society, many scholars suggest that the criminal justice system ought to commit more resources to rehabilitation. Yet, the U.S. prison system stresses punishment more than these other elements. The United States has approximately 4 percent of the global population. But we have roughly one quarter of the global prison population. When sociologists think about whether incarceration "works" or not, our questions are: "works" to accomplish what? Or, "works" for whom?

The Death Penalty

6.4.5 Summarize why sociologists are confident that the death penalty does not actually deter people from committing the crimes associated with this sentence.

Fewer than half of the countries in the world (69) currently have death penalties—countries like Algeria, Benin, China, Mongolia, Thailand, and Uganda. There is only one in the industrialized West: the United States. The European Union will not accept as a new member any country that has the death penalty. As of this writing, the death penalty exists in all but 19 of the states. In 2016, four countries—Iran, Iraq, Saudi Arabia and Pakistan—accounted for 87 percent of all confirmed executions (although China executes thousands but keeps the number a secret). The United States ranks seventh, but it is the only country in the global north (Death Penalty Information Organization 2017). The use of the death penalty has steadily dropped in the United States, particularly in the late 1990s and early 2000s: in 2008, 37 inmates were executed, a 14-year low (Moore 2008). But the decline was short-lived. In 2009, there were 52 executions, 46 in 2010, 43 in 2011 and 2012, and 39 in 2013. In the United States, it is usually invoked only in cases of murder and treason. The U.S. public generally favors the death penalty for adult offenders—by about two to one, with more support among men than women and more among whites than among minorities (see FIGURE 6.6). Americans typically cite the death penalty's value in deterring crime. Research has shown, however, that the death penalty does not deter crimes associated with this penalty.

Many scholars have noted that the death penalty is unjustly applied—illustrating intersectional forms of inequality. For instance, race has been shown to play a major

FIGURE 6.6 The Death Penalty in the United States, 1937–2016

Opinions regarding the death penalty are among the more dividing issues in the United States. And although we tend to think that opinions about issues like this tend to be static, like U.S. opinions regarding abortion, Americans' support for and rejection of the death penalty goes through ebbs and flows. Currently, the majority of Americans are in favor of the death penalty, but opposition has been steadily growing since the mid-1990s. (Opinions depicted here are only for Americans' opinions regarding the death penalty in cases involving convicted murderers).

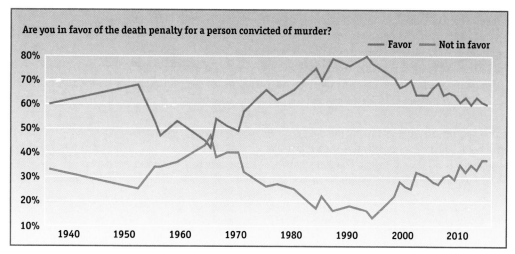

SOURCE: Data from Gallup 2016. "Are you in favor of the death penalty for a person convicted of murder?" Available at http://www.gallup.com/poll/1606/death-penalty.aspx.

role in death penalty sentences: Blacks convicted of murdering whites are most likely to get the death penalty, and whites convicted of murdering blacks are the least likely (Phillips 2008; Paternoster, Brame, and Bacon 2007; Baldus and Woodworth 1998; General Accounting Office 1990). The death penalty, once applied, is irreversible, leading to worries that innocent people might be wrongly executed. In the twentieth century, studies estimate that at least 4 percent of all people who receive the death penalty are innocent (Gross, et al. 2014), and today new techniques of DNA analysis are thinning the ranks of death row.

HOW DO WE KNOW WHAT WE KNOW?

DOES THE DEATH PENALTY ACT AS A DETERRENT TO CRIME?

When we ask that question, we are really concerned with causality. Consider two scenarios. (1) Does knowing about the possibility of going to the gas chamber or electric chair *cause* people to reconsider their murder plans? (2) If killing police officers comes with a mandatory death penalty sentence, do states with these laws see lower rates of cop killings? They might seem like fairly straightforward questions. In fact, you might have an opinion about each of them. But they are challenging questions to answer conclusively with social scientific research. The best way to determine causality is through experiment: Introduce variable A into controlled and experimental contexts and determine if variable B results. If B only happens after A is introduced, and never before A or without A, then we can state with some certainty that A caused B (although, even in this case, we have to rule out potential alternative explanations). But, like many questions that interest us about social life, sociologists can't turn the death penalty on and off to look at the results. Instead, we turn to the somewhat riskier business of *correlation*. We look at places where the death penalty has ended, or where it has been instated, to see what happens to the crime rates associated with serious crime.

Imagine a country that has no death penalty and a murder rate of 0.10 per 1,000 people, significantly higher than that of the United States (0.04). The country decides to institute the death penalty, and within 5 years the death penalty drops 10 percent, to 0.09. Sociologists all over the world would stare at the statistics in amazement: The death penalty (variable A) is correlated with a decrease in the murder rate (variable B)! Is it possible that someone stops to consider the consequences before he sets out to shoot his nuisance of a brother-in-law? Maybe. Correlation cannot prove causality.

Maybe the country is enjoying a period of remarkable economic prosperity, so there is less crime in general. Maybe it has instituted strict gun control laws, so there is no way for anyone to shoot his brother-in-law. Maybe the population is aging, and murder is mostly a young person's activity. We can never know for sure that the death penalty, and not other intervening variables, caused the drop in the murder rate.

Even though a positive correlation is not always a good indication of a causal relationship, the *lack* of correlation is a pretty good indicator of *a lack* of causality. If *B* happens sometimes before *A*, sometimes after *A*, and sometimes without *A*, we can be reasonably sure that the two variables are not causally linked. When real-life countries and states enact death penalty sentences as law, or revoke them, the rate of murder and other serious crime has not been shown to rise or fall in any systematic fashion. There is no significant correlation. In fact, it might actually seem to go the other way. Florida and Texas, the two states with the highest numbers of executions, actually have higher murder rates than states with no death penalty or that have death penalties on the books but few or no executions. States with death penalty laws associated with cop killings have not been shown to have fewer cop killings per capita, suggesting that the laws are not a deterrent.

Of course, no one would seriously make the argument that the death penalty *causes* murders! But neither can anyone make a convincing argument that the death penalty deters murder either.

Therefore, despite what "everybody knows," sociologists conclude that the death penalty has no significant effect on serious crime. What "everybody knows" in this case turns out to be wrong.

---

iSOC AND YOU Understanding Crime and Deviance Institutionally

In this chapter, we've seen how crime and deviance are not inherent properties of certain acts, not properties of certain individuals, but are based on the *interactions* of some people with other people. If people in high school call you a "loser," that could become your *identity*, but what you are aware of at that moment is their collective power to label you as a loser and the *inequality* that makes it harder for you to say "No I'm not." Of course, some people can embrace, even celebrate, an identity as "deviant," but for most of you, being deviant is not a characteristic of your *identity* that you particularly want. The ability of some groups to get their label to stick to you reveals that deviance is based on *interaction*, and reflects social *inequality*. Such interactions and relationships are reproduced through social *institutions*, like the family or education. *Intersecting* identities and inequalities make some people far more likely to be labeled than others.

Conclusion
Deviance and Crime NOW

The main question in deviance and crime is not only why so many people break the rules. It's also why so many people don't. The question of order is the flip side of the question of deviance—and both are of significant interest to sociologists. We may all be deviants, but we're also, most of the time, law-abiding citizens. And we obey the law not only because we are afraid to get caught or deterred by the punishments associated with violations, but because, deep down, we believe that the system of laws is legitimate and that we all will benefit somehow from everyone obeying them.

In the future, we'll continue to obey most of the rules and also decide which ones we can break and justify their breaking to ourselves. Our society will likely continue its anticrime spending spree, and the number of prisoners will continue to spiral upward. The crime rate will shift unevenly; some crimes will increase and some decrease. And we'll continue to debate the age-old questions of guns and the death penalty.

The sociological questions will remain the same: How do people make the sorts of decisions about what laws to obey and which ones to break? Who decides what laws are, how they are to be enforced, and how equally the law is to be applied? How does our understanding of deviance and crime reflect and reinforce the inequalities of our society even as the institutions that administer them—the police, courts, and prisons— also reflect and reinforce those inequalities? What are the possibilities of more equitable understandings and policies?

CHAPTER REVIEW Crime and Deviance

6.1 Thinking Sociologically about Crime and Deviance

Thinking sociologically about crime and deviance often means that we take a step back and ask less about individuals and more about the contexts in which they find themselves. This means that we are critically interested in how individuals come to understand themselves as "deviant" or "criminal." Distinguishing crime from deviance requires understanding how these identities are imposed on us from outside of ourselves, how some people endure this imposition more regularly than others, and how some may more readily accept the label than others. We are considered deviant when we violate a social or moral rule, whether or not it is illegal. However, we can also be considered deviant without doing, saying, or believing anything bad or wrong but just by belonging to the "wrong" group in some circumstances (Hispanic, gay, Jewish, for example) or by having some status that goes against what's considered "normal" (mentally ill, disabled, atheist, being overweight at a fitness club). There is even deviance by association: If you have a friend or romantic partner who belongs to the minority group, you may be labeled as deviant just for being seen with them. When lawmakers consider a deviant act bad enough to warrant formal sanctions, it becomes a crime, and laws are enacted to regulate it. Sociologists are interested in understanding the process that creates these distinctions and categories— how and why that happens—as well as in tracing the consequences of this process.

Each culture develops different types of rules that prescribe what is considered appropriate behavior in that culture. We develop our identity, our sense of ourselves as individuals and our membership in different groups, by our relationship to these rules—which ones we obey, which ones we disobey, and the rationales we develop for our choices. Deviance and crime are defined through interaction: our actions can only be understood as "deviant" or "criminal" in relation to a set of social norms or laws of which they are seen as in violation. These understandings become embedded in institutions such that institutions systematically come to treat different groups in different ways. Over time, this different treatment creates boundaries and barriers between groups and perpetuates inequality in ways that come to feel inevitable, but are in fact socially structured.

6.1 Key Terms

deviance Violating a social or moral rule, or refusing to follow one, whether or not that act is illegal.

mores Informally enforced norms based on strong moral values, which are viewed as essential to the proper functioning of a group.

taboos Address social prohibitions viewed as essential to the well-being of humanity. To break a *mos* is bad or immoral, but breaking a taboo is unthinkable, beyond comprehension.

incest taboo Sigmund Freud identified the taboo that one should not have sex with one's own children as a foundation of all societies.

6.2 Theorizing Crime and Deviance

Emile Durkheim observed that deviance serves society— providing cohesion, drawing people together through shared morality, defining boundaries for behavior. Without this social coherence, there is anomie, a state of disorientation and confusion that results from too little social regulation, in which institutional constraints fail to provide a coherent foundation for action. But why individuals are deviant is another question. Why do they do it? What makes them think they can or should? Most sociological theories stress the interaction of the individual or group that breaks norms or contravenes values with the larger group or society of which they are a part. Travis Hirschi theorized that people are rational actors who perform a rational cost-benefit analysis about becoming deviant, determining how much punishment is worth the degree of satisfaction or prestige the deviance will confer. Edwin H. Sutherland theorized that deviance occurs based on differential association—that is, when an individual receives more prestige and less punishment by violating norms than by following them. Social control theory, a hypothesis posited by Walter Reckless, asserts that people don't commit crimes even if they could probably get away with them due to external social controls on our behavior. There are outer controls—family, friends, teachers, social institutions, and authority figures (like the police)—who influence (cajole, threaten, browbeat) us into obeying social rules; and inner controls—internalized socialization, consciousness, religious principles, ideas of right and wrong, and one's self-conception as a "good person." Self-control theory places the emphasis on inadequate socialization and thus a weakened internal monitor system. Opportunity theory holds that those with more opportunities will be more likely to commit crimes than those with fewer opportunities. Labeling theory emphasizes the process in which deviance is constructed, focusing on the power to define who, and what, is or isn't deviant. Robert K. Merton argued that excessive deviance is a by-product of inequality. When a society promotes certain goals but provides unequal means of acquiring them, there will always be deviance. This is called structural strain theory. Primary deviance passes unnoticed, but deviant identities develop with secondary deviance, which tertiary deviance normalizes. Some sociologists see deviance as social inequality because punished deviants are typically powerless, with their fate justified by the powerful and privileged, who themselves evade similar treatment.

6.2 Key Terms

anomie A term developed by Émile Durkheim to describe a state of disorientation and confusion that results from too little social regulation, in which institutional constraints fail to provide a coherent foundation for action.

differential association Edwin H. Sutherland's theory suggesting that deviance occurs when an individual receives more prestige and less punishment by violating norms than by following them.

structural strain theory Robert K. Merton's concept that excessive deviance is a by-product of inequality within societies that promote certain norms and versions of social reality yet provide unequal means of meeting or attaining them.

social control theory As Walter Reckless theorized, people don't commit crimes even if they could probably get away with them due to social controls. There are outer controls—family, friends, teachers, social institutions, and authority figures (like the police)—who influence (cajole, threaten, browbeat) us into obeying social rules; and inner controls—internalized socialization, consciousness, religious principles, ideas of right and wrong, and one's self-conception as a "good person."

self-control theory In explaining deviance, places the emphasis on inadequate socialization and thus a weakened internal monitoring system.

subculture Group within a society that creates its own norms and values distinct from the mainstream and often its own separate institutions as well.

opportunity theory Cloward and Ohlin's 1960 theory of crime, which holds that those who have many opportunities—and good ones at that—will be more likely to commit crimes than those with few good opportunities.

labeling theory Howard Becker's theory stresses the relativity of deviance, naming the mechanism by which the same act is considered deviant in some groups but not in others. Labels are used to categorize and contain people.

stereotype threat Term coined by Claude Steele to assess the extent to which labels about people "like us" have measurable impacts on their performances. It refers to the variation in performance measured when the belief that people who belong to an identity category you share are worse at a particular task than the comparison group.

stereotype promise Term coined by Jennifer Lee and Min Zhou to address the "promise" of being viewed through the lens of a positive stereotype that leads one to perform in ways that confirms the positive stereotype (the counterpart to "stereotype threat").

primary deviance Any minor, usually unnoticed, act of deviance committed irregularly that does not have an impact on one's self-identity or on how one is labeled by others.

secondary deviance The moment when someone acquires a deviant identity, occurring when he or she repeatedly breaks a norm and people start making a big deal of it, so the rule-breaking can no longer be attributed to a momentary lapse in judgment or justifiable under the circumstances but is an indication of a permanent personality trait.

tertiary deviance Occurs when members of a group formerly labeled deviant attempt to redefine their acts, attributes, or identities as normal—even virtuous.

stigma An attribute that changes you "from a whole and usual person to a tainted and discounted one," as sociologist Erving Goffman defined it. A stigma discredits a person's claim to be normal.

6.3 The Social Organization of Crime

Sociologists study crime as *socially organized*. By this, they mean that different factors associated with society play a role in determining both the type and extent of criminal activity in a given society.

Crime is a form of deviance that has large institutions devoted to prevention and control and a whole field of study, called criminology. Crimes are categorized as being against people, which includes violent crime, or as property crime. We usually conceptualize workplace crime as office theft, or shoplifting, but white-collar crime is actually far more costly to society. Occupational crime and organizational crime are forms of white-collar crime that cost society tremendously more than "regular" crime, although the perpetrators are rarely caught, and, when caught, they don't serve long prison terms; fines and light sentences are more common, in contrast with other property crime. Crime using the Internet is the fastest-growing category. Pervasive computer use has led to cybercrime, from new versions of old crimes, like phishing, to hacking and identity theft. Hate crime is dramatically underreported, so true rates are hidden, but the most common triggers of bias crime is anti-Semitism and racism. When sociologists discuss crime, they are interested in examining the types of social forces that might play a role in producing these outcomes. In some ways, this ought to be a liberating way of looking at an examining crime. Sociologists do not understand a certain type or level of criminal activity to be inevitable.

6.3 Key Terms

crime A deviant act that lawmakers consider bad enough to warrant formal laws and sanctions.

criminology The study of crime that has developed into a subdiscipline separate from the sociology of deviance, with its own special theories about the causes and consequences of different kinds of crimes.

white-collar crime Edward Sutherland's term for the illegal actions of a corporation or people acting on its behalf, by using the authority of their position to commit crime.

occupational crime The use of one's professional position to illegally secure something of value for oneself or for the corporation.

organizational crime Illegal actions committed in accordance with the operative goals of an organization, such as antitrust violations, false advertising, or price fixing.

cybercrime The growing array of crimes committed via the Internet and World Wide Web, such as Internet fraud and identity theft.

organized crime Like corporate or white-collar crime, it is a business operation whose purpose is to supply illegal goods and services to others.

hate crime A criminal act committed by an offender motivated by bias against race, religion, ethnicity, sexual orientation, or disability status. Anyone can commit a hate crime, but perpetrators usually belong to dominant groups (white, Christian, straight) and victims to disenfranchised groups (black, Jewish, Muslim, or gay).

hate groups Groups with beliefs or practices that attack or malign a class of people often due to immutable characteristics associated with the group (like sexual orientation, skin color, ancestry, gender identity).

the "chivalry effect" The sociological thesis that women are treated more leniently for committing certain crimes by police, judges, and juries who are likely to perceive them as less dangerous and their criminal activities less consequential. Women who belong to stigmatized groups—who are black, Hispanic, or lesbian, for instance—are more likely to be arrested and convicted, perhaps because they are not granted the same status as more privileged women in the mainstream.

"sneaky thrills" Jack Katz's concept that crimes like shoplifting, burglary, joyriding, and vandalism are committed by amateurs, mostly adolescents, for the fun of it, not necessarily to acquire money or property. Katz theorized that sneaky thrills offer the adolescent perpetrators an experience similar to sexual experimentation.

sexual scripts A cognitive map about how to have sex and with whom.

6.4 Understanding Crime and Deviance Institutionally

The criminal justice system is a complex of institutions that includes the police and the courts, a wide range of prosecuting and defense lawyers, and also the prison system. Learning to think sociologically about crime necessitates an understanding of some of the primary institutions involved: the police and processes of policing; what happens in courtrooms; what happens in institutions of punishment and "correction" in our society. The United States has high crime rates and stands out from other advanced countries in homicides because of our emphasis on individual economic success to the exclusion of other indicators of success like accomplishment or social relationships, the ever-widening gap between haves and have-nots, and the availability of guns. Crime is differentially distributed by social category.

Men commit far more crimes than women, except for gender-coded crimes like shoplifting. Racial minorities are dramatically overrepresented in the criminal justice system. Young people and the poor are overrepresented as both perpetrators and victims of crime, following the pattern that lower status relates to both more arrests and greater victimization for crimes against both persons and property, compared with those of high status. We must consider and come to understand how different groups are more and less likely to be policed and racially profiled, punished, including mandatory sentencing, incarcerated and re-incarcerated as a result of recidivism, and also examine the multidimensional consequences that stem from these differences.

6.4 Key Terms

racial profiling Stopping and searching minorities because members of minority groups are seen as "more likely" to be criminals. It's more a self-fulfilling prophecy: Believing is seeing.

mandatory sentencing rules Rules enacted across the United States in the early 1990s that were supposed to be tough on crime and eliminate bias in prosecutions and sentencing. The primary result, however, has been an explosion in the prison population.

recidivism An individual's relapse into criminal behavior after having served time or endured some intervention aimed to affect their future behavior. Thus, the "recidivism rate" is the rate at which people who have served time will commit another crime after leaving.

SELF-TEST

〉 CHECK YOUR UNDERSTANDING

1. Belching loudly during meals and picking your nose publicly are violations of _____
   a. folkways.
   b. mores.
   c. taboos.
   d. laws.

2. Goffman identified an attribute that is discrediting, changing us from a normal person to a tainted one, as _____
   a. a taboo.
   b. a stigma.
   c. deviance.
   d. anomie.

3. Pat and Chris are both overweight. Pat acts like a jolly, happy-go-lucky clown. Chris is an activist against negative portrayals of big people, in a group that believes they are superior for rebelling against the unrealistic, damaging body images portrayed in the media. Which of Goffman's strategies for neutralizing stigma are Pat and Chris using?
   a. Pat is using normification; Chris is using minstrelization.
   b. Pat is using minstrelization; Chris is using militant chauvinism.
   c. Pat is using militant chauvinism; Chris is using minstrelization.
   d. Pat is using minstrelization; Chris is using normification.

4. Durkheim's view of deviance is that _____
   a. it is harmful to society because it corrupts the social order, which is why people work to stamp it out.
   b. it is helpful to society, as it gives people who don't fit in a way to join others like themselves in society, where they can conform.
   c. it is harmful to society for violating group norms, and it undermines social unity.
   d. it is helpful to society by bringing people together uniting against it, and it defines the boundaries of what is acceptable.

5. Which theory of deviance emphasizes the process by which deviance is constructed, focusing on the power needed to define deviance?
   a. Control theory
   b. Differential association theory
   c. Labeling theory
   d. Social control theory

6. To be a crime, an act of deviance must _____
   a. be bad in and of itself.
   b. violate a folkway or more.
   c. violate a formal code enacted by a legally constituted body.
   d. All of the answers are necessary for an act of deviance to be a crime.

7. Which theory of crime argued that crime results from inequality and the gap between the goals of society and the means to reach the goals?
   a. Strain theory
   b. Broken window theory
   c. Opportunity theory
   d. Conflict theory

8. When it comes to guns in the United States, the data show _____

   a. about one-third of all households have at least one gun at home.
   b. there are as many guns as there are people in the United States.
   c. we rank in the middle of all countries' rates of deaths by guns, but our rate is nearly double that of the next highest country in the industrialized world.
   d. all of the answers are correct.

Self-Test Answers: 1. a, 2. b, 3. b, 4. d, 5. c, 6. c, 7. a, 8. d

CHAPTER 7

SOCIAL CLASS AND STRATIFICATION: IDENTITY AND INEQUALITY

Social class is demonstrated in lots of ways beyond simply financial good fortune. All manner of social tastes are ways we demonstrate class status to each other. Musical preferences, for instance, are strongly correlated with class status. You can see some of this when you look at the types of crowds different sorts of musical genres draw for live performances—like country music concerts and performances of classical music.

LEARNING OBJECTIVES

In this chapter, using the iSoc framework, you should be able to:

7.1.1 Explain social stratification as both inequitably distributing benefits and rewards and maintained by belief systems.

7.1.2 Recognize how each of the five elements of the iSoc model can be used to examine social class and stratification sociologically.

7.1.3 Distinguish among caste, feudalist, and class systems of social stratification.

7.1.4 Explain the difference between social and structural mobility, and discuss how each of these processes work.

7.2.1 Summarize what it means to understand social class as a fundamental element of identity.

7.2.2 Explain Marx's understanding of class inequality in capitalist societies and why he believed class revolution to be inevitable.

7.2.3 Distinguish among the three dimensions of class Weber defined, and explain why sociologists today prefer "socioeconomic status" to class.

7.2.4 Understand the role that class culture plays in reproducing the class structure of a society.

7.2.5 Distinguish between cultural univores and omnivores and how these relate to class inequality.

7.3.1 Distinguish between the different socioeconomic classes both economically and culturally.

7.3.2 Explain why so many Americans believe they are middle class even though the American middle class appears to be in decline.

7.3.3 Summarize some of the general characteristics of distribution of wealth in the United States and compare them with other nations.

7.3.4 Explain the racial wealth gap and the feminization of poverty in the United States and in global perspective.

7.3.5 Summarize some of what we know about how many people are poor in the United States and who they are.

7.3.6 Explain what it means to understand poverty as a structural rather than a personal or cultural failing.

7.4.1 Distinguish between relative and absolute poverty, and understand income inequality on a global scale.

7.4.2 Explain the distinctions among low-, middle-, and high-income countries.

7.4.3 Distinguish among the core features of market theories, state-centered theories, dependency theories, and world system theory in making sense of global inequality.

7.4.4 Distinguish between "outside" assistance approaches and microcredit approaches to reducing poverty.

7.4.5 Understand what it means to say that Americans have less "class consciousness" than people do in other nations.

Introduction

There's an old British joke that goes something like this:

> Two Oxford professors, a physicist and a sociologist, were walking across a leafy college green. "I say, old chap," said the physicist, "What exactly do you teach in that sociology course of yours?"
>
> "Well," replied the sociologist, "This week we're discussing the persistence of the class structure in America."
>
> "I didn't even know they had a class structure in America," said the physicist. The sociologist smiled. "How do you think it persists?"

Most countries are aware of their own class structure—the physics professor didn't need a sociology course to know that England has social classes. But in the United States, class seems to be invisible. Many people don't seem to believe it exists. Surely, they say, we're an equal-opportunity country. Class is a relic of old European monarchies, where princes scandalize the media by consorting with commoners.

But the United States does have a class structure. Every country does; social class is present in some form in every human society. Even the Old Order Amish, perhaps the most egalitarian society that has ever existed, have three social classes ranked by occupational prestige: traditional farmers, business owners, and day laborers (Kraybill 2001). The details may shift and change somewhat over time, but class structure is omnipresent, always operating in our lives, in ways that are, paradoxically, especially powerful in countries where people don't believe it exists. Their inability to "see," as the joke suggests, helps class persist from generation to generation.

And the entire world has a global class system, in which some countries get far more of their share of the pie than others, and in which different national groups can connect across national boundaries because of their shared culture. Although both global and local class systems seem invisible, sociologists believe that social class remains the single best indicator of your "life chances"—of the sort of life you are likely to have—where you will go to school, what you think, and even whom you will marry (or if you will) and how you like to have sex! Even focusing so much on your individual choices and individual talents is a reflection of your class position. (Middle-class people believe in the meritocracy more than upper-class people.)

This chapter will explore the importance of class in our society—as a source of identity and as a structure of inequality, in both the national and the global arenas.

7.1 Thinking Sociologically about Social Class and Stratification

Social stratification is a topic that is at the core of what sociologists study. Although the term is often associated primarily with class (as we will predominantly be discussing it in this chapter), societies are "stratified" along multiple axes of identity: class, race, gender, age, sexuality, bodily ability, appearance, and more. Coming to understand how societies construct, maintain, and reproduce hierarchies in terms of each of these dimensions of identity is a primary goal for a great deal of sociological research. In this chapter, you will learn more about what social class is, how it is produced in interactions and embedded in institutions, and how social class intersects with other dimensions of identity that make studying it intersectionally necessary to understand how systems of inequality affect the lives and opportunities of different groups in different ways.

In this first section, we will begin by learning more about what social stratification is, how sociologists understand social class, and how this understanding shapes the ways they study it. You will learn about the different systems of stratification that structure different societies around the world and throughout time. And we will consider how to apply the iSoc model to our understanding of social class and social stratification as well. Finally, we will examine one issue to which sociologists studying social class and stratification have dedicated a great deal of attention: the different ways that people and groups move within and between social classes. What are the odds that you will occupy the same social class as your parents or siblings? How likely is it for you to climb out of poverty and become a millionaire? What if you were born rich; what are the odds that you will someday experience poverty?

What Is Social Stratification?

7.1.1 Explain social stratification as both inequitably distributing benefits and rewards and maintained by belief systems.

The system of structured social inequality and the structure of mobility in a society is called **social stratification**. Social stratification is concerned with the ranking of people. Social stratification takes its name from geology. Imagine a society looking very much like the side of a mountain made of sedimentary rock: each layer—or "stratum"—carefully demarcated and sitting on the top of another well-defined layer. Similarly, societies rank people in terms of social status, power, and social standing. The criteria for the ranking, however, vary. In the contemporary United States, for example, perhaps it's the size of your bank account, while in traditional societies, it might be the size of your yam crop. But once you are ranked, you enjoy benefits and rewards considered "appropriate" to your social location and standing.

Simply put, the ways societies organize status and power are socially constructed, but systems of stratification have real life consequences and a self-perpetuating quality. In almost every society, an entrepreneurial genius born in a hovel dies in a hovel and a person of, shall we say, limited ability born in a palace dies in a palace. Although fairy tales celebrate rags-to-riches stories of people moving from hovel to palace, almost no one makes this transition in most societies. Your social position is a matter of birth, passed on from parents to children, from generation to generation. Some societies, mostly extremely wealthy ones, like the United States, allow for some **social mobility**. So entrepreneurial geniuses born into families with little wealth can found mega-successful corporations, or the children of solidly middle-class shop owners can find themselves punching time clocks. But even where social mobility is possible,

social stratification

Taken from the geological term for layers of rock, or "strata," the ranking of people into defined layers. Social stratification exists in all societies and is based on things like wealth, race, and gender.

social mobility

The process of moving between different positions in social hierarchies within society (e.g., from one social class to another).

most people remain at the same social location throughout their lives. If your father was a janitor, it is unlikely that you will one day be the president—even if you get the right education. This is a process sociologists refer to as **social reproduction**.

Social stratification involves inequalities not only in wealth and power but also in belief systems—something sociologists often refer to as **social ideologies**. This means that sociologists who study stratification are interested in the ways societies distribute social benefits and rewards disproportionately, but also in the ways through which these social arrangements are defined as fair, just, and reasonable. The explanation offered for *why* it is fair, just, and reasonable differs from society to society. Often no explanation is offered at all: both the "haves" and the "have-nots" accept the system without question (Crompton 1993; Kerbo 1996; Saunders 1990).

Classical sociologists disagreed on the question of what purpose social stratification might serve. Some, like Durkheim, believed that stratification was a necessary organizing principle of a complex society and that it served to create interdependence among society's members, so that everyone "needed" the activities of everyone else (Filoux 1993). Marx, on the other hand, stressed the ways the stratification system benefited those at the top at the expense of those at the bottom. He spoke of oppression and exploitation, not integration and interdependence (Resnick and Wolff 1987).

In the middle of the twentieth century, many sociologists followed Durkheim, saw stratification as integrative, and claimed that it allowed for significant mobility. For example, Kingsley Davis and Wilbert Moore (1945) argued that as long as some degree of social mobility was possible, stratification is essential to the proper functioning of a society. Some jobs (say, brain surgeon) are extremely important, and other jobs (say, serving hamburgers at the student union) are relatively unimportant. Social stratification, argued Davis and Moore, creates a **meritocracy**—a system in which those who are the most "meritorious" will rise to the top and those who are less so will sink to the bottom. Of course, some will not succeed; *most* will not succeed. But the society benefits from everyone working very hard. Davis and Moore's argument, however, came at an optimistic point in U.S. history. Today, the persistence—and intensification—of class-based inequality has rendered their vision obsolete. Sociologists now understand that social mobility occurs in only a few societies, and it is not common anywhere. Speaking only of the "functions" obscures the ways the inequalities are institutionalized. In most societies that fancy themselves meritocratic, that ideology is largely a myth (see FIGURE 7.1).

Although your class position does provide a foundation for your identity, as a social system, stratification divides us far more than it unites us. Stratification is an institutionalized and intersectional form of inequality. Elites maintain inequality for their own advantage, prohibiting many of the most talented and intelligent people from making favorable contributions to the society and sometimes giving less talented, less intelligent people tremendous amounts of power. Even where some people do get to move up in the rankings, this situation is so infrequent that elites still manage to retain control, and the possibility of mobility ensures that the disenfranchised remain docile: They assume that if they don't succeed, it's their own fault (McAll 1990).

social reproduction

The structures and activities that transmit social inequality from one generation to the next.

social ideologies

The ways through which these social stratification arrangements are defined as fair, just, and reasonable.

meritocracy

Social system in which the greater the functional importance of the job, the more rewards it brings in salary, perks, power, and prestige.

iSoc: The Sociology of Social Class and Stratification

7.1.2 Recognize how each of the five elements of the iSoc model can be used to examine social class and stratification sociologically.

Social class is an incredibly powerful and pervasive system of social stratification in every society. It helps to organize who is understood to own what, how much, and more. It shapes virtually every aspect of our experiences and opportunities in the

FIGURE 7.1 How Americans Stand Out in Understanding Social Class
Social class is less visible in the United States than it is in many other countries around the world. And Americans are much more likely to feel that whether or not they achieve social mobility is largely a matter of individual effort. Those who work harder, Americans think, get ahead. The tenacity of social reproduction is all around us; Americans, however, are much more reticent to believe the hype than are people elsewhere.

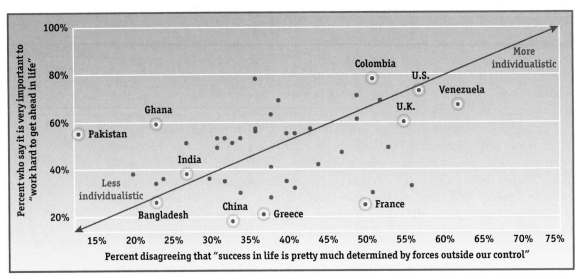

SOURCE: Data from Pew Research Center. Spring 2014 Pew Global Attitudes Survey, Q13b and Q66b. Available at: http://www.pewglobal.org/files/2014/10/Pew-Research-Center-Inequality-Report-FINAL-October-17-2014.pdf..

societies in which we live. But in some societies, social class is less noticed than others. In the United States, social class is less visible than it is in other societies around the world. By that, we mean that people do not necessarily identify with their social class (or they identify with social classes with whom they do not technically belong). Americans don't necessarily see themselves as having something in common with other people who share their class status. Thus, although class is an incredibly dominant and inescapable aspect of our lives, many of us do not recognize class to be the socially deterministic force that it is. Applying the iSoc model to making sense of social class and stratification can help us unpack this paradox that structures our lives in addition to better understanding societies around the world.

IDENTITY—Social class becomes a powerful piece of our identities. It shapes how we come to understand ourselves from a young age. From the value of our homes and belongings, to our understandings of the struggles of people "like us," social class is more than an amount of income, wealth, and possessions. It is a state of being and a body of accumulated knowledge and experiences that shapes the way we look at the world around us and understand our place within it. Understanding social class as an *identity* can help us better appreciate the tenacity with which people cling to class identities as well as their identification with social class to which they do not seem to objectively belong.

INEQUALITY—Class inequality is a ubiquitous form of social *inequality*. Yet it is not always recognized as such. A great deal of social inequality is the result of circumstance—simply having been born into or landed in a working-class or poor family has a lasting impact on your life. Class inequality shapes how long you live, where you live, who your friends are, what kind of education you are likely to receive, where you work and in what kind of job, and more. It's a pervasive form of social inequality with all-encompassing sets of consequences.

INTERACTION—Although we often speak about social class as an objective quality of a group of people (e.g., the working-class, middle-class Americans), class is also cultural, and produced inside *interactions*. It is possible to "perform" a class to which you do not

Here you can see social class written into the landscape of a city—Rio de Janeiro, Brazil.
Look at the extreme contrast between the poor neighborhoods (*favelas*) and the middle-class
neighborhoods.

actually belong. Similarly, there are patterned sets of interactional strategies we all rely
on to reiterate our understandings of class differences—whether that means walking
past homeless people on the street asking for money, to distinguishing ourselves by
the clothes we wear or all manner of consumer habits and leisurely activities. We are
"doing" class whenever we are engaging in behavior that situates us as meaningfully
"different" from other social classes. This tells us an important fact about social class:
It is a system of social stratification defined by much more than dollars and cents. It is
defined by a way of looking at, approaching, and *being* in the social world.

INSTITUTIONS—Social class can be considered a social *institution* insofar as institutions can be understood as persistent patterns in social interaction difficult to meet
solely with collections of individual people. To say that social class is "institutionalized" means examining the patterned ways in which social reproduction takes effect.
If our social class shapes the ways and quality of our interactions with various institutions (indeed, sometimes access itself is, in part, governed by social class), then those
institutions have been organized in ways that help to reiterate and reproduce the class
system. Examining how this takes place and the consequences associated with this
process necessitates an understanding of just how class gets institutionalized in the
first place.

INTERSECTIONS—Examining intersections in social class is important for more than
one reason. For one thing, the effects of class inequality are inequitably distributed
among populations: Some people and groups are more likely to experience the most
harmful effects than others or that experience can be shaped by other social factors as

well (like race, gender, sexuality, age, and more). Understanding the *intersectional* qualities of class and class inequality produces a more complex understanding of social reproduction and inequality.

Considering social class and stratification using the iSoc model can help you better appreciate the different ways that social class operates. Social class shapes our experiences and opportunities in powerful ways and a great deal of research documents the powerful forms of social inequality associated with stratification. But, social class also provides a powerful sense of solidarity; it is a meaningful category of identity that consumes us entirely—even when we are unaware of this process as it happens.

Systems of Stratification

7.1.3 Distinguish among caste, feudalist, and class systems of social stratification.

Societies reproduce social stratification in different ways. Sometimes boundaries are relatively fluid, and sometimes they are etched in stone. The most common systems of social stratification are the caste system, feudalism, and class.

CASTES   Castes, found in many traditional agricultural societies, divide people by occupation: farmers, merchants, priests, and so on. A **caste system** is fixed and permanent; you are assigned to your position at birth, without any chance of getting out. Perhaps the most famous example of a caste system has been India. India had four castes, or *varnas*: *Brahmin* (priests), *Kshatriyas* (warriors and other political elites), *Vaishyas* (farmers and merchants), and *Shudras* (servants), plus the untouchables, a "casteless" group at the bottom of the society. Your *varna* determined not only your occupation but where you could live, whom you could talk to on the street (and the terms you would use to address them), your gods, and even your chances of a favorable afterlife. Modern India prohibits discrimination on the basis of caste and reserves a percentage of government jobs and university admissions to untouchables. However, the traditional system is still strong, especially in rural areas (The Economist 2010). In 2005, the Indian government proposed to reserve 27 percent of seats in the country's best medical school, technology school, and business school—as well as all other major institutions of higher education for the "Other Backward Classes" (OBCs) to help them gain higher levels of representation in these institutions. This resulted in large protests from the upper castes, who claimed they were now the victims of a politically motivated reverse discrimination (Rao 2006). Caste systems organized on the basis of race are referred to as **apartheid**.

caste system

A fixed and permanent stratification system to which one is assigned at birth.

apartheid

A race-based caste system that mandated segregation of different racial groups. In South Africa it was a political system institutionalized by the white minority in 1948 and remained in effect until 1990.

feudalism

A fixed and permanent social structure based on mutual obligation, in which peasants worked the estates belonging to a small group of feudal lords, who fed and protected them. A peasant's only avenue to social advancement was to enter a convent or monastery.

This woman is an untouchable, one of the 160 million people who occupy India's lowest caste. No matter how hard or diligently she works, she won't escape the poverty and discrimination into which she was born. Her experience of social reproduction is probably inescapable despite the fact that caste-based inequality has been illegal in the Indian Constitution for more than 50 years.

In the Oscar-winning film, *Slumdog Millionaire* (2008), 18-year old orphan Jamal Malik comes under suspicion because no one could possibly believe that some poor "slumdog" could possibly know the answers to the questions on "Who Wants to Be a Millionaire?"

FEUDALISM   In medieval Europe, between the eleventh and sixteenth centuries; in nineteenth-century Japan; and in a few other regions, there were a few merchants and "free men," but most of the population consisted of peasants and serfs who worked the estates belonging to a small group of feudal lords. **Feudalism** was a fixed and permanent system: If you were born a lord or a serf, you stayed there your whole life.

SOCIOLOGY AND OUR WORLD

APARTHEID—A CASTE SYSTEM

How is apartheid a caste system of social stratification?

Apartheid is a caste system in which the basis of the caste designation is race. The term derived from the Dutch term for "separate," and politically it involves the geographic, economic, and political separation of the races. It was the common, if informal, system in the southern United States through the first half of the twentieth century, maintained legally by "Jim Crow" laws. In South Africa, the most famous cause of apartheid, the ruling political party, descendants of Dutch immigrants, enacted apartheid laws in 1948. People were required to register as white (someone who was "in appearance obviously a white person"), black (a member of an African tribe), or colored (of mixed descent, plus South and East Asians). (A fourth category was added later, which separated South and East Asians into their own group.) Blacks were forced to live in four separate Mantistans, or "homelands" within approximately 13 percent of South Africa's geographic area, even

Nelson Mandela was the anti-apartheid revolutionary, prisoner, and politician, who served as President of South Africa from 1994 to 1999. President Mandela was the first democratically elected president in South Africa and the first black chief executive.

though they comprised about 75 percent of the population. When they went to "white" South Africa, they had to carry passports and identification papers.

Protests against apartheid began almost immediately, among both blacks and whites. (In 1976, more than 600 high school students were killed in the African townships of Soweto and Sharpesville, when the police finally responded to their protests with bullets.) Finally, after years of protests, riots, strikes, and states of emergency, former dissident Nelson Mandela was elected president in 1994, the homelands were dismantled, and apartheid laws were removed from civil code. Of course, racial prejudice and discrimination still exists in South Africa; some newspaper commentators argue that the end of apartheid has exacerbated racial tensions, as whites who believe that they are now discriminated against in jobs and housing are likely to lash out against blacks (Clark and Worger 2004).

The classic feudal relationship was one of mutual obligation. The feudal lords housed and fed serfs, offered protection inside the castle walls, and decided on their religion and whether they would be educated. Peasants had no right to seek out other employment or other masters. In effect, they were property. Their only avenue to social advancement was to enter a convent or monastery (Backman 2002).

Feudalism endured in Germany through the nineteenth century and in Russia until the Bolshevik Revolution of 1917. A person's wealth—and the taxes owed to the Tsar—was gauged not by how much land that person owned but by how many serfs (or "souls") he owned. Feudalism began to disappear as the class of free men in the cities—artisans, shopkeepers, and merchants—grew larger and more prosperous, and the center of society began to shift from the rural manor to the urban factory. International trade shifted the social world to the city from the countryside, and global networks of commerce—trade, credit, banking, and the like—linked urban centers in new ways that further isolated rural feudal manors. Industrial society dispensed with feudal rankings and ushered in the modern class system.

CLASS SYSTEM Class is the most modern form of stratification. **Class** is based on economic position—a person's occupation, income, or possessions. Of the major forms of stratification, class systems are the most "open"—that is, they permit the greatest amount of social mobility, or, the ability to move up—or down—in class status and

Downton Abbey is a historical period drama television series that first aired in the United Kingdom in 2010 and in the United States in 2011. The show is set on a fictional country estate in Yorkshire and depicts the lives of an aristocratic family and their domestic servants during the first decades of the twentieth century. Feudal society is firmly in decline and the drama illustrates how aristocratic families and estates were managing this transition as the system of social hierarchy was in the midst of revolutionary changes.

class

A group of people sharing the same social position in society. Class is based on income, power, and prestige.

class system

System of stratification in which people are ranked according to their economic position.

achieved status

Status or social position based on one's accomplishments or activities.

ascribed status

Status that is assigned to a person and over which he or she has no control.

rank. **Class systems** are systems of stratification based on economic position, and people are ranked according to **achieved status** (as opposed to **ascribed status**). Each system of stratification creates a belief system or ideology that declares it legitimate, that those at the top "deserve" to be there through divine plan, the natural order of things. Class systems "feel" the most equitable to us today because they appear to justify one's ranking solely on his or her own initiative, hard work, and talent. Yet, as we will see in this chapter, class reproduction is incredibly common in societies organized by class systems as well. *How* and *why* this happens is the subject of an incredible amount of research.

Social Mobility

7.1.4 Explain the difference between social and structural mobility, and discuss how each of these processes work.

Social mobility means the movement from one class to another. And although we often think of social mobility as upward (moving to a higher social class than the one into which you landed by birth or circumstance), social mobility happens in both directions—up and down. It can occur in two forms: (1) intergenerational—that is, your parents are working class, but you became lower, or your parents are middle class, but you became upper class; and (2) intragenerational—that is, you move from working to lower, or from middle to upper, all within your lifetime. One of the most important studies of mobility was undertaken in the 1960s by Peter Blau and Otis Dudley Duncan (Blau and Duncan 1967). In their studies of the U.S. occupational structure, they found little mobility between classes, although they found a lot of mobility within any particular class. People moved up or down a little bit from the position of their parents, but movement from one class to another was extremely rare. Intergenerational mobility seems to have increased since Blau and Duncan (Hout 1984; Solon 1992); however, your parents' social class remains a strong predictor of your own social class.

Much of the upward mobility that Blau and Duncan found was structural—a general upward trend of the entire society, not the result of either intergenerational or intragenerational mobility. **Structural mobility** means that the entire society got wealthier (or poorer). Because of the post–World War II economic boom, many working-class families found themselves enjoying middle-class incomes. Similar structural mobility occurred during the Industrial Revolution, when the labor force shifted from farming/agriculture to manufacturing. More recently, the pattern in the United States has been downward mobility, caused by the decline in manufacturing jobs (40 percent disappeared between 1970 and 2000), coupled with the growth of service jobs. Service jobs tend to pay low wages (averaging about half the wages of manufacturing jobs) and offer few or no benefits (averaging 60 percent less than manufacturing jobs). As a result, many people who grew up or spent most of their lives in the middle class may find themselves working class or even working poor (Uchitelle 2006).

Many Americans are **underemployed**—highly educated and qualified for positions higher than the ones they occupy. On *The Simpsons*, the proprietor of the comic book store defends his bitter outlook on life by saying, "I have a master's degree in folklore and mythology." Millions of Americans have had similar experiences. They acquire college degrees, with dreams of a white-collar job and a middle-class lifestyle, only to find that the jobs simply aren't there. So they take jobs for which they are vastly overqualified in the service industry or as clerical workers, with low salaries, no benefits, and no possibility of career advancement, and some will join the ranks of the working poor. Another way to move down from the middle class is to become a permanent temp or part-time worker. Employers prefer temporary employees, even for contracts that will last years, because "temps" command

structural mobility

A general upward trend of the entire society. Structural mobility means that the entire society got wealthier, as occurred in post–World War II America.

underemployed

People educated and qualified for positions higher than the ones they occupy.

lower salaries and receive neither benefits nor severance pay. Sometimes, employers demote full-time employees to a "part-time" status of 35 hours per week, because employment laws require benefits to be offered only to full-time employees. The result is that employees suffer from the reduced salary and benefits but corporate profits increase (Cummings 2004).

Intergenerational mobility, the kind Blau and Duncan studied, takes place largely within groups, not between them. Your chances of getting ahead or falling behind are largely influenced by family income—that is, by where you started. Only 6 percent of children born to low-income parents make it to the top of the income ladder. Forty-two percent of children in the bottom of the income distribution remain there as adults (Pew Economic Mobility Project 2009). What's more, the children of high-income groups also experience greater income growth: Families with a median income in the top quintile ($100,100 or more) see their children's income grow by 52 percent in a single generation; families with incomes in the bottom quintile ($23,100 or less) see their children's income grow only 18 percent across their working lives (Isaacs 2007). But a significant portion of Americans at both the top and the bottom of the income distribution experience little or no economic mobility at all. Thirty-six percent of children born to parents in the bottom wealth quintile remain in the bottom as adults, and 36 percent of children born to parents in the top quintile remain in the top as adults (Isaacs 2007; Pew Economic Mobility Project 2009).

intergenerational mobility
Changes in social status between different generations within the same family.

HOW DO WE KNOW WHAT WE KNOW?

MOBILITY STUDIES

Blau and Duncan were interested in the relative weight of these ascribed or achieved characteristics to measure the "openness" of the U.S. class system and the amount of mobility in it. In other words, how much does your gender or race (both ascribed characteristics) matter in terms of your ability to be upwardly mobile? How much do the education and work experience you acquire (both achieved characteristics) matter? And, to make things a bit more complicated, what role do ascribed characteristics play in making it more likely that people will obtain certain achieved characteristics?

In their effort to understand the *American Occupational Structure* (the title of their 1967 book, which summarized two decades of research), Blau and Duncan created a "path diagram" of U.S. intergenerational mobility using four key variables: father's level of education, father's occupation, son's level of education, and son's occupation. (These questions were asked only of white men.) One version is shown in the diagram. One of their key findings was that the effects of father's occupation and education were both direct and indirect. They directly confer some advantages and also indirectly enhance their sons' education, which furthers the sons' success as well. Here, the son's education and occupation depend on both *ascriptive* characteristics (the father's occupation and education are fixed, and the son is born with them) and *achieved* characteristics (the "e" refers to external factors). The son's education (an achieved characteristic) is an intervening variable because it affects occupation all by itself, as well as being influenced by his father's education and occupation.

Among their key findings were that 40 percent of the sons of blue-collar workers *moved up* to white-collar jobs. Perhaps even more intriguing, almost 30 percent of the sons of white-collar workers *moved down* to blue-collar jobs. Today, though, we would also question the idea that we can chart "American" mobility patterns by using data drawn only from white men. It is a puzzle sociologists are still trying to solve. But, in a nutshell, sociologists have found that fathers' education and occupation are great predictors of the social class their sons will eventually occupy

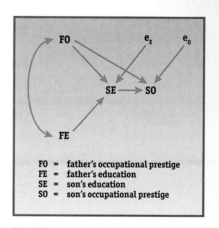

FO = father's occupational prestige
FE = father's education
SE = son's education
SO = son's occupational prestige

SOURCE: Blau, Peter M., and Otis Duncan. *American Occupational Structure*. New York: John Wiley & Sons, 1967.

(those two variables alone accounted for about 40 percent of the variation they discovered!). But the same formula is less predictive of where daughters will end up. And all of this is assuming heterosexual parents whose marriages are intact.

Historically, women have had less opportunity for upward mobility than men because of the types of jobs they were permitted: mostly clerical and service positions that do not offer many opportunities for promotion or increased responsibility. And when they married, they were expected to quit even those jobs or else decrease their hours to part time. Today, many middle-class women still do not pursue careers that afford middle-class lifestyles because they curtail career ambitions for household and child care responsibilities. As a result, if they divorce, they experience downward mobility. Not only do they lose the second (and often higher) income from their husband, they also lose benefits like health care and insurance (Weitzman 1996).

intragenerational mobility

Changes in a person's social mobility throughout the course of a lifetime.

Mobility is also affected by race and ethnicity. White people have higher upward mobility. For example, in every income group blacks are less likely than whites to surpass their parents' family income and more likely to fall down the economic ladder (Isaacs 2007, 2009). Only 31 percent of black children born to middle-income parents end up making more than their parents' family income, compared with 68 percent of white children. And black Americans experience significantly more downward mobility than white people do: Almost half of black children born to middle-income parents fall to the bottom of the income ladder as adults (Pew Economic Mobility Project 2009). Men and women have similar rates of **intragenerational mobility**; that is, the family income of both sons and daughters resembles their parents'. The one big exception is children born to parents on the bottom rung of the economic ladder: 47 percent of daughters born there, stay there, as compared to 35 percent of sons (Pew Economic Mobility Project 2009). But when it comes to mobility between generations—intergenerational mobility—men experience greater upward mobility than women (Pew Economic Mobility Project 2009).

Despite these structural causes of downward mobility, most Americans believe that mobility is largely their fault. In a Pew Foundation study, most Americans believed that downward mobility was attributed to the way we live and the choices we make (Pew Economic Mobility Project 2009). Since the beginning of the twenty-first century, the United States has become less mobile than it has ever been in its history. According to a recent survey, Americans are more likely than they were 30 years ago to end up in the class into which they were born. That doesn't mean that Americans have stopped believing in their own mobility, though. Today, 40 percent of Americans believed that the chance of moving up from one class to another had risen over the last 30 years—the same period when those chances were actually shrinking (Scott and Leonhardt 2005). Even amid the deep recession that began in 2008–2009, the vast majority of Americans, including many hardest hit by the economic downturn—83 percent of African Americans, 86 percent of Hispanics, and 88 percent of young people—still believe it is possible for people to move up in the world (Pew Economic Mobility Project 2009).

---

iSOC AND YOU Thinking Sociologically about Social Class and Stratification
Stratification is the study of social hierarchies. We may all be born equal, but we don't end up equal, do we? Sociologists study the patterns of *inequality* to understand how such inequalities exist, function, and are reproduced over time. Because you construct your *identities* through your membership in groups and your *interactions* within social and historical contexts, inequalities quite literally shape your understanding of who you are. And patterns of inequality that persist—race, class, gender, sexuality, age, etc.—also *intersect* with one another, and become *institutionalized* throughout society.

U.S./WORLD

U.S. MOBILITY IN INTERNATIONAL CONTEXT

The United States has less relative mobility than many other industrialized countries. Internationally speaking, levels of social mobility in the United States are in the middle of the pack—less than many other societies, but more than many as well. Large social welfare bureaucracies, as in social democratic countries in Scandinavia (Norway, Sweden, and Denmark), are often criticized for stifling social mobility because mobility is thought to be based on individual initiative and hard work. But mobility in the Nordic countries is often more than double that of the United States.

Mobility is difficult to measure. But one way of measuring it that sociologists use it to look at how predictive parents' income is of the income that their children go on to make in life. A society with lots of intergenerational mobility would be one with little relationship between your family's class status and the adult income outcomes of children. A child born into poverty, in other words, would have about the same chance of earning a high income later in life as a child born to a wealthy family. Intergenerational earnings elasticity is a measure scholars of stratification use to measure this precisely. This scale proceeds from zero (complete intergenerational mobility) to one (no intergenerational mobility). So, societies with higher scores on intergenerational earnings elasticity have less mobility, while those with lower scores have more mobility.

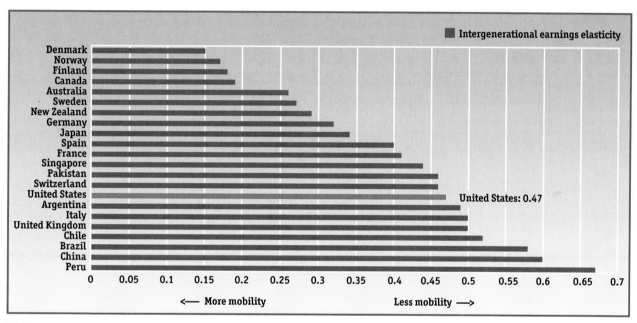

While the United States has an average level of social mobility in international comparison, it's also important to ask where in the class structure that mobility occurs. In the case of the United States, much of our mobility occurs within the middle classes. The bottom and top income groups do not see a lot of movement; in other words, the class positions of the richest and poorest in the United States are much more fixed than those in between. In general, societies with higher levels of income inequality (where the differences between the richest and poorest are the widest) have lower levels of social mobility.

SOURCE: Data from Corak, Miles. "Inequality from Generation to Generation: The United States in Comparison." In Robert S. Rycroft, ed., *The Economics of Inequality, Poverty, and Discrimination in the 21st Century*, 107–123. Santa Barbara, CA: Praeger, 2013.

INVESTIGATE FURTHER

1. Why would social democracies, with large-scale health care, state-supported education, and state-supported childcare and family policies actually *increase* mobility? What other factors might explain the differences in mobility?

7.2 Class Identity and Inequality

We often think about social class in terms of dollars and cents. And certainly, income and wealth are primary components of what it is that we call "social class." And yet, social class is also experienced interactionally and adopted as an identity. By this, I mean that people can identify with social classes to which they do not belong (at least if we're counting who belongs by looking at bank accounts). Think about a famous sports star who started from a humble background and is now signing a multimillion-dollar contract to play on a national stage. What about someone from a working-class background who happens to strike it rich playing the lottery. The odds of either of these happening to any single individual are small. But it might not surprise you if both of these people continued to identify with and as the social class they recently left. This helps us understand that, in some ways, we need to be able to disentangle class identities from income and wealth.

In this section, you will learn more about how sociologists study class identity and what they have learned. For instance, you will consider the ways that sociologists have discovered that all manner of your tastes (from the music you like, to the clothes you wear, to the vacations you desire) are shaped by your class. And tastes play a much more integral role in the reproduction of class inequality than you might have thought. Read on to understand more about the cultural foundations of class identity and class inequality.

Social Class and Identity

7.2.1 Summarize what it means to understand social class as a fundamental element of identity.

Many Americans believe that a class system is a relic from our European past and that it exerts far less influence—if any—in the modern world. After all, the very idea of U.S. democracy is that an individual should be able to rise as far as his or her talents, aspirations, and hard work can take that person.

Yet, we also have seen ample evidence that the importance of class is increasing. The frequent appeals to "Joe the Plumber," "people who shower *after* work, not before," and "working families" in the rhetoric of the 2008, 2012, and 2016 presidential elections suggests important class distinctions within U.S. society and culture. The continued commentary on the rescue and cleanup efforts in New Orleans in the aftermath of Hurricane Katrina exposes the persistent class and racial inequalities in the United States.

Yet if we openly acknowledge class at all, it is usually the class to which we are aspiring, not the class into which we were born. But it turns out your class of origin is a reliable measure of where you will end up. Your class background is just about the

Class inequality often combines other forms of inequality to create a complex hierarchical order. The government's response to Hurricane Katrina in 2005 exposed persistent class and racial inequalities in the United States.

best predictor of many things, from the seemingly important—what college you go to (or if you go to college at all), what job you have—to the seemingly trivial—what your favorite sexual position is, what music you like, and even what you probably had for dinner last night. In that sense, class forms the foundation of your identity, your sense of yourself. Social class is a powerful piece of our identities. And when we analyze social class as an identity in more depth, we have learned that Americans are not necessarily the best judges of the classes to which they might be said to objectively belong. We have opinions about our social class, and sometimes they are at odds with the work we do and the income we earn.

Class also operates on the global level. Just as there are upper-, middle-, and lower-class people, there are upper-, middle-, and lower-class countries. And it is also true that countries come to have global class identities. These, too, shift and change over time—a tycoon country today might be a pauper country tomorrow, and vice versa—but the hierarchy of rich and poor, weak and strong, high status and low status doesn't seem to go away. (We will return to the global dimension of class later in the chapter.)

Theories of Social Class—Marx

7.2.2 Explain Marx's understanding of class inequality in capitalist societies and why he believed class revolution to be inevitable.

The analysis of social stratification in general, and class in particular, is one of the defining interests of the founders of sociology—as well as a central concern among sociologists today.

Karl Marx (1818–1883) was the first social scientist to make class the foundation of his entire theory. Marx argued that human survival depends on producing things. How we, as a society, organize ourselves to do this, and how we distribute the rewards, is what Marx called the **mode of production**—the organization of society to produce what people need to survive. There are many ways to do this. We could imagine a system in which one person owns everything, and everyone else works for him or her. Or we could imagine a system in which everyone owns everything, and you simply take what you need—and leave the rest for others. Or we could imagine a system in which very few people had far more than they could possibly ever need, and the large majority had very little; but, instead of giving the rest away to others who need it, the wealthy would simply throw it away. All of these are systems that organize production, the creation of the goods we need for survival, and the relations of production—the relationships people enter into to facilitate production and allocate its rewards.

Marx argued that, historically, it has always been the case that some people own means of production—the cornfields, the cows, and the factories—and everyone else works for them. With ownership comes control. If you own the only cornfield in town, everyone else has to listen to you or go without corn. From this perspective, and according to Marx, there are two types of people: Owners and workers.

In Marx's day, capitalists (a group he called the "**bourgeoisie**") owned the means of production, only now they owned factories instead of farms, and the working classes (the "**proletariat**") were forced to become wage laborers or go

mode of production
The organization of society to produce what people need to survive.

bourgeoisie
Popularized by Karl Marx, term for the upper-class capitalists who owned the means of production. In Marx's time, they owned factories instead of farms. Today the term is also used to refer to upper-class managers who wield a lot of power.

proletariat
Popularized by Karl Marx, the term for the lower classes who were forced to become wage laborers or go hungry. Today, the term is often used to refer to the working class.

Marx argued that the poor are poor because the rich are rich. Here, a poor woman poses in the doorway of her one room shack with three of her seven children. The despair and depression that often accompany poverty make it difficult to understand how the poor will organize to rise up and take over the system, as Marx predicted.

hungry. They received no share of the profits and lived in perpetual poverty. Ironically, they used their wages to buy the very products that they were helping to manufacture. Capitalism is a system that works in the collective interest of the bourgeoisie because, while workers are paid for their time in the production process, the bourgeoisie are able to make more money from workers' labor than they pay them (sometimes a great deal more). Marx believed that this system was inherently unfair. He also believed that classes were in intractable and inevitable conflict. He predicted that eventually the proletariat would organize, revolt, and overthrow capitalism altogether in favor of a socialist economy where the workers owned the means of production (Smelser 1975).

Theories of Social Class—Weber

7.2.3 Distinguish among the three dimensions of class Weber defined, and explain why sociologists today prefer "socioeconomic status" to class.

Max Weber (1864–1920) doubted that overthrowing capitalism would significantly diminish social stratification. It might address economic inequality, but what about other forms of inequality? In one of his most celebrated essays, "Class, Status and Party" (1946), Weber argued that there were three components to social class: economic (class position), social (status), and political (power). Often, they were interrelated, but sometimes they operated independently: You could be at the top of the economic ladder, but at the bottom of the social ladder, and somewhere in the middle of the political ladder. So, are you a member of the upper, middle, or lower class? Or all three? Social class, as Weber understood it, is a more complex, multidimensional hierarchy. In Weber's theory, stratification is based on these three dimensions: class position, status, and power.

status
One's socially defined position in a group; it is often characterized by certain expectations and rights.

power
The ability to extract compliance despite resistance or the ability to get others to do what you want them to do, regardless of their own desires.

Max Weber was critical of Marx for his exclusive focus on the economy and social class. Some professions, like firefighter for instance, have relatively modest pay but receive an incredible amount of social status. Their "class" position has to do with more than their paycheck alone.

CLASS POSITION It can determine whether you are an owner or a worker; how much money you make (your income); your property, stocks, bonds, and money in the bank (your wealth). Wealth is more important than income because the legal system, with its laws concerning private property and inheritance, ensures that wealth will pass on to your heirs and endow them with a class position similar to yours—or higher. For Weber, "class" is based simply on your relationship to production—what you do for a living and what you earn.

STATUS If class is based on your relationship to the marketplace, **status** is based on your lifestyle. Status refers to other people's evaluation of your lifestyle. People see what you have and how you live and make judgments about how much wealth and power you have. This results in people often buying higher-priced luxury goods—"status symbols"—even if they have a hard time paying for them. In that sense, status is not about what you produce, but what and how you consume. People with higher class positions tend to enjoy higher status, but this is not always the case. And people with lower class positions tend to enjoy lower status. But some people defy easy classification. Some occupations might provide a lot of income, but not be considered particularly high status; whereas other occupations might provide little or modest income, but be considered very high status.

POWER Power is the ability to do what you want to do. This may mean a certain amount of control over your own working situation. People in higher class or status positions can set their own hours, disregard punching time clocks, and work to their own rhythm. Power also resides in your ability to influence the actions of others. People with high power dictate, order, command, or make "requests" that are really commands issued in a nice way, as when a police officer "asks" to see your driver's license. People such as the police officer

SOCIOLOGY AND OUR WORLD

PRESTIGE MEANS NOT HAVING TO DEAL WITH PEOPLE

Why is it that the more occupational prestige you have, the less you have to interact with other people?

In *The System of Professions: An Essay on the Division of Expert Labor* (1988), sociologist Andrew Abbott noticed an interesting workplace phenomenon: the more prestigious the job the less contact with real, live human beings. When you go to a doctor's office, a receptionist (low prestige) greets you, asks you to fill out some forms, and creates or updates your file. Then a nurse (medium prestige) records your weight,

temperature, and blood pressure in the file prepared by the receptionist. The nurse may also ask about your visit and take notes on what brought you in and how you are feeling. Finally, a doctor (high prestige) swoops in, examines you briefly, and gives direction to the nurse, who often completes your treatment. On your way out, the receptionist talks to you again to take your payment and set up another appointment. In the end, you could eas-

ily spend 60 percent of your visit with the receptionist, 35 percent with a nurse, and only 5 percent with the doctor you came to see.

When you walk into a fast-food restaurant for lunch, the person who takes your order (low prestige) will probably take hundreds of other orders that day. If you are dissatisfied with your order, you will go to the manager (medium prestige), who determines the work schedules, checks on the supplies, and handles complaints, but never takes orders from customers. Meanwhile, somewhere far away in a glass-and-steel tower, the CEO (high prestige) makes high-level policy decisions and never sees a customer. We can find so many examples that it seems almost a workplace rule: The higher your prestige, the less you actually have to deal with people.

---

can have a great deal of power but comparatively low class position or social status (Weber 1958). But people with higher class positions and social status tend to have more power. As the tyrannical king tells us in the *Wizard of Id* comic strip, "Remember the Golden Rule: He who has the gold makes the rules."

Class position, status, and power remain the major components of social class. But sociologists after Max Weber have continued to postulate new ones: your social connections, your taste in art, your ascribed and achieved statuses, and so on. Because there are so many components, sociologists today tend to prefer the term **socioeconomic status** (SES) over *social class* to emphasize that people are ranked through the intermingling of many factors: economic, social, political, cultural, and community. Socioeconomic status refers to a position in the social stratification system based on the combined weights of class position, status evaluation, and power.

MEASURING SOCIAL STATUS   The status of your job or occupation is often measured by something sociologists call **occupational prestige**—the degree of status accorded to an occupation. For example, in the United States, college professors enjoy high status, but (unfortunately for them) most don't make much money, compared to other high-status professions. Conversely, accountants, bankers, and real estate brokers have some of the lowest status ratings in the United States, but they tend to command high salaries. High and low status differs from society to society, is sometimes evaluated different even among members of the same society, and changes over time. Status does not pass from generation to generation automatically, like wealth, but it can still be transmitted. Upper-class parents teach their children the social skills expected of people with high status, perhaps an appreciation for classical music or modern art, and send them to exclusive schools and colleges where they can prepare

socioeconomic status (SES)
Your social connections, your taste in art, your ascribed and attained statuses, and more. Because there are so many components, sociologists today tend to prefer the concept of socioeconomic status to that of social class, to emphasize that people are ranked through the intermingling of many factors, economic, social, political, cultural, and community.

occupational prestige
The degree of status accorded to an occupation.

TABLE 7.1 Top 10 Prestigious Occupations

	More Prestige (net)	Has a Great Deal of Prestige	Has Prestige		Less Prestige (net)	Has Not That Much Prestige	Not at All Prestigious
Doctor	90%	51%	39%		10%	6%	4%
Scientist	83%	37%	46%		17%	11%	6%
Firefighter	80%	40%	40%		20%	14%	6%
Military officer	78%	38%	40%		22%	15%	7%
Engineer	76%	22%	54%		24%	16%	8%
Nurse	76%	31%	44%		24%	18%	6%
Architect	72%	20%	52%		28%	19%	9%
Emergency medical technician (EMT)	72%	29%	43%		28%	21%	7%
Veterinarian	71%	24%	48%		29%	20%	9%
Police officer	67%	28%	39%		33%	24%	10%

NOTE: Percentages may not add up exactly to 100 percent due to rounding.

SOURCE: Data from The Harris Poll. 2016. Available at http://media.theharrispoll.com/documents/Prestigious+Occupations_Data+Tables.pdf.

for high-status lives. Meanwhile lower-middle-class and working-class parents teach their children the skills necessary for lives of somewhat lower expectations. Consider how Americans rank the relative prestige of different occupations on a representative survey (see TABLE 7.1).

As you can see, there is some disagreement. But, most people concede that doctor is an occupation with a high degree of occupational prestige—(what Weber called "status"). And doctor is also an occupation that tends to bring in high earnings as well (what Weber called "class"). But some of the occupations on this list might not earn as much money, but still enjoy a great deal of status. Professions considered "noble" are often ranked highly in terms of status. But, why some (like firefighters) are higher than others (like police officers) is not immediately apparent.

Class and Culture

7.2.4 Understand the role that class culture plays in reproducing the class structure of a society.

Class is not only about income and poverty. It's more than standard of living. As Weber recognized, it is equally about lifestyle as well. Sociologists have found that your class position is a pretty reliable indicator not only of how much you have but of *what* you have, what you want to have, and what you think it's important to have. Class helps sociologists predict what sorts of things you do in your spare time, how you raise your children, the kinds of books you read, the TV shows you watch—or whether you watch TV at all. Class even helps sociologists predict how thin or fat you are. Class, it turns out, is cultural: Classes develop different cultural standards—values, norms, and lifestyles.

The French sociologist and social theorist Pierre Bourdieu (1984) was fascinated with the study of the cultural elements of class. Bourdieu is the same sociologist who coined the term **cultural capital** (you encountered this in Chapter 2). He believed that as people gained more distance from necessity (distance from having to worry about food, water, and shelter for instance), class cultures emerge. Bourdieu understood class as placing indelible imprints upon every aspect of our being—it shapes how we look at the world, act and interact within it, and it shapes elements of our most intimate tastes and desires. Bourdieu refers to this process as the **habitus**—the practical

cultural capital
French sociologist Pierre Bourdieu's term for the cultural articles—ideas, artistic expressions, forms of music or literature—that function as resources that people in the dominant class can use to justify their dominance.

habitus
French sociologist Pierre Bourdieu's term for the practical mastery of self that arises, in part, out of class location and distance from necessity.

mastery of self that arises, in part, out of class location and distance from necessity. Bourdieu argued that all manner of preferences, proclivities, and predispositions often thought to constitute our most core "self" are actually products of mult-layered socializing forces that stem, in part, from social class positioning. Thus, for Bourdieu, **tastes** refer to an abstract process through which we all adopt routines, practices, and interests which have their origins in material constraints. Our tastes and interests, in other words, are as stratified as our incomes.

And class does not operate alone. As we'll see in the coming chapters, class intersects with race and ethnicity, as well as other elements of identity. Sometimes, we are more likely to see race or ethnicity—that is, to see differences between groups who are all in the same class—and thus miss opportunities to effectively address some issues of inequality because we fail to notice them. For example, if the only images of poverty that you see in the media are racial and ethnic minorities in America's cities, you might not "see" the rural poverty among whites that might be more common in your region. (The highest percentage of poor people are rural and white, but it's hard to know that by watching the news; see MAP 7.1.)

Some elements of class culture are evident in what we consume: Consumption is one of the chief ways in which we both reveal our class position and also try to hide it. For many Americans, consumption indicates the class to which we aspire, and so because we want to be of a higher class, we consume as if we were, buying those products we associate with "lifestyles of the rich and famous." Many of us who buy shirts with little polo players on them, for example, will never play the actual game of polo. But we wouldn't be caught dead wearing a shirt with a little bowler on it— even though we may actually occasionally go bowling! As Max Weber understood: Class is also often associated with status, with lifestyle.

Class is about more than what we buy and where and what we eat. It's also evident in how we raise our children. Sociologist Annette Lareau (2003) studied a group of third graders, black and white, middle-class and working-class. The wealthier parents were extremely involved in the children's lives and talked constantly with their children; the kids' lives were a blur of sports practices, musical instrument

The upper classes are the prime consumers of high-end luxury brands. Their tastes, however, often trickle down to the middle classes, who consume these same brands as a way to exhibit their mobility and status.

tastes

French sociologist Pierre Bourdieu's term for an abstract process through which we all adopt routines, practices, and interests which have their origins in material constraints.

MAP 7.1 The Intersections Between Poverty and Race in the United States

As you can see, many of those counties who suffer the highest rates of poverty are in states where you might have expected them (depending on where you grew up and what you know about poverty). And although there are more poor white people than there are poor people in other racial and ethnic groups, as a group, white people in the United States are less likely than other racial groups to be poor (they are just a larger part of the U.S. population).

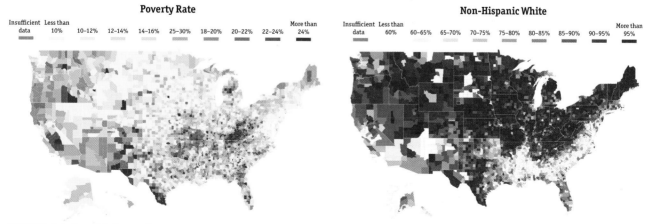

SOURCE: Data from U.S. Census Bureau.

lessons, and family cultural outings. The poorer kids experienced no such parental involvement or structured activities. They spent their time outside school hanging out at home making up games with the neighbors and friends. Lareau argues that both of these styles of parenting have their advantages—middle-class kids are comfortable in a world of adult culture and are far more assertive, while working-class kids can be more creative figuring out what to do with themselves without formal structure. Lareau stresses, however, that these differences are *cultural* differences, and that in a world where those middle-class skills are more heavily valued, classes tend to socialize their children to remain in the class into which they are born. Class culture, then, is a way that class structure is reproduced.

Class, Culture, and Musical Taste

7.2.5 Distinguish between cultural univores and omnivores and how these relate to class inequality.

Class and cultural capital are embedded in all manner of our tastes—from the names we select for our babies, to the clothes we wear, locations we select for vacation, leisurely activities to pursue. And, as Pierre Bourdieu suggested, tastes are one way that we accomplish and reproduce class differences. Saying "*we* like this" and "*they* prefer that" helps us to create divisions in society that are made all the more real when they become associated with income, access to health care, healthy food, and more. Simply put, tastes stratify. But they don't always do so in the ways you might imagine.

For instance, stereotypes of the elite often situate them as having a narrow range of tastes; we imagine that they prefer things that are largely off-limits to many of us as a result of resources, circumstance, or some combination. Sociologist Richard Peterson (1992) refers to people with narrow ranges of tastes as **cultural univores**, as opposed to those with more cosmopolitan tastes—a group he called **cultural omnivores**. We imagine, in other words, that the elite are largely culturally "univorous," that they prefer to consume a rather limited set of cultural objects and experiences, as opposed to the rest of us who we might imagine are a bit less discerning and more open to a larger range of cultural objects and experiences.

Indeed, many social theorists who have studied elite culture suggested that they see other cultural forms as crude, vulgar, or even dishonorable. Peterson argued, however, that this is a completely incorrect understanding of the cultural tastes of the elite and how their tastes play a role in reproducing class inequality. The elite, Peterson showed, are defined not by cultural intolerance in their tastes, but rather, by "omnivorous" consumption habits (Peterson and Kern 1996).

Sociologist Bethany Bryson (1996) discovered that musical tastes were an excellent example of this. Bryson discovered that musical tastes were one means by which people established symbolic boundaries between themselves and people "like them" and people from whom they see themselves as distinct. The most elite economically were better defined by the music they abhorred than by the music they liked. In 1993, the musical genres most exclusively liked by Americans with the least amount of education and lowest earnings potential were gospel, country, rap, and heavy metal. These were the same genres of music most likely to be rejected by Americans with more education. According to Bryson, the elite today no longer only listen to opera and classical music. They've become *culturally omnivorous*, consuming lots of different genres of music. As Bryson puts it, the elite are much more likely to say, "Anything but heavy metal" when asked about their musical tastes today. They consume widely. And, as Bryson's research showed, they are more likely to form class-based identities and communities through rejecting very specific things (rather than *all* things) associated with social classes below them economically.

cultural univores
Sociologist Richard Peterson's term for people with narrow ranges of tastes.

cultural omnivores
Sociologist Richard Peterson's term for people with more cosmopolitan tastes.

iSOC AND YOU Class Identity and Inequality

Social class is among the most dominant mechanisms for social organization and social *inequality*. To sociologists, class is more than "how much money you make." It's a way of life, a foundation for your *identity*. Classes have different cultures, worldviews. Classes can be communities: Your *interactions* with others reproduce your membership in your class, and reveal those of others. Class differences are reproduced throughout all social *institutions* like educational system or the workplace. And class *intersects* with other aspects of inequality to maximize some inequalities and minimize others, and often form networks and communities.

7.3 Class Inequality in the United States

Our class position unites us in common class-based identities. And our class system, as a whole, also divides us into different and unequal groups. Class is one of the fundamental bases of social inequality. Karl Marx divided the world into two simple classes, the rich and the poor. But the sweeping economic and social changes of the past century and the recognition of multiple components to socioeconomic status have pushed sociologists to redefine these class categories and to further delineate others. In this section, you will learn more about what class inequality looks like in the United States—both historically and contemporarily.

We will examine the contemporary class structure of the United States as well as how it has changed and the direction in which it is headed today. And you will also learn to think about the class structure intersectionally. For instance, not all groups are equally likely to be rich, or poor. But how this happens and what the consequences of these intersecting systems of inequality are for Americans is more complicated than you might initially suspect. We will also examine poverty in depth in this section, learning to understand how sociologists have sought to classify who is (and therefore who is not) impoverished and how our rates of poverty and wealth distribution compare with other societies on an international scale.

The American Class System

7.3.1 Distinguish between the different socioeconomic classes both economically and culturally.

Today most sociologists argue for six or more socioeconomic classes in the United States. They are usually divided on the basis of household income because that information is easily obtained in census reports, but bear in mind that there are many other factors, and income is not always the best indicator. Our class position is both an ascribed status (the class we are born into) and an achieved status (the class we end up in). Unfortunately for the myth of American mobility, these are far more likely to be the same than they are to be different. In fact, class is the single best predictor of a person's **life chances**—a person's abilities to have access to material goods (food and shelter) and social resources (health care, education) that together control the quality of life. And class positions in the United States, by almost any measure, have shifted in recent history (see FIGURE 7.2).

One way to divide classes is on the basis of income (because this is information easily obtained on the U.S. Census); but remember that there are other factors and that income is not always the best indicator. We'll consider seven socioeconomic classes and discuss some of their characteristics.

The **upper upper class** are the superrich, with annual incomes of more than $1 million. They include the older established wealthy families, born into massive fortunes that

life chances

A person's abilities to have access to material goods (food and shelter) and social resources (health care, education) that together control the quality of life.

upper upper class

The superrich, with annual incomes of more than $1 million. They include the older established wealthy families, born into massive fortunes that their ancestors amassed during the industrial boom of the nineteenth-century Gilded Age.

FIGURE 7.2 Income Distribution by Class in the United States, 1970-2015

As you can see here, stratification related to income and wealth in the United States has grown immensely over a very short period of time. Each earnings quintile has seen growth over the long run. But, as you can see, that growth has not been equitably distributed between the quintiles. Those at the top have seen much faster growth than those below them. So, their share of the income distribution has grown. And those at the upper end of the top earning quintile in the United States saw the vast majority of those gains made by the top quintile more generally.

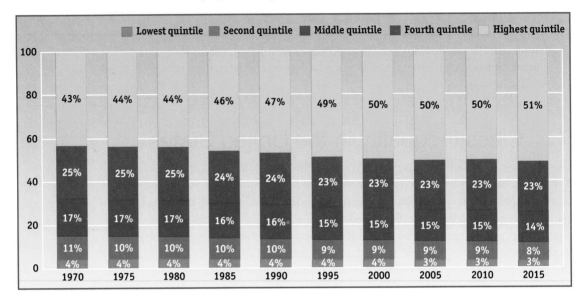

SOURCE: Data from U.S. Census Bureau.

their ancestors amassed during the industrial boom of the nineteenth-century Gilded Age. Although the original fortunes were amassed through steel, railroads, or other industries, recent generations depend on extensive worldwide investments. Many of the superrich amassed their fortunes recently, during the information revolution, in computers and other technology. Bill Gates came from an elite background but was nowhere near even the top 10 percent in income in 1975, when he dropped out of Harvard to found Microsoft. Today, Gates's fortune is close to $453 billion. The superrich are usually invisible to the rest of the world. They have people to do their shopping and other chores. They have private jets, so they rarely stand in line at airports.

The **lower upper class** (with annual household incomes of more than $150,000 but less than $1 million) are the "everyday" rich. They tend to have advanced degrees from high-ranking colleges. Though they have substantial investment incomes, they still have to work: They are upper-level CEOs, managers, doctors, and engineers. Much more visible than the superrich, they still protect their privacy. They do not participate extensively in civic and community organizations. They live in gated communities, vacation at exclusive resorts, and send their children to prestigious private schools.

With household incomes above $80,000 but less than $150,000, the **upper middle class** are the high-end professionals and corporate workers. Most have college degrees. Only a small percentage of their income comes from investments. They tend to be community leaders, active in civic organizations and the arts. The audience in performances of the local philharmonic is likely to be mostly upper middle class (while, for instance, the upper class might be vacationing in Vienna and the lower middle and working classes are at home watching television). The **middle middle class** (with household incomes between $40,000 and $80,000) are the "average" American citizens. Most hold white-collar jobs: technicians, salespeople, business owners, educators, etc. Many blue-collar workers and high-demand service personnel, like police, firefighters, and military, have incomes high enough to place them in the middle class. Most have attended college, and many have college degrees. They

lower upper class

Annual household incomes of more than $150,000 but less than $1 million; they are the "everyday" rich. They tend to have advanced degrees from high-ranking colleges. Though they have substantial investment incomes, they still have to work: They are upper-level CEOs, managers, doctors, and engineers.

upper middle class

With household incomes above $80,000 but less than $150,000, they are the high-end professionals and corporate workers. Most have college degrees. Only a small percentage of their income comes from investments.

middle middle class

Household incomes between $40,000 and $80,000; these are the "average" American citizens. Most hold white-collar jobs: technicians, salespeople, business owners, educators, etc. Many blue-collar workers and high-demand service personnel, like police, firefighters, and military, have incomes high enough to place them in the middle class. Most have attended college, and many have college degrees.

have little investment income but generally enough savings to weather brief periods of unemployment and to provide some degree of retirement security. They are usually able to buy houses, drive new cars, and send their children to college. They tend to have small families and are active in community civic life.

The **working class**—sometimes referred to as the "lower middle class" to avoid the stigma of *not* being middle class in the United States—has a household income between $20,000 and $40,000. They tend to be blue-collar workers, involved in manufacturing, production, and skilled trades, but also include some low-level white-collar workers and professionals (such as elementary school teachers) and some high-level clerical and service industry workers, especially those in two-income households. They make things and build things. They usually have high school diplomas, and many have been to college (but are less likely to have a degree). Their savings are usually minimal, so a few missed paychecks can be devastating, and for retirement they will have to depend on government programs. They can sometimes buy houses, drive inexpensive cars, take occasional vacations, and send their children to public college. The working class are not heavily involved in local civic and community organizations; instead, their social lives revolve around home, church, and maybe some hobby or sports groups. Extended family appears to be extremely important, more significant in the daily lives of the working class than of the middle class or upper class, who usually live farther away from aunts, uncles, and cousins.

The **lower class**—sometimes called the "working poor" to avoid the stigma of being called lower class—has a household income of less than $20,000 per year. They hold unskilled and semiskilled jobs. They are service workers, maintenance workers, clerical workers. They deliver pizzas, wait on customers at retail stores, and clean homes and offices. Most do not have high school diplomas: They have an average of 10.4 years of education, as compared with 11.9 for the working class, 13.4 for the middle class, and 14.3 for the upper class. It's hard to accumulate any money on $20,000 per year, so the lower class usually live from paycheck to paycheck, and even a brief period of unemployment can be catastrophic. And because service jobs rarely include health benefits, illnesses and accidents also have a devastating effect. They often cannot afford houses or cars or college educations for their children. They are not heavily involved in any activity besides making ends meet. They often endure brief stints with poverty as they are so often forced to live one tragedy or misfortune away on a daily basis.

The **underclass** has no income and no connection to the job market. Their major support comes from welfare and food stamps. Most live in substandard housing, and some are homeless. And when we examine homelessness intersectionally, we can see that some groups are much more likely to experience homelessness than others—in absolute numbers, Black men are the single largest group among the homeless. This fact is all the more striking when we realize that black men account for only about 6.2 percent of the U.S. population overall. The underclass more generally has inadequate education, inadequate nutrition, and no health care. They have virtually no possibility of social mobility and little chance of achieving the quality of life that most people would consider minimally acceptable. Most members of the underclass are not born there: They grow up working poor, or working class, or middle class, and gradually move down through a series of firings, layoffs, divorces, and illnesses.

In the United States and other high-income countries, college is a necessary prerequisite for a middle-class life but no longer guarantees it.

working class

With household income between $20,000 and $40,000. They tend to be blue-collar workers, involved in manufacturing, production, and skilled trades, but also include some low-level white-collar workers and professionals (such as elementary school teachers) and some high-level clerical and service industry workers, especially those in two-income households.

lower class

Sometimes called the "working poor"—they have a household income of less than $20,000 per year. They hold unskilled and semiskilled jobs. They are service workers, maintenance workers, clerical workers. They deliver pizzas, wait on customers at retail stores, and clean homes and offices.

underclass

About 4 percent of the U.S. population, this group has no income, no connection to the job market, little education, inadequate nutrition, and substandard housing or none at all. They have no possibility of social mobility and little chance of achieving the quality of life that most people would consider minimally acceptable.

WHAT DO YOU THINK? WHAT DOES AMERICA THINK?

Conflict Between Poor and Rich in the United States

Because capitalist countries are built on a profit-based economy, they can be especially prone to inequality based on economic status, and this inequality often leads to conflict between the rich and the poor.

What do you think?

In your opinion, in America, how much conflict is there between poor people and rich people?

- ○ Very strong conflict
- ○ Strong conflict
- ○ Not strong conflict
- ○ No conflict

What does America think?

In the 2011 survey, the Pew Research Center found two thirds of Americans felt there was either strong or very strong conflict between the rich and the poor (66%). Broken down by race, 74 percent of black Americans, 65 percent of white Americans, and 61 percent of Hispanic Americans stated that there are strong or very strong conflicts between the rich and the poor. With regard to political party, Democrats were the most likely to say the same (73%), followed by Independents (68%), and distantly, by Republicans (55%).

NOTE: For results from the 2011 survey, *n*=2,048. Whites and blacks include only non-Hispanics. Hispanics are of any race.

SOURCE: Data from Morin, Rich. Rising Share of American See Conflict Between Rich and Poor. *Pew Research Center, Social & Demographic Trends*, January 11, 2012. Available at http://www.pewsocialtrends.org/2012/01/11/rising-share-of-americans-see-conflict-between-rich-and-poor/.

THINKING CRITICALLY ABOUT SURVEY DATA

The differences in responses by race and political party are significant. What explains these differences? In sociology, we study the intersections among things like race, class, and political identity. How does the intersection between race and class help explain these survey results?

The Myth of the Middle Class

7.3.2 Explain why so many Americans believe they are middle class even though the American middle class appears to be in decline.

So much for what the social scientists say about the different classes. In our day-to-day lives, most Americans actually believe that class is unimportant and that most Americans are middle class (see FIGURE 7.3). On the other hand, class inequality has never been greater, and it is growing wider, not narrower. How, you might ask, is it possible that both of these facts are true?

For the entire twentieth century, the middle class expanded dramatically, and the classes of the very rich and the very poor declined. (This is true despite the dramatic increase in the gap between the richest and the poorest Americans.) Home ownership has risen, incomes have risen, and many more people own stock through mutual funds, pensions, and retirement accounts than ever before. (This is also true despite the recent economic recession.) To think of it as Marx might have, they thus own at least a fraction of the means of production—and identify not with workers but with owners.

At the same time that boundaries of the middle class are expanding to the breaking point, with many identifying with the middle class (or upper middle class or lower middle class), the lifestyle associated with middle class is in obvious decline: less money, a smaller house or no house, a worse job or no job, and less financial security.

Economist Michael Lind (2004) argues that the middle class has always been a product of social engineering by the government. Today's middle class emerged during the "New Deal" of the 1930s when technological innovation, a home front relatively

FIGURE 7.3 Subjective Class Identification among Americans, 1975–2016

The General Social Survey asks Americans to claim a class identity on one survey question. Survey respondents are asked, "If you were asked to use one of four names for your social class, which would you say you belong in: the lower class, the working class, the middle class, or the upper class?" What these data show is that there have been fluctuations in how Americans self-identify their social class over time. But working class and middle class are the most common subjective identifications and Americans are least likely to self-identify as "upper class." Recently, Americans have been self-identifying as middle class a bit less, and working and lower class a bit more.

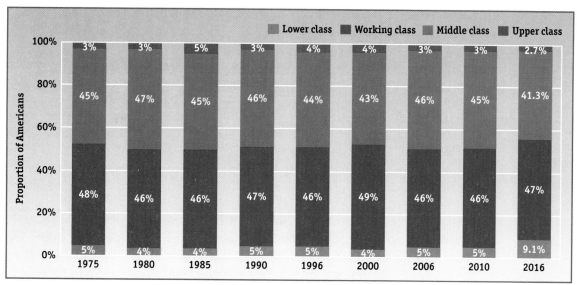

SOURCE: Data from General Social Survey, 1975–2016.

unscathed by war, and a large population of young, well-educated people led to a climate just right for an unprecedented expansion of the middle class. In the early 1970s, a college graduate earned about 45 percent more than a high school graduate. By 2008, that number had jumped to 84 percent more, the result of increased demand for higher skills (Glenn 2008).

But the Great Recession of today has reversed some of these trends. Sociologist Theda Skocpol calls it **"the missing middle"** – the gradual disappearance of the middle class as the nation becomes increasingly polarized into rich and poor (Skocpol 2000). There are several reasons for this. Two of the most important factors, a superior education and a favorable investment climate, have begun to decline in significance. The increases in the percentage of the labor force with college degrees has slowed to less than 5 percent, and America's massive trade deficit and the better-performing economies of Asia and some parts of Latin America make America less attractive for investment. And white-collar jobs are in steady decline. Knowing about computers is no longer key to instant success. The jobs with the biggest numerical gains in the next 10 years in terms of numbers of workers are expected to be in food service, customer service, retail sales, clerical work, and private security.

Class Inequality in Perspective

7.3.3 Summarize some of the general characteristics of distribution of wealth in the United States and compare them with other nations.

At the same time that so many Americans believe they are middle class and believe that the system works for them, the United States is increasingly a nation of richer and poorer. Sociologists measure income inequality in a society by comparing the top incomes with the bottom incomes. In the United States, the top 5 percent earn an average of 11

"the missing middle"

Sociologist Theda Skocpol's term for the gradual disappearance of the middle class as the nation becomes increasingly polarized into rich and poor.

We may be seeing the rise of a new feudalism, with a few elites sitting in their skyscraper condos while the rest of the population—the new serfs—cook, clean, park the cars, and patrol the grounds. Here a man shines the shoes of another man who clearly occupies a higher socioeconomic status. See the ways in which class is also accomplished in interaction as the two men position their bodies relative to one another.

times more than the bottom 20 percent—an earnings disparity that accumulates into mountainous differences between the top and bottom. The Great Recession has pushed this disparity to a record high (Sommeiller and Price 2015). The United States has the most extreme income inequality in the developed world. In fact, the income gap in the United States is the widest of any industrialized country among all countries included in the Organization for Economic Cooperation and Development (OECD), an international organization that measures and assists in economic development (see FIGURE 7.4). And the income gap in the United States has actually been growing.

Even at the top, the gaps are growing enormously. Over the past 35 years or so, the wages and salaries of the top 10 percent of earners have grown nearly 35 percent—about 1 percent a year. That means that being in the top 10 percent did not pay off all that handsomely. In fact, three out of five Americans earning more than $100,000 say they "always or almost always" live from paycheck to paycheck (Pisani 2009). But income at the 99th percentile (the top 1% of earners) rose more than 180 percent during that same period. And income at the 99.99th percentile (the top one-hundredth of 1%) rose nearly 500 percent. That's for those earning more than $6 million a year (Krugman 2006). An old expression promises us, "A rising tide lifts all boats." But nowadays the rising tide lifts only the yachts.

On the other side of the class divide, things are getting significantly worse. The bottom 80 percent of U.S. households held about 7 percent of the liquid financial assets. And the bottom 40 percent of income earners in the United States now collectively own less than 1% of the nation's wealth. More than 1.4 million Americans filed for bankruptcy in 2009—nearly a one-third increase from the year before (MyBudget360 .com 2009). More than one in five American children are living below the poverty line—the highest rate in 25 years. And in 2010, for the first time in U.S. history, more than 40 million people are on food stamps (Snyder 2010).

FIGURE 7.4 **Shares of Income Received by the Bottom and Top 10 Percent, by OECD Nations, 2014**
These relative income measures compare the gap between the top 10 percent of U.S. households and the bottom 10 percent of household incomes in each country to the U.S. median household income in purchasing-power-parity terms.

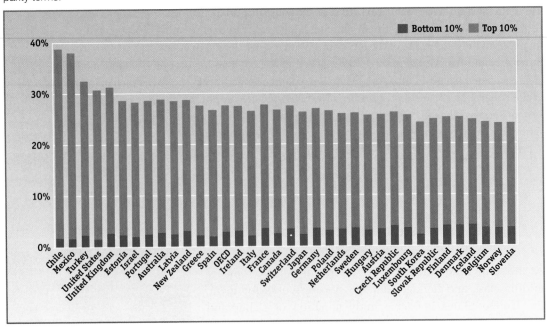

SOURCE: Data from https://www.oecd.org/social/OECD2016-Income-Inequality-Update.pdf.

Intersections with Class, Race, and Gender

7.3.4 Explain the racial wealth gap and the feminization of poverty in the United States and in global perspective.

Class position is based on your position in the economic world. And although it is more flexible than your race or gender statuses that are fixed (or *ascribed*) at birth, it is also less an *achieved* status than we often imagine. For instance, there is less than a 2 percent chance that someone whose parents are in the bottom 60 percent of all earners will ever end up in the top 5 percent. And if you are born in the bottom 20 percent, you have a 40 percent chance of staying there (Hertz 2007). This also means that the historical legacy of racism and the long-term patterns of gender inequality have enormous consequences for class position. Given how little mobility there actually is, the descendants of poor slaves were unlikely to rise very much in the class hierarchy—even over several generations.

It is also true that some African Americans do make it, and at the same time as African Americans are overrepresented among the poor, there is also a growing black middle class, a class of professionals, corporate entrepreneurs, and other white-collar workers. Although the existence of the black middle class in the United States reveals that there is some mobility in American society, its small size also illustrates the tremendous obstacles facing any minority member attempting to be upwardly mobile (see FIGURE 7.5).

And, on the other side, there are significant numbers of poor whites in the United States. Largely in rural areas, former farmers, migrants, and downsized and laid-off white workers have also tumbled below the poverty line. In cities like Flint, Michigan, where a large GM auto manufacturing plant closed, former workers, both white and black, were suddenly and dramatically downwardly mobile. Race may be a predictor of poverty, but poverty surely knows no race. And poverty is stratified by gender and age as well—women and children are disproportionately likely to live in poverty, a fact sociologists refer to as the **feminization of poverty**.

feminization of poverty
A worldwide phenomenon that also afflicts U.S. women, this term describes women's overrepresentation among the world's poor and tendency to be in worse economic straits than men in any given nation or population.

FIGURE 7.5 Median Household Income by Race and Ethnicity, 1967–2016
Median household income averages in the United States, however, mask even greater disparities between whites and people of color. Although the median household income in the United States was $56,516 in 2015, the median income of black households was just two-thirds of that at $36,898. And these numbers only account for income; white households also have dramatically more wealth than do the households of people of color.

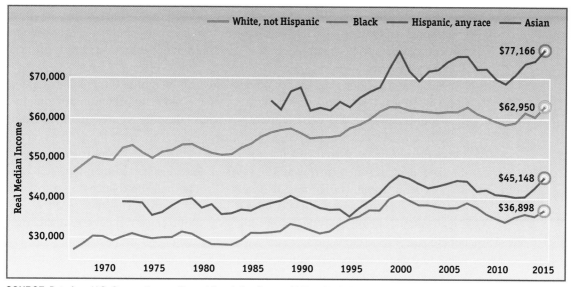

SOURCE: Data from U.S. Census Bureau, Current Population Survey, 1967 to 2016. Available at https://www.census.gov/library/publications/2016/demo/p60-256.html.

As with race, so too with gender. Social scientists often argue that poverty is also being increasingly "feminized"—that is, women compose an increasing number of poor people. The image of the itinerant (male) pauper has largely faded, replaced today by a single mother. This is what sociologists call the "feminization of poverty"—a term meant to convey the gendered shift in the composition of America's poor.

This feminization of poverty has never been more obvious. In 2015, nearly 15 percent of all women in the United States were impoverished, compared with roughly 12 percent of men. Although African American and Hispanic women face proportionally higher poverty rates, the disparity between women and men holds true for all racial and ethnic groups. Women earn less income, as a group, than do men. And the widest gender gap in poverty rates occurs during the childbearing years. Supporting a family is difficult for single mothers because women's salaries are often lower anyway (due to the fact that women are, on average paid less, and because women are disproportionately likely to work in occupations that pay less). As a result, many single mothers leave the labor force, pause their education, or work part time to provide unpaid care to children or elderly or disabled family members. The lack of adequate child support in the United States—from parental leave policies to affordable day care to adequate health care—has only made this problem worse.

And when we consider this issue a bit more intersectionally, these problems are even more acute for women of color and their children. Consider the following statistic from the 2013 Survey of Consumer Finances (a national survey sponsored by the Federal Reserve Board): The median wealth for white households was approximately $142,000 collecting all of their assets in one figure. For black households, that figure was $11,000. It was $13,700 for Hispanic households. This disparity persists even among single woman households. This means that black and Hispanic people are much more likely to live precariously close to financial crisis, and black and Hispanic women especially. Wealth affords people the opportunity to weather tough times, when a part-time employer has fewer hours to offer an employee, for instance, or when a household experiences a spike in monthly bills because of a health crisis or unexpected car trouble.

These facts underscore the importance of thinking about a social problem like poverty from an intersectional perspective. Although poverty is a problem around the world, the magnitude of that problem shifts a great deal and what exactly that problem looks like from your perspective depends on the various groups to which you belong. And the groups most at risk of enduring poverty and the life-threatening consequences associated with it are those also marginalized by other forms of social inequality in society.

Racial and gender gaps in U.S. poverty rates are magnified in the global arena. In poor countries, women suffer double deprivation—the deprivation of living in a poor country and the deprivation imposed because they are women. In high-income countries, women live much longer than men: 8.26 years in France, 7.35 years in Switzerland, 6.55 years in the United States. But in low-income countries, the gap in life expectancy is much narrower: 3.20 years in Zaire, 2.40 years in Sudan, 1.10 years in India. And women suffer most in societies where their life chances are composed entirely of bearing and raising children. Indeed, according to the World Health Organization, pregnancy is the second-highest leading cause of women's death (only behind cardiovascular disease). Every year, approximately 287,000 women die as a result of complications in pregnancy and childbirth, and 99 percent of those women live in developing countries.

Globally, class and race also intersect. The economic south, largely composed of Africans, South Asians, and Latin Americans, is the home to more than four-fifths of all the world's poor—and a similar percentage of the world's people of color. On the other side of the global divide, the predominantly white nations of Europe are among those with the highest standards of living and the lowest levels of poverty. From 1995 to today, wage inequality between the top and bottom earners worldwide has increased by two-thirds. Among developed countries, Germany, Poland, and the United States are the countries where the gap between top and bottom wages has increased most rapidly, although wage inequality has also increased sharply in some countries, including Thailand, Argentina, and China (ILO 2009a, b).

Who Is Poor in America?

7.3.5 Summarize some of what we know about how many people are poor in the United States and who they are.

The poor are probably not who you think they are. As of 2014, the population of the United States was just less than 320 million. And of the 320 million people living in the United States, 46.7 million were living in poverty in 2014 (DeNavas-Walt and Proctor 2015)—that's 14.8 percent of the entire population. In the United States, we gauge poverty with a calculation devised in 1964 by President Lyndon Johnson. When Johnson declared "war on poverty" in the United States as part of his dream of a Great Society, he asked economist Mollie Oshansky to devise a poverty threshold, a minimum income necessary to not be poor. She decided that poverty meant "insufficient income to provide the food, shelter, and clothing needed to preserve health." So, she took the least expensive of the diets, multiplied it by three (one-third food, one-third shelter, one-third clothes), and voilà! She estimated the poverty threshold—or the **poverty line**. The number and proportion of people living in poverty shifts, and just how we define "poverty" to assess who is impoverished has been the subject of much research and debate. Relying on the definition used by the U.S. Census, consider shifts in U.S. poverty over time (see FIGURE 7.6).

Not all poor people are ethnic minorities. The poverty rate for whites is lower (10.1%), compared to that of blacks (26.2%), Hispanics (23.6%), and Asians (12%). However, 31 million whites were poor in the United States in 2014, a number that accounts for

poverty line

Estimated minimum income required to pay for food, shelter, and clothing. Anyone falling below this income is categorized as poor.

FIGURE 7.6 A Profile of Poverty in the United States, 1959–2015

Although the proportion of Americans in poverty (the poverty rate) has fallen over the past half century, the actual numbers of Americans in poverty has increased because of our growing population. Sometimes, proportions can be difficult to make sense of. But, if 13.5 percent of Americans were impoverished in 2015, that amounts to 43.1 million people. Put another way, 43 million people is approximately the size of the entire populations of New York, Florida, and Iowa, combined.

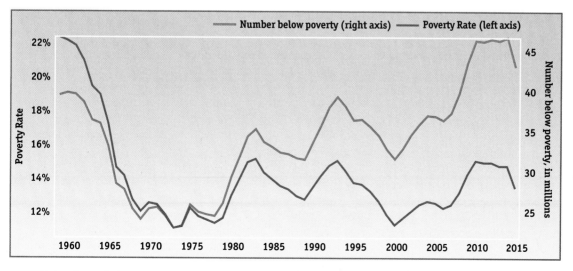

SOURCE: Data from U.S. Census Bureau. Current Population Survey, 1960 to 2015 Annual Social and Economic Supplements. Available at https://www.census.gov/library/publications/2016/demo/p60-256.html.

roughly two-thirds of the more than 46.7 million below the poverty line (DeNavas-Walt and Proctor 2015)

Not all poor people live in the inner city. In fact, the highest percentages of poor people live in the rural South. In 2008, only Louisiana, Mississippi, Texas, and New Mexico had poverty rates above 16 percent, compared to 9.7 percent in the urban north (U.S. Census Bureau 2009). But poverty is becoming more suburban as well; the suburbs are now home to 13.7 million poor Americans, one-third of the nation's total—and rising. Since 2000, the number of American suburban poor has increased significantly as well.

Not all poor people are unemployed. The connection between poverty and the realities of the labor market is complex. Low and stagnant wages keep many from being able to earn enough. In 2014, about 9.5 million people who spent at least half of the year working were in poverty; the "working poor" comprised 6.3 percent of all individuals in the U.S. labor force that year (Bureau of Labor Stastistics 2016). Seventy percent of poor children are in working families (Children's Defense Fund 2016).

Children are more likely than others to be poor. Right now, 18 percent of children (13.3 million) in the United States live in poverty—10 percent of white children, 29 percent of Hispanic children, and 35 percent of black children (Forum on Child and Family Statistics 2009). The child poverty rate in the United States is often two to three times higher than that of other major industrial nations. Children suffer more than adults from limited health care, poor nutrition, and unsanitary living conditions. Plus, low income tends to increase stress and conflict within families, hamper early cognitive development, stifle educational achievement, and increase the likelihood of participation in serious criminal activity (Children's Defense Fund 2016).

Mothers are more likely than others to be poor. The poverty rate among female-headed households is more than six times that of married couple families. About half of all poor families are depending on a mother alone to support them (U.S. Census Bureau 2008).

The elderly are less likely than others to be poor. A generation ago, in 1967, 30 percent of Americans older than age 65 were living in poverty. By 2007, government intervention through such programs as Social Security, subsidized housing and food, and

SOCIOLOGY AND OUR WORLD

THE HIDDEN INJURIES OF CLASS

Why do the working-class and poor in the United States judge themselves by stereotypes of the poor?

In a now-classic study, sociologists Richard Sennett and Jonathan Cobb interviewed working-class and poor men and women whose jobs were difficult, demeaning, low paying, and dead end. Sennett and Cobb expected to hear about hardship and deprivation, but they also heard working-class men judging themselves by middle-class standards. They believed in the American dream, where a poor boy can grow up to be president, where all it takes to get rich is perseverance and hard work. Yet they weren't rich—and they blamed themselves. They thought their "failure" was a matter of laziness, lack of ambition, or stupidity.

How did they ward off despair, when they believed themselves fully to blame for their lives of deprivation? They deferred success from their own lives onto the lives of their children. They were working at difficult, dirty, and dangerous jobs not because they were failures but because they were sacrificing to give their children a better life. They were noble and honorable. Middle-class fathers tried to be role models to their children, saying, in effect, "You can grow up to be like me if you study and work hard." But working-class fathers tried to be cautionary tales: "You could grow up to be like me if you *don't* study and work hard."

Living through one's children proved to be enormously damaging. Fathers were resentful if their children were successful and perhaps even more resentful if they weren't, and all of the deprivation was for nothing. Successful children felt ashamed of their parents, and unsuccessful children felt guilt and despair of their own. Following the American dream can also produce painful feelings.

Medicare lowered the poverty rate to 9.8 percent, a little less than the elderly population in general (12.4%) (U.S. Census Bureau 2008). In 1959, the elderly were the most likely age group to live in poverty (more than one in three people ages 65 or older). But, by 2015, those aged 65 and older became the least likely to live in poverty. Today, children are the most affected age group—roughly 2 in 10 children younger than age 18 are impoverished. And a great deal of this has to do with the fact that women are more likely to be in poverty than are men and there are more single mother households by far than there are single father households. However, poverty places more of a burden on elderly people than others. They are more likely to suffer from chronic illnesses that require expensive treatment. They are more likely to live alone and lack the social support networks that other poor people use to get by. And, as the population ages and people live longer, the government subsidy safety nets will be strained to the breaking point.

Explaining Poverty: Interactions and Institutions

7.3.6 Explain what it means to understand poverty as a structural rather than a personal or cultural failing.

Why are poor people poor? Is it because they are born into poverty, or because they don't work hard enough to get themselves out of it, or because they have some physical, intellectual, or emotional problem that prevents them from getting out?

One common explanation is that people are poor because they lack something—initiative, drive, ambition, discipline. An item in the 1984 General Social Survey stated, "Differences in social standing between people are acceptable because they basically reflect what people made out of the opportunities they had," and 74 percent of respondents agreed! The question has not been on the survey since. But those who agreed were expressing a long-standing belief that people are poor because they are unmotivated and lazy. They do not try hard enough. They don't want to work. Although we often excuse widows, orphans, children, and the handicapped—the "deserving poor"—who can't help it (Katz 1990), Americans continue to believe that the vast majority of poor people are "undeserving" poor.

Sociologists, however, understand poverty differently—as a structural problem, not a personal failing. In fact, it's often that people are unmotivated and lack ambition *because they are poor*, not the other way around. No matter how hard they try and how motivated they are, the cards are so heavily stacked against them that they eventually give up—as would any sensible person. In *Nickel and Dimed* (2001), renowned journalist Barbara Ehrenreich conducted an experiment: to live on minimum wage for a year. "Disguised" as a poor person, she applied for and received jobs as a waitress in Florida, a maid in Maine, and a Walmart employee in Minnesota. At first she worried that she would not be able to maintain the ruse: Surely coworkers would notice her superior intelligence and competence and realize that she wasn't "one of them," or else the boss would notice and fast-track her into a managerial position. But neither happened. She was no smarter and *less* competent than anyone else in minimum wage jobs. Back home as a renowned journalist, she had to conclude that her privileged lifestyle had little to do with her drive, ambition, intelligence, and talent, and much more to do with her social location. Anthropologist Katherine Newman found that poor people actually work harder than wealthy people—often in multiple demeaning, difficult, and exhausting dead-end jobs (Newman 1999).

The poor often work harder than the rich. The working poor often work very hard, but their wages are still inadequate to live on.

culture of poverty

Oscar Lewis's theory that poverty is not a result of individual inadequacies but larger social and cultural factors. Poor children are socialized into believing that they have nothing to strive for, that there is no point in working to improve their conditions. As adults, they are resigned to a life of poverty, and they socialize their children the same way. Therefore poverty is transmitted from one generation to the next.

In 1965, sociologist Oscar Lewis introduced the influential **culture of poverty** thesis (Lewis 1965) that argued that poverty is not a result of individual inadequacies but of larger social and cultural factors. Poor children are socialized into believing that they have nothing to strive for, that there is no point in working to improve their conditions. As adults, they are resigned to a life of poverty, and they socialize their children the same way. Therefore, poverty is transmitted from one generation to the next. This notion of resignation has often been challenged.

Indeed, if you examine FIGURE 7.1 again, you'll note the United States stands out in international comparison when it comes to thinking about class. Americans are much more likely to disagree with the notion that success in life is determined by things outside of our direct control; we're much more likely to say that, if you work hard, you can achieve success. This is an individualistic way of thinking about social class—the notion that we can personally change our fate if only we try hard enough.

Today sociologists know that poverty results from structures of inequality: nationwide and worldwide institutional factors that no one individual has any control over, such as economic change, globalization, racism, discrimination, and governmental policies. We also understand that though people living in poverty are not necessarily resigned to their situation, they face structural disadvantages that are nearly impossible for many people to overcome. They would like to lift themselves out of poverty and lead better lives, but they suffer from: poor nutrition, inadequate education, higher rates of chronic diseases, poor or nonexistent health care, inferior housing, in addition to factors like a greater likelihood of being victimized by crime and a greater likelihood of being labeled criminals.

We may believe that wealth or poverty is an attribute of individuals—those who work hard enough and sacrifice enough get ahead, and those who don't, well, don't—but, in reality, wealth and poverty are structural features of society. Your relative wealth or poverty depends on who you are more than on how hard you work. What's more, wealth and poverty are related to each other. Sociologists have argued that the poor are poor *because* the rich are rich. Maintaining a wealthy (or middle-class) lifestyle requires that some people be poor. People at the top of the social hierarchy have resources that enable them to respond to opportunities when they arise, like choosing a prestigious internship or job even if it doesn't pay or relocating to an expensive city or area to garner better education or experience. Superior resources allow people at the top to weather problems (from illnesses to accidents to lawsuits to unemployment) that ruin the already precarious lives of the poor. Advantages start early and persist throughout life. And they are virtually invisible—unless you don't have them.

---

iSOC AND YOU Class Inequality in the United States
In the United States, class is still the best predictor of everything—from what college you go to, to what kind of job you'll have, to how many children you'll have, to even how long you will live. Class inequality structures our experiences and opportunities. And it is a durable system of inequality, likely to be reproduced across generations. The best predictor of what social class you will occupy when you grow up is the social class in which you started. In short, class is the underground spring from which you draw your *identity*. Class identities are produced in *interaction* with others in a social world based on *inequality*. These interactions are formalized in social *institutions*, which are primary mechanisms through which they are reproduced, and they *intersect* with other forms of inequality.

7.4 Resistance and Change in Class Inequality

In the final section of this chapter, you will learn about class inequality around the world. Today, we live in a global economy. You are more connected to other people in the world than any generation before you has ever been. And the social, cultural, political, and economic structure of your society is more tied to those of other societies around the world than it has ever been. So, studying class today necessitates an understanding of social class around the world. In this section, you will learn more about what class inequality looks like around the world, how sociologists have come up with different theoretical frameworks to attempt to explain global class inequality, and more.

We conclude by discussing political resistance to class inequality. As we have already learned in this chapter, the difference between the rich and the poor is higher in the United States than almost anywhere else on earth. You might think Americans would be among the most politically active when it comes to issues of class inequality. But we're not. What does political resistance to class inequality look like? And how do sociologists understand whether and how it might work? We consider all of these issues and more in this section.

Global Class Inequality

7.4.1 Distinguish between relative and absolute poverty, and understand income inequality on a global scale.

Poverty is one of the most significant structural consequences of class inequality. When sociologists think about poverty, they usually use one of two terms. **Absolute poverty** is when people do not have the ability to sustain their lives and lack the most basic necessities like food and shelter. **Relative poverty** describes those who may be able to afford the basic necessities of life but still are unable to maintain an adequate standard of living. Half the world's population—three billion people—live in absolute poverty, on less than $1.25 a day. In fact, the gross domestic product of the poorest 60 nations in the world—that is, more than one quarter of the world's nations—is less than the wealth of the world's three richest *people* combined (The Economist 2009e; Shah 2007). And yet the actual number of the world's poor has been declining, but not everywhere and not at the same rate everywhere.

Global inequality is the systematic differences in wealth and power among countries. These differences among countries coexist alongside differences within countries. Increasingly, the upper classes in different countries are more similar to each other—especially in their patterns of consumption—than they are to the middle classes in their own countries. The world seems to be developing a global class structure. The same processes we observed in the United States are happening on a global scale. For example, over the past 30 years, the overall standard of living in the world has risen. Illiteracy is down, the infant mortality rate is down, the average income is up, and life expectancy is up, too. But many of these gains are in countries that were high or middle income to begin with, such as the advanced industrial economies of Europe. The standard of living in many of the poorest countries has actually declined. Rich countries are getting richer; poor countries are getting poorer.

The income gap between rich and poor that we see in the United States is becoming the pattern worldwide (see MAP 7.2). The richest 20 percent of the world's population receives about 80 percent of the global income and accounts for 86 percent of total private consumption, while the poorest 20 percent survives on just 1 percent of the global income and accounts for 1.3 percent of private consumption.

Globalization refers to the increased economic, political, and social interconnectedness of the world. It has also resulted in staggering disparities in the basics that provide

absolute poverty

A global problem that afflicts half the world's population, the term for people who are so poor they do not have the ability to sustain their lives and lack the most basic necessities like food and shelter.

relative poverty

The ability of people to afford only the basic necessities of life; those who live in relative poverty are unable to maintain an adequate standard of living.

global inequality

Systematic differences in wealth and power among countries, often involving exploitation of the less powerful by the more powerful countries.

globalization

A set of processes leading to the development of patterns of economic, cultural, and social relationships that transcend geographical boundaries; a widening, deepening, and speeding up of worldwide interconnectedness in all aspects of contemporary life.

MAP 7.2 Income Inequality on a Global Scale

Measuring income inequality around the world is difficult because different countries have different standards of living, levels of average income, and more. The most common measure is the *Gini coefficient*, a measure of how dispersed income in a country actually is. Gini coefficients are between 0 and 1.0. Zero indicates perfect income equality, where income is perfectly equally distributed between everyone in the population. Conversely, a Gini coefficient of 1.0 indicates the maximum level of income inequality (where one person receives all of the income). So, the higher the value of your Gini coefficient, the more income is held by a relatively smaller group of people. Here you can see how different countries rank relative to one another. The United States has a Gini coefficient of .45, which is not far from the income distribution in countries like Rwanda (.47), Saudi Arabia (.46), and Jamaica (.46).

Gini Coefficient

no data 0.25–0.29 0.3–0.34 0.35–0.39 0.4–0.44 0.45–0.49 0.5–0.54 0.55–0.59 >0.60

SOURCE: Data from CIA, The World Factbook. Available at https://www.cia.gov/library/publications/the-world-factbook/rankorder/2172rank.html.

quality of life. The difference between the "haves" and the "have-nots" in our world has never been greater. Consider this example: The $13 billion Americans spend on pet food each year is the same amount it would take to ensure basic health care and nutrition for every person on Earth. Europeans spend more every year on ice cream ($11 billion) than it would take to install water and sanitation for all ($9 billion). Americans spend approximately $12 billion a year on cosmetics, much more than the $8 billion it would take to provide basic education for every person in the world (Aziz 2008).

And the middle class may be disappearing in the United States, as the rich claim a larger share of the pie and the poor grow more numerous. But globally, the opposite is happening. Countries that have long been characterized by the two-class system of rich and poor now see a vibrant and growing middle class. Take, for example, what are now known as the BRIC countries—Brazil, Russia, India, and China. Globally, the middle class is expected to increase by more than 1 billion people over the next decade, especially in China and India (Kharas 2017). (The middle class is defined globally as those making between $10 and $20 per day.)

Although that will unleash a massive amount of entrepreneurial initiative and innovation, there are also potential economic and political problems. For one thing, the rising middle classes have historically been more liberal; indeed, they were called "democracy's secret weapon" because the rich prefer more autocratic or authoritarian systems and the poor tend toward more collectivist or socialist ones. But this new emerging middle class is less likely to be democratic, supporting conservatives like Vladimir Putin in Russia, conservative Islam in Indonesia, and state-control over corporations in Brazil. Economically, the middle class also consumes far more than the classes below it, and the increased demand will both cause the prices of things like steel, gasoline, and food to rise, as well as significant environmental strain as countries try to meet surging demand. Income inequality may also continue to increase, as the gap between skilled and unskilled workers grows.

Classifying Global Class Systems

7.4.2 Explain the distinctions among low-, middle-, and high-income countries.

Social scientists used to divide the world into three socioeconomic categories: high-, middle-, and low-income countries.

HIGH-INCOME COUNTRIES   There are about 40 high-income countries, including the United States ($57,300 per capita GDP), Switzerland ($59,400), Japan ($38,900), and Spain ($36,500). These 40 countries cover 25 percent of the world's land surface and are home to 17 percent of its population. Together they enjoy more than half of the world's total income and control the world's financial markets. Most of these nations' populations live in or near cities. Industry is dominated by large-scale factories, big machinery, and advanced technology; however, these countries are also at the forefront of the Information Revolution, with the most companies that make and sell computers and the most computer users; 72.5 percent of the U.S. population and 76 percent of Switzerland's are on the Internet. Because they have access to better nutrition and expert medical care, residents of these countries tend to have high life expectancies (82 in Japan) and low infant mortality rates (4.23 per 100,000 in Switzerland). And, because the population is mostly urban and well educated, the birth rate tends to be low (9.87 per thousand in Spain) and the literacy rate high (99 percent in Switzerland).

MIDDLE-INCOME COUNTRIES   There are about 90 middle-income countries, divided into high middle-income countries like Portugal ($28,500 per capita GDP), Uruguay ($20,300), and South Africa ($13,500) and low middle-income countries like Brazil ($14,800), Ukraine ($8,200), and China ($14,600). These countries cover 47 percent of Earth's land area and are home to more than half of its population. Only two-thirds of the people live in or near cities. There are many industrial jobs, but the Information Revolution has had only a minor impact: Less than 40 percent of Portugal's residents and 9.4 percent of South Africa's are on the Internet. Demographic indicators vary from country to country: In South Africa, the life expectancy is very low (49.5), but in China it is quite high (71). The infant mortality rate is 4.85 deaths per 1,000 births in Portugal and 23.33 in Brazil. Middle countries are not staying in the middle: They are getting either richer or poorer. (And within those countries, the rich are also getting richer and the poor, poorer.)

LOW-INCOME COUNTRIES   There are about 60 low-income countries, including Jamaica ($9,000 per capita GDP), India ($6,700), Kenya ($3,400), and Somalia ($400). These countries cover 28 percent of the world's land area and are home to 28 percent of its population. Most people

Low-income countries rely on cash crops and subsistence agriculture. Rice farming, pictured here in Vietnam, is especially labor intensive, requiring great care and attention to detail. In fact, rice is one of the most "labor elastic" crops in the world, meaning that more people working and harvesting will produce a higher yield. Most crops have a cutoff; at some point adding more people won't produce more food. Rice is less like that than almost any other crop on earth.

live in villages and on farms, as their ancestors have for centuries; only about a third live in cities. They are primarily agricultural, with only a few sustenance industries and virtually no access to the Information Revolution: There are slightly more than 3 million Internet users among Kenya's 40 million people (12.5%) and 102,000 among Somalia's 10.1 million (1%). They tend to have low life expectancies (50 in Somalia, 58.8 in Kenya), high infant mortality rates (107.4 deaths per 1,000 births in Somalia, 53.5 deaths per 1,000 births in Kenya), high birth rates (43.33 in Somalia, 35.14 per thousand in Kenya), and low literacy rates (61 percent in India, 38 percent in Somalia). Hunger, disease, and unsafe housing frame their lives (CIA World Factbook 2016).

Explaining Global Inequality

7.4.3 Distinguish among the core features of market theories, state-centered theories, dependency theories, and world system theory in making sense of global inequality.

For many years, sociologists weren't worried about the causes of global inequality as much as its cure, how to help the underprivileged countries "get ahead." Today, social scientists are less optimistic and are at least equally concerned with what kinds of social factors work to keep poor countries poor. Different theoretical approaches attempt to explain global inequality in different ways. Below, we'll briefly summarize four dominant approaches sociologists have used.

market theories

Theories that stress the wisdom of the capitalist marketplace. They assume that the best possible economic consequences will result if individuals are free to make their own economic decisions, uninhibited by any form of governmental constraint.

modernization theory

W. W. Rostow's theory focusing on the conditions necessary for a low-income country to develop economically. Arguing that a nation's poverty is largely the result of the cultural failings of its people, Rostrow believed poor countries could develop economically only if they give up their "backward" way of life and adopt modern Western economic institutions, technologies, and cultural values that emphasize savings and productive investment.

state-centered theories

Theories that argue appropriate government policies do not interfere with economic development but that governments play a key role in bringing it about.

Market theories stress the wisdom of the capitalist marketplace. They assume that the best possible economic consequences will result if individuals are free to make their own economic decisions, uninhibited by any form of governmental constraint. The only avenue to economic growth is unrestricted capitalism. By far the most influential market theory was devised by W. W. Rostow, an economic advisor to President Kennedy. His **modernization theory** focuses on the conditions necessary for a low-income country to develop economically. He argued that a nation's poverty is largely the result of the cultural failings of its people. They lack a "work ethic" that stresses thrift and hard work. Rostow suggested that these nations would be able to develop economically only if they give up their "backward" way of life and adopt modern Western economic institutions, technologies, and cultural values that emphasize savings and productive investment. Sociologists have been quick to criticize this theory for its ethnocentrism (using the United States as the "model" for what development should look like), its suggestion that people are responsible for their own poverty, and for ignoring the ways that wealthy countries often take advantage of poor countries and block their economic development. In a global economy, every nation is affected by the others. Nevertheless, Rostow's theory is still influential today (Firebaugh 1996, 1999; Firebaugh and Beck 1994; Firebaugh and Sandu 1998). It is sometimes argued that global free trade, achieved by minimizing government restrictions on business, will provide the only route to economic growth.

Perhaps the solution is not the market, operating on its own, but active intervention by the government (or by international organizations). **State-centered theories** argue that appropriate government policies do not interfere with economic development but that governments play a key role in bringing it about. For proof, they point to the newly developed economies of East Asia, which grew in conjunction with, and possibly because of, government intervention (Appelbaum and Henderson 1992; Cumings 1998). The governments have acted aggressively, sometimes violently, to ensure economic stability: They outlaw labor unions, jail labor leaders, ban strikes, repress civil rights. They have been heavily involved in social programs such as low-cost housing and universal education. The costs have been enormous: horrible factory conditions, widespread environmental degradation, exploitation of female workers, children, and "guest workers" from impoverished neighboring countries. But the economic results have been spectacular: Japan enjoyed an economic growth of 10 percent per year through the 1960s, 5 percent through the 1970s, and 4 percent through the 1980s (followed by a slowdown to 1.8%). It has a national reserve of $664 billion and has donated $7.9 billion in economic aid to other countries.

Dependency theory focuses on the unequal relationship between wealthy countries and poor countries, arguing that poverty is the result of exploitation. Wealthy countries (and the multinational corporations based in them) try to acquire an ever-increasing share of the world's wealth by pursuing policies and practices that block the economic growth of the poor countries. Capitalist countries exploit worker countries (just as Karl Marx predicted), thereby ensuring that the rich get richer and the poor get poorer. The exploitation began with **colonialism**, a political-economic system under which powerful countries established, for their own profit, rule over weaker peoples or countries (Cooper 2005). The most extensive colonialism occurred between 1500 and 1900, when England, Spain, France, and some other European nations exercised control over the entire world. Europeans immigrated in large numbers only to regions with low native populations—the Americas, southern Africa, Australia, and New Zealand—which soon became colonial powers in their own right. Other nations were merely occupied and mined for the raw materials necessary to maintain European wealth—petroleum, copper, iron, sugar, tobacco, and even people (the African slave trade was not finally outlawed until 1830).

After World War II, colonialism gradually ended; today only a few colonial possessions are left, mostly small islands (e.g., Bermuda, Guam, Martinique). However, the exploitation did not end. **Multinational corporations**, often with the support of powerful banks and governments of rich countries, established factories in poor countries, using cheap labor and raw materials to minimize their production costs without governmental interference. Today corporations engage in "offshoring," setting up factories in poor countries where the cost of materials and wages is low. The exercise of power is crucial to maintaining these dependent relationships on the global level. Local businesses cannot compete with the strength of multinational corporations, and former self-subsisting peasants often have no other economic options but to work at near-starvation wages at foreign-controlled mines and factories. Dependency theory has been criticized for being simplistic and for putting all blame for global poverty on high-income countries and multinational corporations. Some social scientists, such as Enrique Fernando Cardoso (also a past president of Brazil) argue that, under certain circumstances, poor countries can still develop economically, although only in ways shaped by their reliance on wealthier countries (Cardoso and Faletto 1978).

World system theory draws on dependency theory but focuses on the global economy as an international network dominated by capitalism. It argues that the global economy cannot be understood merely as a collection of countries, some rich and some poor, operating independently of each other except for a dynamic of exploitation and oppression: It must be understood as a single unit. Rich and poor countries are intimately linked. Immanuel Wallerstein, who founded world system theory and coined the term world economy (1974, 1979, 1984, 2004), argued that interconnectedness of the world system began in the 1500s, when Europeans began their economic and political domination of the rest of the world. Because capitalism depends on generating the maximum profits for the minimum of expenditures, the world system continues to benefit rich countries (which acquire the profits) and harm the rest of the world (by minimizing local expenditures and therefore perpetuating poverty). According to Wallerstein, the world system is composed of

dependency theory
Theory of poverty that focuses on the unequal relationship between wealthy and poor countries, arguing that poverty is caused by policies and practices by the rich that block economic growth of poor countries and exploit workers.

colonialism
A political-economic system under which powerful countries establish, for their own profit, rule over weaker peoples or countries and exploit them for natural resources and cheap labor.

multinational corporations
Large, international companies, also called transnational corporations, that manage production and/or deliver services in more than one country at once. Multinational corporations have a powerful influence in the local economies of the countries in which they operate, and in the global economy.

world system theory
Immanuel Wallerstein's theory that the interconnectedness of the world system began in the 1500s, when Europeans began their economic and political domination of the rest of the world.

Globalization has increased the economic, political, and social interconnectedness of the world. It has also increased some staggering inequalities between the world's rich and its poor.

SOCIOLOGY AND OUR WORLD

PROSTITUTION AND THE WORLD SYSTEM

How can we use world system theory to make sense of global sex trafficking and sex work?

In the world system, it is not only goods and services that flow from periphery to core. People do, too, in the form of slaves, foreign workers, and prostitutes (or sex workers). Interviews with sex workers in dozens of countries around the world reveal that in Japan (core), they tend to come from Korea (semiperiphery) or the Philippines (periphery). In Thailand (semiperiphery), they tend to come from Vietnam or Burma (periphery). In France (core), they tend to come from Turkey or North Africa (semiperiphery). In Germany, they tend to come from Bosnia, Slovenia, or the Czech Republic (semiperiphery). However, in the Czech Republic, they tend to come from Poland, Slovakia, and Hungary (semiperiphery).

Why does a country in the semiperiphery draw sex workers from the semiperiphery? Perhaps the answer lies in relative wealth: The average GDP per capita in the Czech Republic is $23,194, compared to $18,679 in Hungary and $15,800 in Poland. Or perhaps it lies in the mechanics of global "sex tourism", in which people (mostly men) from the core take vacations in periphery or semiperiphery states with the intention of having sex, either with sex workers or with impoverished local "friends" willing to spend the night in exchange for dinner or gifts. Prostitution in the Czech Republic really means Prague, about two hours by train from Dresden and four hours from Munich, a perfect distance for German businessmen to get away for a weekend sex holiday (Kempadoo, Saghera, and Pattanaik 2005).

---

four interrelated elements: (1) a global market of goods and labor; (2) the division of the population into different economic classes, based loosely on the Marxian division of owners and workers; (3) an international system of formal and informal political relations among the most powerful countries, who compete or cooperate with each other to shape the world economy; and (4) the division of countries into three broad economic zones—core, periphery, and semiperiphery.

global commodity chains

Worldwide network of labor and production processes, consisting of all pivotal production activities that form a tightly interlocked "chain" from raw materials to finished product to retail outlet to consumer. The most profitable activities in the commodity chain (engineering, design, advertising) are likely to be done in core countries, while the least profitable activities (mining or growing the raw materials, factory production) are likely to be done in peripheral countries.

World system theory emphasizes **global commodity chains**—worldwide networks of labor and production processes, consisting of all pivotal production activities, that form a tightly interlocked "chain" from raw materials to finished product to retail outlet to consumer (Gereffi and Korzeniewicz 1993; Hopkins and Wallerstein 1996). The most profitable activities in the commodity chain (engineering, design, advertising) are likely to be done in core countries, while the least profitable activities (mining or growing the raw materials, factory production) are likely to be done in peripheral countries. Some low-profit factories (or "sweat-shops") are appearing in core countries, often underground to avoid minimum wage laws; but, paradoxically, they tend to employ mostly immigrants from peripheral countries, who are willing to settle for the poor pay (still better than they would get at home), minimal or nonexistent benefits, and terrible working conditions. World system theory has been criticized for depicting the process as only one way, with goods and services flowing from periphery to core.

Reducing Poverty

7.4.4 Distinguish between "outside" assistance approaches and microcredit approaches to reducing poverty.

When President Johnson declared a "war on poverty" in 1964, he assumed, optimistically, that it was a war that could be won. The ensuing half-century has shown that poverty is a more difficult enemy than anyone originally believed—not because poor people have it so good that they don't want to work to get themselves out of poverty, but because the structural foundations of poverty are so structurally, institutionally, and intersectionally entrenched. A greater proportion of families and children in the United States today live in poverty than in 1973—when the 11.1 percent poverty figure was the lowest ever on record. And poverty rates for blacks and Hispanics greatly exceed the national average. Dramatic structural, demographic, and policy shifts keep the number of poor high but also obscure just how many poor people have struggled to get themselves out of poverty.

Different societies have tried different sorts of strategies to alleviate poverty. Virtually all industrial nations have a **welfare system** that guarantees all citizens the basic structural opportunities to work their way out of poverty: free education, national health care, welfare subsistence, housing allowances. Only the United States does not provide those basic structural requirements, and so poor people spend most of their money on housing, health care, and food. As a result, the United States has the highest percentage of poor people of all industrialized countries.

Efforts to reduce poverty on a global scale have historically relied on "outside" help: the direct aid of wealthier countries, global organizations devoted to the issue, or large-scale philanthropic foundations. The United States spends billions in direct aid to poor nations. And the World Health Organization, the Red Cross and Red Crescent, and other global organizations channel hundreds of billions of dollars to poorer nations. Finally, foundations such as the Ford and Gates Foundations and the Open Society Institute funnel massive amounts of aid to poor nations to improve health care and education and to reduce poverty, disease, and violence. In 2001, the United Nations announced the "Millennium Project"—a global effort to identify the causes of poverty and to eradicate extreme poverty and hunger by 2015. Although the project has seen great gains, extreme poverty and hunger still exist.

This strategy is vital in creating the infrastructure (roads, hospitals, schools) and sustaining agricultural food production (irrigation, seed technologies) that will enable nations to combat poverty. Yet this strategy of direct payments to governments has also received criticism because some of these funds have been terribly misspent by corrupt political regimes, and often little of the money collected actually reaches the poor themselves.

Several newer strategies target local people more directly. In the poorer rural areas of Latin America, the governments of Mexico and Brazil, for example, have embraced "conditional cash transfer schemes" (CCTS) by which the government gives direct payments to poor families of about $50 a month. This may mark the difference between too little food to feed the family and just barely enough. CCTS are "conditional": In return, the beneficiaries must have their children vaccinated and their health monitored and must keep them in school (The Economist 2005c).

In Pakistan, economist Muhammad Yunus has developed a system of **microcredit** by which his bank lends tiny amounts to local poor people. Initially, as a young professor, he loaned a group of women $27 to buy straw to make stools. Over the past 30 years, Grameen Bank has lent $5.72 billion to 6.61 million borrowers—some loans as low as $9—including beggars who wanted to start small businesses or a group of women who needed start-up funds to start a cell phone business or to buy basket-weaving supplies. The bank claims a 98 percent repayment rate (Moore 2006). In 2006, Yunus received the Nobel Peace Prize in recognition of his work to end poverty one person at a time.

Political Resistance to Class Inequality

7.4.5 Understand what it means to say that Americans have less "class consciousness" than people do in other nations.

Marx predicted that as class-based inequality grew more pronounced—as the rich got

welfare system
The basic structural opportunities provided by most countries for people to work their way out of poverty: free education, national health care, welfare subsistence, housing allowances.

microcredit
When a bank lends tiny amounts of money to local poor people.

Microcredit helps individuals pull themselves out of poverty by providing tiny loans—some as little as $9—that enable borrowers to start businesses. Most microcredit participants worldwide are women.

richer and the poor got poorer—eventually the working class would no longer be able to stand the grinding pain of persistent poverty. At that moment, a grand movement of a politically mobilized class would rise up and, being far greater numerically than the rich, they would take over the government and institute a socialist government based on class-equality.

Historically, a mobilized, active, and increasingly radical **labor movement** was celebrated as the vanguard of this class-based social movement that would instill a democratic society (actual rule by the numerical majority). In many countries, that active labor movement became institutionalized in political parties that vie with others for political power. When they get into government (as, for example, the Social Democrats in European countries), they tend to implement policies that benefit the working and middle classes through health care, family supports, and education. Class-based inequality throughout Europe is far lower than it is in the United States and they are much more aware of class inequality than are Americans (having more of what sociologists refer to as **class consciousness**). Nonetheless, those parties are part of the government, and are not interested in toppling it to replace it with some socialist utopia.

The United States has neither a viable political party that represents the interests of the poor and working class nor even a particularly active movement of organized labor (as in unions) outside the political party system. As we will discuss in Chapter 13, unions have been steadily declining in the United States for half a century. Despite the dramatic increase in the gap between the haves and the have-nots, class is a far less significant basis for collective organizing in the United States. Certainly, other foundations of identity and structures of inequality—race, gender, and sexuality, for example—are far more immediate in their claims for our identity. Perhaps it is because Americans experience their class positions not as *social* positions (not, in other words, within a structure of inequality), but rather as an individual "situation" from which we intend to escape. Within this framework, it becomes difficult to organize collectively to oppose class-based inequality.

On the other hand, as we will see in the chapters that follow, class-based inequality rarely exists on its own. Sociologists today speak not of class or race or gender or any other identity as separate and distinct from every other. Rather, sociologists understand how

labor movement
Class-based social movement that would instill a democratic society (actual rule by the numerical majority).

class consciousness
Awareness of social class and class inequality.

Marx's ideas about political resistance to class-based inequality have become plot devices in a great deal of popular media today. The entire Disney movie, *A Bug's Life* is premised on Marx's delineation of classes. The grasshoppers in the film are the bourgeoisie. They extract free labor from the ants in the form of annual crops so that they do not themselves have to work. And, in exchange, they allow ants to live free from their tyranny. The ants (the proletariat) perform this labor unquestioningly for generations, until one ant unites them in the realization that they are much more numerous than the grasshoppers. Acting together, they revolt against them and hierarchies within their own ant society are challenged at the same time—just as Marx theorized.

these different sources of identity and structures of inequality intersect— and through that intersection, become visible to us analytically, as well as a basis for political mobilization.

---

iSOC AND YOU Resistance and Change in Class Inequality

Class is a social construct. It's not inevitable, and class *inequalities* can and do change over time. Therefore, not only is class a basis for *identity*, but class inequality also inspires efforts to reform or resist that inequality. But you can't do it alone. Through your *interactions* with others who are similarly positioned in the class structure of your society, or those whose inequalities *intersect* with your class-based inequality, you can collectively attempt to reduce class inequality, perhaps by reforming social *institutions* to create greater equality or, occasionally, by transforming the very system of class stratification in a society entirely.

Conclusion

Social Class and Stratification NOW

Although to Americans, class is somewhat elusive, it is one of the major features of social life, a near-universal element of society. As a basis of identity, class unites us into communities based on shared symbols, consumption patterns, and languages. And as a feature of social inequality, class divides us into different groups, often separate, and increasingly unequal. As with all the other dimensions of stratification we will discuss in subsequent chapters in more depth—race, gender, age, sexuality—class stratification both unites and divides us. As a nation founded on ideals of mobility—the ability to harness your talents, motivation, and discipline to rise higher in a class hierarchy than your parents did—we tend to experience class identity as a far weaker element of our identity than we do other elements of our backgrounds, such as ethnicity or race. We're aware of class inequality because we believe that an open society should be more permeable, and that we should not be constrained by our class position.

Whether we are looking around the globe or around our neighborhoods, class is a crucial element of social life. Globally, the nations of the world are arrayed hierarchically, from richer to poorer, just as different people in those countries are also organized into class hierarchies. Globally, the gaps between rich and poor seem to be growing, just as it is growing in the United States. Indeed, in the United States, the gap between rich and poor has never been as great as it is today—although in several European countries, the gaps between rich and poor are actually shrinking, as governments step in to redistribute wealth. Can the growing gap between rich and poor—individuals or nations—continue indefinitely? Will something have to give?

Today, class continues to have a remarkable impact on our lives—from the type of education or health care you receive to the type of job you'll have, whom you'll marry, and even how long you'll live and how many children you'll have. The decline in social mobility in the United States makes America increasingly a nation of rich and poor. The gap grows daily. As a result, "being born in the elite in the United States gives you a constellation of privileges that very few people in the world have ever experienced," notes David Levine, an economist who researches social mobility and class in the United States. But, comparatively, "being poor in the U.S. gives you disadvantages unlike anything in Western Europe and Japan and Canada" (cited in Scott and Leonhardt 2005).

Just as class increases in importance and class inequality increases in its impact on our everyday lives and our society, so too do Americans continue to disavow its importance. We may be becoming a nation of rich and poor, but we continue to assert that we're all middle or working class, and that class has little bearing on our lives. Perhaps that Oxford professor from the joke we mentioned at the outset of this chapter was onto something.

CHAPTER REVIEW Social Class and Stratification: Identity and Inequality

7.1 Thinking Sociologically about Social Class and Stratification

Some societies have more obvious class structures, while in others social stratification is less apparent, or, as in the United States, hidden by ideology or beliefs. Nations are globally stratified. Social class is the single-best predictor of the life you will have, as resources, opportunities, and prestige are differentially distributed in ways that are unquestioned or justified. Social mobility is rare. Because social stratification pervades society, sociologists have questioned why it exists and found different answers. Durkheim found that social stratification creates interdependence in complex societies, while Marx's analysis highlighted how social stratification serves the powerful and wealthy at the expense of those at the bottom of the hierarchy. Stratification does provide incentive for achievement in a meritocracy; but, because advancement is rare, stratification mainly justifies the status quo. Historically there have been different social stratification arrangements around the world, including caste systems, feudalism, and, more recently, in industrialized societies, class.

7.1 Key Terms

social stratification Taken from the geological term for layers of rock, or "strata," the ranking of people into defined layers. Social stratification exists in all societies and is based on things like wealth, race, and gender.

social mobility The process of moving between different positions in social hierarchies within society (e.g., from one social class to another).

social reproduction The structures and activities that transmit social inequality from one generation to the next.

social ideologies The ways through which these social stratification arrangements are defined as fair, just, and reasonable.

meritocracy Social system in which the greater the functional importance of the job, the more rewards it brings in salary, perks, power, and prestige.

caste system A fixed and permanent stratification system to which one is assigned at birth.

apartheid A race-based caste system that mandated segregation of different racial groups. In South Africa it was a political system institutionalized by the white minority in 1948 and remained in effect until 1990.

feudalism A fixed and permanent social structure based on mutual obligation, in which peasants worked the estates belonging to a small group of feudal lords, who fed and protected them. A peasant's only avenue to social advancement was to enter a convent or monastery.

class A group of people sharing the same social position in society. Class is based on income, power, and prestige.

class system System of stratification in which people are ranked according to their economic position.

achieved status Status or social position based on one's accomplishments or activities.

ascribed status Status that is assigned to a person and over which he or she has no control.

structural mobility A general upward trend of the entire society. Structural mobility means that the entire society got wealthier, as occurred in post–World War II America.

underemployed People educated and qualified for positions higher than the ones they occupy.

intergenerational mobility Changes in social status between different generations within the same family.

intragenerational mobility Changes in a person's social mobility throughout the course of a lifetime.

7.2 Class Identity and Inequality

Class is a pervasive social force. It forms the foundation of our identities and also conditions our life chances. The kind of life you will have is strongly shaped by your social class. Class also operates on the global level. Just as there are upper-, middle-, and lower-class people, there are upper-, middle-, and lower-class countries. And countries come to have global class identities, as well. These, too, shift and change over time—a tycoon country today might be a pauper country tomorrow, and vice versa—but the hierarchy of rich and poor, weak and strong, high status and low status doesn't seem to go away. Marx analyzed society in terms of production, identifying the inequity and conflict between the class of owners and the class of workers, the bourgeoisie and the proletariat. For Weber, class stratification was not just economic, but composed of dimensions that even today we can observe tend to vary with each other, but don't always go together—social qualities such as prestige, status, occupational prestige, and power. Sociologists today use socioeconomic status (SES) when studying social stratification, which is multidimensional. In the United States, there are at least six socioeconomic statuses, yet we all believe we are middle class, even though the United States has the widest gap between the haves and have-nots of all industrialized nations. Race is a predictor of class here, and globally, as well. Within any society, members of different classes share different cultural experiences, including lifestyles, values, and norms. Bourdieu believed that as people gain more distance from necessity (distance from having to worry about food, water, and shelter for instance), these class cultures develop. Consumption is one of the chief ways in which we both reveal our class position and also try to hide it. For many Americans, consumption indicates the class to which we aspire, not the class to which we belong.

7.2 Key Terms

mode of production The organization of society to produce what people need to survive.

bourgeoisie Popularized by Karl Marx, term for the upper-class capitalists who owned the means of production. In Marx's time, they owned factories instead of farms. Today the term is also used to refer to upper-class managers who wield a lot of power.

proletariat Popularized by Karl Marx, the term for the lower classes who were forced to become wage laborers or go hungry. Today, the term is often used to refer to the working class.

status One's socially defined position in a group; it is often characterized by certain expectations and rights.

power The ability to extract compliance despite resistance or the ability to get others to do what you want them to do, regardless of their own desires.

socioeconomic status (SES) Your social connections, your taste in art, your ascribed and attained statuses, and more. Because there are so many components, sociologists today tend to prefer the concept of socioeconomic status to that of social class, to emphasize that people are ranked through the intermingling of many factors, economic, social, political, cultural, and community.

occupational prestige The degree of status accorded to an occupation.

cultural capital French sociologist Pierre Bourdieu's term for the cultural articles—ideas, artistic expressions, forms of music or literature—that function as resources that people in the dominant class can use to justify their dominance.

habitus French sociologist Pierre Bourdieu's term for the practical mastery of self that arises, in part, out of class location and distance from necessity.

tastes French sociologist Pierre Bourdieu's term for an abstract process through which we all adopt routines, practices, and interests which have their origins in material constraints.

cultural univores Sociologist Richard Peterson's term for people with narrow ranges of tastes.

cultural omnivores Sociologist Richard Peterson's term for people with more cosmopolitan tastes.

7.3 Class Inequality in the United States

Class is one of the fundamental bases of social inequality. Karl Marx divided the world into two simple classes, the rich and the poor. But the sweeping economic and social changes of the past century and the recognition of multiple components to socioeconomic status have pushed sociologists to redefine these class categories and to further delineate others. In the United States, there are at least six socioeconomic statuses, from the upper upper class to the underclass. Still, the United States has the widest gap between the haves and have-nots of all industrialized nations. People of color are significantly more likely to be poor than are other Americans, although there is plenty of poverty among white Americans, particularly in rural parts of the country. There is a gender gap in poverty as well, called "the feminization of poverty." Such gaps are magnified in the global arena. Globally, class and race intersect, and does class and gender. We may believe that wealth or poverty is an attribute of individuals—those who work hard enough and sacrifice enough to get ahead, and those who don't, don't—but, in reality, wealth and poverty are structural features of society. Your relative wealth or poverty depends on who you are more than on how hard you work. Today sociologists know that poverty results from structures of inequality: nationwide and worldwide institutional factors that no one individual has any control over, such as economic changes, globalization, racism, discrimination, and government policies. We also understand that though people living in poverty are not necessarily resigned to their situation, they face structural disadvantages that are nearly impossible for the vast majority of people to overcome. They would like to lift themselves out of poverty and lead better lives, but they suffer from poor nutrition, inadequate education, higher rates of chronic diseases, poor or nonexistent health care, inferior housing, in addition to factors like a greater likelihood of being victimized by crime and a greater likelihood of being labeled criminals.

7.3 Key Terms

life chances A person's abilities to have access to material goods (food and shelter) and social resources (health care, education) that together control the quality of life.

upper upper class The superrich, with annual incomes of more than $1 million. They include the older established wealthy families, born into massive fortunes that their ancestors amassed during the industrial boom of the nineteenth-century Gilded Age.

lower upper class Annual household incomes of more than $150,000 but less than $1 million; they are the "everyday" rich. They tend to have advanced degrees from high-ranking colleges. Though they have substantial investment incomes, they still have to work: They are upper-level CEOs, managers, doctors, and engineers.

upper middle class With household incomes above $80,000 but less than $150,000, they are the high-end professionals and corporate workers. Most have college degrees. Only a small percentage of their income comes from investments.

middle middle class Household incomes between $40,000 and $80,000; these are the "average" American citizens. Most hold white-collar jobs: technicians, salespeople, business owners, educators, etc. Many blue-collar workers and high-demand service personnel, like police, firefighters, and military, have incomes high enough to place them in the middle class. Most have attended college, and many have college degrees.

working class With household income between $20,000 and $40,000. They tend to be blue-collar workers, involved in manufacturing, production, and skilled trades, but also include some low-level white-collar workers and professionals (such as elementary school teachers) and some high-level clerical and service industry workers, especially those in two-income households.

lower class Sometimes called the "working poor"—they have a household income of less than $20,000 per year. They hold unskilled and semiskilled jobs. They are service workers, maintenance workers, clerical workers. They deliver pizzas, wait on customers at retail stores, and clean homes and offices.

underclass About 4 percent of the U.S. population, this group has no income, no connection to the job market, little education, inadequate nutrition, and substandard housing or none at all. They have no possibility of social mobility and little chance of achieving the quality of life that most people would consider minimally acceptable.

"the missing middle" Sociologist Theda Skocpol's term for the gradual disappearance of the middle class as the nation becomes increasingly polarized into rich and poor.

feminization of poverty A worldwide phenomenon that also afflicts U.S. women, this term describes women's overrepresentation among the world's poor and tendency to be in worse economic straits than men in any given nation or population.

poverty line Estimated minimum income required to pay for food, shelter, and clothing. Anyone falling below this income is categorized as poor.

culture of poverty Oscar Lewis's theory that poverty is not a result of individual inadequacies but larger social and cultural factors. Poor children are socialized into believing that they have nothing to strive for, that there is no point in working to improve their conditions. As adults, they are resigned to a life of poverty, and they socialize their children the same way. Therefore poverty is transmitted from one generation to the next.

7.4 Resistance and Change in Class Inequality

Poverty is one of the most significant structural consequences of class inequality. It can be defined as absolute poverty or relative poverty. Global inequality is the systematic differences in wealth and power among countries. These differences among countries coexist alongside differences within countries. Increasingly, the upper classes in different countries are more similar to each other—especially in their patterns of consumption—than they are to the middle classes in their own countries. The world seems to be developing a global class structure. Globalization refers to the increased economic, political, and social interconnectedness of the world. It has also resulted in staggering disparities in the basics that provide quality of life around the world. Social scientists are concerned with global inequality, and study what kinds of social factors work to keep poor countries poor. Different theoretical approaches attempt to explain global inequality, including market theories such as Rostow's modernization theory; state-centered theories; and dependency theories, particularly those focusing on the consequences of colonialism. Sociologists also study the role of multinational corporations, whose factory operations in poor countries help keep rich countries rich and poor countries poor.

Different societies have tried different sorts of strategies to alleviate poverty. Virtually all industrial nations have a welfare system that guarantees all citizens the basic structural opportunities to work their way out of poverty. Only the United States does not provide those basic structural requirements, and so poor people spend most of their money on housing, health care, and food. Modern methods of combating poverty globally focus on local assistance and developing economic independence. Several newer strategies target local people more directly, including conditional cash transfer schemes (CCTS) and microcredit.

7.4 Key Terms

absolute poverty A global problem that afflicts half the world's population, the term for people who are so poor they do not have the ability to sustain their lives and lack the most basic necessities like food and shelter.

relative poverty The ability of people to afford only the basic necessities of life; those who live in relative poverty are unable to maintain an adequate standard of living

global inequality Systematic differences in wealth and power among countries, often involving exploitation of the less powerful by the more powerful countries.

globalization A set of processes leading to the development of patterns of economic, cultural, and social relationships that transcend geographical boundaries; a widening, deepening, and speeding up of worldwide interconnectedness in all aspects of contemporary life.

market theories Theories that stress the wisdom of the capitalist marketplace. They assume that the best possible economic consequences will result if individuals are free to make their own economic decisions, uninhibited by any form of governmental constraint.

modernization theory W. W. Rostow's theory focusing on the conditions necessary for a low-income country to develop economically. Arguing that a nation's poverty is largely the result of the cultural failings of its people, Rostrow believed poor countries could develop economically only if they give up their "backward" way of life and adopt modern Western economic institutions, technologies, and cultural values that emphasize savings and productive investment.

state-centered theories Theories that argue appropriate government policies do not interfere with economic development but that governments play a key role in bringing it about.

dependency theory Theory of poverty that focuses on the unequal relationship between wealthy and poor countries, arguing that poverty is caused by policies and practices by the rich that block economic growth of poor countries and exploit workers.

colonialism A political-economic system under which powerful countries establish, for their own profit, rule over weaker peoples or countries and exploit them for natural resources and cheap labor.

multinational corporations Large, international companies, also called transnational corporations, that manage production and/or deliver services in more than one country at once. Multinational corporations have a powerful influence in the local economies of the countries in which they operate, and in the global economy.

world system theory Immanuel Wallerstein's theory that the interconnectedness of the world system began in the 1500s, when Europeans began their economic and political domination of the rest of the world.

global commodity chains Worldwide network of labor and production processes, consisting of all pivotal production activities that form a tightly interlocked "chain" from raw materials to finished product to retail outlet to consumer. The most profitable activities in the commodity chain (engineering, design, advertising) are likely to be done in core countries, while the least profitable activities (mining or growing the raw materials, factory production) are likely to be done in peripheral countries.

welfare system The basic structural opportunities provided by most countries for people to work their way out of poverty: free education, national health care, welfare subsistence, housing allowances.

microcredit When a bank lends tiny amounts of money to local poor people.

labor movement Class-based social movement that would instill a democratic society (actual rule by the numerical majority).

class consciousness Awareness of social class and class inequality.

SELF-TEST

⟩ CHECK YOUR UNDERSTANDING

1. According to the text, which of the following is true of the United States?

   a. There is no social mobility, as no one changes from the social class into which he or she was born.

   b. There is very little social mobility; relatively few people change social class.

   c. There is a great deal of social mobility.

   d. The United States does not have social classes—everyone is equal.

2. Which of the following systems of stratification is found in the United States?

   a. Caste system

   b. Feudalism

   c. Class system

   d. There is no social stratification in the United States, as everyone is a member of the middle class.

3. Identify Durkheim's view of social stratification and class.

   a. It results from ownership of means of production, which benefits the owners, while those who work for the owners are exploited.

   b. There are many dimensions to social stratification, including power and status, and you can be high on some and low on others.

   c. Stratification integrates society, creating interdependence.

   d. Stratification serves society by rewarding those who make the greatest contribution.

4. Identify Marx's view of social stratification and class.

   a. It results from ownership of means of production, which benefits the owners, while those who work for the owners are exploited.

   b. There are many dimensions to social stratification, including power and status, and you can be high on some and low on others.

   c. Stratification integrates society, creating interdependence.

   d. Stratification serves society by rewarding those who make the greatest contribution.

5. How many social classes have been identified in the United States today, according to the text?

   a. There is only one class—the middle class.

   b. There are no social classes in the United States, as everyone is equal in this country.

   c. There are three.

   d. There are six or more.

6. Of the following, which was identified as being a problem with using the poverty line as an indicator of poverty?

   a. It does not take into account expenses other than food, housing, and shelter, such as medical expenses, child care, and transportation.

   b. It is not corrected for location, and some places have a significantly higher cost of living.

   c. The amount is much too low because the formula counts each of the categories as the same, when some cost much more than others.

   d. All of these are problems with the use of the poverty line as an indicator of poverty identified in the text.

7. Which of the following is not included in the poverty line calculation?

   a. Medical costs

   b. Food

   c. Housing

   d. Clothing

8. Members of which of the following groups are most likely to be poor?

   a. Racial minorities

   b. Ethnic minorities

   c. People living in rural areas

   d. Children

Self-Test Answers: 1. b, 2. c, 3. c, 4. a, 5. d, 6. d, 7. a, 8. d

CHAPTER 8

RACE AND ETHNICITY

Race and ethnicity are often believed to be hard-wired, biological differences. Sociological research helps us understand that racial and ethnic inequality are produced by societies, not by biology. Children have to learn what "race" is and how it organizes their social worlds. And challenging racial and ethnic inequality often demands protest, mass mobilization, and sociologically informed demands for justice.

→ LEARNING OBJECTIVES

In this chapter, using the iSoc framework, you should be able to:

8.1.1 Summarize what sociologists mean when they say that race is a biological fiction with a political function.

8.1.2 Summarize the similarities and differences between race and ethnicity.

8.1.3 Recognize how each of the five elements of the iSoc model can be used to examine race and ethnicity sociologically.

8.1.4 Explain the changing trends in intermarriage and multiracial identities in recent U.S. history.

8.1.5 Explain what it means that sociologists understand the question of who qualifies as a racial "majority" or "minority" member as about much more than the size of different racial and ethnic group populations.

8.2.1 Distinguish among racial prejudice, racial discrimination, and racism relying on "stereotype threat" as an example.

8.2.2 Summarize why sociologists study racism as a systemic, rather than individual, issue.

8.2.3 Identify forms of racial discrimination in social life, and summarize how they work to collectively disadvantage specific racial groups.

8.2.4 Summarize what it means to think about racism "institutionally."

8.2.5 Explain what "color-blind" racism is and how it is different from previous forms of racism.

8.2.6 Understand the historical role that segregation has played in racial inequality in the United States as well as how racial segregation continues to be related to racial inequality today.

8.2.7 Explain how and why we need to think about racial inequality historically to fully understand contemporary forms of racial inequality.

8.2.8 Understand the "matrix of domination" and how this applies to thinking about inequality intersectionally.

8.3.1 Explain how "white people" comprise a historically constructed (and changing) category in U.S. history.

8.3.2 Understand the history of Native Americans in the United States including contemporary struggles and the current resurgence in American Indian identification.

8.3.3 Summarize what the controversy over whether "Hispanic" and "Latino" are racial or ethnic categories indicates about how sociologists study race and ethnicity.

8.3.4 Describe the ways that the history of African Americans' enslavement has shaped their experience in the United States and race relations in the United States more broadly.

8.3.5 Summarize the reasons why the "model minority" stereotype of the Asian American racial and ethnic experience is misleading.

8.3.6 Explain what it means to claim that Muslims and Middle Eastern Americans were "racialized" post September 11th in the United States.

8.3.7 Understand where different people of different ethnicities in the United States came from (and how this has changed) in addition to enduring patterns in ethnic segregation.

8.4.1 Understand what it means (and does not mean) to refer to prejudices as a "self-fulfilling prophecy."

8.4.2 Explain how ethnic diversity within a society is related to "symbolic ethnicity" and rates of genocide and ethnic violence.

8.4.3 Distinguish between "assimilationist" and "pluralist" understandings of ethnic diversity in the United States.

8.4.4 Explain the difference between "multiculturalism" as an ideal and as realized in a society with rich cultural diversity.

8.4.5 Understand the history of movements for racial equality in the United States and their continued significance today.

8.4.6 Recognize the history of opposition to racial inequality in the United States and what role it plays in contemporary racial and ethnic relations today.

Introduction

In his inaugural address, Barack Obama, the nation's 44th president, observed the symbolic milestone his election represented, that "a man whose father less than 60 years ago might not have been served at a local restaurant can now stand before you …" From the segregated South to the Oval Office in the course of a generation is a dramatic shift. Indeed, some claim that this means that the issue of race has all but disappeared. Sociologists are skeptical of this kind of sweeping transformation and have continued to find that race still plays a critical role in organizing social life and inequality.

Obama's election made Michael Kimmel recall my grade school social studies textbook. Race, he learned there, was fixed, permanent, and primordial. There were only three races: "Negroid, Mongoloid, and Caucasoid." Nobody could be a member of any other race, and nobody could belong to more than one race.

To Michael, the most memorable parts of the book chapter were the illustrations. There were three: a black guy in a loincloth, holding a spear, standing in front of a grass hut; an Asian guy in a silk kimono, holding some sort of scroll, standing in front of a pagoda; and a white guy in a business suit, holding a briefcase, standing in front of a skyscraper. They were all men. They were supposed to classify the three races, from *least* to the *most* civilized, technologically sophisticated, inventive, and intelligent. It doesn't take a genius to guess which of the three "races" the illustrator belonged to. In fact, it's never been the case in human history that groups of people attempting to study group hierarchies have not miraculously discovered that the groups they belong to are at "the top" of the hierarchies they create.

But we've come a long way from thinking about race in the way Michael was taught. How do sociologists think about race today?

Sociologists tend not to see fixed, immutable, biologically based characteristics, but the social and cultural ways in which we have come to *see* those characteristics as timeless and universal. Race is less fixed than fluid, less eternal, and more historical. In fact, the concept of race itself is relatively recent, an invention of Europeans in the eighteenth century. Rather than immutable, it is among the parts of our identity that is in greatest flux at the present, as individuals are increasingly biracial or even multiracial. With race, as with other features of social life and identity, believing is seeing: When we believe that there are only a certain number of races, then we will "see" those, and only those, races.

To a sociologist, race is more than a system of classification, a system that categorizes people. It is more than just a basis for our identity. Race is also one of the central bases of social inequality—the unequal distribution of opportunities, rewards, and punishment. Race is among the foremost predictors of your experience in society. Along with class, gender, age, and ethnicity, race is both a foundation of identity and a basis for social inequality—at the individual level, in our society, and around the world.

8.1 Thinking Sociologically about Race and Ethnicity

Just what are race and ethnicity? Although the terms are sometimes used interchangeably, they are based on two different assumptions. Race depends on the assumption of *biological* distinctions; yet sociologists understand it as socially constructed. You can be black or white and live in any country in the world, have any religion, and speak any language. All that matters is your skin color and whatever other physical trait(s) are understood to "count." These distinctions between different groups are more arbitrary than you might think and have been historically relied upon to differentiate and exclude. Similarly, ethnicity defines a *cultural* group, distinct not by biology but by cultural practices and origins. You can belong to any race and have a Swedish ethnicity—if you speak Swedish at home, attend the Swedish Lutheran Church, eat lutefisk (cod soaked in lye and served with bacon fat), and celebrate St. Lucia's Day on December 13 by walking with lit candles on your head, as many young girls still do in Sweden. Though, certainly some groups will have a more challenging time making the claim that they are Swedish than others.

But you might even be Swedish if you do none of these things at all. Few Swedish American students at undergraduate colleges today eat lutefisk or wear crowns of candles! There are likely few, if any, cultural differences between Swedish students and everyone else on campus. In fact, you'd probably never know they are Swedish, except for last names like "Swenson" and a few Swedish flags on dorm room walls. Their Swedish ethnicity resided entirely in how their ancestors might have lived.

Race and ethnicity are among the central elements of your identity. They can be used to predict how—or even *if*—you vote, whom you will marry, how much income and wealth you might earn, and what sort of job you will have when you graduate from college. So, although race and ethnicity are not biological realities, this does not mean that they do not have real consequences and effects. Race and ethnicity can predict your attitudes on birth control, your musical tastes, and whether or not you go to church. Despite repeated, extensive attempts at racial integration, Americans tend to live in segregated neighborhoods, go to segregated churches, make friends almost entirely within their own race or **ethnic group**, and date almost entirely within their own race or ethnic group. (There's an old saying among Protestant clergy that the most segregated time in the United States is every Sunday at 10 o'clock in the morning.)

ethnic group

A group that is set apart from other groups by language and cultural traditions. Ethnic groups share a common ancestry, history, or culture.

In this section, you'll learn how sociologists distinguish between race and ethnicity and why this is sometimes a bit more challenging than you might suspect. We will also explore how sociological understandings of race and ethnicity shape what we are able to know about racial and ethnic identities, interactions, and inequality. To illustrate this, we highlight the ways that sociologists are not only interested in racial and ethnic identities and interactions, but how race and ethnicity become institutionalized in ways that produce understandings of racial and ethnic "minorities" as the "majority." To help make sense of how this framework breaks down, we consider sociological research on people with multiracial identities.

What Is Race?

8.1.1 Summarize what sociologists mean when they say that race is a biological fiction with a political function.

Most cultures divide people into different "types" on the basis of cultural traits—usually "us," the real people, against "them," the cannibals (who eat the "wrong" food), barbarians (who speak the "wrong" language), or infidels (who worship the "wrong" God). But physical appearance was not always part of the equation. Historically, the word *race* meant the same thing as *culture*: The French "race" lived in France and spoke French, and the Russian "race" lived in Russia and spoke Russian. We even refer to the "human race." Not until the eighteenth century, however, did physical attributes become determining factors in "race." In the United States, debates about the morality of "Negro slavery" indicated a concern for skin color that was more important than the different cultures from which slaves were stolen. By the nineteenth century, "race science" tried to give the real people/barbarian division a scientific-sounding gloss, arguing that some "races" were more highly evolved than others. And just as mammals are physiologically different from reptiles and fish, the more highly evolved races differed from the less highly evolved, not only culturally, but physiologically, intellectually, and even morally. What is important to recognize here is that this was done with political, social, and economic goals, such as when "race science" was used to justify the genocide of Native Americans, or slavery.

Today, we use the term *race* to talk about what we think of as *physiological differences* between groups and the term *ethnicity* to refer to *cultural distinctions* between groups. But, neither race nor ethnicity is biological—not in the sense nineteenth-century "race scientists" thought (though their ideas creep into contemporary thinking as well). People of different races are actually far more physiologically similar than different. Genetic makeup, blood type, facial type, skin color, and every other physical attribute vary more within the groups we call races than between them. Neither race nor ethnicity has any basis in biological or genetic fact. In 2000, Craig Venter, one of the lead scientists of the Human Genome Project, which has mapped the human genetic code, concluded that, "the concept of race has no genetic or scientific basis." Race has a *social*, not a biological, origin.

To sociologists, race is socially constructed, not biologically determined. As a socially constructed identity category, **race** refers to a class of individuals who are understood to be differentiated by shared physical characteristics and are believed to share a common genetic ancestry. *Race is a biological fiction with a political function.* Racial categories have been socially invented and "discovered" throughout history as a means of producing hierarchies between "types" of people. Race has always been about more than racial *difference*—from the beginning, distinguishing different races has been a "political" project in that it has been about establishing racial hierarchies ("superior" and "inferior" races). Yet such a perspective remains unpopular; most of us want to believe that race has some "real" foundation in biological facts.

race

Social category, still poorly defined, that depends on an assumption of biological distinction to rate and organize social groups.

Biologically speaking, race isn't "real"—that is, there are no distinct races that are pure and clearly demarcated from others. And there haven't been such things in millennia. Sociologically, however, race is very real. In fact, it is a sociological maxim (first offered by sociologists W. I. Thomas and D. S. Thomas in 1928) that "things that are perceived as real are real in their consequences." Most people believe there are distinct races, with distinct characteristics, and therefore social life is often arranged as though there were. Thus, although people who select "black" or "Asian" when they fill out their race on the U.S. Census will not all share the same genetic material or a common bloodline, it is true that they are likely to share a number of social experiences in common, including the types of places they live, where they shop, political values and beliefs, varying life expectancies, susceptibilities to different types and levels of health concerns, and more.

Our society is organized such that people who occupy distinct racial and ethnic groupings may share a lot in common. That they share experiences and opportunities in common, however, is the result of the organization of our society—not our genes. What race you are impacts what kind of job you may end up having. It might shape whether you are even interviewed or not for jobs to which you apply. Living in a society that treats race as real causes race to have very real impacts on people's life chances, their experiences, and opportunities. Race may be biologically fictitious, but when we invest meaning in racial differences, they have real consequences—they just aren't based on biology.

As hip-hop radio host and digital activist John Randolf (better known by his deejay name, Jay Smooth) put it: "When we grapple with race issues, we're grappling with something that was designed for centuries to make us circumvent our best instincts. It's a dance partner that's designed to trip us up" (Smooth 2011). To sociologists, race is not only an identity; it is a category of identity that powerfully shapes the ways we interact with one another and that has become institutionalized such that it shapes our experiences and opportunities in patterned and unequal ways as well. What this means is that we live in a society organized by race; race is a fundamental component of the ways our lives are organized in the United States and most other societies around the world. And race does more than organize our experiences in society. It is also a system organized by inequality.

What is Ethnicity?

8.1.2 Summarize the similarities and differences between race and ethnicity.

"Race" was initially used to mean something more similar to the ways we might use the term *culture* today (e.g., the German "race"). Today, race has different meanings. But some of the meanings that were once associated with race are today associated with our understanding of "ethnicity." **Ethnicity** refers to a group of people with a shared cultural identity, founded on shared national identity, ancestry, language, religious beliefs, and collections of cultural traditions and practices. There are some similarities and differences between what sociologists call "race" and what they refer to as "ethnicity." But the largest is that ethnicity is something much more fluid in nature—meaning people both classify themselves and are classified by others as a race, but are more likely to "opt in" to various ethnic identities. This means that, in general, ethnicity has a more fluid quality than does race; people's racial identities are more stable over time than are ethnic identities.

Race and ethnicity are related, but the concepts are distinct. In fact, we sometimes use the terms interchangeably, like our penchant to use the terms *black* (a racial category) and *African American* (an ethnic category) as though they mean the same thing. This mix-up occurs because black and African American, as identities, have some overlap—including the perception of shared physiological characteristics like skin

ethnicity

Social category that depends on an assumption of inherent cultural differences to rate and organize social groups.

TABLE 8.1   Distinctions Between Race and Ethnicity

Race	Ethnicity
Singular—you are assumed to only have one	Multiple—you might claim many different backgrounds
Rigid—something we think of as unchanging	Fluid—can change
Compulsory—we are identified in the society in which we live whether we agree with that identification or not (though there is fluidity here as well)	Chosen—we get to select whether or not to identify any origins to which we see ourselves as having a legitimate claim (though not everyone is afforded the "choice")
Physiological—based on perceived biological, physical, or genetic differences	Cultural—based on perceived cultural differences
Ranked—not only about difference, but hierarchy and inequality	Not ranked—need not be ranked

racial ethnicity

An ethnic group believed to also have common psychological characteristics.

color (race) alongside the perception of a common cultural identification (ethnicity). To make sense of this, some sociologists use the concept of **racial ethnicity**, which refers to an ethnic group believed to also have common psychological characteristics. This is why it is common to see sociologists capitalize terms like "White" and "Black"—it's a shorthand way of indicating that we are talking about racial ethnicities rather than only skin color, for example. So, the differences between race and ethnicity are sometimes complicated. But, TABLE 8.1 is a useful way of considering the distinctions between the two.

The United States experienced massive immigration from Southern and Eastern Europe in the first few decades of the twentieth century. Huge numbers of immigrants, many coming from poor peasant backgrounds, came to the United States who were illiterate, impoverished, and from different cultural backgrounds. All of these factors combined made thinking about the process of whether and how they might assimilate to life in the United States an enormous political and social issue. Sociologists use the term **assimilation** to refer to a general process—the decline in cultural distinctions between immigrants and mainstream society. Simply put, assimilation refers to how important an ethnic group feels it is to maintain their ethnic identity. This is related to a similar process—**acculturation**—used to discuss the process of acquiring a new culture and language. Would subsequent generations born to this new wave of European immigrants still identify with their ethnicity? Or, would their ethnicities start to matter to them less over time, as they assimilated into U.S. life?

In general, there are two perspectives regarding this process—the "assimilationist" and the "pluralist" perspectives. Some suggest that assimilation is inevitable. These scholars adopt the **assimilationist perspective**—the idea that as we are around one another for sustained periods of time, ethnic distinctions will gradually erode. They suggest that social factors that might maintain ethnic solidarity will wane over time. So, as residential segregation and occupational specialization decline, and intermarriage, social mobility, and distance in time and generation from the original immigrant group increase, ethnic groups will be less isolated and their ethnic identities will become less important to them (Gordon 1964). Alternatively, other sociologists have pointed out that assimilation is not inevitable. The **pluralist perspective** argues that assimilation is not inevitable and that ethnic identities are not necessarily abandoned as ethnic groups become less isolated. For instance, some sociologists highlighted the fact that many ethnic groups continue to marry others of their ethnic background even after they are many generations removed from immigrating. They also continue to self-identify among their ethnic groups on many surveys (Novak 1973). But, much of this research done on assimilation looked at evidence among white ethnic groups to make claims about how non-white ethnic groups either were (or might be) assimilating. When we consider a process as complex as assimilation intersectionally, race and ethnicity are intertwined such that the same processes do not work in precisely the same ways for ethnic groups not identified as "white" in the United States (Waters 1990).

assimilation

A process of decline in cultural distinctions between immigrants and mainstream society.

acculturation

The process of acquiring a new culture and language.

assimilationist perspective

The idea that as we are around one another for sustained periods of time, ethnic distinctions will gradually erode.

pluralist perspective

This perspective argues that assimilation is not inevitable and that ethnic identities are not necessarily abandoned as ethnic groups become less isolated.

SOCIOLOGY AND OUR WORLD

WHY FILIPINO AMERICANS DON'T IDENTIFY AS ASIAN

The Philippines are part Asia (geographically, anyway); why are young Filipino Americans likely to identify as "Latino"?

When Americans think about "Asians" as a group, Filipino Americans are probably not the first group of people to come to mind. We tend to think of Chinese, Japanese, and Korean populations. You might initially assume that has something to do with the size of the Filipino population in the United States. Perhaps, you might think, there just really aren't that many Filipino people who live in the United States. And maybe that's part of why we don't as readily think of them. But, there are more than 3.5 million Filipino people living in the United States. As a group, Filipinos are the third-largest immigrant group in the United States, trailing only Mexicans and Chinese. But, despite their size, Americans seem to know relatively little about Filipino people and culture. Think about whether you are any different. Can you name a Filipino celebrity or public figure? Can you name a traditional Filipino dish? Do you know anything about Filipino music or culture?

Sociologist Anthony Ocampo found this fascinating and wondered what it meant. To conduct this research, Ocampo interviewed more than 80 Filipino young adults living in Los Angeles, California (in California, Filipinos outnumber every other Asian American group). While he asked about immigration experiences, family, school, and neighborhood dynamics, Ocampo's larger interest was in searching for patterns in how Filipinos carve out a racial identity and space for themselves in a society that struggles to make sense of where Filipinos "belong." In a survey in Los Angeles in 2004, more than 50 percent of respondents identifying as Filipino did not select "Asian" (see figure). But what does this mean? Ocampo wanted to know, if they aren't identifying as Asian, how are they identifying themselves?

In his book, *The Latinos of Asia* (2016), Ocampo discovered that many young Filipino Americans have flexible racial identities. How they racially identify themselves was highly dependent on social and institutional context. Some of them associated being "Asian American" as meaning that they were less culturally assimilated and did not want a racial identity that they felt segregated them from Americans of other racial and ethnic groups. Many of Ocampo's respondents felt they had more in common with Latinos in the United States than they did with "Asian Americans" as a group. Some equated Latino identities with Catholicism and being family-oriented, but even found cultural commonalities beyond these as well. For instance, one of his respondents, Camille (a Filipino) had a Mexican American friend (Alicia) who constantly explained why Camille was "really Mexican." As Alicia put it, "Filipino families are huge just like ours…. Everyone and their mom was there [at family gatherings]. And it wasn't even a special occasion. The moms would shove food down your throat even if you're not hungry. That's just like what Mexican moms do." According to Ocampo, young Filipino Americans are "breaking the rules of race." And they are doing so in patterned ways as they search for racial identities in the United States that feel "right" to them.

What Is Your Racial Background?

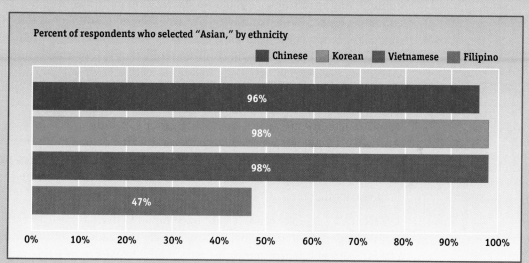

Percent of respondents who selected "Asian," by ethnicity

Chinese   Korean   Vietnamese   Filipino

- Chinese: 96%
- Korean: 98%
- Vietnamese: 98%
- Filipino: 47%

SOURCE: Data from Immigrant and Intergenerational Mobility in Metropolitan Los Angeles Study, 2004.

iSoc: The Sociology of Race and Ethnicity

8.1.3 Recognize how each of the five elements of the iSoc model can be used to examine race and ethnicity sociologically.

As you can better understand at this point, race and ethnicity are less stable than you might have previously thought. And they are simultaneously categories of identity and pervasive mechanisms of social control and inequality. Race and ethnicity simultaneously help us understand who "we" are, and also where "we" fit in the societies in which we live. Racial and ethnic systems of classification and categorization often *feel* natural and inevitable. But part of using the **sociological imagination** is in recognizing that the features and factors that feel intensely relevant to us in terms of understanding who is different from or similar to us are, in important ways, arbitrary. We could just as easily have organized people on the basis of height, whether people's ear lobes are separated or attached, eye color, or some other arbitrary feature of people's bodies. This does not mean that racial and ethnic distinctions are meaningless—but it is a powerful questioning of where that meaning comes from, how it persists, and how different groups benefit and are disadvantaged in the process. Applying the iSoc model to making sense of race and ethnicity helps us to understand just how much a part of our lives and societies race and ethnicity truly are.

IDENTITY—Race and ethnicity are important parts of who we understand ourselves to be. Each shapes how we come to see ourselves from early in our socialization. Sociologists Michael Omi and Howard Winant (1986) understand race and ethnicity as "projects" they refer to as "racial formations." **Racial formations** is a theory that understands race and ethnicity as socially constructed *identities*. This means that both the *content* and *importance* of racial and ethnic categories are determined by the societies in which they exist. Omi and Winant (1986) famously showed how social, economic, and political forces helped to shape the categories of identities themselves as well as their salience in the societies in which they are constructed in the first place.

INEQUALITY—Racial and ethnic *inequality* are simultaneously individual, social, cultural, and institutional problems. As with many forms of social inequality, inequalities based on race and ethnicity are often misunderstood. Racial and ethnic inequality shape your experience in school, where you attend school, the opportunities and constraints you will confront while there. They shape your interactions with others, where you are likely to live, as well as how long you are likely to live. They shape how much education you will likely receive, what kind of job you might eventually acquire, your experiences in the workplace, and more. Racial and ethnic inequality are issues that affect groups of individuals in patterned ways. And when sociologists recognize patterned forms of inequality like this, we are interested in how they might be institutionalized such that societies are organized in ways that work to the continued disadvantage of some and the persistent advantage of others.

INTERACTION—Like class, it's not uncommon to think of race and ethnicity as objective properties of individuals. If you've ever had a tough time figuring out the racial category into which someone fits, you might speak of race this way: "What race (or ethnicity) *are* they?" This understanding of race and ethnicity proceeds from the assumption that race and ethnicity are something that people *have* or *are*. Although some sociological research proceeds from this premise (such as when we ask people to categorize their race or ethnicity on surveys to look at the different experiences of different racial or ethnic groups), we also understand race as a "project" as Omi and Winant (1986) suggested. This means that sociologists are equally interested in

sociological imagination
The ability to see the connection between our individual identities and the social contexts (family, friends, and institutions) in which we find ourselves.

racial formations
A theory that understands race and ethnicity as socially constructed identities. This means that both the *content* and *importance* of racial and ethnic categories are determined by the societies in which they exist.

how race and ethnicity are produced in *interactions*—race and ethnicity as not only properties of self, but performances of self as well. Thus, we are "doing" race and ethnicity throughout our lives. And sociologists are not only interested in examining race and ethnicity as something accomplished in interactions.

INSTITUTIONS—Although sociologists are interested in racial and ethnic *projects*, they are also interested in the ways that social *institutions* shape and encourage some "doings" over others as well as how various "doings" are rewarded and punished in different contexts. To say that race and ethnicity are institutionalized means to recognize the ways that our society is organized around racial and ethnic categories of being. Sociologists studying racial and ethnic inequality are interested in how the experiences of different racial and ethnic groups are powerfully shaped by their interactions with large-scale social institutions, like education, the workplace, the State, and more. This way of understanding racial and ethnic inequality frames them as "systemic," in that they do not always require conscious bias or evil people to be perpetuated.

INTERSECTIONS—The sociology of race and ethnicity is an important field of study. But, sociologists of race and ethnicity today understand that although both are important elements of our identities and powerfully shape our experiences and opportunities, they also need to be understood alongside other identity categories that work alongside race and ethnicity in shaping our lives. What this means is that categories like age, gender, sexuality, class, nationality, citizenship status, and more all *interact* with race and ethnicity in ways that differently shape our experiences of these identities as well as any outcomes we experience associated with them.

Considering race and ethnicity using the iSoc model can help you better appreciate the different ways that both race and ethnicity operate throughout your life. They shape who we understand ourselves to be as well as how others make sense of our identities, actions, and lives. And a great deal of sociological research on race and ethnicity is interested in inequality, marginalization, and structured forms of disadvantage. But sociologists of race and ethnicity also understand that these categories simultaneously provide people and groups with important connections, and a sense of solidarity.

Biracial and Multiracial Identities

8.1.4 Explain the changing trends in intermarriage and multiracial identities in recent U.S. history.

There is no such thing as a "pure" race. Every human group has mixed ancestry, even President Obama, who is literally "African American" (his father was a black African, from Kenya, and his mother was a white American, from Kansas). Even so, interracial romantic relationships have often been considered deviant and forbidden, and research suggests they remain stigmatized today as well (see FIGURE 8.1). Historically, **interracial relationships** were labeled "miscegenation" and punishable by prison sentences in all but nine states until the landmark Supreme Court case in 1967, *Loving v. Virginia*, in which the court ruled that state bans on interracial marriage were unconstitutional. Lawmakers had previously argued that they were against nature and against God's law, that they were an insult to the institution of marriage and a threat to the social fabric (many of the arguments made against same-sex marriage in more recent history in the United States). Children of mixed-race unions were called half-breeds or "mulattos" (black–white) or "mestizos" (white–Indian) and considered morally and intellectually inferior to members of both races.

interracial relationships

Once labeled "miscegenation," a relationship between people of different racial categories.

FIGURE 8.1 Approval of Marriages Between Black and White Americans by Race, 1958–2013
The legal restrictions against intermarriage have been gone for around 50 years, and popular support has shifted considerably. In 1958, 17 percent of white Americans approved of marriages between black and white people, compared with 56 percent of black Americans (Gallup 2013). And although those numbers have shifted significantly since, a racial gap in approval of racial intermarriage remains (specifically regarding Americans' opinions about marriages between black and white Americans): In 2013, 84 percent of white Americans approved of marriages between black and white people, and 96 percent of black Americans approved. So, although a great deal of progress has been made, differences based on race persist.

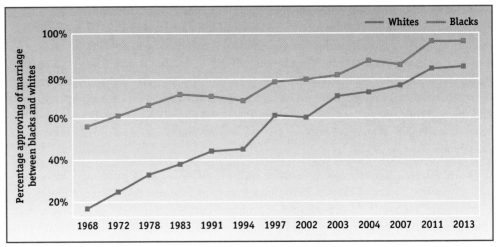

NOTE: From 1968–1978, this question was worded: "… marriages between whites and non-whites." Additionally, the trend for whites here includes Hispanics from 1968–2003; those identified as 'white' here from 2004–2013 are non-Hispanic whites only.

SOURCE: Data from Gallup Survey, 1958–2013. Available at http://www.gallup.com/poll/163697/approve-marriage-blacks-whites.aspx.

It is interesting that just as magazine articles and dire warnings were given to white Americans at the turn of the last century about "race suicide," now some popular magazine articles and films still sidestep interracial romance. In the 2005 hit romantic comedy, *Hitch*, Will Smith plays a professional "date doctor," who helps men learn how to woo and win the women of their dreams. But Smith alleged that in casting the film, producers offered the role to Cuban-American actress Eva Mendes rather than a white actress because a Latina-black relationship was thought to avoid the whole issue of a "real" interracial relationship (Walls 2005). Although interracial relationships have become increasingly common, not all configurations are equally common. For instance, in 2010, roughly 7 percent of married couple households in the United States included spouses of different races (U.S. Census Bureau 2010). And interracial couples are not equally distributed around the United States—regionally, interracial couples are most common in the west and by state, Hawaii (37%), Oklahoma (17%), and Alaska (17%), have the highest proportions of interracial couples.

Interracial marriage rates also vary by racial group. Among newlyweds in 2013, approximately 7 percent of whites, 19 percent of blacks, 28 percent of Asians, and 58 percent of American Indians married someone of another race (Wang 2015). Considering this intersectionally, we should also look at the gender dynamics of these intermarriage rates. For instance, white men's and women's rates of intermarriage for newlyweds in 2013 were the same (7% for both). But more black men (25%) than black women (12%) who married in 2013 married someone of another race while fewer Asian men (16%) than Asian women (37%) married outside their race.

But just because you have parents of two different racial identities does not mean you necessarily identify as "multiracial." In fact, it was not even possible on the U.S. Census until 2000. That was the first time respondents were given the option of selecting more than a single race when filling out the survey. And since then, growing numbers of Americans have begun identifying as multiracial. As of 2010, approximately 2.9 percent of the U.S. population selected more than a single racial category (and while that might not sound like a big percentage, it accounts for approximately 9 million

FIGURE 8.2 Percentage of Racial Groups Reporting Multiple Races, 2010

The two numerically smallest racial groups (American Indian and Alaska Native & Native Hawaiian and Other Pacific Islander) had a large proportion of their racial groups identify as multiracial. Of everyone in the United States claiming Native Hawaiian or a Pacific Islander racial identity, 55.9 percent of them also claimed another racial identity. Compare that with the white population in the United States—only 3.2 percent of people claiming a white racial identity also claim another racial identity.

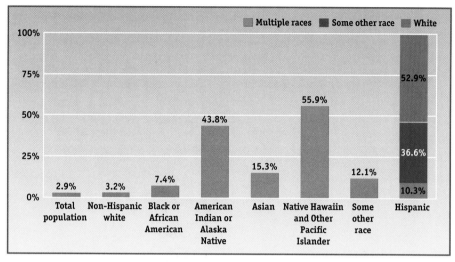

NOTE: Because "Hispanic" is counted as an ethnicity by the Census (and not a race), Hispanic and/or Latino people are not included in the Census tabulations. But, of the approximately 50.5 million Hispanic people identified on the 2010 Census, 5.2 million of them (or 10.3 percent on the figure above) identified as other races of multiple races. They are a significant group of multiracial Americans as well.

SOURCE: Data from U.S. Census Bureau, 2010 *Census Redistricting Data (Public Law 94-171) Summary File*, Table P1. Available at https://www.census.gov/prod/cen2010/briefs/c2010br-13.pdf.

individuals—a number just about the size of the entire population of Sweden). But, as you can see in FIGURE 8.2, everyone is not equally likely to identify as multiracial.

Interracial relationships give rise to new and more complex racial identities. It is still more common for Americans to marry members of their own race than outside of their race. And as intermarriage becomes more common, it is not surprising to hear that multiracial identities are also on the rise (at least since the Census has included questions allowing people to identify as multiracial). Of the approximately 9 million Americans with multiracial identities, more than half of them are younger than age 18 (see the chart). Perhaps *biracial* will become a new ethnicity. In the past, people of mixed races usually just "picked one." One young woman, the daughter of a white mother and a black Cuban father, is Hispanic, white *and* black. "Blacks think I'm black," she says. "Hispanics think I'm Hispanic. Honestly, I don't identify with either bucket." (El Nasser 2010, p. 1). As multiracial identities become more common, how people make sense of them and what kinds of social outcomes are associated with each will be the source of more and new scholarship on the subject.

Minority Groups and "Majority" Groups

8.1.5 Explain what it means that sociologists understand the question of who qualifies as a racial "majority" or "minority" member as about much more than the size of different racial and ethnic group populations.

A racial or ethnic minority group is not defined strictly in terms of its numerical proportion of the population (see FIGURE 8.3). In fact, there are more "minorities" in many places in the United States than the "majority" population. Blacks constitute 71 percent of the population of Allendale County, South Carolina, and 0.3 percent of the population of Blaine County, Montana, but no one would say they are a minority group in only one of those places. And not all groups that are few in numbers are necessarily minorities. There are only 2.8 million people of Swedish ethnicity in the United States (a relatively small number); but according to the most recent Census,

FIGURE 8.3 The Racial and Ethnic Composition of the United States, 1965–2065
As you can see, the racial and ethnic composition of the United States is projected to change fairly dramatically over the course of the next half-century. White people are projected to comprise less than half of the U.S. population by 2042. This has caused some commentators to claim that white people will be the "minority" in this country. Of course, as comedian Hari Kondabolu says of this projection in a stand-up routine, "Forty-nine percent doesn't make you the minority. That's not how math works. Forty-nine percent only makes you the 'minority' if you think the other fifty-one percent are *exactly the same*. The only way that works is if you think it's 'Forty-nine percent white people and fifty-one percent YOU people.' That's the only way that works" (Kondabolu/NPR 2014). This shift results from immigration, but also from the fact that different racial and ethnic groups have different fertility rates. So, those having fewer children will inevitably shrink while groups having more children on average will invariably grow. This shift does not mean that racial inequality will end. But it will probably mean that we'll start to see politicians worrying about the "Asian vote" and the "multiracial vote" in addition to the ways they currently worry about black and Hispanic voters shaping election outcomes.

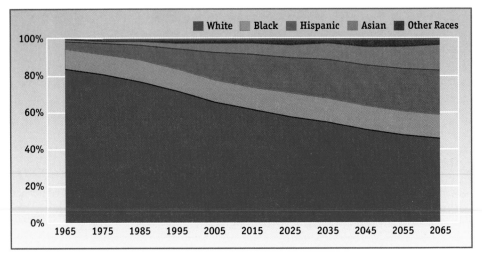

NOTE: Data are here provided in ten-year increments: 1965, 1975, 1985, etc. Data points in between do not necessarily perfectly reflect shifts or projections.

SOURCE: Data from http://www.pewhispanic.org/2015/09/28/appendix-c-population-tables-1965-2065/.

27 percent have graduated from college, 33 percent are in managerial/professional jobs, and their median household income is $42,500, all higher than the national average. Clearly, they are not subjected to significant amounts of discrimination. So, discussing who qualifies as a racial or ethnic "minority" is about more than just numbers.

For a race or ethnic group to be classified as a **minority group**, it needs to have four characteristics:

1. *Differential power.* There must be significant differences in access to economic, social, and political resources. Group members may hold fewer professional jobs and have a higher poverty rate, a lower household income, greater incidence of disease, or a lower life expectancy, all factors that point to lifelong patterns of discrimination and social inequality.
2. *Identifiability.* Minority group members share (or are assumed to share) physical or cultural traits that distinguish them from the dominant group.
3. *Ascribed status.* Membership is non-voluntary—it is something you are born with. Affiliation in many ethnic groups is a matter of choice—you can decide how much of your French heritage, if any, you want to embrace—but you can't wake up one morning and decide to be Japanese.
4. *Solidarity and group awareness.* There must be awareness of membership in a definable category of people, so that there are clearly defined "us" and "them." The minority becomes an **in-group** (Sumner [1906] 2002), and its members tend to distrust or dislike members of the dominant **out-group**. When a group is the object of long-term prejudice and discrimination, feelings of "us versus them" can become intense.

Minority groups and **majority groups** are often constructed in the United States through skin color: dark people versus light people, people "of color" versus people

minority group
A group one is born into, which has a distinguishable identity and whose members have less power and access to resources than other groups in society because of that group membership.

in-group
A group with which you identify and that you feel positively toward, producing a "we" feeling.

out-group
One to which you do not belong and toward which you feel either neutral or hostile; the "they" who are perceived as different from and of lower stature than ourselves.

majority group
A group whose members experience privilege and access to power because of their group membership. With regard to race, lighter-colored skin usually means membership in the majority group.

who are "white." In an interesting linguistic experiment called the Implicit Association Test (see Chapter 5 HOW DO WE KNOW WHAT WE KNOW? How Do We Know We're Socialized to Believe in Racial Inequality?), students were given word association tests, and all of them, regardless of their own race, tended to associate "white" with purity, goodness, and happiness, and "black" with corruption, evil, and sadness (Greenwald, McGhee, and Schwartz 1998; Hofmann et al. 2005). Within racial groups, people who are lighter are privileged over people who are darker (Greenwald and Farnham 2000; Greenwald, McGhee and Schwartz 1998). When the African American sports legend O. J. Simpson was arrested on suspicion of murdering his estranged wife and her companion, he appeared on the cover of *Time* magazine. The photograph was manipulated to make him look considerably darker than he did in real life.

The idea that whiteness is associated with purity, goodness, kindness, and success while blackness is not associated with these qualities is so deeply embedded in our society that it affects everyone, regardless of their race or ethnicity.

Sometimes, people will describe a visit to the "dentist" or the "black dentist." Race is often invisible—to those who are white. Whiteness becomes the standard, the "norm," against which everyone else is measured (like being a man, being heterosexual, or being able-bodied). It's not uncommon for advertisers to offer several versions of a product—the standard, unmarked version, and the "African-American" version or the "Latino" version.

This is why the racial "majority" and "minorities" is about more than just relative proportions of the population. It is also a question of racial and ethnic inequality. Among sociologists studying various forms of social privilege (white privilege, male privilege, heterosexual privilege, etc.), it is a truism that privilege works best when it goes unrecognized—when it remains invisible to those who benefit from its operation.

---

iSOC AND YOU Thinking Sociologically about Race and Ethnicity
Race may be a biological fiction, but it is a sociological reality, with real consequences. Race is, whether you like it or not, a major facet of your *identity*, and a primary social axis of *inequality*. Racial difference and inequality are enacted and reproduced in every *interaction*, and in every social *institution*. And race *intersects* with other aspects of your identity like age, education, class, and more. Race shapes our experiences and opportunities in fundamental ways.

8.2 Racial and Ethnic Inequalities: Interactions and Institutions

Racial and ethnic inequality are pervasive features of social life. And as forms of social inequality, they affect more aspects of our lives than you may realize. They are perpetuated in interactions with others in our society, but they are also institutionalized such that racial and ethnic inequality will be reproduced even absent conscious will or intent. When students initially think about "racism," it is not uncommon to think about collections of people who harbor damaging forms of prejudice and consciously work to perpetuate racial inequality, like the Ku Klux Klan or any number of similar **hate groups**. Sociologists are interested in studying that brand of racism. But we are just as interested in studying racism as an embedded feature of social life; we study the ways that societies are organized around categories of race and ethnicity that systematically work to disadvantage some racial and ethnic groups and privilege others. But this latter form of racial and ethnic inequality is often a new way of thinking about racism for many students. Not only are these forms of inequality more difficult to challenge,

hate groups

Groups with beliefs or practices that attack or malign a class of people often due to immutable characteristics associated with the group (like sexual orientation, skin color, ancestry, gender identity).

they are also more difficult to recognize in the first place. And it is here that sociological research has made important discoveries that can help us better appreciate just how embedded racial and ethnic inequality are as well as how challenging they will be to overcome.

When sociologists study racial and ethnic inequality, they do so with the understanding that racism is best understood as "systemic" in that it shapes not only what stereotypes exist and how prejudice and discrimination are perpetuated by individuals, but also how these forms of inequality become embedded in our social institutions such that they organize all our lives whether we recognize it or not.

In this section, you will learn about how sociologists understand racial and ethnic prejudice and discrimination as well as the ways that they have studied each of these phenomena. To fully understand racial and ethnic inequality today, however, also necessitates putting these systems of inequality into historical perspective. Where racial and ethnic inequality come from, and what role our racial and ethnic histories play in our lives today is equally important. Indeed, as C. Wright Mills explained, honing your sociological imagination requires that you understand the ways that history and biography collide. Some of the ways racial and ethnic inequality were perpetuated in the past are elements of a bygone era. And sociologists recognize this. But we also understand that complex systems of inequality like those based on race and ethnicity shift as they operate in new historical circumstances. And we will also consider some of the ways that racial and ethnic inequality are perpetuated today in new, and often less easily recognizable ways.

Prejudice and Stereotypes

8.2.1 Distinguish among racial prejudice, racial discrimination, and racism relying on "stereotype threat" as an example.

Prejudice is a set of beliefs and attitudes that cause us to negatively "prejudge" people based on their social location. In the classic work on the subject, psychologist Gordon Allport defined prejudice as "a pattern of hostility in interpersonal relations which is directed against an entire group, or against its individual members; it fulfills a specific irrational function for its bearer" (Allport 1954, p. 12). For example, you may decide not to sell your car to an Asian American because you believe they are bad drivers, or you may decline to rent an apartment from a Hispanic owner because you believe the building would be sloppily maintained. **Racism** is an ideology that holds that inequality based on race is justified because of the assumed natural differences between the races. **Discrimination** is a pattern of interactions, a set of behaviors, by which one denies some rewards to some groups based on prejudice. Thus, *prejudice* refers to the attitude that structures our interactions, *racism* to the ideologies that justify those interactions, and *discrimination* to the institutional dynamics at play in determining various outcomes of those interactions.

Often prejudices are based on **stereotypes**—generalizations about a group that are oversimplified and exaggerated and fail to acknowledge individual differences in the group. For instance, if you believe the stereotype that Asians are gifted in science, you will believe that it is true of all Asians, without exception. You will believe that any Asian selected at random will be able to answer scientific questions and will score better on science exams than any person randomly selected from another race. Most likely, however, you will not reason it out in any systematic way; rather, you will just ask an Asian when you have a scientific question or be surprised when you meet an Asian who is an art history major.

prejudice

A set of beliefs and attitudes that cause us to negatively prejudge people based on their social location.

racism

An ideology that holds that inequality based on race is justified because of assumed natural differences between races.

discrimination

A set of actions based on prejudice and stereotypes.

stereotype

Generalization about a group that is oversimplified and exaggerated and that fails to acknowledge individual differences in the group.

For a very long time, racism was taken for granted in U.S. society—so that racist images were casually used in all sorts of places. This ad singing the praises of white paint was made in 1935.

Most stereotypes, like the association of "Asian" and "science" refer to traits that only a small percentage of group members actually possess or that are no more common to group members than to anyone else, so they are simply inaccurate and unfair. Some stereotypes, however, are downright inaccurate: No one (or almost no one) in the group actually possesses the trait.

In the early 1960s, Bull Connor, a sheriff in Alabama, commented that "Blacks are intellectually inferior" and that therefore integration would fail. In the 1980s, Al Campanis, an official with the Los Angeles Dodgers, commented that "Blacks are better athletes." One occasionally hears that blacks are more "naturally" gifted basketball players but that white players are "smarter" or "have a better work ethic." In a content analysis of nearly 24,000 newspaper articles published between 2003 and 2014 addressing race, genetics, and athletics, sociologists Matthew Hughey and Devon Goss (2015), discovered that mainstream journalism continues to advance the notion that black athletic success is the result of genetic traits. Similarly, for years, football quarterbacks were white, on the assumption that you had to be a brilliant tactician, not a powerful athlete, to play the position. There have also been several celebrated cases in which public speakers spoke about these stereotypes, indicating that they believe them to be true, that races and ethnic groups *are* significantly (or biologically) different in their strength, physical power, intelligence, musical ability, or other characteristics. Sometimes these public pronouncements cost them their jobs.

Recently, Brent Staples—an African American columnist for *The New York Times*—described how, as a young graduate student in Chicago, he tried to cope with these stereotypes. When he would walk down the street, looking, as far as he was concerned, like a typical grad student, he noticed that couples would lock their arms or reach for each other's hands when they saw him. Some crossed to the other side of the street, stopped talking, or stared straight ahead. "I tried to be innocuous but didn't know how," he recalled. He was aware that he made white people uneasy when he walked by them. Initially, he said that he took side streets in an attempt to avoid them, so as not to frighten people. Out of nervousness—his nervousness that his mere presence was frightening to them—he took to whistling. And he noticed something: Whistling tunes by the Beatles and especially Vivaldi's "Four Seasons" had an interesting effect. "The tension drained from people's bodies when they heard me. A few even smiled as they passed me in the dark" (Steele 2010). Obviously, a black man whistling baroque music couldn't possibly be a threat. Psychologist Claude Steele uses this as a prime example of the ways that racial stereotypes have measurable effects on peoples' lives. Steele coined the term **stereotype threat** (see Chapter 6 SOCIOLOGY AND OUR WORLD Stereotype Threat and Stereotype Promise) to refer to the variation in performance measured when the belief that people who belong to an identity category you share are worse at a particular task than the comparison group is made salient.

Today, arguments and ideologies associated with racial superiority and inferiority have become more subtle and sophisticated, but no less stereotypic, often with "culture" merely substituted for "biology" as an explanation of the differences. For instance, some suggest that, because of social discrimination, blacks have less stimulating intellectual environments than whites during their formative years, and thus end up with lower levels of intelligence. Others suggest that black parents reward playing basketball instead of cracking books, while the parents of white children reward academic skills—so the black children grow up to be better athletes. This is still stereotyping. No study has demonstrated that black parents regularly discourage their children from getting good grades or that white parents are never obsessed with their children's sports accomplishments. But confronting stereotypes is often more difficult than scientifically disproving them because they didn't require scientific evidence for people to believe them in the first place.

stereotype threat

Term coined by Claude Steele to assess the extent to which labels about people "like us" have measurable impacts on their performances. It refers to the variation in performance measured when the belief that people who belong to an identity category you share are worse at a particular task than the comparison group.

Understanding Racism Sociologically

8.2.2 Summarize why sociologists study racism as a systemic, rather than individual, issue.

Racism describes a set of attitudes, but also implies some institutional framework. This means that when sociologists talk about racism, we are talking about interactions, but we are also interested in examining how social institutions play a key role in structuring interactions in ways that reproduce forms of power and inequality between different racial groups in society. Simply put, racism is prejudice that is systematically (or "institutionally") applied to members of a group. It can be **overt racism**, in speech, manifest in behaviors such as discrimination or a refusal to associate with members of that group. But it can also be **subtle racism**, simply a set of mental categories that we possess about racial "others" based on stereotypes. This means sociologists understand racism in ways that do not require individuals to consciously be aware of how they are promoting racial inequality. Although they study this kind of racism as well, sociologists are more generally concerned with the ways that racial inequality is reproduced in ways that might not feel like they require our active participation.

Racism is a particularly powerful belief system revolving around the idea that members of different racial groups possess different and unequal traits. It involves more than a belief in general stereotypes, but a belief that one race (usually white) is inherently superior to the others. And it is not necessary to belong to the dominant racial group to buy into racism. Race science, with its "evidence" of the superiority

overt racism

Systematic prejudice applied to members of a group in clear, manifest ways, such as speech, discrimination, or a refusal to associate with members of that group.

subtle racism

Systematic prejudice applied to members of a group in quiet or even unconscious ways; a simple set of mental categories that one may possess about a group based on stereotypes.

HOW DO WE KNOW WHAT WE KNOW?

RACE AND INTELLIGENCE

In 1994, Harvard psychologist Richard Herrnstein and public policy analyst Charles Murray resurrected a historical controversy with their book *The Bell Curve: Intelligence and Class Structure in American Life*. They argued that intelligence—measured by the speed with which you learn new skills and adapt to new situations—is the key to social success and that low intelligence is an important root cause of crime, poverty, unemployment, bad parenting, and many other social problems. In other words, intelligent people succeed more often than stupid people. The real controversy came when Herrnstein and Murray presented the results of their research to demonstrate that this essential intelligence is correlated with race: African Americans, on average, scored significantly lower than white Americans on standard intelligence tests. Scientists have known about racial differences on intelligence tests for many years and explain that they are due to cultural bias in the testing instrument or social inequality during the crucial period of primary socialization, rather than to inherent racial differences in the way brains actually process information. But Herrnstein and Murray argue that intelligence is 40–80% inherited, based on genetics. And they claimed to have proven that white Americans are inherently, indeed genetically smarter than black Americans.

Now people got angry. Murray was labeled "America's most dangerous conservative" by the *New York Times Magazine*. (Herrnstein died in 1994.) When conservative columnist Andrew Sullivan published an excerpt in the magazine *The New Republic*, the entire editorial board vehemently protested. When *The Bell Curve* was assigned in college classrooms, some students refused to read it, and some complained of racism to deans and college administrators.

But the most important objection to *The Bell Curve* is that it was just bad science. In *Inequality by Design: Cracking the Bell Curve Myth*, sociologists Claude Fischer and Mike Hout and their colleagues documented the methodological flaws in Herrnstein and Murray's research: Neither "intelligence" nor "race" is a purely biological phenomenon, so their correlation cannot be purely biological either (Fischer et al. 1996). Plus, as we saw in the methodology chapter, demonstrating correlation between two variables cannot tell you the direction or cause of the relationship.

Among other failings, Herrnstein and Murray failed to account for the impact of institutional racism—the structures of discrimination that have nothing to do with individual abilities. Social structures set "the rule of the game" whereby individual differences come to matter. If you have high intelligence but no access to the elite education necessary for social prestige, you might learn the skills of drug dealing or adapt to the new situation of a federal penitentiary rather than going for a Berkeley PhD. On the other hand, if you have low intelligence but the right social connections, you just might inherit the family fortune.

of white people, was quite common 50–60 years ago and still pops up from time to time in academic or popular discussions (along with its opposite, "evidence" of the superiority of black people). But scientific racism has been thoroughly discredited.

We still hear racist sentiments from time to time. For instance, talk radio star Don Imus lost his job in 2007 after referring to the Rutgers women's basketball team as "nappy-headed hos" during the NCAA Women's Basketball Championship in his commentary on a match they played against the University of Tennessee (a team dominated by white women athletes that year). It's a comment that can and should also be understood intersectionally because it was also a group of women athletes who were being evaluated not on the basis of athletic performance but on the basis of appearance (this is an issue we will return to in Chapter 9 on Gender). Although many people defended Imus from claims that he was racist, sociologists understand that his actions can certainly be understood as promoting racial inequality (regardless of whether or not Imus personally identifies as a racist or not). This is why the distinction between "overt" and "subtle" racism is important: Systems of inequality that survive over long periods of time are so challenging to oppose primarily because they are perpetuated in different kinds of ways and exhibit a flexible quality that allows them to adapt to new circumstances in unpredictable ways.

Shock jock radio host, Don Imus, made national headlines in 2007 when reporting on a college women's basketball game. Imus referred to Rutgers' women's basketball team as "nappy headed hos" as he compared their primarily black team roster with the primarily white team roster of the opposing team.

Racial Discrimination

8.2.3 Identify forms of racial discrimination in social life, and summarize how they work to collectively disadvantage specific racial groups.

Discrimination is a set of actions based on prejudice and stereotypes. Discrimination is often studied as a process that negatively affects the group in question. But in practice, discrimination can help as well. For instance, if I believe that Asians are academically gifted, I may ask Asian students more questions in class, assign them more difficult projects or grade their papers more leniently, giving them the "benefit of the doubt." But I may also be especially aware of an Asian student who is disruptive in class. Indeed, this is part of what led Jennifer Lee and Min Zhou to study this phenomenon, something she calls **stereotype promise** (see Chapter 6 SOCIOLOGY AND OUR WORLD Stereotype Threat and Stereotype Promise).

Some acts of discrimination are responses to specific stereotypes. But more often, discrimination occurs as general negative treatment. A waiter or waitress may exercise discrimination against minority customers by waiting on nonminority customers first, rushing them out when they have finished eating, or behaving in an unfriendly or hostile manner. Of course, the victims never know for sure if they are facing discrimination or just bad service. Minority students who get low grades on tests might suspect that the professor is discriminating, but they will never know for sure unless they do some detective work and uncover a pattern of low grades for minority students.

Prejudice and discrimination are not always causally connected. I can be prejudiced but not discriminate—if, for example, none of my friends is discriminating and I don't want to appear different or do something socially unacceptable. Or I can also discriminate without being prejudiced—if all of my friends are discriminating, and I believe that it is "the thing to do" or participate just to go along with what others are doing. Sociological research has shown that many of the perpetrators of hate crimes are no more prejudiced than those who do not commit hate crimes: They are just "going along for the ride" (Boyd, Berk, and Hamner 1996; Craig and Waldo 1996; Morsch 1991).

stereotype promise

Term coined by Jennifer Lee and Min Zhou to address the "promise" of being viewed through the lens of a positive stereotype that leads one to perform in ways that confirms the positive stereotype (the counterpart to "stereotype threat").

SOCIOLOGY AND OUR WORLD

PERCEPTIONS OF PREJUDICE VARY BY ... RACE!

What does it mean to suggest that all of us are affected by racial and racist biases?

How large a role does prejudice play in contemporary U.S. life? Well, it depends on what race you are. According to a 2015 Pew survey, 73 percent of blacks and 44 percent of whites think that racism is still a big problem in the United States, and four and a half times as many whites as blacks thought that we have made necessary changes to give blacks equal rights with whites (Pew Research Center 2015). In another survey, 72 percent of whites thought that blacks overestimated the amount of discrimination they faced, and 82 percent of blacks thought that whites underestimated the among of discrimination that blacks experience (Blow 2009).

Who's right? They both are—but for different reasons and with different consequences. Whites are right that overt discrimination has decreased with the passage of new laws protecting racial minorities. But black people are also right that white people simply don't see everyday discrimination. Project Implicit, a joint research project at Harvard, the University of Virginia and University of Washington, developed a test that measured unconscious and "implicit" bias. Their survey found that, unconsciously, most white people (three-fourths in the survey) have an implicit pro-white/anti-black bias. (Black people, by contrast, split evenly between those who showed a pro-black bias and those who showed a pro-white bias. And black people were the most likely of all races to show no biases at all.)

Can such biases be eliminated? Yes. But research suggests it will take a lot of work. One recent survey found that whites found it "emotionally draining" to work so hard to appear unprejudiced. Many white people avoid all discussion of race entirely so they won't appear prejudiced. This tactic, however, may have backfired because blacks perceived those whites who worked the hardest to avoid talking about race to be the most prejudiced! This also means that white people may be working against a complete understanding of racial inequality because to even address it or learn about it seems to make many white people feel as though they are putting themselves at risk of being seen as perpetuating racism.

(Test your own racial biases at: https://implicit.harvard.edu/implicit/demo/takeatest.html.)

---

sentencing discrimination

Black defendants receive harsher sentences from judges and juries, on average, when compared with white defendants on trial for the same crimes (even when we account for prior offenses and other issues that affect both conviction rates and other decisions regarding sentencing).

Consider one form of discrimination that a variety of social scientific research has documented, but has been stubbornly persistent despite incredible attempts to remedy the problem: **sentencing discrimination**. Black defendants receive harsher sentences from judges and juries, on average, when compared with white defendants on trial for the same crimes (even when we account for prior offenses and other issues that affect both conviction rates and other decisions regarding sentencing). We know this form of discrimination exists; it is well documented and judges are aware of it as well. But, it is also a form of discrimination that exists in the aggregate. For instance, if I'm a judge, and a black man is convicted for committing a crime, it is hard to assess whether the man's race is playing a role in the sentence he receives. But when we add all these cases up, judges and juries discriminate in patterned ways—they punish black defendants with harsher penalties (higher fines, longer prison and jail sentences, and more). Sometimes discrimination is the result of conscious bigotry, but sociologists are equally interested in institutionalized forms of discrimination that do not necessitate deliberate acts on the part of individuals actively acting on various prejudices they harbor.

Institutional Racism

institutional racism

The most subtle and pervasive type of discrimination, it is deeply embedded in such institutions as the educational system, the business world, health care, criminal justice, and the mass media. These social institutions promote discriminatory practices and traditions that have such a long history they just "seem to make sense," and minority groups become the victims of systematic oppression, even when only a few people, or none at all, are deliberately trying to discriminate.

8.2.4 Summarize what it means to think about racism "institutionally."

Racial and ethnic inequality is fueled by stereotypic attitudes, which solidify into an ideology supporting inequality (racism) premised on supposed differences between groups. These differences then become the bases for institutional inequalities—the ways that inequalities are solidified in various social institutions like law, health, workplaces, education, the economy and so on. Attitudes become ideologies which become institutionalized practices, which then reinforce the very stereotypes from which they emerge. **Institutional racism** is the most subtle and pervasive form of racial discrimination, deeply embedded in social institutions like the educational system, the business world, health care, criminal justice, and the mass media. These social institutions promote discriminatory practices and traditions that have such a long history they just "seem to make sense," and minority groups become the victims of systemic oppression, even when only a few people, or none at all, are deliberately trying to discriminate. If unchecked, institutional racism undermines the idea of a society based on individual achievement, merit, and hard work. Democracies must institute laws that prevent it and provide remedies when it happens. But institutionalized forms of inequality are also incredibly difficult to challenge meaningfully.

Think, for example, about where you live. Screening out black applicants for an apartment or house is illegal in the United States. I may be free to behave in a hostile or impolite fashion toward anyone I choose, but I may not deny members of certain minority groups equal access to housing, jobs, public services, and selected social rewards. The Fair Housing Act of 1968 banned discrimination in housing. Nevertheless, unequal access to housing has continued in spite of legislation. African Americans and Latinos are turned down for home loans twice as often as whites with the same qualifications. The HUD Housing Discrimination Against Racial and Ethnic Minorities 2012 Study found that minority renters are told about and shown fewer housing units (homes and apartments) than equally qualified whites. Black renters are told about 11.4 percent fewer housing units compared to whites, Hispanic renters are told about 12.5 percent fewer housing units than whites, and Asian renters are told about 9.8 percent fewer housing units than whites. Minority renters were also less likely to be offered a unit for inspection, and were quoted higher rents. The discrimination rates and types varied from city to city. For example, in Chicago, required payments at move-in are $200 greater for black tenants than white tenants, whereas no difference was found in Atlanta. In Miami and Dallas, white renters are less likely than Hispanic renters to be told that a background check is required, but this is not the case in New York.

A separate consequence of institutional forms of racial discrimination is the dramatic under-representation of minorities in the professions. Slightly more than 4 percent of all corporate board members in *Fortune 100* companies are Latino, and 9.2 percent are black (Alliance for Board Diversity Census 2013). In 2015–2016, only 6.3 percent of all medical school students enrolled in the United States were black and another 5 percent were Latino, and 0.2 percent were Native American, whereas 54 percent were white and 20.5 percent were Asian American (Association of American Medical Colleges 2016).

Institutionally based inequality leads to growing gaps between whites and minorities—gaps widen, rather than shrink, over time. Because whites make more than blacks, are more likely to be in the professions, and more likely to own their own homes, the gap between them has continued to widen, dramatically at times, especially fueled by the housing bubble. Between 1984 and 2007, the **racial wealth gap**—based on total financial assets including home equity—increased by $75,000, from $20,000 to $95,000 (see FIGURE 8.4).

This **racial income gap** holds true for both middle-income and high-income groups, although the gap between high-income whites and blacks is astonishingly high; middle-income whites have far more wealth than high-income blacks. And it is important to look at the *wealth* gap (rather than the *income* gap alone) because it helps us better capture the effects of institutional racism and how a history of racial discrimination and inequality piles up (see FIGURE 8.5).

Although the racial income gap is wide in the United States, the racial wealth gap is even wider. Part of the reason for this is that the wealth gap is wider among the middle

racial wealth gap

Gap in wealth—based on total financial assets including home equity—between blacks and whites. Because whites make more than blacks, are more likely to be in the professions, and more likely to own their own homes, the gap between them has continued to widen.

racial income gap

The gap in income between blacks and whites. The gap between high-income whites and blacks is astonishingly high, and because of the racial income gap over time, even middle-income whites have far more wealth than high-income blacks.

FIGURE 8.4 Racial Wealth Gap Between Black, Hispanic, and White Americans, 1983–2013

The racial wealth gap between white Americans and black and Hispanic Americans has remained consistently wide over the last three to four decades. As of 2013, the median net worth of white family households was almost 10 times higher than Hispanic family households and more than 12 times higher than black family households.

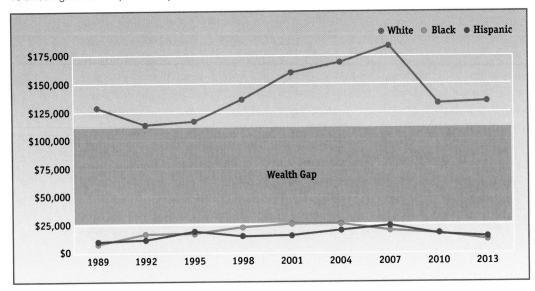

NOTE: Levels net worth are expressed in 2013 dollars.

SOURCE: Data from https://www.federalreserve.gov/econresdata/feds/2015/files/2015076pap.pdf (pages 42–43 – Table 1, Panel b: Medians).

and upper-classes among white and Asian Americans than it is for other groups. So, while middle and upper-class black Americans earn different amount of income each year, the differences between how much wealth they have accumulated are much smaller than the differences between the amounts of wealth middle- and upper-class white Americans have accumulated.

FIGURE 8.5 Median Household Income by Race/Ethnicity, 1967–2016

Although the median income of all U.S. households was between $56,000 and $57,000, you can see that the same figure is different for different racial groups in the United States. By 2015, Asian households had a median income of more than $77,000, non-Hispanic whites earned more than $62,000. But Hispanic and black households in the United States were significantly below the median income for all Americans at $45,148 and $36,898, respectively.

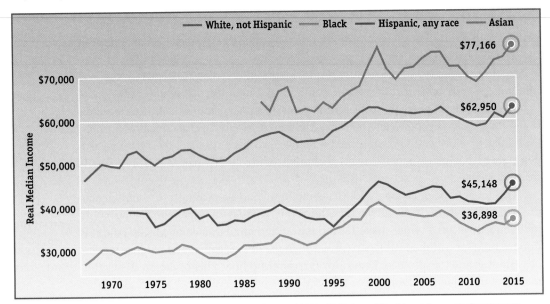

SOURCE: Data from U.S. Census Bureau, Current population Survey, 1968 to 2016 Annual Social and Economic Supplements. Available at https://www.census.gov/library/publications/2016/demo/p60-256.html.

Color-Blind Racism

8.2.5 Explain what "color-blind" racism is and how it is different from previous forms of racism.

One important distinction to remember when it comes to thinking about racism *individually* versus *institutionally* is that, although we think of individuals as discriminating intentionally (though, as sociologists have found, this is not always the case), it makes little sense to think of institutions that way. Rather, institutions discriminate based on race as they rely on policies and practices that put certain racial and ethnic groups at a patterned form of disadvantage (one that tends to accumulate over time). The challenge in understanding racism and racial inequality from a sociological perspective is that it often exists in circumstances that might not initially seem like they would perpetuate racial inequality.

Sociologists have used a variety of different methods to attempt to assess the prevalence of racial inequality in the United States today. In 2008, for the first time in U.S. history, we elected a president who identifies as African American (though, as we discussed previously, President Obama's racial identity is more complex than this). Racial segregation and discrimination are illegal and both reproduce (and are simultaneously produced by) institutional racism more generally. In the post-Civil Rights era, cases of racial discrimination are held to the standard of "strict scrutiny" by the Supreme Court of the United States—a standard which holds that it is never legal to discriminate against people of different races. For comparison, gender discrimination is still only held to a standard of "intermediate scrutiny," meaning that it is legal to discriminate based on gender (under some circumstances). This has led some to suggest that racial prejudice, discrimination, and inequality are elements of a bygone era. Indeed, a superficial analysis of survey data might bear this out. Over the past half-century, Americans have become much more likely to support racial intermarriage, racially integrated schools, and to oppose racially segregated neighborhoods for white people. Yet, surveys also show that white Americans still think about racial inequality in problematic ways.

Sociologist Eduardo Bonilla-Silva (2003) refers to this new form of racism as **color-blind racism**—the process of disregarding race as a method attempting to realize or express equality that has the unintended consequence of reproducing racial inequality in new ways. In fact, alongside the racially progressive views on surveys on the issues mentioned previously, white Americans (as a group) support a set of beliefs that are at odds with racial equality. For instance, when asked about the persistence of racial inequality, roughly 65 percent of whites explained income, housing, and employment inequality as the result of a lack of motivation among black Americans on the General Social Survey in 1977; in 2016, that proportion only dropped to 42.8 percent. It is still true today that white Americans are much more likely to support the statement that many white minorities (Irish, Italian, Jewish) worked their way up in the United States, and that "Blacks should do the same without any special favors." Approximately two-thirds of white Americans supported this statement in 2016. But these survey data seem to be dramatically at odds with those mentioned in the previous paragraph. So, which is it? Are we a racist society or a "post-racial" society?

Sociologists who have sought to disentangle these seemingly contradictory data have done so, primarily using either qualitative research methods or experimental research designs.

Although resume audit studies illustrate that racial inequality can be perpetuated in the labor market even in ways of which we are not entirely aware, what about life outside of work? Another method sociologists have used to study racial

color-blind racism

The process of disregarding race as a method attempting to realize or express equality, it has the unintended consequence of reproducing racial inequality in new ways.

HOW DO WE KNOW WHAT WE KNOW?

DO EMPLOYERS DISCRIMINATE BASED ON RACE?

Employment discrimination is an important source of continued inequality. And it illustrates how inequality can become institutionalized and perpetuated even when we are not necessarily aware of this process while it's going on. The research on employment discrimination is a great example of color-blind racism because it does not necessitate evil individuals, intentionally attempting to promote racial inequality. Rather, implicit biases and prejudices, in the aggregate tell the story of very different job market experiences for white and black people searching for employment in the United States (something we'll also read more about in Chapter 14 on the workplace).

Some of the most fascinating research done on racial employment discrimination has been *experimental*—meaning that sociologists have attempted to run experiments in the social world (a challenging feat by any definition, as we learned in Chapter 4). Resume audit experiments are performed when sociologists submit fictitious resumes to real job listings to see which resumes are contacted and which are not. What this allows sociologists to do is to vary different elements of a resume to test whether there are patterned differences in how employers respond to them—whether any of those fictitious applicants get invited to interview, have their references checked, or offered a position. Beyond that, we can assess whether employers respond in patterned ways to identity-based differences on applications. The classic experiment in this vein is a study by Marianne Bertrand and Sendhil Mullainathan (2004) attempting to assess racial discrimination in the labor market.

Bertrand and Mullainathan sent roughly 5,000 fictitious resumes to slightly more than 1,300 employment advertisements in Boston and Chicago. They also restricted the jobs to which they submitted just a few types of positions to collect a large sample within each of those types. Finally, they varied the fake resumes by quality (some had more experience, education, and expertise than others), gender, and race. And the way they varied the "race" and "gender" of the applications was interesting—they did it by selecting white-sounding and African American-sounding names. Indeed, the title of the paper they published with their results is: "Are Emily and Greg More Employable Than Lakisha and Jamal?" They wanted to find out, in other words, what the effects of race and gender are on the odds of receiving a favorable response when you submit an application for a job.

In Bertrand and Mullainathan's experiment, they discovered that applications coded as "white" with "white-sounding" names received approximately 50 percent more callbacks than applications with "African American-sounding" names, even when controlling for the quality of the application in other respects. Employers did not seem to infer class from applications; but they did discover that resumes with white- and black-sounding names are not treated equally by employers. Whether employers were consciously discriminating against black applicants was not the point of the study. This research showed that they are discriminating whether they are aware of this or not. A separate study, conducted by sociologist Devah Pager (2003), sought to look at the impact that criminal background has on this process as well. She discovered that the stigma of past incarceration does not affect white and black applicants equivalently either. We will discuss Pager's finding in more depth in Chapter 14 on the workplace. This is powerful evidence that labor market discrimination continues to be a serious problem, even if we aren't necessarily aware of every instance that might qualify.

inequality in an era sometimes classified as "post-racial" or "post-racist" is to analyze the ways that people and groups talk about race. One of the most famous studies in this vein is an examination of interviews with white people talking about race, prejudice, and racial inequality in the United States. In his book, *Racism without Racists* (2003), Sociologist Eduardo Bonilla-Silva analyzes long in-depth interviews with white Americans talking about race and racial inequality. Bonilla-Silva identified a set of patterned strategies upon which white people rely that work to perpetuate racial inequality while not necessarily appearing to be openly "racist." What he discovered is that white people rely on a small collection of strategies when discussing race and racism that downplay the enduring role that race plays in structuring social life—what Bonilla-Silva refers to as the "central frames of color-blind racism."

- **Abstract Liberalism**—This tactic involves relying on ideals associated with political and economic liberalism (like "equal opportunity," choice, and individualism) in an *abstract* manner when discussing issues related to race relations. So, whites might employ this tactic when discussing affirmative action if they said things like, "I'm opposed to affirmative action because I'm all for equal opportunity; and that's not fair." It's sounds race-blind. But this only makes sense if we ignore centuries of racism. Similarly, whites often employ ideals like "individualism" and "choice" when talking about segregated neighborhoods and schools. When disconnected from racial realities in the United States, these ideals sound reasonable and as having little to do with race at all.
- **Naturalization**—This strategy is relied on by whites to rationalize racial issues by proposing that they are the result of *natural* differences or *natural* inclinations of people. So, racial segregation (whether between neighborhoods, in workplaces, or even in school cafeterias) can be justified within this framework by explaining that people "naturally gravitate toward people like themselves." This strategy allows whites to avoid discussing racial inequality by simply suggesting (using different language) that different racial and ethnic groups naturally (perhaps even biologically) tend to have different qualities and prefer to be around one another rather than in mixed-race settings.
- **Cultural Racism**—This tactic is similar to "naturalization," but rather than putting the emphasis on nature to explain racial differences, the focus is on culture. Similarly, cultural racism is relied on to suggest that there are natural differences between groups (just that they reside in culture rather than nature). White people are relying on this strategy when they explain, for instance, racial gaps in education by saying something like, "Mexicans just don't value education as much" or when they talk about racial differences in family formation practices by suggesting, "Black people just have too many babies too early."
- **Minimization**—This final strategy refers to the ways that white people suggest that race is no longer the most important factor in determining racial minorities' lives and life chances. Bonilla-Silva discovered that it was common for white people to minimize racial inequality by suggesting things like "Well, it's better now than it used to be" or "There are some racists left; but *most* people aren't racist anymore." This tactic enables white people to accept extreme examples of contemporary racial inequality while simultaneously suggesting that racial minorities are being "too sensitive," or "using race as an excuse."

A great deal of research since Bonilla-Silva's (2003) publication has continued to find similar findings that allows Americans to feel as though racial inequality is (or is close) to being "a thing of the past," while simultaneously excusing and perpetuating it in new ways. This is what sociologists refer to as "color-blind racism," and it is the topic of a great deal of important research.

Racial Segregation

8.2.6 Understand the historical role that segregation has played in racial inequality in the United States as well as how racial segregation continues to be related to racial inequality today.

One of the more dramatic forms of institutional racism and discrimination is when it is enshrined in law. For many years in the United States, physical separation between the white majority and the minority groups (especially African Americans), or segregation, was law. Discrimination means unequal treatment, and in the 1896 *Plessy v. Ferguson* decision, the Supreme Court ruled that "separate but equal" accommodations for blacks and whites were *not* discriminatory.

Racial segregation was so pervasive that races didn't only have separate schools, sections on public transportation and at movie theaters, and water fountains; there were also all manner of spaces and places in society reserved for "Whites only."

residential segregation
Institutional discrimination of housing created neighborhoods, usually with lower quality infrastructure, for whites and other race and ethnic groups.

In fact, they were necessary to cater to the different needs of the races and ensure racial harmony. There were separate neighborhoods, separate businesses, separate sections on buses and in restaurants and movie theatres, separate schools and colleges, even separate washrooms and drinking fountains. In mainstream (that is, white) movies, blacks appeared only as servants and entertainers, but in their own "separate but equal" movies, they played rugged action heroes, mystery sleuths, romantic leads, every imaginable role.

Usually, however, the "separate" meant "inferior." Black schools received only a fraction of the resources of white schools. The black section of the bus was at the back. The black section of the restaurant was in the kitchen.

In the case of the system of apartheid, that inferiority was institutionalized and legal. Apartheid means "separation" (think: apart-ness), and it was a system that mandated segregation of different racial groups. In South Africa, apartheid was a political system institutionalized by the white minority in 1948, and all social life was determined by whether you were one of three races, later expanded to four: white, black, "coloured" (mixed race), or Indian (South and East Asian) (as you read about in Chapter 7). There were separate schools, restaurants, hospitals, churches, drinking fountains—and even separate buses and bus stops.

In the United States, in 1954, the Supreme Court heard the *Brown v. the Board of Education* case and reversed its decision, concluding that "separate but equal" was never equal. So segregation was replaced by legal integration, physical intermingling of the races, which presumably would lead to cultural intermingling and racial equality. Sixty years later, integration has not been entirely achieved. We have integrated washrooms and drinking fountains in the United States, but most people, especially poor blacks and rich whites, continue to live in same-race neighborhoods and attend same-race schools. Segregation continues to separate poor people of color from education and job opportunities and isolate them from successful role models, helping to create a permanent minority underclass (Massey and Denton 1993). Indeed, **residential segregation** remains one of the primary means through which racial inequality is institutionalized and perpetuated. (You can look up racial residential segregation in your hometown online or different cities around the United States at The Racial Dot Map from the University of Virginia, Weldon Cooper Center for Public Service, Demographics Research Groups to explore residential segregation: http://demographics.coopercenter.org/racial-dot-map/).

Visualizing racial segregation in this way is important, because it illustrates an important reality about race relations in the United States today. Not only does residential segregation paint a picture of historical relations of power and inequality between different racial and ethnic groups in this country, but it is a powerful way of looking at the ways that racial inequality endures today. It probably won't surprise many readers to learn that the schools, shopping malls, parks and recreational facilities, and more tend to be higher quality in white neighborhoods when compared with neighborhoods dominated by black, Hispanic, or Asian households. By 2042, white people in the United States will comprise less than half of the population. Yet, the endurance of racial segregation is one way that racial inequality may remain intact through that transition. It is testament to the ways that sociologists think about racial "minorities" and the racial "majority" is about more than just numbers—we draw these distinctions along the lines of power and inequality as well.

SOCIOLOGY AND OUR WORLD

IS LIVING ON THE "WRONG SIDE OF THE TRACKS" A SOCIAL REALITY?

What role does physical infrastructure play in residential segregation?

Like many sayings, living on "the other side of the tracks" was originally quite literal. Different groups were segregated by physical barriers, like railroad tracks. In fact, in U.S. history, it wasn't all that uncommon for black neighborhoods and white neighborhoods to be separated by railroad tracks, turning tracks into permeable, but

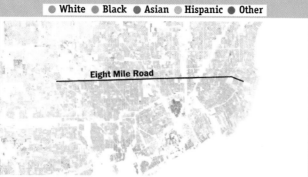

● White ● Black ● Asian ● Hispanic ● Other

Eight Mile Road

Mile Road (made nationally famous in the movie *Eight Mile*—a semi-biographical history of rapper Eminem's struggles and rise to fame in Detroit).

Or look up Shreveport, Louisiana to see how the I-49 divides the city, or how railroads racially divide Hartford, Connecticut; or the way that Delmar

real boundaries in society. And in many cities around the United States, these divisions persist to this day. They are the result of decades of policies that discriminated against different racial and ethnic groups and forms of institutionalized racism. And they also speak to the ways that societies rely on the physical environment to construct boundaries between people.

One thing you might notice is that lots of major cities around the United States have stark lines separating neighborhoods in which black and white people live—and often, those lines are highways, railroads, or other impassable features of infrastructure. Look at the map of Detroit, with Eight

Boulevard divides St. Louis, Missouri; or Main Street in Buffalo, New York; Rock Creek Park in Washington D.C.; or a set of twin rivers and highways in Milwaukee. The roads we travel on and the parks we play in have a racial history as well. And, in many cities around the United States, it is a history that survives in the form of enduring residential segregation that, when viewed from above, can tell us a story about racial segregation and inequality in local spaces.

SOURCE: Badge, Emily and Darla Cameron. "How Railroads, Highways and Other Man-Made Lines Racially Divide America's Cities." *The Washington Post* Wonkblog, July 16, 2015. Available at https://www.washingtonpost.com/news/wonk/wp/2015/07/16/how-railroads-highways-and-other-man-made-lines-racially-divide-americas-cities/.

Thinking Historically about Racial Inequality

8.2.7 Explain how and why we need to think about racial inequality historically to fully understand contemporary forms of racial inequality.

In 1965, President Lyndon Johnson asked employers to "take affirmative action to ensure that applicants are employed, and that employees are treated … without regard to their race, color, creed, or national origin." He established the Equal Opportunity Commission, which administers many affirmative action programs to ensure that minorities get fair treatment in employment applications. Affirmative action programs are controversial. Opponents complain that minority applicants are "stealing jobs" from more qualified white applicants, a form of what some refer to as "reverse discrimination." But this rhetoric relies on an incomplete understanding of why affirmative action programs exist in the first place. Consider the following cartoon, which oversimplifies a complex history of race relations in the United States with an interaction between one white and one black man.

Many white people are unaware of just how much history has advantaged them, and what it really means today. Some whites, for instance, might think that racial

Socially privileged groups are not always aware of the historical legacies of privilege from which they benefit. Here, cartoonist Barry Deutsch attempts to make sense of the logics by which white people in the United States sometimes do not understand how they have been helped by history, while other racial groups are still making up ground.

A CONCISE HISTORY OF BLACK-WHITE RELATIONS IN THE U.S.A.

inequality is less of an issue today and that slavery and racism are largely associated with a distant (if uncomfortable) past. Indeed, this is part of what sociologists today refer to as *color-blind racism*. Yet, when looked at this way, it's not an exaggeration to claim that white males have been the beneficiaries of a 2,000-year "affirmative action" policy that favored them. In an article in *The Nation* (1995), the eminent historian Eric Foner ruminated on his own college experience as a beneficiary of that version of affirmative action:

> Thirty-two years ago, I graduated from Columbia College [the undergraduate college at Columbia University]. My class of 700 was all-male and virtually all white. Most of us were young men of ability; yet had we been forced to compete for admission with women and racial minorities, fewer than half of us would have been at Columbia. None of us, to my knowledge, suffered debilitating self-doubt because we were the beneficiaries of affirmative action—that is, favored treatment on the basis of our race and gender.... [In fact], I have yet to meet a white male in whom favoritism (getting a job, for example, through relatives or an old boys' network, or because of racial discrimination by a union or an employer) fostered doubt about his own abilities....

"Despite our rhetoric," Foner concludes, "equal opportunity has never been the American way. For nearly all our history, affirmative action has been a prerogative of white men" (Foner 1995). Because race has long benefitted white people in the United States, they collect on a legacy of privilege that has passed down through generations of white Americans. The history of race relations in the United States, in other words, continues to play a role in structuring racial inequality today.

legacy of slavery
Those enduring forms of racial inequality that result from generations of systematic, institutionalized, legal forms of racial oppression.

Historians and sociologists discussing the role of history in contemporary forms of racial inequality discuss the **legacy of slavery**—those enduring forms of racial inequality that result from generations of systematic, institutionalized, legal forms of racial oppression. Affirmative action is about your ancestors and the history of the society in which you happen to live. Although you might feel like your GPA, SAT scores, and resume are solely the result of your individual talents, it is also true that some people have had the historical luck of being privy to forms of privilege collected over generations. And programs like affirmative action proceed from the well-founded assumption that the residue of the systematic, and lawful enslavement of an entire racial group will not diminish simply because we decide to open school doors and allow them to apply for the same jobs as everyone else. This history has resulted in what sociologist Joe Feagin (2000) refers to as "*undeserved impoverishment*" and "*undeserved enrichment*." By this, Feagin is making the sociological argument that our resources and status in society are tied to the history of the groups with whom we are identified in our society. Feagin's argument was primarily about distinctions between black and white Americans, but the argument can be applied to other groups as well: like the current struggles of Native Americans in the United States—an issue structured by state-sanctioned genocide in early U.S. history.

Understanding Racial and Ethnic Inequality Intersectionally

8.2.8 Understand the "matrix of domination" and how this applies to thinking about inequality intersectionally.

Race overlaps with other social categories, like ethnicity, age, class, gender, and sexuality. One doesn't stop being a woman when one is marginalized on the basis of, say, religious intolerance or racial stereotypes. Interestingly, stereotypes about stigmatized groups often reinforce each other, because these stereotypes are often remarkably similar: The group in question is considered illogical (childlike), overly emotional, primitive, potentially violent, and sexually promiscuous. Consequently, stereotypes and prejudices often combine, and the effects of racism are compounded by the effects of classism, sexism, heterosexism, and all manner of "–isms."

And, as we have learned throughout this text, sociologists understand that one cannot easily tease apart these different, yet entangled, strands.

As a result, sociologists today discuss **intersectionality**—the ways in which our experiences as members of different groups intersect with one another. Sometimes these experiences reinforce each other; sometimes they contradict each other. But to the sociologist, the key fact is that they are inseparable. One does not stop being African American when one is working-class, woman, or lesbian (Collins 1990). All these experiences taken together comprise what sociologists see as an interlocking system of control in which each type of inequality reinforces the others so that the impact of one cannot be fully understood without also considering the others.

Often, this intersectionality offers a painful reminder of marginality, and the ways in which even the oppressed groups can still hold prejudices. Consider a woman who is black and identifies as lesbian. She might feel that whenever she is around other black people, she is keenly aware that she is lesbian and feel that she doesn't fully "fit in." But when she is around other lesbians, she might remain keenly aware that she is black and feel like she doesn't "fit in" there either. Sometimes, the intersections of different categories of identity leave us feeling marginal—even when we are in a group of "our own." Indeed, in sociologist Mignon Moore's (2006) research on black lesbian identity and community, she discovered that these experiences are felt in patterned ways among black lesbians.

Intersectionality illustrates how the very categories we use to anchor our identities—our race, gender, ethnicity, sexuality and the like—are also the same axes along which social inequality is maintained and reproduced. It shows that comparing oppressions—who is more "oppressed," a Muslim man or a white woman? A black lesbian or an elderly disabled Jewish man?—disregards the ways that each axis of inequality amplifies and reinforces the others.

intersectionality

Sociological term for the ways that different identities "intersect" with one another to shape our social identity and our experience of inequality.

---

iSOC AND YOU Racial and Ethnic Inequalities: Interactions and Institutions
Race and ethnicity are foundations of *identity* and also central axes of social *inequality* in society. You express racial and ethnic identity and reproduce—or challenge—inequalities in *interactions* with other people. Every social *institution*, as well, reproduces these inequalities, whether by stereotypes about different groups or by specific rules that govern activity within the institution. And racial and ethnic identities and inequalities *intersect*, as you've seen, making for complex webs of identity and inequality with other forms of identity (like class, gender, sexuality, age, and more). It's a sociological irony that the very aspects of your identity that make you feel most like you belong can be used to also marginalize you.

8.3 Ethnic Identities in the United States

Although race and ethnicity impact the lives of every racial and ethnic group, it's also true that their lives are impacted in different ways as a result of how they are situated within the racial and ethnic relations in a given society. The histories of how different groups came to a society, the social niches they have historically occupied, whether and how they have been able to assimilate, and more all structure the life options, experiences and opportunities of different racial and ethnic groups in different ways. Relying on language from the iSoc model, ethnicity is—like race—an identity. Ethnicities refer to collections of cultural practices, local knowledge, and traditions. And groups and identities form around pockets of different ethnic practices, knowledge, and traditions. This means that ethnicities are necessarily constituted through practice—through interaction.

The United States has a reputation for being racially and ethnically diverse. But diversity and equality are not the same. The various histories of the different ethnic groups that comprise the ethnic identities in the United States position distinct groups in different ways throughout social life. Indeed, ethnicities have a fluid quality (Gans 1979); they change over time and over the course of some peoples' lives. Sociologists studying ethnicity have attempted to capture this quality in a variety of ways—one of the most obvious is by changing the ethnic categories we offer on surveys to try to accurately capture the ways that people make sense of their own ethnicities. This means, that ethnicities become institutionalized, but it is also a powerful demonstration of how institutionalized forms of identity and interaction can shift—they aren't biologically inevitable; they are socially organized.

Sociologists studying ethnicity and ethnic diversity are equally interested in inequality. In this section, we will briefly examine some of the histories and social forces that have shaped the primary ethnic groups making up the U.S. population today: people from Europe, people from North America, people from Latin America, people from sub-Saharan Africa, people from East and South Asia, and people from the Middle East. Social inequality dramatically shapes the lives of each of these ethnic groups—whether they are advantaged, disadvantaged, or simply marginalized by institutionalized forms of inequality. But to fully appreciate how complex social inequality is, we will also examine it intersectionally. So, we look at how ethnicity intersects with race, national origin, history, and more in this section. It is only by understanding the interconnections between all of these social forces and factors that we can come to better understand this particular system of identity and inequality that shapes all of our lives.

People from Europe

8.3.1 Explain how "white people" comprise a historically constructed (and changing) category in U.S. history.

In a recent U.S. Census, 73.8 percent of the U.S. population was identified as white, most of European ancestry (see FIGURE 8.6). The largest ethnic groups were German

FIGURE 8.6 Percentage of Legal Immigrants Reporting European Origins, 1820–2015
European countries were once the most dominant sources of U.S. immigrant groups. Today, those numbers have grown smaller as people all over the world are pushed and pulled in different ways by the societies in which they live to move to other societies.

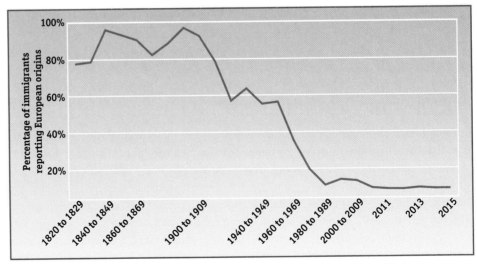

SOURCE: Data from Department of Homeland Security, Yearbook of Immigration Statistics 2015. Available at https://www.dhs.gov/immigration-statistics/yearbook.

(14.9%), Irish (10.8%), English (8%), and Italian (5.5%) (U.S. Census Bureau 2015). We may now call them "European Americans" as a matter of convenience, but really we are saying "white people," referring to race rather than ethnicity. The differences today among many of these groups are far smaller than they once were. The white Non-Hispanic population will experience an 8.2 percent decrease by 2060, changing from 198 million in 2014 to 181 million (U.S. Census Bureau 2015).

But, who qualifies as "white" in the first place has historically depended on much more than skin color alone. It has a history and is the result of social positioning. During the nineteenth century, ethnologists, anthropologists, and sociologists traveled around the world, dividing people into "races" and ordering them from the most to least intelligent, moral, interesting, and evolved. Initially, they "found" hundreds of races and divided them into ten broad categories. Teutonic people (from England, Germany, and Scandinavia) were defined as white, but people from other parts of Europe were not. The U.S. Census used to separate them on surveys and forms. Magazine illustrations, popular songs, and sociology textbooks characterized these "others" as savage, lazy, sexually promiscuous, born criminals, and responsible for the "social disintegration" of the slums. They were denied jobs and places to live. In the South, many were lynched along with blacks. The furor of racial classification in the late nineteenth century and the "discovery" that Europe had inferior and superior races was directly related to a fear of immigration.

Before 1880, most European immigrants were German, French, English, or Scots-Irish. They were mostly middle class and Protestant, and they settled in small towns, where they assimilated quickly into the middle-class, Protestant population. But between 1880 and 1920, 23 million immigrants came to the United States, too fast to disperse and assimilate. Instead, they piled up in cities; in 1900, immigrants and their children made up more than 70 percent of populations of New York, Boston, Philadelphia, and Chicago. They were primarily working-class and poor, they spoke Italian, Polish, or Yiddish, and they were more often Catholic or Jewish (Van Vugt 1999; Walch 1994).

The U.S.–born English-German, Protestant, small-town elite feared these new "primitive" groups (Roediger 1991). By 1924 the door to immigration from most of Europe (not England) slammed shut (Saxton 1971, 1990). Because the immigrants tended to have larger families than the native elites, President Theodore Roosevelt raised the alarm of "race suicide" and urged Anglo-Saxon women to have more children, just as poor and immigrant families were advised to limit the number of children they had. By the 1920s and 1930s, scientists developed theories of *eugenics,* the science of "breeding," and encouraged laws that would help the country breed a superior race (Mowry 1958; Selden 1999). This new racialist "science" was being taught as fact in U.S. universities—an ideology we now teach as a form of what sociologists refer to as **scientific racism**.

Gradually the Irish, the Italians, the European Jews, and other European ethnic groups became categorized as "white." The 1930 census distinguished 10 races (white, Negro, American Indian, Chinese, Japanese, Korean, Filipino, Hindu, Mexican, and Other) and further classified white people into only three types: native white with native white parents; native white with immigrant parents; and immigrant white. The 1940 census distinguished only native white and immigrant white. How did that happen? Historian Noel Ignatiev (1995) maintains that the Irish deliberately positioned themselves in opposition to blacks, visibly participating in the massive anti-black violence in the northeastern United States in the 1840s, to posture for a place at the table of "whiteness." Anthropologist Karen Brodkin (1998) similarly maintains that

Both Irish immigrants and black men were seen as "ape-like" as they are both depicted here in this illustration from a *Harper's Weekly* issue published in 1876.

scientific racism

The science of "breeding," and encouraged laws that would help the country breed a superior race, eugenics.

Jews began to "speak of a mythic whiteness" that both they and the Anglo-Saxons participated in, transcending the separate categories that scientific racism put them in. The Irish and the Jews "chose" to be white and then set about trying to convince native-born Protestant whites that they should be included in the racial category. The idea of the United States as a "melting pot" seemed to work only with Europeans and with some drawbacks: Assimilation meant abandoning cultural traditions. Immigrant parents punished their children for speaking the language from back home, and in a generation or two an entire cultural heritage was nearly forgotten. That was the price they paid for becoming white; a hefty price to be sure, but one that came with a host of new privileges as well.

People from North America

8.3.2 Understand the history of Native Americans in the United States including contemporary struggles and the current resurgence in American Indian identification.

Native Americans (once called "Indians") were the original inhabitants of North America, present from at least 40,000 BCE. When the first Europeans and Africans arrived, there were between 2 and 10 million people living north of the Rio Grande, divided into around 800 linguistic and cultural groups. Some were the nomadic hunter-gatherers of Hollywood-movie myth, but many were settled and agrarian, living in villages as large and prosperous as any villages among the European settlers. Early European settlers usually approached the Native Americans through stereotypes: They were either "noble savages," living without sin in a sort of Garden of Eden or they were "wild savages," uncivilized and bestial. They were systematically deprived of their land and herded onto reservations, if not hunted and killed outright. William Henry Harrison and Andrew Jackson were both elected to the presidency primarily on their prestige as "Indian fighters." Political slogans and illustrations of the day showed them as noble, heroic white men "saving" the United States from the savage Indian threat. This threat was contrived as the excuse to appropriate Native American land and natural resources and especially to clear a path for the transcontinental railroad.

Many of the stereotypes about Native Americans are still intact today. For instance, Native Americans have long been used as mascots for sports teams. Roughly half of all high school, college, and professional teams that used Native American mascots in 1960 have changed their mascots. Despite claims that these mascots are signs of "respect" for the tenacity and ferocity of the Native American tribes—tribes on whose appropriated land the colleges and universities may actually have been built—most Native Americans feel such mascots are insulting and perpetuate racist stereotypes. Consider the campaign (in the photo) produced by the National Congress of American Indians to raise awareness about the mascots with racist depictions of Native Americans. The Cleveland Indians have had a racist stereotype of Native Americans as a mascot since 1932!

In the most recent Census, only about 1.7 percent of the population identified as Native American (either alone or in combination with other races). But many more people have some Native American ancestry (most tribes require one-quarter ancestry to declare an official tribal affiliation). About half live in rural areas, mostly on reservations (see MAP 8.1), and the rest are concentrated in big cities, especially Los Angeles, New York, Seattle, Chicago, and Houston.

Just before the beginning of the 2016 MLB season, ESPN commentator Bromani Jones sported a Cleveland "Caucasians" t-shirt during a network show—an obvious critical reference to the "Indians" logo of the Cleveland team. He received a lot of critical attention for the stunt; many called for him to be fired for taking such a political stance. In his public response he said, "This is the same thing that goes on with the logo for the Cleveland Indians…. To have a problem with the logo of this [gesturing to the shirt] would be to have a problem with the Indians'. But if you're quiet about the Indians' and now you've got something to say about my shirt, I think it's time for some introspection" (Wallee 2016).

HOW DO WE KNOW WHAT WE KNOW?

DO MASCOTS DEPICTING RACIAL STEREOTYPES REALLY MATTER?

Many people defend the use of Native American mascots for sports teams because, proponents claim, it actually denotes respect and admiration for the qualities associated with Native Americans: ferocity, courage, or loyalty. But research actually suggests something quite different. Psychologist Chu Kim-Prieto examined how our brains respond to such images. In two clever experiments, she compared how students answered a survey about a different ethnic group: Asian Americans. (She chose Asian-Americans because stereotypes about them are so different from those about Native Americans.)

In the *first experiment*, students at the University of Illinois filled out a survey about Asian American stereotypes. The surveys had been placed in three different folders, so when each student, randomly assigned to one of three groups, were given the surveys one-third of the students saw lots of images of Chief Illiniwek, the school's mascot, one-third saw a bit letter "I" for Illinois, and one third saw only a blank folder. Those who saw the image of the mascot reported significantly greater endorsement of stereotypes of Asian Americans. In the *second experiment*, students at the College of New Jersey, read one of two generally positive and respectful articles about the University of Illinois both taken from the official university website: either a history of Chief Illiniwek or a description of the university arts center. Once again, those who read about Native Americans were significantly more likely to express stereotypic views of the Asian Americans.

Although previous research suggested that the use of these mascots had deleterious consequences for Native Americans, Kim-Prieto and her colleagues found something a bit more disturbing. "One's reliance on stereotypes appears to be heightened with increased exposure to stereotypes, regardless of whom the stereotypes are portraying," the authors conclude. In other words, exposure to some ethnic stereotypes may lead to greater acceptance of stereotypes of other ethnic groups as well.

The NCAA started a policy in fall 2008 that prohibited collegiate teams from using Native American mascots. The former University of Illinois mascot was mistaken for an actual Native American Chief and even asked to perform weddings.

SOURCE: Kim-Prieto, Chu, Lizabeth Goldstein, Sumie Okazaki, and Blake Kirschner, "Effect of Exposure to an American Indian Mascot on the Tendency to Stereotype a Different Minority Group" in *Journal of Applied Social Psychology*, 43, 3 (March 2010): 534–553.

The largest Native American nation, the Navajo or Dine of Arizona and New Mexico, has 308,296 members and many distinctive cultural institutions, including its own newspaper, radio station, and college. Its language is thriving. But most of the other Native American cultures are slowly dying out. Before the Europeans arrived, California was home to some 300 languages, more than the whole of Europe. Today 50 remain, though few people speak them, almost all of them elderly.

The history of contact between European immigrants and Native Americans left many tribes destroyed, decimated, or displaced onto "reservations" (which were ironically conceived of initially as places to "protect" the Native Americans from further

MAP 8.1 Native American Reservations in the Continental United States

Indian reservation in the United States is technically a legal designation that refers to a land area that is managed by a Native American tribe under a federal organization, the U.S. Bureau of Indian Affairs. Each reservation in the United States is associated with a particular tribe. Yet, not all of the 567 recognized tribes in the United States have a designated reservation—just fewer than 60 percent of them do. And many reservations are fragmented, which has produced different enclaves that create administrative, political, and legal challenges.

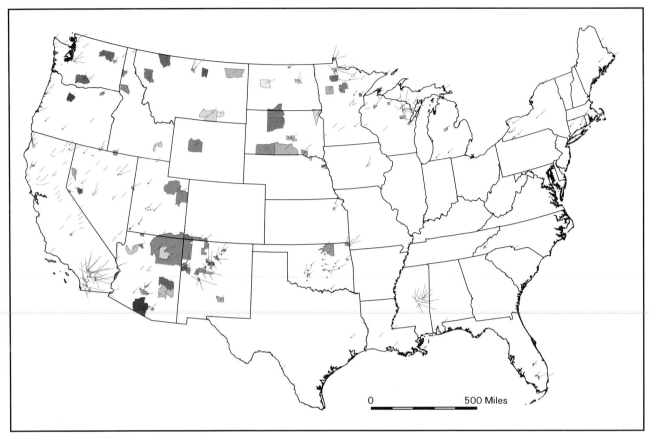

SOURCE: Data from U.S. Bureau of Indian Affairs.

harm by whites who were stealing their land). As a result, today, Native Americans are worse off than other minorities in many measures of institutional discrimination and racism:

- A 65 percent high school graduation rate and 9 percent college attendance rate, far below the national average
- A poverty rate of 32.2 percent, higher than any other ethnic group
- The highest rate of suicide in the 18- to 24-year-old age group of any racial or ethnic group in the United States
- A lower percentage of "current drinkers" than whites and Hispanics, yet a higher rate of alcoholism
- A lower life expectancy than the nation as a whole

SOURCE: Ho, Vanessa, "Native American Death Rates Soar as Most People are Living Longer." *Seattle Post-Intelligencer*, March 12, 2009.)

Reservation life has grown difficult, and funds are scarce for needed services. Many Native American cultures have taken advantage of tax and legal opportunities to open casinos (because reservations are not legally restricted from gambling) as a way to raise money since federal and state funds have all but dried up. This presents Native tribes with a cynical "choice": Either open a casino and feed the nation's gambling addiction or fail to provide needed services for their people.

Nonetheless, many Native Americans continue to embrace their cultural heritage. Indeed, sociologist Joane Nagel (1995) studied a process she refers to as **ethnic renewal** to discuss the process by which ethnic identities are reconstituted and reclaimed after having been discarded earlier. Nagel noticed that between 1960 and 1990, the numbers of Americans selecting an American Indian race on the Census more than tripled. And she showed that the increase was not due to more births, lower death rates, or immigration. Nagel discusses how and why more Americans who might have previously identified as "non-Indian" are changing their racial designation. Nagel argued that this kind of "ethnic switching" had a great deal to do with American Indian political activism among other things. *Pan-Indianism* today emphasizes common elements that run through Native American cultures, creating an identity that goes beyond the individual nations. And it just might make more young people today who might be able to claim Native American ancestry more likely to identify with that ethnic option.

ethnic renewal
Process by which ethnic identities are reconstituted and reclaimed after having been discarded earlier.

People from Latin America

8.3.3 Summarize what the controversy over whether "Hispanic" and "Latino" are racial or ethnic categories indicates about how sociologists study race and ethnicity.

In the most recent Census, 16.8 percent of the U.S. population declared that they were Hispanic or Latino/Latina, with ancestry in Latin America (the Caribbean, Mexico, and Central and South America). Between 2000 and 2010, the Hispanic population has accounted for more than half of all U.S. population growth (Passel, Cohn, and Lopez 2011). Latinos are now the largest ethnic minority group in the United States, and they are growing almost three times faster than the population as a whole (2.9 percent per year versus 1 percent per year in the general population), due both to immigration and higher birth rates. By 2050, the Hispanic population will nearly triple, from 35.6 million to 102.6 million.

Because these regions were originally settled by Native Americans, Europeans, Africans, and Asians, Hispanics may be of any race. Most speak Spanish at home, but they may speak Portuguese, French, Creole, Japanese, Italian, or an Indian language. Most are Roman Catholic, but they can be Protestant (usually Pentecostal), Jewish, Muslim, or followers of an Afro-Caribbean religion like Santería. Some do not approve of dozens of distinct cultures being lumped together into people from a continent, so they prefer to be called Mexican Americans (or Chicanos), Cuban Americans, and so on.

Latinos in the United States come from various countries of origin:

- *From Mexico: 34 million.* This is the most established of the Hispanic subgroups: Just 34 percent are foreign born, and many have had ancestors in California, Arizona, or Texas because those states were once part of Mexico.
- *From Central America: 4.7 million, mainly from El Salvador, Guatemala, Honduras, and Nicaragua.* These people live mostly in California, Texas, Florida, and New York. They tend to be foreign born (70%), and 36 percent immigrated within the past decade. About 22 percent fall beneath the poverty line.
- *From South America: 3.2 million, mainly from Colombia, Ecuador, and Peru.* They tend to be foreign born (76.2%), and 12 percent immigrated within the past four years. Many are well educated and belong to the middle class. About 29 percent of the foreign born have college degrees.

We are a nation of immigrants. President John F. Kennedy said this was the "secret" of America: "a nation of people with the fresh memory of old traditions who dared to explore new frontiers" (Kennedy 1958). Latinos represent the nation's largest ethnic minority (Spanish Harlem, New York City).

- *From Cuba: 1.9 million.* Of this group, 57 percent are foreign born, but most arrived more than a decade ago. Most have settled in Florida. They tend to be more affluent than other Hispanic subgroups. About a third of the foreign-born adults have some college education.
- *From the Dominican Republic: 1.6 million.* More than half live in New York. They are among the most impoverished of the Hispanic subgroups; 26 percent fall below the poverty line.
- *From Puerto Rico: about 4.7 million (not counting the 3.5 million in Puerto Rico itself).* About a third live in New York. They are among the most impoverished of the Hispanic subgroups: 27 percent are below the poverty line (Passel and Suro 2005; U.S. Census Bureau 2015).

SOURCE: U.S. Census Bureau, 2014 ACS Census estimates.

Hispanic Americans are not only the fastest growing minority group in the United States. They also have the fastest-growing rates of college attendance (estimated to

SOCIOLOGY AND OUR WORLD

WHY HISPANIC WENT FROM BEING A RACE TO AN ETHNICITY

The U.S. Census now lists Hispanic/Latino/Chicano as "ethnic" identities rather than "racial" identities. Why did they change and what does it mean?

Previously in the chapter, we learned about how the Census has routinely had to adopt new categories and systems of categorization to make sense of the shifting landscape of racial and ethnic relations in the United States. Sometimes that simply means updating the word we use to designate a racial or ethnic category (Native American, black, and Hispanic have all gone through this sort of transformation). But sometimes that also means adding new categories and getting rid or others (allowing people to identify as more than one race or ethnicity, for instance, only became possible in 2000—you simply couldn't identify as multiracial on the survey prior to that change). Currently, the Census allows people to select "Hispanic, Latino, or Spanish origin" (all lumped together as a single ethnic category), but also asks people to write in their specific ethnicities within this (e.g., Mexican American, Puerto Rican, Cuban, Salvadoran, Columbian, Dominican). People filling out the survey were alerted to the change with the following information: "For this census, Hispanic origins are not races."

The reasons behind these changes are multiple. But one reason that Hispanic/Latino went from being a race to an ethnicity is that the Census is attempting to respond to the ways people think about and classify themselves rather than attempting to force them to adopt the Census method of categorization. And because race is socially constructed, how we draw boundaries between racial and ethnic groups will shift and require new language over time.

Consider the following predicament. Using a nationally representative survey from 2015, The Pew Research Center asked adults identifying as "Hispanic" whether being Hispanic was a part of their racial or ethnic background. Below is what they discovered.

A full 13 percent of Americans identifying as "Hispanic" said they do not know whether being Hispanic is about race or ethnicity. More than half of Americans identifying as Hispanic understand it as both a racial and an ethnic identity. And about 30 percent of Americans identifying as Hispanic understand it as either a racial identity (11%) or an ethnic identity (19%), but not both. It's complicated and it illustrates how even the categories the Census relies on are best understood as moving targets. Indeed, the U.S. Census is presently debating about how the categories will be presented on the 2020 Census.

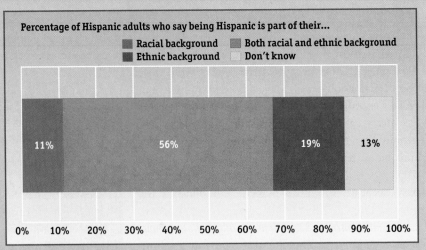

Percentage of Hispanic adults who say being Hispanic is part of their...

- Racial background
- Ethnic background
- Both racial and ethnic background
- Don't know

11%   56%   19%   13%

0% 10% 20% 30% 40% 50% 60% 70% 80% 90% 100%

NOTE: Figures do not add to 100 percent due to rounding.

SOURCE: Data from Gonzalez-Barrera, Ana and Mark Hugo Lopez. "Is Being Hispanic a Matter of Race, Ethnicity or Both?" *The Pew Research Center, Facttank,* June 15, 2015. Available at: http://www.pewresearch.org/fact-tank/2015/06/15/is-being-hispanic-a-matter-of-race-ethnicity-or-both/.

have grown 45 percent between 2005 and 2016, compared with 17 percent of the general population). And they have the fastest-growing rate of affluence. Their disposable income topped $1 trillion in 2010 (Humphreys 2006), and their earnings growth has not yet reached its peak (Moreno 2008). Marketing executives have noticed. Hispanic people appear regularly on television commercials as purveyors of "traditional American values." When Mexican American actor Mario Lopez starred in the teen sitcom *Saved by the Bell*, his character had to be made Anglo: Executives feared that no one would watch a show "with a Mexican in it."

Today, Hispanic actors are still often assigned to play gangsters, thugs, and servants, or else asked to play Anglo, but some, such as Penelope Cruz, America Ferrera, Benicio Del Toro, Antonio Banderas, Salma Hayek, and Jennifer Lopez, have "gone mainstream": They not only refuse to hide their ethnicity, they celebrate it. In South Florida, cable TV offers multiple all-Spanish channels, but they are not marketing only to the Hispanic community. The most popular *telenovelas* (prime-time soap operas) come with English-language subtitles so Anglos can watch too.

People from sub-Saharan Africa

8.3.4 Describe the ways that the history of African Americans' enslavement has shaped their experience in the United States and race relations in the United States more broadly.

In the most recent Census, 13.2 percent of the U.S. population was identified as black or African American, with ancestry in sub-Saharan Africa. The two terms are often used interchangeably, but technically *black* is a race that includes Andaman Islanders, Australian aboriginals, and other people with ancestry from outside sub-Saharan Africa and does not apply to the white, Asian, and Khoisan residents of Zimbabwe or Zaire. African American is an ethnicity, referring to the descendants of black Africans who came to North America as slaves between 1500 and 1820 and who, after slavery, were subject to "Jim Crow" laws that kept blacks and whites separate and unequal. They therefore share a history and cultural traditions. African Americans are the only group to immigrate to the United States against their will, as they were forcibly abducted to serve as slaves in the South and in the Caribbean.

To reinforce that common cultural tradition, some have celebrated June 19, called "Juneteenth," the day that word of the Emancipation Proclamation reached the slaves of the South; others have invented new holidays, like Kwanzaa. Some have fashioned a distinctive dialect of English, sometimes referred to as "Ebonics," with some terms and grammatical structures borrowed from West African languages. The creation of new, and distinctly African American, names is also an invented way to "preserve" traditions. Historically, slaves were named by their masters and likely to bear Anglo names like "Sally" and "Bill"; the power to name your child a more African-sounding name, like, say, "Shaniqua" or "Kadeem," illustrates the power to control the fate of that child. Thus, in the process, they transformed race into ethnicity in its own right. Contemporary immigrants from Nigeria or South Africa may be black, white, or Asian, but they would not be African American. As we discussed, however, while this trend might increase cultural solidarity, it also perpetuates social inequality as "black-sounding" names on resumes have been shown to produce fewer job opportunities (Bertrand and Mullainathan 2003). It's an underappreciated and sometimes less visible form of racial discrimination.

The African American population is expected to experience modest growth by 2050, growing from 40.2 million to 61.4 million.

At the turn of the last century, the great African American sociologist W. E. B. Du Bois said that "the problem of the twentieth century is the problem of the

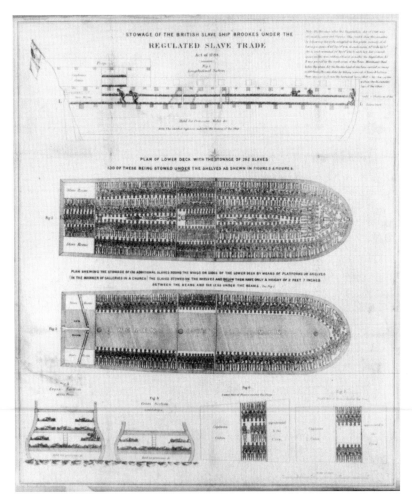

Slaves were crammed into ships for the crossing between Africa and the New World. This plan for the English slave ship Brookes, built in 1781, depicts plans for more than 780 slaves. A bill passed in Parliament in 1788 limited the Brookes to "only" 292 slaves for subsequent voyages.

color line" (DuBois 1903). There are many racial and ethnic minority groups in the United States, and African Americans are not even the largest; yet they have always been the "standard" minority. Studies of prejudice and discrimination often concentrate on white and black, ignoring everyone else, and indeed most of the racist legislation in the United States has been directed primarily if not exclusively against African Americans. The Civil Rights movement of the 1960s did not need to be more specific: Everyone realized that it was about the civil rights of African Americans. Some argue that regardless of what race you identify with in the United States, you have to navigate a racial arena that is shaped by black/white relations and inequality and the difficult past associated with slavery.

Today, African Americans have achieved some measure of political and economic success. There is a sizeable black middle class, with educational background and earnings comparable to those of middle-class whites. Overall, however, African Americans lag behind white non-Hispanic Americans in high school graduation rate by 15 percentage points (Bidwell 2015) and college graduation rate by 24 percentage points (National Student Clearinghouse 2017). Black men's median earnings are 73 percent of what white men earn (women are roughly equal) (Pew Research Center 2016), while 27.4 percent of black people and 9.9 percent of white people are below poverty level (State of Working America 2016). Young black men are eight times more likely to be murdered than are white men, and black women three times as likely as white women (Mortimer 2016, U.S. Department of Justice 2009). In recent years, there has been much debate about paying "reparations" to the descendants of former slaves because they worked for no payment and had their lives torn apart through slavery. (Jews have received reparations from the German and Swiss governments that profited from seizing their assets during World War II, and black South Africans have received reparations for what was lost during apartheid.) Opponents claim that it would be too costly and would result in profiteering by minorities.

People from East and South Asia

8.3.5 Summarize the reasons why the "model minority" stereotype of the Asian American racial and ethnic experience is misleading.

About 4.6 percent of the U.S. population traces its ancestry to East, Southeast, or South Asia. These groups include China (22%), the Philippines (15%), India (15%), Korea (10%), Vietnam (10%), and Japan (9%). Harsh quotas limited immigration before the 1960s, so most are recent immigrants. They differ tremendously in language, religion, and culture, and often they have long-standing ethnic and national conflicts back home (Korea versus Japan, China versus

Vietnam, and so on) that make the umbrella term *Asian American* problematic (see FIGURE 8.7).

Even within a nationality, there are many ethnic differences. People from China may speak Mandarin, Cantonese, or any of a dozen other varieties of Chinese or a hundred local languages. People from India may be Hindu, Muslim, Christian, Buddhist, Sikh, Jain, or atheist. People from Mindanao, the largest and most industrialized island of the Philippines, may look down on people from other islands as uncouth and uncivilized. So even *Chinese American, Indian American*, and *Filipino/a* become a problem. The Asian American population is expected to increase 115 percent by 2050, rising from 14.7 million to 34.3 million, primarily due to immigration (U.S. Census Bureau 2015).

Asian Americans are often depicted as "the model minority." Many measures of discrimination are significant only for blacks, Hispanics, and Native Americans (like school achievement, college enrollments, prison populations); Asian Americans score the same as whites or surpass them. They have the highest college graduation rate of any ethnic group (as you'll read more about in Chapter 13 on education). Though Asian Americans are just less than 6 percent of the labor force, they comprise 21 percent of all U.S. physicians and surgeons, 32 percent of all software developers, and are the most likely group to have graduated from college (Bureau of Labor Statistics 2016). They are less likely to become victims of racially motivated hate crimes than any ethnic group except whites.

Even the stereotypes of Asian Americans are somewhat different. Prejudiced beliefs about blacks and Hispanics mark them as barbaric, unpredictable, violent, and sexually dangerous. *The Bell Curve* and other works claimed that African Americans were genetically inferior to whites, had a lower native intelligence—that is, the arguments were about "nature" and no amount of "nurture" could compensate for their natural inferiority (Herrnstein and Murray 1994). Prejudiced ideas about Asian Americans stereotype them as weak, passive, and asexual. In the mass media, they commonly appear

FIGURE 8.7 Who Make Up "Asians" in the United States?
As with any racial group in the United States, Asians are diverse. Because Asians are also overrepresented among multiracial Americans, you can see here which ethnicities are more and less likely to be represented among multiracial Americans as well.

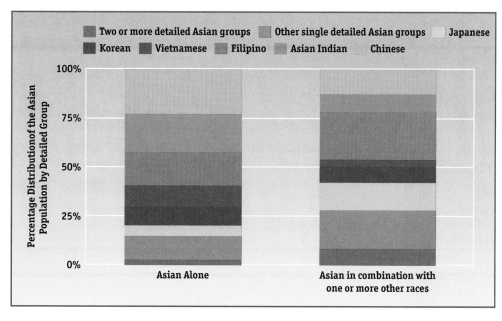

NOTE: Percentages may not add to 100% due to rounding.

SOURCE: Data from U.S. Census Bureau, 2010 Census special tabulation.

At the 2016 Oscars, there was a bit of an outrage after all of the dominant actor nominations were given to white actors. It prompted the social media hashtag #OscarsSoWhite and protest of the event by many high profile black actors. Comedian Chris Rock, also a black American, hosted the event and joked a great deal about racial tensions and white privilege throughout. At one point, three Asian children came on stage under the pretense of bringing out the accountants from a multinational professional services network Rock jokingly blamed for the outcome of the Oscars vote. The joke relied on popular stereotypes about Asians and Asian Americans as smart and American stereotypes about who receives our outsourced jobs and why. Perhaps sensing the joke would cause some discomfort, he followed his joke with, "And if anybody's upset about that joke, just Tweet about it on your phone, which was also made by these kids," joking now about child labor.

not as thugs and drug dealers but as mystical sages and science nerds—stereotypes that are equally unfair but not nearly as threatening (Hamamoto 1994).

Sociologically speaking, the success of Asian Americans, though, is attributed to their incredible work ethic, discipline, and parental influence in addition to several economic niches Asian Americans have come to dominate in the United States (like nail salons and dry cleaning businesses) which has helped solidify their community and shape the assimilation experiences of subsequent waves of immigration. Using the iSoc model, we can see intersections here between race, ethnicity, age, national origin and more in addition to the ways these intersections shape their interactions and identities, play into and navigate systems of inequality, and are perpetuated by becoming institutionalized in the workplace, families, schools, and more. Few would be so consistent as to posit that Asian Americans were genetically superior to other groups. Of course, all of these are broad and false stereotypes. The point is that racist arguments are inconsistent; people refer to whichever one suits their purposes.

Scholars wondering about the "success" of the Asian American population have come up with several explanations. First, most Asian immigrants belonged to the middle class in their home country, so they find it easier to enter the middle class in the United States. In fact, those who were from lower classes did not do especially well at all—class trumps ethnicity (Zhou 2007). They are more likely to be fluent in English. Because there are relatively few of them, they are unlikely to live in segregated neighborhoods and much more likely to marry someone of another racial/ethnic group (Tran and Birman 2010). Finally, if prejudice boils down to light versus dark, they may profit by being, on average, relatively light skinned.

People from the Middle East

8.3.6   Explain what it means to claim that Muslims and Middle Eastern Americans were "racialized" post September 11th in the United States.

The U.S. Census does not give them a separate category, but about 2 million people in the United States trace their ancestry to the Middle East or North Africa. Presently, the Census is considering including "Middle Eastern and North African (MENA)" as an ethnic group in the

Athletes like 2007 All-Star Game MVP Ichiro Suzuki defy stereotypes of Asians as weaklings and submissive nerds.

2020 Census. About 1.5 million are recent immigrants who have arrived since 1970. About one-third of these are Iranian, one-third Turkish, and the other one-third are Arabs, Israelis, Cypriots, and others. There have been two broad migrations of Middle Easterners to the United States:

- Between 1880 and 1920, refugees came here from the failing Ottoman Empire, especially Lebanon, Cyprus, Syria, and Armenia. They were mostly working class and poor, about 75 percent Christian and the rest Muslim or Jewish. They settled primarily in the industrial Northeast and Midwest.
- After 1970, many middle-class Israelis, Arabs, and Iranians immigrated to the United States. Of those, 73 percent were Muslim. They settled primarily in large cities, especially Los Angeles, New York, Chicago, Houston, and Washington, DC.

Members of the first wave of immigration were *assimilationists*; like most other immigrants of the period, they hid or minimized their Middle Eastern ancestry and sought to fit in. During the past 50 years, there has been an increase in efforts to retain separate, distinct, identities as Middle Eastern.

Like Asian Americans, Middle Eastern Americans tend to be a "model minority." They are the most well-educated ethnic group in the United States: Almost half have college degrees, as opposed to 30 percent of white non–Middle Easterners. The median salary of Middle Eastern men is slightly higher than the national mean. However, it is also unfair to depict them as a single group as 30 percent live below the poverty level (Zong and Batalova 2015).

Stereotypes about Middle Easterners tend to be more extreme, and more commonly believed, than stereotypes about other minority groups. Many Americans unaware of the political, cultural, and religious differences in the Middle East tend to believe that all Middle Easterners are Arabs, Muslims, or even Bedouins, who live in tents and ride camels. The men are stereotyped as wide-eyed terrorists; the women as subservient chattel. Even the hero of Disney's *Aladdin* (1993), who was an Arab but evidently not "as Arab" as everyone else, complains of the barbarity of his country: "Where they cut off your ear if they don't like your face, it's pathetic, but hey, it's home." The conventional movie villain was once German, then Russian, then "Euro-terrorist"; now he is a Middle Eastern Arab.

Prejudice and discrimination against Middle Easterners, Arabs, and Muslims increased significantly after the 9/11 terrorist attacks. In 2003, the Pew Forum on Religion and Public Life found 38 percent of respondents would not vote for a well-qualified Muslim for president (a higher percentage than for any minority except gays), and half believed that half or more of all Muslims are anti-American (Pew Forum on Religion and Public Life 2003). The FBI documented an increase of 1,600 percent in hate crimes against Arabs in 2001, jumping from 28 reported crimes in 2000 to 481 in 2001. Crimes were even committed against groups perceived to be either Muslim or Middle Eastern. Sociologists who study this refer to a process called **racialization or ethnicization**— twin processes of ascribing either racial or ethnic qualities to groups who did not identify themselves as such.

racialization or ethnicization
Twin processes of ascribing either racial or ethnic qualities to groups who did not identify themselves as such.

Most recently in the United States, the number of anti-Islamic bias crimes is about 257 incidents, less than half the number of anti-Jewish crimes, which tower atop the list at 664 religion-based incidents (Federal Bureau of Investigation 2015). In most countries of the European Union, intolerance has also increased significantly, first following September 11th and then spiking in different countries in the aftermath of incidents in each. Eighty percent of Muslims in the United Kingdom said they had experienced discrimination in 2001, a jump from 45 percent in 2000 and 35 percent in 1999; hostility increased in Spain and Germany after the Madrid train bombing and in the Netherlands after the murder of filmmaker Theo van Gogh, both in 2004 (International Helsinki Federation for Human Rights 2006). In 2010, a case study of "Islamophobia" in the city of London found the

Ethnic groups compose niche markets that develop their own lifestyles and patterns of consumption. Young Muslim women can embrace the traditional and the modern at the same time.

continuing problem of hate crimes against Muslims is being fueled by mainstream politicians and some sections of the media which are circulating the belief that Muslims are a security threat to the country (Githens-Mazer and Lambert 2010).

A Profile of Ethnicity in the United States

8.3.7 Understand where different people of different ethnicities in the United States came from (and how this has changed) in addition to enduring patterns in ethnic segregation.

Ethnicity, like race, is a fluid concept. We may never agree on ethnic categories as we attempt to navigate the different ways ethnicity is experienced in different historical moments and national and international contexts. But we can attempt to capture images of what ethnicity looks like and make claims surrounding qualities that form an important part of ethnic identities and relations. For instance, global immigration plays a large role in our understandings of immigration. Throughout this section, you've read about the different groups who comprise the major ethnic groups in the United States today. But as you've also read, these groups have shifted over time.

Beyond this, although the United States is often discussed as a "melting pot" where people with different ethnicities can come and all become assimilated into a single, common, uniquely U.S. identity, this has always been untrue (on incomplete, at the very least). For example, were we truly assimilated, you would not expect to see the degree of ethnic segregation that we witness in the United States. And, although some groups remain largely separate and are able to excel and achieve status and success (as some people from South and East Asia have), their assimilation can best be described as "incomplete."

---

iSOC AND YOU Ethnic Identities in the United States

There are few elements of our *identity* that you likely feel more strongly than your race or your ethnicity. It's likely that when you say who or what you are, you list your identity first, followed by a hyphen and the word "American." What you often feel more strongly is the adjective before the hyphen. And of course, that means you already know that not all ethnicities are considered *equal*; in most societies, some ethnicities are ranked above others. Ethnicity is not biological; you have to be taught, socialized, into your ethnic identity, and you do this through *interactions* with others in your group, which teach you how "your people" do it. In some cities, Irish-Americans and Italians-Americans go to different churches, even though they are all Catholic. In this way, ethnicities are reproduced within social *institutions*. And ethnicity *intersects* with other aspects of your identity and social inequality, such as class, or sexuality, or age.

8.4 Resistance and Mobilization to Racial and Ethnic Inequality

Sociologists are also interested in studying the ways that racial and ethnic inequality are both perpetuated and challenged throughout social life. This is a dramatically different way of thinking about racial and ethnic inequality than the forms of nineteenth-century "race science" we discussed at the beginning of the chapter. The largest difference between the ways nineteenth-century "race scientists" understood race, ethnicity and related forms of social inequality compared with sociologists today is that we no longer think about race or ethnicity as biological realities. And whether race is *biological* or *social* can sometimes feel like a philosophical conversation without much consequence. But this difference means that sociologists of race and ethnicity today understand something not possible by those who adopt a biological perspective on race: Sociologists know that racial inequality is not inevitable.

The ways in which we divide people up into different races and ethnicities is, in some ways, completely arbitrary. It's an issue of social organization. And the social organization of race and ethnicity is an issue that can and has been challenged and reworked and will continue to exhibit these qualities in the future as well. Sociological research and theory on race and ethnicity is a powerful way of acknowledging not only that change in racial and ethnic relations is a historical constant, but also of understanding that change is possible on a scale nineteenth-century race scientists couldn't have even imagined.

This section considers research on how racial and ethnic prejudice and discrimination have shifted over time, as well as how and when each are subject to challenge. And change is not unidirectional. There are a variety of data sociologists use to claim that racial and ethnic inequality have been successfully challenged in many ways. And, indeed, this is true. Yet, sociologists are equally interested in the ways that systems of inequality related to race and ethnic identities are also subject to change. Simply put, racial and ethnic inequality is not perpetuated in some finite number of ways at which we can slowly chip away. Rather, racial and ethnic inequality are institutionalized and shape individuals' lives in intersectional ways.

Identities and Interactions: Can Prejudice Be Overcome?

8.4.1 Understand what it means (and does not mean) to refer to prejudices as a "self-fulfilling prophecy."

As we've seen, prejudice is a set of ideas, assumptions that we have about other groups. Is there any way to reduce prejudice? Some social scientists in the 1950s believed that prejudice could be changed by exposure to members of minority groups (Allport 1954). We might believe that Italians are passionate, blacks are lazy, or Jews are greedy because we haven't met enough members of these groups who don't fit the stereotypes. Would increased exposure to groups about which someone held prejudices reduce them?

During the 1960s and 1970s, a huge amount of time and money was invested in busing students from segregated schools, not only to equalize instruction, but to introduce black and white students to each other. It didn't work. Contact alone does not diminish prejudice. People who have never met even one member of another particular group may not be prejudiced, while people who are surrounded by members of the minority group may still be prejudiced. Social psychologist Mark Snyder (1987) found that even awareness of prejudice and desire to change were insufficient. You can realize that prejudice is wrong, and you can try to stop, but you might still believe stereotypes. They are beyond the reach of reason and goodwill. We tend to notice and remember the ways people from minority groups seem to fit a stereotype, whether we want to or not.

One of the problems in combating prejudice is that it is not merely a matter of individual perceptions. Gordon Allport (1954) called prejudice "a self-fulfilling prophecy." We see what we expect to see and don't see what we don't expect to see. Thus, what we see "fulfills" our expectations, and the stereotypes are confirmed. Prejudice exists at work, among friends, in families, and among strangers—even within the group that has been negatively stereotyped. We tend to modify our beliefs and behaviors to correspond to a social role, even if that role is associated with negative stereotypes. In 1997, the anthropologist John Ogbu, wondered why middle-class African American students in affluent Shaker Heights, Ohio, got lower grades than their white classmates (an average of C instead of B). Usually such disparities are explained by economic and social inequalities, but in this case, both groups of students were attending well-funded middle-class schools. He concluded that the black students were afraid of being labeled as "acting white" if they studied too hard or got good grades (Ogbu and Davis 2003). More recent research in inner-city schools suggests an even more compelling picture. It turns out that black *girls* who do well in school are indeed accused of "acting white," but black *boys* who do well are accused of "acting like girls" (Ferguson 2001; Fordham 1996). To make sense of this requires understanding the intersections between gender and racial oppression: For these boys, being seen as a girl is even worse than being seen as white.

However, there is hope. People can and do decrease their prejudice. Mere contact is not enough, but when people of different groups must work together toward a common goal (Miller, Brewer, and Edwards 1985), most measures of prejudice decrease. Other important factors are strong role models that contradict the stereotypes and a decrease in institutional forms of discrimination that make inequality seem normal and natural.

Unfortunately, some evidence suggests that many people are just learning what answers look best on surveys, regardless of how they really feel or react. Discrimination, especially of the "color-blind" variety, seems to be on the rise. In a 2015 Gallup poll, 78 percent of whites believed that blacks and whites were always treated fairly on the job and at work, but only 43 percent of blacks agreed. 30 percent of black respondents said that they had encountered discrimination during the past month, while shopping, at work, while dining out, while using public transportation, or with the police. The percentage increased to 70 percent for young black men, who were especially likely to experience discrimination while shopping (45%) and in interactions with the police (35%). A 1995 survey of the racial climate at Indiana State University (Terre Haute, Indiana) found that 64 percent of black students had heard racial jokes or seen racial graffiti, 55 percent felt they had been left out of social activities, 48 percent had been insulted intellectually, and 47 percent had been called names or racial slurs. Most surprisingly, 40 percent had been insulted in class by a teacher.

Still, it is important to recognize that decreasing prejudice is not the same as decreasing institutional racism. The latter is much more challenging to dismantle given the vested interests among those privileged to maintain the status quo.

Ethnicity: Identity and Conflict

8.4.2 Explain how ethnic diversity within a society is related to "symbolic ethnicity" and rates of genocide and ethnic violence.

Ethnicity is fluid; but it is not equally fluid for everyone. Sometimes ethnic identification is stronger than at other times. For some groups for whom discrimination has largely disappeared, such as the Irish and the Italians, ethnic identity has become mostly a choice (Waters 1990)—or what sociologist Herbert Gans referred to as **symbolic ethnicity** (Gans 1962, 1979). Ethnicity becomes "situational"—to be asserted in times and situations when it will increase their prestige and downplayed or ignored when it may decrease their prestige. Or it becomes symbolic ethnicity, something to participate in on special occasions, like St. Patrick's Day or Passover, but ignored the rest of the time. Just as old ethnicities can fade away, new ethnicities can emerge. More marginalized groups are often presented with less choice when if comes to ethnicity—or what Mary Waters (1990) refers to as "ethnic options." For instance, members of the Yoruba, Ibo, Fulani, and other West African ethnic groups transported to the United States during the slavery era were forcibly stripped of their distinctive cultures, until only a few customs remained, but they banded together to form a new ethnic group—African American. Although their ethnicity changed, this transformation was largely outside of their immediate control.

When several different ethnic groups are present in a single nation, they often compete for power and resources. Because there are around 5,000 ethnic groups in the world trying to share 190 nations, ethnic conflict is common, ranging from discrimination to violence and sometimes even civil war. Since 1945, 15 million people have died in conflicts involving ethnicity to some degree (Doyle 1998). At its most brutal, ethnic conflict can result in **genocide**, the planned, systematic destruction of a racial, political, or cultural group. The most infamous modern example of genocide is the Nazi massacre of 6 million Jews, Gypsies, gays, and other "undesirables" during World War II. But there have been a number of others. Between 1915 and 1923 the Turkish elite of the Ottoman Empire killed more than 1 million ethnic Armenians. In the 1990s, the dominant Hutu ethnic group killed hundreds of thousands of minority Tutsi in Rwanda and Burundi; and a new euphemism for genocide, "ethnic cleansing," arose when majority Serbs killed hundreds of thousands of minority Muslims in Bosnia. War in Kosovo in 1999 was prompted by the charges that Serbian forces were engaging in "ethnic cleansing" of the Kosovar Albanians.

Why do ethnic minorities live in relative harmony in some countries although in others they are at each other's throats? There are no easy answers, but one factor appears to be *heterogeneity*. If there are many ethnic groups in the country, it is less likely that any one will dominate (in a genocidal manner). However, if there are only two or three, it is easier for them to characterize each other as demonic. Another factor is the rights and privileges given to minorities. In countries where ethnic minorities are accepted as ordinary parts of the political structure, they are less likely to compete for resources, real or imagined, and ethnic conflict is less common (Gurr 2000; van Amersfoort 1982). This also often means, however, that social hierarchies are well-established and institutionalized to the extent that groups in relative power have little to worry about the prospect of being "dethroned."

Challenging Institutional Inequalities

8.4.3 Distinguish between "assimilationist" and "pluralist" understandings of ethnic diversity in the United States.

A generation ago, social studies textbooks glowingly described America as a *melting pot*. The United States was praised for its acceptance of difference, lack of prejudice, and our ability to "melt down" all cultural differences into a single, savory American soup. Sociologically, this process seems unlikely because the dominant groups are rarely willing to let their characteristics melt away into the pot. Instead, minority groups were subject to assimilation, many of whom abandon their cultural traditions altogether and embrace the dominant culture. Only a few of their traditions

symbolic ethnicity
Discrimination has largely disappeared and ethnic identity has become mostly a choice to be asserted in times and situations when it will increase their prestige and downplayed or ignored when it may decrease their prestige.

genocide
The planned, systematic destruction of a racial, political, or ethnic group.

WHAT DO YOU THINK? WHAT DOES AMERICA THINK?

The Melting Pot

Often referred to as a melting pot society, the United States boasts a rich variety of ethnic customs and traditions. As a society, we are trying to find a balance between assimilation and division.

What do you think?

Some people say that it is better for a country if different racial and ethnic groups maintain their distinct customs and traditions. Others say that it is better if these groups adapt and blend into the larger society. Which of these views comes closer to your own?

- ◯ It is better for society if groups maintain their distinct customs and traditions.
- ◯ It is better for society if groups adapt and blend into the larger culture.

What does America think?

The responses to this question were split almost in half. About 55 percent of respondents thought it was better if groups adapted and blended into the larger society. White respondents (56%) were more likely to think that than were black respondents (53%), and those who identified as other race were least likely to feel groups should assimilate (42%).

SOURCE: General Social Survey, 2014.

THINKING CRITICALLY ABOUT SURVEY DATA

Why do you think there were only small differences in responses by racial classification? In many areas of the world, the question of assimilation and group difference leads to civil war and even genocide. Why do you think that does not happen in the contemporary United States?

---

entered the pot, mostly food (like pizza) and slang terms (like *pal* for friend, from the Romany word for "brother"). Most traits and traditions were left behind. It was Italian Americans in the process of assimilating, not Italy, that gave us pizza; it was unknown in Palermo until a Pizza Hut franchise opened there. Besides, only white Europeans were invited to melt down. Asians, Native Americans, and Blacks were presented with a different array of options.

Some immigrant groups felt that assimilation was not desirable. They didn't want to lose their distinctive customs, social norms, language, and religion. Why couldn't they continue to speak their native language, read newspapers from home, eat the same food they ate at home, and still be Americans? Maybe in the nineteenth century, when the journey from the homeland to the United States took months and there was little chance of ever returning, assimilation made sense, but now the homeland was only a short plane flight away, and friends and relatives back home as close as a telephone call or e-mail message.

During the 1980s and 1990s, many minority groups proposed pluralism as an alternative to the melting pot. **Pluralism** maintains that a stable society need not contain just one ethnic, cultural, or religious group. The different groups can treat each other with mutual respect instead of competing and trying to dominate each other. Thus, minority cultures can maintain their own distinctiveness and still participate in the greater society without discrimination.

pluralism

Maintains that different groups in a stable society can treat each other with mutual respect and that minority cultures can maintain their own distinctiveness and still participate in the greater society without discrimination.

U.S./WORLD

WHO'S FOREIGN BORN?

The United States proudly calls itself "a nation of immigrants." What percent of the population in the following countries is foreign born—and what percentage of those immigrants are citizens of their new country? Consider this: why is the percentage of foreign-born people higher than the average in the United States and the percentage who are citizens lower than average?

Country	Foreign Born (%)	Those of Them Who Are Citizens (%)
Switzerland	27.7	45.2
Australia	27.3	83.4
Canada	19.8	92.0
Austria	16.2	52.9
Sweden	15.5	84.3
United States	13.0	60.2
Germany	12.8	61.0
Netherlands	11.5	77.8
OECD average	9.3	61.9
Belgium	15.2	61.8
Chile	2.4	—
Czech Republic	7.1	74.8
Denmark	8.2	49.6
Estonia	14.9	38.3
Finland	5.3	66.4
France	11.9	62.4
Greece	6.6	29.1
Hungary	4.3	84.9
Iceland	11	83
Ireland	16.3	56.4
Israel	23.2	—
Italy	9.4	37.4
Japan	1.6	—
Korea	1.9	—
Luxembourg	42.6	22.4
Mexico	0.8	—
Norway	13.2	71.8
Poland	1.8	92
Portugal	8.4	80.7
Slovak Republic	2.9	88.6
Slovenia	14.6	90.6
Spain	14.3	34.3
Turkey	1.2	—
United Kingdom	11.9	66

SOURCE: Data from OECD, OECD Indicators of Immigrant Integration, 2015.

INVESTIGATE FURTHER

1. Only a few countries have higher percentages of foreign-born people than the United States, but the percentage of that group who are citizens of their new country varies dramatically. What might explain the differences between Australia and Switzerland, for example?

2. Why is the percentage of foreign-born people higher than the average in the United States and the percent who are citizens lower than average?

Multiculturalism

8.4.4 Explain the difference between "multiculturalism" as an ideal and as realized in a society with rich cultural diversity.

multiculturalism

The doctrine that several different cultures (rather than one national culture) can coexist peacefully and equitably in a single country.

At its most stable, pluralism becomes **multiculturalism**, in which cultural groups exist not only side by side, but equally. Real multiculturalism seems to be rare—one language, religion, or culture will usually dominate, either by numbers or by status, and people will be drawn to it, even in the absence of institutional discrimination. India, for instance, has 22 official languages, but official communication in the national arena must be conducted in Hindi or English, and for everyday communication people tend to prefer English.

Advocates of multiculturalism like to point out the case of Switzerland, where four linguistic and cultural groups enjoy complete equality under the law. But are they really equal in everyday life? As of 2016, nearly two-thirds (64%) of the population speaks German, 23 percent French, 8 percent Italian, and less than 1 percent Romansch (descended from Latin). Street signs are usually in the local language and German. In Parliament, speeches may be given in any of the national languages, but most politicians choose German, even if they speak something else at home. All schoolchildren must learn a second national language, but schools usually offer only German and French, so learning Italian or Romansch (at least in school) is not an option. Some people outside the German-speaking cantons often pretend that they do not understand German at all, as a way of resisting what they feel is linguistic imperialism by the "dominant" linguistic group. Clearly, the other languages do not enjoy the same prestige.

The U.S. assimilation model meant that English was preferred by society at large as the home language. The dominant culture expected that immigrants would enroll in English classes the moment they arrived; and, even if children were not punished for using their parents' birth language, they might grow up thinking that it was old-fashioned and outdated, a relic of their parents' generation. Today, however, many immigrants continue to speak their "native" language. Spanish is especially popular. The Hispanic preference for speaking Spanish has led to some controversy that speakers of Bengali, Muong, and Byelorussian, by comparison, do not generate. In the United States, 37.6 million people use Spanish

The United States is increasingly multicultural—and our institutions show it. Many American cities now have street signs in several languages, depending on the ethnic composition of the neighborhood. (This picture was taken in Chinatown, in New York City.)

as their everyday language, more than any non-Spanish nation in the world, yet 31 states have laws declaring English their official language and permitting only English in official documents.

But, is it fair to call the United States "multicultural" just because we have a great deal of cultural diversity? Is race, alone, still the defining feature of U.S. social life? Some sociologists, using a more intersectional approach, have tracked two linked phenomena: the rise of a new black middle class (increasing numbers of black professionals, who live in affluent areas and wield significant disposable income) and the development of a permanent black underclass, of chronically

SOCIOLOGY AND OUR WORLD

LEARNING THE LANGUAGE

Why do immigrants moving to the United States today learn English faster than earlier waves of immigrants coming to the United States?

Given the insistence of some groups that English be declared the official language of the United States, and only English taught in schools, and the equally vociferous insistence of other groups to have bilingual education readily available, you might think that immigrants these days are far slower in learning English than previous generations. And you'd be wrong. In their book, *Century of Difference* (2006), sociologists Claude Fischer and Mike Hout show that today's immigrants learn English faster than previous generations.

Perhaps you're thinking that's because they come from English-speaking countries. Fischer and Hout compared recent Spanish-speaking immigrants—and more of them also spoke English when compared with previous generations and waves of Spanish-speaking immigrants to the United States. Why is this? Perhaps it's because those earlier generations were able to live in ethnically and linguistically contained neighborhoods (ethnic enclaves), reading only their own newspapers, shopping at stores owned by members of their ethnic group. Today, by contrast,

just about everyone in the same neighborhood, regardless of ethnicity, shops at the same bodegas, buys vegetables from the same Korean green grocers, and drops their laundry off at the Chinese laundry. So English is the *lingua franca*. Right? But this has effects on native-born Americans as well.

This may also mean that other Americans are more likely today to speak a language other than English. Consider how different age groups responded to the General Social Survey question in 2016: "Can you speak a language other than English?" (see figure). Whether this is a cohort effect cannot be shown here. It is also true that these are self-reports of the ability to speak another language. So, it may be that younger people are more likely to claim they speak a language other than English even if they do so without much proficiency. But it might be the case that immigrants coming to the U.S. are learning English faster than they used to *and* that all Americans are also becoming more likely to be able to speak languages other than English as well.

Ability to Speak a Language Other than English by Age, 2016

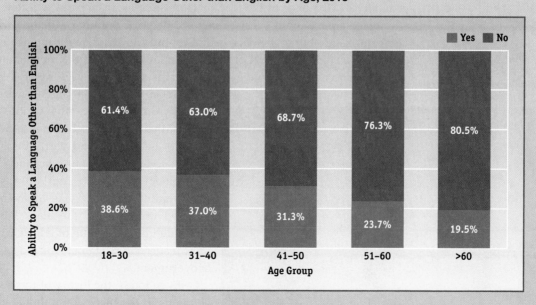

SOURCE: Data from General Social Survey 2016.

life chances

A person's abilities to have access to material goods (food and shelter) and social resources (health care, education) that together control the quality of life.

unemployed or underemployed poor people in the nation's ghettos. In both these cases, sociologists following William Julius Wilson (1978, 1987, 2009), argue that class is a more important predictor than race of your "**life chances**" (the sort of life, job, education, marriage, and health you are likely to have). In other words, race used to be the single most important force in our lives, but now that some blacks have become middle class, and others remain mired in a permanent underclass, class has become the more salient feature in our lives. Because the urban poor are so often people of color, we "see" race more readily than class, but Wilson argues that class actually exerts more social influence over our lives. Race is often a shorthand for class, yes, but it also exerts an independent effect on one's life chances. Even black professionals face discrimination and archaic stereotypic attitudes.

Movements for (and Against) Racial and Ethnic Equality

8.4.5 Understand the history of movements for racial equality in the United States and their continued significance today.

For many years, in the United States and around the world, racial prejudice and institutionalized forms of racial inequality and discrimination went hand in hand. Beginning in the middle of the twentieth century, these barriers began to fall—but not without significant struggle. In 1948, President Harry Truman lifted segregation in the military (today the U.S. military is perhaps the most integrated institution in the country). In 1954, in the case *Brown v. Board of Education of Topeka*, the U.S. Supreme Court ended centuries of legal segregation in education. The next year, a black woman, Rosa Parks, refused to give up her seat in a crowded bus in Montgomery, Alabama, in violation of segregation laws on public transportation. After she was arrested, Rev. Dr. Martin Luther King led a yearlong boycott of the Montgomery bus system, catapulting him to the national stage as the leader of the Civil Rights movement. In 1957, in Greensboro, North Carolina, the "Greensboro Four" attempted to integrate a racially segregated lunch counter at Woolworths.

These events heralded a decade-long struggle that culminated first in the successful passage of the Civil Rights Act in 1964, and successive campaigns for equality in all arenas of U.S. life that continue to this day. Nonviolent campaigns (modeled after Gandhi's resistance to British rule in India) were met with murder, lynching, and shocking police brutality; but the steadying guidance of Dr. King, and the sustaining support of the black church, enabled the movement to consolidate its successes. Notable events—such as the Voting Rights Act (1965) and the March on Washington (1963)—were accompanied by dramatic, and often vicious opposition by Southern police and elected officials. Partly due to its success, and partly because of how long success seemed to take, the Civil Rights Movement splintered into groups following more militant leaders like Malcolm X (assassinated in 1965) and the Black Panther Party (founded in 1968), both of which argued for direct insurrection against an irredeemably racist government.

Even today, the legacy of those movements remains in the black community—in the black church, where so many of the Civil Rights

The Greensboro Four attempted to integrate a lunch counter at Woolworths in 1957. (From right to left: Joseph McNeil, Franklin McCain, Billy Smith, and Clarence Henderson).

leaders began their careers, and in popular culture, where films like *Do the Right Thing* (1989) and political rap like Public Enemy (in the 1980s) or perhaps Kendrick Lamar more recently (both of whom urge listeners to "fight the power"). Indeed, Beyoncé's Super Bowl 50 (2016) performance continued a long tradition of using popular culture to send messages about racial inequality and the continuing fights for social justice and civil rights. Beyoncé's hit single was "Formation" on her newly released album, a song that touched on continued police brutality against the black community, the black Panthers, and Malcolm X. Indeed, the music video for Formation depicted a young black man in a hoodie dancing in front of armed police officers with graffiti in the background reading, "Stop shooting us" referencing the most recent killing of a black man, Mario Woods, in San Francisco, as well as the use of a hoodie in reference to the exoneration of a man in a neighborhood watch who killed an unarmed 17-year-old black boy (Trayvon Martin) in Sanford, Florida, who happened to be wearing a hoodie while walking home at night. After Martin's killer was not sentenced, pleading self-defense, the hoodie became the symbol of an international social movement about racial inequality. The movement has since taken on the slogan "Black Lives Matter" in reference to the disproportionate deaths of black people at the hands of (often white) state authorities. When a case erupted in Ferguson, Missouri, when a white police officer shot and killed 18-year-old Michael Brown, a social movement infrastructure was already in place to make sense of the event in light of disproportionate levels of violence committed against black boys and men.

The early victories of the Civil Rights movement in both making institutional inequality visible and in successfully challenging discrimination in housing, employment and education especially inspired other minority groups to see their experiences as structured social inequality, based more on their social status than on any particular cultural or personality trait that might hold them back. By the late 1960s and early 1970s, groups of Chicano activists, Asian American activists, and Native American activists began to challenge all racial and ethnic forms of discrimination. Globally, the campaigns for racial and ethnic equality have met with dramatic successes. Most nations with long-standing institutionalized discrimination along racial grounds have abandoned those policies.

Racial and ethnic classifications still blight the political landscape, however. The wholesale efforts at genocide in Rwanda, the "ethnic cleansing" by ethnic Serbs in Bosnia and Kosovo, in the 1990s, and the viciously racialist policies in the Sudan and Somalia today expose the ways that ethnic identity can maintain murderous policies. Indeed, the Black Lives Matter movement underway in the United States and beyond today illustrates that while great progress has been made, institutionalized forms of inequality still structure different life chances, experiences, and opportunities for different racial and ethnic groups. The road is inevitably toward greater equality, tolerance of others, and multiculturalism, but the road is filled with obstacles, and the setbacks are many.

Local police throughout the segregated south used dogs and fire hoses to terrorize nonviolent civil rights protesters. This photo was taken in Birmingham, Alabama, in 1965.

Resistance to Racial and Ethnic Equality

8.4.6 Recognize the history of opposition to racial inequality in the United States and what role it plays in contemporary racial and ethnic relations today.

Of course, not everyone supports racial equality. Some people actively oppose it. The mobilization of social movements by so many ethnic and racial minorities mobilized some members of the majority to assert they equality had gone too far, done too much damage to the "real" America, and had resulted in native-born white Americans becoming the new victims of reverse discrimination. Even in the beginning, the Civil Rights movement was met with significant opposition in both the North and the South. Candidates campaigned for elective office on a segregationist ticket; one South Carolina senator, Strom Thurmond, ran for president in 1948 on the "Dixiecrat" ticket, a breakaway from the integrationist Democratic Party, promising to maintain segregation throughout the south. (It was revealed in his last years that he had had a youthful affair with a black woman who had worked for his family and had supported their secret daughter for seven decades.) Thurmond carried four states—Alabama, Mississippi, Louisiana, and South Carolina—the most states ever won by a third-party candidate for president.

Most opposition to racial and ethnic equality remains attitudinal; people might not like the idea of equality, but they rarely do anything more than vote for candidates who think as they do. Some go further, believing that the government is proceeding down the wrong path, or that the government is not doing enough to protect native-born white people. A few join hate groups.

People join hate groups to promote discrimination against ethnic and other minorities, usually because they feel that the main society is not doing a very good job of it. The Know-Nothing Party was formed in 1849 to promote anti-Catholic and anti-immigrant legislation. The Ku Klux Klan (KKK), formed shortly after the end of slavery in 1863, tried to prevent newly freed blacks from acquiring social equality with both political legislation and the more immediate tactics of violence and intimidation. When open discrimination is commonplace in the main society, these groups can acquire a great deal of political power. The Know-Nothings managed to dominate several state legislatures, including Massachusetts, and promoted the sitting president, Millard Fillmore, in the 1852 presidential election (he lost, but not due to an anti-immigrant agenda). At its height in the 1920s, the second Ku Klux Klan had more than 4 million members and was praised by many public figures, including President Warren Harding.

When open discrimination is frowned upon in the main society, it becomes more difficult for hate groups to get laws passed or sponsor successful political candidates. Former KKK Grand Wizard David Duke rose highest, when he captured 55 percent of the white vote in the 1989 Louisiana gubernatorial election, although he had to explain that his KKK membership was a "youthful mistake." Similarly, when Duke supported Donald Trump as a candidate during the 2016 presidential race, Trump denied formal affiliation with Duke and knowledge of the KKK. Hate groups today usually do not hope to legislate discriminatory policies. Instead, they want to make their presence known, win supporters, and promote individual acts of discrimination, especially violence.

Today, many hate groups have moved beyond marching in strange costumes or starting fistfights on talk shows to using up-to-date tools of mass media and marketing: attractive, professionally produced books, music, Web pages, and social networking sites that hide their racist beliefs under a veneer of respectability. In public presentations, they never use racist slurs. They say that they are interested in science, Christianity, or patriotism rather than racism. Many hate groups use the rainbow as a symbol to talk about race relations in the United States ("All of the colors of separate and equal, and that's the way it ought to be"). The number of hate groups in the United States has risen by over 50 percent since 2000. Today there are 892 groups active across the United States (Southern Poverty Law Center 2016). Yet there are perhaps only 50,000 hard-core members of hate groups and no more than 500,000 "fellow travelers," people who read the literature, browse the websites, and agree with racist ideologies (Potok 2006). A more subtle threat of hate groups is to draw attention away from everyday forms of prejudice and discrimination (see FIGURE 8.8).

This increase in hate crimes is not just an American problem. Significant increases in immigrant populations in European countries, coupled with fears of terrorism and the economic downturn, have provoked many into targeting immigrants. Across Europe, national governments are alarmed at the dramatic increases in hate crimes against Muslims.

FIGURE 8.8 Offenses by Bias Motivation, 2005–2015
Although membership in organized hate groups is relatively low, there is an alarming increase in violent crimes in which the victim was chosen because of his or her membership in some minority group. In 2005, the FBI documented 7,163 hate crimes. The most (2,630) were against blacks, and 828 were against whites. The second highest group, however, was anti-Jewish (848). There are more anti-Semitic crimes than against all other religious groups combined. The 128 anti-Islamic crimes, however, are by far the fastest growing type of bias crime.

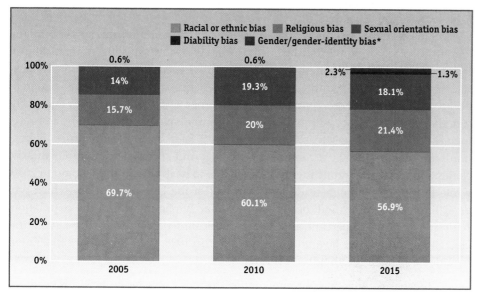

NOTE: The FBI did not categorize hate crimes as biased by gender or gender-identity in 2005 or 2010. So, those data only appear for 2015.

SOURCE: Data from https://www.bjs.gov/content/pub/pdf/hc0309.pdf; https://ucr.fbi.gov/hate-crime.

iSOC AND YOU Resistance and Mobilization to Racial and Ethnic Inequality
Because ethnicity and race are both elements of *identity* and social bases for *inequality*, race and ethnicity are always "political"—that is categorization and inequality are always subject to resistance. Oppositional movements may form to ethnic and racial inequality in the same way that they become part of our lives: People interact with each other, forming stable movements and movement organizations. That is these *interactions* become *institutionalized* in movements and organizations. Making coalitions with others, whose identity and inequality *intersect* with yours can be a viable political strategy. But because ethnicity is so often a community (regularized patterns of interactions among those seen as similar), such coalitions may be difficult.

Conclusion
Race and Ethnicity NOW

Sociologists understand that, as the geneticist Craig Venter wrote, there is no genetic, biological or anatomical foundation for racial classification: Race is a *social* construct. Race has meaning only in the social world, not in the natural world. That doesn't mean race isn't real: Race is a core element of our identity, and a primary mechanism for social stratification, a way that societies are organized unequally. Even more than that, race is not a "thing," a "possession," something you have or are—but also something you do, every day, in every interaction. And race is an element of every institution with which you interact and in which you find yourself.

Every one of us constructs our identity, at least in part, through race and ethnicity. It is one of the most important foundations of identity, an anchor that ties us to family, tradition, and culture. And yet virtually every one of us also wants to be treated as an individual, by our talents and achievements alone. We love it when race and ethnicity give us a sense of belonging and community; we hate it when our race and ethnicity are used against us, to deny us opportunities or to suggest that we received them for reasons other than hard work and merit. Maybe it is simply that we each want to be the ones who decide when race matters and when it doesn't: It should matter when we need to feel the connections among our roots, and it shouldn't matter when we want to be seen as individual trees.

But just as race and ethnicity seem to tie us to one common ancestry, a common identity, a place of blood and birth, those categories are shifting dramatically in the contemporary world. These processes expose the *sociology* of race and ethnicity: The experiences of fixed and essential characteristics are the invention of different groups as they come into contact with each other. (After all, virtually every culture that had no contact with other people did not have an understanding of race; they simply called themselves "human beings.") Race, as an idea, requires interaction with others—that is, it requires not biology but society and culture. And the changes in racial and ethnic identities are liable to be dramatic and lasting. In 2050, white Europeans will constitute less than half of the U.S. population (which will be 420 million), Latinos will occupy approximately one-quarter of the population, African Americans 15 percent, and Asian Americans 8 percent. We will be a multiracial nation; but will we be a multicultural one? In 1998, then-President Bill Clinton heralded a rich and multicultural future:

> Today, largely because of immigration, there is no majority race in Hawaii or Houston or New York City. Within five years, there will be no majority race in our largest state, California. In a little more than 50 years, there will be no majority race in the United States. No other nation in history has gone through demographic change of this magnitude in so short a time. [These immigrants] are energizing our culture and broadening our vision of the world. They are renewing our most basic values and reminding us all of what it truly means to be American.

Ten years later, during the presidential campaign of 2008, this phrase was often repeated in black churches and other cultural centers of the black community: "Rosa sat so that Martin could walk. Martin walked so that Barack could run. Barack ran so that our children can fly." In that slogan, more than half a century was spanned, from Rosa Parks's historic refusal to give up her seat on that segregated bus in Montgomery, Alabama, in 1954, to Rev. Dr. Martin Luther King's historic march across that bridge in Selma, Alabama, on his way to Montgomery, to Barack Obama's historic campaign to become America's first African American president.

Have we arrived? Sociologists would say "Yes and no." We have never, as a society, been more racially and ethnically equal; and yet, we are among the most racially divided nations in the industrial world. Race remains one of the best predictors of where you will end up in your life. A simple increase in numbers does not necessarily bring equality. In a well-known essay, sociologist Norman Glazer (1998) states, "We are all multiculturalists now." Will we start acting like it?

CHAPTER REVIEW Race and Ethnicity

8.1 Thinking Sociologically about Race and Ethnicity

To sociologists, race is socially constructed, not biologically determined. As a socially constructed identity category, race refers to a class of individuals who are understood to be differentiated by shared physical characteristics and are believed to share a common genetic ancestry. *Race is a biological fiction with a political function.* Racial categories have been socially invented and "discovered" throughout history as a means of producing hierarchies between "types" of people. Race has always been about more than racial *difference*—from the beginning, distinguishing different races has been a "political" project in that it has been about establishing racial hierarchies ("superior" and "inferior" races). Yet such a perspective remains unpopular; most of us want to believe that race has some "real" foundation in biological facts. "Race" was initially used to mean something more similar to the ways we might use the term *culture* today (e.g., the German "race"). Today, race has different meanings. But some of the meanings that were once associated with race are today associated with our understanding of "ethnicity." Ethnicity refers to a group of people with a shared cultural identity, founded on shared national identity, ancestry, language, religious beliefs, and collections of cultural traditions and practices. There are some similarities and differences between what sociologists call "race" and what they refer to as "ethnicity." But the largest is that ethnicity is something much more fluid in nature—meaning people both classify themselves and are classified by others as a race, but are more likely to "opt in" to various ethnic identities. In general, ethnicity has a more fluid quality than does race; people's racial identities are more stable over time than are ethnic identities. Race and ethnicity simultaneously help us understand who "we" are, and also where "we" fit in the societies in which we live. Racial and ethnic systems of classification and categorization often *feel* natural and inevitable. It can sometimes be hard to imagine how else we might separate people into different groups. But part of using the sociological imagination is in recognizing that the features and factors that feel intensely relevant to us in terms of understanding who is different from or similar to us are, in important ways, arbitrary.

8.1 Key Terms

ethnic group A group that is set apart from other groups by language and cultural traditions. Ethnic groups share a common ancestry, history, or culture.

race Social category, still poorly defined, that depends on an assumption of biological distinction to rate and organize social groups.

ethnicity Social category that depends on an assumption of inherent cultural differences to rate and organize social groups.

racial ethnicity An ethnic group believed to also have common psychological characteristics.

assimilation A process of decline in cultural distinctions between immigrants and mainstream society.

acculturation The process of acquiring a new culture and language.

assimilationist perspective The idea that when we are around one another for sustained periods of time, ethnic distinctions will gradually erode.

pluralist perspective This perspective argues that assimilation is not inevitable and that ethnic identities are not necessarily abandoned as ethnic groups become less isolated.

racial formations A theory that understands race and ethnicity as socially constructed identities. This means that both the *content* and *importance* of racial and ethnic categories are determined by the societies in which they exist.

interracial relationships Once labeled "miscegenation," a relationship between people of different racial categories.

minority group A group one is born into, which has a distinguishable identity and whose members have less power and access to resources than other groups in society because of that group membership.

in-group A group with which you identify and that you feel positively toward, producing a "we" feeling.

out-group One to which you do not belong and toward which you feel either neutral or hostile; the "they" who are perceived as different from and of lower stature than ourselves.

majority group A group whose members experience privilege and access to power because of their group membership. With regard to race, lighter-colored skin usually means membership in the majority group.

8.2 Racial and Ethnic Inequalities: Interactions and Institutions

Racial and ethnic inequality are pervasive features of social life. They are perpetuated in interactions with others in our society; but they are also institutionalized such that racial and ethnic inequality will be reproduced even absent conscious will or intent. Sociologists are interested in studying hate groups, collections of people who harbor damaging forms of prejudice and consciously work to perpetuate racial inequality, but we are just as interested in studying racism as an embedded feature of social life; we study the ways that societies are organized around categories of race and ethnicity that systematically work to disadvantage some racial and ethnic groups and privilege others.

Racism is a particularly powerful belief system revolving around the idea that members of different racial groups possess different and unequal traits. It involves more than a belief in general stereotypes, but a belief that one race (usually white) is inherently superior to the others. And it is not necessary to belong to the dominant racial group to buy into racism. Prejudice, racism, and discrimination are often based on a stereotype. Overt racism includes discrimination, and is more obvious than subtle racism, which may be unconscious thoughts based on stereotypes. Institutional discrimination is particularly damaging, being pervasive, systematic, sometimes without willful intent. Segregation refers to racial separation; like apartheid, it perpetuates and sanctions discrimination and inequality. In the United States, integration occurred when segregation's inequalities were acknowledged by the Supreme Court, although in reality segregation and inequality continue in many areas of American life, including residential segregation, the racial wealth gap, the racial income gap, and numerous others.

8.2 Key Terms

hate groups Groups with beliefs or practices that attack or malign a class of people often due to immutable characteristics associated with the group (like sexual orientation, skin color, ancestry, gender identity).

prejudice A set of beliefs and attitudes that cause us to negatively prejudge people based on their social location.

racism An ideology that holds that inequality based on race is justified because of assumed natural differences between races.

discrimination A set of actions based on prejudice and stereotypes.

stereotype Generalization about a group that is oversimplified and exaggerated and that fails to acknowledge individual differences in the group.

stereotype threat Term coined by Claude Steele to assess the extent to which labels about people "like us" have measurable impacts on their performances. It refers to the variation in performance measured when the belief that people who belong to an identity category you share are worse at a particular task than the comparison group.

overt racism Systematic prejudice applied to members of a group in clear, manifest ways, such as speech, discrimination, or a refusal to associate with members of that group.

subtle racism Systematic prejudice applied to members of a group in quiet or even unconscious ways; a simple a set of mental categories that one may possess about a group based on stereotypes.

stereotype promise Term coined by Jennifer Lee and Min Zhou to address the "promise" of being viewed through the lens of a positive stereotype that leads one to perform in ways that confirms the positive stereotype (the counterpart to "stereotype threat").

sentencing discrimination Black defendants receive harsher sentences from judges and juries, on average, when compared with white defendants on trial for the same crimes (even when we account for prior offenses and other issues that affect both conviction rates and other decisions regarding sentencing).

institutional racism The most subtle and pervasive type of discrimination, it is deeply embedded in such institutions as the educational system, the business world, health care, criminal justice, and the mass media. These social institutions promote discriminatory practices and traditions that have such a long history they just "seem to make sense," and minority groups become the victims of systematic oppression, even when only a few people, or none at all, are deliberately trying to discriminate.

racial wealth gap Gap in wealth—based on total financial assets including home equity—between blacks and whites. Because whites make more than blacks, are more likely to be in the professions, and more likely to own their own homes, the gap between them has continued to widen.

racial income gap The gap in income between blacks and whites. The gap between high-income whites and blacks is astonishingly high, and because of the racial income gap over time, even middle-income whites have far more wealth than high-income blacks.

color-blind racism The process of disregarding race as a method attempting to realize or express equality, it has the unintended consequence of reproducing racial inequality in new ways.

residential segregation Institutional discrimination of housing created neighborhoods, usually with lower quality infrastructure, for whites and other race and ethnic groups.

legacy of slavery Those enduring forms of racial inequality that result from generations of systematic, institutionalized, legal forms of racial oppression.

8.3 Ethnic Identities in the United States

U.S. citizens have origins in many countries and cultures. Ethnicity changes from generation to generation. The further removed generationally people are from their origins, the fewer the ties to their original culture and to people sharing those traditions. This is how people lose identification with an ethnic group. In a few generations, U.S. citizens with European origins, the largest percentage of Americans, have typically lost identification with their culture of origin. There are few Native American people left in the United States. This group suffers stereotyping and deprivation, with few resources, as a result of "protection" on reservations as their lands were diminished. Although few original tribal cultures remain, their ethnic identity is a source of pride. People with Latin American origins have great diversity due to the numerous countries and languages of origin. Together they are the largest ethnicity in the United States, with the greatest growing affluence and population. People of sub-Saharan African origin, called African Americans, share a unique heritage, having been brought here against their will, abducted and transported as slaves, and later subjected to "Jim Crow" laws. Asian Americans and Middle Eastern Americans, who also hail from numerous countries, often come from middle-class backgrounds originally and tend to be well off and highly educated compared to other U.S. ethnic groups. Both groups suffer from stereotyping, including the tendency to be seen as a "model minority," and the latter group, most recently, have been victims of increased hostility and discrimination.

8.3 Key Terms

scientific racism The science of "breeding," and encouraged laws that would help the country breed a superior race, eugenics.

ethnic renewal Process by which ethnic identities are reconstituted and reclaimed after having been discarded earlier.

racialization or ethnicization Twin processes of ascribing either racial or ethnic qualities to groups who did not identify themselves as such.

8.4 Resistance and Mobilization to Racial and Ethnic Inequality

One of the problems in combating prejudice is that it is not merely a matter of individual perceptions. Prejudice is a self-fulfilling prophecy. We see what we expect to see and don't see what we don't expect to see, even in ourselves. However, people can and do decrease their prejudice, especially when they work together toward a common goal, have strong role models who contradict stereotypes, and see and experience less institutional discrimination, which makes inequality seem normal and natural. Ethnic conflict arises from ethnic diversity in a nation, coupled with differential power and resources. Conflict includes discrimination, violence, civil war, and, at its most extreme, genocide. The more diversity, the less likely that any one ethnicity will be demonized. Conflict is also less likely when ethnic groups are part of a nation's political structure. Instead of conflict, assimilation may occur in a "melting pot," as in the United States, although this results in loss of ethnic identity for minority ethnicities, with dominance of the majority. An alternative is pluralism, which preserves and respects diversity, resulting in multiculturalism, in which cultural groups exist not only side by side, but equally. Real multiculturalism seems to be rare—one language, religion, or culture will usually dominate, either by numbers or by status, and people will be drawn to it, even in the absence of institutional discrimination. So have we arrived? Sociologists would say "Yes and no." We have never, as a society, been more racially and ethnically equal; and yet, we are among the most racially divided nations in the industrial world. Race remains one of the best predictors of where you will end up in your life. A simple increase in numbers does not necessarily bring equality.

8.4 Key Terms

symbolic ethnicity Discrimination has largely disappeared and ethnic identity has become mostly a choice to be asserted in times and situations when it will increase their prestige and downplayed or ignored when it may decrease their prestige.

genocide The planned, systematic destruction of a racial, political, or ethnic group.

pluralism Maintains that different groups in a stable society can treat each other with mutual respect and that minority cultures can maintain their own distinctiveness and still participate in the greater society without discrimination.

multiculturalism The doctrine that several different cultures (rather than one national culture) can coexist peacefully and equitably in a single country.

life chances A person's abilities to have access to material goods (food and shelter) and social resources (health care, education) that together control the quality of life.

SELF-TEST

⟩ CHECK YOUR UNDERSTANDING

1. Which of the following is an action or behavior, rather than a belief or an attitude?

   a. Racism

   b. Prejudice

   c. Stereotype

   d. Discrimination

2. One of your classmates states that members of certain ethnic minorities are bound to get better grades on the exam because they are smarter. Your classmate's statements are examples of _____

   a. racism.

   b. prejudice.

   c. a stereotype.

   d. discrimination.

3. According to sociologists, race _____

   a. is a biological fact.

   b. is a social construct.

   c. depends on country of origin.

   d. follows from culture.

4. Which of the following is not true of minority groups?

   a. Members are always fewer in number than the majority.

   b. The group has less social power than the majority.

   c. Group members have less access to resources than the majority.

   d. All of the above are true of minority groups.

5. Which of the following is true about institutional racism

   a. It is embedded in the education system, the business world, criminal justice, health care, and the mass media.

   b. It can occur when only a few people, or none at all, are deliberately trying to discriminate.

   c. It results from traditions of discriminatory practices that have such a long history they just seem to make sense.

   d. All of the answers are true.

6. In the United States, the fastest-growing ethnic group is comprised of people originating in _____

   a. sub-Saharan Africa.

   b. Asia.

   c. Latin America.

   d. the Middle East.

7. "Ethnic cleansing" is another name for _____

   a. civil war.

   b. genocide.

   c. prejudice.

   d. discrimination.

8. A pluralistic society is one in which _____

   a. everyone comes together in a "melting pot" and ethnic minorities assimilate.

   b. the majority is the standard for what is considered normal and minorities suffer.

   c. there are no minority groups because everyone is similar with a shared ethnicity.

   d. minority groups preserve their distinctive identities and have political participation.

Self-Test Answers: 1. d, 2. c, 3. b, 4. a, 5. d, 6. c, 7. b, 8. d

SEX AND GENDER

Gender is embedded in social institutions to such an extent that one of these images might strike many as "out of place." That is because gender organizes more than our interactions and identities; it is also institutionalized in ways that shape our experiences of inequality in ways that we often learn to take for granted.

→ LEARNING OBJECTIVES

In this chapter, using the iSoc framework, you should be able to:

9.1.1 Summarize the difference between sex and gender and the gender binary.

9.1.2 Recognize how each of the five elements of the iSoc model can be used to examine *sex* and gender sociologically.

9.1.3 Explain why sociologists question the idea that gender differences are primarily the result of biological sex differences.

9.1.4 Understand how the social response to intersex variations of anatomy reveal the social construction of sex and gender.

9.1.5 Describe why and how transgender people help sociologists understand gender and gender

inequality in ways that might be more challenging to discover by only studying cis-gender people.

9.2.1 Using the issue of sex segregation in public restrooms, explain what it means when sociologists claim that our society is organized by gender.

9.2.2 Describe the process of gender socialization and how we learn to look at the world with gender bias.

9.2.3 Summarize the gender similarities hypothesis, and explain how the media help shape androcentric understandings of gender in spite of it.

9.2.4 Describe what "doing gender" means by distinguishing between gender roles and gender relations.

9.2.5 Illustrate your understanding of intersectional analysis by examining the process of gender policing in high school and college.

9.2.6 Explain how gender affects not just our identities, but also our intimate lives and relationships.

9.3.1 Understand gender bias and how it can perpetuate gender inequality even when we do not realize it.

9.3.2 Explain how gender is embedded in the institution of education such that boys and girls have dramatically different experiences in school.

9.3.3 Understand how gender shapes what kind of work we perform (and do not perform) and how this is related to gender inequality.

9.3.4 Illustrate your understanding of how gender shapes our lives by summarizing gender differences in men's and women's attempts to balance work and family.

9.3.5 Explain what sociologists mean when they say that the institution of marriage is "gendered" and how this relates to gender inequality.

9.3.6 Understand how beliefs about inherent differences between women and men can shape concrete outcomes by examining Americans' beliefs about women in politics.

9.3.7 Understand what it means to talk about violence as "gendered."

9.4.1 Illustrate your understanding of gender inequality as a global phenomenon by explaining how gender inequality is related to the process of globalization.

9.4.2 Summarize the goals of the various "waves" of the Women's Movement and how women and men have participated.

9.4.3 Summarize the meaning of feminism and what it means to argue that it takes different forms in different cultural contexts.

9.4.4 Consider the progress toward gender equality made in recent history and how and why gender gaps still exist.

Introduction

Barbie will turn 61 in 2020. First introduced by Mattel in 1959, Barbie quickly became an international icon of femininity. More than 1 billion Barbies have been sold (two dolls every second) in 150 countries.

Barbie dolls were given a voice—literally—in 1992. Among Teen Talk Barbie's phrases were "I love shopping!" and "Math class is tough!" These sentiments suggested a distinctly feminine identity built around looking attractive and steering clear of science and math, where public life takes place in shopping malls.

The idea that men and women have fundamentally different identities and occupy different social worlds pervades many cultures—including ours—today. Men and women "think, feel, perceive, react, respond, love, need and appreciate differently"—so differently that we might as well be from different planets, was how best-selling self-help author John Gray put it in "Men Are from Mars, Women Are from Venus" (Gray 1992: 5), the same year Barbie began to speak.

Yet, you are also probably attending a coeducational school, where you may live in the same dorms, take the same tests, and are graded (you hope) by the same criteria as members of the opposite sex. At home, we live in the same houses, use the same bathrooms, and often watch the same television programs as our opposite-sex family members or spouses. We live in a world of *both* gender difference *and* gender similarity.

Gender is one of the fundamental building blocks of identity. Every society in the world classifies people by whether they are male or female, and a host of social roles and relationships are prescribed as a result. And gender is one of the fundamental ways in which societies organize themselves and distribute resources. Gender inequality is a nearly universal phenomenon; to be a man or a woman means not only difference but also hierarchy.

Gender is expressed in every social *interaction* and embedded in every *institution* in society. Gender is an element of *identity*, a basis for social *inequality* and is experienced *intersectionally*.

Two big questions animate the sociological study of gender. Why do societies differentiate people on the basis of biological sex? And why are societies also based on gender inequality?

Women and men do often appear to be rather different creatures, and yet we are also so similar that we are able to work together, learn together, and even live together. Even Barbie. After all, she's not only been an elementary school teacher, aerobics instructor, nurse, and flight attendant, but also a surgeon, U.S. Army officer, firefighter, police officer, pilot, business executive, astronaut, and three-time presidential candidate!

9.1 Thinking Sociologically about Sex and Gender

Sex and gender are central elements of our identities. And gender plays a key role in our interactions with others as well. Have you ever had the experience of walking past someone and been unable to decide whether they are a man or a woman? Have you ever had to interact with a parent when you are not entirely sure whether his or her child is a boy or a girl? Most of us don't simply shrug our shoulders and move on with our day. We become obsessed with "finding out." And all sorts of things that have both no biological relationship with sex become the features to which we look to provide clues in our search for the answer: boy or girl; man or woman? Sometimes, people whose gender is often mistaken experience anger or frustration from others who interact with them. This is because gender is a central element of social organization, and our ideas about gender are part of an intricate set of cultural expectations that shape how we understand ourselves and everyone else as well.

Part of learning to think sociologically about sex and gender means that you need to unlearn some of the ways many people are taught to think about gender from a young age. Sociological research on sex and gender, for example, challenges the idea that boys and girls or men and women are as different as we tend to think of them. Evidence and research suggests that we are much more similar than we often think. This idea can be challenging to accept (even when sociological research can demonstrate it) because we often like to think about sex and gender as elements of our biology, not our society. Yet, disentangling the two is much more complex than you might first imagine. What we do know is that societies dramatically shape the ways in which we come to understand sex and gender and the discrete categories into which it is often assumed everyone will *naturally* fit. The fact is, we don't. And those individuals and identities that challenge the ways we think about sex and gender are important to sociologists, because they are a powerful illustration of what it means to think of sex and gender as "socially constructed" in the first place.

In this first section, we examine what it means to understand sex and gender from a sociological perspective. To do this, we will challenge you to question some ideas about sex and gender you might not even realize you hold. And you may find that you are much more resistant to this challenge than you thought you might be. But sociologists begin here, because it enables us to understand that sex and gender and systems of social (not biological) organization. And they are embedded in every institution and interaction you have. They are so much a part of the air we breathe, that it's often easy to not even realize they are there in the first place. But this is a key element of the sociological enterprise: to learn to see the ordinary as *extra*ordinary.

What Are Sex and Gender?

9.1.1 Summarize the difference between sex and gender and the gender binary.

Sociologists begin by distinguishing sex from gender. When we refer to **sex** we are talking about the biology of maleness and femaleness—our chromosomal, chemical, anatomical organization. **Gender** refers to the meanings that societies give to the fact of biological difference. Sex is male and female; gender is the cultural understanding of masculinity and femininity—like the idea that women are innately nurturing and cooperative, or the belief that men are inherently aggressive and competitive. Beliefs like these are often presented as related to biological differences between men and women. Indeed, much of social life is constructed around what sociologists refer to as the **gender binary**—the belief that humans come in two types, males who behave in masculine ways and females who behave in feminine ways. But sociological research has shown that the gender binary is better understood as rooted in our culture than our nature. In fact, beliefs about gender vary enormously. This is a more significant fact than you may realize. It is because of this variation that we know that claims about women's "innate" nurturing capacities or men's "inherent" predisposition toward violence are much more complex than they first appear.

Each of the social and behavioral sciences contributes to the study of sex and gender. Anthropologists illuminate the cross-cultural differences, whereas historians focus our attention on the differences over time. Developmental psychologists explore how definitions of masculinity and femininity vary over the course of your life. And it has been sociology's contribution to examine the ways in which our different experiences and different sources of identity and inequality (like class, or race) affect our understandings and experiences of gender.

People both create and internalize gender ideas. And we do so collectively as well as individually. **Gender identity** refers to our understanding of ourselves as male or female, masculine or feminine—what we ourselves believe it means to be a woman or a man. But sociologists are also interested in studying how other identities—like class, age, race, or sexuality—dramatically affect and inflect gender *identity* as well. Sociologists who observe the intersectionality of these identities speak, then, of gender identities as plural: *masculinities* and *femininities*. By understanding gender *identity* as plural, we acknowledge that what it means to a black college student in the Northeast may be different than to a retired white farmer in Kansas. In fact, the differences *among* men and *among* women are often greater than the differences that we imagine *between* women and men. So, for example, although there are small differences between girls and boys in math and language abilities, we all know boys who are adept at languages and can barely learn their times tables and girls who whiz through math class but can't conjugate a Spanish verb.

Like race and ethnicity, gender is not only a matter of cultural difference, but it is also a dynamic system of inequality. **Gender inequality** has two dimensions: the collective power of men over women and the power of some men over other men (by virtue of class inequality or race inequality, for example) and some women over other women (for the same reasons). Making the category of identity plural helps us look at gender "intersectionally," enabling us to understand that all masculinities or femininities are not considered equal. All known societies are characterized by some amount of gender inequality, in which men dominate women. This is called *male domination*, or patriarchy. **Patriarchy** literally means "the rule of the fathers," and although fathers don't rule in every case, men as a group do hold power over women as a group.

sex
A biological distinction; the chromosomal, chemical, and anatomical organization of males and females.

gender
A socially constructed definition based on sex category, based on the meanings that societies attach to the fact of sex differences..

gender binary
The belief that humans come in two types: males, who behave in masculine ways, and females, who behave in feminine ways, which is a belief sociological research has shown is better understood as rooted in our culture than our nature.

gender identity
Our understanding of ourselves as male or female, masculine or feminine.

gender inequality
Gender inequality has two dimensions: the domination of men over women, and the domination of some men over other men and some women over other women.

patriarchy
Literally, "the rule of the fathers"; a name given to the social order in which men hold power over women.

Mark Zuckerberg and Sheryl Sandberg work at the same company—Facebook. Zuckerberg is the Chief Executive Officer. Sandberg is the Chief Operating Officer. That a man and a woman work alongside one another in this capacity is a powerful illustration of some gains in gender equality—women, like Sandberg, are now entering positions that have long been reserved for men. Once there, however, the rules are sometimes a little different for them. One challenge women professionals face at work is *interactional*: how should a "professional woman" appear? What should she wear? Donning jeans, a plain grey t-shirt, and a hooded sweatshirt has long been Zuckerberg's stock and trade. It's part of the way he presents himself as a "man of the people." Sandberg never appears in a professional capacity wearing similar leisure attire. And if she did, would we take her as seriously as we do Zuckerberg? It might seem like a small dilemma, but it's a double bind for professional women that work to reproduce gender *inequality* in ways less easily identified.

And most societies also grant more power and resources to some men and some women. One definition of masculinity or femininity comes to dominate and becomes the standard against which everyone comes to be measured and by which they measure themselves. This is where race and class differences, among other bases of identity and inequality, come in.

The sociologist Erving Goffman described the ideal masculine gender identity in the United States that is still quite current today: "In an important sense, there is only one complete … male in America: a young, married, white, urban, northern, heterosexual, Protestant, father, of college education, fully employed, of good complexion, weight and height, and a recent record in sports" (1963: 128). Because it is certain that all males will, at some point, fail to measure up to all those criteria, Goffman then describes what it feels like to *not* have all those characteristics. "Any male who fails to qualify in any one of these ways is likely to view himself—during moments at least—as unworthy, incomplete, and inferior." This is significant because it illustrates an important fact about gender ideals: no one has to necessarily be able to achieve them for the set of ideals to exert power over groups of people. In fact, some scholars suggest that gender ideals are so powerful precisely because of their unattainability. We internalize prevailing gender ideas, with all of their inequalities, despite the fact that, sometimes, they hurt us.

iSoc: The Sociology of Sex and Gender

9.1.2 Recognize how each of the five elements of the iSoc model can be used to examine *sex* and gender sociologically.

Gender is both a foundation of our identities and a fundamental way that societies organize themselves, allocating tasks and distributing resources. Gender is produced in our interactions and embedded in our institutions, and different groups experience gender in different ways. We briefly consider some of the ways we can rely on the iSoc model in thinking about what kinds of questions sociologists who study sex and gender are interested in as well as considering the different ways that sociologists have learned to look at and study sex and gender in social life.

IDENTITY—Perhaps the first question a parent asks is: "Is it a boy or a girl?" (This, of course, happened in the era before sonograms and ultrasound and genetic testing—that is, through human history up until about 1980 or so). We ask this because we know that the answer sets the infant on one of two different paths. Gender is one of the foundations of our identity; indeed, we are boys or girls before we are pretty much anything else. Much of the socialization process is to ensure that little girls and little boys act in accordance with cultural definitions of masculinity and femininity.

INEQUALITY—Assuming that the genders are different is also often used as a form of justification for the *inequality* between them. The gender division of labor, for instance, has traditionally allocated different social tasks and different economic activities to women and men—and systematically rewarded them differently as well. Gender *inequality* is one of the most durable forms of social inequality, though it has been markedly reduced in recent years.

INTERACTIONS—Gender is not only something that you "have"—a gender identity that results from your socialization. You do not just absorb gender like a sponge or get imprinted with an identity like a puppy. Gender is also a process, something we "do." Many of our *interactions* with others are ways we confirm our gendered identities, producing the very differences we then observe. "Feeling like a man or a woman" doesn't just happen; we make it happen. And every time we do, we participate in justifying beliefs about gender that are embedded in the societies in which we live.

INSTITUTIONS—Although we are more likely to "see" how gender operates at the individual level, or even in a group, sociologists also understand that gender inequalities are embedded in the structure of our social *institutions*. So, for example, the allocation of household tasks like cleaning and cooking reflect, we may believe, natural differences between women and men. But in some countries, the school day has a three-hour lunch break during which time the children cannot stay in school; that is, they must go home. What does that mean for women's employment possibilities, women's economic equality? In the United States, the way we organize professional careers, putting the most intense work time at the beginning of the career, often means women are put at a disadvantage if they also want to start families because we believe that women "naturally" should be the primary caretakers of babies. (We're not saying the decision to stay home is a "bad" one; rather, sociologists are interested in the consequences of decisions like these that we are strongly influenced to make based on the organization of our society.)

INTERSECTIONS—Although gender is one of the central elements of our identity, and one of the major axes along which inequality is organization, gender does not work the same way for every group at all times. Race, class, ethnicity, age, sexuality—all of these and more—combine to shape our experiences of being gendered. Within any one society it may mean different things to be a man or a woman depending on race, religion, region, age, sexuality, class, and other social categories. Gender "*intersects*" with these other categories of identity and is experienced differently as a result.

By now, hopefully you are becoming more familiar with applying the iSoc model to different topics of sociological study. We live in a "gendered" society, which means that our experiences of just about anything you can imagine are structured by gender. Imagine how your life might have been different had you been born or transitioned to be socially recognized as a different gender. Although many experiences and opportunities are shared more equitably between girls and boys today than they have been historically, it remains the case that we live in a society in which gender is understood as a fundamental category of difference.

The Biology of Sex and Gender

9.1.3 Explain why sociologists question the idea that gender differences are primarily the result of biological sex differences.

Most everyday explanations of gender identity and gender inequality begin—and often end—with biology. The observed biological differences between women and men are thought to lead naturally, and inevitably, to the inequality we observe. For example, consider the idea that male upper body strength makes men "naturally" better hunters, or that lactation and pregnancy make females inherently more adept nurturing parents. If these differences are natural, it is thought, at least some amount of gender inequality is inevitable. From this perspective, changes in male–female relations to promote equality would contradict nature's plan.

To a sociologist, however, the opposite is true. It's not that gender difference causes inequality, but that gender inequality actually causes gender difference! This might sound odd. But consider a couple examples. "Everybody knows" that boys are better at math, right? Not so fast. Did you know that in most developed countries, fourth-grade boys are no better at math than fourth-grade girls are, and that in some countries, girls are actually *better* at math? Those countries in which girls are better at math turn out to be those countries that have the highest proportion of women in government, professional women working, and women with college degrees. That is, the more equal women are, the better girls do at math. Research shows that greater inequality leads to greater gender differences in math ability. Or consider the workplace. Gender inequality at work (as measured by the wage gap) is said to be the result of women's "fear of success"; they aren't as assertive, take lower-paying jobs, and don't ask for raises. This too, however, turns out to be untrue. Research shows that when women get the same opportunities in the workplace, they behave just like the men do. Lack of opportunity, not women's different personality, explains workplace inequality.

Sociological analyses of gender identity and gender inequality arose, in part, in response to biological claims of innate gender difference. These arguments rest on three types of evidence: evolutionary adaptation, different brain structures and chemistry, and hormonal differences. Sociologists must be aware of these sorts of arguments because sociological perspectives on sex and gender often run counter to them.

Falling outside of your culture's standard definitions of masculinity or femininity can be uncomfortable at best. But beyond comfort, the consequences of gender nonconformity can be severe, affecting your relationships, job opportunities, safety, and quality of life.

evolutionary imperative

The belief, typically used to justify traditional assumptions about masculinity and femininity, that males and females developed different reproductive strategies to ensure that they reproduce successfully and are able to pass on their genetic material to the next generation.

According to evolutionists, the differences we observe between women and men are the result of thousands of years of evolutionary adaptation (Daly and Wilson 1999; Buss 1995; Dawkins 1978). Males and females, according to this story, developed different "reproductive strategies" to ensure that they reproduce successfully and that they are able to pass on their genetic material to the next generation. This process is called the **evolutionary imperative**. Biologically, so they suggest, the male's part is to inseminate as many females as possible, increasing his chances that his offspring will survive. By contrast, the female must invest a significant amount of energy to ensure that her offspring is born and survives a very long infancy. Thus, the evolutionary argument goes, men are more aggressive, want more casual sex, and avoid commitment; females are nurturing, passive, and desire commitment (Symons 1985). To sociologists, these evolutionary arguments are unpersuasive. They work backward, by observing some difference in sexual behavior among contemporary people and then reasoning back to its supposed evolutionary origin. Proponents of such evolutionary imperatives use selective data and ignore other "natural" behaviors like altruism and cooperation. One could take the same evidence, in fact, and construct an equally plausible evolutionary explanation for exactly the opposite results (Hrdy 1981; McCaughey 2008).

SOCIOLOGY AND OUR WORLD

MONOGAMOUS MASCULINITY, PROMISCUOUS FEMININITY

Are we cherry-picking biological evidence to suggest men are naturally more promiscuous?

One group of evolutionists—evolutionary psychologists—argue that the size and number of reproductive cells lead inevitably to different levels of parental "investment" in children. (Males produce millions of tiny sperm; females produce only a few dozen comparatively huge eggs.) Sarah Blaffer Hrdy (1981) adds a few more biological facts to the mix. Unlike other mammals, she notes, human females conceal estrus; that is, they are potentially sexually receptive throughout their entire menstrual cycle, unlike other female mammals that go "into heat" when ovulating and who are otherwise utterly uninterested in sex. What is the evolutionary reason for this? Hrdy asks. (*Hint:* The female knows that the baby is hers, but the male can never be exactly sure.)

Could it be, she asks, that females might want to mate with as many males as possible, to ensure that all of them (or as many as possible) will provide food and protection to the helpless and dependent infant, thereby increasing its chances of survival? (Remember that infant mortality in those preindustrial cultures of origin was extraordinarily high.) Could it be that females have a natural propensity toward promiscuity to ensure the offspring's survival and that males have a natural propensity toward monogamy, lest they run themselves ragged providing food and protection to babies who may—or may not—be theirs? Wouldn't it be more likely for males to devise a system that ensured women's faithfulness—monogamy—and institutionalize it in marriage and then develop a cultural plan that would keep women in the home (because they might be ovulating and thus get pregnant)? And because it often takes a couple more than one "try" to get pregnant, wouldn't regular couplings with one partner be a more successful strategy for a male than a one-night stand?

Of course, no one would suggest that this interpretation is any more "true" than the one proposed by evolutionary psychologists. What Hrdy revealed is that one can use different (sometimes better) biological evidence and construct the exact opposite explanation. What Hrdy illustrates is that we should be *extremely* cautious in accepting evolutionary arguments about gender. But she also illustrates how readily we often accept arguments that support existing beliefs about gender.

Other research has stressed the importance of sex hormones like testosterone in males and estrogen in females in causing the differences we observe between men and women. But studies on this are equally inconclusive. For example, much hormone research concerns the effect of men's higher testosterone levels on men's greater aggressiveness as compared with women. Higher levels of testosterone *are* associated with increases in aggression. But it is equally true that aggressive behavior actually leads to an increase in production of testosterone. So the hormone could be either cause or effect, which makes it difficult to say that biology caused those changes (see Kemper 1990; Sapolsky 1997).

To a sociologist, biology is not necessarily destiny. But biology does provide the raw material out of which we develop our identities; that raw material is shaped, molded, and given meaning within the culture in which we find ourselves. So, sociologists of gender are best understood as exploring the interaction of biology and culture rather than pretending that something as complicated as personal identity or the social arrangements between women and men can be reduced to either nature *or* nurture.

The Medicalization of Sex and Gender

9.1.4 Understand how the social response to intersex variations of anatomy reveal the social construction of sex and gender.

One major contribution of cross-cultural research has been to challenge the "natural" dichotomy of two biological sexes (male and female) and two gender identities (masculinity and femininity). Some biologists have pointed out that even the simple dichotomy of male and female sex fails to capture all the various possible experiences in between, as for example with people with **intersex traits**, whose genital anatomy is in between male and female types or whose genetics include a mixture of female XX chromosomes and male XY ones. There are a variety of intersex traits that situate some people as not easily categorized as either biologically male or female. In the United States, the division between biological male and biological female is sometimes blurry. A small percentage of people are born intersex—that is, their biological sex is ambiguous enough as to be impossible to categorize as either male or female. One in about 1,500 babies are born with something that qualifies as an intersex trait (Fausto-Sterling 2000). The vast majority of these births are ones involving genital ambiguity; it is far rarer for people to have a chromosomal type other than XX (female) or XY (male), although they do exist. This means that the odds that you know someone who might be classified as intersex to some degree are good. This also means, as with all forms of identity and inequality, that it is an issue that deserves our understanding and respect.

intersex traits
People are said to have intersex traits when their bodies cannot be clearly categorized as fully male or female.

Different cultures have made sense of people that have intersex traits in different ways throughout time. Although acknowledged and revered in some societies throughout time, they have been concealed and medically "managed" in others. And even in societies in which intersex infants are medically managed, it is not always in precisely the same ways (Dreger 1998). For instance, while there are dozens of conditions that qualify bodies as "intersexed," only a small minority of conditions that qualify as intersex require some type of surgical or medical intervention in early infancy or childhood. Yet, it has long been true that intersex infants have undergone surgeries dangerously early in the course of their lives in ways that help preserve the gender binary—that idea that there are two (*and only two*) types of people: men and women.

Infants born with intersex traits is more common than you think. One way we often hear about it is when a professional athlete's sex is called into question. The International Association of Athletics Federations (IAAF) and the International Olympic Committee (IOC) sometimes ask athletes to undergo "sex testing" to determine whether or not they ought to be allowed to compete. Take the case of 18-year-old Caster Semenya, a middle-distance runner from South Africa, who

Semenya is here depicted racing and responding to the sex test she was forced to endure to continue competing alongside other women. What kinds of social pressures might have encouraged Semenya to align her presentation of self with "feminine" comportment and style following her highly publicized "sex verification test"?

literally "ran away" with the world record in the 800-meter race at the 2009 World Championships in Track and Field. After the race, her biological sex was challenged by a defeated rival and the IAAF required Semenya to submit to a sex test. Semenya "passed" her sex test and continues to compete today. Indeed, Semenya ran away with the gold medal for the 800-meter race in the 2016 Olympics in Rio de Janeiro. Sex verification cases brought against athletes by the IAAF are exclusively brought against athletes competing as women. Charges are typically—though not always— brought when the athletes in question begin to break records. Consider the collection of beliefs about gender behind this pattern of sex testing athletes.

Sociologists of sex and gender are interested in studying how societies respond to diversity in sex development because it illustrates the social construction of both gender *and* sex. Like people whose racial and ethnic identities do not neatly map onto available categories mentioned in Chapter 8, people with intersex traits also offer us a powerful picture of how much work it takes to fit everyone into categories that do not actually encompass *everyone*. Some scholarship examines the ways that process of "medicalization" as it relates to sex and gender (Kessler 1998; Fausto-Sterling 2000). **Medicalization** refers to the process by which *human* conditions comes to be defined and treated as *medical* conditions such that they also become subject to medical study, diagnosis, and treatment. For a long time, it was not uncommon for medical professionals to surgically alter intersex bodies such that they conformed to the two-sex system—often without parents, and nearly always without the children themselves, completely understanding what is happening. When this happens, sex has become "medicalized." Today, social activists fighting for the rights of people with intersex traits argue that surgical interventions are dangerous and unnecessary. And sociologists study the social movements and identity-based activism among people with intersex traits and their allies as well (Preves 2003; Davis 2015).

medicalization

The process by which *human* conditions come to be defined and treated as *medical* conditions such that they also become subject to medical study, diagnosis, and treatment.

Portrait of an Indian *Hijra* dressed up for a dancing performance.

Some anthropologists discuss sex and gender in similar ways, suggesting that there may be far more sexes and

MAP 9.1 **Mapping Gender-Diverse Cultures Around the World**
Throughout recorded history, a diversity of cultures around the world have recognized more than two sexes and/or genders. Indeed, in many cultures, individuals occupying a category other than man or woman have been given high social status. In some, more than two genders are not only recognized, but fully integrated into the society. Globally, the variety of ways that different societies have recognized more than two genders is incredible.

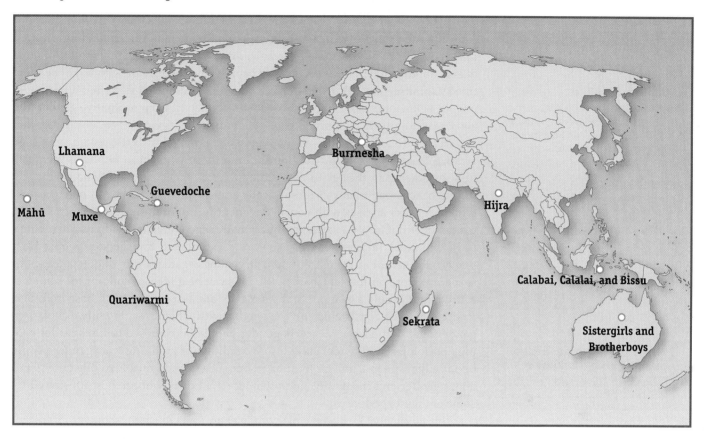

NOTE: This is not an exhaustive list of gender diversity around the world or throughout time.

SOURCE: Data from PBS, *Independent Lens.* "A Map of Gender-Diverse Cultures," August 11, 2015. Available at http://www.pbs.org/independentlens/content/two-spirits_map-html/.

genders out there than we acknowledge. Simply put, some cultures recognize more options than only two; other cultures recognize the possibility of being more than one (see MAP 9.1). Some societies do recognize more than two genders—sometimes three or four. The Navajo appear to have three genders—one for masculine men, one for feminine women, and one called *nadle* for those whose sex is ambiguous at birth. One can be born or choose to be nadle; they perform tasks for both women and men and dress in either men's or women's clothing according to the tasks they are performing. And they can marry either men or women. This illustrates that both sex and gender are best understood across a spectrum—rather than as discrete categories. *Hijras* in India occupy a similar space in Indian society, as a third gender category.

Numerous cultures have a clearly defined gender role for what people who live outside the gender binary as contemporary U.S. society (along with many others) defines it. These are members of one biological sex who take the social role of the other sex, usually a biological male who dresses and acts as a woman. In most cases, they are not treated as freaks or deviants but are revered as special and enjoy high social and economic status; many even become shamans or religious figures (Williams 1986). People with intersex traits are a powerful example of the fact that not everyone fits into the gender binary, but also that our society is organized around a gender binary despite the fact that our bodies and biology sometimes resist the system of sex and gender classification in place.

Transgender Identities: Blurring the Boundaries of Gender

9.1.5 Describe why and how transgender people help sociologists understand gender and gender inequality in ways that might be more challenging to discover by only studying cis-gender people.

transgender

An umbrella term that describes a variety of people, behaviors, and groups whose identities depart from normative gender ideals of masculinity or femininity.

cis-gender people

People whose gender identities are consistent with the identities they were assigned at birth based on sex characteristics.

And although people with intersex traits challenge our understanding of what makes people qualify as male or female, other groups challenge us to think more deeply about gender as well. Consider people who identify or who might be identified as transgender. **Transgender** is an umbrella term that describes a variety of people, behaviors, and groups whose identities depart from normative gender ideals of masculinity or femininity. Transgender people develop a gender identity that is different from the biological sex they were assigned at birth; as a group, they arrange themselves along a continuum from those who act in public as members of a sex other than the sex to which they were assigned, to those who chemically (through hormone therapy) or surgically transform their bodies to be consistent with the gender and sex with which they identify. Importantly, identifying as transgender does not imply a sexual orientation; transgendered individuals can identify as heterosexual, homosexual, bisexual, or asexual. And transgender people are a powerful illustration of just how much gender organizes our understandings of sexuality (more on that in Chapter 10). This can be a foreign concept for some because many people assume that the sex they are assigned at birth based on their anatomy will be consistent with the gender with which they identify. Scholars of gender refer to these people as **cis-gender people** (as opposed to transgender people). Sociologists of gender have a long tradition of studying transgender people because they are in a unique location in our society and are able to illustrate issues about gender and inequality that often affect all of us but are best illustrated by some of their experiences.

This means that, just as people with intersex traits illustrate about sex, transgender people help us to understand gender identity and behavior along a continuum from "our culture's definition of masculine" to "our culture's definition of feminine." Some people feel constrained by gender role expectations and seek to expand these by changing their behavior. Though there are significant penalties for boys who are effeminate ("sissies") and some, but fewer, penalties for girls who are masculine ("tomboys"), many adult men and women continue to bend, if not break gender norms in their bodily presentation. Some may go as far as to use the props of the opposite sex to challenge gender stereotypes; some people find erotic enjoyment in this, and others do it to "pass" into a forbidden world. Again, this runs along a continuum. Some people transgress gender boundaries for fun or for play, like women who wear man-tailored clothing or "power suits" to work. Other people wear full cross-gender regalia, undergo hormone therapy, and sometime surgical procedures as well. And there are many people in-between.

Although transgender remains relatively rare—estimates suggest between 1 in 4500 to 12,000 males, and between 1 in 8,000 to 30,000 females who undergo sex reassignment surgery (Van Kesteren, Gooren, and Megens 1996; Olyslager and Conway 2007)—the implications of such identities and procedures are enormous. For a long time (and in many cultures this remains true today), a discrepancy between one's biological sex and what one experienced internally as one's gender would privilege the body, as if it contained some essential truth about the person. If such conflicts were to be resolved by therapeutic interventions, they would "help" the person accept their body's "truth" and try and adjust their feelings about their gender. Transgender individuals enable us to dissolve what is experienced as an arbitrary privileging of the body at birth as the most important factor in identifying our sex or gender.

Research on transgender people is important because their experiences can often shed light on social issues that affect all of us; they are simply in a better place to highlight these issues. For instance, deciding who "counts" as a man or a woman is accomplished at multiple levels. At one level, it's accomplished in interactions as we socially recognize people as men or women. When we do this, we are typically responding to their *gender*, not their *sex*. But sex and gender are also decided on institutionally. So, for instance, if we consider whether or not someone who identifies as a woman but was assigned "male" at birth ought to be allowed to legally change her driver's license to represent her gender (Meadow 2010), to let her compete against other women in competitive sports, or to allow her to legally use public restrooms for "women," we are talking about institutional—not just individual—recognition. Perhaps not surprisingly, a great deal of collective anxiety is provoked surrounding these issues when we are forced to examine the fact that the criteria we rely on to assess gender are imperfect—something sociologists Laurel Westbrook and Kristen Schilt (2014) call a **gender panic**.

gender panic
Situations in which people react to ruptures in assumptions about gender assumed to be based in our biology by frantically reasserting the supposed "naturalness" of the male/female gender binary.

Interestingly, sociological research suggests that we do not apply the same criteria for assessing sex or gender everywhere. The criteria we apply to determine a

HOW DO WE KNOW WHAT WE KNOW?

JUST HOW MANY TRANSGENDER PEOPLE ARE THERE?

Estimating the size of the transgender population is more difficult than you might think. Currently, there are no nationally representative surveys that ask questions that would enable transgender people to anonymously identify themselves. This is part of the reason that estimates of the size of the population vary so widely. *The Williams Institute*—an independent research think tank conducting rigorous research on issues of gender and sexuality—suggests that the transgender population in the United States is approximately 700,000 people (Gates 2011). This is a higher estimate than other scholars suggest, but a more accurate estimate is challenging to achieve for two separate reasons. First, we lack questions on nationally representative surveys that might help us better enumerate transgender people (Westbrook and Saperstein 2015). Second, existing research suggests that, even if we were able to add a question, the changes necessary are much more complex than simply adding "transgender" as a third option when asking questions about gender (Schilt and Bratter 2015). This means that estimating the size of this population is challenging.

More recently, the U.S. Bureau of the Census published a report attempting to identify people who are likely to be transgender persons based on how they answer other questions that relate to sex and gender *identity* (Harris 2015). As we mentioned in Chapter 1, research on names can tell us more than you might think. In a 2015 report, Benjamin Harris attempted to identify the number of what he refers to as "likely transgender individuals" in the United States by combining Census data with data collected by the Social Security Administration, the latter of which collects three important pieces of data on every citizen with a Social Security Number: first and middle name, sex-coding (male or female), and date of birth. Harris combines these data sets to identify how many adults in the U.S. changed information in their accounts in ways that are consistent with a gender transition. Thus, by linking these data with the Census, Harris was also able to provide some basic demographic characteristics of "likely transgender people" as well as residential patterns.

To identify whether people are likely transgender, Harris first identified people who changed their names from a traditionally male name to a traditionally female name (or vice versa), and then asked whether those people also changed their sex coding (from male to female, or vice versa) in the same direction. Whether a name is "male" or "female" is determined by the proportion of people with that name who have a sex coding of "male" of "female." Some names (like John) are virtually only given to boys, whereas others (like Val) are given to boys and girls in roughly equal numbers. So, he had to think carefully about whether a name change might likely indicate transgender *identity* or not. Although the number of people who qualified as "likely transgender" in Harris's (2015) study was smaller, he was able to produce new knowledge about who transgender Americans are, where they live, and whether they are more likely to pursue legal transitions (measured by name and sex code changes with the Social Security Administration).

Likely Transgender Individuals in the United States

Here you can also see that the people Harris was able to identify as "likely transgender individuals" are not evenly distributed around the United States. That in and of itself is an interesting finding. And it could mean more than one thing. A larger proportion of the population in Washington, Oregon, and Vermont is transgender, for instance, than in Utah, Iowa, and Louisiana.

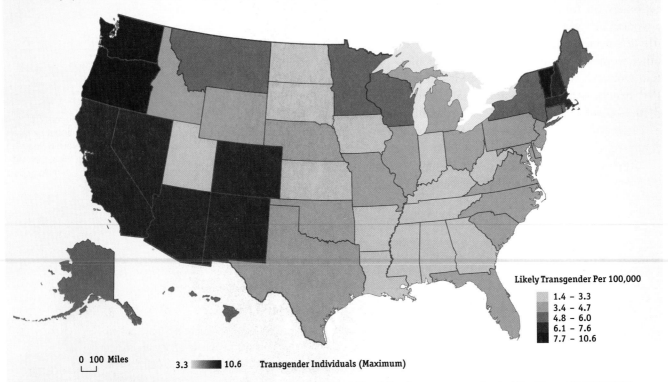

Likely Transgender Per 100,000

- 1.4 – 3.3
- 3.4 – 4.7
- 4.8 – 6.0
- 6.1 – 7.6
- 7.7 – 10.6

0 100 Miles

3.3 ▮▮▮ 10.6   Transgender Individuals (Maximum)

SOURCE: Data from U.S. Census Bureau, as of 2010. Refreshed July 13, 2015. Available at https://www.census.gov/content/dam/Census/library/working-papers/2015/adrm/carra-wp-2015-03.pdf.

person's gender (whether they qualify as a man or woman) vary; they're not the same everywhere. It might seem like a subtle finding, but it has widespread implications. Westbrook and Schilt (2014) analyzed news reporting surrounding gender panics associated with three separate issues having to do with transgender rights. Among their findings, they uncovered two important discoveries. First, they found that the bar for qualifying as men or women in gender-segregated spaces (restrooms, locker rooms, and sports teams, for instance) is higher than gender-integrated spaces (like classrooms, workplaces, or public spaces in general) (Schilt and Westbrook 2009; Schilt 2010). Second, they discovered that the criteria for being considered a man are much less demanding than the criteria to be considered a woman. The real anxiety appears around people who have penises who enter women-only spaces. Not everyone with a penis identifies or is identified as a man, nor do all those without penises identify as women.

This cultural anxiety provoked by penises in "women's" spaces belies a larger investment in a twin set of cultural ideals: the belief that all people with penises are uniquely capable of violence and the belief that those without penises are uniquely vulnerable. So, Westbrook and Schilt's research illustrates that, despite great changes in the public recognition of transgender people and moves toward gender equality, our reactions to the gender panics that transgender people provoke illustrate that we remain invested in cultural beliefs about gender and the gender binary that perpetuate inequality.

FROM SEEING IS BELIEVING TO BELIEVING IS SEEING Consider the ways that eggs and sperm interact with one another to produce a baby. You know this story, right? Millions of tiny sperm make their way into the vagina, racing toward an egg that aimlessly drifts toward them. As the sperm reach the egg, they each attempt to burrow into the egg and eventually one breaks through and, well, you know the rest. Right?

Although this is a simplified version of the story, is it true? Do sperm "race"? Do they "burrow"? Are eggs really as passive as they are portrayed here, aimlessly drifting? Do sperm cells actually behave in culturally masculine ways? Are they competitive with one another? Of course not. In fact, this is a ridiculous question. And on a larger level, it's actually not entirely biologically accurate to tell the story this way. While it does support stereotypes we have about men and women (stereotypes not shared by every society around the world), it misses some important biological facts about eggs and sperm. Anthropologist, Emily Martin, was interested in this story and how it gets perpetuated. Martin (1991) studied the ways sexual reproduction is written about in medical textbooks and found that this pattern in language (active sperm, passive egg) is extremely common, despite the misunderstandings and inaccurate information it supports.

Male reproductive processes are explained as active, incredible, and awe-inspiring in medical textbooks. Conversely, female reproductive processes are explained as passive and, often, wasteful. Is this accurate? Or Martin asked, is it possible that gender stereotypes are affecting the ways we understand and interpret biological processes? Consider what's missed with this version of the story. We don't learn, for instance, that sperm have been shown to be incredibly inefficient swimmers. In fact, were it not for the fibers on the outside of the egg that attract sperm and retract when they attach, it's unlikely sperm would be capable of getting to the egg in the first place. The explanation of the sperm burrowing into the egg also makes it seem as though sperm are the active cells here, each competing to penetrate the egg first. But in fact, the protein bond that forms between the egg and sperm is more accurately understood as a partnership between the two cells (what is sometimes referred to as the "lock-and-key model" for protein bonds in textbooks). Indeed, Martin suggests that we might equally speak of eggs as *enveloping* helpless sperm that they collect after first capturing them with the egg's spindly fibers. Like Hrdy's story-flipping the cultural belief about men's "inherent" promiscuity on its head, this story is no less "true." But it certainly sounds a lot different from the story we're used to hearing about eggs and sperm.

Building on this, sociologist Lisa Jean Moore (2003) studied the depictions of sperm in children's educational books about reproduction. We know how medical students are taught about eggs and sperm. But what about kids? Similar to Martin's (1991) findings, Moore discovered exaggerated metaphors associated with heterosexual romance and fairy tales. It was not uncommon for sperm to be depicted as romantic men, sometimes depicted in tuxedos carrying roses or, once, in armor storming a castle in which an egg is depicted awaiting her "hero" gazing out of the

How were you taught about eggs and sperm and how they interact?

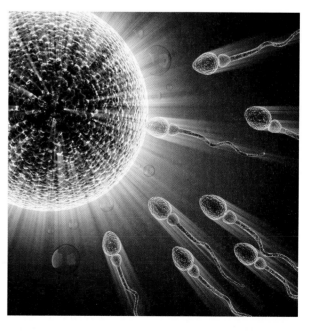

Emily Martin's research discovered that we often anthropomorphize sex cells; we pretend the sperm are masculine (athletic, strong) and eggs are feminine (passive, nurturing). Lisa Jean Moore found that we see these depictions in the ways reproduction is explained to children in books as well. Sperm aren't romantic, are they? So, why are we depicting them bringing roses to eggs?

highest tower. Eggs and sperm do not actually have gender. But we are "gendering" them when we depict and learn about them in these ways.

What these examples illustrate is that beliefs about gender often come to be more than just beliefs. They affect the way we see the world around us. They affect what we look for under a microscope when we think gender should matter. They also affect the ways we selectively interpret our evolutionary ancestry and learn to understand and think about our bodies. We have been socialized and raised in a society in which these cultural beliefs about the gender binary and differences between women and men shape our understanding of just about everything related to gender.

Sociologist Judith Lorber (1993) calls this type of thinking "believing is seeing." Lorber suggests that although we are used to thinking that if we witness or experience something (if we "see" it) then we are forced to reckon with that reality, and believe it—regardless of what we had previously thought. Lorber suggests that our cultural beliefs shape what and how we see things in the first place.

---

iSOC AND YOU Thinking Sociologically about Sex and Gender
Gender is among the most important components of your *identity* – even before you're born! And although you may be taught to think of your gender as fixed and permanent, perfectly consistent with your biological sex, sociologists see gender as more fluid than fixed, and as much socially constructed as based in biology.

9.2 The Social Organization of Gendered Interactions and Inequality

Sometimes, sociological thinking requires us to unlearn some of the ways we have been taught to think about elements of our society and learn to understand them in a new light. Whereas the previous section explores why sociologists understand sex and gender identities as socially constructed, this section considers how the ideas about sex and gender we questioned in the last section become a part of our societies. Beliefs about sex and gender are powerful. They take on material reality when we construct a society based on those beliefs, and they become self-perpetuating. Sex and gender are major identity categories around which our society is stratified. Simply put, women and men live in the same societies; but they have dramatically different experiences of those societies. Gender structures virtually every aspect of our lives, and we participate in this process much more than you might assume.

In this section, you will learn to understand how it is that we come to learn about gender and how you are not only learning, but also teaching others about gender. Sociologists who study gender in this way are primarily interested in how gender is produced inside of our interactions with one another. This means that we need to come to think about gender as both something you can *have* (like a gender identity) and also something that you *do*. And when sociologists study they ways we "do gender," they are also studying how gender inequality gets reproduced within these interactions. And a great deal of sociological research is also interested in how the experience of gender is often refracted through other identity categories as well (like race, class, sexuality, age, and more). Learning to understand gender and gender inequality intersectionally helps sociologists to examine the complexity of gender in our social world.

The Bathroom Problem: Organizing Our World Around Gender

9.2.1 Using the issue of sex segregation in public restrooms, explain what it means when sociologists claim that our society is organized by gender.

To fully appreciate just how much of your life is organized by gender, good sociological thinking means that we have to acknowledge that our lives could be organized differently than they are. Our social interactions, institutions, and even the spaces we occupy are organized in ways that highlight gender differences. Sociologist Erving Goffman (1977) argued that performances of gender are often framed as though they come from within (as a consequence of gender differences), but he believed that it was through this process that gender differences are often produced. It is this same feature of social life that Barrie Thorne (1993) later came to call "borderwork." **Borderwork** refers to the ways that we selectively call attention to gender difference (and ignore all of those moments when boys and girls, men and women are basically the same). Borderwork is an active process in which we all participate; but borderwork can also take on concrete form as we construct environments in which to interact.

borderwork
An active process in which we all participate, it refers to the ways we selectively call attention to gender difference (and simultaneously ignore gender similarities).

Public restrooms are the classic example, and there has been a host of fascinating research and theory on bathroom behavior and bathroom segregation. Sex segregation in public bathrooms is so widespread, it would not be all that surprising if you'd never imagined a world with gender-integrated public restrooms. Goffman was fascinated by gender segregation in public restrooms and what it accomplished; we've actually designed restrooms to have to be sex segregated. Commenting on the lack of things like urinals in homes, Goffman (1977) argued that there is nothing inherent about this. Rather, it reiterates a pattern he finds throughout social life: "a sort of with-then-apart rhythm" that has reverberations throughout social life.

> "The *functioning* of sex-differentiated organs is involved, but there is nothing in this functioning that *biologically* recommends segregation; *that* arrangement is totally a cultural matter.... [T]oilet segregation is presented as a natural consequence of the difference between [men and women], when in fact it is rather a means of honoring, if not producing, this difference" (1977: 316).

Sex segregation in public bathrooms is not necessary, but we have come to think of it as an important feature of modern life. Women and men do a great deal collectively, but we still cling to the idea that there are some things they *must* do separately (even if we're all doing much of the same things in those spaces). We even invented a type of toilet that is then used to justify the *need* for separate rooms—the urinal.

Here, Goffman suggests that although we tend to think that women and men should use different public restrooms, there is nothing inherent about male and female bodies that necessitates different spaces. And while urinals are designed to be used by the male anatomy, we designed them this way and we continue to expect them in precisely one-half of the restrooms in public settings. Rather than thinking about urinals as a natural consequence of differences between men's and women's bodies, Goffman understood something as mundane as toilet design as one of the ways that we honor and celebrate our continued investment in the idea that women and men are completely different from each other.

Gender Socialization: Learning about Gender Difference

9.2.2 Describe the process of gender socialization and how we learn to look at the world with gender bias.

In a critique of biological research on gender differences, Harvard biologist Ruth Hubbard writes:

> If a society puts half its children into short skirts and warns them not to move in ways that reveal their panties, while putting the other half into jeans and overalls and encouraging them to climb trees, play ball, and participate in other vigorous outdoor games; if later, during adolescence, the children who have been wearing trousers are urged to "eat like growing boys" while the children in skirts are warned to watch their weight and not get fat; if the half in jeans runs around in sneakers and boots, while the half in skirts totters about on spike heels, then these two groups will be biologically as well as socially different. (1990, p. 69)

And what if the half in jeans and sneakers, eating heartily, were female, she seems to want us to ask, and the ones in frilly dresses and high heels and on constant diets were males? Would there be complete gender chaos, or would we simply come to believe that boys and girls were "naturally" like that?

gender socialization

The process by which males and females are taught the appropriate behaviors, attitudes, and traits associated with their biological sex in a particular culture.

Gender socialization is the process by which males and females are taught the appropriate behaviors, attitudes, and traits culturally associated with their biological sex (we touched on this in Chapter 5). Of course, the behaviors, attitudes, and traits deemed "appropriate" for boys and girls differ (sometimes subtly and sometimes substantially) from one culture to the next. But the process is the same. Gender socialization begins at birth and continues throughout our lives. Before you know anything else about a baby, you know its sex. Even at the moment of birth, researchers have found, boys and girls are treated differently: girls are held closer and spoken to in softer voices about how pretty they are; boys are held at arm's length, and people speak louder about how strong they appear. Indeed, gender socialization begins during amniocentesis, when babies are in utero as parents select names, paint rooms, and collect different sorts of gendered accessories and objects for boys and girls.

gender bias

The ways we systematically treat men and women (and boys and girls) differently.

From infancy onward, people interact with children based at least as much on cultural expectations about gender as on the child itself. Sociologists refer to the ways that we systematically treat men and women (and boys and girls) differently as **gender bias**. In one now-classic experiment, adults were told that the baby was either a boy or girl, and the adults consistently gave gender-stereotyped toys to the child—dolls and hammers—regardless of the child's reaction to them. However, the babies in the experiment were assigned at random, and the boys were often dressed in pink and the girls in blue. In another classic experiment, adults were shown a videotape of a 9-month-old infant's reaction to a jack-in-the-box, a doll, a teddy bear, and a buzzer. Half the adults were told it was a boy; half were told it was a girl. When asked about the child's emotional responses, the adults interpreted the exact same reaction as fear if they thought the baby was a girl and anger if they thought it was a boy (Condry and Condry 1976). As both of these experiments illustrate, we are often unaware of the ways that we are affected by gender bias and we are equally unaware of when and how we are participating in the gender socialization process. But research shows that we are all affected by gender bias, and we all participate in gender socialization and are gender socialized (even if we are unaware of that fact).

We come to understand and define our own gender and the gender of others by the ways in which gender is organized in the societies in which we live. And virtually every social institution in a society contributes to the process of gender socialization. This means that we encounter gender socialization from our families, our education, the workplace, religious institutions, the media, our peer groups, and much more.

SOCIOLOGY AND OUR WORLD

PINK FOR BOYS AND BLUE FOR GIRLS

If we didn't used to think about boys and girls as such different creatures, why might we have started to?

Little boys and girls were not always dressed differently. In fact, it used to be the opposite of what it is now. Before the late nineteenth century, boys and girls were dressed identically until the age of about 6 or 7, in small skirts and dresses. Their hair—both boys' and girls'—was also kept similarly long. Consider this image of Franklin D. Roosevelt when he was 2½ years old. His white skirt is spread neatly over his lap and the delicate embroidery on the blouse and skirt lay neatly over his shoulders and legs. Young Franklin has shoulder-length hair and dons a smart set of patent leather flats with a strap. This image is from 1884, and by today's standards, Franklin appears to be wearing an outfit intended for a girl. But at the time, this outfit was understood as gender neutral—not particularly masculine or feminine, just a child's outfit. At the time, advice columns in parenting magazines were filled with mothers asking whether their sons were "ready for trousers" and, for those who had made the switch, testimonies from mothers blaming all manner of bad behavior on the pants.

When children began to wear color-coded clothing, the rule at the time was pink for boys and blue for girls. Pink was declared to be "a more decided and stronger color" and thus more suitable for boys, whereas blue was "more delicate and dainty." A debate in the 1910s and 1920s began to reverse that trend, and blue became the boy color and pink the girl color. Historians don't have a firm answer for exactly why the colors switched, but they have identified that this is right around when it happened. And today we dress little girls more like little boys—in overalls, T-shirts, and sneakers (Paoletti 2012).

That we might not recognize all of the ways we were socialized to understand gender differences does not mean we are immune. It's challenging to think about the scale of gender socialization. As Judith Lorber (1994) wrote,

> Talking about gender for most people is the equivalent of fish talking about water.... Gender is so pervasive that in our society we assume it is bred into our genes. Most people find it hard to believe that gender is constantly created and re-created out of human interaction.... Yet gender, like culture, is a human production that depends on everyone constantly "doing gender."

Gender Socialization: Learning about Gender Inequality

9.2.3 Summarize the gender similarities hypothesis, and explain how the media help shape androcentric understandings of gender in spite of it.

When we are socialized into the gender binary, we are socialized to more than just gender *difference*. Gender socialization also plays a role in helping us to understand and accept gender *inequality*. We learn to think about masculinity as more valuable and worthy of status, respect, and attention than femininity. Whether we are talking about boys doing masculinity or girls doing masculinity, masculinity is treated as though it has higher status than femininity. Sociologists refer to this phenomenon as **androcentrism**. Sociologists are interested not only in the ways that gender socialization helps us understand women and men as dramatically different from one another, but also how our collective acceptance of the gender binary helps to justify gender inequality.

This is the double message of gender socialization: You learn difference and inequality simultaneously. After all the differential socialization boys and girls receive, what, then, are the real psychological differences between women and men? A recent review of all available research on gender differences found little or no difference on virtually every other characteristic or behavior a finding Janet Hyde refers to as the **gender similarities hypothesis** (Hyde 2005).

androcentrism
The practice, conscious or not, of placing males or masculinity at the center of one's worldview and treating masculinity as though it has higher status and value than femininity.

gender similarities hypothesis
Janet Hyde's assertion, based on meta-research, that men and women are similar until proven otherwise.

HOW DO WE KNOW WHAT WE KNOW?

WOMEN AND MEN ARE FAR MORE SIMILAR THAN THEY ARE DIFFERENT

Research in any field is best understood as a work in progress. There are few findings in most fields that we are so confident in that we simply don't study anymore—in fields like chemistry, physics, and biology, these are sometimes referred to as "laws." But people are less predictable than atoms and because of this, there are fewer laws in the social sciences than you might expect. Yet, through repeated testing, we do come to be more and less confident in ideas as more research either supports them or calls them into question. One technique that helps us look at a range of research findings on a common topic is what scientists refer to as a *meta-analysis*; it's basically a study of studies. A meta-analysis is a quantitative method that allows scholars to combine results from multiple studies with the hope of identifying patterns that cut across a large body of published research.

As you might imagine, gender differences are a topic that has amassed a sizeable body of research. Meta-analysis allows us to look across that large body of research to see what kinds of differences between men and women appear to be consistent findings. Psychologist Janet Hyde (2005) undertook this project, combining more than 7,000 different studies by scholars assessing more than 100 different measures of gender difference between men and women. Hyde discovered that of all of the differences between men and women studied, the overwhelming majority (over 75% of the studies) found little to no difference at all. On most measures of difference, the size of the difference is so small that when we focus on averages, it sounds like men and women are different. But when we look at actual distributions of men and women, we see that the overlap is greater than a discussion of averages alone might lead us to believe. Consider these overlapping parabolas that represent the distributions of men's and women's self-esteem (Kling et al. 1999).

As Hyde writes, "Clearly, this small effect size reflects distributions that overlap greatly—that is, that show more similarity than difference" (2005: 586–587). It is for this reason that Hyde (2005) proposes the "**gender similarities hypothesis**"—the idea that men and women are similar until proven otherwise. Although this hypothesis might challenge some conventional wisdom about gender, Hyde's work continues to show that it has much more support than the gender differences hypothesis—no matter how hard we might cling to the gender binary notion that men and women *really are* different.

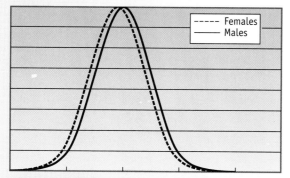

Note. Two normal distributions that are 0.21 standard deviations apart (i.e., d = 0.21). This is the approximate magnitude of the gender difference in self-esteem, averaged over all samples, found by Kling et al. (1999). From "Gender Differences in Self-Esteem: A Meta-Analysis," by K. C. Kling, J. S. Hyde, C. J. Showers, and B. N. Buswell, 1999, *Psychological Bulletin, 125*, p. 484. Copyright 1999 by the American Psychological Association.

Women and Men Are Far More Similar than They Are Different

This graph illustrates the approximate magnitude of gender difference. When it comes to issues like height, self-esteem, strength, and all manner of characteristics, men and women have, on average, slightly different averages (and men's aren't always "higher" than women's). But, as you see here, simply discussing the averages obscures the more general point that most men and women are similar. Although only a quarter of the studies in Hyde's sample produced measurable differences between women and men, the vast majority were, like the difference illustrated here, so small that the difference is, largely, meaningless. Similarity is the real story here.

Despite our similarities, however, we learn to think about gender differences in ways that simultaneously reproduce gender inequality. Consider how the media play a role in our gender socialization. Boys and girls interact somewhat differently with media—everything from social-networking sites to video games, television, movies, and music. And alongside other messages, media content conveys powerful messages about how women and men *should* behave. From Disney and Sesame Street, throughout chick flicks and action movies, TV shows and the advertising we endure in between, we are bombarded with messages about what constitutes "appropriate" behavior for our gender. Sometimes these messages seem contradictory, but they consistently illustrate perhaps the most important lesson of socialization: *our gender performances are being evaluated by others.* And the fact that they are being evaluated (in addition to our awareness of this fact) powerfully impacts the ways we act and understand our identities and actions as well as how we make sense of gender inequality.

Have you ever thought about whether the movies you like are androcentric? Do women play leading roles? Do the women in leading roles interact with other women? Or are women in the movies you like more often relied on to support, highlight, or call attention or affection to the men who star in those films? In 1985, Alison Bechdel—author and illustrator of the queer comic, *Dykes to Watch Out For*—wrote a comic strip that created a more systematic way to think about women's representation in movies and whether the movies we watch portray women in marginal roles and make men's lives appear to matter more. The movie has to satisfy "three basic requirements" to "pass" the Bechdel Test: (1) it must contain at least two women (2) who talk to each other (3) about something other than a man (see the strip).

This is the original strip in which the "Bechdel Test" was first proposed— a strip titled "The Rule" (1985).

FIGURE 9.1 Movies Assessed by the "Bechdel Test," 1970–2015
The "Bechdel Test" is a simple test allowing us to superficially assess the portrayals of girls and women in film. Although it might seem an easy test to "pass," see the proportions of films that have passed and failed over time. Films "passing" are those in which (1) more than one female character is present, (2) who interact with each other, (3) about something other than a man.

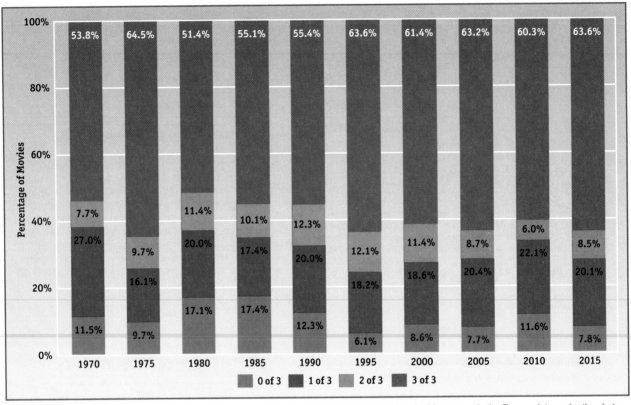

NOTE: 0 of 3 - fewer than two women in the film; 1 of 3 - women in the film never speak to each other; 2 of 3 - women in the film speak to each other, but only about men; 3 of 3 -film passes the Bechdel Test

SOURCE: Data from http://bechdeltest.com/statistics/.

It is a simple enough test that it has been used to assess an incredible number of films on the website BechdelTest.com (you can participate by adding movies you watch at the site). And as a result of this, we have a large sample of films over time to superficially assess women's presence in movies (see FIGURE 9.1).

This does show that more movies are beginning to pass the test. But it is important to remember that "passing" the Bechdel test is a pretty low bar for gender equality in movies. What we do know from the existing data is that movies in genres like Westerns, War, History, and Action tend to fair worse than others on the test and movies that were either written or directed by women or that have women executive producers tend to fair much better. And though those defending Hollywood sometimes claim that movies failing the test simply make more money, existing data suggest that movies passing the test have a marginally *better* return when we control for dollars spent in production. Although movies are only one metric, they are a powerful example of how we are socialized to think about gender inequality in ways that present a certain level of androcentrism or inequality between women and men as either natural, desirable, or both.

Gendered Interactions

9.2.4 Describe what "doing gender" means by distinguishing between gender roles and gender relations.

social construction of gender

The social process by which we construct our gender identities throughout our lives, using the cultural ideas and materials we find around us.

Sociologists speak of gender as socially constructed. The **social construction of gender** means that we construct our gender identities throughout our lives, using the cultural ideas and materials we find around us. Our gender identities are both *voluntary* (we choose to become who we are) and *coerced* (we are pressured, forced, and often physically threatened to conform to certain rules). We don't make up the rules we have to play by, but we often bend them, reinterpret them, and shape them to make them feel like our own.

Sociologists have long borrowed terms and ideas associated with theater as a way of talking about social life. We talk about social *roles*, cultural *scripts, performances*, and more. It's a metaphor we rely on to talk about social life as more organized, directed, controlled, and coerced than many people assume. You need props and lots of rehearsing to get it right; then you try it out on a public stage, and the audience lets you know if you are doing it well—or not. In large part, sociologists understand gender as a performance. We use our bodies, language, and actions all to communicate to others that we are acting our part effectively. This is hard for some people to understand because many people don't feel like they are performing. But when sociologists use the term, we understand gender as a performance at which most of us have had so much practice that we no longer recognize it as a performance—because it no longer feels like work. Think about the first time you ever put on make-up, sat in a skirt, or braided your hair. Or, consider the first time you learned how to tie a tie, sag your pants, or shave your face. When you're learning, these things are challenging. But with time, we become so practiced that it is easy to fail to acknowledge how much work these elements of the performance actually are.

Some psychologists use the term *sex roles* or **gender roles** to define the bundle of traits, attitudes, and behaviors that are associated with biological males and females. Gender roles are the social blueprints that prescribe what you should do, think, want, and look like, so that you can successfully become a man or a woman. We don't all live up to all these prescriptions, but we are often held accountable to them whether we like it or not. Sociologists have suggested, however, that the "role" model of understanding gender ignores several important issues. For one thing, for a long time sociologists assumed that the two gender roles were independent, but otherwise equal: "his" and "hers." The assumption of equality, however, was false: masculinity—and especially the traits associated with it—is more highly valued than femininity. This is what it means to live in an androcentric society. Nor does the term *role* adequately capture gender in its complexity. Sociologists today are more likely to use **gender relations** to emphasize how the definitions of masculinity and femininity are developed in relation to each other and to systems of social power and inequality.

What this amounts to is the fact that gender identity is not something you "get" through socialization. It's not a possession, something you "have." To a sociologist, gender is something you *do* in every single interaction. We are always "doing gender"—performing the activities and exhibiting the traits that are prescribed for us as men and women in the societies in which we live (West and Zimmerman 1987). And we do gender differently in different contexts and interactions. This means that you do gender differently when interacting with your parents compared with, say, a romantic partner. Similarly, you probably do gender very differently in a college classroom compared with a college party. We situationally adapt our performances, and we are so accustomed to doing this that it's easy to neglect to recognize how much work it actually is. Doing gender separates biological sex from gendered behavior; you don't need a male body to "do" masculinity or a female body to "do" femininity (see Transgender Identities: Blurring the Boundaries of Gender). For example, people who have highly gendered jobs—like firefighters or nurses—are doing masculinity or femininity, even if they are female firefighters or male nurses.

Learning to "do" gender is both serious work and, often, associated with play and fun as well.

gender roles

The bundle of traits, attitudes, and behaviors that are associated with biological males and females.

gender relations

Sociologists today are more likely to use gender relations (rather than "role") to emphasize how the definitions of masculinity and femininity are developed in relation to each other and to systems of social power and inequality.

There are many reasons an Afghan family might disguise their daughters as sons: financial need, social pressure, and even the superstition that the practice can give rise to the birth of a boy.

In some cultures, temporary or permanent changes in gender performance are encouraged out of convenience or necessity. For instance, in Afghanistan, girls are not allowed to receive much education, work outside the home, or appear in public without a male chaperone. Certainly, these restrictions affect girls and women; but they can also create additional burdens and problems for their families. Sending your daughter to the store to pick something up is only allowed if she is accompanied by, for example, her brother. Sons are also permitted to work outside the home, which can bring additional income to the family. So, families without sons have additional burdens that families with sons (and particularly families who only have sons) do not. It probably should not be that surprising that some families with only daughters select one to be a boy. In Afghanistan, these children are called a *bacha posh*, which translates to "dressed up as a boy" in Dari. Bacha posh do not provoke huge surprise and most Afghan families understand and accept sex-switched children, both their own and those of others.

We like our categories tidy and orderly; we want biological males to *do* masculinity and biological females to *do* femininity. This is why male nurses are the butt of so many jokes in our culture. They illustrate that gender categories aren't actually as neat and tidy as we often pretend they are. And we're often uncomfortable when people blur those boundaries (whether intentionally or not). Many people enjoy playing with the performance of gender. Cross-dressers, drag performers, and transgender people of all types use various props, signs, and symbols to convince others to see them in a particular way. Some people cross-dress for fun; others take it quite seriously. They remind us that successfully doing gender requires not just the performance, but the evaluation of the performance by others in the interaction.

"Gender Policing" and Gender Accountability

9.2.5 Illustrate your understanding of intersectional analysis by examining the process of gender policing in high school and college.

When sociologists study gender as a performance, they are also interested in what sorts of factors shape that performance. What causes us to perform gender in one way and not another? What causes us to perform one gender rather than the other? And when West and Zimmerman (1987) originally theorized gender as something we are constantly "doing," they were equally interested in those social factors that hold us *accountable* to certain performances rather than others. Sociologists who study this issue sometimes refer to it as **gender policing**—the enforcement of normative gender ideals associated with the gender binary onto individuals. In many contexts, gender

gender policing
The enforcement of normative gender ideals by rewarding normative gender performances and punishing transgressions.

Often, we don't realize how powerful gender boundaries are until we transgress them. In those moments, gender becomes activated in social life—a process sociologists examine who study "gender policing" and its consequences.

performances consistent with normative "masculinity" or "femininity" are encouraged and rewarded, whereas gender transgressive performances are discouraged through punishment or, more often, negative reactions.

The ways in which gender transgressions are "policed" can range from fairly minor illustrations of disagreement, outrage, or disgust to more serious forms of violence and assault. The methods of gender policing also vary depending, at least partially, on the perceived gender of the individual target. Research has long suggested that boys and men are generally policed more frequently and harshly (Kimmel 1994; Pascoe 2007). And although gender policing occurs throughout our lives and in every social context and institution we encounter, the bulk of the scholarship on gender policing has focused primarily on public contexts and among children and young adults. As with socialization (discussed in depth in Chapter 5), this can lead to the mistaken assumption that gender policing is over in adulthood. But sociologists understand this process as lifelong. Consider two stigmatizing labels that we often imagine are restricted to young people's interactions with one another: "fag" and "slut." Sociological research suggests that labels associated with sexuality are among the more ubiquitous insults traded among young people, and they are a primary mechanism of gender policing (Thurlow 2001). Both "fag" and "slut" are simultaneously all about sexuality and have absolutely nothing to do with sexuality at all.

Sociologist C. J. Pascoe (2007) studied the meanings and use of the term *fag* among high school boys. Employing both ethnographic and interview methods, Pascoe was interested in understanding who used the term, how it was used, and what role it played in the culture of young people in the high school in California she studied. Most of Pascoe's research participants in her study of the use of fag among boys said that they would never aim the insult at someone who is "actually gay." Pascoe suggests that this indicates a need for a more nuanced way of understanding sexuality—not as some *thing* inherent in specific bodies or identities, but as a mechanism of gender policing. "Fag" is a gender-policing label boys apply to one another to delineate the boundaries of masculinity. "Slut" is used in similar ways—as a mechanism of gender policing. And most of the research focusing on either is primarily about gender policing and gender and sexual inequality. But, research shows that both of these forms of gender policing need to be understood intersectionally as well to understand the role they play in racial and class inequality, too.

Pascoe discovered that young men's use of fag was a process of gender policing primarily concerned with drawing boundaries around acceptable (and unacceptable) masculinity. Boys hurled the insult at each other in jest, sometimes at random, and as a part of a social game—one in which they were incredibly invested. But it was a "game" primarily played among white boys. Black boys and white boys rely on distinct symbolic resources when doing gender. For instance, paying "excessive" attention to one's clothing or identifying with an ability to dance well put white boys at risk of being labeled a fag according to Pascoe, but worked to enhance black boys' masculine status. As a group, black boys were much less likely to use the term than white boys; and when they did, black boys were much more likely to be punished by school authorities. Black boys were also the only students reported to school authorities for saying *fag* by their peers. White boys, in other words, relied on racial hierarchies to control the meaning of fag; it was interpreted as "playful" and "meaningless" when white boys used the term, but "dangerous" and "harassing" when black boys did.

In a separate study of sexuality in college life, Elizabeth A. Armstrong, Laura T. Hamilton, Elizabeth M. Armstrong, and J. Lotus Seely (2014) investigated the meaning of the term *slut* among college women as a part of a larger research project on party culture in college (Armstrong and Hamilton 2013). Armstrong and colleagues (2014) discovered that slut had a fluid meaning for college women; not all of the women in their study understood the same sorts of behavior as putting someone at risk of receiving the insult. At the institution at which the study was conducted, they found that social status among women fell largely along class lines. "High-status" women were almost entirely upper and upper-middle class. This was at least partially due to the fact that performing the femininity necessary for classification required class resources (joining a sorority, having the "right" kind of body, hair, clothes, etc.). Armstrong and colleagues found that high-status women used slut to refer to a specific configuration of femininity, one they defined as "trashy." Although high-status women rarely actually deployed classist language, their comments relied on understandings of performance of gender stereotypically associated with less-affluent women and allowed them to situate their own sexual behavior and identities as beyond reproach. Armstrong and colleagues (2014) found that performing "classy" or "preppy" femininity (a performance that is simultaneously gendered, raced, sexualized, and classed) worked to shield high-status women from the slut stigma.

Conversely, the low-status women in Armstrong and colleagues' (2014) study understood the label *slut* to be more about sexuality than gender. Lower-class women used slut to stigmatize the sexual behavior of higher-class women (sex outside of relationships). In an analogous way to Pascoe's findings regarding race and the use of fag, these classed differences involving women drawing moral boundaries around femininity were enforced unevenly. Although both groups reconstituted slut to work to their advantage, casual sexual activity posed little reputational risk for high-status women, so long as they continued to perform a "classy" configuration of femininity in the process. Similar to Pascoe's research, high-status women here relied on their gendered performances of class to control the meaning of the insult, such that participation in casual sexual interactions took on a different meaning when coupled with "classy" performances of gender. Here, class worked to insulate high-class women from stigma and punishment just as race worked to insulate white boys in Pascoe's research.

Both studies illustrate important intersections among gender, sexuality, race, and class. Sexual discourses are invoked in a variety of ways throughout social life. They play an integral role in policing gender boundaries. But it is also important to continue to consider the role that sexual discourses play in bolstering boundaries around race and class.

Gender, Friendship, and Love

9.2.6 Explain how gender affects not just our identities, but also our intimate lives and relationships.

Gender difference and gender inequality also have a profound impact on our everyday lives, in our relationships, friendships, marriages, and family life. For instance, during the eighteenth and nineteenth centuries, only men were thought capable of

Although friendships feel natural and like highly personal decisions, who we choose to befriend and what our experiences of friendship are like are dramatically shaped by our society and our social locations within it. Where you sit on the quad and who you sit with is, in part, shaped by your society and how and where you fit within it.

the emotional depth and constancy that true intimacy demanded. These days, though, intimate life is seen largely as the province of women. Women are seen as the relationship experts, capable of the emotional expression and vulnerability that today define intimacy. For centuries it was men who were seen as the experts on relationships; however, intimate life today is largely understood as a "feminine" sphere. How did this change? The Industrial Revolution drove a wedge between home and work, emotional life and rational life. For the first time, most men had to leave their homes for work that was competitive and challenging; success in that dog-eat-dog world required that they turn off their emotions and become competitors. Women's sphere remained the emotional refuge of home and hearth, and things associated with home and hearth began to take on a newly "feminized" meaning. Men learned to separate love and work, while women's work *was* love (Tavris 1992).

As a result, women came to be seen as the experts on love and friendship. (Men became the experts on sex, which we discuss in Chapter 10.) Sociological research on friendship finds that women talk more with their friends, share their feelings more, and even have a larger number of friends in the first place. In some early research on the topic, 75 percent of women could identify a best friend, whereas only 33 percent of men could do so (Rubin 1986). Men tend not to sustain friendships over time but rather pick up new ones in new situations. As sociologists and psychologists understand intimacy to be based on verbal and nonverbal sharing of feelings, mutual disclosure, vulnerability, and dependency, men's friendships can be described as "emotionally impoverished." Yet other elements of masculinity—such as reliability and consistency, practical advice, and physical activity—also provide a solid foundation for friendship. Few sociologists would suggest that women have a monopoly on those qualities that make good friends. Close loving relationships require a good deal of both emotional sharing and practical activity. This is why most sociologists argue that the separation of spheres leaves both women and men unfulfilled. "Who is more loving," sociologist Francesca Cancian (1987) asks rhetorically, "a couple who confide most of their experiences to each other but rarely cooperate or give each other practical help, or a couple who help each other through many crises and cooperate in running a household but rarely discuss their personal experiences?"

One of the most significant changes in the gender of friendship is the gender of our friends. As late as the 1980s, most young women and men could not name a good friend of the opposite sex. Friendships tended to be "homosocial"—within the same sex. Men were friends with other men; women were friends with other women. In the classic movie *When Harry Met Sally*, Harry tells Sally that men and women can't be friends "because sex always gets in the way."

Today, however, few young people are unable to name a friend of the opposite sex. Sex may, sometimes, still "get in the way," but the ability to deal with it has become part of young people's lives. Cross-sex friendships are one indicator of emerging forms of equality between women and men; after all, you generally don't become friends with people who are not your peers—that is, more or less equal (Arnett 2006, Kimmel 2008).

Thinking about friendship and relationships intersectionally, we also know that friendship and love also vary by race and class. Both men and women of color exhibit greater amounts of physical expressiveness, but perhaps slightly lower degrees of emotional disclosure than do middle-class white men. Working-class black and Latino men are more self-disclosing to their friends than upwardly mobile black men, who have fewer friends than their working-class counterparts. This may be due, in part, to the fact that as they move up the economic ladder there are simply fewer of them with whom to make friends (e.g., Franklin 1992, Harris 1992). Cross-race friendships also reflect racial stereotypes of gender. Both black and white people rate their cross-race friendships as "less intimate" than their "same-race" friendships (Aboud, Mendleson, and Purdy 2003). In college, cross-race friendships become more common if one's roommate is of a different race, but classroom integration has been shown to have little effect on encouraging more cross-race friendships (Stearns, Buchmann, and Bonneau 2009).

Racial stereotypes both inspire and inhibit cross-race friendships. For both white boys and girls, black people may be seen as rebellious, and less obedient, and therefore associating with them might increase a white person's status as tough, rebellious, or independent. Interviews with college-aged white men found many placing a high premium on "scoring a black dude" as a friend to enhance a guy's status among his other (white) friends (Kimmel 2008). On the other hand, stereotypes of Asians as especially docile and obedient may inhibit cross-race friendships among boys because rebelliousness and disobedience can be important markers of masculinity, particularly at young ages when other markers are less available. Yet, when it comes to friends, scholarship suggests that white, heterosexual men have the fewest friends of all Americans, and that they are less likely to share secrets and trust even the few friends that they do have (McPherson, Smith-Lovin, and Brashears 2006; Way 2013).

iSOC AND YOU The Social Organization of Gendered Interactions and Inequality

Although it is a core element of our *identity*, sociologists see gender less as something you have, and more as something you create. But you don't create it out of thin air, right? You create it through your *interactions* with others, who guide you toward some activities and away from others. And you create it within a social framework of *inequality* that values some types of gender identities over others, men over women, for example, or cis-gender over transgender. So gender is as much something you *do* as something you have. And the other social identities we construct—race, class, ethnicity, sexuality—all provide the *intersectional* framework in which we do gender.

9.3 Studying Gender Inequality Institutionally and Intersectionally

By now, you are getting used to the fact that when sociologists use the term *gender*, they use it is more than one way. We study gender as an identity that people can have. In survey research, we often treat gender this way, as an unproblematic identity—an independent variable—so that we can assess the effect of that identity on people's lives. But sociologists also think about gender as a verb rather than a noun—gender as something we "do." Beyond that, sociologists also sometimes use the term *gendered* to refer to social processes that shape men's and women's lives differently. When we do this, we are playing with the term *gender* to enable us to examine institutional level processes. So, we're stepping a bit beyond identities and interactions.

For instance, sociological research suggests that the workplace is a gendered institutional context. Men and women, on average, end up in different jobs, doing different kinds of work, for different kinds of pay, and more. And these different experiences are actually part of the structure of the workplace itself. Abstract rules and guidelines in the workplace often differently impact women and men (to say nothing of people who identify outside the gender binary). And when they do, sociologists understand those rules and guidelines themselves as gendered. In examining this process intersectionally, we can also learn to pay attention to the ways that other forms of inequality are connected with gender inequality. To help you understand this way of thinking, we examine how institutional features reproduce gender inequality in ways that are sometimes hard to perceive unless you are actively looking.

We begin by examining a social process that is behind the reason why so few women play in symphony orchestras and why college students routinely give lower scores to women professors on student evaluations. And we examine how similar processes are embedded in every major social institution and reproduce inequality throughout social life.

Gender Bias in Orchestras and Student Evaluations

9.3.1 Understand gender bias and how it can perpetuate gender inequality even when we do not realize it.

Gender inequality is often tricky to study because we don't always see it for what it is. Gender stereotypes affect boys and girls, women and men, throughout their lives in ways that are not only easy to perceive, but also in ways more challenging to actually observe. Sometimes, ideas about natural gender differences prevent us from seeing how much we're doing to make things harder for women and easier for men. And because of this, we sometimes fail to see gender inequality *as* inequality; it often masquerades as a *natural* gender difference. For instance, if we believe men are naturally more competent at, say, building and using tools, do you think this belief might affect whether we hire women for construction work? Remember that when sociologists use the term *gender bias* we are referring to the ways that we systematically treat men and women (and boys and girls) differently.

Proving gender bias is harder than you might think. How do we know that it's gender bias at work and not something else? Here, we'll consider two examples of gender bias relying on data from two sources: symphony orchestras and student evaluations of college professors. Both help to illustrate that gender inequality is often perpetuated in ways that are difficult to perceive. What if employers don't think they are biased against women, but seem to disproportionately hire men anyway? What if students don't think they are biased against women, but seem to rate the women teaching them less favorably than the men? Are they biased against women?

Two economists, Claudia Goldin and Cecilia Rouse (2000), provide one example of this issue in an interesting place—symphony orchestras (see FIGURE 9.2). How musicians tried out for symphony orchestras changed dramatically in the 1970s and 1980s in most major U.S. orchestras. Auditions were made "blind"—the identities of the musicians trying out were concealed from the judges. Generally, this meant that a screen was put up so that judges would not be able to see the person trying out. The screen was actually initially put up to guard against judges selecting only students from the most elite music schools. But screens had an unanticipated consequence as well—suddenly women became much more likely to be selected to join the orchestra based on their auditions. This is something social scientists sometimes refer to as a "natural experiment." It would be unethical to conduct an experiment testing whether gender

FIGURE 9.2 Changes in the Proportion of Women in U.S. Symphony Orchestras, 1940–1996
These data illustrate shifts in the proportion of women in five orchestras between 1940 and 1996. These five orchestras are sometimes referred to as "The Big Five": the New York Philharmonic, the Boston Symphony Orchestra, the Chicago Symphony Orchestra, the Philadelphia Orchestra, and the Cleveland Orchestra. In their research, they found that all major symphony orchestras that began employing blind auditions in the 1970s followed a similar pattern—they started hiring more women.

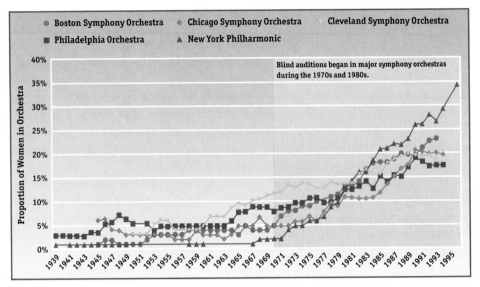

SOURCE: Data from Goldin, Claudia and Cecilia Rouse. "Orchestrating Impartiality: The Impact of Blind Auditions on the Sex Composition of Orchestras." *American Economic Review* 90, 4 (September 2000): 715–741.

bias affected the occupational destinies of *actual* musicians. But because orchestras did this at different times and we can control for a variety of other factors (like the rise in women musicians more generally), blind auditions allow us to see how women fared in different orchestra auditions using different audition strategies.

In 1970, just about 10 percent of major orchestra members were women. By the mid-1990s, women jumped to roughly 35 percent. And the number of new hires for orchestras was actually declining over this period. So, the proportion of *new hires* who were women is even larger than it appears. Goldin and Rouse (2000) were able to show that blind auditions did cause musicians to receive more impartial auditions and for more women playing in major symphony orchestras today. This means that gender bias was present even though people might not have realized it was there. Perhaps beliefs about men's inherent strength impacted how judges listened to men and women playing instruments that appear to rely on strength, like the strings or lifting and holding some of the larger instruments. Perhaps their bias was related to beliefs about the lung capacities of men and women for wind instruments. Regardless, when auditions were made blind, judges stopped hearing gender, and they just listened to and judged the music. Some orchestras have added carpeted walkways for musicians to use walking to their auditioning chair behind the screen to ensure that the sound their shoes make does not impact the judges. In others, musicians are prohibited from even clearing their throat during an audition in case the timbre of the musician's voice can be assumed by the noise, potentially causing judges to guess at the gender. This is just one way gender bias in hiring has been discovered.

It is connected to major institutional practices that might feel "fair." But when we subject them to sociological research and examination, they're often less fair than they might feel. To consider a separate example, think of the evaluation forms you fill out at the end of every college course for your professors (or the ones you will fill out if this is your first semester). Students routinely evaluate their professors in college. And the "scores" professors receive from students in their classes are sometimes used in decisions regarding hiring, firing, and promotions and awards. But are student evaluations biased? Do you assess the women and men who teach you in college in different ways? Might you do this even if you are unaware? Research has shown that you do, and women are much more likely to receive lower student evaluations when compared with the men they work alongside. Women of color are particularly likely be evaluated more negatively, damaging their chances for tenure and promotion (see Lopez and Johnson 2014). Sociologists do not think this means that men are naturally more gifted teachers—rather, it is an indication that women and men are assessed differently, and this difference works to men's collective advantage and to women's collective disadvantage (Arbuckle and Williams 2003; Johnson, et al. 2008).

Women receive lower scores in experimental and real-world research on student evaluations. Is this because students perceive the occupation ("professor") as having a gendered component that they might believe men are more naturally likely to possess? Certainly, professors are likely to be depicted as older, white men in movies. But students don't just give women professors lower scores on average on student evaluations. They also highlight different qualities in women compared with men on their evaluations. Relying on data from the online site RateMyProfessor.com that allows students to anonymously and publicly post reviews of their professors, historian and data visualization expert Ben Schmidt produced a tool that shows how often students use specific words in their reviews of men and women professors by field of study (see FIGURE 9.3).

What we have learned about orchestras and student evaluations is equally true in many other realms of social life and across virtually any social institution you can imagine. We are all affected by gender bias, whether we realize it or not. And

FIGURE 9.3 Frequency of Terms Used in Student Evaluations of Women and Men Professors on RateMyProfessor.com
On RateMyProfessor.com, students are much more likely to use the word "genius" when they are referring to men teaching them (and music professors are more likely to receive the compliment than are professors of criminal justice). Men are also more likely to be reviewed as "funny" than are women. Women professors, on the other hand, are much more likely to be described by students as "disorganized" than are men on the site (and anthropologists are much more likely to receive the critique than are mathematicians).

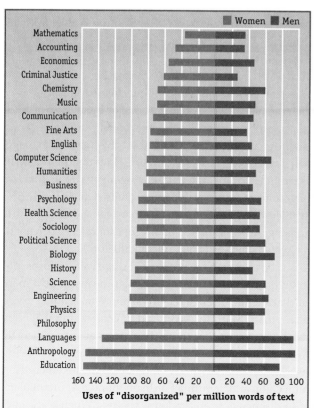

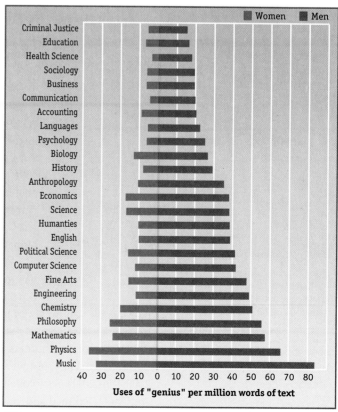

SOURCE: Data from Schmidt, Ben. "Gendered Language in Teaching Reviews" February 20, 2015. Available at http://benschmidt.org/profGender/.

sociological research on gender bias is important because it is a powerful illustration of just how embedded gender inequality is in our society and how much it affects our lives. Next we briefly consider gender in a few major social institutions.

Gender and Education

9.3.2 Explain how gender is embedded in the institution of education such that boys and girls have dramatically different experiences in school.

Remember Barbie's first words in 1992: "Math class is tough!" Her hundreds of millions of owners were learning all about gender—and gender inequality. From the earliest ages, our education teaches us far more than the ABCs. Alongside reading, writing, and arithmetic, we learn important lessons about what it means to be a man or a woman. And these subtle lessons (like Barbie's first words) play an important role in the reproduction of gender inequality. These lessons are part of what sociologists refer to as the hidden curriculum—all the "other" lessons we're learning in school (see Education, Chapter 14). In nursery schools and kindergarten classes, we often find the heavy blocks, trucks, and airplanes in one corner and the miniature tea sets and dolls in another. Subjects are often as gender coded as the outfits toddlers wear.

Previous research focused on how boys were the "preferred" sex in school. Research in the 1990s found that teachers call on boys more often, spend more time with them, and encourage them more. Many teachers expect girls to hate science and math and love reading, and they expect boys to feel exactly the opposite. This led researchers to describe a "chilly classroom climate" for girls, which is a climate that holds girls back from achieving as much as they are capable (see American Association of University Women [AAUW] 2007). In one experiment a teacher conducted on her own class, a teacher decided to treat boys and girls exactly equally; to make sure she called on boys and girls equally, she always referred to the class roster, on which she marked who had spoken. "After two days the boys blew up," she told a journalist. "They started complaining and saying that I was calling on the girls more than them." Eventually, they got used to it. "Equality was hard to get used to," the teacher concluded, and the boys "perceived it as a big loss" (Orenstein 1994: 27).

But in recent years, we've seen boys falling behind. Boys' rates of attendance and their levels of achievement are significantly lower than those of girls. And girls also stay in school, on average, longer than boys. In 2015, 69.2 percent of U.S. students enrolled in college as freshmen immediately following high school. But, 72.6 percent of young women enrolled immediately, whereas only 65.8 percent of men did (U.S. Bureau of Labor Statistics 2016). Girls receive higher grades and more honors; for example, 70 percent of high school valedictorians in 2012 were female.

Why are boys doing so poorly? The answer, it turns out has to do with gender—what boys think it means to be a man.

From the earliest ages, our education teaches us far more than the ABCs. Alongside reading, writing, and arithmetic, we learn important lessons about what it means to be a boy or a girl.

Boys regard academic disengagement as more masculine; if you like school, you must not be a real man (Martino 2008). And in considering this issue intersectionally, sociologists have discovered that these differences are magnified by differences of race and class. Middle-class white boys can often get away with being disruptive in class, but working-class and minority boys might be punished (Ferguson 2000; Rios 2011). Sociologists John Ogbu and Signithia Fordham found that urban black students used race and gender to disengage from academic success. When black girls did well in school they were accused of "acting white" (a phenomenon we discussed in Chapter 8). Black boys, by contrast, were accused of "acting like girls" (Fordham 1996; Noguera 2008; and Ogbu 2003). Asian boys often face a different dilemma; on the one hand, they are considered the "model minority" and particularly smart and studious, although they also seek to act masculine and disengage from school.

Education is often hailed as the major way to get ahead in our lives. And research has shown that gender inequality in education makes that promise more difficult for some to achieve.

The Gendered World of Work

9.3.3 Understand how gender shapes what kind of work we perform (and do not perform) and how this is related to gender inequality.

The work we do is "gendered." We have definite ideas of what sorts of occupations are appropriate for women and which are appropriate for men. These ideas have persisted despite the fact that the workforce has changed dramatically over the past century. The percentage of women working has risen from around 20 percent in 1900 to more than 57 percent today. And this percentage holds for women who have children—even more among women who have children younger than 6 years old (63.9 percent). It is also true among all races, and for every single occupation, from low-paid clerical and sales jobs to all the major professions. Today, women represent a majority of clerical and support workers and also half of students in medical school and more than half of students in law school (American Bar Association 2017; Association of American Medical Colleges 2016; Current Population Survey 2017).

Despite these enormous transformations in women's participation in the workforce, it's also true that traditional ideologies persist about women and work. Women who are highly successful are often thought to be "nontraditional" women, whereas men who are successful are seen as "real men." And these beliefs as biases also translate into practices and concrete consequences: Women are paid less, promoted less, excluded from some positions, and assigned to specific jobs deemed more appropriate for them. Gender discrimination in the workplace was once far more direct and obvious: Women were simply prohibited from entering certain fields. Until the late 1960s, classified advertising was divided into "Help wanted—Male" and "Help wanted—Female." In job interviews, women were asked whether they planned to marry and have children (because that would mean they would leave the job). Can you imagine a male applicant being asked questions like that?

The chief way that gender inequality occurs in the workforce is by occupational sex segregation. **Occupational sex segregation** refers to women's and men's different concentrations in different occupations, different industries, different jobs, and different levels in a workplace hierarchy. Because different occupations are seen as more "appropriate" for one gender or the other, the fact that one job is paid more than another is often seen as resulting from qualities associated with the job, not the gender of the person doing the job. But research has shown that jobs seen as "feminine" are paid less regardless of the kind of work they are performing. Think about it this way: How many of you have worked as a babysitter when you were a teenager? If your experience is like that of our students, most of the women have and many of the men have not. And the women were paid between $5 and $10 an hour, about $20 to $50 a day. Now, how many of you have also shoveled snow or mowed lawns? Most of the men in our classes have done this, but fewer of the women have. Snow shovelers and lawn mowers are paid somewhere around $25 a house and make up to $100 to $150 a day. Why?

Many of you are saying that shoveling snow and mowing lawns is "harder." And by that, you mean the jobs require more physical exertion. But in our society, we usually pay those who use their brawn far *lower* wages than we pay those who use their brains—think of the difference between an accountant and a professional gardener. Besides, the skills needed for babysitting—social, mental, nurturing, caring,

occupational sex segregation
Refers to women's and men's different concentrations in different occupations, different industries, different jobs, and different levels in a workplace hierarchy.

Babysitting and shoveling snow are both examples of gendered work often done by young people. And among young people the work is not equally rewarded. This small example mirrors gender segregation in the workplace more broadly. Jobs dominated by women, as a class, tend to earn less than jobs dominated by men. We learn to take this for granted early on in our lives.

and feeding—are generally considered much more valuable than the ability to lift and move piles of snow. And most people would agree that the consequences of bad babysitting are potentially far worse than those of bad lawn mowing! When grown-ups do these tasks—as lawn mower and baby nurse—their wages are roughly equivalent to each other. What determines the difference is simple: Girls babysit, and boys mow lawns. In this way, occupational sex segregation often hides the fact that gender discrimination is occurring.

dual labor market

The pervasive condition in the United States in which work and workers are divided into different sectors—primary or secondary, formal or informal, and also male or female.

Sex segregation is so pervasive that economists speak about a **dual labor market** based on gender. The idea of a dual labor market is that work and workers are divided into different sectors—primary or secondary, formal or informal, and, in this case, male or female. About 4 out of every 10 American workers work in jobs with at least 75% other male or female employees (Institute for Women's Policy Research [IWPR] 2010). Men and women rarely compete against each other for the same job at the same rank in the same organization. Rather, women compete with other women and men compete with other men for jobs that are already coded as appropriate for one group, but not the other.

Although we might think that different sexes are "naturally" predisposed toward certain jobs and not others, that is not the same everywhere. Most dentists in the United States are male; in Europe, most dentists are female. In New York City, only 49 of the 10,500 firefighters are women, whereas in Minneapolis, 12 *percent* of firefighters are women! The issue is less about the intrinsic properties of the position that determine its wages and prestige and more about which sex performs it—or with which the work is associated. So widespread is this thinking that in occupations from journalism and medicine, to teaching, law, and pharmacy, sociologists have noted a phenomenon dubbed **feminization of the professions**, in which salaries drop as women's participation increases (Menkel-Meadow 1987; Wylie 2000). And not all women are impacted equally. The wage gap between men and women hurts women of color most and benefits white men the most (we discuss the wage gap in more detail in Chapter 12).

feminization of the professions

Widely demonstrated sociological phenomenon in which salaries drop as women's participation increases in a particular job category or profession.

Balancing Work and Family

9.3.4 Illustrate your understanding of how gender shapes our lives by summarizing gender differences in men's and women's attempts to balance work and family.

Women also face discrimination if they try to balance work and family life. If employees who get pregnant, bear children, and take care of them are less likely to get promoted, then women who want to balance work and family will face painful choices. And men may experience such discrimination, too. Men who say they want a better balance between work and family, or want to take parental leave, are often scoffed at by their colleagues and supervisors as not sufficiently committed to their careers; they may be put on an informal "daddy track" and passed over for promotion or high-profile accounts (Kimmel 1993; Jarrell 2007). Consider how gender intersects with race and education in terms of the effect on wages and income (see FIGURE 9.4).

Though nearly all of us, women and men, work for a living outside the home, women also do the great majority of work *inside* the home. Sociologist Arlie Hochschild (1989) called this the **second shift**—the housework and childcare that also needs to be done after a regular working shift is over. Today, childcare, and especially housework, remain largely women's responsibilities. Seeing housework and childcare as "women's work" illustrates gender inequality; women do not have a biological predisposition to do laundry or wash dishes.

second shift

Arlie Hochschild's term for the dual day experienced by working women in which they perform the lion's share of the housework and childcare after a regular working shift is over.

FIGURE 9.4 Median Annual Earnings by Race, Gender, and Educational Attainment, 2014–2016
Men's median earnings are higher than women's in every racial group (though the gap is much larger in some). But, breaking it down by race also shows us some important intersections between race and gender. For instance, white women's median earnings are lower than white men's, but higher than Black and Latino men's at some levels of educational attainment. This chart illustrates that education increases the average earnings of men and women in every racial and ethnic group. Yet, more education appears to help some groups more than others. Paying attention to intersections between race, class, and gender can be challenging—even more so when we realize that inequality produced in one institution (education) has effects on others (work and family). But by attending to these connections we gain a better understanding of wage inequality in the United States.

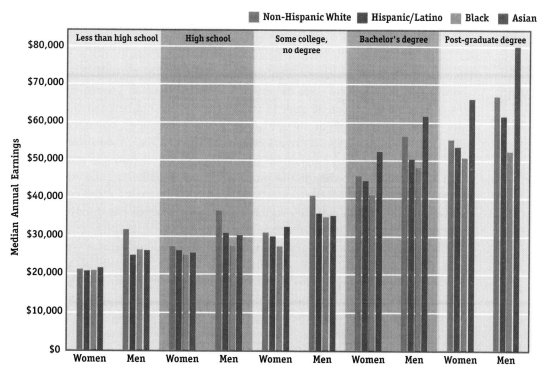

SOURCE: Data from U.S. Census Bureau, Current Population Survey, Annual Social and Economic Supplement, 2014, 2015, and 2016.

Men's share of housework increased somewhat in recent history, largely in response to the increasing numbers of women working outside the home. In the 1920s, 10 percent of working-class women said their husbands spent "no time" doing housework; by the late 1990s, only 2 percent said so (Pleck and Masciadrelli 2004; Pleck 1997). Between the 1960s and today, men's contribution to housework increased from about 15 percent to about 30 percent of the total (Burnett et al. 2010). Still, in an international study of men's share of housework found that U.S. men spend no more time on housework today than they did in 1985 and do only 4 more hours of housework per week than they did in 1965.

Another international study of 20 industrialized countries found that over the past 40 years, men's proportional contribution to family work, including housework, shopping, and childcare—where the most dramatic increases in men's contributions have been found—grew from about one-fifth to about one-third (Claffey and Mickelson 2009; Greenstein 2009; Hook 2006; Knudsen and Wærness 2008; Bianchi, Robinson, and Milkie 2006; Fisher et al. 2006; Sullivan 2006). Today, despite a gradual convergence in the amount of time both women and men spend in paid work and family work, U.S. women spend 60 percent more time on chores than men do—an average of 27 hours a week. International comparisons of seven countries—the United States, Sweden, Russia, Japan, Hungary, Finland, and Canada—revealed that Swedish men do the most housework (24 hours per week) and Japanese men clock the least time (4 hours weekly).

But whether increases in childcare from fathers in heterosexual family households is a sign a serious change is more challenging to say than you might think. Simply claiming that dads are more involved today has its own dangers, as dad becomes the "fun parent." Dad takes the kids to the park or the zoo, they play all afternoon, while mom does the laundry, cleans the house, and makes dinner. "What a great time we had with Dad!" the kids shout as they come home. This is one reason why studying housework and childcare is challenging. It's not simply a matter of how many hours each person logs; different tasks and obligations come with different kinds of consequences and rewards as well (more on this in Chapter 12).

Gender and Marriage

9.3.5 Explain what sociologists mean when they say that the institution of marriage is "gendered" and how this relates to gender inequality.

Heterosexual marriage is also a deeply gendered institution. Consider how we think about it. A woman devises some clever scheme to "trap" a man into marriage. This is why men sometimes jokingly refer to their wives as "the old ball and chain"—basically claiming to be symbolically imprisoned in their marriages. When she succeeds, her friends throw her a shower to celebrate her triumph. The groom's friends stereotypically throw a raucous party, often with strippers or prostitutes, to mark his "last night of freedom." According to this model, marriage is something she wants and he resists—as long as he can. She wins; he loses. This way of thinking about marriage and gender, however, is at odds with sociological research, which has discovered something quite different.

Back in the 1970s, sociologist Jessie Bernard (1972) identified two types of marriage—"his" and "hers." And as Bernard discovered then, and we have documented in more detail since, "his is better than hers." Contemporary research shows marriage still benefits men more than it does women. Married men are happier and healthier than either single men or married women. They live longer, earn more money, and have more sex than single men; they have lower levels of stress and initiate divorce less often than married women. They also remarry more readily and easily. All of these

SOCIOLOGY AND OUR WORLD

WILL YOUNG PEOPLE TODAY PRODUCE A GENDER REVOLUTION IN MARRIAGE TOMORROW?

Do young heterosexuals really want the equal relationships they claim to want with their romantic partners?

Young heterosexual women and men today agree that they want more egalitarian marriages. Sociologist Kathleen Gerson (2010) interviewed 120 young people, aged 18 to 32, of different races and class backgrounds, and found that their preferred marital arrangement was dual-career—sharing childcare and balancing work and family. That is, Gerson discovered no gender difference in what young women and men say they want out of marriage in their lives: They both want an equal relationship and they both have similar ideas about what that means. This could mean that young people today will dramatically alter the way marriage and family life looks in a decade.

But Gerson was skeptical of such an easy explanation. She also asked them what they would choose if they *couldn't* have the more egalitarian marriages they claimed to desire. And here, she discovered a striking gender difference. The overwhelming majority of the women said that their second choice is to simply go it alone. If they were unable to achieve the egalitarian relationship they said they wanted, they'd remain single, adopt a baby, and make a life outside of the institution of marriage. By contrast, the overwhelming majority of the men said their second-choice option would be a more traditional nuclear family arrangement (what Gerson refers to as "neotraditional"), in which men worked outside the home and their wives stayed home and raised the children.

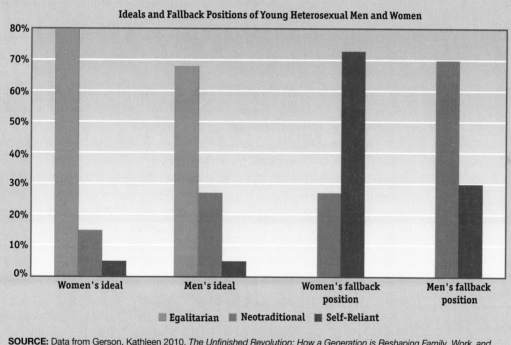

Ideals and Fallback Positions of Young Heterosexual Men and Women

■ Egalitarian   ■ Neotraditional   ■ Self-Reliant

SOURCE: Data from Gerson, Kathleen 2010. *The Unfinished Revolution: How a Generation is Reshaping Family, Work, and Gender in America.* New York: Oxford University Press.

findings suggest that in many ways marriage benefits men in ways it does not benefit women—at least not to the same extent.

Why would this traditional definition of marriage benefit men more than women? Because it is based not only on gender differences between women and men but also on gender inequality. Within the gender division of labor, she works at home, and he does not; outside the home, he works, and so does she (although often not for as many hours). And she provides all the emotional, social, and sexual services he needs to be happy and healthy. "Marriage is pretty good for the goose much of the time," writes a science reporter surveying the field, "but golden for the gander practically all of the time" (Angier 1999).

Of course marriage is also good for women. Married people live longer and healthier lives, have more and better sex, save more money, and are less depressed than unmarried people (Centers for Disease Control and Prevention 2006). But as long as there is gender inequality in our marriages, it will remain a better deal for men. Indeed, in marriage, as at work, gender equality turns out to be a pretty good deal for both women and men. The more egalitarian the marriage, the happier and healthier are both the husbands and wives—and their children (Gottman 1994). (We will address research on same-sex marriages, family dynamics, and more in Chapter 10.)

Gender and Politics

9.3.6 Understand how beliefs about inherent differences between women and men can shape concrete outcomes by examining Americans' beliefs about women in politics.

The gender distribution in U.S. politics is still unequal, with local and state governments tending to have more women representatives than the national government. Part of this has to do with beliefs about women's ability as leaders. See how your own views relate to Americans' opinions when asked whether they agreed with the statement: "Most men are better suited emotionally for politics than are most women." Proportions of Americans agreeing and disagreeing with this statement on surveys have changed over time.

These are huge transformations in Americans' beliefs about gender. It is also true, however, and as you can see, that women's beliefs about the political efficacy of women tend to outpace men's.

These trends are a powerful illustration of the ways that we often harbor cultural beliefs that work to women's disadvantage. For instance, research shows that boys and girls have similar rates of political ambition when they are young. As they reach adolescence, however, girls' political ambition begins to fall just as boys' starts to increase. Although this gap has been closing, a wide chasm persists between the numbers of women and men who deem themselves "fit" for political office (Constantini 1990). Ambition alone, however, does not account for women's absence in politics. They are also much less likely to be recruited to run in the first place, even when we only compare highly qualified men and women with strong backgrounds and connections in political parties (Fox and Lawless 2010).

This is all the more striking when we consider these facts alongside Americans' beliefs about gender differences in the qualities associated with political leadership. Americans consistently rank a set of individual qualities as key to effective political leadership: ability to compromise, being honest and ethical, working to improve the quality of life in the United States, and standing up for one's beliefs. The Pew Research Center (2015) asked a representative sample of Americans about whether they believe that women or men are more likely to exhibit these qualities (or whether people perceive no difference between women's and men's likelihood of exhibiting these qualities; see FIGURE 9.5).

Although the majority of Americans believe that gender is essentially unrelated to the qualities they suggest are the most important to consider in candidates for political leadership, a great deal of Americans do believe in gender differences. And in each case, a greater share of Americans believe that women are more likely to exhibit each of these qualities. We will discuss more about this research in Chapter 13.

WHAT DO YOU THINK? WHAT DOES AMERICA THINK?

Women and Politics

The gender distribution in U.S. politics is still unequal, with local and state governments tending to have more female representatives than the national government.

What do you think?

Most men are better suited emotionally for politics than are most women.

○ Agree
○ Disagree

What does America think?

	Less than High School		High School		College +		Bachelor's Degree		Graduate School	
	Men	**Women**	**Men**	**Women**	**Men**	**Women**	**Men**	**Women**	**Men**	**Women**
Agree	51.28%	46.9%	27.7%	20.6%	25.6%	19.13%	19.6%	11%	17.36%	11.63%
Disagree	48.72%	53.1%	72.3%	79.4%	74.4%	80.87%	80.4%	89%	82.64%	88.37%

SOURCE: Data from General Social Survey 2016.

As you might notice, there appears to be a strong correlation between gender and how people feel about women's and men's emotional suitability for politics. In general, men are more likely than women to agree with the statement. But when we examine how this trend intersects with education, it is also true that those with more education are less likely to agree with the statement. So more men than women agree with the statement in each educational group. But similar proportions of women with only a high school degree disagree with this statement compared with men with a bachelor's degree. Many of these beliefs were put on dramatic display in the 2016 presidential election between Hillary Clinton and Donald Trump.

And when asked directly whether they would vote for a qualified candidate for president who happened to be a woman, there are also differences.

What do you think?

If your party nominated a woman for president, you would vote for her if she was qualified for the job.

○ Agree
○ Disagree

What does America think?

	Less than High School		High School		Some College		Bachelor's Degree		Graduate School	
	Men	**Women**	**Men**	**Women**	**Men**	**Woman**	**Men**	**Women**	**Men**	**Women**
Agree	80.8%	76.48%	90.7%	93.4%	92.83%	93.8%	95.4%	95.9%	96.13%	95.3%
Disagree	19.2%	23.52%	9.3%	6.6%	7.17%	6.2%	4.6%	4.1%	3.87%	4.7%

SOURCE: Data from General Social Survey 2016.

Although it is true that both women and men are much more likely to vote for a woman nominated in their political party than not solely because she is a woman, it is also true that women show a stronger commitment here than men—at least until they receive graduate degrees.

THINKING CRITICALLY ABOUT SURVEY DATA

More respondents said they would vote for a female president than said that women were as emotionally suited for politics as men are. What do you think explains that difference?

FIGURE 9.5 Politics and Business: Public Perceptions of Men and Women as Political Leaders, 2014

When people are asked about their beliefs about women's and men's strengths, Americans tend to think that women are better at most things required of jobs in political office. Despite this fact, women are underrepresented throughout American politics.

Percentage responding men/women in top political positions are better at...

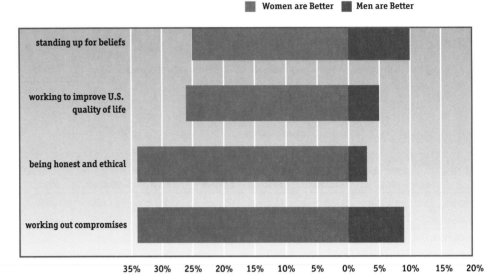

NOTE: The majority of those surveyed claimed there was 'no difference' between women and men on each of the qualities listed. Here, you are only seeing the proportions for individuals who felt women and men are meaningfully better or worse at each of the qualities listed.

SOURCE: Data from Pew Research Center. "Women and Leadership." Pew Research Center, Social & Demographic Trends. January 14, 2015. Available at: http://www.pewsocialtrends.org/2015/01/14/women-and-leadership/.

Domestic violence is a gendered issue. Although both men and women are affected by this social issue, men are dramatically more likely to be perpetrators than victims.

Gender and Violence

9.3.7 Understand what it means to talk about violence as "gendered."

Most violence is "gendered." Whether you're thinking about the gender of the perpetrator, the psychological motivations that lead to violence, or the structural dynamics that institutionalize it, violence is among the most highly gendered social behaviors we know.

Consider perpetrators. In the United States, in 2014, males accounted for 79.8 percent of people arrested for violent crimes: 97.2 percent of people accused of rape, 88.5 percent of those arrested for murder, and 86.1 percent of those arrested for robbery (2014 FBI Uniform Crime Reports 2014). The most consistent pattern with respect to gender, according to the National Academy of Sciences, is the extent to which men's criminal participation in serious crimes at any age greatly exceeds that of women's. This is true across all data sources, of different types of crime, extent of involvement in the criminal activity, or any other measure of participation. And when we examine intersections between gender and age, we can explain nearly all of that violence.

This is most evident in intimate partner violence (IPV), which is something we will examine in more depth in Chapter 11. IPV is highly gendered, and women are far more likely to be physically or sexually assaulted by an intimate partner (husband, ex-husband, boyfriend) than the other way around. (It is true that a small percentage of IPV is female-to-male.) Among heterosexual marriages, spousal homicide and ex-spousal homicide (homicide by an ex-spouse) are disproportionate. For instance, in 2013, 34 percent of female homicide victims were killed by a male intimate partner, compared with only 2.5 percent of male homicide victims being killed by a female intimate partner. More generally, 85 percent of domestic abuse victims are women compared to 15 percent men (FBI Uniform Crime Reports 2014). Men's violence against women is a confirmation of masculinity, a gendered interaction. Violence is one of the ways that boys and men "do gender." And research suggests that boys and men are likely to turn to violence as a resource to do masculinity when they perceive themselves as unable to accomplish masculinity in more socially acceptable forms (Messerschmidt 1999, 2000; Munsch and Willer 2012).

The same is true for men's violence against other men, whether interpersonally or institutionally in war. Institutionalized violence in wars has everything to do with militarism and promoting the ideology of glory and heroism, defined as manly traits (Messerschmidt 2010). The humiliation of the losing side in battle is but the humiliation of the defeat of your opponent in a fistfight—just on a much larger scale. In both cases, one's manhood is confirmed, and the other disconfirmed. It is not a surprise that mass rape of the women of the "losing" side often accompanies warfare; it is the final humiliation of their men.

Even though we have seen dramatic gender convergence on many areas—workforce participation, political ambition, and allocation of family roles—and despite some modest increases in violence among women, violence remains the most consistent and unwaveringly gendered behavior in our society.

---

iSOC AND YOU Studying Gender Inequality Institutionally and Intersectionally
Now you've seen not only how gender is an individual experience, but also how it is profoundly social, that is, constructed through *interactions* on an unequal playing field and embedded within the major *institutions* that compose society: education, politics, the family work, and economics. And you've seen how that seemingly individual experience connects with other facets of your *identity*, like race or sexuality, that are also played out on an unequal field. Violence, then, becomes a way to both express those gender dynamics—*identity* and *inequality*—and also, sometimes, to restore the working arrangements that people believe are supposed to be in place. Not only on a local level, but globally, as well.

9.4 Gender Inequality at the Global and Local Level

Gender inequality exists at different levels in different societies. As we mentioned in Chapter 2, sociologists try to adopt a position of cultural relativism. This means that we try to balance looking at societies from the outside in and from the inside out to avoid perpetuating ethnocentric points of view. To understand gender inequality at a global level means acknowledging two things. First, gender inequality exists in different levels in different societies. So, we can do some cross-cultural comparisons to ask "how much?" gender inequality exists in different societies relative to one another. Sometimes, social scientists use a common set of measures applied to diverse societies to consider them against one another—things like: proportion of women in political positions, the gender wage gap, educational gaps between men and women, maternal mortality rates, and the gender gap in labor force participation. But it is also true that gender inequality exists and is perpetuated in different ways in different cultural contexts.

Scholarship considering gender inequality at the global and local levels is interested in connecting the two. This means that sociologists of sex and gender studying this process add an additional "i" to the iSoc model: international. To understand the intersections between the local and the global means that sociologists examine the ways that societies are connected to each other and how these connections are related to different kinds of gender inequality in different societies. We also consider progress toward gender equality. Although incredible progress was made over the course of the twentieth century, on a great deal of measures, progress seems to have slowed or stalled. In this section, we'll consider what this means and why, despite this, the more general trend has been toward women and men achieving higher levels of similarity on a variety of measures as well.

Understanding Gender Inequality Globally

9.4.1 Illustrate your understanding of gender inequality as a global phenomenon by explaining how gender inequality is related to the process of globalization.

Gender inequality is a global problem. Just about every country in the world treats its women less well than it treats its men (Kimmel, Lang, and Grieg 2000). Everywhere you look, there are gender gaps—from literacy, education, and employment to income, health, and decision making in the developing world, and these gaps are larger in nonindustrialized countries.

Globally, women are disproportionately represented among the world's poor. They are often denied access to critical resources, such as credit, land, and inheritance. Their labor is far less acknowledged and less rewarded. Their health care and nutritional needs are underserved. They have far less access to education and support services. Their participation in decision making at home and in the community can be minimal, but it is routinely lower than men's (UN Development Program [UNDP] 2016). More women around the world are working than ever before, but they face a higher unemployment rate than men, receive lower wages, and number 60 percent of the world's 550 million working poor (i.e., those who do not earn enough to lift themselves and their families above the poverty line of $1 a day) (International Labour Organization 2008).

As a result, gender inequality can be said to hurt women somewhat more in poorer nations than it does in wealthier ones. In rapidly developing nations, like China, a large labor supply means that employers can be picky about whom they hire. As a result, stereotypes often mean persistent gender discrimination. Young ambitious women are routinely denied jobs because their employers suspect they will get pregnant and leave the position. Women are "confused" about their identity, says Qin Liwen, a magazine columnist in Beijing.

> Should I be a 'strong woman' and make money and have a career … but risk not finding a husband or having a child? Or should I marry and be a stay-at-home housewife…? Or should I be a 'fox'—the kind of woman who marries a rich man, drives around in a BMW, but has to put up with his concubines? (Tatlow 2010).

However, gender discrimination in industrial countries is still a significant problem. When the World Economic Forum measured the global gender gap in 2014 and published an international ranking of countries based on measures like women's economic opportunity and participation, political empowerment, educational attainment, and health and well-being, many wealthy countries ranked quite poorly in overall scores. Of 142 countries included in the sample, Japan ranked 104 and Italy 69 (see U.S./World The Global Gender Gap).

Even U.S. women, who are well off by global standards, are badly harmed by discrimination based on sex—and so are their families. If the U.S. gender wage gap were closed so working women earned the same as men for the same jobs, U.S. poverty rates would be cut in half (Murphy and Graff 2005). Globally, 7 out of 10 of the world's hungry are women and girls; in the United States, more than 65 percent of all hungry adults are women (UN World Food Program 2009). Taken together, trends like these have come to be known as the **feminization of poverty**—a term that refers to the disproportionate concentration of economic disadvantage among women, especially among female-headed households. Coined in the 1970s by sociologist

feminization of poverty
A worldwide phenomenon that also afflicts U.S. women, this term describes women's overrepresentation among the world's poor and tendency to be in worse economic straits than men in any given nation or population.

U.S./WORLD

THE GLOBAL GENDER GAP

Each year, the World Economic Forum (WEF), a European-based nonpartisan policy institute, ranks 130 countries on their level of gender *inequality*. The WEF uses four criteria: level of economic participation, educational attainment, health, and political empowerment.

Overall Index Rank

- N/A
- 1–20
- 20–40
- 40–60
- 60–80
- 80–100
- 100–120
- 120–140
- > 140

Explore the map to see where different countries rank on the most recent report. The United States ranked only 45, well behind Iceland (1), Finland (2), Norway (3), Sweden (4), Rwanda (5), Switzerland (11), South Africa (15), France (17), Canada (35) and others.

SOURCE: Data from World Economic Forum, Global Gender Gap Report 2016, The Global Gender Gap Index 2016 Ratings. Available at: http://reports .weforum.org/global-gender-gap-report-2016/rankings/.

INVESTIGATE FURTHER

1. Why do you think the top-ranked countries are all in Scandinavia? And why do you think the countries ranked lowest are in the Middle East and South Asia?

2. If you were a policy maker, how would you mix cultural ideology and social policy to reduce the gender gap?

Diana Pearce (1978), the feminization of poverty is a worldwide phenomenon that also afflicts U.S. women. And in the United States today, women of color are even more burdened by gender inequality because of the ways it intersects with racial inequality. In all the indicators, the racial gap is wide. Like white women, women of color also perform the second shift—the housework and childcare that need to be done after the regular work shift is over. But minority women also tend to hold the lowest-paying, least-rewarding jobs. Recent immigrants may face an additional layer of discrimination.

Moreover, the global economy means the economic condition of both women and men in the United States is linked to that of people in other parts of the world.

Photographer Michael Wolf traveled to Hong Kong to document some of the people working in the toy industry there for a series he calls, "The Real Toy Story." This is one image from the collection.

Driven by U.S.-based multinational corporations, all workers have become part of an international division of labor (see Chapter 12). Corporations scanning the globe for the least expensive labor available frequently discover the cheapest workers are women or children. As a result, the global division of labor is taking on a gender dimension.

Globalization has variously changed the dynamics of global gender inequality. Just as globalization tends to pull us together in increasingly tight networks through the Internet and global cultural production, it also works in ways that push us apart. Globalization has dramatically affected geographic mobility as both women and men from poor countries must migrate to find work in more advanced and industrial countries. This global geographic mobility is extremely sex segregated: men and women move separately. Men often live in migrant labor camps, or dozens pile into small flats, each saving to send money back home and eventually bring the family to live with them in the new country. Women, too, may live in all-female rooms while they clean houses or work in factories to make enough to send back home (Hondagneu-Sotelo 2001).

Additionally, some women and girls are kidnapped or otherwise lured into a new expanding global sex trade, in which brothels are stocked with terrified young girls who borrowed from the traffickers enough money to pay their transportation, believing they were going to work in factories. They are forced into prostitution to repay these debts, and their families are often threatened should they try to escape. Global sex trafficking and global sex "tourism" are among the ugliest elements of globalization (and discussed in more detail in Chapter 10).

Although gender inequality is a worldwide phenomenon, its expressions can and do vary from country to country and from region to region within countries. For instance, in some Muslim countries, like Saudi Arabia, women may not own or drive cars, but in other Muslim countries, like Pakistan and the Philippines, women have been heads of state.

Resistance to Gender Inequality

9.4.2 Summarize the goals of the various "waves" of the Women's Movement and how women and men have participated.

Because sociologists study the links between identity and inequality—whether based on race, class, sexuality, age, or gender—sociologists also study the various movements that have been organized to challenge that inequality and enhance the possibilities of those identities. Many men and women have found the traditional roles that were prescribed for them to be too confining, preventing them from achieving the sorts of lives they wanted. Historically, women's efforts to enter the labor force, seek an education, vote, serve on a jury, or join a union served as the foundation for contemporary women's efforts to reduce discrimination, end sexual harassment or domestic violence, or enable them to balance work and family life. Women soon understood that they could not do these things alone, and their opposition to gender roles became political: They opposed gender inequality.

The modern **Women's Movement** was born to remove obstacles to women's full participation in modern life. In the nineteenth century, the "first wave" of the Women's Movement was concerned with women's *entry* into the public sphere. Campaigns to allow women to vote (suffrage), to go to college, to serve on juries, to go to law school or medical school, or to join a profession or a union all had largely succeeded by the middle of the twentieth century. The motto of the National Woman Suffrage

Women's Movement

The movement to remove obstacles to women's full participation in modern life. From its origins, the Women's Movement has been a global movement, yet each national and cultural expression has sought changes tailored to its specific context.

Association was, "Women, their rights and nothing less! Men, their rights and nothing more!" From its origins, the Women's Movement has been a global movement, yet each national and cultural expression has sought changes tailored to its specific context.

In the 1960s and 1970s, a "second wave" emerged, continuing the struggle to eliminate obstacles to women's advancement but equally determined to investigate the ways that gender inequality is also part of personal life, which includes their relationships with men. In the industrialized world, the second wave focused on public participation—equality in the working world, election to political office—as well as beginning to focus on men's violence against women, rape, the denigration of women in the media, and women's sexuality and lesbian rights. Their motto was, "The personal is political."

Today, a "third wave" has emerged primarily among younger women. Although third-wave feminists share the outrage at institutional discrimination and interpersonal violence, they also have a more playful relationship with mass media and consumerism. While they support the rights of lesbians, many third-wavers are also energetically heterosexual and insist on the ability to be friends and lovers with men. They are also decidedly more multicultural and seek to explore and challenge the *intersections* of gender inequality with other forms of inequality, such as class, race, ethnicity, and sexuality.

Beginning in the 1970s, many men began to express their feeling that traditional definitions of masculinity were restrictive as well. They sought "liberation" from parts of that role—as "success object" or "emotionless rock." "**Men's liberation**" never really took off as a social movement, but many thousands of men have since become involved with groups that promise a more fulfilling definition of masculinity. Unfortunately, this is often to be achieved by returning to traditional, anachronistic, ideas of femininity as well. For example, the evangelical Christian group, the Promise Keepers embraces a traditional nineteenth-century vision of masculinity as responsible father and provider—as long as their wives also return to a traditional nineteenth-century definition of femininity, staying home and taking care of the children.

But today there are also many men who support gender equality. These "profeminist" men believe not only that gender equality is a good thing for women, but that it would also transform masculinity in ways that would benefit men too, enabling them to be more involved fathers, better friends, more emotionally responsive partners and husbands—fuller individuals and human beings.

The Women's March on January 21, 2017, after the election of President Donald Trump may have been the largest mass protest in the history of the United States. The Women's Movement has fought for gender equality throughout U.S. history and continues to do so today.

men's liberation
Beginning in the 1970s, an effort by men to challenge and revise traditional definitions of masculinity.

Fighting Inequality: Movements for Gender Equality

9.4.3 Summarize the meaning of feminism and what it means to argue that it takes different forms in different cultural contexts.

The political position of many young women today, however, is "I'm not a feminist, but …" Most young women subscribe to virtually all the tenets of feminism—equal pay for equal work, right to control their bodies and sexuality—but they believe that they are already equal to men and therefore don't need a political movement to liberate them. For many, the term *feminist* carries too many negative connotations. This led sociologist Jo Reger (2012) to argue that for young people today, feminism is both "everywhere and nowhere."

Feminism is the belief that women should have equal political, social, sexual, economic, and intellectual rights to men. It insists on women's equality in all arenas—in the public sphere, in interpersonal relations, at home and at work, in the bedroom,

feminism
The belief that women should have equal political, social, sexual, economic, and intellectual rights and opportunities to men.

SOCIOLOGY AND OUR WORLD

MEN AND FEMINISM

Are men are part of the movement for gender equality?

The global struggle against gender inequality also engages men. Although in most developing nations, men see and assume the benefits of gender inequality, in some industrial countries, especially the United States, Britain and Australia, some men have begun to protest that they, not women, are really the victims of gender inequality. Women's increased inequality has come, they argue, at the expense of men. These "men's rights" groups are often analogous to those groups of white people who argue that racial progress has left white people the victims of reverse discrimination (as we discussed in Chapter 8). Sociologists of gender are not persuaded; we see that despite enormous strides, gender equality remains a distant goal in every society.

In many countries, there are also men who visibly support gender equality. These men have embraced the feminist vision of gender equality and seek to work with men to end men's violence against women, sexual harassment in the workplace, and guarantee equality in the workplace and at home. Global organizations like the White Ribbon Campaign, begun in Canada in the 1990s, have groups in more than 50 countries working to end men's violence against women. In the United States, organizations such as the National Organization for Men Against Sexism (NOMAS) and Men Can Stop Rape (MCSR) and A Call to Men seek to bring men together to promote gender equality.

On campuses around the country, there are men's organizations working to support the campus women's groups. Groups such as Harvard Men Against Rape and Tulane Men Against Violence actively work to engage men in campus-based activities such as supporting Take Back the Night marches or Vagina Monologues productions or "Walk a Mile in Her Shoes" campaigns to raise men's awareness and to get men involved in the fight to end violence against women.

and the boardroom. As a political theory, feminism rests on two foundations: one an empirical observation and the other a moral stand. The empirical observation is that women and men are not equal; that is, that gender inequality still defines our society. The moral stand is that this inequality is wrong and should change. Feminism is about women's choices and the ability to choose to do what they want with no greater obstacles than the limits of their abilities.

Feminism is also a global movement—with local, regional, and transnational expressions. The United Nations Declaration of 1985 made clear that women's rights were universal human rights and that women's bodily integrity, her sexual autonomy, and her rights to public participation knew no national boundaries. There are several major strands of feminism. Each emphasizes a different aspect of gender inequality and prescribes a different political formula for equality. Global and transnational feminism today brings together the major strands of feminism to challenge women's subordination in society in various contexts and ways. It fuels transnational women's labor organizing and women's rights organizing, for example, and has also become a significant force and voice in organizations with broader or more multiple goals, like international development, violence, and human rights (Walby 2002; Khagram, Riker, and Sikkink 2002; Ferree and Tripp 2006).

Transnational feminism reflects both convergence and variety in its goals and forms around the world. Sociologists and others have found the globalization process fosters increasing agreement on some issues (Moghadam 2000; True and Mintrom 2001; Naples and Desai 2002; Ferree and Mueller 2007), but also increasing variance worldwide in the forms of activism used to protest or address them. For example, there is fairly wide-spread agreement on an agenda that includes women's representation in government and also the issues of abortion and prostitution among women's groups in many parts of the world. However, ownership and activism styles tend to vary by issue. Local, in-formal networks are more likely to develop political actions when it comes to abortion, yet are nearly absent from activism about prostitution, where formal organizations are especially engaged (Ferree and Mueller 2007).

Just as forms of activism vary across issue, the feminist claims that frame each issue also vary—in fact, even more so. For example, there is significant cross-national agreement on the need for women's representation in government, but in some coun-tries the argument is that political representation would combat male domination, and in others, feminists argue that more women in politics would improve wom-en's status. And there is no agreement transnationally on the feminist politics around prostitution.

Challenges to Gender Inequality and the Endurance of Gender Gaps

9.4.4 Consider the progress toward gender equality made in recent history and how and why gender gaps still exist.

Girls' and women's participation in athletics and sports has meant that women are now competing at the most elite levels in most international athletic competitions. When they began competing, the differences between men's and women's world record times were sizeable. But gaps between men and women in athletic achievement have been declining. Women's and men's world records in all sort of sporting competitions are converging. It's one small example of a larger trend in gender relations. Consider the gender gap in world record times in the 1500-meter race (see FIGURE 9.6). You might notice two trends. First, although men's world records are still faster than women's, women's world record times have decreased at a much higher rate than men's. Second, as of the 1980's, it appears as though women's progress converging toward men's world record times seemed to stall. There is more than one way to consider this shift.

FIGURE 9.6 World Record Times in 1500-Meter Running for Women and Men, 1912–2015

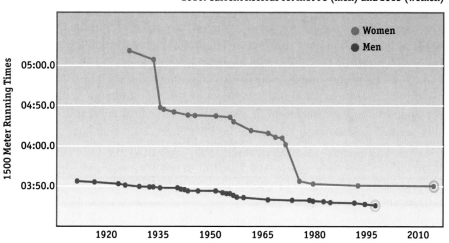

NOTE: Markers indicate the year the record was set.

SOURCE: Data from https://en.wikipedia.org/wiki/1500_metres_world_record_progression.

FIGURE 9.7 Shifts in the Gender Wage Gap, 1940–2012

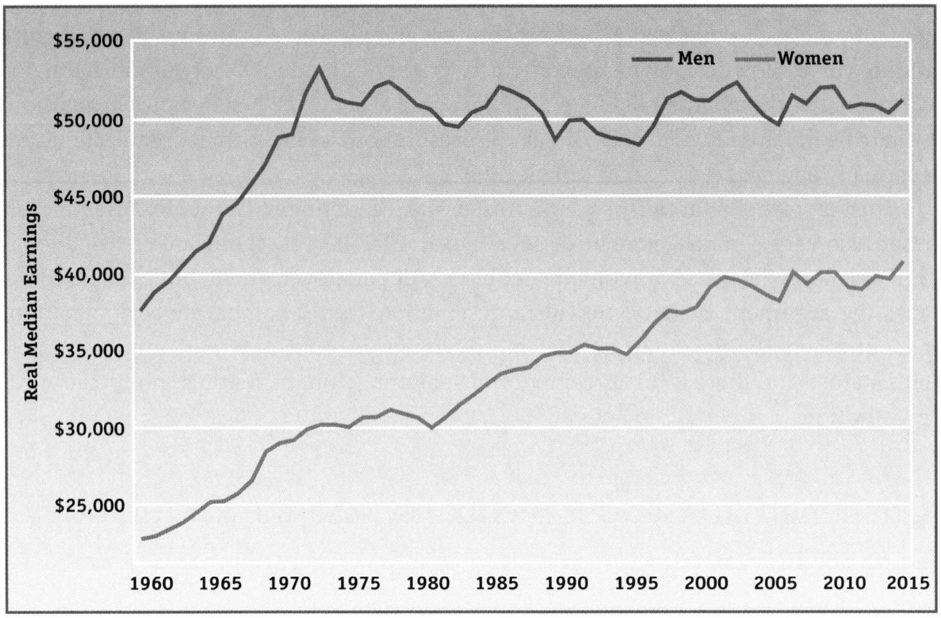

SOURCE: Data from U.S. Census Bureau, Number and Real Median Earnings of Total Workers and Full-Time, Year-Round Workers by Sex and Female-to-Male Earnings Ratio: 1960 to 2014, https://www2.census.gov/programs-surveys/demo/tables/p60/252/table5.pdf and U.S. Census Bureau, Current Population Survey, 2015 and 2016 Annual Social and Economic Supplements.

One way of making sense of the stall in the gap here is that perhaps we are reaching the biological limits of male and female bodies and the gap we still see today is more the result of biology than anything else. What is curious is that gender gaps stalled on a variety of different measures at a similar time.

Consider the gender wage gap. In FIGURE 9.7, you can see how the gender wage gap has closed over time. Similar to the gender gap in world record times for the 1500-meter race, the gender wage gap closed over the course of the twentieth century, and seems to have stalled during the 1980s as well. Additionally, the closing of the gap here seems to have more to do with decreases and stagnation in men's wages than increases in women's wage (a fact we will address in more detail in Chapter 14, on the workplace).

When sociologist Arlie Hochschild discovered what she came to call the "second shift," she also coined another term—the "stalled revolution" (Hochschild 1989). What she discovered was that, despite enormous gains in gender equality in the labor market, heterosexual women had achieved minimal gains on the home front. The **stalled revolution** refers to the fact that, although women are much more likely to earn a living wage on their own, men have not responded in kind and participated more in work around the house. Indeed, although men's weekly hours dedicated to housework in heterosexual couples have increased in recent history (and the hours women spend have been decreasing), a similar gap remains, and progress toward equality seemed to stall at a similar point in time (Sayer 2016). Similarly, we've seen a great deal of progress in college majors become desegregated through the 1980s (England 2010). Look back at the chart illustrating women's representation in films (Figure 9.1) and you'll note that progress on the Bechdel Test appears to stall right around the same time.

As these examples all illustrate, significant gains have been made toward gender equality in relatively recent history; the general trend is one of gender convergence. And when we examine these trends intersectionally, we can also say that some groups of women have benefited from these changes more than others (middle-class, young, heterosexual, white women, for instance). But it's also true that a great deal of the

stalled revolution

The widespread change in gender relations whereby women are much more likely to earn a living wage on their own but men have not responded in kind and participated more in work around the house.

progress toward gender equality seems to have *stalled*. The convergence of all manner of gender gaps began to slow and stall between 1980 and 1990. Sociologists are still at work considering whether, how, and why remaining gaps might be related to a common collection of social factors.

---

iSOC AND YOU Gender Inequality at the Global and Local Level

Gender structures just about any aspect of your life that you can imagine. And yet, precisely how gender structures your life is something differently organized in different societies. Because gender *identity* forms such a foundational component of who we are, it organizes everything from our *interactions* with other people and the various social *institutions* that make up society. But gender identities are constructed within a structure of gender *inequality*. So, although gender affects everyone's experiences and opportunities, girls and women (considered as a group) are systematically, institutionally disadvantaged by this process, and boys and men are advantaged. As we have learned, when we consider this *intersectionally*, it is also true that gender *inequality* impacts everyone in a society and many boys and men suffer from gender *inequality*, too (particularly those marginalized along the lines of race, class, and sexuality). And although gender *inequality* in the United States is something women (and some men, too) have fought for since the United States first came into being, that fight continues today as gender *inequality* shifts and is perpetuated in new ways in a changing society.

Conclusion
Sex and Gender NOW

Sociologists today speak of gender as socially constructed; even biological sex, it turns out, requires some social agreement about what constitutes biology or which aspects of someone's biology should "count" when it comes to sex. Sociologists see gender as a core element of identity—who you are—as well as a primary mechanism for social stratification, or social inequality. This means that gender inequality is often challenging to study because gender is associated with both pleasures and recognition, but also pain, injustice, and enduring forms of inequality. Sociologists observe that gender is not only something that you achieve through socialization, but also something that you "do," every day through social interaction and in every social institution in which you find yourself.

Often, we think that gender differences are the basis for gender inequality: because women and men are different, they have different talents and abilities, different interests, and desires. Thus, the gender inequalities we observe in our institutions—the wage gap, for example—we often assume are the result of women and men making different choices about what is important to them. This is only half-true. It's both that gender differences can be the cause of gender inequality *and* that gender inequality can be the cause of gender difference.

Consider how the iSoc model can be applied to studying sex and gender. The gender identities with which we identify and the sexed identities by which our bodies are classified have real consequences for the kinds of lives we will be able to lead. And gender brings us both pleasure and pain as we often enjoy donning our gender for others and ourselves (by wearing make-up, conditioning our bodies, sporting a beard, etc.). When we do this, we are, quite literally, bringing gender into existence in our interactions. And understanding gender as something we "do" (rather than as an inherent property or something that we "have") means that sociologists understand gender as something we are capable of "doing" differently—though there are many obstacles that exist. This is because sex and gender are also part of systems of inequality, which means that those same identities and interactions are part of a larger structure in society by which they are rewarded (and punished) in different and patterned ways. The various ways we "do" and are expected to do gender become a part of social institutions such that attempting to challenge gendered expectations that are institutionalized can be difficult and sometimes seems impossible. Part of this challenge results from the fact that gender inequality is experienced differently by different people and groups. This is why thinking about intersections between different facets of our identities (like race, class, sexuality, gender, and more) is so important.

There is little doubt that around the world gender inequality is gradually being reduced, in some societies more than others and for some groups more than others.

gender convergence

One of the central social dynamics of gender noted by sociologists today, it refers to the gradual closing of the gender gap in many aspects of social life, rendering women's and men's lives increasingly more equal.

Perhaps one of the central social dynamics of gender is gradual **gender convergence**—many aspects of social life in which a gender gap exists are beginning to close. Women's and men's lives are looking increasingly similar. That doesn't mean, however, that women and men are becoming "the same." Gender convergence means that our activities and our interactions are more similar and more equal. Living in times of great historical transformation, we often forget just how recent are the changes we today take for granted. There are still women who remember when women could not vote, drive a car, serve on a jury, become doctors or lawyers, serve in the military, become firefighters or police officers, join a union, or go to certain colleges. All these changes happened in the twentieth century. At the same time, today, there is significant backlash against gender equality.

The struggle for gender equality has a long history, filled with stunning successes and anguishing setbacks. And sociologists who study sex and gender help us better understand just how wide-reaching gender inequality is. But for women (and the men who are allied with them) who believe in gender equality, there is no going back.

CHAPTER REVIEW Sex and Gender

9.1 Thinking Sociologically about Sex and Gender

Part of learning to think sociologically about sex and gender means that you need to unlearn some of the ways many people are taught to think about gender because we often like to think about sex and gender as elements of our biology, not our society. However, societies dramatically shape the ways in which we come to understand sex and gender and the discrete categories into which it is often assumed everyone will *naturally* fit. Sociologists begin by distinguishing sex from gender. When we refer to sex we are talking about the biology of maleness and femaleness—our chromosomal, chemical, anatomical organization. Gender refers to the meanings that societies give to the fact of biological difference. Sex is male and female; gender is the cultural understanding of masculinity and femininity—like the idea that women are innately nurturing and cooperative, or the belief that men are inherently aggressive and competitive. Gender is both a foundation of our *identities* and a fundamental way that societies organize themselves, allocating tasks and distributing resources. It is produced in our *interactions* and embedded in our *institutions*, and different groups experience gender in different ways. And like race and ethnicity, gender is not only a matter of cultural difference, but it is also

a dynamic system of *inequality*. The observed biological differences between women and men are thought to lead naturally, and inevitably, to the *inequality* we observe. To a sociologist, however, the opposite is true. It's not that gender difference causes inequality, but that gender inequality actually causes societies to construct gender difference to justify it.

9.1 Key Terms

sex A biological distinction; the chromosomal, chemical, and anatomical organization of males and females.

gender A socially constructed definition based on sex category, based on the meanings that societies attach to the fact of sex differences.

gender binary The belief that humans come in two types: males, who behave in masculine ways, and females, who behave in feminine ways, which is a belief sociological research has shown is better understood as rooted in our culture than our nature.

gender identity Our understanding of ourselves as male or female, masculine or feminine.

gender inequality Gender inequality has two dimensions: the domination of men over women, and the domination of some men over other men and some women over other women.

patriarchy Literally, "the rule of the fathers"; a name given to the social order in which men hold power over women.

evolutionary imperative The belief, typically used to justify traditional assumptions about masculinity and femininity, that males and females developed different reproductive strategies to ensure that they reproduce successfully and are able to pass on their genetic material to the next generation.

intersex traits People are said to have intersex traits when their bodies cannot be clearly categorized as fully male or female.

medicalization The process by which *human* conditions come to be defined and treated as *medical* conditions such that they also become subject to medical study, diagnosis, and treatment.

transgender An umbrella term that describes a variety of people, behaviors, and groups whose identities depart from normative gender ideals of masculinity or femininity.

cis-gender people People whose gender identities are consistent with the identities they were assigned at birth based on sex characteristics.

gender panic Situations in which people react to ruptures in assumptions about gender assumed to be based in our biology by frantically reasserting the supposed "naturalness" of the male/female gender binary.

9.2 The Social Organization of Gendered Interactions and Inequality

Sex and gender are major *identity* categories around which our society is organized and also stratified. Simply put, women and men live in the same societies, but they have dramatically different experiences of those societies. Gender is socially constructed, and we both participate in this process and conform to social ideas and expectations. Thus, our gender identities are both *voluntary* (we choose to become who we are) and *coerced* (we are pressured, forced, and often physically threatened to conform to certain rules). Gender is something we "do," and also something to which we are held accountable through both *interactions* and virtually every social institution in a society—our families, our education, the workplace, religious *institutions*, the media, our peer groups, and much more. These forces and structures socialize us into more than just gender differences; we are also helped to understand and accept gender *inequality*. We learn to think about masculinity as more valuable and worthy of status, respect, and attention than femininity.

9.2 Key Terms

borderwork An active process in which we all participate, it refers to the ways we selectively call attention to gender difference (and simultaneously ignore gender similarities).

gender socialization The process by which males and females are taught the appropriate behaviors, attitudes, and traits associated with their biological sex in a particular culture.

gender bias The ways we systematically treat men and women (and boys and girls) differently.

androcentrism The practice, conscious or not, of placing males or masculinity at the center of one's worldview and treating masculinity as though it has higher status and value than femininity.

gender similarities hypothesis Janet Hyde's assertion, based on meta-research, that men and women are similar until proven otherwise.

social construction of gender The social process by which we construct our gender identities throughout our lives, using the cultural ideas and materials we find around us.

gender roles The bundle of traits, attitudes, and behaviors that are associated with biological males and females.

gender relations Sociologists today are more likely to use gender relations (rather than "role") to emphasize how the definitions of masculinity and femininity are developed in relation to each other and to systems of social power and inequality.

gender policing The enforcement of normative gender ideals by rewarding normative gender performances and punishing transgressions.

9.3 Studying Gender Inequality Institutionally and Intersectionally

Sociologists think about gender as a verb rather than a noun—gender as something we "do." Beyond that, sociologists also use the term *gendered* to refer to social processes that shape men's and women's lives differently. When we do this, we are playing with the term *gender* to enable us to examine institutional level processes. *Institutions* shape gender stratification and gender inequality. Educational *institutions* are gendered, conditioning dramatically different experiences for boys and girls in school and different responses to the learning process; gender shapes the workplace—what kind of work we perform (and don't perform) and how these jobs are regarded and compensated; heterosexual marriage is deeply gendered institution, from how marriage is organized and conducted to who is perceived to benefit from it. Most violence is gendered; from the gender of the perpetrator, to the psychological motivations that lead to violence and the structural dynamics that institutionalize it, violence is among the most highly gendered social behavior we know.

9.3 Key Terms

occupational sex segregation Refers to women's and men's different concentrations in different occupations, different industries, different jobs, and different levels in a workplace hierarchy.

dual labor market The pervasive condition in the United States in which work and workers are divided into different sectors—primary or secondary, formal or informal, and also male or female.

feminization of the professions Widely demonstrated sociological phenomenon in which salaries drop as women's participation increases in a particular job category or profession.

second shift Arlie Hochschild's term for the dual day experienced by working women in which they perform the lion's share of the housework and childcare after a regular working shift is over.

9.4 Gender Inequality at the Global and Local Level

Gender *inequality* is a global problem. Just about every country in the world treats its women less well than it treats its men. Along virtually every *institutional* axis there are gender gaps—from literacy, education, and employment to income, health, and decision making; these gaps are larger in the developing world and nonindustrialized countries. However, there are also worldwide efforts to fight gender *inequality*. Feminism is also a global movement—with local, regional, and transnational expressions. The United Nations Declaration of 1985 made clear that women's rights were universal human rights and that women's bodily integrity, her sexual autonomy, and her rights to public participation knew no national boundaries.

9.4 Key Terms

feminization of poverty A worldwide phenomenon that also afflicts U.S. women, this term describes women's overrepresentation among the world's poor and tendency to be in worse economic straits than men in any given nation or population.

Women's Movement The movement to remove obstacles to women's full participation in modern life. From its origins, the Women's Movement has been a global movement, yet each national and cultural expression has sought changes tailored to its specific context.

men's liberation Beginning in the 1970s, an effort by men to challenge and revise traditional definitions of masculinity.

feminism The belief that women should have equal political, social, sexual, economic, and intellectual rights and opportunities to men.

stalled revolution The widespread change in gender relations whereby women are much more likely to earn a living wage on their own but men have not responded in kind and participated more in work around the house.

gender convergence One of the central social dynamics of gender noted by sociologists today, it refers to the gradual closing of the gender gap in many aspects of social life, rendering women's and men's lives increasingly more equal.

SELF-TEST

〉 CHECK YOUR UNDERSTANDING

1. _____ refers to the biological distinction of being male or female, whereas _____ refers to the meanings that society attaches to these biological differences.
   a. gender; sex
   b. feminism; oppression
   c. sex; gender
   d. physiology; sociology

2. As revealed by cross-cultural research, how many gender roles are found in each society?
   a. Only one
   b. Always two
   c. At least three
   d. It varies by society.

3. How prevalent are division of labor by gender and gender inequality today?
   a. Both are universal.
   b. Developing countries have division of labor by gender, whereas industrial societies have gender inequality.
   c. Developing countries have gender inequality, whereas industrial societies have division of labor by gender.
   d. Although both were prevalent in prehistoric societies, neither exist in society today.

4. How are infants of differing sexes treated?
   a. Infants of different sexes are treated identically by adults.
   b. They are treated the same by women but differently by men.
   c. They are treated the same by men but differently by women.
   d. Adults treat infants of different sexes differently.

5. According to the text, for which trait has a significant gender difference been found?
   a. Intelligence
   b. Violence
   c. Extroversion
   d. No significant differences have been found.

6. The second shift Arlie Hochschild wrote about refers to

   a. the overtime a woman would have to work to earn as much as a man does for the same job.

   b. the fact that women get the less desirable shifts in the workplace because of their lower status.

   c. the extra hours working women work, compared with men, because they do the housework, too, after working outside the home.

   d. the next shift in awareness, when women are not only legally recognized as equal but actually treated as such.

7. Which of the following is the result of the "hidden curriculum," according to the text?

   a. Men learn they are expected to like math and science.

   b. Women learn to talk more in class, to fulfill the expectation that women are chattier.

   c. Men learn that reading comes naturally to them, whereas women have to struggle with it.

   d. Both men and women get the message that they are valued equally and have equal potential.

8. Identify which of the following is not one of the principles of feminism identified in the text.

   a. The moral position that inequality is wrong and should change

   b. The empirical observation that men and women are not equal in our society

   c. The fact that male and female biology is inherently different means that they will inevitably have different contributions to make to society.

   d. All of these are principles of feminism that were identified in the text.

Self-Test Answers: 1. c, 2. d, 3. a, 4. d, 5. b, 6. c, 7. a, 8. c

CHAPTER 10

AGE: FROM YOUNG TO OLD

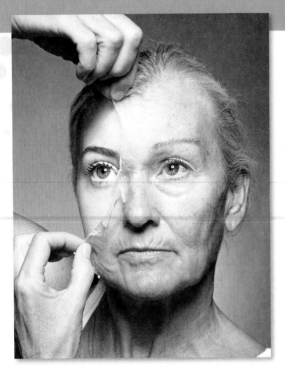

Age is more than a number. Age shapes the sorts of social roles you occupy, it affects your health, and it shapes your social position and status within the society in which you live. As such, aging is much more than a biological process, it's a sociological process as well with wide-ranging implications.

→ LEARNING OBJECTIVES

In this chapter, using the iSoc framework, you should be able to:

10.1.1 Distinguish between chronological age and functional age to understand how sociologists study age and aging.

10.1.2 Recognize how each of the five elements of the iSoc model can be used to examine age sociologically.

10.1.3 Understand what sociologists mean by "life expectancy" and how and why this prediction changes over time.

10.1.4 Understand that the practice of dividing the life span up into different identity-related chunks is a social practice.

10.1.5 Summarize the ways that "children" (as a distinct social group) is a concept that did not always exist.

10.1.6 Explain the social factors that gave rise to adolescence as a distinct stage of the life course.

10.1.7 Describe the ways that young adulthood emerged as a stage of the life course as a result of economic changes.

10.1.8 Summarize some of the ways that society is organized in ways that often make middle age a challenging portion of the life course.

10.1.9 Delineate between the three stages of old age, and describe the social experiences associated with each.

10.2.1 Summarize some of the social forces that produced the "baby boom" and shaped the experience of this generation.

10.2.2 Explain how the smaller size of Generation X (compared to the Baby Boomers) shaped their experience of childhood in different ways from their parents' childhoods.

10.2.3 Explain some of the challenges that Millennials face and how they are related to the structure of society.

10.2.4 Understand how the age structures of societies are changing and what sorts of consequences these changes will produce.

10.3.1 Summarize which age groups are most at risk of poverty and why.

10.3.2 Explain some of the ways that age shapes the types of social interactions we enjoy (or are denied).

10.3.3 Determine some of the ways that inequality shapes who has access to retirement and when.

10.3.4 Summarize the sorts of changes that occurred in U.S. society that have changed who cares for the elderly and how.

10.3.5 Explain what it means that sociologists understand death as a cultural process rather than a biological event.

10.4.1 Define the "expansion of morbidity" and why it is a central problem in many societies today.

10.4.2 Summarize what child labor looks like in the United States.

10.4.3 Understand how the frequency and type of child labor differs around the world.

10.4.4 Summarize how people have attempted to oppose age inequality and how and why they have been successful.

Introduction

Our society is obsessed with youth. Supermodels are over the hill at age 25, and actresses older than 40 are rarely cast as anything but grandmothers. Television, movie, and print advertisements are aimed directly at the 18- to 35-year-old demographic and ignore the interests, tastes, and wallets of anyone older. You can buy hundreds of products designed to eliminate baldness, gray hair, wrinkles, crows' feet, paunches, all of the characteristics of age, but not a single one that promises "distinguished-looking gray hair" or "venerable wrinkles of a life well-lived." We compliment people by saying they are young-looking, as if it is the exact equivalent of strong, healthy, and attractive.

At the same time, our society is growing older. You can hardly pick up a newspaper or magazine without seeing a headline about the Graying of America. The proportion of Americans older than 65 increases every year, while the proportion younger than 35 shrinks. Retirement is no longer a few years at the end of life: When the average person will live to see 79, some can expect to spend nearly a quarter of our lives after age 65 (U.S. Census Bureau 2016). Today, 16.7 percent of Americans 65 and older (11.2 million people) are still working at least part-time, and there's talk of raising the official retirement age to 67 or even 70 (U.S. Census Bureau 2016).

We tend to think either that we're witnessing the "Graying of America" or the "Youth-Obsessed America." But to a sociologist, it's really both. We're graying and youth obsessed at the same time.

Age is one of the bases of our identities, and a central axis of inequality in our society. Unlike other dimensions of identity and inequality, though, age seems more fluid, as we move from one age group into another. And age is part of the structure of every major social institution in our society.

10.1 Age, Identity, and the Stages of Life

What does "old" mean, anyway? Sociologists believe that age is less of a biological condition than a social construction. Depending on the norms of their society, a 15-year-old may play with toy soldiers or fight in real wars, a 20-year-old may receive a weekly paycheck or a weekly allowance, 40-year-olds may be changing the diapers of their children or their grandchildren, and a 60-year-old may be doddering and decrepit or in the robust prime of life. It is not the passing of years but the social environment that determines the characteristics of age. As people have been living longer, who qualifies as "old" shifts. This is why popular media often quips, "sixty is the new forty" and the like. Age is something that is continually redefined in modern societies.

Age and aging are great topics of sociological analysis because, unlike many forms of identity that sociologists examine, age is a source of identity that will continually shift over the course of your life. While most people retain a racial or gender identity throughout their lives (though, by no means everyone, as we learned in Chapters 8 and 9), our age is an identity that is constantly changing. And as our age changes, we confront new age-related problems and institutions in our society. Understanding age as a social identity is the first step toward a sociological understanding of age and aging. And to completely grasp the changes this social identity undergoes necessitates considering the ways that societies divide people up into different groups based on age and how we all collaborate to make those age-related divisions meaningful (in our interactions, our social institutions, and more).

Age and Identity

10.1.1 Distinguish between chronological age and functional age to understand how sociologists study age and aging.

Prior to the twentieth century, people became adults astonishingly early. Girls were allowed to marry at age 14 or even younger, though most would not go through puberty until sometime after their eighteenth birthday. Jewish boys were considered adults at age 13. The Anabaptists of Reformation Europe disapproved of baptizing infants, as the Catholics did, so they baptized only "adults," by which they meant anyone over the age of 14. Today, people seem to postpone adulthood until halfway through their lives. We regularly say "He's 23 years old—just a baby," and even 30-year-olds are often considered immature rather than real grownups. Middle age starts in the 50s, and old age—who knows? The boundaries are pushing upward every year.

With so much change and so much redefinition, one would expect age to diminish in importance as a social category. What does it matter if you graduate from college at age 20 or age 50? If you date someone 20 years older? If your boss at work is 20 years younger than you? Why should the number of years you've been alive make any difference whatsoever? Yet age remains one of our major social identities; we assess ourselves and each other—positively and negatively—based on age as frequently as on class, race, ethnicity, gender, and sexuality. These judgments result in social stratification, for distributing rewards and punishments, and for allocating status and power. Thus, while social stratification often refers to class, societies are stratified by all manner of social identities, including age.

To the sociologist, age is a basis for *identity* and a cause of *inequality*. As an identity, sociologists differentiate between your **chronological age**—a person's age determined by the actual date of birth—and **functional age**—a set of observable characteristics and attributes that are used to categorize people into different age cohorts (though this is more true for some age cohorts than others). Sociologists refer to the forms of social organization that are based on age and through which we pass over the course of our lives as **age grades**. An **age cohort** (sometimes also referred to as an "age set") is a group of people who are born within a specific time period and assumed to share both chronological and functional characteristics. You live in an extremely "age graded" society if age is used as a proxy to segregate different groups.

Traditionally, the sociological study of aging was called **gerontology**, which is the study of phenomena associated with old age and aging. Sociologists now understand

chronological age
A person's age as determined by the actual date of birth.

functional age
A set of observable characteristics and attributes that are used to categorize people into different age cohorts.

age grades
The term sociologists use to refer to the forms of social organization that are based on age and through which we pass over the course of our lives.

age cohort
A group of people who are born within a specific time period and assumed to share both chronological and functional characteristics, as well as life experiences.

gerontology
Scientific study of the biological, psychological, and sociological phenomena associated with old age and aging.

SOCIOLOGY AND OUR WORLD

EDUCATION AS AGE GRADED

Why do we use age as a basis for what students should be learning?

Eugenie de Silva received her Bachelor's degree in May 2013. She studied Intelligence Analysis at the American Military University and graduated with a 4.0 GPA (summa cum laude). Among the sea of students she sat with at graduation, Eugenie was a bit different. She was born in Manchester, England. But other students studied at her university from abroad as well. What made Eugenie distinct in her class was her age—she was 14 years old when she completed her Bachelor's degree. After promptly acquiring a Master's degree as well, Eugenie began pursuing a Ph.D. in Politics at the University of Leicester (England). Eugenie is a child prodigy.

In the United States, and in many other countries, we educate citizens based on age. This is why you spend much of your young life hanging around people who are almost exactly the same age as you are (give or take a few months when you are younger, and a few years as you get older). We assume that people around the same age should be able to comprehend the same sorts of things. This is what makes people like Eugenie so unique—she is notably different from the rest. And, while Eugenie seems incredibly capable of keeping up in the classroom, sometimes students who attend college much earlier than everyone else do struggle socially. The same is sometimes true of older college students, coming back to school to pursue a degree a bit later in life than most.

Of course, we don't have to educate people this way. There are other ways to imagine dividing people up into groups for the purposes of education. Indeed, we already do some "tracking" in schools by dividing students up by ability (something we discuss in more depth in Chapter 13). But divisions by ability tend to take place within age groups for the most part. So, skipping a grade is less common than you might think. And it is part of the reason that age holds so much meaning for people; it is a marker of life stage and a powerful element of social identities.

that such a study, although essential, tells only half the story. While age is a facet of identity at all moments through the life cycle, most of the inequality based on age occurs at the upper and lower ends of the life course—that is, among the young and the elderly. In high-income countries like the United States, older people often wield a great deal of political power, but they still must battle negative stereotypes and limited social services. Children, teenagers, and young adults often lack power, prestige, and resources, but they are seen as filled with potential, and we strive to look like them. Although we tout compassion for our elders and commitment to our kids, our social and economic policies often shortchange or harm both of these vulnerable groups. Today, the study of age and aging in sociology requires that we study both identity and inequality among both the young and the old—as well as everyone in between.

iSoc: The Sociology of Aging

10.1.2 Recognize how each of the five elements of the iSoc model can be used to examine age sociologically.

Aging is something we often think about biologically—as something that *happens to* us, rather than as a system of social organization. And certainly aging is a process that involves our biology as humans. It affects the types of diseases to which our bodies are likely to succumb, it shapes the color of our hair, the wrinkles in our skin, our hearing, our eyesight, the likelihood that we will die soon, and so much more. Aging is, simply put, an embodied experience. But aging is *social* when we recognize that all of these processes happen at different times for different groups. Aging does not affect everyone the same way.

And *age*—as an identity rather than process—is also a social phenomenon. Age is a category in which societies invest a great deal of meaning; importantly, however, not all societies invest precisely the same meaning. And it is this point that requires sociological explanation and study. Just when do you stop being a "child" and start being an "adult"? Certainly, this can be handled with laws (and it is in most societies), but not all societies set the same ages. And, as people have started living longer, we are also increasingly dividing our lives up into more and more meaningful chunks of life that we understand as distinct from each other in important ways. Infants from toddlers, toddlers from kids, kids from "tweens," tweens from teenagers, teenagers from young adults … you get the idea. As you'll see in this chapter, age and aging are best understood sociologically and they both are dramatically influenced by social forces. To best understand how these forces impact age, consider the age and aging within the iSoc model.

IDENTITY—Age is an *identity*. When you're young, small distinctions in age are incredibly important sources of identity. This is why children sometimes count partial years when they tell each other their ages ("I'm four and three-quarters"). As an identity, age is related to social status as well. Turning 21 before most of your friends in college is often a source of status, or being the first among your friends to be able to drive a car, see an R-rated movie, or get a credit card in your own name. Age works as an identity because our society is stratified by age and segregated by age. How old you are matters.

INTERACTIONS—Like other sources of identity, age is also accomplished *interactionally*. This is why parents often tell their children to "Act your age!" Through interacting with other people and social institutions, we all come to learn what this means and also understand that it will change as we get older. Often, we get some practice along the way, as when parents dress their children up for formal events. Children look silly in formal attire (gowns, suits and ties). But it allows them to understand that part of becoming a "grown-up" is a performance and it involves learning the part.

INEQUALITY—As with many of the identities we've analyzed in this book, age is also related to *inequality*. People of different ages are likely to have dramatically different experiences in society. For instance, a larger share of children are in poverty than adults. Age shapes that experience of inequality. Many elderly people are social isolated. Age inequality shapes that experience as well. Because we often imagine age to be a biological phenomenon, it can be easy to forget that society could be organized in ways that did not work better for people of some ages than others. But it could. Not all societies struggle with the same issues of age inequality.

INSTITUTIONS—Every *institution* in society is stratified by age, though to differing degrees and in different ways—the family, religion, the workplace, and school. Age shapes when we start school, the year we have our bat or bar mitzvah or are "confirmed," when we're legally allowed to work and where, and all manner of lines of authority in the family. Age shapes whether we receive an "allowance," "wages," or mere gratitude from those around us for the work we do. But institutions also exist to stop us from working as we get older. When you are young, as a general rule, social institutions afford more power to people older than you. But as you get older, the balance of power shifts and eventually, you may feel that institutions seem to advantage those younger than you.

INTERSECTIONS—Age and aging are also processes that vary a great deal by other social identities, like race, class, and gender, for instance. How long you are likely to live, for instance, is dramatically influenced by your race, your gender, and what social class you happen to occupy. This is an important issue and examining *intersections* with age and aging allows us to show that age inequality is best seen in interaction with other forms of inequality. Everyone ages and everyone has an age; but aging is a process that affects different groups in different ways. To understand how these differences are related to social inequality and the social organization of a society requires us to understand aging as a social process from an intersectional perspective.

So, aging is an interactional process in which each of us is actively participating. Age shapes our understandings of who we are and where we fit into various hierarchies in the societies in which we live. And recognizing this, we realize that, unlike many other systems of inequality, our experience of age inequality changes over the course of our lives. Although most of us will occupy the same racial or gender identity for our entire lives, age is an identity that is constantly changing, and as members of a society stratified by age, we are expected to shift and adapt. But the experiences of people of different ages in different age groups are far from inevitable; rather, they are shaped by social forces and the structure of society.

Thinking about Age Sociologically

10.1.3 Understand what sociologists mean by "life expectancy" and how and why this prediction changes over time.

As we just read, we often think about age biologically. But age is a wonderfully sociological topic. Age is one of the axes of social identity that most societies use to categorize members of a society as members of different groups. And age becomes institutionalized as a means of dividing people such that it shapes our interactions and all manner of social life. And age is also centrally related to social inequality. Consider this: How long will you live? Sociologists refer to this prediction as **life expectancy**— the average number of years that people born in a certain year are predicted to live.

From ancient times through the early modern period of the seventeenth century, the rough division into childhood, adulthood, and old age was sufficient. Beginning about 1800, however, advances in sanitation, nutrition, and medical knowledge pushed up the average life expectancy in the United States and Western Europe. This means that, as a result of changes in society, people are living longer. This general trend, however, is more true for some than others. And we can learn a lot about a society just looking at how long different groups are expected to live compared with one another (see MAP 10.1).

life expectancy
The average number of years a person can expect to live; varies greatly by country and region.

MAP 10.1 Life Expectancy Around the World
The average life expectancy of a baby born in the United States in 1880 was 39.4 years; by 1960, it jumped to 70 years; and by 2014, the average life expectancy of babies born in the United States was 78.9 years. In India in 1881, the life expectancy of a baby was 25.4 years; in 2014, that age increased to 68.4 years. These are big changes. People are living longer. But life expectancies vary wildly around the world, and this variation is a powerful illustration of global inequality. See how life expectancies differ around the world today.

No data
45 – 49
50 – 54
55 – 59
60 – 64
65 – 69
70 – 75
75 – 80
> 80

SOURCE: Data from The World Bank. Accessed 02/17/17. Available at http://data.worldbank.org/indicator/SP.DYN.LE00.IN?end=2014&start=2014&view=map.

Although the United States has among the highest life expectancies of any nation in the world, the different identities you happen to occupy, where you happen to live, and more also influence how long you are expected to live. For instance, the state with the highest life expectancy in the United States is Hawaii (81.3 years). The lowest life expectancies are associated with people born in Oklahoma (75.9 years), Louisiana (75.7 years), Alabama (75.4 years), West Virginia (75.4 years), and Mississippi (75 years). Different life expectancies in different states are not the result of climate; they are related to income, life options, education, nutrition, and access to health services. The states with the largest poor populations are also those with the least access to health care, both issues that cause people to be more likely to die sooner and from circumstances from which they may have been saved had they lived somewhere else or had more resources.

But life expectancy is not only related to social location; it is also dramatically influenced by your social identities. Different groups in the United States, for example, have dramatically different life expectancies. And although life expectancies have been increasing over time for everyone, there are gaps in how long different groups are expected to live that illustrate inequality in society. In iSoc terms, life expectancy intersects with other identities to produce different outcomes for different groups. For instance, white people live longer in the United States than most other racial and ethnic groups. And women live longer than men; though this is primarily because they are less likely to sustain unintentional injury (due to dangerous behavior), having stronger social networks (women are better connected to people), and they take better care of themselves. Men are less likely to regularly visit the doctor, more likely to take risks, and less likely to reach out to others when they need help. All of these factors combine to shorten men's lives.

Although life expectancy is only one issue related to age, it is an important one. As people begin to live longer, they will enter stages in the life course that their parents and grandparents did not have to navigate. Changes in life expectancy necessitate changes throughout society.

The Stages of Life

10.1.4 Understand that the practice of dividing the life span up into different identity-related chunks is a social practice.

life span

The span of time during which a person is alive, which all societies—whether tribal, agrarian, or industrial—have always divided into stages, seasons, or age groups.

age norms

Distinctive cultural values, pursuits, and pastimes that are culturally prescribed for each age cohort.

All societies—whether tribal, agrarian, or industrial—have always divided the **life span** into stages, seasons, or age groups. Age grading is a cultural universal, though different societies divide people up by age in very different ways. Each stage is expected to have its own **age norms**—distinctive cultural values, pursuits, and pastimes that are culturally prescribed for each age cohort. Life stages create predictable social groupings, allowing us to know in advance what to expect from strangers and new acquaintances and how to respond to them. For instance, "children" in our society might be expected to share a fondness for comic books and chocolate milk, differentiating them from teenagers' penchant for pizza and music magazines or an adult's daily dose of financial news and bran cereal.

At the same time that life expectancies increased dramatically, the Industrial Revolution required that most children would grow up to work in factories and offices rather than on farms. They had to go to school to learn to read, write, and do basic arithmetic, and many of them stayed in school well into their teens. They weren't children anymore, but they weren't adults, either. New stages of life were coined to accommodate these changes. The term *adult* entered the English language around 1656. **Adolescence** gained its current meaning, a life stage between childhood and adulthood, late in the nineteenth century. The adjective *teen-age* appeared during the 1920s, and the noun *teenager* in 1941. The stages advanced as well: Adulthood started near the end of the teens, and elderly meant older than 60, then older than 65.

adolescence

A life stage between childhood and adulthood that gained its meaning late in the nineteenth century.

Today, increasing affluence, better nutrition, and more sophisticated medical expertise have increased the average life expectancy (in rich countries). Now, we often become adults at 25 or 30, and "elderly" means well older than 70. With such a longer life expectancy, we need more life stages than "childhood," "adolescence," "adulthood," and "old age." We now divide adulthood and old age into new stages, delineated roughly by decade-length increments:

- 25–35: young adulthood
- 35–45: "young" middle age
- 45–55: middle age
- 55–65: "old" middle age
- 65–75: "young" old age
- 75–85: "old" old age
- 85 and older: "oldest" old age

Of course, the boundaries of these life stages are subject to lots of variation and change.

In most societies, the transitions between life stages are occasions of great importance, marked by important milestones, ceremonies, and rituals. Many nonindustrial societies require grueling **rites of passage**, such as weeks in a sweat lodge or embarking on some "spirit quest" in the wilderness. Today many transitional stages are marked by bar or bat mitzvahs, religious confirmations, high school and college graduations, coming-out parties (for young women entering fashionable society at age 18), and quinceañeras (for 15-year-old girls in Hispanic communities).

Middle-class milestones—like getting a driver's license, being allowed to drink alcohol, going away to college, or getting a first apartment or first job—are also marked by many people. Middle-class adulthood has fewer milestones, and many involve watching children go through the life stages. Late adulthood and the transition to old age are marked by a flurry of retirement ceremonies and sometimes accompanied by cross-country moves.

This Hispanic family poses in celebration of a quinceañera. The word *quinceañera* translates to a girl who is 15 years old. Among Latinos living in the United States, quinceañera is also the name of a coming-of-age ceremony celebrated on a girl's fifteenth birthday.

rites of passage

A marker, often a ceremony, that denotes an important stage in someone's life, such as birth, puberty, marriage, death.

Childhood

10.1.5 Summarize the ways that "children" (as a distinct social group) is a concept that did not always exist.

It might sound odd, but children were simply not always understood as "children"— at least not how we think of them today. When you look at paintings and sculptures from medieval Europe, you may notice a curious phenomenon: Children are portrayed as miniature adults. The artists could certainly look around and see that a 10-year-old differed from a 30-year-old in shape, proportion, and features, but they were responding to a society that did not differentiate childhood as a separate stage of life. Children worked alongside the adults, boys mostly in the fields, girls mostly at home. They were smaller, so they received easier tasks, but there was no conception that childhood should be free of cares or responsibilities. The "miniature adults" had little free time and few toys; and only a tiny percentage went to school. They were not protected from knowledge about sex and death. And because they were not considered innocent, when they committed crimes, they received the same penalty as adults, including the death penalty (Ariès 1965; deMause 1974).

As historian Steven Mintz writes, "Two centuries ago, the experience of youth was very different from what it is today. Segregation by age was far less prevalent, and

Many toys are "practice" for grown-up activities, whether actually being a soldier to hosting a tea party. These kind of toys emerged at a point in history when we began to think of children as different and needing more time for learning and play.

chronological age played a smaller role in determining status. Adults were also far less likely to sentimentalize children as special creatures who were more innocent and vulnerable than adults." (Mintz 2009: 49) Although some scholars disagree, Ariès (1965) and deMause (1974) argue that the Western concept of childhood, as a distinct stage of life, didn't emerge until the Industrial Revolution of the eighteenth century. At that time, children required training outside the home before they could go to work, so schools and apprenticeships became common, and books, toys, and games designed to train children in adult social norms began to appear in large numbers. Protestant theologians argued that children were innocent by nature, so they could not be held accountable for their sins. English common law agreed: Because children were innocent, they could not distinguish between right and wrong, and so they should not receive adult penalties for their crimes. By the nineteenth century, childhood was conceptualized as a time of innocence, and children needed to be protected. Child labor laws went into effect to ensure that children would not be put to work, and compulsory education, the YMCA, Boy and Girl Scouts, and high school sporting activities ensured that their lives would ideally consist of nothing but school and play.

Societies differ about what childhood is really like and therefore the way that society should respond to children. Some cultures believe that children are "little devils"—out of control, animalistic, and in desperate need of discipline if they are to become tame and controllable enough to join society. "Spare the rod and spoil the child." On the other hand, some societies believe that childhood is a time of "innocence"—though this is a historically recent phenomenon. In these societies, children's actions do not carry the same consequences as those of adults (and so we often prosecute juvenile crime differently from adult crimes). Americans subscribe to both ideas—that children are little angels and little devils. Regardless of the position we take, most Americans believe that children should be shielded from information about sex and death.

Most of the concerns over childhood exposure to sex and death (or violence) began near the end of the nineteenth and beginning of the twentieth centuries. In their 1929 study of a typical American community, Middletown, sociologists Robert and Helen Lynd (1929) discovered that nearly half of "little boys" (meaning high schoolers) had attended petting parties (in those days "petting" meant kissing). This statistic was so contrary to his conception of childhood innocence that he blamed it on imitating "sex movies" and "sexually explicit songs," certainly nothing that the teenagers would think of on their own.

Today the "sex movies" and songs are even more explicit, and technological advances make it even more difficult to keep awareness of death, violence, sex, and kissing away from children and teenagers. However, people still react with shock and dismay to the possibility that childhood may not be so innocent after all. They complain that "children are growing up so fast these days," with 14- and 15-year-olds becoming sexually active, wearing makeup, and having body image problems. (It is unclear whether children of previous eras were really all that different, and we may lack good information about it because such knowledge would have certainly been more hidden.)

Adolescence

10.1.6 Explain the social factors that gave rise to adolescence as a distinct stage of the life course.

Before the eighteenth century, people were certainly aware of the physiological transformation that children undergo as they become adults, and they even called it "adolescence." But, as with childhood, they did not recognize it as a distinct stage of the life course. Through the eighteenth century, teenagers were also considered "miniature adults." Then they were considered "big kids," just as innocent and carefree. In fact, through the early twentieth century, they were expected to have the same pastimes and interests as younger children. But as labor became more specialized, children required increasingly specialized training; they had to go to high school. Between 1880 and 1940, the high school graduation rate increased from 2 to 50 percent and the college graduation rate from less than 2 to 9 percent. Faced with postponing adulthood from the early teens to the late teens or even later, adolescence became a new life stage between childhood and adulthood, with its own norms, values, pastimes, and pursuits.

WHAT DO YOU THINK? WHAT DOES AMERICA THINK?

Teen Sex

Rites of passage have cultural and personal significance; one of these rites of passage is becoming sexually active.

What do you think?

For those in their early teens, 14–16 years old, sex before marriage is:
○ always wrong
○ almost always wrong
○ sometimes wrong
○ not wrong at all

What does America think?

While most Americans are opposed to sex between teenagers, the youngest age group here (18- to 30-year-olds) is the most accepting among these. As people age, they become increasingly opposed, such that the oldest respondents appear to be the most conservative in their views concerning sex between teens. Although this trend is true of both men and women, men are less sexually conservative in their opinions about sex among people in their early teens when compared with women in each age group.

Opinions about Sex Outside Marriage Among People in Their Early Teens by Gender and Age, 2014

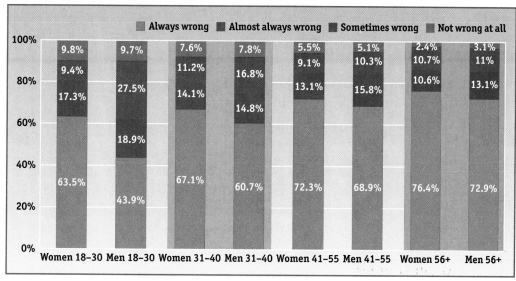

SOURCE: Data from General Social Survey, 2014.

THINKING CRITICALLY ABOUT SURVEY DATA

How do you explain differences between women and men of different age groups here in responses to attitudes about teen sex? How do you explain age differences in responses to attitudes about teen sex?

Young Adulthood

10.1.7 Describe the ways that young adulthood emerged as a stage of the life course as a result of economic changes.

Young adulthood is a transitional stage from adolescence, marking the beginning of our lives as fully functioning members of society. As with other life stages, its lower boundary has been gradually moving forward through the life span, from 18 to 25 to 30 and beyond. Many people still think of themselves (and are treated by others) as "aging adolescents" well into their thirties (see Arnett 2004). On the now-classic TV sitcom *Seinfeld*, Jerry and George famously agree that it's "time to grow up" and act like young adults by getting married and having children (they already have jobs and their own apartments). They were about 40 years old.

Age 40 might be a bit out of the ordinary, but the boundary is moving forward because we're postponing most of the milestones that separate young adulthood from adolescence. Sociologists have identified five milestones that define adulthood: (1) establishing a household separate from our parents; (2) getting a full-time job so we are no longer financially dependent; (3) getting married; (4) completing our education; and (5) having children. Major structural changes in the economy, as well as media images that encourage us to stay young longer, have pushed the age at which we complete these from about 22 to close to 30 (see Arnett 2004, Kimmel 2008). Consider the shift in young adults living at home in the United States today and how this has changed over time (see FIGURE 10.1).

FIGURE 10.1 Proportions of Young Adults (18-34) Living with Their Parents, 1880–2014

For both young men and young women, living with parents was at a low point around 1960 when the economy supported young people moving out on their own at earlier ages. Today, young people live at home with their parents in equal numbers to those living with a romantic partner. Interestingly, the trend is also gendered: Young men are significantly more likely than young women to live at home with their parents into their "young adult years."

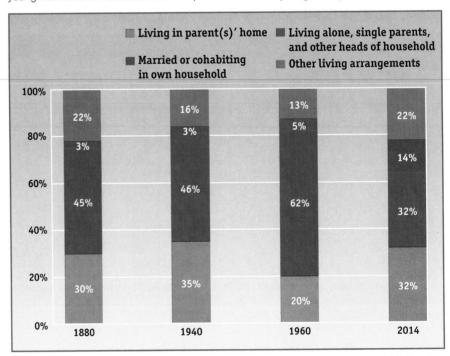

SOURCE: Data from Pew Research Center tabulations of the 1880–2000 decennial censuses and 2010 and 2014 American Community Surveys (IPUMS). Available at http://www.pewsocialtrends.org/2016/05/24/for-first-time-in-modern-era-living-with-parents-edges-out-other-living-arrangements-for-18-to-34-year-olds/.

In 1950, close to half of all women in the United States were married for the first time by age 20 (and men a few years later). By 1975, the median age (when half were married) was 21, and today it's risen to about 27.6 (28.7 for men, 26.5 for women), although these numbers vary by race, ethnicity, class and region (Vespa 2017). We're starting families later, too. In 1970, the average age for women at the birth of their first child was 21.4 in the United States (men weren't asked). Today, it is slightly older than 26, although this too differs by race and ethnicity: American Indian, African American, and Hispanic women tend to be younger than white women when they have a first child, and Asian women tend to be a bit older (Vespa 2017). One of the reasons for the delay for all women is greater gender equality. Since 1970, the percentage of women graduating from college has nearly doubled, and the number in the labor force has gone up from 40 percent to almost 60 percent (Vespa 2017).

The age at first birth differs by race: 24.2 for African Americans, 27 for whites, and 29.5 for Asian Americans. Among Hispanic Americans, the age ranges from 23.7 for Mexican women to 24.1 for Puerto Rican women to 27 for Cuban women (Mathews and Hamilton 2016). It also differs significantly by state, from 23.6 in Mississippi to 28.7 in Massachusetts (Mathews and Hamilton 2016). Both of these correlations probably reflect the lurking variable of socioeconomic class: Well-educated, wealthy and middle-class women are more likely to finish college or start their careers before they think about having children, while poor and working-class women are likely to start having children in their late teens or early twenties. We see the same pattern globally; in wealthy countries, women put off starting their families for several years after adolescence. The average age of a mother when she gives birth for the first time is 30.4 in Switzerland. But in Botswana, the average age of a mother when she gives birth for the first time is 19—and it is younger than 19 in Chad, Angola, Niger, Mozambique, Mali, Malawi, Guinea, Bangladesh, and Uganda (CIA World Factbook 2016).

An extended period of education and training between childhood and adulthood has been required since the Industrial Revolution, but even today, for roughly three quarters of the U.S. population, that training mostly ends at high school graduation, around the age of 18. So why is settling down to jobs, houses, and life partners rarely occurring at age 18 or even at age 22 for everyone anymore? The media have even invented new terms—*twixters* and *boomerang kids*—for people in their twenties, years past their high school or college graduation but still culturally adolescent: living with their parents, having fun, and trying to discover "what they want to do when they grow up."

Putting off all adult responsibilities may be a response to increased longevity: If I'm going to live 20 years longer than my grandparents did, then maybe I have 20 more years to "grow up." But it is also a response to the fluid nature of contemporary adulthood. Most people no longer select a career in their teens, find a job shortly after high school or college, and stick with it for the next 50 years. They change jobs every couple of years and switch careers three or four times in the course of their lives, going back to school for more training between and during each change; thus, "deciding on a career" is not a once-in-a-lifetime event restricted to adolescents but a lifelong process. The milestones that once spelled the entrance to adulthood, definitively and finally, now occur throughout life, so it is little wonder that people feel like adolescents at age 30, 40, 50, or even as old as 60. Just watch the "Frat Pack"—Ben Stiller (52), Jack Black (48), Will Ferrell (50), Vince Vaughn (47), Luke (46) and Owen (49) Wilson, and Steve Carell (55). Or Mick Jagger (74).

Achieving independence from parents is a challenge for young adults today. In a shifting economy that demands more investments in education for many to achieve independence, this often means putting off symbols and markers of adulthood that previous generations might have been able to achieve at younger ages.

Middle Age

10.1.8 Summarize some of the ways that society is organized in ways that often make middle age a challenging portion of the life course.

Because they're starting young adulthood later, people are also starting middle age later, in their 50s instead of their 40s, but eventually they are bound to notice some physiological changes. Thinking *intersectionally* allows sociologists to examine the relationship that many of these have with different social groupings and identities, like race and class. Difficult manual labor obviously ages one more rapidly than working in an office, and painting houses will age you more quickly than painting on a canvas.

If there is a developmental task of middle age, it is this: acceptance. One must accept one's life as it is and "put away childish things"—like the dreams that you will drive a Ferrari, be a multimillionaire, or get to say "you're fired" on national television. Many adults have a difficult time achieving that acceptance; indeed, the constant emphasis on youth and glamour makes it increasingly difficult. The lives they have now are, most likely, the lives they are going to have forever. This leads some middle-aged adults to experience what is sometimes referred to as the "mid-life crisis."

HOW DO WE KNOW WHAT WE KNOW?

WHY MIDDLE AGE CAN BE SO CHALLENGING

Beginning in the 1970s, two best-selling books, *Seasons of a Man's Life* (1978) and *Passages* (1976) popularized the belief that middle-aged men (and to a lesser extent, women) go through a developmental "crisis" characterized by a pressure to make wholesale changes in their work, relationships, and leisure. For men, stereotypical responses to this pressure might include divorcing their wives to date younger women, pursuing lifelong ambitions, changing jobs, buying sports cars, and taking up adventurous and risky hobbies. The idea of midlife crisis was quickly embraced by a large segment of mainstream U.S. culture. Thirty years later, it remains a popular concept, the subject of pop psychology books about finding lifelong fulfillment, and blockbuster films that explore the process and its rewards, including *City Slickers* (1991, 1994), *Groundhog Day* (1993), and *American Beauty* (1999) in the 1990s; *Wonder Boys* (2000), *Sideways* (2004), *Wild Hogs* (2007), *Up In the Air* (2009) and *Greenberg* (2010) more recently.

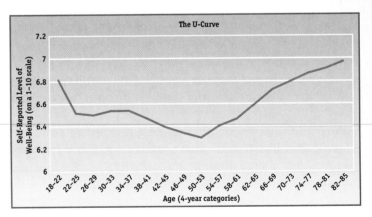

SOURCE: Data from Stone, Arthur, et al. "A snapshot of the age distribution of psychological well-being in the United States," *Proceedings of the National Academy of Sciences of the United States*, 107, 22 (2010): 9985–9990.

Middle age is a time of reckoning. It means coming to terms with what you have done in your life and what you are likely to do with the remainder. It's not uncommon for birthdays between 40 and 50 to be challenging years. A great deal of scholarship has shown that happiness is extremely correlated with age. And the relationship between age and happiness is a U-shaped curve. Life satisfaction declines for the first few decades of life, bottoms out when people are between 40 and 50 years old, and then increases with age (until the very last years when happiness declines again). Today, social scientists sometimes refer to this as the "happiness U-curve." And it is something that has been shown to exist in industrialized nations around the world. This doesn't mean that it is true of everyone's experience; but it is true of most people's experience. Consider how Americans respond to questions about their own well-being by age. We follow the U-curve.

Why is middle age associated with the lowest levels of well-being? Social scientists studying the relationship between age and well-being do not consider it a biological phenomenon; it's a sociological phenomenon. Middle age today is associated with challenging dilemmas. It is around the age when we have to reckon with what we've accomplished so far in life ("Is this all there is?"). And during that time, adults today are likely caring for children while also navigating losing their own parents and struggling with all the financial woes of mid-life throughout. Interestingly, most people emerge out of this stage with a new perspective on life. And, although it's not true for everyone, levels of happiness for many people are higher in old age than they are among the young.

SOURCE: Rauch, Jonathan. "The Real Roots of Midlife Crisis." *The Atlantic* (December 2016). Available at: http://www.theatlantic.com/magazine/archive/2014/12/the-real-roots-of-midlife-crisis/382235/.

In previous generations, parents hoped that they would live long enough to see their children marry. Today they often live to see their grandchildren and great-grandchildren marry. But the increase in life expectancy (people are living longer than they used to) and the delay in childbearing means that many middle-aged adults find themselves in the **"sandwich generation,"** caring for dependent children and aging parents at the same time. For instance, say a woman has a child when she is 33 years old and her own mother is 63. She will have a toddler around the house during her mother's retirement years, and a child requiring care as her mother requires care, too. When her child goes off to college, she will be 51 years old, and her mother will probably still be living at 81. The sandwich generation is often stressed, worried, strapped, and squeezed.

And these pressures may occur during more than one life stage for all involved. The Pew Research Center found that among adults with both aging parents and grown children, 78 percent say their grown children rely on them "frequently" or "sometimes" for emotional support, while 65 percent say the same about their aging parents. Women are more likely to be caregivers than men, providing practical, emotional, financial support, or some combination of these. Overall, types and amounts of care vary not only by gender, but also by age, marital status, race and ethnicity, and income (Parker and Patten 2013). Still, the most recent data available suggest that 91 percent of those in the sandwich generation still feel satisfied with their family lives—about the same percentage as everyone else (General Social Survey 2012).

"sandwich generation"
With the increase in life expectancy and the delay in childbearing, many middle-aged adults find themselves "sandwiched" between caring for dependent children and aging parents at the same time.

Old Age

10.1.9 Delineate between the three stages of old age, and describe the social experiences associated with each.

A hundred years ago, half of the population of the United States was younger than 23 years old, and only 4 percent was 65 or older. But the number of older Americans has increased dramatically: In 2012, they numbered 43 million, or about 14 percent of the population (U.S. Census Bureau 2014). Jerry Gerber and his coauthors (1990) argue that in the next few decades, the dramatic growth in the proportion of people older than age 65 will produce an "age-quake" with similar radical social transformations. By 2050, the elderly will number 83.7 million, more than the entire U.S. population in 1900. They will comprise more than 20 percent of the population of the United States and about 20 percent of the global population (U.S. Census Bureau 2014). The fastest-growing segment will be people 85 and older. By 2050, there will be 17.9 million of them (4.5 percent of the total population).

Three factors have led to the increase in the percentage of the population that is elderly. First, the birth rate has been declining for more than a century. The fact that women have been working outside the home meant that they were unable to raise a large number of children, and advances in birth control technology limit unexpected pregnancies. As a result, the U.S. birth rate is at close to its lowest level since national data have been available and is 147th in the world—1.87 in 2016 (CIA World Factbook 2016).

Second, although the birth rate has been going down, life expectancy has been going up (though the United States still lags behind most wealthy nations). In the United States, it shot up over 20 years during the first half of the century, from 47.3 in 1900 to 68.2 in 1950. Over the last 65 years, life expectancies increased by more than 10 years, to 78.7 hitting record highs for white men (77.1 years) and black men (71.7 years), as well as white women (81.7 years) and black women (78 years) (U.S. Census 2014). Seen from a different perspective, 42 percent of the babies born in 1900 were expected to live past age 65; by 2000 this rate had nearly doubled to 83 percent. Some of these increases were quite dramatic, depending on race and gender. Even occupation plays a role: People with high-prestige jobs, for instance, live longer than those with low-prestige jobs, even after they retire (Bassuk, Berkman, and Amick 2002).

Third, advanced medical treatment also means that some of the major killers of elderly persons are decreasing. The annual death rate from heart disease decreased almost 32 percent in the past decade. Between 2004 and 2014, the death rate from stroke decreased by 28.7 percent, and the actual numbers of people dying from strokes declined by 11.3 percent (American Stroke Association 2017). The death rates for hypertension, Parkinson's disease, and Alzheimer's disease, however, have all increased during that time. Some of the life expectancy increases are quite dramatic, but they also vary significantly by global economic status and by race, gender, and class within countries. Life expectancy for the United States as a whole has been increasing, as it has in the other wealthy countries (OECD 2015). But within that, affluent people have experienced greater gains, widening the gap in life expectancy between rich and poor among Americans and elsewhere (Pear 2008).

In poor countries, however, life expectancy did not rise significantly during the twentieth century. In fact, in sub-Saharan Africa, it actually decreased. In Uganda it is 55.4, in Nigeria it is 53.4, in Zambia it is 52.5, and in Chad it is 50.2 (CIA World Factbook 2016). Not that people are dying of age-related illnesses like heart disease and cancer at the age of 49 or 50; malnutrition and disease, especially HIV, keep most people in these countries from living to see middle age. Worldwide, things are getting higher and lower, better and worse, at the same time.

Finally, a fourth factor that is producing the aging bulge is the historical anomaly of the "baby boom"—the surge of births after World War II—who are now beginning to hit retirement age.

There are three life stages among the elderly. The **"young old,"** ages 65 to 75, are likely to enjoy relative good health and financial security. They tend to live independently, often with a spouse or partner. The **"old old,"** ages 75 to 85, suffer many more health and financial problems. They are more likely to be dependent. The **"oldest old,"** ages 85 and older, suffer the most health and financial problems (Belsky 1990). These experiences, however, are best understood intersectionally. For instance, they vary enormously by class. For the lower classes, aging is often a crisis, in some cases a catastrophe. Working-class and poor people have the greatest number of health problems and the lowest rates of insurance, the least savings and retirement benefits, and the greatest financial needs.

"young old"
The term for people ages 65 to 75.

"old old"
The term for people ages 75 to 85.

"oldest old"
The term for people ages 85 and older.

---

iSOC AND YOU Age, Identity, and the Stages of Life

Although there are no biological exact categories of age, only conceptual ones, age is a primary source of *identity* in many societies. You experience yourself as going through "stages," and, at each stage, there are certain norms about how you are to *interact* with other people and what kinds of roles you are considered responsible for taking on in different social *institutions*. (Think of all the ways you can say "Act your age!" to someone, young or old.) Age is also an axis of *inequality*, as groups are accorded more or less status, depending on their age. There are specific *institutions* that have developed to address the needs of people as they age. And age also *intersects* with other aspects of social life: Not all social groups age the same way.

10.2 Boomers, Busters, and Boomlets: The Generations of Youth

When you happened to be born shapes a great deal about your life. As you learned previously, it shapes what kinds of names your parents might have considered for you (or failed to consider). But when you are born shapes much more than what name you have. It shapes your life trajectory in ways you might not believe. Do you know what one of the best ways to become a millionaire is? Graduate from Harvard Business School. But if you really want to increase your chances, you can't graduate just any year. What year you enter the job market matters enormously for how much you will earn over the course of your life. And if you wanted to be a millionaire, there was one year in particular that offered a perfect storm of opportunities to recently minted MBAs—1949. The Harvard Business School class of 1949 is one of the most successful groups of people in the world. By their twenty-fifth reunion, in 1974, one in five had become a millionaire, roughly half had become chairmen, chief executive officers, and chief operating officers.

Laurence Shames published a book about the class titled, *The Big Time: The Harvard Business School's Most Successful Class & How It Shaped America* (1986). It was wildly popular. It was reviewed in *The New York Times*, was on *Business Week*'s "10-best" list for the entire year, and more. The Shames book was so popular because everyone hoped to glean some insight that might be applied to the rest of us, some small nugget of information that could be applied to our own lives and potentially lead the rest of us to fortune as well. What readers missed is that the success of the Harvard Business School class of 1949 had much less to do with what those students learned and how they applied that in their lives after school. They were so successful because it was 1949. When they graduated in early spring, there were only about 3,000 people in the world with MBA degrees, and of those, only 653 of them graduated from Harvard. They entered the business world at a moment of world-historical opportunity and were able to cash in on their degree in a way that has never since been repeated by so many in a single class. In short, they were lucky—lucky to have been born when they were and in a social class that made attending a new business program at Harvard not inevitable, but much more likely than others.

As this example illustrates, when you are born matters. It shapes what sorts of opportunities you might experience, how long you will likely live, and more. Sociologists who study this break people up into meaningful groups of people born in a given chunk of time who share some experiences, opportunities, and characteristics as a result of being similar ages at critical moments in their lives. Sociologists call these "generations." Your generation is an identity you carry with you whether you think about it or not. It shapes the ways you interact with the world around you, your access to and experience in every social institution in our society, and the kinds and qualities of inequality you will experience. And, must frustratingly of all, it is something that is completely and utterly out of your control. In this section, we profile three recent generations and their experiences in the United States: the "Baby Boomers," "Generation X," and "Millennials."

Baby Boomers

10.2.1 Summarize some of the social forces that produced the "baby boom" and shaped the experience of this generation.

Many GIs returning from World War II took advantage of low-interest student loans, cheap suburban housing, and a hugely expanding economy to enter the middle class, marry, and have children—lots of children. A postwar **baby boom**, lasting from 1946 to 1964, created a big bulge in the populations of Europe and North America

baby boom
This large generation born after the end of World War II between 1946 to 1964 created a big bulge in the populations of Europe and North America and is the biggest age cohort in American history—77 million babies in the United States.

FIGURE 10.2 U.S. Birth Rate, 1940–2015
On this chart, you can see the "baby boom" generation. Between 1946 and 1964, the fertility rate in the United States increased.

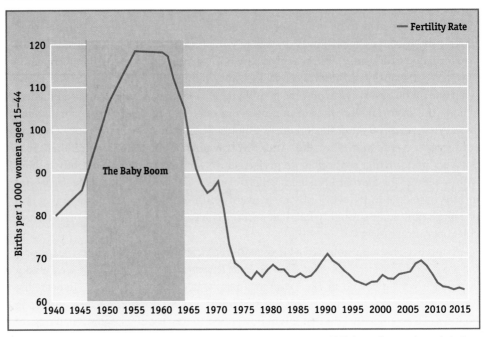

SOURCE: Data from National Vital Statistics Reports, Vol. 66, No. 1, January 5, 2017, https://www.cdc.gov/nchs/data/nvsr/nvsr66/nvsr66_01.pdf.

(see FIGURE 10.2). This created the biggest age cohort in U.S. history—77 million babies in the United States.

Because of the size of this generation, the baby boomers necessitated changes in society. As a group, they reshaped society. As the baby boomers passed through childhood, the United States became a nation wholeheartedly dedicated to child rearing, with new schools and libraries, a surge in children's television and other forms of mass media, and new techniques of child rearing. As the first wave of baby boomers passed through their adolescence beginning around 1960, the United States shifted its emphasis from childhood to adolescence. There was a surge in youth-oriented magazines, movies, television programs, and songs. College attendance soared. The "now" generation, the counterculture, was wholeheartedly dedicated to social and political change, transforming norms, expectations, and ideas. It was an era of expansion—an expanding economy, expanding social rights, and expanding consciousness. The Civil Rights movement, the women's movement, and the gay/lesbian movement all started or increased their momentum while the baby boomers were college students and young adults.

The first boomers hit middle age around 1980, and the United States shifted its emphasis again, from adolescence to middle age. A new era of conservatism began, with concern for the "midlife crisis," and the "now generation" became the "me generation." As of the first years of the twenty-first century, this wave of baby boomers is reaching retirement age, and they promise to have an enormous impact on the Social Security system, health care, and ideas about what it means to be old and even what qualifies as "old" in the first place.

Boomers are often portrayed as a single group with a shared history and similar demographic characteristics. As they are portrayed, they're often imagined to be mostly white, well-educated, liberal, affluent, innovative, and obsessed with self-discovery. But they are actually a diverse group. About 30 percent are people of color (12% black, 10% Hispanic, 4% Asian, and 4% "other"). Twelve percent of early and 15 percent of late boomers are immigrants (including 86% of all foreign-born Latinos and 57% of foreign-born Asians in the country). The economic disparities between white and non-white boomers are as profound as in any other generation. Many members are poor or conservative. The baby boom lasted for 20 years, after all, so the earliest boomers are a full generation removed from the latest (and could even be their parents) (Hughes and O'Rand 2004).

A study by the Pew Research Center (Cohn and Taylor 2010) found that now that those baby boomers have themselves become parents, and even grandparents, nearly 4 in 5 believe that there still is a **generation gap**. But the generation gap remains largest not between Millennials and their Boomer parents, but between Millennials and Boomers as a group—and the Boomers' parents! Take technology. For example, three-fourths of teenagers and half of adults, but only 40 percent of adults ages 65 to 74 use the Internet daily. Only 5 percent of older Americans make most of their telephone calls on a cell phone and 9 percent use them to text; 72 percent of teenagers make all their calls on cell phones and 88 percent text. Boomers use cell phones and text (51%) in proportions more similar to their children than their parents.

But this grand-generational gap is most evident in music. In 1969, the year of Woodstock, rock music was the *least* popular music among adults—44 percent said they disliked it, and only 4 percent said they liked it. Today, it is the most popular genre of music among Millennials (45% listen often), Gen Xers (42%), and Boomers (33%), although Boomers' parents still hate it). Boomers are more likely to like country music than their kids, but not by that much. The only gap? Rap and hip hop. More than two in five Millennials listen often, compared to 15 percent of Gen Xers and 3 percent of Boomers. Kendrick Lamar and Nicki Minaj just don't resonate with those who like Bono or Springsteen.

generation gap
Differences in outlook and opinion that arise between generations.

Generation X

10.2.2 Explain how the smaller size of Generation X (compared to the Baby Boomers) shaped their experience of childhood in different ways from their parents' childhoods.

The generation that followed the baby boom cohort has been called baby busters, or also **Generation X**—those born between 1965 and 1979. There weren't many of them. A society can maintain a stable population with a **fertility rate** of 2.1 (also referred to as the "replacement rate"); that is, 2.1 lifetime births per woman (the 0.1 because typically 5–10 percent of a population does not reproduce). But since 1970, the fertility rate in rich countries has been lower than 2.1, sometimes considerably lower. In 2015, France was the highest of any rich country, at 2.00; the fertility rate was 1.9 in the United Kingdom, Sweden, and the United States, and only 1.4 in Japan, Germany, and Italy (Population Reference Bureau 2014). These countries are stable rather than depopulating because population is determined by many factors besides fertility, including infant mortality, longevity, and immigration.

Still, because we exist in an age-graded society, a shift in the size of generations will have ripple effects throughout the social institutions that structure society. A stable population after years of enormous expansion means school closings, sharp declines in college enrollment, and a decrease in television, movies, and other mass media aimed at children or families. The 10-year-old boomers of 1963 could spend their evenings watching the kid-friendly *My Favorite Martian, Beverly Hillbillies, Ozzie and Harriet*, and *My Three Sons*; even

Generation X
Sometimes called the "baby bust," this generation born after the Baby Boom, between 1965 and 1979, is a small age cohort.

fertility rate
The number of births per 1,000 women ages 15 to 44 in a calendar year.

Because we come into our identities during specific historical moments, generational gaps exist between the young and the old on all sorts of different axes, from clothes and music, to interests, to political ideals, to comfort and familiarity with various technology and media.

The Flintstones was on prime time. In 1973, 10-year-old gen-Xers could watch the more adult-oriented *All in the Family, The Mary Tyler Moore Show, Maude, The Bob Newhart Show,* and *M*A*S*H.* Gen-X often felt like an afterthought compared with the "me generation." Like the boomers, Gen-Xers are often seen as a homogeneous group of white, middle-class, affluent liberals, but they are predictably as diverse as their parents: 12 percent black, 18 percent are Hispanic, and 6 percent are Asian (Taylor and Gao 2014).

Although they are often derided as slackers and whiners, Gen-Xers really are worse off economically than their boomer parents. The average individual income dropped dramatically between the early 1970s and the 1990s, especially during the 1980s when the first gen-Xers were entering the work world. Women's income dropped less sharply than men's (and actually increased a little during the 1980s). This meant that the gender wage gap declined during this period, but the shift in this gap had more to do with men losing income than it did with women gaining income. And when we examine intersections with other categories of identity (like race) the income decline was compounded. Young African Americans lost three times more income than whites between 1972–1973 and 1984–1985, and four times more between 1984–1985 and 1994–1995 (Paulin and Riordan 1998).

Gen-Xers also experienced a decline in educational opportunity and attainment (Paulin and Riordan 1998). In 1972–1973 more than 50 percent of young unmarried persons were college graduates, but by 1984–1985 this had dropped to 30 percent. More Xers were living at home after college, and more were going to college part-time, combining working and education. The costs of independence were simply out of reach of many, if not most, college-age people. And this was a big change compared with the experiences of the parents of the baby boomers. This meant they had children later, were less likely to own homes, and struggled to achieve independence in ways that their parents and grandparents did not. These trends become even more exacerbated among the Millennial generation.

Millennials—Generation Y

10.2.3 Explain some of the challenges that Millennials face and how they are related to the structure of society.

Millennials
The generation of nearly 50 million people born after 1980—the first generation to come into their adulthood in the new millenium.

Since 2000, social scientists have identified a new generation of youth: **Millennials**. The label refers to the nearly 50 million people born after 1980—that is, the first generation to come into their adulthood in the new millennium. Structurally, they are among the most precarious and vulnerable generation of young people ever: Nearly 4 out of 10 are unemployed or out of the workforce (also because so many are in college); only about 60 percent were raised by both parents; 10 percent reported that they recently lost a job. Part of this is the result of very different economic conditions that early versus late Millennials have faced as they come of age. On the other hand, Millennials seem optimistic about their future; they are, in the words of a recent survey, "confident, self-expressive, liberal, upbeat and open to change" (Pew Research Center 2014). They're liberal, but not rebellious; they respect their elders and get along well with their parents. They want to succeed, but family is more important to them than it was to Baby Boomers. Roughly 40 percent are still in school, and they are on track to be the most educated generation ever. They're slightly less religious, somewhat less affiliated with particular denominations, but no less committed to a moral code. And they are also the most racially diverse generation (see FIGURE 10.3).

Millennials are the most media savvy and technologically sophisticated generation in our history. Three-fourths have a profile on a social-networking site (compared to less than one-third of Baby Boomers and only half of Gen Xers). Four out of five have texted within the past 24 hours, compared with just over a third of Baby Boomers (yes, we know, many of you reading this book have texted within the

FIGURE 10.3 **Racial and Ethnic Diversity among Age Cohorts, 2014**

Racial diversity is certainly among the most defining characteristics of the Millennial generation. Millennials account for more than one-quarter of the total racial minority population in the United States. Almost 4 in 10 voting age minorities in the United States are Millennials. And Millennials account for 43 percent of minorities in the United States who are in their prime working ages.

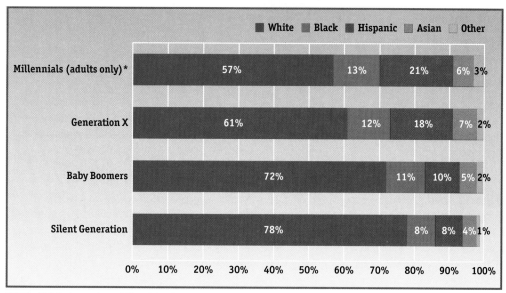

NOTE: *Adults here refer to Millennials who were 18+ years of age in 2014.

SOURCE: Data from http://www.pewsocialtrends.org/2015/03/19/comparing-millennials-to-other-generations/.

past 24 minutes!). And yet, although they interact more on computers and handheld devices, they watch less TV than previous generations: Only 57 percent watched more than an hour in the previous 24-hour period, compared to two-thirds of Gen Xers, and 80 percent of Baby Boomers.

In some parts of the globe, intergenerational conflict occurs as Millennials reject traditional ways of life (United Nations 2005). In Russia and Eastern Europe, this is the first generation to grow up without memories of communism. In newly affluent countries like South Korea, they are the first generation to grow up expecting the same degree of affluence that Western Europe and America enjoys, while their parents and grandparents experienced conditions more representative of the Third World. What this means is that the concerns and conflicts of their parents' generation are largely irrelevant to many Millennials, who may feel that they are being asked to fight their parents' battles.

Despite living in a world very different from the one in which their parents and grandparents grew up, Millennials often need to rely on their parents for longer periods of time than many generations before them. It is much more challenging to be able to move out of your parents' home for good after high school today than it was 20 or 30 years ago. Increasingly, Millennials are moving back in with their parents after college as well, prompting some to label them "Boomerang Kids." Indeed, the rate of young adults living with their parents today has not been this high since the Great Depression. In fact, today, for the first time since the 1880s, more young people are living with their parents than are living with a romantic partner (married or otherwise).

In the United States, those young people without a college education are much more likely to live with their parents than young adults who are college educated. And this trend is not limited to the United States. Young adults across Europe are living with their parents. In 2011, Canada found that more than 4 in 10 young adults in their 20s lived in their parents' homes. In Australia, almost 3 in 10 young adults between 18 and 34 lived with their parents in 2011. In Japan, almost one half of 20- to 34-year-old young adults were living in their parents' homes in 2012!

Millennials are—as a group—politically liberal, more secular than past generations, highly educated, racially diverse, and they are a generation of digital natives

SOCIOLOGY AND OUR WORLD

SONS ARE MORE LIKELY TO LIVE WITH PARENTS THAN DAUGHTERS

Why are young men more likely to live with their parents into adulthood than young women? And why are white young men and women less likely to move in with their parents than other racial groups?

The share of young adults living with their parents today is among the highest over the past century. And interestingly, it's a pattern that is also gendered: Across race and ethnicity, more young men live with their parents than young women.

The 1960s were a low-point in this general pattern for both men and women. And since then, the gap between young men and women has narrowed a bit. This pattern is true of every major racial and ethnic group in the United States.

The one exception to men being more likely to live with their parents than women is Asian Americans. Asian American young women were more likely than Asian American young men to live with their parents between 1900 and 1910, and again between 1930 and 1940. In 1940, for instance, 39 percent of Asian American young women lived with their parents compared with only 27 percent of Asian American young men. This is because "Asian" was a racial classification on the 1940 U.S. Census that encompassed a diverse group of people. The shift was largely due to an increase in living with parents among Japanese American young women—in 1930, 17 percent lived with their parents; by 1940, roughly 49 percent did.

The general trend that we often hear about regarding young people today is that they are more likely to live at home longer than were the baby boomers. But when we examine this trend intersectionally, it becomes clear that this is not only about gender, but also about race. The economic independence we often associate with baby boomers can clearly be seen among whites. All of a sudden, they became dramatically less likely to live at home starting in the 1940s. But among black, Hispanic, and Asian Americans, the trend is different; each of these groups have steadily increased their rates of living with their parents. It is an illustration of why we need to think intersectionally because this shows one instance in which experience and characteristics often associated with generations are sometimes really just the experience of the dominant social group—in this case, white people.

SOURCE: Fry, Richard. "For First Time in Modern Era, Living with Parents Edges Out Other Living Arrangements for 18- to 34-Year-Olds." *Pew Research Center*, 2016. Available at: http://www.pewsocialtrends.org/2016/05/24/for-first-time-in-modern-era-living-with-parents-edges-out-other-living-arrangements-for-18-to-34-year-olds/.

(they've never known anything but life in a digital world). Millennials will encounter new challenges as they enter young adulthood and adulthood. Will they be able to find jobs that help them pay for all of the education they accrue? What sorts of social and political issues will consume their attention and passion? Will the qualities we've just mentioned associated with Millennials change as they get older? Some have labeled the generation following Millennials, **Generation Z** (those born since 2000). And many of the trends that are true of Millennials appear all the more true of the next generation (at least so far).

Generation Z
The generation of people born since 2000.

Global Youth—A Dying Breed?

10.2.4 Understand how the age structure of societies are changing and what sorts of consequences these changes will produce.

Although the United States keeps naming new stages into an ever-expanding process of growing up, and continues to be obsessed with images and ideas of youth, young people in the most developed nations of the world are a declining breed (see FIGURE 10.4). In many rich countries, and especially in Southern and Eastern Europe and Japan, the 1980s and 1990s were periods of falling birth rates. Demographers predict that the percentage of youth worldwide will continue to decline steadily in the wealthiest nations in the world; while the absolute numbers will remain stable, their proportion in the global population will decline by 20 percent as older people live longer and bring up the mean age of the country (He, Goodkind, and Kowal 2016).

People are living longer and having fewer children, both of which bring the average age up. In 2014, the percentage of the world's population that was teenaged or young adult (aged 10 to 24) ranged from a high of 36 percent in Zimbabwe to a low of

FIGURE 10.4 Global Population Distribution Projections by Age Group, 2017 to 2050.
Lower birth rates around the world mean that the average age around the world is increasing.
The group that is projected to grow most rapidly are the elderly—those age 65 and older.

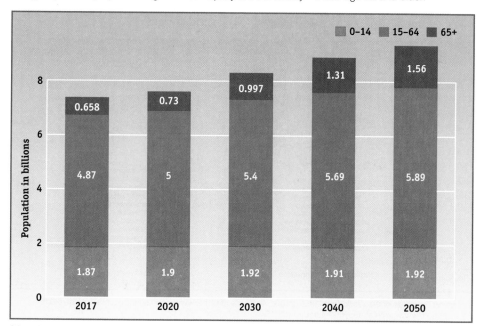

SOURCE: Data from U.S. Census Bureau, International Programs Center, International Database.

14 percent in Italy, with an average of about 26 percent. During the next 50 years, the percentage is expected to decline steadily because both low birth rates and increased life expectancies, until 2050, when youth will account for about 20 percent of the global population (Population Reference Bureau 2014; He, Goodkind, and Kowal 2016).

The distribution of people of different age groups is often represented by a graph called a **population pyramid**, which visualizes the age structure of a population—displaying the proportion of the population in 5- or 10-year age groups as different-sized bars, segregating women and men on different sides of the graph. Many poor countries, like Mexico, have "expansive pyramids" that look like real pyramids. This indicates that the largest share of the population is young. They have a broad base to signify a high fertility rate, and every "block" gets smaller as the age group shrinks as a result of accident, disease, or other mortality factors, until the highest block (the elderly) is very small. Consider the differences between the population pyramids of Mexico, Italy, and Iraq in FIGURE 10.5.

Rich countries often have "constrictive pyramids." The base is not broad because the fertility rate is not high, but there's a big block of middle-aged and older people. Some countries, like Italy, even look somewhat top heavy because the middle and apex of the pyramid are bigger than the base; there are many more people older than age 30 than there are children. A few countries have "stationary pyramids," which look like pillars. Because few people in each age group die of accident or disease, every block is about the same size, beginning to shrink only a little beginning with the 60-year-olds. Demographers predict that while the United States is slightly constrictive now, it will be more stationary by 2030. As we learned in Chapter 8, the higher fertility rates of immigrants in the United States help account for a less-constrictive pyramid than in some other wealthy countries.

Population pyramids also allow us to examine intersections between age and gender, with men on one side and women on the other. If one of the blocks is larger on one end than the other, it means that one sex outnumbers the other in that age group. In the United States, women begin outnumbering men around the age of 70, but in India, they begin outnumbering men around the age of 40.

population pyramid

Type of graph that shows five- or ten-year age groups as different-sized bars, or "blocks."

FIGURE 10.5 Population Pyramids—Mexico, Italy, and Iraq, 2015
One immediately apparent fact you can see here is that Mexico and Iraq have higher fertility rates than Italy. But differently sized population pyramids produce different sorts of age-related issues societies must navigate (like education, health care, care for the elderly, etc.). Italy also has the "tallest" population pyramid here, which is an illustration of life expectancy. So, although the global trend has been a decline in fertility and an aging global population, this is more true of some societies (like Italy) than it is of others (like Iraq).

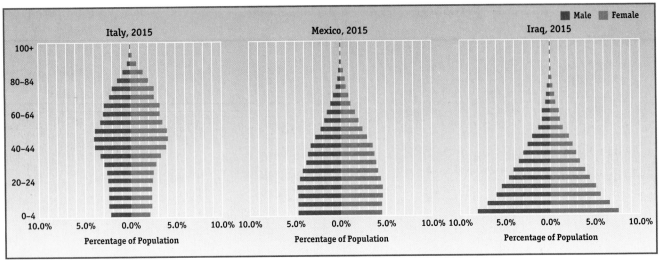

SOURCE: Data from PopulationPyramid.net, "Population Pyramids of the World from 1950–2100." Available at http://www.populationpyramid.net/italy/2015/; http://www.populationpyramid.net/mexico/2015/; and http://www.populationpyramid.net/iraq/2015/.

Demographers use population pyramids to determine current and future social service needs of the society. In the United States, the baby boomer block has been a bulge in the pyramid, working its way upward since the 1950s, allowing demographers to predict a need for more child-oriented facilities, then more colleges and universities, and now more facilities for elderly people.

iSOC AND YOU Boomers, Busters, and Boomlets: The Generations of Youth
Though age is a continuous process, in each person and each society, we ascribe to our own aging process sets of characteristics, specific age cohort *identities*. Each generational group is thought to have its own identity as a group—hippie radical boomers, money-grubbing GenXers—as though a small number of the cohort defines the cohort's entire identity. Norms for *interaction* are prescribed for each cohort, and members of the cohorts interact with different social *institutions*, such as higher education, that are established especially for them. Social *inequalities* based on other aspects of identity—race, class, and sexuality—can be muted or exaggerated within any generational age cohort, and these other identities *intersect* with your experience of age.

10.3 Age and Inequality

Age is also an important social identity in terms of social inequality. How old you are shapes a great variety of different issues related to inequality. Indeed, although the United States is often characterized as youth-obsessed, it is also true that children are more likely to be in poverty than any other age group in the United States. Similarly, while it sometimes might feel like "old age" is more of a medical diagnosis than an identity, our attention to poverty among the elderly in the United States has dramatically shifted the likelihood that people will be impoverished when they die. But much of this transition has meant that our care for the elderly is something no longer handled by family members (as was the case throughout history); now we have institutions that provide care for the elderly. And although this has enabled fewer to finish their lives in poverty, it also means that the elderly have been increasingly segregated from everyone else to a greater extent than at any other point in history. Emerging institutions that provide end-of-life care are also an illustration of a more subtle form of inequality, shaping whether and how people of different ages interact with each other. Indeed, people are living longer today than ever before in world history; but it is also the case that the elderly are much more likely to die among people to whom they are not related.

Age and Poverty

10.3.1 Summarize which age groups are most at risk of poverty and why.

In 1959, 33 percent of elderly men and 38 percent of elderly women in the United States were living below the poverty level. Today, seniors as a whole are more affluent than ever before, in wealth (accumulated net worth) if not in annual income. Elderly households headed by those 65 through 74 have a median net worth of $187,652, and although older white households and older married households have substantially higher net worth than elderly blacks or singles, all older Americans still compare favorably to those younger than age 35—who have a much smaller median net worth of $6,676 (U.S. Census Bureau 2011).

Many elderly people lack the savings, investments, or pensions to be self-supporting after retirement, and the financial turmoil of recent years has eroded what accumulated retirement savings and home equity some may have had (Mermin 2008). Most rich nations provide extensive benefits to their elderly populations, but the United States does not. Consequently, the poverty rate for senior citizens in the United States is about 10 percent—much higher than it is in other rich nations (U.S. Census 2016). The elderly are both richer and poorer than they ever have been.

In old age, inequalities based on race and gender are magnified. While they are age 18 to 64, African Americans and Hispanics are twice as likely to fall beneath the poverty threshold as their white non-Hispanic counterparts, but in the older-than-65 age group, they are *three* times as likely. Elderly women of all races are more likely to be poor than elderly men. When disenfranchised gender and racial categories are combined, the income inequality becomes more pronounced: 21 percent of elderly black and Hispanic women are poor compared with less than 6 percent of elderly white men.

The Social Security program, begun in 1940, improved the financial situation of the elderly. Retired workers receive a monthly stipend based on how much they contributed to the program through their lives. Those who worked consistently throughout adulthood (for employers who participate) might receive $2,000 per month, but gaps in employment history decrease the stipend to a few hundred dollars. As a result of social welfare programs like these, targeting the elderly, their rates of poverty have substantially decreased. And yet, there are still impoverished elderly people. Children are disproportionately more likely to be affected by poverty. In 2015 the poverty rate for children younger than 18 in the United States was 19.7 percent—higher than in any other age group. (By comparison, the poverty rate for adults aged 18 to 64 was less than 12.4 percent and for senior citizens aged 65 and older, less than 9 percent). 43 percent of children (more than 10 million) live in low-income families, defined as income below twice the federal poverty level. The poverty rate for children (like the elderly) also varies by race and ethnicity (see FIGURE 10.6).

Many countries around the world offer "family allowances" for children younger than 18, reasoning that they are unable to work and therefore require support. In France, family allowances cover the cost of childbirth, maternity and paternity leaves, and day care or babysitting services and provide the parents with a small monthly stipend for each child. In the United States, parents are expected to provide full financial support for their children. Federal programs like Aid to Dependent Children (ADC) and Women, Infants and Children (WIC) are available for low-income single parents, but the support is far from adequate and is limited to a total of five years for each child in lifetime benefits.

FIGURE 10.6 Child Poverty Rate by Race, 1976–2013

As with other forms in inequality, age intersects with race to impact the lives of different groups of young people in different ways. In 2013, the poverty rate among white and Asian children in the United States was 10.7 percent and 10.1 percent, respectively. The poverty rate among Hispanic children was roughly three times higher and the poverty rate among black children was almost four times higher than the rates among whites and Asians in the United States.

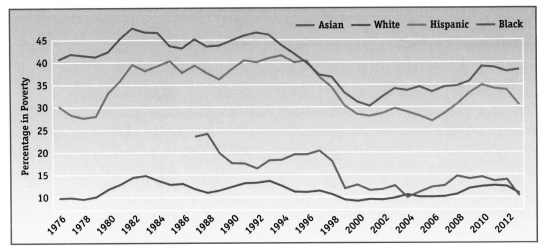

SOURCE: Data from Pew Research Center, "Child Poverty Rate Stable Among Blacks, Drops Among Other Groups;" July 14, 2015. Available at: http://www.pewresearch.org/fact-tank/2015/07/14/black-child-poverty-rate-holds-steady-even-as-other-groups-see-declines/.

Age Inequalities in Interactions

10.3.2 Explain some of the ways that age shapes the types of social interactions we enjoy (or are denied).

In addition to the institutional inequalities of age, older people also experience some interactional problems that are specific to their age situation. As you age, your social networks tend to shrink, as people move away, lose touch, die, or become more concerned with their immediate families. Loneliness is common among all life stages, but as people age, they are particularly vulnerable to social isolation, limited regular interaction with family, friends, and acquaintances (Goldscheider 1990).

Children may leave home and return to visit only occasionally. Retirement closes off work as a source of interaction. The elderly sometimes move to assisted living quarters, nursing homes, or retirement communities hundreds or thousands of miles from home and their long-standing social connections, and health and financial problems limit their ability to establish new ones. Family, friends, and spouses or life partners precede them in death, and negative stereotypes limit their interactions with the younger generation. Many experience social disengagement, a gradual withdrawal from feeling connected to their immediate communities or to the wider world. They may stop watching the news or reading newspapers, and they may keep up only with celebrity gossip. Because women tend to live longer and spend more time without marital partners, they tend to feel the impact of social isolation longer than men. However, they are often more emotionally prepared for it because many did not work outside the home, or worked only part-time, and therefore spent many hours alone through their lives.

This means that the experience of social isolation might differ for men and women. Consider one example. Eric Klinenberg (2003) studied the Chicago heat wave in 1995. In July 1995, temperatures came close to and topped 100° F for multiple days in a row, resulting in more than 700 heat-related deaths. The poor and elderly were among those disproportionately more likely to have been killed because they were not able to afford air conditioning. And among the elderly, men were much more likely to have died in the heat wave than were women. This is an interesting finding for two reasons. Elderly men were much *less* likely to live alone in Chicago at the time (primarily because their spouses more commonly outlived

Retirement in societies that segregate the elderly often means people become less socially engaged as they age, more isolated, and become more withdrawn from the communities in which they used to participate.

them), but older men living alone were disproportionately *more* likely to have died alone as a result of the heat. Why? They didn't do anything or go anywhere. Older women living alone did; they relied on their social relationships and networks in ways older men did not.

Retirement

10.3.3 Determine some of the ways that inequality shapes who has access to retirement and when.

At the other end of the workplace experience looms retirement. Work not only provides money and an opportunity for social interaction, it brings social prestige, personal identity, and a purpose in life. Its end, therefore, can have a devastating impact. We all have heard of people who were in good health yet died within months of their retirement. Perhaps the most poignant story is of cartoonist Charles Schulz, creator of the *Peanuts* comic strip, who died the day he drew Charlie Brown and Snoopy for the last time. (He had announced his retirement because he had cancer.)

Retirement is also a mark of social status. High-status professionals, managers, and sales workers are less likely to retire because their jobs are less physically demanding and more flexible than those of laborers, machine operators, and low-status clerical workers (Hayward and Grady 1990). And while people retire at similar ages all around the world, because life expectancies vary, how many years people are able to spend in retirement also varies greatly (see FIGURE 10.7).

FIGURE 10.7 Life Expectancy and Retirement Years
People retire at different average ages in different societies and have different life expectancies as well. In Mexico, for instance, men retire (on average) almost exactly when most of them will die. Men in Luxembourg, by contrast, enjoy (again, on average) almost two decades of retirement before they die.

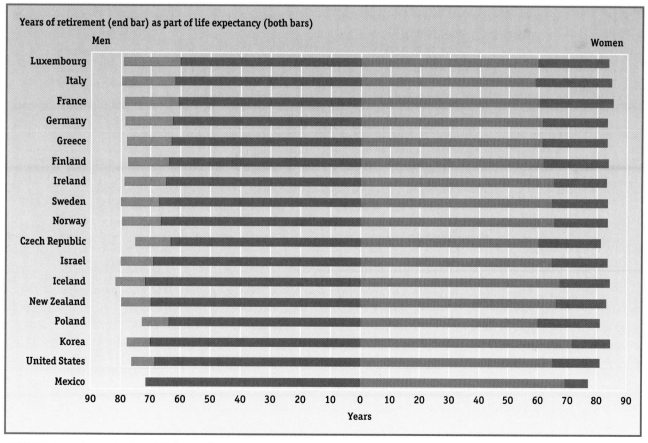

NOTE: Men in Mexico commonly work their entire life.

SOURCE: Data from Organization for Economic Cooperation (OECD); Flowing Data, "Who spends the most years in retirement?" 2011. Available at https://flowingdata.com/2011/04/07/who-spends-the-most-years-in-retirement/.

The idea of retirement as an abrupt transition from work to leisure, however, belongs to the past. Today it is hard to determine who is a retiree and who is not. Many elderly people continue to work, at least on a part-time basis. In fact, an increasing proportion of older Americans may have to delay retirement due to the financial crisis and recession. About 65 percent of workers ages 50 to 61 expect to be working full-time when they reach age 62, and more than 55 percent of workers ages 50 to 64 expect to be working full-time when they reach age 65 (2009 HRS Internet Survey; Mossaad 2010). These numbers represent an increase over those reported in 2008. While labor force participation for both men and women ages 65 and older has been rising, the financial crisis and the recession is likely to accelerate this increase among older Americans (Mossaad 2010).

These trends have been increasing. When AARP asked baby boomers how they envision their retirement over a decade ago, 79 percent said they plan to work in some capacity during their retirement years (AARP 2001). About a decade later as the boomer generation begins to retire, 15.5 percent of the U.S. workforce already consists of those older than 65. Most of those seniors are working part-time, but more than a third are working 35 hours or more. People in many countries are doing and planning the same thing. A 2015 study of attitudes about retirement in a collection of societies that contain over half of the world's people—found that alternating work and leisure was seen by the majority as the ideal "later lifestyle" (HSBC Group 2015).

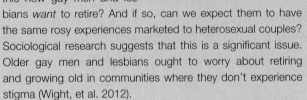

SOCIOLOGY AND OUR WORLD

RETIRING AND GAY? WHERE?

How will sexuality affect the lives of the elderly as more people identifying as gay or lesbian begin to retire?

As the generation of gay men and lesbians that came of age during the Gay Rights movement reach retirement age, it is important to consider how and where they will retire. Are retirement communities for heterosexual individuals and couples heterosexualized in ways that make them unattractive to gay and lesbian individuals and couples? Are they open to sexual diversity? Is this how gay men and lesbians *want* to retire? And if so, can we expect them to have the same rosy experiences marketed to heterosexual couples? Sociological research suggests that this is a significant issue. Older gay men and lesbians ought to worry about retiring and growing old in communities where they don't experience stigma (Wight, et al. 2012).

So, do retirement communities designed with heterosexual individuals' and couples' needs in mind negatively affect the population of gay men and lesbians coming of age? Early research on this topic did find that older gay men and lesbians have a specific set of needs. Some are no different from heterosexual couples and individuals: support during this transition in life, assistance if they are physically disabled, etc. But other issues, like a reduction of social stigmatization, are distinct. But gay men and lesbians should not only worry that social stigmatization that might come from the heterosexual men and women with whom they retire. They also worry that administration and the care staff are potential sources of discrimination (Johnson, et al. 2008). This might mean that prejudice and discriminatory practices are part of many retirement and care communities at a structural level.

As a result, Johnson and colleagues (2008) found that many older gay men and lesbians are interested in gay-friendly or exclusive retirement communities. Many of the gay and lesbian retirement communities that do exist, however, are struggling financially—some have been forced to close their doors. Beyond this, because sexuality is difficult to measure (as we'll see in Chapter 11), it is difficult to determine how financially secure they are and whether this generation of aging sexual minorities will be economically capable of retiring in spaces that protect their psychological well-being.

Elder Care

10.3.4 Summarize the sorts of changes that occurred in U.S. society that have changed who cares for the elderly and how.

Before the twentieth century, family members were expected to take care of their elderly parents, grandparents, aunts, and uncles. The few elderly people with no surviving relatives, or with relatives not interested in caring for them, might find their way into a convent or monastery, but more likely they would end their days as beggars. Today, family members still provide about 80 percent of elder care, providing services estimated at $522 billion per year (National Alliance for Caregiving 2015). However, the birth rate is decreasing, so a much larger proportion of the elderly population has no close relatives, and the increased life expectancy means an increased incidence of health problems severe enough to require professional care. So who is taking on that burden?

Many industrialized societies have institutionalized elder care through a series of nursing homes, hospitals, and other institutions. This means that older people are more segregated than they used to be (something many societies do with children as well). Although the general quality of care is acceptable, it depends significantly on class. In many places, poorly paid staff at underfunded and overcrowded institutions leads to neglect and even elder abuse. In some cases, patients are treated as "inmates" serving a life sentence and are overmedicated and undervalued. Even the best nursing homes "deny the personhood of age" by seeing the aging process as "inevitable decline and deterioration," according to feminist writer Betty Friedan (1993, p. 516).

While these stories may provide fodder for tabloid TV and newspapers, often serving to increase the guilt of the younger generation that placed the elderly there in the first place, the elderly are just as likely to experience abuse and neglect if they stay with their families as if they are in institutions. And most Americans do care about the elderly. According to a survey from the National Alliance for Caregiving (2015), 40 percent of family caregivers consider their situation "highly stressful," another 25 percent of them claim at least moderate levels of stress associated with their care work. For many, this stress is associated with finances; they constantly juggle caregiving with their work and personal commitments: 60 percent work full-time in addition to their caregiving, and 28 percent are raising children younger than 18 (National Alliance for Caregiving 2015). Few have siblings to help out (31 percent believe that caregiving has increased family tension).

They are "squeezed from all sides," negotiating with doctors, outside specialists, part-time caregivers, and their own family, coordinating their own lives and everyone else's lives, feeling guilt and stress over their loved one's decline, and worrying that their loved one is receiving inadequate care. Half of the family caregivers surveyed report that their care recipient had missed meals or suffered poor nutrition, a third were involved in accidents that required emergency room care, and 22 percent were home alone when an emergency occurred.

Most caregivers also have full-time jobs, and so they must "outsource" caregiving while they work. The average family caregiver for someone 50 years or older spends $5,531 per year on out-of-pocket caregiving expenses. Nearly half (47%) of working caregivers say the increase in expenses has caused them to use up all or most of their savings. During the economic downturn in 2009 alone, 1 in 5 family caregivers had to move into the same home with their loved ones to cut expenses (National Alliance for Caregiving 2015). Women who assume caregiver roles are more than 2.5 times more likely to live in poverty than non-caregivers, and the proportion increases dramatically when they are non-white (Wakabayashi and Donato 2006). Other economic consequences are more subtle: Caregiving limits the types of outside jobs one can take and the opportunities for advancement, and women are disproportionately likely to pay these costs.

Aging and Dying

10.3.5 Explain what it means that sociologists understand death as a cultural process rather than a biological event.

In 2005, *USA Today* asked people about their fears of growing old. 52 percent responded "winding up in a nursing home"; 69 percent said "losing mental abilities"; 36 percent said "being alone"; 59 percent said "not being able drive/travel," and 49 percent said "not being able to work/volunteer." Although the survey is not representative, these myths about growing old are persistent, but have little basis in reality.

- *Living in a nursing home.* The vast majority of elderly people maintain their own homes and apartments, and a large percentage live with relatives. Only about 5 percent live in continuous long-term care facilities (LTCF's) or nursing homes. This fear is really about losing independence, and it is true that about 20 percent of people older than age 70 are unable to care for themselves without assistance. (Kinsella and Phillips 2005) However, most are nearing the end of their lives. A person who dies at the age of 80 will spend less than three years in a dependent state (Freedman, Martin and Schoeni 2002).

- *Losing mental abilities.* Alzheimer's is one of several different root causes of senility, a gradual or sudden loss of cognitive function (thinking, reasoning, and memory). But only a small minority of the elderly develop any of the types (National Institute on Aging 2015). Some decline in learning and memory does occur after 70, but usually it is more of a nuisance than a tragedy, forgetting where you left your keys rather than forgetting your children's names. Even "nuisance" memory loss can be combated by continuing to learn and seeking out new experiences.

- *Being alone.* Some degree of loneliness is inevitable as long-term family and friends die or move away, but 71 percent of elderly men and 44 percent of elderly women live with a spouse or romantic partner, and a sizeable percentage live with relatives other than their spouses: 21 percent of white, 43 percent of African American, 49 percent of Hispanic, and 59 percent of Asian elderly (Wilmoth, DeJong and Hmes 1997; Fields and Casper 2001). Many others live with non-relatives.

- *Having nothing to do.* This is usually a characteristic of income rather than age: It takes money to do things. The poor are likely to have nothing to do regardless of their age, but the middle class and affluent elderly tend to be more active in sports, hobbies, and religious and community groups than the middle-aged who are busy with their children and careers.

From ancient societies through the European Middle Ages, poor nutrition, sanitation, and health care meant that the end of life often came in childhood, young adulthood, or middle age. The elderly (which meant anyone older than 40) were not viewed as waiting for an inevitable decline and death, but as very lucky to have cheated death for so long. Today we see a similar pattern in many nonindustrial countries. The leading causes of death offer a clue. In Bangladesh, they are pneumonia, respiratory failure, accidental poisoning, and diarrhea. These diseases and accidents afflict young bodies more often than old, and are fatal only when the immune system is compromised by poor nutrition and health care is inadequate.

In the United States, the leading causes of death are heart disease, cancer, stroke, accidents, and emphysema. These diseases are rare among the young; they come primarily in old age, as the body wears out. Thus, we can conclude that death is common among children and young adults in Bangladesh, but very rare in the United States. Not only do these differences in causes of death reveal global inequalities, so do the meanings we attribute to death and dying, and the ways in which different cultures experience it. For some, it is simply the next phase of life and to be welcomed; for others, it is a "fact" and accepted less readily. Just as different groups view death differently, different cultures have developed different rituals to commemorate death.

Death and mourning are often linked to religious beliefs. There is archeological evidence that the earliest humans stained the bodies of the dead with red ochre before burial, perhaps signaling some belief in an afterlife. Bodies are prepared for some type of removal from the world of the living, either through burial, cremation, or some other event. Ancient Egypt developed sophisticated mechanisms for embalming because only a fully intact body could pass over to the afterlife. Most cultures require some form of funeral and public mourning by relatives and the larger community. In some, mourners are required to be immensely sad, while in others, the immediate family is supposed to celebrate the life passed with merriment and song and a big feast. Chinese funerals can be raucous, multiday affairs, with lots of ritual wailing and bands playing bad music to scare ghosts away. Often people buy paper houses, appliance, cars, and fake money to burn for the deceased to use in the afterlife. Chinese also celebrate "qing ming" which is the day when people clean their ancestor's graves and burn fake money. Chinese are pragmatists ... even in the afterlife!

What's important sociologically is that death is a process, not an event. Death may be the cessation of biological life, but its meaning changes dramatically from culture to culture. It is as much a cultural process as birth, maturation, and aging. Understanding how a group of people experience and explain death can provide a lens through which one can view the entire society.

---

iSOC AND YOU Age and Inequality

Aging is both venerated and degraded. You're told to respect your elders, and when you're young you might say, "I can't wait to be older." Yet culturally, we deny the *identity* of being old as long as we can, and as a result, we don't treat the old particularly well. As you age, the norms of *interaction* change, and the numbers of people with whom you interact begin to dwindle. Aging is also beset by *inequality*, both to the old themselves, and also in the ways that age exaggerates many other *intersecting* aspects of inequality. Entire *institutions*, such as hospitals, nursing homes, and the like, are organized to deal with the problems of old age, and access to these institutions is often structured by other intersecting inequalities.

10.4 Institutional Age Inequalities in Global and Local Perspectives

Inequalities associated with age become embedded in social institutions, such as the workplace, education, health care, and politics. Both young and old experience discrimination in their working lives. For example, employers are often reluctant to hire older workers, believing that they require higher wages and have higher healthcare costs, but also because they believe age-related stereotypes that older workers are more risk-averse, less cooperative and team-oriented, less productive, and less willing to learn than younger workers. All these stereotypes turn out to be false, but that does not mean that they do not have real consequences.

On the other hand, young people face significant hardships entering and staying in the labor force. As the most recently hired, they are often the most readily fired, especially in sectors that institutionally protect workers by seniority. For example, younger workers have been hit hardest during the current recession, as you will learn more about in this section. In addition, young people are subject to age-specific forms of inequality and discrimination such as child labor and trafficking. Although

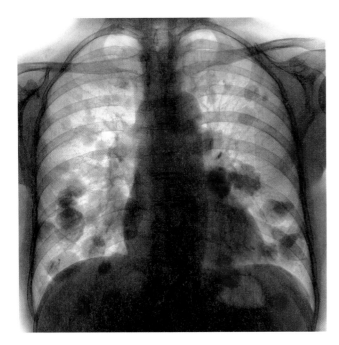

Because people are living longer, they are more likely to be able to do more damage to their lungs from smoking and other activities. As a result, lung cancer has become a larger cause of death than it once was because people are simply more likely to live long enough for it to develop.

sociologists study age as an identity and basis for inequality, they also understand that age is differently experienced by different groups within a society as well as by different societies around the world. In this section, you will learn more about age and inequality in global perspective as well as how age inequality is not only perpetuated interactionally, but institutionally as well.

Aging, Health, and the Life Course

10.4.1 Define the "expansion of morbidity" and why it is a central problem in many societies today.

In 2012, the results from the "Global Burden of Disease Study" were published—a research project conducted over 5 years by almost 500 researchers at over 300 different institutions in 50 countries around the world. It was a monumental effort. They charted the rates of different causes of death in different countries around the world as well as the effects of risk factors associated with illness (like not enough fruit in a diet, childhood abuse or trauma, or low income). And they calculated causes of death and risk factors associated with illness at two points in time (1990 and 2010) to allow them to see how things had changed.

This enabled the study to discover the leading causes of death around the world as well as how those causes have changed. The top two (heart disease and stroke) did not change between 1990 and 2010. Others moved significantly in the rankings. Malnutrition, for instance, was the eleventh-leading cause of death around the world in 1990; by 2010, it had dropped to twenty-first. Other causes of death moved up in the rankings (like diabetes, lung cancer, and car accidents). One thing the study showed was the gains made in fighting causes of death that caused many to die prematurely. But, this has had two consequences. First, it has meant that more people are surviving long enough to die of diseases that disproportionately affect people in old age, like Alzheimer's disease and Parkinson's disease. Second, people have also become more likely to live with health conditions that do not kill them but impact their lives.

So, people's lives are longer, but the years added onto life expectancies around the world are not all years in good health. Things like mental disorders, issues with substance abuse, musculoskeletal pain, loss of vision or hearing all affect people's lives in dramatic ways, but do not necessarily kill people. The study was able to show that we have made fantastic gains in reducing mortality, but they have not been equaled by progress in reducing disability. All of this means that more people will require more care as they get older, and because they are likely to live in diminished health, they will require care for longer periods of time than previous generations. The trend of increasing the amount of years spent in bad health is referred to as the **expansion of morbidity**, and it is likely to be a central challenge to larger numbers of people over the next few centuries in addition to those who provide and pay for their care.

expansion of morbidity

As people are living longer, this trend describes the increasing time they will spend in bad health.

Child Labor in the United States

10.4.2 Summarize what child labor looks like in the United States.

In the United States, we tend to think of child labor as a relic of the distant past, appearing only in Victorian novels like *David Copperfield*. Teenagers may take part-time jobs at McDonald's to supplement their allowances, but strict laws ensure that no job can be hazardous or time consuming or interfere with childhood, a life stage we imagine as "carefree." Children younger than the age of 14 cannot work at all (with a few exceptions, like delivering newspapers, performing, or working for parents). If they are 14 or 15, they can work a maximum of 18 hours per week when school is in session (full-time in summer), and they must go home no later than 7:00 P.M. (9:00 P.M. in summer). And if they are younger than 18, they cannot perform many hazardous tasks, including roofing, meatpacking, demolition, manufacturing explosives, or any job that requires driving a car.

These are the federal guidelines. Many states have laws that differ a bit. For instance, in Connecticut, 16- and 17-year-olds with no school the next day can work until 10:00 P.M. in manufacturing and retail establishments, bowling alleys, pool halls, or photography establishments. They can work until 11:00 P.M. in restaurants and recreational, amusement, and theater establishments, and if they happen to land jobs in

U.S./WORLD

YOUTH UNEMPLOYMENT AROUND THE WORLD

Youth unemployment varies widely around the world. In Japan, only 5.2 percent of young people were unemployed in 2016. But in France, that proportion is almost 25 percent.

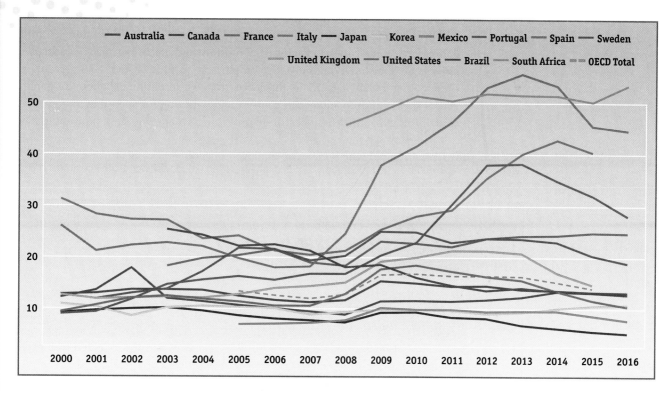

SOURCE: Data from Organization for Economic Cooperation and Development (OECD), 2016. Available at https://data.oecd.org/unemp/youth-unemployment-rate.htm.

INVESTIGATE FURTHER

1. What factors do you think might have contributed to the rise of youth unemployment in some societies (like Spain, or Italy) versus the relative stability of youth unemployment over time in others (like the United States, Korea, or Mexico)?

supermarkets of 3,500 square feet or more, they can work until midnight. But as they become young adults, young people are struggling to find work at much higher rates than are adults.

In the United States, teenagers (ages 14 to 17) are mostly working for extra money rather than to contribute to household income: 30 percent of the teenagers in the highest-income households but only 15 percent in the lowest-income households have jobs (see U.S./WORLD Youth Unemployment Around the World). Of white teenagers, 37.1 percent worked during the school year and 35 percent during the summer, a significantly larger percentage than for African Americans (29% and 28%) or Hispanic youth (31% and 28%). Among the most common jobs were in the leisure and hospitality industry (27%), another 20 percent work in retail, and 11 percent worked in education and health services (Bureau of Labor Statistics 2015).

Child Labor Around the World

10.4.3 Understand how the frequency and type of child labor differs around the world.

Globally, the statistics concerning child labor are different than they are in the United States (see FIGURE 10.8). In 2012, 264 million children aged 5 to 17 were in the workforce, (that's 16.7 percent of the children alive in between those ages). Although this number is enormous, it has actually been declining in recent history: The figure for 2012 is 40 million fewer children than were working in 2008 (305 million children ages 5–17). Throughout that time, boys have continuously been more exposed to work than girls on the whole (18.1 percent of boys ages 5–7 compared to 15.2 percent of girls between those ages).

In sub-Saharan Africa, 1 in 5 children ages 5 to 17 are child laborers (59 million), compared to 1 in 12 in Asia Pacific (77.7 million) and one in fourteen in Latin America and the Caribbean (7.9 million). By comparison, Europe has only 0.3 percent of children younger than age 15 in the labor force (International Labour Organization 2006). These children and adolescents are not working for spending money; they are contributing to family finances, often providing a major source of household income.

FIGURE 10.8 Global Trends in the Number of Employed Children—2008, 2012
While an incredible number and proportion of children are employed around the world, the rate at which children work has been decreasing over time.

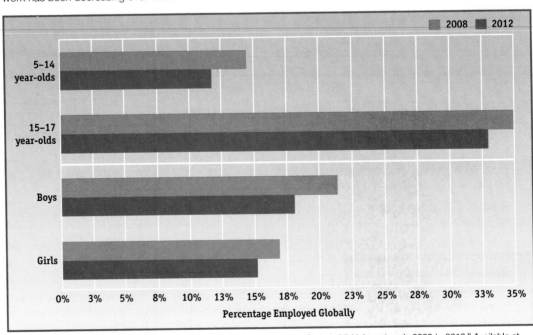

SOURCE: Data from International Labour Organization. Statistical Report "Global child labour trends 2008 to 2012." Available at http://www.ilo.org/ipec/Informationresources/WCMS_IPEC_PUB_23015/lang-en/index.htm.

Their jobs differ considerably from the teen workers in the United States: Almost 60 percent are in agriculture, one third in services (including child care and domestic work), and 7 percent in industry.

Many child laborers work long hours that prohibit them from going to school or having any time for leisure; more than half work for 9 or more hours per day, 7 days a week, with no holidays. Over two-thirds work for no pay, and the others receive a fraction of what adults would receive; one international study (International Labour Organization 2006) found them being paid a sixth of the standard adult wage. About half (85 million) work under hazardous conditions, exposed to dangerous chemicals or using dangerous tools. They do not receive sufficient exposure to fresh air and have little freedom of movement. They may be beaten and abused. More than 20 percent suffer physical injuries; many others suffer irreparable psychological harm.

Their situations vary, and not all are unpleasant or exploitive, but for every 16-year-old studying college chemistry from behind a counter at the family shop, there are a dozen 4-year-olds tied to rug looms to keep them from running away.

THE NEW SLAVERY   Global trafficking transports people far from their homes for forced, bonded, and illegitimate labor. There are about 21 million victims worldwide (nearly three times as many as were victimized by the African slave trade of 1500–1830, discussed in Chapter 8), including over 5.5 million children (International Labour Organization 2012). Most are seeking an escape from poverty; they are likely to be from disenfranchised tribal groups, castes, or minority groups. Many are refugees. They may be lured from their homes with the promise of good jobs or an education overseas, but some are sold by their parents, and some are kidnapped outright. They are crammed onto boats or trucks with insufficient food, water, and air, and transported thousands of miles from home. When their "employers" are threatened with discovery, the children are abandoned in border regions or killed.

The destinations of these children differ depending on region and local culture, but they follow the general trend of globalization: Raw materials and labor flow from the less-developed countries to the more developed (see MAP 10.2).

MAP 10.2 Global Flow of Child Slavery
Examining flows of child slavery around the world is a powerful illustration of global inequality. As a rule, societies that enslave children are taking children from less developed nations.

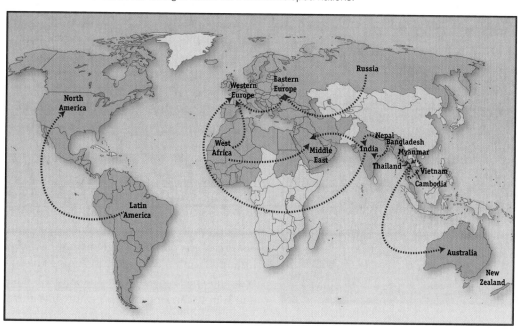

- From Latin America to North America
- From Russia and Eastern Europe to Western Europe
- From West Africa to Western Europe and the Middle East
- From Cambodia, Myanmar, and Vietnam to Thailand
- From Thailand to Australia and New Zealand
- From Nepal and Bangladesh to India
- From India to the Middle East and Western Europe

When the children finally reach their destination, the "good job" turns out to be poorly paying or unpaid domestic, factory, or farm work. They are not permitted to leave their jobs, and if they do, they have nowhere to go. They are in a strange country where they do not speak the language. Their parents are a continent away and have no resources to get them back. They cannot seek other help because they are in the country illegally, with no papers, and the authorities are usually corrupt. They are virtual slaves—if they are lucky. Trafficked children are more likely than others to fall prey to the worst forms of child labor defined by the International Labour Organization (2012).

THE WORST FORMS OF CHILD LABOR   Forced and bonded labor occupies 5.7 million children and adolescents. A little more than 1 million have been trafficked, transported to other regions or countries, and the rest work close to home (International Labour Organization 2006). Most jobs in forced and bonded labor are technically legal, on farms and in factories, but 1.8 million work in the global sex trade, as prostitutes or performers in pornographic videos. Most are girls, but an estimated 10 to 30 percent are boys. Procurers prefer children to adults because they are easy to control and can be promoted to potential clients as virgins and therefore disease free (International Labour Organization 2006).

Another 600,000 are employed in criminal activities other than the sex trade (of course, a sizeable percentage do both). Usually their jobs involve drug manufacture or distribution, but they can also engage in pickpocketing, shoplifting, car theft, and burglary. Most are boys. Procurers prefer them to adults because they can move about freely, cause less suspicion, and receive lenient punishment when caught (International Labour Organization 2006).

Adolescents and children have been commandeered for armed conflicts in Africa, Asia, Latin America, and the Pacific. Some countries permit the conscription of 13- or 14-year-olds, and others simply fail to regulate age limits in conscription process (in Bolivia, 40 percent of the armed forces are younger than 18 years old). Intertribal conflicts and terrorism also draw on underage operatives. Most are boys, but a sizeable number of girls are conscripted as well. A few become soldiers, and the others become servants or camp prostitutes (Beber and Blattman 2010).

An estimated 300,000 soldiers around the world are youth younger than age of 18. Some join fighting groups because they believe in the cause, while others join mainly to sustain themselves with food and protection. Many others are forced to join; they may be abducted or drafted then indoctrinated. While boys are stereotypically assumed to be the better fighters, girls are participating in fighting forces in more than 50 countries, assuming roles as fighters, spies, messengers, lookouts, medics and supply carriers, as well as more traditional

These young boys in South Sudan are surrendering their weapons. UNICEF supports local efforts like this to help child soldiers with the hopes of aiding them in reintegrating into society.

gender roles as captive "wives" or sex slaves, cooks, and domestic servants (Child Soldiers International 2008).

Opposition and Mobilization: The Politics of Age

10.4.4 Summarize how people have attempted to oppose age inequality and how and why they have been successful.

Just as age is a source of identity and the basis for social inequality, it has also become a basis for political mobilization. In the 1960s, young people began to mobilize around their lack of power and control over their lives. Political campaigns to lower the voting age, for example, were carried out mainly by young people who argued that if they are old enough to serve in the military and fight and die for their country they ought to have some electoral say over who gets to send them into harm's way. More recently, youth have organized on issues from anti-war activism, to pro-sex education, to expanded educational access, and younger people have dominated activism in groups including Occupy Wall Street and Black Lives Matter. Young people must come to think of themselves a coherent voting bloc; otherwise, these sorts of decisions are generally made for young people by middle-aged people.

Older people have been more successful in mobilizing for political and social change. For one thing, as the population has aged, and as longevity has increased, older people are increasingly visible—especially as vital and active participants in society. Like other radical groups of the 1960s and 1970s, older people mobilized. When Maggie Kuhn, who worked for the Presbyterian Church, was forced to retire in 1970 at age 65, she took inspiration from the Black Panthers and La Raza, and organized the Gray Panthers. The Gray Panthers were concerned about both ends of age inequality, and advocated for both young people and old. Kuhn believed that teenagers needed to be taken more seriously as well. Their motto was "Youth and Age in Action" and their membership was split between older people and high school and college students. In their early years, they promoted stricter monitoring of industries that relate to older people. They helped to produce a famous critique of the hearing aid industry's practices called "Paying Through the Ear." More recently, they have joined with other groups to advocate for better health care, education, and housing (Brown 1998).

Most efforts by the elderly to mobilize politically have come from more established lobbying efforts and mainstream organizations that advocate for their interests as older Americans. The American Association of Retired Persons (AARP) was founded in 1958 by Dr. Ethel Percy Andrus, a retired teacher who had been lobbying for health care for retirees. Today, with a membership of more than 40 million people, AARP is among the largest membership organizations in the country—more than 10 times the membership of the National Rifle Association (NRA). The success of AARP has been its ability to treat age as both an identity and as a basis for inequality. Whether social movements and organizations associated with young people today will mobilize based on age as well is an open question. We're still waiting to see.

Black Lives Matter protests and activist organizations on college campuses around the United States address an issue important to many young people organizing for change today—systemic racism.

iSOC AND YOU Institutional Age Inequalities in Global and Local Perspectives
The *inequalities* of age are not just reproduced in everyday *interactions*—the way you are treated by doctors, hospitals, and even at the grocery store—they are also exaggerated or muted by other *intersecting* structures of inequality. Age is a significant aspect of global inequality, as both youth and old are more easily subject to exploitation and intersecting inequalities. Some young people never get to experience the *identity* of "youth," as they are subject to "adult-like" work experiences by the time they are supposed to be entering kindergarten. And young people continue to be among those most concerned with social protest and change.

Conclusion

Youth and Aging NOW

A recent issue of the AARP magazine had rock star Bruce Springsteen—once the symbol of rebellious youth who was "born to run"—on the cover. The cover captures some of the paradoxes of the sociology of age: Both an identity and a basis for inequality, age is also constantly in transition, as one generation's youthful rebel becomes the next generation's wise elder.

We often think of age as a biological process, as simple maturation, a chronology. And yet culturally, we think of age as a progression through certain stages or categories— childhood, adolescence, adulthood, and the like. These stages vary so much from one culture to the next that sociologists understand age as a social phenomenon. Like gender and race, our age may be a biological phenomenon, but what it *means* to be any particular age is a sociological question. In that sense, age is a facet of identity. And, as we've seen, it is constantly shifting as societies change. The adolescent was an invention of the early twentieth century; the "emerging adult" between adolescence and adulthood was invented at the beginning of the twenty-first. People are still the same ages; but what it means to be 14 or 20 differs.

As a foundation of our identity, age is also an axis of inequality, a mechanism by which societies allocate goods and rewards. In our society, the middle aged have more power than either the very young or the very old. That's why there are social movements for youth and for the aged. Rarely are there political organizations demanding more power for the middle aged.

As both a foundation of identity and inequality, the meaning of age varies even within our society—by race, class, and gender. Take the example of the teenager, a social invention, as we've seen. The idea of the teenager itself is a product of suburban, middle-class white people. When we learn to understand age and inequality intersectionally, we can better explain why the same "boys will be boys" or tolerance for "teen hijinks" among white, middle-class teens is quite different when teens of color participate; those kids could go to jail for doing what other "teenagers" do.

Many of our social institutions are organized by age as well. In most cases, it feels so natural—school for young people, workplaces for the middle aged, families for two generations living together—that we forget just how

Bruce Springstein, once a pop cultural symbol of youth, virility, and rebellion, is here featured on the cover of the American Association of Retired Persons (AARP) magazine. It's a powerful testament to the ways age transforms our status in society.

different it is in other places. Some cultures segregate people by age—children's huts in some cultures, for example, or dorms on an Israeli kibbutz. Identifying people by age is a way that the media, for example, both enables us to feel part of a larger community, and serves to divide us from one another.

To sociologists, then, age is a social phenomenon—a foundation of identity, a mechanism for inequality, a dynamic of interactions and an element of our institutions. How will it develop in the twenty-first century? The status of elders may rise as baby boomers start hitting retirement age, and because boomers grew up at the start of the information revolution, they will have the computer expertise that previous cohorts of the elderly lacked. Aging will continue to change. Having "come of age" during the tumultuous 1960s, baby boomers will likely continue to organize around age-related issues. But will the young, who are always difficult to organize into a social movement based on age?

What is certain is that young people and old people are constantly changing the meaning of age in our society. In the future we will certainly live longer lives, and children will delay assuming full adult responsibilities for longer and longer periods; that is, we will be both old and young for a longer amount of time. It remains to be seen whether living longer will enable all of us to also live better and whether the rich will live longer and happier lives while the poor will live shorter, unhappier lives.

CHAPTER REVIEW Age: From Young to Old

10.1   Age, Identity, and the Stages of Life

What is "old" and "young"? Sociologists view age as a social construction, meaning it is not the number but the social environment that determines what age means. Age of marriage and other social expectations depends on the meanings society gives to age. Children used to be viewed as adults very early; today they are postponing adulthood until much later. Age is one of society's major social identities and is a basis for inequality. Most inequality based on age affects either the very young or the very old. All societies divide members by age, and individuals are sorted into age cohorts, groups in which people experience similar life experiences and norms for behavior. With increased life expectancy and laws about child labor, age groups and definitions have changed. Transitions between age stages are often marked by rites of passage and other milestones, although the tasks and milestones of age groups are now blurred and have lost some meaning.

10.1 Key Terms

chronological age A person's age as determined by the actual date of birth.

functional age A set of observable characteristics and attributes that are used to categorize people into different age cohorts.

age grades The term sociologists use to refer to the forms of social organization that are based on age and through which we pass over the course of our lives.

age cohort A group of people who are born within a specific time period and assumed to share both chronological and functional characteristics, as well as life experiences.

gerontology Scientific study of the biological, psychological, and sociological phenomena associated with old age and aging.

life expectancy The average number of years a person can expect to live; varies greatly by country and region.

life span The span of time during which a person is alive, which all societies—whether tribal, agrarian, or industrial—have always divided into stages, seasons, or age groups.

age norms Distinctive cultural values, pursuits, and pastimes that are culturally prescribed for each age cohort.

adolescence A marker, often a ceremony, that denotes an important stage in someone's life, such as birth, puberty, marriage, death.

rites of passage Rituals or ceremonies that mark important transitions between life stages.

"sandwich generation" With the increase in life expectancy and the delay in childbearing, many middle-aged adults find themselves "sandwiched" between caring for dependent children and aging parents at the same time.

"young old" The term for people ages 65 to 75.

"old old" The term for people ages 75 to 85.

"oldest old" The term for people ages 85 and older.

10.2 Boomers, Busters, and Boomlets: The Generations of Youth

When you happened to be born shapes a great deal about your life—what sorts of opportunities you might experience, how long you will likely live, and more. Sociologists who study this break people up into meaningful groups of people born in a given chunk of time who share some experiences, opportunities, and characteristics as a result of being similar ages at critical moments in their lives. Sociologists call these "generations," which is an *identity* you carry with you whether you think about it or not. It shapes the ways you *interact* with the world around you, your access to and experience in every social *institution* in our society, and the kinds and qualities of *inequality* you will experience. The biggest age cohort in U.S. history is the Baby Boomers, those born roughly between 1946 and 1964. Because they are such a large group, their presence changed society in many ways. When they were children, the nation was focused on child rearing. When they were adolescents, the culture focused on that stage of life. The Boomers themselves changed the landscape of society with their active participation in the Civil Rights, women's, and gay rights movements. When the boomers became middle aged, the concerns of society shifted into a new era of conservatism. Now the boomers are redefining what it means to be old. The baby boomers were followed by Generation X, those born between 1965 and 1979.

A smaller cohort, the culture focused less on them, and individuals in this generation experienced a decline in their standard of living. Since 1980, social scientists have identified a new generation of youth—Millennials; born after 1980, they are the first generation to come into their adulthood in the new millennium. Structurally, they are among the most precarious and vulnerable generation of young people ever. On the other hand, Millennials are, in the words of a recent survey, "confident, self-expressive, liberal, upbeat and open to change." Some have labeled the generation following Millennials, Generation Z (those born since 2000), and many of the trends that are true of Millennials appear all the more true of the next generation (at least so far). Although the United States keeps naming new stages into an ever-expanding process of growing up, and continues to be obsessed with images and ideas of youth, young people in the most developed nations of the world are a declining breed. Demographers predict the percentage of youth worldwide will continue to decline steadily in the wealthiest nations in the world; while the absolute numbers will remain stable, their proportion in the global population will decline by 20 percent as older people live longer and bring up the mean age of the country.

10.2 Key Terms

baby boom This large generation born after the end of World War II between 1946 to 1964 created a big bulge in the populations of Europe and North America and is the biggest age cohort in American history—77 million babies in the United States.

generation gap Differences in outlook and opinion that arise between generations.

Generation X Sometimes called the "baby bust," this generation born after the Baby Boom, between 1965 and 1979, is a small age cohort.

fertility rate The number of births per 1,000 women ages 15 to 44 in a calendar year.

Millennials The generation of nearly 50 million people born after 1980—the first generation to come into their adulthood in the new millennium.

Generation Z The generation of people born since 2000.

population pyramid Type of graph that shows five- or ten-year age groups as different-sized bars, or "blocks."

10.3 Age and Inequality

How old you are shapes a great variety of different issues related to inequality. Although the United States is often characterized as youth-obsessed, it is also true that children are more likely to be in poverty than any other age group in the country. While it sometimes might feel like "old age" is more of a medical diagnosis than an identity, our attention to poverty among the elderly in the United States has dramatically shifted the likelihood that people will be impoverished when they die. But much of this transition has meant that our care for the elderly is something no longer handled by family members (as was the case throughout history); now we have institutions that provide care for the elderly. And while this has enabled fewer to finish their lives in poverty, it also means that the elderly have been increasingly segregated from everyone else to a greater extent than at any other point in history. Loneliness is common among all life stages, but as people age, they are particularly vulnerable to social isolation, limited regular interaction with family, friends, and acquaintances.

10.4 Institutional Age Inequalities in Global and Local Perspectives

Inequalities associated with age become embedded in social institutions, such as the workplace, education, health care, and politics. Both young and old Americans experience various sorts of discrimination in their working lives. Globally, child labor is different than it is in the United States. In the United States, teenagers (ages 14 to 17) work mainly for extra money rather than to contribute to household income, but around the world almost 17 percent of all children ages 5 to 17—some 264 million children—are in the workforce. Although this number is enormous, it has actually been declining since at least 2008. Many child laborers work long hours that prohibit them from going to school or having any time for leisure; over half work for 9 or more hours per day, 7 days a week, with no holidays. More than two-thirds work for no pay, and the others receive a fraction of what adults would receive. About half work under hazardous conditions, exposed to dangerous chemicals or using dangerous tools. They do not receive sufficient exposure to fresh air and have little freedom of movement. They may be beaten and abused. Over 20 percent suffer physical injuries; many others suffer irreparable psychological harm.

10.4 Key Terms

expansion of morbidity As people are living longer, this trend describes the increasing time they will spend in bad health.

SELF-TEST

⟩ CHECK YOUR UNDERSTANDING

1. Which of the following is not one of the causes for the increase in the percentage of elderly in the U.S. population?
   a. Decline in birth rate
   b. The large cohort of baby boomers reaching retirement age
   c. Increased life expectancy
   d. All of the answers are relevant factors.

2. Who lives longer, men or women?
   a. Women
   b. Men
   c. Men live longer in developing countries but women live longer in industrial countries.
   d. Women live longer in developing countries but men live longer in industrialized countries.

3. What factors contribute to the differences in life expectancy in different U.S. states?
   a. Income and education
   b. Nutrition and access to health care
   c. Both a and b are factors.
   d. Neither a nor b are factors.

4. Why is middle age associated with the lowest levels of well-being?
   a. It can be a time of reckoning about what we will do or attain in life.
   b. It can be a time when people are "sandwiched" between child-rearing and caring for elderly parents.
   c. Both a and b are correct.
   d. It is not associated with low levels of well-being.

5. Which of the following characteristics are associated with the Millennials?
   a. They are born after 2000 in the new millennium.
   b. They are among the most precarious and vulnerable generations of young people ever in the United States.
   c. They are rebellious, suspicious of elders, and care about success more than anything else in life.
   d. All of the answers are correct.

6. By looking at population pyramids, sociologists can see _____
   a. the distribution of different age groups.
   b. many poor countries have "expansive" pyramids, which indicate that most of the population is young.
   c. many rich countries have "constrictive" pyramids, with larger shares of middle-aged and older people than young people.
   d. All of the answers are correct.

7. When it comes to youth employment _____
   a. in the United States, a larger percentage of teenagers in the lowest-income households have jobs as compared with the percentage of those in the highest-income households.
   b. globally, more than 260 million children ages 5 to 17 are in the workforce, close to 17 percent of the children alive in between those ages.
   c. girls have continuously been exposed to more work than boys.
   d. All of the answers are correct.

8. Globally, millions of children are forced into forms of labor including _____
   a. the sex trade.
   b. criminal activity such as shoplifting, car theft, and burglary.
   c. armed conflict
   d. All of the answers are correct.

Self-Test Answers 1. d, 2. a, 3. c, 4. c, 5. b, 6. d, 7. b, 8. d

CHAPTER 11

THE BODY: HEALTH AND SEXUALITY

We typically think of bodies as *biological*—as truly separate from the *social*. But, sociologists know that bodies are both the raw materials from which societies are made as well as impacted dramatically by the societies in which they reside. Put another way, bodies play a key role in shaping our opportunities and experiences, but so too are they shaped by those opportunities and experiences.

LEARNING OBJECTIVES

In this chapter, using the iSoc framework, you should be able to:

11.1.1 Summarize the ways that beauty is socially constructed in ways that support existing systems of inequality in societies.

11.1.2 Recognize how each of the five elements of the iSoc model can be used to examine bodies and embodiment sociologically.

11.1.3 Understand how tattoos and cosmetic surgery are means by which people use their bodies to craft identities.

11.1.4 Explain the ways that gender inequality is expressed through gendered forms of body dissatisfaction.

11.1.5 Understand how public reactions to transgender people are a powerful illustration of our collective investment in embodied understandings of gender.

11.1.6 Explain why concerns about obesity are framed as about "health," but often have more to do with socially constructed body ideals and embodied forms of inequality.

11.1.7 Describe the ways bodily ability related to social inequality and how disabilities intersect with other social identities (like race, class, and age).

11.1.8 Provide an example of what it means to say that inequality is embodied illustrating your understanding.

11.2.1 Distinguish between epidemiology and social epidemiology.

11.2.2 Explain what it means to study health inequality intersectionally.

11.2.3 Understand how global inequality affects health and well-being around the world.

11.2.4 Describe the ways that health and well-being as well as health inequality are also perpetuated interactionally.

11.2.5 Summarize some of the forms of inequality from which the mentally ill suffer.

11.2.6 Explain what it means to say that health inequalities are also institutionalized, providing an example to illustrate your understanding.

11.3.1 Understand the origins of research on sexuality in the social sciences.

11.3.2 Distinguish between the three dimensions of sexuality, and explain why drawing this distinction helps sociologists explain how sexualities are socially constructed.

11.3.3 Define sexual scripts, and explain why understanding sexual scripts is among the most important components of sexual socialization.

11.3.4 Understand that what qualifies as "sexual" varies wildly by society.

11.3.5 Understand that the notion of "having" a sexual identity is a historically recent idea.

11.3.6 Explain the sexual double standard and the "masculinization" of sex.

11.3.7 Summarize what sociologists have learned about contemporary gender and sexual inequality by examining the social phenomenon of "hooking up."

11.3.8 Explain some of the different ways that sexual inequality is perpetuated around the world.

11.3.9 Summarize some of the reasons for and consequences of the LGBT movement becoming much more mainstream today than it once was.

Introduction

The untimely death of Michael Jackson in 2009 left the music world saddened by the loss of a great talent. But Jackson's physical transformation over the course of his career was deeply disturbing to many people. Each stage of his career seemed to be accompanied by a correspondingly new physical persona.

We think of our bodies as a possession, something uniquely and distinctly ours. "It's *my* body," says transgender theorist Susan Stryker, "I live here. I don't rent. And that means I can do with it whatever I want." As a result, we also consider our bodies to be a "project"—something that we can "work" on, a canvas of our own creation.

On the other hand, we also think our bodies are biological entities, subject to natural processes such as aging, health, maturation, and decay. We experience ourselves to be driven by "urges," or needs that seem to come from inside the body but outside our control. Sometimes we even think parts of our bodies have a mind of their own.

Sex, for example, is among our most intimate and private bodily experiences. We rarely discuss our sexual experiences honestly with family and friends. We may think of our desires as irrational, out-of-control impulses, some too shameful to even utter. Yet sex is also pretty much everywhere we look. References to sex and the sexual body are sprinkled liberally through our daily conversations. Sex is everywhere—online, in books and magazines, on TV, and in movies and music. And these images reflect cultural notions of what is sexy to people, and they also help shape our personal experiences and expressions of sexual desire as well.

And when it comes to sexual identities, we think of them as fixed and permanent—something we are, not something we become. At the same time, though, we debate about whether or not members of sexual minorities identities can teach our children without trying to "recruit them" and offer "conversion" therapies to help gays become heterosexual.

So which is it—public or private? Bodies, health, and sexuality as biologically fixed or malleable and changing? To the sociologist, the answer to these questions is rarely one or the other. It's both. Bodies, health, and sex are all simultaneously both private and public. They are central parts of your identity, and they evolve and change over the course of your life. What you desire, what you do, and what you think about what you do are all social. What's more, bodies, health, and sexuality are not only building blocks of your identity, but they are also important axes of inequality. How you have sex, and with whom, is not only a matter of moral scrutiny; it may actually be illegal. It is in the social arena that you learn what sorts of desires are "normal" or permissible, and what sorts are not. Who is likely to be unhealthy and who has access to care often intersects with various other forms of inequality. What our bodies look like, how we care for them, and what they are forced to endure are all questions of *social*, not *biological*, organization.

Understanding what it means to examine and study bodies, health, and sexuality from a sociological perspective requires an ability to think about some of the most intimate elements of who we are as structured by social forces that are often beyond our immediate control.

11.1 Embodying Identities and Inequality

At first glance, finding someone attractive might feel purely instinctive. You experience an immediate "gut reaction" of interest, without even thinking about it. But if our sexual desires were operated purely on instinct, the standards of physical attractiveness would be the same across human cultures and throughout history; and, with a few exceptions (like big eyes, a symmetrical face), they are not. They change dramatically from culture to culture. Indeed, what a society defines as "beautiful" often has much more to do with power and inequality in that society than it does with biology. Beauty is best understood with the sociological concept of "distinction"—a sociological process wherein certain groups endeavor to distinguish themselves from various "others." Distinction is a social process, and it works to produce and reproduce understandings of difference and, along with those understandings, the concomitant status, power, and comforts that accompanies being situated as "on the right side" of this distinction. So, fatness was beautiful in societies where food was in short supply. As food became more abundant (but healthy food less so or more costly), new understandings of beauty emerged.

Our bodies are projects that are intimately related to our identity. And as such, bodies are tied to inequalities as well. How beautiful your body is understood to be by others in your society doesn't only determine how likely you are to get a date to your senior prom, but it also plays a role in how you are treated by healthcare professionals, it affects your odds of getting a job, it shapes our interactions with others, and much more. This is why sociologists who take the body seriously are interested in the social processes whereby inequalities become, quite literally, *embodied*. Bodies intersect with other forms of inequality and inequalities are played out on the body in terms of life expectancy, health, sexuality, and more. In this section, you'll learn more about what this means and how to think more sociologically about bodies relying on the iSoc perspective.

Thinking Sociologically about Beauty

11.1.1 Summarize the ways that beauty is socially constructed in ways that support existing systems of inequality in societies.

What we think of as "beautiful" varies around the world. And it changes over time as well. At one time, weight was a signifier of class position: If you were heavy it meant you were upper class, because you could afford large quantities of food.

Beauty ideals change over time. One way of seeing these changes is by going to a museum and looking at portraits of beautiful bodies. On the left is the famous painting by Artemisia Gentileschi, *The Sleeping Venus* (1625–1630). Italian artist and actress, Anna Utopia Giordano reimagines famous paintings by altering the bodies to be consistent with twenty-first century beauty ideals. See the image on the right for Giordano's reimagining of Gentileschi's painting. What changed? Look up Giordano online and see the other Venuses she altered as well.

Today, weight and class vary together, but in the opposite direction: Obesity is often correlated with being poorer. Throughout the world though, the differences are interesting. Slender bodies are challenging to achieve in the most affluent societies in the world and fat bodies are challenging to achieve in the most impoverished societies in the world.

Social status becomes inscribed on bodies in multiple ways. Consider strong muscles and tanned skin on white bodies. During the nineteenth and twentieth centuries, throughout Europe and in the United States, strength and tan skin were signs of lower status among men and women. Having a strong body and tan skin was an indication of the kind of work you did to make a living. The elite did not work much at all and could afford to stay out of the sun. Thus, pale and plump bodies were in vogue. This is why the nudes painted by artists in the Renaissance look a little heavy by today's standards.

iSoc: The Sociology of Bodies and Embodiment

11.1.2 Recognize how each of the five elements of the iSoc model can be used to examine bodies and embodiment sociologically.

IDENTITY—Our Bodies, Ourselves was the best-selling guide to women's health first published in the 1970s. The equation between the body and the self was evident then —and is even more evident today. Bodies are often seen as a living canvas, and we can shape and sculpt it to express our selves. *Identity* is expressed through the body—in sickness and in health, and regardless of what we do with our bodies sexually. Bodies are markers of identity. Similarly, health is intimately connected with identity. Sociologists examine the ways that health and illness define our identities in enduring ways. Coping with cancer is more than a biological and medical struggle, it's a social struggle as well. And being a "cancer survivor" is not merely a medical fact about a patient; it becomes a powerful point of reference in a patient's life course, an identity they may identify with for the rest of their lives (even if the cancer never returns). Similarly, sexuality is about much more than sexual behavior; it is also about how we *identify* ourselves sexually and how we are identified by others. People did not always understand themselves to have "sexual identities." But we do today, and they are deeply connected to our social experience.

*INEQUALITY—*All bodies are not seen as equal. Some bodies are more valued and receive higher rewards. Not just by race, or size, or any other marker of the body, but also its relative conformity to standards of beauty. Attractive people make more money. Attractive men are more likely to be listened to, but attractive women are often thought to be less smart. And those who are sexual minorities have historically been discriminated against. So, your bodies and your sexualities are also ranked hierarchically, expressing social inequality. And health is no different. Becoming ill may be a biological reality, but risk factors associated with which groups and societies are more likely to become ill is the product of social organization. And how societies navigate individuals whose health has failed them often reproduces many of the same systems of *inequality* we have learned about in the preceding chapters.

INTERACTION—We don't just "have" bodies, health, or sexuality, we "do" them, too— that is, our bodies and our perceptions of them are the product of *interactions*. Heavy or skinny, tall or short, healthy or ill, cis-gender or transgender, LGBTQ or heterosexual— these aren't just labels for properties we have, they are processes by which we come to be who we are through interactions with others. We learn how to inhabit our bodies, how to use them, what they are like through our interactions with other people. And we do it constantly, all the time.

INSTITUTIONS—Just think of all the different *institutions* that are organized to facilitate our relationships with our bodies, to keep them healthy, fit, beautiful, to shape them, transform them, heal them. Our bodies are constantly engaged with a host of institutions from hospitals to spas, from sports fields to cosmetic surgeon's offices. These institutions circumscribe the possibilities of embodied action. Schools, workplaces, homes: Wherever we find ourselves, our experiences of our bodies, our health, and our sexualities are organized, expressed, and subject to rules and regulations.

INTERSECTIONALITY—All these elements (bodies, health, sexualities) combine and collide in different ways, and they *intersect* with other forms of identity and inequality as well, like those based on race, class, gender, nationality, and more. Our class position structures the possibilities of medically or surgically transforming our bodies. Our standards of beauty and appropriate bodily activity are structured by our race, sexuality, and disability status. Each element of our identity is also placed inside social hierarchies: Put them all together and they combine in different ways.

Embodying Identity—Tattoos and Cosmetic Surgery

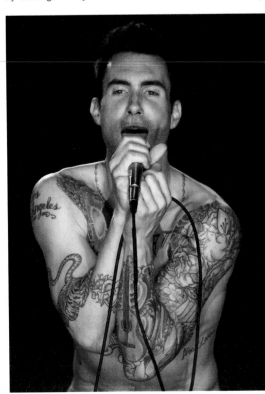

Pop star Adam Levine poses here displaying his tattooed arms. Today, about half of young people with tattoos only have one, and only one in five has more than six tattoos. The fact that visible tattoos are increasingly a part of pop star identities is one way of considering their popularity more generally.

11.1.3 Understand how tattoos and cosmetic surgery are means by which people use their bodies to craft identities.

Virtually all of us spend some time and energy in some forms of bodily transformation: We wear clothing we think makes us look good, or jewelry, or other adornments. But until recently, relatively few people in the United States had tattoos, pierced their bodies, or received cosmetic surgery. These practices have a history of being associated with "deviant" groups and subcultures until relatively recently, though they were far more common in other cultures. Today, body piercing involves far more than the earlobes and can include the tongue, eyebrows, navel, nose, lips, nipples, and even the genitals. Increasing numbers of young people are also getting tattoos. Cosmetic surgery is more of a norm than it has ever been (much more so in some societies than others). Given their vaguely "naughty" character in American society, tattoos and piercings denote a slight sexualized undertone—if only because they indicate that the bearer is aware of his or her body as an instrument of pleasure and object of desire.

Tattoos have long been a way to decorate the body among people in North and South America, Mesoamerica, Europe, Japan, China, Africa, and elsewhere. Their decline in Europe occurred with the spread of Christianity (Sanders 1989). Today, however, tattoos have become quite common. Millennials have the most tattoos, according to a 2010 Pew Research Report. About 3 in 10 have at least one, and half of those with tattoos have between two and six, with 18 percent having more than six tattoos. Not far behind, 32 percent of Gen Xers have a tattoo. However, only 15 percent of Baby Boomers and 6 percent of those older than Baby Boomers have one. Tattoos are more common in the South than other regions of the country, twice as common among whites and Latinos as among African Americans, and more common among gay, lesbian, and bisexual Americans than among many other groups (Harris Poll 2016). Overall, about 23 percent of all Americans between 18 and 50 have at least one tattoo, more than double the prevalence in 1985—making tattoos slightly more common in the United States than DVD players (Rian 2008; Pew Research Center 2010). Sociologists have studied people with tattoos (women especially) as a way of learning more about **social stigma** and a process sociologists refer to as **gender policing**.

Tattoos are seen as a way people can design and project a desired self-image (Atkinson 2003). In cultures becoming increasingly image-oriented, tattooing is conscious **identity work**. Tattoo design and placement are often sexually charged; more than a third of tattoo wearers say it makes them feel more rebellious, and almost a third say it makes them sexier. (On the other hand, almost 4 in 10 non-tattoo wearers think it makes other people less sexy.) Although this mystique may attract people to

social stigma
Disapproval or discontent with a person or group that differs from cultural norms, which often serves to distinguish that person or group from other members of a society.

gender policing
The enforcement of normative gender ideals by rewarding normative gender performances and punishing transgressions.

identity work
The concern with and performance of physical, symbolic, verbal, and behavioral self-representations designed to be taken as part of one's identity.

SOCIOLOGY AND OUR WORLD

HOW WOMEN WITH INK ILLUSTRATE GENDER POLICING

What do the experiences of women with tattoos tell us about all women's experiences of body surveillance and gender inequality?

In the research she conducted for her book, *Covered in Ink: Women, Tattoos, and the Politics of the Body* (2015), sociologist Beverly Yuen Thompson started with a simple premise—is it different for women to collect tattoos than men? Tattoos have become increasingly popular and "mainstream." But being *heavily* tattooed still has, so Thompson suggested, an aura of masculinity. In her interviews with heavily tattooed women, she found a pattern of comments they all claimed to systematically confront, often from men. It wasn't uncommon for her to hear women say they'd heard comments from men like, "You're such a pretty girl; why would you do something like *that* to your body?" Her interviewees took from this that they were being told, first, that their tattoos made their bodies ugly, and second, that women's bodies *should* be pretty.

So, these women's experiences are a profound statement about gender policing more generally, particularly how it applies to women's bodies. Most of the women agreed that although tattooing has become more

This tattoo enthusiast poses for photo at Hong Kong International Tattoo Convention in 2015. Today, about half of young people with tattoos only have one, and only one in five has more than six tattoos. But are certain tattoos more "masculine"?

popular, normative tattoos for women are small, cute, and easily concealed. Thompson studied women who violated this gendered inking mandate and writes about the negative social sanctions associated with this transgression in her book. Many reported that strangers approached them and touched them without permission; many reported being worried that they would lose their job were they unable to conceal them at work properly. Many reported negative reactions from parents and grandparents, and it wasn't uncommon for Thompson to hear women coming into the parlor to get tattoos after breaking up with men who did not want them to alter their bodies.

As these experiences all attest, women face significant social stigma, shame, and all manner of social sanctions for transgressing gendered beliefs about tattoos and tattooing. Thompson also shares some of her findings in a documentary film, *Covered*, which you can access online at Vimeo: https://vimeo.com/94019352.

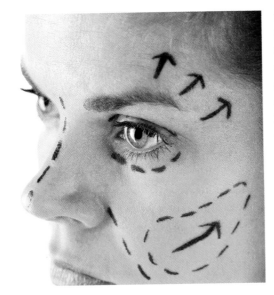

Cosmetic surgery is a growing industry and while nonsurgical procedures vastly outnumber surgical procedures, both have become much more common in the United States over the past 20 years.

tattoos, it turns out that tattooing and piercing are also associated with other deviant behaviors—marijuana or other drug use, arrest, or even cheating on a college exam or binge drinking—though, only when the wearer has a lot of body art: those with four or more tattoos and seven or more piercings (Koch, et al. 2010). This might be why 70 percent of Millennials with tattoos say that their tattoos are able to be easily hidden by clothing (Pew Research Center 2010). More conventionally, the motivation for middle-class people to "get inked" today has a lot to do with social groups. Tattoos are increasingly seen to symbolize traits valued by peers, including environmental awareness, athletic ability, artistic talent, and academic achievement (Harris Poll 2016; Irwin 2001). Of course, gangs and other marginalized groups also continue to use tattoos as specific markers of identity.

Another form of bodily transformation—indeed, one of the fastest-growing means—is cosmetic surgery. According to the American Society of Plastic Surgeons, the total number of cosmetic procedures increased more than 500 percent since 1997, to 13.6 million procedures and more than $15 billion spent on those procedures in 2016 alone (American Society for Aesthetic Plastic Surgery 2016). Reality television shows like *Extreme Makeover* make cosmetic surgery increasingly normal; one survey found these shows influenced about 80 percent of cosmetic surgery patients (Singer 2007). Though women continue to be the primary consumers of such cosmetic surgery at 91 percent, men have gone from 54,845 in 1992 to roughly 2.8 million in 2016 and now comprise 9.3 percent of all surgical procedures. Teenagers are also having more plastic surgery, especially liposuctions, breast augmentations, tummy tucks, eyelid surgeries, and rhinoplasties ("nose jobs"). In 2016, the most common surgical procedure for those 18 and younger was ear surgery, and breast augmentation for those ages 19–34 (American Society of Aesthetic Plastic Surgery 2016). (Though things like Botox far outnumber these more invasive types of surgeries.)

Once the preserve of wealthy whites, cosmetic surgery has become increasingly common among non-whites and the middle class. The number of people of color seeking cosmetic surgery tops three million a year, four times what it was 10 years ago. Today, white people account for just about three-quarters of all cosmetic surgeries in the United States. The remainder are made up of Hispanic (9.7%), African American (7.3%), Asian (5.5%) and other races (2.1%) (American Society of Plastic Surgeons 2016). Historically, cosmetic surgery was performed to "minimize" those ethnic characteristics that stood out—"Jewish noses" or "Irish ears," for example—to better assimilate into American society. Today, such assimilationist impulses ("Asian eyelids" or "Iranian noses," for example) are accompanied by procedures that exaggerate ethnic differences, such as buttock lifts among Dominican women who want to accentuate "Latin curves" (Dolnick 2011).

And it is not just the United States that is witnessing accelerated growth in cosmetic procedures. Europe accounts for more than one-third of all cosmetic procedures performed worldwide, second only to the Americas. The popularity of different procedures, however, does vary by country. For instance, in 2014 the United States and Brazil accounted for more than one-third of all cosmetic procedures performed on breasts in the entire world (21% and 14%, respectively). And, although South Korea's population is less than 20 percent of the U.S. population, their rate of cosmetic procedures on faces and heads was only 77 percent of the U.S. rate in 2014 (ISAPS 2015).

- In Japan, South Korea, Singapore, Colombia, Russia, and Romania, eyelid surgery is the most common operation.
- In Brazil, Argentina, and Germany, liposuction is the most popular.
- In Spain, Italy, Great Britain, Sweden, Norway, and Slovenia, breast augmentation is the top procedure performed.
- In Jordon, Lebanon, Cyprus, Turkey, Taiwan, and France, nose reshaping tops the list.

Why eyelid surgery across Asia? Why nose work in the Middle East? Perhaps we are seeing an emerging global standard of beauty as a result of globalization. Not only are people living and working in more multinational settings, but also Western images long exported worldwide by magazines, movies, and television have been accelerated in recent years by the addition of satellite TV, the Internet, and more. Like globalization in other arenas, some influence goes both ways, and global beauty standards are interpreted locally as well, but the dominant tendency has been for beauty standards to trend from West to East (Gimlin 2002; Guterl and Hastings 2003). As we learned previously in this chapter, standards of beauty have long been associated with power differences within societies; international trends related to cosmetic surgery indicate that this is no less the case when describing differences between societies.

Gender and Body Dissatisfaction

11.1.4 Explain the ways that gender inequality is expressed through gendered forms of body dissatisfaction.

In 1954, Miss America was 5'8" and weighed 132 pounds. Today, the average Miss America contestant still stands 5'8", but now she weighs just 117 pounds. In 1975, the average female fashion model weighed about 8 percent less than the average American woman; by 1990 that disparity had grown to 23 percent. And though the average American woman today is 5'4" tall and weighs 167 pounds, with a waist circumference of 37 inches, the average model is 5'11" and weighs 117 pounds. (Men's average height is 5 feet 9 ½ inches, with a 39.7-inch waist and weighs 195 pounds.) No wonder 42 percent of girls in first through third grades say they want to be thinner, and 81 percent of 10-year-olds are afraid of being fat. Almost half of 9- to 11-year-olds are on diets; by college the percentage has nearly doubled (National Center for Health Statistics 2016; Gimlin 2002; Robbins 2008).

Many girls are preoccupied with their **body image**. And young women are particularly concerned with their weight. Research on adolescents suggests that a large majority consciously trade health concerns in their efforts to lose weight. As a result, increasing numbers of young women are diagnosed with either anorexia nervosa or bulimia every year. Anorexia nervosa involves chronic and dangerous starvation dieting and obsessive exercise; bulimia typically involves "binging and purging" (eating large quantities and then either vomiting or taking enemas to excrete them). These are serious problems, often requiring hospitalization, which can, if untreated, threaten a girl's life. To a sociologist, they represent only the farthest reaches of a continuum of preoccupation with the body that begins with such "normal" behaviors as compulsive exercise or dieting. This is why feminist scholar, Susan Bordo (1993 [1985]), suggested thinking about anorexia as "the crystallization of culture"—rather than considering it abnormal and evidence of psychopathology. Bordo sought to highlight some of the social and cultural forces that shape all girls' and women's understandings of their bodies.

Although rates of anorexia and bulimia are higher in the United States than in any other country—close to 4 percent of girls in the United States experience one or the other, more than 10 times the rate for European countries—rates among American girls vary by race or class (Eating Disorders Hope 2017; Fitzgibbon and Stolley 2000; U.S. Department of Health and Human Services 2006). This is not to say that boys and men are not also dissatisfied with their bodies. But they are more likely to struggle with different issues.

Although men have long been concerned about appearing strong, the emphasis on big muscles seems to increase as an obsession

body image
The subjective picture or mental image of one's own body.

Middle-class white girls are especially concerned about their weight (body image varies by race and class). And they learn to think about their bodies in this way at a young age. At one end of the continuum are fad diets and efforts to stay in shape. At the other end, however, lie more dangerous, and potentially lethal, eating disorders.

One way that Pope, et al. (2000) tried to measure shifts in the cultural pressure boys and men might confront to obtain more heavily muscled bodies came from an analysis of action figures over time.

Adonis complex

The belief that men must look like Greek gods, with perfect chins, thick hair, rippling muscles, and washboard abdominal muscles.

transgender

An umbrella term that describes a variety of people, behaviors, and groups whose identities depart from normative gender ideals of masculinity or femininity.

during periods when men are least likely to actually have to use their muscles in their work (Gagnon 1971; Glassner 1988). Today, successful men's magazines like *Men's Health* encourage men to see their bodies as women have been taught to see theirs—as ongoing works-in-progress. In part, this coincides with general concerns about health and fitness, and in part it is about looking young in a society that does not value aging (as we learned in Chapter 10). But more than that, it also seems to be about gender.

Many men experience what some researchers have labeled "muscle dysmorphia," a belief that one is too small, or insufficiently muscular. Harvard psychiatrist Harrison Pope and his colleagues call it the **Adonis complex**—the belief that men must look like Greek gods, with perfect chins, thick hair, rippling muscles, and washboard abdominal muscles (Pope, Phillips, and Olivardia 2000).

The standards for men, like those for women, are becoming increasingly impossible to achieve. If the 1974 GI Joe action figure had been 5'10" tall, he would have had, proportionally, a 31-inch waist, a 44-inch chest, and 12-inch biceps—strong and muscular but at least within the realm of the possible. If the 1999 GI Joe is still 5'10" tall, his waist has shrunk to 28 inches, his chest has expanded to 50 inches, and his biceps are now 22 inches—nearly the size of his waist! Such proportions are nearly impossible to obtain and illustrate shifts in body expectations for boys and men, too (Pope et al. 2000).

Changing Identity by Changing the Gendered Body: Embodying Transgender Identities

11.1.5 Understand how public reactions to transgender people are a powerful illustration of our collective investment in embodied understandings of gender.

Many people who modify their bodies—through surgery or ornamentation—do so to conform more readily to their culture's definitions of the healthy, young, or beautiful body. That means their efforts generally emphasize or exaggerate their biological sex characteristics (such as breast surgery for women or pectoral implants for men). But some people develop body modification techniques, ranging from ornamentation to surgery also, that are designed to minimize, or even eradicate, some bodily trait, because they feel that that bodily characteristic actually contradicts who they feel they really are. **Transgender** is an umbrella term that describes a variety of people, behaviors, and groups whose identities depart from normative gender ideals. Transgender individuals develop a gender identity that is different from the biological sex they were assigned at birth; they exist along a continuum from those who act in public as members of the sex other than the sex they were born, to those who chemically (hormone therapy) or surgically (sex confirmation surgeries) transform their bodies. Transgender does not, however, imply a sexual orientation; thus, transgender individuals can identify as heterosexual, homosexual, bisexual, or asexual.

Think of gender identity and behavior along a continuum from "our culture's definition of masculine" to "our culture's definition of feminine." Some people feel constrained by gender role expectations and seek to expand these by changing their behavior. Though there are significant penalties for boys who are effeminate ("sissies") and some, but fewer, penalties for girls who are "tomboys," many adult men and women continue to bend, if not break gender norms in their bodily presentation. Some may go as far as to use the props of the opposite sex to challenge gender stereotypes;

some people find erotic enjoyment in this, others do it to "pass" into a forbidden world. Again, this runs along a continuum: At one end are women who wear man-tailored clothing and power suits to work; at the other end are those men and women who wear full cross-gender regalia as a means of mockery and the pleasure of transgression.

Some people, though, feel that their biological sex doesn't match their internal sense of gender identity. Many transgender people feel trapped in a body they feel does not illustrate their identity. Although psychology has long collected transgender persons under the diagnosis "gender identity disorder," the most recent publication of the American Psychiatric Association's *Diagnostic and Statistical Manual* (DSM-V) replaced this term with "gender dysphoria." For a long time, transgender people have lobbied to have this changed as it presented all transgender people as mentally ill, as having a "disorder." Although still imposing a diagnosis, the new term illustrates some changes in cultural understandings of transgender identity and institutional attempts at transgender recognition.

Historically, transgender identities were quite rare; in 1980, only about 4,000 people in the world had undergone these surgical interventions (what were called "sex reassignment surgeries" and are now more respectfully referred to as "gender confirmation surgeries"), almost all of them biological males seeking to become women. New medical and surgical procedures facilitated both male-to-female and female-to-male transgender operations, and the inclusion of gender confirmation operations as procedures to be covered by Medicare (1978) and the listing of transsexualism in the DSM-III in 1980 allowed for insurance coverage for surgeries. The increased visibility of transgender people within the gay and lesbian movement has also increased the viability of surgical interventions as viable options for transgender people.

Despite these gains, transgender persons also struggle with diverse forms of discrimination and inequality. Although 18 states and about 200 municipalities protect transgender people from discrimination in employment or housing, there are no current federal laws that protect transgender people from such discrimination, let alone from harassment and assault. Transgender people experience significant discrimination in some predictable arenas; until 2014, they were not protected from being fired after their transition, but presently, they have no protection if their children are taken away and may struggle to retain spousal rights like medical decisions and legal power. They are disproportionately targeted for street harassment, hate mail, verbal threats, and assault. And when we examine this intersectionally, it also appears to be the case that black and non-white transgender women are among the most common victims of violence (Schilt and Westbrook 2009). Currently, there are 19 states (and the District of Columbia and Puerto Rico) that ban discrimination based on gender identity expression (three other states ban discrimination based on sexual orientation but not against transgendered people.) In October 2009, President Barack Obama passed The Matthew Shepard Act, which expands the 1969 U.S. federal hate-crime law to include crimes motivated by actual or perceived gender, sexual orientation, gender-identity, or disability.

Although transgender individuals are relatively rare (something we discussed in Chapter 9), the implications of gender confirmation surgery and of the forms of inequality from which they collectively suffer are enormous. Previously, a discrepancy between one's biological sex and what one experienced internally as one's gender would privilege the body, as if it contained some essential truth about the person. If such conflicts were to be resolved by therapeutic interventions, they would "help" the person accept their body's "truth" and try and adjust their feelings about their gender. Contemporary surgical techniques, technologies and therapies, however, enable us to dissolve what is experienced as an arbitrary privileging of the body at birth, and give

Transgender actress and activist, Laverne Cox, made a huge media splash starring in her role in *Orange Is the New Black*. Since then, Cox has been on talk shows and speaks at venues around the world about transgender rights and recognition. In 2014, Cox became the first transgender person even on the cover of *Time* magazine. Although this is a historical shift in the recognition of transgender people, whether transgender rights will keep pace remains to be seen.

more weight to who we feel we are. And yet, the forms of inequality that continue to plague transgender people belie an incredible investment in embodied understandings of gender that leave little room for transgression or challenge.

Obesity and Fatness

11.1.6 Explain why concerns about obesity are framed as about "health," but often have more to do with socially constructed body ideals and embodied forms of inequality.

In the United States, we're getting fatter. In 1990, 11.3 percent of Americans were obese; by 2008, it was 34 percent (obesity is measured as having a body mass index [BMI] of over 30 [Flegal, et al. 2010]). About one out of three Americans younger than age 19, and about two-thirds of all adults, qualify as overweight or obese (Hellmich 2006). About 6 percent of Americans are "morbidly obese," which is so fat that they qualify for radical surgery (Flegal, et al. 2010). If current trends continue, by 2030, most American adults—a projected 86 percent—will be overweight or obese (Liang, Caballero, and Kumanyika 2008). The U.S. military reports that more than a quarter of recruitment-age Americans are "too fat to fight" (Badger 2010).

Globally, obesity is a growing health problem, the mirror image of hunger and starvation. The World Health Organization reported that in 2014 1.9 million adults (18 years and older) were overweight (World Health Organization 2016). Beyond this, there are already as many over-nourished people as undernourished around the world (BBC 2008; Crister 2003; Newman 2004). Despite their connection, we think of starvation and obesity very differently. We have pity for the hungry and donate significantly to charities that minister to hunger. We have contempt for the obese and believe it is their fault, a moral failure of sorts, that they are fat.

Obesity is an important issue to examine sociologically. Like many social problems, obesity and fatness is often examined by looking at individuals rather than the social forces that impact individuals' lives, decisions, and well-being. Sociologists Abigail Saguy and Kjerstin Gruys (2010) conducted a content analysis of a decade of news reporting on eating disorders and obesity (between 1995 and 2005). One thing they discovered is that there were a lot more articles on fatness than on issues of eating disorders. The media paid more attention to obesity during the period they analyzed. But they also noted that that is a fairly recent phenomenon. As you can see from the figure, reporting on fatness has increased dramatically when compared with journalism on eating disorders.

Saguy and Gruys (2010) discovered that fatness was most often presented as an individual problem, a moral failing on the part of fat individuals. As one article in their sample read: "You can't pick your parents, but you can pick what you eat and how often you exercise." Obesity is most commonly framed in the media as a problem of lifestyle choice and a lack of individual effort and control (Boero 2007). Eating disorders, by contrast, were much more commonly framed as issues beyond an individuals' control—either resulting from psychological issues, a disease or disorder, or cultural forces and pressures to obtain certain bodily ideals (see FIGURE 11.1).

What research on fatness has discovered is that the so-called "obesity epidemic" is greatly exaggerated by changing ideas and ideals surrounding cultural beliefs in what bodies *should* look like. Obesity today is invoked as a **moral panic** that provokes media coverage and policy because it is assumed that social control is slipping away (Boero 2012). Although wealthy countries worry about obesity, poor countries worry about malnutrition and starvation. Developing countries, particularly those that are realizing economic gains as a result of globalization, are in between, seeing waistlines expand with economic development that includes urbanization, less exercise,

moral panic

The process of arousing social concern that the well-being of society is threatened by a particular issue.

Obesity has become a global problem. And although it is a larger issue in industrialized consumer societies, it is not limited to them. And when we think of fatness as an individual problem worthy of blame, a moral failure on the part of "lazy" individuals, we fail to appreciate just how social this problem actually is.

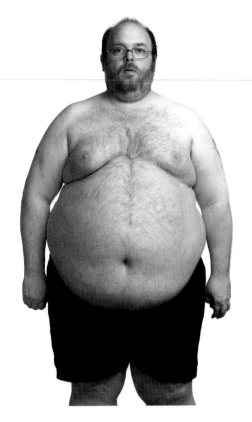

FIGURE 11.1 Number of News Articles Containing "Obesity," "Overweight," "Anorexia," and "Eating Disorder," 1950–2016

As you might notice here, the use of the terms *obesity* and *overweight* has become much more common in news articles when compared with articles including key terms often associated with reporting on eating disorders, like *eating disorder* and *anorexia*. This chart displays raw numbers of articles published in newspapers (including online sources), state and federal cases, and law reviews between 1950 and 2016. Here, you can see Saguy and Gruys' finding magnified. Their study examined this trend between 1995 and 2005 and you can see the emergence of the moral panic surrounding obesity on this graph. But look at how the trend they discovered has proceeded since 2005!

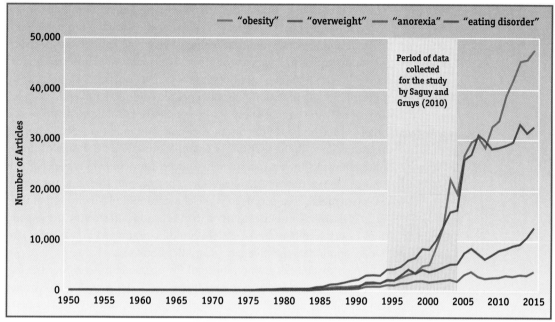

SOURCE: Data from LexisNexis.

and high-fat foods that are cheap, prepackaged, and readily available. Yet within the developed countries, the rich are significantly thinner than the poor. The wealthier you are, the more likely you are to eat well and exercise regularly; poorer people eat more convenience foods with high fats and suffer more weight-related illnesses, like diabetes.

In fact, there are a great deal of health-related concerns associated with thin bodies as well. And although we are often led to believe that fat bodies pose more health risks than thin bodies, research on the matter suggests that it depends what kinds of risks we are talking about. In fact, a **meta-analysis** of research studying the relationship between body mass index and the risk of premature death discovered that people categorized as "obese" or "overweight" are the *least* likely to die prematurely (Flegal, et al. 2013). So, if we defined "normal weight" by risk of premature death, then it might make more sense to produce reality shows helping people gain weight. Currently, "normal weight" is defined in ways that do not acknowledge body diversity and produces social and medical stigmas associated with fatness in the process.

meta-analysis

A quantitative analysis of several separate but similar experiments or studies conducted to test the pooled data for statistical significance.

The "Disabled" Body

11.1.7 Describe the ways bodily ability relates to social inequality and how disabilities intersect with other social identities (like race, class, and age).

According to the Americans with Disabilities Act of 1990 (ADA), a **disability** is "a physical or mental impairment that substantially limits one or more major life activities." A person is considered to have a disability if he or she: has difficulty performing certain functions (seeing, hearing, talking, walking, climbing stairs, and lifting and carrying), has difficulty performing activities of daily living, or has difficulty with certain social roles (doing school work for children, working at a job and around the house for adults). A person who is unable to perform one or more activities, who uses

disability

According to the Americans with Disabilities Act of 1990, disability is "a physical or mental impairment that substantially limits one or more major life activities."

Sarah Reinersten was the first woman leg amputee to compete in the Ironman World Competition in 2005 in Kona, Hawaii—in competition against able-bodied people. Born with a bone-growth disorder, Reinersten's leg was amputated when she was 7 years old. In 2005, she crossed the finish line of one of the most grueling endurance competitions on earth—the Ironman World Competition—in slightly more than 15 hours.

an assistive device to get around, or who needs assistance from another person to perform basic activities is considered to have a severe disability. By these definitions, nearly 20 percent of the all Americans have one or more disabilities (Brault 2012)

The number of Americans with a physical or mental disability has increased in recent years. This is because of several factors. First, advances in medical technologies means that many people who might not have survived with their disabilities are now living longer lives. In addition, those medical breakthroughs are enabling the survival of people born with disabilities that would earlier have been fatal. Third, life-expectancy continues to rise for everyone, and some disabilities, such as arthritis, are age related. Disabilities are not always visible, nor are they necessarily "disabilities" in that many disabled people could live full and "normal" lives if only the larger society would cooperate. Disabilities do not reside solely in the bodies of the disabled person, but rather emerge through a relationship with the society. For example, the standard design of streets and sidewalks makes it extremely difficult for people in wheelchairs or walkers to use the same sidewalks as other people. The standard design of buses means that people in wheelchairs cannot use them. Is that their fault? Disabilities are the result of an interaction between the person and the society. In other words, society could be organized in ways that better accommodate the diversity of abilities bodies have.

And disabilities do not affect all groups equally. Consider the fact that disability rates vary dramatically by age (see figure). Disability rates do not vary much among younger people. But, at mid-life, disability rates start to vary more dramatically. The change in disability rates between people ages 5–17 and people 18–64 is an increase of 5 percent. But the next age range (older than 65) is associated with an 25 percent increase in the disability rate (see FIGURE 11.2).

Most disabilities are not present at birth; they are the result of accidents, disease, and war. One powerful illustration of this is that, as of 2015, roughly 4.26 million veterans receive compensation for service-related disabilities. Some disabilities are the result of industry and pollution. The highest rates of disability by county in the United States are in coal mining regions; the highest rates in cities are in those cities near oil refineries. Globally, poorer countries have higher rates of disability, caused by malnutrition as well as accidents

FIGURE 11.2 Prevalence of Any and Severe Disabilities and Needs for Assistance by Age, 2015
The older people get, the more likely they are to suffer from a disability. Although around 5 in 100 children in the United States younger than the age of 17 have severe disabilities, more than 1 in 3 people older than 65 are living with disabilities.

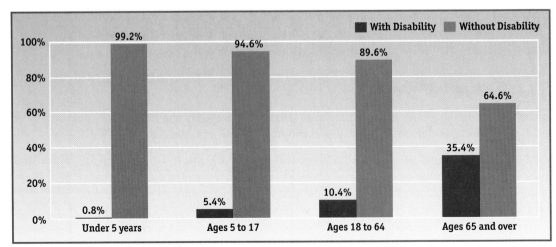

SOURCE: Data from Kraus, Lewis. (2017). 2016 Disability Statistics Annual Report. Durham, NH: University of New Hampshire. Available at https://disabilitycompendium.org/sites/default/files/user-uploads/2016_AnnualReport.pdf.

and disease. In Brazil, 18.9 percent of the population is disabled; in Ecuador, about 13.6 percent; in the Philippines, more than 28 percent (World Health Organization 2011). Across the developing world, approximately 1 of every 10 people are disabled, according to the World Health Organization and some of the most recent data we have available.

Disabilities are unevenly distributed by race and class within the United States as well. African Americans have significantly higher levels of disability than whites, but Asians and Latinos have lower rates than whites. The poor have more disabilities than the rich. Disabilities not only reflect existing social inequalities by race and class, but disabilities are, themselves, the basis for further discrimination. People with disabilities are employed at a fraction of the rate as people without disabilities. According to the World Health Survey which analyzes data from 51 separate countries (including the United States), the employment rate for men with disabilities is 52.8 percent and 19.6 percent for women with disabilities (compared to 64.9 percent and 29.9 percent, respectively, for men and women without disabilities). Similar findings were discovered in a survey for OECD nations who found that the employment rate for persons with disabilities across 27 countries was approximately 44 percent, compared to 75 percent among persons without disabilities (World Health Organization 2011). The Americans with Disabilities Act (1990) made it illegal to discriminate against people with disabilities in public accommodations. As a result, buses were adapted to accommodate people in wheelchairs, ramps replaced high curbs at street corners, and landlords built ramps to accommodate disabled tenants. "Black people fought for the right to ride in the front of the bus," said one disability activist. "We're fighting for the right to get on the bus" (cited in Shapiro 1993: 128.)

Many people find themselves feeling uncomfortable and even angry around people with disabilities, as if somehow the disability is contagious. But people with disabilities are increasingly integrated into society. In addition to their efforts to overcome discrimination, they actively participate in sports like wheelchair basketball tournaments, marathon races, and the Paralympics. One of Michael and Amy's family members is a good example. Diagnosed with rheumatoid arthritis at age 2, she came perilously close to death several times in early childhood. As a result of the medication she has taken for 25 years, several other systems failed, and she is now blind as well. She has had spinal fusion surgery twice to compensate for deteriorating discs and complete knee replacements in both knees. She also graduated near the top of her class in high school and majored in psychology at Princeton, where her books were read to her on tape or offered in Braille. Since then, she has sailed in regattas for the blind and won races in New Zealand and Newport, Rhode Island.

Embodied Inequality

11.1.8 Provide an example of what it means to say that inequality is embodied illustrating your understanding.

Discussing the bodies of transgender identities or bodies we think of as "disabled," or fat makes it clear that the body is not simply a canvas on which we write (or revise) our identities. It is also the basis for social inequality. In some cultures, bodies are marked— with tattoos or piercings—as symbols of inequality. Jews in Nazi concentration camps had numbers tattooed on their forearms—at least those who weren't murdered immediately upon arrival. Slaves have also historically been branded or tattooed. And across North Africa, young girls are subject to genital cutting which both marks their entry into their culture as women, and also makes them marriageable in a male-dominated culture. (In some cases, female genital mutilation, or FGM, removes the clitoris, rendering the woman more marriageable because she would, so the theory goes, be unable to pursue sexual pleasure on her own if she couldn't actually "enjoy" it.)

In most cases, it is the nonconforming, "deviant" body that is the object of discrimination. As we have already learned, fat people are frequently victims of discrimination, and targets of remarkable hostility and stigma. Obese children are 60 percent more likely

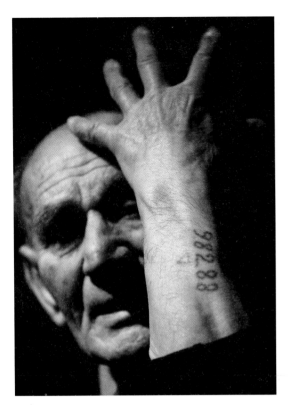

Leon Greenman survived time in six different Nazi concentration camps (including Auschwitz) during World War II. Here, he shows the prison number that Nazis tattooed on his arm at the Jewish Museum in London. Since 1946, he has recounted this experience at the museum where he conducts educational events.

reciprocal effects

A dynamic cause-and-effect relationship in which two or more social phenomena can be shown to be both cause and effect, for example, fatness and social class.

positive discrimination

The provision of special opportunities to those with certain characteristics than to those without them, typically to a disadvantaged group.

negative discrimination

The provision of less-favorable treatment to those with certain characteristics, typically to a disadvantaged group, than to those without them.

appearance-based discrimination

Prejudice or discrimination based on physical appearance and particularly physical appearance believed to fall short of societal notions of beauty.

to be bullied in primary school; simply "overweight" children are 13 percent more likely (Lumeng, et al. 2010). One study even discovered that 11 percent of couples in a survey said they would abort a fetus if it were predisposed toward obesity (Rhode 2010). They are the victims of special hostility, as if their weight were a moral failing, evidence of a lack of self-control. (Obesity is the result of the interplay of lifestyle and genetics, rarely entirely one or the other.) Consider the strong correlation between obesity and social class. This relationship is an important illustration of what social scientists refer to as **reciprocal effects**. For instance, it is both true that poor people are disproportionately likely to be fat and that fat people are disproportionately likely to be poor in the United States. That is, fatness can cause poverty (as fat people are discriminated against, which makes obtaining a job more challenging) and poverty can cause fatness (as poor people are much more likely to have to rely on less healthy food options to sustain themselves). Research shows that both of these relationships are true. It is an important illustration of why understanding intersections among different forms of inequality matters.

More generally, our embodied identities are also the basis for inequality and discrimination. Having lots of visible tattoos or piercings may be grounds for employment discrimination. A spokesperson for the Society for Human Resource Management explains that "people make decisions based on image" and, employers "can't afford to lose business because a guy has something [a tattoo design] crawling up his neck." Several major companies, such as Walmart, Bank of America, and Disney permit visible tattoos, as long as they are not deemed offensive on a case by case basis. On the other hand, some patrons of certain public places are being asked to cover their tattoos if employees deem them offensive or harmful to children (Baker 2010).

Historically, the disabled have faced diverse sources of discrimination—without protections from workplace or housing discrimination and constant threats of harassment, bullying, and assault. Since 1990, the Americans with Disabilities Act has protected people with disabilities from discrimination. This has led to dramatic changes in access, such as ramps on sidewalks and, if necessary, houses, and apartments, hotel accommodations, as well as prohibitions against discrimination in employment and public accommodation.

Even whether we are attractive or not can be the basis for discrimination and inequality—both positive and negative. Research has shown that beauty pays ... well, most of the time. In general, attractive people experience **positive discrimination**. Research reveals that people who are judged physically attractive by others are happier, healthier, and make more money. Conversely, the less attractive are, for instance, likely to receive longer prison sentences than physically attractive people put on trial. One recent longitudinal study found that looks and brains and personality are the best predictors of long-term financial gain (Judge, Hurst and Simon 2009).

On the other hand, being beautiful can also lead to **negative discrimination** as well. In one recent experiment, men and women students imagined themselves as job recruiters and were asked to evaluate candidates, whose resumes and photographs they reviewed. The highly attractive recruiters showed no biases either way, but the average-looking women recruiters were significantly more negative toward the attractive women candidates (though more positive toward attractive men candidates). The average looking men recruiters were slightly more negative toward attractive job candidates who were men (Agthe, Spörrle, and Maner 2010). Legislating this type of discrimination—**appearance-based discrimination**—is challenging because we also know that beauty is socially constructed. So, proving someone hired or fired you because of your appearance is more difficult than you might assume (Rhode 2010).

Bodies and embodiment are difficult to understand apart from considering the types of inequality different kinds of bodies confront. And as many of these examples illustrate, studying bodies and embodiment sociologically necessitates an understanding of health and well-being. Like so many valued resources, health and well-being too are not equally distributed throughout the population in most societies. We turn now to sociological research on health and well-being.

---

iSOC AND YOU Embodying Identities and Inequality

Our bodies *are* ourselves. Bodies are a significant element of *identity*. You can decorate it, shape it, and change it. How you look affects your *interactions* with others—the types of job you'll have, how much money you'll make, and myriad other things. Some bodies are preferred over others, leading to *inequalities* based on physical characteristics. Entire *institutions* have developed to help you transform or at least improve your body. And your embodied identity, and the inequalities that shape your body's movement in social space, *intersects* with other aspects of your identity, such as race or gender.

11.2 Understanding Health and Illness Sociologically

A major concern of sociologists has been to understand health and illness, from the personal experience of being sick to the institutional arrangements that societies develop to care for the sick, to the political issues that surround health care, such as health insurance and prescription drug coverage. The World Health Organization (WHO) defines "health" as a state of complete mental, physical, and social well-being, not simply the absence of disease. But when social scientists study health, they typically do so using a negative health standard; that is, we are healthy when we are *not sick*. Statistically, the presence of a fever, pain, or illness that interferes with our daily lives means we are not healthy. Anyone who has ever been sick can tell you that it transforms your daily lives.

But health is not only a biological issue; it is also a sociological issue. Consider that your age, race, gender, class, and sexuality all affect not only the likelihood that you are in good health, but also the kinds of health concerns with which you are likely to struggle during your lives. Simply put, health and illness vary; they vary by nationality, age, gender, race, and more. And health and illness are most completely understood within a sociological model. Although we often think about health and illness as objective states our bodies occupy, they are also identities we inhabit. For instance, fighting cancer is an incredibly challenging process, necessitating treatments that not only affect our bodies, but also our identities. Think of how those who survive cancer sometimes come to understand themselves as occupying a new identity—cancer survivor. We have events, fundraisers, support groups, and more that construct this identity and imbue it with status and meaning. And we learn about these new identities and roles through interactions.

Health and illness also meaningfully relate to social institutions. In fact, some forms of mental health "illnesses" or "disorders" can lead to "institutionalization." Social institutions play an important role in defining health and illness, and in structuring the social expectations associated with health and illness throughout society. Think, for instance about bringing a "sick note" to a teacher for missing class. This is one way institutions recognize and authorize illness. And finally, health and illness are also powerful sources of social inequality. When we examine each intersectionally,

In 2010, Debrahlee Lorenzana filed a lawsuit against her former employer, Citibank, claiming they fired her for being "too beautiful." Apparently, someone had actually looked at her Facebook page and thought she would distract male workers from doing their job.

it becomes clear that different groups in society struggle with very different health concerns—and these often exacerbate existing hierarchies in status and inequality.

Health and Inequality

11.2.1 Distinguish between epidemiology and social epidemiology.

epidemiology

The study of the causes and distribution of disease and disability.

social epidemiology

The study of both biomedical elements of disease and the social and behavioral factors that influence its spread.

mortality rate

The death rate as a percentage of the population.

morbidity rate

The rates of new infections from disease.

disease incidence

How many new cases of a disease are reported in a given place during a specified time frame.

disease prevalence

The distribution of the disease over different groups of the same population.

Health and illness are among the most profoundly social experiences we have. For one thing, not everyone gets sick with the same illnesses in the same ways. Health and illness are not randomly distributed around the world, in the United States, or even within individual communities. They vary enormously by nationality, race, gender, and age. The study of the causes and distribution of disease and disability is called **epidemiology**. This includes all the biomedical elements of disease and also social and behavioral factors that influence the spread of disease. The focus on these social and behavioral factors is called **social epidemiology**.

All health researchers begin with baseline indicators, such as the **mortality rate**, which is the death rate as a percentage of the population, and the **morbidity rate**, which indicates the rates of new infections from disease. Epidemiologists then attempt to understand the **disease incidence**—that is, how many new cases of a disease are reported in a given place during a specified time frame—and the **disease prevalence**, which usually refers to the distribution of the disease over different groups of the same population. For example, when a new disease like SARS is discovered, or a new epidemic of the flu breaks out, epidemiologists will try and track the spread of the disease and will try and observe its effect on different groups (race, age, region) to assess the risks of different groups and even suggest policies that may inform the sorts of precautions people might take. Measures of health care include:

- *Life Expectancy*: an estimate of the average life span of people born in a specific year.
- *Infant Mortality Rate*: the number of deaths of infants younger than 1 year of age per 1,000 live births in a given year.
- *Maternal Mortality Rate*: the number of deaths of pregnant or new mothers either before, during, or immediately following childbirth, per 1,000 births in a given year.
- *Chronic Diseases*: long-term or lifelong diseases that develop gradually or are present at birth (rates are calculated as proportion to the population * per 1,000, 100,000, or 1 million).
- *Acute Diseases*: diseases that strike suddenly and may cause severe illness, incapacitation, or even death.
- *Infectious Diseases*: diseases that are caused by infectious agents such as viruses or bacteria.

Often, outbreaks of different diseases are also associated with patterned social responses, which is why the Center for Disease Control and Prevention has to carefully plan out not only protecting the population from disease, but also managing the ways in which information about the disease and how it is spread, measure to consider for protection, as well as particularly vulnerable populations is shared with the public. Consider the moral panic incited in 2014 by the presence of cases of the Ebola virus in the United States—a deadly virus that kills approximately half of all people who contract it. In September 2014, a man traveled from Liberia to Dallas, Texas. He did not display symptoms when leaving Liberia, but he started to develop them 4 days after arriving in the United States. He died from the disease on October 8, 2014. Throughout October, two more cases of Ebola were discovered in people who had provided care for the initial patient. Additionally, a separate case was diagnosed in New York City in a medical aid worker who had been participating in Doctors Without Borders in Guinea. And there was a flurry of media attention surrounding these events.

Following these much-publicized cases, other forms of inequality began to emerge as well, prompting what some began referring to as "Ebola racism." As one Liberian man from Monrovia put it, "People, once they know you are Liberian—people assume you have the virus in your body" (Brown and Constable 2014). Many suggested that the panic associated with the disease exacerbated existing forms of social inequality based on race, nationality, immigrant status, and more. Indeed, social scientists conducting an extensive review of the research on stigma and discrimination related to Ebola discovered that attitudes toward Ebola in recent history were strikingly similar to initial perceptions of persons with HIV/AIDS; there was a great deal of misinformation, misperceptions about causes, indicators of who might be ill, and more (Davtyan, et al. 2014). It was a powerful illustration of the ways in which diagnoses associated with health and illness are not only made by medical practitioners. Social diagnoses can be equally powerful in terms of shaping identities and interactions.

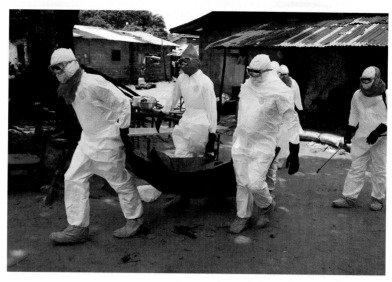

The Liberian health department removes the body of a woman suspected of dying of the Ebola virus from her home in August 2014 in Monrovia, Liberia. Teams collected bodies from all over, where the Ebola epidemic killed more than 1,000 people in four West African countries during 2014.

Thinking Intersectionally about Health Inequality

11.2.2 Explain what it means to study health inequality intersectionally.

Not everyone has equal access to good health and well-being. Different groups in society are more and less likely to live greater portions of their lives in good health. A simple way of thinking about this is that inequality has health outcomes, and those outcomes shift over the course of our lives. Our health changes as we age. Not only does our general health decline, but also our susceptibility to various illnesses shifts. For example, men ages 25 to 44 are twice as likely to die of HIV or unintentional injury as they are to die of heart disease or cancer. But, by ages 45 to 64, heart disease and cancer are about 20 times more likely to be the cause of death than either HIV or unintended injury.

In the United States and throughout the world, the wealthier you are, the healthier you are. People in more developed countries live longer and healthier lives, and in every country, the wealthy live longer and healthier lives. Of course, wealthy people are not immune to illness simply because they are wealthy. But they have better nutrition, better access to better quality health care, and better standards of living—and these all lead to healthier lives. And just as being wealthy is a good predictor of being healthy, so too is being poor a good predictor of being ill. Lower class people work in more dangerous and hazardous jobs, with fewer health insurance benefits, and often live in neighborhoods or in housing that endangers health (peeling lead-based paint, exposed and leaky pipes which attract disease-bearing rodents or insects, unsanitary water and food supplies, for example). Stated most simply, inequality kills. And sometimes, this is simply the result of nutritious food being in short supply (see MAP 11.1).

Poor urban blacks have the worst health of any ethnic group in the United States, with the possible exception of American Indians. One third of all poor black 16-year old girls in urban areas will not reach their 65th birthdays. High rates of heart disease, cancer, and cirrhosis of the liver make African American men in Harlem less likely to reach age 65 than men in Bangladesh (Epstein 2003). Latinos die of several leading causes of death at far higher rates than do whites, including liver disease, diabetes, and HIV. Racism itself is harmful to health: The stress brought about by discrimination and inequality may contribute to the higher rates of stress-related diseases and hypertension, and mental illness (Waitzkin 1986; Brown 2003; Jackson and Stewart 2003). Although research suggests some medicines may be more or less effective depending on the patient's race, poverty explains far greater health disparities (Braveman, et al. 2011).

Not only do class, race, and age affect health and illness, but so, too does gender. Before the twentieth century, women's life expectancy was slightly lower than men's,

MAP 11.1 Food Scarcity in the United States, 2015

This map illustrates where you can find what some scholars refer to as "food deserts" in the United States—areas in which a substantial share of residents are low income and have limited access to a supermarket or large grocery store. In these locations, it is difficult to obtain affordable, good-quality fresh food. To map this, the U.S. Department of Agriculture relies on data from the Census, showing where there are significant proportions of low-income residents who are 1 mile or more away from a supermarket in urban areas and at least 10 miles from a supermarket in rural areas.

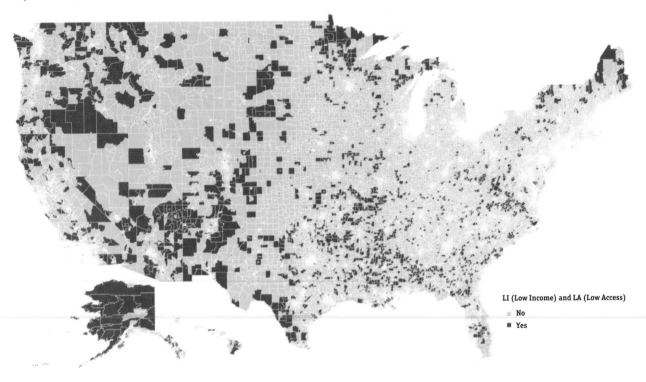

LI (Low Income) and LA (Low Access)

▪ No

▪ Yes

SOURCE: Data from U.S. Department of Agriculture (USDA), Economic Research Service, 2015. Available at http://www.ers.usda.gov/data-products/food-access-research-atlas/go-to-the-atlas.aspx#.UUDJLTeyL28.

largely as a result of higher mortality rates during pregnancy and childbirth. Through the twentieth century, though, women have been increasingly outliving men, so that today American women's life expectancy is 80 years, and men's is 78 years. In the highly developed countries, women outlive men by about 5 to 8 years, but they outlive men by less than 3 years in the developing world. In general life expectancy for both women and men has been increasing at a rate of 2.5 years per decade—with no end in sight. But why do women in the advanced countries outlive men now? For one thing, improvements in prenatal and maternal health care during pregnancy and childbirth save many lives. But another reason may be the gender of health. Norms of masculinity often encourage men to take more health risks and then to discourage them from seeking healthcare services until after an illness has progressed. As health researcher Will Courtenay put it:

> "A man who does gender correctly would be relatively unconcerned about his health and well-being in general. He would see himself as stronger, both physically and emotionally than most women. He would think of himself as independent, not needing to be nurtured by others. He would be unlikely to ask others for help…. He would face danger fearlessly, take risks frequently, and have little concern for his own safety" (Courtenay 1998, p. 21).

Or, as one Zimbabwean man put it, "real men don't get sick" (in Foreman 1999 p. 22). In FIGURE 11.3, you can see the ratio of male to female age-adjusted death rates for the 10 leading causes of death for the total population in the United States in the year 2013, by race.

Note that most of the causes of death with the highest differential by sex are those most closely associated with gendered behavior, not biological sex: accidents, suicide,

FIGURE 11.3 Leading Causes of Death in the United States, by Sex and Race, 2013

Race, class, and gender intersect with one another to produce patterns in inequality that can be seen in data on leading causes of death. Look at how prevalent the leading causes of death are by race and gender in the United States. What disparities between groups to do you see? And what might account for them?

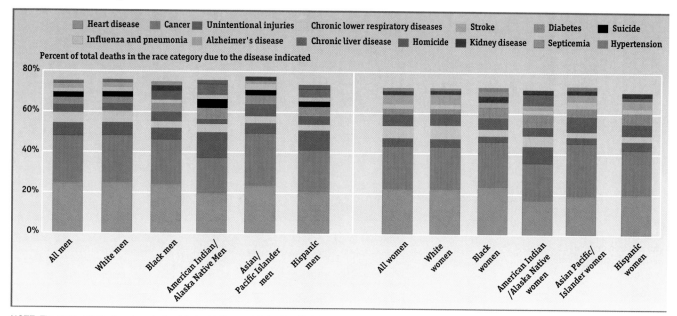

NOTE: The white, black, American Indian/Alaska Native, and Asian/Pacific Islander race groups include persons of Hispanic and non-Hispanic origin. Persons of Hispanic origin may be of any race.

SOURCE: Data from Centers for Disease Control and Prevention, 2013. Available at http://www.cdc.gov/men/lcod/2013/index.htm; http://www.cdc.gov/women/lcod/2013/index.htm.

chronic liver disease (drinking). Similarly, women are more likely to die of diseases that strike in old age (like Alzheimer's disease) because they are more likely to live long enough to acquire it. Similarly, the largest racial disparities here are associated with inequality rather than biological difference. Homicide ranks among the top-10 leading causes of death for black men, Hispanic men, and American Indian and Alaskan Native men, but not white or Asian men in the United States. These differences in leading causes of death by gender and race illustrate very different realities each of these groups experiences. They may live in the same society, but their experiences of and in that society are shaped by inequality in different ways.

Another reason for the disparities between women's and men's health has been the success of the women's health movement. Beginning in the 1970s with a critique of a male-dominated healthcare industry that seemed relatively uninterested in women's health issues, the women's health movement has brought increasing awareness to certain illnesses such as breast cancer that overwhelmingly affect women (a tiny number of men get breast cancer per year). In addition, the movement has also spurred new interest in women wresting control over pregnancy, labor, and childbirth from the medical establishment, sparking increased interest in natural childbirth, a wider variety of reproductive and neonatal healthcare options, and the breastfeeding of newborn babies.

The Global Distribution of Health and Illness

11.2.3 Understand how global inequality affects health and well-being around the world.

Globally, the problem of health and inequality is enormous (see MAP 11.2). The wealthier the country, the healthier its population. In the poorest countries, high rates of poverty also mean there are high rates of infectious diseases, malnutrition, and starvation. In the United States, for instance, roughly 6.5 children out of every 1,000 will not survive to age 5. In Finland the rate is almost one-third what it is in the United States at 2.3. In Haiti, roughly 69 out of every 1,000 children will die before their fifth birthday. And in Somalia, 136.8 children will die before they reach the age of 5. That's a rate of more than 1 out of every 10

MAP 11.2 Under-Five Mortality Rate Around the World, 2015

One measure of health and well-being in a society is the rate of mortality among the youngest people in the society (those 5 and younger). Societies with more resources have among the lowest rates of mortality among young people around the world, although those with less are less able to protect one of the most vulnerable populations from death—children.

Child Mortality Rate
(for children under age 5,
per 1,000 in the population)

- < 10
- 10–14.9
- 15–29.9
- 30–44.9
- 45–59.9
- 60–74.9
- 75.9–89.9
- 90–104.9
- 105–119.9
- > 120

SOURCE: Data from UNICEF. Monitoring the Situation of Children and Women. World Health Organization, World Bank Group, United Nations, 2015. Available at: http://data.unicef.org/child-mortality/under-five.html.

In the developing world, a major cause of death is infectious disease, a great number of which are transmitted by unclean water. And access to clean water is a challenge for many in the developing world. This Indian woman fills a container with clean drinking water from a government water supply tanker.

children—more than 20 times higher than the U.S. rate and almost 60 times higher than the rate in Finland (UNICEF 2015). And when we look at the actual numbers of children who will not live to the age of 5, more than one-half of those children can be accounted for by just five countries—India, Nigeria, Pakistan, the Democratic Republic of the Congo, and China.

The cause of death for most people in the developed world is chronic diseases—such as heart attacks, cancers, and others—more than one-half of all deaths in the developing world are the result of infectious diseases or complications during pregnancy and childbirth to either the mother or the baby. But even some wealthy countries do not manage to safeguard health for their citizens or take care of the ill or fragile in their populations. Despite the fact that the U.S. healthcare system is among the world's most advanced, the United States does not rank particularly high on many of the most basic health indicators. We rank 42nd in life expectancy, and 56th in infant mortality (CIA World Factbook 2016).

In fact, when comparing wealthy countries, there is considerable variation in the levels of health achieved. To look at the amount of money spent on health care, one would think the United States is the healthiest country in the industrialized world. Today, U.S. health expenditures equal $9024 per person per year while Japan spends just $4152 (in U.S. dollars). Australia spends $4177 (Peter G. Peterson Foundation 2016). Yet life expectancy in Japan is the highest in the most industrialized countries of the world and life expectancy in the United States is among the lowest of all these countries. Australia enjoys the sixth highest life expectancy of the top-10 countries (OECD 2015). Canada spends $4506 per capita, yet the average Canadian's life expectancy is also more than 2 years longer than the average American's (CIA World Factbook 2016). Moreover, on many measures of healthcare quality, the United States ranks at the bottom when compared with other developed countries, including Canada, Britain, and Australia.

Sickness and Stigma

11.2.4 Describe the ways that health and well-being as well as health inequality are also perpetuated interactionally.

Our experience of illness may be individual, but the way we understand our illness and the way we act is deeply socially patterned. In a still relevant formulation, sociologist Talcott Parsons described what he called the **sick role** to describe not how we "get" sick, but how we learn to "be" sick. Sickness, in other words, is not simply a disease or condition; it is a mode of interaction, a social role we learn to occupy and with which we learn to interact. According to Parsons, the individual is not responsible for being sick. Getting sick is not a moral failure; the origins of illness are seen as coming from outside the individual's control. As a result, the sick individual is entitled to certain privileges, including a withdrawal from normal responsibilities, and the expectation that others will exhibit compassion and sympathy, often in the form of care-taking behaviors. However, such rights and privileges of the ill are not indefinite; they are, according to Parsons, temporary. The sick person must actively make an effort to get better, by seeing a doctor, taking medication, and doing whatever therapies a medical expert prescribes (Parsons 1951).

Other sociologists refined the idea of the sick role. Eliot Friedson (1970), specified three different types of sick roles:

- The *conditional* sick role. This concerns individuals who suffer from an illness from which they will recover. This is the most typical sick role. As long as the sick person plays his or her part (tries to get better), then other aspects of the role (relief from work or family obligations, expectation of compassion) will follow.
- The *unconditionally legitimate* sick role. This concerns those people who have either long-term or incurable illnesses, such as certain forms of cancer, and who are unable to get better by their own behavior. They are therefore entitled to occupy the sick role for as long as they are ill with no moral disapproval.
- The *illegitimate* sick role. This may concern those people who do nothing to improve their situation, or people who are believed to be ill because of something they, themselves did. Those who suffer from sexually transmitted infections (STIs) may be seen by some as bringing the disease on themselves, and therefore are not entitled to play the sick role. Initially, those suffering from HIV/AIDS were seen by many as occupying an illegitimate sick role. But after three decades and serious political campaigning, most people now see those with HIV as occupying an unconditionally legitimate sick role.

The example of HIV also illustrates some limitations of this theory. What happens when the sick person believes he or she is legitimately ill, but others do not? What happens when those who don't think you are sick include your family, your boss, or your medical insurer? What happens when doctors and patients disagree? How do the general cultural values informing health care figure in? Can the sick role actually empower some patients to take on their doctors and treatment options? The sick role assumes that all members of a society agree, and obviously this is not always the case (Shilling 2002). Other sociologists use these possible conflicts among different people to examine the ways that illness operates within social life. For example, in modern

sick role

Talcott Parsons' coinage to describe how we learn to "be" sick; it is a social role we learn to occupy and with which we learn to interact.

society, people are living longer, and they are also living with chronic illnesses that would have killed people just a few years ago. How do people negotiate their social lives—work, family life, friendships, sexuality—in the face of such chronic illness? What effect does illness have on people's identity?

Sociologists Juliet Corbin and Anselm Strauss (1985) identified three types of "work" that individuals do to manage their illnesses within an overall context of identity management. *Illness work* consists of the things we do to manage the actual illness—the timing of medicine, treating pain, cycles of doctors and hospital appointments, and the like. *Everyday work* consists of what we do in the rest of our life—family life, friendship networks, routine household responsibilities, as well as our actual jobs. Finally, individuals also perform *biographical work* to interpret for themselves and others the impact the illness has had on their life. This latter form of work involves crafting an identity around our health and well-being. We revise and rewrite our identities constantly, especially in the light of new information such as a chronic illness.

Some illnesses leave a person doubly affected. Not only do people who have these illnesses suffer from the illness itself, but they also suffer from discrimination

SOCIOLOGY AND OUR WORLD

CRIMINALIZING SICKNESS?

Is being sick a crime?

Sociologists have long been interested in the ways that different categories of health and illness are produced, regulated, and subject to social control. Increasingly, sociologists are focusing on how sicknesses are controlled not only by medical authorities and institutions, but by legal authorities as well. This shows how stigma can become "institutionalized." Through this process, some sicknesses come to be "criminalized" such that people who suffer from

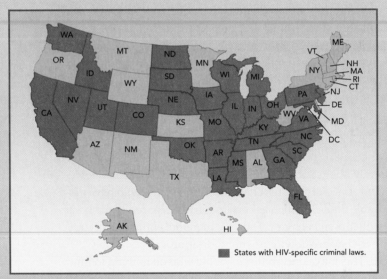

| States with HIV-specific criminal laws.

States with HIV-specific Criminal Statutes, 2015
SOURCE: Data from Centers for Disease Control and Prevention, 2015.

them can be punished by law for being sick. Sociologist Trevor Hoppe (2013) studies this process in relation to the criminalization of HIV. Although a great deal of political activism and education has endeavored to reduce the stigma associated with HIV diagnoses, Hoppe is interested in examining the ways in which stigma associated with HIV has become institutionalized in the form of HIV disclosure laws. Although these laws are advertised as being in the interest of public health, Hoppe shows how they are used to unfairly punish groups of people who are effectively criminalized for being sick. Consider the number of states with HIV-specific criminal laws on the books (see map).

Hoppe conducted a content analysis of the court proceedings of 58 cases in Michigan between 1992 and 2010 involving

a defendant who was being tried in violation of public disclosure laws surrounding HIV. Although controlling the spread of disease is important, Hoppe discovered that these laws serve a much more moral purpose of not simply socially stigmatizing individuals with HIV, but legally stigmatizing them as well. The legislation relied on stereotypes of HIV-carriers as dangerous, morally repugnant people whose disease meant that they were a

risk to public health. Few diseases have been criminalized in the way that HIV/AIDS has. It is one of the most stigmatizing illnesses someone can have. And legislation exists that both prevents discrimination against persons with HIV/AIDS (like workplace and housing discrimination, for instance) as well as other types of legislation that criminalize those with HIV/AIDS.

Indeed, in 1989, at the tail end of the AIDS epidemic, the Michigan House Legislative Analysis wrote, "Criminalization could actually foster the spread of HIV infection by driving it underground, impeding cooperation from infected individuals both in counseling and testing and in partner notification" (quoted from Hoppe 2013; see also Hoppe 2017). Yet, Michigan (and many other states) continues to try people for being sick.

because they have it. Those who suffer from mental illness, alcohol or drug addiction, physical or mental disabilities, or HIV also suffer from social stigma. People who have these types of illnesses struggle against social expectations and prejudices. Ironically, people who suffer from these illnesses constitute the majority of Americans.

The dominant trends in dealing with these stigmatized illnesses are de-institutionalization and medicalization. **De-institutionalization** means the re-integration of the sick back into society, instead of isolating them in separate places like mental institutions. Isolation was understood as further contributing to the illness; integration, it is believed, will facilitate recovery. Thus, for example, the number of children with learning disabilities who are "mainstreamed" in regular classes has expanded rapidly, and "Special Education" classes are now reserved for those with severe handicaps. **Medicalization** refers to the process by which *human* conditions come to be defined and treated as *medical* conditions such that they also become subject to medical study, diagnosis, and treatment (Conrad 1992). For example, childbirth, a perfectly natural, healthy process, has become "medicalized"; once managed by midwives or other lay personnel, pregnancy and childbirth are now managed by doctors, mainly in hospitals, and often involves equipment and drugs (and often maternity leave is characterized as a "disability"). Similarly, death is now seen as a medical moment, rather than the natural destiny of all living things.

Mental Illness

11.2.5 Summarize some of the forms of inequality from which the mentally ill suffer.

We once thought people who acted strange were deviant or weird, or perhaps evil and "possessed" by demons. Now we're more likely to think they have a treatable medical condition—a "mental illness." A **mental illness** refers to any impairment of thought, mood, or behavior that can be attributed to a psychiatric disease, disorder, or condition. Mental illnesses are among the least understood illnesses, precisely because the body seems to be "normal" and yet behavior and expression are often not at all normal. The causes of mental illness are as varied as the causes of bodily illnesses. In some cases, genetic factors before birth affect brain chemistry or neurological development; in other cases, mental illness can be caused by trauma (either physical or psychological), side effects of other diseases (AIDS-related dementia), chemical imbalances in the brain (schizophrenia), or even aging.

The definition of any illness is strongly affected by social construction. Since the 1960s, studies have found the ways odd or mentally ill people are perceived by the medical profession as well as the public depends a great deal on the label that is attached to their behavior (Scheff 1974). In fact, in one landmark study, Rosenhan (1973) found if we are told a person is "a mental patient" or "mentally ill," we may perceive their behavior as strange, no matter what they do. Those defined as mentally ill or even merely strange or neurotic are strongly stigmatized in our society. Studies of public attitudes consistently find that the public fears people with mental health problems (Martin, Pescosolido and Tuch 2000) and desires to be socially distant from them (Abrecht, Walker, and Levy 1982). Indeed, there is a persistent fear among Americans that the mentally ill are violent, criminal, and dangerous. Yet, research has consistently shown that the mentally ill are much more likely to be the victims of violence and crime than the perpetrators—so much so that the American Psychological Association repeatedly releases statements to that effect.

Since the 1960s, sociologists have encouraged mental health practitioners to reconsider the nature of mental illness. Many argued that the label "mental patient" or "mentally ill" had become too powerful, and that people were being kept in asylums who might be able to live in society if properly supervised. At the same time, new drugs were developed that were proving effective against a number of disorders. These factors resulted in the **de-institutionalization movement** of the 1970s: Patients

de-institutionalization

The re-integration of the sick back into society, instead of isolating them in separate places like mental institutions.

medicalization

The process by which *human* conditions comes to be defined and treated as *medical* conditions such that they also become subject to medical study, diagnosis, and treatment.

mental illness

Among the least understood illnesses, any impairment of thought, mood, or behavior that can be attributed to a psychiatric disease, disorder, or condition.

de-institutionalization movement

In the 1970s, advocates sought to relocate patients to "half-way" houses and community-based organizations to help reintegrate them into society, yet care alternatives were plagued by disorganization and under-financing, and many severely and persistently mentally ill people were left without essential services resulting in increasing numbers of mentally ill people on the streets or in prisons because there is no place else for them to go.

WHAT DO YOU THINK? WHAT DOES AMERICA THINK?

MacArthur Mental Health Module

Read the following vignettes and indicate whether you would be willing, unsure, or unwilling to move next door to this person, spend an evening socializing with them, make friends with them, work alongside them at your job, or be willing to have this person marry into your family. Sociologists sometimes rely on vignettes like these to assess how people might feel about or interpret a given social interaction, individual, or circumstance.

VIGNETTE 1:

Emily is a white woman, who has completed her Bachelor's degree. Up until a year ago, life was pretty okay for Emily. But then things started to change. She thought that people around her were making disapproving comments and talking behind her back. Emily was convinced that people were spying on her and that they could hear what she was thinking. Emily lost her drive to participate in her usual work and family activities and retreated to her home, eventually spending most of her day in her room. Emily became so preoccupied with what she was thinking that she skipped meals and stopped bathing regularly. At night, when everyone else was sleeping, she was walking back and forth in her room. Emily was hearing voices even though no one else was around. These voices told her what to do and what to think. She has been living this way for 6 months.

What do you think?

How would you feel about moving next door to Emily?
- ◯ I would be willing.
- ◯ I am unsure.
- ◯ I would be unwilling.

How would you feel about spending an evening socializing with Emily?
- ◯ I would be willing.
- ◯ I am unsure.
- ◯ I would be unwilling.

How would you feel about making friends with Emily?
- ◯ I would be willing.
- ◯ I am unsure.
- ◯ I would be unwilling.

How would you feel about working alongside Emily at your job?
- ◯ I would be willing.
- ◯ I am unsure.
- ◯ I would be unwilling.

How would you feel about Emily marrying into your family?
- ◯ I would be willing.
- ◯ I am unsure.
- ◯ I would be unwilling.

What does America think?

This vignette was written to describe someone with symptoms that might indicate they suffer from schizophrenia, a psychological condition that can produce these kinds of thoughts and actions. When a random, representative sample of Americans were presented with this vignette on the General Social Survey in 1996, 37 percent said that they would either "definitely" or "probably" be unwilling to move next door to Emily; 49 percent said they would be unwilling to spend an evening socializing with Emily; 34 percent stated they would be unwilling to be friends with Emily; 64.1 percent said they would be unwilling to work alongside Emily at their job; and 72.2 percent said that they would be unwilling to allow Emily to marry into their family.

You can consider how you answered the questions associated with the scenario and compare your answers with these results to consider your own biases and prejudices about people with mental health issues.

VIGNETTE 2:

Jeremiah is a black man, who has completed high school. For the last 2 weeks Jeremiah has been feeling really down. He wakes up in the morning with a flat, heavy feeling that sticks with him all day long. He isn't enjoying things the way he normally would. In fact, nothing seems to give him pleasure. Even when good things happen, they don't seem to make Jeremiah happy. He pushes on through his days, but it is really hard. The smallest tasks are difficult to accomplish. He finds it hard to concentrate on anything. He feels out of energy and out of steam. And even though Jeremiah feels tired, when night comes he can't get to sleep. Jeremiah feels pretty worthless, and very discouraged. Jeremiah's family has noticed that he hasn't been himself for about the last month, and that he has pulled away from them. Jeremiah just doesn't feel like talking.

What do you think?

How would you feel about moving next door to Jeremiah?
- ◯ I would be willing.
- ◯ I am unsure.
- ◯ I would be unwilling.

How would you feel about spending an evening socializing with Jeremiah?
- ◯ I would be willing.
- ◯ I am unsure.
- ◯ I would be unwilling.

How would you feel about making friends with Jeremiah?
- ◯ I would be willing.
- ◯ I am unsure.
- ◯ I would be unwilling.

How would you feel about working alongside Jeremiah at your job?
- ◯ I would be willing.
- ◯ I am unsure.
- ◯ I would be unwilling.

How would you feel about Jeremiah marrying into your family?   ○   I am unsure.
  ○   I would be willing.   ○   I would be unwilling.

What does America think?

This vignette was written to describe someone with symptoms that might indicate they suffer from a depressive disorder. When a random, representative sample of Americans were presented with this vignette on the General Social Survey in 1996, 22.9 percent said that they would either "definitely" or "probably" be unwilling to move next door to Jeremiah; 37.8 percent said they would be unwilling to spend an evening socializing with Jeremiah; 23.1 percent stated they would be unwilling to be friends with Jeremiah; 48.6 percent said they would be unwilling to work alongside Jeremiah at their job; and 60.6 percent said that they would be unwilling to allow Jeremiah to marry into their family.

You can consider how you answered the questions associated with the scenario and compare your answers with these results to consider your own biases and prejudices about people with mental health issues.

One thing you'll note is that different conditions prompted different reactions. So, Americans were less unwilling to interact with someone with a depressive disorder than with schizophrenia. But you might also note that the patterns in where they were unwilling to interact were similar. Americans were most opposed to working alongside people with mental health issues, allowing people with mental health issues to marry into their families, and to spend the evening socializing with people with mental health issues.

SOURCE: Data from General Social Survey, MacArthur Mental Health Module, 1996. Available at http://www.indiana.edu/~icmhsr/docs/Americans'%20 Views%20of%20Mental%20Health.pdf.

THINKING CRITICALLY ABOUT SURVEY DATA

In 1996, the MacArthur Mental Health Module included a selection of vignettes on the General Social Survey that sociologists could rely on to assess how people might feel about or interpret a given social interaction, individual, or circumstance with respect to perceptions and opinions about people with mental health issues. How do you explain the finding that Americans are more willing to "be friends" with someone with a mental health issue than to "spend an evening socializing" with them? And why are Americans less willing to work with people with mental health issues than they are to consider being friends with them or socializing with them?

were relocated to "half-way" houses and community-based organizations to help re-integrate them into society. By the 1990s, the number of patients in mental hospitals had decreased by 80 percent from what the number was 40 years earlier (Mechanic and Rochefort 1990). Yet care alternatives were plagued by disorganization and under-financing, and many severely and persistently mentally ill people were left without essential services (Mechanic and Rochefort 1990). One effect has been increasing numbers of mentally ill people on the streets or in prisons, because lack of treatment and supervision has abetted their committing a crime or because there is no place else for them to go (Kupers 1999).

At the same time as deinstitutionalization re-integrated the mentally ill into "normal" life, mental illness began to be redefined more biologically, and treated more medically, especially with drugs. Mental illness was "medicalized." Instead of people who have "problems," they are increasingly seen as patients with symptoms. Insurance companies and managed care require that most psychological problems be treated not with therapy or counseling but with prescription medication, which is significantly cheaper. Fewer people are being institutionalized, but there have been dramatic increases in the writing of prescriptions. Despite all of this, the mentally ill continue to suffer prejudice. Large numbers of Americans say they would ostracize people with mental health problems. A majority of Americans express an unwillingness to have people suffering from these problems as coworkers, largely because they fear the "disturbing behavior" more often directly observed by the public. Wealthier people have long been more likely to say they would avoid the mentally ill (and those with the least income are also among the most likely to suffer from mental health issues). But urban residents recently emerged as significantly more likely to do so than in the past. What's more, the label of "mental illness" only increases desires for social distance.

Understanding mental illness is increasingly important, not only because so many mentally ill people have been de-institutionalized, but because more than half of Americans will develop a mental illness at some point in their lives, according to a recent survey. In part, this is the result of ever-expanding definitions of mental illness, but it also indicates an increased awareness of the prevalence of mental illness (Carey 2005).

Health as a Social Institution

11.2.6 Explain what it means to say that health inequalities are also institutionalized, providing an example to illustrate your understanding.

A crucial sociological aspect of health and illness is the set of institutions that are concerned with health care. From medical professionals (and their respective professional organizations) to hospitals, medical insurance companies, and pharmaceutical companies—health care is big business. The combined spending on health care in the United States in 2015 was $3.2 trillion—17.5 percent of the Gross Domestic Product (National Center for Health Statistics 2017). This makes health care the second-largest industry after the military.

As we've seen, the United States has both the most advanced healthcare delivery system in the world and one of the most inequitable and expensive among industrial nations. The United States is the only industrialized nation that does not guarantee coverage for essential medical services, rations care by income, race, and health, and allows for-profit insurance companies to exclude people who need care. In the United States in 2014, the number of Americans without health coverage accounts for approximately 10.4 percent of the U.S. population (or 33 million people). But, within this group, non-Hispanic whites have the lowest uninsured rate (see FIGURE 11.4). More than 3,000 Americans lose their health insurance every day. As the great television journalist Walter Cronkite said, "America's healthcare system is neither healthy, caring, nor a system."

Many of the problems in the U.S. healthcare system derive from its scale and size. Health care is a massive enterprise, involving every American, every single

FIGURE 11.4 Percentage of U.S. Adults without Health Insurance
In 2016, whites had the lowest uninsured rate at 6.9 percent. Blacks (12.5%) had higher uninsured rates, and Hispanics had the highest of all in 2016 at 27.4 percent.

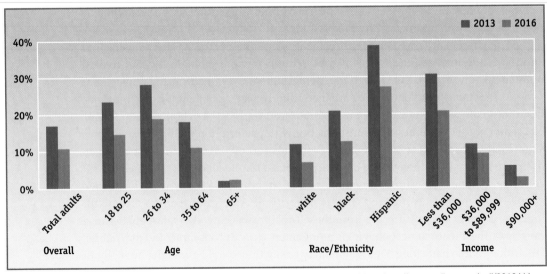

SOURCE: Data from Gallup-Healthways. Well-Being Index, January 9, 2017. Data available at http://www.gallup.com/poll/201641/uninsured-rate-holds-low-fourth-quarter.aspx).

government (state, local, federal) and a host of corporations and professions (doctors, hospitals, medical technology, drugs, insurance). This system is also the product of competing values. As we saw earlier, in Chapter 1, Americans hold two different types of values, and these often collide. On the one hand, we believe that "all men are created equal" and that "human life is sacred." These values would push us towards supporting policies that would make basic health care a basic human right, not a privilege of the rich or the employed. On the other hand, we believe hard work should be rewarded, individual initiative and entrepreneurship should be unimpeded, and government should neither control profits nor tax Americans to pay for the welfare of those most in need. These values would lead us to "rationing" health care to those who can best afford it.

We hold both sets of values, but tend to weigh them differently. In the abstract, we probably prefer to keep spending and taxation low, but our values change if we or a loved one is suddenly in urgent need of medical care. Then, we want "the best" treatment options available, regardless of the cost.

Institutionally, the healthcare industry reflects intersecting inequalities of race, ethnicity, and gender. Women and minorities are clustered in the more "service-oriented" areas, while white men are concentrated in the more technically demanding and prestigious occupations. The gender and racial distribution of healthcare professionals thus resembles all other professions, in which the closer you are to actually interacting with and touching the body of another person, the lower your status tends to be. On the other hand, the more technically proficient you are, and the more distant you are from actually being forced to interact with people the higher your status (see Abbott 1981).

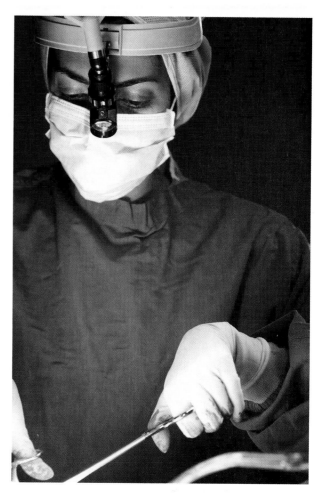

Although women are much more likely to go to medical school today than they were in recent history, some specialties still have few women. For instance, only about one in five surgeons in the United States are women, and surgery remains one of the highest status (and paying) specialties in medicine.

Part of racial or gender inequality in the health professions may seem like personal preferences because different groups of people might make different career choices. But it turns out that personal preferences are themselves shaped by institutional processes. For example, surgery is one of the most gender-skewed subfields of medicine, with far higher percentages of men than women. Personal choice about working hours, stressful conditions, and dedication to career? When sociologists asked medical students about possible careers in surgery, they found that the women and men were very similar. Before they undertook their surgical rotation, neither expressed much concern about the long workloads, or about the possible conflicts with family time; indeed, the women med students were *less* likely to cite those problems than were men. But after their rotation, the women were turned off by the "old boys' club" mentality, the sex discrimination by male surgeons, and the idea that a "surgical personality" had to be "masculine" (Nagourney 2006).

Such inequalities may actually be bad for your health. Patients are more likely to trust doctors who share their race or ethnicity—and trusting patients are more likely to follow medical advice and seek regular care. This may be especially true for minorities, who may distrust other doctors because of past discrimination and substandard care. Yet 86 percent of whites have white doctors, and only 60 percent of blacks and Hispanics do (LaVeist and Nuru-Jeter 2002). There aren't enough minority doctors to go around.

---

iSOC AND YOU Understanding Health and Illness Sociologically

Health is a profoundly individual experience, and also a profoundly social experience. More than 17 percent of the gross domestic product in the United States is devoted to health care, and Americans spent more than $3 trillion on health care—a far higher percentage than any other country. Being well or sick involves learning the norms of illness, a "sick role," which, over time, can become a part of your *identity*. Health and illness affect every aspect of your *interactions* with others. Access to health care, quality of care, and expense all correlate with *intersecting* social *inequalities*. Health care is a gigantic business, involving many different social *institutions*. The poor are sicker and receive less (and lower quality) care. One pundit commented that our current system "comforts the comfortable and afflicts the afflicted."

11.3 The Social Organization of Sexuality and Sexual Inequality

One of the ways we experience our bodies as distinctly private and personal is sexually. And yet few experiences are also more social. Once considered simply a biological "urge," social scientists now understand sexuality to be among the most important and complex components of identity—and one of the most hotly debated bases for inequality. Sexuality is interactional, it's institutionalized, and it intersects with just about every element of identity you can imagine.

Consider the following. At the 2017 Golden Globe Awards, Ryan Gosling, Ryan Reynolds, and Andrew Garfield were all in the running for Best Performance by an Actor in a Motion Picture. Gosling was announced as the winner and immediately, Reynolds and Garfield turned toward one another and locked lips as Gosling took the stage to make his speech. The moment went viral on social media because both Reynolds and Garfield were understood to be heterosexual. Some people thought it was "hot," others thought it might be an indication that their sexualities were perhaps different than they assumed. Later, interviewed on Stephen Colbert's late night show about the interaction, Garfield was pressed about his comfort kissing another man and kissed Stephen Colbert before discussing the event. Britney Spears and Madonna shared a similar kiss on stage, while the pop anthem that helped propel Katie Perry to international stardom was the hit, "I Kissed a Girl, and I Liked It." Most of these performers identify as heterosexual. So, what's going on? Sure, these are publicity stunts, attempts to grab our attention. But, what do they mean?

The sexual interaction that Garfield and Reynolds participated in publicly is something different from their sexual identities. And it grabbed headlines and our attention, because we like to think that sexual behavior and sexual identity match up neatly for everyone. But, sexuality, like so many aspects of social life, is just a lot more complicated than that. Sociologists know that our sexualities are socially organized. Everything from what we find sexual to who to how we imagine sexual interactions taking place is dramatically shaped by society, to a much greater extent than you may think. In this section, we will unpack these dynamics in detail and rely on the iSoc perspective to help us understand how sociology can help us better understand one of the most intimate aspects of the human experience: sex and sexuality.

Researching Sexuality

11.3.1 Understand the origins of research on sexuality in the social sciences.

Human beings are curious about sex, and we have been conducting "sex research" since the beginning of time. In the Middle Ages, adventurous aristocrats collected anecdotes about sexual activity for their personal gratification, and religious leaders collected them for a (presumably) more spiritual reason, using confessions about sexual activity as a window into immorality of all sorts (Foucault 1979). By the eighteenth century, sex was seen as draining the body of its energy, and any sexual behavior that was not procreative (especially masturbation) should be avoided entirely.

In the late nineteenth century, sex research was gradually taken over by scientists, who sought to observe sex without moral condemnation. After World War II, the center of sex research moved from Europe to the United States. At Indiana University, a zoologist named Alfred Kinsey (1884–1956) had been asked to teach a new course on Sexuality and Marriage. Realizing there was little reliable information, he set about gathering data on American sexual behavior.

Kinsey was determined to study sexual behavior, unclouded by morality. Eventually, he and his colleagues at the Institute for Sex Research collected sexual histories from 18,000 Americans. His books were for many years the definitive works on American sexual behavior (Kinsey, Pomeroy, and Martin 1948; Kinsey et al. 1953).

In order not to confuse behaviors with identities or ideology, Kinsey asked what sorts of "outlets" people used to have orgasms: masturbation, oral sex, anal sex, or coitus? With male or female partners? How often? Under what circumstances? Kinsey's results were surprising, and his books caused enormous controversy. What he exposed was a wide gulf between Americans' professed morality surrounding sexual behavior and their actual behaviors. Among his most shocking findings were:

1. The higher your socioeconomic class, the more sex you have. People at the time believed that the working-class was more sexually active and aware ("earthy"); but Kinsey found that the middle class had sex more often, and with a greater variety of techniques.
2. Women enjoy sex. The "common knowledge" of the era taught that women did not enjoy sex, and engaged in it only to please their husbands. However, women were as interested in sex as men, and most had orgasms (although primarily achieved through masturbation).
3. Extramarital affairs are not extremely rare. Kinsey discovered that 50 percent of married men and 26 percent of married women had at least one extramarital partner.

But by far the most controversial finding concerned same-sex behavior. In the 1950s, it had been assumed that homosexuality was a severe, and extremely rare, psychiatric disorder (indeed, the term *homosexual* was initially a psychiatric diagnosis and sexual "disorder"). Kinsey found a great deal of variation in practices, so much that he classified his respondents along a 7-point continuum, from 0 (exclusively heterosexual outlets) through 6 (exclusively same-sex outlets). Although only about 5 percent of the men in his sample were ranked at 6 (only same-sex experiences), less than half of the adult men in the sample (45 percent) ranked at 0 (exclusively heterosexual behavior). Among women, less than 3 percent were ranked at 6, and roughly two-thirds of the women in the sample (66 percent) ranked at 0.

It wasn't until the 1990s, however, that America got a definitive, scientific survey of sexual behavior. A team of researchers at the National Opinion Research Center (NORC) at the University of Chicago undertook the most comprehensive study of sexual behavior in American history (Laumann et al. 1994). Their findings were as controversial as Kinsey's, but in the opposite direction: Instead of huge amounts of nonprocreative sexual activity, they found much smaller amounts than Kinsey did. Only 25 percent of men and 10 percent of women reported having had an extramarital affair—less than half of Kinsey's percentages. The percentage of people with exclusive same-sex experiences was similar, about 5 percent of men and less than 3 percent of women, but the percentage with both same-sex *and* heterosexual experiences declined dramatically. It seemed that no one but gay men and lesbians were having same-sex experiences anymore.

Why such different findings? Is it possible that after all the changes in American culture since the 1950s—the birth control pill, the sexual revolution, feminism, gay liberation, the legalization of abortion—we had actually become *more* sexually conservative?

Not really. Kinsey did not draw a random sample of Americans to survey, as NORC did. He drew "convenience samples" of groups he believed he could persuade to take the survey. His respondents included a large number of college students, prisoners, psychiatric patients, and even his own personal friends. It is possible that they had more variety in their sexual experiences to begin with—something that may have made them more likely to agree to participate in his study in the first place.

Additionally, the historical context of the study may also have determined the behavior. Many of the men in his sample had been in the military during World War I and World War II, when visiting a prostitute was a common form of recreation for soldiers and sailors on leave. In the 1990s, a relatively small proportion of the men were veterans of any war. The same-sex behavior may have declined because with the rise of gay liberation, straight men in the 1990s might have been more sensitive to being labeled "gay" than their 1940s counterparts and if so, may have been less likely to engage in recreational sex with each other. In the same way, gay men were likely to "come out" at an early age, and not experience so much social pressure to sleep with women. So, paradoxically, sexual orientation and behavior were more closely aligned in the 1990s than they had been in the 1940s.

Americans had been shocked by the high rates of variant sexual behaviors reported by Kinsey; in the 1990s, they were equally shocked at the relatively low rates of variant sexual behaviors found by the NORC study. Critics of both studies believed that people would not tell the whole truth: Kinsey's critics believe they would omit instances of unconventional sexual behavior to make their life history sound more "normal," and the NORC study's critics suggest that they would invent instances of unconventional sexual behavior because they were afraid of being labeled "prudes" in an era of sexual liberation. But the NORC researchers built in elaborate statistical checks to catch people who were untruthful, and untruthful surveys were discarded from the analysis. It appears, after all, that Americans were much more sexually conservative than Kinsey discovered—the majority having their sexual experiences with committed partners "appropriate" to their age and sexual orientation.

What Is Sexuality?—The Social Ingredients of Sexuality

11.3.2 Distinguish between the three dimensions of sexuality, and explain why drawing this distinction helps sociologists explain how sexualities are socially constructed.

As you will recall from the gender chapter (Chapter 9), scientists draw a distinction between sex, referring to one's physiology (typically, but not always, male or female), and gender, which refers to the social and cultural meanings associated with being male, female, or something else. Sex is biological, standard across the human species, but gender is a social construction that differs from culture to culture and across time. And sociologists navigate similar questions when studying sexuality. This is challenging for many reasons, not the least of which is that sexuality *feels* instinctive—we all experience sexual urges and desires as residing inside our bodies.

When we discuss "**sex**" in the context of sexuality, we are not referring to one's biological sex but rather sexual behavior, or "sexual conduct"—the things people do from which they derive sexual meanings. Think of sex as whatever people do to

sex
A biological distinction; the chromosomal, chemical, and anatomical organization of males and females.

experience sexual pleasure. For sociologists, **sexuality** refers to three separate (but related) things: **sexual desire**, **sexual behavior**, and **sexual identity**. We experience sexual desires, we engage in sexual behaviors, and we identify ourselves with sexual identities. It is easy to assume that all of these elements of sexuality match up in the ways we might logically expect them to. But the sociologically interesting fact is that, for many people, they don't. This means that, for instance, measuring the size of the lesbian, gay, and bisexual population in the United States is more challenging than you might think (Savin-Williams 2006; Gates 2011). Which measure should we use: desire, behavior, or identity?

Not every society has conducted representative surveys asking people about their sexualities. But among those that have, there is limited evidence to suggest that there is a higher proportion of lesbian, gay, and bisexual people living in the United States than in many other societies. Yet, it is also true that estimates vary widely by survey. In considering how we might ask questions about sexuality on surveys, it is important to remember that the various dimensions of sexuality do not always match up as neatly as we might expect. This means that many people experience same-sex desires who never participate in any sexual behavior consistent with those desires. People also participate in sexual behavior that might seem to contradict their sexual identities. For instance, if someone identifies as *heterosexual*, but also has sex with someone who shares his or her gender identity or sex they might qualify as "same-sex oriented" in some degree as a result of their sexual behavior or desires, but not their sexual identity. Or, if someone identifies as lesbian, but has also been sexually intimate with men, then they have also participated in sexual behavior that we might consider to be inconsistent with their sexual identity.

Sociologist Jane Ward provides an interesting example with her research on populations of men who advertise in the "casual encounters" section of Craigslist—a website dedicated to classified advertisements for jobs, services, items wanted or for sale, and for personal advertisements as well. Ward (2008) collected advertisements from heterosexual-identifying men seeking sexual interactions with other heterosexual-identifying men. Her sample of advertisements was collected in California, and most of the advertisements were posted by white straight men seeking to be sexually intimate with other white straight men. Although some might question their sexual identities, Ward is interested in how these men make sense of their same-sex desires and their interest in participating in same-sex sexual behavior as consistent with a *heterosexual* identity. Ward discovered that by relying on specific cultural references and resources these men framed themselves as authentically heterosexual despite their interest in same-sex sex. This provides just one example of the multiple ways that sexual desires, behavior, and identities are often much more fluid than we might assume they would be.

Regardless of how we measure sexuality, both gender and sexual minorities are a population that is quite literally on the move. Between 2012 and 2016, the proportion of Americans who identified as lesbian, gay, bisexual, or transgender (LGBT) jumped from 3.5 percent to 4.1 percent of the U.S. population. That might not sound like a lot when listed in this way. But consider it in terms of actual numbers. That means that in those 5 years, the LGBT-identifying population in the United States went from around 8.3 million people to more than 10 million people (Gates 2017). That's a huge shift in a population in a really short period of time. And when a shift like this happens, sociologists want to know how and where it occurred. In this case, that means that we're interested in knowing which groups in society account for this shift. Was everyone more likely to identify as LGBT over this period of time, or was the shift exaggerated among some groups and absent among others. In this case, the changes really boil down to three: The increase can be accounted for by women, people of color, and those with a college education. Consider the three graphs in FIGURE 11.5 to see these shifts.

sexuality
An identity we construct that is often based on our sexual conduct and often intersects with other sources of identity, such as race, class, ethnicity, age, or gender.

sexual desire
Any intense sexual feelings associated with specific environmental, cultural, or biological stimuli.

sexual behavior
Any behavior that brings sexual pleasure or release (typically, but not always, involving sex organs).

sexual identity
Typically, it is understood to refer to an identity that is organized by the gender of the person (or persons) to whom we are sexually attracted. Also called "sexual orientation."

FIGURE 11.5 U.S. Adults Identifying as LGBT, 2012–2016

As you can see, the proportion of women identifying as LGBT increased at a much steeper rate than it did for men. The same is true of Asian and Hispanic people in the United States who identify as LGBT. And although we see an increase among all education groups, those with a college degree saw the largest increase. This is big news as it is a powerful illustration of how much can change in a relatively short period of time.

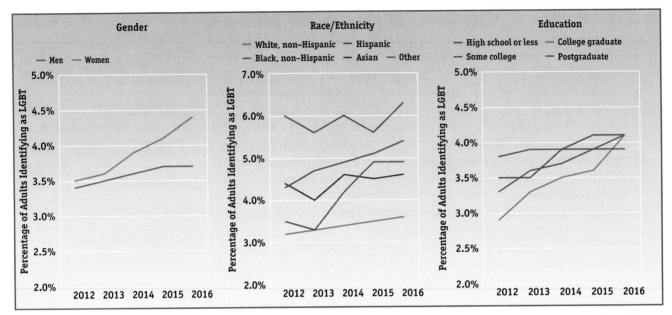

SOURCE: Data from Gates, Gary J. "In U.S., More Adults Identifying as LGBT," *Gallup*, January 11, 2017. Available at: http://www.gallup.com/poll/201731/lgbt-identification-rises.

Studying Sexual Interactions: Sexual Scripts

11.3.3 Define sexual scripts, and explain why understanding sexual scripts is among the most important components of sexual socialization.

Our identities may derive from the biological sex of the person whom we desire or with whom we have sex; that is, we may consider ourselves *heterosexual, homosexual, bisexual*.

Because sexual desire, sexual behavior, and sexual identity are so social, they are subject to values about their "correctness" and norms governing their enactment and even their expression. Some behaviors and identities are pronounced proper and others immoral or unnatural. There is therefore significant inequality based on sexual identity and sexual behavior. Sexual behavior is, in this sense, no different from all the other behaviors in our lives. We learn it from the people and institutions and ideas around us and assemble it into a coherent narrative that comes to be our sexuality and that shapes and gives meaning to our sexual interactions and identities as well.

Every culture develops **sexual scripts**, sets of ideas and practices that answer the basic questions about sex: With whom do you have sex? What do you do? What do you like? How often? Why? These scripts form the basic social blueprint for our sexual desires, behaviors, and identities (Gagnon and Simon 1967). Over the course of childhood and adolescence, even through adulthood, your understanding of your culture's sexual scripts begins to cohere into a preference. This is your **sexual socialization**.

There are four ways in which sexuality can be understood as socially constructed:

1. Sexuality varies enormously from one culture to the next.
2. Sexuality varies within any one culture over time.
3. Sexuality varies among different groups in society. Race, ethnicity, age, and religion—as well as gender—all construct your sexualities.
4. Sexual behavior changes over the course of your life. What you might find erotic as a teenager may not be a preview of your eventual sexual tendencies; sexual tastes develop, mature, and change over time.

sexual scripts

A cognitive map about how to have sex and with whom.

sexual socialization

The process by which your sexual scripts begin to cohere into a preference and sexual identity.

Sexual scripts are those cultural guidelines that help us understand what sexual interactions are and are not. Kissing is, in many cultures around the world, considered an act of sexual intimacy. But, we also have sexual scripts that govern kissing, which is why kissing is not *always* sexual. Parents kiss their children, friends sometimes kiss one another, siblings might kiss. Kissing others on the cheek and even lips is, in some cultures, a simple gesture intended to indicate that you are meaningfully (though not necessarily sexually) connected with someone. It's an interactional ritual associated with all sorts of relationships (similar to handshakes, slapping high five, or hugs).

Desires and Behaviors

11.3.4 Understand that what qualifies as "sexual" varies wildly by society.

Sexual behavior differs widely from culture to culture. Some practices, like oral–genital and genital–genital contact, occur everywhere, but others are extremely rare. Even within the same society, different groups have vastly different incidences of specific sexual activities. In the United States, for instance, sadomasochism or S&M (deriving sexual pleasure from inflicting or receiving pain), is much more popular among whites and Asian Americans than among African Americans. Like sexual desire, sexual behavior is monitored and policed by social institutions, which are constantly giving us explicit messages about what is "desirable" and what is "bad," "wrong," and "deviant."

In the contemporary United States, genital–genital contact is often presented as the most natural, normal, and fulfilling sexual behavior; other behaviors are often considered "not really sex" at all. Sexual behavior refers not only to what you do sexually but with whom you do it, how, how often, when, where, and so on. Sexual customs display a dizzying array that, taken together, imply that sexual behavior is anything but organized around reproduction alone. Where, when, how, and with whom we have sex vary enormously within cultures as well as from one culture to another.

For example, Ernestine Friedel, an anthropologist, observed dramatic differences in sexual customs between two neighboring tribes in New Guinea (1975). One, a highland tribe, believes that heterosexual intercourse makes men weaker and that women threaten men with their powerful sexuality. Many men who would otherwise be interested in women prefer to remain celibate rather than risk the contact. As a result, population remains relatively low, which this culture needs because they have no new land or resources to bring under cultivation.

Not far away, however, is a very different culture. Here, people enjoy sex and sex play. Men who have sex with women worry about whether their partners are sexually satisfied, and they get along relatively well. They have higher birth rates, which is manageable because they live in a relatively abundant and uncultivated region, where they can use all the hands they can get to farm their fields and defend themselves.

American sexual behavior looks something like this: Take the typical American couple, Mr. and Mrs. Statistical Average. They're white, middle-aged, heterosexual, and married. They have sex once or maybe twice a week, at night, in their bedroom, alone, with the lights off, in the "missionary position"—the woman on her back, facing the man who lies on top of her. The encounter—from the "do you want to?" to kissing, foreplay, and intercourse (always in that order) and finally to "Goodnight, sweetheart"—lasts about 15 minutes.

Now consider other cultures: Some cultures believe that having sex indoors would contaminate the food supply because they live in one large room; they only have sex outdoors. Some cultures have sex two or three times a night, others perhaps once a month—or less. Some cultures

Most scientists now agree that sexual identity is the result of the interaction of biological, cultural, and social influences. But one thing is clear: In industrialized countries, there is increased acceptance of all sexual identities. The founding charter of the European Union prohibits discrimination based on sexual identity.

practice almost no foreplay at all but proceed directly to intercourse in every sexual interaction; others prescribe several hours of touching and caressing, in which intercourse is a necessary but sad end to the proceedings. While for us, kissing is a virtually universal initiation of sexual contact—"first base," as it is often known—other cultures find it disgusting because of the possibility of exchanging saliva. "Putting your lips together?" say the Siriono of the Brazilian Amazon. "But that's where you put food!"

Among heterosexuals in our culture, men are supposed to be the sexual initiators, and women are supposed to be sexually resistant. How different are the Trobriand Islanders, where women are seen as sexually insatiable and take the initiative in heterosexual relations. Or a culture in Brazil where the women commit adultery, not men, but they justify it by saying that it was "only sex." The men in that culture secretly give the women anaphrodisiacs to reduce their sexual ardor. These are but a few examples. When questioned about them, people in these cultures give the same answers we would. "It's normal," they'll say. Sexual norms can take many forms, but none is more "natural" than any other.

Sexual behavior can occur between people of the same gender or different genders, alone or in groups. It can be motivated by love or lust, money or reproduction, anger, passion, stress, or boredom. For example, some cultures forbid same-sex behavior and endorse only sexual activity between men and women. Some cultures develop elaborate rituals to credit the behaviors the culture endorses and to discredit those of which it disapproves.

Same-sex activity is treated differently from culture to culture. In the 1940s, anthropologist Clyde Kluckhohn surveyed North American Indian tribes and found same-sex behavior accepted in 120 of them and forbidden in 54 (this is not to say that it did not occur; it was simply considered "bad" or "wrong") (Kluckhohn 1949). In the West, same-sex marriage has become legal only recently, but some traditional cultures (Lango in East Africa, Koniag in Alaska, and Tanala in Madagascar) have permitted it for thousands of years.

The Sexual Identity Binary

11.3.5 Understand that the notion of "having" a sexual identity is a historically recent idea.

Norms about sexual behavior govern not only our sexual conduct but also how we develop a *sexual identity*. Our sexual identities cohere around a preference—for a type of person or a specific behavior. These preferences are more flexible than we typically think. Take, for example, sadomasochism or S&M. Although this preference for specific behaviors is often understood as "deviant" sexual behavior, most Americans have experienced erotic stimulation of some kind from either inflicting or receiving pain (biting, scratching, slapping). Some percentage will find that they like that experience so much that they want to do it again, and a smaller percentage will actually incorporate it into their sexual script, as a preference. An even smaller percentage will find that they *really* like it, enough to make it a requirement of sexual conduct, and a tiny fraction will find that they can be aroused only through this behavior.

Typically, we understand sexual identity (or, sometimes, orientation) to refer to an identity that is organized by the gender of the person (or persons) to whom we are sexually attracted. If you are attracted to members of the opposite sex, you are presumed to be heterosexual; if you are attracted to members of your own sex, you are presumed to be gay or lesbian. If you are attracted to both, you are bisexual. For all these orientations, the organizing principle is how your gender contrasts with or complements the gender of your potential partners.

Worldwide, the most common sexual identity is **heterosexuality**, sexual behavior between people of different genders. *Hetero* comes from the Greek word meaning "different." In most societies, heterosexuality is considered "normal," which means that it is seen as occurring naturally. In most societies, heterosexuality is also "normative," meaning that those who do not conform to it are often seen as deviant and subject to sanction. Sociologists use

heterosexuality

The most common sexual identity worldwide, it is organized around sexual attraction between people of different sexes.

the term **heteronormativity** to refer to this duality—the ideology by which heterosexuality is simultaneously understood as both *normal* and *normative*. Although it is seen as normal, heterosexuality is learned within culture—it takes more work than you might realize to get an entire group of people to learn to think of one sexual identity as "normal."

Although our sexual behavior may have very little to do with the institution of marriage, we typically understand heterosexual behavior only in relation to marriage. As a result, surveys often list only three types of heterosexual sexual behavior: "pre-marital" (which takes place before marriage); "marital" (sex within the confines of a marriage); and "extramarital" (sex outside the confines of marriage). The wording is problematic as it assumes that all sexual activity takes place in relation to marriage. And although many people might think that all sexual activity *should* take place in relation to marriage, when sociologists are studying the world, we examine the world as it really is. Even if a college student, for example, doesn't even think about marriage when deciding whether or not to have heterosexual relations, it will be understood as fitting into one of those three categories. (To be more accurate, we use the term *nonmarital* instead of *premarital* elsewhere in this book.)

The term **homosexuality** refers to sexual desires or behaviors with members of one's own sex. This comes from the Greek word *homo*, which means "same." As we have seen, homosexuality has been documented in most cultures, but sometimes it is praised, and sometimes it is condemned or even presumed not to exist.

Whether you are gay or lesbian, heterosexual, or bisexual, sounds straightforward: Gay men and lesbians are attracted to members of the same sex, heterosexuals to the opposite sex, and bisexuals to both. But again, sexual orientation turns out to be far more complex. As we learned, many people who identify as heterosexual engage in same-sex practices, and many who identify as gay engage in heterosexual practices. Their identity is derived from the people and institutions around them and assembled into a coherent narrative and experiences that don't fit are left out: The lesbian who has sex with men may explain it as "trying to fit in" rather than evidence she is "really" bi-sexual, and the heterosexual man who enjoys same-sex activity may explain it as "fool-ing around," irrelevant to his heterosexual identity.

Most societies around the world and throughout time have gotten along fine without any sexual identities at all. There were desires and behaviors, but the very idea that one's desire or behavior was part of the foundation of one's sexual identity dates to the middle of the nine-teenth century, when the terms *heterosexual* and *homosexual* were first used as nouns (describing identities) rather than as adjectives (describ-ing behaviors). That distinction between behaviors and identities is cru-cial in some cultural prohibitions. In some cases, it is the identity that is understood as "problematic," not the behaviors—you can do pretty much what you want; just don't make it the basis of your identity. In other cases, it is the behaviors that are "troubling," not the identity. The Roman Catholic Church's official position on homosexuality—love the sinner, hate the sin—is an example of the latter.

SEXUAL IDENTITIES OUTSIDE THE BINARY: BISEXUALITY AND ASEXUALITY We're so used to the gay-straight dichotomy that we often believe that you have to be one or the other: gay/straight sounds as natural and normal as young/old, rich/poor, black/white. And like many dichotomies, thinking of sexuality only in terms of *gay* and *straight* leaves a lot of people out. Consider **bisexuality**—a sexual identity organized around attraction to both women and men.

First, bisexuality in not indiscriminate. Imagine a man who is at-tracted to men in some circumstances and women in others. Or maybe he falls in love with men, but feels a sexual attraction only toward women, or vice versa. Or maybe he has had sex only with women, but

heteronormativity
Sociological term to refer to the ideology by which heterosexuality is simultaneously understood as both *normal* and *normative*.

homosexuality
A sexual identity organized around sex-ual desire for members of one's own sex. In colloquial terms, homosexuals are often called "gay."

bisexuality
A sexual identity organized around attraction to both women and men.

Michael Sam, *People* Magazine, May 26, 2014. Sam was the first American football player to come out as gay before being drafted to the NFL. While no longer playing in the NFL, his story was held up by many as a powerful illustration that sexual diversity can be found everywhere.

FIGURE 11.6 Proportions of LGBT Persons by Relationship Type and the Importance of Sexual Orientation to Their Identity
Some data suggest that bisexuals are less attached to their sexual identities than are gay men and lesbian women. And data also show that people identifying as bisexual are most commonly in committed relationships with partners of the opposite sex.

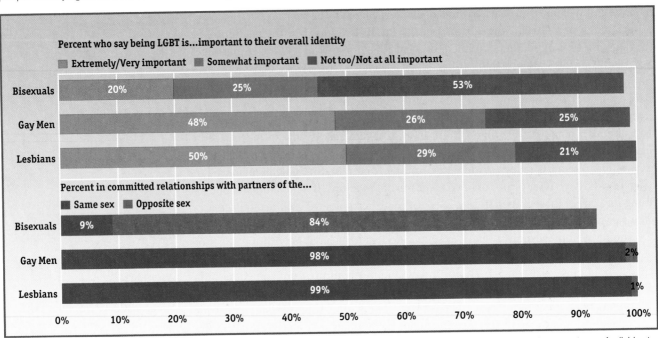

SOURCE: Data from Pew Research Center, February 20, 2015. "Among LBGT Americans, bisexuals stand out when it comes to identity, acceptance. Available at: http://www.pewresearch.org/fact-tank/2015/02/20/among-lgbt-americans-bisexuals-stand-out-when-it-comes-to-identity-acceptance/.

he wouldn't say no if Taylor Lautner or Michael B. Jordan called. The variety of experiences differs considerably. Second, few understand you. Tell a date that you are bisexual, and you may get weird looks, a lecherous request to "watch" sometime, or outright rejection. Your straight friends might believe that you are really straight but "confused," "just experimenting," or "going through a phase." Your gay friends believe that you're really gay but too frightened to admit it. Third, despite the jokes and the invisibility, you may also have a great deal of pride. Bisexuals often argue that they are more spiritual, or more psychologically developed, than gay or straight people because they look at a person's character and personality rather than at trivial details like gender. They may be exaggerating a bit: Most bisexuals are just as attracted to certain physical types, and not as attracted to others, just as gay and straight people are. They just include some men and women in the category of "people to whom I'm attracted" (see FIGURE 11.6).

Identifying as a bisexual requires a coming-out process, a realization that both your same-sex and opposite-sex relations "count." Few organizations exist specifically for bisexuals, and scholars have paid less attention to them than to gay and straight identifying people—though this has been changing in the past decade or so. But bisexuals still have a long way to go before the average person stops assuming automatically that a new acquaintance must be gay or straight (Burleson 2005; Fox 2004; Rust 1995, 1999; Storr 1999; Tucker 1995; Weinberg, Williams, and Pryor 1994). And this is all the more interesting when we realize that bisexuals might just be as large of a group as gay men and lesbian women combined.

There are other sexual identities based more on sexual behaviors than the gender of your partner. For example, some people may experience erotic attraction to specific body parts (partialism) or to objects that represent sexual behaviors (fetishism). Or they may become sexually aroused by the presence of real or imagined violence and power dynamics (sadomasochism) or find that they can be aroused only when having sex in public (exhibitionism) or when they observe others having sex (voyeurism). Although many of these behaviors are present in routine sexual experiences—the fear of getting caught, wearing sexy clothing, biting and pinching—only a small percentage of the population make them the only activities in their sexual repertoire.

And some people state they have no sexual desire for anyone. They aren't gay/lesbian or heterosexual, they aren't bisexual either; they're **asexual**. Some estimates suggest that about 4 percent of men and women self-identify as asexual (Poston and Baumle 2006), while other studies have found that about 1 percent of people report experiencing no sexual desire at all (Bogaert 2004). People who are asexual are not the same as people who are celibate. Asexuals experience little or no sexual desire, but they still might have sex to please their partner or spouse, or to go along with convention. Celibate people may feel a significant amount of sexual desire; they just choose not to act on it.

Friends, family, and the medical establishment are quick to diagnose asexuals as confused, conflicted, suffering from a hormone deficiency, or traumatized by child abuse. But asexuals counter that their sexuality is not a problem that needs to be cured; rather, it is a perfectly valid sexual orientation. Asexuals have their own organizations, like Asexuality Visibility and Education Network (AVEN), websites (www.asexuality.org) slogans, coming-out stories, and lots of merchandise to buy (Harris 2006). As with many identities that challenge the rigidness of the ways we learn to think about identity categories (remember multiracial identities?), they are often under-acknowledged, misrepresented, and struggle with a variety of concerns related to rights, respect, and recognition.

asexuality

A sexual identity organized around having no sexual desire for anyone.

Women's sexuality has changed enormously in the past 50 years. Once, a woman active with many sexual partners would have been universally despised. But, today, characters like *Glee*'s Brittany Susan Pierce, Hannah Horvath from HBO's *Girls*, or Ilana Wexler from Comedy Central's *Broad City* are expanding the ways women's sexual appetite and agency are presented.

The Gendered Construction of Sexual Interactions

11.3.6 Explain the sexual double standard and the "masculinization" of sex.

How do Americans construct their sexual identities? The single-most important organizing principle of sexuality is *gender*. Men and women are raised to have different attitudes toward sexual desire, behavior, and identity. One might say that there are "his" and "her" sexuality. For many years, it was assumed that only men experienced sexual desire at all; women were interested in romance and companionship, but not sex (so the theory held). Women who flirted with men were not expressing sexual desire but trying to "ensnare" men into marriage or buying them something.

Although today many people agree that women have some degree of sexual desire, they consider it inappropriate to express openly. Men are expected to express how "horny" they are; women are not. Men who have a lot of sex are seen as "studs," and their status rises among their peers. Women who have a lot of sex are seen as "sluts," and their status falls. "Women need a reason to have sex," commented comedian Billy Crystal. "Men just need a place."

Whether gay or heterosexual, sexual behaviors, desires, and identities are organized more by the gender of the actor than by the genders of those toward whom he or she might be erotically inclined. That is to say, on all available measures, gay and straight men are far more similar to each other than either is to gay or straight women. Men are socialized to express a "masculine" sexuality, and women are socialized to express a "feminine" sexuality, regardless of their sexual orientation.

And "his" and "her" sexuality are not considered equal. In our culture, the **sexual double standard** encourages men to pursue sex as an end in itself, to seek a lot of sex with many different partners, outside of romantic or emotional commitment. And women are taught to consider sex with one partner and only in the context of an emotional relationship. As one young woman recently told a researcher, "Guys can have sex with all the girls and it makes him more of a man, but if a girl does then all of a sudden she's a 'ho' and she's not as quality of a person" (Armstrong, Hamilton and England 2010). Men are expected to have a lot of sex to demonstrate their masculinity; women are expected to say no.

sexual double standard

The social standard that encourages men to pursue sex as an end in itself, to seek a lot of sex with many different partners, outside of romantic or emotional commitment, and teaches women to consider sex with one partner and only in the context of an emotional relationship.

HOW MANY SEX PARTNERS DO PEOPLE HAVE?

For decades, sex researchers have noticed something strange: Men and women report different numbers of partners. A recent survey found that men reported a median number of seven sexual partners over the course of their lives, while the number of partners for women was four. How can this be? After all, it's a mathematical impossibility for men to average almost twice the number of partners that women average (if they are exclusively heterosexual anyway). Perhaps one reason is what we might call the *"stud versus slut" effect*: men might overestimate their numbers to appear more like a "stud" while women might underestimate their numbers to appear less like a "slut."

For example, about 10 percent of Americans have sex outside of their marriages in any given year—though the percentages change quite a bit depending upon exactly how the question is asked. In face-to-face interviews, about 1 percent of women admit to being unfaithful; on anonymous computer surveys, about 6 percent of women say they have. It might also be that men are picking partners from outside the surveyed population in numbers far greater than women (going to sex workers or having sex in other countries when they travel, for instance). There's also a problem with *retrospective analysis*: people's memories are notoriously bad at explaining exactly what happened. In fact, memory often reveals more about what people either believe happened or may want to have happened—or even what they believe should have happened (even if it didn't).

All of these issues may contribute to the disparity between men and women when we ask "How many?" But it turns out that this difference shows up only about some groups and only when they are asked some types of questions. For the 90 percent of Americans who have had 20 or fewer sexual partners over their lifetime, the discrepancy between men's and women's responses is close to 1—that is, they report basically the same number of partners. And if you ask men and women how many different partners they had in the last year, the ratio is—again—close to 1.

The entire discrepancy, it seems, is a result of measurement errors among the remaining 10 percent of Americans who claim more than 20 sexual partners over their lives. Four-fifths of those who have had more than 20 partners report their numbers in round numbers (25, 50, and 100, rather than 63, 87, or 114, for example). And men tend to round up and women tend to round down. When you have had that many partners, most people just don't keep an exact count—not precisely anyway.

It may simply be that the force of normative expectations associated with the "studs versus sluts" effect really only come into effect for some groups (like those with 20 or or more sexual partners) and only when they are asked certain questions (Morris 1993; Parker-Pope 2008).

As a result, the highest rates of sexual activity occur among gay men (masculine sexuality times two), and the lowest rates among lesbians (feminine sexuality times two). Gay men have an average of more than 30 partners during their lifetime, whereas lesbians have fewer than three. Gay men have the lowest rates of long-term committed relationships, straight men next, then straight women, and finally, lesbians have the highest rates. Thus, it appears that men—gay or straight—place sexuality at the center of their lives, and that women—gay or straight—are more interested in affection and caring in the context of a long-term love relationship.

In recent years, there has been increased convergence in women's and men's sexual attitudes and behaviors. Women's sexuality is becoming increasingly similar to men's; in fact, we might even speak of a **"masculinization" of sex**. The masculinization of sex includes sexual intercourse starting earlier (see FIGURE 11.7), the pursuit of pleasure for its own sake, increased attention to orgasm, increased numbers of sexual partners, the interest in sexual experimentation, and the separation of sexual behavior from love. These are partly the result of the technological transformation of sexuality (from birth control to the Internet) and partly the result of the sexual revolution's promise of greater sexual freedom with fewer emotional and physical consequences (see Parker-Pope 2008; Pew Research Center 2006; Rubin 1990; Schwartz and Rutter 1998).

"masculinization" of sex

The shift in gendered sexual scripts toward a masculine model of sexuality that emphasizes the pursuit of pleasure for its own sake, increased attention to orgasm, increased numbers of sexual partners, interest in sexual experimentation, and the separation of sexual behavior from love.

FIGURE 11.7 Proportion of Youth Who Have Had Sex by Age and Gender

Today, the proportion of boys and girls and young men and women who have had sex are much more similar than they were at throughout the twentieth century. In 1925, among high school age youth in the United States, less than 10 percent of women admitted to having sex and about half of men did. The rates have increased among both boys and girls, men and women, but the rate of increase has been much steeper for girls and women (which accounts for why the proportions of boys and girls and young men and women are as similar as they are today).

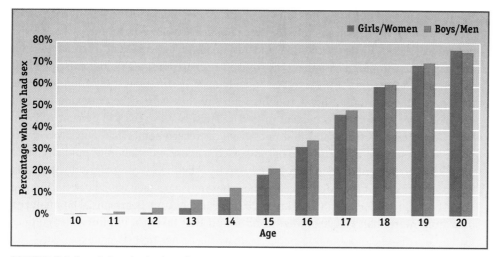

SOURCE: Data from Guttmacher Institute. September 2016. "U.S. Teen Sexual Activity: The proportion of adolescents who have had sex increases rapidly by age. Available at https://www.guttmacher.org/fact-sheet/american-teens-sexual-and-reproductive-health#1.

Convergence on Campus: Hooking Up and Sexual Consent

11.3.7 Summarize what sociologists have learned about contemporary gender and sexual inequality by examining the social phenomenon of "hooking up."

Similar to the moral panic induced by "dating" at the outset of the twentieth century, a moral panic emerged surrounding "**hooking up**" in the twenty-first century. The same concerns are largely recycled—the notion that with less rules, young people will run wild and fewer will eventually marry. "Hooking up" is interesting language because it's a term that deliberately defies specific definition—it's not just vague; it's *intentionally* vague. It can refer to a great variety of different relationships and interactions. Indeed, this is part of the power of the term. One set of researchers defines it as "a sexual encounter which may nor may not include sexual intercourse, usually occurring on only one occasion between two people who are strangers or brief acquaintances" (Lambert 2003, p. 129). Although that seems to cover most cases, it fails to include those heterosexuals who hook up more than once or twice, or "sex buddies" (acquaintances who meet regularly for sex but rarely if ever associate otherwise), or "friends with benefits" (friends who do not care to become romantic partners but may include sex among the activities they enjoy together).

Hooking up is fairly common—in the most comprehensive study of 14,000 students on 19 campuses, 72 percent of all students reported at least one hookup by senior year—but it is not the only behavior in collegiate sexual repertoire. By senior year, 40 percent of those who had ever hooked up had engaged in fewer than 3; another 40 percent had engaged in between 4 and 9 hookups, and only 20 percent in 10 or more. Nor does it always include intercourse: Only about one-third engaged in intercourse in their last hook up. Another third had engaged in oral sex or manual stimulation of the genitals. And 20 percent had engaged only in kissing and non-genital touching (Armstrong et al. 2010). On many campuses, the sexual marketplace—gay and straight—is organized around groups of same-sex friends who go out together to meet appropriate sexual partners in a casual setting like a bar or a party. Party scenes feature hooking up as the standard mode of sexual interaction. Almost all hooking up involves more alcohol than sex: Men averaged

hooking up

A deliberately vague term for a sexual encounter that can refer to a great variety of different relationships and interactions, may nor may not include sexual intercourse, and usually occurs on only one occasion between two people who are strangers or brief acquaintances. Although that seems to cover most cases, it fails to include those heterosexuals who hook up more than once or twice, or "sex buddies" (acquaintances who meet regularly for sex but rarely if ever associate otherwise), or "friends with benefits" (friends who do not care to become romantic partners but may include sex among the activities they enjoy together).

orgasm gap

Term for the pattern of pleasure discrepancy between women and men that often occurs between hook-up sex and relationship sex.

4.7 drinks on their most recent hookup, women 2.9 drinks (England, Shafer, and Fogerty 2008; Kimmel 2008; Wade 2017). And some of the most recent research on the topic suggests that up to one-third of college students remain outside of "hookup culture," but are largely unaware of the fact that so many are abstaining (Wade 2017). Research on college hookups also shows a significant **orgasm gap** between heterosexual encounters in relationships versus hookups, suggesting they may be less sexually liberating than some suggest.

If hooking-up culture is the dominant campus sexual culture, then "abstinence pledgers" may represent a counterculture. Abstinence campaigns encourage young people to take a "virginity pledge" and refrain from heterosexual intercourse until marriage (the campaigns assume that gay and lesbian students do not exist). At first glance, such campaigns appear to be somewhat successful. One study found that the total percentage of high school students who say they've had heterosexual sex had dropped from more than 50 percent in 1991 to slightly more than 45 percent 10 years later. Teen pregnancy and abortion rates have decreased somewhat, and proponents point to the success of abstinence-based sex education and elaborate publicity campaigns in a 10 percent drop in teen sexual activity. Abstinence campaigns do appear to have *some* effect, but they do not offset the other messages teenagers hear. Sociologist Peter Bearman and Hannah Brückner (2001; Brückner and Bearman 2005) analyzed data from more than 90,000 students and found that taking a virginity pledge does lead an average heterosexual teenager to delay his or her first sexual experience—by about 18 months. But, such pledges have also been found to have some adverse effects on sexual health as well, as those who do have sex among this group are less likely to use contraceptives, have similar rates of sexually transmitted infections as their non-pledging peers, and are more likely to engage in oral and anal sex as well. And the

HOW DO WE KNOW WHAT WE KNOW?

WHY HOOKING UP MIGHT BE LESS EMPOWERING THAN YOU THINK

When young people are asked what qualifies as "hooking up," there is a general agreement that it refers to a sexual interaction that is more than a hug, but how much more is unclear. Setting the moral issues aside, one question asked by scholars and popular commentators alike is what "hooking up" means for women—does it empower them and authorize women's sexuality and sexual desire, or should it be understood as disempowering for women? Elizabeth Armstrong, Paula England, and Allison Fogarty (2012) set out to answer this question by looking at sexual intimacy among heterosexual college students in relationships and those hooking up. Armstrong and colleagues conducted a large-scale survey of 21 separate colleges and universities around the United States and also interviewed more than 80 women at two of those universities to supplement the data collected by the survey. They wanted to assess whether sex among "hook ups" was really as enjoyable (at least sexually speaking) for women as sex in relationships. How did they measure the level of enjoyment? By the presence or absence of orgasms.

They discovered, perhaps not surprisingly, that men are more likely to achieve orgasm in heterosexual encounters than are women—whether those encounters happen inside of relationships or not. But, for women, relationship sexual encounters were much more likely to be associated with their own sexual pleasure—heterosexual women achieve orgasm more often in relationships than hookups. Armstrong and colleagues (2012) refer to this pattern as the "orgasm gap." They discovered that the reason for this pleasure discrepancy for women between relationship sex and hookup sex was related to two separate issues: *sexual practices* and *gendered beliefs* about who is entitled to receive sexual pleasure. In terms of practices, their data showed that specific sexual practices, prior experience with a sexual partner, and level of perceived commitment were associated with a higher likelihood of orgasm for women—and also much more likely to occur inside relationships than in hookups. But interview data also showed that the orgasm gap is related to beliefs as well: Both men and women questioned women's entitlement to achieving orgasm in hookups (but not men's), but also strongly believed in women's entitlement to sexual pleasure in relationships (as well as men's).

And although "hooking up" is a term that often makes us think of heterosexual relationships, some research has begun to consider whether hooking up is experienced differently among people participating in same-sex intimacy as well. Research on same-sex "hookups" finds that these interactions may provide opportunities to explore same-sex desires less possible (for some) outside of this context (Rupp, et al. 2014).

pledges were effective only for students up to age 17. By the time they are 20 years old, more than 90 percent of both boys and girls are sexually active.

The pledges were not effective at all if a significant proportion of students at the school was taking them. That is, taking the pledge seems to be a way of creating a "deviant" subculture, or a counterculture, what Bearman and Brückner called an "identity movement"—add "virgins" to the Goths, jocks, nerds, preps, theater kids, and rappers. Additionally, sociologists have found that when pledgers do have heterosexual intercourse, they are *far less likely* to use contraception. Another survey of 527 never-married heterosexual students at a large midwestern university found that 16 percent had taken virginity pledges but that 61 percent of them had broken their pledge before graduating from college (Lipsitz, Bishop, and Robinson 2003; Rosenbaum 2009).

Because abstinence-based programs are often used instead of actual sex education, there is not wide agreement in exactly what "counts" as keeping your pledge. In one recent survey of 1,100 college freshmen, 61 percent believed they were still abstinent if they had participated in mutual masturbation; 37 percent if they had had oral sex; and 24 percent if they had had anal sex. On the other hand, 24 percent believed that kissing broke their abstinence pledge (Bearman and Brückner 2001; Lipsitz et al. 2003). As a result, one recent study found abstinence-only programs had no impact on teen sexual activity or rates of unprotected sex (Trenholm et al. 2008). A secondary analysis of data gathered from more than 1,700 heterosexual teenagers nationwide found that those who received abstinence-only education (24 percent of the students) were 50 percent *more* likely to report a pregnancy than those who received comprehensive sex education, which includes information about birth control (Kohler, Manhart, and Lafferty 2008).

SOCIOLOGY AND OUR WORLD

WHAT HAPPENS TO MEN WHO WAIT?

How do young Christian men pledging abstinence perform masculinity if being heterosexually active is a key component of contemporary masculinities?

Abstinence pledges are so counter to the sexual norms among young people, that they have become the foundation of groups and identities. It would be easy to assume that young heterosexual men who take abstinence pledges are emasculated and teased by peers. But, scholarship studying young men pledging abstinence until marriage has discovered that one of the ways that young men "save face" is by continually discussing and identifying just how difficult it is to wait. Sociologist Amy Wilkins (2009) refers to this as young men enacting "collective processes of temptation." The young Christian men in Wilkins' study who pledged abstinence were not simply waiting to have sex, they were continually—indeed, strategically—emphasizing how difficult the waiting was. And this constant discussion about temptation is one way that these men were able to uphold the cultural notion that men are "sex-crazed" even in the absence of actually having or pursuing sex.

Another sociologist, Sarah Diefendorf, wanted to know what actually happens in the sex lives of men who wait. A lot of scholarship has compared the rates for pledgers and everyone else associated with safe sex, unintended pregnancy, and more. Another body of scholarship has examined how pledgers construct meaningful gender and sexual identities out of a professed decision to *not* have sex. Diefendorf (2015) examines something else: She wanted to know what kinds of sexual support young men pledging abstinence received before marriage and how that support paid off in their marriages.

To study this, she conducted interviews, focus groups, and ethnographic observations with young Christian men who were part of a large nondenominational church. The men in her study joined a church group that met weekly to support each other in their decisions to be abstinent. She was interested in the support they offered each other in the group. But, Diefendorf also came back 3 years later and connected with the men again—after all but one of the men in the group had married. Before marriage, these men talked about challenging topics with each other; they had honest conversations about avoiding pornography, masturbation, and all sorts of things many young men do not openly discuss in this way with each other. They supported each other, had "accountability partners" and checked in with one another when someone was finding it challenging to keep the pledge.

After marriage, however, Diefendorf discovered that most of these men still really struggled with issues related to talking about sexuality. Because they understood sex as "sacred" men felt it was inappropriate to discuss with friends or peers; but because sex is sacred to these men, they were also not able to have open, frank conversations about their sex lives with their spouses. Diefendorf (2015) found that the support these men provided for one another navigating a challenging issue in any relationship was really only present before they might actually have a real need for it. After marriage, those support networks disappeared and the men were left to fend for themselves.

Although abstinence-only sex education has little or no effect on reducing rates of abortion, unwanted pregnancy, or sexually transmitted infections, comprehensive sex education lowers rates on all three measures (Boonstra 2014; Dailard 2001; Darroch, Landry, and Singh 2000; Kaiser Family Foundation 2000; Kirby 2001; Kohler et al. 2008; Landry, Kaeser, and Richards 1999). Globally, those countries with the most comprehensive sex education have far lower rates of unwanted pregnancies and sexually transmitted infections (Guttmacher Institute 2015; Sullivan/Anderson 2009; United Nations 2008). In the United States, however, it is also true that students are increasingly receiving no sex education on a variety of topics that research has shown actually impacts sexual behavior. Students receive less sex education on a variety of topics today than they did in 2000. Sex education is, to be sure, a controversial issue in the United States. But, many young people today are more likely to need to rely on the Internet or their peers when learning about sex.

Sexual Inequality: Attitudes, Prejudice, and Discrimination

11.3.8 Explain some of the different ways that sexual inequality is perpetuated around the world.

You might not personally be a fan of any specific sexual behavior, but how do you feel about people who are? During the past 40 years, the General Social Survey has asked a number of questions about attitudes toward various sexual behaviors, and although disapproval of interracial and same-sex relationships has declined considerably, many attitudes have remained fairly stable. Consider the shifts in the ways Americans think about premarital sex, extramarital sex, and same-sex sex over the last four decades (see FIGURE 11.8).

FIGURE 11.8 Proportion of Americans Defining Premarital Sex, Extramarital Sex, and Same-Sex Relations as "Always Wrong" or "Almost Always Wrong"
Americans have changed their opinions about lots of issues related to sexuality. Here you can see the proportions of Americans who felt that the following were either "almost always wrong" or "always wrong": sex before marriage, extramarital sex, and same-sex sexual relations. As a group, Americans remain most opposed to extramarital sex, and they have greater opposition to same-sex sex than to premarital sex. And although Americans have become slightly more opposed to extramarital sex over this time and slightly more accepting of premarital sex, the real change is toward much greater levels of acceptance of same-sex sex, particularly after 1990.

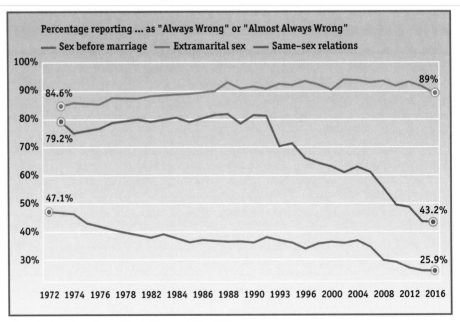

SOURCE: Data from General Social Survey, 1972–2016.

Yet, even the consistency in attitudes toward some kinds of sex (like premarital and extramarital) may be deceiving. For one thing, there is often a wide gap between those moral positions we take with regard to *other* people's behaviors and those we take with regard to *our own* behaviors. Also, attitudes may describe a position without telling us much about how someone actually applies that moral position in everyday life. Take, for example, attitudes about homosexuality. In 1973, 79.2 percent of Americans believed that "sexual relations between two adults of the same sex" was "always wrong" or "almost always wrong." By 2016, that proportion has dropped to 43.2 percent (see FIGURE 11.8). But what if these people discovered that a close friend at work, a family member, or someone else to whom they are close had come out as gay? Would they cut off ties, leave them out of the community, shun them? Or would they be polite and tolerant to gay co-workers or relatives and even make gay friends? In other words, their negative attitude does not necessarily predict negative behavior. Attempting to predict how people will behave using the attitudes they profess on surveys is tricky business. But these numbers do show a shift in public acceptance or tolerance toward same-sex sexual identities, relationships, behaviors, and desires.

When sociologists are studying attitudes about sexuality and toward people with different sexual identities, we often rely on the term "**homophobia**." While the concept of *phobia* is used in relation to fear (think arachnophobia, fear of spiders; claustrophobia, fear of small places; or acrophobia, fear of heights), homophobia is a concept used to measure a wide variety of **sexual prejudice** toward people identifying with sexual identities other than heterosexual (Herek 2000). And that prejudice can take a variety of different forms—anything from distrust to disgust to hatred to violence. That is, there is a spectrum of sexual prejudice and different forms of **sexual discrimination** based on that prejudice.

Increasingly, a great deal of scholarship suggests that we are in the middle of what sociologist Suzanna Walters (2014) calls "**the tolerance trap**." Trends on all manner of public opinion polls collecting data on Americans' attitudes about gay and lesbian sex, sexual identities, same-sex marriage, and more have taken a decidedly liberal turn. And when we turn to the world of popular culture, "gay friendly" is a media buzzword. From Chris Colfer's depiction of a gay teen struggling with bullying and finding his place in a high school in *Glee* to co-stars Eric Stonestreet and Jesse Tyler Ferguson's portrayals of a married gay couple with an adopted daughter in *Modern Family* to out and proud Ellen DeGeneres receiving a major day-time talk show (*The Ellen Show*), gay rights and recognition appear to be at hand. Walters (2014), however, argues that these examples are better seen as *sexual tolerance* than *sexual equality*. Although there have been enormous gains in popular, political, and cultural "inclusion," Walters points out that these gains have largely taken place alongside the persistence of anti-gay laws and legislation, the spate of suicides by queer youth, homophobic bullying and violence, and more.

Consider one example. Sociologists Long Doan, Annalise Loehr, and Lisa Miller (2014) conducted a survey experiment among a nationally representative sample of Americans concerning sexual inequality. They started with the notion that many forms of inequality and prejudice take on new forms—often forms that are less easy to detect using the traditional attitudinal measures associated with prejudice. For instance, most of the measures that we use to detect sexual prejudice are associated with what Doan, Loehr, and Miller (2014) refer to as *formal rights*—legal protections that the government grants to privileged groups (like rights to marriage, property, etc.). But, less research considers people's opinions about what Doan and colleagues (2014) refer to as *informal privileges*—those interactional advantages that dominant groups receive when compared with minority groups.

These sorts of informal privileges are not conferred legally; rather, they arise interactionally and play a role in sustaining the belief (even if only subtly) that dominant groups are somehow inherently superior. One *informal privilege* heterosexual couples are often granted is that their public displays of affection are widely accepted. In their

homophobia

A concept used to measure a range of sexual prejudices toward people identifying with sexual identities other than heterosexual, anything from distrust to disgust to hatred to violence.

sexual prejudice

Negative attitudes about an individual or group based on sexual identity.

sexual discrimination

Discrimination against a person on the grounds of sex or sexual identity.

"the tolerance trap"

Suzanna Walters' concept to capture the co-existence of enormous gains in popular, political, and cultural "inclusion" of gay people with the persistence of anti-gay laws and legislation, the spate of suicides by queer youth, homophobic bullying and violence, and more.

MAP 11.3 LGBTI Rights in the World

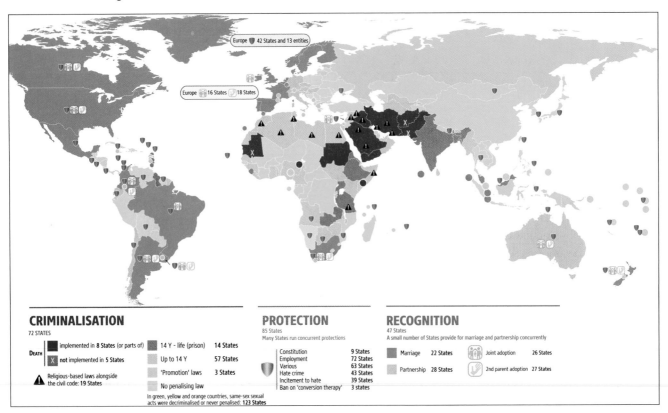

SOURCE: International Lesbian and Gay Association (ILGA). Available at http://ilga.org/downloads/2017/ILGA_WorldMap_ENGLISH_Overview_2017.pdf.

survey, they discovered that heterosexual, gay, and lesbian Americans are all support-ive of marriage equality (a formal right)—though lesbian women and gay men were *more* supportive than heterosexuals. Regarding informal privileges for same-sex cou-ples, heterosexuals showed much *less* support than did gay men and lesbian women. Heterosexuals were less supportive of same-sex couples holding hands in public or kissing in public. These findings are consistent with a lot of work on modern prejudice of different forms (gender, racial, age-related, etc.). Indeed, a great deal of scholarship suggests that as structural forms of discrimination are legally outlawed and begin to decline, these sorts of interaction-based forms of inequality may become much more important sources of continued advantage for dominant groups—a finding that illus-trating that inequality may be simultaneously declining *and* being perpetuated in new and less easily identifiable ways.

Yet it is also true that when we look at rights, protections, and forms of legal recog-nition around the world, it is clear that formal rights are important to continue to ad-dress as well. Consider the different laws affecting LGBT people in different societies around the world (see MAP 11.3).

Resistance to Inequality: The LGBT Movement

11.3.9 Summarize some of the reasons for and consequences of the LGBT movement becoming much more mainstream today than it once was.

In response to sexual inequality, people with minority sexual orientations often band together, both to find suitable partners and to escape the hostility of the main-stream society. If there are enough of them and they manage to find each other, they can form their own subcultures, with their own gathering places, social hierarchies, norms, values, and group cohesion. Sometimes they can even work to change so-cial disapproval. Gay men and lesbians have probably been the most successful at creating social change. Thirty to 40 years ago, the mass media commonly carried articles about crazy "homosexuals." How could anybody engage in such behavior? Today it is just as likely to carry articles about crazy homophobes. How could anyone be so prejudiced? This is a big change in a short time. What happened?

The gay movement happened. As early as the nineteenth century, there were gay neighborhoods in some large cities, such as Paris, Berlin, and New York, but most people with same-sex interests believed that they were alone (Chauncey 1993). Medical science believed there were probably only a few thousand homosexuals, mostly in psychiatric hospitals. That changed during World War II, where gay and lesbian soldiers found each other, and realized that there were many more than anyone thought (the Kinsey Report of 1948 helped also). However, they still faced oppression. If a man sat next to you in a bar and offered to shake hands, he could be an undercover police officer, who would count the handshake as a "homosexual overture" and arrest you. An arrest for "homosexuality" could get you fired, kicked out of your apartment, sent to prison, or sent to a psychiatric hospital (where you could be subject to electroshock therapy and forced castration). In the 1950s, gay men and lesbians began forming organizations such as the Mattachine Society, One, Incorporated, and the Daughters of Bilitis, to petition for the end of police harassment.

The 1969 Stonewall Riots, three days of resistance to police harassment in New York City, led to the formation of the Gay Liberation Front. More gay rights groups followed, until by 1975, there were hundreds: student groups, religious groups, political groups, social groups, groups for practically any interest you could imagine, in practically every city and town in the United States, until a whole new social movement emerged, the Gay Rights Movement. They were not apologetic. They were loud, in-your-face, "out and proud," staging sit-ins, marches, and media "zaps," shouting rather than whispering, demanding rather than asking: We are not crazy! We are not criminals! We are an oppressed minority!

And they were extremely successful. During the next few years, sodomy laws were thrown out in half of the U.S. states, the American Psychiatric Association removed homosexuality from its list of disorders, a dozen Christian denominations voted to allow gay people full membership, and a new term, *homophobia*, was coined to describe antigay prejudice (Armstrong and Crage 2006).

In 1977, the top-rated TV sitcom, *Three's Company*, was based on the premise that a straight guy, Jack Tripper (John Ritter), could pretend to be gay so a conservative landlord will let him share an apartment with two girls. (That premise would have been impossible a few years earlier.) By 2004, *Queer Eye for the Straight Guy* choreographed complete makeovers for straight men (to make them more appealing to women), courtesy of five "fabulous" gay culture experts. Today, there are gay characters on dozens of shows, and gay themed shows on network television as well as cable, from pathbreaking earlier hits like *Will and Grace* and *The L Word*, to more recent shows including—but hardly limited to—*Glee*, *Gossip Girl*, and *Greek* to *This is Us*, *Jane the Virgin*, *One Day at a Time*, and more.

Why was the gay rights movement so successful at affecting change? One answer may be the connections with people who do not identify as gay. The movement arose simultaneously with the youth counterculture of the late 1960s, when millions of college-aged people were protesting all sorts of injustices, from the Vietnam War to gender and racial inequality. Gay rights activists at the time were mostly college aged and members of that same counterculture. One of their early slogans was "We are your children." Political and social leaders were faced, for the first time, with gay men and lesbians who looked and acted like other young people, who could indeed be their children.

In fact, the gay rights movement may have been too successful to remain a counterculture or a subculture; it is now part of the mainstream culture. Many strictly gay social institutions are struggling to survive. Gay bookstores are going out of business

SOCIOLOGY AND OUR WORLD

GAY MEN AND LESBIANS CONGREGATE, BUT NOT ALWAYS TOGETHER

Is the fact that gay neighborhoods ("gayborhoods") are in decline a sign of progress toward sexual equality or not?

Although groups of gay men and lesbians have sought living spaces organized around sexual identity for a long time, neighborhoods actively recognized as "gayborhoods" by others is something arguably more recent. Sociological research on gayborhoods asks a few different kinds of questions: How and why do gay neighborhoods emerge? What kinds of factors shape their growth and endurance? What kinds of processes and forces threaten their existence? A variety of social forces account for the emergence of gayborhoods. Sociologist Amin Ghaziani (2014) discusses the pivotal role that World War II played in their emergence. As men and women came home—some after being dishonorably discharged from service (as a result of their sexuality)—they settled in port cities like San Francisco. But, gayborhoods were also emerging before WWII as well. Yet, these early, largely urban, gay enclaves were distinguished by their unpublicized nature. They were spaces to which people with same-sex desires could go to locate one another.

Gay neighborhoods post-WWII in the United States, however, were marked by a shift toward the development of increasingly formalized urban gay districts in some of the larger U.S. cities. Indeed, many cities with nationally recognized gayborhoods have begun to treat them as natural resources to be marketed to tourists. The Philadelphia Gay Tourism Caucus even produced a map delineating the boundaries of the gayborhood, complete with historical sites of community activism and noteworthy gay-run establishments. And Philadelphia is not alone.

Yet, Ghaziani also finds that many U.S. gayborhoods are in decline. And part of the reason for this is that they have achieved some of their political goals—so much so that gayborhoods have become vibrant sources of urban culture. Yet, Ghaziani also argues that this process is "uneven and incomplete." Certain populations within the LGBT community might benefit from the assimilation of gay spaces in ways others will not be able to. Similarly, in Jane Ward's (2003) analysis of West Hollywood's pride celebration, she discovered that as the events became increasingly mainstream, they have lost much of their political character in favor of celebrations of definitions of gay culture that inevitably marginalize portions of the gay community. Thus, whether to discuss the demise of gayborhoods as an indication of a general decline of sexual inequality or as a vital resource that may be less available to those most in need depends, in part, on which members of the LGBT community you are talking about.

because gay-themed books are increasingly available at every bookstore. Why join a gay church, when gay people are welcomed in the church down the street? It is not that antigay prejudice and discrimination no longer exist but that they can now be fought more effectively within mainstream social institutions. It may often be the case that the more successful a social movement is, the less it is felt to be needed.

---

iSOC AND YOU The Social Organization of Sexuality and Sexual Inequality
Sexuality is a central part of your *identity* and an essential component of how you *interact* with others. It's far more than what you do, with whom, and why. It's a basis for *inequality*, as some sexualities are seen as legitimate and others as "deviant." And the ways sexualities are viewed and understood also become *institutionalized* as sexuality is legislated and codified in formal and informal norms, roles and expectations in every major social institution (from families, to schools, to workplaces, to places of religious worship, and beyond). And, as with other forms of inequality, sexual inequality can exaggerate or offset, perhaps, other *intersecting* facets of inequality.

Conclusion

Bodies, Health, and Sexualities NOW

The body has always been a site of identity and belonging. It has also been a primary means by which societies rank people and thus reproduce inequality. Just think of the different ways you might get a tattoo: to show you belong to a specific group, to express your individuality, to show you are a risk-taker, or to be marked in prison or even a concentration camp. Just as bodies are mutable, you experience what you "do" with them to reveal something important about yourself. There are few things more social than the individual body.

Yet the body is also a site of inequality. You might read people's identities through their bodily performance; indeed, it is through interaction that you come to understand how others see you. In sickness and in health, bodies are social: You learn how to "be" sick, what the rules are, how to interact with others, and how institutions will organize and shape that experience.

There are few experiences more personal that sexuality—what you do with your body and why you do it. Yet there are also fewer experiences that are more social, learning how to be sexual, how to organize your sexuality, what's prescribed and what's proscribed, even what feels good! How you are sexual, with whom, and how that becomes part of your identity—or even whether or not it does—are profoundly social experiences, and therefore organized within a framework of social inequality, through interactions, and within institutions. And as such, the body is a component of your social identity that intersects with all the others (like race, class, gender, sexuality, ability, nationality, and more).

The body has become more mutable, as technologies and social attitudes shift. Just as we now understand gender to be less categorical (male and female) and more a spectrum ranging across a variety of measures, so too with the body of the future: you will experience greater choices about what bodies can and should do, and yet these will be, as they always have been, subject to ever-shifting norms and values.

CHAPTER REVIEW The Body: Health and Sexuality

11.1 Embodying Identities and Inequality

Bodies are often seen as a living canvas, and we can shape and sculpt it to express our selves. Bodies are markers of identity, but all bodies are not seen as equal. Some bodies are more valued and receive higher rewards. Not just by race, or size, or any other marker of the body, but also its relative conformity to dominant standards of beauty, health, sexuality. What's more, we don't just "have" bodies, or have a sexuality, we "do" them—that is our bodies and our perceptions of them are the product of interactions. Heavy or skinny, tattooed or not, cis-gender or transgender, LGBT or heterosexual—these aren't just labels for properties we have, they are processes by which we come to be who we are. We learn how to inhabit our bodies, how to use them, what they are like, through our interactions with other people. And we do it constantly, all the time, as elements of our identities combine and collide in different ways. Bodies are social texts, written on by social forces and social groups, as well as by ourselves.

11.1 Key Terms

social stigma Disapproval or discontent with a person or group that differs from cultural norms, which often serves to distinguish that person or group from other members of a society.

gender policing The enforcement of normative gender ideals by rewarding normative gender performances and punishing transgressions.

identity work The concern with and performance of physical, symbolic, verbal, and behavioral self-representations designed to be taken as part of one's identity.

body image The subjective picture or mental image of one's own body.

Adonis complex The belief that men must look like Greek gods, with perfect chins, thick hair, rippling muscles, and washboard abdominal muscles.

transgender An umbrella term that describes a variety of people, behaviors, and groups whose identities depart from normative gender ideals of masculinity or femininity.

moral panic The process of arousing social concern that the well-being of society is threatened by a particular issue.

meta-analysis A quantitative analysis of several separate but similar experiments or studies conducted to test the pooled data for statistical significance.

disability According to the Americans with Disabilities Act of 1990, disability is "a physical or mental impairment that substantially limits one or more major life activities."

reciprocal effects A dynamic cause-and-effect relationship in which two or more social phenomena can be shown to be both cause and effect, for example, fatness and social class.

positive discrimination The provision of special opportunities to those with certain characteristics than to those without them, typically to a disadvantaged group.

negative discrimination The provision of less-favorable treatment to those with certain characteristics, typically to a disadvantaged group, than to those without them.

appearance-based discrimination Prejudice or discrimination based on physical appearance and particularly physical appearance believed to fall short of societal notions of beauty.

11.2   Understanding Health and Illness Sociologically

Health is unequally distributed in society, varying by social factors like nationality, wealth, race, gender, and age. Life expectancy also varies dramatically by social location. In the United States and globally, it is largely true that the wealthier you are, the healthier you are. In wealthier nations chronic diseases are the main cause of death, but in the poorest countries, high rates of poverty also mean there are high rates of infectious diseases, malnutrition, and starvation. The United States ranks low on numerous indicators of health as compared to other industrialized countries and is still the only industrialized nation that does not provide health care to all its citizens as a right. Our experience of illness may be individual, but the way we understand our illness and the way we act is deeply socially patterned. We learn what's called "the sick role"—that is, how to "be" sick. However, not all members of a society agree on the proper performance of this role, and not all illnesses are seen the same way by society. Indeed, some illnesses leave people doubly affected by their condition. Those who suffer from mental illness, alcohol or drug addiction, physical or mental disabilities, or HIV not only suffer from the illness itself, but they also suffer from social stigma and discrimination because they have it.

11.2 Key Terms

epidemiology The study of the causes and distribution of disease and disability.

social epidemiology The study of both biomedical elements of disease and the social and behavioral factors that influence its spread.

mortality rate The death rate as a percentage of the population.

morbidity rate The rates of new infections from disease.

disease incidence How many new cases of a disease are reported in a given place during a specified time frame.

disease prevalence The distribution of the disease over different groups of the same population.

sick role Talcott Parsons' coinage to describe how we learn to "be" sick; it is a social role we learn to occupy and with which we learn to interact.

de-institutionalization The re-integration of the sick back into society, instead of isolating them in separate places like mental institutions.

medicalization The process by which *human* conditions comes to be defined and treated as *medical* conditions such that they also become subject to medical study, diagnosis, and treatment.

mental illness Among the least understood illnesses, any impairment of thought, mood, or behavior that can be attributed to a psychiatric disease, disorder, or condition.

de-institutionalization movement In the 1970s, advocates sought to relocate patients to "half-way" houses and community-based organizations to help reintegrate them into society, yet care alternatives were plagued by disorganization and under-financing, and many severely and persistently mentally ill people were left without essential services resulting in increasing numbers of mentally ill people on the streets or in prisons because there is no place else for them to go.

11.3   The Social Organization of Sexuality and Sexual Inequality

We consider sex to be biological, and sexuality to be personal and private, but sociologists also see sexuality as a social construction, an important component of identity, and the arena where social negotiation, control, and inequality play out in the sexual script we learn and in sexual socialization. Sexual behavior varies widely, but there is social control at all levels about what is considered normal and what is deviant, which varies widely by culture. We usually think about sexual identity in terms of sexual binary—we are either heterosexual or homosexual—but bisexuality, asexuality, and sexual behaviors as well as sexual identities diverge from this limited, heteronormative model. Our expectations for gendered behavior are so powerful that, regardless of our choice of sexual partners, we often conform to the sexual double standard. However, this is changing as there is an increasing masculinization of sex for women. Hooking up is common on campuses.

Teens are taking abstinence pledges, but sex education is much more effective at preventing negative consequences of sexual behavior. Overall, the greater the equality between men and women, the happier everyone is with their sex lives. Not only gender, but race, age, and culture exert an influence on sexuality. Homophobia is still a pervasive ideology justifying heterosexism and fueling sexual prejudice and sexual discrimination.

11.3 Key Terms

sex A biological distinction; the chromosomal, chemical, and anatomical organization of males and females.

sexuality An identity we construct that is often based on our sexual conduct and often intersects with other sources of identity, such as race, class, ethnicity, age, or gender.

sexual behavior Any behavior that brings sexual pleasure or release (typically, but not always, involving sex organs).

sexual desire Any intense sexual feelings associated with specific environmental, cultural, or biological stimuli.

sexual identity Typically, it is understood to refer to an identity that is organized by the gender of the person (or persons) to whom we are sexually attracted. Also called "sexual orientation."

sexual scripts A cognitive map about how to have sex and with whom.

sexual socialization The process by which your sexual scripts begin to cohere into a preference and sexual identity.

heterosexuality The most common sexual identity worldwide, it is organized around sexual attraction between people of different sexes.

heteronormativity Sociological term to refer to the ideology by which heterosexuality is simultaneously understood as both *normal* and *normative*.

homosexuality A sexual identity organized around sexual desire for members of one's own sex. In colloquial terms, homosexuals are often called "gay."

bisexuality A sexual identity organized around attraction to both women and men.

asexuality A sexual identity organized around having no sexual desire for anyone.

sexual double standard The social standard that encourages men to pursue sex as an end in itself, to seek a lot of sex with many different partners, outside of romantic or emotional commitment, and teaches women to consider sex with one partner and only in the context of an emotional relationship.

"masculinization" of sex The shift in gendered sexual scripts toward a masculine model of sexuality that emphasizes the pursuit of pleasure for its own sake, increased attention to orgasm, increased numbers of sexual partners, interest in sexual experimentation, and the separation of sexual behavior from love.

hooking up A deliberately vague term for a sexual encounter that can refer to a great variety of different relationships and interactions, may nor may not include sexual intercourse, and usually occurs on only one occasion between two people who are strangers or brief acquaintances. Although that seems to cover most cases, it fails to include those heterosexuals who hook up more than once or twice, or "sex buddies" (acquaintances who meet regularly for sex but rarely if ever associate otherwise), or "friends with benefits" (friends who do not care to become romantic partners but may include sex among the activities they enjoy together).

orgasm gap Term for the pattern of pleasure discrepancy between women and men that often occurs between hook-up sex and relationship sex.

homophobia A concept used to measure a range of sexual prejudices toward people identifying with sexual identities other than heterosexual, anything from distrust to disgust to hatred to violence.

sexual prejudice Negative attitudes about an individual or group based on sexual identity.

sexual discrimination Discrimination against a person on the grounds of sex or sexual identity.

"the tolerance trap" Suzanna Walters' concept to capture the co-existence of enormous gains in popular, political, and cultural "inclusion" of gay people with the persistence of anti-gay laws and legislation, the spate of suicides by queer youth, homophobic bullying and violence, and more.

SELF-TEST

⟩ CHECK YOUR UNDERSTANDING

1. Tattooing is seen as a form of identity work because

  a. nearly a third of tattoo wearers say it makes them feel sexier.

  b. tattooing and piercing are associated with deviant behaviors.

  c. tattoos are increasingly seen to symbolize traits valued by peers, from environmental awareness, to athletic ability, to artistic talent, to academic achievement.

  d. All of the answers are correct.

2. Sociologists see obesity and social class as having reciprocal effects because
   a. overweight people are less likely to work hard to succeed.
   b. fatness can cause poverty and poverty can cause fatness.
   c. fatness can cause social discomfort, which can cause more eating.
   d. All of the answers are correct.

3. Which of the following are learned along with cultural standards and sexual scripts?
   a. Sexual desire
   b. Sexual behavior
   c. Sexual identity
   d. All of the answers are correct.

4. Which of the following is most effective in reducing negative consequences of sexual behavior, including rates of abortion, unwanted pregnancy, and sexually transmitted infections, according to the text?
   a. Abstinence-based education
   b. Government-subsidized free birth control
   c. Comprehensive sex education
   d. All have been shown to be equally effective.

5. All of the following statements are true EXCEPT:
   a. Our sexual identities cohere around a preference, but these preferences are more flexible than we typically think.
   b. Bisexuality and asexuality confirm the sex-gender binary.
   c. There are sexual identities based more on sexual behaviors than the gender of your partner.
   d. The single most important organizing principle of sexuality is gender.

6. Sociological research shows that, in general, the wealthier you are, the healthier you are. Which of these reasons is NOT true:
   a. Wealthy people have better genes.
   b. Poorer people do more dangerous jobs.
   c. Wealthy people have better access to preventive health care.
   d. Poorer people have fewer choices about diet and lifestyle.

7. The pioneering survey research by Alfred Kinsey:
   a. found that homosexual behavior was far more common among men than anyone had believed.
   b. found that middle-class people had more sex, more often, and with a greater variety of techniques than working-class people.
   c. over-sampled college students and prisoners, which might have skewed his data.
   d. All of the above are correct.

8. In describing progress toward sexual equality, sociologists find
   a. there is a tolerance trap, where enormous gains in popular, political, and cultural inclusion are accompanied by anti-gay laws and legislation and homophobic bullying and violence.
   b. heterosexual couples enjoy informal privileges such as public displays of affection, whereas same-sex couples experience less tolerance for holding hands in public or kissing in public.
   c. inequality may be simultaneously declining and being newly perpetuated in less easily identifiable ways.
   d. All of the answers are correct.

Self-Test Answers: 1. d, 2. b, 3. d, 4. c, 5. b, 6. a, 7. d, 8. d

FAMILIES

Families are more diverse today than ever before in history and the family as a social institution has undergone more transformation during your parents' and grandparents' lives than it has over the last few hundred years. Sociologists know that the "family" is a constantly evolving social ideal and institution that shifts and adapts to changing circumstances, desires, and ideas. For these reasons and more, this is an exciting time to be studying families.

→ LEARNING OBJECTIVES

In this chapter, using the iSoc framework, you should be able to:

12.1.1 Explain why defining "the family" is so challenging and why sociologists rely on a broad and flexible definition.

12.1.2 Distinguish between different systems of kinship, and explain the role of marriage in social reproduction.

12.1.3 Recognize how each of the five elements of the iSoc model can be used to examine families sociologically.

12.1.4 Summarize the external forces that affected the emergence of families as well as how they have changed over time.

12.1.5 Understand when and why the nuclear family emerged as well as why thinking of it as a "traditional" family form is historically inaccurate.

12.1.6 Explain why sociologists today argue that family diversity is the new norm when it comes to family forms.

12.2.1 Summarize shifts in courtship and dating in the United States since the late 1800s through today distinguishing between "calling," "dating," and "hookups."

12.2.2 Explain the role that marriage has played in societies in the past and how that role has changed in some contemporary societies.

12.2.3 Summarize gay and lesbian families' existence throughout history as well as how legal transformations have affected them in the United States and beyond.

12.2.4 Understand what it means that Americans are more open to racial intermarriage as an ideal than a practice.

12.2.5 Summarize what we can learn from the facts that people are delaying marriage for longer periods of time.

12.2.6 Explain both why cohabitation has become more common and what we can learn when we understand the groups among which it is the most and least common.

12.2.7 Understand what sociologists can learn from trends in solitary living and what these trends indicate about shifts in family life in the United States.

12.2.8 Explain how the rise in nonmarital choices is related to a changing relationship among sex, marriage, and reproduction in society.

12.3.1 Understand how parents' time spent with their children has changed and what we know about gender differences in parenting abilities and practices.

12.3.2 Summarize shifts in single-parent families and the role of grandparents in recent history among U.S. families.

12.3.3 Summarize the different types of adoption, and understand the stigma that many adoptive families face.

12.3.4 Explain which groups of Americans have seen the largest increases in childlessness and why.

12.4.1 Summarize some of what sociologists know about divorce in the United States in international perspective.

12.4.2 Understand why sociologists are less sure that divorce produces negative outcomes for children than we might think.

12.4.3 Explain what Cherlin means by the "marriage-go-round" and how it relates to both remarriage and blended families.

12.4.4 Understand how intimate partner violence impacts American families and relationships in international perspective.

12.4.5 Summarize what we know about inter- and intragenerational family violence.

Introduction

Almost daily, we hear some political pundit predict the end of the family. The crisis of the family is so severe that in 2000, the U.S. Congress passed a Family Protection Act, as if the family were an endangered species, like the spotted owl. Divorce and remarriage have never been more common. Millions of children are growing up with single parents or in blended households. Millions of young adults are putting off marriage until their 30s, or cohabiting instead of getting married, or opting to stay single. People are selecting household arrangements today that would mystify our ancestors. Even the staid U.S. Census Bureau has given in and added the category "cohabiting partners" to the old list of single, married, widowed, or divorced. Only 51 percent of Americans older than age 18 are now married—compared with almost 75 percent 50 years ago.

On the other hand, the family has never been more popular. Suddenly, everyone seems to want one: single people, gay men and lesbians, even the elderly and widowed. Prime-time sitcoms have made a staple of both lovably dysfunctional nuclear families (like *The Middle*), fractured divorced families (*Two and a Half Men* and *Parenthood*), where ex-spouses try to navigate a postnuclear world, or combinations of single, engaged, and married couples laughably explore their similarities and differences (*Terms of Engagement*), or even a variety of families and single people (*Modern Family* and *Suburgatory*). And the wedding industry generates sales of about $50 billion every single year.

The family is in crisis. The family has never been more popular.

The great novelist Thomas Wolfe said "You can't go home again." A few years earlier, the poet Robert Frost wrote that "Home is the place where, when you have to go there, they have to take you in." We believe both statements—in part, sociologists understand, because both are true. The family has never been more popular in part *because* it is in crisis—and all the cultural media, from TV to movies to pop songs, are trying to reassert its predominance in an increasingly individualized and global world. And the family is in crisis in part *because* of those institutional forces, like the global marketplace and its ideology of individualism, which constitute the dominant ideology around the world.

One thing is certain: The family is hardly a separate realm from the rest of society. It is a political football, tossed around by both liberals and conservatives, who appeal to it abstractly and develop policies that shape and mold it concretely. It is the foundation of the economy. And it is the basic building block of society. Always has been. Probably always will be.

What is the family? Where did it come from? Is it still necessary? How do sociologists understand the forces that hold it together and the forces that pull it apart?

12.1 The Family as a Social Institution

Unlike most animals, human beings are born helpless. For the first few years of their lives, they require round-the-clock care; and, for the first decade, they require nearly constant supervision, or they won't survive to adulthood. But even after they learn basic survival skills, humans are still not qualified to make their own way in the world—an adult has to provide for all of their needs for 10 or 15 years or more. You are born into or otherwise land in the group that will care for you in early life—and your survival depends on that group. This group is, of course, the family.

Family is a cultural universal in that families exist in every society. This does not mean, however, that all families look alike—indeed, what qualifies as a "family" differs by society, sometimes dramatically. But definitions of family differ considerably within societies as well. These distinctions between all of the various interactions, relationships, and people who comprise what we think of as "family" are important to consider as sociologists examine the role that families play in society and for individuals. For better or worse, sociologists have found that the family you land in when you are young (whether by birth, choice, or chance) plays a profound role in determining what the rest of your life will look like. And it is for this reason that sociologists understand the family to be among the primary social institutions in every society.

To call the family a "social institution" means that we recognize that families are formal systems of roles, norms, and values, and that, as a social institution, families help to meet the needs of a society that would be almost impossible to meet with individuals acting alone. As an institution, the family has been subject to incredible change. Indeed, it's not an exaggeration to say that there has been more change in the American family over the course of your parents' and grandparents' lives than at any other point in human history. It has, quite literally, transformed.

Families as Kinship Systems

12.1.1 Explain why defining "the family" is so challenging and why sociologists rely on a broad and flexible definition.

What and who actually comprise "the family" is a more difficult question than you might think. In the most common sense, families are defined as "groups of people related by blood or marriage." But, this definition does not really capture everyone who we consider to be "related" to us. Have you ever known someone who refers to a family friend as "Aunt" or "Uncle" even they don't actually legally or biologically meet the definition? Have you ever heard of a family babysitter who helps out so much and becomes so much a part of a family's routine that they are considered "one of the family"? Do you have a friend you consider to be almost a sibling? Each of these relationships illustrates relationships that are left out if we use the "blood and marriage" definition.

families
The basic unit in society, these social groups are socially understood as either biologically, emotionally, and/or legally related.

family of origin
The family a child is born or adopted into, with biological parents or others who are responsible for his or her upbringing.

family of procreation
The family one creates through marriage or cohabitation with a romantic partner, to which one chooses to belong.

kinship systems
Cultural groupings that locate individuals in society by reference to their families, typically mapped as a network from closest (mother, father, siblings) to a little more distant (cousins, aunts, uncles) to increasingly distant (second-cousins twice removed).

matrilineal
Tracing one's ancestry through the mother and maternal side of the family.

patrilineal
Tracing one's ancestry through the father and paternal side of the family.

bilateral
Tracing one's ancestry through both parents, rather than only the mother (see *matrilineal*) or only the father (see *patrilineal*).

The core element of all these definitions is the fact of relatedness. And this is how sociologists define **families**—groups of people who are logically, biologically, legally, or emotionally *related* to each other. And that is why the idea of the family has become such a political hot potato. "Relatedness" is everything. Excluding some people from establishing that relationship prevents them from being in a family. Rather than coming up with some arbitrary definition of what families *should* be, sociologists study what families *are*—and in doing so, we recognize that what they are will shift. So, for instance, under the "blood or marriage" definition, gay and lesbian couples failed to legally qualify as "family members" in most states in the United States until the *Obergefell v. Hodges, 2015* Supreme Court decision that the fundamental right to marry should be constitutionally guaranteed to same-sex couples as well. We do not use this example to suggest that those couples were not families before 2015 and that now they are. Rather, gay and lesbian couple families previously existed at an emotional level, and now are institutionalized at the legal level as well.

Yet even that "group of people related by blood or marriage" comes in an enormously varied number of types. Chances are that you will occupy at least two different family units during your lifetime. While you are a child, you belong to a **family of origin**—the family you are born or adopted into—with your biological parents or others who are responsible for your upbringing. When you grow up, if you marry or cohabit with a romantic partner, you now also belong to a **family of procreation**, which is the family to which you *choose* to belong. Families usually have some rationale, real or imaginary, for being together. Every human society has divided the adults into cooperative groups who take charge of the care and feeding of the children. This is the origin of the family, but certainly, modern families come in more types than this alone—think of single parents with children, spouses without children, and several generations living together, for instance.

Families provide us with a sense of history, both as individuals and as members of a particular culture. Families themselves are part of what sociologists call **kinship systems**—cultural forms that locate individuals in the culture by reference to their families. Kinship systems are groupings that include all your relatives, mapped as a network from closest (mother, father, siblings) to a little more distant (cousins, aunts, uncles) to increasingly distant (your second-cousin twice removed). Your kinship system can be imagined as a "family tree" providing a sense of history.

Family trees can be organized in several ways to ground you in that history, depending on how you trace your descent, where you live, and whom you marry. These different ways of constructing a family tree give you a different cognitive map of the world and your place in it. Your line of descent can be **matrilineal** (everyone related to you is traced through the mother's side of the family), **patrilineal** (everyone related to you is traced through only the father's side of the family), or **bilateral** (those related to you are traced through both parents' families equally). As you are beginning to understand, families are not simply an expression of love between people who want to have children. They are fundamental cultural institutions that have as much to do with economics, politics, and sex as they do with raising children. As the fundamental unit of society, the social functions of the family and the regulation of sexuality have always been of interest to sociologists.

Families also come with rights and obligations. So, families ensure the regular transfer of property and establish lines of succession. If you receive loans for college, part of what you are required to declare is your parents' income, as that factors in when considering how much financial assistance you will need. As a parent, this financial obligation is implied in these rules. Families then bear the economic and emotional burden of raising only the children that belong to them (Malinowski [1927] 1974). All of this and more is why we understand family as such a complex concept that requires a flexible definition.

Sex, Marriage, and Family

12.1.2 Distinguish between different systems of kinship, and explain the role of marriage in social reproduction.

Who counts as family varies from culture to culture and over time. And who gets to marry whom also varies. Mom, Dad, brother, sister, son, or daughter are always off limits, except in a few cases of ritual marriage (the ancient Egyptian pharaohs married their sisters). But uncles and nieces commonly married each other through the nineteenth century, and first cousins are still allowed to marry in most countries in Europe and 26 of the U.S. states. In the Hebrew Bible, God struck Onan dead because he refused to have sex with his widowed sister-in-law and thereby produce an heir for his brother. But nowadays an affair with one's sister-in-law would be thought of as creepy at best.

No society allows its members to marry or have sex with just anyone they might take an interest in, but the specifics of who can marry whom vary from place to place and over time. The most common arrangement is **monogamy**, which is marriage between two people. Most monogamous societies allow men and women to marry each other because it usually takes one of each to make a baby, but same-sex monogamy is probably more common than you might think. Historian John Boswell (1995) found evidence of same-sex marriages existing alongside male-female marriages even in early Christian Europe. Many societies have instituted some form of **polygamy**, or marriage between three or more people, although most of those allow monogamy as well. The most common form of polygamy is **polygyny**, one man with two or more women, because a man can have children with several women at the same time. Among the Yoruba of northern Nigeria, women can have only one husband, but *they* can have as many wives as they want, so they practice a type of same-sex polygyny: One woman marries two or more women (Roscoe 2001). **Polyandry**, one woman marrying two or more men, is rare, but it has been documented in Tibet and a few other places where men are absent for several months of the year.

Only a few societies practice **group marriage**, two or more men marrying two or more women, with children born to anyone in the union "belonging" to all of the partners equally. Group marriages appeared from time to time in the 1960s counterculture, but they rarely lasted long (Hollenbach 2004). Today, the term **polyamory** is used to describe committed relationships among three or more people, and many who self-identify as polyamorous say they would choose multipartnered marriage if it were legal (Schippers 2016). Marriage does more than ensure that the proper people are responsible for the upbringing of the child; it ensures that when the child grows up, he or she will know who is off limits as a marriage partner. Almost every human society enforces **exogamy**: Marriage to (or sex with) members of your family unit is forbidden. This is the **incest taboo**, which Sigmund Freud argued was the one single cultural universal (since, social scientists have identified others—as we discussed in Chapter 2). Without it, lines of succession and inheritance of property would be impossible.

Marriage is also a primary mechanism of *social reproduction* (see Chapter 7). Sex, marriage, and family play a critical role in reproducing boundaries between groups because most people practice what sociologists call "endogamy" rather than "exogamy." **Endogamy** refers to marriage within one's own social group. We tend to marry people who are more like us than not. So, marriage between people of the same race is more common than marriages between people of different races. We tend to marry people within our religious groups, with similar amounts of education, who grew up belonging to a similar social class, and more. As we will see in this chapter, these forms of family formation play a central role in the reproduction of inequality (and privilege) in society.

Monogamous relationships are often presented as more than simply a cultural norm, but biologically destined. Monogamy, however, is a social institution, only one of many possibilities observed around the world and throughout history.

monogamy
Marriage between two (and only two) people.

polygamy
Marriage between three or more people. (*See polygyny* and *polyandry*.)

polygyny
The most common form of polygamy, a marriage between one man and two or more women.

polyandry
Rare form of polygamy in which one woman marries two or more men.

group marriage
Rare marriage arrangement in which two or more men marry two or more women, with children born to anyone in the union "belonging" to all of the partners equally.

polyamory
Committed relationships among three or more people.

exogamy
Marriage among people who belong to meaningfully different social groups (race, religion, social class, etc.)

incest taboo
Sigmund Freud identified the taboo that one should not have sex with one's own children as a foundation of all societies.

endogamy
The strong tendency to marry within one's own social group (often with the same race, religion, class, educational background for instance).

iSoc: The Sociology of Families

12.1.3 Recognize how each of the five elements of the iSoc model can be used to examine families sociologically.

Society could not exist without families; it's equally true that families could not exist without society. Families are a central social institution, a core element of what comprises a society in the first place. Indeed, families are so central, that "the family" is often a metaphor for other groups; you've probably heard someone say that your school is a family, or your country, or a "family style" restaurant. "When you're here, you're family." Obviously, the advertisers think that's it's a good thing to be family. The metaphor implies a certain kind of relationship that we imbue with great significance. Sociologists who study families do so by examining families within the different dimensions of the iSoc model.

IDENTITY—Your family is the first arena in which you develop your *identity*. Families are primary institutions of socialization, not only teaching you table manners and right from wrong, but also what it means to be a member of a family in the first place. One of Michael's earliest childhood memories was, at around 7 years old, having his grandfather tell him to stop shouting to his friends at the beach. "Why?" he asked. "Because we're Kimmels, and Kimmels don't raise their voice," his grandfather replied. Learning what it means to be "an Aronson" or "a Bridges" for that matter implies that we understand families as central elements of our identities—who we understand ourselves to be. It is in your family that you first understand that your needs will not always be the first to be met, and that you have to compromise and share. Families provide an identity anchor: Your family gives you a ready-made history, a sense of where you come from and who you are. (Michael still rarely raises his voice.) Think about it this way: Blaming your parents for your problems is the surest sign that you know your identity is, at least partly, derived from your family life.

INEQUALITY—Families derive their sense of themselves largely through participation in various communities: Your race, class, or ethnicity is often interwoven into your family's sense of itself. Families are centrally related to *inequality*, and in more ways than one. Social inequalities are the bricks and mortar of family life, defining how the family works, or doesn't work, what roles you have to play in the family, and how the family gets along. Some family dynamics reproduce existing inequalities at a micro level: Poorer families have more children, for example, which often leads to less mobility, increasing the likelihood of a second generation of poverty—what sociologists call *social reproduction*. Families navigate social inequality in complex ways: They both perpetuate and are defined by forms of inequality; but they also exist to shield us from other forms of inequality. They involve lines of power and authority, but are also among the most intimate relationships we will ever have.

INTERACTIONS—Social interactions with others in your family are often the prototype for how you will interact with others throughout your life. You learn how to deal with authority figures by interacting with your parents, how to deal with colleagues and fellow workers by interacting with your siblings or cousins. Is your younger brother or sister a "servant" who you get to boss around, or a vulnerable younger person who needs and deserves your protection? How does your older brother or sister treat you? What's more, in some family forms, you observe how men and women are supposed to interact with each other, what their roles and expectations are. Does dad do much housework? Does mom work outside the home? When is it okay to raise your voice? Does anybody hit anybody else? Although it's true that many people who engage in family violence were raised in violent homes, there are many more who were raised in violent homes who are not violent. It's not inevitable, but it's a family interaction that can shape what you think is "normal." This means that in an important sense, families are something that we produce in *interaction* with one another—and as such, they are continually being defined and redefined through this ongoing and dynamic process.

INSTITUTIONS—At its origins, the family also served the functions of virtually every other social *institution*: It was a church, an economic unit (the family farm, a son apprenticing to his father's trade), a school (you were taught at home), and more. Today, the family interacts with every other social institution, bringing you into those institutions and establishing a connection with them. You go to religious services *with* your family, they help with your homework (or homeschool you) and sometimes provide your first educational instruction. Family budgets are a cornerstone of every economy, and members of families tend to vote similarly. As such, the family should be sociologically understood as *both* a core social institution *and* the primary way you first interact with other social institutions.

INTERSECTIONS—Not all families are alike and not all families are created equal. Examining *intersections* within and between families means studying the ways that black families might be meaningfully different from Filipino American families. It also means examining the different experiences and understandings of families shaped by things like social class, sexuality, age, and more. Examining intersections allows sociologists to examine why and how people experience families as well as whether some groups might have greater access to realizing the families they want or need. It is a powerful lens that allows us to examine identity and inequality and take into account the complexity inherent in understanding that not everyone experiences family in precisely the same way.

The iSoc model helps sociologists examine the various dimensions of families and family life as well as what role they play in society. Family is an important social institution to learn about, and often fun, because we've all got one. The family you land in—whether by birth, choice, or chance—shapes your future more than you may realize; families shape your experiences and opportunities over the entire course of your life. And sociologists have been studying families since they've been studying anything at all.

A Brief History of "The Family"

12.1.4 Summarize the external forces that affected the emergence of families as well as how they have changed over time.

You've probably seen this type of exhibit in a book, movie, or television show. Natural history museums often display lifelike dioramas of other cultures—Eskimo, Polynesian, Amazonian—and also displays that portray the evolution of modern society through the Neolithic, Paleolithic, and Pleistocene ages. These sorts of dioramas are often depicted in exactly the same form. In the front, a single male, poised as a hunter or fisherman. Behind him, by a fire toward the back of the tableau, sits a single woman, cooking or preparing food, surrounded by several small children. Dioramas depicting animals often depict animal families in a shockingly similar form. A single male—lion, gorilla, whatever—standing proudly in front, a single female and offspring lounging in the back waiting for him to bring home fresh meat.

Most of these animals actually live in larger groupings, extended families, and cooperative bands. And lionesses, for instance, do most of the hunting (and caring for the young) while the males lounge about lazily most of the day. Similarly, every family throughout human history was not a nuclear family unit, a residential arrangement of only two generations, the parents and their children. Indeed, the nuclear family emerged only recently, within the past few

Family forms and the relationships within families are often assumed to have existed for all of human history. This is why images and exhibits depicting early humans often situate them as having had family arrangements, roles, and relationships that depict stereotypes of men's and women's roles in the family. These depictions, however, are historically inaccurate; they do not portray early human families and societies as they actually existed.

thousand years, and still doesn't apply universally across race, class and cultural lines. For most of human existence, our family forms have been quite varied and significantly larger, including several generations and all the siblings all living together. Exhibits in the museum like those described here are not historically accurate reflections of human (or animal) history. Rather, they are better understood as normative efforts to make the contemporary nuclear family appear to have been eternal and universal, to read it back into history and across species—in a sense, to rewrite history so that the family didn't have a history but instead to pretend it had always been the way it is. Nothing could be further from the truth. Families have developed and changed enormously over the course of human history.

Families evolved to socialize children, transmit property, ensure legitimacy, and regulate sexuality. They also evolved as economic units. Because children went to work alongside the adults for much of human history, they contributed to the economic prosperity of the family; in fact, the family became a unit of economic production. Property and other possessions were passed down from the adults of the family to the children. Occupation, religion, language, social standing, and wealth were all dependent on kinship ties.

In all agrarian societies, including Europe and the United States as late as the nineteenth century, the household has been the basic economic unit. Production—and consumption—occurred within the household. Everyone participated in growing and eating the crops, and the excess might be taken to market for trade. There was no distinction between family and society: Family life *was* social life. Families performed a whole range of functions later performed by other social institutions. The family was not only a site of economic production and consumption. It was:

- *A school.*   Any reading and writing you learned was at your parents' knee.
- *A church.*   The head of the household led the family prayers; you might see the inside of a "real" church or temple once or twice a year.
- *A hospital.*   Family members knew as much as there was to know about setting broken bones and healing diseases.
- *A daycare center.*   There were no businesses or religious or community organizations to take care of children, so someone in the family had to do it.
- *A police station.*   There were no police to call when someone wronged you, so you called on your family to take care of the situation.
- *A retirement home.*   If you had no family to take care of you in your old age, you would end up in debtor's prison or begging on the streets.

extended family

The family model in which two or three generations live together: grandparents, parents, unmarried uncles and aunts, married uncles and aunts, sisters, brothers, cousins, and all of their children.

Obviously, all these functions cannot be met by the nuclear family model. The most common model in the premodern era was the **extended family**, in which two or three generations lived under the same roof or at least in the same compound. No one left the household except to marry into another family, until the group got too big for the space available and had to split up. And even then, they would build a new house nearby, until eventually everyone in the village was related to everyone else.

The Origins of the Nuclear Family

12.1.5   Understand when and why the nuclear family emerged as well as why thinking of it as a "traditional" family form is historically inaccurate.

Just as families are no longer concerned exclusively with socializing children, marriage developed far more functions than simple sexual regulation, ensuring that parents and children are socially aware of and tied to one another. Marriage could also validate a gentleman's claim to nobility and establish that a boy had become a man. It could form a social tie between two families or bring peace to warring tribes. In the Middle Ages, European monarchs often required their children to marry the child of a monarch next door, on the theory that you are unlikely to go to war with the country that your son or daughter has married into. (It didn't work—by the seventeenth century, all of the European monarchs were second or third cousins, and they were virtually constantly invading each other).

Marriage has also come to represent a distinctive emotional bond between two people. In fact, the idea that people should select their own marriage partner is actually a recent phenomenon. For thousands of years, parents selected partners to fulfill their own economic and political needs or those of the broader kinship group. Arranged marriages are still the norm in a number of countries. People still fall in love—romantic love is practically universal across human societies—but not necessarily with the people they intended to marry. The tradition of courtly love, praised by the troubadours of medieval France, was actually about adultery, falling in love with someone else's spouse (De Rougemont 1983). Only about 200 years ago did men and women in Western countries begin to look at marriage as an individual affair, to be decided by the people involved rather than parents, church, and state.

Like the **companionate marriage**, in which individuals choose their marriage partners based on emotional ties and love, the nuclear family is a relatively recent phenomenon. It emerged in Europe and the United States late in the eighteenth century. Its emergence depended on certain factors, such as an economy capable of supporting a single breadwinner who could earn enough in the marketplace to support the family (the "**family wage**") and sufficient hygiene and health so that most babies would survive with only one adult taking care of them. Historians like Carl Degler (1980) trace the new nuclear family, as it emerged in the white middle class between 1776 and 1830, and Christopher Lasch (1975) suggests the theory of **progressive nucleation** to explain how it gradually superseded the extended family and became the norm. During the nineteenth century, industrialization and modernization meant that social and economic needs could no longer be met by kin. It became customary for children to move far from their parents to go to school or look for work. With no parents around, they had to be responsible for their own spouse selection; and, when they married, they would have to find their own home. Eventually adult children were expected to start their own households away from their parents, even if they were staying in the same town. When they had children of their own, they were solely responsible for the child rearing; the grandparents began to play smaller, less formal roles.

The change was not always beneficial: In every generation, husbands and wives had to reinvent child-rearing techniques, starting over from scratch, with many possibilities for mistakes. Indeed, anthropologist Margaret Mead (1978) commented that never before in history had anyone ever asked families to do all of this with so little help and support. As she wrote, "With no relatives, no support, we've put it in an impossible situation." Today, we often think that spouses should be our most intimate relationships in every aspect of the word. It's not uncommon to expect our spouses to fulfill us in every way, from best friend to most romantically intimate relationship in our lives. We've asked marriages to live up to an ideal that may be unrealistic for many. So, it shouldn't be all that surprising that many perceive their marriages to fall short of this ideal (Coontz 2005).

The nuclear family is also a more highly "gendered" family—roles and activities are allocated increasingly along gender lines. On the one hand, because the nuclear family was by definition much smaller than the extended family, the wife experienced greater autonomy. On the other hand, in her idealized role, she was increasingly restricted to the home, with her primary role envisioned as childcare and household maintenance. She became a "housewife." Because the home was seen as the "women's sphere," middle-class women's activities outside the home began to shrink. The husband became the "breadwinner," the only

companionate marriage
The (historically recent) idea that people should select their own marriage partner based on compatibility and mutual attraction.

family wage
Arising in the nineteenth century, the term refers to a wage sufficient for a single wage earner to support a family (spouse and children).

progressive nucleation
Christopher Lasch's idea that industrialization and modernization made it customary for children to be independent from their parents in going to school, looking for work, and choosing a spouse, increasingly reducing extended family arrangements and promoting the nuclear family model of household structure and child-rearing.

Romantic love is virtually universal, found in all cultures. But it is not always seen as the most important ingredient for marital relationships. This couple in Bali, Indonesia, is waiting for the religious ceremony at their wedding. They may have married for love or may be part of an arranged marriage organized by their parents. In many societies that practice arranged marriage, this tradition is not the only method of "getting hitched."

SOCIOLOGY AND OUR WORLD

WHY SEPARATE SPHERES MEANT "MORE WORK FOR MOTHER"

Why did shifts in the family and the emergence of "labor-saving" technologies have the combined effect of producing *more* work for mothers?

In 1983, historian Ruth Schwartz Cowan published a landmark study of how industrialization changes family life—*More Work for Mother: The Ironies of Household Technology from the Open Hearth to the Microwave* (1983). Cowan was able to show that an industrialized workplace meant that men reduced the type of work and amount of hours spent working when compared with their preindustrial counterparts. The story for women, however, is more complex. Cowan showed that the work required of women did not shift in the same way. You might think that modern appliances, like vacuums, cupboards, refrigerators, microwaves, and more would have made work at home easier. But Cowan showed that, actually, indeed ironically, household technology did everything but make women's work at home any less of a burden.

From the start, household technology was marketed this way. "Time-saving" was a popular promise attached to new-fangled items being marketed to make life at home "easier." In the 1890s and later, many feminists welcomed household appliances as labor-saving devices that would free women to pursue more independent and political

A gift in a million...for a wife in a million!

General Electric 1949 Two-door Refrigerator-Home Freezer Combination

GENERAL ELECTRIC

lives. Sewing machines and washing machines were demonstrated at suffrage events. In fact, however, Cowan shows that the labor "saved" by household technology not only failed to save women time spent doing household labor, but it also actually produced new kinds of labor. This happened for two reasons. First, a great deal of labor-saving household technology performed work that had historically been performed by husbands and servants (for families who could afford servants) in the first place. Second, shifts in household technology actually transformed the *norms* (see Chapter 2) of household cleanliness, creating new expectations associated with keeping house. Dressers meant that clothes had to be put away. Cupboards meant that dishes would be stored out of reach of children, shifting tasks children had historically participated in within the division of household labor onto mothers—like setting the table for a meal. Vacuum cleaners made cleaning the floor easier, yes; but they also helped to usher in new standards of cleanliness for floors at a historical moment when fewer people were responsible for cleaning them than ever before in American history.

one in the family who was supposed to go to work and provide economic support for the household. (Of course, families of lesser means could not always survive on the salary of a single earner, so wives often continued to work outside the home.)

As the attention of the household, and especially the mother, became increasingly centered on children, they were seen as needing more than food, clothing, education, and maybe a spanking now and then. They were no longer seen as "little savages," barbarians who needed civilizing, or corrupt sinners who would go to Hell unless they were baptized immediately. Instead, they were "little angels," pure and innocent, born "trailing clouds of glory" as they descended from heaven. Therefore, they had to be kept innocent of the more graphic aspects of life, like sex and death, and they needed love, nurturing, and constant care and attention. The number of children per family declined, both because they would no longer be providing economic support for the family and because each child now required a greater investment of time and emotional energy.

In modern societies, children don't often work alongside their parents, and the family has become a unit of consumption rather than production; its economic security is tied to the workplace and the national economy. Instead, the major functions of the family are to provide lifelong psychological support and emotional security.

Family Diversity

12.1.6 Explain why sociologists today argue that family diversity is the new norm when it comes to family forms.

The contemporary American **nuclear family**—the breadwinning husband, his homemaker wife, and their 2.2 children, who live in a detached single-family house in a suburb we call Anytown, USA—developed historically. But even today, it is only one of several family forms. Families vary not only from culture to culture but also, intersectionally, within our society, by class, race, ethnicity, and more. As each racial and ethnic group has a different history, for instance, their family units developed in different ways, in response to different conditions. For example, how can we understand the modern African American family outside the deliberate policies of slavery whereby families were broken up and husbands, wives, and children deliberately sold to different slave owners, so as to dilute the power of family as a tie of loyalty to something other than the master?

We tend to think of the nuclear family when we picture a generic family in our mind and discuss this family form as traditional, as in "the traditional family." But as far as traditions go, however, this one has a shockingly short history and was never as much of a norm as we seem to remember it was.

nuclear family

The presumed model of the modern American family structure consisting of a breadwinning husband, homemaker wife, their children, and no extended family members.

matrifocal

Families centered on mothers.

Sociologists are interested in the diversity of family forms by race and ethnicity—as well as other axes of diversity, like sexuality, and social class. Some racial and ethnic differences are now so well documented that to enumerate them sounds almost like a stereotype. And to be sure, each ethnic group exhibits wide variation in family form. Many of these differences may be as much a result of class as they are of specific ethnic culture. For example, working-class families—regardless of the family's ethnic background—are less stable than middle-class families and more likely to be "**matrifocal**" (centered around mothers). As a result, sociologists are also interested in the process by which one family form became the standard against which all other family forms were measured—and found wanting. Think about this intersectionally. Although these family adaptations might be more popularly associated with ethnic minorities, they are also seen among the white working class, which suggests that they are less "ethnic" adaptations to a white family "norm" and more class adaptations to a middle- and upper-class family "norm" (Wilson 1987). As each ethnic group develops a stable middle class, their families have often come to resemble the companionate-marriage nuclear family of the white middle class. This is not evidence suggesting that the nuclear family form is inevitable, but that it is *expensive*—without significant governmental support, it cannot flourish.

The contemporary American family is the result of deliberate social policies beginning in the first decades of the twentieth century. These policies held up a specific model as normal and natural and then endeavored to fulfill that vision by prohibitions on women's entry into the workplace or pushing them out once they found their way there, ideologies of motherhood and birth control to limit family size, a "eugenics" movement that demanded that all new immigrants conform to a specific standard of marriage and family, and a new educational and child-rearing ideology that specified how parents should raise their children. American families have always been subject to deliberate policies to encourage certain types of families and discourage others, a process that continues today.

The end of World War II saw the largest infusion of government funding toward the promotion of this new nuclear family—the interstate highway system that promoted flight to the suburban tract homes, the massive spending on public schools in those suburbs, and policy initiatives coupled with ideologies that pushed women out of manufacturing work and back into the home, while their veteran husbands were reabsorbed into the labor force or went to college on the GI Bill.

The family form that finally emerged in the 1950s is what is sometimes now referred to as the "traditional family"—a nuclear family form that took a great deal of

FIGURE 12.1 Proportion of U.S. Households, by Type (1940–2016)

As you can see, married couples used to occupy a larger proportion of American households than they do today. And much of this shift is a result of a dramatic decline in married couples with children households (married couples without children saw much smaller decreases). This household type was always less of a norm than we are sometimes led to imagine.

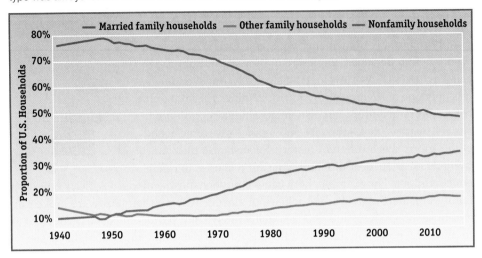

NOTE: According the the U.S. Census, "other family households" refers to households in which the householder was living with children or other relatives but had no spouse present. "Nonfamily households" refers to households in which the householder is living either alone or with nonrelatives only.

SOURCE: Data from U.S. Census Bureau, Current Population Survey, Annual Social and Economic Supplement, selected years, 1940–2016.

We often look back to the 1950s as an era when the "traditional family" was intact. Indeed, contemporary family forms are often weighed against the family form that we saw on family sitcoms aired around the United States in the 1950s and 1960s, like *Leave It to Beaver* (1957–1963) depicting a fictional family—The Cleavers—with a working dad (Ward), stay-at-home mom (June), and two children, both boys (Wally and Beaver).

social organization to produce. And it was not only aided by social policies, but simultaneously idealized in our culture as well in classic situation comedies of the 1950s and early 1960s like *Father Knows Best* and *Leave It to Beaver* on that newly emergent and culturally unifying medium: television. These policies promoting this family form, coupled with the ubiquity with which the nuclear family was presented in Americans in popular culture gave the impression that nearly everyone lived in nuclear families. That was far less the case than is popularly imagined, as historian Stephanie Coontz (1992) in her classic analysis, *The Way We Never Were: American Families and the Nostalgia Trap* (see FIGURE 12.1).

The nuclear family form was more possible in the 1950s and 1960s because of a wartime economy that enabled an unprecedented proportion of American families to thrive off of a single wage. This means that the nuclear family was far less a naturally emergent evolutionary adaptation and far more the anomalous result of deliberate social planning and social and cultural engineering. Today, the new norm in family life is diversity, according to sociologist Philip Cohen. As Cohen (2014) writes, "Some of the new diversity in work-family arrangements is a result of new options for individuals, especially women and older people, whose lives are less constrained than they once were. But some of the new diversity also results from economic changes that are less positive, especially the job loss and wage declines for younger, less-educated men since the late 1970s." And although family diversity leads to family inequality in the United States—in that some family forms have an easier time existing than others—this is by no means inevitable. For instance, in the United States, families with unmarried mothers are disproportionately likely to be poor. But this is not true in Nordic countries like Denmark, Finland, or Norway. Similarly, the children of single mothers fare much worse on education outcomes than children of married couples in the United States But that discrepancy is not true of the children of single mothers in every society. So, although it can sometimes be tempting to conclude that family diversity and family inequality are inevitably connected and that some family forms will always be privileged, sociological research suggests that societies can be organized in ways that enable diverse family forms to exist and thrive.

---

iSOC AND YOU The Family as a Social Institution

The family, institutionally, is a primary source of your *identity*, because it anchors you in tradition and culture, connects you to a past, and provides a foundation for social *interaction*. Families work as social *institutions* because they accomplish something for all of us that we could not easily accomplish on our own. But families also reflect and reproduce *intersecting* social *inequalities*, so that family form, structure, and even the ways in which family members interact vary significantly by race or class or ethnicity. What's more, families themselves are hardly egalitarian—older people have power over younger ones, sometimes gender inequality is also present, and even siblings are hardly an egalitarian citizenry under the rule of the adult parents. It is in the family that we first learn how to interact with those who have more or less power than we do. Over time, the family has remained a primary institution, but functions it once held have been transferred to other institutions: the workplace, schools, and religious institutions.

12.2 Forming Families

Sociologists study the variations in the family form and also the processes by which we form families. To most of us, it probably seems pretty straightforward: After a few years of dating, you become increasingly serious with one special someone, you fall in love, you gradually realize that this one is "it," and you decide to marry. Historically, this has been a process known as courtship, the intensification and institutionalization of an intimate relationship from meeting to marrying to mating. And it is so common, so casually assumed, we often have no idea just how unusual and recent this process is.

In this section, we consider the process of family formation from the iSoc perspective. Our family relationships are important elements of our identities. This is why Facebook allows us to identify these connections as "special" on their site. You can identify siblings, parents, aunts, uncles, and more. And these identifications imbue those relationships and interactions with special and symbolic meaning. But you can also identify as "married," "in a relationship," or even "it's complicated." Relationships are core parts of our identities. Some of these relationships become institutionalized—like marriage. Marriage is not in our genes, it's a relationship form that societies created, and that relationship has changed as societies change. And marriage is only one type of "family" relationship. Sociologists who study marriage and the family, however, are also interested in studying inequality—marriage can be seen as a mechanism promoting love and care, but also as a social relationship that often works to reproduce existing forms of inequality in a society. It is through understanding family formation processes intersectionally that we can fully appreciate how different groups engage in different family formation practices, and these practices powerfully shape virtually every aspect of our lives.

Courtship and Dating

12.2.1 Summarize shifts in courtship and dating in the United States since the late 1800s through today distinguishing between "calling," "dating," and "hookups."

In the famous musical *Fiddler on the Roof*, a drama that centers on the breakdown of a traditional Jewish family in a small Russian village in the late nineteenth century, as each of the three daughters chooses to marry an increasingly troublesome man, the girls' parents reminisce about their courtship. "The first time I met you was on our wedding day," Golde tells her husband, Tevye. That was not uncommon. So, he asks if she loves him. "Do I what?!?" she answers. Courtship was largely unknown in ancient

Dating and courtship in college has been partly replaced with a "hook up" culture, in which groups of friends socialize and then individuals may pair off later. Hooking up usually entails few, if any, expectations of an actual relationship.

dating
A courtship practice that arose in the 1920s in which young adults participated in recreational activities in pairs rather than groups prior to engaging in long-term commitments to one another.

calling system
A process by which a young man (a "suitor") would obtain permission for access to a young woman, and ascertain her interest in forming a romantic attachment, all beginning with a request to "call," or visit her at home, initially under the watchful eyes of her parents and extended family.

society. Marriages were arranged, and children often were betrothed (promised, engaged) as toddlers. But even in the days when marriages were arranged by parents, children often had a voice in the selection process, and they found ways to meet and evaluate potential partners so they could make their preferences known. By the turn of the twentieth century, they were classmates at coed high schools, and they formed romantic bonds with people that their parents didn't even know. But the process of change was slow, and not without its challenges. And it is equally true that courtship has not transformed in this way everywhere or even for every group in the United States.

The custom of **dating**, engaging in recreational activities in pairs rather than groups and with the goal of establishing or strengthening a romantic commitment, did not arise until the 1920s. Before that time, a separate system of courtship existed among Americans that scholars now refer to as "calling." Within the **calling system** of courtship, young men ("suitors") might confront young women in a public setting and inquire as to whether they might "call" on the young ladies at a later date. At this moment, young women could politely decline or express interest. At a later time, if the young man had received an invitation, he would report to her residence. The parents (or a servant if the family could afford one) would answer the door, and the man would state that he was there to "call" on the young woman in question. This presented another opportunity for young women to turn down men's advances. If she was interested, the young man and woman would be seated in a room to themselves to have a "private" conversation ("private" in quotes because the whole of the encounter was organized to take place under the watchful eyes and ears of parents). By modern standards, this would have qualified as a "date"—though it's probably dramatically different from any date on which young people reading this book will have been.

Dating emerged as a system of courtship that directly challenged aspects of early twentieth century courtship rituals. Children of working-class immigrants in major American cities were trying to distance themselves from the old-fashioned supervised visits that their parents insisted on, and fortunately they enjoyed both a great deal of personal freedom and a wide range of brand-new entertainment venues (Bailey 1989). Although many fashions and trends begin among the elite and filter down to lower classes, dating is an interesting example of how this process is capable of going both ways. By the 1930s, the custom had spread to the middle class. College-aged men and women participated in a process called "rating and dating," whereby they were rated on their desirability as a date and would ask or accept dates only with people of similar ratings. Dating was based on physical attractiveness, social desirability, and other qualities—not family name and position. Most importantly, dating was supervised and scrutinized by one's peer group, not one's parents—an enormous transformation (Nock 2003; Waller 1937).

College and high school became the time of unparalleled freedom for American youth and were increasingly taken up by dating and courtship. Campus wits joked that girls were attending college just to get their "Mrs." degree. By the 1950s, parents were eagerly awaiting their son or daughter's first date as a sign of their entry into adulthood. There were many stages: casual dating, "going steady" (dating only one person), being "pinned" (wearing a class ring or pin as a sign of commitment), and finally becoming engaged. Boys and girls were supposed to begin dating early in high school and date many people over the period of years, perhaps going steady several times, until they found "the one" to marry. But not for too many years. "Still dating" in the late 20s was considered sad and slightly unwholesome. In the 1970s, the increased incidence of divorce sent many people in their middle years into the world of dating again, until there was little stigma about dating at the age of 30, 40, or 50.

SOCIOLOGY AND OUR WORLD

DATING IN JAPAN

Why is dating so much more important to young people in the United States than it is in Japan?

In 1955, parents arranged 63 percent of all marriages in Japan. In 1998, the percentage had dropped to 7 percent (Retherford, Ogawa, and Matsukura 2001). A 2011 survey finds a slight rise in the rate of arranged marriages, at 10 percent (Millward 2012). However, in the wake of the 2011 tsunami and earthquake, arranged marriages seem to be back on the rise. Yet, relative to the United States, Japan has not developed a strong dating culture. You're not expected to bring a date to every recreational activity, and if you're not dating anyone at the moment, your friends don't feel sorry for you and try to fix you up. The expectation that dating leads to marriage is also absent. Japanese television and other mass media don't glorify marriage and ridicule or pity single people, as American television often does (Orenstein 2001).

More recent research suggests that some of this is shifting, but not without challenge. There is a new label—"parasite singles"—that targets dating women out of fears associated with the economic and demographic future of Japan (Rosenberger 2007). Recent economic stagnation has resulted in children living with their parents and relying on their parents' income and savings for longer periods of time because fewer are able to afford to live on their own. And the marriage rate dropped alongside this shift as well.

In 2001, schoolgirls around the world were asked whether they agreed with the statement that "everyone should be married." Three-quarters of American schoolgirls agreed. But 88 percent of Japanese schoolgirls disagreed (Coontz 2005). As singlehood and dating are increasingly recognized and stigmatized in Japan, it will be interesting to see what the future holds.

Today it seems that everyone is dating. Kindergarteners go on "play dates," married couples go on "date nights," and the recently widowed or divorced are encouraged to date again almost immediately. Internet "dating sites" are among the Web's most popular, and your potential dates are neatly categorized by age, gender, race, and sexual orientation. Yet, it also sometimes seems that no one is dating. On campuses, the preferred mode of social and sexual interaction is "hooking up," which is so loose and indiscriminate that its connection to dating and mating has been lost (we discussed this last trend in more depth in Chapter 11).

Shifting Contexts for Family Formation

12.2.2 Explain the role that marriage has played in societies in the past and how that role has changed in some contemporary societies.

Marriage is the most common foundation for family formation in the world. The marriage of two people is universal in developed countries, although there are significant variations among different cultures. Marriage is not identical to a nuclear family, although the two tend to go together. One can imagine, for example, marriage as a relationship between two people who are, themselves, embedded in an extended family or a communal child-rearing arrangement (such as the *kibbutz*). Sociologically, its universality suggests that marriage forms a stable, long-lasting, and secure foundation for the family's functions—child socialization, property transfer, legitimacy, sexual regulation—to be securely served.

Marriage is also a legal arrangement, conferring various social, economic, and political benefits on the married couple. This is because the state regards marriage—that is, stable families—as so important that it is

With the proliferation of automobiles alongside shifts in courtship, a new consumer economy emerged geared toward young people. Driving to a local restaurant on a date was initially thought of as deviant and American parents worried about the decline of young people's morality. Companies like Coca-Cola eagerly attempted to shape the ways young people spent this income they were dedicating toward courtship, inventing the "Coke date" and encouraging young people with advertisements to go on a date and share a Coke.

Brighten every bite with Coke! Only Coca-Cola gives you that cheerful lift...that cold crisp taste! No wonder it's the real refreshment...anytime...anywhere you're driving! Pause...for Coke!

SIGN OF GOOD TASTE

willing to provide economic and social incentives to married couples. As a result, people who have been legally excluded from marrying—the mentally ill, gays and lesbians—have sought to obtain that right as well.

And marriage is certainly not the only living arrangement for people in society. In America over the past century, the number of adults living alone increased by more than 20 percent, single parents and children by more than 20 percent, unmarried partners by well more than 60 percent, and unmarried partners with their children by nearly 90 percent. In several developing countries, marriage is also occurring later and bringing with it numerous positive social outcomes. In industrialized countries like the United States, the implications of the shift toward later marriage and less marriage are a source of extensive sociological research and social debate.

Many heterosexual women in the United States and Europe change their names when they get married, taking their husband's name as their new last name. Although most family forms in the United States are examples of *bilateral kinship*, name sharing is an example of how we may symbolically uphold patrilineal ideals. But not all heterosexual married women take their husbands' last names. A study in 2010 showed that a woman taking their husband's last name (or hyphenating her name) was perceived as meaningfully different than women who kept their own names. Women with changed names were perceived as more caring, dependent, and emotional, but less intelligent, competent, and ambitious than women who kept their last names. A job applicant who took her husband's name was less likely to be hired and her salary lower, costing her more than $470,000 over her working life (Noordewier, Ruys, and Stapel 2010).

Marriage varies widely by race, ethnicity, education, and income. Two-thirds (66 percent) of white women older than 18 who make more than $100,000 a year are married, whereas only 29 percent of black women older than 18 who earn less than $20,000 per year are married (Raley, Sweeney, and Wondra 2015). However, this is actually a misleading use of the statistics because you are comparing rich white women to poor black women, not rich to rich or poor to poor. Do poor white women have the same rate of marriage as poor black women? We don't know from this sentence. Census 2014 data shows that 66 percent of white women making more than $100,000 are married, whereas 45 percent of black women making more than $100,000 are married; and between 43 and 70 percent (depends on level of income) of white women making less than $20,000 are married, whereas between 23 and 34 percent of black women making less than $20,000 are married.

Marriage, itself, has changed. It no longer necessarily signifies adulthood or conveys the responsibilities and commitment it once did—at least not for everyone. People are putting off marriage, living together in romantic relationship outside of marriage, or opting for singlehood in larger numbers. On the other hand, marriage has become more desirable than ever before, bringing together couples from varying backgrounds and repeat performers and inspiring many who've been excluded to fight for the right to marry. Some of these changes are temporary, like delayed marriage and, in most cases, cohabitation (which often leads to marriage). Others, like singlehood, have become more permanent and less transitory.

Same-Sex Marriage and LGBT Family Forms

12.2.3 Summarize gay and lesbian families' existence throughout history as well as how legal transformations have affected them in the United States and beyond.

Same-sex couples have been cohabiting for hundreds of years, although sometimes societal pressures forced them to pretend that they were not couples at all. In the seventeenth and eighteenth centuries, for example, middle-class men often "hired" their working-class partners as valets or servants, so they could live together without question. Sometimes they pretended to be brothers or cousins. In the eighteenth and nineteenth centuries, it was so common for women to spend their lives together that there was a special name for their bonds, "Boston marriages." Though gay and lesbian couples have been socially, culturally, and legally prohibited from forming families, this does not mean they haven't been forming families. In anthropologist Kath Weston's (1996) classic ethnography of gay and lesbian families in *Families We Choose: Lesbians, Gays, Kinship*, she studied family formation patterns among gay men and lesbian women living in the San Francisco bay area, showing that they produced networks of what anthropologists used to call **fictive kin**—people whom we form kinship ties and networks with who are not legally or biologically tied to us as kin. Gay and lesbian people have long been producing families, whether the rest of society recognized them as families or not.

Recent sociological research allows us to paint a portrait of the typical lesbian or gay couple, at least the ones who are open:

- *They're urban.*   More than half of gay and lesbian couples live in just 20 U.S. cities, including gay meccas or "gayborhoods" like Los Angeles; San Francisco; Washington, D.C.; New York; and Atlanta. Though there is some evidence to suggest that gayborhoods are, more recently, in decline (Ghaziani 2014).
- *They're well educated and make more money.*   They tend to have higher educational attainments and higher incomes than men and women in heterosexual marriages.
- *They are less likely to have children.*   Almost half of married couples versus 27 percent of lesbian couples and 11 percent of gay male couples are living with children of their own. And that number is higher when we only consider gay and lesbian people younger than age 50 (Gates 2013). Many are the products of previous heterosexual marriages, although artificial insemination and adoption are increasingly common.
- *They tend to be more egalitarian.*   They are more likely to share decision making and allot housework more equally than married couples and have less conflict as a result (Allen and Demo 1995; Carrington 2002).
- *They are not always interested in marriage.*   Although same-sex marriage remains a symbolic political battleground for many same-sex couples, there are many for whom marriage is not desirable for an array of personal and political reasons (Bernstein and Taylor 2013; Baumle and Compton 2016, 2017).

And, until 2015, they were not permitted to marry in most of the United States. In 2012, for instance, 25 states had a constitutional amendment restricting marriage to one man and one women, 11 states had a law (not affecting their constitution) restricting marriage to a man and a woman, and the United States is debating a federal constitutional amendment to ban gay marriage. However, 2011 to 2012 proved to be a significant year for same-sex couples as California lifted its ban on same-sex marriage and New York, Maryland, and Washington all legalized same-sex marriages; Delaware, Hawaii, Illinois, and Rhode Island started granting civil union rights to same-sex couples, and Maine and New Jersey included ballot initiatives in November 2012 to amend the state constitution and legalize same-sex marriage. In states that did not allow gay and lesbian couples to marry, these couples lacked access to family hospital visitation rights, family inheritance, and more than 1,000 other rights that heterosexual couples enjoyed. Until 2015, gay and lesbian families were legally prohibited from forming marital family households.

Part of the reason that the Supreme Court ruled that same-sex couples could now legally marry in 2015 is because of you. When we write "you" here, we don't necessarily mean you personally—but "you" collectively. People's opinions about same-sex marriage have been on the move in recent history (see FIGURE 12.2).

When we examine how age intersects with people's opinions about same-sex marriage, opponents are significantly older than supporters. Among college students, the support for same-sex marriage is even stronger. In 2009, 64.9 percent of entering college

fictive kin

Similar to "urban tribes," the term refers to people with whom we form kinship ties and family networks even though they are not legally or biologically tied to us as kin.

FIGURE 12.2 Americans' Attitudes Toward Same-Sex Marriage, 2001–2017

Opposition to same-sex marriage has been steadily declining. In 2011, the lines crossed for the first time in history and more Americans support legal same-sex marriage than oppose it. The Supreme Court decision in *Obergefell* v. *Hodges* (2015) granting same-sex couples the right to marry followed public opinion trends as well.

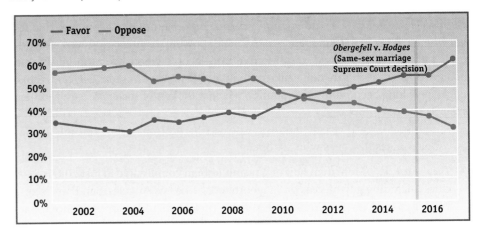

SOURCE: Data from Pew Research Center. Available at http://www.pewforum.org/fact-sheet/changing-attitudes-on-gay-marriage/.

freshman supported same-sex marriage; that percentage climbed to 71.3 percent by 2011 (Higher Education Research Institute at UCLA 2012). Same-sex marriage is now legal in the United States. And as of this writing, same-sex couples can marry or enter into civil partnerships with the same rights as heterosexual couples in most European countries and can enter into civil partnerships with most of the same rights as heterosexual couples in nine others, including Brazil, France, Israel, South Africa, and Switzerland (see MAP 12.1).

It is important to remember that, as is the case for heterosexual people and couples, marriage is not the only way to form a family. But it is a family form and relationship in which many societies are culturally, legally, and politically invested. So, while the legality of gay marriage in the United States is an important illustration of how definitions of family change at the legal level, it's important to acknowledge that not everyone wants to get married (whether gay or straight).

Interracial Marriage

12.2.4 Understand what it means that Americans are more open to racial intermarriage as an ideal than a practice.

Through most of the history of the United States, marriage or sexual relations between men and women of different races were illegal. Not until the Supreme Court's *Loving v. State of Virginia* decision in 1967 were men and women of different races legally permitted to marry in all U.S. states. There were serious fines, penalties, and prison sentences for not only individuals participating in an interracial marriage, but often, also for those officiating such marriages (see TABLE 12.1).

Social barriers still place dating, courtship, and marriage within clear racial categories. However, interracial marriage (one form of "exogamy") is evolving from virtually nonexistent to merely atypical: While only 6.3 percent of married heterosexual couples are interracial, 12.5 percent of unmarried heterosexual couples and 13.3 percent of unmarried same-sex couples are interracial. Today, 4.3 percent of the population of the United States claims ancestry in two or more races, and between 1980 and 2013 the share of U.S. couples with spouses of different races increased from 1.6 percent to 6.3 percent (Pew Research Center 2015). Moreover, nearly two-thirds of Americans (63%) say it "would be fine" with them if a member of their own

MAP 12.1 Same-Sex Marriage Law Around the World

Much more of the world allows gay and lesbian couples to marry than used to. Among those that do allow gay marriage, the United States passed federal legislation later than many of the other countries. It's also still true, however, that gay marriage remains illegal in many nations around the world.

Not	Legal	Legal in some
Legal	nationwide	jurisdictions

SOURCE: Data from Pew Research Center, "Gay Marriage around the World, June 26, 2015. Available at http://www.pewforum.org/2015/06/26/gay-marriage-around-the-world-2013/.

TABLE 12.1   Interracial Marriage in U.S. States, 1913

These are state laws restricting interracial marriage in a collection of U.S. states in 1913.

	Forbidden Marriages	Status of Marriage	Maximum Penalty
Alabama	White person and Negro or *descendant* of a Negro to the third generation, inclusive, though one ancestor in each generation be white. Constitution forbids marriage of white person with Negro or descendant of Negro.		Imprisonment 2–7 years for each party.
Arizona	Persons of Caucasian blood or their descendants with Negroes, Mongolians, or their descendants.	Void.	
Arkansas	Between a white, a Negro, or mulatto.	Void.	
California	White person with Negro, mulatto, or Mongolian.	Void. No license to be issued.	
Colorado	White person with Negro or mulatto, except in portion of state derived from Mexico.		Fine $500 or imprisonment 2 years.
Delaware	White person with Negro or mulatto (as enrolled).	"Unlawful."	Fine $100 or imprisonment 30 days.
Florida	White with a Negro (one-half or more Negro blood). Constitution specifies persons of Negro descent to fourth generation, inclusive.	Full and void.	Imprisonment 10 years or fine $1000.
Georgia	White persons with persons of African descent.	"Forever prohibited, null and void."	For officiating, fine, imprisonment, 6 months, and work in a chain gang, 12 months.
Idaho	White person with Negro or mulatto.	Illegal and void.	For solemnizing, fine $300 and imprisonment 3 months.
Indiana	White person with person having one-half or more Negro blood.	Void.	Imprisonment 10 years and fine $100.
Kentucky	White person with Negro or mulatto.	Prohibited and void.	Fine $5000.

SOURCE: Charles Davenport, *State Laws Limiting Marriage Selection Examined in the Light of Eugenics.* Eugenics Record Office, Cold Spring Harbor, NY, 1913, p. 28.

family were to marry someone outside their own racial or ethnic group (Wang 2012). And 2 years later 37 percent of Americans said that "having more people of different races marrying each other was a good thing for society" (Wang 2015). Blacks are twice as likely as whites to have an immediate family member in an interracial marriage, and Latinos and Hispanics fall in the middle of those two groups. The most common interracial couple in the United States is a white husband married to an Asian wife (14 percent of all interracial couples).

Despite the increasing frequency of interracial marriage, many couples still face disapproval—sometimes even from the members of their own families. And although almost half of all Americans think that allowing interracial marriage will make the world a better place, rates of interracial marriage and dating among heterosexual couples in the United States are much lower. Collecting generalizable data on dating relationships is difficult. But, as online dating becomes more popular in the United States, social scientists can begin to examine some of these questions in more detail. One thing we have learned is that although most Americans seem to favor interracial relationships when asked about them on surveys, they are less likely to become involved in an interracial relationship themselves than you might think. One online dating site (OkCupid.com) makes some of the data associated with their users public. So, we can begin to examine patterns in beliefs and behaviors surrounding interracial intimacy in the United States.

For instance, a small proportion of OkCupid.com users think that racial intermarriage is a bad idea—(from 2008 and 2014, that proportion of users fluctuated between just less than 8 percent of users to roughly 3 percent). And the proportion of OkCupid users who state that they strongly prefer to date someone of their own race dropped from roughly 42 percent of users to approximately 30 percent during that period. Yet, women's and men's rates of reply vary by race, and heterosexual identifying people on the site are most likely to respond to people of the same race. (You can see the reply rates by race at http://blog.okcupid.com/index.php/your-race-affects-whether-people-write-you-back/.) Interestingly, the pattern of interracial avoidance that we see among heterosexual users of OkCupid.com is less pronounced among individuals using the site to search for same-sex intimacy and relationships.

What all of these trends illustrate is that while Americans' openness to interracial relationships has been increasing, particularly in relatively recent history, their participation in interracial relationships has not increased at the same rate. More Americans are in interracial relationships than ever before. But, given the level of racial and ethnic diversity in the United States, Americans still tend to marry people of their own racial background. It's a pattern that persists despite Americans' professed openness to interracial relationships. And although Americans do express openness to interracial relationships, many interracial couples still face societal disapproval, sometimes even from family and friends.

Delayed Marriage

12.2.5 Summarize what we can learn from the facts that people are delaying marriage for longer periods of time.

Marriage is a relationship structured by age in virtually every society in which it exists. But just how young is too young is a question that differs by society. Girls can get married as young as 14 in Nicaragua (15 for boys), but both girls and boys have to wait until they are 20 in Myanmar. In some societies—like the United States—young women and men are legally allowed to marry at the same age. But in many, the ages for women and men (or boys and girls, depending on age) are different.

Early marriage—usually arranged by parents—is still the rule in sub-Saharan Africa and South Asia. One in three women alive today entered a marriage before the age of 15 (UNICEF 2014). Almost half of all child brides live in Southern Asia;

56 percent of young women in South Asia are married before the age of 18. In West and Central Africa, it's 46 percent; in Latin America and the Caribbean, 30 percent (UNICEF 2014). More than half of all girls younger than 18 are married in some countries, including Bangladesh, Chad, India, and Nepal (The 2014 UNICEF report notes these countries as more than 50 percent: Niger 77 percent, Bangladesh 74 percent, Chad 69 percent, Mali 61 percent, Central African Republic 60 percent, India 58 percent, Guinea 58 percent, Ethiopia 58 percent, Burkina Faso 52 percent, and Nepal 52 percent.) The prevalence of child marriage is decreasing significantly around the world. Since 1970, the median age of first marriage has risen substantially worldwide—for men from 25.4 years to 27.2 and for women from 21.5 to 23.2 (U.N. Population Fund [UNFPA] 2005). In 1985, 33 percent of all women ages 20 to 24 had been married or in union before age 18, and we have seen a slight and steady decline since then (see FIGURE 12.3).

In the United States, young people are experiencing longer periods of independent living while working or attending school before marriage. In 1950, the median age of first marriage was slightly older than 20 for women, and just younger than 23 for men; in 2015, the median ages are 27.8 for women and older than 29.7 for men (U.S. Census Bureau, American Communities Survey 2015a, 2015b). Yet, this statistic is a little misleading because it presents the idea that heterosexual men's and women's ages at first marriage have been steadily increasing in the United States. Remember, however, that the 1950s and 1960s were a unique period in American history. So, comparing heterosexual women's and men's median age at first marriage now with that period creates a picture of marriage that looks a bit different if we wind back the clock a bit. In 1900, the median ages at first marriage for women and men were 22.0 and 26.1, respectively.

A 25-year-old American man today is far more likely to be single and childless than he would have been 50 years ago—or even 25 years ago. Among 25-year-old women, the fastest-growing demographic status is single, working, childless, head of household (Fussell and Furstenberg 2006). The United States still has one of the industrial world's *lowest* ages at first marriage. Differences among black, white, and foreign-born populations in education and labor market opportunities have narrowed since the 1960s, creating more similarities between the lives of people of color and their white peers. However,

FIGURE 12.3 Child Marriage Rates Around the World
Although it's true that child marriage is still legal in many countries around the world (and sometimes practiced despite not being legal), it's also true that it is decreasing. The decline is primarily as a result of a decline in women marrying before they reach age 15—somewhat less so among women marrying after 15, but before they reach 18.

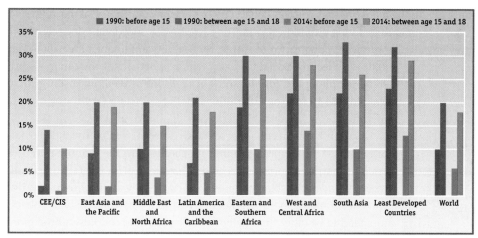

SOURCE: Data from UNICEF Data: Monitoring the Situation of Women and Children, 2015. Available at http://www.data.unicef.org/corecode/uploads/document6/uploaded_pdfs/corecode/Child-Marriage-Brochure-HR_164.pdf.

significant educational and economic gaps and inequalities, in addition to cultural differences, mean that different groups will continue to first marry at different ages.

Cohabitation

12.2.6 Explain both why cohabitation has become more common and what we can learn when we understand the groups among which it is the most and least common.

cohabitation

Once called "shacking up" or "living in sin," now more often called just "living together," the sociological term for people who are in a romantic relationship but not married living in the same residence.

One reason some people are delaying marriage longer is that they are moving in together before marriage in larger numbers. Sociologists use the term **cohabitation** to refer to unmarried people in a romantic relationship living in the same residence. Research on cohabitation primarily considers heterosexual couples as it is often compared with marital relationships (and, until 2015, gay and lesbian couples did not have the option to marry one another at the federal level). A few decades ago, when nonmarital sex was illegal in most states, cohabitation was virtually impossible—landlords wouldn't rent to people unless they were related by blood or marriage; hotel managers could lose their license if they rented rooms to unrelated people. Today, cohabitation has become commonplace, largely lacking in social disapproval (Jayson 2008). The number of Americans currently cohabitating climbed to about 8 million in 2016, up 29 percent since 2007 (Stepler 2017; Teachman 2003). Nearly 32 percent of young adults ages 18 to 34 were living with a partner as of 2014, either married or cohabitating (Fry 2016), and in the first decade of the twenty-first century, unmarried couple households grew by almost 42 percent (Waggoner 2016).

Globally, cohabitation is most common in liberal countries—in Sweden, for instance, it is four times as prevalent as in the United States. That is largely because those countries provide universal health care and education to everyone. So, you don't need to get married to be covered by your spouse's health plan or to ensure your children can go to university. However, it is rare in more conservative countries and remains illegal in some. As cohabitation becomes more common, it may also begin to be a relationship form undertaken in more patterned ways—to be "institutionalized." Currently, cohabitation does not have a set cultural script all cohabiting couples are encouraged to follow. For instance, should cohabiting couples share finances? If you're about to begin a cohabiting relationship, should you meet your partner's parents and families? Or are you allowed to live together not knowing each other's families?

In the 1980s, sociologists thought of cohabitation as a stage of courtship, somewhere between dating and marriage—some even referred to it as "trial marriage." Women cohabitors were found to be more likely to desire marriage than men (Blumstein and Schwartz 1983), but about 25 percent did not expect to marry the man they were currently living with (Fowlkes 1994; Seltzer 2001). Today, with more extensive information about cohabitors and more sophisticated research methods, many researchers are working to understand the many reasons couples cohabit before marriage or in lieu of marriage.

For some, their living situation has nothing to do with marriage. More than one million elderly Americans cohabit, for example, for a significant financial reason (older people collecting Social Security will lose benefits if they marry). But some people opt to cohabit for other reasons as well, prompting some sociologists to see the cohabiting relationship as a family form in its own right.

Gay and lesbian cohabitors tend to diverge from many of these patterns, in several respects coming much closer to the demographics of straight married couples. Part of this has to do with the fact that, until recently, gay and lesbian couples were not legally allowed to marry. But consider some of the differences. As a group, gay and lesbian cohabitors tend to be older than heterosexual cohabiting couples. A little more than half of gay cohabitors and straight married couples pay a mortgage on a home they own, as compared with only one third of opposite-sex

Almost half of people ages 25 to 40 in the United States have cohabited, and 60 percent of all marriages formed from the 1990s on began with cohabitation.

FIGURE 12.4 Household Earnings by Couple Employment Status and Marital Status among Heterosexual Couples, 2016

Heterosexual cohabiting couples are less likely to rely on a single income than are heterosexual married couples. Among married couples, more than one in five are relationships in which the husband earns at least $50,000 more than the wife. This income disparity is much less common in cohabiting households. And equal relationships come with more benefits for both partners (indeed, egalitarian couples are happier and healthier on most measures). As a result of this, there are a larger share of people in unmarried households in every income category in which both partners are employed (as you can see). Although less than 1 in 10 heterosexual cohabiting households earning more than $100,000 annually are ones in which only the man is working, about twice that proportion of heterosexual married couples earning more than $100,000 a year are ones in which only the husband is employed. Couples in which both partners are in the labor force also face fewer "exit costs" should they decide to divorce. This is a different way of thinking about divorce than you might be used to. But research suggests that part of this trend is the result of higher levels equality inside of heterosexual cohabiting relationships.

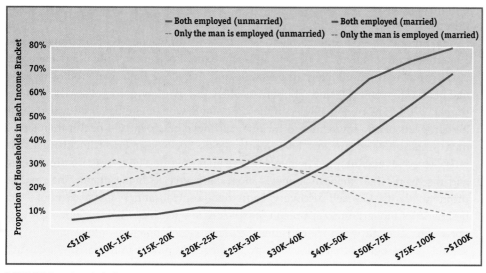

SOURCE: Data from U.S. Census Bureau, Current Population Survey, 2016 Annual Social and Economic Supplement.

cohabitors. On average, gay and lesbian cohabitors tended to be better educated and more affluent than their straight counterparts (Elliott and Dye 2005).

So, gay and lesbian cohabitors were, on average, better educated and more affluent than opposite-sex cohabitors (see FIGURE 12.4). But part of this may also have had to do with the fact that they are more likely to be older as well—age is correlated with education and income as well. In these ways, opposite-sex cohabitors are different from same-sex cohabitors. But in other ways, they are similar. For instance, opposite-sex cohabitors are similar to straight married couples when it comes to raising kids—just shy of half of each group have kids in the home. Today, 4 percent of children in the United States are living with two unmarried parents: 68 percent are white; 39 percent are Hispanic; and 21 percent are black (U.S. Census Bureau 2015).

Just over a decade ago, researchers found that cohabitation before marriage increased the risk of divorce (Teachman 2003). Today, researchers find the odds of divorce among women who married their only cohabiting partner are significantly lower than among women who never cohabited before marriage—but they are higher for those who cohabit with a romantic partner more than once. The risk seems to be a higher risk of divorce if one cohabits many times or does not cohabit at all (Lichter and Qian 2008; Teachman 2003). But whether that increased risk of divorce has something to do with the experience of cohabitors is less easy to identify. For instance, it could be—and many sociologists agree—that the type of person who is willing to cohabit will also be someone who is more likely to condone divorce. This means that it may have nothing to do with the experience of cohabitation at all. Some evidence also suggests that heterosexual cohabiting relationships may also exhibit more equality between women and men (see FIGURE 12.4).

Living Alone

12.2.7 Understand what sociologists can learn from trends in solitary living and what these trends indicate about shifts in family life in the United States.

Not long ago, people who were "still not married" by their late 20s were considered deviant. Men were considered "big babies," who "refused to grow up" and "settle down." Women were "old maids," thought to be too unattractive or socially inept to attract a husband. But singlehood has become commonplace, if not exactly respectable. Just more than half of all Americans ages 25 and over are not married or cohabiting. This represents a historic milestone: More than half of all households in the United States do not have a couple living there. More than 60 percent of all unmarried Americans have never been married. And the trend differs for different groups.

In Europe, the percentage of households with only one occupant ranges from 39 percent in Germany to 24 percent in Ireland and 7 percent in Bulgaria (Klinenberg 2012). Women are more likely to be single and live alone than men. Today, roughly half of all U.S. women 18 and older are married and living with a spouse (U.S. Census Bureau 2015). But, among singles in the U.S., single women are better educated, have higher levels of employment and income, and have better mental health than single men (Catalyst 2009; Fowlkes 1994; Marks 1996). Sociologist Eric Klinenberg (2012) interviewed several hundred people who live alone (a group he refers to as **singletons**) and discovered that modern living is more conducive to living alone. The practice promotes things like self-discovery, individual control, and personal freedom—all hallmarks of modern life. As a result, people are less fearful of living alone than they once were. Though when we consider the identity of "singleton" intersectionally, we should also recognize that not every group is equally drawn to live alone or capable of living alone—and these differences tell us an important story of about inequality as well (see FIGURE 12.5).

singletons

Modern term for people living alone, often by choice.

FIGURE 12.5 Proportions of Men and Women Living Alone by Age Group, 2016
Although the percentage of single people is rising for all Americans (presently 27 percent of all households have only one occupant), those rates vary considerably between different groups. Consider how gender and age intersect to make living alone more and less likely for different age groups of men and women in the United States. Among the young, men are more likely to live alone than women. But that changes when men and women get old, and much of this has to do with health disparities making it more likely that women will live longer than men.

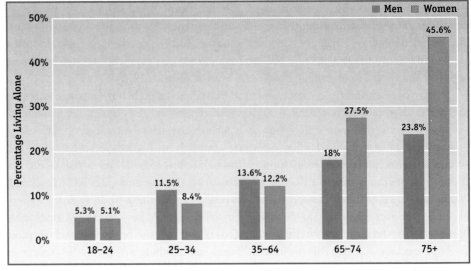

SOURCE: Data from U.S. Census Bureau, Current Population Survey, Annual Social and Economic Supplement, 1967–2016.

Unmarried people are, unsurprisingly, far more social than married couples. They eat in restaurants more often, and mingle with friends more regularly than do married people. Far from finding that being single causes your social networks to shrink, Klinenberg (2012) found that, instead, single people have large and diverse social networks. This is an interesting finding, because it also says something about marriage. We don't often think of marriage as isolating and as cutting off social networks and ties; in fact, this is more likely a popular stereotype of singlehood. But Klinenberg's findings suggest that being single is not what it used to be—at least in the places where being a "singleton" is currently in vogue.

Thinking Sociologically about Nonmarital Choices

12.2.8 Explain how the rise in nonmarital choices is related to a changing relationship among sex, marriage, and reproduction in society.

Sociologists offer numerous explanations for the increases in delayed marriage, singlehood, and cohabitation. First, these changes are partially explained by new practices, such as courtship and dating. After all, arranged marriages usually take place when the children are younger. But courtship and dating are linked to the worldwide increase in the status of women. Although it's true that arranged marriages affected both boys and girls, increased individual choice of marriage partners enables more women to seek educational and economic advancement and increases choices for women. Second, these changes tend to be associated with higher levels of education—for both men and women.

Third, these changes are partially explained by changing sexual behaviors and attitudes, especially increased acceptance of "premarital sex." For a long time, sexual activity before marriage was referred to as "premarital" because it was assumed that the couple involved would be in a serious, committed relationship and intend to marry. Some view sex as an appropriate conclusion to a first date. Still others "hook up" and don't even go as far as dating. Therefore, a more precise term might be **nonmarital sex**—sex that is not related to marriage (see FIGURE 12.6).

nonmarital sex
Sex outside of marriage.

FIGURE 12.6 Shifts in the Timing and Sequence of Sex, Marriage, and Reproduction in the United States
Although not all sex leads to marriage or reproduction (nor is it intended to), one of the largest shifts in the family in the latter half of the twentieth century has to do with a greater separation of sex, marriage, and reproduction than has ever existed in human history. The gap between first sex and first marriage and birth for both women is wider today than it has ever been before.

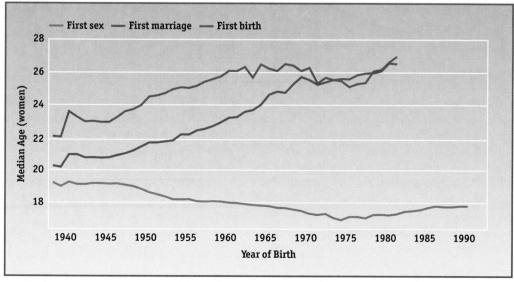

SOURCES: Data from The Guttmacher Institution; Finer and Filbin (2014).

Separating sex, marriage, and reproduction is a world historical event. In wealthy countries, especially in northern Europe, nonmarital sex has become increasingly acceptable, even during the teen years (Schalet 2011). These countries provide sex education and health care services aimed at equipping young people to avoid negative consequences of sex by encouraging contraceptive use. In the United States, public attitudes toward nonmarital sex have changed significantly over the past 20 years. In a national survey in the early 1970s, 37 percent of respondents said that nonmarital sex is always wrong. By 1990 this number had fallen to 20 percent (Michael et al. 1994). More recently, according to the General Social Survey, half of Americans agree that nonmarital sex is "not wrong at all," and just about one in four Americans agrees that it is "always wrong." However, attitudes differ by race and ethnicity (as well as by age). Nearly half (42%) of blacks say premarital sex is wrong, as compared to 32 percent of whites and 33 percent of Hispanics. According to a Pew survey, nearly two-thirds of whites say unmarried couples having children is bad for society, whereas 58 percent of blacks and 45 percent of Hispanics do (Pew Research Center 2007).

American social and political institutions reflect this complex picture and have changed slowly. As a result, rates of teen pregnancy and sexually transmitted infections (STIs) are much lower in Europe than in the United States, although their rates of sexual activity are no higher (Alan Guttmacher Institute, 2014). Living outside of marriage is more possible today than ever before. The relationship between sex, marriage, and reproduction is a *social* arrangement. And, as such, it will shift over time and as other elements of society change as well.

SOCIOLOGY AND OUR WORLD

IS THERE A SHORTAGE OF "MARRIAGEABLE" MEN TODAY?

Just what makes men "marriage material"?

The idea that some guys are not really "marriage material" is widespread in popular culture. It's possible to use the phrase precisely because it doesn't really seem to mean one thing. But sociologist William Julius Wilson (1987) gave the idea a measureable quality and a sociological name. He referred to this issue as men's "marriageabilty" and suggested that we measure men's relative marriageability by economic stability. That is, Wilson proposed that economic stability was a basic benchmark by which we could assess men's relative value as marital partners (among heterosexual relationships).

Wilson discovered that when we consider a stable income as the primary factor in considering whether men might be understood as "marriage material" by women who might consider a relationship with them, lower-class women (particularly lower-class *black* women) faced a dearth of marriageable men. Because of endogamy, we know that most people marry others within their own social class and race.

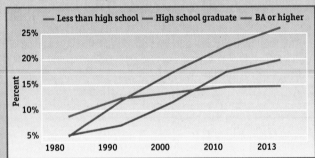

Percentage of 40-year-old Women Never Married by Education, 1980–2013

— Less than high school — High school graduate — BA or higher

Data from U.S. Census Bureau, American Community Survey (ACS).

And education is something sociologists often use as a proxy for social class (because the two are so correlated with one another). So, women with less education face smaller pools of men they might consider marrying (if income earned or even income potential is a characteristic by which heterosexual women assess men's suitability as marital partners).

What we do know is that the proportion of women who have never married by the time they hit their 40th birthday is on the rise in recent history. But that increase has been steeper for women with the least education in the United States. Indeed, today, more than one quarter of 40-year-old women with less than a high school education have never married. Perhaps the "marriageable men" are in the shortest supply among this group. What do you think?

SOURCE: Bridges, Tristan and Melody L. Boyd. "On the Marriageability of Men." *Sociology Compass* 10,1 (2016): 48–64.

iSOC AND YOU Forming Families
The choices you make about the type of family you will form, including whether you will even form a family, are profoundly social. Your *identity* (based on race, class, gender, age, sexuality, etc.) structures your choices; where you live creates or constrains options and possibilities. Your choices, although your own, are patterned in response to your own identity, your *interactions* with others, and existing social *inequalities*. And they are expressed in and through social *institutions*, like religion or education. All these structured possibilities *intersect*, forming, at once, a set of possibilities that is both unique to you and profoundly socially structured.

12.3 Children, Parents, and Parenting

Just as children have never been so important in our cultural values, parents have never been considered so important in the lives of their children. More people have wanted to become parents than ever before, including some who would rarely have considered parenting just 20 or 30 years ago: teenagers, 50-year-olds, gay and lesbian couples, infertile heterosexual couples. Ironically, even though parents are thought to be so utterly decisive in the outcomes of their children's lives, we also seem to believe that it's all hereditary, and socialization plays a very minor role in how our children turn out. Of course, to a sociologist, both sides are true: Parental socialization of children is enormously important, and parents also overestimate the control they have over their children's lives and social destinies. The questions, as you've learned in this book, are not whether or not parents are important or biology trumps socialization, but in which arenas and under what circumstances does parental influence make a decisive difference, and does it make the same differences among all groups around the world?

And although it's true that children have never been so valued and desired, it's equally true that they have never been so undervalued and neglected. Children around the world are facing poor health care, compromised education, and the lack of basic services. In the United States, families get virtually no financial assistance to raise their children, although they receive a lot of advice about having them. The core relationship of the family has always been between parents and children. Yet today that bond has been both loosened by other forces pulling families apart (like technology and overscheduling) and tightened by ideas that only parents know what is best for their children. It may be the case that the less time parents spend with their children, the more we insist that they spend time together.

In this section, we will examine family identities, interactions, and relationships in more detail. Lots of sociological research considers the relationships between parents and children. But, increasingly, people are opting to not have children (either by choice or necessity); and sociologists are equally interested in those people. Because the care of children has been a historical function of families, people who form families without children often have to form identities as people without children—"childless" or "childfree." We conclude the section considering who these people are and what it means that this group is growing.

Gender, Sexuality, and Parenting

12.3.1 Understand how parents' time spent with their children has changed and what we know about gender differences in parenting abilities and practices.

Pretty much every single household has a **domestic division of labor**, the allocation of some tasks to some people, and other tasks to other people. Although the majority of women are now working outside the home, numerous studies (including

domestic division of labor
The ways couples divide up all of the chores and obligations necessary to run a household.

HOW DO WE KNOW WHAT WE KNOW?

MEASURING TIME SPENT

People are often shockingly wrong about how much time they dedicate to various tasks. In general, we tend to overestimate how much time it takes to do things we dislike and underestimate how much time we spend on tasks we enjoy. So, people routinely overestimate how much time they spend on laundry, cleaning bathrooms, working out and underestimate how much time they spend watching television, napping, eating, or doing any number of tasks that provide them with joy.

Asking about how people use their time has been a mainstay on surveys dealing with households and family life. Social surveys often ask people to assess how much time they spend on all manner of mundane tasks in their lives—everything from shopping, sleeping, watching television, attending to their children, and household labor is divided up into an astonishing number of variables. This is one way sociologists try to create concrete evidence to assess (among other things) the division of household labor. When we ask people to estimate the number of hours they spend on different tasks around the house, we proceed from an assumption: that people can provide meaningful information or that their responses are an accurate (or approximately accurate) portrayal of the time they actually spend. Research has shown, however, that people either lie about how they use their time when asked or, more likely, that most of us don't really realize how we use our time and aren't good at providing that information when asked (Bianchi, Robinson, and Milkie 2006). This is why time diary studies came into being; they produce a more accurate picture of how people use their time.

Relying on more objective measures of time use, sociologists have been able to calculate shifts in the average time spent by heterosexual couples with children on core tasks related to maintaining a family household: paid work, housework, and childcare. Consider how mothers' and fathers' time spent on these various activities has changed over the past half-century.

About 5.2 million married women are stay-at-home mothers, staying out of the workforce to care for their children (younger than age 15). However, there are only about 199,000 married stay-at-home fathers (U.S. Census Bureau 2016). (Importantly, these numbers only consider heterosexual married couples and don't include gay men/women or those who are single parents.) On the other hand, American fathers are more active and involved parents than ever before. Today's new fathers (those between 20 and 35 years old) do far more childcare than their own fathers did and are willing to decline job opportunities if they include too much travel or overtime (Pleck and Masciadrelli 2004). The cultural meanings of fatherhood are on the move. Think about it this way. We use the terms mother and father as both nouns and verbs—you can be a mother, but you can also "mother" someone or be thought of as particularly "motherly." When we use mother as a verb, we mean "to nurture" or "to care for." But think about father. "To father" someone is best understood as having contributed genetic material that helped produce them in the first place. Fathering today, however, is much more than this.

As you might notice in the figure, fathers are, on average, working outside the home for pay for more hours a week than are women. But those hours have declined, and for mothers, paid work hours have increased. And although fathers do more hours of housework and mothers do less today than they did in 1965, it's also true that less hours are dedicated to housework in general. And many of those hours are taken up by an increase in childcare among both fathers *and* mothers.

Changes in Time Use for Parents Between 1965 and 2011

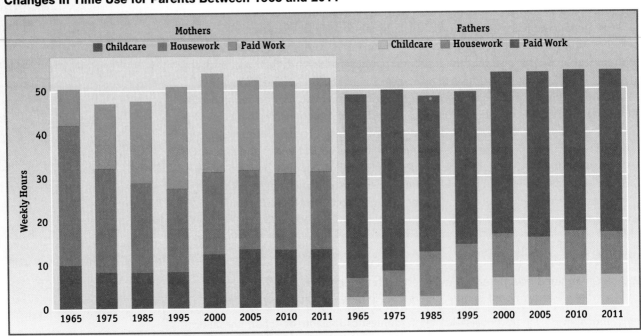

SOURCE: Data from 1965–2000 various early time use surveys (Bianchi, et al. 2006). 2003–2011 data from the American Time Use Survey, Pew Research Center; available at http://www.pewresearch.org/data-trend/society-and-demographics/parental-time-use/.

time study diaries) have confirmed that domestic work remains "women's work." Most people agree with the statement that housework should be shared equally between both partners, and more men in heterosexual couple households are sharing some of the housework and childcare, especially when the woman's earnings are essential to family stability (Perry-Jenkins and Crouter 1990). But still, the women in heterosexual couple households do about two-thirds of the housework (Bianchi et al. 2000; Sullivan and Coltrane 2008). That includes childcare. Mothers spend much more time than fathers interacting with their children. They do twice as much of the "custodial" care, the feeding and cleaning of the children (Sullivan and Coltrane 2008). A survey of American secondary students revealed that 75 percent of girls but only 14 percent of boys who planned to have children thought that they would stop working for a while, and 28 percent of girls but 73 percent of boys expected their partner to stop working or cut down on work hours (Bagamery 2004).

It seems obvious to many people that children need *both* a mother and a father. It's just plain common sense, counseled by therapists, ordained by religious figures, and even enshrined into law, as when a 2006 New York State Court of Appeals decision against same-sex marriage claimed, definitively, that "it is better, other things being equal, for children to grow up with both a mother and a father. Intuition and experience suggest that a child benefits from having before his or her eyes, every day, living models of what both a man and a woman are like." (Hernandez v Robles 2006).

For a long time, this seemed so self-evidently true that few researchers have actually looked for any empirical confirmation. But two sociologists did, and the results are somewhat surprising. Tim Biblarz and Judith Stacey (2010) actually compared the outcomes for children in two-parent families with same or different sex parents, as well as single-mother and single-father families. When they looked at the findings of all the empirical studies published since 1990, they found some differences, but not the ones you might have expected. The big difference wasn't between the different sex parents (a mom and dad) and all the other families. The big difference was between those families with one parent or two.

The children in two-parent families—regardless of whether that meant two moms, two dads, or one of each—had roughly equivalent outcomes on child's happiness, psychological adjustment, and school achievement. The findings, the two sociologists conclude, have "not identified any gender-exclusive parenting abilities"—women are not naturally better suited than men, and women and men don't have naturally different parenting competencies. What's more, when gender *is* a factor in parenting, it tends to favor women—that is, lesbian coparents tend to outperform heterosexual married parents on most measures of quality of parenting. They conclude that "no research supports the widely held belief that the gender of parents matters for child well-being." What children need is lots of love, support, and time—and that can come in many different arrangements and gendered packages. It's not the *form* of the family, as much as the *content* of its relationships.

Single Parents and Grandparents

12.3.2 Summarize shifts in single-parent families and the role of grandparents in recent history among U.S. families.

During the first half of the twentieth century, the primary cause of single-parent families was parental death. By the end of the century, most parents were living—but many were living elsewhere. As of 2014, about 34 percent of children in the United States are being raised in single-parent families, the vast majority of them in single-mother households, (Livingson 2014). Single-parent families have become more common among all demographic groups, but the greatest increases have been among less-educated women and among African American families (Sidel 2006; U.S. Census Bureau 2008a). Roughly, one in five white, non-Hispanic children live with a single parent, one in three Hispanic children live with one parent, and one in two black children live with one parent.

time diary studies
Research method that measures how people allocate their time during an average day by having subjects regularly record their activities in a diary, log, or other record.

Sometimes the parents are cohabiting, but most often one parent lives elsewhere and does not contribute to the day-to-day emotional and economic support of the child.

Most single parents are not so by choice. The pregnancy may have been an unexpected surprise that prompted the father to leave, or the relationship ended, leaving one parent with custody. Young, unprepared mothers predominate: Nearly 90 percent of teenage mothers are unmarried, but about 30 percent of mothers aged 30 to 44 are unmarried (U.S. Department of Health and Human Services 2016). Teen moms have the highest poverty rate of any demographic group in the United States, and those who do marry are much more likely to get divorced: 50 percent of women who marry before age 18 are divorced within 10 years, as compared with only 15 percent of those who marry between the ages of 25 and 29. At the same time, an increasing number of women are choosing single motherhood, either through fertility clinics and sperm banks or through adoption. White college-educated women lead this trend, many of whom are in professional and managerial jobs (Bock 2000; DeParle 1993; Hertz 2006; Mattes 1994).

Single mothers predominate both because it is easier for a father to become absent during the pregnancy and because mothers are typically granted custody in court cases. Although mothers predominate, the gender disparity varies from country to country. Among the countries for which data are available, Belgium has the smallest proportion of women who are the single parent ("only" 75 percent—that is, 25 percent of single parents are the fathers) with Norway, Sweden, and Finland close behind. Estonia has the largest (95%). Those countries in which women's status is higher tend to have lower percentages of women who are single parents. Even so, single mothers do not necessarily raise their children single-handedly. They are often interdependent with friends, family, and other members of their social networks, sharing support and care-work (DePaolo and Trimberger 2008; Hertz 2006). And, grandparents remain an important source of aid for single- and multiparent households alike.

The number of grandparents raising their grandchildren has grown from 957,000 in 1970 to more than 2.9 million by 2016. Currently 1 in 10 grandparents in the United States lives with their grandchildren. The number of multigenerational families living in grandparents' homes with at least one parent present has grown even more, from 2.4 million in 1970 to 4.3 million today. In 2012, 7 million children lived with a grandparent in either a parent or grandparent-maintained household; 4.5 million of these children lived in a grandparent maintained household (Wiltz 2016).

What happened to the parents? Often the father has abandoned the child, and the mother is incompetent, in prison, or on drugs. Courts are much more likely to grant custody of a child to a blood relative than to a legal stranger. Grandparents can even legally adopt their grandchildren, in effect becoming their parents.

Adoptive Parents

12.3.3 Summarize the different types of adoption, and understand the stigma that many adoptive families face.

When Angelina Jolie and Madonna each adopted babies from orphanages in Africa, they were ridiculed for trying to "save the world" one baby at a time. These Hollywood celebrities were not an elite vanguard, but latecomers to a well-worn trend in the industrial world. In the United States alone, about 135,000 children are adopted each year—about 2 percent of all children (Child Trends 2012).

Historically, adoption was considered an option to resolve an unwanted pregnancy—that is, it was about the biological mother. For centuries, all over Europe, foundling hospitals (those that received unwanted newborn babies) enabled mothers to anonymously leave babies at a back door or on the steps, and nuns would find willing families to raise the children as their own. Today, however, the interest has shifted to the adoptive families, as more and more people who want to have children use various services to adopt. Adoption has shifted from being about "helping a girl in trouble" to "enabling a loving family to have a child."

There are many different types of adoptions, including:

- *Foster care adoption:* Adoption of children in state care for whom reunification with their birth parents is not feasible for safety or other reasons.
- *Private adoption:* Adoption either through an agency or independent networks.
- *Intercountry adoption:* Adoption of children from other countries by U.S. citizens. The top three countries for international adoption in 2011 were China (2,231 adoptions), South Korea (260), and Russia (303) (U.S. State Department 2016). These numbers have been falling from an adoption peak in the United States in the 1970s primarily because laws surrounding international adoption have become more strict in the intervening years.
- *Transracial adoption:* Adoption of a child of a different race from the adopting parents; this involves about 10 to 15 percent of all domestic adoptions and the vast majority of intercountry adoptions.

Intercountry adoption (ICA) is often also transracial adoption.

Motivations for adoption vary. The couple may be incapable of conceiving a child themselves; they may be infertile or gay. Some single women adopt, whereas others use assisted reproductive technologies to become pregnant. In some cases, fertile couples adopt because they choose to adopt. Adoption seems to have largely beneficial effects for all concerned (birth parents, adoptive parents, and adoptees). However, a sizeable minority of birth parents characterize their adoption experiences as traumatic, and many birth parents and adoptees spend significant time trying to locate each other and experience some reunions or closure in their relationships. The number of adoptions by nonrelatives has declined sharply since 1970. The availability of birth control and legal abortion has meant that fewer women are having unwanted children, and adoption is still stigmatized in the United States; it is popularly perceived, as one sociologist put it, as "not quite as good as having your own" (Fisher 2003).

SOCIOLOGY AND OUR WORLD

HOME ECONOMICS, ADOPTION, AND CORNELL'S "PRACTICE BABIES"

What can we learn about intersecting forms of inequality from a consideration of the value of Cornell's "practice babies" on the adoption market?

During the first half of the twentieth century, it was not uncommon for elite universities to acquire newborn infants from local orphanages. The infants were delivered to home economics programs so that women at these elite institutions could learn the most up-to-date "science of mothering." The babies were often referred to as "practice babies" and young women took turns living in "practice apartments" not only learning about how to take care of children, but also received actual practice on a real live one while they were doing it.

Cornell babies were returned to orphanages typically after a year or so, at which point they became available for adoption

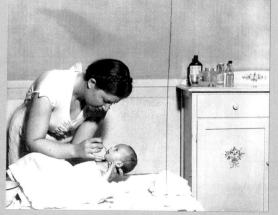

and were, by all testimonies, in great demand. Newly adoptive parents were excited to find a baby cared for by the latest methods in the science of childcare. Sometimes Cornell's babies were referred to as "Domecon babies" (short for "domestic economics"). The Home Economics program at Cornell University trained women in childcare sciences from 1919 to 1969. You can go to the University library website and find images of the notes young women studying there took on children, meticulously documenting their development.

Childfree versus Childless

12.3.4 Explain which groups of Americans have seen the largest increases in childlessness and why.

Childlessness is becoming increasingly common (see FIGURE 12.7). In 1976, about 10 percent of women ages 40 to 44 (near the end of their childbearing years) had never conceived a child. According to the U.S. Census Bureau, that percentage grew to 20 percent in 2005, and as of 2016, has dropped to 15 percent (Livingston 2015; U.S. Census Bureau 2016). Today one in five women in America is remaining childless throughout her life, twice the proportion of just a generation ago (U.S. Census Bureau 2016, Livingston 2015). Sociologists draw an important distinction between "childless" and "childfree" women; research shows that women with more income and job experience are more likely to forego children by choice ("**childfree**") than by necessity ("**childless**") (Blackstone and Stewart 2012, 2016). Women reaching their forties without children is a growing portion of our population, but they are not growing at the same rate among all groups of women. Indeed, middle- and upper-class women dominate the group of women who are older than 40 years old and do not have children. And increases in the proportion of women never married by the time they reach their 40th birthday has been shown to contribute to increases in childlessness among some groups (Hayford 2013).

Because class is an important predictor of childlessness, so too is education. The more education a woman has, the more likely she is to bear no children. The proportion of childless women with graduate or professional degrees is about 1 in 5; for those with less than a high school diploma, it's less than 1 in 10 (Livingston 2015). The longer women put off children, the more likely they are to opt out of having children altogether, perhaps because they become accustomed to a childfree lifestyle. And trends in the United States toward later childbearing and the growing proportion of childless women are in tune with patterns across developed countries (Ebener et al. 2015).

Race is also significant when it comes to living childfree. White women are the most likely to be childless, at 17 percent; Hispanic women are the least likely to remain childless, at only 10 percent. (The number of children a Hispanic woman has,

childfree

A term for women and men who forego having children as a personal choice.

childless

A term for women and men who forego having children out of necessity.

FIGURE 12.7 Percent of Childless Women Ages 40–44, 1976–2014

As you can see here, the proportion of women between the ages of 40 and 44 who have never had children has increased over the last four decades. In 1976, approximately 1 in 10 women reached the age of 44 without having children. By 2014, that figure jumped to just shy of 1 in 7 women—a big change in a relatively short period of time.

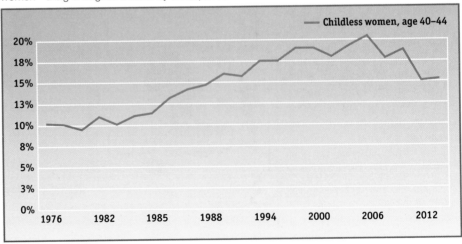

SOURCE: Data from U.S Census Bureau, Current Population Survey, June 1976–2014.

however, decreases sharply depending on how many generations her family has lived in the United States.) Fifteen percent of black women and 13 percent of Asian American women are childless (Livingston 2015). Part of the reason for this relationship between race and childlessness needs to be contextualized intersectionally. For instance, the middle- and upper-class women likely to remain childfree into their 40s are also more likely to be white, have higher levels of education, and be privileged as a result of their class status. So, rather than thinking of one of these factors as primarily responsible for explaining increasing rates of childlessness among educated, class-privileged, white women, sociologically speaking, it is the combination of these factors that combines to produce this net difference.

People have many reasons for remaining "childfree by choice," from concern about overpopulation to a desire to concentrate on their career to just not liking children or feeling they were not important to a happy marriage. In one study, women said they enjoyed the freedom and spontaneity in their lives, and some others gave financial considerations, worries about stress, relationships too fragile to withstand children, being housebound, and diminished career opportunities. Men were more likely to cite more economic considerations, including commitment to career and concern about the financial burden (Arnoldi 2007; Gerson 1985; Lunneborg 1999; Scott 2009).

WHAT DO YOU THINK? WHAT DOES AMERICA THINK?

Attitudes Toward Abortion

A central function of the institution of the family is to produce new members of society. Hence, family planning is a key element of the institution. Whether, and when, to have children is a personal or family decision, yet this decision is informed by societal norms and laws. Let's look at how you and other Americans view abortion and at how attitudes toward abortion have changed or not over time.

What do you think?

Do you think it should be possible for a pregnant woman to obtain a legal abortion if:

1. The woman's own health is seriously endangered by the pregnancy?
   - ○ Yes
   - ○ No
2. She is married and does not want any more children?
   - ○ Yes
   - ○ No
3. The family has a low income and cannot afford any more children?
   - ○ Yes
   - ○ No
4. She became pregnant as a result of rape?
   - ○ Yes
   - ○ No

What does America think?

In 1972, 87.4 percent of respondents said "yes" to women having the legal right to an abortion if their health was seriously endangered by the pregnancy. By 2016, 89.2 percent responded "yes" to the same question. It's a circumstance under which the largest share of Americans are supportive of abortion as a legal option. During the same period of time, Americans became slightly less supportive of women's right to an abortion if the pregnancy was the result of sexual assault. Similarly, Americans became less supportive of low income women's right to terminate pregnancies if they feel they cannot afford more children. Conversely, when asked whether married women should be legally allowed to obtain an abortion if they do not want any more children, Americans have become *more* supportive between 1972 and 2016.

Percentage of Americans Who Support Women's Right to Legal Abortion by Circumstances, 1972–2016

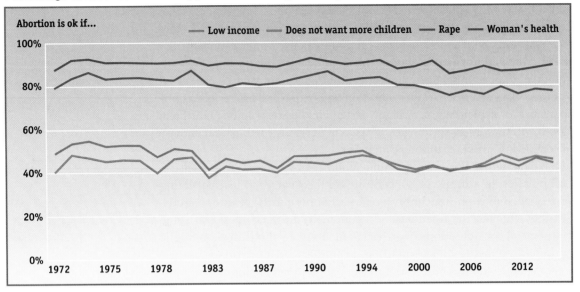

SOURCE: Data from General Social Survey, 1972–2016.

THINKING CRITICALLY ABOUT SURVEY DATA

Why do you think Americans have such different opinions about whether women ought to have the right to an abortion under different circumstances? What kinds of stereotypes associated with race, gender, and class do you think might intersect to impact Americans' opinions about abortion legislation?

iSOC AND YOU Children, Parents, and Parenting

The decision to be a parent or not, how many children to have, and when to have them feel like personal decisions, but they are structured, and even "predictable." No, sociologists can't predict your actual individual decision. But if we know your race, class, age, region, and family background—that is, if we know a bit about your *identity*—we can predict a likelihood that these intimate and personal decisions will result in a certain pattern. That's because these aspects of your identity also reflect existing social *inequalities*, and that your decisions depend also on social *institutions* that work in ways that encourage or discourage these kinds of choices. If you live somewhere with adequate schools, health insurance and care, and religious influences, you'd be more likely to have a child earlier, for example. Your *interactions* with others shape your individual decisions, and all these factors *intersect* with one another to form a kind of matrix of patterned individual decision making.

12.4 Family Transitions, Inequality, and Violence

Although we have already examined family diversity and transformations in family formation practices, families transform after they are formed as well. Sociologists are interested in studying the family as a dynamic social institution—one that shifts and changes over time. As such, sociologists are equally interested in how families change and what those changes mean for family members. Not all families remain legally intact forever. Indeed, separation and divorce are central elements of contemporary family life. Considering how these changes impact our family identity and alter family interactions are important questions to sociologists of the family.

And once separated and divorced, the creation of new families is possible once again. Sociologists are interested in examining the rise of "blended families," resulting from subsequent marriages. How are blended families different? What kinds of experiences and interactions are unique to blended family forms? Are they happier? Do they involve new and more challenging struggles and dilemmas?

Finally, because sociologists are always interested in understanding social inequality; we are equally interested in experiences of family inequality. This means that sociologists study the darker side of family life as well, including diverse forms of family violence. Understanding the ways that our identities are formed at the intersection of connections with many different groups, sociologists are always interested to examine how different groups have distinct experiences of family transitions, violence and more. In this section, relying on the iSoc model, we examine these transitions and forms of family inequality in more detail.

Separation and Divorce

12.4.1 Summarize some of what sociologists know about divorce in the United States in international perspective.

Through most of European and American history, marriage was a lifelong commitment. Period. Divorce and remarriage were impossible. Though couples could live separately and find legal loopholes to avoid inheritance laws, they could never marry anyone else. In the sixteenth century, the English King Henry VIII had to behead two wives, divorce two others, found a new church (the Anglican Church), and close all the monasteries in England to get out of marriages he didn't like. Today, it's a little bit easier. **Divorce** is the legal dissolution of a marriage. Grounds for divorce may vary from "no-fault" divorces, in which one party files for divorce, to those divorces that require some "fault" on the part of one spouse or the other (adultery, alienation of affection, or some other reason). Divorces are decrees that dissolve a marriage; they do not dissolve the family. Parents must still work out custody arrangements of children (if they have children), alimony payments, child support. If you know anything about divorce in the United States, you might know that we have a higher divorce rate than many other countries around the world. The **divorce rate** is a measure of the proportion of marriages that end in divorce (see U.S./WORLD Divorce Rates in International Comparison).

In the United States, the divorce rate rose steadily from the 1890s through the 1970s (with a dip in the Depression and a spike after World War II). During the past 30 years, it has fallen significantly, along with marriage rates overall (see FIGURE 12.8). The annual national divorce rate is at its lowest since 1970, marriage is down 30 percent, and the number of unmarried couples living together is up tenfold since 1960 (The State of Divorce 2007; U.S. Census Bureau 2011). These trends are led by the middle class. At the lower end of the scale, however, the picture is reversed, leading some sociologists to describe a "divorce divide" based on class and race (Martin 2006).

Whatever these different sociological dimensions, some commentators broadly blame divorce for nearly every social ill, from prostitution (where else are divorced men to turn?) to serial murder (evidently watching their parents break up has kids reaching for the nearest pickax). More moderate voices worry that quick and easy divorce undermines the institution of the family, forcing the divorced adults to start courting again when they should be engaged in child rearing and teaching children that dysfunction is the norm. Sociologists understand that both statements are, at least, partially true. Some people believe that the easy availability of divorce weakens our belief in the institution of marriage. On the other hand, sociologists often counter that divorce makes families stronger by allowing an escape from damaging environments and enabling both parents and children to adapt to new types of

divorce
The legal dissolution of a marriage.

divorce rate
A social scientific measure of the proportion of marriages that end in divorce.

U.S./WORLD

DIVORCE RATES IN INTERNATIONAL COMPARISON

Divorce rates have been falling around the world since 1980. But they are still higher in some places than others. The United States has one of the highest divorce rates in the industrialized world. But, thinking about what the "right" divorce rate ought to be for a society is a social decision. The optimal murder rate, for instance, is zero. But divorce is different in important ways - not all divorce, for instance, is bad. Divorce is difficult, but also helps some people exit bad marriages. But, how much divorce is the "right" rate for a society is the subject of a great deal of disagreement.

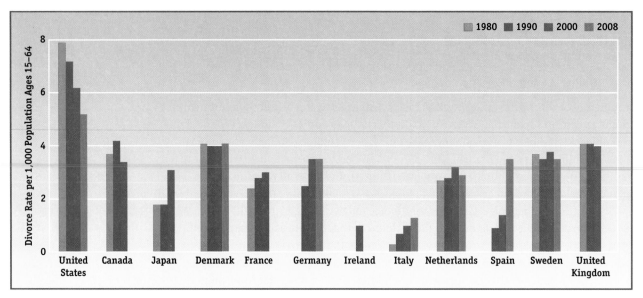

SOURCE: Data from U.S. Bureau of Labor Statics, updated and revised from "Families and Work in Transition in 12 Countries, 1980–2001," *Monthly Labor Review*, September 2003, with national sources, some of which may be unpublished.

INVESTIGATE FURTHER

1. Why does the divorce rate vary so much? What holds families together, and what pulls them apart?

2. Does making divorce more difficult to obtain good or bad for society?

relationships. Indeed, examining who wants out of marriages can tell us a lot about a marital relationship more generally.

Who usually wants the divorce? On the average, men become more content with their marriages over time, while women become less content; the wife is usually the one who wants out (Coontz 2005). Stanford University's "How Couples Meet and Stay Together" (HCMST) is a nationally representative survey of American adults organized by sociologist Michael Rosenfeld. Although many people assume that women are more likely to initiate breakups in heterosexual relationships, Rosenfeld discovered that this is true only among heterosexual marriages. They discovered that women initiate roughly about 7 out of every 10 divorces in the United States. But in dating relationships, men and women are equally likely to initiate a separation. So, it's not that women are more likely to leave relationships; rather, women are more likely to leave heterosexual marital relationships. Less is known about lesbian, gay, and bisexual

FIGURE 12.8 More Education, Less Divorce

As the graph illustrates, talking about the "divorce rate" as a static number conceals the fact that marriages are becoming both more and less stable for different groups. Sociologists today understand that it might make more sense to talk about divorce rates (in the plural) to allow us to examine how separation and divorce intersect with other categories of identity. As you can see here, those with more education become progressively *less* likely to divorce, producing what demographer Steven P. Martin calls "the divorce divide."

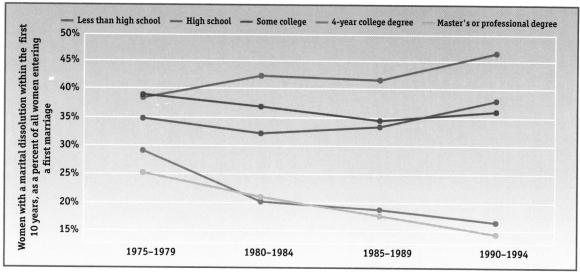

SOURCE: Data from "Trends in Marital Dissolution by Women's Education in the United States" by Steven P. Martin, Demographic Research, December 13, 2006 15 (20): 537–560.

individuals and divorce as same-sex marriage was only legalized at the federal level in 2015. But, Rosenfeld's HCMST survey specifically oversampled lesbian, gay, and bisexual Americans in the hopes of answering this question some day as well.

After Divorce

12.4.2 Understand why sociologists are less sure that divorce produces negative outcomes for children than we might think.

Married couples opt for divorce for all sorts of reasons, and the divorce itself can be easy or hard. So it is understandable that research on the impact of divorce on the husband and wife is mixed. Some studies find that people are happier after their divorce than before (Wilson and Oswald 2005). Others find psychological scars that never heal unless the divorcees remarry (Johnson and Wu 2002). Still others find that individual attitudes make the difference in well-being after a divorce (Amato and Sobolewski 2001). And a great deal of sociological research on divorce has been dedicated to divorces among heterosexual couples with children to answer the question of what kind of impact divorce has on children. We discuss all of this here. But we'll begin with the couple.

In the 1960s, sociologist Jessie Bernard found that "there are two marriages, his and hers—and his is better than hers" (Bernard 1972). The same is true for divorce. There are differences between men's and women's divorce, and, in general, his is better than hers. In a large majority of divorces, women's standards of living decline, while men's go up. Those men who are used to being the primary breadwinner may suddenly find that they are supporting one (plus a small amount for child support) on a salary that used to support a whole family. Those women who are more accustomed to being in charge of the household, with a secondary, part-time, or even no job, may suddenly find that their income must stretch from being a helpful supplement to supplying most of the family's necessities.

SOCIOLOGY AND OUR WORLD

INSTANT DIVORCE

What factors put you at risk of getting divorced and what things might shield you from divorce?

Does religion "cause" divorce? It's a silly question, right? It's true, though, that aside from Nevada (the state that is the home of the "instant divorce"), the states that have the highest divorce rates include many of those in the Bible Belt. The average divorce rate in the United States is 3.2 per every 1,000 people. The states with the highest rates, however, were: Arkansas, Nevada, Oklahoma, West Virginia, Florida, Wyoming, Idaho, Alaska, Alabama, Kentucky, Tennessee, and Colorado. Those states with the lowest rates were: Iowa, Illinois, Maryland, Massachusetts, Pennsylvania, Wisconsin, Texas, and New York (CDC 2016).

How would a sociologist explain this? First, divorce varies by income: Lower-income people have significantly higher divorce rates than wealthier people. (This makes sense: Higher income shields you from greater money problems, and lower rates of money worries means lower marital conflict.) The states with the highest divorce rates also have the lowest household incomes. But, religion also plays a role. The states with the lowest divorce rates have the highest percentages of Catholics and Jews and the lowest percentages of evangelical Protestants. Jews have very low divorce rates, and Catholics have a lower rate than Protestants because they are, technically, prohibited from getting a divorce.

It's also true that the likelihood of divorce increases as the age of marriage decreases: The younger you are when you get married, the more likely is divorce. And high divorce states have lower ages at first marriage—in part because they also are states that mandate abstinence-only sex education, which means they have the highest rates of teen pregnancy and therefore so-called "shotgun" marriages (Bryner 2009). In recent history, however, rates of teen pregnancy have declined (Boonstra 2014). Simply put, if you wanted to get divorced, you can increase your chances significantly by living in a Southern state, being poor, evangelical, taking an abstinence pledge, and getting married young.

It is crucial to remember that the breadwinning husband with an income-supplementing or stay-at-home wife has rarely been an option for many minority families. Black women, for example, have a longer history of workforce participation than women of other races (Page and Stevens 2005). Divorce plays an even bigger economic role for black households than for whites in the United States, partly because of this difference. Although family income for whites falls about 30 percent during the first 2 years of divorce, it falls by 53 percent for blacks (Page and Stevens 2005). Three or more years after divorce, white households recoup about one-third of the lost income, but the income of black families barely improves. This may have to do with the fact that when divorce occurs, the probability of black mothers working does not change, whereas recently divorced white women have an 18 percent greater probability of working (Page and Stevens 2005).

After a divorce among heterosexual parents, children of all races and ethnicities are still more likely to live with the mother, and the father visits on specified days or weeks. Not only do the children have to navigate this new living situation, but many will also soon move to a new home, enroll in a new school, and face the stress and depression of a mother who has suddenly entered or reentered the workforce as the primary breadwinner. And that's when the divorce is amicable. At times there is open hostility between the mother and father, with each telling the children how horrible the other is or even trying to acquire full custody, with many potential negative outcomes.

Psychologist Judith Wallerstein (2000) studied 131 children of 60 couples from affluent Marin County, California, who divorced in 1971. She followed these children through adolescence and into adulthood, when many married and became parents of their own. She found a sleeper effect: Years later, their parents' divorce is affecting the children's relationships. They fear that their relationships will fail, fear betrayal, and, most significantly, fear any change at all. Divorce, she argued, was bad for children—both immediately and later in their lives. Couples, politicians argued, should, indeed, stay together, "for the sake of the children." However, Wallerstein's findings have been quite controversial—and, in fact, have been disconfirmed by most sociological studies. After all, Wallerstein studied only children who came to see her as a therapist—that is, she based her findings on those children who were already having difficulties *before their parents divorced*. And she studied children only in wealthy ultraliberal Marin County, California. She attributed their subsequent problems in relationships to their parents' divorce, when it is just as plausible that it was the conflict between the parents that led to both the divorce *and* the children's problems. Staying together might have been the worst imaginable outcome.

Sociological research consistently finds that children are resilient and adapt successfully to their parents' divorces. Mavis Hetherington (2002), for example, studied more than 2,500 children from 1,400 families over a period of 30 years and found that the fear of a devastating effect of divorce on children is exaggerated, with 75–80 percent of children coping reasonably well. Other scholars agree that, although parental divorce increases the risk of psychological distress and relationship problems in adulthood, the risks are not great (Amato 2003; see also Ahrons 2004).

Perhaps the outcome of divorce depends less on whether one gets a divorce and more on how civilly the parents behave toward each other and how much ongoing investment they maintain in their children's lives. That is to say, what's better for children is explained less well by whether the parents are married or divorced and better by the quality of the relationships the parents have with their children—and with each other.

Divorce is rarely a "pleasant" experience, but its impact varies significantly by race, gender, and class. Women's standard of living declines more sharply than men's (which may even rise). Poor and minority women's standards of living decrease even more, and they recoup that lost income more slowly than do white women—if ever.

Remarriage and Blended Families

12.4.3 Explain what Cherlin means by the "marriage-go-round" and how it relates to both remarriage and blended families.

At least half of all children will have a divorced and remarried parent before they turn 18 (Ahrons 2004). Indeed, the share of all children living in two-parent households is, today, smaller than it has been in more than 50 years. Almost 3 in 10 children today do not live in this type of household, but fewer of those parents are married today. One in 4 children today live with only one parent, up from less than 1 in 10 in 1960 (Pew Research Center 2015). And these children face different issues, depending on how old they are, the role that their parents have, which parent remarries, and whether it's the **custodial parent** (the parent with whom they live; see FIGURE 12.9). Typically, they must adjust to a new residence and a new school and share space with new siblings. The classic media example is an old television sitcom (and subsequent movies), *The Brady Bunch*—two parents who each had three children from previous relationships who meet, fall in love, and move each of their families in together. Sociologists refer to families like these as **blended families**.

In many blended families, finances become a divisive issue, placing significant strains on the closeness and stability of blended families (Korn 2001; Martinez 2005). Several studies have found that children in blended families—both stepchildren and their half-siblings who are the joint product of both parents—do worse in school than children raised in traditional two-parent families (Ginther 2004). And some research suggests that boys tend to have a more difficult time coping with half- or stepsiblings than girls do (Tillman 2008).

Although the dynamics of blended families tend to be similar across class and race, the likelihood of blending families tends to be far more common among the middle classes, where parents have sufficient resources to support these suddenly larger families. Lower-class families may be "blended" in all but name: They may cohabit with other people's children but not legally formalize it by marrying. But when they do formalize this, it often involves **remarriage**—a term sociologists use for people entering a new marriage after leaving at least one previous marriage by divorce.

Although we have already learned that the United States has one of the highest divorce rates in the industrialized world, fewer people are as aware of another rate on

custodial parent

The parent whose residence is considered a "primary residence" for the child or children after separation or divorce.

blended families

Families formed when two divorced or unmarried parents with children marry (with stepparents, stepsiblings, and possibly half-siblings as well).

remarriage

The term sociologists use for people entering a new marriage after leaving at least one previous marriage by divorce.

FIGURE 12.9 Living Arrangements for U.S. Children, 1960–2014
View the transformation in the composition of households with children since 1960. It's a lot of change in a relatively short period of time.

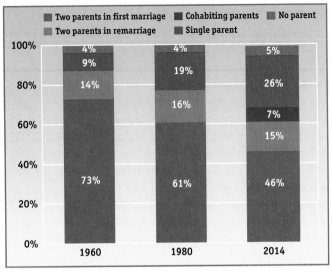

NOTE: Based on children under 18. Data regarding cohabitation are not available for 1960 and 1980; in those years, children with cohabiting parents are included in "one parent." For 2014, the total share of children living with two married parents is 62 percent after rounding. Figures do not add up to 100 percent due to rounding.

SOURCE: Data from Pew Research Center analysis of 1960 and 1980 decennial census and 2014 American Community Survey (IPUMS). Available at http://www.pewsocialtrends.org/2015/12/17/1-the-american-family-today/#fn-21212-3.

marriage rate

The annual number of marriages in a given geographical area per 1,000 inhabitants.

which the United States similarly stands out. The United States also has the highest **marriage rate**—the rate depicting the number of people who do or will eventually marry (see U.S./WORLD Divorce Rates in International Comparison).

People in the United States are simply much more likely to marry than are people in other parts of the world. And although we have a higher divorce rate than many of our peer countries, we also have among the highest remarriage rates in the world (Cherlin 2009). So, even when our marriages fail, we are much more likely to find someone new and try again. The sociologist Andrew Cherlin (1992) famously referred to remarriage as an "incomplete institution" because he realized that remarriages often do not follow a standards set of norms. Deciding whether a formal wedding is necessary is less defined among remarriages. Whether couples should unite their finances is more uncertain among remarriages than first marriages as well. And, as you might guess, these features also mean that remarriages have a higher divorce rate than do first marriages as well.

In Cherlin's (2009) more recent study, he wanted to better understand the state of marriage and the family among Americans today by attempting to explain what our high divorce rate, marriage rate, and remarriage rate mean about how Americans understand families and the institution of marriage more generally. Cherlin suggests that in American culture, marriage and individualism are contradictory cultural goals for many Americans. Our cultural model of marriage stresses the ideas that: Marriage is among the best ways to exist, marriage should be permanent and loving, and that divorce should be a last resort. But our cultural model of individualism stresses competing ideals: Our primary obligation is to ourselves, individuals must make choices to better their own lives, and people dissatisfied with their relationships are justified in leaving them. As a group, Americans show strong support for all of these ideas. Cherlin shows, however, that they result in what he calls the "marriage-go-round." We get married because we believe it is a great way to live. But we evaluate our marriage individualistically

("What is this marriage really doing for me?"), and as a result are likely to leave them. But once we leave one, because marriage is an ideal for many Americans, we're likely to jump right back in.

Intimate Partner Violence

12.4.4 Understand how intimate partner violence impacts American families and relationships in international perspective.

The famous American historian Christopher Lasch spoke of the family as a "haven in a heartless world," but for some the family is a violent nightmare. In many families, the person who promised to love and honor you is the most likely to physically assault you; the one who promised to "forsake all others" is also the most likely to sexually assault you; and the one who is supposed to protect you from harm is the one most likely to cause that harm. **Intimate partner violence (IPV)** represents violence, lethal or nonlethal, experienced by a spouse, ex-spouse, or cohabiting partner; boyfriend or girlfriend; or ex-boyfriend or ex-girlfriend. It is commonly called "domestic violence," but because some does not occur in the home, IPV is the preferred term. IPV is the single major cause of injury to women in the United States. It is also true, however, that like other forms of violent crime, rates of intimate and family violence have been declining since the 1990s.

intimate partner violence (IPV)
Violence between people who either are or were in a sexual or romantic relationship with one another. It is commonly called "domestic violence," but because some does not occur in the home, IPV is the preferred term.

Almost one-third of women in the United States (27.3 percent or approximately 32.9 million) have experienced rape, physical violence, or stalking by an intimate partner at some point in their lifetime. One in 3 women (31.5%) has experienced physical violence by an intimate partner and nearly 1 in 10 (8.8%) has been raped by an intimate partner in her lifetime. Approximately 4.0 percent, of women in the United States reported experiencing these forms of violence by an intimate partner in the 12 months prior to taking the survey (Breiding, et al. 2014).

When we examine how IPV intersects with categories beyond only gender, we can learn that it is more common among the poor (women in households with annual incomes below $7,500 have the highest rates of IPV) and the young (women aged 20 through 24 have the highest rates, followed by women aged 25 through 34). Young women are also more likely to suffer dating assaults: 1 in 10 American adolescents reports being a victim of dating violence, with 13 percent of high school girls (compared to 7.4 percent of boys) reporting physical dating violence and 14.4 percent reporting sexual violence by a dating partner (compared to 6.2 percent of boys) (Kann, et al. 2014). In the United States, IPV knows no class, racial, or ethnic bounds. Yet there are some differences by race and ethnicity, as well as class and age (see FIGURE 12.10). Some research suggests that racial and ethnic differences disappear when social class is taken into account (Cazenave and Straus 1979; Leeder 2003).

Gay men and lesbians endure IPV as well. Yet we have less data documenting the extent of this. There are a dozen empirical studies that point to higher rates of IPV among gay men and lesbian women, but also nationally representative data, such as the National Intimate Partner and Sexual Violence Survey, which recently found that 40.4 percent of all lesbian women report intimate partner violence during their lifetime, and 25.2 percent of gay men do, compared to 32.3 percent of heterosexual women and 28.7 percent of heterosexual men. The rate of reported IPV is even higher among bisexual adults, at 56.9 percent for bisexual women and 37.3 percent for bisexual men (Brown and Herman 2015).

Globally, the problem of family violence is widespread. A study released in 2006 by the World Health Organization found that rates of IPV ranged from a low of 15 percent of women in Japan to a high of 71 percent of women in rural Ethiopia. (Rates in the European Union and United States were between 20 percent and 25

FIGURE 12.10 Intimate Partner Violence Against Women, by Age Group, Race, and Marital Status, 1993–2010

Intimate partner violence varies significantly by age. Younger women (18–24) have the highest rates of being victimized. And, although rates of victimization have declined among all age groups of women in the United States since 1993, women between 18 and 49 now face similar rates of intimate partner violence. Intimate partner violence also varies by race. But race is not as predictive as it is often presented. The most recent data suggest that black and white women have the highest rates of victimization, and Hispanic and other raced women have lower rates, on average. Marital status is also related to intimate partner violence. As with age and race, intimate partner violence against women has declined since 1993, but women who are separated but not divorced from their husbands face much higher rates of violence than do married, divorced, and never married women.

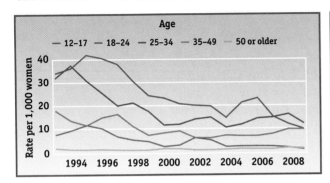

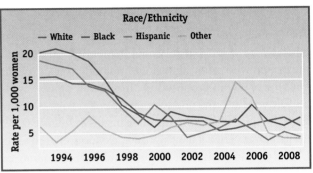

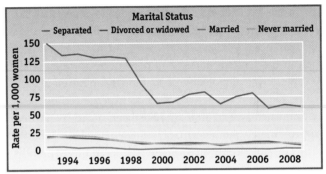

NOTE: Estimates based on two-year rolling averages. Includes rape or sexual assault, robbery, aggravated assault, and simple assault committed by current or former spouses, boyfriends, and girlfriends.

SOURCE: Data from Bureau of Justice Statistics, National Crime Victimization Survey, 1993–2010.

percent.) In 6 of the 15 sites of study, at least 50 percent of the women had been subjected to moderate or severe violence in the home at some point. Perhaps more telling, the majority of the 25,000 women interviewed in the study said that it was the first time they had ever spoken of the abuse to anyone (García-Moreno et al. 2006).

The single greatest difference in rates of IPV is by gender. According to the Bureau of Justice Statistics, about 80 percent of all victims of domestic violence are women (Truman and Morgan 2014; see Kimmel 2002). The gender imbalance of intimate violence is staggering. Of those victims of violence who were injured by spouses or ex-spouses, women outnumber men by about five to one. Eight times as many women were injured by their boyfriends as men injured by girlfriends. And boyfriends and girlfriends are almost twice as likely as spouses to commit IPV and almost four times as likely as ex-spouses. But it is also the case that violence is experienced differently by women and men. For instance, between 2003 and 2012, 65 percent of violent crimes against women were committed by people they knew compared with only 29 percent by strangers (the similar statistics for men are 34 percent and 55 percent). In the same study, 37 percent of women were shown to have experienced serious domestic violence, compared with 10 percent of men (Truman and Morgan 2014).

HOW DO WE KNOW WHAT WE KNOW?

GENDER SYMMETRY IN IPV

Despite dramatic gender differences, there are some researchers and political pundits who claim that there is "gender symmetry" in domestic violence—that rates of domestic violence are roughly equal by gender (see, for example, Brott 1994). One reason this symmetry is underreported is because men who are victims of domestic violence are so ashamed they are unlikely to come forward—a psychological problem that one researcher calls "the battered husband syndrome" (Steinmetz 1978).

But a close look at the data suggests why these findings are so discordant with the official studies by the Department of Justice and the FBI. Those studies that find gender symmetry rely on the "conflict tactics scale" (CTS) developed by family violence researcher and sociologist Murray Straus and his colleagues over 30 years. The CTS asked couples if they had ever, during the course of their relationship, hit their partner. An equal number of women and men answered "yes." The number changed dramatically, though, when they were asked who initiated the violence (was it offensive or defensive?), how severe it was (did she push him before or after he'd broken her jaw?), and how often the violence occurred. When these three questions were posed, the results shifted back: The amount, frequency, severity, and consistency of violence against women are far greater than anything done by women to men.

There were several other problems with the CTS as a measure (see Kimmel 2002). These problems included:

1. *Whom did they ask?*   Studies that found comparable rates of domestic violence asked only one partner about the incident. But studies in which both partners were interviewed separately found large discrepancies between reports from women and from men.
2. *What was the time frame?*   Studies that found symmetry asked about incidents that occurred in a single year, thus equating a single slap with a reign of domestic terror that may have lasted decades.
3. *Was the couple together?*   Studies that found gender symmetry excluded couples that were separated or divorced, although violence against women increases dramatically after separation.
4. *What was the reason for the violence?*   Studies that find symmetry do not distinguish between offensive and defensive violence, equating a vicious assault with a woman hitting her husband to get him to stop hitting the children.
5. *Was "sex" involved?*   Studies that find symmetry omit marital rape and sexual aggression; because a significant amount of IPV occurs when one partner doesn't want to have sex, this would dramatically change the data.

Of course, women can be—and are—violent toward their husbands and partners. Criminologists Martin Schwartz and Walter DeKeseredy estimate that women commit as much as 3 to 4 percent of all spousal violence (Schwartz and DeKeseredy 2008). But research such as this requires that we look more deeply at the questions asked. Sometimes, the answers are contained in the questions.

Family Violence between Generations

12.4.5 Summarize what we know about inter- and intragenerational family violence.

In addition to violence between domestic partners, there is also a significant amount of intergenerational and intragenerational violence in families. *Inter*generational violence refers to violence between generations, such as parents to children and children to parents. *Intra*generational violence refers to violence within the same generation—that is, sibling violence.

Sibling violence goes beyond routine sibling rivalry. Earlier reports found that as many as 80 percent of American children had engaged in an act of physical violence toward a sibling (Straus and Gelles 1990). In a recent sociological study, David Finkelhor and his colleagues (2006) found that 35 percent of all children had been attacked by a sibling in the previous year. Of these, more than a third were serious attacks. The consequences of sibling violence can be severe. Children who were repeatedly attacked were twice as likely to show symptoms of trauma, anxiety, and depression, including sleeplessness, crying spells, thoughts of suicide, and fear of the dark (Butler 2006). Finkelhor and his colleagues found that attacks did not differ by class or race or even by gender, although boys were slightly more likely to be victims than girls. They occurred most frequently on siblings ages 6–12 and gradually tapered off as the child entered adolescence.

Sometimes, children use violence against their parents. Though, rates of child-to-parent violence decrease as the child ages; it is more often younger children who hit their parents. Injuries to parents are rare, but they do happen. And when parents react to a child's violence with violence, the child has learned a lesson that could last a lifetime.

elder abuse

The physical, sexual, psychological, and financial abuse and neglect of people of a vulnerable age.

A significant amount of family violence occurs towards the elderly. The term **elder abuse** was coined in 1988 by a Congressional Committee investigating the problem. Elder abuse consists of physical, sexual, psychological, and financial abuse and neglect. It is estimated that about 10 percent of the nation's 40 million Americans older than age 65 have experienced one or more of these forms of elder abuse (Lachs and Pillemer 2015). Financial mistreatment is the most common form of reported elderly abuse, followed by potential neglect, emotional abuse, and sexual abuse (Acierno, et al. 2010; New York City Department for the Aging 2011). This seems to be the result of different life-expectancy rates for women and men; because women outlive men, they are more likely to be victimized. And women are more likely to be the caretakers of the elderly as well. Because the elderly often have smaller support systems and fewer resources, the impact of the abuse is magnified. Like young children, they are more vulnerable and dependent, and sometimes a single incident is enough to trigger a downward spiral to serious illness, depression, or despair (Burgess and Hanrahan 2006).

child abuse

Actions on the part of parents or caretakers that result in physical, emotional, or psychological harm (or the risk of such harm) to children.

child sexual abuse

The sexual exploitation of children.

The rates of parental violence against children are significantly more serious. In recent years, American society has also been vitally concerned about the problem of **child abuse** (violence against children) and **child sexual abuse** (the sexual exploitation of children). According to the Department of Health and Human Services, rates of victimization and the number of victims have been decreasing in the first decades of the twenty-first century. An estimated 686,000 children were determined to be victims of child abuse or neglect for 2012 (the last year for which there are data). Seventy-eight percent of child victims were neglected by their parents or other caregivers (U.S. Department of Justice 2015). The United States has rates that are significantly higher than rates in other English-speaking countries such as Australia, Canada, and Great Britain, partly, but not entirely, because of the higher rates of child poverty in the United States (poverty is a significant risk factor). Rates of child abuse and child sexual abuse vary significantly by class but less by race or ethnicity.

Globally, the problem of child abuse and neglect is equally serious—and includes forms of abuse that are not found in the economic North. In 2006, the United Nations commissioned the first global investigation into child abuse. They found that between 80 and 98 percent of children suffer physical punishment in their homes, with a third or more experiencing severe physical punishment resulting from the use of implements. Despite these global differences, it is equally true that Americans are far more accepting of violence against children than they may realize. More than half of all American parents believe that **corporal punishment**, including spanking, is acceptable; and one-third of parents have used corporal punishment against their adolescents (Straus 2005). These numbers are significantly less than the 94 percent who supported the use of corporal punishment in 1968 and the two-thirds who used it with adolescents in 1975 (Straus 2005). But it is still the case that more than 9 in 10 parents used corporal punishment with toddlers, and they did so, on average, three times a week. Consider how support for corporal punishment has changed over time (see FIGURE 12.11).

corporal punishment

Punishment that is physical, often involving hitting someone.

Not all groups agree with corporal punishment to the same extent. For instance, in recent history political ideologies have become much more correlated with beliefs in corporal punishment than they were in the 1980s. Today, roughly 80 percent of Republicans support corporal punishment of children, while only approximately 60 percent of Democrats do (General Social Survey 2016). There is also an incredible

FIGURE 12.11 Percentage of Americans who "Agree" or "Strongly Agree" with Spanking as an Important Form of Discipline for Children, 1986–2016
Although the proportion of Americans who support corporal punishment as a form of discipline for children has declined over the past 30 years, the majority of Americans still agree or strongly agree with the statement: "that it is sometimes necessary to discipline a child with a good, hard spanking."

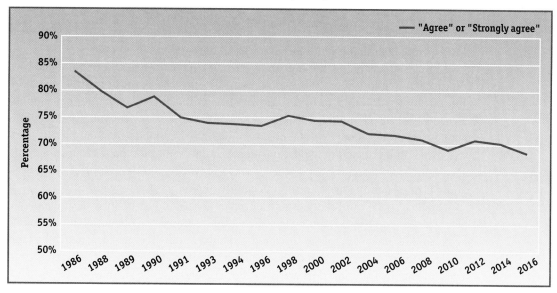

SOURCE: Data from General Social Survey, 1986–2016

regional divide. Americans living in the South are the most supportive of corporal punishment while those living in the West and Northeast are the least supportive. Thinking about corporal punishment intersectionally, it is also the case that support varies by gender and race—though some of this is confounded by other systems of inequality. For instance, black Americans are much more supportive of spanking children than are white Americans. But it is also the case that black people in the United States, as a group, have less income and education than do white people. And people with more education and more income are less supportive of spanking. So, whether the differences in opinion between black and white Americans concerning spanking are due to race, education, or class is more complex than it might at first appear. Though, it is also true that the majority of all Americans support corporal punishment of children in every region of the United States, among every race, of every political persuasion, and more. And this too, is a profound statement concerning our beliefs in violence against children.

---

iSOC AND YOU Family Transitions, Inequality, and Violence
Family transitions are experienced so personally, so individually, that it's hard sometimes to recognize how they fit into patterns. Some of these transitions have become easier to resist as markers of your *identity*. For example, saying you are a "divorcee" or "a battered woman" was a way of identifying yourself, but these are increasingly experienced as only one part of your identity today. Violence—whether between partners, or between adults and children—follows distinct patterns, as does support for such practices. Family transitions lead to different experiences in *institutions*, based on social *inequality*: The rich, for example, have an easier time aging than the poor. Their interactions with social *institutions* like hospitals and government bureaucracies go more smoothly and they receive a set of patterned advantages as a result. Whether forming or dissolving families, social inequalities *intersect* to create the patterns sociologists study and observe.

Conclusion

Families NOW

In the first line of his novel *Anna Karenina*, the great Russian novelist Leo Tolstoy wrote, "Happy families are all alike; every unhappy family is unhappy in its own way." How unsociological! Families, happy or unhappy, are as varied as snowflakes when viewed close up and as similar around the world as all the sand in the desert.

Families are as old as the human species. We have always had them; indeed we couldn't live without them. They are among the most basic social institutions and a cultural universal found in every known society. But it's equally true that families have always been changing, adapting to new political, social, economic, and environmental conditions. Some expectations of family may be timeless; yet families have always been different, and new relationships, arrangements, and patterns are emerging all over the world today, just as they always have been. Today, "typical" American family is not a family form of one type. Family diversity is the new norm.

Families shape our identities and our experiences of inequality at a fundamental level. The families we start out in have an enormous impact on our social life. So, at one level, families play a big role in social reproduction and help reproduce inequality (and privilege) from one generation to the next. But, families are also there to shield us from social inequality. They are supposed to be those to whom we can turn when we have nowhere else to go. This is a characterization of the family that is not true of every family, however. Indeed, although we often imagine the family as shielding us from hardships in the rest of society, research on family violence shows that families harm people as well. This is part of why an intersectional understanding of family life is so important.

The idea of "the family" elicits a strong reaction from most people. We conjure an image—either of our own family or some family "ideal" we imagine. Sociologists who study the family study families not as we might want them to be, or as some people believe they *should* be. Rather, we study families as they actually are. And this necessitates being comfortable with recognizing that this reality will change over time and will be very different for different people and groups.

CHAPTER REVIEW Families

12.1 The Family as a Social Institution

The family is changing as social structures change, alarming some people and yet causes nostalgia, even as alternatives develop, but it has changed before. Unlike premodern families, we move from our family of origin to a separate residence with our family of procreation. Family is more than a nuclear family, including kinship systems traced by matrilineal descent, patrilineal descent, and bilateral descent. Families serve many social functions, including care of the children and economic transfer by establishing legitimacy, as well as regulation of sexual activity and procreation through variations besides monogamy, including polygamy, polygyny, polyandry, and even group marriage. Exogamy is the one constant. The nuclear family is a recent phenomenon. The extended family was the norm before the modern era. Before companionate marriage, spouses were selected by parents to solidify family position. The role of marriage and of spouses and children within the marriage changed in the modern era, moving from a practical unit of economic production to an isolated nuclear unit organized around emotional connection.

12.1 Key Terms

families The basic unit in society, these social groups are socially understood as either biologically, emotionally, and/or legally related.

family of origin The family a child is born or adopted into, with biological parents or others who are responsible for his or her upbringing.

family of procreation The family one creates through marriage or cohabitation with a romantic partner, to which one chooses to belong.

kinship systems Cultural groupings that locate individuals in society by reference to their families, typically mapped as a network from closest (mother, father, siblings) to a little more distant (cousins, aunts, uncles) to increasingly distant (second-cousins twice removed).

matrilineal Tracing one's ancestry through the mother and maternal side of the family.

patrilineal Tracing one's ancestry through the father and paternal side of the family.

bilateral Tracing one's ancestry through both parents, rather than only the mother (see *matrilineal*) or only the father (see *patrilineal*).

monogamy Marriage between two (and only two) people.

polygamy Marriage between three or more people. (*See polygyny* and *polyandry*.)

polygyny The most common form of polygamy, a marriage between one man and two or more women.

polyandry Rare form of polygamy in which one woman marries two or more men.

group marriage Rare marriage arrangement in which two or more men marry two or more women, with children born to anyone in the union "belonging" to all of the partners equally.

polyamory Committed relationships among three or more people.

exogamy Marriage among people who belong to meaningfully different social groups (race, religion, social class, etc.)

incest taboo Sigmund Freud identified the taboo that one should not have sex with one's own children as a foundation of all societies.

social reproduction The social structures, processes, and activities that transmit inequality from one generation to the next.

endogamy The strong tendency to marry within one's own social group (often with the same race, religion, class, educational background for instance).

extended family The family model in which two or three generations live together: grandparents, parents, unmarried uncles and aunts, married uncles and aunts, sisters, brothers, cousins, and all of their children.

companionate marriage The (historically recent) idea that people should select their own marriage partner based on compatibility and mutual attraction.

family wage Arising in the nineteenth century, the term refers to a wage sufficient for a single wage earner to support a family (spouse and children).

progressive nucleation Christopher Lasch's idea that industrialization and modernization made it customary for children to be independent from their parents in going to school, looking for work, and choosing a spouse, increasingly reducing extended family arrangements and promoting the nuclear family model of household structure and child-rearing.

nuclear family The presumed model of the modern American family structure consisting of a breadwinning husband, homemaker wife, their children, and no extended family members.

matrifocal families Families centered on mothers.

12.2 Forming Families

Historically, families selected mates for children who had little say in the matter. Courtship is a recent development. Individual choice and peers have become important in rating and dating, and courtship has become ritualized, with specific steps often leading to marriage. Today hookups often replace dating in college. In less developed parts of the world, arranged marriages persist, and girls are married off at early ages; but, in the developed world, we are increasingly marrying later, and there are alternatives to marriage, including being paired in cohabitation, and greater acceptability of nonmarital sex, with more people remaining single. Marriage today varies widely by race, ethnicity, education, and income. And marriage, itself, has changed. It no longer necessarily signifies adulthood or conveys the responsibilities and commitment it once did. Social barriers still place dating, courtship, and marriage within clear racial categories, but interracial marriage is becoming more common. Same-sex unions are legal. And, just like heterosexual couples, gay and lesbian couples who marry do so in diverse ways.

12.2 Key Terms

dating A courtship practice that arose in the 1920s in which young adults participated in recreational activities in pairs rather than groups prior to engaging in long-term commitments to one another.

calling system A process by which a young man (a "suitor") would obtain permission for access to a young woman, and ascertain her interest in forming a romantic attachment, all beginning with a request to "call," or visit her at home, initially under the watchful eyes of her parents and extended family.

fictive kin Similar to "urban tribes," the term refers to people with whom we form kinship ties and family networks even though they are not legally or biologically tied to us as kin.

cohabitation Once called "shacking up" or "living in sin," now more often called just "living together," the sociological term for people who are in a romantic relationship but not married living in the same residence.

singletons Modern term for people living alone, often by choice.

nonmarital sex Sex outside of marriage.

12.3 Children, Parents, and Parenting

Child-rearing is also changing. More people have wanted to become parents than ever before, including some who would rarely have considered parenting just 20 or 30 years ago:

teenagers, 50-year-olds, gay and lesbian couples, infertile heterosexual couples. Women still do the majority of childcare as well as housework, but men are increasingly involved as parents as the majority of all parents now work outside the home. More than a quarter of all children are raised in single-parent homes, most of these female headed; single-parent families have become more common among all demographic groups, but the greatest increases have been among less-educated women and among African American families. Some older well-educated women are actively choosing to become single parents, and, at the same time, the choice to live "child-free" is becoming more common. Family formation through adoption has shifted from being about "helping a girl in trouble" to "enabling a loving family to have a child."

12.3 Key Terms

domestic division of labor The ways couples divide up all of the chores and obligations necessary to run a household.

time diary studies Research method that measures how people allocate their time during an average day by having subjects regularly record their activities in a diary, log, or other record.

childfree A term for women and men who forego having children as a personal choice.

childless A term for women and men who forego having children out of necessity.

12.4 Family Transitions, Inequality, and Violence

Separation and divorce are central elements of contemporary family life. In the United States, the divorce rate rose steadily from the 1890s through the 1970s, but during the past 30 years, it has fallen significantly, along with marriage rates overall. Sociological factors associated with higher rates of divorce include living in a Southern state, being poor, evangelical, taking an abstinence pledge, and getting married young. Children of divorced parents fare worse on a number of social indicators, from performance in school, to psychological well-being, to all manner of behavioral problems and outcomes, when compared with households in which the parents' marriage is intact. However, when children in divorced households are compared with those who live with parents in high-conflict marriages, sometimes divorces were associated with decreasing levels of behavioral issues. One in four children today live with only one parent, and at least half of all children will have a divorced and remarried parent before they turn 18, many of them living in "blended families" resulting from subsequent marriages. Sociologists also study the darker side of family life, including diverse forms of family violence. In the United States, Intimate Partner Violence (IPV) knows no class, racial, or ethnic bounds. IPV is the leading cause of injury to women and is more common among young poor women, often including dating violence. Although women are by far the most common victims, men, particularly gay men, suffer, as well. Violence also occurs between and across generations in families. Sibling violence, which occurs most between ages of 6 and 12, has severe consequences and does not vary by gender, race, or class. Elder abuse occurs most often in the home, by family members. Child abuse is epidemic globally, and often legal, and even in the United States it is tacitly accepted.

12.4 Key Terms

divorce The legal dissolution of a marriage.

divorce rate A social scientific measure of the proportion of marriages that end in divorce.

custodial parent The parent whose residence is considered a "primary residence" for the child or children after separation or divorce.

blended families Families formed when two divorced or unmarried parents with children marry (with stepparents, stepsiblings, and possibly half-siblings as well).

remarriage The term sociologists use for people entering a new marriage after leaving at least one previous marriage by divorce.

marriage rate The annual number of marriages in a given geographical area per 1,000 inhabitants.

intimate partner violence (IPV) Violence between people who either are or were in a sexual or romantic relationship with one another. It is commonly called "domestic violence," but because some does not occur in the home, IPV is the preferred term.

elder abuse The physical, sexual, psychological, and financial abuse and neglect of people of a vulnerable age.

child abuse Actions on the part of parents or caretakers that result in physical, emotional, or psychological harm (or the risk of such harm) to children.

child sexual abuse the sexual exploitation of children.

corporal punishment Punishment that is physical, often involving hitting someone.

SELF-TEST

⟩ CHECK YOUR UNDERSTANDING

1. According to the text, historically, families served as which of the following?
   a. Production units and consumption units
   b. Consumption units and emotional units
   c. Emotional units and production units
   d. production units & cultural units.

2. Historically the most common family arrangement has been the
   a. fictive kinship.
   b. nuclear family.
   c. extended family.
   d. group marriage.

3. The term for the requirement that people marry outside their own family is
   a. polyandry.
   b. exogamy.
   c. legitimacy.
   d. polygamy.

4. Mutual ties of obligation and support among non-blood relations that develop in poor communities, for example, are referred to as
   a. honorary aunties.
   b. blood brothers.
   c. godparents.
   d. fictive kinship.

5. Which of the following is not declining in incidence?
   a. Marriage
   b. Childbirth
   c. Single-parent households
   d. All of these are in decline.

6. Globally, attitudes toward same-sex marriage are
   a. largely unknown, due to taboos.
   b. becoming more restrictive.
   c. becoming more accepting.
   d. remaining unchanged.

7. The nuclear family emerged as a result of
   a. industrialization.
   b. birth control.
   c. Social Security.
   d. immigration.

8. In modern society, the primary role of the family is
   a. production.
   b. consumption.
   c. emotional support.
   d. procreation.

Self-Test Answers: 1. a, 2. c, 3. b, 4. d, 5. c, 6. c, 7. a, 8. c

CHAPTER 13

EDUCATION

Education is both a primary mechanism of social mobility and of social reproduction. Sociologists who study education know that schools both help and hurt. Although they offer enormous and vital opportunities, many existing inequalities (like class inequality, for instance) get reproduced within an institution designed to help people overcome them—education.

→ LEARNING OBJECTIVES

In this chapter, using the iSoc framework, you should be able to:

13.1.1 Explain the difference between the manifest and hidden curriculum.

13.1.2 Recognize how each of the five elements of the iSoc model can be used to examine education sociologically.

13.1.3 Briefly summarize the historical origins of education.

13.1.4 Understand that many social issues today require basic types of literacy, but that a great deal of what we learn privileges the knowledge and accomplishments of some groups in society at the expense of others.

13.2.1 Explain what it means to argue that education is inequitably distributed throughout a population using the United States as an example.

13.2.2 Understand how education inequality varies around the world.

13.2.3 Summarize some of the ways that education is improving around the world.

13.3.1 Explain what "school effects" are, and summarize some of why they are challenging to study.

13.3.2 Describe the ways that different types of educational institutions in the United States help perpetuate inequality using private schools as an example.

13.3.3 Understand what it means that tracking is both a response to educational inequality as well as involved in the reproduction of educational inequality.

13.3.4 Summarize the relationship between parents' socioeconomic status and student educational outcomes as well as how that relationship varies by race.

13.3.5 Summarize some of the ways that gender inequality is institutionalized within education.

13.4.1 Understand how higher education has changed in recent history and who has benefitted from these changes and how.

13.4.2 Explain the ways that we can assess just how prepared Americans are to attend college after leaving high school.

13.4.3 Understand how social identities like class and race shape who attends college as well as what students' experiences will be like once admitted.

13.4.4 Review some of the ways that different types of higher educational institutions aimed at making higher education more accessible may exacerbate the very problems they were designed to redress.

Introduction

Education, as we often hear, is "the great equalizer." By studying hard, staying in school and applying yourself, you can gain the knowledge and skills you need to get ahead. Education can enable a poor person to get out of poverty and can catapult you into ranks of the wealthy and powerful. It's the purest form of meritocracy; the smartest cream always rises to the surface. Sometimes, when you hear parents or teachers talk admiringly about education, it sounds as though getting a college degree is like winning the lottery.

Talk to others and it sounds like you're in prison. Education is the best predictor of your eventual position in the socioeconomic hierarchy; but the best predictor of your education turns out not to be your motivation or intelligence but your parents' level of education. Education keeps you where you are, keeps the structures of inequality (based on class, race, or gender) in place. In fact, education is what makes that inequality feel like a meritocracy, so you have no one to blame.

So why do it? It depends on whom you ask. Teachers often subscribe to the meritocracy idea and contend that education builds critical reasoning skills, the ability to grapple with issues, weigh evidence, and make informed decisions in a changing society. It is valuable in itself. Students are often more cynical, interested in learning the skills they will need to get or keep a job.

Does education level the playing field and facilitate mobility or does it freeze things where they are and maintain the status quo? Should education teach you how to think, or how to make a living? Is it the road to the good life, or does it turn us into overintellectualized snobs, corrupting goodness and simple virtues?

To a sociologist, it's all this and more. Education is intrinsically interesting and valuable for its own sake. And you can gain useful skills to build your job credentials. It is a path to mobility for many—it's how to "get ahead." But education is, at the same time, one of the most central institutions involved in the reproduction of structured social inequality.

13.1 Education and Society

Education emerged as a mechanism of ensuring that all members of a society collected a common body of knowledge and skills to participate as full members of that society. And in this way, education is sometimes referred to as the "great equalizer." But, as with every major social institution, education is also centrally involved in the reproduction of social inequality. Although education is more "open" than it was a half-century ago, it is still true that where you live, what race you are, how much money your parents make, and more, structure both the quantity and quality of education you are likely to receive. Of course, this is not universally true. But the cases of students who defy this generalization are exceptions to a larger rule.

Sociologists interested in studying education are interested in the role that education plays in social life and what role education plays in perpetuating or challenging social inequality. Sociologists of education want to know how parents make decisions about where to send their children to school. They are interested in how students get divided by race, class, ability, and more and what role these divisions play in shaping the rest of young people's lives. They want to know who goes to college and what they get out of that experience while there and beyond. They are interested in the ways teachers and students interact with each other and what role these interactions play in shaping the experiences and opportunities of students belonging to different social groups.

The sociology of education is an enormous subfield within sociology. Sociologists studying this topic are united by a common focus on this central institution. They are interested in the social promise of education in combatting many of the forms of inequality sociologists are interested in more generally. But they have also found a great deal of evidence suggesting that education is often socially organized and set up in ways that leave systems of social inequality and hierarchy unchallenged and reproduced.

Education in Social Context

13.1.1 Explain the difference between the manifest and hidden curriculum.

Every day in the United States, about 71 million people gather in auditoriums, classrooms, and laboratories, in the open air and in online chat rooms, to learn things from some 5.1 million teachers, instructors, and professors (U.S. Department of Education 2016). Students can learn an endless variety of subjects: Babylonian cuneiform and nuclear physics, short-story writing and motorcycle repair, conversational Portuguese and managerial accounting, symphony conducting and cartoon animation, existential philosophy and the gender politics of modern Japan.

Most people spend a quarter of their lives (or even more) becoming *educated*. If you live to be 70, you will devote 19 percent of your life to preschool, elementary school, and high school, and another 6 percent to college (assuming you graduate in four years). A Ph.D. might easily take another 8 years. You would then finish your education at age 30, with 43 percent of your life already behind you.

Education doesn't end at high school, college, or graduate school. Many people return to school after they received their degree, for additional degrees, courses, and certificates. Some want to learn a new skill or develop a new interest. And many others depend on education for their livelihood: They become teachers, administrators, and service personnel; they write and publish textbooks; they build residence halls and manufacture three-ring binders; they open restaurants and clothing shops in college towns to draw student business. In the United States, we spent approximately $620 billion on elementary and secondary schools in 2012–2013 and another $517 billion on colleges and universities in 2013–2014 (U.S. Department of Education 2016).

Why do we do it? How does it work? How does it both enable and restrict our own mobility? Sociologists define **education** as a social institution through which society provides its members with important knowledge—basic facts, job skills, and cultural norms and values. It provides socialization, cultural innovation, and social integration. It is accomplished largely through schooling, formal instruction under the direction of a specially trained teacher (Ballantine 2001).

Like most social institutions, education has both manifest (clearly apparent) and latent (potential or hidden) functions. The manifest function is the subject matter: reading and writing in grade school, sociology and managerial accounting in college. Latent functions are by-products of the educational process, the norms, values, and goals that accrue because we are immersed in a specific social milieu. Education teaches both a subject and a **hidden curriculum**: individualism and competition, conformity to mainstream norms, obedience to authority, passive consumption of ideas, and acceptance of social inequality (Gilborn 1992).

education

A social institution through which society provides its members with important knowledge—basic facts, information, job skills, as well as cultural norms and values and lessons in socialization, cultural innovation, and social integration.

hidden curriculum

A means of socialization through which education not only creates social inequalities but makes them seem natural, normal, and inevitable.

In addition to the formal curriculum in class, students also participate in a "hidden curriculum" in which they learn social lessons about hierarchy, peer pressure, and how to act around the opposite sex. Here, students demonstrate having learned to be obedient to authority by raising their hands before speaking in class.

In addition to teaching a subject matter and various sorts of hidden norms and values, education establishes relationships and social networks, locating people within social classes. Randall Collins (1979) notes that the United States is a **credential society**: You need diplomas, degrees, and certificates to "qualify" for jobs; you can open a medical practice only if you have an MD degree, regardless of how smart you are; and you have to pass the state bar exam to practice law, regardless of how much law you know. Diplomas, degrees, certificates, examination scores, college majors, and the college you graduate from say "who you are" as much as family background. They tell employers what manners, attitudes, and even skin colors the applicants are likely to have. They provide gatekeeping functions that restrict important and lucrative jobs to a small segment of the population.

credential society

A society based more on the credentialing aspects of education—diplomas, degrees, and certificates—than any substantive knowledge.

iSoc: The Sociology of Education

13.1.2 Recognize how each of the five elements of the iSoc model can be used to examine education sociologically.

Education is one of every society's most fundamental institutions. It is the foundation of our identities, a major vehicle for reproducing inequality, and one of the primary arenas in which we learn the basics of social interaction.

IDENTITY—Starting at around age 3 or 4, your first nonfamilial social role is that of "student." It is through your education that you come to define yourself socially, and to locate yourself in the wider social world. It is through your educational experiences that you develop your first *identity* "label"—whether it's geek or jock or Goth or stoner—that comes to define who you are. Education is the social arena in which you also accumulate the credentials necessary to create an identity, a professional identity like doctor or lawyer or accountant. Next to the family, education is a primary agent of socialization—one in which you spend the majority of your waking hours for the first quarter of your life.

INEQUALITY—Education is the primary way that people in our society can change their class position. (Well, that and winning the lottery.) You might believe that if you get a good education you can rise in the social hierarchy. Many of you are in college now for that reason: You need education to get a good job, to earn enough to buy a nice house. Many of your parents did not go to college, and they worked hard and saved money to enable you to do so on the promise that education is a vehicle for upward mobility. That is, you believe that education *can* be an "equalizer"—something capable of challenging enduring systems of *inequality* based on race, class, education, and more.

But, it is equally true that education is the great un-equalizer, making existing inequalities based on race or class or gender appear to be inequalities based on individual aptitude or simply the willingness (or lack of it) to work hard. Some groups have consistently enjoyed more educational success than others. Women received less elementary and secondary education than men through the nineteenth century and were all but excluded from higher education until the early twentieth century. The vast majority of high school dropouts come from low-income families, and the vast majority of college students come from high-income families. There is a consistent "funneling" of educational success, as class, gender, and race and ethnicity all act as filters through which some people pass and others do not. Indeed, your race, gender, class, and more all affect how much and what type of education you are likely to receive. And education is among the primary indicators of your country's position in the global arena.

INTERACTIONS—Schools are the testing grounds for social *interaction*. They're the place where you learn your place, so to speak—the way you are supposed to interact with those above and below you in social hierarchies of various kinds. You learn to understand the proper way to interact with those in authority and also with those whom you believe are your inferiors. In addition to the academic curriculum, there is often a "hidden curriculum" in which status hierarchies develop that are entirely independent of academic achievement (indeed, in some schools, high academic achievement might consign you to a very low status group.) You learn how to give and receive deference, and many of our schoolyard experiences involve conflicts over whether or not deference is due to you or to the other person. Schools also formally introduce and often legitimate hierarchies based on gender, race, age, and class, as you are taught what sorts of displays and performances are "appropriate" for your identity.

INSTITUTIONS—Educational institutions are among the central social *institutions* in any society. They exhibit formal structural arrangements of any organization, and enable the society to channel people into different occupational and professional fields based on talent and ability (as well as by race, class, gender, and sexuality). They also serve an important function in maintaining social order: Can you imagine what society would be like with 32 million children running around every single day? What the job market would be like if children needed jobs too, and if every parent had to care for their own children? By siphoning off the youngest one-fourth of our population into a full-time job of going to school, the rest of the society can run far more smoothly.

INTERSECTIONS—Education stratifies; it separates groups from one another based on level of degree, type of institution, number of years completed, and more. But stating this fact alone fails to account for the ways that different groups interact with education as a social institution. For instance, in the United States, women currently earn a larger share of the bachelor's degrees awarded each year than do men. But, the gender gap in degrees awarded differs by racial and ethnic group as well as by class. And failing to recognize the ways that race, class, and gender all interact to produce different educational realities for distinct groups of Americans will invariably leave us with only a partial understanding. Making sense of *intersections* in education means paying attention to the ways that different configurations of identities are treated differently, have distinct outcomes, and experience education in diverse ways. Understanding education intersectionally complicates our understandings of the role that education plays in the reproduction of inequality in society.

The iSoc model helps sociologists understand the ways that education is both a vehicle for mobility and reinforces the status quo, a prime way you create and maintain your identities as well as an institutionalized arrangement that predetermines your future experiences and opportunities. Education is often treated individually. Your educational successes and struggles are measured this way. Grades are given out to individuals, not to whole classes, for instance. But sociologists think of education at the level of collective social life. Although individuals may struggle, we want to know whether and how specific groups of individuals seem to collectively struggle in patterned ways when compared to others. This means looking beyond individuals and examining the ways education intersects with your social identities in ways that shape your educational experiences and opportunities much more than you may realize.

A Brief History of Education

13.1.3 Briefly summarize the historical origins of education.

For most of human history, there were no schools. Your parents taught necessary skills, or they hired you a tutor. Sometimes people with special skills opened academies, where you could pay tuition to study philosophy, music, or art. But there was no formal, structured system of education. In many cultures, schools developed out of a need to train religious leaders. In ancient Babylonia, priests in training went to school so they could learn to read sacred texts and write the necessary rituals. In India, *gurukuls*, connected to temples and monasteries, offered instruction in Hindu scriptures, theology, astrology, and other religious topics (Ghosh 2001). In China, citizens who wanted to become civil servants on any level had to pass a series of "imperial examinations." Examinations were theoretically open to anyone, but only the wealthy could afford the years of preparation necessary for even the lowest exam (Chaffee 1985; Gernet 1982).

European schools also developed to teach priests and other religious workers necessary subjects, like Latin, theology, and philosophy. We still call the highest academic degree a PhD, or "doctor of philosophy." When the Protestant Reformation began to teach that all believers—not just priests—should be able to read and interpret the Bible, many churches began to offer children instruction in reading and writing. By the sixteenth century, formal schooling for children was available in many European countries, though only the wealthy had enough money and free time to participate (Bowen 1976; Boyd and King 1978). The United States was among the first countries in the world to set a goal of education for all of its citizens, under the theory that an educated citizenry was necessary for a democratic society to function. Yet the founding fathers disagreed about its purpose. Some believed that education would enable citizens to use reason to protect their freedom and to challenge government policies; others thought education should teach citizens to accept the social order, to be, as Daniel Webster argued, "citizens educated to be humble, devout, and submissive to legitimate authority" (Urban and Wagoner 2003, p. 79). This tension in the purpose of education between free-thinking rebels and docile obedient participants persists, in some form, to the present day.

A free public education movement began in 1848, and soon there were free, tax-funded elementary schools in every state, with about half of young people (ages 5 to 19) attending (Urban and Wagoner 2003). They often attended for only a few years or for only a few months of the year, squeezed in between their duties at home, and instruction was very basic—"reading, writing, and arithmetic." By 1918, every state had passed a mandatory education law, requiring that children attend school until they reached the age of 16 or completed the eighth grade, and a variety of new subjects were available, including higher levels of mathematics, science, social studies, foreign languages, art and music, and "practical subjects" like bookkeeping and typing. By the mid-1960s, a majority of American adults were high school graduates. Today about 8 of 10 have high school diplomas (see FIGURE 13.1).

FIGURE 13.1 Proportion of Americans 25 and Older with High School or College Degrees, 1940–2016

In 1940, only about 1 in 4 Americans 25 years and older completed a high school education. That same year, only 1 in 20 had completed college. By 2015, the proportion of Americans 25 years of age and older with a high school degree was just shy of 1 in 9 and roughly 1 in 3 had completed college.

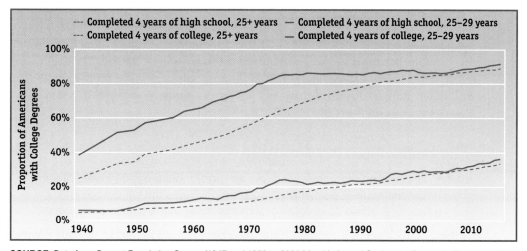

SOURCE: Data from Current Population Survey (1947 and 1952 to 2002 March), Annual Social and Economic Supplement to the Current Population Survey (2003 to 2016) (noninstitutionalized population, excluding members of the Armed Forces living in barracks); 1950 Census of Population and 1940 Census of Population (resident population). Available at: https://www.census.gov/data/tables/2016/demo/education-attainment/cps-detailed-tables.html.

Educational opportunity and retention are organized by class and race. Lower-income and minority students are far more likely to drop out than middle-class and white students. The highest dropout rate is among lower-income Hispanic girls.

Why did education expand so much? As industry expanded in the mid-nineteenth century, occupations became more differentiated, and work skills could no longer be passed down from parents to children. There was a great need for specialized education in the skills necessary for the modern workforce, especially English composition, mathematics, and the sciences. Abstract learning in subjects such as history and Latin did not provide immediate work skills, but they did signify that the student had the cultural background necessary to move into the middle class (Willis et al. 1994). They were not only the key to advancement; they were the key to impressing people.

As education became universal, more and more scholars began experimenting with how people learn. Was rote memorization effective? Problem solving? Practical experience? For instance, one school of thought—Pragmatism—taught the value of practical experience: actually using a foreign language for everyday conversations, for instance, instead of translating passages from great works of literature. During the 1960s, *affect*, or feelings, became nearly as significant in educational theory as *cognition*, or intellect. Students learned self-esteem, how to recognize and handle emotions, how to manage conflict, often to the detriment of more practical skills. A backlash in the 1980s and 1990s moved the curriculum "back to basics," and rote memorization returned as an appropriate way to learn.

Before the Civil War, abolitionist Frederick Douglass (c. 1818–1895) stated that learning to read and write would be the "road to liberation" for oppressed minorities. Education theorist Horace Mann (1796–1859) believed that education could be "the great equalizer," eliminating class and other social inequalities as everyone gained access to information and debate. For this goal to be met, however, all citizens in the country must be educated. On the college level, the United States ranks among the best-educated countries in the world, with the highest graduation rate for adults older than 35 (one in three adults now has a bachelor's degree) and boasts the majority of the world's best universities. Among younger Americans ages 25 through 34, only South Korea, Japan, Israel, and Canada have higher proportions who have attained a postsecondary degree between 2001 and 2015 (National Center for Education Statistics 2016). And on the high school level, although our graduation rate has started to increase slightly since 2010, after declining for the past four decades, with racial and ethnic minorities graduating at lower rates than whites, the United States ranked at the bottom of the OECD's countries for graduation rates in 2014. The United States has more dropouts and underpreparedness than any other industrialized country, and we are falling behind in math, science, and problem-solving skills (OECD 2014).

The Sociology of Education

13.1.4 Understand that many social issues today require basic types of literacy, but that a great deal of what we learn privileges the knowledge and accomplishments of some groups in society at the expense of others.

Is there really a set of information that everyone should know? Or is it all a matter of personal preference? Who should decide which types of knowledge or which skills are important enough that everyone should be forced to learn? Is the person who can discuss Shakespeare's *The Tempest* but has never seen an episode of

Star Trek really better educated than the person who can argue the merits of Kirk versus Picard but looks for the remote when Shakespeare's play is performed on PBS? Are they more qualified for white-collar jobs? Better able to select a candidate on Election Day? E. D. Hirsch Jr. thinks so. A University of Virginia professor of humanities, Hirsch caused some controversy with his *Cultural Literacy: What Every American Needs to Know* (1988). He argued that the modern school curriculum, with its emphasis on diversity, is depriving children of the background that they need to be effective American citizens. They learn trivia, rather than a sound core curriculum.

So what do Americans need to know? Hirsch compiled a 600-plus-page *Dictionary of Cultural Literacy* (Hirsch, Kett, and Trefil 2003). He doesn't reveal much about his criteria for inclusion: He selected items that are not too broad or too narrow, that appear frequently in national periodicals, and that have found "a place in our collective memory," as Hirsch put it. It sounds like an outline of the "hidden curriculum," a reproduction of elite knowledge, and indeed there is little authored by or even about minorities, very little about non-Western cultures. *Star Trek* is mentioned, as well as *Batman* and the *Peanuts* comic strip. However, most of the entries have to do with "high culture," elite knowledge. For example, here are some things that every "educated person" should know according to Hirsch:

- "The Ballad of Reading Gaol," a poem by Oscar Wilde
- Absurdist playwright Samuel Beckett
- François Rabelais, who wrote the sixteenth-century masterpiece *Gargantua and Pantagruel*
- Thomas Aquinas, whose *Summa Theologica* is a classic of medieval theology
- Novelist Sir Walter Scott
- William Gladstone, prime minister of England during the Victorian era

How many did you know? How many did your *instructor* know? Why are these more important to know than, let's say, the lyrics to a Bob Dylan or Aretha Franklin song or who Lord Voldemort or Lisbeth Salander are? Why is *Peanuts* a more important comic strip to know about, but *The Boondocks* (one of the first mainstream comic strips satirizing African American culture) is not?

And what about **scientific literacy**—the capacity to understand scientific concepts and processes necessary for complete participation in economic, civic, and cultural life? Scientific literacy in the United States has more than doubled over the past three decades, but, still, only about 28 percent of Americans are scientifically savvy and alert, according to Jon D. Miller, director of the Center for Biomedical Communications at Northwestern University Medical School (Miller 2007). Miller's research found that: (1) Most American adults do not understand what molecules are; (2) fewer than a third can identify DNA as the key to heredity; (3) only about 10 percent know what radiation is; and (4) one in five Americans believes the sun revolves around the Earth! He attributes this ignorance to poor education. Many high schools require only a year of two of "general science" that does not provide adequate instruction in everyday scientific concepts. Colleges are little better, often requiring only two or three "general interest courses" to fill their science requirements.

A more recent representative survey of Americans conducted by The Pew Center asked respondents to take an interactive quiz to assess basic scientific knowledge (see FIGURE 13.2).

Low scientific literacy undermines our ability to take part in the democratic process today. One can't be an effective citizen without it, given that we are facing such issues as stem-cell research, infectious diseases, nuclear power, and global warming. Indeed, to completely understand many of the issues we vote for today requires basic scientific literacy.

scientific literacy
The capacity to understand scientific concepts and processes necessary for complete participation in economic, civic, and cultural life.

FIGURE 13.2 A Brief Summary of Americans' Understandings of Basic Scientific Knowledge
In 2014, the Pew Research Center conducted a nationally representative survey of Americans, asking a series of multiple choice questions about basic scientific terms and concepts to get a sense of the scientific literacy of the American public. For instance, one question asked was, "What does a light-year measure?" with the following answers: brightness, time, distance, weight. The figure here lists the proportion of Americans answering each question correctly.

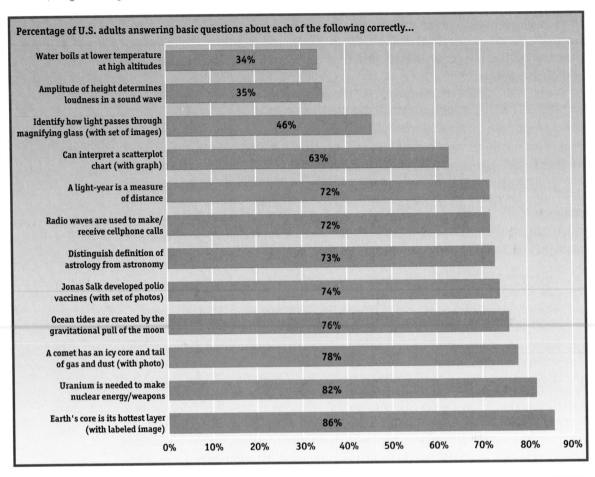

SOURCE: Data from Pew Research Center, American Trends panel (wave 6). Survey of U.S. adults conducted August 11 – September 3, 2014. Available at http://www.pewinternet.org/2015/09/10/what-the-public-knows-and-does-not-know-about-science/.

iSOC AND YOU Education and Society
Education is one of the primary social *institutions*. It's the largest single work-place in the United States, and a source of potential mobility for teachers and students alike. It's where you learn how to *interact* with others who are not in your family. It's also the setting in which you begin to shape and test out your *identity* through your interactions with others. It's where you must go if you are going to move up in society (to be socially "mobile"), but where social *inequalities* also end up getting reproduced as well. Like other forms of social inequality, educational inequalities express and *intersect* with each other.

13.2 Education as a Mechanism of Social Inequality

Societies with different rates of education fare differently economically as well. In general, the better educated a society, the better off it is economically. That might seem like a simple and intuitive correlation, but figuring out how to educate members of your society in a systematic way, ensuring they all can achieve the same set of expectations, and presenting them with similar educational opportunities is more complex. Additionally, what works for some members of a society might not work for everyone. Or, to put it more precisely, it might not work in exactly the same ways. How to educate members of a society is a pressing question in every major society around the world.

Education is a social institution whose aim is to pass on the important knowledge and skills from one generation to the next. But as we've already learned, that isn't all education passes on. Social inequalities that shaped the lives of previous generations are also part of educational institutions as well. As such, education plays a central role in social reproduction, passing on the social inequalities of one generation to the next as well. Understanding how and why this happens necessitates a consideration of educational inequality both between societies as well as within societies.

Students achieve better outcomes in Finland, for instance, than they do in the United States. But as with wealth, understanding education inequality also means considering how education is distributed throughout the population. In some societies, the difference between the most- and least-educated members is smaller than in others. And, like the difference between the richest and poorest in the United States, our education gap is also wide. Understanding this gap helps us appreciate the role that education plays in perpetuating social inequality.

Education and Inequality

13.2.1 Explain what it means to argue that education is inequitably distributed throughout a population using the United States as an example.

If education doesn't make you smarter, at least it makes you richer. The higher your level of education, the higher your income will likely be. The same holds true in other countries. In fact, education is a good predictor of economic growth. The better educated your citizenry, the more likely your nation is to experience economic growth (see FIGURE 13.3). Although men at all levels of education earn more than equally educated women, and whites earn more than racial and ethnic minorities, the relative earnings of all people of greater education are higher than those with lesser educational attainment (OECD, Education at a Glance 2016).

But is this because educated people get paid more or because people who are already in the upper classes have enough resources to make sure their children go further in their education and because upper-class people value education more and therefore push their children? Most of us believe that education is a ticket to social mobility. And it's partly true. Over the course of American history, different groups of immigrants—for example, Jews, Koreans, and Cubans—have successfully used educational advancement as a vehicle for social mobility for the entire ethnic group. But education is also one of the primary vehicles by which society reinforces social inequalities based on race, ethnicity, class, and gender. As long as we believe that education is a strict **meritocracy**—the best get ahead—we believe that different educational outcomes are based on characteristics of those individuals or those groups: They try harder and do more homework, or their culture rewards educational achievement more than other groups.

Educational inequality refers to the extent to which different groups lack access to the educational opportunities and experiences systematically made more available to other groups. Some nations provide very few opportunities for public education, like South Africa and Peru. Other societies provide a great deal of opportunity and access, but do not apply it evenly to everyone in the society—meaning that some get a great deal of education, while others receive very little. The United States is a good

meritocracy

Social system in which the greater the functional importance of the job, the more rewards it brings in salary, perks, power, and prestige.

educational inequality

The extent to which different groups lack access to the educational opportunities and experiences systematically made more available to other groups.

FIGURE 13.3 How Is Education Related to Economic Growth Around the World?

This graph plots education against economic growth. The vertical axis is a measure of economic growth (annual growth in per capital GDP between 1960 and 2000). And the horizontal axis depicts average test scores assessing mathematical and scientific aptitudes internationally. The graph illustrates that those societies with higher average levels of education were also societies that experienced higher rates of economic growth.

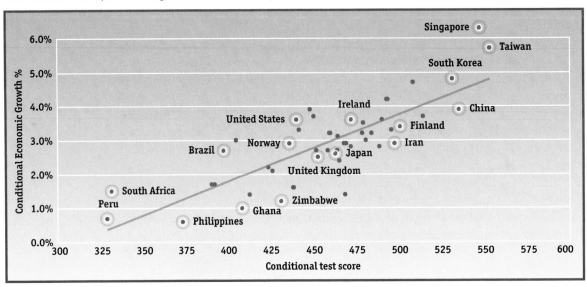

SOURCE: Data from Hanushek, Eric A. and Ludger Woessmann. 2013. "Do Better Schools Lead to More Growth? Cognitive Skills, Economic Growth, and Causation." Journal of Economic Growth 17 (4): 267–321.

example of this type of society. Like the wealth gap in the United States, the gap between those with the most and least education in the United States is among the widest gaps in the world.

To consider the ways that education is unequally distributed, consider the rates of high school graduation in the United States. In 2014, the U.S. Department of Education boasted that the high school graduation rate had been climbing since 2010 and was currently at 81 percent. Depending on how you spin this figure, it might look like something to celebrate or something to collectively mourn. What was not mentioned in the press releases is the range of high school graduation rates around the United States. County-level data collected by the U.S. Census Bureau's American Community Survey show that the high school graduation rates for people 25 and older ranged from 46.7 percent to 98.7 percent. This is the difference between growing up somewhere where you have less than a 1 in 2 chance of graduating high school compared with growing up where someone not graduating is virtually unheard of (see MAP 13.1).

As you can see, education in the United States is unevenly distributed throughout the population. Education is concentrated—or perhaps it is more appropriate to say that the lack of education is concentrated. And education is strongly correlated with income. So, it shouldn't be all that surprising to note that poverty rates are higher where rates of high school graduation are lower. Yet, the process by which this happens is reciprocal. Lower rates of education produce lower earnings; but lower earnings also shape the likelihood that children will receive a great deal of education.

Through this process, education not only creates social inequalities but makes them seem natural, normal, and inevitable (Bowles 1976; Lynch 1989; Margolis 2001). Of course, some teachers and administrators deliberately introduce stereotypes, marginalization, and exclusion into their lesson plans. But the problem goes much deeper than that. Educators need not *try* to reproduce social

MAP 13.1 U.S. High School Graduation Rate

One way of visualizing how education intersects with other forms of identity and inequality is to examine where educational inequality seems to impact the largest shares of actual people. Education is strongly related to income. So, it should not surprise us that those areas of the United States associated with the highest poverty rates and lowest rates of income are also areas with lower education rates. These rates use U.S. Census data from the American Community Survey to show high school graduate rates for people 25 and older throughout the United States.

Percent with at least a high school diploma

| Less than 50% | 50–75% | 75–80% | 80–85% | 85–90% | 90–95% | 95–100% |

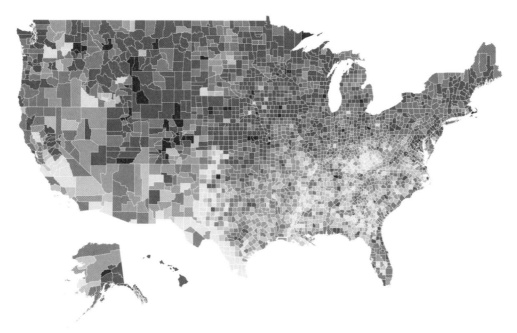

SOURCE: Data from U.S. Census Bureau, 2010–2014 American Community Survey estimates.

inequalities. They are reproduced in textbooks, in test questions, and in classroom discussions.

The most important lessons of the hidden curriculum actually take place outside the classroom, on the playground, in the cafeteria, in the many informal interactions that take place during every school day, from kindergarten through college. Students learn which of their peers are "supposed" to dominate and which are "supposed" to be bullied, beaten, laughed at, or ignored. They learn about gender hierarchies (call a boy a "girl" to humiliate him, or "gay" to humiliate him even more). They learn about racial hierarchies. They learn about class hierarchies, sexual hierarchies, hierarchies of bodily ability and appearance, and much more. They are learning lessons about social status. And the lessons they learn will influence their future decisions, whether they are in the boardroom or the courtroom, whether they are applying for a job or doing the hiring, regardless of how often the formal curriculum includes units on diversity.

Education Inequality on a Global Scale

13.2.2 Understand how education inequality varies around the world.

Education is a major interest to sociologists precisely because it is one of the primary vehicles of **social reproduction**. Education is the main way for any particular individual to be socially mobile and move up in the social hierarchy; but it is also the way that the social system, as a whole, reproduces the inequalities of race or class or gender

social reproduction

The structures and activities that transmit social inequality from one generation to the next.

that already exist. And, what's more, that some people use the educational system to rise in the hierarchy actually serves, at times, to legitimate the inequalities that the educational system as a whole reinforces. Some suggest, for instance, that if you don't make it it's not because of your membership in one of the groups that are discriminated against, but because you, individually, didn't try hard enough. Paradoxically, just as challenges to inequality have opened education up to groups historically denied entrance, their very entrance sometimes provides a new justification to close those doors to others.

Research confirms the funneling effect of the educational system. Just consider this intersectionally when we examine high school graduation rates by gender and race. Although the U.S. rate for on-time graduation is 82 percent overall, that proportion varies a great deal by gender and race (see FIGURE 13.4) (U.S. Department of Education 2015).

Financial barriers play a large part in these differences: 83.6 percent of high school students from families in the highest-income group enroll in college, whereas only 63.6 percent of middle-income students do. For the lowest-income group, it is 57.8 percent. From there, the funnel continues to narrow. Fewer minorities are able to complete a 4-year college degree within 6 years. Although 62.9 percent of white students graduate with a bachelor's degree within that time, only 40.8 percent of blacks and 52.9 percent of Hispanics do (National Center for Education Statistics 2016). Then when it comes to the advanced degrees that enable workers to garner increasingly higher wages in today's global knowledge economy, only 22.5 percent of blacks and 15.5 percent of Hispanics 25 and older have attained bachelor's degrees, as compared to 32.8 percent of whites and 53.9 percent of Asian Americans (Ryan and Bauman 2016). Dropout rates follow a similar pattern. The Hispanic dropout rate is particularly troubling because that group is a top driver to future workforce growth. 12.7 percent of Hispanics ages 16 to 24 are high school dropouts, as compared with about 7.5 percent of blacks and 4.3 percent of whites (National Center for Education Statistics 2015). There are many causes for this disparity: low incomes, a language barrier, and low-quality schooling that discourages participation.

FIGURE 13.4 High School Graduation Rates by Gender and Race/Ethnicity, 1972–2014

In 1972, a great deal of the jobs available to men did not require a college education. In fact, many jobs wouldn't have required a high school education. But as women moved into the workplace in greater numbers, the jobs available to them demanded more education. So, it's not surprising the women receive high school degrees at higher rates than men. Today, however, fewer jobs in the United States are available to people without high school degrees. And although a gender gap exists between all racial and ethnic groups in the United States, this gap is largest among black and Hispanic people.

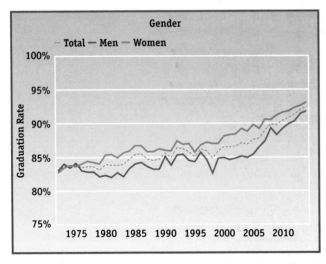

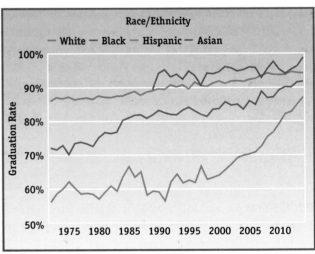

SOURCE: Data from U.S. Department of Commerce, Census Bureau, Current Population Survey (CPS), October, 1972 through 2014. (This table was prepared March 2016.)

These gaps matter for lots of reasons. But consider one. **Educational homogamy** is one of the chief mechanisms of the social reproduction of inequality—the penchant to marry people who share our level of education. People with bachelor's degrees are extremely likely to marry other people with bachelor's degrees. People with PhDs marry other people with PhDs. And people with only a high school education are most likely to marry other people with only a high school education. In fact, about three in four Americans that are in heterosexual marriages are married to someone who shares their level of education almost exactly. In other words, education shapes our interactions and identities in fundamental ways. And when we pair up in these ways, we amplify the effects of social inequality because education is significantly correlated with wealth. Those with more education and wealth are most likely to marry each other. And this amplifies the differences between them and those with less education and wealth.

educational homogamy

Marriage between people who are similar to one another in educational attainment.

These dynamics are true globally as well. In low- and middle-income nations like India, Uganda, and Malawi, boys and girls may spend several years in school, but their learning is limited to the practical knowledge they need to farm or perform other traditional tasks. They don't have time for much else. A child in a high-performing country such as Norway, by contrast, can expect an average of 12.6 years of education, double that of a child in El Salvador, four times as much as a child in Sierra Leone, and nine times that of a child in Niger (U.N. Development Program 2016). Yet progress has been made in the past decade. With the major exception of Africa, most children around the world now receive some primary education, and the chance of a child continuing from primary school into the secondary grades is more than 80 percent in most countries. Beyond that, however, enrollment percentages drop dramatically in most regions of the world. In China, Malaysia, and Mexico, for example, the 87 percent of students who are enrolled at the secondary level drops to under 30 percent in the tertiary level (The World Bank 2014).

Gender also determines educational opportunity. One in three children worldwide lives in a country that does not ensure equal access to education for boys and girls. And in all countries without gender parity, it is girls who are disadvantaged. Gender disparity is even more widespread at the secondary level; in fact, the magnitude of inequity increases by educational level. Ironically, while disadvantages for girls in secondary education are common in low-income countries, girls tend to outnumber boys in high-income countries, including the United States (The World Bank 2009).

As a result of these trends more generally, the literacy rate is extremely low in poor countries. Among the Arab states, 14 percent of men and 30 percent of women were not literate as of 2013. Globally, 40 percent of sub-Saharan Africans, 32 percent of South and West Asians, and 8 percent of Latin Americans are illiterate (UNESCO 2015). When most citizens cannot read and write at ordinary levels, they cannot compete in the global marketplace, and their nations remain impoverished. What's more, where women are better educated, children fare better in health, growth, and survival. Educated mothers are more likely to get prenatal care, to ensure children are immunized, and to provide a healthy diet, among other factors. One study of 65 countries found that increasing

Some developing countries have made enormous strides in education. China now boasts very high enrollments in primary grades and almost 96.4 percent literacy (CIA World Factbook 2015). And yet enrollment drops considerably after ninth grade, especially in poorer regions, and there are large gender gaps.

the proportion of girls educated at the secondary level would result in a drop of weather-related deaths (like flooding) as well as the numbers of people affected by droughts. Increasing the proportion of girls educated has also been shown to drop the infant mortality rate (Save the Children 2014).

A REPORT CARD ON EDUCATION IN THE UNITED STATES Once the world leader in education, the United States spends more per child on education than any other country. Yet, like U.S. spending on health care, we might not rank where you'd imagine given the resources dedicated. In recent years, the U.S. international rank in reading and math performance has been slipping. We are no longer among the top 10 in either. Every year, the OECD cooperates with nations around the world to assess student performance around the world. The comparisons between nations are based on aggregate test scores in 76 different countries. It's an important indicator of the quality of education around the world and also a sobering reminder of education inequality on a global level.

Each year, the 76 nations are ranked according to two separate scores: one for student performance in math and science and a separate score for reading. Data on reading were collected most recently in 2012, while math and science scores were assessed in 2015. Year to year, different countries move around in ranking. But the overall trend and relative ranking of each nation has tended to remain the same. Although Americans receive more education than people in many other parts of the world, we do not fare as well as we often believe we should on measures of student achievement. Indeed, on an assessment of universal basic skills in OECD nations, the United States ranks 29th in terms of student achievement. And the U.S. ranking is more the result of gaps in mathematical skills than reading and scientific competencies when compared with other nations.

The United States is not among the leaders in education internationally. You might find this surprising as so many of the world's most elite educational and research institutions are found in the United States. But part of this has to do with educational inequality in the United States. The scoring for each nation is done in the aggregate; it's an average score. From that piece of data, we do not see the range. Do most student scores in a given nation hover right around the national average? Is there an enormous range or a small one? The United States certainly has high-achieving students as well. But we also have a large proportion of low-achieving students. This tells us that there are two important ways we need to think about education inequality—there is inequality *between* societies, but *within* societies as well.

Understanding Educational Improvement

13.2.3 Summarize some of the ways that education is improving around the world.

A number of developing nations have begun intensive efforts to improve education, from grade school through university and professional schools. India has the world's youngest population, with 500 million people ages 18 and younger. If they could be educated, they would prove a formidable economic force. Government spending on education has grown rapidly. As a result, approximately 90 percent of all Indian children are enrolled in primary school. The literacy rate was up to 74 percent in 2011—from 53 percent in 1995. The number of Indians attending colleges and universities almost doubled in the 1990s. However, there is wide variation in literacy rates by location—wealthy districts have 93 percent literacy and poorer, rural ones have 63 percent—and especially by sex: The best districts have female literacy rates of 91 percent, whereas the worst have 52 percent (Census India 2011), and dropout rates are still high in India as well, with 40 percent of children dropping out of school by eighth grade (Bajoria and Braunschweiger 2014).

In the 1980s, China also planned for universal education for grades 1 through 9 by 2000. As a result, there was an immense expansion of the educational system. Enrollment is high—at least through grade nine—so the literacy rate is 92 percent nationally, and 99.7 percent among young adults (ages 15 to 24) (UNESCO 2015). There has also been a massive university expansion, especially at the doctoral level; China is catching up to the United States particularly in doctorates awarded in science and engineering (National Science Foundation 2008). And these more general trends toward more education have been true around the world as well. If we consider literacy as one measure of education, consider the differences in literacy rates among the elderly around the world (see MAP 13.2). Rates are vastly improved among the world's youth, though disparities remain.

These indicators illustrate that education is a global issue and is improving on an international scale. But it is also true that a great deal of educational inequality remains. Not all nations are improving, nor are they all improving at the same rate. And beyond this, these rates are still reported as averages and tell us little about education inequality *within* nations—an issue we turn to in the next section.

MAP 13.2 Literacy Rates Around the World, by Age Group, 2015

This map does not have data for all societies around the world. The literacy rate in the United States and many European nations, for instance, are not listed here. These data are not reported by UNESCO. But data from the U.S. Census suggest that the U.S. literacy rate is approximately 86 percent—14 percent are not literate. In actual numbers, that amounts to roughly 32 million Americans who cannot read. Globally, young people are learning to read at much higher rates than the elderly. This is one indication of education change around the world. Certainly, reading today is much more of a necessity than it might have been 80 years ago. In many countries, to meaningfully participate in the economy requires basic reading knowledge. And although rates of change are still uneven, the general trend is toward increasing literacy.

Literacy rate for age 65+

| No data | Less than 10 | 10–20 | 20–30 | 30–40 | 40–55 | 55–65 | 65–75 | 75–90 | >90 |

SOURCE: Data from United Nations Educational, Scientific, and Cultural Organization (UNESCO).

---

iSOC AND YOU Education as a Mechanism of Social Inequality

Education is both a way to challenge *inequality* and among the most primary mechanisms by which inequality is reproduced. Both globally and locally, education can promote mobility and keep you stuck where you are. *Institutionally*, education can provide the social skills to *interact* with people in new ways, enable you to construct and reconstruct your *identity*, and complicate existing *intersectional* inequalities. Considered another way, education shapes the kinds of inequalities that you are likely to endure, but the collection of inequalities you endure also impact both the amount and type of education you receive. This is what social reproduction looks like.

13.3 Institutional Differences, Interactions, and Inequality

Did you apply to more than one college? It's not uncommon for college applicants to select their "top choice." That might mean that you spent a bit more time on the application, awaited the news with a bit more anxiety, and so on. Students also often apply to schools they think of as "safety schools"—institutions they feel like they are a sure bet compared with others. Embedded in these tough decisions a belief that *where* you get a degree is at least as important as whether or not you get one at all. And it probably won't shock readers to hear that, in general, those fears are true. You're much more likely to become a CEO or to become a best-selling author if you attended Harvard than you are if you attended your local community college. And, in general, we all casually appreciate these status differences between institutions. We may not be aware of precisely where our institution is ranked—but we know who its peers are and aren't.

But college feels different because it involves an application process. Most students don't have to apply to get into elementary, middle, or high school. Yet, even at these earlier points in your educational career, a great deal of sociological research has asked whether some schools are better than others. And if so, which qualities associated with schools matter the most. Identifying the institutional ingredients that seem to be key to student success is important. This section considers institutional differences and identifies some of the patterned ways in which social inequality is perpetuated by education. We will examine intersections among race, class, and gender and consider the ways that social identities shape young people's educational experiences and opportunities.

How Much Does Your School Matter?

13.3.1 Explain what "school effects" are, and summarize some of why they are challenging to study.

In 1954, the Supreme Court of the United States declared state laws that established separate public schools for black and white students to be unconstitutional in *Brown v. the Board of Education*. It was a historic 9–0 vote against laws preserving segregation. Chief Justice Earl Warren famously stated, "separate educational facilities are inherently unequal." It was a landmark case and was used to argue that *de jure* racial segregation was in violation of the Equal Protection clause of the Fourteenth Amendment. This case was an important victory for the Civil Rights Movement, helping to articulate just how and why the idea of "separate but equal" was an enactment of racial inequality. Indeed, Justice Warren claimed that "separate" is "*inherently* unequal." What the decision did not spell out was any kind of specific method by which schools ought to go about ending school **segregation** in favor of **integration**—only suggesting that

segregation

The practice of physically separating whites from other races by law and custom in institutions and communities.

integration

The physical intermingling of the races organized as a concerted legal and social effort to bring equal access and racial equality through racial mixing in institutions and communities.

each state does so "with all deliberate speed." It is noteworthy that integration began with students, not teachers.

But nearly a decade later, U.S. schools remained highly segregated. Achievement gaps between the achievements of white and black students had remained high, too—indeed, these gaps persist today. And the general thinking was that achievement gaps between black and white students were the result of differences between the types of schools black and white students were attending. People generally think that what kind of school you go to matters. It's not hard to assume that students attending overcrowded urban schools in extremely impoverished districts would fare worse than students attending elite private schools in some of the most privileged districts. It doesn't only matter *that* you get an education—it matters *where*, too. Doesn't it?

Roughly 10 years after the Supreme Court decision, the U.S. government commissioned one of the largest sociological studies ever undertaken. The principal scholar associated with this study was the sociologist James Coleman. The resulting report is probably the most important study of education in the twentieth century. The report was titled, the "Equality of Educational Opportunity" (Coleman, et al. 1966), but it is generally referred to now as "The Coleman Report." The study itself was monumental. Roughly 650,000 students were surveyed from more than 3,000 separate schools. The study examined school facilities, quality of textbooks, classroom sizes, curricula, school administration, and all types of extracurricular activities available at each school in the study.

The results of the study shocked everyone, even Coleman himself. The biggest finding was that differences between schools in terms of school resources didn't seem to matter. The characteristics they measured of individual schools only explained a small amount of the educational outcomes for students. Whether your school had new textbooks or not, enough supplies and materials or too many, appeared to not matter. What Coleman found mattered a great deal—more than anything else, in fact—was two things: (1) the family backgrounds of individual students and (2) the student peers with whom students attended school and interacted.

It was an enormous controversy and fueled an intense debate among social scientists about **"school effects".** The report is commonly cited as evidence that increased school funding will have little impact on student achievement—a scary prospect; it makes inequality in educational outcomes appear almost inevitable. But it didn't take long for research to show that student outcomes are meaningfully shaped by school characteristics. One of the most famous studies conducted addressed this by examining class size. Some small, private, liberal arts colleges put extremely low caps on classroom sizes. Tristan attended Colorado College, where classes were capped at 25 students when he attended. He took a few classes in which fewer than 10 students were enrolled. Contrast this with students enrolled in large lecture courses at big state institutions with classes larger than 300 students. That's a big difference—but does the difference *matter*?

One of the best-known studies of school characteristics is a **longitudinal study** conducted over 4 years by the Tennessee State Department of education, starting in 1985, "Project STAR" (Word et al. 1990). In an experimental design, students and teachers were assigned to one of three types of classrooms for a period of 4 years (kindergarten through third grade). Some were assigned to classes with 22–26 students and some were assigned to classes with only 13–17 students. The study kept students and teachers in these class sizes for 4 years and then a variety of scholars analyzed differences in student outcomes. Interestingly, they were interested in both short- and long-term outcomes (even though students moved out of experimental classroom designs starting in fourth grade). Those students in smaller classes initially showed high test scores and were less likely to be cited for disciplinary problems in the classroom. But not only that, the effects of that small class size early on also appeared to stick with

"school effects"

The term for research demonstrating the ways student outcomes are meaningfully shaped by school characteristics.

longitudinal study

An observational research method in which data is gathered for the same subjects repeatedly over a period of time that can extend over years or even decades.

SOCIOLOGY AND OUR WORLD

SINGLE-SEX SCHOOLING AND STUDENT SUCCESS

What do you think are the benefits and costs of single-sex schools?

Among the proposed remedies for gender inequality in education has been the resurgence of single-sex education. At one time, many of America's most elite private colleges and universities were single sex, but beginning in the late 1960s, virtually all of the all-male schools and about half of the all-female colleges and universities went coed. This was based on the notion that women and men were perfectly capable of being educated in the same classes, reading the same texts, and being graded by the same criteria. In the 1990s, the last all-male military institutions (Virginia Military Institute and The Citadel) were ordered by the Supreme Court to admit women.

No sooner than these colleges and universities went coed, there was a movement to separate girls and boys in public high schools, especially in STEM fields, where girls' levels of achievement were lagging behind that of boys. Separating boys and girls was perceived to be a method that would encourage both boys and girls to learn more effectively. In the early 2000s, many school districts experimented with these single-sex classes, although many were challenged by the American Civil Liberties Union (ACLU), which considered them a form of sex discrimination. As we saw when discussing race, "separate but equal" generally isn't equal.

In these suits, the ACLU charged organizations supporting single-sex education with perpetuating stereotypes. What do you think? Here is an extract from the National Association for Single Sex Public Education (an organization promoting single sex education in the United States):

> Girls and boys differ fundamentally in the learning *style* they feel most comfortable with. Girls tend to look on the teacher as an ally. Given a little encouragement, they will welcome the teacher's help. A girl-friendly classroom is a safe, comfortable, welcoming place. Forget hard plastic chairs: put in a sofa and some comfortable beanbags… The teacher should never yell or shout at a girl. Avoid confrontation. Avoid the word 'why.'… Girls will naturally break up in groups of three and four to work on problems. Let them. Minimize assignments that require working alone.

We assume that most of the women reading this will be deeply insulted by these stereotypes. Bean bag chairs? Seriously? But aren't you guys equally insulted? Are you only capable of learning when the teacher yells at you and constantly asks why, forces you to sit in uncomfortable chairs, and never ever lets you work with others? The number of schools educating students in sex-segregated classrooms is currently on the rise in the United States, increasing 24 percent between 2007 and 2012. And the vast majority of schools educating students in single-sex environments do not advertise this to parents and prospective students. This means that many students find themselves in deliberately sex-segregated educational settings despite not having voluntarily elected to participate.

them. Those students were also more likely to graduate high school and were more likely to indicate that they intended to attend college. Some school characteristics do matter; class size is a big one. And Project STAR discovered that the benefits of being in a smaller class early on were most pronounced for marginalized student populations: students from lower-class households and non-White students (Mosteller 1995). So, institutional differences do matter. But which ones and why is still the subject of a great deal of research.

Social Inequality and Institutional Differences

13.3.2 Describe the ways that different types of educational institutions in the United States help perpetuate inequality using private schools as an example.

The types of schools and the uneven distribution of resources for schools result in often dramatic differences in student achievement. One in nine American schoolchildren attends a private school, which most of us believe are superior to public schools. Though when we consider these numbers intersectionally, those proportions change dramatically by race and ethnicity and class as well. The evidence to support the belief that private schools offer a superior education is far from clear, although parents, children, and even public school teachers all believe that private schools offer a better education.

Today 10 percent of American children, roughly 5.4 million, attend private schools (National Center for Education 2014). White students are twice as likely to attend private schools as black students, and their numbers are increasing: Only 58 percent of white students were enrolled in public school in 2007–2008, 9 percentage points less than a decade before.

Slightly more than two-thirds of the 33,366 private schools in the United States are run by religious bodies. The Roman Catholic Church runs the most (7,115), and interdenominational fundamentalist Protestants come in a close second, but there are also schools affiliated with Presbyterians, Mormons, Lutherans, Orthodox Jews, and many others. There are usually no restrictions about the religious background of the students, but religious instruction is required, along with chapel and other religious services. Most of the 10,635 secular private schools are prestigious (expensive), modeled after British boarding schools, with many advantages in educational quality and school-based social networks. They draw an elite group of students, and their graduates go on to equally prestigious and expensive private universities.

Many people believe that a private school provides better education, and send their children if they can afford it. Thirty-six percent of U.S. Congress members and 46 percent of U.S. Senators with school-age children sent them to private schools (Heritage Foundation 2009). In Florida, nearly 40% of lawmakers, nearly four times the state average, send their school-aged children to private schools. But when the lawmakers are on education committees, the percentage rises to 60 percent (survey by Matus 2005). Even public school teachers believe that private schools are superior—nationwide, more than one in five public school teachers choose private schools for their own children, almost twice the state average (Perry 2013).

Other than the prestige, what is the attraction of private education? Advocates argue that smaller class sizes and lower student-teacher ratios facilitate learning. Discipline is better, and thus there is a more focused and orderly environment for learning. And private schools are safer (Coleman, Hoffer and Kilgore 1982; Chubb and Moe 1990).

Tracking

13.3.3 Understand what it means that tracking is both a response to educational inequality as well as involved in the reproduction of educational inequality.

Sometimes, however, students from different backgrounds do end up in the same schools. Indeed, this is one of the initial ways that racially segregated schools were desegregated. To overcome the effects of residential segregation on school demographics, students were bused to districts away from their homes to forcibly desegregate their schools. Perhaps not surprisingly, busing was met with a great deal of protest and anxiety on all sides. Movies like *Remember the Titans* (2000) celebrate this as a period in American history where we overcame racial tensions and started to more meaningfully address racial inequality. In the film, Denzel Washington plays a black high school football coach who moves to a new city with his family to coach at a desegregated white school in Alexandria, Virginia.

And, although it may have put students from different backgrounds into the same schools, students from different backgrounds don't always end up in the same classrooms. This is the result of a process education scholars refer to as "tracking." **Tracking**, or grouping students according to their ability, is common in American schools. Some schools do not have formal tracking, but virtually all have mechanisms for sorting students into groups that seem to be alike in ability and achievement (Oakes 1985). It makes intuitive sense—the idea is that students learn best when they are learning alongside other students with similar abilities.

Whether the tracking is formal or informal, strong **labeling** develops. Individuals in the low-achievement, noncollege preparatory, or manual track often come to be

tracking

Common in American schools, it is the term for grouping students according to their academic abilities.

labeling

Often associated with self-fulfilling prophecy and stereotyping, labeling theory describes how self-identity and behavior of individuals may be determined or influenced by the terms used to describe or classify them.

labeled "Dummies" or "Greasers" by both teachers and other students, and even among themselves. They are not only labeled, they are treated as if they are stupid or incompetent, thus affecting their self-image and ultimately affecting their achievement in a self-fulfilling prophecy. The negative impact of tracking mostly affects minority students (Oakes 1990).

self-fulfilling prophecy
The social phenomenon that when we expect something to happen, it often does.

The term **self-fulfilling prophecy** was coined by Merton (1949/1968) for a curious phenomenon: When you expect something to happen, it usually does. We've seen this before with racial stereotypes (see Chapter 8). And Rosenthal and Jacobson (1968/1992) found it among San Francisco school children as well. Farkas (1990a, 1990b, 1996) found that girls and Asian-Americans got better grades than boys and black and Latino students, even when they all had the same test scores. They concluded that girls and Asian Americans signaled that they were "good" students; they were eager to cooperate, quickly agreed with what the teacher said, and demonstrated they are trying hard. These characteristics, coveted by teachers, were rewarded with better grades.

In addition, because the funds go mostly toward the educational needs of the high-track students, the low-track students receive poorer classes, textbooks, supplies, and teachers. Gamoran, et al. (1995) confirmed Oakes' finding that tracking reinforces previously existing inequalities for average or poor students, but found it has positive benefits for "advanced" students. The correlation between high educational achievement and race is not lost on the students. In a speech before the National Democratic Convention in 2004, soon-to-be-President Barack Obama denounced "the slander that a black child with a book is 'acting white.'" He was paraphrasing research by Berkeley anthropologist John Ogbu (1997), which demonstrates that even people who suffer from stereotyped images often believe them. Minority children, especially boys, believe that good school performance is a challenge to their ethnic identity, or a betrayal. They *are supposed to* perform poorly.

Pedro Noguera (2008) found a positive correlation between self-esteem and school achievement: Students who feel good about themselves perform better. Only one group showed no correlation: African American boys. They are so disconnected from school that raising their self-esteem has no effect on how well they do. This illustrates that educational inequality is not only perpetuated between institutions, but within them as well.

Understanding Educational Inequality Intersectionally

13.3.4 Summarize the relationship between parents' socioeconomic status and student educational outcomes as well as how that relationship varies by race.

Parents say they switch to private schools—or want to—because of the crumbling buildings, overcrowded classrooms, bare-bones curriculum, and poor instruction in many public schools today. Unfortunately, those parents most able to afford private schools probably live in districts where the public schools are actually pretty good. Because education is funded largely by local property taxes, wealthier neighborhoods, and communities have more money to spend on schools than poorer ones. Public schools in wealthy neighborhoods can afford state-of-the-art labs and libraries, small classes, and highly paid teachers. It is the poor neighborhoods that have the crumbling buildings, overcrowded classrooms, and overworked, underpaid teachers. The pattern holds up in every city and every state, reproducing the same class privileges that we find in the public/private school divide (Oakes 1990). Indeed, data show that in the United States, there is a strong correlation between social class and academic achievement. Students in school districts where parents are wealthier are, on average, performing better than their peers in poorer districts. A new report out of Stanford University attempts to illustrate these facts in an accessible way (Reardon 2016).

Although James Coleman was unable to find meaningful differences in student outcomes associated with specific school characteristics, subsequent research has shown that where you go to school matters. Students in Lexington school district in Massachusetts are performing 3.8 grade levels *above* average; the median family income there is $163,000. That's a big difference from students in the Birmingham City school district in Alabama where students are, on average, performing 1.8 grade levels *below* average and the median family income is $30,000. But this is also a dramatic illustration of Coleman's finding of what does matter about schools: your own family background and the family backgrounds of your peers.

This shows us that class matters, but what about race? In The Coleman Report, they discovered that black students fared much better, on average, in majority-white schools and they also discovered that lower-class students fared better in schools where the majority of students came from families in higher socioeconomic classes. Reardon's work illustrates that racial achievement gaps are still incredibly pronounced, even within single school districts. One issue is that black and Hispanic students are both significantly more likely to come from lower socioeconomic households and have, on average, lower levels of academic achievement. There are large gaps between white students and their black and Hispanic classmates. And much of this is the result of continued segregation. Integration in U.S. classrooms peaked in 1988, then began to reverse when the 1991 Supreme Court ruling allowed the return of neighborhood schools. In 1998, more than 70 percent of black students attended intensely segregated schools. The most dramatic (and largely ignored) trend affects Hispanic Americans. In 1968, a little more than 20 percent of Hispanic students were enrolled in intensely segregated schools—by 1998, more than a third were. Hispanics face serious levels of segregation by race and also poverty, with particularly large increases in segregation in the West, the first area in the nation to have predominantly minority public school enrollment (Orfield 2004).

School segregation is strongly associated with poverty for all groups: Nearly 90 percent of intensely segregated black and Latino schools have student bodies with concentrated poverty (Orfield 2004). **Concentrated poverty** means students with worse health care, lower nutrition, less-educated parents, more frequent moves, weaker preschool skills, and often limited English skills. They have two strikes against them in their quest for educational excellence already, and then they must contend with outdated textbooks, inadequate facilities, overcrowded classrooms, and, often, inexperienced and noncredentialed teachers.

concentrated poverty
The extreme density of socio-economic deprivation in a particular area.

This is why examining sociological issues intersectionally is so important. Inequalities have a tendency to pile up on certain populations while other groups collected concentrated accumulations of diverse forms of advantage. Consider differences between races in levels of educational attainment for adults, age 25 and older in the United States (FIGURE 13.5).

On this chart, Hispanic and Asian Americans stand out. They're what social scientists refer to as "outliers" in the data. Hispanic Americans stand out here because their levels of educational attainment appear to be disproportionately lower than every other racial and ethnic group, while Asian Americans' levels of educational attainment appear to surpass other groups by a large margin. Sociologists examining facts like these will ask questions like: Are all groups identified as "Hispanic" equally at risk of lower educational attainment? Are some worse off than others? And as you can see in FIGURE 13.6, there is a lot of variation between different ethnic groups among those identified as "Hispanic" or "Latino" on the American Communities Survey.

FIGURE 13.5 Educational Attainment by Race among Adults Age 25 and Older, 2013

Here, you can see the effects on education of race and class inequality. By the time they reach 25, there are large differences between educational attainment among different racial and ethnic groups in the United States. Although only 8 percent of white Americans have less than a high school education by this age, 16 percent of black Americans and 35 percent of Hispanic Americans have less than a high school education. This matters because education remains an important predictor of future mobility, and thus, is here a primary engine in the reproduction of racialized forms of educational inequality.

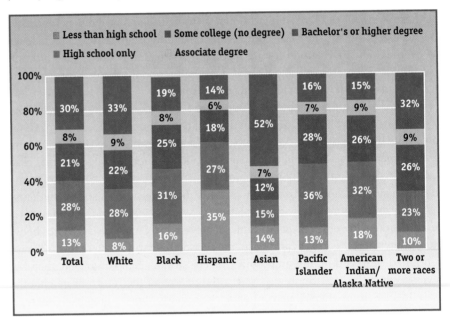

NOTE: Percentages within groups may not add up to 100 percent because of rounding.

SOURCE: Data from U.S. Department of Commerce, Census Bureau, American Community Survey. 2013. See Digest of Education Statistics, table 104.40.

Although a great deal of these discrepancies have to do with school segregation; students from different racial and ethnic backgrounds are largely segregated into different schools, and those schools are associated with very different kinds of outcomes for long-term educational attainment. But research has also shown that racial disparities persist even within the same school districts by race. The research by Reardon discovered that those gaps are among the most pronounced in some of the most affluent school districts. Even in districts where white students and black and Hispanic peers came from families with remarkably similar class backgrounds, white students still out-performed black and Hispanic students. This difference might possibly be the result of tracking. It could be that white students are simply much more likely to be recognized as "gifted" and placed on higher tracks early on in their education than are black and Hispanic students. And this placement gives them an early advantage and has cumulative effects over the course of their education. It's a telling example of just how entrenched educational inequality is and how challenging it is to overcome. We need much more than desegregation to ensure that students from all socioeconomic backgrounds, races, and ethnicities are presented with similar educational opportunities that will provide more equitable educational outcomes.

THE RACIAL ACHIEVEMENT GAP In *No Excuses: Closing the Racial Gap in Learning* (2003), Abigail and Stephan Thernstrom argue that African American educational underachievement stems from a variety of factors:

- Low birth weight, which can impair intellectual development
- High number of single-parent families led by young mothers unprepared to give children good educational guidance

FIGURE 13.6 Educational Attainment among Hispanic/Latino People Age 25 and Older, by Ethnicity, 2013

On this chart we see that when it comes to educational attainment, there is a great deal of within-group variation among Hispanic Americans. About one in three South Americans in the United States has a bachelor's degree or more, and only 1 in 10 Mexicans in the United States has the same level of educational attainment (and even fewer among Salvadorans).

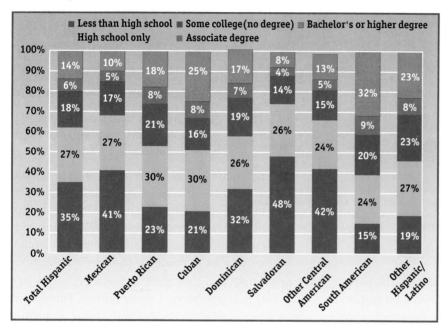

NOTE: Percentages within groups may not add up to 100 percent due to rounding.

SOURCE: Data from U.S. Department of Commerce, Census Bureau, American Community Survey. 2013. See Digest of Education Statistics, table 104.40.

- Inadequate funding
- Difficulty recruiting good teachers to work in schools attended primarily by black students

By contrast, Ronald Ferguson (2001) studied middle- and upper-middle-class students in Ann Arbor, Michigan, a wealthy, well-educated community, the site of the University of Michigan. Students in the city's three high schools had an average SAT score in 2004 of 1,165, more than 100 points higher than the national average. In 2003, they had 44 National Merit finalists. Eighty-five percent of high school seniors go on to 4-year colleges and universities. Quite an elite bunch! Even in middle-class college-bound high schools, African American students typically had a C average, white students a B. African Americans typically scored 100 points below white students on the SAT. Why?

Some of the reasons Ferguson found were environmental. For instance, even in the same community and the same schools, the African American students were less affluent: Only about one in five were upper-middle class or upper class, compared to almost three in four of the white students. But there was more. The parents of African American students lacked access to the networks white parents had to trade information about the best teachers, classes, and strategies for success. They felt less entitled, less able to be demanding and advocate for their children. So, white parents were more likely to advocate for their children in terms of grades, but also in terms of helping to ensure their children were on elite tracks, aimed at elite futures.

Teachers often misread signals from the black students. In high-stress, high-achievement schools, students who are trying hard and not doing well

Grades reflect both students' achievement and teachers' expectations. In one study, girls and Asian Americans received better grades than other students—even when their test scores were the same. The researchers concluded that this was because they conformed to teachers' perceptions of how good students behave.

perceive themselves as failures. Many felt that it is better to act as though you are simply uninterested in doing well than to acknowledge that you are struggling. Teachers see laziness and indifference, lower their expectations, and give students less support—which Ferguson found matters a great deal to minority students. They then try harder to pretend that they are uninterested, resulting in a self-fulfilling prophecy.

Gender Inequality in Education

13.3.5 Summarize some of the ways that gender inequality is institutionalized within education.

Education also reproduces other kinds of inequality—like gender inequality. And the primary mechanisms through which this is accomplished are gender stereotypes. In the hidden curriculum, teachers, administrators, and peers require us to conform to narrow definitions of what it means to be a "boy" or a "girl," and they punish deviance, subtly or not. However, education also allows us to move beyond stereotyping: The classroom is perhaps the only place where a boy can be praised for being quiet and studious and a girl can be praised for knowing the answer.

In their book, *Failing at Fairness* (1994), David and Myra Sadker documented some of the subtle ways teachers reinforce both gender difference and gender inequality. They named it the **chilly classroom climate** for girls, describing that class materials used often reflect stereotyped differences between women and men, boys and girls. Because of such disparities, there has been an effort to increase the number of active girls in schoolbooks and also in children's media more generally. And there have also been dramatic changes outside the classroom. Title IX legislation forbids discrimination against girls and women in all aspects of school life. As a result, many elementary and secondary schools have increased funding for girls' sports, allowing more girls the opportunity to participate. And contrary to some expectations, girls have shown they love sports, too.

Still, one of the chief lessons taught in school is what it means to be a man or a woman. Schools are organizations that produce gender identity—rewarding conformity and punishing nonconformity, both in the formal curriculum, and in informal interactions. Gender conformity—adhering to normative expectations about masculinity or femininity—is carefully scrutinized. We get messages everywhere we look—in the content of the texts we read, the rules we are all supposed to follow, and the behaviors of teachers and administrators as role models. But it is most significantly taught by peers, who act as a sort of "**gender police**," enforcing the rules. Step out of line, even the tiniest bit, and your friends and other students will let you know, clearly and unequivocally, that you have transgressed. Do it again, and they may begin to doubt you as a potential friend. Do it consistently, and you will be marginalized as a weirdo, a deviant, or, most importantly, as "gay."

Every American teenager knows that the most constant put-down in our high schools and middle schools these days is "that's so gay!" Ordinarily this **gay-baiting**—calling people or something they do "gay" as a way of ridiculing them or putting them down—has little to do with sexual orientation. It means that

chilly classroom climate

The subtle ways teachers reinforce both gender difference and gender inequality through class materials and interaction dynamics that often reflect stereotyped differences between women and men, boys and girls.

"gender police"

Student peers who act to enforce gender rules against transgressions large and small.

gay-baiting

Calling people or something they do "gay" as a way of ridiculing them or putting them down. Usually applied to men, it has little to do with sexual orientation, but instead accuses them of acting or appearing insufficiently masculine.

you don't think he is acting sufficiently masculine (Pascoe 2007). The constant teasing and bullying that occur in middle schools and high schools have become national problems (Juvonen, Graham, and Schuster 2003; Olweus 1993; Klein 2013; Pascoe 2013). Bullying is not one single thing but a continuum stretching from hurtful language through shoving and hitting to criminal assault and school shootings. Harmful teasing and bullying happen to more than one million schoolchildren, both boys and girls, each year. The evidence of bullying's ubiquity alone is quite convincing. In one study of middle- and high-school students in midwestern towns, 88 percent reported having observed bullying, and 77 percent reported being a victim of bullying at some point during their school years. In another, 70 percent had been sexually harassed by their peers; 40 percent had experienced physical dating violence, 66 percent had been victimized by emotional abuse in a dating relationship, and 54 percent had been bullied. Many middle- and high-school students are afraid to go to school; they fear locker rooms, hallways, bathrooms, lunchrooms, and playgrounds, and some even fear their classrooms.

As social media have become a larger part of young people's lives, bullying too has gone virtual. This makes bullying more visible and often more challenging to oppose. Today, students hear messages about "appropriate" and "inappropriate" uses of social media. But as with many forms of new technology and media, young people are often a bit ahead of adults.

SOCIOLOGY AND OUR WORLD

RANDOM SCHOOL SHOOTINGS

Why is it that school shootings are so overwhelmingly likely to be committed by boys and men?

On April 16, 2007, Seung Hui Cho, a 23-year-old student at Virginia Tech, murdered two students in a dorm, waited about an hour, and then calmly walked to an academic building, chained the entrance, and started shooting methodically. In the end, he killed 30 students and faculty before shooting himself—the deadliest school shooting by an individual in our nation's history. Although obviously mentally disturbed, he had managed never to be ill "enough" to attract serious attention. In the time between the shootings, he recorded a video in which he fumed about all the taunting, teasing, and being ignored he had endured and how this final conflagration would even the score. In February, 2008, a 27-year-old former student at Northern Illinois University, Stephen Kazmierczak, opened fire on a crowded lecture hall at Northern Illinois University, killing four students before turning the gun on himself.

And then there was Columbine High School in Littleton, Colorado. The very word *Columbine* has become a symbol; kids today talk about someone "pulling a Columbine." The connection between being socially marginalized, picked on, and bullied every day propelled Eric Harris and Dylan Klebold deeper into their video-game-inspired fantasies of a vengeful bloodbath. On April 20, 1999, Harris and Klebold brought a variety of weapons to their high school and proceeded to walk through the school, shooting whomever they could find. Twenty-three students and faculty were injured, and 15 died, including one teacher and the perpetrators.

What all these boys—virtually all school shooters have been boys—have in common is a self-justifying narrative of victimization. All claimed to have been bullied, taunted, teased—maliciously, routinely, and with absolute impunity. Their actions came from a sense of "aggrieved entitlement"—they felt they had been wronged and sought revenge. One boy, Luke Woodham, who killed two classmates in 1997, said, "I am not insane. I am angry. I killed because people like me are mistreated every day. I am malicious because I am miserable." Another boy, Michael Carneal, told psychiatrists weighing his sanity that "people respect me now" (Blank 1998).

Several recent works emphasize the serious psychiatric disorders of these rampage shooters. Although it's true that they did have serious psychological problems, a sociological perspective also considers the patterns of these shootings and the similarities among the perpetrators. What's more, we don't profile only the shooters, but also the schools: Did the schools have any characteristics in common? Students understand these common characteristics, even if some observers do not. In a national survey of teenagers' attitudes, 86 percent of teenagers said that they believed that the school shootings were motivated by a desire "to get back at those who have hurt them" and that "other kids picking on them, making fun of them, or bullying them" were the immediate causes. Other potential causes, such as violence on television, movies, computer games or videos, mental problems, and access to guns, were significantly lower among the adolescents' ratings (Gaughan, Cerio, and Myers 2001).

To avoid being bullied, most students struggle to ensure that nothing they do transgresses a gender boundary. And although the stereotypes they confront in the classroom, on the playground, and in their textbooks might seem easily surmountable, they pile up. And they come to affect the ways students think about themselves, their educational achievements, and abilities. Gender inequality shapes classroom interactions, is institutionalized in classroom practices and materials, and comes to help students form gendered identities as students that shape future educational opportunities goals, and trajectories.

---

iSOC AND YOU Institutional Differences, Interactions, and Inequality

How does social *inequality* come to appear "normal," something that we take for granted and even accept? Part of the answer is that inequality is embedded in social *institutions* and, becomes harder to see. Dramatic inequalities between and among schools can sometimes mask how those schools themselves reflect existing, *intersecting* inequalities based on things like class or race. Your *interactions* with others, students and teachers, play a role in both producing and reflecting these inequalities. And thus, your educational *identity* (your ability to succeed or fail as a student) that you use to "move up" or "stand still" becomes more easily seen as your "fault" as an individual than the predictable outcome of an unequal institutional system. Education is institutionalized in ways that cause predictable paths of success for some, and educational paths of struggle and failure for others.

13.4 Higher Education

Ask an American "where did you go to school?" and they will tell you, more often than not, where they went to college or university. We get much of our identity from associating with our school. You're probably institutionally "branded" right now, reading this in a T-shirt or sweatshirt with the name of your school on it. By contrast, if you ask an Australian where they went to school, they'll tell you which *high school* they attended. Australia has an elaborate system of private schools for high school, but virtually everyone goes to large public universities.

Where you go to college matters; both in terms of your identity and also because your college provides access to informal networks that can help you get a job or find a place to live. While in school, you'll read the same books, and take exams that are pretty similar, no matter where you go—this book alone is being used at more than 100 colleges and universities—but the outcomes will be enormously different because of the "social capital" you would acquire at some schools and not others. Indeed, your social interactions and the friendships and networks your form with professors, administrators, and your peers are just as valuable for securing a future for yourself as the knowledge you encounter in your college classrooms. Higher education is access, mobility, and entry, and it is also a sorting process that enables those at the top to stay there. So, higher education is a social institution that provides participants with a social identity, but simultaneously plays a key role in reproducing social inequality.

What's more, higher education has become even more important in our society, both as a source of identity and a mechanism of inequality. It is the institution in which you will spend the majority of the first quarter of your life, and the place where you will learn how to interact as a grownup citizen in your society.

A Brief History of Changes in Higher Education

13.4.1 Understand how higher education has changed in recent history and who has benefitted from these changes and how.

In 1949, there were 2.4 million college students in the United States. Fifty years later, there were 16 million. The population of the country had doubled during that period, but the proportion of the population going to college increased by 800 percent. About one in four Americans now has a college degree. And it is not merely a matter of intellectual interest: Today people need bachelor's degrees, and sometimes master's degrees, to get jobs that would have required a high school diploma or less 50 years ago. What happened?

In 1949, college degrees were simply unnecessary. A high school diploma qualified you for almost every job, and if you needed additional training, you could apply directly to a law or medical school. The wealthy went to college to "become educated," learn the social skills, and build the social networks necessary for an upper-class life (Altbach 1998; Lucas 1996; Rudolph 1990).

After World War II, GI loans brought many of the returning soldiers to college for the first time. Most were the first in their families to attend college, and they weren't quite sure what to expect. Some studied "liberal arts" such as English, history, and philosophy, but most wanted courses directly related to the jobs they would get afterward. Colleges filled the need with job-oriented majors and courses. Employers, faced with a glut of applicants more qualified than usual, began to require more advanced degrees for entry-level jobs: Why hire someone with just a high school diploma for the typist job, when there were a dozen applicants with college degrees? Majors and career paths became more specialized: Why hire someone with an English degree for the advertising job, when there were a dozen applicants who majored in advertising? Today most students still major in one of the liberal arts, but job-oriented majors are very popular.

And what initially appeared to be a "gender gap" between college attendance and graduation rates for women and men looks more complex when we consider race and ethnicity as well (see FIGURE 13.7). In 2014, approximately 40.2 percent of 18- to 24-year-old white men were enrolled in college compared with 44.2 percent of white women in the same age group. That's a four percent gap. But look at the gap among black and Hispanic women and men. Black women were enrolled at a rate 8.1 percent higher than black men in 2014. And Hispanic women were enrolled at a rate 9.1 percent higher than Hispanic men in the same year. And these are only *enrollment* rates—so, this does not provide information about *graduation* rates. Not all students who enroll in college will ultimately leave with a degree. And the likelihood of leaving with a degree is lower for racial and ethnic minority students (particularly men) as well as students from lower class backgrounds.

Preparing for College

13.4.2 Explain the ways that we can assess just how prepared Americans are to attend college after leaving high school.

Though college is rapidly becoming a necessity for middle-class and even working-class lives, the quality of American higher education is in question. Student readiness and achievement are both low. Among industrialized countries, American 15-year-olds rank 35 out of 64 in math literacy and 27 out of 64 in science (Desilver 2017). They fall behind most Scandinavian countries, Singapore, South Korea, Japan, Canada, Australia, New Zealand, Slovakia, and the Czech Republic. Thirty-seven percent of American high school graduates have college-ready skills in reading and mathematics (National Assessment of Education Progress 2015). About 60 percent of all college

FIGURE 13.7 Total Undergraduate Enrollment in Degree-Granting Two and Four-Year Postsecondary Institutions with Projections, by Gender and Race, 1970–2017

More Americans are receiving a college education than ever before in history. But when we examine some of the ways that education intersects with other aspects of our identity, it becomes quickly clear that this is truer for some groups than others. For instance, although the gender wage gap still works to men's collective benefit, women have been earning more bachelor's degrees than men for over 35 years—and the gap is growing. Yet, the gender gap is also different for different groups.

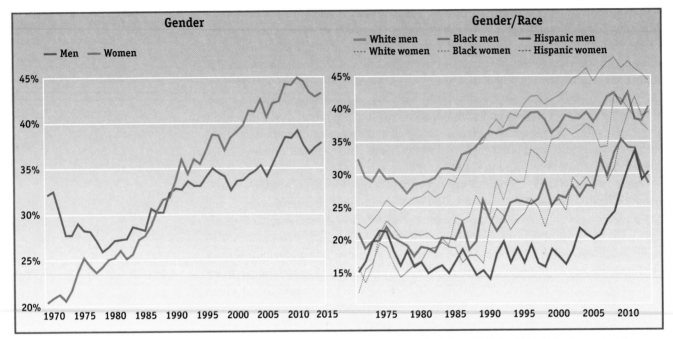

SOURCE: Data from National Center for Education Statistics, and W. Hussar Projections of Education Statistics to 2017. Available at http://nces.ed.gov/programs/digest/d15/tables/dt15_302.60.asp?current=yes.

freshmen are required to take remedial English or math (The National Center for Public Policy and Higher Education 2010).

Because they are unprepared for college, it is understandable that they are not prepared to graduate within the traditional four years. Smaller college endowments (which mean less scholarship money) and a widening gap between federal grant stipends and tuition costs mean that most students must work, part-time or full-time, and classes and studying compete with their work schedules. In 2002, a national study attempted to measure the college-readiness rates across the United States. Only slightly more than 60 percent of all college freshmen actually receive a bachelor's degree within six years of enrolling. The 6-year rate varies from a high of about two-thirds of students in Massachusetts and Maryland to a low of approximately one-third of students in New Mexico and Louisiana, and roughly one in five in Alaska (National Center for Education Statistics 2017). Part of what this tells us is that not all college students are adequately prepared to receive a college education.

In assessing students' preparedness for college, Greene and Winters (2005) relied on three criteria: Students must (1) graduate high school with a regular diploma, (2) have the minimum level of academic coursework represented on their transcripts (associated with the least selective 4-year institutions), and (3) be able to read at a basic level (see MAP 13.3).

On the other hand, there is also evidence that we are no less prepared than we used to be. For example, the average SAT scores are about the same today as they were in 1976. As you can see in FIGURE 13.8, contrary to common opinion, scores on the SAT test (the Scholastic Aptitude Test, taken by most high school students who intend to go to college) have not been in a downward spiral. During the 40 years, the mean score on the verbal section has stayed about the same, and the mean score on the math section jumped in the beginning of the twenty-first century, but the gains were short-lived.

Could it be that American students are doing about the same as they have been for decades, but that the rest of the world is catching up?

MAP 13.3 Rates of College Preparedness, by State

Just as rates of high school completion vary around the United States, so too do rates of preparedness for college. So, as we have a national conversation about the high costs of college and whether the investment is "worth it" for students attending, attention is sometimes diverted away from whether students ready to attend are truly prepared. Consider how prepared students were for college around the United States as of 2002. What, if anything, do you think might have changed since?

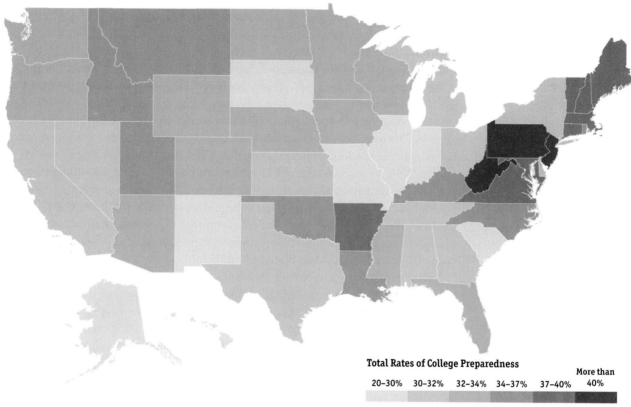

Total Rates of College Preparedness

| 20–30% | 30–32% | 32–34% | 34–37% | 37–40% | More than 40% |

SOURCE: Data from Greene, Jay P., Winters, Marcus A., Public High School Graduation and College Readiness Rates: 1991–2002, "Education Working Paper," No. 8, February 2005. Available at https://www.manhattan-institute.org/pdf/ewp_08.pdf.

FIGURE 13.8 Average SAT Scores of High School Seniors in the United States, 1976–2014

Whether students are prepared to go to college or not and just how prepared they might be can be assessed by looking at average SAT scores over time. Average SAT scores have been falling. Part of this is the result of more students taking the test and new populations applying to go to college.

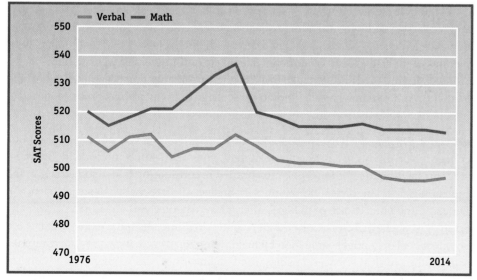

SOURCE: Data from College Entrance Examination Board, 2005; National Center for Education Statistics, 2016.

Higher Education and Inequality

13.4.3 Understand how social identities like class and race shape who attends college as well as what students' experiences will be like once admitted.

High school graduation is only the rim of the funnel of educational privilege. Of those minorities and lower- and working-class persons who graduate from high school, few go on to college. Of those who do attend college, few graduate from college. And so on. By the time they turn 24, 77 percent of people from wealthy families but just 9 percent of people from low-income households have a bachelor's degree (Pell Institute 2015).

Although colleges and universities have become much more diverse than they used to be in terms of race and ethnicity, they have simultaneously become less diverse when it comes to social class. The class barrier to higher education is actually increasing. The proportion of students from upper-income families attending the most elite colleges declined dramatically after World War II, but it is growing again. For instance, in 2014, social class dramatically influenced the likelihood that students would enter college immediately following high school. Eighty-one percent of students from high-income families enrolled in college directly following high school—a rate 17 percentage points higher than students from middle-income families (64 percent), and 29 percentage points higher than students from low-income families (52 percent) (National Center for Education Statistics 2017).

And it is not just elite colleges. Across the spectrum, colleges are drawing more members from upper-income households and fewer from average or below-average income households. Because the income gap between the college educated and the noncollege educated was 66 percent in 1997 (up from 31 percent in 1979) (The Economist 2005e), it seems that the universities are reproducing social advantage instead of serving as an engine of mobility.

The poorer students are priced out of the market for higher education by soaring tuition increases (which means that financial aid is extending farther up the income ladder than it used to). We might think, "Oh, there are always scholarships for the smart ones," but being smart is not a replacement for having money. Seventy-eight percent of the top achievers from low-income families go to college. But 77 percent of the *bottom* achievers from high-income families also manage to get in ("Dreams Only Money Can Buy," 2003). The cost of higher education has increased more than 13-fold since 1978. Part of this is the result of inflation; but, when compared with the consumer price index (a statistical estimate of inflation that relies on changes in the prices of a sample of representative items purchased by most U.S. households), it becomes clear that the price of college has increased a great deal more than the price of almost anything else. Consider FIGURE 13.9.

Although higher education is supposed to be "the great equalizer," rising costs and fees associated with attending college have recreated new forms of class segregation even as colleges and universities celebrate their efforts to "open their doors" with pictures of diverse groups of students on college and university website homepages. Students from class disadvantaged backgrounds are simply much less likely to be able to attend. And research has also shown that college does not always produce the same rewards for students from lower-class backgrounds.

GENDER SEGREGATION IN HIGHER EDUCATION Do you already know your college major? If you're a new college student, you might still be undecided. But most students have an idea of the type of major they're considering (e.g., "something in the humanities," "a language," "economics or business," "pre-med," "a social science"). Do you think your choice of major is affected by whether you are a man or woman? Sociologist Shelley Correll (Correll 2001) wanted to figure this out. We know that there is a great deal of gender segregation by major. Men congregate in majors like computer science, the physical sciences, business, and engineering. And women tend to congregate in education, foreign languages, and English. And, perhaps unsurprisingly, this

FIGURE 13.9 Growth in the Cost of Higher Education, 1976–2017

The costs of everything associated with going to college have grown over the past four decades. But the price of college tuition has grown at a much higher rate than other costs. This means that young people are encountering an economy today that increasingly demands higher levels of educational credentials, but also charges students more to receive those credentials than ever before.

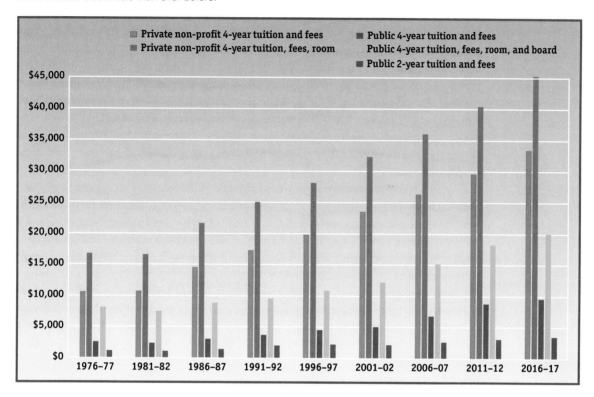

SOURCE: Data from The College Board, Annual Survey of Colleges; NCES, IPEDS data. Available at: https://trends.collegeboard.org/college-pricing/figures-tables/tuition-and-fees-and-room-and-board-over-time-1976-77_2016-17-selected-years.

SOCIOLOGY AND OUR WORLD

THE CHOSEN

College admissions committees use students' "character" to decide who is admitted—and this often allows them to admit more white middle- and upper-class applicants than they otherwise would.

Sociologist Jerome Karabel graduated from Harvard University and now teaches at the University of California at Berkeley (and served on the admissions committee), so he may be the ideal person to write *The Chosen: The Hidden History of Admission and Exclusion at Harvard, Yale, and Princeton* (2005). He examined a century of admissions decisions at these three Ivy League schools to determine who gets in—and how.

Prior to the 1920s, all applicants who met high academic standards were accepted. The administration of these schools became concerned about the increasing numbers of well-qualified Jewish applicants (20 percent of the Harvard freshman class of 1918): How could they maintain a Protestant majority if they admitted everyone with a rash of As? Instead, they established admissions committees and limited the "super bright" to about 10 percent of available spots. For the rest, grades were

less important than "character": manliness, congeniality, leadership potential, and other qualities they believed were lacking among Jewish men.

Other universities followed the example of the Big Three; and, for the rest of the century, admissions committees from the top to the bottom tier of universities regularly rejected applicants whom they believed belonged to an "undesirable" race, ethnic background, religion, or socioeconomic status. "Character" was further delineated by looking at applicants' extracurricular activities and soliciting letters of recommendation. That system is still in place today. Though no admissions committee would dare ask about an applicant's race or religion today, they still weed out applicants with the wrong "character," and that rarely means the children of wealthy alumni.

shapes subsequent occupational segregation as women and men are, on average, pursuing different types of study while in college.

Correll wanted to know whether and how gender might play a role in shaping early career-relevant decisions among college students selecting majors. To test this, she was interested in measuring student competence in mathematics, that might lead to careers in engineering, math, and the physical sciences—fields shown to be particularly resistant to women's entrance. But Correll was not only interested in students' actual mathematical competence; she also wanted to know how competent they felt they were. As we discussed in Chapter 9, cross-national studies of gender differences in mathematical aptitude have shown biological explanations incorrect (boys don't have a biological advantage in math). Despite this, there is a widespread belief that boys are good at math and girls are not. And Correll wanted to know whether this widespread gender belief influenced the ways young women and men considered their own competence, or not.

What Correll discovered helps to explain some of the reasons that gender segregated fields of study remain gender segregated. Women and men are assessing themselves differently, in gender-biased ways. She discovered that when comparing men and women with the same test scores and grades in math classes (objective measures of mathematical ability), they do not perceive themselves as having the same ability. Men are systematically more likely to assess themselves as competent than are women. Grades did impact students' perceptions of their abilities; those with higher grades, in general, perceived themselves as more capable. But grades were a stronger predictor for women than for

HOW DO WE KNOW WHAT WE KNOW?

HOW UNIVERSITIES REPRODUCE CLASS INEQUALITY

Students develop a subculture that their professors (and their parents!) often find foreign and even a bit disconcerting. According to this stereotype, student life revolves around drinking, partying, playing video games and online poker, watching pornography on the Internet, sports, and sleeping. At many colleges, it appears that academic life—studying, homework, reading in the library, doing research—is almost an incidental afterthought, the least important part of a student's day. Occasionally, a professor goes "underground" and lives in a dorm or fraternity or sorority house for a semester and writes an exposé of campus life, designed to shock adults into paying attention to student culture (see Moffatt 1989; Nathan 2005; Armstrong and Hamilton 2013).

Sociologists Elizabeth Armstrong and Laura Hamilton (2013) performed one such ethnography at a university they call "Midwestern University" (a pseudonym for the large research university where they conducted their research). Armstrong and Hamilton conducted an ethnographic research project in which they followed a group of students through their college careers and beyond—a study that involved moving into the dorms with them. And much of the difficulty students navigated in their study surrounded student's *social* lives at college just as much as their *academic* lives. In the late 1980s, anthropologist Michael Moffatt similarly moved into the dorms at Rutgers and wrote a scathing exposé of campus life (Moffatt 1989)—a world of indiscriminate drunken sex, copious drinking, no studying but lots of sleeping, and a lack of serious intellectual engagement. College, he wrote, is really about the pursuit of "fun."

But "fun" at college, just like the cost of admission, comes with an additional price tag—and not one that all students are equally able to afford. Armstrong and Hamilton (2013) discovered that there were basically two pathways offered through college—the *party pathway* and the *mobility pathway*. Students from middle- and upper-class families may not actually need to be as academically motivated in college to succeed afterward. Indeed, the social networks they produce in the party scene may be integral to succeeding after college as well. For the least-prepared and least-advantaged students, however, Armstrong and Hamilton found that the party scene can be truly devastating. Some end up socially isolated while pursuing their studies. Others are pulled in to the social scene but struggle to keep up financially and sometimes opt into easier majors that require less work. Unfortunately, after college, middle- and upper-class students were able to tap into existing family networks to help set them on a career path, while lower-class students faced lower rates of graduation and higher rates of transferring to community colleges.

Lower-class students in Armstrong and Hamilton's study were left with difficult options—participating in the party scene even though it came at a much higher cost for them than their class-privileged peers or foregoing the party scene and facing social isolation, unlikely to yield the social networks they might have expected to be a part of the college experience.

men. In other words, women with lower than average grades in math classes were likely to assess themselves as lacking what it takes to proceed with the major. Men with the same grades were much less likely to view their abilities in the same light.

This results in a curious scenario. There are few women who major in engineering and math, but they tend to be among the top of their class. It's not because women don't need help and resources. Rather, it is the result of women with average scores and grades leaving to pursue a major in which they might be more likely to perceive themselves as competent.

The Transformation of Higher Education

13.4.4 Review some of the ways that different types of higher educational institutions aimed at making higher education more accessible may exacerbate the very problems they were designed to redress.

The "traditional" college experience celebrated in the Hollywood film—a leafy residential campus, ivy climbing on grand nineteenth-century buildings at a private 4-year liberal arts college—has never captured the majority of students' experience in higher education. Those small, private, liberal arts colleges account for only about 16 percent of all higher-education students. "State" and "Tech" are far more common than Yale and Harvard. About half of all students attend colleges that charge less than $9,500 a year in tuition—that is, those that are publicly funded (College Board 2016).

More than 40 percent of all students attend 2-year or community colleges (College Board 2016). Unlike the traditional 4-year liberal arts curriculum, the community college attracts a far more diverse student body, especially in terms of class and age. The overwhelming majority of community college students are **first-generation students** (meaning that their parents did not go to college), making them truly an expression of the American belief that everyone deserves a chance. On the other hand, community colleges also reproduce the very inequalities they attempt to address. They have no endowments and minuscule resources, pay their faculty far less than 4-year schools and work them harder, and have far more part-time faculty who receive no benefits. Although 46 percent of U.S. undergraduates go to community colleges, 2-year schools receive less than one-tenth of the money that 4-year schools get from the federal government (Fitzpatrick/Austin 2009). In that sense, too, they are a case study in the sociology of education: both challenging and reproducing inequalities at the very same time (see also Goldrick-Rab 2016).

One of the dominant recent educational trends, in primary and secondary education as well as in higher education, has been the spread of the marketplace. For centuries, colleges and universities were a sort of refuge from the market, a place where the pursuit of dollars didn't interfere with the pursuit of knowledge. Not anymore. Traditional universities are not-for-profit organizations. However, an increasing number of proprietary or **for-profit universities** have arisen in recent years (McMillan Cottom 2017). They have some advantages over traditional universities: The cost is comparatively low, the university rather than the professors owns the curriculum, and students can graduate relatively quickly. They omit or severely curtail the traditional social activities of a college; their facilities are usually very limited; and their degrees lack the prestige of a degree from a traditional university. However, many students today are far more interested in developing practical, job-related skills than a "total college experience," and they have found proprietary schools a viable alternative.

The University of Phoenix, the largest for-profit university in the United States, is also the largest university in the United States, period. It has 345,300 students on 239 campuses and various satellite campuses around the world, including some in China and India, and enrollment is growing at 25 percent per year. Phoenix is the brainchild

first-generation students
Students whose parents did not go to college.

for-profit universities
Business ventures offering higher education courses attuned to adult learners seeking practical, job-related skills.

WHAT DO YOU THINK? WHAT DOES AMERICA THINK?

Confidence in Education

Not everyone experiences the educational system in the same way.

What do you think?

As far as the people running the education system are concerned, would you say you have a great deal of confidence, only some confidence, or hardly any confidence at all in them?

- ○ A great deal
- ○ Only some
- ○ Hardly any

What does America think?

Data from 2016 show that 57 percent of all respondents have "only some" confidence in the educational system. Slightly more than 25 percent have "a great deal" of confidence, and 17 percent have "hardly any." Differences by race were significant and interesting. Black respondents were far more likely than white respondents to have confidence in the education system. And this is partially explained by education as well as we have learned that different racial groups have different average levels of education. On the whole, those with more education are much less likely to say they have a "great deal" of confidence in the people running the education system in the United States. It is those with the least amount of education who express the most faith in the people running education in the United States.

SOURCE: Data from General Social Survey, 2016.

THINKING CRITICALLY ABOUT SURVEY DATA

The differences in the survey response by race were striking. Explain why you believe blacks—who are underserved by the educational system—have more confidence in the system than whites.

of John Sperling, a Cambridge University–educated economist turned entrepreneur. While teaching at a state university, he noticed that the curriculum was designed for "traditional" 18- to 22-year-old students and ignored adult learners. But, in the new economy, people 10 or 20 years past high school often decide that they need college, and those with degrees often return to update their skills or retool their résumés. Sperling decided to found a new university catering to working adults, with convenient class schedules, many centers in conveniently located areas instead of one giant central campus (beginning in the 1990s, entire degrees could be taken online), and an emphasis on practical subjects that will help them build careers.

Nontraditional students now account for 95 percent of the Phoenix student body. The average student age is 34 years old, hoping to enhance their job possibilities rather than broaden their intellectual interests, and not particularly interested in immersing themselves in the traditional college environment. In some ways, the University of Phoenix has proved more successful than traditional colleges in meeting the needs of nontraditional students.

However, as institutions for higher learning, for-profits strip the university of its other functions. There are no science labs, and no faculty members that do research; nor are professors protected by tenure or any forms of academic freedom. Faculty members are paid only to teach, and they are paid hourly wages that don't approach the salaries of professors at most colleges and universities. In a sense, these private universities separate the different dimensions of higher education and concentrate on some while ignoring others. At present, for-profit colleges only graduate 28 percent of their students within 6 six years, compared with 56 percent at public not-for-profit institutions. And, after they complete their education, students graduating from for-profit institutions are

College is no longer the sole domain of traditional-age students. Adult learners older than 23 years old now make up about 10 percent of all college students—and more than 90 percent at some for-profit schools.

not only more likely to be unemployed, but their unemployment lasts longer than students graduating from public institutions. Surveys also show that for-profit students are less happy with their education than are students at public universities (McMillan Cottom and Goldrick-Rab 2012). Indeed, University of Phoenix is presently part of a class-action law suit by students and has been investigated by the Federal Trade Commission for deceptive marketing practices that attempt to lure students with false promises for their futures.

---

iSOC AND YOU Higher Education

Higher education provides a great institutional case study of how education is both a route to mobility and a mechanism to freeze you in place. Higher education is a social *institution* that provides participants with a social *identity*, but simultaneously plays a key role in reproducing social *inequality*. Your *interactions* with others, from informal friends to serious formal networking, will structure the possibilities for your future, both formally and informally. Education can facilitate the collision of *intersecting* inequalities or bring them into an overwhelming harmony.

Conclusion
Education NOW

Americans have always had the optimistic faith that education leads to a secure future, to happiness, to success. Chances are that you have this faith. That's why you are here, enrolled in a college class, reading this book. But the first country in the world to institute mass education for all of its citizens may be the first to sell it out. Literally, to corporate interests, but also to those millions who were denied education, or found that it did not lead to a secure future at all.

Like every social institution, education is always going to be both an arena for the grounding of identity and a mechanism for the perpetuation of inequality. Some members of underprivileged groups will acquire the skills necessary to move up in the social hierarchy of our society. Most will not. Some members of majority groups will acquire the skills necessary to combat injustice. Most will not. Inequality will certainly be criticized, in uncounted thousands of lesson plans and essay-exam questions. But it will also be made to appear natural and inevitable.

CHAPTER REVIEW Education

13.1 Education and Society

We typically spend more than a quarter of our lives getting an education. The educational system serves manifest and latent functions, providing content in subjects and a socializing environment advancing values, goals, and norms. This hidden curriculum includes obedience to authority, conformity, individualism, and competition. In a credential society, you need diplomas, degrees, and certificates to "qualify" for jobs, and these markers of educational attainment say "who you are" as much as family background, providing gatekeeping functions that restrict important and lucrative jobs to a small

segment of the population. For most of human history, there were no schools. Your parents taught necessary skills, or they hired you a tutor. Sometimes people with special skills opened academies, where you could pay tuition to study philosophy, music, or art. But there was no formal, structured system of education. In Europe, when the Protestant Reformation began to teach that all believers—not just priests—should be able to read and interpret the Bible, many churches began to offer children instruction in reading and writing. By the sixteenth century, formal schooling for children was available in many European countries, though only the wealthy had enough money and free time to participate. The United States was among the first countries in the world to set a goal of education for all of its citizens, under the theory that an educated citizenry was necessary for a democratic society to function. Yet the Founding Fathers disagreed about its purpose. Some believed that education would enable citizens to use reason to protect their freedom and to challenge government policies; others thought education should teach citizens to accept the social order. Today there remains considerable debate about the content and function of an education. Is there really a set of information that everyone should know? Or is it all a matter of personal preference? Who should decide which types of knowledge or which skills are important enough that everyone should be forced to learn? What constitutes a good education—understanding of high culture, insight into everyday processes, images and events, scientific literacy?

13.1 Key Terms

education A social institution through which society provides its members with important knowledge—basic facts, information, job skills, as well as cultural norms and values and lessons in socialization, cultural innovation, and social integration.

hidden curriculum A means of socialization through which education not only creates social inequalities but makes them seem natural, normal, and inevitable.

credential society A society based more on the credentialing aspects of education—diplomas, degrees, and certificates—than any substantive knowledge.

scientific literacy The capacity to understand scientific concepts and processes necessary for complete participation in economic, civic, and cultural life.

13.2 Education as a Mechanism of Social Inequality

Most of us believe that education is a ticket to social mobility. And it's partly true. Over the course of American history, different groups of immigrants have successfully used educational advancement as a vehicle for social mobility for the entire ethnic group. But education is also one of the primary vehicles of social reproduction, whereby society reinforces and passes on social inequalities based on race, ethnicity, class, and gender from one generation to the next. As long as we believe that education is a strict meritocracy—the best get ahead—we believe that different educational outcomes are based on characteristics of those individuals or those groups: They try harder and do more homework, or their culture rewards educational achievement more than other groups. However, the fact that some people use the educational system to rise in the hierarchy actually serves, at times, to legitimate the inequalities that the educational system as a whole reinforces. Some suggest that if you don't make it it's not because of your membership in one of the groups that are discriminated against, but because you, individually, didn't try hard enough. Paradoxically, just as challenges to inequality have opened education up to groups historically denied entrance, their very entrance sometimes provide a new justification to close those doors to others. Research confirms a funneling effect of the educational system, and these dynamics are true globally as well. A number of developing nations have begun intensive efforts to improve education, from grade school through university and professional schools.

Education is a global issue and is improving on an international scale. But, it is also true that a great deal of education inequality remains. Not all nations are improving, nor are all of those improving at the same rate. And beyond this, these rates are still reported as averages and tell us little about education inequality *within* nations around the world.

13.2 Key Terms

meritocracy Social system in which the greater the functional importance of the job, the more rewards it brings in salary, perks, power, and prestige.

educational inequality The extent to which different groups lack access to the educational opportunities and experiences systematically made more available to other groups.

social reproduction The structures and activities that transmit social inequality from one generation to the next.

educational homogamy Marriage between people who are similar to one another in educational attainment.

13.3 Institutional Differences, Interactions, and Inequality

Many institutional ingredients are crucial to student success in school. More than 50 years after the Supreme Court case *Brown v. Board of Education* articulated how and why the idea of "separate but equal" was an enactment of racial inequality, U.S. schools remain highly segregated. Achievement gaps between the achievements of white and black students persist today as well. School effects are significant: The types of schools and the uneven distribution of resources for schools result in often dramatic differences in student achievement. Still, studies find rather modest differences in achievement between students in public and private schools, and those differences are actually explained by demographic variables, such as parents' education, income, and other factors. When researchers control for these factors, no appreciable differences were found. Indeed, data show that in the United States, there is a strong correlation between social class and academic achievement; public schools in wealthy neighborhoods that can afford state-of-the-art labs and libraries, small classes, and highly paid teachers offer students significant educational opportunities that those in poor neighborhoods with crumbling buildings, overcrowded classrooms, and overworked, underpaid teachers lack. In virtually every city and every state, students in school districts where parents are wealthier are, on average, performing better than their peers in poorer districts. Within well-resourced schools of any kind, not all students end up in the same types of classrooms. Tracking is common in American schools and promotes labelling. Individuals in the low-achievement, noncollege preparatory, or manual track often come to be labeled "Dummies" or "Greasers" by both teachers and other students, and even among themselves. They are not only labeled but are also treated as if they are stupid or incompetent, thus affecting their self-image and ultimately affecting their achievement in a self-fulfilling prophecy. In addition, because the funds go mostly toward the educational needs of the high-track students, the low-track students receive poorer classes, textbooks, supplies, and teachers.

13.3 Key Terms

segregation The practice of physically separating whites from other races by law and custom in institutions and communities.

integration The physical intermingling of the races organized as a concerted legal and social effort to bring equal access and racial equality through racial mixing in institutions and communities.

"school effects" The term for research demonstrating the ways student outcomes are meaningfully shaped by school characteristics.

longitudinal study An observational research method in which data is gathered for the same subjects repeatedly over a period of time that can extend over years or even decades.

tracking Common in American schools, it is the term for grouping students according to their academic abilities.

labeling Often associated with self-fulfilling prophecy and stereotyping, labeling theory describes how self-identity and behavior of individuals may be determined or influenced by the terms used to describe or classify them.

self-fulfilling prophecy The social phenomenon that when we expect something to happen, it often does.

concentrated poverty The extreme density of socio-economic deprivation in a particular area.

chilly classroom climate The subtle ways teachers reinforce both gender difference and gender inequality through class materials and interaction dynamics that often reflect stereotyped differences between women and men, boys and girls.

"gender police" Student peers who act to enforce gender rules against transgressions large and small.

gay-baiting Calling people or something they do "gay" as a way of ridiculing them or putting them down. Usually applied to men, it has little to do with sexual orientation, but instead accuses them of acting or appearing insufficiently masculine.

13.4 Higher Education

Although colleges and universities have become much more diverse than they used to be in terms of race and ethnicity, they have simultaneously become less diverse when it comes to social class. The proportion of students from upper-income families attending the most elite colleges declined dramatically after World War II, but it is growing again. Because in the 1920s, all applicants who met high academic standards were accepted. But when increasing numbers of highly-qualified Jewish applicants began gaining admission, elite colleges limited the "super bright" to about 10 percent of available spots. For the rest, grades were less important than "character": manliness, congeniality, leadership potential, and other qualities they believed were lacking among Jewish men. Other universities followed the example of the Big Three, and, for the rest of the century, admissions committees from the top to the bottom tier of universities regularly rejected applicants whom they believed belonged to an "undesirable" race, ethnic background, religion, or socioeconomic status. Today, across the spectrum, colleges are drawing more members from upper-income households and fewer from average or below-average income households, effectively reproducing social advantage instead of serving as an engine of mobility. At many of these 4-year colleges, academic life—studying, homework, reading in the library, doing research—has become almost an incidental afterthought, the least important part of a student's day. But "fun" at college comes with an additional price tag—and not one that all students are equally able to afford. The party scene leaves lower-class students with difficult options—participating in the party scene even though it comes at a much higher cost for them than their class-privileged peers or foregoing the party scene and facing social isolation, unlikely to yield the social networks they might have expected to be a part of the college experience. This "traditional" college has never captured the majority of American students' experience in higher education anyway. Community colleges attract a far more diverse student body than the four-year liberal arts institutions, especially in terms of class, age, and first-time college attendance. On the other hand, community colleges also reproduce the inequalities they attempt to address. They have no endowments and minuscule resources, pay their faculty far less than 4-year schools and work them harder, and have far more part-time faculty who receive no benefits.

13.4 Key Terms

first-generation students Students whose parents did not go to college.

for-profit universities Business ventures offering higher education courses attuned to adult learners seeking practical, job-related skills.

SELF-TEST

〉CHECK YOUR UNDERSTANDING

1. All of the following are part of the "hidden curriculum" *except*

  a. passive consumption of ideas.

  b. acceptance of social inequality.

  c. competition.

  d. acumen.

2. When it comes to scientific literacy, which of the following facts do the largest proportion of Americans know?

  a. the earth's core is its hottest layer.

  b. that radio waves are used to make cell phone calls.

  c. how light passes through a magnifying glass.

  d. the difference between astrology and astronomy.

3. Sociologists understand that education

  a. is never a good predictor of economic growth.

  b. can promote self-fulfilling prophecies that affect student achievement.

  c. reverses the funneling effect through which social inequalities are reproduced.

  d. All of the answers are correct.

4. School bullying

  a. is pervasive.

  b. has gone virtual, often involving social media.

  c. is defined along a continuum stretching from hurtful language through shoving and hitting to criminal assault and school shootings.

  d. All of the answers are correct.

5. College education today

  a. gives access to generalized information found only in certain books.

  b. has become somewhat more diverse racially and ethnically, but less so in terms of social class.

  c. almost always prioritizes studying, homework, reading in the library, doing research, making social life and the party scene almost an incidental afterthought.

  d. All of the answers are correct.

6. Normative gender expectations about masculinity and femininity

  a. are absent from education as a result of Title IX legislation.

  b. are rarely present anymore in the texts assigned to read in school.

  c. are not usually modeled by teachers or administrators.

  d. are often taught and policed by peers, both in groups and through digital and social media channels.

7. From a sociological perspective, random school shootings

  a. are not as random as they might seem.

  b. are largely perpetrated by boys as compared to girls.

  c. are often motivated by a desire to get back at those the shooters feel have hurt, mistreated, or picked on them.

  d. All of the answers are correct.

8. Research on college preparation finds that

  a. American high school students' readiness for college and achievement in college are both low.

  b. the vast majority of college students are able to graduate in four years.

  c. a college education today is effectively combating social disadvantage and serving as an engine of social mobility.

  d. All of the answers are correct.

Self-Test Answers: 1. d, 2. a, 3. b, 4. d, 5. b, 6. d, 7. d, 8. a

14

ECONOMY AND WORK

What you do for work can be many things. In a very meaningful way, work is a means to an end for everyone. Work is labor, and lots of kinds of work feels laborious during the actual "working." But, work can be a meaningful form of identity as well; it's a symbol you rely on to project an image of yourself out into the world. This is why we so often meet new people (especially as adults) and start by asking, "And what do you *do*?"

LEARNING OBJECTIVES

In this chapter, using the iSoc framework, you should be able to:

14.1.1 Understand what it means to think of the economy as a social institution.

14.1.2 Recognize how each of the five elements of the iSoc model can be used to examine work and the economy sociologically.

14.1.3 Distinguish among agricultural, industrial, consumer, and postindustrial economies.

14.1.4 Summarize the different forms of work that organize postindustrial economies in contrast to industrial economies.

14.1.5 Explain what sociologists mean when they suggest that globalization is responsible for connecting societies around the world more than ever, while also making us feel less connected than ever before.

14.1.6 Summarize the defining qualities of a capitalist economic system.

14.1.7 Distinguish between socialist and communist economic systems, and explain how both differ from capitalism.

14.1.8 Explain why economic protest throughout history has primarily been related to the extent to which governments intervene in the economy.

14.2.1 Explain the difference between "Theory X" and "Theory Y" for understanding people's relationship to work.

14.2.2 Distinguish between the different types of jobs today, and consider the ways that different groups tend to dominate in different types of work.

14.2.3 Understand the difference between minimum and "living" wages as well as some of the challenges associated with each.

14.2.4 Distinguish between part-time and contingent work.

14.2.5   Explain why unpaid work has been present throughout history and how it is inequitably distributed in the United States.

14.2.6   Understand what it means to suggest that the informal economy is "organized" and that it represents a significant portion of economic activity in every society.

14.2.7   Distinguish among the three types of unemployment, and understand how each type puts different groups at risk.

14.3.1   Explain why increased workplace diversity has not necessarily led to workplace equality.

14.3.2   Understand the meaning of tokenism and how it operates in workplaces.

14.3.3   Summarize what the gender pay gap is and how it has changed over time.

14.3.4   Understand how occupational segregation contributes to the unequal distribution of status and economic rewards associated with different kinds of work.

14.3.5   Understand how work–family balance dilemmas are experienced in gender-specific ways that work to women's collective disadvantage in the workplace.

14.3.6   Distinguish between emotional and aesthetic labor, and understand how this work disproportionately impacts the work lives of women and people of color.

14.3.7   Explain some of the ways lesbian and gay employees are disadvantaged in the workplace as a result of their sexuality.

Introduction

Americans spend an average of 34.4 hours per week working. That's 18 percent more time at work than in France, 20 percent more than in the Netherlands, Norway, or Denmark, and 23 percent more than in Germany, but about 15–20 percent less than in Mexico, Korea, Costa Rica, Greece, or Chile (OECD 2016). The differences come to hundreds of hours per year. An American who works full-time from age 18 to age 65, with 3 weeks off for vacations and holidays each year, will spend about 92,000 hours (52 weeks in a year means 49 full-time work weeks with 3 weeks of vacation; 47 years working full-time between 18 and 65 years of age; and 40-hour minimum full-time work week: 92,120 hours of work) doing things that are more likely to be boring, degrading, and physically exhausting than they are fun, interesting, and exciting. Why do we do it? The answer to that question, of course, depends on who you happen to be asking.

Ask a janitor or a sales clerk, and you are likely to hear: *for the money*. No one gets a free ride: Food, clothing, and shelter all come with price tags. You have to support yourself, your family. Work is, well, *work*, not play. Unless you win the lottery, you just have to find some way to get through each day. Maybe you can think about your real life after hours, with family, friends, and leisure.

Ask a photojournalist or a trial lawyer, and you are likely to hear: *for the satisfaction*. A job is a "calling," the fulfillment of talent, skill, training, and ambition, not something you *do* but something you *are*. Even when the work day is supposedly over, you are constantly getting new ideas or thinking about problems. There is no "after hours." This *is* your life.

Clearly, our motivations for working are a bit of both of these sentiments. For most of us, it's a combination of the two. The janitor and the sales clerk probably find some degree of worth, meaning, and satisfaction in their jobs in addition to paychecks, and the photojournalist and the trial lawyer would be far less likely to consider their jobs a "calling" if they weren't paid. Whether we feel we must "work to live" or find so much meaning in our jobs that we "live to work," everyone performs some kind of work. And our relationship with that work is structured by who we are and what we have done over the course of our lives.

A job provides both identity and financial support. Both sales clerks and lawyers are engaged in various markets, where people buy, sell, and trade what they have—resources, things, their abilities to work, and their skills—to others. The economy is the social arena in which they do that. Given that we spend so much of our lives in that arena, sociologists understand the economy as one of the primary social institutions of social life. And, just like the family and education, you'd think that such important institutions would be stable, secure, and relatively equal. Yet as just about everyone in the world could tell you, the economy is unstable, insecure, and responsible for inequality on a massive scale. Our jobs often feel insecure, our prosperity is precarious, and our sense of continuity between generations as tenuous as ever in history. And it's all connected: When we hear that the stock market in Asia goes down a few points, everyone on Wall Street braces for a bad day. Little ripples in Singapore or Spain send shock waves back to San Francisco and New York. And vice versa. The global economy has never been more connected—but neither has our place in it ever felt more local and fragmented.

14.1 Economy and Society

We all need material resources to survive, like food, clothing, and shelter. But an adequate quality of life requires more, like transportation, communication, education, medical care, and entertainment. A vast array of goods and services is available to meet these needs: cars, cell phones, college classes, daycare, diapers, magazine subscriptions, microwave ovens, postage stamps, and psychiatric appointments. One person or household could never produce everything, so we must organize collectively to produce and distribute resources. The result is an economy.

The economy of the society in which you happen to live shapes more of your life than you may realize. As a social institution, it is among the most all-encompassing in society. When economies shift and transform, so too do societies and the lives of everyone living in them. Whether you realize it or not, your identity is meaningfully related to the economy. The jobs you've had (and the occupations you soon will) become core elements of your identity. And these identities shape our interactions. Jobs shape who we interact with as well as how.

But economies shape much more of our lives than simply who we understand ourselves to be. They also provide a structure within which social inequality affects different groups in different ways. For this reason, economies are also fraught and subject to protest and change. In this section, we explain what precisely an economy is and then address economic transformations and how those transformations produce dramatically different societies in their wake.

economy

A set of institutions and relationships that manage capital.

capital

Natural resources, manufactured goods, and professional services.

Children learn from a young age to imagine themselves doing different types of work, and in so doing, they form early career aspirations. Typically, this begins as play. But this kind of "play" also establishes early relationships with jobs, careers, and occupational sectors that help to shape the kinds of work children perform when they grow up.

What Is an Economy?

14.1.1 Understand what it means to think of the economy as a social institution.

An **economy** is a set of institutions and relationships that manages natural resources, manufactured goods, and professional services. These resources, goods, and services are called **capital**. The major economic theories of the world diverge around a central question—whether the people serve the economy or the economy serves the people. British empiricists like John Locke (1689/1988) and Thomas Hobbes (1658/1966) believed that no economy could ensure that everyone has adequate resources. Therefore, people must compete with

each other. We are motivated by rational self-interest, a desire to meet our own material needs even though we see others going without. Economies form when individuals band together to protect their common resources or to make their competition more congenial and predictable. If asked why they work, they will answer, like the janitor and sales clerk: *for the money.*

Adam Smith (1776/2000), the greatest theorist of capitalism, argued that social life involves much more than individuals striving for social gain: People cooperate as often as they compete. There are many good samaritans, many altruistic acts, and many collective struggles over fairness and justice. If you ask them why they work, they will answer, like the photojournalist and the trial lawyer: *for the satisfaction.*

Karl Marx (Marx and Engels 1848/1998) believed that both answers were true—and therein lay the problem. Marx believed that an economic system based on private property divided people into two unequal and competing classes: The upper class worked because they achieved satisfaction by owning all the goods and services and controlling politics and social life. The working class worked because they had to—because they were, in effect, slaves to the upper classes. Eventually, he believed, if the workers controlled and owned everything, everyone would work for the pleasure of it.

By contrast, Émile Durkheim (1893/1997) argued that, in modern societies, we are all interdependent: Every person must depend on hundreds or thousands of others for goods and services. Thus, economies are not an isolating, divisive force at all, but a unifying force. They foster strong social ties and create social cohesion through networks of mutual interdependence—what Durkheim referred to as **organic solidarity**.

There is some truth to all these theories. Every economic system requires some degree of competition and some degree of cooperation. An economy is essential to the common good, but it can also serve to emphasize or exacerbate the gap between rich and poor—it provides the structure of **social stratification**. This means that economies work in ways that help draw boundaries between, for instance, middle-class and working-class people, those who own a home versus those who rent an apartment, those who drive a car versus those who take the bus. The economy shapes the lives of everyone. And as such, it is a powerful source of identity; but it is also one of the key social institutions responsible for social inequality.

organic solidarity

Émile Durkheim's argument that, in modern societies, we are all interdependent; thus, economies are not an isolating, divisive force, but a unifying force that foster strong social ties and create social cohesion through networks of mutual interdependence.

social stratification

Taken from the geological term for layers of rock, or "strata," the ranking of people into defined layers. Social stratification exists in all societies and is based on things like wealth, race, and gender.

iSoc: The Sociology of Work

14.1.2 Recognize how each of the five elements of the iSoc model can be used to examine work and the economy sociologically.

Whether you live to work or you work to live, few people could deny that our economic experiences are among the most crucial social experiences we have. Indeed, the economy is a social institution that shapes virtually every aspect of your life. As a field, sociology was founded during a moment of economic transformation. Scholars struggling to make sense of these changes understood that the shift to an industrial economy (about which you'll learn shortly) didn't simply change what people did for "work." It changed just about everything you can imagine.

IDENTITY—If you ask an adult to tell you about themselves, they're very likely to start by telling you what they do for a living. Indeed, this is so much the case, that all we have to ask to learn about someone's occupation is, "What do you *do*?" Of course, we all "do" many things; but the assumption here is about the work we do. Our jobs are a crucial part of our *identities*, whether we are auto mechanics, baristas at coffee shops, yoga instructors, or chief executive officers. From the time you are a child, you're taught to prepare for a job. And throughout your life, your job will provide an important sense of your identity. (That's why unemployment is often as much a psychological issue as it is a financial one.) More than that, though, our participation in the economy constructs and expresses our identity in other ways besides our occupations. For example, we express ourselves often through our patterns of consumption: What kind of car you drive, the team logo on your baseball hat, the brand of t-shirt you are wearing, the perfume or cologne you prefer, the beer you drink—all these, you probably believe, say something about who you are as a person. It is through your experience with both production and consumption that you create an economic identity.

INEQUALITY—The economy is a major mechanism for social *inequality*. This inequality may have nothing to do with you: It is still the case that the best predictor of your eventual class position is your father's occupation (for children in heterosexual parent families). The economy, in fact, is probably the biggest engine of social inequality: How much money you make in your job determines what sorts of things you can buy, how you live, how healthy you are, and even how old you're likely to be when you die. Every society is comfortable with this fact; economic inequality is pretty much a cultural universal, and that is certainly the case in all industrial societies. How much inequality is tolerable or desirable, however, is the subject of heated political debate.

INTERACTIONS—Most economic models assume that people act rationally, in their own self-interest, in the marketplace. You work hard, play by the rules, hoping to make a good living and someday, even, get ahead. You shop carefully, for the best quality at the best price. Of course, sociologists know that people have all kinds of motivations that guide their experiences in the economic sphere. Although some people choose their careers, others fall into jobs because a friend works there, or because you think it might be interesting or well paid. And while some of you shop for bargains, some of you also will pass up a cheaper pair of jeans of equal quality, if you can afford the higher priced one with the right label on it—even if it costs more. It's not "rational" (in the economic sense), but it sure makes sense to you. What's more, our *interactions* with others in the economic arena—from fellow workers to supervisors or bosses, to clients and customers, to other consumers—are the interactions that define and construct our social lives. These other people are among the most important people besides your family members and close friends with whom you will interact.

INSTITUTIONS—We interact in economic *institutions* every single day, whether we are working in a corporation, shopping, traveling, or just sitting around watching television. Sometimes, it might even feel like economic systems completely dominate your life. You may interact more with corporations than you do with other people—especially if your interactions with other people are on computers or smartphones. Economic institutions are the places you go to answer just about every single need or desire you have. Sometimes they can be as local and personal as a small Ma and Pa grocer on the corner; other times they can be massive multinational corporations, with branches all over the world, employing millions of people worldwide.

INTERSECTIONS—How we interact with the economy is also powerfully shaped by the various intersecting identities we occupy. So, your race, gender, sexuality, age, social class, family background, education, and more all shape your relationship with the economy. Another way of thinking about this is to say that economic inequality is inequitably distributed throughout the population. So, whether you are black or white shapes the likelihood that you will endure poverty as does whether you are a man or woman. Whether you happen to be a citizen of the United States or Sierra Leon shapes your relationship with the economy. A focus on *intersections* examines the ways that the economy intersects with our multiple identities in ways that powerfully shape our economic experiences and opportunities.

As with previous chapters, considering the economy and work from an iSoc perspective means understanding how, when, and why sociologists stress different lenses in this framework. Most good sociology combines different lenses within the iSoc model when studying economic realities.

The Changing Economy

14.1.3 Distinguish among agricultural, industrial, consumer, and postindustrial economies.

The first human societies, tens of thousands of years ago, were nomadic hunter–gatherer groups of roughly 20 to 40 people. They had few rules about the production and distribution of capital. Sometimes a particularly talented or interested person might specialize in a task, like making pottery or spears, but otherwise everyone worked together to provide food, shelter, and clothing, and there were few other material resources available (nomads can't own a lot) (Panter-Brick, Layton, and Rowley-Conwy 2001). Then came the **Agricultural Revolution**.

THE AGRICULTURAL ECONOMY.   Around 10,000 years ago, people living along the great rivers in Mesopotamia, Egypt, and China learned how to plow the land and grow regular, predictable crops of rice, wheat, or corn. No longer nomadic, they could acquire more goods. And because agriculture is far more productive (more food produced per hour of work) than hunting and gathering, not everyone had to be involved in providing food, shelter, and clothing for the group. Farmers could use their surplus crops to pay professional potters, builders, or priests. As a result, a **division of labor** emerged. Sometimes a village might have a surplus of pottery makers and start exchanging its pottery with a village downstream, which had a surplus of spear makers. **Markets**, regular exchanges of goods and services, began, and with them the economy became a social institution. The agricultural economy, with its characteristics of permanent settlements, job specialization, and intergroup trade, lasted for thousands of years, through the great empires of Greece, Rome, China, and Mesoamerica (Cameron and Neal 2002; Cipolla 1994; North and Thomas 1976).

THE INDUSTRIAL ECONOMY.   Before 1765, all work was done by human or animal muscle, except for an occasional windmill or waterwheel. Then James Watt marketed the first reliable, high-functioning steam engine, and the era of the machine began. Within a century, hundreds of new machines powered by steam or electricity appeared, including lithographs, telegraphs, steam locomotives, sewing machines, slot machines, lawn mowers, and refrigerators. By 1900, there were typewriters, phonographs, electric stoves, and automobiles. The **Industrial Revolution** ushered in a new economy, based on factory production: the **industrial economy**. This economy differed from agricultural economies in five ways (Hobsbawm 2000; Oshima 1986; Stearns 2001):

1. *Power.*   Machines were powerful: They could do 100 times the work of human or animal muscles.
2. *Centralization.*   Manufacturing required bulky, expensive machines unfeasible for home use, so most jobs moved away from family farms to centralized offices and factories. For the first time, people had to leave home in the morning and *go to work*, juggling two distinct worlds.
3. *Specialization.*   Instead of a toy maker hammering, sewing, and painting every toy from start to finish, perhaps taking 2 entire days to complete one doll, it

Agricultural Revolution
The transition from a society dependent on hunting and gathering for food to one that maintains a diet cultivated through farming.

division of labor
The assignment of different tasks to different people to improve efficiency in production.

markets
The regular exchange of goods and services within an economy.

Industrial Revolution
The rapid development of industry that occurred in numerous countries in the eighteenth and nineteenth centuries reorganized the production and distribution of goods from the quaint system of craft production, in which apprentices learned trades and entered craft guilds, to large-scale factory production in which only the very few owned the factories and many workers had only their ability to work to sell to the highest bidder.

industrial economy
Economy based on factory production and technologies.

would be more efficient for one person to do nothing but affix arms. Where 20 start-to-finish toy makers could produce 10 dolls in a day, 20 specialized toy makers could produce 600.

4. *Wage labor.* Instead of being paid for the end result of their labor, workers got a regular paycheck in exchange for performing a specific task. Usually they never saw the end result. They received the same pay, no matter how successful their product was, while the handful of people who owned the factories kept all the profits.

5. *Separation of work and home.* The family farm was both home and workplace. But the coming of the industrial factory meant that home and work became separate social spheres, with enormous consequences for both realms.

With industrialization came the decline of agriculture as a livelihood. In 1700, before the Industrial Revolution, 60 percent of all workers in the United States were involved in the three Fs (farming, fishing, and forestry). As late as 1900, it was 30 percent. Today, the three Fs occupy less than 1 percent of the American workforce. Of course, there is little need for more workers. In 1880, a typical farmer could grow enough food to sustain five people (about the size of the typical farm family). Today's high-tech agribusiness specialists can feed about 80 people apiece.

Industrialization ushered in large-scale factories, assembly-line production, and more routinized labor, and thus transformed the experience of work itself. Assembly line at a generator factory of the Ford Motor Company.

THE MODERN CONSUMER ECONOMY.   As more efficient machines and assembly lines streamlined manufacturing production, the emphasis of industrial economies shifted from **production** (how to get more goods produced) to **consumption** (how to make decisions about what goods to buy from the plethora made available). Advanced economies focus more on what we buy than on what we make. As a result, advertising became an essential part of business. Products received brand names, trademarks, slogans, and spokespeople. General stores were replaced by department stores like Harrod's in London and Wanamaker's in the United States. In 1904, Macy's, on Herald Square in New York City, was advertised as "the largest store on Earth," with nine stories, 33 elevators, four escalators, and a system of pneumatic tubes. "Window shopping," looking through shop windows for items that one would like to possess, became a pastime (Lancaster 1995).

In 1899, Thorstein Veblen coined the term **conspicuous consumption** to mark the shift to this **consumer economy** in which social status was based on accumulating possessions and showing them off. Veblen argued that the real symbols of wealth were those that made it look as though you didn't have to work. So, fashions like long fingernails, high heels, and tight skirts for women were a sign that they were pampered and didn't need to work; and wealthy men were shown sailing, skiing, and otherwise experiencing the leisure that only true wealth can bring.

THE POSTINDUSTRIAL ECONOMY.   Industrial economies have flourished for more than 200 years (Mathias and Pollard 1989). Industrialized—or "developed"—nations remain the world's economic leaders. Perhaps the simplest way to determine how rich or poor a country is would be to compare the percentage of its labor force involved in agriculture to the percentage in industry. In Switzerland, it's 3.4 percent agriculture, 23.4 percent industry. In Chad, it's 80 percent agriculture, 20 percent industry and services (CIA World Factbook 2014). Worldwide, jobs are shifting to the services sector, although unevenly, with developed economies seeing far greater increases in employment in services and declines in agriculture (see FIGURE 14.1).

The bulk of job growth around the world is happening in the service sector. Indeed, industrial employment has been slowing for a while and is predicted to stabilize at around 22 percent of the global workforce by 2019. And much of the

production
The creation of value or wealth by producing goods and services.

consumption
The purchase and use of goods and services.

conspicuous consumption
Thorstein Veblen's term to describe a new form of prestige based on accumulating and displaying possessions.

consumer economy
An economy driven by consumer spending.

FIGURE 14.1 Employment Growth by Sector, 2000–2014 (or latest year), OECD average

"Health and Social Work" is just one portion of the services sector. But, as you can see here, it is a sector associated with some of the most economic growth within the services sector.

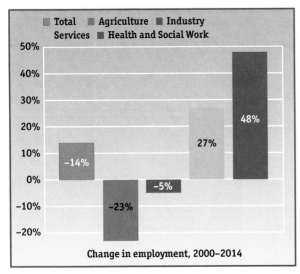

Change in employment, 2000–2014

NOTE: This visualizes average growth in 30 OECD countries for which data are available (excluding Chile, France, Japan, and the United States).

SOURCE: Data from James, Chris. 2016. "Health and Inclusive Growth: Changing the Dialogue." High-Level Commission on Health Employment and Economic Growth (the Commission). Available at: http://www.who.int/hrh/com-heeg/Health_inclusive_growth_online.pdf.

knowledge work

One defining element of the postindustrial economy; it is work that produces ideas and information as a new form of capital.

rootlessness

The experience of having few or no ties and no real place in society, often as the result of economic and/or social change.

knowledge economy

An economy oriented around knowledge, and the quantity, quality, and accessibility of information, rather than on the production of commodities.

remaining jobs here are in construction; manufacturing jobs continue to decline around the world. The world's most advanced economies still account for the majority of manufacturing jobs in the world. But current projections suggest that manufacturing jobs will comprise less than 12 percent of all jobs by 2019. Industrial employment is not predicted to grow any time soon (International Labour Organization (ILO) 2015). Three social changes characterize these emerging "postindustrial" economies: **knowledge work**, globalization, and **rootlessness** (Bell 1976; Kumar 1995; Vallas 1999). And it is to these intersecting issues that we now turn.

Knowledge Work

14.1.4 Summarize the different forms of work that organize postindustrial economies in contrast to industrial economies.

Postindustrial economies shift from production of goods to production of ideas. In 1940, during the peak of the industrial economy, roughly half of all U.S. workers were working in factories. By 1970, that figure was 31 percent. Today, with automation, outsourcing, and the decline of production, blue-collar jobs (production, natural resources, and maintenance of various types) now comprise 13.6 percent of total U.S. employment (Baker and Buffie 2017). At the same time, 40 percent are white-collar (management and the professions) and more than 40 percent are pink-collar (jobs composed predominantly of women) service and office/clerical jobs. Across all these categories, more than 40 percent of Americans are now employed as contingent workers, that is, temporary, contract-based, or on-call employees. They may not receive employer-provided health or retirement benefits or job protections such as the right to a leave under the federal Family Medical Leave Act without losing their job (Government Accountability Office 2015). These shifts have affected more than work; it has had an impact on attitudes, lifestyles, and worldviews.

Postindustrial economies are sometimes also called knowledge economies. A **knowledge economy** is less oriented around the actual production of a commodity and more concerned with the idea of the commodity, its marketing, its distribution, and its relationship to different groups of consumers. It is focused on the quantity, quality, and accessibility of information rather than on the production of goods. For example, a toy company may require very few people to attach doll arms on the assembly line, but it requires many people to conduct market research, direct TV commercials, design tie-in websites, negotiate with government and parental groups, and acquire global distribution rights. Postindustrial workers work not in factories, but in R&D (research and development), finance, investment, advertising, education, and training. They manipulate words and numbers rather than tools. In a knowledge economy, ideas, information, and knowledge have become the new forms of capital (Adler 2001; Powell and Snellman 2004).

Because knowledge-based workers now design, develop, market, sell, and service, they need classes in public speaking, technical writing, global business management, computer programming, and Web design. That is, they need to go to college—at least. The proportion of American workers doing jobs that call for complex skills has grown three times as fast as employment in general, and other economies are moving in the same direction, raising global demand for educated workers. International assessments by the U.S. Department of Education find that Americans are way behind other developed countries in the actual competencies our students achieve and suggest that in key areas from literacy, to math, to technological skills, U.S. high school graduates look something like the high-school dropouts in other developed countries (U.S. Department of Education 2016; Emanuel 2016).

In the **postindustrial economy**, some countries and some groups of people race down the "information superhighway" while others do not even have a paved road. What happens to people with limited education in a postindustrial economy? Fifty years ago, they would have become blue-collar workers. Assembly-line work did not require a lot of education, and it paid nearly as much as many white-collar jobs. But now, instead of finding assembly-line work, they are stuck in low-paying service jobs that offer less money and fewer benefits than jobs on the assembly line. They cannot afford houses in the same neighborhoods as the white-collar workers. Often, they cannot afford houses at all. The gap between "comfortable" and "barely getting by" shrank during the industrial economy, but today it is growing again (Krugman 2002).

postindustrial economy

An economy that shifts from the production of goods to the production of ideas.

Globalization and Rootlessness

14.1.5 Explain what sociologists mean when they suggest that globalization is responsible for connecting societies around the world more than ever, while also making us feel less connected than ever before.

In addition to knowledge economies, postindustrial economies are often called *global economies* (Hirst 1997). They have produced a global division of labor, creating networks of interconnected workers while simultaneously dividing them along socioeconomic lines. As we mentioned in Chapter 1, **globalization** is a process of interaction and integration among the people, companies, and governments of different nations, a process driven by international trade and investment and aided by information technology. Different societies experience this differently, but there is no doubt that globalization affects the environment, culture, political system, and economic development and prosperity everywhere.

Global production refers to the fact that corporations derive raw materials from all over the world and use manufacturing and assembly plants in many different countries, using international labor forces. **Global distribution** ensures that these products are marketed and distributed all over the world as well. The products we buy are likely made of materials from several countries, assembled in another country, packaged in and distributed by yet another, with advertising campaigns and marketing schemes drawn from yet another.

During the Industrial Revolution, the raw materials may have been drawn from other countries, but the entire manufacturing and marketing processes were located in the industrial country. Now, however, the process is fragmented, and each economic function may be located in another country, or several countries. This has also led to **outsourcing**, the contracting out to another company of work that had once been done internally by your company. Initially, technology and IT were outsourced to cheaper call centers in developing nations like India and China. Then, production line jobs began to move overseas where labor was cheaper and factories could be built without bowing to environmental regulations. Now even white-collar jobs like sales and service have also been outsourced.

Although research, development, production, and distribution occur in many different countries, the "knowledge labor" tends to occur in wealthier countries, whereas unskilled and semiskilled factory work takes place in poorer countries. Indeed, although the world has become wealthier, that growth in wealth has been inequitably

globalization

A set of processes leading to the development of patterns of economic, cultural, and social relationships that transcend geographical boundaries; a widening, deepening, and speeding up of worldwide interconnectedness in all aspects of contemporary life.

global production

A term that describes how, in a global economy, goods are manufactured from raw materials and produced in factories all over the world in complex production chains and international labor forces.

global distribution

A term that describes how the products we buy are likely made of materials from several countries, assembled in another country, packaged and distributed from yet another, with advertising campaigns and marketing schemes drawn from yet another.

outsourcing

Also called *offshoring*, it refers to the practice of contracting out any phase(s) of product development that had once been done internally to lower-wage countries or groups.

SOCIOLOGY AND OUR WORLD

CARDBOARD: A GOLDMINE IN A GLOBALIZED WORLD

What types of global interactions and relationships are necessary to make an organization like Nine Dragons Paper Co. profitable?

Have you ever heard of Nine Dragons Paper Co.? You've probably held their product in your hands recently. Nine Dragons recycles paper and turns it into cardboard. Driven by paper shortages in China, Zhang Yin travelled to the United States with her husband. They drove around the country in a minivan requesting paper from garbage dumps. Now, her company purchases paper waste from the United States and Europe, ships it to China, recycles that paper into corrugated cardboard and sells it to Chinese companies to package and ship products around the world. It's no exaggeration to suggest that if you bought something shipped from China, it was probably shipped in Nine Dragons cardboard. And after you threw that box away, Nine Dragons shipped it right back to China and turned it into a new box.

It was a smart idea for a business—smarter than you might realize actually because Zhang Yin is among the top-25 richest people in China with a net worth upward of $4.4 billion. Just for comparison, that makes Yin almost 1.5 times as wealthy as Oprah Winfrey and more than 3 times as wealthy as Sheryl Sandberg!

Zhang Yin's success is testament to the power of globalization. She started with a problem in China—a paper shortage. Rather than finding new forests to cut down for more paper, Yin realized that there was more than enough paper in the world. Someone just needed to find a way to get that paper and recycle it into the forms needed. Globalization and existing chains of global production and distribution were necessary to make this company possible.

---

shared by people around the world. Even on the global level, the gap between rich and poor is increasing as globalization reinforces or even increases the stark inequalities of income and wealth around the world (see MAP 14.1).

Examining global production on an international scale illustrates that some nations have seen much more economic growth than others. But MAP 14.1 tells us little about **income distribution**—how a nation's income is distributed among the population—within each individual nation, of the level of economic stratification in different societies. What it does is give us a better understanding of where economic growth is occurring by visualizing differences in the **gross domestic product** around the world.

Globalization links owners and managers into an interlocking system of a managerial elite; often managers from Sri Lanka and Belgium will have more in common with each other (consumption patterns, tastes in art and music, and so on) than either will with the working-class in his or her own country. However, although the elite at the top become more integrated and cohesive, the working classes will remain fractured and distant from each other, asserting local, regional, and cultural differences as a way to resist integration. In this way, also, the globalizing rich become richer and the globalized poor become poorer.

Industrial economies move workers from home to factories, and postindustrial economies move them out into the wide, wide world. The production of ideas does not require all of the workers to be in the same building or even on the same continent. And the technologies of globalization make this ever more possible. A decade ago, they could phone in their ideas and fax their presentations; now they can transmit entire volumes by instant message, e-mail, Internet, and other digital media. And when you call for technical support, you may be speaking to someone on another continent.

"Rush-hour traffic" is quickly becoming a meaningless term because many people don't have to be in some physical location called "work" every day between 9:00 and

income distribution

How a nation's income is distributed among the population—within each individual nation, of the level of economic stratification in different societies. What it does is give us a better understanding of where economic growth is occurring.

gross domestic product

The total value of goods produced and services provided in a country during one year.

MAP 14.1 Global Gross Domestic Product (GDP)

As you can see, the growth in global gross domestic product (GDP) has not been equally experienced around the world. This is why it is true that the GDP has increased incredibly over the last half-century, but it is also true that the gap between the richest and poorest societies in the world has grown significantly in recent history.

2016 (Trillions)
- No data
- 0 – 0.05
- 0.05 – 0.1
- 0.1 – 0.2
- 0.2 – 0.5
- 0.5 – 0.8
- 0.8 – 1.0
- 1.0 – 2.0
- 2.0 – 4.5
- > 4.5

SOURCE: Data from World Bank and OECD national accounts. Available at http://data.worldbank.org/indicator/NY.GDP.MKTP.CD?end=2015&start=1960& view=map&year=2015).

5:00. They are on the road constantly, en route between home, office, meetings, and the airport. Service workers *are* stuck in some physical location; but their day might begin at 11:00 AM, 4:00 PM, or midnight, or they could work a "split shift," with 4 hours in the morning and 4 hours in the evening. So, the streets are always crowded.

Even time becomes meaningless to the postindustrial worker. Clients and coworkers live in every part of the globe, so there is no "quitting time." Work can happen any time of the day or night. As a result, the 200-year-old distinction between home and work, livelihood and leisure, is fading away. This has led to an increasing sense of "rootlessness"— the notion that people today have fewer ties to a particular place or community. It's more likely today than ever before in history that you might work "with" coworkers who you will never meet in person at a "workplace" of your own choosing. This economic shift comes with a host of consequences—both positive and negative. And when we examine them intersectionally, sociologists have shown that the negative consequences associated with this transformation have been disproportionately felt by those already marginalized by existing inequalities.

Economic Systems—Capitalism

14.1.6 Summarize the defining qualities of a capitalist economic system.

All societies must deal with three fundamental economic issues: (1) *production*, making sure that the society produces the things that people want and need; (2) *distribution*, making sure that these products find their way into places where people can access them; and (3) *consumption*, ensuring that people can actually use the products that the society produces. An **economic system** is a mechanism that deals with the production, distribution, and consumption of goods and services in a particular society.

Capitalism is a profit-oriented system based on the private or corporate ownership of the means of production and distribution. It arose in the Netherlands and Britain during the sixteenth century, when private investors began to fund the wealth-accumulating journeys of traders, explorers, and eventually colonists. Individual companies competed with each other for customers and profits with no government interference. Classical capitalism has three basic components:

economic system

A mechanism that deals with the production, distribution, and consumption of goods and services in a particular society.

capitalism

An economic system in which free individuals pursue their own private interests in the marketplace. In laissez-faire capitalism, markets freely compete without government intervention. State capitalism requires that the government use a heavy hand in regulating and constraining the marketplace, and welfare capitalism creates a market-based economy for most goods and services, yet also has social welfare programs and government ownership of essential services.

- *Private ownership* of the means of production (natural resources and production machinery).
- *An open market* with no government interference. Kings and queens (and later prime ministers and presidents) should "*laissez-faire,*" or keep their hands off.
- *Profit* (receiving more than the goods cost to produce) as a valuable goal of human enterprise.

Each of these varies enormously, even among capitalist countries. In the United States, most people believe that the *political system* of democracy would be impossible without the *economic system* of capitalism. But capitalism has also turned out to be compatible with other political forms. Fascist Italy and the Communist former Soviet Union acted as capitalist nations in the global marketplace. The state simply kept most of the profits.

In fact, democracy and capitalism often contradict each other. Capitalism, after all, frees individuals to pursue their own private interests in the marketplace; it promotes unconstrained liberty. Democracy, on the other hand, constrains individual liberty in the name of the common good. For instance, in capitalism, it makes sense for a factory to toss its toxic waste into the nearest river: The money saved on proper waste disposal can go into the stockholders' pockets, maximizing profits. But in a democracy, concern for the common good (unpolluted rivers) requires the factory to dispose of its toxic waste properly, limiting its individual liberty and reducing its profits. Indeed, Americans today are divided over the question of governmental regulation of business and industry. As a result of the tension, capitalism in democratic countries has developed in different ways, in an attempt to balance individual liberty and the common good or, as the issue is sometimes framed, freedom and responsibility.

laissez-faire capitalism

The original form of capitalism, theorized by Adam Smith, "laissez-faire" means "to leave alone" in French; under this system, governments would leave the marketplace alone to organize the economy, without government interference. (Smith believed that there were natural limits to people's greed.) Markets should be able to compete freely to sell goods, acquire raw materials, and hire labor. No government interference is necessary: The "invisible hand" of supply and demand creates a self-regulating economy.

Capitalist economic systems are organized around private ownership, open markets, and economic profit. This concern with economic profit and growth shapes your experience in capitalist economic workplaces in every possible way.

The original form of capitalism, theorized by Adam Smith, "laissez-faire" means "to leave alone" in French; under this system, governments would leave the marketplace alone to organize the economy, without government interference. (Smith believed that there were natural limits to people's greed.) Markets should be able to compete freely to sell goods, acquire raw materials, and hire labor. No government interference is necessary: The "invisible hand" of supply and demand creates a self-regulating economy. **Laissez-faire capitalism** dominated in Europe and North America through the nineteenth century, but it has proved ineffective in preventing economic crises. Thus, the relationship between the government and economy can no longer be a question of whether or not the government should be involved in economic life. Today, the questions are how much should the government be involved? In what sectors? In what ways?

U.S./WORLD

THE PROSPERITY OF NATIONS: NATIONS WITH THE HIGHEST PER CAPITA INCOME, 2016

The most economically prosperous nations in the world offer extensive state-sponsored safety nets to provide essential services to everyone in the society. Access to basic necessities like transportation and health care are important features of prosperous societies.

Luxembourg	$105, 829
Switzerland	79,577
Norway	79,497
Macau	67,012
Ireland	65,879
Qatar	60,732
Iceland	57,888
United States	57,293
Denmark	53,242
Singapore	53,053

The United States is certainly the largest society listed here in terms of population. Yet, societies in the top five have much higher per capital incomes than does the United States. And, interestingly, all five of them have much more extensive socialized systems of social welfare that provide *more* for everyone in society. Perhaps this is more easily done in less populous societies than the United States with more strict immigration laws and restrictions on citizenship. But it is also true that these data suggest that providing more for everyone in a society has positive effects felt by *everyone* in that society—not only those most in need of the assistance.

SOURCE: Data from International Monetary Fund, "Projected GDP Per Capita Ranking," 2016–2020. Available at http://statisticstimes.com/economy/projected-world-gdp-capita-ranking.php.

INVESTIGATE FURTHER

1. What elements of a welfare capitalist economy can you identify in the United States?
2. What role might they play in helping people acquire income in capitalist economies?

But laissez-faire capitalism is only one system of capitalism. Another, **state capitalism**, requires that the government use a heavy hand in regulating and constraining the marketplace. Companies may still be privately owned, but they must also meet government-set standards of product quality, worker compensation, and truth in advertising. In turn, the government provides some economic security to companies to avoid catastrophic losses and controls foreign imports to help local companies compete in world markets. This system is still common in the rapidly developing countries of the Pacific Rim, such as South Korea and Singapore.

Most contemporary capitalist countries also include extensive social welfare programs, and the government regulates some of the most essential services, such as transportation, health care, and the mass media (Barr 2004; Esping-Anderson 1990; Stephens and Huber 2001). This is called **welfare capitalism**. As a hybrid system—private ownership (capitalism) and a state-sponsored safety net (socialism)—welfare capitalist countries are the most prosperous; of the top-10 countries in per capita income, all but two have some version of welfare capitalism.

The U.S. economy incorporates elements of all three forms of capitalism. Many companies seek to operate with as little government regulation as possible and set up corporate headquarters so they do not have to pay taxes in the United States

state capitalism
A version of capitalism that requires that the government use a heavy hand in regulating and constraining the marketplace.

welfare capitalism
A version of capitalism in most contemporary capitalist countries, it is concerned with the welfare of the worker as well as profits and includes such policies as collective bargaining and industrial safety codes while the government regulates some of the most essential services, such as transportation, health care, and the mass media.

(*laissez-faire*). Companies like Walmart resist the unionization of their workers and undermine minimum wage regulations. Other industries, like the airlines and automobile manufacturers, agree to fare regulation or automotive emission controls in return for a more stable economic environment (*state capitalism*) and the promise that if they go bankrupt, as AIG and General Motors did in 2008 and 2009, the government will bail them out. And the massive public sector—federal, state, and local bureaucracies and political systems—work as a kind of *welfare capitalism*, attempting to ensure that everyone obtains at least a minimum standard of living.

Economic Systems—Socialism and Communism

14.1.7 Distinguish between socialist and communist economic systems, and explain how both differ from capitalism.

Although capitalism became the dominant economic system in the West by the end of the eighteenth century, it was not without its detractors. Utopians argued that it would be more equitable to *cooperate* instead of *compete*, so that everyone could share the goods and services. In the nineteenth century, many socialist communes were founded in the United States, where all property was commonly owned and all decisions made as a collective body. However, it was never attempted on a national level. Karl Marx argued that the pursuit of rational self-interest was inhumane and oppressive. The **bourgeoisie** (owners) kept all the profits for themselves, while the **proletariat** (workers) had no choice but to work for them at wages barely enough to ensure survival. Marx hypothesized that the huge economic gap between the groups would cause increasing hostility and resentment and would eventually result in violent revolution.

Marx proposed to adapt socialism to national governments by ensuring that workers rather than owners controlled the means of production and that everyone would be treated fairly. Strong government controls would be put into place to ensure equitable distribution of resources. Thus, **socialism** is the exact opposite of laissez-faire capitalism, offering:

- *Collective (public sector) ownership.*   Private property is limited, especially property used to generate income. Goods and services are available equally to all, regardless of individual wealth.
- *Collective goals.*   Capitalism celebrates profit as the entrepreneurial spirit, but socialism condemns profit as greed. Individuals should concentrate on the common good.
- *Central planning.*   Socialism operates through a "command economy." The government controls all production and distribution.

On the national level, many countries, both rich and poor, have socialist economies, but they allow for a degree of entrepreneurship, some profit, and differences in individual wealth, resulting in a "democratic socialism" that looks and feels more like welfare capitalism (Lichtheim 1982; Rose and Ross 1994). In Sweden, for instance, about 12 percent of economic production is "nationalized" (state controlled), and the rest is in private hands. High taxation, aimed especially at the rich, funds a wide range of social welfare programs for everyone, including universal health care and childcare. Scholars differ on whether this economy should be classified as *socialist* or *capitalist* as clearly it has elements of both economic systems.

Many people confuse socialism with a separate economic system—communism. But communism is *not* socialism. Marx believed that socialism was a necessary transition from the economic oppression of capitalism to the ideal economic system of communism. **Communism** is an economic system based on collective ownership of the means of production and is administered collectively, without a political apparatus to ensure equal distribution. It is utopian, and Marx believed that communism

bourgeoisie
Popularized by Karl Marx, term for the upperclass capitalists who owned the means of production. In Marx's time, they owned factories instead of farms. Today the term is also used to refer to upper-class managers who wield a lot of power.

proletariat
Popularized by Karl Marx, the term for the lower classes who were forced to become wage laborers or go hungry. Today, the term is often used to refer to the working class.

socialism
Economic system in which people are meant to cooperate rather than compete, share goods and services, own property collectively, and make decisions as a collective body.

communism
Envisioned as the ideal economic system by Karl Marx, communism would produce and distribute resources "from each according to his or her ability, to each according to his or her need," erasing social inequalities along with crime, hunger, and political strife.

could be achieved only after many years of socialism. Socialism requires strong government intervention, but in a communist state, government is abolished. Socialism retains a difference between high-status and low-status work, so the janitor receives a lower salary than the physician, but in the communist state, the principle of distribution will become "from each according to his or her ability, to each according to his or her need." Thus, the janitor and the physician will receive the same stipend for personal expenses. Social inequalities will disappear, along with crime, hunger, and political strife.

Strangely, communist ideas did not take hold in industrialized, capitalist countries where the gap between owners and workers was most evident, but in agricultural countries, usually after revolutions or civil wars, such as in Russia (1917), China (1949), Vietnam (1954), Cuba (1959), and Yemen (1969). These countries usually called themselves socialist rather than communist because the government had not yet "withered away" in the manner Marx predicted. But as time passed, the governments never withered away. Bureaucracy and regulation actually expanded, until the governments were stronger and more centralized than in capitalist countries. And social and class divisions remained strong (Muravchik 2002; Pipes 2001). What happened? A failure to think intersectionally. Sociologists explain that social stratification isn't simply a matter of economics. It involves power and status as well as wealth (and power and status are related to a diverse set of social identities beyond social class). So simply eliminating income disparities will not result in paradise. In fact, the communist governments created a new class of political elite. In the Soviet Union, about 10 percent of the population in 1984 belonged to the Communist Party. Called the *nomenklatura*, they got to shop in the best stores, send their children to the best schools, vacation at exclusive resorts, and travel abroad (Taylor 1987; Voslensky 1984).

The worker's paradise that Marx envisioned never happened and probably never could. After half a century of trying, most of the communist governments of the world

WHAT DO YOU THINK? WHAT DOES AMERICA THINK?

The Rich and Taxes

Some Americans think taxation is handled in an unfair way. For instance, some think the rich should pay more taxes than they do, whereas others maintain that the rich contribute to society in other ways, such as providing jobs and revenue for middle- and working-class Americans.

What do you think?

"Some wealthy people don't pay their fair share." How much does this statement bother you with regard to the federal tax system?
"Some poor people don't pay their fair share." How much does this statement bother you with regard to the federal tax system?
"The amount you pay in taxes." How much does this statement bother you with regard to the federal tax system?

- ○ A lot
- ○ Some
- ○ Not too much/Not at all

What does America think?

Data from a Pew Research Center study showed that 61 percent of respondents were bothered a lot by the feeling that some wealthy people don't pay their fair share; 18 percent were bothered some; and 20 percent weren't bothered too much or not at all. Approximately 20 percent of respondents were bothered a lot by the feeling that some poor people don't pay their fair share; 22 percent were bothered some; and 56 percent weren't bothered too much or not at all. Finally, 27 percent of respondents were bothered a lot by the amount they pay in taxes; 26 percent were bothered some; and 46 percent weren't bothered much or not at all. Americans, as a group, tend to be more bothered by the sense that corporations and the wealthy are not paying fair amounts of taxes than they are about how much they pay individually or how much those with the least means pay in taxes.

Americans' Frustrations with the Tax System, 2015

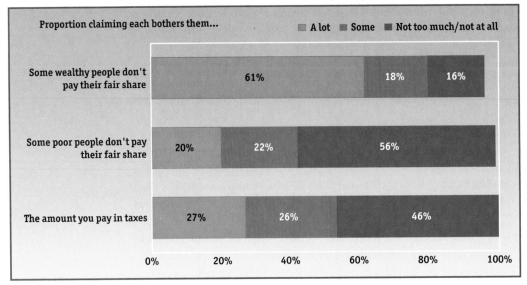

Proportion claiming each bothers them...		■ A lot ■ Some ■ Not too much/not at all

Some wealthy people don't pay their fair share: 61% | 18% | 16%

Some poor people don't pay their fair share: 20% | 22% | 56%

The amount you pay in taxes: 27% | 26% | 46%

0%   20%   40%   60%   80%   100%

SOURCE: Data from The Pew Research Center, 2015. Available at http://www.pewresearch.org/fact-tank/2015/04/10/5-facts-on-how-americans-view-taxes/.

THINKING CRITICALLY ABOUT SURVEY DATA

How do you think responses might differ if they were broken down by social class? In other words, how do you think race and class intersect in ways that might shape the opinions of people when asked about taxation in the United States?

have shifted to some form of capitalism. Today there are only five communist countries left (China, Cuba, Laos, North Korea, and Vietnam), and all except North Korea are decentralizing government controls and encouraging entrepreneurship (Hall 1994; Oh and Hassig 2000; Schopflin 1993).

Economies and Politics: Protest and Change

14.1.8 Explain why economic protest throughout history has primarily been related to the extent to which governments intervene in the economy.

Smith may have believed that the best relationship between government and economy is "laissez-faire," leaving the market alone to regulate itself, no society in the history of the world has actually ever practiced that. It's impossible for governments not to get involved in the economy. For one thing, there's too much money at stake; governments want some of it to create the infrastructure that enables markets to work well in the first place.

In 1979, the government bailed out the Chrysler automobile company with a $1.5 billion loan, because, politicians reasoned, three big domestic car companies are better than two, and would lead to lower prices for cars. In 2008, President George W. Bush bailed them out again, this time for $4 billion. During the financial crisis of 2008, President Bush declared that some banks and institutions were "too big to fail"—that their failure would severely weaken the entire economy—and that, therefore, the government had to

In April 2009, hundreds of protestors crowded the streets in financial district in New York City to protest the governmental bailouts of the banks and financial institutions responsible for the economic recession in the first place. Many disagreed with the decision to save these financial institutions.

intervene. Governments are always intervening in the marketplace. The U.S. government pays massive subsidies to farmers to either stimulate or suppress production of certain crops (encouraging them to grow crops that experience shortages or discouraging them from growing crops for which there is a surplus). Governments regulate labor markets also, providing a stable and secure labor market for corporations, providing unemployment insurance and other benefits so that out-of-work workers don't riot. So the question is never whether or not the government should intervene in the economy. Governments do intervene. The sociological questions are: How much? In whose interests? When and where do they intervene? And these questions are invariably political.

Throughout history, social movements have arisen to steer the economy in a different direction, or to change the government so as to free up the economy or to constrain it. Several of the great historical revolutions were triggered by the government's efforts to tax people (as in the English Revolution, which began as a tax revolt) or refusing to regulate the market (as in the French Revolution, when the king refused to intervene in the market to keep bread prices low). It is difficult to mount a social movement simply against an economic system; instead such protests are almost always mobilized against economic *policies*—that is, against the ways in which governments intervene in the economy to control and regulate economic life, or to advocate for greater intervention. Some of the great social movements in American history were inspired by economic protests. The Populist movement of the late nineteenth century sought to expand government intervention in the agricultural economy by constraining and regulating some of the financial practices of large banks. So, too, does the current Occupy movement seek government regulation of financial institutions that offered impossible mortgages to unsuspecting home buyers, and then packaged those mortgages up as assets and offered them to investors, all the while betting against those same investments.

In every economy, some win and others lose. Some economies are more zero-sum than others; some try an enable most people to win a little bit, and others consider the economy a winner-take-all contest. Some governments want to stand back and watch the contest; others seek only to level the playing field in the present moment. More interventionist governments acknowledge that the playing field has been terribly skewed and that one side has made up all the rules, and that, therefore, state action is needed to give the other side a bit of a boost.

---

iSOC AND YOU Economy and Society

The economy is one of the primary social *institutions*, like education or family or government. Economies organize the production and distribution of goods and services; that is, they are both based on and also shape the *interactions* among different groups of actors. Your position in the economy is a significant element of your *identity*. You may even define yourself by your job. Though there are numerous ways economies could be organized, they all reflect different sorts of *inequalities*: Some people have more than others. Economic inequality often coincides with other forms of inequality, like, say, race or gender, but not entirely. As such, economic inequality is also *intersectional*.

14.2 Institutionalizing Inequality at Work

Since the beginning of human society, our working lives have occupied the majority of our waking hours. From sunup to sundown, people in nonindustrial cultures have hunted and gathered, planted and sown, fished and farmed to provide for their society's members. This is still true today for most of the world's population. In contemporary industrial and postindustrial economies, it was only in the early twentieth century that we cut the "work day" to 8 hours. And political movements in Europe are suggesting cutting the work week from 40 to 35 hours and the work day to 7 or even 6 hours a day. In that sense, we work fewer hours today than ever before.

At the same time, we constantly hear how we are working longer and harder than ever before. Top-level managers in corporations and young lawyers in large firms often log 100-hour work weeks. Countless CEOs boast about virtually living in their offices. Americans are working harder and longer than residents of all but a handful of other industrialized nations. Sociologists understand that both these phenomena are true: The organization of our economies makes it possible for us to work fewer hours and also often makes it necessary for us to work longer hours. Part of the answer lies in just what qualifies as "work" in the first place. Most of what we think of as work is a part of formal economic exchange. But "work" encompasses much more than this. Another piece of this answer requires us to examine intersections in our identities which shape what kinds of work we might perform.

In this section, we will learn about research on worker productivity and just how challenging it is to study. We will also distinguish between different types of jobs and the different groups that tend to occupy them. And finally, we examine those least likely to be able to find work and least able to support themselves.

Studying the Way We Work

14.2.1 Explain the difference between "Theory X" and "Theory Y" for understanding people's relationship to work.

In the early days of mass production, the assembly line basically imagined workers as machines. People were simply trained to do a task with scientific precision and then asked to do it repeatedly. No one really cared whether the workers felt challenged, bored, intimidated, or humiliated. As industrialization progressed, management scientists began to research how we respond to the workplace, to coworkers, to bosses, and to labor itself. Happier workers, who felt less bored and more valued, it turned out, were more productive—and that spelled higher profits. But assembly-line production didn't always make for the happiest workers.

The earliest experimental study of work productivity was conducted between 1927 and 1932 at the Western Electric Hawthorne factory in Chicago. Researcher Elton Mayo chose six female assembly-line workers and assigned an observer to watch them, ask for their input, and listen to their complaints. Then he made a variety of environmental changes, including breaks of various lengths, different quitting times, different quotas, a day off, and a free lunch. To his surprise, almost every change increased productivity. And when he changed things back to the default, productivity increased again (Mayo 1933)!

Mayo concluded that the changes themselves weren't responsible for the increase in productivity. It was that the workers had some input. The workers chosen for the experiment had no boss telling them the "proper" procedure. They were allowed to work in their own way; in fact, the observer displayed a keen interest in their individual work styles. They were treated as intelligent, creative individuals rather than as mindless machines.

Hawthorne effect

The alteration of behavior by the subjects of a study because of their awareness of being observed.

The **Hawthorne effect** soon became a standard in management textbooks: People alter their behavior in response to becoming aware that they are being observed. The employees at Western Electric, in others words, became more productive because they were being watched—not necessarily for any of the reasons Mayo had initially suspected. Except for one small problem: It wasn't exactly true. Economist Steve Levitt, coauthor with Steven Dubner of the best-selling book *Freakonomics* (2005), looked at Mayo's original data and found something interesting. The lighting was changed on

FIGURE 14.2 How Much Do We Work?

Americans work long and hard—but not as long as some countries, and lots longer than others. How many hours per year does the average employed person work in these selected countries? What sorts of factors influence how long we work? What would we do with the 362 extra hours that Norwegians have every year? That's approximately 15 full 24-hour days, or more than 45 working (8-hour) days!

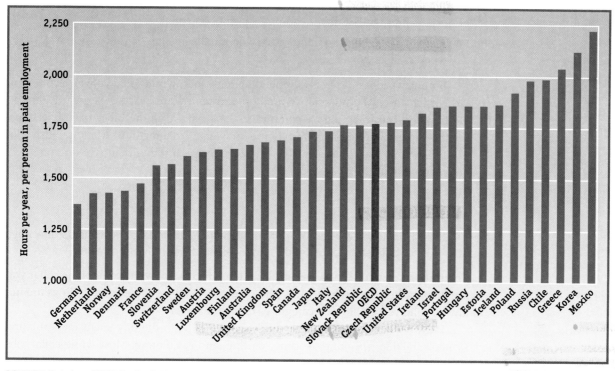

SOURCE: Data from OECD Factbook 2015–16: Economic, Environmental and Social Statistics. Available at http://www.keepeek.com/Digital-Asset-Management/oecd/economics/oecd-factbook-2015-2016/hours-worked_factbook-2015-54-en#.WNk90fkrLIV#page2.

a Sunday, so that the change would take effect on Monday when workers returned to work. But Levitt found that productivity *always* went up on Mondays, whether there was a change of lighting or not (*The Economist* 2009a).

In 1960 Douglas McGregor published *The Human Side of Enterprise*, about two theories of work (McGregor, 1960/2005). Theory X assumes that people naturally dislike work, so they will slack off unless they are coerced and threatened. On the assembly line, a line supervisor must be watching them at all times. In white-collar jobs, they must fill out time sheets, goals statements, and allocation lists. Theory Y is based on the assumption that people naturally like work, so they will do it if they feel they are a valued part of a team (as in the Hawthorne effect). The job of the supervisor is to create team spirit, solve problems, and offer advice, not monitor productivity. On the assembly line, there should be suggestion boxes and team meetings. White-collar workers might go on retreats where they fall backward into each other's arms to learn trust. McGregor argued that both theories are valid and can increase productivity, depending on the task and the maturity and responsibility of the workers. The biggest mistake of management is to implement Theory X all the time and never consider the possibility of Theory Y.

Sociologist Michael Burawoy (1980) wondered why so many people work so hard, making only their managers rich. It's not a desire for promotion because people work just as hard at dead-end jobs. It's not fear of being fired. Why don't they slack off or rebel against the oppressive system? Why do they care? To find out, he took a blue-collar job at "Allied Corporation" and carefully observed both management and workers. He found that management engaged in three strategies designed to **manufacture consent**, by which workers came to embrace a system that also exploited them.

manufacture consent

The production of values and emotions (in addition to the actual things they produce) that bind workers to their company.

- *Piece-rate pay system.* The workers competed with each other to produce the highest quotas. Though the "prizes" were only minor pay raises, workers devoted a lot of time to "making out," strategizing new ways to increase their production. Even Burawoy found himself working harder.
- *Internal labor market.* Increasing job mobility within the company gave the workers the illusion that their dead-end jobs had potential.
- *Collective bargaining.* Unions gave workers the illusion that they, as individual workers, held power.

Buroway's ideas have been applied to many jobs, white collar as well as blue collar. For instance, in academia, promotion and tenure are based to a great extent on publications, but often tenure committees look only at the number of publications, not the quality. So professors find their own way of "making out." Many publish a lot of short articles that do not involve extensive research rather than working on a big, meaningful project.

Types of Jobs

14.2.2 Distinguish between the different types of jobs today, and consider the ways that different groups tend to dominate in different types of work.

There are several different types of jobs, often categorized by the color of the collar you are thought to wear—white, blue, pink, green. Of course, these color codings are not always followed, but the job categories remain relatively stable.

white-collar work

Knowledge-based work, requiring considerable education, in which a typical day is spent manipulating symbols: talking, speaking, reading, writing, and calculating.

White-collar work is knowledge-based work, with the day spent manipulating symbols: talking, speaking, reading, writing, and calculating. Most white-collar jobs require considerable education, usually a bachelor's degree and, today, often a master's degree. In 1900, only about 16 percent of American workers had white-collar jobs, but today that figure is almost three times that proportion. "Professionals" are among the elite of the white-collar jobs—a category including doctors, lawyers, and teachers as well as scientists, engineers, librarians, architects, artists, journalists, and entertainers. Professions can generally be distinguished from other jobs by four characteristics:

1. *Theoretical knowledge.* You must have not only technical training in a skill but also a theoretical understanding of a field. Architecture became a profession only when it became less about constructing buildings and more about understanding the dynamics of inhabited space.
2. *Self-regulating practices.* Other jobs have procedures, but professions observe a "code of ethics."
3. *Authority over clients.* Based on their extensive training, professionals are qualified to advise their clients and expect them to obey directions. You expect that your doctor knows more than you do about your rash.
4. *Community orientation.* Rather than merely seeking personal income, the professional has a duty to the community.

Alongside the professionals are the white-collar workers in business. Business administration remains the most popular college major, comprising nearly 2 in every 10 of all bachelor's degrees awarded in 2015 (U.S. Department of Education, National Center for Education Statistics 2016). Yet only about 67,000 American workers are actually employed in management, business, and financial occupations (Bureau of Labor Statistics 2016). Because white-collar jobs offer the highest salaries and the most opportunity for advancement, many sociologists, including C. Wright Mills (1959), have argued that white-collar workers are more in agreement with capitalism than blue or pink-collar workers. However, contemporary scholars note that, in the postindustrial economy, most white-collar jobs are becoming more regimented and bureaucratic, and white-collar workers are experiencing a decay in autonomy, creativity, and advancement potential similar to that of the blue-collar workers as well (Fraser 2001).

The term *blue collar* was first coined in 1951 for jobs involved with production rather than knowledge, because factory workers traditionally wore blue jumpsuits. In 1900, 60 percent of American workers were blue collar. Today that proportion is less than a quarter of working Americans. There are several types of **blue-collar work**—like natural resource and construction, factory work, and skilled crafts work. Natural resource and construction work includes farming, fishing, and forestry, plus the construction trades (electricians, bricklayers, plumbers), and also auto and airplane repair, heating, air conditioning, and refrigeration. Only a minority of Americans perform this type of work (around 1 in 10), the vast majority of whom are men.

The term *pink collar* was coined by Louise Kay Howe (1977). Howe found that jobs in offices, restaurants, and stores—such as secretary, wait staff, or sales clerk—were often held by women. And collectively, **pink-collar work** is low in both pay and prestige. Some highly experienced and lucky pink-collar workers can work their way up to the salary of a white-collar job, but most barely make a living wage, like the factory workers of the nineteenth century. Many of the most dominant pink-collar jobs are in clerical and sales work. These are jobs in office production: typists, file clerks, data entry clerks, receptionists, secretaries, administrative assistants, and office managers, plus cashiers, insurance agents, and real estate agents. The mostly women who occupy these jobs today are also disproportionately likely to be white.

A growing sector of work in the United States is **service work**. This category includes food preparation and service, personal services (hair stylists, launderers, childcare workers), and maintenance workers (janitors, garbage collectors), plus police officers and firefighters. Service jobs are more equally divided by gender as a group, though men and women are often found in different service sectors. Service work is also age oriented: It includes the oldest and the youngest workers, like the retirees who greet you at Walmart and the local teenagers who are flipping your burgers at a fast food restaurant. Service jobs include many of the lowest paid, least prestigious occupations, and the ones with fewest—if any—health and retirement benefits.

Finally, as the global economy continues to change, a new type of job has begun to emerge. **Green-collar work** refers to jobs in those industries that are involved with new and renewable energy. Today green-collar workers are installing solar panels, retrofitting buildings to make them more efficient, constructing transit lines, refining waste oil into biodiesel, erecting wind farms, repairing hybrid cars, and building green rooftops. Green-collar jobs refute the notion that environmental health comes at the expense of economic expansion.

Presidential candidates perennially promise to bring manufacturing jobs back to the United States. But, in our service economy, there are increasingly fewer opportunities for this kind of work. And the jobs replacing this work require dramatically different sets of skills and educational credentials.

blue-collar work
Jobs involved with production rather than knowledge.

pink-collar work
Louise Kay Howe's coinage for types of employment traditionally held by women, especially in relatively low pay service positions, such as secretarial, sales clerks, and wait staff.

service work
A growing sector of work in the United States, this category includes food preparation and service, personal services (hair stylists, launderers, childcare workers), and maintenance workers (janitors, garbage collectors), plus police officers and firefighters.

green-collar work
A new category of advanced manufacturing jobs, it denotes work involved in environmental and renewable energy industries.

Wages: High, Minimum, and Living

14.2.3 Understand the difference between minimum and "living" wages as well as some of the challenges associated with each.

The **minimum wage** in the United States is $7.25 per hour. (That's the federal mandate; some states may have higher rates. And, increasingly some cities have increased the minimum wage as high as $15 per hour.) But those earning $7.25 bring

minimum wage
The lowest wage permitted by law.

in about $58 a day. Maybe that could sustain a teenager living at home; but a person living alone, without parental support, could never acquire adequate food, clothing, and shelter for that amount (and don't even think about supporting children). Millions of U.S. adults earn minimum wage or less today, and those numbers include people working in service and office jobs. Additionally, almost half of people earning minimum wage in the United States are employed full-time. And these figures also do not take into account a much larger number of workers in the United States who will spend at least half of their work lives in jobs at or near minimum wage. It is these workers, plus the 25 million more who earn a dollar or two an hour above the minimum wage, who sociologists refer to as the **working poor**.

working poor
Working people whose income nevertheless falls below the poverty line.

The real value of the minimum wage (that is, its equivalent in the contemporary workplace) rose through the 1960s to a high of $7.18 (in 1968). It fell steadily during the Reagan and Bush presidencies, to a low point of $4.80 (in 1989). President Clinton raised it to $5.89, but it fell again under George W. Bush. All the while, worker productivity, corporate profits, and CEO pay have increased significantly. To consider who earns these wages as well, see FIGURE 14.3.

An obvious solution would be to raise the minimum wage—to at least $8.00 per hour, the minimum necessary for a single full-time worker to acquire adequate food, clothing, shelter, and transportation (but not health insurance, which most low-income jobs don't offer anyway). Opponents argue that raising the minimum wage will hurt businesses, fuel inflation, increase unemployment, and ultimately harm low-skill workers. But several studies reveal that the costs to businesses, even small businesses, would be minimal. And they would save on recruitment, training, and retention costs; reduce turnover and absenteeism; and improve quality of work, all positively affecting profits (Sklar, Mykyta, and Wefald 2001).

living wage
A minimum income necessary for a worker to meet his or her basic needs.

More than 130 municipalities around the country have legislated "**living wage**" ordinances since 1994, including big cities such as New York, Chicago, Boston, Detroit,

FIGURE 14.3 Who Earns Minimum Wage?
While white people are the largest population of people earning minimum wage, it's important to remember that white people are also the largest racial group in the United States. Here, we can see what proportion of different age groups earn minimum wage (or less), by gender. And we can also see what proportion of different racial and ethnic groups earn minimum wage (or less), by gender. When sociologists examine issues like this intersectionally, we want to know more than raw numbers. We're interested in whether different groups (like women or racial or ethnic minorities) are disproportionately more likely to endure this hardship or not.

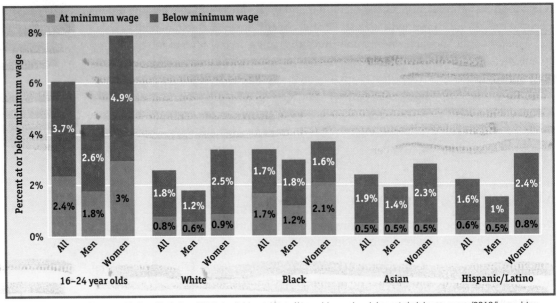

SOURCE: Data from Bureau of Labor Statistics, 2016. Available at https://www.bls.gov/opub/reports/minimum-wage/2016/home.htm.

HOW DO WE KNOW WHAT WE KNOW?

THE POOR WORK HARDER THAN THE RICH

One of the most enduring myths in Western culture is the myth that people are poor because they don't work hard enough. Consistently, sociologists have debunked this myth by surveys of hours worked, comparisons that show the minimum wage fails to come close to helping people live above the poverty line, and other methods. Recently, though, sociologists and journalists have gone deeper into the work lives of working people and found something somewhat startling: Poor people work much harder than rich people.

Sociologist Katherine Newman (1999) sent teams of her graduate students into minimum-wage jobs, like flipping burgers in a fast-food restaurant she called "Burger Barn." The researchers were surprised to see just how honest and hard-working the workers were, but also noted how workers had to scramble frantically to try and put a few dollars aside for the future because they had neither health benefits nor retirement plans. The workers were proud to work, in fact, preferring to make it on their own than rely on public assistance. Journalist Barbara Ehrenreich (2001) went even further: She took 6 months and worked in a variety of entry-level jobs that define low-wage service work in the global economy. She worked as a cleaning woman in Maine, as a waitress in Key West, and as an "associate" in a Walmart in Minneapolis.

At Walmart, Ehrenreich had to stay late (and off the books) to clean up and arrive early (off the books) to set up. Working two jobs, she could not afford rent on an apartment and ended up, as did the other women she worked with, living out of a car or in a run-down weekly rate motel, eating soup out of cans she heated on a hot plate (studies have found that even basic groceries are more expensive in poor neighborhoods [Talukdar, 2008]). Ehrenreich had to wear an adult diaper because she was not permitted to take bathroom breaks during her shift. She often relied on the kindness of strangers, as her coworkers were always offering to share what little they had. Only the working poor, she sadly concluded, actually believe in the Protestant work ethic—that if you work hard enough, you can make it in America. The middle class has long since abandoned such illusions.

"Most civilized nations," Ehrenreich concludes, "compensate for the inadequacy of wages by providing relatively generous public services such as health insurance, free or subsidized childcare, subsidized housing and effective public transportation." What, she wonders at the end of the book, does that say about us?

Cleveland, Los Angeles, and Miami. Some foreign cities, such as Toronto, Canada, have long had fair wage standards in place; in 2007, London, England, began a major living wage campaign (Jackson 2007). Although there are "living wage" ordinances nationwide, actual minimum wages are different. Often, people regard living wage ordinances as symbolic, as local governments fail to actually adjust minimum wage regularly/accordingly.

Part-Time and Contingent Work

14.2.4 Distinguish between part-time and contingent work.

Globalization has shifted much industrial production to the developing world, and many manufacturing plants in the United States and Europe have closed. Alongside this shift, displaced workers search for work in a new economic climate and much of the work available to new and seasoned employees is part-time. About 18 percent of the American workforce is employed **part-time** (fewer than 30 hours per week) (U.S. Bureau of Labor Statistics 2017). The percentage has remained fairly stable, between 17 and 20 percent, for the past 25 years. Women are currently almost twice as likely as men to work part-time (Bureau of Labor Statistics 2015). Globally, part-time workers are becoming increasingly common, ranging from slightly more than 4 percent of the workforce in Russia, Romania, and Hungary to 38.5 percent in the Netherlands. Women remain the primary part-time workers (OECD 2016).

Many people work part-time by choice because they want to attend to other commitments (part-time jobs have been traditional for high school and college students for years). However, more than a quarter of part-timers want full-time work but are prevented by the lack of suitable jobs, transportation, childcare problems, or by employers who keep them just below the 35-hour-per-week limit to avoid paying

part-time work
Form of employment that carries fewer hours than a full-time job. In the United States, part-time work is generally considered to be 30 hours per week or less.

full-time salaries and benefits. A surge in part-time employment began as a result of the weak economy: The number of Americans who saw their full-time jobs cut to part-time doubled at the onset of the Great Recession in 2008, to 3.7 million—the largest figure since the U.S. government began tracking such data more than a half-century ago (Newman and Pedulla 2010). In the United States, the vast majority of those working at or below minimum wage are part-time employees. Often, to make ends meet, they must take a part-time job in addition to a full-time job, or two or three part-time jobs.

Many employers have discovered the economic benefit of replacing permanent employees with employees hired to do a specific project or for a specific time period, or to be "on call," working only when their services are needed. As much as 40 percent of the American workforce may currently perform **contingent labor**, depending on how their "alternative work" is classified. Some work as freelancers or independent contractors; some are "on-call" workers who work only when called to work; others are limited contract workers or "temps" (General Accountability Office 2015). The ranks of temporary works have been swelling since the mid-1990s, both in the United States and globally. More than twice as many temps are employed in the United States as in any other country, but they are on the rise elsewhere, including emerging markets such as Brazil, South Africa, and Mexico (Coe, Johns, and Ward 2008; Stern 2009).

Because there is no presumption of permanent employment, employers of contingent workers in the United States are not required by law to offer retirement pensions; cost-of-living raises; paid holidays, vacations, or sick leave; or health insurance. They need not find more work for employees who have finished their duties early or pay overtime if their duties take longer than expected. They can lay off employees at any time without investing in expensive severance packages.

The characteristics of these workers vary widely. Independent contractors tend to be middle aged, white, and men, while temporary workers tend to be young, ethnic minority, and women. A large percentage of independent contractors, on-call workers, and contingency workers have white-collar jobs in management, the professions, or sales, but temporary workers are overrepresented in low-skill, low-paying jobs. The new "gig economy" seems to offer both workers and owners significant benefits. Owners enjoy the savings on health care and other benefits for workers not employed full-time, but only contingently. Workers enjoy the flexibility, the ability to set their own hours, and manage their time. Just don't get sick.

contingent labor
Provisional group of workers who work on a contract, project, or other nonpermanent basis.

The new "gig economy" offers many new benefits to employers and workers. But the flexibility often comes at a cost. For instance, Uber drivers are responsible for their own vehicles and take on the risks associated with wear, tear, and increased likelihoods of accidents and tickets. They also do not receive any additional benefits aside from wages and tips, making health care and retirement perennial issues for "gig" workers.

Unpaid Work

14.2.5 Explain why unpaid work has been present throughout history and how it is inequitably distributed in the United States.

For most of human history, all work was unpaid. People provided their own food, clothing, housing, and entertainment. For jobs that were too big for one person or household, favors could be called in from friends and family. Sometimes people bartered something they had for something they needed. With the advent of capitalism, most of the goods and services that families or groups used to provide for themselves, from clothing to entertainment to police protection, increasingly became someone's job and required pay. But we still do a tremendous amount of unpaid work.

The best example of continued unpaid work is taking care of our own household—doing the dusting, vacuuming, dishwashing, food preparation, and so on. It is denigrated as "women's work," assumed to be the domain of full-time "housewives," even though husbands, unmarried partners, relatives, and friends all sometimes stay home to take care of the household, while someone else "goes to work" to provide the financial support. Before capitalism, there was no division between work and home: Everything took place at or near home. But as the division between home and work grew, and men began to work in the public arena for wages, they began to perceive themselves as "breadwinners," solely responsible for the economic vitality of the household, for "putting food on the table."

The idea that unpaid household labor had nothing to do with "real" economy was set in stone as early as the 1920s. The ideology of **separate spheres** became implanted in the American imagination and structurally instituted as workplaces began to tear men out of the home, leaving women behind. Domestic labor lost the status of "work" and became a part of the heterosexual marital bond. Women were presumed to have found household labor similar to the work involved in wrapping a present, a "labor of love"—technically work, but worth it to please their husbands.

separate spheres

A set of beliefs that coalesced as a distinct ideology in Europe and North America during the Industrial Revolution, it assigned to women and men distinct and virtually opposite functions, duties, characteristics, and activities in society.

The Informal Economy

14.2.6 Understand what it means to suggest that the informal economy is "organized" and that it represents a significant portion of economic activity in every society.

Working for wages is not the only way that people work. In fact, much of our labor is not for wages at all. Economists have identified several "alternatives" to the wage-labor system. Many people depend on informal, under-the-table, off-the-books work for a substantial part of their income. This **informal economy** includes several types of activities. Although some people are uncomfortable thinking of crimes as drug dealing, sex work, shoplifting, gambling, car theft, and burglary as part of the underground economy, studies of arrests have found that most perpetrators think of themselves as "taking care of business." They "go to work" as deliberately as someone with an office job. They follow rules, procedures, protocols, and a code of ethics; they take occupational risks (such as being injured or going to prison). "Informal" does not mean "unorganized." Nationally and globally, billions of dollars of goods, services, and money change hands through complex networks of crime families, gangs, corrupt officials, smugglers, and money-launderers (Portes, Castells, and Benton 1989).

Illegal immigration fosters another type of informal economy. Illegal immigrants are particularly vulnerable to unscrupulous entrepreneurs who offer sweatshop working conditions at well below minimum wage. Although some manage to find white-collar jobs or are self-employed, the majority of illegal immigrants take service jobs, including maids, cooks, and groundskeepers. Indeed, unauthorized workers hold twice the percentage of service, production, and construction jobs as native-born workers do. The average income of an "undocumented family" is a little more than $30,000, well below the median income in the United States of about $54,000. Yet, collectively, unauthorized immigrant workers pay nearly $12 billion in state and local taxes (Gee, Gardner, and Wiehe 2016; Passel and Cohn 2015).

Most often, however, neither the work nor the worker is illegal; the informal economy comes into play only because the money is undeclared and therefore untaxed. A waiter receives an average of $30 in tips

informal economy

Refers to economic activities and income that are partially or fully outside government regulation, taxation, and observation.

The informal economy includes work most often paid in cash or services with no benefits and often includes workers in restaurants and bars, farm workers, housecleaners, and childcare workers.

every night, but at income tax time, he reports only his official salary, not the extra $7,500. A collector buys a vase at a garage sale for $5 and sells it on eBay for $100, pocketing the money but forgetting about it at tax time. People fix cars, do laundry, mow lawns, babysit informally for friends and neighbors, adding perhaps $60 to their pocketbooks this week and $80 next week, resulting in an extra $4,000 at the end of the year that the IRS doesn't know about.

The size of the informal economy varies among countries and regions. In many developing countries, the informal economy amounts to more than 50 percent of the gross domestic product. In India, 83 percent of workers are informal; in sub-Saharan Africa, about 76 percent are (Barta 2009). In the high-income countries of the OECD, it is about 15 percent (OECD 2008a). Every socioeconomic class participates in the informal economy, but the $95 profit that the collector made on the eBay vase is a negligible contribution to a middle-class income (and the IRS is unlikely to be terribly concerned about it). However, money earned off the books and under the table may easily double a $7.25 per hour minimum wage income. The working poor are likely to depend on the informal economy for their everyday survival; in many developing countries, the informal economy is the only safety net people have.

Unemployment

14.2.7 Distinguish among the three types of unemployment, and understand how each type puts different groups at risk.

Even when the economy is functioning as smoothly as possible, there are always some people out of work, looking for work, or unable to work. Some people work only during some times of the year and not others; others are in between jobs, looking for a new position; others cannot find work in their field or are somehow disqualified from some jobs. Social scientists typically distinguish among three different types of unemployment; the first two tend to be more temporary than the last:

1. *Seasonal unemployment* refers to the changes in demand for workers based on climate or seasonal criteria. For example, demand for agricultural labor drops dramatically after the harvest, and demand for workers in the tourist industry during "high season" for tourists.

2. *Cyclical unemployment* is a response to normal business cycles of expansion and contraction. During periods of economic expansion, demand for labor increases, and the unemployment rate goes down. But during recessions and economic downturns, demand for labor goes down.

3. *Structural unemployment* refers to more permanent conditions of the economy. In some cases, it may be caused by a mismatch—say, between the skills needed by employers and the skills possessed by workers or between the geographic locations of employment and the location of potential workers. In the 1980s and 1990s, more than 10 million American workers lost their jobs as a result of structural shifts in the economy, including the transformation of the auto and steel industries, the rise of high-technology jobs, and through the "outsourcing" of many jobs.

Countries measure unemployment by counting people who are actively looking for jobs. The **unemployment rate** takes that number as a percentage of all employable workers (that means that the unemployment rate is lower than the actual number of people who do not have jobs, as some people simply give up and don't look for jobs. Part-time workers are also not included in

During the Great Depression, millions of male breadwinners suddenly needed free coffee and doughnuts themselves, as the nation's unemployment rate hit 25 percent in 1934. During the Great Recession of 2008–2011, the unemployment rate topped 10 percent.

the unemployment rate). In 2007, the unemployment rate in the United States was 4.4 percent. By July 2009, however, it had more than doubled, to 9.5 percent. It peaked at 10 percent in December 2009, at the height of the Great Recession. The current unemployment rate is around half the rate it was at the 2009 peak.

Globally, although more people are working than ever before, so, too, are more people unemployed. The International Labor Organization (ILO) estimates that as much as 6.2 percent of the global workforce is unemployed, or an estimated 205 million people worldwide in 2010; this compares to 6.3 percent in 2009, but is still well above the rate of 5.6 percent in 2007 (The World Bank 2016).

unemployment rate

The measure of the prevalence of unemployment, it is calculated by dividing the number of unemployed individuals by all individuals currently in the labor force.

SOCIOLOGY AND OUR WORLD

THE SOCIOLOGY OF THE RECENT GLOBAL RECESSION

How did intersecting systems of inequality shape the experiences of different groups with unemployment during the recent global recession?

"In Epidemic of Layoffs, No One Is Immune," read one headline about the dramatic increase in unemployment during the current recession. Yet, when we examine economic inequality intersectionally, it becomes clear that some are more immune than others. Although the nightly news may have focused on laid-off Wall Street brokers, the national reality looks quite different. The most vulnerable employees are, it turns out, the most "vulnerable" to unemployment. The current unemployment rate for those workers older than 25 who have a bachelor's degree or more is 2.6 percent—less than half the national rate. For college-educated and white workers, the rate is 2.4 percent (Bureau of Labor Statistics 2016). But the unemployment rates vary dramatically by gender, race, and education.

In part, unemployment trends in recent U.S. history are the result of the decline of manufacturing jobs. Those jobs have seen steeper declines in recent history than have sales and service jobs. But it also indicates the sociological observation that periods of economic crisis reveal the lines of inequality already in

place and put occupational segregation in stark relief. Recovery can either remedy or reproduce these inequalities (Karabell 2009). Young people have been especially hard hit. Unemployment for people between 16 and 24 is roughly double that of all workers (if we don't take into account race; it's three to four times as high for black and Hispanic young people and three times as much for Asian American young people between ages 16 and 19), although some of those are seasonally unemployed when not in school.

Even if the rich are not getting richer, the poor are getting *much* poorer. People in developing countries are harder hit by the current downturn than those in wealthier countries. The continuing high cost of food and the dramatic drop in demand for raw materials have dramatically affected many in the developing world. Nearly three of four Mexicans say food prices have affected them "a great deal" (compared with one-third of U.S. residents and one-fourth of Canadians). And more than 9 of 10 Kenyans say they are greatly affected (BBC World Service 2009).

Unemployment Rates, 2016

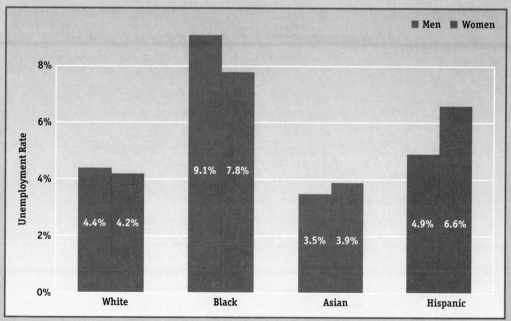

SOURCE: Data from Bureau of Labor Statistics, 2016. Available at https://www.bls.gov/cps/cpsaat03.pdf and https://www.bls.gov/web/empsit/cpsee_e16.htm.

---

iSOC AND YOU Institutionalizing Inequality at Work

What you do for work is a key component of your *identity*. In a typical workday you will *interact* with others who are in different roles and doing different things. In your experience in economic *institutions*—whether factories or offices or labs or on work sites—you will experience *inequalities* based on the kind of work you do, as well as intersecting inequalities based on other social criteria.

14.3 Workplace Identities, Interactions, and Inequalities

Workplaces have become more diverse spaces over the latter half of the twentieth century. There's no doubt about that. That means that men are more likely today to work alongside women than ever before in history. People of different races are more likely to have the same jobs than ever before too. It has not been a seamless transition. Indeed, workplaces and workplace dynamics have had to change as a result of these shifts toward increasingly diverse work settings. Because of these changes, challenges to inequality are increasingly likely to be concerned with work settings themselves—policies regarding sexual harassment, racial discrimination, and more represent some of the ways we attempt to acknowledge and challenge inequality in the workplace.

Your gender, racial, and sexual identities shape your workplace interactions in ways you might not assume—both in terms of the work expected of you and the work from which you are excused. In this section, we examine the ways that increases in workplace diversity are associated with a move toward workplace equality, but have also been associated with new forms of workplace inequality as well. We will examine wage gaps, job discrimination, and segregation, and explain how sociologists have discovered that the new forms of workplace inequality are sometimes difficult to identify, necessitating new language to help us examine taken-for-granted workplace realities that distribute workplace obligations and opportunities inequitably across groups. This research helps us better understand the realities of inequality in the workplace today.

Workplace Diversity

14.3.1 Explain why increased workplace diversity has not necessarily led to workplace equality.

Domestic comedy movies from the 1950s often began at a suburban train station, where a crowd of white middle-class men, all dressed in identical gray suits, prepared for their work day in the big city. And, in fact, the middle-class work world in 1950 was nearly that homogeneous. In 1950, white men occupied more than 90 percent of white-collar jobs in the United States. More recently, men's share of managerial positions has shrunk to 61 percent (Bureau of Labor Statistics 2016). Women and ethnic minorities have been steadily catching up. As we learned in Chapter 8, during the next 50 years, the numbers of Hispanics and Asian Americans in the United States will triple, whereas the white non-Hispanic population will increase a mere seven percent. The United States will become a "majority minority" nation, with more than half the population belonging to ethnic minority groups. This shift will necessarily produce a corresponding increase in racial diversity in the workforce (see FIGURE 14.3). Coupled with increases in women's workforce participation, this means that white men may soon become a minority in the workplace.

This means that the workforce will become more diverse for more people. Certainly, occupational segregation and discrimination will continue to produce different workplace realities for different groups. But that scene from 1950s movies is a scene of the past. Getting to work means going out into that diversity. Behind this increasingly diverse workplace, however, is a larger reality of economic inequality in which the earnings gaps between the have and the have nots are growing, and this growth will continue to produce class-based segregation, even as other kinds of segregation are challenged. Consider the subway system in New York City. Along each subway line, earnings can range from poverty to a great deal of wealth. And this range means that subway cars may be filled with people from across the class divide as they proceed down the line, but the stops the rich and poor get on and off at may overlap less than you'd think.

As the composition of the U.S. workforce becomes increasingly racially diverse, so too will many U.S. workplaces. Yet, sociologists are also concerned with studying the ways that gender and racial segregation and discrimination in the workplace often work to resituate socially dominant groups in positions of wealth, power, and authority.

Racial Diversity

14.3.2 Understand the meaning of tokenism and how it operates in workplaces.

Higher representation does not necessarily result in equality in the workplace. The salaries of people of color consistently lag behind those of white men, for instance. For every dollar that white men earn, black and Hispanic men earn 65 cents, black women 58 cents, and Hispanic women 48 cents. Two problems are becoming increasingly common in the racially diverse workforce—*tokenism* and the *glass ceiling*.

When only a few members of a minority group occupy a job, they often believe (and are treated as if) they were hired as **tokens**, as representatives of their group rather than individuals. They are hypervisible—everything they say or do is taken as what group members *always* say or do. If they get angry, for instance, their coworkers will conclude that everyone in the group gets angry easily. Their failures will be taken as evidence that the group as a whole is incompetent. Under constant pressure to reflect well on their group, tokens must be on guard at all times. Indeed, research has shown that tokens must consistently outperform their coworkers just to be perceived as equal (Moss-Kanter 1977; Yoder 1991).

Think about a time when you were the only member of some group in a larger group. You could have been the only woman or man, white person or person of color, straight or gay or bisexual, old or young, Christian, Muslim, or Jew—whatever set you apart. Let's say you were the only Latino. At some point, someone turns to you, innocently enough, and asks, "Well, how do Latinos feel about this?" At that moment, you become invisible as an individual, but you are hypervisible only as a member of the group. Of course, the only sensible answer is, "How should I know? I'm just an individual. I can only answer for myself. But I bet there are sociologists who have surveyed Latinos, and we can find out what most of them think about the question."

And while workplaces are becoming more diverse, it is also the case that as you climb workplace hierarchies, that diversity slows down. It is for this reason that scholars sometimes refer to the **glass ceiling** in workplaces—an invisible barrier that seems to continue to protect the positions at the upper echelons of the workplace for men, and often, straight white men. Hillary Clinton routinely said she was at work "cracking the highest glass ceiling in America" while campaigning for president in 2016. And the women most likely to break through are most often privileged on the basis of race (see FIGURE 14.4). We address this more next.

token

Representative of a traditionally disenfranchised group whose hypervisibility results in constant pressure to reflect well on his or her group and to outperform co-workers just to be perceived as equal.

glass ceiling

An unofficially acknowledged barrier to advancement in a profession, especially affecting women and members of minorities.

FIGURE 14.4 Proportion of *Standard & Poor*'s 500 Board Seats Held by Women, by Race, 2014

Men still occupy the vast majority of board seats for the most powerful companies (more than 80 percent). And though women have broken through this glass ceiling, white women have been much more likely to make this transition than have women of color. Of the 19.2 percent of S&P 500 board seats occupied by women, more than 80 percent of them are occupied by white women. Yet, as we climb higher, the proportion of women drops dramatically. For instance, although women occupy almost 1 in 5 board seats at S&P 500 companies, they occupy fewer than 1 in 20 CEO positions at those same companies.

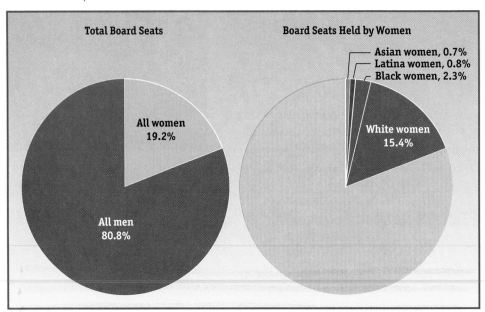

SOURCE: Data from Catalyst, "Statistical Overview of Women in the Workforce." Available at http://www.catalyst.org/knowledge/statistical-overview-women-workforce.

Gender Diversity: Wage Inequality

14.3.3 Summarize what the gender pay gap is and how it has changed over time.

In 1900, less than 20 percent of American women (age 15 and older) worked outside the home. Today more than half do, and the percentage is increasing worldwide. And women's employment is highest in poor countries, where everyone who can work does. Over the second half of the twentieth century, the U.S. workforce has quite literally transformed. Some of the largest transformations have to do with gender. In 1950, of the almost 60 million people working in the United States, less than one in three was a woman. Two things have changed today: The workforce has expanded considerably and women comprise a much larger proportion of workers. Some of this change has been brought on by a move toward gender equality; but the majority of this change is the result of economic shifts—structural transformations that have caused people to have to adapt to keep up with a changing society. Consider FIGURE 14.5.

The increase in the number of women in the workforce during the past 50 years has been called **the quiet revolution** because its consequences have been gradual but wide-ranging—a transformation of consumer patterns, workplace policies, dating and relationship norms, parenting practices, household maintenance, and self-concepts for both men and women. But that transformation is incomplete. Men and women are still not equal, either in the workplace or at home. Indeed, just because women and men are working in more equal numbers today does not spell workplace equality.

You may have heard of the **gender wage gap**—the difference in the amounts of wages provided to women and men for performing the same work with comparable sets of credentials. You may already know that women earn less than men. As of 2014, women employed in full-time jobs earned a median weekly income of $719; the median income for men working full-time was $817. Women's median earnings were approximately 83 percent of men's in 2014. As you can see in FIGURE 14.6, this is a

the quiet revolution
Gradual but wide-sweeping changes that have resulted from the increase in the number of women in the workforce during the past 50 years, transforming consumer patterns, workplace policies, dating and relationship norms, parenting practices, household maintenance, and self-concepts for both men and women.

gender wage gap
The consistent, worldwide difference between what men are paid and what women are paid for the same labor.

FIGURE 14.5 Number of U.S. Workers and Proportions of Men and Women, 1948–2016

From this figure, you can see two things: There are a lot more people working in the United States today than there were a half-century ago and the proportion of those people who are women have been steadily increasing that entire time.

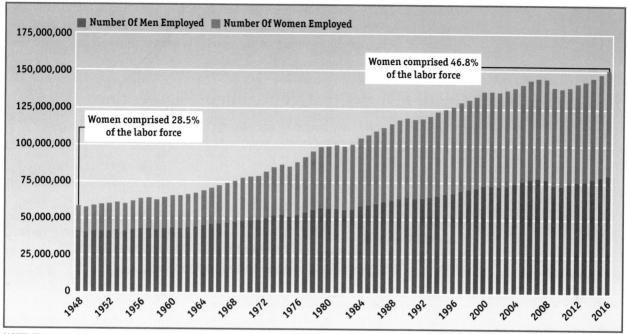

NOTE: These numbers reflect annual averages for employment status of the civilian noninstitutional population, 16 years and older.

SOURCE: Data from U.S. Bureau of Labor Statistics, Current Population Survey.

big increase from the first year the Census has data allowing a comparison of men's and women's income—in 1979, women's median income was 62 percent of men's. But, you may also notice that the rate of change has slowed. The gap is noticeable across all racial divisions, although it is smaller for blacks and Hispanics than for whites and Asians. The gap varies considerably by geographic location and by age; it is much smaller among young workers (25 to 34) than middle-aged and older ones.

FIGURE 14.6 Median Annual Earnings by Gender, 1960–2014

Overall, the gender pay gap has decreased over the last half century. But, you may also notice here that changes in the gender wage gap seemed to stall out at the end of the 1980s. It is also important to understand that the pay gap varies extensively by race as well.

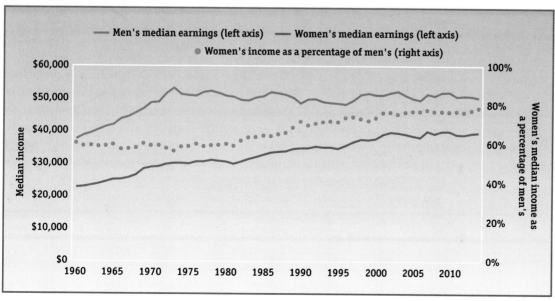

NOTE: All figures are expressed in 2014 dollars.

SOURCE: Data from U.S. Census Bureau, Current Population Survey, Annual Social and Economic Supplements.

As you can see, once we begin to examine intersections between gender and other identities, the pay gap can change dramatically. For instance, the pay gap between white men and black women is much larger than the gap between white men and white women. This does not mean the gender pay gap is not meaningful. What it does mean is that gender is only one way to measure pay inequality. And, as much as one variable can explain anything in social life, gender is among the most important variables to consider when looking at pay inequality.

Gender Diversity: Occupational Segregation

14.3.4 Understand how occupational segregation contributes to the unequal distribution of status and economic rewards associated with different kinds of work.

One of the largest reasons that the gender pay gap is reproduced is that it is actually harder to recognize than you might think. For a variety of reasons, directly comparing women and men in the workplace is more challenging than you might assume. And chief among those is that, although similar numbers of women and men are leaving for work every day, they are not headed to the same places—not exactly anyway. Sociologists refer to this phenomenon as **occupational sex segregation**.

occupational sex segregation

Refers to women's and men's different concentrations in different occupations, different industries, different jobs, and different levels in a workplace hierarchy.

Consider the following fact. There are more than 500 separate occupational categories listed on the U.S. Census—the categories we use to tell the Census what kind of work we do. Of those more than 500 occupations, about one-third of the more than 70 million women in the U.S. workforce can be accounted for by only 10 of those occupations (these are the jobs referred to as "pink collar work"). You can probably guess many of the occupations on that list—among them are: secretaries and administrative assistants, primary and middle school teachers, nurses, retail sales workers, customer service representatives, and cashiers. About half the world's workers are in sex-segregated occupations. In the United States, men comprise 98 percent of construction workers and 97 percent of airline pilots, for instance, whereas women comprise 76 percent of cashiers and 75 percent of clerical workers. Although the overall sex segregation declined significantly in the 1970s, there is evidence of a recent slowdown and resegregation of jobs within broad occupations (Charles and Grusky 2004; Padavic and Reskin 1994/2002).

Occupational segregation is one reason that makes giving an overall number to represent the gender wage gap challenging. So, sociologists are also interested in examining the gender wage gaps of different kinds of occupations to see where pay gaps are the largest and smallest. For instance, those jobs with some of the highest average incomes also have among the highest gender wage gaps. In 2014, women CEOs earned only 70 percent of what CEOs who happened to be men earned (U.S. Department of Labor, Bureau of Labor Statistics 2016). These are also jobs that are heavily dominated by men—only 4.1 percent of CEOs for major S&P 1500 companies are women. In fact, there are more CEOs for S&P 1500 companies whose first name is "John" than there are women CEOs at all (Wolfers 2015). Among physicians and surgeons, women earned only 62 percent of what men earned in 2014 (Bureau of Labor Statistics 2016). Women who enter occupations dominated by men tend to receive less money and are often segregated within those professions as well (among physicians, pediatrics is one example).

Sometimes this is referred to as the glass ceiling. Although women have been making small gains consistently for half a century, white men still control nearly all of the top jobs in corporate America. Women comprise more than half of all managers and professionals but less than 16 percent of the *Fortune 500* corporate officers, only about 6 percent of the top earners, and only 3 percent of the CEOs (Catalyst 2009; Jones 2009). Women of color fare worse: They comprise only one corporate officer of every 100 (Catalyst 2003) (see FIGURE 14.4). And women at the top are paid less, too. A 2008 study of more than 3,200 companies in North America found women CEOs earn 15 percent less than men

FIGURE 14.7 Women as a Proportion of Different Economic Sectors, 1972–2017
Occupational segregation by gender can be seen simply by looking at the proportions of women and men working in different economic sectors. And here you can see how this has shifted over time. In fact, a great deal of the economic growth over the last 50 years in the United States has been in economic sectors that either were or are becoming more dominated by women (education and health services, for instance, or professional and business services). Economic sectors that were dominated by men 50 years ago and continue to be today are associated with jobs that are in increasingly short supply (like manufacturing and construction).

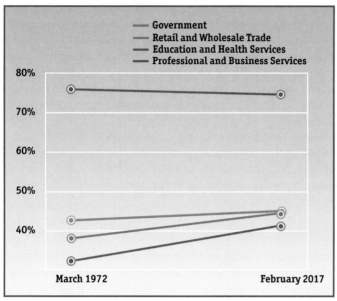

SOURCE: Data from Bureau of Labor Statistics.

in the same jobs (Jones 2009). The Glass Ceiling Commission observes: "The world at the top of the corporate hierarchy does not yet look anything like America." Men, however, don't have quite the same experience when they participate in jobs dominated by women. Sociologist Christine Williams (1992) showed that men doing "women's work" receive more, on average, than do the women doing that work—a phenomenon she refers to as the **glass escalator**. Subsequent scholarship suggests that this advantage seems to be primarily experienced by white men (Wingfield 2009).

Gender inequality in the workplace looks different today not only because of occupational segregation. It is also as a result of the transformations in the U.S. economy more generally. Economic sectors historically dominated by men have, on average, shrunk in recent history. There are fewer of those jobs than there used to be. Meanwhile, sectors dominated by women have grown quite a bit. Consider FIGURE 14.7.

Manufacturing has been declining in the United States throughout the latter half of the twentieth century and into the twenty-first. Meanwhile, jobs requiring more education have increased. And a great deal of those require service and care work. Men continue to dominate some of the smaller sectors of the economy; but those that have seen the most growth are jobs in which women and men work together in roughly equal numbers or pink-collar industries in which women dramatically outnumber men.

glass escalator
Christine Williams's phrase for her research finding that men doing "women's work" receive more, on average, than do the women doing that work.

Gender and Work–Family Dynamics

14.3.5 Understand how work–family balance dilemmas are experienced in gender-specific ways that work to women's collective disadvantage in the workplace.

Our family lives also reinforce workplace gender inequality. Beginning in 2002, for the first time, the majority (51 percent) of married male–female couples in the United States were dual income (perhaps not surprisingly because the middle-class lifestyle that used to be feasible on one income now takes two). As women break into the ranks

HOW DO WE KNOW WHAT WE KNOW?

WORKPLACE DISCRIMINATION

Although new laws and regulations try to reduce the amount of workplace discrimination based on gender or sexuality, old stereotypes persist, keeping economic gender or sexual equality elusive. One way to see these dynamics is to observe what happens when people—not their workplaces—change. In a fascinating study, sociologist Kristen Schilt and economist Matthew Wiswall examined earnings records of recent male-to-female and female-to-male transgender people. Because they are really still the same people, their experiences reveal something about gender dynamics in the workplace.

Schilt and Wiswall found that average earnings for female-to-male employees increased slightly following their sexual reassignment surgery, but the wages of male-to-female transgender people fell by nearly one-third! Becoming socially recognized as a woman led several transgender women to lose authority and prestige as well as wages—along with increased harassment and often termination. On the other hand, becoming socially recognized as a man brought a slight increase in respect and authority (Schilt and Wiswall 2008).

Transgender employees offer an important illustration of gender inequality in the workplace, particularly when we examine the ways they receive different treatment as they go from being socially recognized as being one gender to becoming seen to be another. Their experiences help sociologists studying gender inequality in the workplace to examine forms of inequality that cisgender persons might take for granted or not recognize as inequality.

of the top earners, salary differences sometimes upset the traditional designation of the men as "breadwinners" among heterosexual couples. Indeed, 29 percent of women in dual-wage households earn *more* than their husbands (Chalabi 2015). Though, among heterosexual couples in which wives out-earn their husbands, the average is to bring in two-thirds of the family income; among husbands who out-earn their wives bring in, on average, more than four-fifths of the household income.

However, household maintenance is still widely assumed to be a woman's job. A Western woman spends an average of 10 hours per week on household maintenance and a man about 5 hours. Sociologists have found that living arrangements don't change the average much: Two women living together will still spend about the same amount of time, as will two men. When men and women marry, the woman will perform 50 percent more housework than the man, even if they are both working full-time outside the home (Couprie 2007). Once children arrive, the gap actually grows. American mothers do three times as much housework as men, spending 17 hours a week on average, while fathers spend just 6 (Seward et al. 2006).

The United States ranks below a number of wealthy nations in the percentage of mothers in the labor force, with 70 percent of all mothers of children younger than 18 in the workforce (U.S. Bureau of Labor Statistics 2015). In other nations, the percentage ranges from 83 percent (Sweden) to 30 percent (Turkey). For many years, working mothers have been struggling to make corporate culture see children not as "problems" or distractions but as part of "business as usual." Yet, research has consistently documented a **motherhood penalty** by which women receive a host of consequences in the workplace for being parents. For instance, working mothers are perceived as less competent and are offered lower starting salaries than are women without children. Men, conversely, do not face these workplace penalties associated with parenthood; indeed, some work finds that men receive workplace benefits (Correll, Benard, and Paik 2007). Research continues to find that this and other forms of **workplace discrimination** continue to put socially marginalized groups at a disadvantage in the workplace.

As parents, mothers often want more flexibility in their hours and in their career paths, more options, updated criteria for success. Recently some men have joined them, reframing the issue from "women's right to work" to "parenting and the workplace." Employers could benefit significantly from accommodating working parents of either sex. The skills one learns from parenting, including communication, emotional

motherhood penalty

In the workplace, mothers encounter systematic disadvantages in pay, perceived competence, and benefits relative to childless women.

workplace discrimination

A form of discrimination based on race, gender, religion, national origin, physical or mental disability, and age by employers.

availability, multitasking, efficient organization, and patience, are valuable in the twenty-first-century workplace (Crittenden 2005). Levine (1997) found that "working fathers," or fathers heavily invested in their children's daily lives, perform better and are more comfortable in a diverse workplace than the traditional "breadwinners."

Emotional and Aesthetic Labor and Inequality

14.3.6 Distinguish between emotional and aesthetic labor, and understand how this work disproportionately impacts the work lives of women and people of color.

Workplaces have always been complete with occupational requirements that might not necessarily have been listed on the job advertisement, but are nevertheless central requirements associated with the job. **Emotional labor** refers to the process of managing your feelings and emotional expressions as a part of your job. If you have ever held a position in the service industry, this is a form of work you are familiar with—whether you recognized it as work or not. Emotional labor can take two general forms: expressing an emotion you may not actually feel or suppressing an emotion you may strongly feel.

Sociologist Arlie Hochschild (1983) coined the term *emotional labor* in a study on flight attendants—an industry dominated by women. Hochschild not only talked with flight attendants, but also observed their required education at training programs. Formally, the job of a flight attendant is to maintain passenger compliance and order throughout the flight, and to help save passengers' lives in the event of a crash or malfunction. But a big part of their job that Hochschild was interested in had nothing to do with these formal qualities associated with their work. She wanted to know more about the obligations associated with flight attendants' emotional management during work. Flight attendants are expected to manage their emotions according to a set of demands placed on them by their employers. Because women are disproportionately in field associated with service and **care work**, they are also much more likely to have to endure the costs associated with emotional labor as well. Consider this excerpt from Hochschild's book, *The Managed Heart: Commercialization of Human Feeling* (1983):

> The young trainee sitting next to me wrote on her notepad, "Important to smile. Don't forget smile." The admonition came from the speaker in the front of the room, a crewcut pilot in his early fifties, speaking in a Southern drawl. "Now girls, I want you to go out there and really *smile*. Your smile is your biggest *asset*. I want you to go out there and use it. *Really* smile. Really *lay it on*."

Smiling isn't something that was suggested to flight attendants in their training. It's a workplace obligation. The services flight attendants were trained to provide in flight were not all the work they were being asked to perform. As Hochschild put it, "the emotional style of offering the service is part of the service itself." Although not everyone loves their job, flight attendants were quite literally being asked to appear as though they do whatever their actual feelings. And Hochschild was interested in examining what kinds of different **feeling rules** different kinds of jobs require. This can be an awkward experience, and Hochschild discovered that emotional labor was an underacknowledged form of workplace inequality that disproportionately affected women's work lives.

Similarly, sociologists have subsequently examined a separate kind of work based on appearance norms associated with different jobs—**aesthetic labor**. Although emotional labor is concerned with workplace demands on how employees *feel*, aesthetic labor helps us examine demands on the ways employees *look* and *act*. For instance, Christine Williams and Catherine Connell (2010) interviewed employees in retail positions with low pay and no benefits. They were interested in examining the types of labor practices that might attract middle-class workers to what are, objectively speaking, relatively "bad" jobs. Drawn to these jobs by discounts on brands they already like, upscale retail stores attract employees that embody the "look" and "feel" they

emotional labor
Arlie Hochschild's phrase for the process by which workers are expected to manage their feelings in accordance with organizationally defined rules and guidelines.

care work
All tasks that directly involve care processes done in service of others.

feeling rules
Arlie Hochschild's term for socially shared norms that influence how people should demonstrate how they feel in different settings.

aesthetic labor
Christine Williams and Catherine Connell's term for employment practices designed to attract middle-class workers to relatively poor, low-wage retail jobs by attempting to attract employees who embody the look and feel they are attempting to sell without necessarily appearing to do so.

SOCIOLOGY AND OUR WORLD

ARE SOME EMOTIONS OFF LIMITS FOR NON-WHITE EMPLOYEES?

How do feeling rules work in ways that produce gendered and racialized experiences of inequality in the workplace?

The majority of research on emotional labor has examined the ways that it reproduces gender inequality in the workplace. But diversity in the workplace is not only measured along gender lines. Less research considers whether racial minorities have demands on their emotional labor that differ in any way from white employees. Sociologist Adia Harvey Wingfield (2010) conducted an interview study with black professionals to study this issue in more detail. She discovered that feeling rules in the workplace are not only gendered, but are also racialized, imposing additional restrictions and obligations on black employees.

Although all employees are expected to control their emotional outbursts in the workplace, Wingfield discovered that this expectation seemed acutely felt by black professionals. The black professionals in Wingfield's study felt obligated to express pleasantness beyond what they felt was required of their white colleagues. But, more than that, they also discussed the need to conceal irritation and anger in ways not required of the white people they worked alongside. As one of her interviewees put it, "It's more how they [whites] express those emotions. I couldn't yell at people. I would have some kind of note in my file, but I have seen how white folks get away with that stuff. And nobody says anything!"

Sadly, although the black professionals in Wingfield's recognized this as a form of workplace inequality, they also expressed subtle pressures to keep quiet. This suggests that when we consider emotional labor, we need to do so intersectionally to understand that different groups and subsets of groups experience distinct emotional obligations that create very different workplace experiences.

are attempting to sell without necessarily appearing to do so. This aesthetic labor demanded in these jobs was premised on social inequality and often meant that young, conventionally gendered, thin or "fit" bodied, white men and women were more likely to both seek out these jobs and acquire them. As Williams and Connell write, "Aesthetic labor offers a justification for employment discrimination that blames the worker, and not the employer, for sorting workers on the basis of gender, race, and class" (2010: 372).

Sexual Diversity

14.3.7 Explain some of the ways lesbian and gay employees are disadvantaged in the workplace as a result of their sexuality.

family wage

Arising in the nineteenth century, the term refers to a wage sufficient for a single wage earner to support a family (spouse and children).

lavender ceiling

Refers to workplace discrimination that hampers or prevents LGBTQ people from being promoted.

The workplace originated in a heterosexual division of labor: the male husband/father/breadwinner and the female wife/mother/domestic worker. Early decisions about wages and benefits assumed a single breadwinner for the entire family—and assumed that he was not only male but heterosexual. This is why the pay offered to men was referred to as a **family wage**. Many companies continue to assume that all of their employees, stockholders, and customers are heterosexual. There are no federal regulations barring discrimination on the basis of sexual orientation, so employers can refuse to hire gay men and lesbians or fire them at any time. As a result, most gay or lesbian employees must pretend that they are heterosexual, but even those who are out tend to bump up against what is sometimes called the **lavender ceiling**.

Corporate culture is built around the assumption of heterosexuality, with conversations and jokes from the boardroom down to the loading dock focused on husbands and wives, other-sex boyfriends and girlfriends, and the attractiveness of various movie stars. Employees who refuse to participate are perceived as cool, distant, and snobbish, not "team players." Employees who mention same-sex partners, interests, and experiences are perceived as "problems." As a result, they are more easily passed over at promotion time. Despite the stereotype that all gay men are sophisticated interior designers living in Manhattan high-rise apartments, for example, gay and lesbian salaries lag behind those of heterosexual workers (Raeburn 2004).

Some changes have occurred recently. For instance, more than half of all *Fortune 500* companies offer benefits for same-sex partners, and more than 400 include sexual orientation in their nondiscrimination policies. Yet, only a handful of CEOs are openly gay or lesbian (Petroff 2014).

SOCIOLOGY AND OUR WORLD

DO YOU HAVE A "GAY" RESUME?

Are job applicants who are LGBTQ discriminated against for having resumes that "out" them?

As you already read in Chapter 8, research has consistently shown that job applicants with "white-sounding" names are much more likely to receive interviews and job opportunities than are applicants with "black-sounding" names (Bertrand and Mullainathan 2004; Pager 2003). Sociologist Emma Mishel (2016) was interested in whether sexuality might also produce job discrimination in the application process. Although previous work has indicated race on applications by varying names (Jamal versus James, for instance), Mishel wanted to find a similar way to indicate sexuality.

For this experiment, Mishel sent out women's resumes to more than 800 jobs in four states dominated by women (administrative work, clerical and secretarial positions). She sent two fictitious resumes to each position. The two resumes were generally comparable, aside from one small detail related to work experience on each. Both women listed work experience as a secretary for a university organization. But, one resume listed the university's lesbian, gay, bisexual, and transgender (LGBT) organization as her administrative experience, whereas the other listed administrative experience in a non-LGBT (but similarly progressive) university organization. She wanted to know whether this small detail might affect the likelihood that either of the women were contacted for follow-up interviews.

The resumes that listed an LGBT organization as administrative experience received approximately 30 percent fewer callbacks than did the resumes with non-LGBT administrative experience. Although Mishel found some regional variation based on where different jobs were located, her finding was consistent throughout the sample of jobs that received the resumes. This one small detail made potentially LGBT women applicants almost one-third less likely to be pursued for a position. This finding does not even begin to address pay inequities in the workplace. Rather, Mishel is interested in whether queer women are less likely to even get a job to begin with.

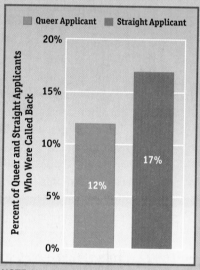

NOTE: N=1,550. Difference between the two callback rates is statistically significant at p<0.01.

SOURCE: Data from Mischel, Emma. "Discrimination against Queer-Perceived Women." *Contexts* blog. February 22, 2016. Available at: https://contexts.org/blog/discrimination-against-queer-perceived-women/.

---

iSOC AND YOU Workplace Identities, Interactions, and Inequalities
The workplace is both a source of *inequality* (class) and an expression of inequality. And your social *identity*—race gender, sexuality, age, etc.—plays a critical role in how you interact with the workplace as a social *institution*. Your identities shape what kinds of work you do, but also shape your experience in those jobs in ways that reproduce existing lines of *inequality* in society. Your *interactions* with others within economic *institutions* are patterned by these other sources of *identity* and inequality. And they all *intersect* in ways that often emphasize some forms of inequality and mute others.

Conclusion

Work and Economy NOW

The workplace as we know it today was created by the needs of an industrial economy. But now we are moving into a postindustrial, knowledge-based economy. The stereotypic office workplace, 9 to 5 workday, and single-field career are all fast becoming obsolete for the vast majority of Americans. What sorts of new arrangements will arise to take their place? Today, only a small percentage of workers will perform a single job throughout their lives, changing only to move up to positions of greater authority (such as teachers becoming principals). Instead, they will develop a portfolio of skills and credentials that they will use to move horizontally, between jobs in many different career fields. Sometimes they will even occupy different jobs simultaneously.

The increased flexibility means that workers will have more control over their work and more creativity. However, they will have no job security because employers will be able to hire and fire them at will. And productivity will suffer because training and recruitment will be never ending: Workers will devote more time and energy to learning new skills and finding work than actually *doing* work.

In the future, we'll be more mobile. At present, such mobility is an option only for white-collar workers; the blue and pink collars are left behind. Also, it is unclear what benefits the white-collar employees will receive as mobility becomes more common. Greater flexibility, perhaps? More creativity? Greater autonomy? They will be working and playing at the same moment, answering personal and professional e-mails, watching movies while checking figures, surfing the Web while videoconferencing. Does this blurred boundary between work and leisure increase the quality of either? Or does it eat into private lives, cause higher stress, and create an army of slaves to e-mail?

And what will be the shape of the new economy as the world emerges from the current recession? Will the gap between rich and poor countries close significantly, or will it continue to widen? The global boom of the 1990s and early 2000s benefited the wealthy and the super-wealthy and actually left those below the top 10 percent in worse economic shape than they had been in the 1980s. In a lighter moment, former President George W. Bush addressed his constituency as "the haves and the have-mores." But what about the swelling ranks of the "have-nots"? Will they have had enough and rebel, or will they find relatively comfortable places at the economic table?

In the future, will we be working more and enjoying it less, or working less and enjoying it more? Will the economy be the engine of spectacular wealth or grinding poverty? To the sociologist, the answer is both. It will depend on whom you talk to, where they live, and what they do for a living.

CHAPTER REVIEW Economy and Work

14.1 Economy and Society

The economy of the society in which you live shapes more of your life than you may realize. Economies shaped who we understand ourselves to be and provide a structure within which social inequality affects different groups in different ways. As a social institution, the economy is among the most all-encompassing in society. When economies shift and transform, so too do societies and the lives of everyone living in them. Economy is vital to society, managing and distributing capital. Whether we view people as self-interested rationalists in competition, as did John Locke and Thomas Hobbes, or idealist and cooperative, as did Adam Smith, or some split between the two, as did Karl Marx, we are, as Émile Durkheim observed, interdependent, relying on one another for goods and services that we cannot provide on our own. Economies unify us through connections, even as they are sources of identity that divide us through inequality. Economies began with agriculture, resulting in stability and surplus, leading to exchange in a market. The Industrial Revolution led to dramatic changes to society in an industrial economy, where work became wage labor for specialized jobs outside the home in centralized locations with powered machinery. With increasing efficiency, economic emphasis moved from production to consumption, and ultimately consumerism and conspicuous consumption. Our postindustrial economy is a knowledge economy, as the nature of work has changed, with global production, global distribution, and outsourcing. Less developed countries do the less-skilled work, while developed nations join the managerial elite for whom work is no longer dictated by time or place. Each society has an economic system, which may include capitalism, which is dominant in the West and compatible with many political systems, such as socialism, communism, or some variation.

14.1 Key Terms

economy A set of institutions and relationships that manage capital.

capital Natural resources, manufactured goods, and professional services.

organic solidarity Émile Durkheim's argument that, in modern societies, we are all interdependent; thus, economies are not an isolating, divisive force, but a unifying force that foster strong social ties and create social cohesion through networks of mutual interdependence.

social stratification Taken from the geological term for layers of rock, or "strata," the ranking of people into defined layers. Social stratification exists in all societies and is based on things like wealth, race, and gender.

Agricultural Revolution The transition from a society dependent on hunting and gathering for food to one that maintains a diet cultivated through farming.

division of labor The assignment of different tasks to different people to improve efficiency in production.

markets The regular exchange of goods and services within an economy.

Industrial Revolution The rapid development of industry that occurred in numerous countries in the eighteenth and nineteenth centuries reorganized the production and distribution of goods from the quaint system of craft production, in which apprentices learned trades and entered craft guilds, to large-scale factory production in which only the very few owned the factories and many workers had only their ability to work to sell to the highest bidder.

industrial economy Economy based on factory production and technologies.

production The creation of value or wealth by producing goods and services.

consumption The purchase and use of goods and services.

conspicuous consumption Thorstein Veblen's term to describe a new form of prestige based on accumulating and displaying possessions.

consumer economy An economy driven by consumer spending.

knowledge work One defining element of the postindustrial economy; it is work that produces ideas and information as a new form of capital.

rootlessness The experience of having few or no ties and no real place in society, often as the result of economic and/or social change.

knowledge economy An economy oriented around knowledge, and the quantity, quality, and accessibility of information, rather than on the production of commodities.

postindustrial economy An economy that shifts from the production of goods to the production of ideas.

globalization A set of processes leading to the development of patterns of economic, cultural, and social relationships that transcend geographical boundaries; a widening, deepening, and speeding up of worldwide interconnectedness in all aspects of contemporary life.

global production A term that describes how, in a global economy, goods are manufactured from raw materials and produced in factories all over the world in complex production chains and international labor forces.

global distribution A term that describes how the products we buy are likely made of materials from several countries, assembled in another country, packaged and distributed from yet another, with advertising campaigns and marketing schemes drawn from yet another.

outsourcing Also called *offshoring*, it refers to the practice of contracting out any phase(s) of product development that had once been done internally to lower-wage countries or groups.

income distribution How a nation's income is distributed among the population—within each individual nation, of the level of economic stratification in different societies. What it does is give us a better understanding of where economic growth is occurring.

gross domestic product The total value of goods produced and services provided in a country during one year.

economic system A mechanism that deals with the production, distribution, and consumption of goods and services in a particular society.

capitalism An economic system in which free individuals pursue their own private interests in the marketplace. In laissez-faire capitalism, markets freely compete without government intervention. State capitalism requires that the government use a heavy hand in regulating and constraining the marketplace, and welfare capitalism creates a market-based economy for most goods and services, yet also has social welfare programs and government ownership of essential services.

laissez-faire capitalism The original form of capitalism, theorized by Adam Smith, "laissez-faire" means "to leave alone" in French; under this system, governments would leave the marketplace alone to organize the economy, without government interference. (Smith believed that there were natural limits to people's greed.) Markets should be able to compete freely to sell goods, acquire raw materials, and hire labor. No government interference is necessary: The "invisible hand" of supply and demand creates a self-regulating economy.

state capitalism A version of capitalism that requires that the government use a heavy hand in regulating and constraining the marketplace.

welfare capitalism A version of capitalism in most contemporary capitalist countries, it is concerned with the welfare of the worker as well as profits and includes such policies as collective bargaining and industrial safety codes while the government regulates some of the most essential services, such as transportation, health care, and the mass media.

bourgeoisie Popularized by Karl Marx, term for the upperclass capitalists who owned the means of production. In Marx's time, they owned factories instead of farms. Today the term is also used to refer to upper-class managers who wield a lot of power.

proletariat Popularized by Karl Marx, the term for the lower classes who were forced to become wage laborers or go hungry. Today, the term is often used to refer to the working class.

socialism Economic system in which people are meant to cooperate rather than compete, share goods and services, own property collectively, and make decisions as a collective body.

communism Envisioned as the ideal economic system by Karl Marx, communism would produce and distribute resources "from each according to his or her ability, to each according to his or her need," erasing social inequalities along with crime, hunger, and political strife.

14.2 Institutionalizing Inequality at Work

Traditionally people worked as long as there was daylight. In the modern age, that workday has shortened, but Americans work longer hours than other developed nations. Research and theories abound addressing why we work and what makes us work harder, including the Hawthorne Effect, Theory X and Theory Y, and manufactured consent, which considers how workers are bound to the company through values and emotion and strive to maximize productivity. White-collar workers do knowledge work, and higher education is required; professions are the most prestigious knowledge jobs. Blue-collar production jobs are male dominated, whereas pink-collar jobs, including clerical positions, are female dominated, with less pay and prestige. A new category of advanced manufacturing jobs, called "green-collar," has emerged

in industries involved with new and renewable energy. Service jobs include many of the lowest paid, least prestigious occupations, and the ones with fewest—if any—health and retirement benefits. Women hold the majority of these jobs. Minimum wages are not enough to live on, and the working poor suffer enormous hardship. Some places have mandated a higher "living wage" instead. The ranks of part-time and contingent "on-call" workers have been swelling since the mid-1990s; these workers include temps, as well as unemployed seasonal workers and workers experiencing cyclical unemployment. Unpaid work includes household labor, which historically is not recognized because it was assumed that men supported their wives, who worked for love. The working poor often rely on working off the books in the underground or informal economy. Globally, although more people are working than ever before, so, too, are more people unemployed. Both nationally and globally, some workers are more vulnerable to layoffs and unemployment than others.

14.2 Key Terms

Hawthorne effect The alteration of behavior by the subjects of a study because of their awareness of being observed.

manufacture consent The production of values and emotions (in addition to the actual things they produce) that bind workers to their company.

white-collar work Knowledge-based work, requiring considerable education, in which a typical day is spent manipulating symbols: talking, speaking, reading, writing, and calculating.

blue-collar work Jobs involved with production rather than knowledge.

pink-collar work Louise Kay Howe's coinage for types of employment traditionally held by women, especially in relatively low pay service positions, such as secretarial, sales clerks, and wait staff.

service work A growing sector of work in the United States, this category includes food preparation and service, personal services (hair stylists, launderers, childcare workers), and maintenance workers (janitors, garbage collectors), plus police officers and firefighters.

green-collar work A new category of advanced manufacturing jobs, it denotes work involved in environmental and renewable energy industries.

minimum wage The lowest wage permitted by law.

working poor Working people whose income nevertheless falls below the poverty line.

living wage A minimum income necessary for a worker to meet his or her basic needs.

part-time work Form of employment that carries fewer hours than a full-time job. In the United States, part-time work is generally considered to be 30 hours per week or less.

contingent labor Provisional group of workers who work on a contract, project, or other nonpermanent basis.

separate spheres A set of beliefs that coalesced as a distinct ideology in Europe and North America during the Industrial Revolution, it assigned to women and men to distinct and virtually opposite functions, duties, characteristics and activities in society.

informal economy Refers to economic activities and income that are partially or fully outside government regulation, taxation, and observation.

unemployment rate The measure of the prevalence of unemployment, it is calculated by dividing the number of unemployed individuals by all individuals currently in the labor force.

14.3 Workplace Identities, Interactions, and Inequalities

Workplaces have become more diverse spaces over the latter half of the twentieth century. The U.S. white-collar workforce used to be homogeneously middle-class white males. Women and minorities are catching up in representation but lag behind in wages and representation at the top. As one climbs workplace hierarchies, diversity on all axes slows down. Scholars sometimes refer to this as the glass ceiling—an invisible barrier that seems to continue to protect the positions at the upper echelons of the workplace for men, and often, straight white men. Inequality includes occupational segregation by gender, as well as the pay gap in the workplace along gender and racial lines. There is also inequality in domestic unpaid labor, with women earning less and working more, and workplace discrimination by sexual orientation and LGBTQ identification. A number of other labor practices affect workplace equality, including a motherhood penalty, unequal burden of emotional labor, and feeling rules that impose additional restrictions and obligations on employees based on race.

14.3 Key Terms

token Representative of a traditionally disenfranchised group whose hypervisibility results in constant pressure to reflect well on his or her group and to outperform co-workers just to be perceived as equal.

glass ceiling An unofficially acknowledged barrier to advancement in a profession, especially affecting women and members of minorities.

the quiet revolution Gradual but wide-sweeping changes that have resulted from the increase in the number of women in the workforce during the past 50 years, transforming consumer patterns, workplace policies, dating and relationship norms, parenting practices, household maintenance, and self-concepts for both men and women.

gender wage gap The consistent, worldwide difference between what men are paid and what women are paid for the same labor.

occupational sex segregation Refers to women's and men's different concentrations in different occupations, different industries, different jobs, and different levels in a workplace hierarchy.

glass escalator Christine Williams's phrase for her research finding that men doing "women's work" receive more, on average, than do the women doing that work.

workplace discrimination A form of discrimination based on race, gender, religion, national origin, physical or mental disability, and age by employers.

motherhood penalty In the workplace, mothers encounter systematic disadvantages in pay, perceived competence, and benefits relative to childless women.

emotional labor Arlie Hochschild's phrase for the process by which workers are expected to manage their feelings in accordance with organizationally defined rules and guidelines.

care work All tasks that directly involve care processes done in service of others.

feeling rules Arlie Hochschild's term for socially shared norms that influence how people should demonstrate how they feel in different settings.

aesthetic labor Christine Williams and Catherine Connell's term for employment practices designed to attract middle-class workers to relatively poor, low-wage retail jobs by attempting to attract employees who embody the look and feel they are attempting to sell without necessarily appearing to do so.

family wage Arising in the nineteenth century, the term refers to a wage sufficient for a single wage earner to support a family (spouse and children).

lavender ceiling Refers to workplace discrimination that hampers or prevents LGBTQ people from being promoted.

SELF-TEST

〉CHECK YOUR UNDERSTANDING

1. Economies are born of rational self-interest, according to
   a. John Locke and Thomas Hobbes.
   b. Adam Smith.
   c. Karl Marx.
   d. Emile Durheim.

2. Collective goals and central planning are hallmarks of which political system?
   a. Capitalism
   b. Socialism
   c. Communism
   d. All of the political systems listed.

3. The original founding tenet of capitalism was "laissez-faire," which translates as
   a. "to leave alone."
   b. "the body politic."
   c. "free profit."
   d. "fair laziness."

4. Corporate culture is built around the assumption of heterosexuality, but even those gay and lesbian employees who are out tend to confront
   a. occupational segregation.
   b. the lavender ceiling.
   c. the glass escalator.
   d. emotional labor.

5. When few members of a minority occupy a job, they often feel like tokens, which means they are
   a. hyper-visible, so that whatever they do is taken as what group members always do.
   b. seen as unusual individuals, never as members of their minority group.

   c. seen as evidence that anybody can achieve whatever they achieve on the job.
   d. able to under-perform their peers and still be perceived as equals.

6. Theoretical knowledge, self-regulating practices, and community orientation are hallmarks of
   a. white-collar jobs.
   b. blue-collar jobs.
   c. pink-collar jobs.
   d. professions.

7. Research in which sociologists and journalists joined the working poor revealed that
   a. most people working low-paying jobs are poor because they have poor work ethics and are lazy.
   b. most of the money the poor earn is spent on things like lottery tickets, alcohol, and eating out at fast food restaurants.
   c. the poor have strong work ethics but don't make enough to survive; still, they would rather work than take a handout.
   d. America provides few social services so as to encourage workplace participation because the poor would rather receive subsidies or welfare benefits than work.

8. In which of the following is the greatest percentage of working women found?
   a. In Western developed countries
   b. In the poorest countries
   c. In the wealthiest countries
   d. In European developed countries

Self-Test Answers: 1. a, 2. b, 3. a, 4. b, 5. a, 6. d, 7. c, 8. c

POLITICS AND RELIGI

In the United States, political and religious life are understood as segregated from one another ("separation of church and state"). But the truth is that religious and political life share a great deal in common and, as social institutions, they overlap far more than we sometimes recognize. Just consider the rapt attention commanded by sermons at mega-churches and the religious-like zeal produced by a political candidate running for president.

→ LEARNING OBJECTIVES

In this chapter, using the iSoc framework, you should be able to:

15.1.1 Summarize the similarities, differences, and interactions between politics and religion as social institutions.

15.1.2 Recognize how each of the five elements of the iSoc model can be used to examine politics and religion sociologically.

15.1.3 Summarize some of the ways that religion and politics are separate social institutions and how a concept like "civil religion" helps us understand that they are connected in some way in every society.

15.2.1 Explain the differences among Weber's three types of authority.

15.2.2 Summarize the qualities that characterize "authoritarian" political systems.

15.2.3 Summarize the qualities that characterize "democratic" political systems.

15.2.4 Explain how and why corruption and bureaucracy are endemic problems in many political systems.

15.2.5 Summarize some of the ways that political systems often end up representing existing inequalities between groups of people in society, providing examples from the United States.

15.2.6 Describe the U.S. political system, and explain the trend toward increasing polarization of Americans' political views.

15.2.7 Understand how age, education, class, race, and gender shape political parties and voting behavior.

15.2.8 Understand the level of political participation among Americans in an international context.

15.2.9 Distinguish between different forms of political change.

Understand key differences between classical theorists in their understandings of the role of religion in social life.

15.3.2 Distinguish between the different types of religious groups that sociologists classify and study.

15.3.3 Explain key differences between the major world religions and understand their relative popularity around the world.

15.3.4 Summarize the dual processes of secularization and religious resurgence on a global scale.

15.3.5 Describe some of the reasons that the United States fails to follow larger patterns related to economic growth, development, and rates of religious beliefs and participation.

15.3.6 Summarize the ways that religion intersects with nation, region, age, and race in the United States in ways that help explain recent shifts in religious identification.

15.3.7 Explain some key changes in the population of religiously unaffiliated in the United States and around the world in recent history.

15.4.1 Describe some of the political elements of religious traditions and beliefs.

15.4.2 Explain how religion pervades our everyday lives, identities, and interactions in subtle and often taken-for-granted ways.

15.4.3 Explain how politics pervades our everyday lives, identities, and interactions in subtle and often taken-for-granted ways.

Introduction

In 2005, a 24-year-old graduate of Oregon State University, Bobby Henderson (a physics major), weighed in on the debate between evolutionary science and creationism. Henderson wrote an open letter to the Kansas State Board of Education about his professed belief in a Flying Spaghetti Monster who had the ability to change the results of scientific tests and experiments demonstrating support for the scientific perspective in this debate. In the letter Bobby wrote that he looked forward "to the time when these three theories are given equal time in our science classrooms across the country, and eventually the world; one third time for Intelligent Design, one third time for Flying Spaghetti Monsterism, and one third time for logical conjecture based on overwhelming observable evidence."

Henderson never received a response from his letter and decided to post it on the Internet. Soon, Pastafarianism became an online sensation. The Flying Spaghetti Monster has become recognized as the official deity of this "religion." In reality, Pastafarianism was intended as satire—"Pastafarians" are part of a social movement that opposes the teaching of creationism or "intelligent design" in public schools. Since 2005, Pastafarianism has been legally recognized as a religion in both the Netherlands and New Zealand. In fact, in April 2016, the first state-sanctioned Pastafarian wedding was performed in New Zealand. In the United States, however, federal courts have ruled "The Church of the Flying Spaghetti Monster" is not a real religion.

Of course, we know that Pastafarianism is silly. We know they don't really believe in a flying spaghetti monster influencing the world around us. It's satire—a critique of organized religion, its irrationality and its influence. That he needed to address such a letter to a government entity though also illustrates just how *political* religion is. Religions are organized sets of beliefs in which groups of people profess faith and share in rituals that illustrate their shared commitment to that faith. But religion is also meaningfully connected with law in many societies. The federal court that ruled that Pastafarianism not be considered a religion in the United States put it this way:

> This is not a question of theology. The Flying Spaghetti Monster Gospel is plainly a work of satire meant to entertain while making a pointed political statement. To read it as religious doctrine would be little different from grounding a 'religious exercise' on any other work of fiction.

In the United States, religious groups, organizations, and religions themselves are subject to various legal accommodations. The freedom to practice religion is part of our political philosophy and codified in law. As Pastafarianism illustrates so well, religion is deeply connected with political life. Although there is a formal "separation of church and state" in the U.S. Constitution, religion and political life are and always have been deeply intertwined with each other. As social institutions, they each play a powerful role in structuring the moral fabric of our society, organizing social order around shared common values that shape the ways we understand ourselves and the societies in which we live.

15.1 Politics, Religion, and Social Life

The separation of church and state is a hallmark of American democracy. Although we often view religion and politics as competing world views, separate and distinct social institutions and arenas, sociologists recognize that there are many similarities as well. Both are organized and coherent systems of authority that are organized into social institutions. Both make claims to govern our conduct: Politics governs our society, regulating and distributing social responsibilities and obligations, and religion orients people toward social interaction in this world as an expression of its beliefs in the next world. Both political and religious institutions function as organizations, with clear rules about how one gets promoted, how to deal with bosses, and the like.

However, there are also many differences between the two institutions. They fulfill different sorts of needs that every society must navigate, from basic questions about social organization like "Do we need a leader?" or "Who's in charge?" to more complex questions about the meaning of our lives and experiences. In this section, you'll learn about some of these interconnections between these two central social institutions in every society, and you will also learn more about how we can best understand politics and religion by focusing on each relying on the iSoc perspective.

Politics and religion are often understood as institutions—features of our social organization that accomplish something we would be unable to accomplish on our own. But they are also both meaningfully related to our identities, and as such, to the various inequalities associated with each of the different identities we happen to occupy as well. Politics and religion have long been of interest to sociologists, from our classical theorists who endeavored to make sense of different systems of solidarity, authority, and control all the way to contemporary social scientists who track belief systems around the world or run political polls ahead of elections to attempt to predict which candidates will win and lose.

Comparing Politics and Religion

15.1.1 Summarize the similarities, differences, and interactions between politics and religion as social institutions.

Religion refers to a set of beliefs about the origins and meaning of life, usually based on a belief in the existence of a supernatural power. It is primarily concerned with the big questions of existence, such as: What is the meaning of life? Where did I come from? Where am I going? The emphasis of politics is less concerned with the "hereafter." **Politics** is the art and science of government. And both religion and politics are about three things: power, government, and authority. **Power** refers to the ability to make people do what you want them to do—whether they want to do it or not (such as paying your taxes or giving a portion of your income to the church). But

religion
A set of beliefs and practices relating to the origins and meaning of life, usually based on a belief in the existence of a supernatural power.

politics
The art and science of government.

power
The ability to extract compliance despite resistance or the ability to get others to do what you want them to do, regardless of their own desires.

government

The organization and administration of the actions of the inhabitants of communities, societies, and states.

authority

Power that is perceived as legitimate, by both the holder of power and those subject to it.

both of these social institutions are also about **government**—the organization and administration of the actions of the inhabitants of communities, societies, and states. Finally, politics and religion organize **authority**—power that is perceived as legitimate by both power holders and those who are subjected to it. If politics and religion are working well, it is through government (either political or religious) that power is transformed into authority.

Sociologists have always wondered about power: how we get it, how we use it, why some of us have so much of it and some of us have so little (Faulks 2000; Lukes 1986; Orum 2000). Back in the nineteenth century, Karl Marx saw power as purely a characteristic of social class. The owners of the means of production had complete control over the workers' tasks, schedules, and salaries. The workers had no power at all. They had no control over their wages or working conditions and could vote only for candidates who were handpicked by the factory owners. And Marx saw religion as an institution that helped put them at ease (promising rewards in another life), helping to stave off organized rebellion against this inequality.

Politics and religion both change over time. There are new interpretations of the revealed message, new emphases, or even new revelations. Political systems are established, overthrown, replaced, and upheld. Change in political or religious institutions almost never proceeds as a smooth, uncontroversial change from one set of beliefs to another. Instead, change is precipitated by dramatic challenges to and breaks with accepted wisdom. In religion, these ruptures generally come when a new prophet or charismatic leader draws people away from established institutions. In politics, these breaks come from social movements, revolutions, civil wars, and international pressure.

iSoc: The Sociology of Politics and Religion

15.1.2 Recognize how each of the five elements of the iSoc model can be used to examine politics and religion sociologically.

IDENTITY—Just how much does politics or religion shape your *identity*, your sense of yourself as a person? For some, one or both of these issues are important parts of who they imagine themselves to be. Perhaps not as important as, say race, or ethnicity, but political and religious affiliation is considered central to identity to a significant number of Americans. Even if you don't consider party affiliation a central component of your identity, many people label themselves as "liberal" or "conservative" as markers of who they are—integral components of their social identities (Greene 1999). Beyond this, the political system in which you live shapes your sense of yourself. For example, perhaps you consider yourself a pretty optimistic person, who believes that with hard work, discipline, and a little bit of luck, one can really succeed in life. If you lived under a totalitarian regime, that optimism could get you arrested, even tortured or killed. Some political regimes require certain emotions from their citizenry, and refusal to exhibit the proper affect can get you in trouble. Or, consider religion. One of the major purposes of religion is to provide you with an anchor for your identity, a grounding and a purpose for your life here on earth, and a vision of what happens when you die. Our religious identities are so important that most Americans still try to marry within their faith communities and live among people who share those beliefs. Indeed, more Americans profess to be "very religious" than any other industrial nation on earth. Participation in either a political or a religious institution can be a secure grounding for your identity.

INEQUALITY—Religions tend to see the world as the unfolding of a divine plan, so efforts to change society may break with that divine plan. As a result, religions tend to be conservative, emphasizing the moral significance of existing *inequalities*. And yet, religious organizations and groups also sometimes play an invaluable role helping those less fortunate and understanding this assistance as one piece of a set of social obligations organized by their religion. Similarly, politics is a world of inequalities—both reproducing them and also developing strategies to alleviate them. Like many religions, some political systems enshrine inequality as either divine or natural law; for example, aristocratic and authoritarian regimes empower some people (nobility, government officials) over others. At the same time, politics is also a world where competing interests of different groups are weighed and balanced, and existing inequalities may be challenged and, sometimes, overcome. For example, virtually every single right that Americans who were not native-born, white, male and middle class (property owners) had to be fought for politically, and required political institutions to change, from the right to vote, go to school, get a job, join a union, or buy or rent a house, to such esoteric rights as the right to drive a car, open a bank account in your name, get a passport.

INTERACTIONS—Both politics and religion rely on the processes of *interaction* to advance their perspectives and to sustain their institutions. Christian religious groups, for example, meet ritually, every Sunday, to create and sustain the sense of community that enables them to feel part of something bigger than themselves; other religious groups like Orthodox Jews do it every day, and some Muslims do it several times a day. Creating political change also relies on interactions. A famous feminist slogan held that "the personal is political." That is, all seemingly personal interactions were also "political" in the sense that they expressed gender, race, class, ethnicity, age, or sexuality—each of which is a core element of identity and inequality. The way you interact with your teachers (obedient and passive or defiant and resistant), or with someone you are interested in dating, or even your family members all are shaped and given meaning by political dynamics. Our interactions, whether inside the officially designated "political" arena of voting, or with people we know or encounter in everyday life, are organized by political dynamics, like the laws that constrain our individual behavior.

INSTITUTIONS—One of the key similarities between politics and religion is that even though they may have antithetical ideas about things, they still are organized into similar sorts of *institutions*. Institutions of faith and governance are arenas that organize and disseminate ideas, organize rules of conduct for members, maintain hierarchies of different roles and positions, and provide opportunities for individuals to follow bureaucratic career paths. Political and religious institutions unite members in shared belief systems. They organize social values and members of societies become invested in those belief systems in various ways. Political institutions engage with you as a citizen—enacting laws to govern individual and collective behavior, regulating excesses, adjudicating problems, enforcing those laws and punishing offenders, and promoting the interests of that society against the interests of other societies through both military and diplomatic courses of action. Religious institutions engage you as a member or as an outsider. Just about every single day you interact with a political or religious institution—attending religious service, obeying speed limits and traffic signals (or not!), paying sales tax for your mocha latte, or even if someone says "Bless you" after you sneeze.

INTERSECTIONS—The ways that we interact and are connected with political and religious institutions in society is also dramatically influenced by the *intersecting* identities that we occupy. Women and racial and ethnic minorities in the United States, for instance, are underrepresented in our political governance. Anyone can run for elected office, but white men hold the majority of political offices in our society. Race, gender, and sexuality are also intertwined with religious identities and institutions. Judaism is a religious tradition, but Jew is also an ethnicity. Many religious traditions are also primarily associated with certain groups. Indeed, religious identities intersect with political identities, gender, sexuality, race, class, ethnicity, age, national origin, and much more. It is only through understanding these intersections that we can fully appreciate the diverse ways that all of our lives are affected by politics and religion, but we are not all equally affected, nor are we all affected in all of the same ways.

Just How Separate Are Church and State?

15.1.3 Summarize some of the ways that religion and politics are separate social institutions and how a concept like "civil religion" helps us understand that they are connected in some way in every society.

In modern secular societies, politics and religion are understood to be separate social realms. This is not true of every society in the world today, but it is true of the United States. The "separation of church and state" is a phrase Thomas Jefferson used (among others) to express the sentiments entailed by the "Establishment" and "Free Exercise" clauses of the First Amendment to the Constitution of the United States of America: *"Congress shall make no law respecting an establishment of religion, or prohibiting the free exercise thereof."* According to the U.S. Constitution, the state should not have the power to determine people's religious beliefs, practices, or establishments. Church and state are separate. But are they really? Sociologists interested in politics and religion have discovered that the answer to this question is both yes and no.

In some societies, religion and politics are deeply connected to one another. In others, they are legally considered separate. Consider the law, passed in France in summer 2016, that prohibited women from wearing "burkinis" (a neologism that refers to the full burkas that some Muslim women wear at the beach, including while swimming). Is this an example of separation of church and state, or an example of the state preventing the "free exercise" of religion? Depends on whom you ask!

Or consider laws regarding blasphemy and apostasy. In the United States, you are allowed (by law) to convert to a different religion; you are allowed (again, by law) to abandon religion all together if you choose. Certainly, you might anger your parents, relatives, friends, and face a variety of pressures and concerns from people in your life. But you wouldn't be brought before a court, arrested, or thrown in jail for this decision. Similarly, in the United States, you are allowed by law to insult or display a general contempt or lack of reverence for religious figures, symbols, deities, and all manner of things considered "sacred" by religious groups. These acts will undoubtedly provoke all sorts of reactions, from frustration and anger, to sadness and contempt. And this does not mean these acts are without consequence; it means that the acts in and of themselves are not punished in the political realm—they are not punished by law.

You may read this and think, "Of course I'm allowed to change religions" or "No one can arrest me if I take the Lord's name in vain." But if you are, that's because you are taking for granted this separation. **Apostasy** and **blasphemy** might strike you as historical artifacts. If you are able to take this for granted, it is because you live in a society that understands religion and politics as separate social realms, social institutions with some overlap to be sure, but limited. That separation is not true of every society in the world.

In the societies highlighted in MAP 15.1, the right to practice religion freely, to abstain from religious practice, and actively and publicly condemn religion and religious beliefs are not enjoyed by everyone. In December 2015, legal authorities in Sudan charged 25 men with apostasy (the act of abandoning their faith, an act that can include converting to another faith). The men faced the death penalty in court for following an interpretation of Islam different from the government sanctioned interpretation. As of 2014, 26 percent of societies had laws or policies against blasphemy; 13 percent had laws or policies penalizing apostasy (Theodorou 2016). These are extreme examples of societies with less separation between religious and political institutions. Other societies have state-sanction religions, for instance, but allow people to publicly speak out against those religions or religious traditions. For instance, Ireland is a Catholic nation; Catholicism is taught in public schools—public schools are Catholic schools. But you can't be arrested for converting to another religion, not practicing Catholicism, or professing a different faith, or even for publicly challenging the Catholic Church.

apostasy
The abandonment or renunciation of a religious belief.

blasphemy
Speaking profanely about God or sacred things.

civil religion
Robert Bellah's term for the values that hold societies together that are expressed through "religious-like" practices—defining moral and ethical boundaries through ritualized practices (like the Pledge of Allegiance in the United States).

Here, a young Muslim woman wearing a burkini sits by the beach in Dubai, India.

MAP 15.1 The Geography of Apostasy and Blasphemy
The right to abstain from religion, to abandon a religious tradition, or to speak out publicly against religious beliefs might strike many as a relic of history. But many societies still have laws that restrict citizen's abilities to do exactly this.

- Neither apostasy or blasphemy laws
- Apostasy laws
- Blasphemy laws
- Both apostasy and blasphemy laws

NOTE: Countries with an apostasy or a blasphemy law, rule, or policy at some level of government during calendar year 2014.
SOURCE: Data from Theodorou, Angelina E. "Which Countries Still Outlaw Apostasy and Blasphemy?" *The Pew Research Center, FactTank*. July 29, 2016. Available at: http://www.pewforum.org/2016/06/23/trends-in-global-restrictions-on-religion/.

Although it may be easy to consider the United States as a very different place, politics and religion are deeply connected in every society. Sociologist Robert Bellah understood this. There's a temptation to look at societies that are more secular as "less religious." But Bellah understood that the values that hold societies together are expressed through "religious-like" practices—defining moral and ethical boundaries through ritualized practices. Bellah (1967) referred to these practices as **civil religion**. He suggested that modern secular societies develop a set of secular rituals that create the same kinds of emotional bonds between people that are created by religion in societies where religion plays more of a central role in organizing everyone's life. Bellah suggests that the qualities associated with religious practice are a part of every society—the emotional bonds and collective effervescence created by religious rituals are not absent from life in more secular societies or societies with laws regarding the separation of political and religious life. They simply take on different forms

Professing faith in a certain religion is not required to run for political office in the United States or many other societies, nor is your religion a factor that can be held against you in a court of law in the United States. Yet, we

The sort of emotional bonds and vibrancy characteristic of religious ceremony is also part of the fabric of everyday life. Consider the collective feeling you get while standing (or refusing to stand) for the National Anthem before sports events. Why do we watch with crowds?

do continually express faith in our societies through religious-like practices and rituals that create similar kinds of emotional bonds to religious ceremonies and rituals. Although teaching religion and religious beliefs is not allowed in public schools in the United States, for instance, children in preschool and kindergarten begin to learn the Pledge of Allegiance (even before they understand what it means). Standing up in unison, holding our hands over our hearts, and removing our hats in respect of the national anthem being sung or played before athletic contests and events is another expression of civil religion. Sitting together to watch fireworks on the Fourth of July is no different. These rituals create the same kinds of moral and emotional bonds that help us to understand ourselves as members of the moral community that make up our society. The point is that, no matter how separate we think religion and politics *should* be, politics and religion are deeply connected in every society—whether by law, custom, or through civil religion and religious-like practices—and produce the same sorts of connections between members of a society.

---

iSOC AND YOU Politics, Religion, and Social Life

Your politics and religion are central components of your *identity*. This is why we can ask, "What are your politics?" as though they are fundamental aspects of who we are. Similarly, what religion you profess—or even whether or not you have a religion—is understood to reveal something important about you. These *identities* structure many of your *interactions*, including the people with whom you are likely to interact as well as those you are more likely to avoid. Religious *institutions* can provide education, recreation, as well as the opportunity to worship collectively with others. Political *institutions* help provide shared belief systems and, sometimes, help coordinate our beliefs and put them into action in the service of our societies. Yet, religion and politics can also determine access to resources—that is, they are a powerful basis for *inequality* as well. As such, they *intersect* with other aspects of your identity to structure your opportunities and experiences in the society in which you live.

15.2 Politics

The great German leader Otto von Bismark once quipped "politics is the art of the possible, the attainable—the art of the next best." Though it might be difficult to believe in the current political climate, he meant that politics is about compromise, negotiation, and interaction. Sociologists are interested in how people organize themselves to run their society, so that the basic social and economic tasks of the society can be fulfilled efficiently, fairly, and safely. And politics play a critical role in this process. There are several political systems that have developed and the United States has borrowed from others to form a distinct political system, complete with its own problems.

Politics is about all of this and more; it is a central social institution necessary for societies to achieve the kinds of negotiation and compromise required by living in groups. But compromise does not always work in everyone's interest in equal ways. In fact, politics play a critical role in the social reproduction of every kind of social inequality. Paradoxically, however, politics are also a critical element of every major challenge to social inequalities. They are a central social institution in every society, and you play a role in politics in your society, even if it is a role you are unaware that you are playing. Whether you participate or not, vote in local and national elections or abstain and feel like your vote makes no difference, whether you join political protests or critique them when they are given voice in the media from your living room couch, you are a part of the political institution in your society.

Politics: Class, Status, and Power

15.2.1 Explain the differences among Weber's three types of authority.

No society has ever been built around pure coercion. A few have come close—the slave society of the antebellum South, for example, or Romania under Nicolai Ceausescu. But such societies have always been vastly inefficient because they must expend almost all of their resources on keeping people in line and punishing dissidents. And even there, the leaders must supplement coercion with other techniques, like persuasion and indoctrination. All of this takes times and resources away from accomplishing anything else as a society.

That's why Max Weber (1978) argued that power is not a simple matter of absolutes. Few of us have total power over others, so force won't work. And few of us have no power at all, so we rarely have to resort to trickery. Most often, people do what we want them to do willingly, not because they are being coerced or tricked. Drivers who obey the speed limits are probably not worried about being fined—after all, hundreds of cars are zooming past them at 90 mph without punishment. Instead, they have decided that they want to obey the speed limit, because they're good citizens, and that's what good citizens do.

In most societies, cultures, subcultures, families, and other groups, coercion remains a last resort, while by far the most common means of exercising power is authority. Authority is power that is perceived as legitimate, by both the holder of power and those subject to it. People must believe that the leader is entitled to make commands and that they should obey. Political leadership comes from authority. And sociologists know that authority comes in more than one type. Weber argued that leaders exercise three types of authority: **traditional authority**, **charismatic authority**, and **legal-rational authority**.

Traditional authority is a type of power that draws its legitimacy from tradition. We do things this way because we have always done them this way. In many premodern societies, people obeyed social norms for hundreds, sometimes thousands, of years. Their leaders spoke with the voice of ancient traditions, issuing commands that had been issued a thousand times before. They derived their authority from who they were: the descendants of kings and queens, or perhaps the descendants of the gods, not from their educational background, work experience, or personality traits.

Traditional authority is very stable, and people can expect to obey the same commands that their ancestors did. Its remnants still exist today in many social institutions, including religion, government, and the family, where we obey some rules because we have always done so. But even in ancient times, large-scale political, economic, and social changes sometimes occurred, such as invasion, war, or natural disaster, and new generations faced situations and challenges unknown to their ancestors, putting a great strain on traditional authority. That's when a second form, charismatic authority, would emerge.

Charismatic authority is a type of power in which people obey because of the personal characteristics of the leader. Charismatic leaders are so personally compelling that people follow them even when they have no traditional claims to authority. Indeed, they often ask their followers to break with tradition. We read in the New Testament that Jesus frequently said "it is written, but I say unto you," contrasting traditional authority (Jewish law) with charismatic authority (his teachings).

Charismatic leaders are often religious prophets, but even when they are not, their followers can be as passionate and devout as religious believers. Some presidents, like Franklin D. Roosevelt and John F. Kennedy, developed a popularity that cannot be explained by their performance in office alone. Many other political leaders of the past and present depend, to some degree, on charisma in addition to other types of authority. Charisma is morally neutral; as a personal quality, it can be found across the ethical spectrum: Adolf Hitler, Mohandas Gandhi, Osama bin Laden, and Nelson Mandela all possessed personal qualities that elicited obedience from their followers.

But pure charisma is also unstable because it is located in the personality of an individual, not a set of traditions or laws. And because they defy other forms of

traditional authority

Dominant in premodern societies, the form of authority that people obeyed because they believed their society had always done things that way; derives from who the leaders are: the descendants of kings and queens, or perhaps the descendants of the gods, not from their educational background, work experience, or personality traits.

charismatic authority

Form of authority derived from the personal appeal of a specific leader.

legal-rational authority

Form of authority where leaders are to be obeyed not primarily as representatives of tradition or because of their personal qualities but because they are voicing a set of rationally derived laws.

authority, charismatic leaders rarely live long; they are exiled (like the Dalai Lama in 1959), assassinated (like Mohandas Gandhi or John F. Kennedy), or imprisoned (like Nelson Mandela). When they are gone, their followers are faced with a crisis. How do you maintain the emotional high that you felt when the leader was with you? Weber argued that after the leader's departure, a small group of disciples will create a set of rules and regulations by which one can continue being a follower. Thus, charismatic authority is replaced by the rules, regulations, and rituals of legal-rational authority.

In the third form of authority, *legal-rational authority*, leaders are to be obeyed, not primarily as representatives of tradition or because of their personal qualities, but because they are voicing a set of rationally derived laws. They must act impartially, even sacrificing their own opinions and attitudes in obedience to the laws of the land. Legal-rational authority has become the most common form of authority in contemporary societies. In fact, many argue that modern government would be impossible without it. Governments operate under a set of regulations flexible enough to withstand changing social situations. Traditional authority is unable to handle much change without breaking down. And no leader, however charismatic, would today be able to sway tens of millions of people of diverse socioeconomic classes, races, religions, and life situations, on the basis of his or her personality alone.

Authoritarian Political Systems

15.2.2 Summarize the qualities that characterize "authoritarian" political systems.

political systems

The term for how group leaders exercise their authority. Virtually all political systems fall into one of two categories, "authoritarian" or "democratic."

authoritarian political system

When power is vested in a single person or small group. Sometimes that person holds power through heredity, such as in a monarchy, sometimes through force or terror, as with totalitarian regimes.

monarchy

One of the first political systems; rule by a single individual (*mono* means "one," and *archy* means "rule"), typically hereditary.

Political systems determine how group leaders exercise their authority. Virtually all political systems fall into one of two categories, authoritarian or democratic. In an **authoritarian political system**, power is vested in a single person or small group. That person holds power sometimes through heredity, sometimes through force or terror.

One of the first political systems was the rule by a single individual, or **monarchy** (*mono* means "one," and *archy* means "rule"). The rule of an individual was legitimized by traditional authority. The rulers of ancient Egypt, China, Japan, and Peru all claimed that their families descended from the gods. Medieval monarchs derived their power from divine right: They were not literally descended from God, but their power was based on God's will. By the time of the Renaissance, most of the kings and queens of Europe were "absolute monarchs." Their word was law, even when their word contradicted the law of the land. It might be illegal for the average person to commit murder, but the king or queen could call for the execution of anyone, for any reason or for no reason (so it made sense to stay on his or her good side).

Gradually a more egalitarian climate began to prevail. We can find traces of "rule of the people" as early as the English Magna Carta (1215), which established government as a relationship between monarchy and the people. During a relatively short period, the English Civil War and revolutions in France, America, and Haiti either deposed hereditary rulers or made them answerable to parliaments of elected officials (Birn 1992; Wedgwood 1990; Winks and Kaiser 2003). Other kingdoms became "constitutional monarchies" peacefully, adopting constitutions and electing parliaments with the full support of the kings or queens. A constitutional monarchy may still have a hereditary ruler, but he or she functions as a symbol of the country and a goodwill ambassador, whereas elected officials make the everyday political decisions based on the principles embedded in a constitution. Today only a few absolute monarchies remain, such as in Kuwait, Saudi Arabia, and Swaziland, but even those countries often legislate a system of checks to keep the rulers from overstating their power.

Today, the forms of authoritarian political systems that are more common are totalitarian and dictatorial. Under **totalitarianism**, political authority is extended over all other aspects of social life—including culture, the arts, and social relations. Any political system may become totalitarian when no organized opposition is permitted and political information is censored. Secret police and paid informers closely monitor

totalitarianism

A political system in which no organized opposition is permitted and political information is censored.

the people to ensure that they remain loyal to a rigidly defined ideology. Propaganda, misinformation, and terror are used to ensure obedience (Arendt 1958/1973).

Other than the brutal attempts to control the thoughts and behaviors of their citizens, modern totalitarian governments have little in common. They can start out as democracies (Nazi Germany), constitutional monarchies (Italy under Mussolini), or socialist states (the Soviet Union under Stalin). They span economic systems, although free-enterprise capitalism is uncommon because it is difficult to control. They tend to be more common in rich nations than in poor nations because they are expensive to maintain—in 2016, *The Korean Times* (2016) reported that North Korea used 23.8 percent of its resources on the military in 2015 alone. Or they can be **dictatorships**, in which one person, with no hereditary claim, can come to power, by military takeover or by being elected or appointed.

Although dictators rule by violence, they often have significant popular support. Adolf Hitler arriving at a rally in Nuremberg in 1936.

Democratic Political Systems

15.2.3 Summarize the qualities that characterize "democratic" political systems.

The great British statesman Winston Churchill once commented that democracy is the worst form of government—except for all the others. Democracy is messy and noisy, and order is difficult because, in its basic idea, democracies aim to give everyone a political voice. **Democracy** (from *demos*, or people) puts legislative decision making into the hands of the people rather than a single individual or a noble class. Pure democracy, or **participatory democracy**, with every person getting one vote and the majority ruling, can work only in very small, homogeneous units, like classrooms, families, communes, clubs, churches, and small towns. If many people participate, it becomes impossible to gather them all together for decision making. If the population becomes heterogeneous, simple majority rule obliterates the needs of minorities.

The idea of democracy originated in ancient Greece, but vanished when ancient Greece became part of the Roman Empire (510–23 BCE). It reappeared during the Enlightenment (1650–1800), when philosophers began to argue that all human beings have natural rights, including the right to select their own political leaders. Because nation-states were too big for participatory democracy, they developed the theory of **representative democracy**, in which citizens elect representatives to make the decisions for them. Representative democracy requires an educated citizenry and a free press. High-speed communication and transportation are also helpful; during the nineteenth century, it took weeks to calculate the popular votes in presidential elections and months before everyone in the country was informed of the results. That is part of the reason why, in practice, there are often several steps between the people and the decisions (such as an electoral college) to minimize chaos while things get counted.

In 1900, there were only a few democracies in the world, and none with **universal suffrage** (voting for all adults, both men and women). Today slightly more than 60 percent of the world's nations are democracies, twice the percentage just 20 years ago, and another 20 percent are constitutional monarchies, all with universal suffrage (see FIGURE 15.1). Yet, measuring which societies ought to qualify as "democracies" and which fail to meet the criteria is more challenging than it might at first appear. The remaining 20 percent of the world's nations are a mixture of colonies, territories, absolute monarchies, communist states, Islamic republics or other forms of theocracy (rule by a religious group), military juntas, and dictatorships, plus one ecclesiastical state (Vatican City) and a couple states with no central government (Somalia, which is in chaos after 20 years of civil war; and Iraq, which is under U.S. occupation as of this writing).

dictatorship

A type of totalitarian political system in which power is held by one person, who may or may not have a hereditary claim on power, usually with military support.

democracy

Derived from the Greek word *demos* (people); puts legislative decision making into the hands of the people rather than a single individual or a noble class.

participatory democracy

Also called "pure democracy," a political system in which every person gets one vote and the majority rules.

representative democracy

System in which citizens elect representatives to make the decisions for them; requires an educated citizenry and a free press.

universal suffrage

Granting of the vote to any and all citizens who meet specified, universal criteria, such as legal citizenship and a minimum age.

FIGURE 15.1 Numbers of Democracies and Autocracies Around the World, 1915–2015
Over the twentieth century, you can see the growth in democracies around the world (political systems that seek to invest the people with political power and authority) alongside the growth and decline of autocratic political systems governed by single individuals with absolute power and authority.

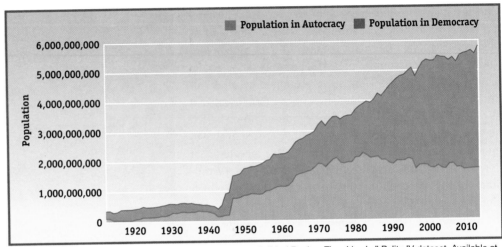

SOURCE: Data from Our World in Data, "World Population by Political Regime They Live In," Polity IV dataset. Available at https://ourworldindata.org/democracy/.

But even these countries are experiencing strong pressure toward democratization from both home and abroad. Globalized mass media constantly put rich people on display as examples of "ordinary" citizens of the United States, Japan, or Western Europe, thereby associating democracy with wealth, privilege, and power. International humanitarian agencies often associate democracy with freedom and condemn autocracies as necessarily oppressive. The only way to resist the pressure is to strictly censor outside media, thereby transforming the state into a totalitarian regime.

HOW DO WE KNOW WHAT WE KNOW?

MEASURING DEMOCRACY

Sociologists generally agree that democracy is a "good thing" and that the more democratic a society is, the better life is. But there is less agreement about how to actually measure democracy. After all, a society in which the majority rules could be one with no tolerance for anyone not in the majority, or one with lots of tolerance. Social scientists have developed three different methods to measure democracy:

(1) *Survey-based data*   identify public perceptions of democracy. These surveys ask questions related to democracy, human rights, and responsive government. Two surveys that use these surveys are the Global Barometer Surveys and World Values Surveys, which now contain data on 55 and 100 countries, respectively (see http://www.worldvaluessurvey.org/WVSContents.jsp and http://www.jdsurvey.net/gbs/gbs.jsp).

(2) *Standards-based data*   use specific political ideals as their basis, and measure the extent to which those ideals have been realized. These ideals might include the constraints on executive behavior, the extent of "polyarchy" or rule by many different people, competitiveness of the nomination process, or the extent of violations of individual rights (torture, terror, political imprisonment, disappearances). FIGURE 15.1 uses this approach to define democracies. Freedom House offers a 7-point scale of political and social liberties that have measured different countries since 1972 (see www.freedomhouse.org).

Another standards-based measure was offered by Finnish researcher Tatu Vanhanen, who measures contestation and participation. Contestation is measured by the smallest political parties' share of the vote and participation is measured by voter turnout. These are multiplied together and divided by 100 to yield an "index of democratization" for 187 countries (Vanhanen 2000). These data are available at https://www.prio.org/Data/Governance/Vanhanens-index-of-democracy/.

(3) *Events-based data*   count specific events that promote or impede democracy. These might include both negative acts of discrimination, corruption, violations of human rights, and positive events, like voter turnout and free and fair elections. Events can be tallied from newspapers or magazines, or from nongovernmental organization networks and human rights testimonies.

Problems with Political Systems I: Corruption and Bureaucracy

15.2.4 Explain how and why corruption and bureaucracy are endemic problems in many political systems.

Democracies are messier than authoritarian systems; populations in open societies are more difficult to control. But both authoritarian and democratic systems are prone to the same types of problems. Corruption and bureaucracy are chief among the challenges associated with political systems.

An international agency, Transparency International (www.transparency.org), ranks the corruption of nations on a scale of 0 (highly corrupt) to 10 (not corrupt) on the basis of three variables:

1. Outside interests donate large sums of money to elected officials.
2. New members of parliament or Congress obey special interest groups rather than the views of the people they are supposed to represent.
3. Officials misuse government funds or the power of their office for personal gain.

Corruption seems to have little to do with whether the country is democratic or authoritarian. For instance, Papua New Guinea, which rated a 10 on democratic institutions, ranked a 2.2 in corruption; and Kuwait, which rated a 7 on democratic institutions, ranked 4.6 in corruption. Instead, corruption seems to be characteristic of poor nations, where there are few economic opportunities, so people use their political influence to make money or exercise illicit power.

As we saw in Chapter 3, bureaucracies develop in all complex societies. Politically, Weber argued that bureaucracies were antagonistic to democracy. In a democracy, after all, one is elected to a fixed term (and with contemporary "term limits," these are increasingly short terms). This means that elected officials do not become "entrenched" but are constantly subordinate to the will of the people. By contrast, **bureaucracies** are staffed by people who are appointed, often for a "life tenure," which means that they are accountable to no one but the bureaucracy itself. Bureaucracies therefore almost always suffer from "bureaucratic entrenchment" (Weber 1978). In the United States, for instance, most people who operate the government are never elected by anyone and not directly accountable to the people, and there are many possibilities of mismanagement, inefficiency, and conflict of interest (Etzioni-Halevy 1983). The administrative staffs of organizations often wield enormous influence over policies, as do lobbyists and other interested groups.

Political power and authority also intersect with other forms of social and cultural power and authority. A separate problem with political systems is that they often end up reproducing lines of power and inequality in a society. For example, the rich have far more political clout than the poor. Every U.S. president elected in the past 100 years has been wealthy when elected, and most were born into that wealth. In recent years, several enormously wealthy men, like Michael Bloomberg (the current mayor of New York City and sixth wealthiest person in the world) or Donald Trump, have spent hundreds of millions of their own dollars to run for public office. Corporations and special interest groups spend millions, sometimes billions, of dollars on lobbying and **political action committees (PACs)**, often leaving the average citizen's concerns far behind. As a result, the average citizen often feels that neither party is doing what is needed, that no one is listening to "people like me." Minorities feel particularly slighted by their parties and by the party system (Kittilson and Tate 2004).

The interconnections between the wealthy and the powerful have been a major area of research interest to sociologists. Beginning in 1969, G. William Domhoff

bureaucracy

Originally derived from the French word *bureau*, or office, a formal organization characterized by a division of labor, a hierarchy of authority, formal rules governing behavior, a logic of rationality, and an impersonality of criteria.

political action committees (PACs)

A type of partisan political organization that is not subject to the same regulations as political parties, that attempt to influence elections and mobilize public opinion.

Republican presidential candidate Donald Trump speaks in front of a capacity crowd at a rally for his campaign on April 10, 2016, in Rochester, New York.

began to document these connections between corporate executives and elected officials. What he found was that formal mechanisms for influence, such as lobbying organizations or PACS, show only a moral public side of influence. In many cases, the private side is far more important. Members of the corporate elite are graduates of the same elite prep schools and Ivy League colleges as the legislators and political officials they seek to influence. They all send their children to the same schools and are even members of the same social organizations or fraternities. Thus, their influence is also powerfully exerted informally: A corporate CEO calls up his "old school chum" who happens to be a senator, and after chatting about their families, mentions his interest in a particular bill. Domhoff even found that the top-level corporate CEOs and political power brokers go away together each year on a retreat to a camp in northern California, where they spend the weekend partying (Domhoff 1967, 1974). This fact means that groups that have historically held political power and authority are likely to continue to represent those with political power and authority.

Problems with Political Systems II: Reproducing Intersectional Forms of Inequality

15.2.5 Summarize some of the ways that political systems often end up representing existing inequalities between groups of people in society, providing examples from the United States.

Very often, the groups who occupy political leadership are also those groups most privileged within society more generally. For instance, the representation of women and minorities in elected offices is small. Put another way, men (and white men in particular) are dramatically overrepresented in political office. Consider how these proportions have changed over the course of the latter half of the twentieth century (see FIGURE 15.2).

As of 2016, of 535 seats in Congress, 104 were women—just 19.4 percent (only 24 of them were women of color—18 black, 9 Latina, and 6 Asian American/Pacific Islanders). Only 17 percent (91 members) were racial minorities: 46 African American (44 in the House, 2 in the Senate); 32 Latinos (29 in the House, 3 in the Senate), 11 Asian Americans and Pacific Islanders (10 House, 1 Senate), and two American Indians in the House. The 111th Congress that began in January 2009 saw the first openly gay candidate to be elected as a freshman; he joined three others, all of whom came out once they were already serving as members. On the state and local levels, the situation is similarly unequal.

The commonsense explanation for the underrepresentation of minorities in high government positions is simple: discrimination. Either minorities lack the financial resources to successfully run for office or else voter prejudice keeps them from being elected. Prejudices about the "qualifications" of various minorities to adequately represent the majority often induce people to vote for "majority" candidates. This, though, raises another question: If the minorities cannot adequately represent the majority, how can the majority claim to adequately represent the minorities? If democracy is defined as the rule of the majority, what happens to those who are not in the

FIGURE 15.2 Proportion of U.S. Women in Positions of Political Leadership, 1965–2017

Although there has been tremendous growth in women's political leadership in the United States over the last half-century, some of that growth has slowed, and at some levels of political office, seems to have reversed. Sociologists are interested in both what drives women's political leadership as well as what kinds of outcomes a society like the United States might have if the political leadership represented more of the diversity of the society it participates in governing.

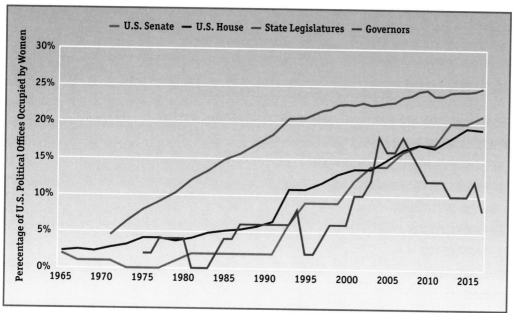

SOURCE: Data from Brown, Anna. "The Data on Women Leaders." The Pew Research Center, March 17, 2017. Available at: http://www.pewsocialtrends.org/2017/03/17/the-data-on-women-leaders/#us-senate.

majority? Will there be, as some sociologists predicted, a "tyranny of the majority," in which power becomes a zero-sum game and the winners get it and the losers don't, or will there be protections of the minorities to ensure they are not trampled politically? (Of course, middle-aged wealthy white men, who dominate all elected offices, are the statistical *minority* of all voters. By a landslide.)

Discrimination does not, however, explain what happens in countries with multiple electoral systems, combining "winner-take-all" (the U.S. practice) with proportional representation. In a **proportional representation** system, each party would receive a proportion of the legislative seats and thus would be more likely to govern "from the center" and build coalitions. This would tend to increase minority representation because coalitions of minority groups can form a majority. Countries that use proportional representation elect many times more women to their legislatures than winner-take-all systems (Rule and Hill 1996).

proportional representation

In contrast to the winner-take-all system used in the United States, proportional representation gives each party a proportion of the legislative seats based on the number of votes its candidates garner.

The Political System of the United States

15.2.6 Describe the U.S. political system, and explain the trend toward increasing polarization of Americans' political views.

In the U.S. political system, citizens are protected as individuals from the exercise of arbitrary control by the government. But individual citizens have little impact on changing the system. Individuals must band together at every level—local, state, and national—to hope to sway policies and affect political change. And even then, it is only through one's elected representatives that change can be accomplished. The system is so large and complex that organized bureaucratic political parties dominate the political landscape. **Political parties** are groups that band together to petition for political changes and to support candidates to elected office. Most of the world's democracies have many parties: Germany has 7, Japan 12, France 17, Italy 11 and other minority parties, and Argentina 12 major and numerous provincial parties. Usually, however, only two or at most three dominate in parliament

political parties

Groups that band together to petition for political chances or to support candidates for elected office.

U.S./WORLD

WOMEN IN PARLIAMENT

The percentage of women in national legislatures varies enormously around the world. The highest rates tend to be among the most developed European nations, but these societies do not represent all of the highest rates of women's political representation around the world. Some developing countries, like Rwanda and South Africa, have fairly new constitutions, which require higher percentages of women.

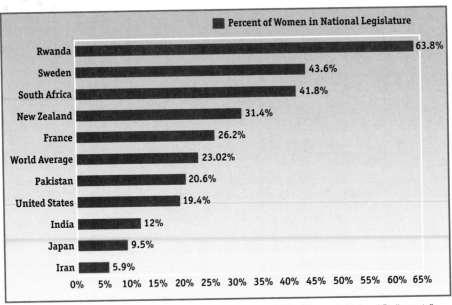

Percent of Women in National Legislature

Country	Percent
Rwanda	63.8%
Sweden	43.6%
South Africa	41.8%
New Zealand	31.4%
France	26.2%
World Average	23.02%
Pakistan	20.6%
United States	19.4%
India	12%
Japan	9.5%
Iran	5.9%

SOURCE: Data from The World Bank (2016), "Proportion of Seats Held by Women in National Parliaments". Available at http://data.worldbank.org/indicator/SG.GEN.PARL.ZS?view=map&year=2016.

INVESTIGATE FURTHER

1. What might explain the differences in the number of women in elected office?

2. What sorts of policies might a country adopt in order to increase women's representation—assuming that increasing women's representation is a positive goal?

or Congress. British elected officials traditionally belong to either the Labour Party or the Conservative Party; there are many other parties, but the most popular among these other parties, the Liberal Democrats, occupy only 1.2 percent of the seats in parliament.

With only two major political parties, the United States is something of an anomaly among democratic nations. Sociologists generally attribute the fact that most other countries have many more political parties to the winner-take-all electoral system in the United States. With legislative representation based on proportional voting, as in Europe, for example, smaller parties can gain seats, have influence, and even be included in coalition governments. In the United States, it doesn't make sense to spend money and launch major campaigns if you are a third (or fourth, and so on) party because if you don't win, you get nothing, no matter how many votes you received. Republicans and Democrats tend to have different platforms (opinions about social and economic concerns) and different ideas about the role of government in the first place.

According to conventional thinking, the Republicans run "against" government, claiming that government's job should be to get out of the way of individuals and off the back of the average taxpayer. Democrats, by contrast, believe that only with active government intervention can social problems like poverty or discrimination be solved.

It is the proper role of government to provide roads, bridges, and other infrastructure, as well as services such as welfare, health insurance, and minimum wages to those who cannot fend for themselves.

But political parties are not the only organized groups that influence political decisions in the United States or elsewhere. Individuals, organizations, and industries often form **interest groups** to promote their interests among state and national legislators and often to influence public opinion. *Protective groups* represent only one trade, industry, minority, or subculture: Labor unions are represented by the AFL-CIO, African Americans by the NAACP, women by NOW, and conservative Christians by Focus on the Family. *Promotional groups,* however, claim to represent the interests of the entire society: Greenpeace tries to preserve the planet's ecology, and Common Cause promotes accountability in elected officials (Grossman and Helpman 2001; Miller 1983). Increasingly, interest groups do not try to represent an entire political agenda. Instead, they fight for or against a single issue, like gun control. As the number of "hot-button" issues has become more visible in the media, the number of interest groups has increased. As a result of widespread public suspicion, interest groups are also subject to restriction. They must be registered, and they must submit detailed reports of their activities.

Both sides point to the other side's failures as evidence that their own strategy is better. To a sociologist, however, this question—whether the government should intervene in personal life or not—is a good example of how framing the issue as "either–or" misses the most important issues. It's always both, and both parties believe that the government should both intervene in private life and stay out of it. It is rather *where* they want to stay out of your life and *where* they want to intervene that is the question.

> **interest groups**
> An organized group that tries to influence the government to adopt certain policies or measures.

American Political Parties: Examining Intersections

15.2.7 Understand how age, education, class, race, and gender shape political parties and voting behavior.

What makes people affiliate with—that is, join, support, or vote for—Republicans, Democrats, or a third party? As we've discussed, politics is about more than beliefs; your political beliefs also comprise a political identity. Surprisingly, it's not often the issues, and rarely the "great divide" of government intervention versus hands off. Just like so many aspects of our social identities, people are socialized into party affiliation. They vote to express their group identity. It is an interactional ritual that solidifies their understandings of themselves and others. We tend to feel as though political beliefs and identities are individual issues. But sociologists and pollsters know that political beliefs are extremely tied to group identifications. Put in iSoc terms, political identification intersects with other elements of our social identities. Consider this: If you were to tell me your age, educational background, class, race, and gender, I would be able to predict who you are going to vote for with considerable accuracy (Burdick and Brodbeck 1977; Popkin 1994; see FIGURE 15.3).

Party affiliation tends to follow from:

1. *Class.* Poor, working-class, lower-middle-class, and blue-collar trade unionists have historically tended to be Democrats, while wealthy, upper-middle-class, white-collar individuals have tended to be Republicans. In 2008, Republican John McCain beat the Democrat Barack Obama among households earning between $100,000 and $200,000 a year, although he lost by 6 percentage points among highest-earning households more than $200,000 per year. In 2016, Trump did better with union households than any

Interest groups organize to lobby around specific issues.

FIGURE 15.3 Who Voted and How in 2016

Gender, race, and education played a big role in the 2016 presidential election. Different groups in U.S. society are often treated as separate units during election season and candidates vie for the "black vote" or "women's vote" hoping to curry favor with entire swaths of people based on one element of their identity. See how people voted by race, gender, and educational attainment in the 2016 presidential election.

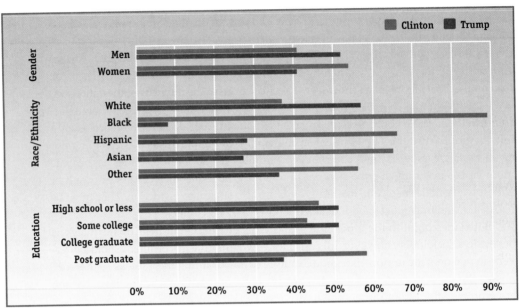

NOTE: Proportions do not add to 100 percent because people who either did not answer or supplied an answer other than Clinton or Trump are not shown here. The education/race intersection only considers whether respondents have a college degree or not.

SOURCE: Data based on exit polls conducted by Edison Research for the National Election Pool, as reported by CNN. Available at http://www.cnn.com/election/results/exit-polls.

Republican since Ronald Reagan in 1980 and also beat Clinton handily among voters earning $100,000 to $200,000 a year.

2. *Education.* Historically, the lower educational levels go Democratic because low education correlates with class, while college graduates have tended to be higher in the class system and thus vote Republican. However, the party affiliation of high school graduates has shifted, and the dramatic gap among the college-educated has also been reduced. Those with higher degrees beyond a bachelor's tend to vote Democratic. In 2008, Obama beat McCain at every education level, and most decisively among those with no high school (63 percent to 35 percent) and those with postgraduate degrees (58 percent to 40 percent). But in 2016, Donald Trump drew most of his support from noncollege-educated white men.

3. *Race.* Since the 1930s, most racial and ethnic minorities have been Democratic. Before 2008, the percentage had been declining as more minorities became more affluent and professional. But Obama received a majority of minority votes in 2008, including 67 percent of Latinos, 95 percent of African Americans, and 62 percent of Asian Americans (Limonic 2008). Whites were the only group that voted for McCain over Obama (55 percent to 43 percent). In 2016, 58 percent of white voters voted for Trump, as compared with 37 percent for Clinton, and Clinton drew fewer minority voters than Obama had: 88 percent of black voters and 65 percent of Latinos overall.

4. *Gender.* Women are more likely than men to vote Democratic, but again the percentages have been declining (54 percent in 2000, 51 percent in 2004, 41 percent in 2009). The decrease has occurred primarily among white women. In 2008, women voted for Obama over McCain 56 percent to 43 percent, but women of color overwhelmingly supported Obama; the Democrat won 96 percent of black women and 68 percent of Latinas. Only white women preferred McCain, by a

margin of 53 percent to 46 percent. In 2016, Trump matched McCain's share of 53 percent of white women, while only 43 percent voted for Clinton, a smaller share than had supported Obama.

5. *Age.* When they vote, younger people tend to lean Democratic. In 2008, only voters older than 65 preferred McCain, by 53 percent to 45 percent. Among the youngest voters, 18 to 29, Obama got 95 percent of black votes, 76 percent of Latinos, and 54 percent of whites. In 2016, more 18- to 29-year-olds voted for Trump (48%) than Clinton (43%), including 9 percent of black voters and 24 percent of Latinos in this age group.

Political Participation versus Political Apathy

15.2.8 Understand the level of political participation among Americans in an international context.

What does political participation mean to you? When sociologists think about political participation, we're talking about a specific collection of behaviors. In general, **political participation** refers to any action or behavior that either aims to affect or has the consequence of influencing governmental action. There are lots of ways to be a political actor. But not all members of a society are politically active. Some people are, politically speaking, "apathetic." **Political apathy** refers to the indifference of a member of a society with regard to their attitude toward political activities. Consider how you rate compared with other Americans. Are you politically engaged?

Popular culture often presents Americans as politically apathetic; as a nation of people who love to complain, but don't always show up for the polls when it actually counts. In general, Americans' political participation (measured by voting behavior) is highest during presidential elections. So, more Americans vote for president than come to vote for their town's sheriff or elected justices of local area courts. But, even in a presidential election, voting turnout varies quite a bit. In 2016, for instance, 57 percent of the voting-age population actually cast a ballot in the presidential election that elected President Donald Trump into office. This was slightly lower than the 2012 election. The proportion is higher if we're only looking at the proportion of people who voted who were registered to vote in the first place. But, is that a lot of political

political participation

Refers to any action or behavior that either aims to affect or has the consequence of influencing governmental action.

political apathy

Refers to the indifference of a member of a society with regard to their attitude toward political activities.

WHAT DO YOU THINK? WHAT DOES AMERICA THINK?

Voting and Citizenship

If you are a registered voter, you are among the slightly more than 145 million other registered voters in the United States. Yet, just being registered to vote does not mean that all 145 million Americans are actually voting in each election in which they are eligible to vote. Registering to vote and voting are only two ways of being a politically engaged and active citizen.

What do you think?

Are you a registered voter?

Have you ever voted in a presidential election?

Have you ever voted in a nonpresidential election?

Have you ever participated in a protest?

Have you ever written to your Congressman or Congresswoman?

Have you ever volunteered to work on a political campaign?

How would you answer each question listed above with regard to voting and citizenship?

○ Yes

○ No

What does America think?

If you are a registered voter, you are among the slightly more than 145 million other registered voters in the United States; that is approximately 53.6 percent of the voting-age population (18 years or older). So, just about 1 in 2 Americans eligible to vote is actually registered to vote in the United States. That number might sound low for a democratic nation. But, we have a significantly higher proportion of our voting-age population registered to vote than does Switzerland (38.6 percent), but much lower than Belgium, a nation where almost 90 percent of the voting-age population is registered to vote (Desilver 2016).

Yet, just being registered to vote does not mean that all 145 million Americans are actually voting in each election in which they are eligible to vote. In general, Americans are more likely to vote in national elections than they are in other elections. In the 2012 presidential election, roughly two-thirds (67 percent) of registered voters in the United States actually turned up and voted. Nonpresidential elections receive far fewer voters. And that rate is much higher than the rates of Americans who vote in regional and local elections.

Of course, registering to vote and voting are only two ways of being a politically engaged and active citizen. For instance, a 2013 poll collected by the Associated Press found that about 10 percent of Americans have ever participated in a protest. Perhaps this means that the majority of Americans feel they have nothing to protest, or perhaps it means that 9 in 10 Americans do not participate politically in this way even if they are dissatisfied. Yet, a survey of U.S. college freshmen suggests growing support for activism on college campuses. In 2015, 9.5 percent of college freshmen expected to participate in protests and political demonstrations while in college. But that number differed dramatically by race. For instance, 66 percent of black college freshmen expected to participate in political demonstrations and protests while in college compared with only 7.1 percent of white college freshmen (Eagan, et al. 2015).

Many Americans might not take to the streets in protest but may still be politically active in other ways. For instance, among Democrats, 34 percent had contacted an elected official in the past 2 years in 2014; among Republicans, the same figure was 42 percent. And surveys show that those most likely to have contacted an elected official are those at the ideological poles of political debate (consistently liberal or conservative across a range of issues) (Pew Research Center 2014). And although Democrats are *less* likely to contact elected officials than are Republicans in the United States, they are *more* likely to have worked or volunteered for a political campaign. Twelve percent of Democrats who hold very unfavorable views of the Republican party have volunteered for a political campaign compared with only 9 percent of Republicans (Pew Research Center 2014).

THINKING CRITICALLY ABOUT SURVEY DATA

What kinds of social factors might shape the ways different groups in the United States opt to participate or resist participation in political life? Try to think of three social barriers that might make it more difficult for some people to participate in these ways politically than for others.

participation or too little? Sociologists use comparative data here to consider how one society might behave different than others. Looking at the facts here alone might not be enough for you to feel like you can make an argument without relying too much on your opinion. But consider how the United States fared in that recent election compared to other Organization for Economic Co-operation and Development (OECD) countries' recent voting behavior (see FIGURE 15.4).

If you look at the United States in terms of the proportion of the voting age population who actually turned up to cast a vote in 2012 for the presidential election, it is among the bottom of this collection of nations. The U.S. voter turnout wasn't as bad as Switzerland (who saw fewer than 40 percent of their voting age population show up to vote in 2015), but they voted far less than Belgians (who, in 2014, saw almost 90 percent of the voting age population participate in their most recent election). But when we look at these data another way, the United States ranks significantly higher. Part of the reason for this is not that Americans are particularly politically apathetic. Certainly some of them are—and are allowed to be according to the laws of the society.

But, just showing these data as the proportion of the voting age population who show up to vote (people 18 and older) disguises another reality that shapes political participation in the United States: the distinction between the **voting-age population** and the **voting-eligible population**. The former is asking what proportion of people 18 and older voted. The latter is asking what proportion of people 18 and older who are not prohibited from voting showed up to vote. Consider one example: felons (remember our discussion of incarceration in the United States we considered in

voting-age population

Term for proportion of people 18 and older who therefore can vote.

voting-eligible population

Term for the proportion of people 18 and older who are not prohibited from voting.

FIGURE 15.4 Voting Behavior in National Elections in OECD Countries

The United States ranks low on the list of OECD nations for voting behavior in national elections. Slightly more than half of the voting age population in the United States vote in national elections. A much higher proportion of registered voters are voting in national elections in the United States, which tells us that a significant portion of the voting age population in the United States is not actually registered to vote in elections. This gap makes us stand out internationally in comparison with other OECD nations.

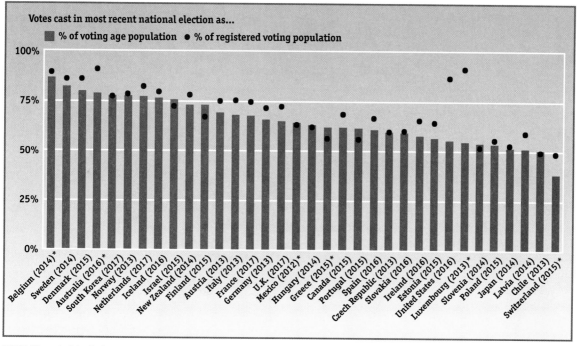

NOTE: The asterisks (*) denote countries in which laws make voting compulsory. In one case (Switzerland), a single canton (Swiss state) has compulsory voting while the others do not.

SOURCE: Data from Desilver, Drew. "U.S. Voter Turnout Trails Most Developed Countries." *Pew Research Center*, August 2, 2016. Available at: http://www.pewresearch.org/fact-tank/2016/08/02/u-s-voter-turnout-trails-most-developed-countries/.

Chapter 6?). **Felony disenfranchisement** is one of the consequences associated with a felony conviction in the United States. Presently, the United States is among the most-punitive societies in the world when it comes to denying people convicted of a felony the right to vote. Whether your right to vote will be restricted if you commit a felony or not depends which state you committed the felony in and in what year (as these laws change) (see MAP 15.2).

As of 2010, 5.85 million Americans were forbidden from voting because of state laws restricting the voting rights for those convicted of felony-level crimes (Uggen, Shannon, and Manza 2012). That's a significant proportion of the voting-age population. And because we know that black and Latino Americans are disproportionately incarcerated in the United States (meaning that there are a disproportionate number of them in prison compared to their overall proportion of the U.S. population), this also means that already marginalized groups are disproportionately *under*represented in elections. So, political participation is also inequitably distributed among the U.S. population; some groups are much more likely to have their voting rights revoked than others as a result of felony disenfranchisement laws. It's a powerful example of how examining the intersections of identities can help sociologists examine some of the ways social inequality gets reproduced from one generation to the next.

So it might be the case that the United States is more politically apathetic than many other nations (if we measure political participation with voting rates). But it also might be the case that the United States would see much higher rates of political participation if the society did away with laws that deny that quality of democracies that makes them unique as a political system—universal suffrage—to some because of their criminal history.

felony disenfranchisement
Punitive U.S. policy that denies people convicted of a felony the right to vote even after a sentence has been served. The presence of restrictions, and their extent, vary by the state in which the felony was committed and the year in which it was committed.

MAP 15.2 Felony Disenfranchisement Laws in the United States by State, 2016

Some states limit the abilities of people convicted of felonies from voting in elections. A few states have no restrictions on voting (like Maine). Others restrict persons convicted of felony who are in prison from voting (like New York, Colorado, and California). Other states restrict persons convicted of felonies who are either in prison, on parole, or on probation. And the most extreme policies in the United States restrict persons convicted of felonies from ever voting again (like Nevada, Arizona, and Florida).

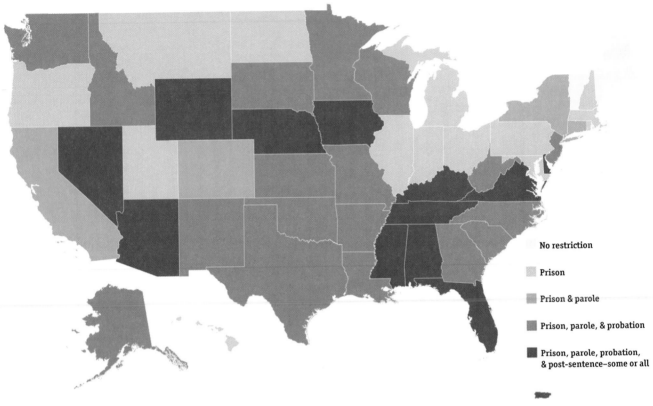

No restriction

Prison

Prison & parole

Prison, parole, & probation

Prison, parole, probation, & post-sentence–some or all

SOURCE: Data from Chung, Jean. May 10, 2016. *The Sentencing Project*, "Felony Disenfranchisement: A Primer," Figure A. Available at http://www.sentencingproject.org/publications/felony-disenfranchisement-a-primer/.

Political Change

15.2.9 Distinguish between different forms of political change.

Political life is not merely a matter of the major political institutions: political parties, voting, and elections. History shows us that some groups find their objectives or ideals cannot be achieved with this framework—or are actively blocked by it. They need to develop "unorthodox" political action. Some types of efforts for political change, social movements and revolutions, are internal; others, like war and terrorism, are attempted from outside the society.

When people seek to effect change, they may engage in political revolutions, but more commonly they start **social movements**—collective attempts to further a common interest or secure a common goal through action outside the sphere of established institutions. They may try to influence public opinion with advertising campaigns or by convincing a celebrity to act as their spokesperson. They may try to get legislators' attention through marches, sit-ins, media "zaps" (invasions of televised media events), Internet protests, boycotts, or work stoppages. Or they may try more colorful (and illegal) methods of getting their points across, like animal-rights activists who splash blood on actors wearing fur coats (McAdam 1996; Meyer, Whittier, and Robnett 2002; Morris and Mueller 1992; Tarrow 1998).

Today there are thousands of social movements, dedicated to supporting every imaginable political agenda. Many social movements are international and rely heavily on use of information technology to link local campaigners to global issues. They

social movement

Collective attempt to further a common interest or secure a common goal through action outside the sphere of established institutions.

are as evident a feature of the contemporary world as the formal, bureaucratic political system they often oppose.

Social movements vary by the type of issues around which they mobilize, their level of organization, and their persistence over time. Some social movements change over the course of their lives. Some become more limited in focus, others more expansive. Some morph into political parties to sustain themselves over time. Movements such as the labor movement or the Civil Rights movement began as more limited in focus, trying to better working conditions and raise the minimum wage, or to ensure the right to vote, but both became broad-based movements that have been sustained over time by large organizations and a wide variety of issues. Today, some organized social movements like the labor movement are in decline. Others, like the Civil Rights, Women's Movement, and Environmental Movement have continued to press for reforms in a wide variety of arenas.

Social movements often use colorful and creative methods to get their point across—and garner significant media exposure for their cause in the process. Here "Code Pink," an all-women anti-war protest organization, confronts Edward Liddy, CEO of American International Group (AIG) at his company's bailout hearing in Washington in 2009.

Revolution, the attempt to overthrow the existing political order and replace it with a completely new one, is the most dramatic and unorthodox form of political change. Many social movements have a revolutionary agenda, hoping or planning for the end of the current political regime. Some condone violence as a revolutionary tactic; many terrorists are hoping to start a revolution. Successful revolutions lead to the creation of new political systems (in France, Russia, Cuba, and China), or brand-new countries (Haiti, Mexico, and the United States). Unsuccessful revolutions, on the other hand, often go down in the history books as terrorist attacks (Defronzo 1996; Foran 1997).

revolution
The attempt to overthrow the existing political and social order of a society and replace it with a new one.

Previous sociologists believed that revolutions had either economic or psychological causes. Marx believed that revolutions were the inevitable outcome of the clash between two social classes. As capitalism proceeded, the rich would get richer and the poor would get poorer, and eventually the poor would become so poor that they had nothing else to lose, and they would revolt. This is called the **immiseration thesis**. Talcott Parsons (1966) and other functionalists maintained that revolutions were not political at all and had little to do with economic deprivation. They were irrational responses by large numbers of people who were not sufficiently connected to social life to see the benefits of existing conditions and thus could be worked into a frenzy by outside agitators. This theory is clearly wrong. Revolutions are almost never caused by mass delirium but by people who want a change in leadership.

immiseration thesis
Karl Marx's theory that, as capitalism proceeded, the rich would get richer and the poor would get poorer, and that eventually the poor would become so poor that they had nothing else to lose and would revolt.

A number of sociologists showed that revolutions were just a type of social movement, rationally planned, with mobilization strategies, grievances, and specific goals in mind (see, for example, Gamson 1975; Paige 1975; Tilly 1978; Zald and McCarthy 1987). But Marx was also wrong—especially about which groups would revolt. It is not people with nothing left to lose, but people who are invested in the social system and have something at stake. Don't expect a revolt from the homeless and unemployed but from the lower middle classes in the cities and the middle-rung peasants in the countryside. Political scientist Ted Robert Gurr (1971) coined the term **relative deprivation** to describe how misery is socially experienced by constantly comparing yourself to others. You are not down and out: You are worse off than you used to be (*downward mobility*), or not as well off as you think you should be (*rising expectations*), or, perhaps, not as well off as those you see around you.

relative deprivation
Describes how misery is socially experienced by constantly comparing yourself to others. You are not down and out: You are worse off than you used to be (downward mobility), not as well off as you think you should be (rising expectations), or, perhaps, not as well off as those you see around you.

SOCIOLOGY AND OUR WORLD

SOCIAL MOVEMENTS AND THE MEDIA

How do social movements attempt to use the media to get their messages out to the public?

Social movements eager to educate the public about the issue(s) they are organizing to promote or challenge often rely on media portrayals of their movements and missions to get their messages out. Indeed, it is no exaggeration to say that many activist groups today equate political success with media success—that is, getting their message in the media in the way they'd intended is a primary goal for many activist groups and movements. Sociologist Sarah Sobieraj (2011) ethnographically studied a collection of roughly 50 different organizations over two campaign cycles in 2000. She took field notes, interviewed activists, went to association events and meetings, read and analyzed the contents of the pamphlets and literature they produced, handed out, and put online. But Sobieraj also interviewed journalists and analyzed the news articles written on the various efforts of the organization, groups, and associations she studied.

Sobieraj had a variety of research questions, but some of the central questions that intrigued her were: How do activist groups and associations attempt to court media attention? How do they try to ensure that the message they want to convey in the media is understood? How do journalists interact with activist groups and decide what's "newsworthy" and what's just noise?

The organizations, associations, and groups Sobieraj studied were all incredibly concerned with crafting "soundbites" for the media—concise phrases, packed with information about their cause. They knew they needed these because they had to be prepared for various organization members to be interviewed, and they wanted to create a consistent message so that journalists would present their idea and their movement in the way they were attempting to be presented. In a media-driven age, this is a smart idea. It helps ensure that anyone interviewed can provide the same soundbite and provides more assurance for them that the message they want to convey won't get lost in translation as it travels from the streets to newsstands. Protesters and activists were trying to respond

to suggestions that they more explicitly frame themselves as "newsworthy" for the media—that this is the more effective path to media inclusion. So, they do things that might qualify as newsworthy (like staging a protest) and then try to demonstrate that their ideas are credible through professional-caliber media work and training. This, Sobieraj discovered, however, was not a path to media inclusion. In fact, their stories were rarely reported on in the ways they'd intended. All of their efforts failed to generate "news." But why?

What Sobieraj (2011) discovered is that activists and journalists were actually speaking different languages. The activists thought they were making things easier for the journalists by prepackaging their messages. But when journalists came across prepackaged claims and soundbites, they failed to see activists as "newsworthy." As Sobieraj writes, "When journalists looked at activists they weren't looking for talking points, they were looking for *authenticity*" (2011: 83). And prepackaged talking points and events that seemed staged to court media attention were not understood as "authentic" enough to merit the kind of reporting activist groups seeking media attention were actually after. Today, Sarah Sobieraj's book—*Soundbitten: The Perils of Media-Centered Activism* (2011)—is taught at some journalism schools in an effort to help news workers and journalists recognize when, how, and why people and groups attempt to court media attention to amplify their political voice.

coup d'état
The violent replacing of one political leader with another; often doesn't bring with it any change in the daily life of the citizens.

Sociologists typically distinguish among different types of revolutionary events, along a continuum from the least dramatic change to the most. A **coup d'état** simply replaces one political leader with another but often doesn't bring with it any change in the daily life of the citizens. (Some coups do bring about change, particularly when the new leader is especially charismatic, as in Argentina under Juan Perón.) A **political revolution** changes the political groups that run the society, but they still draw their strength from the same social groups that supported the old regime. For example, the English Revolution between 1640 and 1688 reversed the relationship between the

The immediate aftermath of Iran's disputed election in June 2009 witnessed two new developments in social movements in that country. First, women led the street protests for the opposition candidate Mirhossein Mousavi, and second, governmental repression was so significant that activists used Twitter and YouTube to broadcast their activities to the rest of the world.

king and aristocracy on the one hand and the elected parliament on the other, but it didn't change the fact that only property owners were allowed to vote. Finally, a **social revolution** changes, as Barrington Moore (1966) put it, the "social basis of political power"—that is, it changes the social groups or classes that political power rests on. Thus, for example, the French Revolution of 1789 and the Chinese Revolution of 1949 swept away the entire social foundations of the old regime—hereditary nobility, kings and emperors, and a clergy that supported them—and replaced them with a completely new group, the middle and working classes in the French case and the peasantry in the Chinese case.

In Hebrew and Arabic, the standard word for *hello* and *goodbye* is *shalom* or *salaam*, meaning "peace." **War** was so common in the ancient world that the wish for peace became a clichéd phrase, like the English *goodbye* (an abbreviated version of the more formal "God be with you"). By some estimates, there were nearly 200 wars in the twentieth century, but they are increasingly hard to pin down. The old image of war, in which two relatively evenly matched groups of soldiers from opposing states try to capture each other's territory, has become increasingly meaningless in the days of long-range missiles, drones, smart bombs, and ecoterrorism. However, war still occurs as a standard, perhaps inevitable characteristic of political life and political change. The frequency of war suggests that it is an inevitable problem of human societies, but extensive research has found no natural cause and no circumstances under which human beings will inevitably wage war. But sociologist Quincy Wright (1967) identified five factors that serve as root causes of most wars.

1. *Perceived threats.* Societies mobilize in response to threats to their people, territory, or culture. If the threats are not real, they can always be manufactured, such as the claim that Saddam Hussein possessed weapons of mass destruction, which was the pretext for the war in Iraq in 2002.
2. *Political objectives.* War is often a political strategy. Societies go to war to end foreign domination, enhance their political stature in the global arena, and increase wealth and power.
3. *"Wag the dog" rationale.* When internal problems create widespread unrest, a government may wage war to divert public attention and unify the country behind a common, external enemy.
4. *Moral objectives.* Leaders often infuse military campaigns with moral urgency, rallying people around visions of, say, "freedom" rather than admitting they

political revolution

Changes the political groups that run the society, but they still draw their strength from the same social groups that supported the old regime.

social revolution

Revolution that changes the social groups or classes on which political power rests.

war

A state of armed conflict between different nations, different states within a nation, or different groups within a nation or state.

fight to increase their wealth or power. They claim that wars are not acts of invasion but heroic efforts to "protect our way of life." The enemy is declared "immoral," and morality and religion are mobilized for the cause.

5. *Absence of alternatives.* Sometimes, indeed, there is no choice. When one country is invaded by another, war may be difficult to avoid.

terrorism

Using acts of violence and destruction (or threatening to use them) as a political strategy.

Terrorism is another strategy attempting to produce political change. **Terrorism** means using acts of violence and destruction against military or civilian targets (or threatening to use them) as a political strategy. For instance, an individual or group interested in acquiring independence for the Basque people of northern Spain might engage in terrorism in the hope that the Spanish government will acquiesce to their demands for autonomy. Frequently, however, terrorism has no specific political goal. Instead, it is used to publicize the terrorists' political agenda or simply to cause as much damage to the enemy as possible. Interviews with terrorists who bomb abortion clinics reveal that they do not believe that their actions will cause the Supreme Court to reverse the *Roe v. Wade* decision; they simply want to kill abortion doctors. Similarly, when al-Qaeda orchestrated the 9/11 attacks, they did not expect Americans to embrace their extremist form of Islam; they simply wanted to hurt Americans (Hoffman 1998; Juergensmeyer 2003). Terrorism can be used *by* the regime in power to blot out all dissent, but usually we think of terrorism as the actions *against* the existing regime. Usually terrorists have little or no political authority, so they use terror to promote or publicize their viewpoints, just as nonviolent groups might use marches and protests. Although terrorism is not new, recent technological advances have made weapons easier to acquire or produce and communication among terrorist groups easier, so that terrorism is increasingly common. According to the U.S. State Department's annual Country Reports on Terrorism, in 2015 there were 11,774 terrorist attacks worldwide, resulting in 28,328 deaths (U.S. State Department 2016). This was an overall decrease since 2014. And more than half of these attacks took place in five countries (Iraq, Afghanistan, India, Pakistan, and Nigeria), and almost 75 percent of all deaths took place in five countries (Iraq, Afghanistan, Pakistan, Nigeria, and Syria; see FIGURE 15.5).

FIGURE 15.5 The Effects of Terrorism in the United States, 1995–2014

Rhetoric about the "War on Terror" can make terrorist acts feel like they are incredibly common. But the numbers of terrorist attacks each year in the United States are relatively low. And although the attack in 2001 stands out here in terms of U.S. fatalities resulting from terrorist acts, in most years in the U.S. fatalities as a result of terrorism are extremely low.

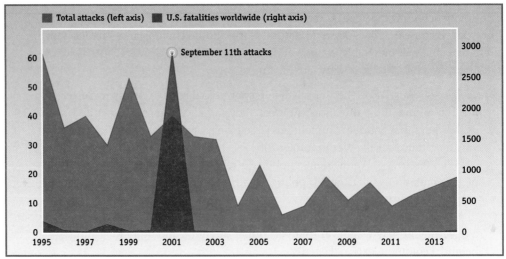

SOURCE: Data from National Consortium for the Study of Terrorism and Responses to Terrorism (START). "American Deaths in Terrorist Acts." October, 2105. Available at: https://www.start.umd.edu/pubs/START_AmericanTerrorismDeaths_FactSheet_Oct2015.pdf.

Democratic societies reject terrorism in principle, but they are especially vulnerable to terrorists because they afford extensive civil liberties to their people and have less extensive police networks (as compared with totalitarian regimes). This allows far more freedom of expression, freedom of movement, and freedom to purchase terrorist weaponry. So too is terrorism always a matter of definition. It depends on who is doing the defining—one person's terrorist might be another's "freedom fighter." Whether we are examining marches on Washington, revolutions to overthrown political regimes, wars, or terrorist organizations or tactics, sociologists have examined the diverse range of forms of action attempting to mobilize political change.

---

iSOC AND YOU Politics

Politics helps you define yourself, not just as a member of a political party, but in relation to others as a citizen. Citizenship itself is a type of *identity* that defines and prescribes your *interactions* with others. Yet not everyone is an equal citizen; political *institutions* organize and often legitimate social inequality. Not everyone participates, not everyone has an equal opportunity to participate, and some people are actually prohibited from participating. Unequal political rights are intertwined with one another, illustrating some of the ways that social *inequalities intersect* with each other as well.

15.3 Religion

As an organized set of ideas, a coherent theology or ideology, religion has long been a way in which people ground their identities, as, say, Christians or Muslims. It often offers a more deeply felt identity than political affiliation: People can change their political parties easily and people barely notice, but if you convert (change your religion) it's a very big deal. Religion informs our interactions and imbues them with meaning; it provides ready-made hierarchies of the saved and unsaved, those who are close to the God or gods, and those who are out of favor.

As a social institution, religion operates like most other institutions. It provides rules of conduct, which are often followed less by the leaders than by the followers. Religious organizations, like churches, are hierarchical organizations in which mobility is contingent on certain kinds of performance measures, not as much by how ardently you believe. There are bureaucratic rules to follow just as there are in political institutions and workplaces.

But why do we "have" religion? Why do we "need" religion? What purpose does religion serve in our society? Sociologists are less interested in proving the truth or falsity of particular theological doctrines (they are, by definition, unprovable), but rather in understanding how religion functions in our everyday lives.

Classical Theories of Religion

15.3.1 Understand key differences between classical theorists in their understandings of the role of religion in social life.

Sociologists have long been fascinated by how religion operates in a society. After all, religion is a **cultural universal**—that is, it exists in every single culture. No human society has yet been discovered that lacks an organized, coherent system of beliefs about a spiritual world. However, religions vary tremendously. Some have no gods, some have many, and some have only one. Some believe in a heaven or a hell, some in reincarnation, some in both, and some do not believe in an afterlife at all. Sociologists are less interested in debating the truth of religious doctrine than in the function of religion. Why do all societies have one? What does religion *do* for the society?

cultural universal

One of the rituals, customs, and symbols that are evident in all societies.

Similar to the ways that Catholics and Protestants drink wine in church as a religious ritual, reaffirming their faith, Hindus do not eat beef or pork. Here, a Hindu man bows to a decorated cow as a ritual way of receiving the blessings of God during one of the largest religious gatherings on earth, held every 12 years—the Maha Kumbh Mela, celebrated over 55 days and attracting more than 100 million people in India.

sacred

Holy moments that evoke a sense of reverence and unity.

profane

That which is not sacred or Biblical, or not concerned with religion or religious purposes.

sacrilegious

That which is profane, blasphemous, impious, irreverent, or sinful.

ritual

Enactment by which members of a culture engage in a routine behavior to express their sense of belonging to the culture.

civil religion

Robert Bellah's term for the tendency of modern, secular societies to develop secular rituals that create the intense emotional bonds among people that used to be accomplished by religion.

For Émile Durkheim, religion served to integrate society, to create a sense of unity out of an enormously diverse collection of individuals. Religion provides a sort of social glue that holds society together, binding us into a common destiny and common values. Durkheim suggested that every society is organized around understandings of what is **sacred** versus what is **profane**. Not every society understands the same actions, objects, and ideas as sacred or as profane; but every society has this distinction. Hindus believe that cows are *sacred* animals—that they represent all other animals and is an earthly symbol representing life and vitality. For this reason, most Hindus do not eat beef and doing so would be **sacrilegious**. Yet, beef is eaten in many societies around the world among people who do not identify as Hindu. To Hindus, cows (and thus, beef) are sacred. To others, cows are profane. Yet in either of these belief systems, religious beliefs work to hold a society together.

To understand the social mechanism by which religion works to hold societies together, Durkheim went back to the origins of society. He surmised that primitive cultures were so overcome by the mystery and power of nature—lightning striking a tree, for instance—that they would come together as a group. These events were seen as sacred—holy moments that evoked that sense of unity. Cultures then try to recreate these moments in **ritual**—solemn reenactments of the sacred events. Rituals would remind individuals that they are part of a whole that is greater than the sum of its parts. Durkheim's emphasis on what holds a society together is important to sociologists who study modern societies, where the greater complexity and diversity pose many challenges to social unity. As we read previously in this chapter, this is what led sociologist Robert Bellah (1967) to suggest that modern, secular societies develop what he calls a **civil religion** in which secular rituals create the intense emotional bonds among people that used to be accomplished by religion. Standing up for our national anthem at a baseball game is different from standing in line at mass to accept wine and bread as the body and blood of a deity, but—from a sociological perspective—both rituals serve to unite a group of people around a sacred belief system.

Although Durkheim saw the positive aspects of religion as social glue, other classical sociologists have explored religion as a form of control. As we've seen, religion attempts to answer basic questions of human existence, which are profound and terrifying, but also provides a way to organize one's life in preparation for the next world. Yet a successful transition to the next life requires obeying specific cultural norms: Do not eat pork (if you're Jewish or Muslim), do not drink alcohol (if you're Muslim or Pentecostal). Religion offers a spiritual justification for why you should obey the rules and not try to make any changes. Marx believed that religion kept social change from happening by preventing people from revolting against the miserable conditions of their lives. In feudal society, Marx argued, religion served as a sort of ideological "blinder" to the reality of exploitation. Because the lords of the manor owned everything, including the rights to the labor of the serfs, anyone could tell that there was brutal inequality. So how could the lords stay in power? How come the serfs didn't revolt? Marx argued that religion provided a justification for inequality. For example, the belief in the "Great Chain of Being," in which all creatures, from insects to kings, were arranged on a single hierarchical arrangement ordained by God, justified the dominion of those at the top over those at the bottom. Marx called religion "the opiate of the masses," a drug that made people numb to the painful reality of inequality.

Weber, by contrast, argued that religion could be a catalyst to change. Weber's earliest work considered why capitalism developed in Western Europe in the way that it did. After all, he noted, capitalist economic activity (profit-maximizing buying and selling) had certainly existed as the dominant economic form of life in other times and places—notably in ancient China, ancient India, and among the ancient Jews. But none of these societies sustained capitalist activity. Only western Europe, in the fifteenth and sixteenth centuries, broke out of feudalism, its established social order, by developing instead a type of capitalism that was self-sustaining. Why? Weber reasoned that it might have had something to do with the impact of religious ideas on economic activity. In the other three cases, religious ideas interfered with economic life, restrained trade, and made it more difficult for capitalism to become a self-sustaining system. He noticed that Protestant countries (Britain, Holland, Germany, the United States) had advanced earlier and further than Catholic countries such as Italy, Portugal, Spain, and France.

Perhaps the Protestant Reformation had freed individuals from constraints and enabled each individual to develop his or her relationship to God directly, without priests or churches as intermediaries. Although Catholicism offered certainty—believers were certain they were going to heaven if they fulfilled the sacraments—Protestantism offered only insecurity; one could never know God's plan. This insecurity led Protestants, especially Calvinists, to begin to work exceptionally hard in this life to reduce the insecurity about where they might be going when they die. Thus, Weber argued, individuals began to work harder and longer, to approach economic life rationally, through careful calculation of costs and benefits, and to resist the temptation to enjoy the fruits of their labor—which led to rapid and dramatic accumulation of capital for investment. These practices, which are religious in origin, eventually enabled capitalism in the West to become self-sustaining. Yet, Weber was pessimistic about the future of this economic activity. Without the original ethical and religious foundation, Weber predicted, we would become trapped in an "iron cage" of routine, senseless economic acquisition.

All three of these classical theorists shared several sociological insights. First, although we may experience our religious beliefs as individuals, religion is a profoundly *social* phenomenon. And they all believed that **religiosity**, the extent of one's religious practice, dedication and belief, typically measured by attendance at religious observances or maintaining religious practices, would decline in modern societies. None, for instance, would have predicted that religion would be as important to Americans as it is today.

religiosity

Sociological term for the numerous aspects of an individual's religious activity, dedication, and belief. A more colloquial term would be "religiousness."

Religious Groups

15.3.2 Distinguish between the different types of religious groups that sociologists classify and study.

There are many forms of religious organizations. Some are small scale, with immediate and very personal contact; others are larger institutions with administrative bureaucracies that rival those of complex countries. These differ not only in size and scale but also in their relationship to other social institutions, the level of training for specific roles within the religion, and the levels of administration (see TABLE 15.1).

TABLE 15.1   Types of Religious Organizations

	Cult	Sect	Denomination	Ecclesia
Size	Small	Small	Large	Universal
Wealth	Poor	Poor	Wealthy	Extensive
Beliefs	Strict	Strict	Diversity Tolerated	Diversity Tolerated
Practices	Variable	Informal	Formal	Formal
Clergy	Untrained	Some training	Extensive training	Extensive training
Membership	Emotional commitment	Accepting doctrine	Birth/decision to join	By belonging to a society

The International Society of Krishna Consciousness (or Hare Krishnas) is considered a cult in the United States. In India, however, it is an established Hindu sect.

cult

The simplest form of religious organization, characterized typically by fervent believers and a single idea or leader.

sect

A small subculture within an established religious institution. Like cults, they break from traditional practices, but unlike cults, they remain within the larger institution.

denomination

A large-scale, extremely organized religious body with an established hierarchy, methods for credentialing administrators, and much more social respect than either a cult or a sect.

The simplest form of religious organization, a **cult**, forms around a specific person or idea drawn from an established religion. It is often formed by splitting off from the main branch of the religion. Cults are distinguished by the measure of loyalty they extract from members. Typically small, cults are also composed of deeply fervent believers. Members of cults leave behind their membership in older religious institutions and often live on the margins of society. Thus, they typically run afoul of local and national governments. And that may mean violent repression, such as the 1993 raid on the Branch Davidian compound outside Waco, Texas. And some cults can develop murderous messianic tendencies as well. In 1995, a cult called Aum Shinrikyo (Supreme Truth) released sarin gas on the Tokyo subway during the morning rush hour, killing 12 people and injuring thousands of others.

But some cults do persist and can develop into religious sects. A **sect** is a small subculture within an established religious institution. Like cults, they break from traditional practices, but unlike cults they remain within the larger institution. For example, the Jehovah's Witnesses are usually classified as a Christian sect. Sects typically arise when some members of an established religious institution believe that the institution is drifting from its true mission, becoming sidetracked by extraneous, more "worldly" pursuits. Like cults, many sects are short-lived. This is generally the case either because the initial *charismatic leader*—a person whose extraordinary personal qualities touch people deeply enough to motivate them to break with tradition—leaves the group, or because they encourage reforms within the established religious institution. Yet, some sects become "established sects" and develop their own formal institutional arrangements within a larger religious institutional framework (see Yinger 1970). In Christianity, the Church of Jesus Christ of Latter-day Saints (Mormons) or the Amish are established sects. Hasidic Jews are a Jewish established sect; the Druze in Lebanon are an independent established sect with ties to Islam. The International Society of Krishna Consciousness (the Hare Krishnas) may be considered a cult in the United States, but it is an established sect in India.

Different from both cults and sects, a religious **denomination** is a large-scale, extremely organized religious body. It has an established hierarchy, methods for credentialing administrators, and much more social respect than either a cult or a sect. Members of cults and sects are often subject to prejudice and discrimination in the mainstream society, but members of denominations are usually considered "normal." The various Pentecostal churches were considered cults or sects as long as their members were mostly poor, urban, and African American; but once they began to gain white middle-class converts, they quickly became denominations. In the United States, the overwhelming majority of the population belongs to one of the denominations of Christianity. The largest is the Evangelical Protestant denomination (25.4 percent). Almost 50 percent of all Americans claim membership in a Protestant denomination (chiefly Methodist, Baptist, Presbyterian, or Lutheran). Twenty percent of Americans identify as Catholic. There are 5.9 million Jews in the United States (1.9 percent), 3 million Muslims (0.9 percent), 2 million Buddhists (0.7 percent), and 1 million Hindus (0.7 percent) (Pew Research Center 2015).

With some 2,000 cults, sects, and denominations in the United States, how do you decide which one to join? Most people adopt the religion of their parents, and stay with it throughout their lives, with little conscious choice. Like our social class, we land in religious traditions through our families. Many denominations accept new members at birth, or offer membership at such a young age that one could scarcely be said to carefully weigh alternatives. A third of the U.S. population has changed

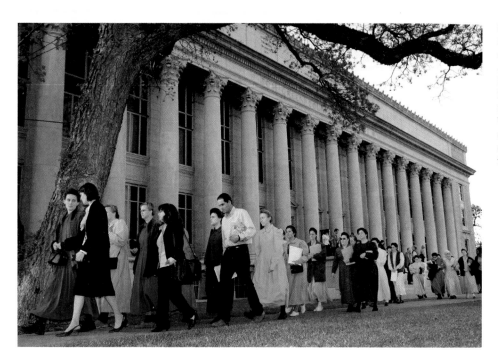

Sects are smaller subcultures within denominations. The compound of the Fundamentalist Church of Jesus Christ of Latter-day Saints, a Mormon splinter group, was raided in April 2008, and 416 children were removed from the polygamous sect's West Texas ranch by officials. The children were placed in temporary custody of the state, but later returned to their families.

denominations, but they usually do not walk into a strange church or temple and say "I want to join you." Most commonly, they adopt the religion of a friend or romantic partner (Pew Research Center 2015).

There is one more formal religious organization, the **ecclesiae**, or religion so pervasive that the boundary between state and church is nonexistent. In such societies, the clerical elite often serve as political leaders or at least formal advisors to political leaders. Everyone in the society belongs to that faith by birth, not individual decision, and those who do not belong to the faith cannot become citizens. Until the French Revolution, the clergy in France was one of the two pillars on which the monarchy rested (the other was the nobility). Today, the Muslim clerics in Saudi Arabia and the Shi'ite mullahs in Iran are nearly identical with political leadership. Such merging of politics and religion is not inevitable. Some societies with established state churches remain remarkably free of clerical influence in political matters. In Sweden, for instance, the Lutheran Church has official status, but it exerts virtually no influence on political decision making. Politics and religion are institutions with deep ties in every society, but some attempt to sever these ties more than others.

ecclesiae

A political assembly of the faithful in which the clerical elite often serve as political leaders or at least formal advisors to political leaders. Everyone in the society belongs to that faith by birth, not individual decision, and those who do not belong to the faith cannot become citizens.

Religions of the World

15.3.3 Explain key differences between the major world religions and understand their relative popularity around the world.

Sociologists are not only fascinated by religion as a cultural universal, but they are also interested in the remarkable diversity of religious belief and practice. In most places, local, traditional religions have given way to **world religions**, religions with a long history, well-established traditions, and the flexibility to adapt to many different cultures.

Three of the world's major religions, Judaism, Christianity, and Islam (plus a few smaller ones) are called **Western religions** because, while they originated in the Middle East, their adherents are largely among Western nations. They all trace their spiritual ancestry to the same event: About 2000 BCE, a nomadic tribe living in ancient Mesopotamia recognized that their god, Yahweh, was not specific to their tribe, but was the god of all the world. (In the Bible, it is Abraham who is the first ethical monotheist, a believer in only one God who is concerned that you act morally in

world religions

Religions with a long history, well-established traditions, and the flexibility to adapt to many different cultures.

Western religions

Three of the world's major religions—Judaism, Christianity, and Islam (plus a few smaller ones)—are called "Western" because, although they originated in the Middle East, their adherents are largely among Western nations.

U.S./WORLD

RELIGIOUS TRADITION AND VARIATION AROUND THE WORLD

Religious traditions vary incredibly throughout the world. And they vary in two key ways in which sociologists are interested. Different societies have different dominant religious traditions. So, in some societies most people are Hindu, or Muslim, or Christian, or Buddhist, for instance. But societies also vary in how dominant the most dominant religious traditions are. For instance, a little more than three-quarters of the U.S. population identify as Christian. It's the dominant religious tradition in the United States. Mexico and Brazil also share Christianity and the dominant religious tradition, but in those nations, Christianity is much *more* dominant.

- Christian
- Muslim
- Buddhist
- Unaffiliated
- Hindu
- Jewish
- Folk Religion

SOURCE: Data from Pew Research Center, "Global Religious Landscape. Table: Religious Composition by Country" (2010) and "Christians are the Largest Religious Group in 2015." Available at http://www.pewforum.org/files/2012/12/globalReligion-tables.pdf and http://www.pewforum.org/2017/04/05/the-changing-global-religious-landscape/pf_17-04-05_projectionsupdate_grl310px/.

On this map, you can see the dominant religions in societies around the world. Some societies have much more religious diversity than others, whereas others are almost uniformly dominated by a single religious tradition. The United States falls somewhere between these two poles. We have a dominant religion by a large margin in the population, but we also have enough religious diversity that identifying with and practicing another religion puts you in good company with about one in five other Americans who are not Christian.

INVESTIGATE FURTHER

1. Why do you think the United States is neither dominated by a single religious tradition nor is it a fully religiously pluralist society? What social, institutional, and historical factors might give rise to the unique religious composition of the United States?

this world.) They eventually founded Judaism (after Judea, where they settled), and they tried to follow God's law as revealed in the Torah, his sacred book. Christianity arose 2,000 years later out of a protest against the "corruption" of Judaism, and Islam 600 years after that as a protest to the "corruption" of both, so all three religions share many beliefs and practices. Because Christianity and Islam emerged from these critiques of previous religions, they share several characteristics:

- They are exclusive: They believe they have the one true faith.
- They are evangelistic: They want you to choose their faith.
- There is only one god (although sometimes there are intermediaries, like saints and angels).
- There is usually a heaven and a hell, where we will experience eternal joy or torment.
- There is a sacred book, usually revealed by God, which followers are expected to read and obey.
- Believers are expected to attend regular worship services, held on the holiest day of the week.
- A messiah is coming to save us. (For Christians, he has already come, but he's coming back; the Shi'ite is the only Muslim denomination that believes this.)

The influence of Judaism and Christianity spread west, through Europe, although the influence of Islam spread east and south, throughout the Arabian Peninsula and into India and Central Asia. Today, of course, all three religions have adherents worldwide (see U.S./WORLD Religious Tradition and Variation Around the World). Today there are about 14 million Jews in the world (0.2 percent of the world's population), 2.2 billion Christians (about one-third of all the world's people), and roughly 1.6 billion Muslims (roughly 20 percent of the world's population).

All three of these religions are divided into various denominations and sects, based on interpretations of their religious texts. Some interpret these texts liberally and thus enable religious belief to casually coexist with modern life. Others are more demanding. At the extreme ends of all these religions are fundamentalist groups, which claim to be the purest and truest followers of their religion. **Fundamentalism** tries to return to the basic precepts, the "true word of God," and live exactly according to his precepts.

Three other major religions of the world, Hinduism, Buddhism, and Confucianism (plus some minor ones), are called **Eastern Religions** because they arose in Asia, although, like the Western Religions, they have adherents around the world. They have many beliefs and practices in common, some of which might baffle people raised in a Western religion. They are not doctrinally exclusive: It may be possible to practice Buddhism, Hinduism, Confucianism, Taoism, and any other religion you want, all at the same time. There are many gods (although often religious scholars interpret them as emanations of a single god). There is no heaven or hell, just an endless series of reincarnations until you achieve enlightenment (except in Confucianism). There is no specific sacred book, although sometimes there are vast libraries of sacred texts to be revered. And there are no regular worship services. Temples are used for special rituals. Today there are one billion Hindus (14 percent of all religious adherents), 94 percent of whom live in India; 488 million Buddhists (7 percent of all adherents), mostly in East Asia; and it is hard to determine the number of adherents of Confucianism because officially no religions are practiced in mainland China.

Eastern religions tend to be somewhat more tolerant of other religions than Western religions. Without the

Fundamentalism
Forms of religion that uphold belief in strict, literal interpretations of scripture.

Eastern Religions
Three other major religions of the world—Hinduism, Buddhism, and Confucianism (plus some minor ones)—are called "Eastern" because they arose in Asia, although, like the Western Religions, they have adherents around the world.

Buddhist priests practice meditation and a strict physical and spiritual discipline to reach enlightenment.

privileged access to revealed truth—by which conversion of nonbelievers is a mission of love—there is not as much need for coerced conversion or the bloody religious wars that have appeared for millennia in the West.

Thinking about Religion Sociologically: Secularization or Resurgence?

15.3.4 Summarize the dual processes of secularization and religious resurgence on a global scale.

secularization

The process of moving away from religious spirituality and toward the worldly.

Early sociologists believed that as societies became more modern, religion would decline. Individuals, and society as a whole, would no longer need it, and so society would become increasingly secular. **Secularization**—the process of moving away from religious spirituality and toward the worldly—was assumed to be the future of religion around the world. Marx believed that as capitalism developed, we would all become rational individuals, interested only in self-interest and the bottom line. Capitalism, he wrote, would "drown the heavenly ecstasies of religious fervor" in the "icy water of egotistical calculation." Weber believed that religious ideas had a way of becoming applied in the everyday world, and that this process made religious ideas less mysterious and special, which in turn, led to their becoming less meaningful to us. And Durkheim thought religion would decline because society, itself, would perform the functions of religion—ensuring group cohesion and providing meaning and social control. The secularization hypothesis was so well accepted that it became a sort of truism; no one contradicted it because it seemed so "right."

Over the years, sociologists amassed a lot of empirical data to support the theory of secularization. But it didn't happen as sociologists had predicted. For one thing, religion has not declined worldwide, despite the dramatic modernization of societies and the technological breakthroughs of the past century. Religious adherence is prospering in a wide variety of different societies. In fact, the majority of countries in the world, the majority of the global population, is experiencing religious resurgence (see FIGURE 15.6).

Worldwide, more than 8 in 10 people identify with a religious group. In 2015, there were approximately 6.1 billion religiously affiliated adults and children in the world, a number that represented 84 percent of the global population (Pew Research Center 2017). In fact, Christianity is not only the world's largest religion today, but, in some regions, particularly in the developing world, it is the fastest-growing religion as well; though overall, Islam is projected to grow at a faster rate over the next few decades than is Christianity (Pew Research Center 2017). Increasingly, trends such as this rapid growth of Christianity in the global south and both comparatively high rates of fertility among Muslims and their increased immigration to Western nations are shaping both public attitudes and government policies around the world.

In the developing world, religion continues to hold enormous sway over the society. For many years, sociologists believed that a society's adherence to religious beliefs was one of the major cultural barriers to modernity. But religion offers an alternative to modern society, which people may regard as corrupt—and corrupting. For example, Buddhism or Confucianism propose radical disengagement with the material world (transcendence), and others offer a parallel spiritual world that enable you to live in the world but not succumb to it (like, for example orthodox Judaism). Other religions, such as some groups of fundamentalist Muslims or Christians demand fervent engagement with the world as a way to redirect society away from such corruption.

From a European perspective, the secularization thesis is more valid than it is in the United States; religious affiliation, belief in God, and church attendance in Europe

FIGURE 15.6 Projected Shifts in Religious Populations Around the World, 2010–2050

Other than Buddhists, populations in every major world religion in the world today are projected to increase by 2060. Yet much of this change is the result of global population growth more generally. So, although the number of Christians is predicted to increase from 2.28 billion to more than 3 billion by 2060, they are not predicted to make up a larger share of the global population than they do currently. Meanwhile, Muslims are projected to grow in both number and in proportion—from 24 percent to 30 percent of the global population by 2060.

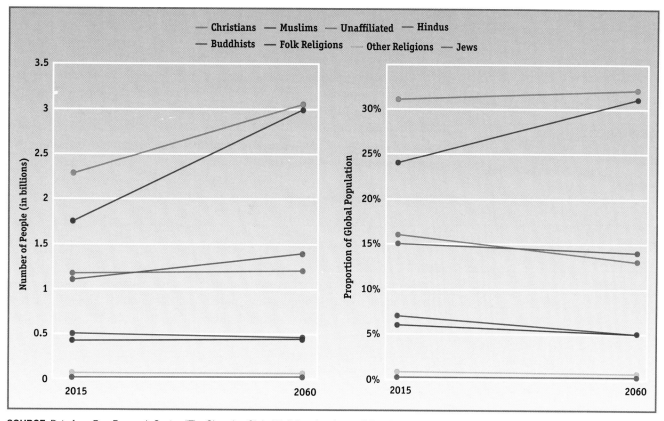

SOURCE: Data from Pew Research Center. "The Changing Global Religious Landscape." *Pew Research Center, Religion & Public Life*, April 5, 2017. Available at http://www.pewforum.org/2017/04/05/the-changing-global-religious-landscape/.

are but a fraction of what they were a century ago. Were it not for one very big exception, one might say that the more industrially and technologically developed a society is, the lower its rates of religious beliefs. In those industrial countries where the government provides the most extensive social safety net (health care, retirement benefits), rates of church attendance have decreased most dramatically. Church attendance throughout Scandinavia is at an all-time low, and most people who do attend are elderly. The lowest level of church attendance is in Denmark, where only 3 percent of the population report attending church on a weekly basis. Even in Italy, the seat of the Roman Catholic Church, attendance is at record lows—though this may be in part due to the fact that the proportion of the population who are baptized as Catholic has been declining in recent history (Pew Research Center 2013).

Indeed, in general, societies that are wealthier are less religious. So, for instance, the percentage of the population who say that religion plays a "very important" role in their lives decreases as the gross domestic product of societies increase (see U.S./WORLD How Important is Religion as a Socializing Force?—Chapter 5). The more money societies have, the less religious they tend to be. This is one of those social relationships that is true of *almost* every society in the world, and the United States is a real outlier here. We are much more religious than other societies with similar levels of wealth (Gao 2015).

The big exception to the rule concerning industrialization, technology, and wealth on the one hand, and religion on the other is the United States. Although scientific and economic progress has continued virtually unabated, so too has religious affiliation. The United States has about 10 percent fewer non-believers than even the state of Israel, let alone European countries (Gallup 2015). The United States always has been a strongly religious country, and we continue to be. It stands alone among wealthy, industrialized countries in its embrace of religion. Nearly 6 in 10 Americans say religion plays a *very* important role in their lives. Considered in international comparison, about 1 in 10 Japanese feel the same way, and the statistic is less than 1 in 20 in Britain, France, and South Korea (Gao 2015).

theory of religious economy

The hypothesis that societies that restrict supply of religion—whether that is through imposed state religions or state-sponsored secularization—are the main causes of drops in religiosity. Simply put, the more religions a society has and acknowledges, the more likely the population is to be religious.

Part of the answer to this sociologically puzzle about Americans' enduring religious zeal, despite economic progress is that we have greater religious diversity than do many other nations with whom we share similar levels of industrialization and wealth. And, according to Stark and Bainbridge's (1985, 1987) **theory of religious economy**, the fact that we have more options when it comes to religion than many other societies might explain our enduring faith.

Religion in the United States

15.3.5 Describe some of the reasons that the United States fails to follow larger patterns related to economic growth, development, and rates of religious beliefs and participation.

Around the time the United States was founded, Thomas Jefferson confidently predicted that people would eventually think of the Bible as a book of myths, like Greek mythology. Yet faith in the literal truth of the Bible remains strong, and the United States remains one of the world's most churchgoing societies. Why have rates of religious belief and participation declined in every European country but not in the United States?

SOCIOLOGY AND OUR WORLD

IS RELIGIOUS PLURALISM RESPONSIBLE FOR AMERICANS' ENDURING RELIGIOUS BELIEFS?

Could it be that because Americans have more religious options, they are more likely to hold onto religion, despite other trends typically associated with secularization in other societies?

Sociologists Rodney Stark and William Sims Bainbridge (1985, 1987) thought about the puzzle of American religiosity from a different perspective. Taking an economic perspective, they considered every society to be complete with a *religious economy*—the social arena within which different "religious suppliers" (like, say Catholicism, Buddhism, Judaism, or Islam) attempt to meet the demands of the collection of "religious consumers" who make up that society. Societies dominated by a single religious tradition offer only a small collection of religious "products" and "services." Societies accepting of and acknowledging a diversity of religious traditions and religions have a more competitive religious economy. It's a metaphor that might cause some to cringe because it treats religion as a "product" and those who practice or identify with a particular religious tradition as "consumers."

This was Stark and Bainbridge's answer to the sociological puzzle about why the United States is not more secular than it is. The United States is an outlier on a global stage when it comes to this aspect of our society. Stark and Bainbridge suggested that it is precisely the fact that there is so much religious diversity in the United States that accounts for Americans' enduring

religiosity, despite social shifts that have led to secularization in virtually every other nation on earth. We're an outlier. According to the *theory of religious economy*, societies that restrict supply of religion—whether that is through imposed state religions or state-sponsored secularization—are the main causes of drops in religiosity. Simply put, the more religions a society has and acknowledges, the more likely the population is to be religious. Just as big box stores cause us to buy more because we're more likely to find the exact products we're looking for, more religious options cause us to be more likely to find a religious tradition that suits us.

The theory is not without its critics in the field. And sociologists generally find *rational choice theory* (a theory that dominates economic explanations of social behavior) problematic. But, it is one provocative answer to the puzzle of the endurance of American religiosity and why the United States has bucked the secularization trend that seems to have led to less religious identification in virtually every other society. We explore some other explanations in the next section.

One factor might be that the United States has been, since its inception, more than simply a nation of immigrants; it's actually a nation of *religious* immigrants. Since the Pilgrims were kicked out of England, the United States has always been a haven for those who were constrained from practicing their religion elsewhere—European Jews, Chinese Christians, Russian Orthodox believers, and so on (see FIGURE 15.7). As some nations become increasingly secular, those who are religious may seek a haven in the United States. As a result, increased religiosity and increased secularism coexist.

Another factor is that the United States has been swept up in several waves of increased religious passion. There were two Great Awakenings, one in the 1720s and one in the 1820s, which witnessed a democratization of religion. These were reformist movements, telling Americans that God was less interested in fancy churches and ornaments than in the sincerity of an individual's beliefs. This may have increased Americans' individual commitment to a more personal relationship with their religious beliefs. Many observers consider this the Third Great Awakening in U.S. history, a religious revival that further democratizes spirituality, making a relationship with the sacred attainable to even greater numbers of Americans, and with even less effort or religious discipline. For example, although more Americans are deeply religious, they commit to religious organizations only as long as they like them; one in three Americans has switched denomination according to a Gallup poll.

Still a third factor has been the way that American religious institutions have grown as providers of social support and cultural interaction. In Europe, churches are often tourist attractions, but locals rarely set foot inside. During one of the author's first trips to London, he thought it might be a good idea to attend a service in Westminster Abbey. But services are held in the Abbey only on Sundays; every other day they're held in a tiny basement chapel—with about 30 people in attendance. Even the great cathedrals of Europe, like Notre Dame in Paris, or St. Peter's in Rome, or the Cathedral of Seville, have sparse attendance at mass—and then the congregation is composed largely of tourists.

FIGURE 15.7 How Americans Describe Their Religious Identity

Approximately 70.6 percent of Americans identify as Christian (though they are broken up into different religious traditions here). The next largest group, who comprise 22.8 percent of Americans, are those who declare no religious identification ("unaffiliated"). The majority of this group identify as "nothing in particular" (15.8 percent of Americans), and the remaining people here are divided between agnostics (4 percent) and atheists (3.1 percent).

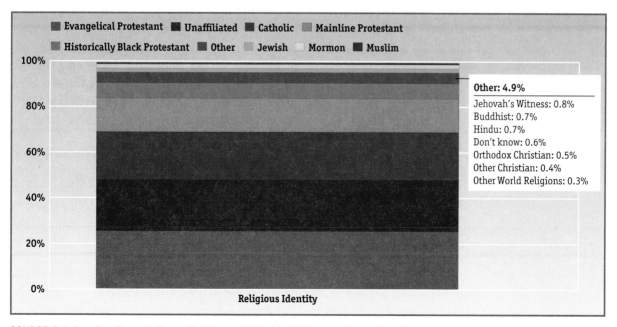

SOURCE: Data from Pew Research Center, "Religion and Public Life, Religious Landscape Study," 2014. Available at http://www.pewforum.org/religious-landscape-study/.

Church attendance in all industrialized countries except the United States is at or near all-time lows. Even in Italy, home of the Pope, church attendance is significantly less than it has been in several centuries. At this evening mass in St. Peter's Basilica in Rome, many of the people are actually tourists.

U.S. churches, by contrast, are almost always full. Churches are often the social and cultural center of the town. Every night there are groups that meet there, from Alcoholics Anonymous to Bible study to social gatherings for divorced parents. Religious institutions not only run parochial schools, but many organize preschool and daycare facilities (these are provided by the government in European countries). Churches sponsor soccer leagues and wilderness retreats, picnics, and bingo nights. They have become the social—as well as the spiritual—hub of U.S. communities, especially important as other civic supports have declined.

Perhaps one of the other reasons religion is so strong in the United States is, ironically, *because* of its separation from political life. The separation of church and state, the prohibitions on school prayer, and the general global trend toward secularization make religiosity something of a rebellion against the dominant culture. Portraying oneself as a minority, whose status as a victim of state persecution, is almost always a good way to recruit new members. Finally, it may be that the assumptions that one had to choose between religious and secular life were invalid. Americans hold religious beliefs in ways that can fit readily into an otherwise secular life. American religious beliefs are modified so that we can be both sacred and secular. Christian bookstores are open on Sundays; children come to church dressed in their soccer uniforms (Gibbs 2004).

Thinking Intersectionally: Religious Diversity in the United States

15.3.6 Summarize the ways that religion intersects with nation, region, age, and race in the United States in ways that help explain recent shifts in religious identification.

Just as the United States has become more racially and ethnically diverse, so too has it come to have more religious diversity. It is still the case that Christianity is the dominant religion in the United States—roughly 7 in 10 Americans today identify as Christian. But, even in very recent history, between 2007 and 2014, the Christian share of the American population fell by almost 8 percent! That's a huge shift in a relatively short period of time.

As you can see in FIGURE 15.8, the decline among Protestants and Catholics is primarily accounted for by increases among non-Christian faiths in the United States (including Jews, Muslims, Hindus, Buddhists, among other world religions and faiths) as well as an incredible increase among the religiously unaffiliated (a group we will return to shortly). This contrasts sharply with projected shifts in this population on a global scale. By 2060, the religiously unaffiliated are projected to shrink as a proportion of the world population, but this trend does not appear to describe the United States.

And when we examine this trend intersectionally, it's also true that Christianity is becoming more diverse even as it is in decline in the United States. Non-Hispanic whites account for a smaller share of both Protestants and Catholics in the United States than they did in recent history, shares that have been primarily taken up by Hispanic Americans. As of 2014, racial and ethnic minorities make up 41 percent of Catholics, 24 percent of Evangelical Protestants, and 14 percent of Mainline Protestants.

Religious identity intersects with every other form of identity and can be examined as a significant intersection. For instance, religion powerfully intersects with age. Older people in the United States are more religious than are younger people. And, although more religious groups in the United States today are aging (meaning that the average age of people identifying with various religious traditions is on the rise), the religiously

FIGURE 15.8 Shifts in Religious Identity in the United States, 2007–2014

Although non-Christian faiths in the United States have become a slightly larger share of the population, the biggest change in recent history in the United States is the increasing proportion of people who claim to be religiously unaffiliated—from 16.1 percent of the U.S. population in 2007, to 22.8 percent of the population by 2014. This is a big shift in a short period of time.

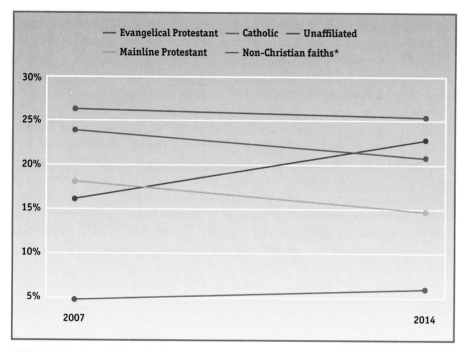

NOTE: *Includes Jews, Muslims, Buddhists, Hindus, other world religions, and other faiths. Those who did not answer the religious identity question, as well as groups whose share of the population did not change significantly, including the historically black Protestant tradition, Mormons, and others, are not shown.

SOURCE: Data from Pew Research Center, 2014 Religious Landscape Study, conducted June 4–Sept. 30, 2014. Available at http://www.pewforum.org/2015/05/12/americas-changing-religious-landscape/.

unaffiliated are comparatively young. More than that, those unaffiliated with any religious tradition in the United States are actually getting *younger* over time. In 2014, the median age of the religiously unaffiliated was 36 years (meaning half of them are 36 or older and half are 36 or younger). Just for comparison, the median age for Catholics in the United States is 49, and for Mainline Protestants that figure is 52 (Pew Research Center 2015).

But it is also true that religious beliefs, adherence, and attendance vary greatly around the United States. So, not only are we religiously diverse, but that diversity is also expressed geographically in the United States. Although about 83 percent of Americans are either absolutely or fairly certain that God exists, those who share this belief are not evenly distributed around the United States—there are more of them in some areas and less in others. For instance, 88 percent of people share this belief in Texas, 89 percent in Louisiana, and 91 percent in Mississippi. But only 67 percent of people in Vermont are either absolutely or fairly certain than God exists (Pew Research Center 2015). In general, those who profess a stronger belief in God tend to have less education and tend to live in states with lower levels of income. Regionally speaking, the South, tends to have the highest rates of belief in God.

On the Religiously Unaffiliated

15.3.7 Explain some key changes in the population of religiously unaffiliated in the United States and around the world in recent history.

The population of people in the world that are not formally affiliated with any religious tradition, or actively accept a belief system that explicitly denounces belief in a religious tradition or a deity is growing. This means that people identifying as **atheist**,

atheist

A person who does not believe in the existence of God.

agnostic
A person who claims neither faith nor disbelief in God, usually asserting that nothing is known or can be known about the existence or nature of God.

or **agnostic**, or people who do not identify with any religious tradition when asked are all on the rise. In the most recent estimates, the religiously unaffiliated worldwide account for approximately 16 percent of the global population, or 1.1 billion people. It is also important to note, though, that there is a lot of diversity even among the religiously unaffiliated. For instance, although 7 percent of religiously unaffiliated people in China believe in God or a higher power, 30 percent of French unaffiliated shared this belief, and 68 percent of the religiously unaffiliated in the United States believe in either God or a higher power. Twenty-seven percent of the people who are religiously unaffiliated in the United States also claim to go to church at least once a year.

And although the proportion of the religiously unaffiliated population in the United States has been increasing, the majority of the world's religiously unaffiliated people are in Asia and the Pacific (see MAP 15.3). Indeed, North America only accounts for roughly 1 in 20 religiously unaffiliated people on earth (Pew Research Center 2012).

And age is meaningfully related to religious affiliation throughout the world, but not always in the same direction. For instance, in Latin America, North America, and Europe, the religiously unaffiliated have a median age *below* that of the median age in the region (they are, as a group, slightly younger than those around them). This

MAP 15.3 The Global Distribution of the Religiously Unaffiliated
The United States accounts for only 5.2 percent of the world's 1.1 billion religiously unaffiliated people. A full three-quarters (76.2 percent) of religiously unaffiliated people live in Asia and the Pacific (partially because so many people live there). So, although they are more numerous, they are a smaller proportion of the population (about one in five) than the religiously unaffiliated are in Europe and the United States (roughly one in six in both).

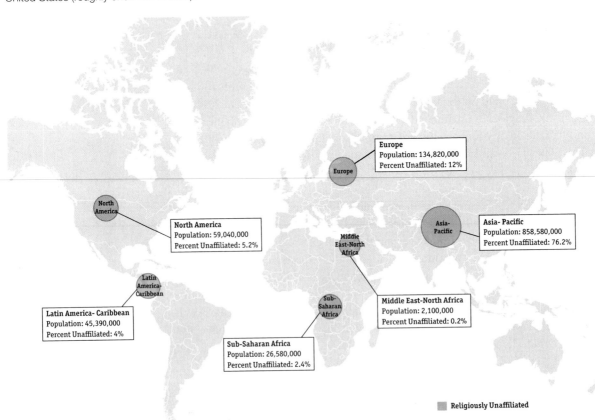

Europe
Population: 134,820,000
Percent Unaffiliated: 12%

North America
Population: 59,040,000
Percent Unaffiliated: 5.2%

Asia-Pacific
Population: 858,580,000
Percent Unaffiliated: 76.2%

Latin America- Caribbean
Population: 45,390,000
Percent Unaffiliated: 4%

Middle East-North Africa
Population: 2,100,000
Percent Unaffiliated: 0.2%

Sub-Saharan Africa
Population: 26,580,000
Percent Unaffiliated: 2.4%

Religiously Unaffiliated

NOTE: Population estimates are rounded to the ten thousands. Percentages may not add up to 100 due to rounding.
SOURCE: Data from Pew Research Center. "The Global Religious Landscape: Religiously Unaffiliated." *Pew Research Center, Religion & Social Life*, December 18, 2012. Available at: http://www.pewforum.org/2012/12/18/global-religious-landscape-unaffiliated/.

is the case in the United States, so it might make sense to those of you reading this from the United States. Younger people are less religious in the United States. So, it might not be all that surprising to read that younger people are less attracted to religion in general in the United States than are older individuals. That trend, however, is not true everywhere in the world. In Asia and the Pacific, and sub-Saharan Africa, for instance, the religiously unaffiliated have a median age *above* that of the median age of the region (they are, as a group, slightly older than those around them). The median age of people living in Asia and the Pacific is 29 years old, but the median age of religiously unaffiliated people in that region of the world is 35 years old (Pew Research Center 2012).

And although it is the case that the United States remains a global outlier in the high level of religiosity it exhibits compared to the wealth of the society (as we saw previously), it is also the case that those unaffiliated with any religion are a growing population here as well. For instance, Americans have always rated religion as very important in their lives on a variety of measures (religious attendance rates, statements regarding the importance of religion in Americans' lives, ranking the importance of God in Americans' lives on a scale from 1 to 10, etc.). Today, the religiously unaffiliated in the United States account for just less than one-quarter of the population (Pew Research Center 2015). The religiously unaffiliated comprise people who identify as atheist, agnostic, or nothing in particular when it comes to religious identity. And each of those groups has grown in recent history (see FIGURE 15.9). But who are they?

In general, those identifying as atheist are more likely to be men (68 percent of U.S. atheists) and more likely to be young in the United States (their median age is 34, compared with the U.S. median age of 46). Because religion intersects with other forms of identity, we also know that atheists are much more likely to identify politically as Democrat (69 percent of U.S. atheists) or politically liberal (56 percent of U.S. atheists). And as a group, they support opinions consistent with those political beliefs—for example, more than 9 in 10 U.S. atheists favor same-sex marriage (92%) and legal abortion (87%), and 74 percent feel that government aid to the poor does more good than harm. Atheists are also more educated and wealthier than are average Americans. A higher proportion of white Americans identify as religiously unaffiliated (20%) than black or Hispanic Americans (15 percent and 16 percent, respectively). And atheism is more common among the unmarried as well as those living in specific regions of the United States—the West and the Northeast United States (Pew Research Center 2012).

Americans more generally, have complicated feelings about atheists as a group. About one in two Americans claim they would be less likely to vote for a presidential candidate who did not believe in God. As a group, Americans like atheists less than they like members of most other religious groups. In 2014, on a scale from 1 to 100, when Americans were asked to describe how cold or warm they felt toward members of different religious groups, atheists received an average rating of 41. Evangelical Christians received a 61 on the same survey; Muslims received a 40 (Lipka 2016). Overall in the United States, however, there is a growing warmth toward all religious groups, including atheists, that crosses regional, age, and partisan lines (Pew Research Center 2017).

FIGURE 15.9 Growth Among the Religiously Unaffiliated in the United States, 2007–2014
The religiously unaffiliated in the United States do not necessarily see themselves as a single homogenous group of individuals. For instance, here you can see how those who contribute to the rise in those unaffiliated with religion are distinct from one another. The majority do not identify as "atheist" or "agnostic," but simply consider themselves "nothing in particular" when it comes to religion. Indeed, by 2014, almost 16 percent of Americans felt this way.

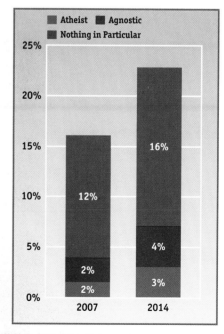

SOURCE: Data from Pew Research Center. "2014 Religious Landscape Survey," conducted June 4–September 30, 2014. Available at http://www.pewforum.org/2015/05/12/chapter-1-the-changing-religious-composition-of-the-u-s/#atheists-and-agnostics-make-up-a-growing-share-of-the-unaffiliated.

iSOC AND YOU Religion

Religious affiliation is a primary source of *identity* (even among those unaffiliated with religion), for some as important as ethnicity, race, or class. And, as such, it's a source of *inequality* as not all religious groups, practices, and beliefs are treated equally. Religion can often prescribe our *interactions* with others, and can also differentiate in our interactions with those who share a faith and those who don't. Thus, religious inequality is related to other *intersecting* aspects of inequality. The United States may be a religiously diverse nation, but it is also not truly inclusive of people of all faiths.

15.4 Politics and Religion in Everyday Life

Politics and religion are social institutions that either organize or impact every other institution in society and imbue them with meaning. But politics and religion do not only take place at the macro level, we also experience each in our individual lives and interactions. Politics is a social arena in which relations of power and authority are established and provided legitimacy. But we experience these lines of power and authority in our everyday lives as well. Religion establishes distinctions between what is sacred and profane. But this doesn't only affect the ways we worship. It impacts our moral understanding of the world around us and it helps us to learn to identify our community of believers—those who share the same values we do and whose beliefs are organized around a common set of symbols and shared rituals.

In that sense, both religion and politics are profoundly social. In discussing the Church of the Fling Spaghetti Monster (Gilsinan 2016), religious studies professor Douglas Cowan noted that "nothing is inherently sacred; it's sacred by virtue of the fact that people agree that it's sacred." In that sense, even if we believe that our deity precedes the world, it still requires the world to agree that this is so.

Religion as Politics

15.4.1 Describe some of the political elements of religious traditions and beliefs.

Religion has always been "political"—indeed, manifesting the vision of one's religious beliefs in the political arena is often an essential part of the religion. The great religious leaders, like Moses, Jesus, and Muhammad, found out firsthand that existing authorities find new religious beliefs threatening to their political control. Thus, although religion and politics are separate social institutions, they intersect a great deal.

Throughout the twentieth and twenty-first centuries, religion has been embroiled in political debates on all sides of the political spectrum. In the former Soviet Union or in China today, just professing religion could be threatening to social control by the Communist party, providing an alternative authority structure. In twentieth-century Latin America, **liberation theology** within the Catholic Church was a source of popular mobilization against ruthless political dictators. Liberation theology focuses on Jesus not only as savior but as the savior of the poor and oppressed and emphasizes the Christian mission of bringing justice to the poor.

Most commonly, religious mobilization has aimed to move society to the political right, to restore a conservative agenda of a "Christian America" or an "Islamic Republic." In contemporary America, the mobilization of the Christian right has had an enormous effect on everyday life, from the sorts of books one can read in classrooms and libraries, to whom one can fall in love with. A few Muslim countries have

liberation theology

A movement in Christian theology, developed mainly by Latin American Roman Catholics, that focuses on Jesus not only as savior but as the savior of the poor and emphasizes liberation from social, political, and economic oppression.

instituted **shari'a**, or the Islamic law outlined in the *Koran*, which, when strictly interpreted, includes such penalties as cutting off the hand for robbery and death by stoning for adultery.

Often, religious beliefs lead to supporting or opposing specific policies. For example, 49 percent of Americans believe that natural disasters like earthquakes and floods are a sign that "end of times/apocalypse" is fast approaching. They'd be unlikely to want to allocate funds for relief or prevention if they believe it's God's ways of communicating with us (Jones, Cox, and Navarro-Rivera 2014).

The secular side also exerts an influence. Although we often hear about religious institutions being intolerant of political diversity, it is also common for secular politics to be intolerant of religious diversity. In the United States, Jehovah's Witnesses have been fined or jailed for refusing to salute the flag. In 2003, French President Jacques Chirac banned the wearing of any religious symbols in French public schools—including Catholic crucifixes, Jewish yarmulkes, Muslim chadors, and Sikh turbans (Sciolino 2004). Although the constitutional principle of the separation of church and state was meant to protect liberty and ensure democracy in the United States, it also enabled religion and politics to develop and expand separately. In recent years, however, the boundaries between the two have become increasingly blurry, and several political debates currently strain their happy coexistence, such as evolution versus creationism, school prayer, and embryonic stem-cell research.

Everyday Religion

15.4.2 Explain how religion pervades our everyday lives, identities, and interactions in subtle and often taken-for-granted ways.

Even though many of us claim to be highly religious, our knowledge of the dominant U.S. religions is rather limited. More than half of Americans (58%) cannot name even five of the Ten Commandments, and just under half know that Genesis is the first book of the Bible. And 12 percent of Americans believe that Joan of Arc was Noah's wife (she was really an early-fiftteenth-century war heroine and political martyr) (McKibben 2005). It may be that the dramatic rise of evangelical Christianity in the United States—nearly 40 percent of Americans identify themselves as "born-again" Christian or evangelical—has less to do with its doctrinal rigidity and more to do with how well it sits with other "American" values. In America, God is intimately involved in the smallest details of your everyday life. (Forget that old idea of a distant, abstract, and judgmental God; in the American version, God is close enough to be your best friend.) "While more Americans than ever consider themselves born again, the lord to whom they turn rarely gets angry and frequently strengthens self-esteem," according to sociologist Alan Wolfe (2003, p. 3).

Like our consumer economy, some evangelical religious organizations have "supersized," so that today, many Americans worship in megachurches such as Houston's Lakewood Church (52,000 weekly attendance) or Chicago's Willow Creek Community Church (17,000 weekly attendance). If these mainstream pop-culture renditions of Protestantism seem either too remote or too commercial, other smaller churches offer a relaxed experience in "house churches" where ministers are likely to wear blue jeans and speak to congregants informally (see Leland 2004). All are relatively "seeker friendly," offering spiritual redemption and psychological therapy in the same package. With congregations numbering in the tens of thousands on any given Sunday, American megachurches are less somber religious affairs and more like a mixture of arena rock concerts and old-time tent preaching.

However, it is important to remember that Christians—even American born-again Christians—do not all agree on major issues. In a recent survey, sociologists Andrew

shari'a

Islamic religious law, outlined in the *Koran*, which, when strictly interpreted, includes such penalties as cutting off the hand for robbery and death by stoning for adultery.

Evangelical megachurches have "supersized" religion in the United States. At Lakewood Church, in Houston, Texas, about 52,000 attend weekly services.

Greeley and Michael Hout found that conservative Christians are not all likely to vote Republican. Rather, it is more apt to say that religion intersects with class identity—poorer Protestants are less likely to vote Republican than wealthier ones. Nor do Christians as a group universally oppose abortion (only 14 percent oppose it in all circumstances and 22 percent are prochoice); and a large majority support sex education in school (Heimlich 2010; Pew Research Center 2015).

Overall, Americans are highly fluid in our religious affiliation; We change affiliation early and often. About half of all American adults have changed religions at least once in their lifetime, and many of those do so more than once (Pew Research Center 2015). The group that has grown the most is those Americans who have left their religion to become unaffiliated, and they have done so for a range of reasons. Many former Catholics and former Protestants say they drifted away from their religions. Two-thirds of former Catholics and half of former Protestants say they stopped believing in its teachings. Large numbers also left their religions because they see religious people as judgmental, hypocritical, or insincere; because they see many religions, not just one, as offering some truth; or because they feel religious organizations focus too much on rules, on money, or on power, and not enough on spirituality and truth. A smaller proportion, about one-third of unaffiliated Americans, left their religion because they believe science had proved religion a superstition (Pew Research Center 2015).

Most churches in the United States are populated by whites *or* blacks; rarely do they worship together. As Dr. Martin Luther King Jr. once put it, "The most segregated hour of Christian America is 11 o'clock on Sunday morning." Just as the white church has been, for centuries, an important social institution, so too has the black church evolved as one of the central institutions of the African American community. Actually, to speak of a singular "black church" in America is a bit misleading; the "black church" is really the vast array of black churches, usually Protestant, that have developed over the course of U.S. history. The massive importation of African slaves in the seventeenth and eighteenth centuries (discussed in more detail in Chapter 8) was coupled with efforts to crush their traditional African-based religions (which were seen as a threat to their enslaved status) and to convert them to Christianity. Often slaves were required to attend church with their white masters but relegated to the balconies. Consider the proportions of racial and ethnic groups

FIGURE 15.10 Distribution of Race and Ethnicity by U.S. Religious Groups, 2014
Among the most racially diverse religions in the United States today are Seventh-day Adventists, Muslims, Jehovah's Witnesses, and Buddhists, though Catholics and those claiming "nothing in particular" are not far behind. Take a moment to consider how religion intersects with race in the United States.

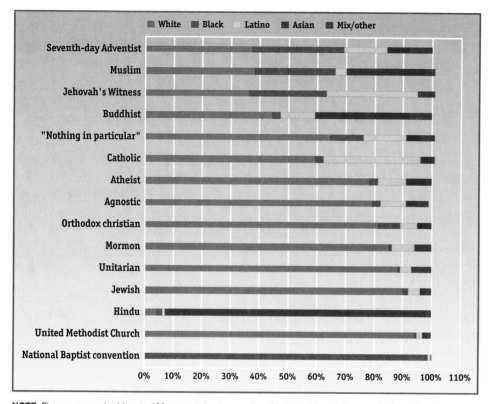

NOTE: Figures may not add up to 100 percent due to rounding. Blacks, whites, Asians, and others/mixed include only those who are not Latino. Latinos include people of all races.

SOURCE: Data from Pew Research Center, "2014 Religious Landscape Study". Available at http://www.pewresearch.org/fact-tank/2015/07/27/the-most-and-least-racially-diverse-u-s-religious-groups/.

in the United States associated with each religious group (see FIGURE 15.10). As you can see, Seventh-day Adventists, Muslims, Jehovah's Witnesses, Buddhists, and the religiously unaffiliated are the *most* racially diverse religious groups in the United States today.

Today the black church remains influential, both as a source of religious inspiration and for political mobilization (Battle 2006; Billingsley 1999). Ministers like Jesse Jackson mounted serious campaigns for the presidency; ministers are often powerful orators who inspire and mobilize. The black church's contribution to American society has been enormous, including being the origins of soul and gospel music (Sam Cooke and Aretha Franklin got their start in gospel groups).

Everyday Politics

15.4.3 Explain how politics pervades our everyday lives, identities, and interactions in subtle and often taken-for-granted ways.

Most political activity does not occur in political caucuses and voting booths, through large-scale social movements, or even through the violence of war, terrorism, and revolution. Politics happens in everyday situations that have nothing to do with candidates. In 1969, Carol Hanisch wrote an article for the book *Feminist Revolution* ([1969] 1979) titled "The Personal Is Political," arguing that even the most intimate, personal actions make a political statement: "Personal problems are political problems," she concluded. Or, to put it another way, every problem is a political problem. This is not so different from C. Wright Mills' (1959) distinction between *private troubles* and *public issues* that we addressed in Chapter 1. For example, you are making a political statement when:

- Someone makes a racist, sexist, or homophobic comment, and you agree, disagree, or stay silent.
- You make a friend who belongs to a different race, gender, or sexual orientation, or who doesn't.
- A company exploits the workers in its foreign factories, but you buy its products anyway, or refuse to buy its products, or don't know about it.
- You seek out a "green" product, or don't, or don't notice whether it is environmentally friendly.

In short, you are "being political" all the time. Just as civil religion allows us to connect in religious-like ways even when we're participating in things that might not seem all that "religious," political behavior is no different. **Everyday politics** is not a replacement for organized political groups. In fact, the two complement each other. Small, seemingly inconsequential everyday acts have a cumulative impact, creating grassroots support for the legislative changes for which political groups lobby. These acts also express political identity, enhance solidarity, and promote social change (Scott 1987).

Frequently, groups with little formal power still attempt to resist what they perceive as illegitimate or dictatorial authority, using symbolic and cultural expressions. For example, historian Kenneth Stampp found that instead of being docile and helpless, American slaves were constantly rebelling in numerous small symbolic ways: breaking

everyday politics

Small-scale political acts in the context of everyday life that connect us to political life just as civil religion allows us to connect in religious-like ways even when we're participating in things that might not seem all that "religious."

SOCIOLOGY AND OUR WORLD:

PEOPLE ESPOUSE POLITICAL OPINIONS EVEN WHEN THEY DON'T HAVE AN OPINION

Why do people champion political opinions in public even when they don't know what they're talking about?

In 1987, sociologist Nina Eliasoph was interested in the ways that people staked a claim to a political identity in their everyday lives. Opinion polls, for instance, proceed from an assumption; they proceed from the assumption that everyone can and does have an opinion about the topics those creating surveys are asking about. Yet, people often have incomplete knowledge about the things we ask them to espouse opinions about; sometimes they may have no knowledge at all and we're simply asking them what they think. If you know nothing about the science regarding climate change and globalization, does your opinion about it really matter? Can you still have an opinion?

Conducting around 100 interviews with people on the street, Nina Eliasoph tested this idea. Confronting people on the street with a recording device, Eliasoph asked people to mobilize a political opinion on the spot surrounding a variety of issues germane to the time of her interviews (the Iran-Contra affair, or the stock market, or an upcoming congressional vote concerning aid to the contras in Central America). She confronted them, stated the political issue and demanded an opinion: "What do you think about it?" she asked. Everyone she interviewed had to mobilize a political presentation

of self, on the spot, often in front of friends and strangers. And Eliasoph wanted to study the different ways people accomplished this.

Some people mobilized a presentation that was meant to be interpreted in jest, lest they say something inaccurate or illustrate themselves un- or underinformed about important political issues in public. Some confessed to being underinformed. Some mobilized political opinions about things they clearly had no knowledge about. Others who were uninformed found another way of performing a political self; they claimed to be uninformed on principle. One thing Eliasoph questioned was the role that context plays in political opinions. Where we are when we're asked to mobilize our political identity matters. Whether we're alone in our living room filling out a survey or out on the street being asked to "take a position" on an issue in front of people we know or don't know might dramatically shape the types of opinions we share. This is just one more reason that opinion polls are challenging to read; they're asked in a very specific context and deciphering how those contexts might shape the opinions given is too great a task for what we are often asking opinion polls to do.

tools, stealing from their owners, and working really slowly (Stampp 1956). When Estonia was under Soviet occupation in the 1980s, citizens would pretend they spoke only Estonian or put signs on hotels in Russian that said "No Vacancy" (Suny 1985). In France and Spain, schools in Brittany, Catalonia, or the Basque country often teach subjects in the local language rather than French or Spanish, to preserve local traditions.

---

iSOC AND YOU Politics and Religion in Everyday Life

Religion and politics—"church and state"—are supposed to be separate, at least according to the U.S. Constitution. But sociologists understand them as intimately connected. Both provide organized *identities* and offer *institutions* that shape and govern the sorts of *interactions* you are likely to have. However, religion and politics are both also sources of *inequality*, and both provide ideologies that justify the differing aspects of *intersecting* inequalities that often must confront it. As with other social institutions (like family and education), the social paradox of politics and religion is that both are important spaces to respond to and challenge inequality while they each also play critical roles in reproducing forms of inequality. And understanding politics and religion sociologically requires an appreciation of this paradox.

Conclusion
Politics and Religion NOW

Though Thomas Jefferson urged Americans to keep politics and religion separate, sociologists have understood how deeply intertwined they have always been, and how each functions in society in similar ways. In many ways, politics are religious, as we see political rituals such as singing the national anthem or reciting the Pledge of Allegiance—or even shouting "USA! USA!" at your political opponents—as experiences that unite us as a community. And religion is political too, providing a guide for action in the secular world. These political and religious interactions are ways you tell yourself who you are.

Both religion and political affiliations help you create and ground your identity; many of you see your religious identity as a central aspect of who you understand yourself to be. And both politics and religion serve as mechanisms for sorting people into categories and ranking those categories into unequal groups. In this way, politics and religion are integrally related to forms of social inequality that shape not only our beliefs and governance, but our struggles, opportunities, and health in dramatic ways. And finally, both religious and political institutions—from churches to legislatures and local governments—provide you with rules to live by and a rationale for those rules. They tell you how to join the club and how to rise on its ladder. To be sure, religion and politics are also very different from each other. But they share many similarities as well.

Will religion and politics move further apart, separating at last church and state as the founding fathers envisioned, or will they become more intertwined, as those very efforts to separate them actually serve to connect them? By now you know the sociologist's reply to pretty much every "either/or" question. "Yes."

CHAPTER REVIEW Politics and Religion

Politics and Religion

15.1 Politics, Religion, and Social Life

Although we often view religion and politics as competing world views, separate and distinct social institutions and arenas, sociologists recognize that there are many similarities as well. Both are organized and coherent systems of authority that are organized into social institutions. Both make claims to govern our conduct. Both political and religious institutions function as organizations, with clear rules about how one gets promoted, how to deal with bosses and the like. However, there are also many differences. Religion is a set of beliefs about the origins and meaning of life, usually based on a belief in the existence of a supernatural power. Politics is the art and science of government. Still, both religion and politics are about three things: power, government, and authority. Power refers to the ability to make people do what you want them to do—whether they want to do it or not (such as paying your taxes or giving a portion of your income to the church). Both of these social institutions are also about government—the organization and administration of the actions of the inhabitants of communities, societies, and states. Finally, politics and religion organize authority—power that is perceived as legitimate by both power holders and those who are subjected to it. If politics and religion are working well, it is through government (either political or religious) that power is transformed into authority.

15.1 Key Terms

religion A set of beliefs and practices relating to the origins and meaning of life, usually based on a belief in the existence of a supernatural power.

politics The art and science of government.

power The ability to extract compliance despite resistance or the ability to get others to do what you want them to do, regardless of their own desires.

government The organization and administration of the actions of the inhabitants of communities, societies, and states.

authority Power that is perceived as legitimate, by both the holder of power and those subject to it.

apostasy The abandonment or renunciation of a religious belief.

blasphemy Speaking profanely about God or sacred things.

civil religion Robert Bellah's term for the values that hold societies together that are expressed through "religious-like" practices—defining moral and ethical boundaries through ritualized practices (like the Pledge of Allegiance in the United States).

15.2 Politics

The two main kinds of political systems are authoritarian political systems, including monarchy and totalitarianism, and democracy, which includes participatory democracy and representative democracy. Universal suffrage is increasing. Problems associated with political systems include corruption, bureaucratic entrenchment, and underrepresentation of minorities and the undue influence of money and power. A solution to the latter problem is proportional representation. In the U.S. political system, as in most democratic societies with elected representatives, an individual cannot effectively change the system, so we become members of a political party. Unlike other countries, there are mainly only two parties in the United States, with third parties having little influence. Party affiliation is typically based on class, education,

race, gender, and age. An interest group, also called a special interest group, pressure group, or lobby, promotes its interests among state and national legislators and often influences public opinion. Political change can occur through political parties, interest groups, or social movements, the term for the ways that people organize collectively. A revolution is the most extreme form of social movement, seeking to replace the existing order. Marx supposed that class inequality would drive the underclass to revolution through the immiseration thesis, but the fact that people experience relative deprivation suggests otherwise. Other changes include coup d'état, a change in the head of state; political revolution, when another political group supplants the previous ruling group; and, more fundamental to society as well as more dramatic, social revolution. War seems to be an inevitable part of political systems, and although it isn't predictable when a war will occur, a number of root causes have been identified underlying wars. Many different kinds of groups engage in acts of terrorism, for different reasons, with increasing frequency made possible by ease of access to technology. Those in power, or those opposed, may commit terrorist acts.

15.2 Key Terms

traditional authority Dominant in premodern societies, the form of authority that people obeyed because they believed their society had always done things that way; derives from who the leaders are: the descendants of kings and queens, or perhaps the descendants of the gods, not from their educational background, work experience, or personality traits.

charismatic authority Form of authority derived from the personal appeal of a specific leader.

legal-rational authority Form of authority where leaders are to be obeyed not primarily as representatives of tradition or because of their personal qualities but because they are voicing a set of rationally derived laws.

political systems The term for how group leaders exercise their authority. Virtually all political systems fall into one of two categories, "authoritarian" or "democratic."

authoritarian political system When power is vested in a single person or small group. Sometimes that person holds power through heredity, such as in a monarchy, sometimes through force or terror, as with totalitarian regimes.

monarchy One of the first political systems; rule by a single individual (*mono* means "one," and *archy* means "rule"), typically hereditary.

totalitarianism A political system in which no organized opposition is permitted and political information is censored.

dictatorship A type of totalitarian political system in which power is held by one person, who may or may not have a hereditary claim on power, usually with military support.

democracy Derived from the Greek word *demos* (people); puts legislative decision making into the hands of the people rather than a single individual or a noble class.

participatory democracy Also called "pure democracy," a political system in which every person gets one vote and the majority rules.

representative democracy System in which citizens elect representatives to make the decisions for them; requires an educated citizenry and a free press.

universal suffrage Granting of the vote to any and all citizens who meet specified, universal criteria, such as legal citizenship and a minimum age.

bureaucracy Originally derived from the French word *bureau*, or office, a formal organization characterized by a division of labor, a hierarchy of authority, formal rules governing behavior, a logic of rationality, and an impersonality of criteria.

political action committees (PACs) A type of partisan political organization that is not subject to the same regulations as political parties, that attempt to influence elections and mobilize public opinion.

proportional representation In contrast to the winner-take-all system used in the United States, proportional representation gives each party a proportion of the legislative seats based on the number of votes its candidates garner.

political parties Groups that band together to petition for political chances or to support candidates for elected office.

interest groups An organized group that tries to influence the government to adopt certain policies or measures.

political participation Refers to any action or behavior that either aims to affect or has the consequence of influencing governmental action.

political apathy Refers to the indifference of a member of a society with regard to their attitude toward political activities.

voting-age population Term for proportion of people 18 and older who therefore can vote.

voting-eligible population Term for the proportion of people 18 and older who are not prohibited from voting.

felony disenfranchisement Punitive U.S. policy that denies people convicted of a felony the right to vote even after a sentence has been served. The presence of restrictions, and their extent, vary by the state in which the felony was committed and the year in which it was committed.

social movement Collective attempt to further a common interest or secure a common goal through action outside the sphere of established institutions.

revolution The attempt to overthrow the existing political and social order of a society and replace it with a new one.

immiseration thesis Karl Marx's theory that, as capitalism proceeded, the rich would get richer and the poor would get poorer, and that eventually the poor would become so poor that they had nothing else to lose and would revolt.

relative deprivation Describes how misery is socially experienced by constantly comparing yourself to others. You are not down and out: You are worse off than you used to be (downward mobility), not as well off as you think you should be (rising expectations), or, perhaps, not as well off as those you see around you.

coup d'état The violent replacing of one political leader with another; often doesn't bring with it any change in the daily life of the citizens.

political revolution Changes the political groups that run the society, but they still draw their strength from the same social groups that supported the old regime.

social revolution Revolution that changes the social groups or classes on which political power rests.

war A state of armed conflict between different nations, different states within a nation, or different groups within a nation or state.

terrorism Using acts of violence and destruction (or threatening to use them) as a political strategy.

15.3 Religion

Sociologists have long been fascinated by how religion operates in a society. After all, religion is a cultural universal—that is, it exists in every single culture. Émile Durkheim suggested that every society is organized around understandings of what is sacred versus what is profane. Not every society understands the same actions, objects, and ideas as sacred or as profane; but every society has this distinction. Although Durkheim saw the positive aspects of religion as social glue, other classical sociologists have explored religion as a form of control. Karl Marx believed that religion kept social change from happening by preventing people from revolting against the miserable conditions of their lives. Max Weber, by contrast, argued that religion could be a catalyst to change. There are many forms of religious organizations, including cults and sects. Although secularization—the process of moving away from religious spirituality and toward the worldly—was assumed to be the future of religion, in the majority of countries in the world, the majority of the global population, is experiencing religious resurgence. Increasingly, trends such as this rapid growth of Christianity in the global South and increased Muslim immigration to Western nations are shaping both public attitudes and government policies around the world. Although Europe is increasingly secularized, the United States stands alone among wealthy, industrialized countries in its embrace of religion. Nearly six in ten Americans say religion plays a *very* important role in their lives. Still, even though many Americans claim to be highly religious, our knowledge of the dominant U.S. religions is rather limited, and, overall, Americans are highly fluid in our religious affiliation—we change affiliation early and often. And, at the same time, Americans identifying as atheist, or agnostic, or people who do not identify with any religious tradition when asked, are all on the rise.

15.3 Key Terms

cultural universal One of the rituals, customs, and symbols that are evident in all societies.

sacred Holy moments that evoke a sense of reverence and unity.

profane That which is not sacred or Biblical, or not concerned with religion or religious purposes.

sacrilegious That which is profane, blasphemous, impious, irreverent, or sinful.

ritual Enactment by which members of a culture engage in a routine behavior to express their sense of belonging to the culture.

civil religion Robert Bellah's term for the tendency of modern, secular societies to develop secular rituals that create the intense emotional bonds among people that used to be accomplished by religion.

religiosity Sociological term for the numerous aspects of an individual's religious activity, dedication, and belief. A more colloquial term would be "religiousness."

cult The simplest form of religious organization, characterized typically by fervent believers and a single idea or leader.

sect A small subculture within an established religious institution. Like cults, they break from traditional practices, but unlike cults, they remain within the larger institution.

denomination A large-scale, extremely organized religious body with an established hierarchy, methods for credentialing administrators, and much more social respect than either a cult or a sect.

ecclesiae A political assembly of the faithful in which the clerical elite often serve as political leaders or at least formal advisors to political leaders. Everyone in the society belongs to that faith by birth, not individual decision, and those who do not belong to the faith cannot become citizens.

world religions Religions with a long history, well-established traditions, and the flexibility to adapt to many different cultures.

Western religions Three of the world's major religions—Judaism, Christianity, and Islam (plus a few smaller ones)—are called "Western" because, although they originated in the Middle East, their adherents are largely among Western nations.

Fundamentalism Forms of religion that uphold belief in strict, literal interpretations of scripture.

Eastern Religions Three other major religions of the world—Hinduism, Buddhism, and Confucianism (plus some minor ones)—are called "Eastern" because they arose in Asia, although, like the Western Religions, they have adherents around the world.

secularization The process of moving away from religious spirituality and toward the worldly.

theory of religious economy The hypothesis that societies that restrict supply of religion—whether that is through imposed state religions or state-sponsored secularization—are the main causes of drops in religiosity. Simply put, the more religions a society has and acknowledges, the more likely the population is to be religious.

atheist A person who does not believe in the existence of God.

agnostic A person who claims neither faith nor disbelief in God, usually asserting that nothing is known or can be known about the existence or nature of God.

15.4   Politics and Religion in Everyday Life

Religion has always been "political"—indeed, manifesting the vision of one's religious beliefs in the political arena is often an essential part of the religion. Thus, although religion and politics are separate social institutions, they intersect a great deal. Throughout the twentieth and twenty-first centuries, religion has been embroiled in political debates on all sides of the political spectrum. In the former Soviet Union or in China today, just professing religion could be threatening to social control by the Communist party, providing an alternative authority structure. In twentieth-century Latin America, liberation theology within the Catholic Church was a source of popular mobilization against ruthless political dictators. A few Muslim countries have instituted shari'a, or the Islamic law outlined in the Koran, which, when strictly interpreted, includes such penalties as cutting off the hand for robbery and death by stoning for adultery. In the contemporary United States, the mobilization of the Christian right has had an enormous effect on everyday life. Although the constitutional principle of the separation of church and state was meant to protect liberty and ensure democracy in the United States, in recent years, the boundaries between the two have become increasingly blurry, and several political debates currently strain their happy coexistence, such as evolution versus creationism, school prayer, gay marriage, and embryonic stem-cell research. In addition to organized Western and Eastern religions, Americans also enjoy a variety of New Age beliefs and practices often defined simply and pluralistically as "spirituality." Overall, Americans are highly fluid in our religious affiliation; we change affiliation early and often. The group that has grown the most is those Americans who have left their religion to become unaffiliated. We are also engaged in "being political" all the time through everyday politics. These small, seemingly inconsequential everyday acts have a cumulative impact, creating grass-roots support for the legislative changes for which political groups lobby as well as expressing political identity and enhancing solidarity.

15.4 Key Terms

liberation theology A movement in Christian theology, developed mainly by Latin American Roman Catholics, that focuses on Jesus not only as savior but as the savior of the poor and emphasizes liberation from social, political, and economic oppression.

shari'a Islamic religious law, outlined in the *Koran*, which, when strictly interpreted, includes such penalties as cutting off the hand for robbery and death by adultery.

everyday politics Small-scale political acts in the con of everyday life that connect us to political life just as civ religion allows us to connect in religious-like ways even when we're participating in things that might not seem all that "religious."

SELF-TEST

〉 CHECK YOUR UNDERSTANDING

1. Which classical figure discussed the historical progression and types of authority found in society?
   a. Durkheim
   b. Marx
   c. Weber
   d. Goffman

2. Charismatic authority is found
   a. in authoritarian political systems.
   b. in democratic political systems.
   c. in religious movements.
   d. Charismatic authority may be found in any of these systems.

3. In which of the following is corruption more often found, according to the text?
   a. Authoritarian governments
   b. Democratic governments
   c. Richer nations
   d. Poorer nations

4. In which type of nation are acts of terrorism more likely to occur?
   a. In totalitarian regimes, where people are likely to strike out against harsh rulers
   b. In poor nations, where there are great numbers of "have nots"
   c. In democratic nations, where there is unchecked freedom
   d. Terrorism is equally likely to occur in all of the nations.

5. A small nation experienced a change in leadership when the nation's leader was arrested by the military police and replaced by a general in the military. The buses and trains continued to run, schools remained open, and there was no change in business or industry. This is an example of

   a. a coup d'état.
   b. political revolution.
   c. social revolution.
   d. terrorism.

6. All three classical theorists discussed in the text agreed that:
   a. religious belief is natural and religiosity would increase over time.
   b. religious belief is social and religiosity would decline in modern society.
   c. religious belief is social and religiosity would increase with globalization.
   d. religious belief is natural and religiosity would decline in modern society.

7. When it comes to characteristics of religious nations
   a. religion tends to hold little sway in developing nations.
   b. without exception, the more technologically and industrially developed a society is, the lower its rates of religious belief.
   c. the secularization thesis is more valid in Europe than in the United States.
   d. wealthier nations and poorer ones tend to be equally religious.

8. Studies of American religiosity find that
   a. about half of all Americans have changed religions at least once, and many of those more than once, in their lifetime.
   b. more than half of Americans can't name five of the Ten Commandments.
   c. very few churches in the United States are racially integrated; most congregations are predominantly black or white.
   d. all of the answers are correct.

Self-Test Answers: 1. c, 2. d, 3. d, 4. c, 5. a, 6. b, 7. c, 8. d

CHAPTER

16

SOCIOLOGY OF ENVIRONMENTS: THE NATURAL, PHYSICAL, AND HUMAN WORLD

The physical environments in which societies are located impact those societies just as societies impact physical environments. Drinking water is a simple example. Potable water is produced by feats of engineering, chemistry, infrastructure, and social organization. But *who* has access to water and what kind of water is related to systems of social inequality. Here, a resident of Flint Michigan brings a baby bottle full of contaminated drinking water to a House Oversight and Government Reform committee hearing addressing why and how a working-class town in Michigan lost access to safe drinking water.

→ LEARNING OBJECTIVES

In this chapter, using the iSoc framework, you should be able to:

16.1.1 Recognize how each of the five elements of the iSoc model can be used to examine populations and environments from local and global perspectives sociologically.

16.1.2 Distinguish between fertility and fecundity, and understand why demographers can learn a good

deal about a society simply by examining shifts in the fertility rate.

16.1.3 Explain the distinction between emigration and immigration, and understand what distinguishes push factors from pull factors in explaining migration.

16.1.4 Understand what we can learn about societies by examining their net migration rates over time.

16.1.5 Understand what we can learn about a society by examining its population pyramid.

16.1.6 Understand why the world population has increased so dramatically in recent history and what social forces will slow it down.

16.1.7 Describe how social theorists have made predictions about the size and growth of populations.

16.1.8 Understand some of the ways that societies have sought to intervene in population dynamics and affect population growth.

16.2.1 Explain the meaning of population density and how different areas might differ on this measure.

16.2.2 Summarize the origin of "suburbs" and how the people living in suburban areas has changed over time.

16.2.3 Understand why sociologists were worried about urbanization and its impact on social relationships, identities, and interactions.

16.3.1 Summarize what it means to examine the natural world from a sociological perspective.

16.3.2 Explain how energy consumption varies around the world.

16.3.3 Describe what Charles Perrow means by "normal accidents" using the Chernobyl nuclear power plant disaster as an illustration.

16.3.4 Understand the scale of lost natural resources on earth and how humans and societies contribute to the problem.

16.3.5 Describe some of the ways that pollution, garbage, and climate change are as much social issues as they are environmental issues.

16.3.6 Understand how "manufactured risks" and "external risks" are unevenly distributed within and between societies in ways that exacerbate existing inequalities.

16.3.7 Define environmental inequalities, and understand how these forms of inequalities intersect with other forms of social inequality.

16.3.8 Describe the key groups in environmental politics, and understand some of the successes and challenges associated with the movement.

Introduction

Flint, Michigan, is a small city (about 30 square miles) with about 100,000 residents roughly 70 miles northeast of Detroit. In 2015, the median household income was just shy of $25,000—more than $30,000 less annually than the median income in the United States that year. About one-third of the residents of Flint are white, more than 50 percent are black, and only slightly more than 1 in 10 of Flint residents that are 25 years old or older have a bachelor's degree or more. The most recent Census estimate calculated that approximately 41.2 percent of Flint's population lives in poverty. So, compared to the national average, Flint residents are disproportionately black, disproportionately poor, and few have chosen or been able to pursue higher education. They are a community of people with tough jobs, and more than 1 in 10 are without health care. Consider this the backstory.

In April 2014, unbeknownst to the majority of Flint residents, the city changed source of water it used to provide water to the population. They had been using water from Lake Huron and the Detroit River that was treated by the Detroit Water and Sewage Department. But in 2014, they started collecting water from the Flint River. The officials charged with making this switch had failed to apply a basic technology used in water treatment—corrosion inhibitors. These are the chemical compounds used in your drinking water that drastically decrease the level of corrosion of the pipes through which the water travels to get to your faucet. Without proper corrosion inhibitors, you'd be drinking a lot more corroded metal, and in Flint's case, that meant that their water quickly became contaminated with lead.

Almost immediately, Dr. Mona Hanna-Attisha, the director for pediatric residency at Hurley Children's Hospital in Flint, noticed some terrifying changes in the children she was treating. She led a research team to study the crisis. And on September 24, 2015, the team released a study confirming everyone's worst fears. Between 2013 and 2015, the numbers of infants and children with elevated lead levels in their blood doubled.

Using Flint hospital records, Dr. Hanna-Attisha and her colleagues were able to show that the spike in blood-lead levels neatly correlated with the switch to using water from Flint River (Hanna-Attisha, et al. 2015). A spokesman from the Michigan Department of Environmental Quality (DEQ) initially dismissed the study, publicly claiming, "Repeated testing indicated the water tested within acceptable levels." He was wrong and later apologized publicly to Dr. Hanna-Attisah. As all of this shows, the Flint water crisis is a problem of enormous infrastructural scale. But it wasn't until January 2016 that the governor of Michigan declared the city of Flint to be in a state of emergency.

This is an environmental problem, to be sure. Metal corrodes when left untreated. And most U.S. citizens benefit from not worrying whether their water is safe to drink. Certainly, Flint residents felt that way in 2014. But this environmental crisis was socially produced—it was the result of people's decisions—and its impact was social, affecting some people and not others. Sociologists are interested in examining which populations are more and less at risk of environmental crises like this. Flint residents are poor, they're undereducated, and a larger share of them are black when compared with the U.S. population as a whole. They are a socially marginalized group. When sociologists see problems like this, we want to know: Why did this happen in Flint? And why are we so much less likely to hear about problems like this happening in communities with Americans with household incomes dramatically *above* the U.S. median household income? Do the education, race, and class characteristics of Flint residents have anything to do with this social problem?

Understanding environmental disasters like the water crisis in Flint, Michigan sociologically requires thinking sociologically about the environment. People may live in a *natural* world, but our interactions with the world around us are inherently *social*. Everything from where we live, to whether our homes are near landfills, or whether we risk our health at work is part of an elaborate process of social organization. And like so many forms of social inequality, once we begin to understand them intersectionally, we realize that certain groups are more at risk than others. Sociologists endeavor to better understand how and why this happens.

16.1 The Human Environment

Humans are a *social* species. We want—and need—to be around other people most of the time. People who go off by themselves on purpose are often considered strange, socially inept, or even psychologically disturbed.

demography

The scientific study of human populations; one of the oldest and most popular branches of sociology. Demographers are primarily concerned with the statistics of birth, death, and migration.

A major part of our environment is the mass of other people around us, simply doing what people do: being born and growing up, moving into town and leaving town, getting sick and getting well, living and dying. **Demography** is the scientific study of human populations and one of the oldest and most popular branches of sociology. Demography is used to understand health, longevity, and even political representation because the Census is the basis for allocation of congressional seats. Demographers are primarily concerned with the statistics of birth, death, and migration (Yaukey and Anderton 2001; Preston, Heuveline, and Guillot 2001). So, demographers study macro-level changes in societies and populations within and across societies.

As we addressed in Chapter 1, the iSoc perspective is best thought of as a series of lenses that sociologists use to focus on different aspects of society. Similarly, we discussed the various research methods on which sociologists rely in Chapter 4 as best understood as different optical devices into which sociologists insert the various iSoc lenses to see societies and social processes in different ways. From this perspective, demographic research relies on the most "zoomed out" view of society. And like every sociological research method, we can learn things from demographic research that could not be learned in any other way. Although the intricacies of human social interaction are less visible from this perspective, the structural backdrop that shapes those interactions, and the macro-level consequences that social interactions can produce is put into stark relief. In this section, we will consider how populations grow as well as how they move about the world. As we live in an increasingly "global" world, population too is best understood globally. We will examine just how large the population of the world is, how it got to be as big as it is as well as where those numbers are headed. And we also examine the flow of populations around the world. Human environments encourage people to leave some societies and to attempt to join others. And sociologists are interested in understanding the diverse causes and consequences of these social processes.

iSoc: The Environment

16.1.1 Recognize how each of the five elements of the iSoc model can be used to examine populations and environments from local and global perspectives sociologically.

Human beings are surrounded by environments—natural, human, and built. These environments are the *contexts* in which we form our identities, the material (natural and social) from which we develop our social institutions, and also the resources that we distribute within society, at different levels of inequality. Environments are deeply connected with societies, social interactions, and social inequality. In society, we interact with our environment; more than that, our society *is* our environment as well. But what kind of relationship you have with the environment is also a product of the status you occupy within your society.

IDENTITY—Who we are depends on the various environments in which we find ourselves. How different might you be, for example, if you lived in a desert or in a rainforest—how might you see the world differently? If you live in an inhospitable climate with scarce resources and a large population, you might develop an assumption that people are basically aggressive and competitive; if you lived in a smaller population, in a land where food was abundant and the weather temperate, you might think human beings were basically loving and generous. Our *identities*, formed within and through our cultures, are also the result of a complex interaction with the various environments societies endure.

INEQUALITY—Our relationships to our environments both reflect existing social *inequalities* and create them. For example, the wealthy claim larger shares of the natural and built environments, have more access, and can shield themselves from the more dangerous elements. Consider one small example: In the United States, living on a hillside overlooking the ocean might be the place for the upper class to live—commanding views, relative isolation. But in Latin America, the hillsides of major cities are often the worst slums because the land is unstable and susceptible to earthquakes and mudslides during the rainy season. Around the world, the wealthy live longer and better than the poor. This has been true throughout time. For instance, today, the upper floors of expensive apartment builds are often reserved for the elite; penthouse floors often require elevator keys that enable precious few to even visit those floors. But in ancient Rome, living on the ground floor of a building housing multiple families was more valuable (families living on the street level would have been the first to get out of the building in case of a fire). As a group, the wealthy also tend to be happier: Although we believe that money can't buy happiness, it does seem to buy the things that make many people happy.

INTERACTIONS—The different environments in which we find ourselves are the context of our *interactions,* and also shape those interactions. In society, we produce the environment—building in some places, farming, fishing and foresting in others—and allocate access to it based on unequal position in society. These human decisions become the arenas in which we interact with each other; social inequalities even determine those with whom we are likely to interact in the first place. Consider the different ways that inequalities produce segregation in societies. People with different amounts of money live in different contexts, even when they live in the same societies. Our environments help shape the people with whom we will likely interact, and those with whom we are less likely to be in contact.

INSTITUTIONS—Our social *institutions*—from, for example, education, family, and religion—arise through our interactions with our environments. In some cases, they mediate our interactions with others; interactions take place through social institutions like schools or religious institutions. Economic institutions develop to produce and distribute the goods and services of a society; political institutions develop to make sure that these goods and services are produced and distributed in accord with social values (which could be to legitimate inequalities or to promote greater equality). Elements of environments are also associated with various risks, and social institutions also exist to distribute that risk throughout a population.

INTERSECTIONS—To fully appreciate the degree to which environmental inequality and risks are inequitably distributed among populations requires thinking about a society *intersectionally*. Those groups with the least resources, who have less social status, and are marginalized by various forms of social inequality also, often, are more likely to be negatively affected by the environment. So, socially marginalized populations are more likely to have garbage dumps by their homes or oil pipelines going through their communities. And although these are socially manufactured risks, these groups are also more likely to live in areas more likely to be affected by naturally occurring risks as well, like earthquakes, tornados, hurricanes, and more. Thinking intersectionally about environments involves examining which groups within a society are impacted by environmental change or hardship. A great deal of sociological research shows that environments often compound existing inequalities, making life harder for groups whose lives are already more challenging as a result of the organization of a society.

The environment is a complex and all-encompassing issue to examine sociologically. In this chapter, we will explain some of the diverse kinds of sociological research that examines environments sociologically. And, like previous chapters, we rely on the iSoc perspective to help us better understand the various ways that societies are, at base, elaborate interactions between humans and environments. Sociologists rely on iSoc to examine patterns in these interactions, to identify consequences associated with particular interactions, and to trace the ways such interactions lead to social change.

Population and Its Institutions

16.1.2 Distinguish between fertility and fecundity, and understand why demographers can learn a good deal about a society simply by examining shifts in the fertility rate.

fertility
The number of children a woman bears.

fecundity
The maximum number of children a woman could have during her child-bearing years.

Demographers use two birth measurements: **fertility** (the number of children that a woman has) and **fecundity** (the maximum number of children that she could possibly have). Women are physically capable of having a child every 9 months, so in the years between menarche (the onset of menstruation) and menopause (the end of menstruation) they could give birth more than 20 times (their fecundity). However, in the United States, women have an average of 1.87 children each (their fertility) (CIA World Factbook 2016). (Men are not counted because they could produce thousands of children if they found enough partners. King Sobhuza II of Swaziland [1899–1982] fathered 210 children with his 70 wives.)

Demographers measure fertility with the number of live births in the country per year. They measure fecundity with the **fertility rate**, the number of children who would be born to each woman if she lived through her childbearing years with the average fertility of her age group. Poor countries often have a fertility rate of four or more (it's 6.62 in Niger), while in rich countries, the fertility rate often drops to less than two (1.6 in Canada) (CIA World Factbook 2016). Very high fertility rates often spell trouble: Children do not contribute to the economy until they are older, but they must be fed, clothed, educated, and given health care, all of which add additional burdens on already impoverished families. Women with so many children may still participate in the labor force, relying on older children or other kin to look after younger children, but it still strains the family economy. As the children grow into adulthood, there will not be enough jobs to accommodate them, resulting in widespread unemployment. On the other hand, more children also mean more potential support for aging and infirm parents.

> **fertility rate**
> The number of births per 1,000 women ages 15 to 44 in a calendar year.

Very low fertility rates also cause problems for societies, suggesting that the population is aging faster than it can be replenished with new births. Fewer people participate in the workforce as they grow old or retire, but at the same time they continue to require housing, food, transportation, and health care, again putting a strain on the economy. The low number of births in the United States means that in about 20 years there will not be enough adult workers to fill critical jobs in business and technology, putting the country at an economic disadvantage. On the other hand, lower birth rates mean that adults have far more geographic and occupational mobility.

Of course, everyone dies sooner or later, but the **mortality rate**, or the number of deaths per year for every thousand people, can tell demographers a great deal about the relative health of the country. In the United States, the mortality rate is 8.2; every year, a little over eight people in every thousand die. Most wealthy nations range between 8 and 12. Strangely, poor nations can have either higher or lower mortality rates. A low mortality rate, as in Guatemala (4.70) or Tonga (4.90), does not necessarily mean that the people there enjoy a high **life expectancy** (the average number of years a person can expect to live). In fact, in Guatemala, it's rather low, 70.3 for men and 74.4 for women (CIA World Factbook 2016). It usually means that the fertility rate is so high that the proportion of older people in the population goes down. In the United States, about 15 percent of the population is 65 or older. It's 4.4 percent in Guatemala and 6.35 percent in Tonga (CIA World Factbook 2016). See U.S./WORLD Life Expectancy Changes in the United States and Select Countries since 1813 to view life expectancy around the world and over time. It is important to remember, however, that like any valuable resource in a society, life expectancy is not always evenly distributed within a given society. That is, some groups have higher life expectancies than others even in the same society.

> **mortality rate**
> The death rate as a percentage of the population.

> **life expectancy**
> The average number of years a person can expect to live; varies greatly by country and region.

A higher mortality rate, as in Lesotho (14.90) or Bulgaria (14.5), usually signifies that, due to famine, war, or disease, many people do not live to see old age (CIA World Factbook 2016). AIDS is causing a significant decline in population growth in many low-income countries. Demographers are also especially interested in the **infant mortality rate**, the number of deaths per year in each thousand infants up to one year old. As you might expect, the infant mortality rate is extremely low in wealthy countries (3.3 in France), and extremely high in poor countries, especially in sub-Saharan Africa: It's 88.4 in the Central African Republic and 76.5 in Angola (CIA World Fact Book 2016). Because infants are more vulnerable to disease and malnutrition than adults or older children, the infant mortality rate correlates with the effectiveness of the country's health care, the level of nutrition, and innumerable other quality of life factors. The infant mortality rate serves as a proxy for the overall health of the country and can guide policy makers in their allocation of funds for hospitals, medical care, and pregnancy counseling.

> **infant mortality rate**
> The number of deaths per year per 1,000 infants (up to 1 year old) in a population.

U.S./WORLD

LIFE EXPECTANCY CHANGES IN THE UNITED STATES AND SELECT COUNTRIES SINCE 1813

Social scientists have enough knowledge and data now that we can make predictions about how long you will live from the moment you are born. Those predictions vary more than you might think by society.

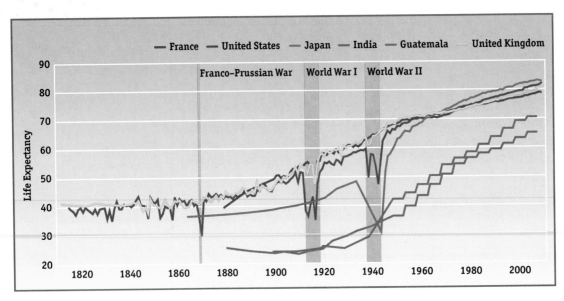

The general trend almost everywhere on earth when it comes to life expectancy has been toward longer lives. In the United States, the life expectancy of a baby born in 1880 was 39.4 years; babies born in the United States in 2016 were expected to live to 78.8. All of the societies listed here follow the same trend. The dramatic drop in life expectancy for Japan in 1945 is a powerful illustration of the devastating effects of the two atomic bombs the United States dropped on Hiroshima and Nagasaki Japan during World War II. Although you can see the trend toward longer lives in all of the societies depicted here, you can also see that longevity has increased more dramatically in some societies (like the United States and Japan) than it has in others (like Guatemala, India, and Nigeria).

SOURCE: Data from Zijdeman, Richard, "Life Expectancy at Birth (both genders), Clio Infra. Our World in Data, "Life Expectancy." Available at https://ourworldindata.org/life-expectancy/.

INVESTIGATE FURTHER

1. Can you think of two or three social forces that might account for this larger trend toward longer lives around the world?

2. Can you think of two or three social forces that might account for the large discrepancies between the different societies depicted here?

Populations on the Move

16.1.3 Explain the distinction between emigration and immigration, and understand what distinguishes push factors from pull factors in explaining migration.

emigration

Outflow of people from one society to another.

immigration

The number of people entering a territory each year for every 1,000 people in population.

In addition to people being born and dying, demographers are interested in their physical movements, as they leave one territory (**emigration**) and take up permanent residence in another (**immigration**). People emigrate and immigrate voluntarily or involuntarily. Most wealthy countries have sizeable populations of voluntary immigrants. In 2014, the United States gained 1,016,000 foreign nationals. Within the OECD (the Organisation for Economic Co-operation and Development, the organization of the world's 30 most-developed nations), Germany had the largest influx of migrants (with 1,342,500), followed by the United States, The United Kingdom (504,000), Korea (407,000), and Japan (336,000) (OECD 2017).

In 2016, 65.6 million people emigrated from their home territory involuntarily. Some 22.5 million are refugees; 40.8 million were displaced by political strife and war; and another 2.8 million were seeking asylum. And in 2016, for the third consecutive year, the country hosting the highest number of those refugees was Turkey (hosting more than 2.9 million refugees), following by Pakistan, Lebanon, the Islamic Republic of Iran, and Ethiopia (see FIGURE 16.1). As of 2015, more than half (54 percent) of those 65.3 million refugees worldwide came from only three nations: Somalia, Afghanistan, and the largest group from the Syrian Arab Republic (UNHCR 2016).

Voluntary migrants usually have two sets of motives for their move, called **push factors** (reasons they want to leave their home territory in the first place) and **pull factors** (reasons they want to settle in this particular territory). The most common push factors are a sluggish economy, political and cultural oppression, and civil unrest—not enough to force them to leave, but enough to make their lives at home miserable. A slight downturn in one country's economic fortunes often leads to a rise in immigration in others. The most common pull factors are the opposite: a good economy, political and cultural tolerance, and civil stability. Because rich nations offer superior jobs and education and a great degree of political and cultural tolerance, they tend to receive the most voluntary migrants.

push factors

Reasons voluntary migrants want to leave their home territory, the most common of which are a sluggish economy, political or cultural oppression, and civil unrest.

pull factors

Reasons voluntary migrants want to settle in a particular territory, the most common of which are a strong economy, political and cultural tolerance, and civil stability.

FIGURE 16.1 Where Refugees Around the World Found Asylum, 2016
Refugees typically find asylum in societies neighboring those from which they are leaving. This is a dramatic illustration of just how globally interconnected societies are today and how geopolitical concerns in one society are of concern to others, particularly those who happen to be located in geographically close proximity. Here you can see where refugees from the major countries producing refugees in 2016 went to find asylum. More than 1 in 10 found safety in a country neighboring the society they left behind.

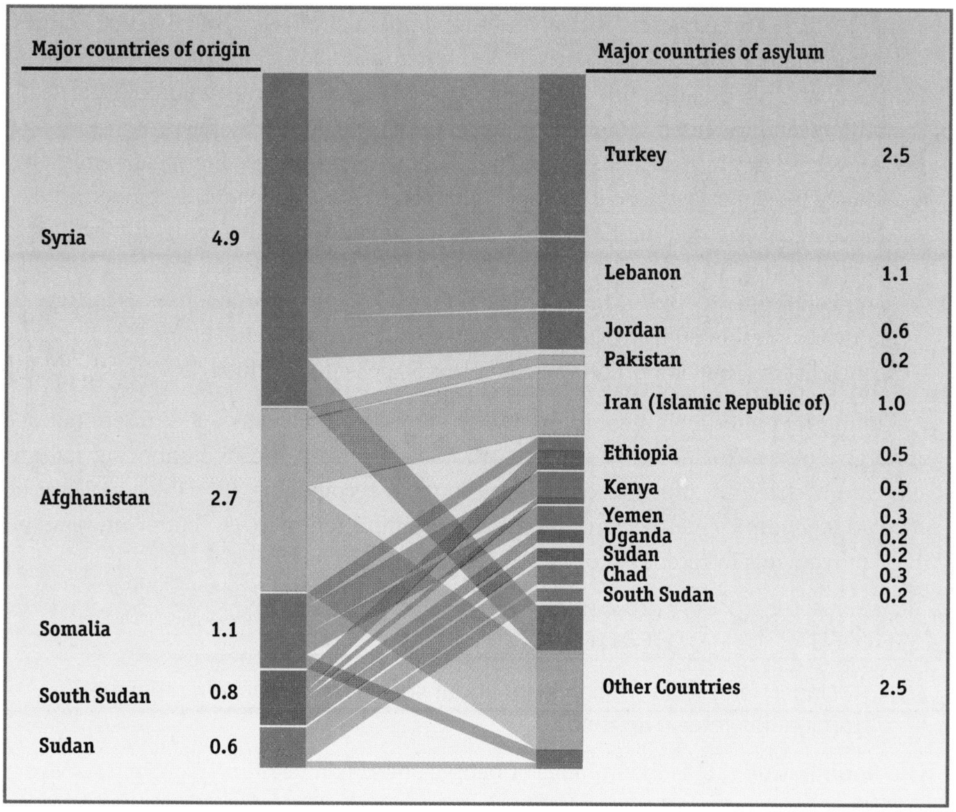

Major countries of origin		Major countries of asylum	
Syria	4.9	Turkey	2.5
		Lebanon	1.1
		Jordan	0.6
		Pakistan	0.2
		Iran (Islamic Republic of)	1.0
		Ethiopia	0.5
Afghanistan	2.7	Kenya	0.5
		Yemen	0.3
		Uganda	0.2
		Sudan	0.2
		Chad	0.3
		South Sudan	0.2
Somalia	1.1		
South Sudan	0.8	Other Countries	2.5
Sudan	0.6		

SOURCE: Data from The United Nations Refugee Agency (UNHCR), "Global Trends: Forced Displacement in 2016," Fig.8:21. Available at http://www.unhcr.org/en-us/statistics/unhcrstats/5943e8a34/global-trends-forced-displacement-2016.html.

Many refugees cluster in places where their ethnic group has gained a foothold. There are more than 250,000 Hmong, political refugees from Laos, in the United States, almost all in a few cities in California, Minnesota, and Wisconsin. Here, Hmong third graders join a class in St. Paul, Minnesota.

Another extremely important pull factor is having someone you know in the territory to which you intend to immigrate. People don't like start afresh in areas where they know no one and where possibly no one speaks their language or understands their culture. So, when they have a choice, they often move to where family and friends are already located. Many relocate to follow a romantic partner.

There have been four major flows of immigration in modern history (Pagden 2001):

1. Between 1500 and 1800, as Europe began to establish colonial empires around the world, millions of English, French, Spanish, and Portuguese citizens emigrated to the sparsely settled regions of North and South America, South Africa, and Oceania. Some were forced to leave as punishment for a crime, but most chose to leave voluntarily, drawn by the promise of wealth or political and religious freedom in the colonies.

2. At about the same time, Europeans transported more than 11 million East and West Africans to their New World colonies in North and South America and the Caribbean to work as slaves. Eventually they came to form a substantial part of the population of the United States, the Caribbean, and many regions of South America, especially Brazil. Because they maintained so much cultural continuity with their African homeland, they are now sometimes called "The African Diaspora" (Gomez 2004; Thornton 1998).

3. Beginning in about 1800, East Asians began to emigrate from China and to a lesser extent other countries, with motives similar to those of the Europeans who settled the New World (Takaki 1998). They immigrated to major cities in the United States, Latin America, Africa, and the Middle East. Today Brazil has the largest population of Japanese ancestry (1.5 million) outside of Japan. In the newly independent United States, this was an era of rapid westward migration of European settlers, and the often-violent displacement of indigenous peoples.

4. Between about 1880 and 1920, millions of Southern and Eastern Europeans emigrated as they faced increasing political and economic strife as their countries modernized. High school textbooks in the United States tend to portray only immigrants arriving at Ellis Island, but they also settled in Canada, South Africa, Australia, New Zealand, and Latin America. By 1914, 30 percent of the population of Argentina was foreign born and speaking Italian, Russian, Polish, Czech, English, Yiddish, and German. In some districts, the proportion was as high as 50 percent (Shumway 1993).

Immigration today is a complex and evolving social process. As different nations undergo political turmoil and political and social unrest, their neighboring nations adapt to a changing globalized political context, recognizing that they too will be affected (see http://metrocosm.com/global-immigration-map/ to better understand these movements in recent history [2010–2015]).

Studying Immigration

16.1.4 Understand what we can learn about societies by examining their net migration rates over time.

The **immigration rate** is the number of people entering a territory each year for every 1,000 people already in the population in that territory. The **emigration rate** is the opposite, the number of people leaving per 1,000 people in that territory's population. (Note that demographic trends are often discussed per 100,000 in the population—like

immigration rate

The number of people entering a territory each year for every 1,000 people in the population.

emigration rate

The number of people leaving a territory each year for every 1,000 in the population.

the rate of violent crime, for instance. Because migration is more common, rates of migration use a smaller denominator.) However, few territories are so terrible that they cannot attract at least a few immigrants, or so wonderful that no one ever decides to emigrate (although some authoritarian states forbid their citizens from emigrating). Therefore, demographers study the changing population by examining the **net migration rate**, the difference between the immigration and emigration rates in a given year.

Because rich countries offer the greatest educational and job opportunities and the most freedom from oppression, more people want to move to them than to leave, so they tend to have positive net migration rates (8.0 in Spain, 6.6 in Norway, 3.9 in the United States, and 1.5 in Germany). A negative net migration rate means that more people are emigrating than immigrating, suggesting that the country is too poor to offer many jobs or else is undergoing a political crisis (–0.10 in Iran, –1.7 in Mexico, –5.2 in Gaza Strip, and –13.4 in Jordan).

Internal migration means moving from one region to another within a territory. The average American moves 11.3 times during his or her life—more for young, middle-class professionals (Chalabi 2015). Most of these migrations occur within the same city or to adjacent cities, as people seek bigger and better residences while staying "close to home." Young college-educated people are more likely to move and to move longer distances. Married or single, they have fewer long-term responsibilities to tie them to a place, no kids to take out of school or houses to put up on the market. Also, people looking for jobs that require a college degree often conduct a regional or national job search instead of a local search. By income group, the affluent are the most likely to move (Cohn and Morin 2008). Although most Americans have moved at least once in their lifetime, a significant portion—nearly 40 percent—have never left the place they were born. Overall, U.S. internal migration has been drifting downward for decades; less than 12 percent of Americans moved between 2013 and 2014 (U.S. Census 2015). Just like neighboring nations, states in the United States have push and pull factors that shape Americans' decisions about internal migration. One way of visualizing this is to consider the share of the people born in a given state who still live there (a quality demographers sometimes refer to as state "stickiness") alongside the share of a state's current residents who came from other states (state "magnetism") (see TABLE 16.1).

Internal and international migrations are regulated by similar push and pull factors: People want jobs and freedom. Two million African Americans moved from the rural South to the urban North between 1900 and 1940, to escape stagnating rural economies and oppressive Jim Crow laws. Another five million moved north between 1940 and 1970 (Lemann 1992). Since World War II, there has been an ongoing migration of young gay men and lesbians from small towns to big cities, to escape from the homophobia and heterosexism back home (Weston 1995). This simultaneous *push* (discrimination) and *pull* (attraction of a community) created and sustained the now well-established gay areas in San Francisco, New York, Miami, Atlanta, and other major cities (see Levine 1979; Ghaziani 2014). Today, internal migration in the United States follows a similar pattern to migration more generally. States, cities, and regions heavily invested in economic sectors that are stagnating and declining tend to have shrinking population; those people tend to follow opportunity toward places with more economic prospects.

The International Olympic Committee selected 10 refugees to compete at the 2016 Olympic Games. Here, refugee Olympian Yusra Mardini is seen training for the games in Berlin after fleeing Syria. Mardini fled Syria with her sister after their home was destroyed during the Syrian civil war. They crossed the Aegean Sea in a boat meant to hold 7 people holding 20 refugees. During the trip, the motor stopped working, and Mardini, her sister, and two other refugees got out and and swam, pulling the boat for more 3 hours to get everyone safely to Greece.

net migration rate
The difference between immigration and emigration rates in a given year.

internal migration
Moving from one region to another within a territory.

TABLE 16.1 Tracking Migration in the United States: How "Magnetic" or "Sticky" Is Your State?

You can see *push* and *pull* factors impacting population movement within societies as well. Consider this figure looking at mobility between states in the United States. States with high levels of "magnetism" are those that have pull factors helping to cause people to move to them (along the right side of the table). Conversely, states with high levels of "stickiness" are those people who are hesitant to leave; meanwhile, states with low levels of "stickiness" have at least modest levels of push factors that make people less attached to remaining inside the state's boundaries. So, for instance, in California, about one-third of the residents come from out of state to live there (causing it to rank in the lower half of states on "magnetism"), whereas more than two-thirds of adults born in California still live in California (causing it to rank high on the "stickiness" scale).

← (low) Magnetism (high) →	
Alabama	Arizona
California	Florida
Illinois	Georgia
Indiana	Maryland
Kentucky	North Carolina
Louisiana	Oregon
Massachusetts	South Carolina
Michigan	Tennessee
Minnesota	Virginia
Missouri	Washington
Ohio	
Pennsylvania	
Texas	
Utah	
Wisconsin	
Iowa	Alaska
Maine	Arkansas
Mississippi	Colorado
Nebraska	Delaware
New York	District of Columbia
North Dakota	Idaho
Rhode Island	Kansas
South Dakota	Montana
West Virginia	Nevada
	New Hampshire
	New Mexico
	Vermont
	Wyoming

↑ (low) Stickiness (high) ↑ / ↓ (low) Stickiness (high) ↓

Neither "Magnetic" Nor "Sticky"

Connecticut

Hawaii

New Jersey

Oklahoma

NOTE: This table only considers U.S.-born adults age 18 and older. State *magnetism* is calculated by residents born outside of a state/total state population. State *stickiness* is calculated by residents born in a state and living in the same state/residents born in the state and living elsewhere in the United States.

SOURCE: Data from U.S. Census Bureau, American Community Survey, 2005–2007.

An influx of new immigrants, either internal or international, can provide new talent for the community, but it also puts a strain on the local infrastructure, as utility companies, school districts, real estate, and retailers try to deal with the influx. Meanwhile, the territories losing population experience a loss of talent, failed businesses, deserted downtowns, and a "sinking ship" feeling. Today, global migration is a politically volatile issue. Millions of immigrants from less-developed countries pour into industrial countries in North America, Europe, and Australia—though, the nations accepting the most immigrants internationally are still in the Middle East and Africa. As the global economy slows down, however, immigrants are vulnerable targets for political opposition and economic protectionism, especially if they have entered the country illegally.

Population Composition

16.1.5 Understand what we can learn about a society by examining its population pyramid.

Comparing births and deaths, emigration and immigration, can give demographers only a partial understanding about what's going on in a country or region. They also want to know the **population composition**—that is, the comparative numbers of different groups in the population (by age, race, ethnicity, and sex/gender for instance). For instance, one aspect of populations that demographers study is the **sex ratio**—the ratio of males to females in a population. The male-to-female ratio is never 50:50. Due to physiological differences in X and Y chromosomes, 104–105 boys tend to be born for every 100 girls (this is what demographers refer to as the **natural sex ratio**). A significantly lower birth ratio suggests that environmental pollution is having an impact on the human body at the chromosomal level (Davis, Gottlieb, and Stampnitzky 1998). A significantly higher ratio, especially in countries where boys are strongly preferred over girls—for instance, China (115), India (112), South Korea (107), Singapore (107) and Guam (106)—suggests to demographers that women are terminating pregnancies after finding out that they are carrying girls. This practice is called **sex-selective abortion**. (Hvistendahl 2011).

After birth, the ratio of men to women decreases in every age group because men are more likely to die in accidents, warfare, and of certain diseases. If the ratio is too high or not high enough, demographers conclude that the country is especially unpleasant or unattractive for men or women. During the middle years of life (ages 15 to 64), the highest disproportion of men to women occurs in countries that draw a substantial number of male foreign workers (for instance, in 2016, there were 3.41 men for every woman in Qatar). Countries that lose many men to foreign employment tend to have a disproportionate number of women (in 2016, there were 0.91 men for every woman in Puerto Rico).

The distribution of people of different age groups can best be represented by a graph called a **population pyramid** (which you may remember from Chapter 10), which shows 5- or 10-year age groups as different-sized bars, or "blocks." These graphs are quick demographic profiles of the age and gender composition of populations. But, we can also look at population pyramids for larger populations (see FIGURE 16.2).

You read about population pyramids in Chapter 10. It's important that population pyramids are also divided by sex, with men on one side and women on the other. If one of the blocks is larger on one end than the other, it means that one sex outnumbers the other in that age group. In the United States, women begin outnumbering men around the age of 55–59, but in Iraq, they begin outnumbering men around the age of 45. Demographers use population blocks to determine current and future social service needs of the society. In the United States, the baby boomer block has been a bulge in the pyramid, working its way upward since the 1950s, allowing demographers to predict a need for more child-oriented facilities, then more colleges and universities, and now more facilities for elderly people.

population composition

The comparative numbers of men and women and various age groups in an area, region, or country.

sex ratio

The ratio of males to females in a population.

natural sex ratio

Refers to the fact that physiological differences in X and Y chromosomes result in a male-to-female ratio at birth that is never 50:50. The natural sex ratio is 104–105 boys born for every 100 girls.

sex-selective abortion

A procedure in which women terminate pregnancies after finding out that they are carrying girls.

population pyramid

Type of graph that shows 5- or 10-year age groups as different-sized bars, or "blocks."

FIGURE 16.2 Global Population Pyramid, 2016
Population growth on a global scale is still increasing rapidly, though that growth is projected to slow around 2050. The world population is currently more than 7 billion people; By 2050, it is projected to grow to more than 10 billion.

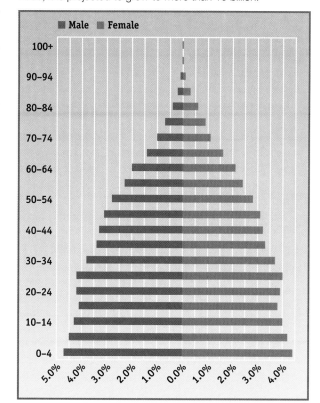

SOURCE: Data from Btlas, "Population Pyramids of the World, 2016." Available at http://www.populationpyramid.net/world/2016/.

SOCIOLOGY AND OUR WORLD

"MISSING WOMEN" AND "SURPLUS MEN"

Why enough couples deciding that they only want to give birth to boys can produce consequences they might not imagine.

How societies care for the elderly differs greatly by society. In China, for instance, a long cultural practice has been that your son's wife would care for you and your spouse in your old age. This meant that having sons was important in Chinese society, not only to carry on the family name, but also to help safeguard your own health and happiness in old age. According to this tradition, sons have a kind of value to a couple that daughters do not. Attach this cultural practice to a widespread androcentric ideology that privileges men over women (an ideal that exists on a global scale), and technological innovations that enable couples to determine the sex of a child early enough in a pregnancy that abortion is still possible. And imagine that all of this takes place in a society that is deeply concerned with halting population growth, pursuing the most restrictive birth control policy ever pursued—only allowing couples to have one child. China's "one-child policy" was introduced in 1979 and finally phased out in 2015. During this period of time, Chinese couples were—as a group—more likely to practice sex-selective abortion, terminating pregnancies when the fetuses were determined to be female.

Sex-selective abortion has been studied by demographers for a long time. Two of the nations with some of the highest rates of sex selective abortion are China and India. This is significant because these are also the two most populous nations on earth—collectively they account for more than one-third of the global population. Indian demographer and philosopher Amartya Sen famously labeled this social problem as the problem of the "missing women" (Sen 1990, 1992). The French demographer Christophe Guilmoto has sought to more carefully calculate the number of women "missing" as a result of sex-selective abortion. And, in 2005, he calculated that if Asia's sex ratio were normal (or "natural"), the continent would have an additional 163 million females. Put another way, ultrasound technology and subsequent abortions claimed more than 160 million female lives—and that's only Asia! Just for scale, that is a figure that is about the same size as the female population of the United States today.

The practice is studied in a couple different ways. Demographers can look at the nation-specific sex ratios to see whether any societies are giving birth to significantly more or fewer girls or boys than would be predicted by a natural sex ratio (in practice anything over 106 or under 104 is understood to be the result of human or environmental intervention). But, often sex-selective abortion is region specific as well.

Another way demographers attempt to figure out whether sex-selective abortion is happening in societies (and on what kind of scale) is to examine sex and birth order. If couples who already have a daughter or two daughters get pregnant for a second or third time, they are no more or less likely to have a boy than they were for the first or second pregnancy; those odds don't change. But, if second born children are more likely than firstborn children to be boys and if third-born children are more likely to be boys than second-born children, then we know that sex selection is happening. It's for this reason that we know that sex-selective abortion is not an issue in China and India alone. In fact, immigrants from Southeast Asia in other parts of the world sometimes continue the practice—desiring fewer children than previous generations, which produces increased pressures to ensure a child is male. And some research suggests that, among the economic elite in the United States, sex selection by birth order may also be occurring.

And the flip side of the problem of "missing women" is something demographers refer to as "surplus men." History shows us that societies with surplus populations of men have not been desirable places to live. In fact, sex-selective abortion has given rise to a host of issues individual couples might never have imagined. As this population of boys has grown older, there are fewer girls in the population that they might marry. Sex crimes, prostitution, and bride buying and bride napping all occur in societies near those with severely upset sex ratios. And because the two most populous nations struggle with this issue, for the first time in the history of the world, some demographers suggest that the sex ratio of the entire globe is outside "natural" limits—now at 107 males born per every 100 females. It's a pressing social problem and it demands sociological thinking. It's the result of cultural pressures that shape private decisions about families and futures.

Explaining Populations Sociologically

16.1.6 Understand why the world population has increased so dramatically in recent history and what social forces will slow it down.

Cities and countries grow or shrink for a variety of reasons: **natural population increase** (the number of births every year subtracted by the number of deaths), immigration and emigration, and changing boundary lines when territories are annexed or lost. But the world as a whole grows for only one reason, natural increase; and it is growing fast, at a rate of 1.13 percent per year. As of this writing, there are 7.5 billion people living on Earth, but by the time this book is published, it will probably be 7.6–7.7 billion. If you are 20 years old today, you can expect to see the world's population reach 8 billion before your 40th birthday and 9 billion long before you retire (Department of Social and Economic Affairs 2015).

How did we get so many people? And what are we going to do with them? For thousands of years, more children meant greater prosperity. They started working alongside their parents as soon as they could walk, thus adding to the family's economic productivity. Women were pregnant as often as they could be. With a high infant mortality rate and virtually no effective medical care, only about half of the babies born survived to age 14 (Kriedte 1983). So it was prudent to have as many children as possible to ensure that a few would survive to maturity. In modern societies, however, most children survive to adulthood. So, it is imprudent to give birth to more than you expect to raise. And rather than being seen as an economic asset, children today are understood as an economic burden. Thus, although parents used to attempt to imagine whether or not they could afford *not* to have children, today, parents are much more likely to question whether they can afford to have kids. For the first 20 years or so of their lives, parents provide their room, board, braces, medicine, school supplies, books, toys, and probably an allowance, while at least in the middle classes the children contribute little or nothing to the family budget (they may have a part-time job, but it's usually for their own spending money).

Even where industrialized countries find children an economic liability, in the absence of social safety nets like Social Security and elderly care facilities, people may want large families to ensure care in their old age. High fertility may be encouraged for religious or political reasons. Also, if women's opportunities are limited, childbearing, especially at an early age, is one of the few roles open to them.

Low infant mortality plus the prestige of large families meant that beginning about 1750, the world's population started to inch upward. Then the inch became a foot. Not only the population itself, but the rate of increase started to climb. It was this climb that sparked the growth of demography as a field of sociological study. In 1900, the world's population was about 1.7 billion. By the twenty-first century, it had more than quadrupled to more than 7 billion, due to plummeting infant and maternal mortality rates (the result of improved health care for both pregnant women and their infants and of better neonatal nutrition) and dramatically increased longevity. Although the peak slowed a bit after 1970 because of a declining fertility rate in rich countries and the world pandemic of HIV/AIDS, we are still adding 83 million people each year, or the equivalent of the entire population of the United States every 4 years (though this rate will slow significantly when the baby boomers start to die; see FIGURE 16.3).

Ninety-six percent of the population growth is taking place in poor countries. For instance, Uganda, one of the poorest countries in the world, added 3.25 percent to its population in 2015 alone (World Bank 2015). This means that the people having the most children are precisely the ones least economically capable of providing for them. Many rich countries, on the other hand, have a stable population, and some are in

natural population increase
Simple calculation of the number of deaths every year subtracted from the number of births.

FIGURE 16.3 Population Growth Around the World: 1960 to 2015

Population growth between 1960 and the early 1970s was steep. But since then, global population growth has slowed. And population growth is projected to slow even more as we get closer to a global population of 10 billion. Yet, it is also true that population growth is uneven. Some societies are growing rapidly, others are shrinking, and some are starting to stabilize. In general, the less-developed societies in the world are growing at faster rates than are the more-developed societies. This means that much of the population growth around the world is happening in societies with fewer resources and infrastructure to manage their growing populations. See how the population growth rates for the United States compare with South Africa, Italy, Ethiopia, Brazil, Japan, and India.

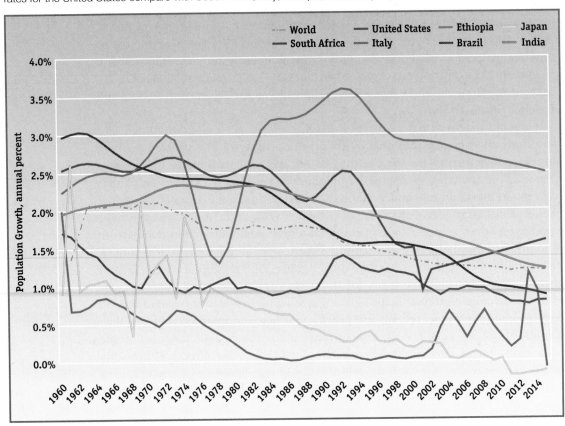

SOURCE: Data from The World Bank, "Population Growth (annual %)." Available at: http://data.worldbank.org/indicator/SP.POP.GROW?end=2015&start=1960&view=chart.

decline. Demographers consider a population growth rate of 0.4 percent or so stable; but, in 33 of the 50 countries in Europe, the growth rate is lower than that, and in 20 of those 33 countries it is actually shrinking. The birthrate and immigration rate are too low to replace those who die and emigrate.

Population Bombs and Booms

16.1.7 Describe how social theorists have made predictions about the size and growth of populations.

Thomas Robert Malthus (1766–1834), an English economist and clergyman, was one of the first to suggest that population growth might spin out of control and lead to disaster (1798/1999). Though the population of England was only about 6 million at the time, **Malthusian theory** held it would increase by geometric progression, doubling in each generation—a man and a woman would have four children, and those four would have eight, and those eight sixteen, and so on. However, because farmland has a limited fertility, even with new technology, food production can only increase by arithmetic progression—20 tons becomes 40, then 60, then 80, and so on. Eventually— and quite rapidly—there would be more people than food, leading to starvation on a global level.

Malthusian theory

Developed by the English economist and clergyman Thomas Robert Malthus (1766–1834), the theory held that population would increase by geometric progression, doubling with each generation—while the food supply would only increase arithmetically, ultimately leading to mass starvation, environmental disaster, and eventual human extinction.

Although in principle his theory made sense, Malthus failed to foresee several cultural trends. First, the birthrate in England began to drop around 1850 as children were increasingly seen as an economic liability and people began to use birth control. Malthus failed to imagine that people would voluntarily opt to have fewer children. Also, Malthus underestimated human ingenuity—irrigation, fertilizers, pesticides, and selective breeding have greatly increased farm productivity. So the population did not increase quite as fast as he thought, and there has been no global starvation. Yet, in rich countries, the problem is often quite the opposite; we consume far more than we need to survive.

Karl Marx was highly critical of Malthus's basic assumption that population growth would be a source of hardship for the masses. He argued that unequal distribution of resources was a far more significant factor. To Marx, the problem was that the rich get richer and the poor get babies. The political question was not how to reduce the number of babies but how to get the poor some of those riches. But Marx has been criticized for failing to take uneven population growth into account as a contributing factor in global inequality. For example, India is the second-most populous country in the world, with 1.324 billion people in 2016. Its population increases by 16 million per year, with an expected 50 percent increase by 2050. It currently faces a severe water shortage. And water, unlike food, is not a resource that can be redistributed.

Paul Ehrlich published *The Population Bomb* (1968), which put a modern take on Malthus. He argued that even a moderate 1.3 percent population increase would soon spin out of control. Before the year 3000, he predicted, Earth's population would grow to 60 million billion, or 100 people for each square yard of the world, including the oceans and mountaintops. Of course, we would run out of food and usable water long before that. Ehrlich predicted that the first mass starvations would begin in the 1990s. He turned out to be slightly off as well. Millions of people are malnourished across the world, but not nearly as many as he predicted. Erlich later argued that an increased population combined with an alarming depletion of natural resources can only lead to chaos. His solution was a global effort to achieve **zero population growth**—where the number of births does not exceed the number of deaths. This would involve not only global stability in population but a decrease in poor countries and a redistribution of resources to those countries.

Frank Notestein (1945) argued that population growth is tied to technological development. **Demographic transition theory** holds that the population and technology spur each other's development. This transition has three stages:

1. *Initial stage.* The society has both a high birth rate and a high death rate, so the population size remains stable or else grows very slowly. Preindustrial societies were all at this stage.

2. *Transitional growth stage.* Industrialization leads to a better food supply, better medical care, and better sanitation, all resulting in a decrease in mortality at all age levels. However, the social status of large families has not decreased, so the birth rate remains high, and the population explodes.

3. *Incipient decline stage.* Social forces and cultural beliefs catch up with technology. Both the birthrates and death rates are low, so population growth returns to minimal levels. Zero population growth is rare, but many industrialized countries like Iceland and Germany are coming close.

zero population growth
Paul Erlich's modern solution to Malthus's concerns, it entails a global effort to ensure that the number of births does not exceed the number of deaths, providing global population stability, a decrease in poor countries, and a redistribution of resources to those countries.

demographic transition theory
A population theory that shows that the transition from high birth and death rates to lower birth and death rates as a country or region develops from a preindustrial to an industrialized economic system.

Migration and fertility rates also affect the age demographics of a society. Puerto Rico loses 0.54 percent of its population every year, becoming older and grayer.

This theory has been criticized as not explaining all shifts in population size for two reasons. First, it always works in the same direction, from high fertility/high mortality to high fertility/low mortality as technology increases, and then to low fertility/low mortality as social norms catch up. However, there have been many instances in history where the mortality rate moved from low to high, such as the periods immediately after the fall of the Roman Empire and the Mayan Empire. In contemporary sub-Saharan Africa, the high rate of HIV infection is offsetting the birthrate and causing countries to move backward, from stage two to stage one (high fertility/high mortality). Second, it is not technology that causes a decrease in the mortality rate—but rather the *society*, the changes in personal and public health practices and institutions. Several major medical discoveries in the eighteenth and nineteenth centuries led to little change in the mortality rate. But when the public accepted the **germ theory of disease**, and therefore they began to sterilize implements, pasteurize their milk, immunize their children, wash their hands, and bathe regularly—then the mortality rate declined.

germ theory of disease

The theory that some diseases are caused by microorganisms that invade humans, animals, and other living hosts. Their growth and reproduction within living hosts causes disease.

HOW DO WE KNOW WHAT WE KNOW?

LIFE EXPECTANCY AND INTERSECTIONALITY

You can go online or to an encyclopedia and find the life expectancy for men and women and different ethnic and occupational groups in every country in the world. But how do we know that a baby born today is likely to live to be 61, or 66, or 78, or 100? It's not easy.

First we have to find the crude death rate, the percentage of people of each age who were alive last year but are dead this year. For instance, if last year's records indicated that there were 1,000,000 people of age 30, and this year there are 900,000 people of age 31, then 30-year-olds have a 90 percent chance of seeing their 31st birthday, and their crude death rate is 10 percent. From this we can construct a life table, a list of the probabilities that persons of age X will live to see age $X + 1$, $X + 2$, and so on. To find the life expectancy of the population, we take the mean of all the probabilities for a person of age 0 (a newborn baby).

Notice that the measure of life expectancy cannot predict the future. In fact, in practice, life expectancy changes every year (as we discussed in more detail in Chapter 10). If the life expectancy in the country is 75, that doesn't mean that newborn babies will live for 75 more years, or that people who are 30 now have 45 years left to live. It is really a measure of how long people are living at this moment in time. It's a snapshot of what is true today—whether or not it is true tomorrow or in years to come is not something we can predict. Below, consider the life expectancies for black and white men and women born in 1904, 2004, and 2015.

Life Expectancies at Birth by Race and Sex: 1904, 2004, and 2015 (in Years)

Subgroup	1904	2004	2015
White males	46.6	75.7	77.7
White females	49.5	80.8	82.2
Black males	29.1	69.8	72.9
Black females	32.7	76.5	78.9

SOURCE: Data from U.S. Census 2015. Available at: https://www.census.gov/population/projections/data/national/2014/summarytables.html.

We can see disparities between these four groups. In general, women are projected to outlive men and white people outlive black people in the United States. But predicting how long you will actually live is more difficult. Demographers provide group-level projections. It doesn't mean that all baby boys born in 2015 will live to see 77 (or beyond). But, it is our best guess based on the data available at the moment—and that prediction changes each year as populations grow older.

The Politics of Human Environments

16.1.8 Understand some of the ways that societies have sought to intervene in population dynamics and affect population growth.

Population dynamics are not simple cycles of birth and death, in and out migration, growth and decline. They are profoundly social events, shaped by the social, economic, and political contexts in which they take place. Different groups of people, who find themselves in different places in a class, race, or gender hierarchy, for example, not to mention in different societies around the globe, experience these demographic processes in distinct ways. Demographic shifts record the gradual movement of social inequalities.

Take, for example, efforts to combat the population explosion. Which groups should have fewer babies—and which groups, if any, should have more? A number of organizations and nations have come together to try to decrease the population explosion. In the United States, Population Connection promotes the replacement level of only two children per family. The organization's website contains updates and policy briefs about different pressing environmental issues and has branches on many college campuses.

But how can countries develop strategies to reduce population? In China, a family planning law was mandated in 1979. Although known worldwide as a one-child policy, it was actually calculated by neighborhoods rather than couples: Each neighborhood was told the maximum number of births it can have per year. The policy was relaxed in 2015 (now allowing couples to have two children). Between 1980 and 2015, if a couple wanted to have a child, they had to apply for a "pregnancy permit." They may have been permitted to have more than one, if the neighborhood has not met its quota, and if there are extenuating circumstances (such as if they work on a farm, if their first child was a girl, if their first child was disabled, and so on); or they may not be permitted to have a child at all. Illegal pregnancy meant losing privileges, paying fines, and even losing their jobs. Globally, some commentators worried about compromising personal freedom, and others worried about women accidentally getting pregnant and then being forced to have an abortion. From a population-level perspective, however, China was extraordinarily successful at controlling the size of its population. China reduced its growth rate to 0.49 percent annually, a rate roughly one quarter of other poor nations.

---

iSOC AND YOU The Human Environment

Your *identity* depends on the various environments in which you find yourself. These environments—human, social, natural—shape your lives, the people with whom you will *interact*, and the sorts of *institutions* in which these interactions take place and to which you will have access. Your ability to interact in these environments will be shaped by dramatic *inequality*—in access, ownership, and resources. From where you live, to how well you live, even to how long you'll live will be shaped by these social inequalities. Inequalities based on access to resources also *intersect* with each other, forming a complex "matrix" of inequalities in which we are each individually situated.

16.2 The Urban Environment

In the U.S. farming town of Dekalb, Illinois, only 65 miles from downtown Chicago, Illinois live people who have never ventured to the city—not to go to a Cubs game or the Art Institute, not to shop at Macy's. When questioned about this, they seem surprised—who in their right mind would want to go into Chicago? It's crowded, dirty, ugly, expensive, and dangerous. Meanwhile, in the high-rise condos of Chicago's Gold

Coast live people who have never ventured more than 5 miles west of the Loop. When they are questioned, they also seem surprised—where else is there to go? They're surrounded by nonstop excitement, cultural diversity, artistic innovation, and economic promise. Beyond Chicago there is nothing but small towns stuck in the 1930s, populated by narrow-minded bigots. Urban and rural are not only qualities of populations, they are also social identities that come with unique sets of social interactions desired by some much more than others.

We think of cities as the capitals of civilization—culturally alive, commercially dynamic, exciting. We also think of cities as the centers and incubators of many of our most central social problems—crime, poverty, and racial and ethnic antagonism. But it's not one or the other—it's both. The two sets of social issues are linked and interacting. To a great extent, one cannot exist without the other. And rural and urban communities today exist in tension while also relying on one another for mutual interdependence. Yet it is also true that the social inequalities that affect urban and rural residents differ in both kind and degree. Poverty, for instance, is often depicted as an issue associated with urban life. Yet, the poor live in rural communities as well. In this section, we examine the history of shifts toward more urbanization in many societies around the world and discuss the ways that this process currently exists on a truly global scale. Just what qualifies as "the city" is an expansive territory whose meaning and boundaries are constantly being called into question and pushed.

The City and the Countryside

16.2.1 Explain the meaning of population density and how different areas might differ on this measure.

When people depend on farming for sustenance and don't have cars, they must live within walking distance of their farmland. Throughout most of human history, and in many undeveloped countries today, they have lived in villages scattered across the farmlands, with a population of only a few hundred, so small that everyone knows everyone else and is probably related through blood and marriage. Between 8000 and 5000 BCE, technological innovations in agriculture began to produce food surpluses, so some people could take on nonfarming jobs, mostly as priests and artisans. They could live in larger settlements— but not too much larger because 99 percent of the population had to be within walking distance of the fields or cattle. Many archaeologists name Çatalhöyük, in modern-day Turkey, as the first city. In 7000 BCE, it was home to 10,000 people—a tiny village today, but then by far the most populous settlement in the world (Mumford 1968; Yoffee 2005).

Most ancient cities grew up along major rivers, where enough food could be produced to feed a large nonfarming population. Still today, the global population is most dense around bodies of water. One Egyptian farmer living along the fertile Nile delta could easily feed five to seven families, but even so, cities tended to be small. Most had no more than 10,000 residents. At the end of the first century BCE, a few cities in China and India reached a population of 300,000, and Rome was probably unique throughout the ancient world for its population of nearly 1,000,000. The number of "large" cities stayed about the same throughout the Middle Ages and the Renaissance. For all of their fame as centers of Western civilization, European cities were surprisingly small. Of the 10 most populous cities in the world in 1500, 4 were in China, 3 in the Middle East, and 2 in India. Only 1 was in Europe: Paris, with a population of 185,000 (about the size of Little Rock, Arkansas, today). Beijing, China, number one, had a population of 672,000 (about the size of Memphis, Tennessee, today) (Chandler 1987).

Cities, both ancient and modern, are often situated near major waterways—for trade, hygiene, and agriculture. This 1853 painting depicts the ninth-century Assyrian palaces of Ashurnasirpal II.

When the Industrial Revolution began around 1750, agricultural productivity increased exponentially, farming jobs began to diminish (a trend that continues today), and manufacturing took precedence. Factories needed hundreds of workers all in the same place, so thousands of people left the farms to move to the city (another trend that continues today). England and Western Europe became urbanized first and then the United States. The Founders of the United States conceived of the United States as a nation of "gentlemen farmers," living on rural estates with their families and servants, with only a few towns scattered about. In 1790, only 5.1 percent of the population was urban. New York, the biggest city, had a population of 33,000. Philadelphia had 28,500 people, and Boston 18,000 (U.S. Census Bureau 1998). These were small towns even by eighteenth century standards; compare them to Paris, which had a population of 525,000 in 1790.

The former colonial empires in Africa, Asia, and Latin America urbanized more slowly. By 1900, 9 of the 10 most populous cities in the world were located in Europe or the United States; the most populous, London, had a population of 6.4 million. Today we can tell rich from poor countries by the percentage of the population that lives in urban areas rather than rural areas: 97.9 percent in Belgium, 93.5 percent in Japan, 82.6 percent in the United Kingdom, as opposed to 39.9 percent in Mali, 33.6 percent in Vietnam, and 19.5 percent in Ethiopia (CIA World Factbook 2016). **Population density** refers to the number of people within a defined area (usually a square kilometer). Consider how population density varies around the world and within individual societies as well (see MAP 16.1).

population density
The number of people per square mile or kilometer.

MAP 16.1 Percentage of Population Living in Urban Areas, by Nation, 2016

Although population density varies within an individual society—for instance, more people live in New York City than some of the smaller rural cities in upstate New York—we can also compare population densities by considering the proportions of populations around the world living in urban areas within societies. Here you can see that the United States has a high rate of urbanization, but not nearly as high as countries like Iceland, Japan, or Argentina.

Percent of Population Living in Urban Areas: No data, 0–30%, 30–40%, 40–50%, 50–60%, 60–70%, 70–80%, 80–90%, 90–100%

SOURCE: Data from Population Reference Bureau, 2016. Available at: http://www.worldpopdata.org/map.

Ironically, where urbanization is high, people moving from rural areas have their choice of many cities, but where urbanization is low, there are fewer choices. Thus, poor countries with a high rural population are more likely to have megacities (cities with populations of 10 million or more). Only 5 of the world's 28 megacities are in the United States or Western Europe, but more than half are in poor countries. The rest are mainly from Asia and South America. The top 10 are (in order): Tokyo, Delhi, Shanghai, Mexico City, Mumbai, Sao Paulo, Osaka, Beijing, New York-Newark Area, and Cairo (United Nations 2014).

Estimates of the population of the city itself are often misleading because suburbs and adjacent cities can double or triple the urbanized population, and in some regions the cities have blurred together into gigantic megacities. For instance, Chicago had an "official" population of about 2.72 million in 2013, but the PMSA (Primary Metropolitan Statistical Area), including all of the outlying suburbs and cities, brought it up to 9.46 million that same year. Thus, sociologists more often use "urban agglomerations"—a central city and neighboring communities linked to it, for example, by continuous built-up areas or commuters.

The number of people in a city is not always a good measure of what it feels like to live there. Does it feel crowded? Are the houses crammed together, or are there wide spaces between them? Is every inch of land built up, or are there open areas, such as parks, lawns, and public squares? Are the streets narrow and clogged with cars? But a better measure of how crowded a city feels is population density. Generally, older cities will have a larger population density, because they were constructed before the automobile allowed cities to spread out. Older neighborhoods will be denser than newer neighborhoods.

The most densely populated cities in the world are constricted; that is, there is no place for them to expand outward. Malé, capital of the Maldive Islands, is the most densely populated city on Earth, with 46,525 people per square mile. The total population of 103,693 (these numbers are for Malé the city; Malé the island has much higher numbers, its population density [122,000/sq. mile for 92,555 people total] is crammed onto a small atoll in the Indian Ocean). By contrast, New York has a population density of 27,532 (except on the island of Manhattan, which goes up to 70,951).

The more recently the city was founded, the lower the population density: Oklahoma City, founded in 1889, has a population density of 872 per square kilometer. Though cities with low population densities don't feel as crowded, they have a downside. Everything is scattered, so it takes time and gas to get anywhere. For example, Phoenix (1.45 million in 2017) and Philadelphia (1.53 million in 2017) are roughly comparable in total population, but the population density in Philadelphia (11,457 people per square mile) is more than four times that of Phoenix (2,937 per square mile). As a result, these two cities might feel completely different to live in. And in Phoenix, you'd better have a car.

THE COUNTRYSIDE The U.S. Census Bureau used to define *urban* as living in an incorporated area with a population of 2,500 or more. However, so many people live in unincorporated areas adjacent to big cities or small towns that have been engulfed by big cities that many demographers suggest a change from a simple dichotomy of city and countryside to a rural–urban continuum, nine levels from number 1 (county in a metropolitan area with one million people or more) to number 9 (counties not adjacent to a major metropolitan area and with no city more than 2,500). By that figure, 93.9 percent of the U.S. population was rural in 1800, 60.4 percent in 1900, 54.5 percent in 1910, and 19.3 percent in 2010 (Ratcliffe, et al. 2016).

Globalization increasingly impoverishes more rural areas, both by concentrating agricultural enterprises into larger and larger agribusinesses and by locating engines of industrial development in or near urban areas. Poverty and hunger are the ironic consequences of farm foreclosures and economic concentration in urban areas.

globalization
A set of processes leading to the development of patterns of economic, cultural, and social relationships that transcend geographical boundaries; a widening, deepening, and speeding up of worldwide interconnectedness in all aspects of contemporary life.

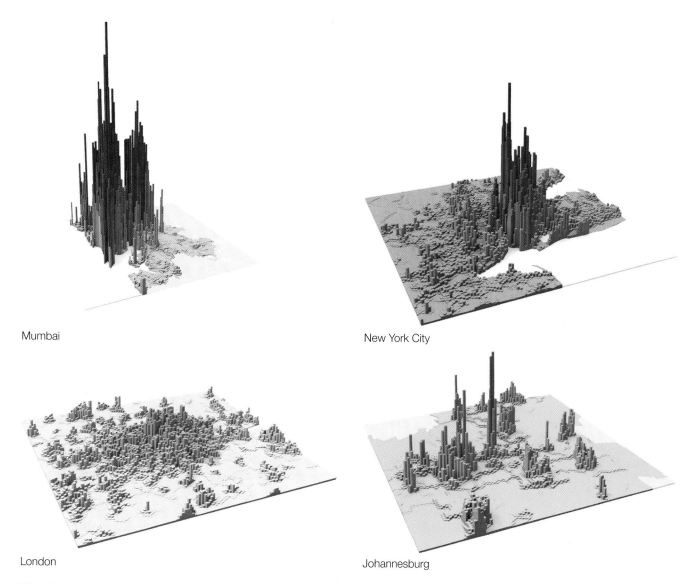

Mumbai

New York City

London

Johannesburg

Visualizing Population Density in Four Cities
These visualizations help provide a better sense of just how crowded different heavily populated cities are around the world. For instance, in 2015, London had a population of 8.6 million; New York City's population was around 8.5 million; Mumbai, India, had a population of more than 20 million people; and Johannesburg, South Africa's population was only 4.4 million. So, Johannesburg has a population of about half the size of New York City and London, whereas Mumbai's population is more than double the size of either. But those numbers don't provide a sense of how differently crowded each of these cities might feel. For instance, London and Johannesburg are spread out and not bordered by water. So, in terms of population density, London might *feel* more like Johannesburg than New York City and New York City might *feel* a bit more like Mumbai than London when you're just thinking about how many people are located in how small of a space.

Rural areas have higher rates of poverty than do urban areas, and rural Americans are more likely than city dwellers to use food stamps—despite the relative proximity to the production of actual food (National Rural Health Association 2006)—a fact related to Amartya Sen's research on food distribution as the more likely source of food scarcity than food supply (Sen 1981). Rural areas in the United States also have increasingly higher suicide rates than cities—with all their urban alienation (National Association for Rural Mental Health 2007).

Yet the scale and speed of migration from the countryside to cities have slowed in rich countries like the United States and in the European Union compared with poor and developing nations, especially in Asia and Africa. The United Nations reports that today's global urban population of 3.9 billion will rise to nearly 6 billion by 2045, when more than two out of three people worldwide will live in cities (United Nations 2014). This surge of migrants will generally come into urban environments whose minimal infrastructure, squalid slums, and air and water pollution already make them fundamentally difficult and dangerous places to live and work.

Suburbs: Identity and Inequality

16.2.2 Summarize the origin of "suburbs" and how the people living in suburban areas has changed over time.

Before the twentieth century, members of the upper classes always had at least two houses, one in the city and the other in the country, for weekend and summer visits (one of the most popular magazines for the upper class is entitled *Town and Country*). Everyone else had to live a mile or two at most from where they worked. Once Henry Ford's mass production made automobiles affordable, people could live much farther from work. What's more, the rapid migration of large numbers of blacks from the rural South to northern cities in the decades after the Civil War led to racial fears of crime and violence. The white middle classes began moving out of the cities altogether, into outlying areas called **suburbs**, where their houses were separate from the others, with front and back yards, just like upper-class estates, instead of the cramped apartments and townhouses of the cities. The first suburbs in the United States were thus a response to shifting race relations at the turn of the twentieth century. Those who could get out of the city—and away from northward migrating black people, newly arriving immigrants, and working class laborers—did so.

suburb

A residential community outside of a city but always existing in relationship to the city.

And shifts in gender relations impacted these movements as well. As urban women sought entry into the paid labor force, schools, and the voting booth, the suburbs promised to preserve the traditional nuclear family arrangements of a male breadwinner and housewife mother. The expression "a man's home is his castle" arose during this period (Jackson 1987). The first mass-produced suburb, Levittown, opened in an unincorporated area on Long Island in 1951. By the time it was finished in 1958, there were 17,311 houses, plus shopping areas, churches, and recreation centers. Men may have needed to commute to the city, but women moving to the suburbs never had to set foot in cities again!

Suburbia has also received its share of detractors. Folksinger Malvina Reynolds complained that the suburbs were made of "Little Boxes," that were "all made out of ticky-tacky, and they all look just the same," not only the houses, but the people too: identical families, white, middle-class, heterosexual, husband, wife, 2.5 kids. Many comedies of the 1950s begin with long lines of cars driven by identically dressed wives, who drop identically dressed husbands off at the train station for their identical commutes into the city. Suburbs were criticized as deadening, soul destroying, isolated. They created a generation of robots—of "men in gray flannel suits" and "Stepford wives." But people still moved there in huge numbers.

Why? Safety, or presumed safety—because cities were increasingly seen as crime infested, poor, and populated by more "dangerous" minorities. Comfort—one could have a larger home, with all the new technological amenities, like televisions and barbecue pits. Ease of life—including the ability to have a car. Suburbs promised "the good life," and Americans followed the call.

Federal policies and programs after World War II propelled the suburbanization of America. The GI Bill, federal mortgage programs, the creation of the interstate highway system, and massive infusions of public funds for commuter railroads and local schools provided the opportunity to move to the suburbs. The desire for a better life, and home ownership, combined with **"white flight"** provided the motive. By the 1960s, suburbs grew at four times the rate of cities.

"white flight"

Term for the pattern of movement by white people out of cities to escape immigrants and minorities.

Once suburban areas had their own jobs and amenities, they were no longer simply "bedroom communities," empty during the day as the workers trekked into the city for their jobs. They became cities in their own right, called "edge cities," with their own economic focus (often high tech). Sometimes they are called "beltway cities," because they are clustered around the interstate highways that loop around major cities. You might live in the edge city of Grand Prairie, Texas, and work in Fort Worth, 22 miles away, though you are actually in a suburb of Dallas, 13 miles away. But it hardly matters because you depend on the nearby edge cities of Irving and Arlington to shop. Downtown is just for jury duty.

Recently, the tide has begun to shift once again, in what may represent a sea change in the relationship between city and suburb. An analysis of Census data from the first decade of the twenty-first century suggests that as many younger, educated white people move to the city to find jobs and relationships, the suburbs are becoming increasingly home to the poor, minorities, and the elderly. Suburbs still "tilt white," but it is actually true that a majority of *all* racial and ethnic groups in large metropolitan areas now live outside the city. Suburban Asian and Hispanic Americans topped 50 percent in 2000, and among black Americans rose to more than 50 percent in 2010, up 7 percent during the past decade. And suburbs now have the largest poor population in the country (Yen 2010).

The post–World War II era witnessed the greatest migration of black Americans from the South to northern cities—and the great migration of whites from those cities to newly developed suburbs. William Levitt saw suburbanization as political, as well as residential. "No man who owns his own home … can be a Communist," he said.

REVITALIZING DOWNTOWN Just as the suburbs have been changing, so, too, has the city (see FIGURE 16.4). During the 1980s and 1990s, many cities attempted to revitalize their downtowns with hip shops, restaurants, and entertainment venues that would attract suburbanites looking for an evening of fun. Some especially hip young professionals even moved back in search of diversity and excitement, buying cheap houses and renovating them. Sometimes they took over whole downtown neighborhoods, raising the property values so much that poor and even middle-class people could no longer afford to live there (a process called **gentrification**). More commonly, cities annexed the suburbs, and any outlying areas that might become suburbs, so they could charge property tax.

Suburbs and edge cities are increasingly difficult to distinguish from inner cities. They have their own problems with traffic, crime, congestion, and pollution. Edge cities often have greater ethnic diversity than inner cities, despite "white flight" (Palen 1995).

As suburbs expanded outward, it was inevitable that they would meet the suburbs of adjacent cities, until they all combined into one gigantic city, a **megalopolis**. This is a social process, but one that occurs on a grand scale. These expanded metropolitan areas contain about two-thirds of the U.S. population and 53 percent of its jobs and generate about 63 percent of the gross domestic product (OECD 2013). Megalopolises span hundreds of miles. You can drive from Nashua, New Hampshire (north of Boston), to Fairfax, Virginia (south of Washington, D.C.), through 10 states and a bewildering number of city and county jurisdictions, without ever hitting unincorporated territory. Because of their scale, megalopolises face enormous structural problems. Their sheer size compounds the problems of air and water pollution, traffic congestion, crime, and joblessness. Civic improvement projects are often stalled

gentrification
The process by which poorer urban neighborhoods are "upgraded" through renovation and development, often pushing out long-time residents of lesser means who can no longer afford to live there.

megalopolis
A term coined by Jean Gottmann in 1961 to describe the integration of large cities and sprawling suburbs into a single organic urbanized unit, such as "Bo Wash," the Boston to Washington, D.C., corridor that includes New York and Philadelphia as well as the suburbs.

FIGURE 16.4 U. S. Cities and Prosperity

The United States claims 18 of the 25 highest-income world metro areas.

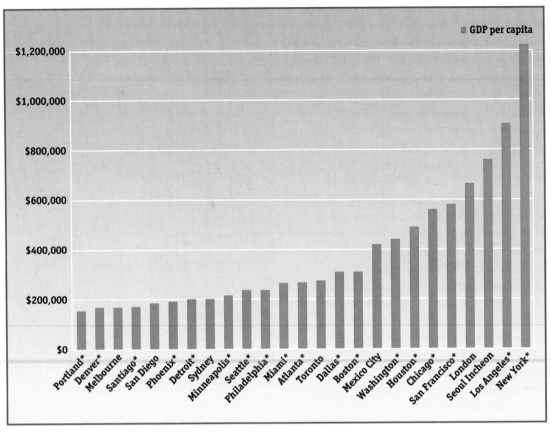

NOTE: *U.S. cities.

SOURCE: Data from OECD Regions at a Glance 2013—U.S. Profile. Available at https://www.oecd.org/governance/regional-policy/Country-statistics-profile-United-States.pdf.

by red tape, as different jurisdictions argue over whose responsibility they are. And megalopolises are a microcosm of what is happening on a global scale as well.

Understanding Urban Life Sociologically

16.2.3 Understand why sociologists were worried about urbanization and its impact on social relationships, identities, and interactions.

Many early sociologists were fascinated and appalled by life in cities. Ferdinand Tönnies (1855–1936) theorized that families, villages, and perhaps neighborhoods in cities formed through *gemeinschaft*, or "commonality" (1957). They shared common norms, values, and beliefs. They had an instinctive trust; they worked together because they cared for each other. Instead, cities and states formed through *gesellschaft*, or "business company." They had differing, sometimes contradictory, norms, values, and beliefs. They had an instinctive mistrust. They worked together toward a definite, deliberate goal, not because they cared for each other but because everyone was acting to his or her own self-advantage. Most sociologists today translate *gemeinschaft* and *gesellschaft* as "community" and "society," as two underlying motives for cementing bonds between people. Moving to the city undermines kinship and neighborhood, the traditional sources of social control and social solidarity. The personal freedom that the city provides comes at the cost of **alienation**.

gemeinschaft
Social relations based on close personal and family ties.

gesellschaft
Social relations based on impersonal relations and formal organization, detached from traditional or sentimental concerns.

alienation
The state or experience of estrangement from a group to which one should belong.

The concepts of *gemeinschaft* and *gesellschaft* have been used most frequently to compare small towns and villages, where presumably everyone is one big happy family, with big cities, where presumably interpersonal connections are based on manipulation and fear. However, they can also be used to compare the "big happy family" of inner cities with the "isolation" of the suburbs.

Shortly after Tönnies, Émile Durkheim theorized that village life was so much nicer because there was little division of labor. Almost everyone did the same work; they shared norms and values. Durkheim called this **mechanical solidarity**, a connection based on similarity. In the cities, by contrast, everyone was different: They worked at different jobs, they had different norms and values, and they disagreed on what was right and wrong. What held them together was what he called **organic solidarity**—connections based on interdependence. Organic solidarity was more stable than (if not as "nice" as) mechanical solidarity because this interdependence meant that each individual was necessary to the functioning of the whole.

After working with the villagers of the Yucatan, anthropologist Robert Redfield (1941) decided that the division was not a matter of settlement size or division of labor but between rural (or "folk") and urban social networks. Folk societies are certainly characterized by homogeneity and a low division of labor, but, more importantly, the social networks are based on family. Family is everything. There are no friends or acquaintances. People who are not related to you by blood or marriage are by default enemies, unless you create sorts of fictional kinship ties in clans (presumed descent from a common ancestor) or in the common tradition of "blood brothers."

mechanical solidarity

Émile Durkheim's term for a traditional society where life is uniform and people are similar. They share a common culture and sense of morality that bonds them.

organic solidarity

Émile Durkheim's term for a modern society where people are interdependent because of the division of labor; they disagree on what is right and wrong but share solidarity because the division of labor causes them to be mutually dependent on each other.

SOCIOLOGY AND OUR WORLD

THE URBAN VILLAGE

How and why do people make crowded cities feel like smaller communities thought to be absent in these spaces?

Herbert Gans (1962, 1968) disagreed with human ecologists. He found that social networks are around the same size in both the city and the small town. You do not try to make friends with the potentially millions of people around you. You find community in a series of smaller worlds, people who share your tastes, interests, and socioeconomic background, just as you would in a village. Consider the hit comedy "New Girl" starring Zoey Deschanel; a group of friends move to the city, have to find roommates to make it work financially, and end up becoming something like family members to one another (with some bumps along the way). Even slums, which to outsiders seem so threatening and merciless, can provide a strong sense of belonging to people.

Gans (1968) found five types of people in the city:
- Cosmopolites—artists and intellectuals
- Young, single professionals—people who would later be called "yuppies" (young urban professionals, a term coined in the 1980s)
- Ethnic villagers—immigrants
- The deprived—poor, often ethnic minorities
- The trapped—poor elderly people

Sociologists from Émile Durkheim to Georg Simmel to Jane Jacobs argued that, although frequently criticized as alienating and impersonal, urban neighborhoods are teeming with life and foster the development of cohesive communities.

In urban societies, family is less important. Geographic mobility is greater, as is the emphasis on "chosen" communities—workplaces, neighborhoods—over kinship. You might call your mother on her birthday and see the entire family over the Christmas holidays. "Secondary relationships"—friendships, work relationships—are more significant. In villages, kinship ties ensured that the person walking toward you would not rob or murder you. In cities, there was no such guarantee. There had to be rules of courtesy (folkways and mores), and there had to be laws. The origins of the rituals such as shaking hands (to show you had no weapons) began in these new environments of strangers.

In "The Metropolis and Mental Life" (1902/1971), the great German sociologist Georg Simmel worried about the overstimulation of the city environment. You are surrounded by so many sights and sounds, so many other humans, that you can't pay attention to everything. So, you pay attention to nothing. You develop a "blasé attitude." It is not that you are cold and unfeeling; it's that you have only enough brain cells to concentrate on your immediate concerns. If someone falls to the sidewalk in front of you, for instance, you might pass him or her by, assuming that someone in authority will provide the necessary assistance.

On the other hand, in *The Death and Life of Great American Cities* (1961), urban analyst Jane Jacobs found that busy streets were not a source of overstimulation at all. Life happened on the street: Children played there; neighbors sat on stoops to gossip with each other; there was a sense of solidarity and belonging. In contrast, in the suburbs no one knew anyone else, and the streets were deserted except for people hurrying from their cars into their houses. Even deviance is under control in the city. Although many strangers are coming and going all the time, they are under constant scrutiny by people in the houses, who are making sure that nothing bad happens. But in the suburbs, no one is peering through windows, and deviance might more easily go undetected.

GLOBAL URBANIZATION For many years, urbanization was considered a sign of development, a sure sign that the nation was becoming richer and more prosperous. Recent trends suggest a more complicated picture. In 2014, 80 percent of the population of Latin America lived in urban areas, about the same as in the industrialized United States. Nearly half lived in cities with over one million inhabitants, and there are seven cities with more than 5 million: Mexico City, São Paulo, Buenos Aires, Rio de Janeiro, Lima, Bogota, and Santiago. But the vast numbers of individuals moving to the city did not find sudden wealth. Indeed, a 2008 U.N. report found that approximately one-third of the population of Latin America (33.2%) live in poverty and many of them are in urban areas—a slight decrease from 36 percent in 2007 (United Nations 2008). These vast neighborhoods in these cities lack adequate sanitation, housing, utilities, and police protection.

Many cities around the world have global rather than local ties (Chase-Dunn 1985). They are command centers not only of their own countries but also of the global economy. They are intimately involved in innovation and creation, producing not manufactured goods but information. They are more interdependent on each other than on the countries where they happen to be located. And they share a common **culture of consumption**. In New York, London, Tokyo, and, to a lesser extent, the second tier of global cities—Jakarta, Milan, Singapore, Rio de Janeiro—businessmen and -women armed with high-tech communication devices hold meetings in board rooms, read the *Financial Times* in English, and relax with U.S. mass culture. Globalization is

culture of consumption
A culture driven and defined by consumption choices and behaviors.

a social process—the multiplication and expansion of economic, political, and cultural connections around the world. And, like other social processes, it is uneven, affecting some more than others, and more beneficial (or detrimental) to some over others.

In 1991, Saskia Sassen introduced the term **global city** (Sassen 1991). She noted that New York, London, and Tokyo are actually located in three different countries on three different continents, with two languages in common use. As such, one might expect significant cultural differences. However, they have so many multinational ties that their exact location is much less meaningful than we might initially assume. There are 2,500 foreign banks and financial companies in New York, employing one-quarter of all of the city's financial employees. National boundaries make little sense when the horizon of expectation for a city resident is the entire world.

global city
Saskia Sassen's term for cities around the world—New York, London, and Tokyo, for example—marked by so many multinational ties that their physical location within a country has a diminished impact on their social and cultural outlook and practices.

Global cities take similar form as transnational businesses and corporations do business around the world. Here, the skylines of Tokyo, Japan (*bottom*), and New York City (*top*) illustrate that while their skylines are distinct, as Saskia Sassen suggests, the look and feel of global cities is often more similar than different.

iSOC AND YOU The Urban Environment

Rural, urban, suburban or something in between—your relation to the city will have an enormous impact on your *identity*. Where you live—the density of the population, its diversity—will shape the sorts of *interactions* you have, and the newness of the ideas floating around. Access to social *institutions* like schools, hospitals, marketplaces (and what kinds and qualities) will all be structured through *inequality*. And these inequalities *intersect* so that race, and class, and gender and age all impact the quality and longevity of your life. Some of you will move to the city for its opportunities, and others will leave because of its noise and its inequalities. (Michael and Amy were raised in the suburbs, but their son was raised in Brooklyn and says he's a "city boy.")

16.3 The Natural Environment

We've seen how the population and the built environments are deeply social processes. But even the natural environment itself is profoundly social. The natural environment provides the material for us to construct our social and individual identities. The type of environment you live in—cold or hot, lush or barren—will shape your view of human nature, your religious beliefs, and your identity. The way you and your community interact with each other and with that environment will structure how you organize yourselves to live in the conditions you find yourselves in. These arrangements are the bases of inequality, the unequal distribution of those natural resources. Social institutions are set up to protect, manage, and control the environment as well.

There is a near-infinite number of ways we could organize ourselves to adapt to the conditions we find to ensure our survival. Over time, these arrangements become the social institutions that define our lives and shape our identities. Family size and structure depends on the natural environment's ability to provide; harsh conditions yield smaller families. Scarcity also requires stronger governments, armies and educational institution to train young people to develop new technologies.

In that sense, the natural environment is not something "out there," a passive collection of stuff waiting for you to use it. It's the very stuff of life—of *social* life. It's how we create ourselves, and is thus an active player in social life.

Understanding the Natural World Sociologically

16.3.1 Summarize what it means to examine the natural world from a sociological perspective.

Sociologists understand that the natural environment—the physical world, or more precisely, animals, plants, and the material substances that make up the physical world—is also organized into **ecosystems**, which are interdependent systems of organisms and their environment. Even if you have lived in Los Angeles your whole life and have never seen an open space other than a vacant lot, you are still participating in biological and geological ecosystems. You still breathe the air of the natural world. You drink its water, eat its food, and depend on its natural resources as raw materials for your manufactured products. Local natural disasters like fires and floods can disrupt your life as quickly as human warfare, and there are global environmental changes, slow-moving disasters, that threaten to disrupt all human life on the planet.

Early sociologists often theorized that the social world was a subcategory of the natural world. Herbert Spencer (1820–1903) argued that biological, social, psychological, and moral systems are all interrelated (2002). Others tried to analyze the impact of social life on the natural world. Ellsworth Huntington argued that Northern Europeans were so "advanced" because they lived in a tough climate, with harsh winters and the need to grow crops (1915/2001). Because they had to struggle to survive, they became industrious and hardworking. Meanwhile, people in tropical climates never had to worry about winter, and they could pick fruit right off the trees, so they became fat and lazy. He was wrong; sustenance in the tropics is no easier than in the north. There were "primitive" hunter–gatherers in the cold climates and advanced technological civilizations in the tropics.

After the first few decades of sociological thought, however, social sciences tended to ignore the environment, leaving it to the biologists, the geologists, and maybe the geographers. Sociology was about people, they figured, so why bother to worry about air and water pollution? Supplies were limitless, and even if they weren't limitless on Earth, we would soon be moving into space to mine the asteroid belt.

ecosystem
An interdependent system in which the animals, plants, and the material substances that make up the physical world live.

Then, during the 1970s, people began to envision Earth not as an infinite space, but as a small, fragile community, "Spaceship Earth" (Schnaiberg 1980). Keep digging up iron and pumping out oil, and eventually there won't be any left. And, if we weren't going to be moving out to other planets, we had to make sure Earth stayed amenable for human life. The two most public environmental concerns of the 1970s were conservation, avoiding the depletion of natural resources, and pollution, avoiding "fouling our nest" (Schnaiberg 1980).

At the same time, some sociologists began to criticize the discipline for being too "anthropocentric," or focused on human beings (Catton and Dunlap 1978). They began to look at the social production of conservation and pollution, how issues were framed as problems, how public perceptions and public policy could change, and the success or failure of environmental movements (Buttel 1987). They looked into the role of technology in causing and potentially solving environmental problems (Bell 2004; Hannigan 1995; King 2005). Finally, they looked at the problems themselves, what impact they were having on social relations, and how they might change social life in the future.

Energy and Other Resources

16.3.2 Explain how energy consumption varies around the world.

In 1900, even if your house was wired for electricity, you couldn't do much with it besides turn on electric lights. In 1930, you might have a telephone and radio; in 1960, an electric refrigerator, oven, and television set. In 2016, you would have a microwave oven, two or three television sets, a stereo system, a game console, several cell phones, a DVD player, a personal computer or two in addition to a tablet, perhaps an air conditioner or two, and, in the garage, at least two cars. Our perceived energy needs have skyrocketed. Sociologists want to know: What are the social implications of dependence on oil and the search for sustainable energy sources, like solar and hydroelectric? What sorts of political arrangements and business environments promote reliance of which types of energy (Rosa, Machlis, and Keating 1988; Smil 2005)?

The United States is by far the world's largest energy consumer, but not when consumption is calculated on a per-capita basis (total amount of energy consumed divided by the population). In 2013, the United States consumed nearly 97 quadrillion Btu (British thermal units) of energy per capita; those countries with rates approaching and exceeding U.S. per-capita rates tend to be either very cold (Norway), oil-producing nations (Kuwait, Norway, Qatar, United Arab Emirates), or small, under-populated remote countries with very small and very wealthy populations where any essential service requires lots of energy to transport and provide (Netherlands Antilles, U.S. Virgin Islands, Gibraltar). Only about 10 percent of energy consumed in the United States comes from renewable sources like nuclear, hydroelectric, geothermal, solar, or wind generators. The other 90 percent of our energy comes from nonrenewable resources, especially oil and natural gas, by-products of millions of years of fossilization that stayed in the ground, undisturbed, until very recently. This is similar to global rates of consumption; worldwide, 11.6 percent (in 2012, projected 2.6 percent annual rise) of the energy supply is from

Many of the new electronic gadgets that populate middle-class American homes consume greater and greater amounts of energy. And there are increasing numbers of technological devices that populate our lives. Indeed, they have become a primary mode of social interaction among many Americans.

renewable sources like tide, solar, wind, and geothermal. In 2020, the EIA projects that 13.8 percent of the worldwide energy supply will be from renewable sources (U.S. Energy Information Administration 2016a, 2016b).

Americans are 4.4 percent of the world's people, yet the United States consumes at least 18 percent of every type of energy and generates 3.28 times the world average per capita of carbon dioxide (CO_2) emissions, or 14.5 percent of the world total annually (World Bank 2013). Americans use about 19.4 million barrels of oil per day, far more than any other country in the world (U.S. Energy Information Association 2016d). Most wealthy countries use less than 2 million. At current levels of consumption, presuming no dependence on foreign oil, we have enough for 20 years (Roberts 2005), though new methods of extraction attempt to stave off reliance on foreign oil further. In 2015, Americans consumed 27.31 trillion cubic feet (Tcf) of natural gas, again far more than any other country in the world, nearly twice as much as number two (Russia with 15.2 trillion Tcf). At current levels of consumption, we have enough for 93 years (U.S. Energy Information Association 2016c).

In addition, the United States produces 2.638 tetrawatt-hours of nuclear energy per million in the population per year, about the same as Bulgaria produces. Because the United States has invested so little in nuclear power in the past decades, our plants are old and inefficient, and there has been little effort to remain competitive. This small investment is partly the result of political opposition to nuclear power, especially following the disasters at Three Mile Island, Pennsylvania, in 1979 and Chenobyl in what was then the Soviet Union in 1986.

Environments, High-Risk Technology, and "Normal Accidents"

"normal accidents"

Seemingly trivial errors within complex systems that have cascading effects and the potential to create much larger events with severe consequences.

16.3.3 Describe what Charles Perrow means by "normal accidents" using the Chernobyl nuclear power plant disaster as an illustration.

Nuclear disasters are rare. And when they occur, it is not uncommon to seek answers, to assign blame, and to attempt to figure out how to ensure that something like that does not happen again. To be sure, they are not annual events. Disasters like the Chernobyl nuclear power plant explosion in 1986, or, more recently, the power plant explosion at the Fukushima power plant in March 2011 following the tsunami caused by the Tōhoku earthquake that same month and year are relatively rare. But the consequences that flow from them are long-lasting, and cut across national boundaries. Sociologist Charles Perrow (1984), however, argues that accidents like these are inevitable by-products of extremely complex systems and environmental processes.

Perrow refers to such systemic failures within complex systems as "**normal accidents**"—seemingly trivial errors within complex systems that have cascading effects and the potential to create much larger events with severe consequences. Technological disasters like nuclear power plant "energy accidents" are not, according to Perrow, the result of isolated equipment malfunctions or small acts of incompetence on the part of

In this satellite view, the Fukushima Dai-ichi Nuclear Power plant after a massive earthquake and subsequent tsunami on March 14, 2011, in Futaba, Japan. Japanese officials reported that a fire at the stricken Fukushima nuclear power plant released radioactive material into the air in the chaos wrought by the earthquake and tsunami that left at least 10,000 people dead in northeastern Japan following the disaster.

Power operators train using a control room simulator at the Bruce B nuclear power plant in Tiverton, Ontario, Canada, on Monday, April 28, 2008. The room gives some sense of the scale of complexity involved in nuclear power plant technology.

system operators. Rather, Perrow identified three separate conditions that make a system much more likely to endure a "normal accident":

1. The system is *complex*—as social life becomes more complex, we are increasingly likely to have to place faith in complicated systems we do not fully understand.
2. The system is *tightly coupled*—as systems become more complex, they often also become more interrelated such that a minor problem in one part of the system can have cascading (and often unanticipated) effects throughout the system.
3. The system has *catastrophic potential*—this refers to the capacity of a system to produce wide scale disastrous effects.

Safeguards are in place in all systems involving high-risk technology. Yet, technology is changing all of the time, and these changes pose new risks despite safeguards. For instance, new nuclear reactor technology is often developed in the interest of safety—and yet, new technology invariably poses greater risks, at least initially, as operators will necessarily have less training and experience with the new design. Indeed, many normal accidents involving nuclear reactor technology happened when people were operating relatively new technology.

Planning for increases in human errors, it is also common to build in engineering redundancies that aim to help ensure safety by making plausible human errors more difficult to actually carry out. Yet, engineering redundancies pose new sets of risks and probabilities associated with normal accidents. For instance, engineering redundancies may be designed to make accidents as a result of human error less likely, but they also result in the production of a system that is *more* complex. Perrow showed that increases in complexity make high-risk technologies more prone to human error and resulting accidents.

Vanishing Resources

16.3.4 Understand the scale of lost natural resources on earth and how humans and societies contribute to the problem.

Globally, forests are being depleted at the rate of one acre per second, depriving the world of a gigantic natural storage capacity for harmful carbon dioxide. Forests are unique in their capability to convert carbon dioxide during photosynthesis into carbon compounds that are then stored in wood, vegetation, and soil humus, a process called "carbon sequestration." Through this natural process, the world's forests store about one trillion tons of carbon—about one-and-a-half times the total amount found

deforestation
The clearing of forests for crops and development.

greenhouse effect
Caused by gases such as carbon dioxide (CO_2) and methane, a phenomenon in which earth's atmosphere traps radiation emitted by the sun, causing the planet's surface to warm.

biodiversity
The variety of life in the world or in a particular habitat or ecosystem.

desertification
The process by which fertile land becomes desert, usually as a result of deforestation, drought, or indiscriminate human use for agriculture, such as intensive farming, overgrazing, or repeated burning.

in the atmosphere. **Deforestation**, the clearing of these forests for crops and development, accounts for about 12 percent of all human-made emissions of carbon dioxide in the atmosphere—just under the amount produced by the United States (20%), the world's second largest polluter (China is first at 22%).

Deforestation is often accomplished by burning, contributing in significant ways to the **greenhouse effect** (Bonnicksen 2000). And, of course, the products that the forests might provide are also gone forever. The depletion of tropical rain forests is particularly disturbing because they cover only 7 percent of Earth's surface but account for up to 80 percent of the world's plant species, most of which have not been tested for medicinal effect. Just as globalization is reducing the level of *cultural* diversity we find around the world, deforestation is reducing the global level of **biodiversity**—a problem whose consequences are difficult to quantify because we may never know what benefits we are losing in the process. Deforestation also results in the loss of topsoil because the cleared land is quick to erode. Covering huge stretches of land with concrete buildings and roads also increases erosion because there is nowhere for rainwater to go but onto undeveloped land. An estimated 75 billion tons of topsoil is being lost per year, transforming arable land into desert (a new study reports 75 million/year and claims topsoil will vanish in 60 years at current rates. Source: http://www.businessgreen.com/business-green/news/2257313/fertile-topsoil-lost-globally). The process of desertification can be seen in many parts of the world, especially sub-Saharan Africa.

Desertification, combined with the increased water use necessary for an increased population, means that the world is quickly losing groundwater—water tables are falling in large swaths of many countries around the world, including the Great Plains and Southwest of the United States, most states in India, the entire northern half of China, and throughout the north of Mexico (Brown 2005). According to a 2009 report, about 2.4 billion people live in "water-stressed" countries like China (Thomas, Krishnan, and Leung 2010).

A final natural resource that we are quickly depleting is animal and plant species—our biodiversity. We don't know exactly how many species there are; new ones are discovered every day. But we do know that species are becoming extinct at a rate 1,000 times greater than before technological civilization, at a rate of approximately 100 per day, usually as their natural environment is destroyed and they cannot adapt to their new surroundings. Worldwide, 22 percent of the world's mammals are threatened with extinction—a result of both habitat and hunting (International Union for Conservation of Nature 2016). In the United States, the Fish and Wildlife Service lists 1,120 endangered animals, including such "common" animals as the brown bear, fox, otter, prairie dog, and red squirrel, as well as 748 endangered plants. Only a few hundred species have a specific economic or aesthetic value to humans, but we won't know which ones do and which do not if they disappear before we can test them. More important, however, is the contribution every species, even the most seemingly insignificant, makes to the delicate balance of an ecosystem. When an insect species goes extinct, the plant that it pollinated will die out soon, a process that will, in turn, put stress on populations of animals that subsisted on that plant and so on.

Environmental Threats

16.3.5 Describe some of the ways that pollution, garbage, and climate change are as much social issues as they are environmental issues.

The natural environment is not only natural, but it is also "social" in that there is a constant interaction between the natural and the built environments, between people and the places where they live (and don't live), and between nature and culture. Social institutions manage our relationship with our environments as well. And the environment is today threatened by several human-created problems.

POLLUTION There are three major sources of water pollution: domestic waste, industrial waste, and agricultural runoff. Indoor plumbing in urban areas means a huge amount of human waste, which is usually treated with toxic chemicals and then dumped into the nearest river. Many industrial processes require huge amounts of water, which is then dumped, along with more toxic chemicals. The petroleum industry is particularly problematic; every year billions of gallons of oil are routinely deposited into the ocean during tank cleaning and other operations. Agricultural runoff includes not only topsoil but toxic pesticides and fertilizers. When it all ends up in the water supply, it can cause a huge number of unspecified health problems in humans. Increases in energy consumption are also often associated with accompanying increases in pollution. Yet, energy consumption is also correlated with increasing levels of prosperity. So, for instance, societies and nations that were earlier to industrialize have among the highest levels of oil consumption in the world, but they are also able to provide more for the populations consuming that oil.

Air pollution is concentrated in urban areas, the result of carbon monoxide, sulfur dioxide, and nitrogen oxide from cars, heaters, and industrial processes. These gases have a profound impact on the lungs and circulatory system; breathing the air in downtown Tokyo is the equivalent of smoking a pack of cigarettes every day. The gases have similar negative effects on every animal trying to breathe the same air, and when toxic gases combine with water molecules in the air, they can return to Earth as acid rain; enter lakes, rivers, and oceans through groundwater runoff; and destroy ecosystems. Or they can rise up to the ozone layer, a band of oxygen isotopes 10 to 30 miles above Earth's surface, and bond with it, eliminating the effectiveness of this layer in shielding Earth from ultraviolet radiation.

GARBAGE In 2014, the Environmental Protection Agency estimated that the United States produced 258 million tons of municipal solid waste, or MSW (household waste and waste from civic maintenance, like mowing parks and sweeping streets). More than 89 million tons of this MSW were recycled and composted, resulting in an annual recycling rate of 34.6 percent (U.S. Environmental Protection Agency 2016). Many other countries are not as good at recycling. In poor countries, it typically doesn't happen at all: 100 percent of the waste goes into landfills. Although rich countries have improved recycling rates over the last decade—65 percent of municipal waste is recycled in Germany, 59 percent in South Korea, 55 percent in Belgium, 50 percent in Sweden, 43 percent in the United Kingdom—landfills remain the predominant treatment for municipal waste throughout the OECD (OECD 2015). More than 90 percent of municipal waste was landfilled in numerous countries, including New Zealand, Chile, Turkey, and Mexico (OECD 2015).

Landfills pose two major problems. First, most of the garbage isn't biodegradable. Petroleum-based products, plastics, and styrofoam stay there forever, which means that the landfills fill up. A third of American landfills are already full, and by 2020, four-fifths of them will be full. There will be no place to put the garbage anymore. When the garbage is biodegradable, it degrades into toxic chemicals, which seep into the groundwater and increase water pollution or into the air to increase air pollution. Degrading waste also increases the world's heat level, contributing to global climate change. A particularly problematic kind of waste comes as a by-product

Garbage is among the most immediate environmental concerns, especially in countries with high levels of consumption. The United States dumps more than half of its garbage in landfills, but soon those landfills will be "land-full."

WHAT DO YOU THINK? WHAT DOES AMERICA THINK?

Environmental Threats and Science

A great deal of controversy surrounds the topic of environmental threats.

What do you think?

Many of the claims about environmental threats are greatly exaggerated.

- ○ Strongly agree
- ○ Agree
- ○ Neither agree nor disagree
- ○ Disagree
- ○ Strongly disagree

What does America think?

About 36 percent of respondents agreed or strongly agreed with this statement, and almost 45 percent disagreed or strongly disagreed. Age, education, gender, and race differences were not significant.

What do you think?

Modern science will solve our environmental problems with little change to our way of life.

- ○ Strongly agree
- ○ Agree
- ○ Neither agree nor disagree
- ○ Disagree
- ○ Strongly disagree

What does America think?

Almost 50 percent of respondents disagreed or strongly disagreed with this statement, although almost 25 percent agreed or strongly agreed. Education, age, gender, and race are not statistically significant.

SOURCE: General Social Survey, 2010.

THINKING CRITICALLY ABOUT SURVEY DATA

Would you have expected social class differences in response to these questions (if so, in which direction)?
How might it challenge beliefs about different groups' opinions to learn that neither class, age, race, nor gender correlate with the most recent nationally representative responses to these questions?

of nuclear energy. Nuclear reactors produce waste that will be radioactive for thousands of years.

CLIMATE CHANGE Since the nineteenth century, the global temperature has increased by about 0.85 degrees Celsius (1.53 degrees Fahrenheit), primarily because carbon dioxide, aerosols, and other gases released by human technology are prohibiting heat from escaping. Many regions are already seeing an environmental impact: in Alaska and Canada, permafrost is thawing; 90 percent of the world's glaciers are in retreat. Because most of the world's major cities are on or near the ocean, a rise in the sea level due to melting glaciers and ice sheets could be catastrophic—like Hurricane Katrina with 200 million refugees. Other possible effects include a proliferation of hurricanes and extreme weather events, droughts and desertification, shortages of fresh water, and the further extinction of species as their ecosystems are destroyed. Only a few pseudo-scientists doubt the credibility of claims about "global warming"; in the scientific community there is as much consensus about climate change as there is for evolution—that is to say, unanimous consensus. But sociologists ask different questions. Sociologists study the social ramifications of such climate shifts—where people will move, how they will survive, which groups are most affected and how—or even *if* they will survive. In addition, sociologists study the sides of the "debate" about climate change: Why do certain groups line up on different sides on this question? What is at stake in the political debate? Research on what social psychologists refer to as the **backfire effect** can help us understand why some are so resistant to hearing evidence that disproves beliefs they hold.

backfire effect
The name given to the social scientific finding that, confronted with evidence challenging their beliefs, people tend to reject the evidence and become even more attached to their challenged belief.

HOW DO WE KNOW WHAT WE KNOW?

WHY FACTS ABOUT CLIMATE CHANGE DO NOT CHANGE PEOPLE'S OPINIONS ABOUT CLIMATE CHANGE

We live in a world with an incredible amount of information. However, not all information is equally accurate. And it would be easy to imagine that when we hold a belief and are confronted with facts at odds with those beliefs, we would then alter our opinions to incorporate that new information for a more accurate understanding of the world around us. But this is not actually the typical response to confronting facts that challenge our deeply held beliefs. In fact, research shows that when your deepest convictions are challenged by contradictory evidence, your beliefs get stronger. Misinformed people do not, as a rule, change their minds when presented with the facts; more than that, they often become even more attached to their beliefs. Social scientists studying this refer to it as the backfire effect (Nyhan and Reifler 2010).

Beliefs about climate change are a great example. Climate change is a complex science; but it's also a topic about which people have opinions. Yet, opinions about climate change are a bit different than opinions about, for instance, whether chocolate or vanilla ice cream is more delicious. We can objectively measure climate change; your personal preference for chocolate or vanilla is more of an individual idiosyncrasy.

To study this, Nyhan and Reifler (2010) conducted a series of experiments in which participants came in and were asked to read newspaper articles that had been altered (the participants were unaware of the alterations). The articles contained statements from political figures that reinforced some kind of widespread misinformation. Some of the participants (the experimental group) read articles that also included corrective information immediately following the factually inaccurate or misleading statement by the political figure, while others (the control group) did not read this corrective

information. Following this, participants were asked to answer a series of factual questions and questions about their personal opinions.

Their findings might not surprise you at this point, but the consequences of them might be greater than you'd first imagine. Nyhan and Reifler (2010) discovered that how people responded to the factual corrections to statements made by political figures varied systematically by how ideologically committed they already were to the beliefs that such facts supported. Among those who believed the popular misconception in the first place, more information and actual facts challenging those beliefs did not cause people to change their opinions; in fact, it often had the effect of strengthening those ideologically grounded beliefs. It's an important sociological puzzle, with profound implications. How are we to create a well-informed electorate (a key principle of democratic societies) if the very act of informing them does little to change their beliefs and subsequent behavior?

Yet, more recent research building on the "backfire effect" has discovered that, for many issues, attempts to build empathy may have a stronger influence on changing people's opinions than challenging them with facts (e.g., Brockman, Kalla, and Sekhon 2016). So, when confronting people's beliefs about gay marriage, asking them how they might feel if their child or sibling came out and was seeking such a union might be a more powerful way of persuading them than citing facts about the lack of adverse effects on children with gay parents or some other measure. Similarly, when challenging people's opinions on climate change, we might start by asking them to consider how their own lives or the lives of people they know and love might be impacted and how that would make them *feel*, regardless of what they *believe*.

The Sociology of Environmental Disasters

16.3.6 Understand how "manufactured risks" and "external risks" are unevenly distributed within and between societies in ways that exacerbate existing inequalities.

environmental disaster

A sudden environmental change that results in a major loss of life and/or property; it can originate in nature, be human-orchestrated, or be a combination of the two.

manufactured risks

Risks produced by the process of modernization, especially through advances in science and technology.

external risks

Risks produced by the natural environment, and thus, largely outside of human control (e.g., earthquakes, floods, hurricanes, and tornados).

An **environmental disaster** is a sudden environmental change that results in a major loss of life and property. It can be human orchestrated, such as a terrorist attack, or it can originate in nature, such as an earthquake or flood. And sometimes, it is some combination of the two. It can be human orchestrated, such as a terrorist attack (**manufactured risks**), or it can originate in nature, such as an earthquake or flood (**external risks**). And sometimes, it is some combination of the two. Bioterrorism would involve unleashing a deadly disease like anthrax and causing a "natural" epidemic. A flu pandemic would involve the natural adaptability of the influenza virus, promoted by human factors like public health conditions, social mores and practices, and travel. The operative term is "sudden," so that it comes on people with little or no warning.

For many years, sociologists were not much interested in disasters. They were interested in the social upheaval of wars and migration more than in fires and floods. One of the earliest sociological studies of a disaster was Kai T. Erikson's *Everything in Its Path* (1978), about the human response to a dam that burst and flooded Buffalo Creek in Logan County, West Virginia. One might expect survivors to experience long-term psychological trauma after losing many of their loved ones and everything they owned, but Erikson probed more deeply to investigate how they lost their individual and communal identity: the "furniture of self" had vanished.

In 1995, a weeklong heat wave in Chicago was responsible for more than 700 deaths in the city. This was not a sudden catastrophe, but many were woefully unprepared. But why? Sociologist Eric Klinenberg (2002) investigated the social conditions that led to and compounded the disaster. He found the obvious, that many poor and elderly people—and most of them black women—had no air conditioning. Some were not aware of the neighborhood "cooling systems" or were afraid to go to them. Others did not realize that they were in danger; the news media downplayed the disaster, treating it as little more than a human-interest story. They were un- or underinformed.

Yet, it is also true that the lives lost to external risks have decreased over time (see FIGURE 16.5). As you can see in the figure, epidemics, droughts, and extreme temperatures killed large populations of people in the first half of the twentieth century. But advances in science and technology have made us better able to predict these events and to coordinate our efforts to reduce their toll on human lives. Today, droughts remain the leading cause of death among naturally occurring catastrophes.

Yet, it is also true that deaths as a result of environmental causes are not equally distributed between societies. Some nations are much more likely to lose lives in environmental disasters than others. And, among the most correlated variables with deaths resulting from environmental causes is poverty. As a rule, the more impoverished a society, the more likely that people will die in environmental disasters.

For instance, Haiti suffered a devastating earthquake on January 12, 2010, just 10 miles outside Haiti's most populous city, Port-au-Prince. The earthquake registered as a 7 on the magnitude scale used to assess earthquake strength and potential for damage. Estimates of the death toll ranged from 100,000 to 160,000, though this number may be higher as many people have since died from related injuries sustained during the quake. Less than one month later, on February 27, 2010, Chile endured an earthquake that registered 8.8 on the magnitude scale (significantly more devastating). That earthquake occurred a bit farther away from a more populous city in Chile, but the difference in lives lost is substantial. Following the earthquake, Chile's President, Michelle Bachelet, claimed that more than 700 people died as a result of the disaster, a number—like Haiti—that would rise over time as related injuries led to deaths for more.

FIGURE 16.5 Global Death Rate from Natural Disasters, 1900–2013

The death toll of natural disasters has dramatically declined over the last century. As you can see here, the major causes of death as a result of natural disaster since 1900 have been disease, drought, and extreme temperatures.

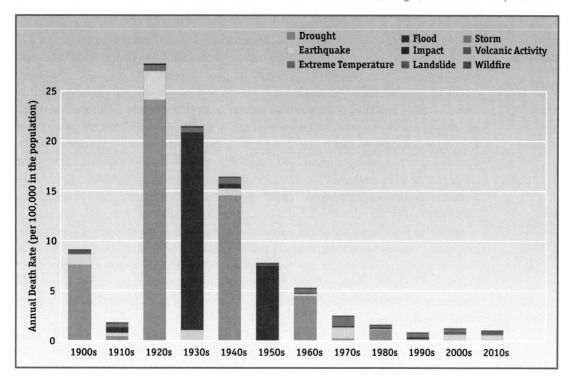

SOURCE: Data from The OFDA/CRED International Disaster Database, www.emdat.be, Universite Catholique de Lovain, Brussels, Belgium. Available at *Our World in Data*, https://ourworldindata.org/natural-catastrophes/.

Why the difference in lives lost? Part of it has to do with the locations of each disaster relative to highly populous areas in each society. But Chile is also a wealthier society with a history of earthquakes, while Haiti is a poor society that had virtually no disaster relief services available. As a society, Chile was more prepared for such an event in the first place because more of Chile's infrastructure was built to withstand and protect people from such an event. Haiti had none of this social and architectural infrastructure in place and is still recovering from this disaster. For similar reasons, poorer areas within a single society are more devastated during natural disasters—like New Orleans after Hurricane Katrina.

More recently, in September 2017, two back-to-back earthquakes struck Mexico City, Mexico (a city with a population of around 9 million people). The first (Sept. 8) registered 8.2 on the Richter Scale, while the second (Sept. 19) registered 7.1. As of writing this, hundreds of people have been declared dead and scores more are still missing, trapped beneath the rubble of fallen buildings and collapsed infrastructure. Earthquakes are natural occurrences, but, as with all natural disasters, their impacts are felt in social ways. Here is where sociology can help us understand the social consequences of natural disaster.

This photo was taken on September 20, 2017 of a building that partially collapsed on vehicles outside as a result of the second earthquake (on September 19) in Mexico City.

Environmental Inequalities

16.3.7 Define environmental inequalities, and understand how these forms of inequalities intersect with other forms of social inequality.

environmental inequalities

The ways that different groups in society experience uneven exposure to environmental risks and hazards.

environmental justice

The idea that all groups, people, and communities are entitled to equal protections by environmental health laws and regulations.

environmental racism

A type of discrimination where people of low-income or minority communities are forced to live in close proximity of environmentally hazardous or degraded environments (like landfills, toxic waste, pollution, or urban decay).

Holly Doll, of Mandan, an enrolled member of the Standing Rock Sioux Tribe, holds a protest sign outside the state's capitol building, in Bismarck, N.D., Saturday, Oct. 29, 2016. Doll and more than 60 other demonstrators voiced their opposition to an oil pipeline crossing an under water source that lies on the reservation land.

Sociologists interested in studying **environmental inequalities** study the ways that different groups in society experience uneven exposure to environmental risks and hazards. Those most exposed are also commonly systematically excluded from environmental decision-making processes as well. The *causes* of environmental inequality are social and political—not biological. As such, environmental inequality is not best understood as an *environmental* issue—it is a social issue. Environmental inequalities are perpetuated by social structures and political and economic institutions. And as forms of inequality, they intersect with all of the other various inequalities that shape social life. And understanding environmental inequalities sociologically helps us better understand what is required to achieve **environmental justice**. Seen this way, the Flint water crisis we addressed at the beginning of this chapter is an illustration of an elaborate lapse in environmental justice and a powerful example of environmental inequality. And although sociological research cannot necessarily predict where the next Flint water crisis will be, we do know that it's likely to happen to communities that share a similar demographic profile to Flint: undereducated, poor, non-white, and living on the outskirts of a recognizable municipal region (so-called "extraterritorial jurisdictions").

A recent study conducted in North Carolina was able to quantify this. They were interested in whether race was a significant predictor for water service access, controlling for both social class (by property value) and population density. The study discovered that, in North Carolina, as black populations within census blocks increased, the odds of being excluded from municipal water services also increased (Gibson, et al. 2014). This means that those communities will be more likely to rely on private wells for drinking water, sources that pose elevated environmental risks associated with contamination. In other words, race is a significant predictor of access to healthy drinking water. Sociologists refer to this particular type of environmental inequality as an example of **environmental racism**.

And although the levels of lead in people's blood were extraordinarily high, a recent analysis discovered that there are, quite literally, thousands of areas in the United States with higher levels of lead poisoning than in Flint at the height of the water crisis. Flint's crisis is real. As an analysis by Reuters notes, "Flint is no aberration. In fact, it doesn't even rank among the most dangerous lead hotspots in America." The chief indicator that correlated with elevated levels of lead poisoning in children remains social class (which are areas that are often disproportionately occupied by households of people of color as well)—the working-class and poor in the United States are at an elevated risk (Pell and Schneyer 2016).

Impoverished communities of color in the United States have historically had to deal with more pollution than other Americans. And this is not a peculiar property of social life in the United States. Environmental inequalities are simply another form of inequality through which marginalized groups in every society often suffer environmental consequences as well. As we learned from

the Flint water crisis, environmental injustice often happens when public officials make poor decisions and ignore residents' complaints. Understanding and better appreciating the environmental consequences of systems of social inequality can better help us imagine new forms of social justice that diverse groups need and deserve.

The Politics of Environments

16.3.8 Describe the key groups in environmental politics, and understand some of the successes and challenges associated with the movement.

The natural world, the built environment, and human populations all inhabit the same planet and exist in a complex web of mutual interaction. "Paving paradise to put up a parking lot" as folk singer Joni Mitchell once sang, may solve some problems, but often creates new ones in the process. Today, the delicate balance among human populations, the built environment and the natural world often feels fragile and imperiled, as the world's animal and plant species shrink, its forests disappear, lakes and rivers dry up, and food becomes scarce. At the same time, the dire predictions of widespread famine and disease have not (yet) come about. Like so many forms of inequality we have examined, the delicate balance is simultaneously fragile and resilient.

The environment has also become political. Even as far back as the nineteenth century, there was an **environmental movement**—or, rather, two movements. One group, *conservationists* wanted to manage America's natural resources for long-term use and exploitation. Another group of *protectionists* sought to protect the land for its own sake, and urged the setting aside of land and resources to be protected from human exploitation. Even today, American policy has also sought to balance these two competing claims. For example, the creation of the vast National Park System, undertaken by President Theodore Roosevelt, was inspired by protectionist John Muir, founder of the Sierra Club. This same protectionist impulse created federally protected marshlands, forests, and other fragile habitats like the Arctic National Wildlife Refuge in Alaska. On the other side, conservationists have overseen those companies that have been given permission to extract vital minerals and otherwise commercially develop federally protected lands.

This split between conservationists and protectionists also polarizes the environmental movement around the world. In some poorer countries, economic development and high levels of employment depend on the exploitation of the country's valuable natural resources. On the other hand, the Brazilian rain forest and the Arabian Peninsula's oil fields are finite resources, and will not last forever. In 1972, the United Nations held its first Conference on the Human Environment in Stockholm, Sweden, and representatives from all over the world began a discussion of the global implications of environmental change. Some environmentalists, believing that the major political parties were failing to see the connections of environmental issues with other social issues, such as energy policy, poverty, and social welfare organized new political parties—such as the "Green Party."

Environmental politics often collide with economic priorities. Opposition to environmental conservation often comes from corporations, who seek to avoid further regulation of their activities, and from white workers, especially white male workers, who fear the loss of jobs if environmental regulations prohibit or curtail industries such as coal mining, gas and oil drilling, and mineral extraction—industries dominated by white men. During periods of economic recession, environmental concerns often take a backseat to policies promoting employment and corporate expansion, leading to the perception that environmental concerns are an issue only for the affluent—a so-called "luxury social issue."

environmental movement

In the United States, the environmental movement has organized itself around two different claims, both still with us in policies and organizations today: *conservationists*, who want to manage the United States's natural resources for long-term use and exploitation, and *protectionists*, who seek to protect the land for its own sake and urge the setting aside of land and resources to be protected from human exploitation.

Caribou running, Arctic National Wildlife Refuge, Alaska. Public concern about whether we should disturb reserves like these for oil drilling or pipelines, public grazing for farmers, and more mean that social battles over the environment are ongoing.

The dramatic success of former Vice-President Al Gore's book and movie, *An Inconvenient Truth*, (for which he won the Nobel Peace Prize in 2006), has raised environmental consciousness, especially among young people, across the country. Odds are your classroom has separate containers for recycling paper and plastic and metal, replaced incandescent light bulbs with eco-friendlier compact fluorescents, and serves vegetarian food as an option in the school cafeteria. Twenty years ago, these were largely unheard of. Some of you are driving hybrid or electric vehicles (you even get a tax break if you buy one!). And you can also get a tax break if you install energy-efficient windows (or roofs, doors, insulation, ac/heating units), heat your pools/hot tubs with solar power, or buy Energy Star appliances.

---

iSOC AND YOU The Natural Environment
People construct their *identities* through their interactions with others within the context of the natural environment. You will be a different person if you live in the Artic or alone in a cabin by a stream, if you live in a teeming city like Mexico City. You will feel differently, *interact* with different people. And yet those interactions will still be organized by *unequal* access to the natural environment, inequalities that *intersect* with each other, and unequal experiences in the *institutions* that organize and regulate those resources.

Conclusion
Environments NOW

What do we do now? Do we sit alone in our room, waiting for the next hurricane, earthquake, tornado, nuclear accident, or biological pandemic, or a more gradual catastrophe caused by global warming, air pollution, desertification, or overpopulation? Do we play video games, eat nachos, and await the impending Apocalypse?

If the explosion of Deepwater taught us anything, it is that we should be prepared and that we can anticipate disasters like Horizon and the resulting BP oil spill, the earthquake, tsunami and nuclear meltdown at Fukushima, or Hurricane Katrina and their aftermaths. Part of this involves using sociology to help us identity who is at risk of what kinds of external and manufactured risks associated with social life put those populations in and out of harm's way. With foresight and planning, we can avoid some catastrophes altogether and greatly reduce the impact of others. And one of the most important tools we have is the recognition of how the natural, urban, and human worlds *intersect* with one another to create a human experience that is simultaneously natural *and* social. Nature is nurture; that is, the natural world does not exist except in relationship to the social and built worlds. City and countryside create each other. People are simultaneously part of the ecosystem and also its greatest threat. Ignoring the interconnections nearly always leads to disaster. But, recognizing and working with them may lead to a future in which we are better able to care for our growing global population.

CHAPTER REVIEW Sociology of Environments: The Natural, Physical, and Human World

16.1   The Human Environment

Sociologists study not only our social environment but also the interplay of the social and physical environment because the human, the urban, and the natural are interdependent. Demography considers data on birth and death. Demographers look at fertility, fecundity, and fertility rate to understand a country. A low birth rate, as found in wealthy nations, means a country can't replace adults to care for the aging, although mobility increases, while poor nations have high birth rates, so there aren't enough resources for the children, or jobs for adults, although more children provide for aging parents. Mortality rate and life expectancy give insight into a nation's health. Infant mortality rate correlates with many quality-of-life factors and indicates how effective health policies are. Demographers look at population changes, including immigration rate, emigration rate, net migration rate, and internal migration and consider the push and pull factors behind these population changes. Economic opportunity and freedom in a region or nation is a pull, whereas oppression, discrimination, and lack of opportunity exert a push. The population composition and population pyramid are revealing. The former varies as a result of preferential selection for boy babies, environmental toxins, immigrant laborers, or wars; the latter by fertility and mortality. Despite other factors, with natural population increase, the world's population is growing. In traditional society, children contribute to wealth, but few survive to adulthood, so birthrates are high; but, in modern society, children are expensive but also likely to survive. The population began to grow when prestigious large families combined with low mortality, but today almost all population growth is in poor nations. Changes in childbearing and agricultural production allowed us to avoid the disaster foretold by Malthusian theory. For Marx, the unequal distribution of resources was the main problem. One solution proposed to impending disaster resulting from overpopulation was zero population growth. Demographic transition theory implicates technology as a partner in population growth, through three stages of technological development and population changes, although this has been criticized for ignoring instances where the patterns differ and the theory doesn't fit and, when it does, overlooking the influence of social changes.

16.1 Key Terms

demography   The scientific study of human populations; one of the oldest and most popular branches of sociology. Demographers are primarily concerned with the statistics of birth, death, and migration.

fertility   The number of children a woman bears.

fecundity   The maximum number of children a woman could have during her childbearing years.

fertility rate   The number of births per 1,000 women ages 15 to 44 in a calendar year.

mortality rate   The death rate as a percentage of the population.

life expectancy   The average number of years a person can expect to live; v͏~ies greatly by country and region.

infant mortality ⟶er of deaths per year per 1,000 infants (͏ulation.

emigration   Ou ⟶ ͏other.

immigration ⟶ each year f

push factors home ter econom

pull facto partic econc

immig eac

emig e

net migr and emigration

internal migration   Moving ͏ within a territory.

population composition   The comparative numbͯ of men and women and various age groups in an area, region, or country.

sex ratio   The ratio of males to females in a population.

natural sex ratio   Refers to the fact that physiological differences in X and Y chromosomes result in a male-to-female ratio at birth that is never 50:50. The natural sex ratio is 104–105 boys born for every 100 girls.

sex-selective abortion   A procedure in which women terminate pregnancies after finding out that they are carrying girls.

population pyramid   Type of graph that shows 5- or 10-year age groups as different-sized bars, or "blocks."

natural population increase   Simple calculation of the number of deaths every year subtracted from the number of births.

Malthusian theory   Developed by the English economist and clergyman Thomas Robert Malthus (1766–1834), the theory held that population would increase by geometric progression, doubling with each generation—while the food supply would only increase arithmetically, ultimately leading to mass starvation, environmental disaster, and eventual human extinction.

zero population growth Paul Erlich's modern solution to Malthus's concerns, it entails a global effort to ensure that the number of births does not exceed the number of deaths, providing global population stability, a decrease in poor countries, and a redistribution of resources to those countries.

demographic transition theory A population theory that shows that the transition from high birth and death rates to lower birth and death rates as a country or region develops from a preindustrial to an industrialized economic system.

germ theory of disease The theory that some diseases are caused by microorganisms that invade humans, animals, and other living hosts. Their growth and reproduction within living hosts causes disease.

16.2   The Urban Environment

Human settlements for most of our history were small villages amid farmland; people could walk to their nearby fields. Surplus allowed larger villages, but ancient cities were quite small by modern standards and few in number. They were typically located on rivers to provide food for the bigger populations. Urbanization began in Europe with industrialization, as workers moved to work in factories. America began with few small cities and large farms but exceeded other parts of the world in the move to urbanization, as a result of industrialization. Urbanization correlates with wealth worldwide, with wealthier cities being more urban and having more large cities, while the poorest nations have rural populations and few, but very large, cities. Newer cities have lower population density. Globalization has taken a toll on the countryside, and in many poor nations, cities are swelling as people move from the countryside into cities. The suburb developed in the United States with the automobile enabling white flight from cities swelling with immigrants and minorities. Gentrification drew affluent people back into cities. About two-thirds of Americans now live in a megalopolis. Sociologists often prefer villages to cities. Ferdinand Tönnies emphasized the connection and trust people had living together in villages, in *gemeinschaft*, or "commonality," while people in cities and suburbs organized by *gesellschaft* or "business company," and were isolated, mistrustful, self-interested, and without connection. Émile Durkheim found villages had mechanical solidarity, while cities had organic solidarity. Anthropologists found the nature of the social network, kin or non-kin, is responsible for the observed differences, rather than size of community or work. Cities may lead us to withdraw and isolate ourselves from the barrage of stimulation or to participate in the vibrant social life around us. Human ecology studies these phenomena. Herbert Gans found social networks were the same size, whether urban or rural; city dwellers just found smaller groups for belonging.

He identified five types of city dwellers. For many years, urbanization was considered a sign of development, but recent trends suggest the global picture is complex. In some large cities in Latin America, people are poorer, not wealthier, and the gap between rich and poor is great. Vast neighborhoods lack adequate sanitation, housing, utilities, and police protection. Global cities, the command centers of economic globalization, have so many multinational ties that their physical location is relatively meaningless. Culturally, they share less with the countries in which they happen to be located than with other global cities, with whom they share a common culture of consumption.

16.2 Key Terms

population density The number of people per square mile or kilometer.

globalization A social process wherein economic, political, and cultural connections multiply and expand around the world. Like other social processes, it is uneven, affecting some more than others, and benefiting some over others.

suburb A residential community outside of a city but always existing in relationship to the city.

"white flight" Term for the pattern of movement by white people out of cities to escape immigrants and minorities.

gentrification The process by which poorer urban neighborhoods are "upgraded" through renovation and development, often pushing out long-time residents of lesser means who can no longer afford to live there.

megalopolis A term coined by Jean Gottmann in 1961 to describe the integration of large cities and sprawling suburbs into a single organic urbanized unit, such as "Bo Wash," the Boston to Washington, D.C., corridor that includes New York and Philadelphia as well as the suburbs.

gemeinschaft Social relations based on close personal and family ties.

gesellschaft Social relations based on impersonal relations and formal organization, detached from traditional or sentimental concerns.

alienation The state or experience of estrangement from a group to which one should belong.

mechanical solidarity Émile Durkheim's term for a traditional society where life is uniform and people are similar. They share a common culture and sense of morality that bonds them.

organic solidarity Émile Durkheim's term for a modern society where people are interdependent because of the division of labor; they disagree on what is right and wrong but share solidarity because the division of labor causes them to be mutually dependent on each other.

culture of consumption A culture driven and defined by consumption choices and behaviors.

global city Saskia Sassen's term for cities around the world—New York, London, and Tokyo, for example—marked by so many multinational ties that their physical location within a country has a diminished impact on their social and cultural outlook and practices.

16.3 The Natural Environment

Sociologists understand that the natural environment—the physical world, or more precisely, animals, plants, and the material substances that make up the physical world—is organized into ecosystems, which are interdependent systems of organisms and their environment. Herbert Spencer conceptualized interrelated subsystems, including the biological, psychological, social, and moral. Ellsworth Huntington saw climate and human behavior as related; he wrongly assumed life was easier in the tropics, with readily available food, and harder in the north, resulting in northern industriousness, ignoring the facts of hunter–gatherers in the north and advanced technology in the south. The 1970s brought renewed interest in the ecosystem and environmental concerns, including conservation and pollution. Energy is particularly important now. Sociologists consider how business and political relationships relate to energy policy and use. The energy consumption of the United States, and its contribution to global carbon dioxide levels, one of crucial gasses that causes the greenhouse effect that induces climate change, is huge. In the United States, as in the rest of the world, only a small percentage of energy is produced from renewable sources, despite many decades of information and scientific knowledge about the catastrophic effects of climate change on people and societies worldwide. Another environmental concern is deforestation. Forests are vital for carbon sequestration, the natural storage of carbon dioxide in plants and trees as part of photosynthesis that keeps even more of this potent greenhouse gas from accumulating in the air. Deforestation removes potential pharmaceutical species; burning increases greenhouse gas; arable land becomes desert when topsoil is washed away in a process called desertification; and more water is then needed, further depleting the water table. These and other manmade environmental impacts are already reducing the earth's biodiversity. Other human-created ecological problems include air pollution, resulting in health problems; garbage storage; and the devastating consequences of climate change. Sociologists are studying sudden disasters—how they disrupt our lives and why we aren't prepared or don't recognize them when they are occurring. They are also studying environmental inequalities, analyzing the ways different groups in society experience uneven exposure to environmental threats, and environmental racism, a type of discrimination that occurs when poor and minority communities are forced to live in closer proximity to environmental hazards. We humans are a part of nature. We have a social world, and we modify our environment, but we are also part of the natural world, all of which have an impact on one another. We can best prepare for disaster by recognizing how human, physical, and urban worlds are interconnected. By understanding, and acting on what we know, we can create better futures, but research shows that time is running short.

16.3 Key Terms

ecosystem An interdependent system in which the animals, plants, and the material substances that make up the physical world live.

"normal accidents" Seemingly trivial errors within complex systems that have cascading effects and the potential to create much larger events with severe consequences.

deforestation The clearing of forests for crops and development.

greenhouse effect Caused by gases such as carbon dioxide (CO_2) and methane, a phenomenon in which earth's atmosphere traps radiation emitted by the sun, causing the planet's surface to warm.

biodiversity The variety of life in the world or in a particular habitat or ecosystem

desertification The process by which fertile land becomes desert, usually as a result of deforestation, drought, or indiscriminate human use for agriculture, such as intensive farming, overgrazing, or repeated burning.

backfire effect The name given to the social scientific finding that, confronted with evidence challenging their beliefs, people tend to reject the evidence and become even more attached to their challenged belief.

manufactured risks Risks produced by the process of modernization, especially through advances in science and technology.

external risks Risks produced by the natural environment, and thus, largely outside of human control (e.g., earthquakes, floods, hurricanes, and tornados).

environmental disaster A sudden environmental change that results in a major loss of life and/or property; it can originate in nature, be human-orchestrated, or be a combination of the two.

environmental inequalities The ways that different groups in society experience uneven exposure to environmental risks and hazards.

environmental justice The idea that all groups, people, and communities are entitled to equal protections by environmental health laws and regulations.

environmental racism A type of discrimination where people of low-income or minority communities are forced to live in close proximity of environmentally hazardous or degraded environments (like landfills, toxic waste, pollution, or urban decay).

environmental movement In the United States, the environmental movement has organized itself around two different claims, both still with us in policies and organizations today: *conservationists*, who want to manage the United States's natural resources for long-term use and exploitation, and *protectionists*, who seek to protect the land for its own sake and urge the setting aside of land and resources to be protected from human exploitation.

SELF-TEST

⟩ CHECK YOUR UNDERSTANDING

1. Which of the following is commonly used as an indicator of a nation's health policies, and general quality of life overall?
   a. Population composition
   b. Infant mortality rate
   c. Net migration rate
   d. Mortality rate

2. *Gemeinschaft* is found in:
   a. cities.
   b. suburbs.
   c. villages.
   d. All have *gemeinschaft*.

3. Gans's "urban village" refers to
   a. suburbs.
   b. rural town centers.
   c. global cities.
   d. social groups and neighbors.

4. According to Émile Durkheim, villages have _____, whereas cities have _____.
   a. mechanical solidarity; organic solidarity
   b. *gemeinschaft; gesellschaft*
   c. organic solidarity; mechanical solidarity
   d. *gesellschaft; gemeinschaft*

5. The return of the middle class and professionals to urban centers is referred to as
   a. "white flight."
   b. gentrification.
   c. urban villages.
   d. urbanization.

6. All of the following were identified in the text as important benefits of forests, *except*
   a. carbon sequestration.
   b. habitat for diverse species.
   c. increased carbon dioxide emissions.
   d. prevention of erosion.

7. Americans are 5 percent of the world's population, but they
   a. generate five times the world average of carbon dioxide emissions.
   b. consume at least 25 percent of every type of energy.
   c. use far more oil and natural gas per day than any other country in the world.
   d. All of the answers are correct.

8. The Flint water crisis is an example of
   a. normal accidents.
   b. desertification.
   c. environmental inequalities.
   d. all of the answers are correct.

Self-Test Answers: 1. b, 2. c, 3. d, 4. a, 5. b, 6. c, 7. d, 8. c

color-blind racism The process of disregarding race as a method attempting to realize or express equality, it has the unintended consequence of reproducing racial inequality in new ways.

communism Envisioned as the ideal economic system by Karl Marx, communism would produce and distribute resources "from each according to his or her ability, to each according to his or her need," erasing social inequalities along with crime, hunger, and political strife.

companionate marriage The (historically recent) idea that people should select their own marriage partner based on compatibility and mutual attraction.

compositional fallacy An error in logic that results when comparing two groups that are different, assuming they are the same, and drawing an inference based on that false assumption.

concentrated poverty The extreme density of socioeconomic deprivation in a particular area.

confirmation bias The tendency to interpret new evidence as confirmation of our existing beliefs.

conflict theory Theoretical approach that stresses the competition for scarce resources and unequal distribution of those resources based on social status (such as class, race, gender).

confounding variables The elements that impede accurate measurements of the impact of one variable on another.

conspicuous consumption Thorstein Veblen's term to describe a new form of prestige based on accumulating and displaying possessions.

consumer economy An economy driven by consumer spending.

consumption The purchase and use of goods and services.

content analysis Research method in which one analyzes artifacts (books, movies, TV programs, magazine articles, and so on) instead of people.

contingent labor Provisional group of workers who work on a contract, project, or other nonpermanent basis.

control group In an experiment, the comparison group that will not experience the manipulation of the independent variable (the experimental group). Having a control group enables sociologists to compare the outcomes of the experiment to determine if the changes in the independent variable had any effects on the dependent variable.

corporal punishment Punishment that is physical, often involving hitting someone.

correlation The term for the fact of some relationship between two phenomena.

counterculture Subculture that identifies itself through its difference and opposition to the dominant culture.

coup d'état The violent replacing of one political leader with another; often doesn't bring with it any change in the daily life of the citizens.

credential society A society based more on the credentialing aspects of education—diplomas, degrees, and certificates—than any substantive knowledge.

crime A deviant act that lawmakers consider bad enough to warrant formal laws and sanctions.

criminology The study of crime that has developed into a subdiscipline separate from the sociology of deviance, with its own special theories about the causes and consequences of different kinds of crimes.

crowd An aggregate of individuals who happen to be together but experience themselves as essentially independent.

cult The simplest form of religious organization, characterized typically by fervent believers and a single idea or leader.

cultural capital French sociologist Pierre Bourdieu's term for the cultural articles—ideas, artistic expressions, forms of music or literature—that function as resources that people in the dominant class can use to justify their dominance.

cultural diffusion The spreading of new ideas through a society, independent of population movement.

cultural diversity The vast differences between the cultures of the world as well as the differences in belief and behavior that exist within cultures.

cultural imperialism The deliberate imposition of one country's culture on another country.

cultural omnivores Sociologist Richard Peterson's term for people with more cosmopolitan tastes.

cultural relativism A position that all cultures are equally valid in the experience of their own members.

cultural tool kit A repertoire of habits, skills, and styles from which people construct their identities.

cultural universal One of the rituals, customs, and symbols that are evident in all societies.

cultural univores Sociologist Richard Peterson's term for people with narrow ranges of tastes.

culture Both the material basis for social life and the sets of values and ideals that we understand to define morality, good and evil, appropriate and inappropriate.

culture lag The relatively gradual process by which nonmaterial elements of culture catch up with changes in material culture and technology.

culture of consumption A culture driven and defined by consumption choices and behaviors.

culture of poverty Oscar Lewis's theory that poverty is not a result of individual inadequacies but larger social and cultural factors. Poor children are socialized into believing that they have nothing to strive for, that there is no point in working to improve their conditions. As adults, they are resigned to a life of poverty, and they socialize their children the same way. Therefore poverty is transmitted from one generation to another.

culture shock A feeling of disorientation when the cultural markers that we rely on to help us know where we are and how to act have suddenly changed.

culture wars Often symbolic clashes of ideas, symbols, or values between groups who support certain changes and those who want to resist change.

custodial parent The parent whose residence is considered a "primary residence" for the child or children after separation or divorce.

cybercrime The growing array of crimes committed via the Internet and World Wide Web, such as Internet fraud and identity theft.

data   The plural of datum. Data are systematically collected and systematically organized bits of information.

dating   A courtship practice that arose in the 1920s in which young adults participated in recreational activities in pairs rather than groups prior to engaging in long-term commitments to one another.

deductive reasoning   Reasoning that logically proceeds from one demonstrable fact to the next. It often moves from the general to the more specific.

deforestation   The clearing of forests for crops and development.

de-institutionalization   The re-integration of the sick back into society, instead of isolating them in separate places like mental institutions.

de-institutionalization movement   In the 1970s, advocates sought to relocate patients to "half-way" houses and community-based organizations to help reintegrate them into society, yet care alternatives were plagued by disorganization and under-financing, and many severely and persistently mentally ill people were left without essential services resulting in increasing numbers of mentally ill people on the streets or in prisons because there is no place else for them to go.

democracy   Derived from the Greek word *demos* (people); puts legislative decision making into the hands of the people rather than a single individual or a noble class.

demographic transition theory   A population theory that shows that the transition from high birth and death rates to lower birth and death rates as a country or region develops from a preindustrial to an industrialized economic system.

demography   The scientific study of human populations; one of the oldest and most popular branches of sociology. Demographers are primarily concerned with the statistics of birth, death, and migration.

denomination   A large-scale, extremely organized religious body with established hierarchy and methods for credentialing administrators, and much more social respect than either a cult or a sect.

dependency theory   Theory of poverty that focuses on the unequal relationship between wealthy countries and poor countries, arguing that poverty is caused by policies and practices by the rich that block economic growth of poor countries and exploit workers.

dependent variable   The variable whose change depends on the introduction of the independent variable.

desertification   The process by which fertile land becomes desert, usually as a result of deforestation, drought, or indiscriminate human use for agriculture, such as intensive farming, overgrazing, or repeated burning.

detached observation   A perspective that constrains the researcher from becoming in any way involved in the event he or she is observing. This reduces the amount that the researchers' observations will change the dynamic that they are watching.

deviance   Violating a social or moral rule, or refusing to follow one, whether or not that act is illegal.

dictatorship   A type of totalitarian political system in which power is held by one person, who may or may not have a hereditary claim on power, usually with military support.

differential association   Edwin H. Sutherland's theory suggesting that deviance occurs when an individual receives more prestige and less punishment by violating norms than by following them.

disability   According to the Americans with Disabilities Act of 1990, disability is "a physical or mental impairment that substantially limits one or more major life activities."

discourse analysis   Is more interested in patterns of portrayal evident in a collection of "texts" that might be difficult to quantify.

discrimination   A set of actions based on prejudice and stereotypes.

disease incidence   How many new cases of a disease are reported in a given place during a specified time frame.

disease prevalence   The distribution of the disease over different groups of the same population.

division of household labor   The ways couples divide up all of the chores and obligations necessary to run a household.

division of labor   The assignment of different tasks to different people to improve efficiency in production.

divorce   The legal dissolution of a marriage.

divorce rate   A social scientific measure of the proportion of marriages that end in divorce.

domestic division of labor   The ways couples divide up all of the chores and obligations necessary to run a household.

double consciousness   W. E. B. Du Bois term for the social experience of black Americans as divided, often against oneself, as "two unreconciled strivings; two warring ideals in one dark body, whose dogged strength alone keeps it from being torn asunder."

dramaturgical model   Erving Goffman's conception of social interaction as like an actor preparing to perform a part in a play.

dramaturgy   Erving Goffman's conception of social life as being like a stage play wherein we all work hard to convincingly play ourselves as "characters," such as grandchild, buddy, student, employee, or other roles.

dual labor market   The pervasive condition in the United States in which work and workers are divided into different sectors—primary or secondary, formal or informal, and also male or female.

dyad   A group of two people, the smallest configuration defined by sociologists as a group.

Eastern Religions   Three other major religions of the world—Hinduism, Buddhism, and Confucianism (plus some minor ones)—are called "Eastern" because they arose in Asia, although, like the Western Religions, they have adherents around the world.

ecclesiae   A political assembly of the faithful in which the clerical elite often serve as political leaders or at least formal advisors to political leaders. Everyone in the society belongs to that faith by birth, not individual decision, and those who do not belong to the faith cannot become citizens.

economic system   A mechanism that deals with the production, distribution, and consumption of goods and services in a particular society.

economy   A set of institutions and relationships that manage capital.

ecosystem   An interdependent system in which the animals, plants, and the material substances that make up the physical world live.

education   A social institution through which society provides its members with important knowledge—basic facts, job skills, and cultural norms and values and lessons in socialization, cultural innovation, and social integration.

educational homogamy   Marriage between people who are similar to one another in educational attainment.

educational inequality   The extent to which different groups lack access to the educational opportunities and experiences systematically made more available to other groups.

ego   Freud's term for the balancing force in the psyche between the id and the superego; it channels impulses into socially acceptable forms.

elder abuse   The physical, sexual, psychological, and financial abuse and neglect of people of a vulnerable age.

emigration   Outflow of people from one society to another.

emigration rate   The number of people leaving a territory each year for every 1,000 in the population.

emotional labor   Arlie Hochschild's phrase for the process by which workers are expected to manage their feelings in accordance with organizationally defined rules and guidelines.

endogamy   The strong tendency to marry within one's own social group (often with the same race, religion, class, educational background for instance).

The Enlightenment   Also called "The Age of Reason," theorists challenged the established social order, like the rule of the monarchy and hereditary aristocracy, and the ideas that justified it, like the "divine right of kings." It was during the Enlightenment of the seventeenth and eighteenth centuries that the idea of the "individual" took shape.

environmental disaster   A sudden environmental change that results in a major loss of life and/or property; it can originate in nature, be human-orchestrated, or be a combination of the two.

environmental inequalities   The ways that different groups in society experience uneven exposure to environmental risks and hazards.

environmental justice   The idea that all groups, people, and communities are entitled to equal protections by environmental health laws and regulations.

environmental movement   In the United States, the environmental movement has organized itself around two different claims, both still with us in policies and organizations today: *conservationists*, who want to manage the United States's natural resources for long-term use and exploitation, and *protectionists*, who seek to protect the land for its own sake and urge the setting aside of land and resources to be protected from human exploitation.

environmental racism   A type of discrimination where people of low-income or minority communities are forced to live in close proximity of environmentally hazardous or degraded environments (like landfills, toxic waste, pollution, or urban decay).

epidemiology   The study of the causes and distribution of disease and disability.

ethnic cleansing   The mass expulsion or killing of members of an unwanted ethnic or religious group in a society.

ethnic enclaves   Ethnically and linguistically contained neighborhoods.

ethnic group   A group that is set apart from other groups by language and cultural traditions. Ethnic groups share a common ancestry, history, or culture.

ethnic renewal   Process by which ethnic identities are reconstituted and reclaimed after having been discarded earlier.

ethnicity   Social category that depends on an assumption of inherent cultural differences to rate and organize social groups.

ethnocentrism   The use of one's own culture as the reference point by which to evaluate other cultures; it often depends on or leads to the belief that one's own culture is superior to others.

ethnography   A type of field method in which the researcher inserts him- or herself into the daily world of the people he or she is trying to study to understand the events from the point of view of the actors themselves.

ethnomethodology   The study of the social knowledge, codes, and conventions that underlie everyday interactions and allow people to make sense of what others say and do.

everyday politics   Small-scale political acts in the context of everyday life that connect us to political life just as civil religion allows us to connect in religious-like ways even when we're participating in things that might not seem all that "religious."

evolutionary imperative   The belief, typically used to justify traditional assumptions about masculinity and femininity, that males and females developed different reproductive strategies to ensure that they reproduce successfully and are able to pass on their genetic material to the next generation.

exogamy   Marriage among people who belong to meaningfully different social groups (race, religion, social class, etc.).

expansion of morbidity   As people are living longer, this trend describes the increasing time they will spend in bad health.

experiment   A research process that is performed under controlled conditions to examine the validity of a hypothesis by carefully varying conditions between groups.

experimental group   In an experiment, the group that will experience the experimental condition being measured to examine what happens. *See control group.*

extended family   The family model in which two or three generations live together: grandparents, parents, unmarried uncles and aunts, married uncles and aunts, sisters, brothers, cousins, and all of their children.

external risks   Risks produced by the natural environment, and thus, largely outside of human control (e.g., earthquakes, floods, hurricanes, and tornados).

face work   In dramaturgical theory, the possible performance of ourselves, because when we make a mistake or do something wrong, we feel embarrassed, or "lose face."

fad   Short-lived, highly popular, and widespread behavior, style, or mode of thought.

families   The basic unit in society, these social groups are socially understood as either biologically, emotionally, and/or legally related.

family of origin   The family a child is born or adopted into, with biological parents or others who are responsible for his or her upbringing.

family of procreation   The family one creates through marriage or cohabitation with a romantic partner, to which one chooses to belong.

family wage   Arising in the nineteenth century, the term refers to a wage sufficient for a single wage earner to support a family (spouse and children).

fashion   A behavior, style, or idea that is more permanent and often begins as a fad.

fecundity   The maximum number of children a woman could have during her childbearing years.

feeling rules   Arlie Hochschild's term for socially shared norms that influence how people should demonstrate how they feel in different settings.

felony disenfranchisement   Punitive U.S. policy that denies people convicted of a felony the right to vote even after a sentence has been served. The presence of restrictions, and their extent, vary by the state in which the felony was committed and the year in which it was committed.

feminism   The belief that women should have equal political, social, sexual, economic, and intellectual rights and opportunities to men.

feminization of poverty   A worldwide phenomenon that also afflicts U.S. women, this term describes women's overrepresentation among the world's poor and tendency to be in worse economic straits than men in any given nation or population.

feminization of the professions   Widely demonstrated sociological phenomenon in which salaries drop as women's participation increases in a particular job category or profession.

fertility   The number of children a woman bears.

fertility rate   The number of births per 1,000 women ages 15 to 44 in a calendar year.

feudalism   A fixed and permanent social structure based on mutual obligation, in which peasants worked the estates belonging to a small group of feudal lords, who fed and protected them. A peasant's only avenue to social advancement was to enter a convent or monastery.

fictive kin   Similar to "urban tribes," the term refers to people with whom we form kinship ties and family networks even though they are not legally or biologically tied to us as kin.

field   Any site where the interactions or processes you want to study are taking place, such as an institution like a school or a specific community.

field experiments   The experimental examination of an intervention in a naturally occurring environment rather than in the laboratory.

first-generation students   Students whose parents did not go to college.

folkway   One of the relatively weak and informal norms that are the result of patterns of action. Many of the behaviors we call "manners" are folkways.

for-profit universities   Business ventures offering higher education courses attuned to adult learners seeking practical, job-related skills.

functional age   A set of observable characteristics and attributes that are used to categorize people into different age cohorts.

Fundamentalism   Forms of religion that uphold belief in strict, literal interpretations of scripture.

gay-baiting   Calling people or something they do "gay" as a way of ridiculing them or putting them down. Usually applied to men, it has little to do with sexual orientation, but instead accuses them of acting or appearing insufficiently masculine.

gemeinschaft   Social relations based on close personal and family ties.

gender   A socially constructed definition based on sex category, based on the meanings that societies attach to the fact of sex differences.

gender bias   The ways we systematically treat men and women (and boys and girls) differently.

gender binary   The belief that humans come in two types: males, who behave in masculine ways, and females, who behave in feminine ways, which is a belief sociological research has shown is better understood as rooted in our culture than our nature.

gender convergence   One of the central social dynamics of gender noted by sociologists today, it refers to the gradual closing of the gender gap in many aspects of social life, rendering women's and men's lives increasingly more equal.

gender identity   Our understanding of ourselves as male or female, masculine or feminine.

gender inequality   Gender inequality has two dimensions: the domination of men over women, and the domination of some men over other men and some women over other women.

gender panic   Situations in which people react to ruptures in assumptions about gender assumed to be based in our biology by frantically reasserting the supposed "naturalness" of the male/female gender binary.

"gender police"   Student peers who act to enforce gender rules against transgressions large and small.

gender policing   The enforcement of normative gender ideals by rewarding normative gender performances and punishing transgressions.

gender relations   Sociologists today are more likely to use gender relations (rather than "role") to emphasize how the definitions of masculinity and femininity are developed in relation to each other and to systems of social power and inequality.

gender roles   The bundle of traits, attitudes, and behaviors that are associated with biological males and females.

gender similarities hypothesis   Janet Hyde's assertion, based on meta-research, that men and women are similar until proven otherwise.

gender socialization   Process by which males and females are taught the appropriate behaviors, attitudes, and traits associated with their biological sex in a particular culture.

gender wage gap   The consistent, worldwide difference between what men are paid and what women are paid for the same labor.

generalizability Also called external validity or applicability; the extent to which the results of a study can be generalized to the general population.

generalized other The organized rules, judgments, and attitudes of an entire group. If you try to imagine what is expected of you, you are taking on the perspective of the generalized other.

generation gap Differences in outlook and opinion that arise between generations.

Generation X Sometimes called the "baby bust," this generation born after the Baby Boom, between 1965 and 1979, is a small age cohort.

Generation Z The generation of people born since 2000.

genocide The planned, systematic destruction of a racial, political, or ethnic group.

gentrification The process by which poorer urban neighborhoods are "upgraded" through renovation and development, often pushing out long-time residents of lesser means who can no longer afford to live there.

germ theory of disease The theory that some diseases are caused by microorganisms that invade humans, animals, and other living hosts. Their growth and reproduction within living hosts causes disease.

gerontology Scientific study of the biological, psychological, and sociological phenomena associated with old age and aging.

gesellschaft Social relations based on impersonal relations and formal organization, detached from traditional or sentimental concerns.

glass ceiling An unofficially acknowledged barrier to advancement in a profession, especially affecting women and members of minorities.

glass escalator Christine Williams's phrase for her research finding that men doing "women's work" receive more, on average, than do the women doing that work.

global city Saskia Sassen's term for cities around the world—New York, London, and Tokyo, for example—marked by so many multinational ties that their physical location within a country has a diminished impact on their social and cultural outlook and practices.

global commodity chains Worldwide network of labor and production processes, consisting of all pivotal production activities that form a tightly interlocked "chain" from raw materials to finished product to retail outlet to consumer. The most profitable activities in the commodity chain (engineering, design, advertising) are likely to be done in core countries, while the least profitable activities (mining or growing the raw materials, factory production) are likely to be done in peripheral countries.

global distribution A term that describes how the products we buy are likely made of materials from several countries, assembled in another country, packaged and distributed from yet another, with advertising campaigns and marketing schemes drawn from yet another.

global inequality Systematic differences in wealth and power among countries, often involving exploitation of the less powerful by the more powerful countries.

global production A term that describes how, in a global economy, goods are manufactured from raw materials and produced in factories all over the world in complex production chains and international labor forces.

global village Marshall McLuhan's term for his vision of the way global electronic media would unite the world through mutual interaction and involvement.

globalization A set of processes leading to the development of patterns of economic, cultural, and social relationships that transcend geographical boundaries; a widening, deepening, and speeding up of worldwide interconnectedness in all aspects of contemporary life.

government The organization and administration of the actions of the inhabitants of communities, societies, and states.

green-collar work A new category of advanced manufacturing jobs, it denotes work involved in environmental and renewable energy industries.

greenhouse effect Caused by gases such as carbon dioxide (CO_2) and methane, a phenomenon in which earth's atmosphere traps radiation emitted by the sun, causing the planet's surface to warm.

gross domestic product The total value of goods produced and services provided in a country during one year.

group Collection of individuals who are aware that they share something in common and who interact with one another on the basis of their interrelated roles and statuses.

group cohesion The degree to which individual members of a group identify with each other and with the group as a whole.

group marriage Rare marriage arrangement in which two or more men marry two or more women, with children born to anyone in the union "belonging" to all of the partners equally.

groupthink Irving Janis's term for social process in which members of a group attempt to conform their opinions to what they believe to be the consensus of the group, even if, as individuals, they may consider that opinion wrong or unwise.

habitus French sociologist Pierre Bourdieu's term for the practical mastery of self that arises, in part, out of class location and distance from necessity.

hardcore members The small number of group members, the "inner circle," who wield a great deal of power to make policy decisions.

hate crime A criminal act committed by an offender motivated by bias against race, ethnicity, religion, sexual orientation, or disability status. Anyone can commit a hate crime, but perpetrators usually belong to dominant groups (white, Christian, straight) and victims to disenfranchised groups (black, Jewish, Muslim, or gay).

hate groups Groups with beliefs or practices that attack or malign a class of people often due to immutable characteristics associated with the group (like sexual orientation, skin color, ancestry, gender identity).

Hawthorne effect The alteration of behavior by the subjects of a study because of their awareness of being observed.

heteronormativity Sociological term to refer to the ideology by which heterosexuality is simultaneously understood as both *normal* and *normative*.

heterosexuality The most common sexual orientation worldwide, it is sexual attraction between people of different sexes.

hidden curriculum A means of socialization through which education not only creates social inequalities but makes them seem natural, normal, and inevitable.

homophobia A concept used to measure a range of sexual prejudices toward people identifying with sexual identities other than heterosexual, anything from distrust to disgust to hatred to violence.

homosexuality A sexual identity organized around sexual desire for members of one's own sex. In colloquial terms, homosexuals are often called *gay*.

hooking up A deliberately vague term for a sexual encounter that can refer to a great variety of different relationships and interactions, may nor may not include sexual intercourse, and usually occurs on only one occasion between two people who are strangers or brief acquaintances. Although that seems to cover most cases, it fails to include those heterosexuals who hook up more than once or twice, or "sex buddies" (acquaintances who meet regularly for sex but rarely if ever associate otherwise), or "friends with benefits" (friends who do not care to become romantic partners but may include sex among the activities they enjoy together).

hypothesis A testable prediction for an event or phenomenon that assumes a relationship between two or more variables.

id Sigmund Freud's label for that part of the human personality that is pure impulse, without worrying about social rules, consequences, morality, or other people's reactions.

ideal type The abstract mental concept of what a pure version of a social phenomenon, such as a bureaucracy, would look like.

identity The unique combination of group affiliations and social characteristics that each individual develops.

identity work The concern with and performance of physical, symbolic, verbal, and behavioral self-representations designed to be taken as part of one's identity.

immigration The number of people entering a territory each year for every 1,000 people in population.

immigration rate The number of people entering a territory each year for every 1,000 of the population.

immiseration thesis Karl Marx's theory that, as capitalism proceeded, the rich would get richer and the poor would get poorer, and that eventually the poor would become so poor that they had nothing else to lose and would revolt.

impression management Erving Goffman's term for our attempts to control how others perceive us by changing our behavior to correspond to an ideal of what they will find most appealing.

incest taboo Sigmund Freud identified the taboo that one should not have sex with one's own children as a foundation of all societies.

income distribution How a nation's income is distributed among the population—within each individual nation, of the level of economic stratification in different societies. What it does is give us a better understanding of where economic growth is occurring.

independent variable In an experimental study, the agent of change, the ingredient that is added to set things in motion.

inductive reasoning Research in which one reasons to a conclusion about all or many members of a collectivity based on examination of only a few members of that class. Loosely, it is reasoning from the specific to the general.

industrial economy Economy based on factory production and technologies.

Industrial Revolution The rapid development of industry that occurred in numerous countries in the eighteenth and nineteenth centuries reorganized the production and distribution of goods from the quaint system of craft production, in which apprentices learned trades and entered craft guilds, to large-scale factory production in which only the very few owned the factories and many workers had only their ability to work to sell to the highest bidder.

industrial societies Those societies driven by the use of technology to enable mass production, supporting a large population with the capacity for a high division of labor.

infant mortality rate The number of deaths per year per 1,000 infants (up to 1 year old) in a population.

informal economy Refers to economic activities and income that are partially or fully outside government regulation, taxation, and observation.

"informed consent" An act of Congress in 1970 made this a requirement of research. Only after all adult subjects of research (or the parents of minors) are clearly informed about its object and assured of confidentiality can they consent to participate. And only then can research proceed.

in-group A group with which you identify and that you feel positively toward, producing a "we" feeling.

in-group heterogeneity The social tendency to be keenly aware of the subtle differences among the individual members of your group.

institutional racism The most subtle and pervasive type of discrimination, it is deeply embedded in such institutions as the educational system, the business world, health care, criminal justice, and the mass media. These social institutions promote discriminatory practices and traditions that have such a long history they just "seem to make sense," and minority groups become the victims of systematic oppression, even when only a few people, or none at all, are deliberately trying to discriminate.

institutional review boards (IRBs) A committee established to review and approve research involving human subjects, it works to ensure that researchers comply with standards and ethics in conducting their research.

integration The physical intermingling of the races organized as a concerted legal and social effort to bring equal access and racial equality through racial mixing in institutions and communities.

interest groups An organized group that tries to influence the government to adopt certain policies or measures.

intergenerational mobility Changes in social status between different generations within the same family.

internal migration Moving from one region to another within a territory.

interracial relationships   Once labeled "miscegenation," a relationship between people of different racial categories.

intersectionality   Sociological term for the ways that different identities "intersect" with one another to shape our social identity and our experience of inequality.

intersex traits   People are said to have intersex traits when their bodies cannot be clearly categorized as fully male or female.

intervening variable   A variable that may not have been measured, but is responsible for the presumed relationship between independent and dependent variables in research.

interview   Research method in which a researcher asks a small group of people open-ended questions.

intimate partner violence (IPV)   Violence between people who either are or were in a sexual or romantic relationship with one another. It is commonly called "domestic violence," but because some does not occur in the home, IPV is the preferred term.

intragenerational mobility   Changes in a person's social mobility throughout the course of a lifetime.

iron cage   While Weber contended that rationality can free us from the theocratic past, he also argued that rationality can imprison us in an utterly dehumanized and mechanized world he termed "the iron cage."

kinship systems   Cultural groupings that locate individuals in society by reference to their families, typically mapped as a network from closest (mother, father, siblings) to a little more distant (cousins, aunts, uncles) to increasingly distant (second-cousins twice removed).

knowledge economy   An economy oriented around knowledge, and the quantity, quality, and accessibility of information, rather than on the production of commodities.

knowledge work   One defining element of the postindustrial economy; it is work that produces ideas and information as a new form of capital.

labeling   Often associated with self-fulfilling prophecy and stereotyping, labeling theory describes how self-identity and behavior of individuals may be determined or influenced by the terms used to describe or classify them.

labeling theory   Howard Becker's term stresses the relativity of deviance, naming the mechanism by which the same act is considered deviant in some groups but not in others. Labels are used to categorize and contain people.

labor movement   Class-based social movement that would instill a democratic society (actual rule by the numerical majority).

laissez-faire capitalism   The original form of capitalism, theorized by Adam Smith, "laissez-faire" means "to leave alone" in French; under this system, governments would leave the marketplace alone to organize the economy, without government interference. (Smith believed that there were natural limits to people's greed.) Markets should be able to compete freely to sell goods, acquire raw materials, and hire labor. No government interference is necessary: The "invisible hand" of supply and demand creates a self-regulating economy.

language   An organized set of symbols by which we are able to think and communicate with others; the chief vehicle by which human beings create a sense of self.

latent functions   The unintended consequences of an action or event.

lavender ceiling   Refers to workplace discrimination that hampers or prevents LGBTQ people from being promoted.

law   One of the norms that has been organized and written down. Breaking this norm involves the disapproval not only of immediate community members but also of the agents of the state, who are charged with punishing such norm-breaking behavior.

leader   People in charge, whether they were elected, appointed, or just informally took control of a group.

legacy of slavery   Those enduring forms of racial inequality that result from generations of systematic, institutionalized, legal forms of racial oppression.

legal-rational authority   Form of authority where leaders are to be obeyed not primarily as representatives of tradition or because of their personal qualities but because they are voicing a set of rationally derived laws.

liberation theology   A movement in Christian theology, developed mainly by Latin American Roman Catholics, that focuses on Jesus not only as savior but as the savior of the poor and emphasizes liberation from social, political, and economic oppression.

life chances   A person's abilities to have access to material goods (food and shelter) and social resources (health care, education) that together control the quality of life.

life expectancy   The average number of years a person can expect to live; varies greatly by country and region.

life span   The span of time during which a person is alive, which all societies—whether tribal, agrarian, or industrial—have always divided into stages, seasons, or age groups.

Likert scale   The most common form of survey coding; arranges possible responses from lowest to highest.

living wage   A minimum income necessary for a worker to meet his or her basic needs.

local culture   The cultural norms, roles, values, expectations, and beliefs that shape distinct social contexts.

longitudinal study   An observational research method in which data is gathered for the same subjects repeatedly over a period of time that can extend over years or even decades.

looking-glass self   Cooley's term for the process of how identity is formed through social interaction. We imagine how we appear to others and thus develop our sense of self based on the others' reactions, imagined or otherwise.

lower class   Sometimes called the "working poor"—they have a household income of less than $20,000 per year. They hold unskilled and semiskilled jobs. They are service workers, maintenance workers, clerical workers. They deliver pizzas, wait on customers at retail stores, and clean homes and offices.

lower upper class   Annual household incomes of more than $150,000 but less than $1 million; they are the "everyday" rich. They tend to have advanced degrees from high-ranking colleges. Though they have substantial investment incomes, they still have to work: They are upper-level CEOs, managers, doctors, and engineers.

macro-level analysis   Analysis of the large-scale patterns or social structures of society, such as economies or political systems.

majority group   A group whose members experience privilege and access to power because of their group membership. With regard to race, lighter-colored skin usually means membership in the majority group.

Malthusian theory   Developed by the English economist and clergyman Thomas Robert Malthus (1766–1834), the theory held that population would increase by geometric progression, doubling in each generation—while the food supply would only increase arithmetically, ultimately leading to mass starvation, environmental disaster, and eventual human extinction.

mandatory sentencing rules   Rules enacted across the United States in the early 1990s that were supposed to be tough on crime and eliminate bias in prosecutions and sentencing. The primary result, however, has been an explosion in the prison population.

manifest functions   The intended consequences of an action or event.

manufacture consent   The production of values and emotions (in addition to the actual things they produce) that bind workers to their company.

manufactured risks   Risks produced by the process of modernization, especially through advances in science and technology.

markers of adulthood   Specific life stages that define who qualifies as an "adult," such as finishing school, getting a job, moving out of the parental home, marrying, and having a child.

markets   Regular exchange of goods and services within an economy.

market theories   Theories that stress the wisdom of the capitalist marketplace. They assume that the best possible economic consequences will result if individuals are free to make their own economic decisions, uninhibited by any form of governmental constraint.

marriage rate   The annual number of marriages in a given geographical area per 1,000 inhabitants.

"masculinization" of sex   The shift in gendered sexual scripts toward a masculine model of sexuality that emphasizes the pursuit of pleasure for its own sake, increased attention to orgasm, increased numbers of sexual partners, interest in sexual experimentation, and the separation of sexual behavior from love.

mass media   Any of the means of communication, such as books, newspapers, magazines, comic books, films and DVDs, radio, television, CDs and MP3s, and a range of digital and social media platforms, that reach large numbers of people.

master status   An ascribed or achieved status presumed so important that it overshadows all of the others, dominating our lives and controlling our position in society.

material culture   The physical objects and spaces that people use to define their culture, including homes, cities, mosques, factories, works of art, clothes and fashions, books and movies, as well as the tools they use to make them.

matrifocal   Families centered on mothers.

matrilineal   Tracing one's ancestry through the mother and maternal side of the family.

matrix of inequality   The various and overlapping intersections of inequality an individual might experience based on age, race, ethnicity, class, gender, sexuality, religion, and the like.

McDonaldization   The homogenizing spread of consumerism around the globe.

mechanical solidarity   Émile Durkheim's term for a traditional society where life is uniform and people are similar. They share a common culture and sense of morality that bonds them.

media   The plural form of "medium," it is the term for the ways that we communicate with each other, from voice to gestures to methods of mass communication like publishing, broadcasting and the internet.

medicalization   The process by which *human* conditions come to be defined and treated as *medical* conditions such that they also become subject to medical study, diagnosis, and treatment.

megalopolis   A term coined by Jean Gottmann in 1961 to describe the integration of large cities and sprawling suburbs into a single organic urbanized unit, such as "Bo Wash," the Boston to Washington, D.C., corridor that includes New York and Philadelphia as well as the suburbs.

men's liberation   Beginning in the 1970s, an effort by men to challenge and revise traditional definitions of masculinity.

mental illness   Among the least understood illnesses, any impairment of thought, mood, or behavior that can be attributed to a psychiatric disease, disorder, or condition.

meritocracy   Social system in which the greater the functional importance of the job, the more rewards it brings in salary, perks, power, and prestige.

meta-analysis   A quantitative analysis of several separate but similar experiments or studies conducted to test the pooled data for statistical significance.

microcredit   When a bank lends tiny amounts of money to local poor people.

micro-level analysis   Analysis of small-scale social patterns, such as individual interactions or small-group dynamics.

middle middle class   Household incomes between $40,000 and $80,000 these are the "average" American citizens. Most hold white-collar jobs: technicians, salespeople, business owners, educators, etc. Many blue-collar workers and high-demand service personnel, like police, firefighters, and military, have incomes high enough to place them in the middle class. Most have attended college, and many have college degrees.

Millennials The generation of nearly 50 million people born after 1980—the first generation to come into their adulthood in the new millennium.

minimum wage The lowest wage permitted by law.

minority group A group one is born into, which has a distinguishable identity and whose members have less power and access to resources than other groups in society because of that group membership.

"the missing middle" Sociologist Theda Skocpol's term for the gradual disappearance of the middle class as the nation becomes increasingly polarized into rich and poor.

mode of production The organization of society to produce what people need to survive.

modernization theory W. W. Rostow's theory focusing on the conditions necessary for a low-income country to develop economically. Arguing that a nation's poverty is largely due to the cultural failings of its people, Rostrow believed poor countries could develop economically only if they give up their "backward" way of life and adopt modern Western economic institutions, technologies, and cultural values that emphasize savings and productive investment.

"modernization theory" of name trends Stanley Lieberson's explanation for the reduction in pressures associated with social institutions like extended family rituals or religious rituals associated with the naming of children—trends that led to more name diversity.

monarchy One of the first political systems; rule by a single individual (*mono* means "one," and *archy* means "rule"), typically hereditary.

monogamy Marriage between two (and only two) people.

moral panic The process of arousing social concern that the well-being of society is threatened by a particular issue.

morbidity rate The rates of new infections from disease.

mores Informally enforced norms based on strong moral values, which are viewed as essential to the proper functioning of a group.

mortality rate The death rate as a percentage of the population.

motherhood penalty In the workplace, mothers encounter systematic disadvantages in pay, perceived competence, and benefits relative to childless women.

multiculturalism The doctrine that several different cultures (rather than one national culture) can coexist peacefully and equitably in a single country.

multinational corporations Large, international companies, also called transnational corporations, that manage production and/or deliver services in more than one country at once. Multinational corporations have a powerful influence in the local economies of the countries in which they operate, and in the global economy.

naming laws The laws some countries have that legally restrict the names parents can give their children.

nation-states A sovereign state whose citizens or subjects are relatively homogenous in factors such as language or common descent.

natural population increase Simple calculation of the number of deaths every year subtracted from the number of births.

natural sex ratio Refers to the fact that physiological differences in X and Y chromosomes result in a male-to-female ratio at birth that is never 50:50. The natural sex ratio is 104–105 boys born for every 100 girls.

negative discrimination The provision of less-favorable treatment to those with certain characteristics, typically to a disadvantaged group, than to those without them.

net migration rate The difference between immigration and emigration rates in a given year.

network effects The sociological idea that we end up sharing a lot in common with people with whom we share a social network.

nonmarital sex Sex outside of marriage.

nonmaterial culture Often just called "culture," the ideas and beliefs that people develop about their lives and their world.

nonverbal communication The communication with others that occurs without words, including apparent behaviors such as facial expressions and less obvious messaging including posture and the spatial distance between two or more people.

norm One of the rules a culture develops that defines how people should act and the consequences of failure to act in the specified ways.

norm of reciprocity The social expectation that people will respond to us favorably, or with hostility or indifference depending upon how we interact with them.

"normal accidents" Seemingly trivial errors within complex systems that have cascading effects and the potential to create much larger events with severe consequences.

normative organization A voluntary organization wherein members serve because they believe in the goals of the organization.

nuclear family The presumed model of the modern American family structure consisting of a breadwinning husband, homemaker wife, their children, and no extended family members.

objectivity A posited ideal for social science researchers, it is a perspective that is free of bias, judgment, or prejudice.

observer effect The direct effect that observation can be shown to have on the phenomenon being observed.

occupational crime The use of one's professional position to illegally secure something of value for oneself or for the corporation.

occupational prestige The degree of status accorded to an occupation.

occupational sex segregation Refers to women's and men's different concentrations in different occupations, different industries, different jobs, and different levels in a workplace hierarchy.

"old old" The term for people ages 75 to 85.

"oldest old" The term for people ages 85 and older.

operationalization The process of attempting to define the topic of your study into measurable factors.

opportunity theory Cloward and Ohlin's 1960 theory of crime, which holds that those who have many opportunities—and good ones at that—will be more likely to commit crimes than those with few good opportunities.

organic solidarity Émile Durkheim's term for a modern society where people are interdependent because of the division of labor; they disagree on what is right and wrong but share solidarity because the division of labor makes them dependent on each other.

organization A formal group of people with one or more shared goals.

organizational crime Illegal actions committed in accordance with the operative goals of an organization, such as antitrust violations, false advertising, or price fixing.

organizational culture The system of norms and values, routines and rituals, symbols and practices that governs an organization.

organizational positions Rosabeth Moss Kanter's term to describe the gendered expectations for behavior within organizations. The differences in men's and women's behaviors have far less to do with their characteristics as individuals than with the "characteristic images of the kinds of people that should occupy" particular positions. People who do occupy them, whether women or men, exhibited those necessary behaviors.

organized crime Like corporate or white-collar crime, it is a business operation whose purpose is to supply illegal goods and services to others.

orgasm gap Term for the pattern of pleasure discrepancy between women and men that often occurs between hook-up sex and relationship sex.

out-group One to which you do not belong and toward which you feel either neutral or hostile; the "they" who are perceived as different from and of lower stature than ourselves.

out-group homogeneity The social tendency to believe that all members of an out-group are exactly the same.

outsourcing Also called *offshoring*, it refers to the practice of hiring out any phase(s) of product development to lower-wage countries or groups.

overt racism Systematic prejudice applied to members of a group in clear, manifest ways, such as speech, discrimination, or a refusal to associate with members of that group.

paradigm An example, pattern, or model, especially an outstandingly clear or typical example or archetype.

participant observation Sociological research method in which one observes people in their natural habitat.

participatory democracy Also called "pure democracy," a political system in which every person gets one vote and the majority rules.

part-time work Form of employment that carries fewer hours than a full-time job. In the United States, part-time work is generally considered to be 30 hours per week or less.

patriarchy Literally, "the rule of the fathers"; a name given to the social order in which men hold power over women.

patrilineal Tracing one's ancestry through the father and paternal side of the family.

peer group Our group of friends and wider group of acquaintances who have an enormous socializing influence, especially during middle and late childhood.

peer review A process by which other scholars in the field are asked to anonymously evaluate one's research before it is published, to ensure it meets the standards of sociological research.

pink-collar work Louise Kay Howe's coinage for types of employment traditionally held by women, especially in relatively low pay service positions, such as secretarial, sales clerks, and wait staff.

pluralism Maintains that different groups in a stable society can treat each other with mutual respect and that minority cultures can maintain their own distinctiveness and still participate in the greater society without discrimination.

pluralist perspective This perspective argues that assimilation is not inevitable and that ethnic identities are not necessarily abandoned as ethnic groups become less isolated.

political action committees (PACs) A type of partisan political organization that is not subject to the same regulations as political parties, and attempt to influence elections and mobilize public opinion.

political apathy Refers to the indifference of a member of a society with regard to their attitude toward political activities.

political participation Refers to any action or behavior that either aims to affect or has the consequence of influencing governmental action.

political parties Groups that bands together to petition for political chances or to support candidates for elected office.

political revolution Changes the political groups that run the society, but they still draw their strength from the same social groups that supported the old regime.

political systems The term for how group leaders exercise their authority. Virtually all political systems fall into one of two categories, "authoritarian" or "democratic."

politics The art and science of government.

polyamory Committed relationships among three or more people.

polyandry Rare form of polygamy in which one woman marries two or more men.

polygamy Marriage between three or more people. (*See* polyandry and polygyny.)

polygyny The most common form of polygamy, a marriage between one man and two or more women.

popular culture The culture of the masses, the middle and working classes, that includes a wide variety of popular music, nonhighbrow forms of literature, any forms of spectator sports, and other popular forms of entertainment, like television, movies, and video games.

population composition The comparative numbers of men and women and various age groups in an area, region, or country.

population density The number of people per square mile or kilometer.

population pyramid Type of graph that shows five- or ten-year age groups as different-sized bars, or "blocks."

positive discrimination   The provision of special opportunities to those with certain characteristics than to those without them, typically to a disadvantaged group.

postindustrial economy   Economy that shifts from the production of goods to the production of ideas.

poverty line   Estimated minimum income required to pay for food, shelter, and clothing. Anyone falling below this income is categorized as poor.

power   The ability to extract compliance despite resistance or the ability to get others to do what you want them to do, regardless of their own desires.

predictability   The degree to which a correct prediction of a research outcome can be made.

prejudice   A set of beliefs and attitudes that cause us to negatively prejudge people based on their social location.

primary deviance   Any minor, usually unnoticed, act of deviance committed irregularly that does not have an impact on one's self-identity or on how one is labeled by others.

primary group   One such as friends and family, which comes together for expressive reasons, providing emotional support, love, companionship, and security.

primary socialization   A culture's most basic values, which are passed on to children beginning in earliest infancy.

production   The creation of value or wealth by producing goods and services.

profane   That which is not sacred or Biblical, or not concerned with religion or religious purposes.

progressive nucleation   Christopher Lasch's idea that industrialization and modernization made it customary for children to be independent from their parents in going to school, looking for work, and choosing a spouse, increasingly reducing extended family arrangements and promoting the nuclear family model of household structure and child-rearing.

proletariat   Popularized by Karl Marx, the term for the lower classes who were forced to become wage laborers or go hungry. Today, the term is often used to refer to the working class.

proportional representation   In contrast to the winner-take-all system used in the United States, proportional representation gives each party a proportion of the legislative seats based on the number of votes its candidates garner.

pull factors   Reasons voluntary migrants want to settle in a particular territory, the most common of which are a strong economy, political and cultural tolerance, and civil stability.

purposive sample   Sample in which respondents are not selected randomly and are not representative of the larger population but are selected precisely because they possess certain characteristics that are of interest to the researcher.

push factors   Reasons voluntary migrants want to leave their home territory, the most common of which are a sluggish economy, political or cultural oppression, and civil unrest.

qualitative methods   Inductive and inferential means to drawing sociological understanding, usually about less tangible aspects of social life, such as the actual felt experience of social interaction.

quantitative methods   Numerical means to drawing sociological conclusions using powerful statistical tools to help understand patterns in which the behaviors, attitudes, or traits under study can be translated into numerical values.

the quiet revolution   Gradual but wide-sweeping changes that have resulted from the increase in the number of women in the workforce during the past 50 years, transforming consumer patterns, workplace policies, dating and relationship norms, parenting practices, household maintenance, and self-concepts for both men and women.

race   Social category, still poorly defined, that depends on an assumption of biological distinction to rate and organize social groups.

racial ethnicity   An ethnic group believed to also have common psychological characteristics.

racial formations   A theory that understands race and ethnicity as socially constructed identities. This means that both the *content* and *importance* of racial and ethnic categories are determined by the societies in which they exist.

racial income gap   The gap in income between blacks and whites. The gap between high-income whites and blacks is astonishingly high, and because of the racial income gap over time, even middle-income whites have far more wealth than high-income blacks.

racial profiling   Stopping and searching minorities because members of minority groups are seen as "more likely" to be criminals. It's more a self-fulfilling prophecy: Believing is seeing.

racial wealth gap   Gap in wealth—based on total financial assets including home equity—between blacks and whites. Because whites make more than blacks, are more likely to be in the professions, and more likely to own their own homes, the gap between them has continued to widen.

racialization or ethnicization   Twin processes of ascribing either racial or ethnic qualities to groups who did not identify themselves as such.

racism   An ideology that holds that inequality based on race is justified because of assumed natural differences between races.

random sample   A sample chosen by an abstract and arbitrary method, such as tossing a piece of paper with each person's name on it into a hat.

rationality   A chief interest of Max Weber, who argued that rationality was the foundation of modern society—an escalating process of order and organization with dire consequences.

recidivism   An individual's relapse into criminal behavior after having served time or endured some intervention aimed to affect their future behavior. Thus, the "recidivism rate" is the rate at which people who have served time will commit another crime after leaving.

reciprocal effects   A dynamic cause-and-effect relationship in which two or more social phenomena can be shown to be both cause and effect, for example, fatness and social class.

reference group   A group toward which one is so strongly committed, or one that commands so much prestige, that we orient our actions around what we perceive that group's perceptions would be.

relative deprivation Describes how misery is socially experienced by constantly comparing yourself to others. You are not down and out: You are worse off than you used to be (downward mobility), not as well off as you think you should be (rising expectations), or, perhaps, not as well off as those you see around you.

relative poverty The ability of people to afford only the basic necessities of life; those who live in relative poverty are unable to maintain an adequate standard of living.

reliability Means that another researcher can use the same data you used and would find similar results.

religion A set of beliefs and practices relating to the origins and meaning of life, usually based on a belief in the existence of a supernatural power.

religiosity Sociological term for the numerous aspects of an individual's religious activity, dedication, and belief. A more colloquial term would be "religiousness."

remarriage The term sociologists use for people entering a new marriage after leaving at least one previous marriage by divorce.

replication One of the main principles of the scientific method, replication is the ability of an entire experiment or study to be duplicated by others.

representative democracy System in which citizens elect representatives to make the decisions for them; requires an educated citizenry and a free press.

representative sample A sample that is scientifically designed to accurately reflect a larger population.

research methods The processes used to systematically collect and analyze information from the social world for the purposes of sociological study and understanding.

residential segregation Institutional discrimination of housing created neighborhoods, usually with lower quality infrastructure, for whites and other race and ethnic groups.

resocialization The process of learning a new set of beliefs, behaviors, and values that depart from those held in the past.

reverse causality Refers either to a direction of cause-and-effect contrary to the presumed relationship between variables or to a two-way causal relationship in, as it were, a loop (a relationship sociologists refer to as "reciprocal").

revolution The attempt to overthrow the existing political and social order of a society and replace it with a new one.

rites of passage A marker, often a ceremony, that denotes an important stage in someone's life, such as birth, puberty, marriage, death.

ritual Enactment by which members of a culture engage in a routine behavior to express their sense of belonging to the culture.

role Behavior expected of people who have a particular status.

role conflict What happens when we try to play different roles with extremely different or contradictory rules at the same time.

role exit The process we go through to adjust when leaving a role that is central to our identity.

role performance The particular emphasis or interpretation each of us gives a social role.

role strain The experience of difficulty in performing a role.

rootlessness The experience of having few or no ties and no real place in society, often as the result of economic and/or social change.

sacred Holy moments that evoke a sense of reverence and unity.

sacrilegious That which is profane, blasphemous, impious, irreverent, or sinful.

sample A limited group of research subjects whose responses are statistically developed into a general theme or trend that can be applied to the larger whole.

"sandwich generation" With the increase in life expectancy and the delay in childbearing, many middle-aged adults find themselves "sandwiched" between caring for dependent children and aging parents at the same time.

Sapir-Whorf hypothesis A theory that language shapes our reality because it gives us a way to talk about the categories of life that we experience.

"school effects" The term for research demonstrating the ways student outcomes are meaningfully shaped by school characteristics.

scientific literacy The capacity to understand scientific concepts and processes necessary for complete participation in economic, civic, and cultural life.

scientific racism The science of "breeding," and encouraged laws that would help the country breed a superior race, eugenics.

second shift Arlie Hochschild's term for the dual day experienced by working women in which they perform the lion's share of the housework and childcare after a regular working shift is over.

secondary analysis Analysis conducted using data previously collected by others for other reasons.

secondary deviance The moment when someone acquires a deviant identity, occurring when he or she repeatedly breaks a norm and people start making a big deal of it, so the rule breaking can no longer be attributed to a momentary lapse in judgment or be justifiable under the circumstances but is an indication of a permanent personality trait.

secondary group Coworkers, club members, or another group that comes together for instrumental reasons, such as wanting to work together to meet common goals. Secondary groups make less of an emotional claim on one's identity than do primary groups.

secondary socialization Occurring throughout the life span, it is the adjustments we make to adapt to new situations.

sect A small subculture within an established religious institution. Like cults, they break from traditional practices, but unlike cults, they remain within the larger institution.

secularization The process of moving away from religion and toward the worldly.

segregation The practice of physically separating races by law and custom in institutions and communities.

self-control theory In explaining deviance, places the emphasis on inadequate socialization and thus a weakened internal monitoring system.

self-fulfilling prophecy The social phenomenon that when we expect something to happen, it often does.

sentencing discrimination Black defendants receive harsher sentences from judges and juries, on average, when compared with white defendants on trial for the same crimes (even when we account for prior offenses and other issues that affect both conviction rates and other decisions regarding sentencing).

separate spheres A set of beliefs that coalesced as a distinct ideology in Europe and North America during the Industrial Revolution, it assigned to women and men distinct and virtually opposite functions, duties, characteristics, and activities in society.

service work A growing sector of work in the United States, this category includes food preparation and service, personal services (hair stylists, launderers, childcare workers), and maintenance workers (janitors, garbage collectors), plus police officers and firefighters.

sex A biological distinction; the chromosomal, chemical, and anatomical organization of males and females.

sex ratio The ratio of males to females in a population.

sex-selective abortion A procedure in which women terminate pregnancies after finding out that they are carrying girls.

sexual behavior Any behavior that brings sexual pleasure or release (typically, but not always, involving sex organs).

sexual desire Any intense sexual feelings associated with specific environmental, cultural, or biological stimuli.

sexual discrimination Discrimination against a person on the grounds of sex or sexual identity.

sexual double standard The social standard that encourages men to pursue sex as an end in itself, to seek a lot of sex with many different partners, outside of romantic or emotional commitment, and teaches women to consider sex with one partner and only in the context of an emotional relationship.

sexual identity Typically, it is understood to refer to an identity that is organized by the gender of the person (or persons) to whom we are sexually attracted. Also called *sexual orientation.*

sexual prejudice Negative attitudes about an individual or group based on sexual identity.

sexual scripts A cognitive map about how to have sex and with whom.

sexual socialization The process by which your sexual scripts begin to cohere into a preference and sexual identity.

sexuality An identity we construct that is often based on our sexual conduct and often intersects with other sources of identity, such as race, class, ethnicity, age, or gender.

shari'a Islamic religious law, outlined in the *Koran*, which, when strictly interpreted, includes such penalties as cutting off the hand for robbery and death by stoning for adultery.

sick role Talcott Parsons' coinage to describe how we learn to "be" sick; it is a social role we learn to occupy and with which we learn to interact.

singletons Modern term for people living alone, often by choice.

small world problem The name for sociological research conducted by Milgram and others that suggests human society is a small network characterized by short paths between strangers. The research is often associated with the phrase "six degrees of separation" (although Milgram himself did not use that phrase).

"sneaky thrills" Jack Katz's concept that crimes like shoplifting, burglary, joyriding, and vandalism are committed by amateurs, mostly adolescents, for the fun of it, not necessarily to acquire money or property. Katz theorized that sneaky thrills offer the adolescent perpetrators an experience similar to sexual experimentation.

social construction of gender The social process by which we construct our gender identities throughout our lives, using the cultural ideas and materials we find around us.

social control theory As Walter Reckless theorized, people don't commit crimes even if they could probably get away with them due to social controls. There are outer controls—family, friends, teachers, social institutions, and authority figures (like the police)—who influence (cajole, threaten, browbeat) us into obeying social rules; and inner controls—internalized socialization, consciousness, religious principles, ideas of right and wrong, and one's self-conception as a "good person."

Social Darwinism A model of social change that saw each succeeding society as developing through evolution and the "survival of the fittest."

social desirability bias The term social scientists use to describe a form of response bias wherein people being studied tend to present themselves in a manner they believe will be perceived favorably.

social epidemiology The study of both biomedical elements of disease and the social and behavioral factors that influence its spread.

social fact Émile Durkheim's term for the values, norms, and structures that transcend individuals, exercising social control over them, and amenable to scientific study.

social forms A special task of sociology is to study the forms of social interaction apart from their content. Georg Simmel assumed that the same social forms—competition, exchange, secrecy, domination—could contain quite different content and that the same social content could be embodied in different forms. Each social form, according to Simmel, would have distinctive properties.

social groups A collection of individuals bound by a common social identity or by some shared goal and purpose.

social ideologies The ways through which these social stratification arrangements are defined as fair, just, and reasonable.

social inequality The social process by which valued goods, opportunities, and experiences are unequally distributed throughout a population.

social institutions Patterned sets of interactions that work to meet collective needs that are not easily met by individuals working alone. They include such social arenas as markets, families, schools, corporations, factories, and prisons.

social interaction   The foundation for societal groups and relationships and the process of how people behave and interact with each other.

social mobility   The process of moving between different positions in social hierarchies within society (e.g., from one social class to another).

social movement   Collective attempt to further a common interest or secure a common goal through action outside the sphere of established institutions.

social network   Often conceived as a web of social relationships, a type of group that is both looser and denser than a formal group but connects people to each other, and, through those connections, with other people.

social reactions and collective evaluation   Alongside considering how acts correspond with normative expectation, we also consider the social reactions and evaluations of groups. This produces four distinct types of deviance: negative; positive; deviance admiration; and rate busting.

social reproduction   The structures and activities that transmit social inequality from one generation to the next.

social revolution   Revolution that changes the social groups or classes that political power rests on.

social role   Sets of behaviors expected of a person who occupies a certain social status.

social scripts   Term for a sequence of expected behaviors in a given situation.

social solidarity   Émile Durkheim's term for the moral bonds that connect us to the social collectivity.

social stigma   Disapproval or discontent with a person or group that differs from cultural norms, which often serves to distinguish that person or group from other members of a society.

social stratification   Taken from the geological term for layers of rock, or "strata," the ranking of people into defined layers. Social stratification exists in all societies and is based on things like wealth, race, and gender.

social structure   A complex framework composed of both patterned social interactions and institutions that together organize social life and provide the context for individual action.

social ties   Refer to the social connections or relationships between individuals and groups.

socialism   Economic system in which people are meant to cooperate rather than compete, share goods and services, own property collectively, and make decisions as a collective body.

socialization   The process by which we become aware of ourselves as part of a group, learn to communicate with others, and learn how to behave as expected.

society   An organized collection of individuals and institutions, bounded by space in a coherent territory, subject to the same political authority, and organized through a shared set of cultural expectations and values.

socioeconomic status (SES)   Your social connections, your taste in art, your ascribed and attained statuses, and more.

Because there are so many components, sociologists today tend to prefer the concept of socioeconomic status to that of social class, to emphasize that people are ranked through the intermingling of many factors, economic, social, political, cultural, and community.

sociological imagination   The ability to see the connection between our individual identities and the social contexts (family, friends, and institutions) in which we find ourselves.

sociology   The study of human behavior in society.

stalled revolution   The widespread change in gender relations whereby women are much more likely to earn a living wage on their own but men have not responded in kind and participated more in work around the house.

state capitalism   A version of capitalism that requires that the government use a heavy hand in regulating and constraining the marketplace.

state-centered theories   Theories that argue appropriate government policies do not interfere with economic development but that governments play a key role in bringing it about.

status   One's socially defined position in a group; it is often characterized by certain expectations and rights.

stereotype   Generalization about a group that is oversimplified and exaggerated and that fails to acknowledge individual differences in the group.

stereotype promise   Term coined by Jennifer Lee and Min Zhou to address the "promise" of being viewed through the lens of a positive stereotype that leads one to perform in ways that confirms the positive stereotype (the counterpart to "stereotype threat").

stereotype threat   Term coined by Claude Steele to assess the extent to which labels about people "like us" have measurable impacts on their performances. It refers to the variation in performance measured when the belief that people who belong to an identity category you share are worse at a particular task than the comparison group.

stigma   An attribute that changes you "from a whole and usual person to a tainted and discounted one," as sociologist Erving Goffman (1963) defined it. A stigma discredits a person's claim to be normal.

stratified sample   Sample in which research subjects are divided into proportions equal to the proportions found in the population at large.

"the strength of weak ties"   Mark Granovetter's discovery that weak ties are valuable precisely because they provide new information that is often less available from strong ties.

strong ties   Term used by Mark Granovetter to characterize those people in your interpersonal network who actually know you.

structural functionalism   A sociological paradigm that contends that all social life consists of several distinct, integrated levels that enable the world—and individuals who are within it—to find stability, order, and meaning.

structural holes A concept from social network research, the term refers to a gap between two networks of individuals who have complementary sources to information.

structural mobility A general upward trend of the entire society. Structural mobility means that the entire society got wealthier, as occurred in post–World War II America.

structural strain theory Robert K. Merton's concept that excessive deviance is a by-product of inequality within societies that promote certain norms and versions of social reality yet provide unequal means of meeting or attaining them.

subculture Group within a society that creates its own norms and values distinct from the mainstream and usually its own separate social institutions as well.

subjectivity The complex of individual perceptions, motivations, ideas, and emotions that give each of us a point of view.

subordinate Individual or group that possesses little or comparatively less social power.

subtle racism Systematic prejudice applied to members of a group in quiet or even unconscious ways; a simple set of mental categories that one may possess about a group based on stereotypes.

suburb A residential community outside of a city but always existing in relationship to the city.

superego Freud's term for the internalized norms, values, and "rules" of our social group that are learned from family, friends, and social institutions.

superordinate Individual or group that possesses social power.

survey Research method in which one asks a sample of people closed-ended questions and tabulates the results.

symbol Anything—an idea, a marking, a thing—that carries additional meanings beyond itself to others who share in the culture. Symbols come to mean what they do only in a culture; they would have no meaning to someone outside.

symbolic ethnicity Discrimination has largely disappeared and ethnic identity has become mostly a choice to be asserted in times and situations when it will increase their prestige and downplayed or ignored when it may decrease their prestige.

symbolic interactionism Sociological perspective that examines how individuals and groups interact, focusing on the creation of personal identity through interaction with others. Of particular interest is the relationship between individual action and group pressures.

systematic sample A type of sample that starts at a random position on a list and selects every *n*th unit (skip interval) of a population until the desired sample size is reached.

taboos Address social prohibitions viewed as essential to the well-being of humanity. To break a *mos* is bad or immoral, but breaking a taboo is unthinkable, beyond comprehension.

tastes French sociologist Pierre Bourdieu's term for an abstract process through which we all adopt routines, practices, and interests which have their origins in material constraints.

terrorism Using acts of violence and destruction (or threatening to use them) as a political strategy.

tertiary deviance Occurs when members of a group formerly labeled deviant attempt to redefine their acts, attributes, or identities as normal—even virtuous.

tetrad A group of four people.

theory of religious economy The hypothesis that societies that restrict supply of religion—whether that is through imposed state religions or state-sponsored secularization—are the main causes of drops in religiosity. Simply put, the more religions a society has and acknowledges, the more likely the population is to be religious.

time diary studies Research method that measures how people allocate their time during an average day by having subjects regularly record their activities in a diary, log, or other record.

token Representative of a traditionally disenfranchised group whose hypervisibility results in constant pressure to reflect well on the group and to outperform co-workers just to be perceived as equal.

"the tolerance trap" Suzanna Walters' concept to capture the co-existence of enormous gains in popular, political, and cultural "inclusion" of gay people with the persistence of anti-gay laws and legislation, the spate of suicides by queer youth, homophobic bullying and violence, and more.

total institution An institution that completely circumscribes your everyday life, cutting you off from life before you entered and seeking to regulate every part of your behavior.

totalitarianism A political system in which no organized opposition is permitted and political information is censored.

tracking Common in American schools, it is the term for grouping students according to their academic abilities.

traditional authority Dominant in premodern societies, including ancient Egypt, China, and Mesoamerica, the form of authority that people obeyed because they believed their society had always done things that way; derives from who the leaders are: the descendants of kings and queens, or perhaps the descendants of the gods, not from their educational background, work experience, or personality traits.

transgender An umbrella term that describes a variety of people, behaviors, and groups whose identities depart from normative gender ideals of masculinity or femininity.

triad A group of three people.

triangulation A research technique that uses cross-verification to ensure the validity of conclusions. When several research methods are used to the study of the same phenomenon, researchers can be more confident with a result.

underclass About 4 percent of the U.S. population, this group has no income, no connection to the job market, little education, inadequate nutrition, and substandard housing or none at all. They have no possibility of social mobility and little chance of achieving the quality of life that most people would consider minimally acceptable.

underemployed People educated and qualified for positions higher than the ones they occupy.

unemployment rate   The measure of the prevalence of unemployment, it is calculated by dividing the number of unemployed individuals by all individuals currently in the labor force.

universal suffrage   Granting of the vote to any and all citizens who meet specified, universal criteria, such as legal citizenship and a minimum age.

upper middle class   With household incomes above $80,000 but less than $150,000, they are the high-end professionals and corporate workers. Most have college degrees. Only a small percentage of their income comes from investments.

upper upper class   The superrich, with annual incomes of more than $1 million. They include the older established wealthy families, born into massive fortunes that their ancestors amassed during the industrial boom of the nineteenth-century Gilded Age.

utilitarian organization   An organization, like the college we attend or the company we work for, whose members belong for a specific, instrumental purpose or tangible material reward.

validity   The extent to which a concept, conclusion, or question is well-founded, and measures what a researcher thinks it is measuring.

value   If norms tell us how to behave, values tell us why. Values constitute what a society thinks about itself and so are among the most basic lessons that a culture can transmit to its young.

voting-age population   Term for proportion of people 18 and older who therefore can vote.

voting-eligible population   Term for the proportion of people 18 and older who are not prohibited from voting.

war   A state of armed conflict between different nations, different states within a nation, or different groups within a nation or state.

weak ties   Granovetter's term for people in your interpersonal network whom you may not know personally, but perhaps you know *of* them, or they know *of* you.

welfare capitalism   A version of capitalism in most contemporary capitalist countries, it is concerned with the welfare of the worker as well as profits and includes such policies as collective bargaining and industrial safety codes while the government regulates some of the most essential services, such as transportation, health care, and the mass media.

welfare system   The basic structural opportunities provided by most countries for people to work their way out of poverty: free education, national health care, welfare subsistence, housing allowances.

Western religions   Three of the world's major religions—Judaism, Christianity, and Islam (plus a few smaller ones)—are called "Western" because, although they originated in the Middle East, their adherents are largely among Western nations.

"white flight"   Term for the pattern of movement by white people out of cities to escape immigrants and minorities.

white-collar crime   Edward Sutherland's term for the illegal actions of a corporation or people acting on its behalf, by using the authority of their position to commit crime.

white-collar work   Knowledge-based work, requiring considerable education, in which a typical day is spent manipulating symbols: talking, speaking, reading, writing, and calculating.

Women's Movement   The movement to remove obstacles to women's full participation in modern life. From its origins, the Women's Movement has been a global movement, yet each national and cultural expression has sought changes tailored to its specific context.

working class   With household income between $20,000 and $40,000. They tend to be blue-collar workers, involved in manufacturing, production, and skilled trades, but also include some low-level white-collar workers and professionals (such as elementary school teachers) and some high-level clerical and service industry workers, especially those in two-income households.

working poor   Working people whose income nevertheless falls below the poverty line.

workplace discrimination   A form of discrimination based on race, gender, religion, national origin, physical or mental disability, and age by employers.

world religions   Religions with a long history, well-established traditions, and the flexibility to adapt to many different cultures.

world system theory   Immanuel Wallerstein's theory that the interconnectedness of the world system began in the 1500s, when Europeans began their economic and political domination of the rest of the world.

young adulthood   The life stage at which people are clearly no longer children or adolescents, but have not yet reached full adulthood either.

"young old"   The term for people ages 65 to 75.

zero population growth   Paul Erlich's (1968) modern solution to Malthus's concerns, it entails a global effort to ensure that the number of births does not exceed the number of deaths, providing global population stability, a decrease in poor countries, and a redistribution of resources to those countries.

AARP. *Baby Boomers Envision Their Retirement.* Washington, DC: AARP, 2001.

Abbate, Janet. *Inventing the Internet.* Cambridge, MA: MIT Press, 2000.

Abbott, Andrew. "Status and Status Strain in the Professions." *American Journal of Sociology,* 86, no. 4 (1981): 819–835.

Abbott, Andrew. *The System of Professions: An Essay on the Division of Expert Labor.* Chicago, IL: University of Chicago Press, 1988.

Aboud, F., Morton Mendelson, and Kelly Purdy. "Cross-Race Peer Relations and Friendship Quality." *International Journal of Behavioral Development,* 27 no. 2, (March 2003): 165–173.

Acierno, Ron, Melba A. Hernandez, Ananda B. Amstadter, Heidi S. Resnick, Kenneth Steve, Wendy Muzzy, and Dean G. Kilpatrick. "Prevalence and Correlates of Emotional, Physical, Sexual, and Financial Abuse and Potential Neglect in the United States: The National Elder Mistreatment Study." *American Journal of Public Health,* 100, no. 2 (2010): 292–297.

Aday, Sean, Henry Farrell, Marc Lynch, John Sides, John Kelly, and Ethan Zuckerman. *Blogs and Bullets: New Media in Contentious Politics.* Washington: USIP, 2010. Available at: https://www.usip.org/publications/2010/09/blogs-and-bullets-new-media-contentious-politics

Adler, Jerry. "The New Naysayers." *Newsweek,* September 11, 2006.

Adler, Paul S. "Market, Hierarchy, and Trust: The Knowledge Economy and the Future of Capitalism." *Organization Science,* March–April 2001: 214–234.

Agthe, M., Matthias Spörrle, and Jon K. Maner. "Don't hate me because I'm beautiful: Anti-attractiveness bias in organizational evaluation and decision making." *Journal of Experimental Social Psychology,* 46, no. 6 (2010): 1151–1154.

Ahrons, Constance. *We're Still Family: What Grown Children Have to Say about Their Parents' Divorce.* New York: HarperCollins, 2004.

Alan Guttmacher Institute. "American Teens' Sexual and Reproductive Health," May 2014. Available at: https://www.guttmacher.org/sites/default/files/pdfs/pubs/FB-ATSRH.pdf

Albrecht, Gary L., Vivian G. Walker, and Judith A. Levy. "Social Distance from the Stigmatized." *Social Science & Medicine,* 16, no. 14 (1982): 1319–1327.

Allan, Emilie Andersen, and Darrell J. Steffensmeier. "Youth Underemployment and Property Crime: Differential Effects of Job Availability and Job Quality on Juvenile and Young Adult Arrest Rates." *American Sociological Review,* 54 (1989): 107–123.

Allen, K. R., and D. H. Demo. "The Families of Lesbians and Gay Men: A New Frontier in Family Research." *Journal of Marriage and the Family,* 57 (1995): 111–127.

Alliance for Board Diversity. "Missing Pieces: Women and Minorities on Fortune 500 Boards." *Alliance for Board Diversity Census,* August 15, 2013. Available at: http://theabd.org/Reports.html

Allport, Gordon. *The Nature of Prejudice.* New York: Anchor, 1954.

Altbach, Philip. *American Higher Education in the Twentieth Century: Social, Political, and Economic Challenges.* Baltimore, MD: Johns Hopkins University Press, 1998.

Amato, Paul R. "Reconciling Divergent Perspectives: Judith Wallerstein, Quantitative Family Research, and Children of Divorce." *Family Relations,* 52, no. 4 (2003): 332–339.

Amato, Paul R., and Juliana M. Sobolewski. "The Effects of Divorce and Marital Discord on Adult Children's Psychological Well-Being." *American Sociological Review,* 66 (2001): 900–921.

American Academy of Arts and Sciences. "Public Research Universities: Changes in State Funding," 2015. Available at: https://www.amacad.org/multimedia/pdfs/publications/researchpapersmonographs/PublicResearchUniv_ChangesInStateFunding.pdf

American Association of University Women (AAUW). *Women's Educational Gains and the Gender Earnings Gap.* Washington, DC: AAUW, 2007.

American Bar Association. "A Current Glance at Women in the Law." *American Bar Association, Commission on Women in the Profession,* January, 2017. Available at: http://www.americanbar.org/content/dam/aba/marketing/women/current_glance_statistics_january2017.authcheckdam.pdf

American Society for Aesthetic Plastic Surgery. "2016 Cosmetic Surgery National Bank Statistics." 2016. Available at: http://www.surgery.org/sites/default/files/ASAPS-Stats2016.pdf

American Society of Plastic Surgeons. *Cosmetic Surgery Procedures,* 2016. Available at: www.plasticsurgery.org

American Sociological Association. "Bachelor's Degrees Awarded in Sociology, By Gender, 1966–2014. Available at http://www.asanet.org/research-and-publications/research-sociology/trends/bachelors-degrees-awarded-sociology-gender-1966-2014

American Stroke Association. Heart Disease and Stroke Statistics 2017: At-a-Glance. *American Heart Association/American Stroke Association*. 2017. Available at: https://www.google.com/url?sa=t&rct=j&q=&esrc=s&source=web&cd=2&ved=0ahUKEwiugNGclPfTAhVq_IMKHTJyC34QFggvMAE&url=https%3A%2F%2Fwww.heart.org%2Fidc%2Fgroups%2Fahamah-public%2F%40wcm%2F%40sop%2F%40smd%2Fdocuments%2Fdownloadable%2Fucm_491265.pdf&usg=AFQjCNGufUkxrZtPZ6_aRQE4Yau3vdzI0A&sig2=44CEDc2xjBJi7dWVj-ZLgQ

Anderson, E. "The Code of the Streets." *Atlantic Monthly*, 273, May 1994, 81–94.

Anderson, Elijah. *Streetwise: Race, Class and Change in an Urban Community*. Chicago, IL: University of Chicago Press, 1992.

Anderson, Elijah. *Code of the Street: Decency, Violence, and the Moral Life of the Inner City*. New York: W. W. Norton, 2000.

Anderson, Hannah, and Matt Daniels, 2016. Film Dialogue from 2,000 Screenplays, Broken Down by Gender and Age. Available at: https://pudding.cool/2017/03/film-dialogue/index.html

Angier, Natalie. *Woman: An Intimate Geography*. Boston: Houghton-Mifflin, 1999.

Angle, John. "A Mathematical Sociologist's Tribute to Comte: Sociology as Science." *Footnotes*, February 2007.

APA. Incarceration Nation. American Psychological Association Newsletter, 45, No. 2, (October 2014): 56.

Appelbaum, Richard P., and Jeffrey Henderson. *States and Development in the Asian Pacific Rim*. Newbury Park, CA: Sage, 1992.

Arbuckle, Julianne, and Benne D. Williams. "Students' Perceptions of Expressiveness: Age and Gender Effects on Teacher Evaluations." *Sex Roles*, 49, no. 9–10 (2003): 507–516.

Arendt, Hannah. *The Origins of Totalitarianism* (1958). New York: Harcourt, 1973.

Ariès, Philippe. *Centuries of Childhood: A Social History of Family Life*. New York, NY: Vintage, 1965.

Armstrong, Elizabeth and Suzanna Crage. "Movements and Memory: The Making of the Stonewall Myth." American Review of Sociology 71, no.5 (2006): 724–751.

Armstrong, Elizabeth, and Laura Hamilton. *Paying for the Party: How College Maintains Inequality*. Cambridge: Harvard University Press, 2013.

Armstrong, Elizabeth A., Laura Hamilton, and Paula England. "Is Hooking Up Bad for Young Women?" *Contexts*, 9, no. 3 (2010): 22–27.

Armstrong, Elizabeth A., Laura T. Hamilton, Elizabeth M. Armstrong, and J. Lotus Seeley. "'Good Girls': Gender, Social Class, and Slut Discourse on Campus." *Social Psychology Quarterly*, 77, no. 2 (2014): 100–122.

Armstrong, Elizabeth A., Paula England, Alison C. K. Fogarty. "Accounting for Women's Orgasm and Sexual Enjoyment in College Hookups and Relationships." *American Sociological Review*, 77, no. 3 (2012): 435–462.

Arnett, Jeffrey Jensen. *Emerging Adulthood: The Winding Road from the Late Teens through the Twenties*. New York: Oxford University Press, 2004.

Arnett, Jeffrey Jensen. "Emerging Adulthood: Understanding the New Way of Coming of Age." In *Emerging Adults in America: Coming of Age in the 21st Century* (pp. 3–19). Washington D.C.: American Psychological Association, 2006.

Arnoldi, Ben. "America Becomes a More 'Adult-Centered' Nation." *The Christian Science Monitor*, July 10, 2007.

Asch, Solomon. "Opinions and Social Pressure." *Scientific American*, 193, no. 5 (1955): 31–35.

Association of American Universities Campus Climate Survey on Sexual Assault and Sexual Misconduct, 2015. Available at: https://www.aau.edu/key-issues/aau-climate-survey-sexual-assault-and-sexual-misconduct-2015

Association of American Medical Colleges. "AAMC Facts & Figures: Diversity in Medical Education." 2016. Available at: http://www.aamcdiversityfactsandfigures2016.org/

Association of American Medical Colleges, 2016. "Number of Female Medical School Enrollees Reaches 10 Year High." 2016. Available at: https://news.aamc.org/press-releases/article/applicant-enrollment-2016/

Atkinson, Michael. *Tattooed: The Sociogenesis of a Body Art*. Toronto, Ontario: University of Toronto Press, 2003.

Ayres, Irving, and Peter Siegelman. "Race and Gender Discrimination in Bargaining for a New Car." *American Economic Review*, 85, no. 3 (1995): 304–321.

Aziz, Mir Adnan. *An Era of Disparity*. New York: Global Policy Forum, 2008.

Backman, Clifford R. *The Worlds of Medieval Europe*. Oxford, UK: Oxford University Press, 2002.

Badge, Emily, and Darla Cameron. "How Railroads, Highways and Other Man-Made Lines Racially Divide America's Cities." *The Washington Post* Wonkblog, July 16, 2015. Available at: https://www.washingtonpost.com/news/wonk/wp/2015/07/16/how-railroads-highways-and-other-man-made-lines-racially-divide-americas-cities/

Badger, Emily. "Tomorrow's G.I. Joe May Be Too Fat to Fight." *Pacific Standard*, June 29, 2010. Available at: https://psmag.com/social-justice/tomorrows-gi-joe-may-be-too-fat-to-fight-18214

Bagamery, Anne. "Hearing Tomorrow's Workers." *International Herald Tribune*, April 14, 2004.

Bailey, Beth L. *From Front Porch to Back Seat: Courtship in Twentieth Century America*. Baltimore, MD: Johns Hopkins University Press, 1989.

Bajoria, Jayshree, and Amy Braunschweiger. "Q&A: Talking Discrimination and School Dropout Rates in India." *Human Rights* Watch, April 22, 2014. Available at: https://www.hrw.org/news/2014/04/22/qa-talking-discrimination-and-school-dropout-rates-india

Baker, Dean, and Nick Buffie, "The Decline of Blue-Collar Jobs, In Graphs." *CEPR Blog*, February 17, 2017: http://cepr.net/blogs/cepr-blog/the-decline-of-blue-collar-jobs-in-graphs.

Baker, Sandra. "Dallas-Fort Worth Businesses Wrestle with Issues raised by Patron's Tattoos." *Dallas Star-Telegram.* July 4, 2010. Available at: http://www.star-telegram.com/living/family/moms/article3825762.html

Baldus, D. C., and G. Woodworth. "Race Discrimination and the Death Penalty: An Empirical and Legal Overview." In J. Acker, R. M. Bohm, and C. S. Lanier, eds., *America's Experiment with Capital Punishment* (pp. 385–416). Durham, NC: Carolina Academic Press, 1998.

Ballantine, Jeanne H. *The Sociology of Education: A Systematic Analysis.* Upper Saddle River, NJ: Prentice-Hall, 2001.

Banyai, Istvan. *Zoom.* New York, NY: Puffin Books, 1998.

Barber, Benjamin. *Jihad vs. McWorld: How Globalization and Tribalism Are Reshaping the World.* New York: Crown, 1996.

Barr, Nicolas. *The Economics of the Welfare State.* New York: Oxford University Press, 2004.

Barta, Patrick. "The Rise of the Underground." *The Wall Street Journal*, March 14, 2009.

Bassuk, Shari S., Lisa F. Berkman, and Benjamin C. Amick II. "Socioeconomic Status and Mortality among the Elderly: Findings from Four U.S. Communities." *American Journal of Epidemiology*, 155, no. 6 (2002): 520–533.

Battle, Michael. *The Black Church in America: African American Christian Spirituality.* London: Blackwell, 2006.

Baumle, Amanda K., and D'Lane R. Compton. *Legalizing LGBT Families: How the Law Shapes Parenthood.* New York, NY: NYU Press, 2016.

Baumle, Amanda K., and D'Lane R. Compton. "Love Wins?" *Contexts*, 16, no. 1 (2017): 30–35.

BBC News. "Obesity: In Statistics." January 2, 2008. Available at: http://news.bbc.co.uk/2/hi/health/7151813.stm

BBC World Service. "Economic System Needs 'Major Changes': Global Poll." June 2009.

Bearman, Peter S., and Hannah Brückner. "Promising the Future: Virginity Pledges and First Intercourse." *American Journal of Sociology*, 106, no. 4 (2001): 859–912.

Beber, Bernd, and Christopher Blattman. "The Industrial Organization of Rebellion: The Logic of Forced Labor and Child Soldiering." Unpublished manuscript, 2010. Available at: http://federation.ens.fr/ydepot/semin/texte0910/BLA2010IND.pdf

Becker, Howard S. *Outside: Studies in the Sociology of Deviance.* New York: The Free Press, 1966.

Becker, Howard S. "Becoming a Marihuana User." *American Journal of Sociology*, 59, no. 3 (1953): 235–242.

Bell, Daniel. *The Coming of Post-Industrial Society: A Venture in Social Forecasting.* New York: Basic Books, 1976.

Bell, Michael Mayerfield. *An Invitation to Environmental Sociology.* Thousand Oaks, CA: Pine Forge Press, 2004.

Bellah, Robert N. "Civil Religion in America." *Journal of the American Academy of Arts and Sciences*, 96, no. 1 (Winter, 1967): 1–21.

Belsky, J. K. *The Psychology of Aging: Theory, Research and Intervention.* Pacific Grove, CA: Brooks/Cole, 1990.

Berger, Peter L., and Thomas Luckmann. *The Social Construction of Reality: A Treatise in the Sociology of Knowledge.* New York: Anchor Books, 1966.

Bernard, Jessie. *The Future of Marriage.* New York: World, 1972.

Bernstein, Mary, and Verta Taylor, eds. *The Marrying Kind?: Debating Same-Sex Marriage within the Lesbian and Gay Movement.* Minneapolis, MN: University of Minnesota Press, 2013.

Berri, David, and Simmons, Rob. "Race and the Evaluation of Signal Callers in the National Football League." *Journal of Sports Economics*, 10, no. 1 (2009): 23–43.

Bertrand, Marianne, and Sendhil Mullainathan. "Are Emily and Greg More Employable than Lakisha and Jamal? A Field Experiment on Labor Market Discrimination." Working Paper. *National Bureau of Economic Research*, July 2003. NBER Working Paper No. 9873. Available at: http://www.nber.org/papers/w9873

Bertrand, Marianne, and Sendhil Mullainathan. "Are Emily and Greg More Employable Than Lakisha and Jamal? A Field Experiment on Labor Market Discrimination." *American Economic Review*, 94, no. 4 (2004): 991–1013.

Bettie, Julie. *Women Without Class: Girls, Race, and Identity.* Berkeley, CA: University of California Press, 2003.

Bianchi, S. M., M. A. Milkie, L. C. Sayer, and J. P. Robinson. "Is Anyone Doing the Housework? Trends in the Gender Division of Household Labor." *Social Forces*, 79 (2000): 191–228.

Bianchi, Suzanne M., John P. Robinson, and Melissa A. Milkie. *Changing Rhythms of American Family Life.* New York: Russell Sage Foundation Publications, 2006.

Biblarz, Timothy J., and Judith Stacey. "How Does the Gender of Parents Matter?" *Journal of Marriage and Family*, 72, no. 1 (2010): 3–22.

Bidwell, Alan. "Racial Gaps in High School Graduation Rates are Closing." *U.S. News and World Report*, March 16, 2015. Available at: https://www.usnews.com/news/blogs/data-mine/2015/03/16/federal-data-show-racial-gap-in-high-school-graduation-rates-is-closing

Bieber, Irving, Toby Bieber, Cornelia Wilbur, and Alfred Rifkin. *Homosexuality: A Psychoanalytic Perspective.* New York: Basic Books, 1962.

Billingsley, Andrew. *Mighty Like a River: The Black Church and Social Reform.* New York: Oxford, 1999.

Birdsong, David, ed. *Second Language Acquisition and the Critical Period Hypothesis.* Mahwah, NJ: Lawrence Erlbaum, 1999.

Birn, Raymond. *Crisis, Absolutism, Revolution: Europe, 1648–1789.* New York: Harcourt, 1992.

Blackstone, Amy, and Mahala Dyer Stewart. "Choosing to Be Childfree: Research on the Decision Not to Parent." *Sociology Compass*, 6, no. 9 (2012): 718–727.

Blackstone, Amy, and Mahala Dyer Stewart. "'There's More Thinking to Decide': How the Childfree Decide Not to Parent." *The Family Journal*, 24, no. 3 (2016): 296–303.

Blair Loy, Mary. "Work Without End? Scheduling Flexibility and Work-to-Family Conflict among Stockbrokers." *Work and Occupations,* 36 (2009): 279–317.

Blank, J. "The Kid No One Noticed." *U.S. News and World Report,* December 1998, 27.

Blau, Judith R., and Peter M. Blau. "The Cost of Inequality: Metropolitan Structure and Violent Crime." *American Sociological Review,* 47, no. 1 (February 1982): 114–129.

Blau, Peter. *Exchange and Power in Social Life.* New York: Wiley, 1964.

Blau, Peter M., and Otis Duncan. *American Occupational Structure.* New York: John Wiley & Sons, 1967.

Blow, Charles. "Gay? Whatever, Dude." *The New York Times,* June 4, 2010. Available at: http://www.nytimes.com/2010/06/05/opinion/05blow.html

Blow, Charles. "A Nation of Cowards?" *The New York Times,* February 21, 2009, p. A21. Available at: http://www.nytimes.com/2009/02/21/opinion/21blow.html

Blumstein, Philip, and Pepper Schwartz. *American Couples.* New York: William Morrow, 1983.

Boaz, Franz, Handbook of American Indian Languages (Washington, D.C.: Government Printing Office, 1911). Available at: https://archive.org/details/handbookamerica00fracgoog.

Bock, Jane. "Doing the Right Thing? Single Mothers by Choice and the Struggle for Legitimacy." *Gender & Society,* 14, no. 1 (2000): 62–86.

Boero, Natalie. "All the News That's Fat to Print: The American 'Obesity Epidemic' and the Media." *Qualitative Sociology,* 30, no. 1 (2007): 41–60.

Boero, Natalie. *Killer Fat: Media, Medicine, and Morals in the American "Obesity Epidemic."* New Brunswick, NJ: Rutgers University Press, 2012.

Bogaert, A. F. "Asexuality: Its Prevalence and Associated Factors in a National Probability Sample." *Journal of Sex Research,* 41 (2004): 279–287.

Bonilla-Silva, Eduardo. *Racism without Racists: Color-Blind Racism and the Persistence of Racial Inequality in America.* Lanham, MD: Rowman & Littlefield Publishers, 2003.

Bonnicksen, Thomas. "Forests Can Give Us Breathing Room on Kyoto Rules." *Houston Chronicle,* November 15, 2000.

Boonstra, Heather. "What is Behind the Decline in Teen Pregnancy Rates." *Alan Guttmacher Institute,* 2014. Available at: https://www.guttmacher.org/gpr/2014/09/what-behind-declines-teen-pregnancy-rates

Bordo, Susan. "Anorexia Nervosa: Psychopathology as the Crystallization of Culture." In *Unbearable Weight: Feminism, Western Culture, and the Body* (pp. 139–164). Berkeley, CA: University of California Press, 1993 [1985].

Boswell, John. *Same-Sex Unions in Premodern Europe.* New York: Vintage, 1995.

Bourdieu, Pierre. Distinction: *A Social Critique of the Judgment of Taste.* Cambridge, MA: Harvard University Press, 1984.

Bourgois, Philippe. *In Search of Respect: Selling Crack in El Barrio.* New York: Cambridge University Press, 1995.

Bowen, *James. A History of Western Education: Civilization of Europe, Sixth to Sixteenth Century.* New York: Palgrave Macmillan, 1976.

Bowles, Samuel. *Schooling in Capitalist America: Educational Reform and the Contradictions of Economic Life.* New York: Basic Books, 1976.

Boyd, Elizabeth A., Richard A. Berk, and Karl A. Hamner. "Motivated by Hatred or Prejudice: Categorization of Hate-Motivated Crimes in Two Police Divisions." *Law and Society Review,* 30, no. 4 (1996): 819–850.

Boyd, W., and E. King. *History of Western Education.* Lanham, MD: Littlefield Adams, 1978.

Brault, Matthew W. "Americans with Disabilities: 2010." *U.S. Census Bureau, Current Population Reports,* July 2012. Available at: https://www.census.gov/prod/2012pubs/p70-131.pdf

Braveman, Paula A., Shiriki Kumanyika, Jonathan Fielding, Thomas LaVeist, Luisa N. Borrell, Ron Manderscheid, and Adewale Troutman. "Health Disparities and Health Equity: The Issue Is Justice." *American Journal of Public Health,* 1101, Supp 1 (2011): S149–S155.

Breiding, Matthew J., Sharon G. Smith, Kathleen C. Basile, Mikel L. Walters, Jieru Chen, and Melissa T. Merrick. "Prevalence and Characteristics of Sexual Violence, Stalking, and Intimate Partner Violence Victimization—National Intimate Partner and Sexual Violence Survey, United States, 2011." *Center for Disease Control and Prevention, Surveillance Summaries,* September 5, 2014. Available at: http://www.cdc.gov/mmwr/preview/mmwrhtml/ss6308a1.htm?s_cid=ss6308a1_e

Bridges, Tristan, 2016. "Why Popular Boy Names are More Popular than Popular Girl Names." *Feminist Reflections,* blog. Available at: https://thesocietypages.org/feminist/2016/02/25/why-popular-boy-names-are-more-popular-than-popular-girl-names/

Bridges, Tristan, and Melody L. Boyd. "On the Marriageability of Men." *Sociology Compass,* 10, no. 1 (2016): 48–64

Brockman, David E., Kalla, Joshua, and Sekhon, Jasjeet S. *The Design of Field Experiments with Survey Outcomes: A Framework for Selecting More Efficient, Robust, and Ethical Designs* (December 7, 2016). Available at SSRN: https://ssrn.com/abstract=2742869

Broda, Christian, Ephraim Leibtag, and David E. Weinstein. "The Role of Prices in Measuring the Poor's Living Standards." *Journal of Economic Perspectives,* 23, no. 2 (2009): 77–97.

Brodkin, Karen. *How Jews Became White Folks and What That Says about Race in America.* New Brunswick, NJ: Rutgers University Press, 1998.

Brott, Armin. "The Battered Statistic Syndrome." *Washington Post,* July 31, 1994.

Brown, DeNeen and Pamela Constable. "West Africans in Washington say they are Being Stigmatized because of Ebola Fear." The Washington Post, October 16, 2014. Available at: https://www.washingtonpost.com/local/

west-africans-in-washington-say-they-are-being-stigmatized-because-of-ebola-fear/2014/10/16/39442d18-54c6-11e4-892e-602188e70e9c_story.html.

Brown, Lester R. *Outgrowing the Earth: The Food Security Challenge in an Age of Falling Water Tables and Rising Temperatures.* New York: Norton, 2005.

Brown, Michael E., ed. *Theories of War and Peace.* Cambridge, MA: MIT Press, 1998.

Brown, Taylor N. T., and Jody L. Herman. "Intimate Partner Violence and Sexual Abuse among LGBT People: A Review of Existing Research." *The Williams Institute,* November 2015. Available at: http://williamsinstitute.law.ucla.edu/wp-content/uploads/Intimate-Partner-Violence-and-Sexual-Abuse-among-LGBT-People.pdf

Brown, Tony N. "Critical Race Theory Speaks to the Sociology of Mental Health: Mental Health Problems Produced by Racial Stratification." *Journal of Health and Social Behavior,* 44 (September 2003): 292–301.

Brückner, Hannah, and Peter Bearman. "After the Promise: The STD Consequences of Adolescent Virginity Pledges." *Journal of Adolescent Health,* 36, no. 4 (2005): 271–278.

Bryner, Jeanna. "Teen Birth Rates Higher in Highly Religious States." MSNBC.com, September 16, 2009. Available at: www.msnbc.msn.com/id/32884806

Bryson, Bethany. "Anything but Heavy Metal": Symbolic Exclusion and Musical Dislikes. *American Sociological Review,* 61, no. 5 (1996): 884–899.

Bumpass, Larry, and H. Lu. "Trends in Cohabitation and Implications for Children's Family Contexts in the United States." *Population Studies,* 54 (2000): 29–41.

Burawoy, Michael. *Manufacturing Consent.* Chicago, IL: University of Chicago Press, 1980.

Burdick, Eugene, and Arthur J. Brodbeck. *American Voting Behavior.* Westport, CT: Greenwood Press, 1977.

Bureau of Justice Statistics. "Law Enforcement." *Office of Justice Programs,* 2014. Available at: https://www.bjs.gov/index.cfm?ty=tp&tid=7

Bureau of Justice Statistics, "National Prisoner Statistics, 1978–2015." Available at https://www.bjs.gov/content/pub/pdf/p15.pdf.

Bureau of Justice Statistics. "Prisoners in 2015." Office of Justice Programs, 2016. Available at: https://www.bjs.gov/index.cfm?ty=pbdetail&iid=5869.

Bureau of Justice Statistics. "Rape and Sexual Assault among College-age, 1995–2013." *Office of Justice Programs,* December 11, 2014. Available at: Females https://www.bjs.gov/index.cfm?ty=pbdetail&iid=5176

Bureau of Labor Statistics. The Employment Situation—July 2015. *U.S. Department of Labor,* August 7, 2015. Available at: https://www.bls.gov/news.release/archives/empsit_08072015.pdf

Bureau of Labor Statistics. "Labor Force Characteristics by Race and Ethnicity, 2015." *United States Department of Labor,* September, 2015. Available at: https://www.bls.gov/opub/reports/race-and-ethnicity/2015/home.htm

Bureau of Labor Statistics. "Monthly Labor Review, 2016." U.S. Department of Labor, 2016. Available at: https://www.bls.gov/opub/mlr/2016

Burger, Jerry. "Replicating Milgram: Would People Still Obey Today?" *American Psychologist,* 64, no. 1 (2009): 1–11.

Burgess, A., and N. Hanrahan. "Identifying Forensic Markers in Elderly Sexual Abuse." Washington, DC: National Institute of Justice, 2006.

Burke, Lindsey, "How Members of the 111th Congress Practice Private School Choice," The Heritage Foundation, April 20, 2009: http://www.heritage.org/education/report/how-members-the-111th-congress-practice-private-school-choice

Burleson, William E. *Bi America: Myths, Truths and Struggles of an Invisible Community.* London: Harrington Park Press, 2005.

Burnett, S. B., C. J. Gatrell, C. L. Cooper, P. Sparrow. "Well-balanced families?: A gendered analysis of work-life balance policies and work family practices." *Gender in Management: An International Journal,* 25, no. 7 (2010): 534–549.

Burroughs, Edgar Rice. *Tarzan of the Apes.* New York: A. L. Burt, 1914.

Burton, Linda M., Diane Purvin, and Raymon Garrett-Peters. 2009. "Longitudinal Ethnography: Uncovering Domestic Abuse." In *The Craft of Life Course Research,* edited by Glen H. Elder, Jr and Janet Z. Giele (pp. 70–92). New York, NY: The Guilford Press.

Buss, David M. "Evolutionary Psychology: A New Paradigm for Psychological Science." *Psychological Inquiry,* 6, no. 1 (1995): 1–30.

Butler, Katy. "Beyond Rivalry: A Hidden World of Sibling Violence." *New York Times,* February 28, 2006.

Buttel, Frederick H. "New Directions in Environmental Sociology." *Annual Review of Sociology,* 13 (1987): 465–488.

Califano, J. A. "A Punishment-Only Prison Policy." *America* (February, 1998): 3–4.

Cameron, Rondo, and Larry Neal. *A Concise Economic History of the World.* New York: Oxford University Press, 2002.

Campbell-Kelly, Martin. *From Airline Reservations to Sonic the Hedgehog: A History of the Software Industry.* Cambridge, MA: MIT Press, 2004.

Cancian, Francesca. *The Feminization of Love.* New York: Cambridge University Press, 1987.

Cancian, Francesca M. *Love in America: Gender and Self-Development.* Cambridge, UK: Cambridge University Press, 1987.

Candland, D. K. *Feral Children and Clever Animals: Reflections on Human Nature.* New York: Oxford University Press, 1993.

Cannon, Angie. "DWB: Driving While Black." *U.S. News and World Report,* March 15, 1999, 72.

Caplow, Theodore. Rule Enforcement without Visible Means: Christmas Gift Giving in Middletown. *American Journal of Sociology,* 89, no. 6 (1984): 1306–1323

Cardoso, Fernando, and Ernesto Faletto. *Dependency and Development in Latin America.* Berkeley: University of California Press, 1978.

Carey, Benedict. "Most Will Be Mentally Ill at Some Point, Study Says." *The New York Times*, June 7, 2005. Available at: http://www.nytimes.com/2005/06/07/health/most-will-be-mentally-ill-at-some-point-study-says.html?_r=0

Carey, Kate B., Sarah E. Durney, Robyn L. Shepardson, and Michael P. Carey. "Incapacitated and Forcible Rape of College Women: Prevalence Across the First Year." *Journal of Adolescent Health,* 56, no. 6 (2015): 678–680.

Carnes, Mark. *Secret Ritual and Manhood in Victorian America.* New Haven, CT: Yale University Press, 1989.

Carrington, Christopher. *No Place Like Home: Relationships and Family Life among Lesbians and Gay Men.* Chicago, IL: University of Chicago Press, 2002.

Caruso, Eugene M., Dobromir A. Rahnev, and Mahzarin R. Banaji. "Using Conjoint Analysis to Detect Discrimination: Revealing Covert Preferences in Overt Choices." *Social Cognition,* 27, no. 1 (February 2009): 128–137.

Casper, Lynne M., and Suzanne M. Bianchi. *Continuity and Change in the American Family.* Thousand Oaks, CA: Sage Publications, 2002.

Catalyst. *Women of Color in Corporate Management: Three Years Later.* New York: Catalyst, 2003. Available at: www.catalystwomen.org

Catalyst. "Quick Takes: Single People." New York: Catalyst, 2009.

Catton, William Jr., and Riley E. Dunlap. "Environmental Sociology: A New Paradigm." *The American Sociologist,* 13 (1978): 41–49.

Cazenave, N., and M. Straus. "Race, Class, Network Embeddedness and Family Violence: A Search for Potent Support Systems." *Journal of Comparative Family Studies*, 10, no. 3 (1979), 282–300.

Celebrity Net Worth. Accessed May 4, 2017. Available at: http://www.celebritynetworth.com/richest-celebrities/actors/daniel-radcliffe-net-worth/

Census India. "6. State of Literacy," 2011. Available at: http://censusindia.gov.in/2011-prov-results/data_files/india/Final_PPT_2011_chapter6.pdf

Centers for Disease Control and Prevention (CDC). *Healthy People, 2010.* Atlanta: Centers for Disease Control, 2006.

Centers for Disease Control and Prevention (CDC). 2013. Available at http://www.cdc.gov/men/lcod/2013/index.htm; http://www.cdc.gov/women/lcod/2013/index.htm

Centers for Disease Control and Prevention (CDC). 2013. "CDC Report: Mental Illness Surveillance Among U.S. Adults." Accessed May 17, 2017. Available at: https://www.cdc.gov/mentalhealthsurveillance/

Centers for Disease Control and Prevention (CDC). National Survey of Family Growth. Available at http://www.cdc.gov/nchs/nsfg/key_statistics/s.htm#sexualactivity; CDC, NCHS Data Brief, No. 232, January 2016, available at https://www.cdc.gov/nchs/data/databriefs/db232.pdf

Central Intelligence Agency, "Mother's Mean Age at First Birth," The World Factbook, 2016: https://www.cia.gov/library/publications/the-world-factbook/fields/2256.html

Chaffee, John. *The Thorny Gates of Learning in Sung China: A Social History of Examinations.* New York: Cambridge University Press, 1985.

Chalabi, Mona. "How Many Women Earn More than their Husbands?" *Fivethrityeight.com*, March, 2015. Available at: https://fivethirtyeight.com/datalab/how-many-women-earn-more-than-their-husbands/

Chalabi, Mona. "How Many Times Does the Average Person Move?" *FiveThirtyEight.com*, January 29, 2015. Available at: https://fivethirtyeight.com/datalab/how-many-times-the-average-person-moves/

Chambliss, William J. *Power, Politics and Crime.* Boulder, CO: Westview Press, 2000.

Chambliss, William J., and Marjorie Zatz, eds. *Making Law.* Bloomington: Indiana University Press, 1993.

zChang, Jeff. *Total Chaos: The Art and Aesthetics of Hip-Hop.* New York: Basic Civitas Books, 2007.

Charles, Maria, and David B. Grusky. *Occupational Ghettos: The Worldwide Segregation of Women and Men.* Stanford, CA: Stanford University Press, 2004.

Chase-Dunn, Christopher. "The System of World Cities." In M. Timberlake, ed., *Urbanization in the World Economy* (pp. 269–292). Beverly Hills, CA: Sage, 1985.

Chauncey, George. *Gay New York: Gender, Urban Culture, and the Making of the Gay Male World, 1890–1940.* Unknown edition. Basic Books, 1993.

Cherlin, Andrew J. *Marriage, Divorce, Remarriage: Revised and Enlarged Edition.* Cambridge, MA: Harvard University Press, 1992.

Cherlin, Andrew J. *The Marriage-Go-Round: The State of Marriage and the Family in America Today.* New York, NY: Vintage, 2009.

Child Soldiers International. Global Report, 2008. *Coalition to Stop the Use of Child Soldiers,* 2008. Available at: https://www.child-soldiers.org/Handlers/Download.ashx?IDMF=26c0549d-aa35-4f1a-8e34-5956f8e2ec51

Child Trends. "Foster care: Indicators on children and youth," Child Trends Data Bank (April 2012).

Children's Defense Fund. "Child Poverty in America." Washington, DC: September 16, 2016. Available at: www.childrensdefense.org/library/data/child-poverty-in-america-2015.pdf

Christakis, Dimitri A. "Early Television Exposure and Subsequent Attention Problems in Children." *Pediatrics,* April 2004.

Christakis, Nicholas A., and James H. Fowler. *Connected: The Surprising Power of Our Social Networks and How They Shape Our Lives.* New York, NY: Little, Brown, 2009.

Chubb, John E., and Terry M. Moe. 1990. "America's Public Schools: Choice Is a Panacea." *The Brookings Review* 8 (1990): 4–12.

CIA World Factbook. "Field Listing: Labor Force – by Occupation." *The World Factbook,* 2014. Available at: https://www.cia.gov/library/publications/the-world-factbook/fields/2048.html

CIA World Factbook. "Field Listing: Literacy." *The World Factbook*, 2015. Available at: https://www.cia.gov/library/publications/the-world-factbook/fields/2103.html

CIA World Factbook. Country Comparison: GDP–Per Capita (PPP). *The World Factbook*, 2016. Available at: https://www.cia.gov/library/publications/the-world-factbook/rankorder/2004rank.html

CIA World Factbook. Country Comparison: Life Expectancy at Birth. *The World Factbook*. 2016. Available at: https://www.cia.gov/library/publications/the-world-factbook/rankorder/2102rank.html

CIA World Factbook. Country Comparison: Total Fertility Rate. *The World Factbook*. 2016. Available at: https://www.cia.gov/library/publications/the-world-factbook/rankorder/2127rank.html

CIA World Factbook. "Field Listing: Age Structure." *The World Factbook*, 2016. Available at: https://www.cia.gov/library/publications/the-world-factbook/fields/2010.html

CIA World Factbook. "Field Listing: Death Rate." *The World Factbook*, 2016. Available at: https://www.cia.gov/library/publications/the-world-factbook/fields/2102.html

CIA World Factbook. "Field Listing: Infant Mortality Rate." *The World Factbook*, 2016. Available at: https://www.cia.gov/library/Publications/the-world-factbook/fields/2091.html

CIA World Factbook. "Field Listing: Total Fertility Rate." *The World Factbook*, 2016. Available at: https://www.cia.gov/library/publications/the-world-factbook/fields/2127.html

CIA World Factbook. "Field Listing: Urbanization." *The World Factbook*, 2016. Available at: https://www.cia.gov/library/publications/the-world-factbook/fields/2212.html

CIA World Factbook. "Infant Mortality." *The World Factbook*, 2016. Available at: https://www.cia.gov/library/publications/the-world-factbook/rankorder/2091rank.html

CIA World Factbook. "Life Expectancy at Birth." *The World Factbook*, 2016. Available at: https://www.cia.gov/library/PUBLICATIONS/the-world-factbook/rankorder/a.html

Cipolla, Carlo M. *Before the Industrial Revolution.* New York: Norton, 1994.

Claffey, Sharon T., and Kristin D. Mickelson. "Division of Household Labor and Distress: The Role of Perceived Fairness for Employed Mothers." *Sex Roles,* 60, no. 11–12 (2009): 819–831.

Clark, David D. *Analysis of Return Rates of the Inmate College Program Participants.* Albany: State of New York Department of Correctional Services, 1991.

Clark, Nancy, and William H. Worger. *South Africa: The Rise and Fall of Apartheid.* Nashville, TN: Longmans, 2004.

Clinton, William J. Commencement Address at Oregon State University, Portland, Oregon, June 13, 1998. Available at: http://www.presidency.ucsb.edu/ws/?pid=56140

Cloward, Richard A., and Lloyd E. Ohlin. *Delinquency and Opportunity: A Theory of Delinquent Gangs.* New York: The Free Press, 1960.

Coder, J., L. Rainwater, and T. M. Smeeding. 2001. "Poverty Across States, Nations, and Continents." In K. Vleminckx and T. M. Smedding (eds.), *Child Well-Being, Child Poverty, and Child Policy in Modern Nations: What Do We Know?* (pp. 33–74). Bristol, UK: Policy Press; Toronto, Canada: University of Toronto Press.

Coe, Neil M., Jennifer Johns, and Kevin Ward. "The Embedded Transnational: The Internationalisation Strategies of the Leading Transnational Temporary Staffing Agencies." *Working Paper 10, Geographies of Temporary Staffing Unit.* Manchester, UK: University of Manchester, May 2009.

Cohen, Patricia. "As Ethnics Panels Expand Grip, No Research Field Is Off Limits." *New York Times,* February 28, 2007, pp. 1, 15.

Cohen, Philip. "Big Name Drops in the News." *Family Inequality (blog).* December 12, 2012. Available at: https://familyinequality.wordpress.com/2012/12/10/big-name-drops-in-the-news/

Cohen, Philip. "Family Diversity is the New Normal for America's Children." *Council on Contemporary Families, Brief Reports,* September 4, 2014. Available at: https://contemporaryfamilies.org/the-new-normal/

Cohn, D'Vera, and Rich Morin. "Who Moves? Who Stays Put? Where's Home?" *Pew Research Center, Social & Demographic Trends,* December 17, 2008. Available at: http://www.pewsocialtrends.org/2008/12/17/who-moves-who-stays-put-wheres-home/

Cohn, D'Vera, and Paul Taylor. Baby Boomers Approach 65—Glumly. *Pew Research Center, Social & Demographic Trends.* December 20, 2010. Available at: http://www.pewsocialtrends.org/2010/12/20/baby-boomers-approach-65-glumly/

Cole, David. "When Race Is the Reason." *The Nation,* March 15, 1999, pp. 22–24.

Cole, T. B. "Rape at U.S. Colleges Often Fueled by Alcohol." *Journal of the American Medical Association,* 296 (August 2, 2006): 504–505.

Coleman, Kenneth, ed. *A History of Georgia.* Athens: University of Georgia Press, 1991.

Coleman, James S., Ernest Q. Campbell, Carol J. Hobson, James McPartland, Alexander M. Mood, Frederic D. Weinfield, and Robert L. York. "Equality of Educational Opportunity." *U.S. Department of Health, Education, and Welfare,* 1966. Available at: http://files.eric.ed.gov/fulltext/ED012275.pdf

Coleman, James, Thomas Hoffer, and Sally Kilgore. "Cognitive Outcomes in Public and Private Schools." *Sociology of Education,* 55, no. 2 (1982): 65–76.

Coley, Richard, and Paul E. Barton. *Locked Up and Locked Out: An Educational Perspective on the U.S. Prison Population.* Princeton, NJ: Educational Testing Service, 2006.

College Board. "Trends in College Pricing 2016." *Trends in Higher Education Series,* 2016. Available at: https://trends.collegeboard.org/sites/default/files/2016-trends-college-pricing-web_0.pdf

Collins, Patricia Hill. *Black Feminist Thought: Knowledge, Consciousness, and the Politics of Empowerment.* New York, NY: Routledge, 1990.

Collins, Randall. *The Credential Society: A Historical Sociology of Education and Stratification.* New York: Academic Press, 1979.

Common Sense Media. "Landmark Report: U.S. Teens Use an Average of Nine Hours of Media Per Day, Tweens Use Six Hours," *CommonSenseMedia.org*, November 3, 2015a. Available at: https://www.commonsensemedia.org/about-us/news/press-releases/landmark-report-us-teens-use-an-average-of-nine-hours-of-media-per-day#

Common Sense Media. "The Common Sense Census: Media Use by Tweens and Teens." *Thrive Foundation for Youth,* 2015b. Available at: ttps://www.commonsensemedia.org/sites/default/files/uploads/research/census_executivesummary.pdf

Condry, J., and S. Condry. "Sex Differences: A Study in the Eye of the Beholder." *Child Development,* 47, 1976.

Connell, Catherine. *School's Out: Gay and Lesbian Teachers in the Classroom.* Berkeley, CA: University of California Press, 2014.

Conrad, Peter. "Medicalization and Social Control." *Annual Review of Sociology,* 18, no. 1 (1992): 209–232.

Cookson, Peter W. Jr., and Caroline Hodges Persell. *Preparing for Power: America's Elite Boarding Schools.* New York: Basic Books, 1985.

Cooky, Cheryl, Michael Messner, and Michela Musto. "It's Dude Time!": A Quarter Century of Excluding Women's Sports in Televised News and Highlights Shows. *Communication & Sport,* 3, no. 3 (2015): 261–287.

Cooley, Charles Horton. *Human Nature and the Social Order* (1902). New York: Transaction, 1983.

Cooley, Charles Horton. *On Self and Social Organization* (1909). Hans Joachim-Schubert, ed. Chicago, IL: University of Chicago Press, 1990.

Coontz, Stephanie. *Social Origins of Private Life: A History of American Families, 1600–1900.* New York: Verso, 1988.

Coontz, Stephanie. *The Way We Never Were: American Families and the Nostalgia Trap.* New York, NY: Basic Books, 1992.

Coontz, Stephanie. *Marriage: A History.* New York: Viking, 2005.

Cooper, Frederick. *Colonialism in Question: Theory, Knowledge, History.* Berkeley: University of California Press, 2005.

Corbin, Juliet, and Anselm Strauss. "Managing Chronic Illness at Home: Three Lines of Work." *Qualitative Sociology,* 8, no. 3 (1985): 224–247.

Correll, Shelley. "Gender and the Career Choice Process: The Role of Biased Self-Assessments." *American Journal of Sociology,* 106, no. 6 (2001): 1691–1730.

Correll, Shelley J., Stephen Benard, and In Paik. "Getting a Job: Is There a Motherhood Penalty?" *American Journal of Sociology,* 112 (2007): 1297–1338.

Coser, Lewis A. *The Functions of Social Conflict.* Glencoe, IL: The Free Press, 1956.

Costantini, Edmond. "Political Women and Political Ambition: Closing the Gender Gap." *American Journal of Political Science,* 34, no. 3 (1990): 741–770.

Costello, B. J., and P. R. Vowell, "Testing Control Theory and Differential Association: A Reanalysis of the Richmond Youth Project Data." *Criminology,* 37, no. 4 (1999): 815–842.

Couprie, Helene. "Time Allocation within the Family: Welfare Implications of Life in a Couple." *Economic Journal,* January 2007: 1–12.

Courtenay, Will H. "College Men's Health: An Overview and a Call to Action." *Journal of American College Health,* 46, no. 6 (1998): 279–290.

Cox, Daniel, Robert P. Jones, Juhen Navarro-Rivera. "I Know What You Did Last Sunday: Measuring Social Desirability Bias in Self-Reported Religious Behavior, Belief, and Identity." Paper presented at the Public Religion Research Institute, May 17, 2014. Available at: https://www.prri.org/academic/study-know-last-sunday-finds-americans-significantly-inflate-religious-participation/

Cowan, Ruth Schwartz. *More Work for Mother: The Ironies of Household Technology from the Open Hearth to the Microwave.* New York, NY: Basic Books, 1983.

Craig, Kellina M., and Craig R. Waldo. "So, What's a Hate Crime Anyway? Young Adults' Perceptions of Hate Crimes, Victims and Perpetrators." *Law and Human Behavior,* 20, no. 2 (April 1996): 113–129.

Crister, Greg. *Fat Land: How Americans Became the Fattest People in the World.* Boston: Houghton Mifflin, 2003.

Crittenden, Ann. *The Price of Motherhood: Why the Most Important Job in the World Is Still the Least Valued.* New York: Metropolitan Books, 2001.

Crittenden, Ann. *If You've Raised Kids, You Can Manage Anything.* New York: Gotham, 2005.

Crompton, Rosemary. *Class and Stratification: An Introduction to Current Debates.* Cambridge, UK: Polity, 1993.

Cross, Harry, Genevieve Kenney, Jane Mell, and Wendy Zimmerman. *Employer Hiring Practices: Differential Treatment of Hispanic and Anglo Job Seekers.* Washington, DC: The Urban Institute Press, 1990.

Cumings, Bruce. *Korea's Place in the Sun.* New York: W. W. Norton, 1998.

Cummings, H. J. "Permanent Temps." *Chicago Tribune,* 2004 (June 8), 12.

Current Population Survey, 2017. "Employed Persons by Detailed Occupation, Sex, Race and Hispanic or Latino Origins." Labor Force Statistics from the Current Population Survey, Bureau of Labor Statistics, 2017. Availabe at: https://www.bls.gov/cps/cpsaat11.htm

Currie, Elliot. *Confronting Crime: An American Challenge.* New York: Pantheon, 1985.

Dahlgreen, Will. "You Are Not Alone: Most People Believe that Aliens Exist." *YouGov US*, September 28, 2015. Available at: https://today.yougov.com/news/2015/09/28/you-are-not-alone-most-people-believe-aliens-exist/

Dailard, C. "Sex Education: Politicians, Parents, Teachers and Teens." *The Guttmacher Report on Public Policy*, 4, no. 1 (2001): 9–12.

Daley, Suzanne. "Greek's Wealth is Found in Many Places, Just Not on Tax Returns." *The New York Times*, May 2, 2010, pp. 1, 20.

Daly, Kathleen. "Neither Conflict Nor Labeling Nor Paternalism Will Suffice: Intersections of Race, Ethnicity, Gender, and Family in Criminal Court Decisions." *Crime and Delinquency*, 35 (1989): 136–168.

Daly, Kathleen, and M. Chesney-Lind. "Feminism and Criminology." *Justice Quarterly*, 5 (1988): 497–538.

Daly, Martin, and Margo Wilson. "Darwinism and the Roots of Machismo." Scientific American 10 (1999): 8–14.

Daly, Martin, and Margo Wilson. *The Truth about Cinderella: A Darwinian View of Parental Love.* New Haven, CT: Yale University Press, 1999.

Darroch, J. E., David Landry, and Susheela Singh. "Changing Emphases in Sexuality Education in U.S. Public Secondary Schools, 1988–1999." *Family Planning Perspectives*, 32, no. 5 (2000): 204–211, 265.

Davenport, Charles. *State Laws Limiting Marriage Selection Examined in the Light of Eugenics.* Eugenics Record Office, Cold Spring Harbor, NY, 1913.

Davis, Devra Lee, Michelle B. Gottlieb, and Julie R. Stampnitzky. "Reduced Ratio of Male to Female Births in Several Industrial Countries: A Sentinel Health Indicator?" *Journal of the American Medical Association*, 279, no. 13 (April 1998).

Davis, Georgiann. *Contesting Intersex: The Dubious Diagnosis.* New York, NY: NYU Press, 2015.

Davis, Kingsley, and Wilbert E. Moore. "Some Principles of Stratification." *ASR*, 10, no. 3 (1945): 242–249.

Davtyan, Mariam, Brandon Brown, and Morenike Oluwatoyin Folayan. "Addressing Ebola-Related Stigma: Lessons Learned from HIV/AIDS." *Global Health Action.* 7 (2014): 1–4. Available at: http://journals.co-action.net/index.php/gha/article/view/26058

Dawkins, Richard. *The Selfish Gene.* New York, NY: Oxford University Press, 1978.

De Rougemont, Denis. *Love in the Western World.* Princeton, NJ: Princeton University Press, 1983.

Death Penalty Information Organization. Executions and Death Sentences Around the World, 2017. Available at: https://deathpenaltyinfo.org/death-penalty-international-perspective#interexec

Defronzo, James. *Revolutions and Revolutionary Movements.* Boulder, CO: Westview Press, 1996.

Degler, Carl N. *At Odds: Women and the Family in America from the Revolution to the Present.* New York: Oxford University Press, 1980.

Dellaposta, Daniel, Yongren Shi, and Michael Macy. "Why Do Liberals Drink Lattes?" *American Journal of Sociology*, 120, no. 5 (2015): 1473–1511.

DeMause, Lloyd. *The History of Childhood.* New York, NY: Psychohistory Press, 1974.

DeNavas-Walt, Carmen, and Bernadette D. Proctor. Income and Poverty in the United States: 2014. *U.S. Census Bureau, Current Population Reports*, September 2015. Available at: https://www.census.gov/content/dam/Census/library/publications/2015/demo/p60-252.pdf

DePaolo, Bella, and E. Kay Trimberger. "Single Women." *Sociologists for Women in Society Fact Sheet,* Winter 2008. Available at: www.socwomen.org/wint08_fs.pdf

DeParle, Jason. "Census Reports a Sharp Increase in Never-Married Mothers; Puncturing Stereotypes of Out-of-Wedlock Births." *New York Times,* July 14, 1993.

Department of Social and Economic Affairs. "Total Population by Sex (Thousands)." *United Nations,* 2015. Available at: https://esa.un.org/unpd/wpp/DataQuery/

Desilver, Drew. "U.S. Students' Academic Achievement Still Lags That of Their Peers in Many Other Countries." *Pew Research Center, FactTank,* February 15, 2017. Available at: http://www.pewresearch.org/fact-tank/2015/02/02/u-s-students-improving-slowly-in-math-and-science-but-still-lagging-internationally/

Desilver, Drew. "U.S. Voter Turnout Trails Most Developed Countries." *The Pew Research* Center, August 2, 2016. Available at: http://www.pewresearch.org/fact-tank/2016/08/02/u-s-voter-turnout-trails-most-developed-countries/

Deux, Kay, and Lawrence S. Wrightsman. *Social Psychology,* 5th ed. Pacific Grove, CA: Thomson/Brooks Cole, 1988.

DeVault, Marjorie. Producing Family Time: Practices of Leisure Activity Beyond the Home. *Qualitative Sociology,* 23, no. 4 (2000): 485–503.

Dickens, Charles. *A Tale of Two Cities.* Leipzig: Bernhard Tauchnitz, 1859.

Diefendorf, Sarah. "After the Wedding Night: Sexual Abstinence and Masculinities over the Life Course." *Gender & Society,* 29, no. 5 (2015): 647–669.

DiMaggio, Paul, and Filiz Garip. "How Network Externalities Can Exacerbate Intergroup Inequality." *American Journal of Sociology,* 116 (2011): 1887–1933.

Doan, Long, Annalise Loehr, and Lisa R. Miller. "Formal Rights and Informal Privileges for Same-Sex Couples: Evidence from a National Survey Experiment." *American Sociological Review,* 79, no. 6 (2014): 1172–1195.

Dolnick, Sam. "Ethnic Differences Emerge in Plastic Surgery." *The New York Times*, February 18, 2011.

Domhoff, G. William. *Who Rules America?* Englewood-Cliffs, NJ: Prentice-Hall, 1967.

Domhoff, G. William. *The Bohemian Grove and Other Ruling Class Retreats.* New York: Harper and Row, 1974.

Domhoff, G. William. *Who Rules America? Power and Politics,* 4th ed. Boston: McGraw-Hill, 2002.

Doyle, Roger. "Ethnic Groups in the World." *Scientific American,* 279, no. 3 (1998): 30.

Drake, Bruce. "Incarceration Gap Widens between Blacks and Whites." *Pew Research Center,* September 6, 2013. Available at: http://www.pewresearch.org/fact-tank/2013/09/06/incarceration-gap-between-whites-and-blacks-widens/

"Dreams Only Money Can Buy." *BusinessWeek,* April 14, 2003, 66.

Dreger, Alive. *Hermaphrodites and the Medical Invention of Sex.* Cambridge: Harvard University Press, 1998.

The Drug Policy Alliance. "The Drug War, Mass Incarceration and Race," 2016. Available at: https://www.drugpolicy.org/sites/default/files/DPA%20Fact%20Sheet_Drug%20War%20Mass%20Incarceration%20and%20Race_(Feb.%202016).pdf.

DuBois, W. E. B. *The Philadelphia Negro* (1899). Elijah Anderson and Isabel Eaton, eds. Philadelphia: University of Pennsylvania Press, 1996.

DuBois, W. E. B. *The Souls of Black Folk* (1903). Bartleby.com, 1999.

Duggan, Maeve. "Gaming and Gamers," Pew Research Center, December 15, 2015: http://www.pewinternet.org/2015/12/15/gaming-and-gamers/

Duneier, Mitchell. *Sidewalk.* New York: Farrar, Straus and Giroux, 1999.

Durkheim, Émile. *The Division of Labor in Society* (1893). New York: The Free Press, 1997.

Durkheim, Émile. *The Rules of the Sociological Method* (1895). New York: The Free Press, 1997.

Durkheim, Émile. *Suicide* (1897). New York: Penguin Classics, 2007.

Eagan, Kevin, Ellen Bara Stolzenberg, Abigail K. Bates, Melissa C. Aragon, Maria Ramirez Suchard, and Cecilia Rios-Aguilar. *The American Freshman: National Norms, Fall 2015.* Cooperative Institutional Research Program at the Higher Education Research Institute at UCLA. 2015. Available at: https://www.insidehighered.com/news/2016/02/11/survey-finds-nearly-1-10-freshmen-plan-participating-campus-protests

Eating Disorders Hope. Statistics, 2017. Svailable at: https://www.eatingdisorderhope.com/information/statistics-studies

The Economist. "Caste in Doubt." 2010 (June 12), 46.

The Economist. "Mind the Gap." 2005c (June 11).

The Economist. "Secrets of Success." 2005e (September 8).

The Economist. "In Search of a New Economy." 2008b (November 6).

The Economist. "Light Work: Questioning the Hawthorne Effect." 2009a (June 4).

The Economist. "Special Report on the New Middle Classes." 2009d (February 14), 6.

The Economist, "The Underworked American." 2009e (June 13), 40.

The Economist. "Flushing Away Unfairness." July 10, 2010. Available at: http://www.economist.com/node/16542591

Edelman, Benjamin. "Red Light States: Who Buys Adult Online Entertainment?" *Journal of Economic Perspectives,* 23, no. 1 (Winter, 2009): 209–220.

Edin, Kathryn, and Maria Kefalas. *Promises I Can Keep: Why Poor Women Put Motherhood Before Marriage.* Berkeley, CA: University of California Press, 2005.

Edwards, S. S. M. "Neither Bad nor Mad: The Female Violent Offender Reassessed." *Women's Studies International Forum,* 9 (1986): 79–87.

Egley, Arlen Jr., and Christina E. O'Donnell. *Highlights of the 2007 National Youth Gang Survey.* Washington, DC, Office of Juvenile Justice and Delinquency Prevention, 2009.

Ehrenreich, Barbara. *Nickel and Dimed: On (Not) Getting by in America.* New York: Owl Books, 2001.

Ehrlich, Paul. *The Population Bomb.* New York: Ballantine Books, 1968.

Eisenstein, Elizabeth. *The Printing Revolution in Early Modern Europe.* New York: Cambridge University Press, 1993.

Ekman, Paul, and Wallace V. Friesen. *Facial Action Coding System: A Technique for the Measurement of Facial Movement.* Palo Alto, CA: Consulting Psychologists Press, 1978.

El Nasser, Haya. "Multiracial no longer boxed in by the Census." *USA Today* (March 3, 2010): 1.

Eliasoph, Nina. "Political Culture and the Presentation of a Political Self." *Theory and Society,* 19 (1990): 465–494.

Elliot, Jane. *The Eye of the Storm.* DVD, 1970. ABC News, New York.

Elliott, Diana B., and Jane Lawler Dye. "Unmarried Partner Households in the United States." A paper presented at the Annual Meeting of the Population Association of America, Philadelphia, March 31–April 2, 2005.

Emanuel, Gabriel. "America's High School Graduates Look Like Other Countries' High School Drop-Outs." *All Things Considered, NPR,* March 23, 2016. Available at: http://www.npr.org/sections/ed/2016/03/10/469831485/americas-high-school-graduates-look-like-other-countries-high-school-dropouts.

England, Paula. The Gender Revolution: Uneven and Stalled. *Gender & Society,* 24, no. 2 (2010): 149–166.

England, Paula, Emily Fitsgibbons Shafer, and Alison C. K. Fogerty. "Hooking Up and Forming Romantic Relationships on Today's College Campus." In Michael Kimmel and Amy Aronson (eds.), *The Gendered Society Reader* (pp. 531–547). New York: Oxford University Press, 2008.

Epstein, Helen. "Ghetto MIASMA: Enough to Make You Sick?" *The New York Times Magazine,* October 12, 2003. Available at: http://www.nytimes.com/2003/10/12/magazine/ghetto-miasma-enough-to-make-you-sick.html

Ericson, Richard V., and Keven D. Haggerty. *Policing the Risk Society.* Oxford, UK: Clarendon Press, 1997.

Erikson, Erik. *Identity and the Life Cycle: Selected Papers.* Chicago, IL: University of Chicago Press, 1959.

Erikson, Kai T. *Everything in Its Path: Destruction of Community in the Buffalo Creek Flood.* New York: Simon & Schuster, 1978.

Esping-Anderson, G. *The Three Worlds of Welfare Capitalism.* Princeton, NJ: Princeton University Press, 1990.

Etzioni, Amitai. *A Comparative Analysis of Complex Organization: On Power, Involvement, and Their Correlates.* Revised and enlarged ed. New York: Free Press, 1975.

Etzioni-Halevy, Eva. *Bureaucracy and Democracy: A Political Dilemma.* London: Routledge and Kegan Paul, 1983.

Evans, Peter B., and James E. Rauch. "Bureaucratic and Growth: A Cross-National Analysis of the Effects of 'Weberian' State Structures on Economic Growth." *American Sociological Review,* 64 (1999): 748–765.

Farber, Susan L. "Identical Twins Reared Apart." *Science,* 215 (February, 1982): 959–960.

Farkas, G. *Human Capital or Cultural Capital? Ethnicity and Poverty Groups in an Urban School District.* New York: Aldine, 1996.

Farkas, G., D. Sheehan, and R. P. Grobe. "Coursework Mastery and School Success: Gender, Ethnicity, and Poverty Groups within an Urban School District." *American Educational Research Journal,* 27, no. 4 (1990b): 807–827.

Faulks, Keith. *Political Sociology: A Critical Introduction.* New York: NYU Press, 2000.

Fausto-Sterling, Anne. *Sexing the Body: Gender Politics and the Construction of Sexuality.* New York, NY: Basic Books, 2000.

FBI Uniform Crime Reports. *Federal Bureau of Investigation,* 2016. Available at: https://ucr.fbi.gov/?came_from=https%3A//ucr.fbi.gov/crime-in-the-u.s/2016/crime-in-the-u.s.-2016

FBI Uniform Crime Reports. "Uniform Crime Reports, Crime in the United States." *U.S. Department of Justice,* 2014. Available at: https://ucr.fbi.gov/crime-in-the-u.s/2013/crime-in-the-u.s.-2013/tables/table-43

Feagin, Joe R. 2000. *Racist America: Roots, Current Realities, and Future Reparations.* New York: Routledge.

Federal Bureau of Investigation. "2014: Crime in the United States." 2014. Available at: https://ucr.fbi.gov/crime-in-the-u.s/2014/crime-in-the-u.s.-2014/persons-arrested/main

Federal Bureau of Investigation. "Police Employee Data," 2014. Available at: https://ucr.fbi.gov/crime-in-the-u.s/2014/crime-in-the-u.s.-2014/police-employee-data/main

Federal Bureau of Investigation. Crime in the United States, 2015. Available at: https://ucr.fbi.gov/crime-in-the-u.s/2015/crime-in-the-u.s.-2015/tables/table-42

Federal Bureau of Investigation. 2015 Hate Crime Statistics. Available at: https://ucr.fbi.gov/hate-crime/2015/tables-and-data-declarations/1tabledatadecpdf

Federal Bureau of Prisons. "Inmate Gender." *U.S. Federal Bureau of Prisons,* April 29, 2017. Available at: https://www.bop.gov/about/statistics/statistics_inmate_gender.jsp

Federal Bureau of Prisons. "Offenses." *U.S. Department of Justice,* 2017. Available at: https://www.bop.gov/about/statistics/statistics_inmate_offenses.jsp

Federal Trade Commission. "Identity Theft Tops FTC's Consumer Complaint Categories Again in 2014." February 27, 2015. Available at: https://www.ftc.gov/news-events/press-releases/2015/02/identity-theft-tops-ftcs-consumer-complaint-categories-again-2014

Feminist Majority Foundation. "FMF Study Shows Increase In Nationwide Single-Sex Public Education." *Feminist Newswire,* December 23, 2014. Available at: http://feminist.org/blog/index.php/2014/12/23/fmf-study-shows-increase-in-nationwide-single-sex-public-education/.

Ferguson, Ann Arnett. *Bad Boys: Public Schools in the Making of Black Masculinity.* Ann Arbor: University of Michigan Press, 2000.

Ferree, Myra, and Mueller, C. M. "Feminism and the Women's Movement: A Global Perspective." In *The Blackwell Companion to Social Movements.* New York: Wiley. 2007.

Ferree, Myra Marx, and Aili Mari Tripp, eds. *Global Feminism: Transnational Women's Activism, Organizing, and Human Rights.* New York, NY: NYU Press, 2006.

Fields, Jason, and Lynne M. Casper. "America's Families and Living Arrangements: March 2000." *Current Population Reports,* 2001: 520–537.

Filoux, J. C. "Inequalities and Social Stratification in Durkheim's Sociology." In S. P. Turner, ed., *Émile Durkheim: Sociologist and Moralist.* London: Routledge: 211–228, 1993.

Fingerhut, Hannah. "In Both Parties, Men and Women Differ Over Whether Women Still Face Obstacles to Progress." *Pew Research Center, Fact Tank,* August 16, 2016. Available at: http://www.pewresearch.org/fact-tank/2016/08/16/in-both-parties-men-and-women-differ-over-whether-women-still-face-obstacles-to-progress/

Finkelhor, David, Heather Turner, and Richard Ormrod. "Kid Stuff: The Nature and Impact of Peer and Sibling Violence on Younger and Older Children." *Child Abuse and Neglect,* 20 (2006): 1401–1421.

Firebaugh, Glen. "Does Foreign Capital Harm Poor Nations? New Estimates Based on Dixon and Boswell's Measures of Capital Penetration." *American Journal of Sociology,* 102, no. 2 (1996): 563–575.

Firebaugh, Glen. "Empirics of World Income Inequality." *American Journal of Sociology,* 104, no. 6 (1999): 1597–1630.

Firebaugh, Glen, and Frank D. Beck. "Does Economic Growth Benefit the Masses? Growth, Dependence, and Welfare in the Third World." *American Sociological Review,* 59, no. 5 (1994): 631–653.

Firebaugh, Glen, and Dumitru Sandu. "Who Supports Marketization and Democratization in Post-Communist Romania?" *Sociological Forum,* 13, no. 3 (1998): 521–541.

Fischer, Claude S., and Michael Hout. *Century of Difference: How America Changed in the Last One Hundred Years.* New York, NY: Russell Sage Foundation, 2006.

Fischer, Claude, Michael Hout, Martin Sanchez-Jankowski, Samuel R. Lucas, Ann Swidler, and Kim Voss. *Inequality by Design: Cracking the Bell Curve Myth.* Princeton, NJ: Princeton University Press, 1996.

Fisher, Allen. "Still 'Not Quite as Good as Having Your Own'? Toward a Sociology of Adoption." *Annual Review of Sociology,* 29 (2003): 335–361.

Fisher, Kimberley, Muriel Egerton, Jonathan I. Gershuny, and John P. Robinson. "Gender Convergence in the American Heritage Time Use Study (AHTUS)." *Social Indicators Research,* 2006.

Fitzgibbon, Marian, and Melinda Stolley. "Dying to Be Thin— Minority Women: The Untold Story." *Nova,* 2000. Available at: www.pbs.org/wgbh/nova/thin/minorities.html

Fitzpatrick/Austin, Laura. "Can Community Colleges Save the U.S. Economy?" *Time,* July 10, 2009, 48–51.

Flegal, Katherine M., Margaret D. Carroll, Cynthia L. Ogden, and Lester R. Curtin. "Prevalence and Trends in Obesity Among US Adults, 1999–2008." *JAMA,* 303, no. 3 (2010): 235–241.

Flegal, Katherine, Brian K. Kit, Heather Orpana, and Barry I. Graubard. "Association of All-Cause Mortality with Overweight and Obesity Using Standard Body Mass Index Categories: A Systematic Review and Meta-analysis." *JAMA,* 309, no. 1 (2013): 71–82.

Fleisher, M. S., and J. L. Krienert. "Life-Course Events, Social Networks, and the Emergence of Violence among Female Gang Members." *Journal of Community Psychology,* 32 (2004): 607–622.

Foner, Eric. "Hiring Quotas for White Males Only." *The Nation,* June 26, 1995, 924.

Foote, Christopher, and Christopher Goetz. "Testing Economic Hypotheses with State-Level Data: A Comment on Donohue and Levitt (2001)." *Federal Reserve Bank of Boston Working Paper,* November 2005.

Foran, John. *Theorizing Revolutions.* New York: Routledge, 1997.

Fordham, Signithia. *Blacked Out: Dilemmas of Race, Identity, and Success at Capital High.* Chicago, IL: University of Chicago Press, 1996.

Foreman, M. *AIDS and Men: Taking Risks of Taking Responsibility.* London: Zed Books, 1999.

Forum on Child and Family Statistics. "America's Children: Key National Indicators of Well-Being, 2009." *Federal Interagency Form on Child and Family Studies,* 2009. Available at: https://www.childstats.gov/pdf/ac2009/ac_09.pdf

Foucault, Michel. *A History of Sexuality, Volume 1.* New York, NY: Random House, 1979.

Fowlkes, M. R. "Single Worlds and Homosexual Lifestyles: Patterns of Sexuality and Intimacy." In A. S. Rossi, ed., *Sexuality across the Life Course* (pp. 151–184). Chicago, IL: University of Chicago Press, 1994.

Fox, Richard L., and Jennifer L. Lawless. "If Only They'd Ask: Gender, Recruitment, and Political Ambition." *The Journal of Politics,* 72, no. 2 (2010): 310–326.

Fox, Ronald C., ed. *Current Research in Bisexuality.* London, UK: Harrington Park Press, 2004.

Fox, Stephen R. *The Mirror Makers: A History of American Advertising and Its Creators.* Urbana: University of Illinois Press, 1997.

Franklin, Clyde. "'Hey Home'—'Yo, Bro': Friendship among Black Men." In Peter Nardi, ed., *Men's Friendships.* Newbury Park, CA: Sage Publications: 201–214, 1992.

Fraser, Jill Andresky. *White Collar Sweatshop: The Deterioration of Work and Its Reward in Corporate America.* New York: W. W. Norton, 2001.

Freedman, Vicki A., Linda G. Martin, and Robert F. Schoeni. "Recent Trends in Disability and Functioning among Older Adults in the United States." *Journal of the American Medical Association,* 288, no. 24 (2002): 3137–3146.

Freeman, Colin L., Harding, John H., Quigley, David, Rodger, Mark (2010). "Structural Control of Crystal Nuclei by an Eggshell Protein" *Angewandte Chemie International Edition,* Volume 49, Issue 30: 5135–5137

Friedan, Betty. *The Fountain of Age.* New York, NY: Simon and Schuster, 1993.

Friedel, Ernestine. *Women and Men: An Anthropologist's View.* New York: Holt, Rinehart, 1975.

Friedman, Thomas. *The Lexus and the Olive Tree: Understanding Globalization.* New York: Farrar Straus and Giroux, 2000.

Friedman, Thomas. *The World Is Flat: A Brief History of the Twenty-First Century.* New York: Farrar, Straus and Giroux, 2005.

Friedson, Eliot. *Professional of Medicine: A Study of the Sociology of Applied Knowledge.* New York, NY: Dodd, Mead, 1970.

Fry, Richard. "For First Time in Modern Era, Living with Parents Edges Out Other Living Arrangements for 18- to 34-Year-Olds." *Pew Research Center,* 2016. Available at: http://www.pewsocialtrends.org/2016/05/24/for-first-time-in-modern-era-living-with-parents-edges-out-other-living-arrangements-for-18-to-34-year-olds/

Fry, Richard, and Jeffrey Passel. In Post-Recession Era, Young Adults Drive Continuing Rise in Multi-Generational Living. *Pew Research Center,* July 17, 2014. Available at: http://www.pewsocialtrends.org/2014/07/17/in-post-recession-era-young-adults-drive-continuing-rise-in-multi-generational-living/. General Social Survey, 1994.

Fuller, Margaret. *Woman in the Nineteenth Century* (1845). Donna Dickenson, ed. New York: Oxford University Press, 1994.

Fussell, Elizabeth, and Frank Furstenberg. "The Transition to Adulthood during the 20th Century: Race, Nativity and Gender." In Richard R. Settersten Jr., Frank F. Furstenberg, and Ruben G. Rumbaut (eds.), *On the Frontier of Adulthood: Theory, Research and Public Policy.* Chicago, IL: University of Chicago Press: 29–75, 2006.

Gagnon, John. "Physical Strength, Once of Significance." *Impact of Science on Society,* 21, no. 1 (1971): 31–42.

Gagnon, John, and William Simon. *Sexual Conduct.* Chicago, IL: Aldine, 1967.

Gallup. Minority Rights and Relations poll, conducted June 13–July 5, 2013. Available at: http://www.gallup.com/poll/163697/approve-marriage-blacks-whites.aspx.

Gallup. "Are you in favor of the death penalty for a person convicted of murder?" 2016. Available at http://www.gallup.com/poll/1606/death-penalty.aspx

Gallup-Healthways. Well-Being Index, January 9, 2017. Available at: http://www.gallup.com/poll/201641/uninsured-rate-holds-low-fourth-quarter.aspx

Gallup International. "Losing Our Religion? Two Thirds of People Still Claim to Be Religious." *Worldwide Independent Network of Market Research, Gallup International,* April 13, 2015. Available at: http://www.wingia.com/web/files/news/290/file/290.pdf

Galvin, Gaby. "Education Secretary Urges States to Ban Corporal Punishment in Schools." *U.S. News and World Report,* November 22, 2016. Available at https://www.usnews.com/news/education-news/articles/2016-11-22/education-secretary-urges-states-to-end-use-of-corporal-punishment

Gamoran, Adam, Martin Nystrand, Mark Berends, and Paul C. LePore. "An Organizational Analysis of the Effects of Ability Grouping." *American Educational Research Journal,* 32, no. 4 (1995): 687–715.

Gamson, William. *The Strategy of Social Protest.* New York: Dorsey Press, 1975.

Gans, Herbert. *The Urban Villagers.* New York: The Free Press, 1962.

Gans, Herbert. *People and Places.* New York: The Free Press, 1968.

Gans, Herbert J. *Deciding What's News: A Study of CBS Evening News, NBC Nightly News, Newsweek, and Time.* New York: Random House, 1979.

Gao, George. How do Americans stand out from the rest of the world? *Pew Research Center FactTank,* March 12, 2015. Available at: http://www.pewresearch.org/fact-tank/2015/03/12/how-do-americans-stand-out-from-the-rest-of-the-world/

García-Moreno, Claudia, Henrica A. F. M. Jansen, Mary Ellsberg, Lori Heise, and Charlotte Watts. *WHO Multi-Country Study on Women's Health and Domestic Violence against Women.* Geneva: World Health Organization, 2006.

Garfinkel, Harold. *Studies in Ethnomethodology.* Englewood Cliffs, NJ: Prentice Hall, 1967.

Garrett, M. T. "Understanding the 'Medicine' of Native American Traditional Values: An Integrative Review." *Counseling & Values,* 43, no. 2 (1999): 84–99.

Gates, Gary. "LGBT Parenting in the United States." *The Williams Institute,* February 2013. Available at: williamsinstitute.law.ucla.edu/wp-content/uploads/LGBT-Parenting.pdf

Gates, Gary J. "How Many People are Lesbian, Gay, Bisexual and Transgender?" *The Williams Institute,* April 2011. Available at: http://williamsinstitute.law.ucla.edu/wp-content/uploads/Gates-How-Many-People-LGBT-Apr-2011.pdf

Gates, Gary J. "In U.S., More Adults Identifying as LGBT." *Gallup,* January 11, 2017. Available at: http://www.gallup.com/poll/201731/lgbt-identification-rises

Gaughan, E., J. Cerio, and R. Myers. *Lethal Violence in Schools: A National Survey Final Report.* Alfred, NY: Alfred University, 2001.

Gee, Lisa Christensen, Matthew Gardner, and Meg Wiehe. "Undocumented Immigrants' State and Local Tax Contributions." *The Institute on Taxation & Economic Policy,* 2016. Available at http://www.itep.org/pdf/immigration2016.pdf

General Accounting Office. *Death Penalty Sentencing: Research Indicates Pattern of Racial Disparities.* Washington, DC: GAO, 1990.

General Accounting Office. "Contingent Workforce: Size, Characteristics, Earnings, and Benefits," April 2015. Available at: http://www.gao.gov/assets/670/669899.pdf

General Social Survey, MacArthur Mental Health Module. 1996. Available at http://www.indiana.edu/~icmhsr/docs/Americans'%20Views%20of%20Mental%20Health.pdf.

Gerber, Jerry, Janet Wolff, Walter Klores, and Gene Brown. *Lifetrends: The Future of Baby Boomers and Other Aging Americans.* New York: Macmillan, 1990.

Gereffi, Gary, and Miguel Korzeniewicz, eds. *Commodity Chains and Global Capitalism.* Westport, CT: Praeger, 1993.

Gernet, Jacques. *History of Chinese Civilization,* J. R. Foster (trans.). Cambridge, UK: Cambridge University Press, 1982.

Gerson, K. (2003, December 21). "Working Moms Heading Home? Doesn't Seem Likely." *The Oakland Tribune,* Op-Ed, December 21, 2003.

Gerson, Kathleen. *Hard Choices: How Women Decide about Work, Career and Motherhood.* Berkeley: University of California Press, 1985.

Gerson, Kathleen. *The Unfinished Revolution: Coming of Age in a New Era of Gender, Work, and Family.* New York, NY: Oxford University Press, 2010.

Ghaziani, Amin. *There Goes the Gayborhood?* Princeton, NJ: Princeton University Press, 2014.

Ghosh, Suresh. *The History of Education in Ancient India.* New Delhi, India: Munshiram Manoharlal Publishers, 2001.

Gibbs, Nancy. "And on the Seventh Day We Rested?" *Time,* August 2, 2004, 90.

Gibson, Jacqueline Macdonald, Nicholas DeFelice, Daniel Sebastian, and Hannah Leker. Racial Disparities in Access to Community Water Supply Service in Wake County, North Carolina. *Public Health Services and Systems Research,* 3, no. 3 (2014): 2–7.

Gilborn, D. "Citizenship, 'Race,' and the Hidden Curriculum." *International Studies in the Sociology of Education,* 2 (1992): 57–73.

Gilligan, Carol. *In a Different Voice: Psychological Theory and Women's Development* (1982). Cambridge, MA: Harvard University Press, 1993.

Gilman, Charlotte Perkins. *Herland* (1915). Denise D. Knight, ed. New York: Penguin, 1998.

Gilman, Charlotte Perkins. *Women and Economics* (1898). Michael Kimmel and Amy Aronson, eds. Berkeley: University of California Press, 1998.

Gilsinan, Kathy. "Big in Europe: The Church of the Flying Spaghetti Monster." *The Atlantic*, November 2016, p. 23.

Gimlin, Debra. *Body Work: Beauty and Self- Image in American Culture*. Berkeley: University of California Press, 2002.

Ginther, Donna K. "Family Structure and Children's Educational Outcomes: Blended Families, Stylized Facts, and Descriptive Regressions." *Demography*, 41, no. 4 (November 2004): 671–696.

Githens-Mazer, Jonathan and Robert Lambert. *Islamophobia and Anti-Muslim Hate Crime: A London Case Study*. European Muslim Research Centre (EMCR)—University of Exeter, 2010. Available at: http://alkawni.com/wp-content/media/documents/reports_on_islam/islamophobia_and_anti-muslim_hate_crime.pdf

Gladwell, Malcolm. "The Cool Hunt." *The New Yorker*, March 17, 1997.

Glassner, Barry. *Bodies*. New York: Putnam, 1988.

Glazer, Nathan. *We're All Multicultural Now*. Cambridge: Harvard University Press, 1998.

Glenn, David. "Supply Side Education." *The Chronicle Review*, July 25, 2008.

Goffman, Erving. *The Presentation of Self in Everyday Life*. New York: Anchor Books, 1959.

Goffman, Erving. *Asylums*. New York: Doubleday, 1961.

Goffman, Erving. *Stigma: Notes on the Management of a Spoiled Identity*. Englewood Cliffs, NJ: Prentice-Hall, 1963.

Goffman, Erving. "The Arrangement between the Sexes." *Theory and Society*, 4, no. 3 (1977): 301–331.

Goldenberg, Suzanne. "Hispanic Names Make Top 10 in America." *The Guardian*, November 20, 2007.

Goldin, Claudia, and Cecilia Rouse. "Orchestrating Impartiality: The Impact of 'Blind' Auditions on Female Musicians." *American Economic Review*, 90, no. 4 (2000): 715–741.

Goldrick-Rab, Sara. *Paying the Price: College Costs, Financial Aid, and the Betrayal of the American Dream*. Chicago, IL: University of Chicago Press, 2016.

Goldscheider, Frances K. "The Aging of the Gender Revolution: What Do We Know and What Do We Need to Know?" *Research on Aging*, 12, no. 4 (1990): 531–545.

Goldspink, David. "Why Women Outlive Men." 2005. Available at: www.thenakedscientist.com/html/content/news/news/405

Gomez, Michael A. *Reversing Sail: A History of the African Diaspora*. New York: Cambridge University Press, 2004.

Gonzalez-Barrera, Ana and Mark Hugo Lopez. "Is Being Hispanic a Matter of Race, Ethnicity or Both?" *The Pew Research Center, FactTank*, June 15, 2015. Available at: http://www.pewresearch.org/fact-tank/2015/06/15/is-being-hispanic-a-matter-of-race-ethnicity-or-both/

Gooch, Brad. "Spiritual Retreats: Om-ward Bound." *Travel & Leisure*, October 5, 2002.

Goode, Erich. "The Ethics of Deception in Social Research: A Case Study." *Qualitative Sociology*, 19 (1996a): 11–33.

Goode, Erich. "Gender and Courtship Entitlement: Responses to Personal Ads." *Sex Roles*, 34, no. 3–4 (1996b): 141–169.

Goode, Erich. "Sexual Involvement and Social Research in a Fat Civil Rights Organization." *Qualitative Sociology*, 25 (Winter 2002): 501–534.

Goode, Erich. *Deviant Behavior*, 7th ed. Englewood Cliffs, NJ: Prentice-Hall, 2004.

Goode, William J., "A Theory of Role Strain." *American Sociological Review*, 25 (1960): 483–496.

Gordon, M. *Assimilation in American life: The Role of Race, Religion, and National Origins*. New York: Oxford University Press, 1964.

Gottfredson, G. D., and D. C. Gottfredson. *Gang Problems and Gang Programs in a National Sample of Schools*. Ellicott City, MD: Gottfredson Associates, 2001.

Gottfredson, Michael R., and Travis Hirschi. "National Crime Control Policies." *Society*, 32, no. 2 (January–February 1995): 30–36.

Gottman, John. 1994. *Why Marriages Succeed or Fail*. New York, NY: Simon and Schuster.

Government Accountability Office, "Contingent Workforce: Size, Characteristics, Earnings and Benefits," April 2015. Available at: http://www.gao.gov/assets/670/669899.pdf

Granovetter, Mark. *Getting a Job: A Study of Contacts and Careers*, 2nd ed. Chicago, IL: University of Chicago Press, 1995.

Granovetter, Mark. "The Strength of Weak Ties." *American Journal of Sociology*, 78, no. 6 (May 1973): 1360–1380.

Granovetter, Mark. *Getting a Job: A Study of Contacts and Careers*. Cambridge, MA: Harvard University Press, 1974.

Gray, John. *Men Are from Mars, Women Are from Venus*. New York: HarperCollins, 1992.

Gray, Lee. *From Ascending Rooms to Express Elevators: A History of the Passenger Elevator in the 19th Century*. Mobile, AL: Elevator World, Inc., 2002.

Greene, Jay P., and Marcus Winters. *Public High School Graduation and College-Readiness Rates: 1991–2002*. New York: Manhattan Institute, 2005.

Greene, Steven. Understanding Party Identification: A Social Identity Approach. *Political Psychology*, 20, no. 2 (1999): 394–403.

Greenstein, Theodore N. "National Context, Family Satisfaction, and Fairness in the Division of Household Labor." *Journal of Marriage and Family*, 71, no. 4 (2009): 1039–1051.

Greenwald, A. G., and S. D. Farnham. "Using Implicit Association Test to Measure Self- Esteem and Self Concept." *Journal of Personality and Social Psychology*, 79 (2000): 1022–1038.

Gregory, Kia. "It's a Worldwide Dance Craze, but It's Not the Real Harlem Shake." *The New York Times*, February 28, 2013. Available at: http://www.nytimes.com/2013/03/01/nyregion/behind-harlem-shake-craze-a-dance-thats-over-a-decade-old.html

Griffin, Gary A., and Harry F. Harlow. "Effects of Three Months of Total Social Deprivation on Social Adjustment and Learning in the Rhesus Monkey." *Child Development*, 37, no. 3 (September 1966): 533–547.

Gross, Samuel, Barbara O'Brien, Chen Hu, and Edward Kennedy. "Rate of false conviction of criminal defendants who are sentenced to death." *Proceedings of the National Academy of Sciences*, 111, no. 20 (2014): 7230–7235. Available at: http://www.pnas.org/content/111/20/7230

Grossman, Gene M., and Elhanan Helpman. *Special Interest Politics.* Cambridge, MA: MIT Press, 2001.

Gurr, Ted Robert. *Why Men Rebel.* Princeton, NJ: Princeton University Press, 1971.

Gurr, Ted Robert. *Peoples versus States: Minorities at Risk in the New Century.* Washington, DC: U.S. Institute of Peace, 2000.

Guterl, F. and M. Hastings. "The Global Makeover: How We Are Remaking Ourselves and—in the Process—Creating a New Global Standard of Beauty." *Newsweek, International Edition*, October 19, 2003.

Guttmacher Institute. "Teen Pregnancy Rates Declined in Many Countries Between the Mid-1990s and 2011." *Alan Guttmacher Institute*, 2015. Available at: https://www.guttmacher.org/news-release/2015/teen-pregnancy-rates-declined-many-countries-between-mid-1990s-and-2011

Guttmacher Institute. "U.S. Teen Sexual Activity: The proportion of adolescents who have had sex increases rapidly by age. September 2016. Available at https://www.guttmacher.org/fact-sheet/american-teens-sexual-and-reproductive-health#1.

Habermas, Jürgen. *On Society and Politics: A Reader*, Steven Seidman, ed. Boston, MA: Beacons Press, 1989.

Hagan, John, and Ruth D. Peterson. *Crime and Inequality.* Stanford, CA: Stanford University Press, 1995.

Hall, G. Stanley. *Adolescence: Its Psychology and Its Relations to Physiology, Anthropology, Sociology, Sex, Crime, Religion, and Education.* New York: D. Appleton and Company, 1904.

Hall, J. A. "After the Fall: An Analysis of Post-Communism." *British Journal of Sociology*, 45, no. 4 (1994): 14–23.

Hamamoto, Darrell Y. *Monitored Peril: Asian Americans and the Politics of TV Representation.* Minneapolis: University of Minnesota Press, 1994.

Hamedani, MarYam G., Hazel Rose Markus, and Alyssa S. Fu. "In the Land of the Free, Interdependent Action Undermines Motivation." *Psychological Science*, 24, no. 2 (2013): 189–196.

Hanisch, Carol. "The Personal Is Political." *Feminist Revolution*, March 1969, 204–205.

Hanna-Attisha, Mona, LaChance, Jenny, Sadler, Richard Casey, and Champney Schnepp, Allison. "Elevated Blood Lead Levels in Children Associated with the Flint Drinking Water Crisis: A Spatial Analysis of Risk and Public Health Response." *American Journal of Public Health,* 106, no. 2 (2015): 283–290.

Hannigan, John. *Environmental Sociology: A Social Constructionist Perspective.* New York, NY: Routledge, 1995.

Hannon, Lance, Robert DeFina, and Sarah Bruch. "The Relationship Between Skin Tone and School Suspension for African Americans." *Race and Social Problems,* 5, no. 4 (2013): 281–295.

Harlow, Harry F., Robert O. Dodsworth, and Margaret K. Harlow. "Total Social Isolation in Monkeys." *Proceedings of the National Academy of Sciences of the United States of America,* 54, no. 1 (July 1965): 90–97.

Harlow, Harry F., Margaret K. Harlow, Robert O. Dodsworth, and G. L. Arling. "Maternal Behavior of Rhesus Monkeys Deprived of Mothering and Peer Associations in Infancy." *Proceedings of the American Philosophical Society*, 110, no. 1 (February 1966): 58–66.

Harlow, Harry F., and Stephen J. Suomi. "Social Recovery by Isolation-Reared Monkeys." *Proceedings of the National Academy of Sciences of the United States of America*, 68, no. 7 (July 1971): 1534–1538.

Harris, Benjamin Cerf. "Likely Transgender Individuals in U.S. Federal Administrative Records." Working Paper Number: CARRA-WP-2015-03. *U.S. Census Bureau*, May 4, 2015. Available at: http://www.census.gov/srd/carra/15_03_Likely_Transgender_Individuals_in_ARs_and_2010Census.pdf

Harris Interactive and CareerBuilder.com. "Forty-Five Percent of Employers Use Social Networking Sites to Research Job Candidates," August 19, 2009. Available at http://www.careerbuilder.com/share/aboutus/pressreleasesdetail.aspx?ed=12%2F31%2F2009&id=pr519&sd=8%2F19%2F2009

Harris, Lynn. "Asexual and Proud!" Salon.com, May 26, 2006. Available at: www.Salon.com

Harris, Shanette. "Black Male Masculinity and Same Sex Friendships." *Western Journal of Black Studies*, 16, no. 2 (1992): 74–81.

Harris Poll. 2016. Available at http://media.theharrispoll.com/documents/Prestigious+Occupations_Data+Tables.pdf.

Harris Poll. "Americans' Belief in God, Miracles, and Heaven Declines," December 16, 2013. Available at: http://www.theharrispoll.com/health-and-life/Americans__Belief_in_God__Miracles_and_Heaven_Declines.html

Harris Poll. Tattoo Takeover: Three in Ten Americans Have Tattoos, and Most Don't Stop at Just One. *The Harris Poll*, February 10, 2016. Available at: http://www.theharrispoll.com/health-and-life/Tattoo_Takeover.html

Harwood, W. S. "Secret Societies in America." *North American Review*, 164, May 1897.

Hayford, Sarah R. "Marriage (Still) Matters: The Contribution of Demographic Change to Trends in Childlessness in the United States." *Demography,* 50, no. 5 (2013): 1641–1661.

Hayward, M. D., and W. R. Grady. "Work and Retirement among a Cohort of Older Men in the United States, 1963–1983." *Demography,* 27, no. 3 (1990): 337–356.

He, Wan, Daniel Goodkind, and Paul Kowal. An Aging World: 2015. *U.S. Census Bureau, International Population Reports,* March 2016.

Health and Retirement Study. "2007 Internet Survey." *HRS Internet Survey,* July 2009.

Healy, J. *Endangered Minds: Why Children Don't Think and What We Can Do about It.* New York: Simon & Schuster, 1990.

Healy, Kieran. "America is a Violent Country." July 20, 2012. Available at https://kieranhealy.org/blog/archives/2012/07/20/america-is-a-violent-country/

Heckert, Alex, and Druann Maria Heckert. Using an Integrated Typology of Deviance to Analyze Ten Common Norms of the U.S. Middle Class. *Sociological Quarterly,* 45, no. 2 (2004): 209–228.

Heckert, D. M. and Best, A. (1997), Ugly Duckling to Swan: Labeling Theory and the Stigmatization of Red Hair. Symbolic Interaction, 20: 365–384.

Heimlich, Russell. "Favor Legalizing Medical Marijuana." *Pew Research Center, Fact Tank,* April 9, 2010 http://www.pewresearch.org/daily-number/favor-sex-education-in-public-schools/

Hellmich, Nanci. "33% of Kids Tip Scales Wrong Way." *USA Today,* April 5, 2006, A-1.

Hemenway, David. Quoted in Wirzbicki, Alan, "Gun Control Efforts Weaken in the South." *The Boston Globe,* September 4, 2005. Available at: www.boston.com/news/nation/article/2005/09/07/gun.control/

Hening, Benjamin J. "The World in 2016." May 11, 2016. Available at http://www.viewsoftheworld.net/?p=4822

KOF Index of Globalization, 2016. Available at http://globalization.kof.ethz.ch/

Herek, Gregory M. "The Psychology of Sexual Prejudice." *Current Directions in Psychological Science,* 9, no. 1 (2000): 19–22.

Heritage Foundation. "How Members of the 111th Congress Practice Private School Choice," by Lindsey Burke. The Heritage Foundation, April 20, 2009.

Hernandez v Robles; 855 N.E. 2d, NY 2006.

Herrnstein, Richard, and Charles Murray. *The Bell Curve: Intelligence and Class Structure in American Life.* New York: The Free Press, 1994.

Hertz, Rosanna. *Single by Chance, Mothers by Choice.* New York: Oxford University Press, 2006.

Hertz, Tom. "Trends in the Intergenerational Elasticity of Family Income in the United States." *Industrial Relations,* 46, no. 1 (January 2007): 22–50.

Hetherington, Mavis. *For Better or for Worse: Divorce Reconsidered.* New York: W. W. Norton, 2002.

Heuser, R. L. *Fertility Tables for Birth Cohorts by Color: United States, 1917–73.* Rockville, Md.: National Center for Health Statistics, DHEW Publication No. (HRA) 76–1152. 1976.

Hickey, Walt. "The Dollar-And-Cents Case Against Hollywood's Exclusion of Women." *FiveThirtyEight.com* (blog). April 1, 2014. Available at: https://fivethirtyeight.com/features/the-dollar-and-cents-case-against-hollywoods-exclusion-of-women/

Higher Education Research Institute at UCLA. "The American Freshman." *Cooperative Institutional Research Program,* January 2012. Available at: https://www.heri.ucla.edu/PDFs/pubs/TFS/Norms/Briefs/Norms2011ResearchBrief.pdf

Hirsch, E. D. *Cultural Literacy: What Every American Needs to Know.* New York: Vintage, 1988.

Hirsch, E. D., Joseph F. Kett, and James Trefil. *Dictionary of Cultural Literacy.* Boston, MA: Houghton Mifflin, 2003.

Hirschi, Travis. *Causes of Delinquency.* Berkeley, CA: University of California Press, 1969.

Hirschi, Travis and Michael Gottredson. "Age and the Explanation of Crime." American Journal of Sociology 89, no. 3 (1983): 552–584.

Hirst, Paul. "The Global Economy—Myth and Realities." *International Affairs,* 73 (1997): 409–425.

Ho, Vanessa. "Native American Death Rates Soar as Most People Are Living Longer." *Seattle Post-Intelligencer,* March 12, 2009.

Hobbes, Thomas. *Leviathan* (1658). New York: Modern Library, 1966.

Hobsbawm, E. J. *The Age of Revolution, 1776–1848.* New York: Anchor, 1962.

Hobsbawm, Eric J. *The Age of Capital.* London, UK: Widenfeld and Nicholson, 2000.

Hochschild, Arlie. *The Second Shift.* New York: Viking Press, 1989.

Hochschild, Arlie Russell. *The Managed Heart: Commercialization of Human Feeling.* Berkeley, CA: University of California Press. 1983.

Hoffman, Bruce. *Inside Terrorism.* New York: Columbia University Press, 1998.

Hofmann, Wilhelm, Bertram Gawronski, Tobias Gschwendner, Huy Le, and Manfred Schmitt. "A Meta-Analysis of the Correlation between the Implicit Association Test and Explicit Self-Report Measures." *Personality and Social Psychology Bulletin,* 31, no. 10 (October 2005): 1369–1385.

Hollenbach, Margaret. *Lost and Found: My Life in a Group Marriage Commune.* Albuquerque: University of New Mexico Press, 2004.

Hondagneu-Sotelo, Pierrette. *Domestica: Immigrant Workers Cleaning and Caring in the Shadows of Affluence.* Berkeley, CA: University of California Press, 2001.

Hook, Jennifer L. "Care in Context: Men's Unpaid Work in 20 Countries, 1965–2003." *American Sociological Review*, 71, no. 4 (2006): 639–660.

Hoover, Stewart, Lynn Schofield Clark, and Lee Rainie. "Faith Online." *Report of the Pew Center on the Internet and American Life, 2004*. Washington, DC: Pew Center.

Hopkins, Terence, and Immanuel Wallerstein. *The Age of Transition: Trajectory of the World System, 1945–2025*. London: Zed Books, 1996.

Hoppe, Trevor. "Controlling Sex in the Name of 'Public Health': Social Control and Michigan HIV Law." *Social Problems*, 60, no. 1 (2013): 27–49.

Hoppe, Trevor. *Punishing Disease: HIV and the Criminalization of Sickness*. Berkeley, CA: University of California Press, 2017.

Hout, Michael. "Status, Autonomy and Training in Occupational Mobility." *American Journal of Sociology*, 89 (1984): 1379–1409.

Howe, Louise Kay. *Pink Collar Workers: Inside the World of Women's Work*. New York: Putnam, 1977.

Howell, J. C., A. Egley Jr., and D. K. Gleason. "Modern Day Youth Gangs." *Bulletin, Youth Gang Series*. Washington, DC: U.S. Department of Justice, Office of Juvenile Justice and Delinquency Prevention, 2002.

Hrdy, Sarah Blaffer. *The Woman That Never Evolved*. Cambridge, MA: Harvard University Press, 1981.

Hrdy, Sarah Blaffer. *Mother Nature: A History of Mothers, Infants, and Natural Selection*. New York: Pantheon, 1999.

HRS Internet Survey. Health and Retirement Study, 2009. Available at: hrsonline.isr.umich.edu/index.php?p=avail

HSBC Group. The Future of Retirement: Choices for Later Life. *HSBC Group, Global Report*, 2015. Available at: http://www.hsbc.com/~/media/hsbc-com/newsroomassets/2015/pdf/global-report-artwork.pdf

Hubbard, Ruth. "The Political Nature of Human Nature." In Deborah Rhode, ed., *Theoretical Perspectives on Sexual Difference*. New Haven, CT: Yale University Press, 1990 63–73.

Hughes, Diane, James Rodriguez, Emilie P. Smith, Deborah J. Johnson, Howard C. Stevenson, and Paul Spicer. "Parents' Ethnic-Racial Socialization Practices: A Review of Research and Directions for Future Study." *Developmental Psychology*, 42, no. 5 (2006): 747–770.

Hughes, Everett C. "Dilemmas and Contradictions of Status." *American Journal of Sociology*, 50 (1945): 353–354.

Hughes, Mary Elizabeth, and Angela M. O'Rand. *The American People Census 2000: The Lives and Times of the Baby Boomers*. New York, NY: Russell Sage Foundation, 2004.

Hughey, Matthew W., and Devon R. Goss. "A Level Playing Field? Media Constructions of Athletics, Genetics, and Race." *The ANNALS of the American Academy of Political and Social Science*, 661, no. 1 (2015): 182–211.

Humphreys, Jeffrey. "The Multicultural Economy 2006." *Georgia Business and Economic Conditions*, 66, no. 3 (2006).

Humphreys, Laud. *Tearoom Trade: Impersonal Sex in Public Places*. New York: Transaction, 1970.

Hunt, G., K. Joe-Laidler, and K. MacKenzie. "Moving into Motherhood: Gang Girls and Controlled Risk." *Youth & Society*, 36 (2005): 333–373.

Huntington, Ellsworth. *Civilization and Climate* (1915). Honolulu: University Press of the Pacific, 2001.

Hvistendahl, Mara. *Unnatural Selection: Choosing Boys Over Girls, and the Consequences of a World Full of Men*. New York, NY: PublicAffairs, 2011.

Hyde, Janet. "The Gender Similarities Hypothesis." *The American Psychologist*, 60, no. 6 (2005): 581–592.

Ignatiev, Noel. *How the Irish Became White*. New York, NY: Routledge, 1995.

Ingraham, Christopher. "A Decade of Bad Press Hasn't Hurt Fraternity Membership Numbers." *The Washington Post, Wonkblog*, March 9, 2015. Available at: https://www.washingtonpost.com/news/wonk/wp/2015/03/09/a-decade-of-bad-media-attention-hasnt-hurt-fraternity-membership-numbers/?utm_term=.9fd3d9c87d05

Institute for Women's Policy Research (IWPR). "Young Women Now Less Likely to Work in Same Jobs as Men; Wage Gap Continues Due to Occupational Segregation." August 31, 2010. Available at: https://iwpr.org/young-women-now-less-likely-to-work-in-same-jobs-as-men-wage-gap-continues-due-to-occupational-segregation/

International Center for Democracy and Electoral Assistance. "Compulsory Voting," *International IDEA*, 2017. Available at: http://www.oldsite.idea.int/vt/compulsory_voting.cfm.

International Helsinki Federation for Human Rights. *Report: Human Rights in the OSCE Region*. Helsinki, Finland: International Helsinki Federation for Human Rights, 2006.

International Labour Organization (ILO). *Facts on Child Labor, 2006*. Available at: www.ilo.org/wcmsp5/groups/public/—dgreports/dcomm/documents/publication/wcms_067558.pdf

International Labour Organization (ILO). *Global Employment Trends*. Geneva: International Labour Office: 2008.

International Labour Organization (ILO). *Global Employment Trends*. Geneva: International Labour Office, January 2009a.

International Labour Organization (ILO). *Global Wage Report 2008/09*. Geneva: International Labour Office, 2009b.

International Labour Organization. Statistical Report "Global child labour trends 2008 to 2012." Available at http://www.ilo.org/ipec/Informationresources/WCMS_IPEC_PUB_23015/lang--en/index.htm

International Labour Organization. ILO Global Estimate of Force Labour: Results and Methodology. *International Labour Office (ILO)*, 2012. Available at: http://apflnet.ilo.org/resources/ilo-global-estimate-of-forced-labour-2012-results-and-methodology/at_download/file1

International Labour Organization (ILO). *World Employment Social Outlook: Trends 2015*. Available at http://www.ilo.org/wcmsp5/groups/public/@dgreports/@dcomm/@publ/documents/publication/wcms_337069.pdf.

International Lesbian and Gay Association (ILGA). June 2016. Available at http://ilga.org/downloads/03_ILGA_WorldMap_ENGLISH_Overview_May2016.pdf; http://ilga.org/what-we-do/lesbian-gay-rights-maps/

International Monetary Fund. "Projected GDP Per Capita Ranking," 2016–2020. Available at http://statisticstimes.com/economy/projected-world-gdp-capita-ranking.php

International Union for Conservation of Nature. 2016. Available at: https://www.iucn.org/

Internet World Stats. "Internet Usage Statistics: World Internet Users and 2017 Population Stats," *Internet World Stats,* 2017. Available at: http://www.internetworldstats.com/stats.htm

Irwin, Katherine. "Legitimating the First Tattoo: Moral Passage through Informal Interaction." *Symbolic Interaction,* 24 (2001): 49–73.

Isaacs, Julia. *Economic Mobility of Black and White Families.* Washington DC: The Brookings Institution, 2007.

Isaacs, Julia. "Economic Mobility of Families across Generations." In Haskins, Ron, Julia Haskins, and Isabel V. Sawhill, eds., *Getting Ahead on Losing Ground: Economic Mobility in America.* Washington, DC: Center on Children and Families, 2009 (15–26).

Isaacson, Walter. *Einstein: His Life and Universe.* New York: Simon and Schuster, 2007.

ISAPS. "ISAPS International Survey on Aesthetic/Cosmetic Procedures Performed in 2014." *International Survey on Aesthetic/Cosmetic Procedures,* 2015. Available at: https://www.isaps.org/Media/Default/global-statistics/2015%20ISAPS%20Results.pdf

Ito, Mizuko, Heather Horst, Matteo Bittanti, Danah Boyd, Becky Herr-Stephenson, Patricia G. Lange, C. J. Pascoe, and Laura Robinson. *Living and Learning with New Media: Summary of the Findings of the Digital Youth Project.* Chicago, IL: John D. and Catherine T. MacArthur Foundation, November, 2008.

Jackson, Andrew. "Fighting Poverty through Municipal Wage Ordinances." *Progressive Economics Forum,* July 18, 2007.

Jackson, Kenneth. *Crabgrass Frontier: The Suburbanization of America.* New York: Oxford University Press, 1987.

Jackson, Pamela Braboy, and Quincy Thomas Stewart. "A Research Agenda for the Black Middle Class: Work Stress, Survival Strategies and Mental Health." *Journal of Health and Social Behavior,* 44 (September 2003): 442–455.

Jacobs, Jane. *The Death and Life of Great American Cities.* New York: Vintage, 1961.

Janis, Irving L. *Victims of Groupthink.* Boston, MA: Houghton-Mifflin, 1972.

Jarrell, Anne. "The Daddy Track." *Boston Globe,* July 7, 2007.

Jayson, Sharon. "Living Together No Longer 'Playing House.'" *USA Today,* July 28, 2008.

Johnson, David R., and Jian Wu. "An Empirical Test of Crisis, Social Selection, and Role Explanations of the Relationship between Marital Disruption and Psychological Distress: A Pooled Time-Series Analysis of Four-Wave Panel Data." *Journal of Marriage and Family,* 64 (2002): 211–224.

Johnson, Michael J., Nick C. Jackson, J. Kenneth Arnette, and Steven D. Koffman. "Gay and Lesbian Perceptions of Discrimination in Retirement Care Facilities." *Journal of Homosexuality,* 49, no. 2 (2005): 83–102.

Johnson, Stefanie K., Susan Elaine Murphy, Selamawit Zewdie, and Rebecca J. Reichard. "The Strong, Sensitive Type: Effects of Gender Stereotypes and Leadership Prototypes on the Evaluation of Male and Female Leaders." *Organizational Behavior and Human Decision Processes.* 106, no. 1 (2008): 39–60.

Johnson, Steven. *Everything Bad Is Good for You.* New York: Riverhead Books, 2005.

Jones, Del. "Women CEOs Gain Slowly on Corporate America." *USA Today,* January 2, 2009.

Jones, James H. *Bad Blood: The Tuskegee Syphilis Experiment.* New and Expanded Edition. Revised edition. New York, NY: Free Press, 1993.

Jones, Robert P., Daniel Cox, and Juhem Navarro-Rivera. "Believers, Sympathizers, and Skeptics: Why Americans are Conflicted about Climate Change, Environmental Policy, and Science." *PRRI/AAR Religion, Values, and Climate Change Survey Findings,* 2014. Available at: http://publicreligion.org/site/wp-content/uploads/2014/11/2014-Climate-Change-FINAL.pdf

Judge, Timothy A., Charlice Hurst, and Lauren S. Simon. "Does It Pay to Be Smart, Attractive, or Confident (or All Three)? Relationships among General Mental Ability, Physical Attractiveness, Core Self-Evaluations, and Income." *The Journal of Applied Psychology* 94, no. 3 (2009): 742–755.

Juergensmeyer, Mark. *Terror in the Mind of God: The Global Rise of Religious Violence.* Berkeley: University of California Press, 2003.

Juvonen, Jaana, Sandra Graham, and Mark Schuster. "Bullying among Young Adolescents: The Strong, the Weak and the Troubled." *Pediatrics,* 112, no. 6 (December 2003): 1231–1237.

Kaestle, Carl F., H. Damon-Moore, Katherine Tinsley, Lawrence C. Stedman, and William Vance Trollinger Jr. *Literacy in the United States: Readers and Reading Since 1880.* New Haven, CT: Yale University Press, 1993.

Kaiser Family Foundation. *Sex Education in America: A View from Inside the Nation's Classrooms.* Menlo Park, CA: Henry J. Kaiser Family Foundation, 2000.

Kann, Laura, Steve Kinchen, Shari L. Shanklin, Katherine H. Flint, Joseph Hawkins, William A. Harris, Richard Lowry, Emily O'Malley Olsen, Tim McManus, David Chyen, Lisa Whittle, Eboni Taylor, Zewditu Demissie, Nancy Brener, Jemekia Thornton, John Moore, and Stephanie Zaza. "Youth Risk Behavior Surveillance–United States, 2013." *Center for Disease Control and Prevention, Surveillance Summaries,* June 13, 2014. Available at: http://www.cdc.gov/mmwr/preview/mmwrhtml/ss6304a1.htm?s_cid=ss6304a1_w

Kanter, Rosabeth M. *Men and Women of the Corporation.* New York: Basic Books, 1977.

Karabel, Jerome. *The Chosen: The Hidden History of Admission and Exclusion at Harvard, Yale, and Princeton.* Boston: Houghton-Mifflin, 2005.

Karabell, Zachary. "We Are Not in This Together." *Newsweek,* April 20, 2009, 30–31.

Katz, E., and Lazarsfeld, P. F. *Personal influence: The part played by people in the flow of mass communications.* New York, NY: The Free Press, 1955.

Katz, Jack. *Seductions of Crime: Moral and Sensual Attractions in Doing Evil.* New York: Basic Books, 1988.

Katz, Michael. *The Undeserving Poor.* New York: Pantheon, 1990.

Keay, Douglas. "AIDS, Education, and the Year 2000: An Interview with Margaret Thatcher." *Woman's Own,* September 23, 1987, 14.

Kempadoo, Kamala, Jyoti Saghera, and Bandana Pattanaik, eds. *Trafficking and Prostitution Reconsidered: New Perspectives on Migration, Sex Work, and Human Rights.* Boulder, CO: Paradigm Publishers, 2005.

Kemper, Theodore. *Testosterone and Social Structure.* New Brunswick, NJ: Rutgers University Press, 1990.

Kennedy, John F., *A Nation of Immigrants* (1958) (New York: Harper Perennial, 2008).

Kennedy, Randall. *Nigger: The Strange Career of a Troublesome Word.* New York: Pantheon, 2002.

Kenny, C. "What Resource Curse?" *Foreign Policy,* December 6, 2010. Available at http://foreignpolicy.com/2010/12/06/what-resource-curse/.

Kerbo, Harold R. *Social Stratification and Inequality: Class Conflict in Historical and Comparative Perspective.* New York: McGraw-Hill, 1996.

Kessler, Suzanne J. *Lessons from the Intersexed.* New Brunswick, NJ: Rutgers University Press, 1998.

Khagram, S., J. Riker, and K. Sikkink, 2002. *Restructuring World Politics: Transnational Social Movements, Networks, and Norms.* Minneapolis, MN: University of Minnesota Press.

Khan, Shamus. *Privilege: The Making of an Adolescent Elite at St. Paul's School.* Princeton, NJ: University of Princeton Press, 2011.

Kharas, Homi. The Unprecedented Expansion of the Global Middle Class: An Update. *The Brookings Institution,* February 2017. Available at: https://www.brookings.edu/wp-content/uploads/2017/02/global_20170228_global-middle-class.pdf

Kiersz, Andy. "Here and the Most Millionaire-Filled States in America." *Business Insider,* January 16, 2014. Available at: http://www.businessinsider.com/map-states-where-millionaires-live-2014-1

Kim-Prieto, Chu, Lizabeth Goldstein, Sumie Okazaki, and Blake Kirschner. "Effect of Exposure to an American Indian Mascot on the Tendency to Stereotype a Different Minority Group" in *Journal of Applied Social Psychology,* 43, no. 3 (March 2010): 534–553.

Kimmel, Michael. "What Do Men Want?" *Harvard Business Review,* April, 1993.

Kimmel, Michael. "Masculinity as Homophobia." In *Theorizing Masculinities,* edited by Harry Brod and Michael Kaufman (pp. 119–141). Thousand Oaks, CA: Sage, 1994.

Kimmel, Michael. "'Gender Symmetry' in Domestic Violence: A Substantive and Methodological Research Review." *Violence against Women,* 8, no. 11 (2002): 1332–1363.

Kimmel, Michael. *Guyland: The Perilous World Where Boys Become Men.* New York: Harper-Collins, 2008.

Kimmel, Michael. "The Bigotry of the Binary: The Case of Caster Semenya." *The Huffington Post,* August 24, 2009. Available at: http://www.huffingtonpost.com/michael-kimmel/the-bigotry-of-the-binary_b_267572.html

Kimmel, Michael, James Lang, and Alan Grieg. *Men, Masculinities and Development.* New York: U.N. Development Program (UNDP), 2000.

King, Leslie. *Environmental Sociology: From Analysis to Action.* Lanham, MD: Rowan & Littlefield, 2005.

Kingston, Lindsey N., and Kathryn R. Stam. "Online Advocacy: Analysis of Human Rights NGO Websites." *Journal of Human Rights Practice,* 5, no. 1 (2013): 75–95.

Kinsella, Kevin, and David R. Phillips. *Global Aging: The Challenge of Success.* Washington, DC: Population Reference Bureau, 2005.

Kinsey, Alfred C., Wardell B. Pomeroy, and Clyde E. Martin. *Sexual Behavior in the Human Male.* New York: W. B. Saunders Company, 1948.

Kinsey, Alfred C., Wardell B. Pomeroy, Clyde E. Martin, and Paul H. Gebhard. *Sexual Behavior in the Human Female.* New York: W.B. Saunders Company, 1953.

Kirby, D. *Emerging Answers: Research Findings on Programs to Reduce Teen Pregnancy.* Washington, DC: Campaign to Prevent Teen Pregnancy, 2001.

Kirkpatrick, David. *The Facebook Effect: The Real Inside Story of Mark Zuckerberg and the World's Fastest Growing Company.* New York: Virgin Books, 2010.

Kirp, David. "After the Bell Curve." *The New York Times Magazine,* July 23, 2006, 15–16.

Kitsuse, John. "The New Conception of Deviance and Its Critics." In Walter A. Gove, ed., *The Labelling of Deviance: Evaluating a Perspective* (pp. 381–392). Thousand Oaks, CA: Sage Publications, 1980.

Kittilson, Miki C., and Katherine Tate. "Political Parties, Minorities and Elected Office: Comparing Opportunities for Inclusion in the U.S. and Britain." University of California, Irvine: Center for the Study of Democracy, Paper 04–06, 2004. Available at: http://repositories.cdlib.org/csd/04-06

Klein, Jessie. 2013. *The Bully Society: School Shootings and the Crisis of Bullying in America's Schools.* New York, NY: NYU Press.

Klinenberg, Eric. *Heat Wave: A Social Autopsy of Disaster in Chicago.* Chicago, IL: University of Chicago Press, 2002.

Klinenberg, Eric. *Going Solo: The Extraordinary Rise and Surprising Appeal of Living Alone.* New York, NY: Penguin Books, 2012.

Kling, K. C., Hyde, J. S., Showers, C. J., & Buswell, B. N. "Gender differences in self-esteem: A meta-analysis." *Psychological Bulletin,* 125 (1999): 470–500.

Kluckhohn, Clyde, *Mirror for Man: The Relation of Anthropology to Modern Life* (New York: Whittlesey House, 1949).

Knudsen, Knud, and Kari Wærness. "National Context and Spouses' Housework in 34 Countries." *European Sociological Review,* 24, no. 1 (2008): 97–113.

Koch, Jerome R., Alden E. Roberts, Myrna L. Armstrong, and Donna C. Owen. "Body Art, Deviance, and American College Students." *The Social Science Journal* 47, no. 1 (2010): 151–161.

Kohlberg, Lawrence. *Stages of Moral Development as a Basis for Moral Education.* Cambridge, MA: Harvard University Center for Moral Education, 1971.

Kohlberg, Lawrence and Carol Gilligan. *The Adolescent as Philosopher: The Discovery of the Self in a Postconventional World* (1971). New York: Daedalus.

Kohler, P. K., L. E. Manhart, and W. E. Lafferty. "Abstinence-Only and Comprehensive Sex Education and the Initiation of Sexual Activity and Teen Pregnancy." *Journal of Adolescent Health,* 42, no. 4 (April 2008): 344–351.

Kohn, Melvin. "Social Class and the Exercise of Parental Authority." *American Sociological Review,* 24 (June 1959a): 352–366.

Kohn, Melvin. "Social Class and Parental Values." *American Journal of Sociology,* 64 (January, 1959b): 337–351.

Kohn, Melvin. "Social Class and Parent-Child Relationships: An Interpretation." *American Journal of Sociology,* 68 (January 1963): 471–480.

Kohn, Melvin. *Class and Conformity.* Chicago, IL: University of Chicago Press, 1977.

Kohn, Melvin. "On the Transmission of Values in the Family: A Preliminary Formulation." In Alan C. Kerckhoff, ed., *Research in Sociology of Education and Socialization: A Research Annual* (Vol. 4, pp. 3–12). Greenwich, CT: JAI Press, 1983.

Kohn, Melvin. "Social Structure and Personality: A Quintessentially Sociological Approach to Social Psychology." *Social Forces,* 68 (September 1989): 26–33.

Kohn, Melvin, with Carrie Schoenbach. "Social Stratification, Parents' Values, and Children's Values." In Dagmara Krebs and Peter Schmidt (eds.), *New Directions in Attitude Measurement* (pp. 118–151). Berlin, Germany: Walter de Gruyter, 1993.

Kohn, Melvin, with Kazimierz Slomczynski and Carrie Schoenbach. "Social Stratification and the Transmission of Values in the Family: A Cross-National Assessment." *Sociological Forum,* 1 (Winter 1986): 73–102.

The Korean Times. "N. Korea Spends Quarter of GDP on Military from 2002–2012: US Data," January 4, 2016.

Available at: http://www.koreatimes.co.kr/www/news/nation/2016/01/485_194556.html

Korn, Donald Jay. "Yours, Mine, OURS." *Black Enterprise,* October 2001.

Kraybill, Donald B. *The Riddle of Amish Culture.* Baltimore: Johns Hopkins University Press, 2001.

Kreager, Derek A., and Jeremy Staff. "The Sexual Double Standard and Adolescent Peer Acceptance." *Social Psychology Quarterly* 72, no. 2 (2009): 143–164.

Kriedte, Peter. *Peasants, Landlords, and Merchant Capitalists.* New York: Cambridge University Press, 1983.

Kristof, Nicholas. "Temperatures Rise, and We're Cooked." *The New York Times, Sunday Review,* Sept. 11, 2016, p. 11.

Kroll Global Fraud and Risk Report. 2016. Available at: http://www.kroll.com/en-us/fraud-report-confirmation

Krugman, Paul. "The End of Middle-Class America." *The New York Times Magazine,* October 20, 2002, 62–67, 76–78, 141.

Krugman, Paul. "Graduates versus Oligarchs." *New York Times,* February 22, 2006, A-31.

Kumar, K. *From Post-Industrial to Post-Modern Society: New Theories of the Contemporary World.* Oxford, UK: Blackwell, 1995.

Kupers, Terry. *Prison Madness: The Mental Health Crisis Behind Bars and What We Must Do About It.* San Francisco, CA: Jossey-Bass, 1999.

Kurki, Leena. "International Crime Survey: American Rates About Average." *Overcrowded Times,* 8, no. 5 (1997): 4–7.

Kutateladze, Besiki L., Nancy R. Andiloro, Brian D. Johnson, and Cassia C. Spohn. "Cumulative Disadvantage: Examining Racial and Ethnic Disparity in Prosecution and Sentencing." *Criminology* 52, no. 3 (2014): 514–551.

Lachs, Mark S., and Karl A. Pillemer. "Elder Abuse." *New England Journal of Medicine,* 373, no. 20 (2015): 1947–1956.

Lambert, Tracy. "Pluralistic Ignorance and Hooking Up." *Journal of Sex Research,* 40, no. 2 (May 2003): 129.

Lancaster, B. *The Department Store: A Social History.* London, UK: Leicester University Press, 1995.

Landry, D. J., L. Kaeser, and C. L. Richards, "Abstinence Promotion and the Provision of Information about Contraception in Public School District Sexuality Education Policies." *Family Planning Perspectives,* 31, no. 6 (1999): 280–286.

Lane, Harlan. *The Wild Boy of Aveyron.* Cambridge, MA: Harvard University Press, 1979.

Lareau, Annette. *Unequal Childhoods: Class, Race and Family Life.* Berkeley: University of California Press, 2003.

Lasch, Christopher. "The Family and History." *New York Review of Books,* 8 (November 13, 1975): 33–38.

Lauer, Robert H., and Jeanette C. Lauer. *Marriage and Family: The Quest for Intimacy,* 5th ed. New York: McGraw-Hill, 2003.

Laumann, Edward O., John H. Gagnon, Robert T. Michael, and Stuart Michaels. *The Social Organization of Sexuality: Sexual Practices in the United States.* Chicago, IL: University of Chicago Press, 1994.

LaVeist, Thomas A., and Amani Nuru-Jeter. "Is Doctor-Patient Race Concordance Associated with Greater Satisfaction with Care?" *Journal of Health and Social Behavior,* 43, no. 3 (2002): 296–306.

Lee, Jennifer and Min Zhou. *The Asian American Achievement Paradox.* New York, NY: Russell Sage Foundation, 2015.

Leeder, Elaine J. *The Family in Global Perspective: A Gendered Journey.* Thousand Oaks, CA: Sage, 2003.

Leland, John. "Hip New Churches Sway to a Different Drummer." *New York Times,* February 18, 2004, A-1, 17.

Lemann, Nicholas. *The Promised Land: The Great Black Migration and How It Changed America.* New York, NY: Vintage, 1992.

Lemert, Edwin. *Human Deviance, Social Problems and Social Control.* Englewood Cliffs, NJ: Prentice-Hall, 1972.

Lenhart, Amanda. Cell Phone and American Adults. *Pew Research Center, Internet & Technology,* September 2, 2010. Available at: http://www.pewinternet.org/2010/09/02/cell-phones-and-american-adults/

Leonhardt, David. "Money Doesn't Buy Happiness. Well, on Second Thought." *New York Times,* April 16, 2008, C1, C7.

Levine, James A. *Working Fathers.* New York: Perseus Books, 1997.

Levine, L. W. *Highbrow/Lowbrow: The Emergence of Cultural Hierarchy in America.* Cambridge, MA: Harvard University Press, 1988.

Levine, Martin. "Gay Ghetto." *Journal of Homosexuality,* 4, no. 4 (Summer 1979).

Levinson, Daniel J. *The Seasons of a Man's Life.* New York, NY: Alfred Knopf, 1978.

Levitt, Steven, and Stephen Dubner. *Freakonomics.* New York, NY: William Morrow, 2005.

Lewis, Oscar. *Five Families: Mexican Case Studies in the Culture of Poverty.* San Francisco: HarperCollins, 1965.

LexisNexis. LexisNexis Academic, 2016. Available at: www.lexisnexis.com

Liang, Lan, Benjamin Caballero, and Shiriki Kumanyika. "Will All Americans Become Overweight or Obese? Estimating the Progression and Cost of the U.S. Obesity Epidemic." *Obesity,* 16, no. 7 (July 2008): 1583–1602.

Liazos, Alexander, "Nuts, Sluts, and Perverts: The Poverty of the Sociology of Deviance." *Social Problems,* 20, no. 1 (Summer 1972): 103–120.

Lichtblau, Eric. "Hate Crimes Against American Muslims Most Since Post-9/11 Era." *The New York Times,* September 17, 2016. Available at: https://www.nytimes.com/2016/09/18/us/politics/hate-crimes-american-muslims-rise.html

Lichter, Daniel T., and Zhenchao Qian. "Serial Cohabitation and the Marital Life Course." *Journal of Marriage and Family,* 70 (2008): 861–878.

Lichtheim, George. *Marxism.* New York, NY: Columbia University Press, 1982.

Lieberson, Stanley. *A Matter of Taste: How Names, Fashion, and Culture Change.* New Haven, CT: Yale University Press. 2000.

Liebow, Elliot. *Tally's Corner.* Boston: Little, Brown, 1968.

Limonic, Laura. "Latinos and the 2008 Presidential Elections: A Visual Data Base." New York: Center for Latin American, Caribbean and Latino Studies, CUNY Graduate Center, 2008.

Lind, Michael. "Are We Still a Middle-Class Nation?" *Atlantic Monthly,* 293, no. 1 (2004), 120–129.

Lipka, Michael. "10 Facts about Atheists." *Pew Research Center, FactTank,* June 1, 2016. Available at: wresearch.org/fact-tank/2016/06/01/10-facts-about-atheists/

Lipsitz, Angela, Paul D. Bishop, and Christine Robinson. "Virginity Pledges: Who Takes Them and How Well Do They Work?" Presentation at the Annual Convention of the American Psychological Association, August 2003.

Livingston, Gretchen, 2014. "Fewer than Half of U.S. Kids Today Live in a 'Traditional' Family" December. PEW Research Center briefing, available at: http://www.pewresearch.org/fact-tank/2014/12/22/less-than-half-of-u-s-kids-today-live-in-a-traditional-family/

Livingston, Gretchen. "Childlessness: Childlessness Falls, Family Size Grows among Highly Educated Women." *Pew Research Center, Social & Demographic Trends,* May 7, 2015. Available at: http://www.pewsocialtrends.org/2015/05/07/childlessness/

Locke, John. *Two Treatises of Government* (1689), ed. Peter Laslett. New York: Cambridge University Press, 1988.

Loehlin, John C., and Robert C. Nichols. *Heredity, Environment, and Personality.* Austin: University of Texas Press, 1976.

Lofland, John. "Collective Behavior: The Elementary Forms." In Russell Curtis Jr. and Benigno Aguirre, eds., *Collective Behavior and Social Movements.* Boston, MA: Allyn and Bacon, 1993: 70–75.

Lopez, Maria Pabon, and Kevin R. Johnson. "Presumed Incompetent: Important Lessons for University Leaders on the Professional Lives of Women Faculty of Color." *Berkeley Journal of Gender, Law & Justice,* 29, no. 2 (summer 2014): 388–405.

Lorber, Judith. "Believing Is Seeing: Biology as Ideology." *Gender & Society* 7, no. 4 (1993): 568–581.

Lorber, Judith. *Paradoxes of Gender.* New Haven, CT: Yale University Press, 1994.

Lubienski, Sarah Theule, and Christopher Lubienski. 2006. "School Sector and Academic Achievement: A Multilevel Analysis of NAEP Mathematics Data." *American Educational Research Journal* 43, no. 4 (2006): 651–698.

Lucas, Christopher J. *American Higher Education: A History.* New York: Palgrave Macmillan, 1996.

Luker, Kristin. *Salsa Dancing into the Social Sciences.* Cambridge, MA: Harvard University Press, 2008.

Lukes, Steven. *Power.* New York, NY: NYU Press, 1986.

Lumeng, Julie C., Patrick Forrest, Danielle P. Appugliese, Niko Kaciroti, Robert F. Corwyn, and Robert H. Bradley. "Weight Status as a Predictor of Being Bullied in Third Through Sixth Grades." *Pediatrics,* 125, no. 6 (2010): 1301–1307.

Lunneborg, Patricia. *The Chosen Lives of Child-Free Men.* Westport, CT: Bergin & Garvey, 1999.

Lynch, Kathleen. *The Hidden Curriculum: Reproduction in Education, a Reappraisal.* London, UK: Falmer Press, 1989.

Lynd, Robert S., and Helen Merrell Lynd. *Middletown: A Study in Contemporary American Culture.* New York, NY: Harcourt Brace, 1929.

MacArthur Foundation. *Living and Learning with New Media: Summary of Findings from the Digital Youth Project.* Chicago, IL: MacArthur Foundation, 2008.

Maffesoli, Michel. *The Time of the Tribes: The Decline of Individualism in Mass Society* (1988). Thousand Oaks, CA: Sage, 1996.

Magazine Publishers of America. *Magazine Media Factbook 2016/17.* Available at: http://www.magazine.org/sites/default/files/MPA-FACTbook201617-ff.pdf

Malinowski, Bronislaw. *Sex and Repression in Savage Society* (1927). New York, Plume, 1974.

Malthus, Thomas Robert. *An Essay on the Principle of Population* (1798). New York: Oxford University Press, 1999.

Margolis, Eric, ed. *The Hidden Curriculum in Higher Education.* New York: Falmer Press, 2001.

Marks, N. "Flying Solo at Midlife: Gender, Marital Status and Psychological Wellbeing." *Journal of Marriage and the Family,* 58 (1996): 917–932.

Martens, Jens. "A Compendium of Inequality: The Human Development Report 2005." Global Policy Forum, 2005.

Martin, Emily. "The Egg and the Sperm: How Science Has Constructed a Romance Based on Stereotypical Male-Female Roles." *Signs: Journal of Women in Culture and Society,* 16, no. 3 (1991): 485–501.

Martin, J. K., B. A. Pescosolido, and S. A. Tuch. "Of fear and loathing: The role of disturbing behavior, labels and causal attributions in shaping public attitudes toward persons with mental illness." *Journal of Health and Social Behavior,* 41, no. 2 (2000): 208–233.

Martin, Karin A., and Emily Kazyak. "Hetero-Romantic Love and Heterosexiness in Children's G-Rated Films." *Gender & Society,* 23, no. 3 (2009): 315–336.

Martin, Steven. *Growing Evidence for a "Divorce Divide"? Education, Race, and Marital Dissolution Rates in the U.S. since the 1970s.* New York: Russell Sage Foundation, 2006.

Martinez, Michael. "Blended Families Face Difficult Financial Decisions." *AP Business Wire,* June 17, 2005.

Martino, Wayne John. "Male Teachers as Role Models: Addressing Issues of Masculinity, Pedagogy and the Re-Masculinization of Schooling." *Curriculum Inquiry,* 38, no. 2 (2008): 189–223.

Marx, Karl. *Capital* (1867). David McLellan, ed. New York: Oxford University Press, 1998.

Marx, Karl, and Friedrich Engels. *The Communist Manifesto: A Modern Edition* (1848). E. J. Hobsbawm, ed. New York: Verso, 1998.

Marx, Patricia. "About Face." *The New Yorker,* March 23, 2015, pp. 50, 51. Available at: http://www.techinsider.io/south-korea-is-the-plastic-surgery-capital-of-the-world-2015-9.

Massey, Douglas S., and Nancy A. Denton. *American Apartheid.* Cambridge, MA: Harvard University Press, 1993.

Mathews, T. J., and Brady E. Hamilton. Mean Age of Mothers Is on the Rise: United States, 2000–2014. *Center for Disease Control, National Center for Health Statistics.* January 2016. Available at: https://www.cdc.gov/nchs/data/databriefs/db232.pdf

Mathias, Peter, and Sidney Pollard. *The Cambridge Economic History of Europe, Vol. 8: The Industrial Economies: The Development of Economic and Social Policies.* Cambridge, UK: Cambridge University Press, 1989.

Mattes, Jane. *Single Mothers by Choice: A Guidebook for Single Women Who Are Considering or Have Chosen Motherhood.* New York: New York Times Books, 1994.

Matus, Ron. "Public Officials, Private Schools." *St. Petersburg Times,* April 6, 2005, 1A.

Mayo, Elton. *The Human Problems of an Industrial Civilization.* New York: Macmillan, 1933.

McAdam, Doug, ed. *Comparative Perspectives on Social Movements: Political Opportunities, Mobilizing Structures, and Cultural Framings.* Cambridge, UK: Cambridge University Press, 1996.

McAll, Christopher. *Class, Ethnicity, and Social Inequality.* Montreal, Quebec, Canada: McGill-Queen's University Press, 1990.

McCabe, Janice. Friends with Academic Benefits. *Contexts,* 15, no. 3 (2016): 22–29.

McCarthy, Justin. "In U.S., Socialist Presidential Candidates Least Appealing." *Gallup Polls,* June 22, 2015. Available at: http://www.gallup.com/poll/183713/socialist-presidential-candidates-least-appealing.aspx

McCaughey, Martha. *The Caveman Mystique: Pop-Darwinism and the Debates Over Sex, Violence, and Science.* New York, NY: Routledge, 2008.

McGregor, Douglas. *The Human Side of Enterprise* (1960). New York: McGraw-Hill, 2005.

McKibben, Bill. "The Christian Paradox." *Harper's Magazine,* August, 2005.

McMilan Cottom, Tressie. *Lower Ed: The Troubling Rise of For-Profit Colleges in the New Economy.* New York, NY: The New Press, 2017.

McMillan Cottom, Tressie, and Sarah Goldrick-Rab. "The Education Assembly Line: The Problem with For-Profits." *Contexts* 11, no. 4 (2012): 14–21.

McPherson, M., L. Smith-Lovin, and M. E. Brashears. "Social Isolation in America: Changes in Core Discussion Networks Over Two Decades." *American Sociological Review,* 71 (2006): 353–375.

Mead, George Herbert. *Mind, Self and Society.* Chicago: University of Chicago Press, 1967.

Mead, Margaret. *Sex and Temperament in Three Primitive Societies* (1935). New York: Harper Perennial, 2001.

Mead, Margaret. "Interview." *New Realities,* June 1978.

Meadow, Tey. "'A Rose Is a Rose': On Producing Legal Gender Classifications." *Gender & Society,* 24, no. 6 (2010): 814–837.

Mechanic, David, and David A. Rochefort. "Deinstitutionalization: An Appraisal of Reform." *Annual Review of Sociology,* 16, no. 1 (1990): 301–327.

Meissner, Christian A., John C. Brigham, and David A. Butz. "Memory for Own- and Other-Race Faces." *Applied Cognitive Psychology,* 19 (January 2005): 545–567.

Menkel-Meadow, Carrie. *The Comparative Sociology of Women Lawyers: The "Feminization" of the Legal Profession.* Menlo Park, CA: Institute for Social Research, 1987.

Mermin, Gordon B. T. *Wealth Accumulation Over the Life Cycle.* Washington, DC: The Urban Institute, 2008.

Merton, Robert K. "Discrimination and the American Creed," 1949. In Sociological Ambivalence and Other Essays, pp. 189–216. New York: The Free Press, 1976.

Merton, Robert K. "Social Structure and Anomie." *American Sociological Review,* 3 (October 1938): 672–682.

Merton, Robert K. *Social Theory and Social Structure* (1949). New York: The Free Press, 1968.

Messerschmidt, James W. "Making Bodies Matter:: Adolescent Masculinities, the Body, and Varieties of Violence." *Theoretical Criminology,* 3, no. 2 (1999): 197–220.

Messerschmidt, James W. "Becoming 'Real Men': Adolescent Masculinity Challenges and Sexual Violence." *Men and Masculinities,* 2, no. 3 (2000): 286–307.

Messerschmidt, James W. *Hegemonic Masculinities and Camouflaged Politics: Unmasking the Bush Dynasty and Its War Against Iraq.* Boulder, CO: Paradigm Publishers, 2010.

Metzl, Jonathan, and Kevin McLeish. "Mental Illness, Mass Shootings and the Politics of American Firearms." *Journal of American Public Health,* 105, no. 2 (2015): 240–249.

Meyer, David S., Nancy Whittier, and Belinda Robnett, eds. *Social Movements: Identity, Culture, and the State.* Oxford, UK: Oxford University Press, 2002.

Meyer, J. W., and Brian Rowan. "Institutional Organizations: Formal Structure as Myth and Ceremony." *American Journal of Sociology,* 83 (1977): 340–363.

Michael, R. T., J. H. Gagnon, E. O. Laumann, and G. Kolata. *Sex in America: A Definitive Study.* Boston: Little, Brown, 1994.

Milgram, Stanley. "Behavioral Study of Obedience." *Journal of Abnormal and Social Psychology,* 67 (1963): 371–378.

Milgram, Stanley. *Obedience to Authority; An Experimental View.* New York: Harper and Row, 1974.

Milgram, Stanley. "The Small World Problem." *Psychology Today* (May 1967).

Miller, Jon. "Science Literacy and Pseudo-Science." *American Association for the Advancement of Science Symposium,* February 27, 2007.

Miller, Lisa. "The Clash of the Yogis." *Newsweek,* May 15, 2010.

Miller, N., M. B. Brewer, and K. Edwards. "Cooperative Interaction in Desegregated Settings: A Laboratory Analog." *Journal of Social Issues,* 41, no. 3 (1985): 63–75.

Miller, Stephen. *Special Interest Groups in American Politics.* Piscataway, NJ: Transaction Publishers, 1983.

Miller, Walter B. "Lower Class Culture as a Generating Milieu of Gang Delinquency." In Marvin E. Wolfgang, Leonard Savitz, and Norma Johnston, eds., *The Sociology of Crime and Delinquency.* New York: Wiley, 1970. Originally published in *Journal of Social Issues,* 14 (1958): 5–19.

Mills, C. Wright. *White Collar: The American Middle Classes.* New York: Oxford University Press, 1959: 6.

Millward, David. "Arranged Marriages Make Comeback in Japan." *The Telegraph,* April 16, 2012.

Milner, Murray Jr. *Freaks, Geeks, and Cool Kids: American Teenagers, Schools and the Culture of Consumption.* New York: Routledge, 2006.

Ministry of Justice, 2015. Race and the Criminal Justice System, 2014. London: Ministry of Justice. Available at: https://www.gov.uk/government/statistics/race-and-the-criminal-justice-system-2014

Mintz, Steven. "American Childhood As a Social and Cultural Construction." In Barbara Risman and Virginia Rutter, eds., *Families as They Really Are* (pp. 48–58). New York, NY: W. W. Norton, 2009.

Mishel, Emma. 2016. "Discrimination against Queer Women in the U.S. Workforce: A Resume Audit Study." *Socius,* (2016): 1–13.

Moffatt, Michael. *Coming of Age in New Jersey.* New Brunswick, NJ: Rutgers University Press, 1989.

Moghadam, Valentine. "Islamic Feminism and its Discontents." *Signs,* 27, no. 4 (Summer, 2002): 1135–1171.

Molotch, Harvey. *Where Stuff Comes From: How Toasters, Toilets, Cars, Computers and Many Other Things Come to Be as They Are.* New York, NY: Routledge, 2003.

Moore, Barrington. *Social Origins of Dictatorship and Democracy: Lord and Peasant in the Making of the Modern World.* Boston, MA: Beacon Press, 1966.

Moore, J. W., and Hagedorn, J. M. "Female Gangs: A Focus on Research." *Bulletin, Youth Gang Series.* Washington, DC: U.S. Department of Justice, Office of Juvenile Justice and Delinquency Prevention, 2001.

Moore, Lisa Jean. "'Billy, the Sad Sperm with No Tail': Representations of Sperm in Children's Books." *Sexualities,* 6, no. 3–4 (2003): 277–300.

Moore, Mignon. "Lipstick or Timberlands: Meanings of Gender Presentation in Black Lesbian Communities." *Signs,* 32, no. 1 (2006): 113–139.

Moore, Molly. "Micro-Credit Pioneer Wins Peace Prize." *Washington Post,* October 14, 2006, A1.

Moore, Solomon. "Executions and Death Sentences in United States Dropped in 2008, Report Finds." *New York Times,* December 11, 2008.

Moreno, Jenalia, "Study Finds Growing Latino Affluence—Young Hispanics." *Houston Chronicle,* May 23, 2008, 14.

Morin, Rich. Rising Share of American See Conflict between Rich and Poor. *Pew Research Center, Social & Demographic Trends,* January 11, 2012. Available at: http://www.pewsocialtrends.org/2012/01/11/rising-share-of-americans-see-conflict-between-rich-and-poor/

Morris, Aldon D., and Carol McClurg Mueller, eds. *Frontiers in Social Movement Theory.* New Haven, CT: Yale University Press, 1992.

Morris, Martina. "Telling Tails Explain the Discrepancy in Sexual Partner Reports." *Nature,* 365, no. 6445 (1993): 437–440.

Morsch, James. "The Problem of Motive in Hate Crimes: The Argument against Prescriptions of Racial Motivation." *Journal of Criminal Law and Criminology,* 82, no. 3 (Autumn 1991): 659–689.

Mortimer, Caroline. "Black Americans are being killed at 12 times the rate of white people in the developed world." *The Independent,* July 8, 2016. Available at: http://www.independent.co.uk/news/world/americas/black-americans-12-times-more-likely-murdered-developed-country-dallas-shooting-statistics-a7127596.html

Moss-Kanter, Rosabeth. *Men and Women of the Corporation.* New York: Basic Books, 1977.

Mossaad, Nadwa. "The Impact of the Recession on Older Americans." *Population Reference Bureau,* 2010.

Mosteller, Frederick. "The Tennessee Study of Class Size in the Early School Grades" *Critical Issues For Children and Youths,* 5, no. 2 (1995): 113–127.

Mowry, George. *The Era of Theodore Roosevelt and the Birth of Modern America.* New York, NY: Harper, 1958.

Mumford, Lewis. *The City in History: Its Origins, Its Transformations, and Its Prospects.* New York, NY: Harvest Books, 1968.

Mumola, Christopher J., and Jennifer Karberg. *Drug Use and Dependence, State and Federal Prisoners, 2004.* Washington, DC: U.S. Department of Justice, October 2006 (NCJ213530).

Munsch, Christin L., and Robb Willer. "The Role of Gender Identity Threat in Perceptions of Date Rape and Sexual Coercion." *Violence Against Women,* 18, no. 10 (2012): 1125–1146.

Muravchik, Joshua. "Marxism." *Foreign Policy,* 133 (November–December, 2002), 36–38.

Murdock, George P. *Social Structure.* New York: Macmillan, 1949.

Murphy, Evelyn, and E. J. Graff. *Getting Even: Why Women Don't Get Paid Like Men—and What to Do About It.* New York, NY: Simon and Schuster, 2005.

Mustard, David B. "Racial, Ethnic, and Gender Disparities in Sentencing: Evidence from the U.S. Federal Courts." *Journal of Law and Economics,* 44 (2001): 285–314.

MyBudget360.com. 1.1 Million Americans Filed for Personal Bankruptcies in 2009 a Jump of 32 Percent from 2008. *MyBudget360.com,* 2009. Available at: http://www.mybudget360.com/141-million-americans-filed-for-personal-bankruptcies-in-2009-a-jump-of-32-percent-from-2008-more-and-more-average-americans-resorting-to-bankruptcy-even-with-tougher-rules-to-file/

NAACP. "Criminal Justice Fact Sheet," 2016. Available at: http://www.naacp.org/criminal-justice-fact-sheet/

Nagel, Joane. "American Indian Ethnic Renewal: Politics and the Resurgence of Identity." *American Sociological Review* 60, no. 6 (1995): 947–965.

Nagourney, Eric. "Surgery Remains 'Macho' Field, Survey Finds." *The New York Times,* April 18, 2006. Available at: http://www.nytimes.com/2006/04/18/health/18spec.html

Naples, Nancy A., and Manisha Desai. *Women's Activism and Globalization: Linking Local Struggles and Global Politics.* New York, NY: Routledge, 2002.

Nathan, Rebekah. *My Freshman Year.* Ithaca, NY: Cornell University Press, 2005.

National Alliance for Caregiving. Caregiving In the U.S. *AARP, Public Policy Institute,* June 2015. Available at: www.caregiving.org/wp-content/uploads/2015/05/2015_CaregivingintheUS_Executive-Summary-June-4_WEB.pdf

National Assessment of Educational Progress (NAEP). "The Nation's Report Card, 2015." *U.S. Department of Education, Institute of Education Sciences,* 2015. Available at: https://nces.ed.gov/nationsreportcard/

National Association for Rural Mental Health. "Suicide Rates in Rural Areas," 2007. Available at: www.highplainsmentalhealth.com/news.asp?ID=73

National Association for Single Sex Public Education. "Learning Style Differences." *NASSPE,* 2014. Available at: http://www.singlesexschools.org/research-learning.htm

National Center for Education Statistics. "Table 219.70. Percentage of high school dropouts among persons 16 to 24 years old (status dropout rate), by sex and race/ethnicity: Selected Years, 1960-2014." *IES > NCES,* 2015. Available at: https://nces.ed.gov/programs/digest/d15/tables/dt15_219.70.asp

National Center for Education Statistics. "Table 326.10. Graduation rate from first institution attended for first-time, full-time bachelor's degree-seeking students at 4-year postsecondary institutions, by race/ethnicity, time to completion, sex, control of institution, and acceptance rate: Selected cohort entry years, 1996 through 2008." *IES > NCES*, 2015. Available at: https://nces.ed.gov/programs/digest/d15/tables/dt15_326.10.asp

National Center for Education Statistics. "Table 603.20 (Digest 2016): Percentage of the population 25 to 64 years old who attained any postsecondary degree, by age group and country, Selected years, 2001 through 2015." *National Center for Educational Statistics*, October 18, 2016. Available at: https://nces.ed.gov/programs/digest/d16/tables/dt16_603.20.asp

National Center for Education Statistics. "Graduation Rates." *National Center for Education Statistics, IES > NCES*, 2017. Available at: https://nces.ed.gov/fastfacts/display.asp?id=40

National Center for Education Statistics. "Immediate College Enrollment Rate." *National Center for Education Statistics, IES > NCES*, updated March 2017. Available at: http://nces.ed.gov/programs/coe/indicator_cpa.asp

National Center for Education Statistics. "Private School Enrollment." *IES > NCES, National Center for Education Statistics*. Updated March 2017. Available at: http://nces.ed.gov/programs/coe/indicator_cgc.asp

National Center for Health Statistics. "Body Measurements." *Center for Disease Control and Prevention*, 2016. Available at: https://www.cdc.gov/nchs/fastats/body-measurements.htm

National Center for Health Statistics. "Health Expenditures." *Centers for Disease Control and Prevention*, 2017. Available at: http://www.cdc.gov/nchs/fastats/health-expenditures.htm

National Center for Public Policy and Higher Education. "Beyond the Rhetoric: Improving College Readiness Through Coherent State Policy," 2010. Available at: http://www.highereducation.org/reports/college_readiness/gap.shtml

National Center for Victims of Crime. 2015. Available at: http://victimsofcrime.org/docs/default-source/ncvrw2015/2015ncvrw_stats_stalking.pdf?sfvrsn=2

National Council of La Raza. *Lost Opportunities: The Realities of Latinos in the Criminal Justice System*. Washington, DC, 2004.

National Council on Crime and Delinquency. *U.S. Rates of Incarceration: A Global Perspective*. Washington, DC: 2006.

National Crime Victimization Survey. *Bureau of Justice Statistics*, 2014. Available at: https://www.bjs.gov/index.cfm?ty=dcdetail&iid=245

National Gang Center. National Youth Gang Survey Analysis, 2012. Available at: https://www.nationalgangcenter.gov/survey-analysis/prevalence-of-gang-problems.

National Institute of Justice. "Gun Violence, 2017. Available at: https://nij.gov/topics/crime/gun-violence/Pages/welcome.aspx

National Institute on Aging. 2014–2015 Alzheimer's Disease Progress Report: Advancing Research Toward a Cure. *U.S. Department of Health and Human Services*, December

2015. Available at: https://www.nia.nih.gov/sites/default/files/2014-2015_alzheimers-disease-progress-report.pdf

National Public Radio. "Guns in America—By the Numbers." *NPR*, January 5, 2016. Available at: http://www.npr.org/2016/01/05/462017461/guns-in-america-by-the-numbers

National Retail Federation, 2016. National Retail Security Survey, June 2016: https://nrf.com/system/tdf/Documents/retail%20library/NRF_2016_NRSS_restricted-rev.pdf?file=1&title=National%20Retail%20Security%20Survey%202016.

National Rural Health Association. "Farm Bill Reauthorization: Implications for the Health of Rural Communities." Issue paper, November 2006.

National Science Foundation. "Global Trends in Higher Education in Science and Engineering." Science and Engineering Indicators, 2008. Available at www.nsf.gov/statistics/seind08/c2/c2s5.htm#c2s54

National Student Clearinghouse Research Center. "Completing College: A National View of Educational Attainment Rates by Race and Ethnicity." April 26, 2017. Available at: https://nscresearchcenter.org/signaturereport12-supplement-2/

National Vital Statistics Reports. "Births: Final Data for 2015." National Vital Statistics Reports 66, no. 1 (January 5, 2017): 1–69. Available at: https://www.cdc.gov/nchs/data/nvsr/nvsr66/nvsr66_01.pdf.

National White Collar Crime Center."National Public Survey on White Collar Crime," 2010. Available at: www.nw3c.org.

NationMaster. "Media > Televisions: Countries Compared." *Nationmaster.com*, 2003. Available at: http://www.nationmaster.com/country-info/stats/Media/Televisions

Neal, Derek and Armin Rick. "The Prison Boom and the Lack of Black Progress after Smith and Welch." NBER Working Paper No. 20283, *The National Bureau of Economics Research*, July 2014. Available at: http://www.nber.org/papers/w20283.pdf

Newman, Cathy. "Why Are We So Fat?" *National Geographic*, August 2004.

Newman, Katherine. *No Shame in My Game: The Working Poor in the Inner City*. New York: Alfred A. Knopf, 1999.

Newman, Katherine, and David Pedulla, "Inequality in America." *The Nation*, July 19, 2010, p. 18.

Newport, Frank. "Most Americans Still Believe in God." *Gallup, Social Issues*, June 29, 2016. Available at: http://www.gallup.com/poll/193271/americans-believe-god.aspx

Newton, Michael. *Savage Girls and Wild Boys: A History of Feral Children*. New York: Thomas Dunne Books, 2003.

New York City Department for the Aging. "Under the Radar: New York State Elder Abuse Prevalence Study," May 2011. Available at: http://ocfs.ny.gov/main/reports/Under%20the%20Radar%2005%2012%2011%20final%20report.pdf

Nielson. "U.S. Homes Add Even More T.V. Sets in 2010," *Neilsen NewsWire*, April 28, 2010. Available at: http://www.nielsen.com/us/en/insights/news/2010/u-s-homes-add-even-more-tv-sets-in-2010.html

Nisbet, Robert A. *The Social Bond: An Introduction to the Study of Sociology.* New York, NY: Alfred A. Knopf, 1970.

Nock, Steven. "The New Chronology of Union Formation: Strategies for Measuring Changing Pathways." Paper prepared for Office of the Assistant Secretary for Planning and Evaluation, HHS, November 2003. Washington, DC: Health and Human Services.

Noguera, Pedro. *The Trouble with Black Boys.* New York, NY: John Wiley and Sons, 2008.

Noguera, Pedro, Aída Hurtado, and Edward Fergus. *Invisible No More: Understanding the Disenfranchisement of Latino Men and Boys.* London, UK: Routledge, 2013.

Noordewier, M., F. van Horen, K. I. Ruys, and D. A. Stapel. "What's in a Name? The Effects of Marital Name Change" in *Basic and Applied Social Psychology*, 32 (Winter 2010): 17–25.

North, Douglas, and Robert Paul Thomas. *The Rise of the Western World: A New Economic History.* Cambridge, UK: Cambridge University Press, 1976.

Notestein, Frank. "Population—The Long View." In P. W. Schultz, ed., *Food for the World*. Chicago, IL: University of Chicago Press: 36–57, 1945.

Novak, M. *The Rise of the Unmeltable Ethnics*, New York, NY: Macmillan, 1973.

Nyhan, Brenden, and Jason Reifler. When Corrections Fail: The Persistence of Political Misperceptions. *Political Behavior* 32 (2010): 303–330.

Oakes, Jeannie. *Keeping Track: How Schools Structure Inequality.* New Haven, CT: Yale University Press, 1985.

Oakes, Jeannie. *Multiplying Inequalities: The Effects of Race, Social Class, and Tracking on Opportunities to Learn Mathematics and Science.* Santa Monica, CA: RAND Corporation, 1990.

Ocampo, Anthony C. *The Latinos of Asia: How Filipino Americans Break the Rules of Race.* Stanford, CA: Stanford University Press, 2016.

OECD. Pisa 2012 Results in Focus. Available at: http://www.oecd.org/pisa/keyfindings/pisa-2012-results-overview.pdf.

"OECD Regions at a Glance 2013—United States Profile." *Organization for Economic Cooperation and Development*, 2013. Available at: https://www.oecd.org/governance/regional-policy/Country-statistics-profile-United-States.pdf

OECD. "Education at a Glance 2014: OECD Indicators," 2014. Available at: https://www.oecd.org/edu/Education-at-a-Glance-2014.pdf

OECD. "Life Expectancy at Birth." *OECD Data*, 2015. Available at: https://data.oecd.org/healthstat/life-expectancy-at-birth.htm

OECD. *Universal Basic Skills: What Countries Stand to Gain*, OECD Publishing, average of mathematics and science. 2015. Available at: http://www.keepeek.com/Digital-Asset-Management/oecd/education/universal-basic-skills_9789264234833-en#page38.

OECD. Education and Skills Today, "Education Post-2015." Available at http://oecdeducationtoday.blogspot.com/2015/05/education-post-2015.html

OECD. "Education at a Glance 2016." *Organization for Economic Cooperation and Development*, September 15, 2016. Available at: http://www.oecd.org/edu/education-at-a-glance-19991487.htm

OECD. "Environments at a Glance, 2015." *OECD Indicators*, 2016. Available at: http://www.keepeek.com/Digital-Asset-Management/oecd/environment/environment-at-a-glance-2015_9789264235199-en#page49

OECD. *OECD Employment Outlook 2016.* Paris: OECD, 2016. Available at: http://www.oecd.org/els/oecd-employment-outlook-19991266.htm

OECD. Life Expectancy at Birth. *Organization for Economic Cooperation and Development.* 2016. Available at: https://data.oecd.org/healthstat/life-expectancy-at-birth.htm

OECD. "Other National R & D Expenditure By Field of Science and By Type of Cost, OECD." Organization for Economic Cooperation and Development, 2017. Available at: https://stats.oecd.org/Index.aspx?DataSetCode=ONRD_COST

OECD. "Part Time Employment Rates." *Organization for Economic Cooperation and Development*, 2016. Available at: https://data.oecd.org/emp/part-time-employment-rate.htm

OECD. "International Migration Database." *Organization for Economic Cooperation and Development*, OECD.Stat, June 5, 2017. Available at: https://stats.oecd.org/Index.aspx?DataSetCode=MIG

Ogbu, John. "Understanding the School Performance of Urban Blacks: Some Essential Background Knowledge." In H. J. Walhberg, O. Reyes, and R. P. Weissberg, eds., *Children and Youth: Interdisciplinary Perspectives.* Thousand Oaks, CA: Sage Press, 1997.

Ogbu, John. *Black American Students in an Affluent Suburb: A Study of Academic Disengagement.* New York, NY: Taylor & Francis, 2003.

Ogbu, John, and A. Davis. *Black American Students in an Affluent Suburb: A Study in Academic Disengagement.* Mahwah, NJ: Lawrence Erlbaum Publishers, 2003.

Ogburn, William F. *Social Change with Respect to Culture and Original Nature* (1922). New York, NY: Dell, 1966.

Oh, Kongdan, and Ralph C. Hassig. *North Korea: Through the Looking Glass.* Washington, DC: The Brookings Institution Press, 2000.

Olweus, Dan. *Bullying at School: What We Know and What We Can Do.* New York, NY: Blackwell, 1993.

Olyslager, Femke, and Lynn Conway. "On the Calculation of the Prevalence of Transsexualism." In *World Professional Association for Transgender Health 20th International Symposium, Chicago, Illinois*, 2007. Available at: http://citeseerx.ist.psu.edu/viewdoc/download?doi=10.1.1.692.8704&rep=rep1&type=pdf

Omi, Michael, and Howard Winant. *Racial Formation in the United States.* New York, NY: Routledge, 1986.

Orenstein, Peggy. *Schoolgirls.* New York: Doubleday, 1994.

Orenstein, Peggy. *Flux: Women on Sex, Work, Love, Kids, and Life in a Half-Changed World.* New York, NY: Academic Press, 2001.

Orfield, Gary. *Brown at 50: King's Dream or the Plessy Nightmare.* Cambridge, MA: Harvard University Press, 2004.

Organization for Economic Cooperation and Development (OECD). "Competition Policy and the Information Economy." Global Forum on Economic Competition, December 2008a.

Organization for Economic Cooperation (OECD); Flowing Data, "Who spends the most years in retirement?" 2011. Available at: https://flowingdata.com/2011/04/07/who-spends-the-most-years-in-retirement/

Orum, Anthony M. *An Introduction to Political Sociology,* 4th ed. Englewood Cliffs, NJ: Prentice-Hall, 2000.

Oshima, Harry T. "The Transition from an Agricultural to an Industrial Economy in East Asia." *Economic Development and Cultural Change,* 34, no. 4 (July 1986): 783–809.

Owen, Robert Dale. *Moral Physiology; or, A Brief and Plain Treatise on the Population Question* (New York: Wright and Owen, 1831)

Padavic, Irene, and Barbara F. Reskin. *Women and Men at Work* (1994). Thousand Oaks, CA: Pine Forge Press, 2002.

Pagden, Anthony. *Peoples and Empires: A Short History of European Migration, Exploration, and Conquest, from Greece to the Present.* New York, NY: Modern Library, 2001.

Page, Marianne, and Ann Huff Stevens. "Understanding Racial Differences in the Economic Costs of Growing Up in a Single-Parent Family." *Demography,* 42, no. 1 (February 2005): 75–90.

Pager, Devah. "The Mark of a Criminal Record." *American Journal of Sociology,* 108, no. 5 (2003): 937–975.

Paige, Jeffrey. *Agrarian Revolutions.* New York: The Free Press, 1975.

Palen, J. John. *The Suburbs.* New York: McGraw-Hill, 1995.

Panter-Brick, Catherine, Robert H. Layton, and Peter Rowley-Conwy. *Hunter-Gatherers: An Interdisciplinary Perspective.* Cambridge, UK: Cambridge University Press, 2001.

Paoletti, Jo B. *Pink and Blue: Telling the Boys from the Girls in America.* Bloomington, IN: Indiana University Press, 2012.

Parker, Kim, and Eileen Patten. "The Sandwich Generation: Rising Financial Burdens for Middle-Aged Americans." *Pew Research Center,* (January 30, 2013). Available at: http://www.pewsocialtrends.org/2013/01/30/the-sandwich-generation/

Parker-Pope, Tara. "Love, Sex and the Changing Landscape of Infidelity." *New York Times,* October 28, 2008.

Parsons, Talcott. *The Structure of Social Action.* New York: The Free Press, 1937.

Parsons, Talcott. *The Social System.* New York: The Free Press, 1951.

Parsons, Talcott. *Societies: Evolutionary and Comparative Perspectives.* Englewood Cliffs, NJ: Prentice-Hall, 1966.

Pascoe, C. J. *"Dude, You're a Fag": Masculinity and Sexuality in High School.* Berkeley, CA: University of California Press, 2007.

Pascoe, C. J. "Notes on a Sociology of Bullying: Young Men's Homophobia as Gender Socialization." *QED: A Journal in GLBTQ Worldmaking* 1 (2013): 87–103.

Passel, Jeffrey S., and D'Vera Cohn. "Share of Unauthorized Immigrant Workers in Construction, Production Falls Since 2007." Pew Research Center, Hispanic Trends, March 26, 2015. Available at: http://www.pewhispanic.org/2015/03/26/share-of-unauthorized-immigrant-workers-in-production-construction-jobs-falls-since-2007/

Passel, Jeffrey S., and Roberto Suro. "Rise, Peak, and Decline: Trends in U.S. Immigration 1992–2004." Pew Hispanic Center Reports on Immigration, September 2005. Philadelphia, PA.

Passel, Jeffrey S., D'Vera Cohn, and Mark Hugo Lopez. "Hispanics Account for More than Half of Nation's Growth in Past Decade." *Pew Research Center, Hispanic Trends,* March 24, 2011. Available at: http://www.pewhispanic.org/2011/03/24/hispanics-account-for-more-than-half-of-nations-growth-in-past-decade/

Paternoster, Raymond, Robert Brame, and Sarah Bacon, eds. *The Death Penalty: America's Experience with Capital Punishment.* New York, NY: Oxford University Press, 2007.

Patten, Eileen. "Racial, Gender Wage Gaps Persist in U.S. Despite Some Progress." *Pew Research Center,* July 1, 2016. Available at: http://www.pewresearch.org/fact-tank/2016/07/01/racial-gender-wage-gaps-persist-in-u-s-despite-some-progress/

Paulin, Geoffrey, and Brian Riordan. "Making It Their Own: The Baby Boom Meets Generation X." *The Monthly Review* (February 1998): 10–21.

PBS/Frontline. "Merchants of Cool." Airdate February 27, 2001.

Pear, Robert. "Gap in Life Expectancy Widens for the Nation." *New York Times,* March 23, 2008: 44.

Pearce, Diana. "The Feminization of Poverty: Women, Work, and Welfare." *Urban and Social Change Review,* 11 (1978): 28–36.

Pell, M. B., and Joshua Schneyer. "The Thousands of U.S. Locales where Lead Poisoning is Worse than in Flint." *Reuters—Off the Charts,* December 19, 2016. Available at: http://www.reuters.com/investigates/special-report/usa-lead-testing/#interactive-lead

Pell Institute, 2015. Indicators of Higher Education Equity in the United States. Philadelphia, Pell Institute. Available at: http://www.pellinstitute.org/downloads/publications-Indicators_of_Higher_Education_Equity_in_the_US_45_Year_Trend_Report.pdf

Pennycock, Alastair. "Language, Localization, and the Real: Hip-Hop and the Global Spread of Authenticity." *Journal of Language, Identity & Education,* 6, no. 2 (2007): 101–115.

Perrow, Charles. *Normal Accidents: Living with High-Risk Technologies.* New York, NY: Basic Books, 1984.

Perry, A. "Brief History: The Resource Curse." *Time,* June 28, 2010. Available at: http://content.time.com/time/magazine/article/0,9171,1997460,00.html

Perry, Mark J. "Why do public school teachers send their own children to private schools at a rate 2X the national average?" *American Enterprise Institute,* October 9, 2013. Available at: http://www.aei.org/publication/why-do-public-school-teachers-send-their-own-children-to-private-schools-at-a-rate-2x-the-national-average/

Perry-Jenkins, M., and A. C. Crouter. "Implications of Men's Provider Role Attitudes for Household Work and Marital Satisfaction." *Journal of Family Issues,* 11, no. 2 (1990): 136–156.

Peter G. Peterson Foundation, 2016. "Per Capita Health Care Costs—International Comparisons," 2016.

Peter, Laurence J., and Raymond Hull. *The Peter Principle: Why Things Always Go Wrong.* New York: William Morrow, 1969.

Peterson, Richard A. "Understanding Audience Segmentation: From Elite and Mass to Omnivore and Univore." *Poetics,* 21, no. 4 (1992): 243–258.

Peterson, Richard A., and Roger M. Kern. "Changing Highbrow Taste: From Snob to Omnivore." *American Sociological Review,* 61, no. 5 (1996): 900–907.

Petroff, Alanna. "Tim Cook Isn't the Only Openly Gay CEO." *CNN Money,* Oct. 14, 2014. Available at: http://money.cnn.com/2014/10/30/news/gay-ceos-tim-cook/

Pew Center on the States, Public Safety Performance Project. *One in 100: Behind Bars in America 2008.* Philadelphia, (published by The Pew Charitable Trusts); 2008.

Pew Economic Mobility Project. "Opinion Poll on Economic Mobility and the American Dream." 2009. Available at: www.economicmobility.org/poll2009

Pew Forum on Religion and Public Life. "Religion and Politics: Contention and Consensus," 2003. Available at: http://pewforum.org/publications/surveys/religion-politics.pdf

Pew Research Center. *A Barometer of Modern Morals: Sex, Drugs and the 1010.* Philadelphia: The Pew Charitable Trusts, 2006.

Pew Research Center, Spring 2014 Global Attitudes survey. Q13b & Q66b. Available at http://www.pewresearch.org/fact-tank/2015/03/12/how-do-americans-stand-out-from-the-rest-of-the-world/

Pew Research Center. "As Marriage and Parenthood Drift Apart, Public is Concerned about Social Impact." *Pew Research Center, Social & Demographic Trends,* July 1, 2007. Available at: http://www.pewsocialtrends.org/2007/07/01/as-marriage-and-parenthood-drift-apart-public-is-concerned-about-social-impact/

Pew Research Center. Millennials: Confident, Connected, Open to Change—Executive Summary. *Pew Research Center, Social & Demographic Trends,* February 24, 2010. Available at: http://www.pewsocialtrends.org/2010/02/24/millennials-confident-connected-open-to-change/

Pew Research Center. "Muslim Population of Indonesia." *Pew Research Center, Religion & Public Life,* November 4, 2010. Available at: http://www.pewforum.org/2010/11/04/muslim-population-of-indonesia/

Pew Research Center. "The Global Religious Landscape: Religiously Unaffiliated." *Pew Research Center, Religion & Social Life,* December 18, 2012. Available at: http://www.pewforum.org/2012/12/18/global-religious-landscape-unaffiliated/

Pew Research Center. "'Nones' on the Rise." *Pew Research Center, Religion & Public Life,* October 9, 2012. Available at: http://www.pewforum.org/2012/10/09/nones-on-the-rise/

Pew Research Center. "During Benedicts Papacy, Religious Observance Among Catholics in Europe Remained Low but Stable." *Pew Research Center, Religion & Public Life,* March 5, 2013. Available at: http://www.pewforum.org/2013/03/05/during-benedicts-papacy-religious-observance-among-catholics-in-europe-remained-low-but-stable/

Pew Research Center. "Millennials in Adulthood." *Pew Research Center, Social & Demographic Trends,* March 7, 2014. Available at: http://www.pewsocialtrends.org/2014/03/07/millennials-in-adulthood/

Pew Research Center. Millennials into Adulthood: Detached from Institutions, Networked with Friends. *Pew Research Center, Social & Demographic Trends,* March 7, 2014. Available at: http://www.pewsocialtrends.org/2014/03/07/millennials-in-adulthood/#low-on-social-trust-upbeat-about-the-nations-future

Pew Research Center. "Section 5: Political Engagement and Activism." June 12, 2014. Available at: http://www.people-press.org/2014/06/12/section-5-political-engagement-and-activism/

Pew Research Center. "Women and Leadership: Public Says Women are Equally Qualified, But Barriers Persist." *The Pew Research Center,* January 14, 2015. Available at: http://www.pewsocialtrends.org/2015/01/14/women-and-leadership/

Pew Research Center. "Across Racial Lines, More Say Nation Needs to Make Changes to Achieve Racial Equality." *Pew Research Center, U.S. Politics & Policy,* August 5, 2015. Available at: http://www.people-press.org/2015/08/05/across-racial-lines-more-say-nation-needs-to-make-changes-to-achieve-racial-equality/

Pew Research Center. "America's Changing Religious Landscape." *Pew Research Center, Religion and Public Life,* May 12, 2015. Available at: http://www.pewforum.org/2015/05/12/americas-changing-religious-landscape/

Pew Research Center. "Among LBGT Americans, bisexuals stand out when it comes to identity, acceptance. February 20, 2015. Available at: http://www.pewresearch.org/fact-tank/2015/02/20/among-lgbt-americans-bisexuals-stand-out-when-it-comes-to-identity-acceptance/

Pew Research Center. "Blacks Express Less Confidence than Whites in Local Police to Treat Blacks and Whites Equally." Available at http://www.pewresearch.org/fact-tank/2015/04/28/blacks-whites-police/

Pew Research Center. "Child Poverty Rate Stable Among Blacks, Drops Among Other Groups;" July 14, 2015. Available at: http://www.pewresearch.org/fact-tank/2015/07/14/black-child-poverty-rate-holds-steady-even-as-other-groups-see-declines/

Pew Research Center. "Gay Marriage around the World," June 26, 2015. Available at http://www.pewforum.org/2015/06/26/gay-marriage-around-the-world-2013/

Pew Research Center. "Multiracial in America. Chapter 1: Race and Multiracial Americans in the U.S. Census." *Pew Research Center, Social & Demographic Trends*, June 11, 2015. Available at: http://www.pewsocialtrends.org/2015/06/11/chapter-1-race-and-multiracial-americans-in-the-u-s-census/#fn-20523-15

Pew Research Center. "Parenting in America: 1. The American Family Today." *Pew Research Center, Social & Demographic Trends*, December 17, 2015. Available at: http://www.pewsocialtrends.org/2015/12/17/1-the-american-family-today/#fn-21212-3

Pew Research Center. "Religious Landscape Study." *Pew Research Center, Religion & Public Life*, 2015. Available at: http://www.pewforum.org/religious-landscape-study/

Pew Research Center. Teen Relationships Survey, Sept. 25–Oct. 9, 2014 and Feb. 10–March 16, 2015. Available at http://www.pewinternet.org/2015/08/06/teens-technology-and-friendships/

Pew Research Center. "Women and Leadership." *Pew Research Center, Social & Demographic Trends*. January 14, 2015. Available at: http://www.pewsocialtrends.org/2015/01/14/women-and-leadership/

Pew Research Center. "Americans Express Increasingly Warm Feelings Toward Religious Groups." *Pew Research Center, Religion & Social Life*, February 15, 2017. Available at: http://www.pewforum.org/2017/02/15/americans-express-increasingly-warm-feelings-toward-religious-groups/

Pew Research Center. "The Changing Global Religious Landscape." *Pew Research Center, Religion & Public Life*, April 5, 2017. Available at: http://www.pewforum.org/2017/04/05/the-changing-global-religious-landscape/

Pew Research Center, American Trends panel (wave 6). Survey of U.S. adults conducted August 11–September 3, 2014. Available at http://www.pewinternet.org/2015/09/10/what-the-public-knows-and-does-not-know-about-science/

Phillips, Scott. "Racial Disparities in the Capital of Capital Punishment." *Houston Law Review*, 45 (October 2008): 441–464.

Piaget, J. *The Child's Conception of the World*. London, UK: Routledge and Kegan Paul, 1928.

Piaget, J. *The Moral Judgment of the Child*. London, UK: Kegan Paul, Trench, Trubner and Co., 1932.

Piaget, J. *The Origins of Intelligence in Children*. London, UK: Routledge and Kegan Paul, 1953.

Piaget, J. *The Child's Construction of Reality*. London, UK: Routledge and Kegan Paul, 1955.

Piper, Abraham. "First Known Photograph of Someone Giving the Finger, 1886." *TwentyTwoWords.com*, Accessed April 27, 2017. Available at: http://twentytwowords.com/first-known-photograph-of-someone-giving-the-finger-1886-3-pictures/

Pipes, Richard. *Communism*. London, UK: Weidenfeld and Nicolson, 2001.

Pisani, Joseph. More Upper-Income Workers Living Paycheck to Paycheck. *CNBC.com*, September 16, 2009. Available at: http://www.cnbc.com/id/32862851

Pleck, Joseph H. "Paternal Involvement: Levels, Sources, and Consequences." In M. E. Lamb, ed., *The Role of the Father in Child Development*, 3rd ed. (pp. 66–103). New York, NY: John Wiley, 1997.

Pleck, Joseph H., and Masciadrelli, Brian. "Paternal Involvement in U.S. Residential Fathers: Levels, Sources, and Consequences." In M. E. Lamb, ed., *The Role of the Father in Child Development*, 4th ed. (pp. 222–271). New York, NY: Wiley, 2004.

Pollak, Otto. *The Criminality of Women* (1950). Westport, CT: Greenwood, 1978.

Ponemon Institute. *Cost of Cyber Crime Study: United*. Traverse City, MI: Ponemon Institute LLC, October 2013. Available at: https://media.scmagazine.com/documents/54/2013_us_ccc_report_final_6-1_13455.pdf

Pope, Harrison, Katharine Phillips, and Roberto Olivardia. *The Adonis Complex: The Secret Crisis of Male Body Obsession*. New York, NY: The Free Press, 2000.

Popkin, Samuel L. *The Reasoning Voter: Communication and Persuasion in Presidential Campaigns*. Chicago, IL: University of Chicago Press, 1994.

Population Reference Bureau. Total Fertility Rate, 1970 and 2014. *Population Reference Bureau*. 2014.

PopulationPyramid.net. "Population Pyramids of the World from 1950–2100." Available at http://www.populationpyramid.net/italy/2015/; http://www.populationpyramid.net/mexico/2015/; and http://www.populationpyramid.net/iraq/2015/

Portes, A., M. Castells, and L. A. Benton. *The Informal Economy: Studies in Advanced and Less Developed Countries*. Baltimore, MD: Johns Hopkins University Press, 1989.

Poston, Dudley L., and Amanda K. Baumle. "Patterns of Asexuality in the United States." Paper presented at the Annual Meeting of the American Sociological Association, Montreal, Canada, August 11, 2006.

Potok, Mark. *The Year in Hate, 2005*. Montgomery, AL: Southern Poverty Law Center, 2006. Available at: www.splcenter.org/intel/intelreport/article.isp?aid=627

Powell, Walter W., and Kaisa Snellman. "The Knowledge Economy." *Annual Review of Sociology*, 30 (August 2004): 199–220.

Preston, Samuel H., Patrick Heuveline, and Michel Guillot. *Demography: Measuring and Modeling Population Processes*. Malden, MA: Blackwell Publishers, 2001.

Preves, Sharon E. *Intersex and Identity: The Contested Self.* New Brunswick, NJ: Rutgers University Press, 2003.

Prison Policy Initiative. "Mass Incarceration, the Whole Pie, 2017." *Prisonpolicy.org,* 2017. Available at: https://www.prisonpolicy.org/reports/pie2017.html

Putnam, Robert. *Bowling Alone: The Collapse and Revival of American Community.* New York, NY: Simon and Schuster, 2001.

Pyrooz, David C. and Cary Sweeten. "Gang Membership Between Ages 5 and 17 Years in the United States." *Journal of Adolescent Health,* 56, no. 4 (2015): 414–419.

Quattrone, G. A. "On the Perception of a Group's Variability." In S. Worchel and W. Austin, eds., *The Psychology of Intergroup Relations,* 2nd ed. Chicago: Nelson-Hall: 25-48, 1986.

Quinney, Richard. *Class, State, and Crime: On the Theory and Practice of Criminal Justice.* New York: David McKay, 1977.

The Racial Slur Database. Data, April 19, 2017. Available at http://www.rsdb.org/

Radway, Janice. *A Feeling for Books: The Book-of-the-Month Club, Literary Taste, and Middle-Class Desire.* Chapel Hill, NC: University of North Carolina Press, 1999.

Raeburn, Nicole C. *Changing Corporate America from the Inside Out: Lesbian and Gay Workplace Rights.* Minneapolis, MN: University of Minnesota Press, 2004.

Raley, Kelly R., and Megan M. Sweeney. "What Explains Race and Ethnic Variation in Cohabitation, Marriage, Divorce, and Nonmarital Fertility?" Los Angeles, CA: California Center for Population Research, September, 2007.

Raley, Kelly R., Megan M. Sweeney, and Danielle Wondra. "The Growing Racial and Ethnic Divide in U.S. Marriage Patterns." *Future Child* 25, no. 2 (Fall 2015): 89–109.

Rao, S. L. "Too Many Bosses: The UPA has a Cabinet with Many Insubordinate Ministers." *The Telegraph, Calcutta, India,* June 5, 2006. Available at: http://www.telegraphindia.com/1060605/asp/opinion/story_6293323.asp

Ratcliffe, Michael, Charlynn Burd, Kelly Holder, and Alison Fields. "Defining Rural at the U.S. Census. *American Community Survey and Geography Brief,* 2016. Available at: http://www2.census.gov/geo/pdfs/reference/ua/Defining_Rural.pdf

Rauch, Jonathan. "The Real Roots of Midlife Crisis." *The Atlantic* (December 2016). Available at: http://www.theatlantic.com/magazine/archive/2014/12/the-real-roots-of-midlife-crisis/382235/

Rawlings, M. Keith, R. J. Graff, R. Calderon, S. Casey-Bailey, and M. Pasley. "Patient and Provider Differences in What They Perceive as Having 'Had Sex': Implications for HIV/AIDS Prevention." Poster 889, 42nd Annual Meeting of the Infectious Diseases of America. Boston, MA: September, 2004.

Raymond, Nate. "Justice Department Objects to White Collar Sentencing Reforms." Reuters News Service, 2015. Available at: http://www.reuters.com/article/us-usa-fraud-sentencing-idUSKBN0M82SZ20150312

Reardon, Sean F. "The Landscape of Socioeconomic and Racial/Ethnic Educational Inequality." *Stanford University,* 2016. Available online: https://cepa.stanford.edu/sites/default/files/may-sreardon.pdf

Reaves, Brian A. "Local Police Departments 2013: Personnel, Policies, Practices," Bureau of Justice Statistics. *U.S. Department of Justice,* 2015. Available at: https://www.bjs.gov/content/pub/pdf/lpd13ppp.pdf.

Reckless, Walter. *American Criminology: New Directions.* New York, NY: Appleton-Century-Crofts, 1973.

Redfield, Robert. *Folk Cultures of the Yucatan.* Chicago, IL: University of Chicago Press, 1941.

Reger, Jo. *Everywhere and Nowhere: Contemporary Feminism in the United States.* New York, NY: Oxford University Press, 2012.

Resnick, Stephan A., and Richard D. Wolff. *Knowledge and Class: A Marxian Critique of Political Economy.* Chicago, IL: University of Chicago Press, 1987.

Retherford, Robert D., Noahiro Ogawa, and Rikiya Matsukura. "Late Marriage and Less Marriage." *Population and Development Review,* 27, no. 1 (2001): 65–78.

Rhode, Deborah L. *The Beauty Bias: The Injustice of Appearance in Life and Law.* New York, NY: Oxford University Press, 2010.

Rian, Shari. "Social Stigma Drives Some Women to Remove Tattoos." *The Los Angeles Times,* July 21, 2008. Available at: http://latimesblogs.latimes.com/booster_shots/2008/07/social-stigma-d.html

Rideout, Victoria J., Ulla G. Foehr, and Donald F. Roberts, Kaiser Family Foundation Study. "GENERATION M2: Media in the Lives of 8-to-18 Year-Olds: 9 (January 2010). Available at https://kaiserfamilyfoundation.files.wordpress.com/2013/01/8010.pdf.

Riesman, David. *The Lonely Crowd: A Study of the Changing American Character.* New Haven, CT: Yale University Press, 1961.

Rios, Victor M. *Punished: Policing the Lives of Black and Latino Boys.* New York, NY: NYU Press, 2011.

Ritzer, George. *The McDonaldization of America.* Thousand Oaks, CA: Pine Forge Press, 1996.

Robbins, Sarah. "Is Your Body Normal?" *Glamour,* July 2008, 98.

Roberts, Paul. *The End of Oil: On the Edge of a Perilous New World.* New York, NY: Mariner Books, 2005.

Robertson, Lindsay. "South Carolina Lt. Governor Andre Bauer Compares His State's Poor Children to "Stray Animals." *New York Magazine,* January 23, 2010. Available at: http://nymag.com/daily/intelligencer/2010/01/south_carolinas_lt_governor_co.html

Robinson, Dwight E. "Fashions in Shaving and Trimming of the Beard." *American Journal of Sociology,* 81, no. 5 (1976): 1133–1141.

Robson, David. "There Really Are 50 Eskimo Words for 'Snow'." *The Washington Post, Health & Science,* January 14, 2013.

Rochlin, Michael, "The Heterosexual Questionnaire." In Kimmel, Michael Kimmel and Michael Messner, eds., *Men's Lives,* 9th ed (New York: Pearson, 2013).

Roediger, David. *The Wages of Whiteness: Race and the Making of the American Working Class*. New York, NY: Verso, 1991.

Rogers, J. W., and M. D. Buffalo. "Fighting Back: Nine Modes of Adaptation to a Deviant Label." *Social Problems*, 22 (1974): 101–118.

Rosa, Eugene, A., Gary E. Machlis, and Kenneth M. Keating. "Energy and Society." *Annual Review of Sociology*, 14 (1988): 149–172.

Roscoe, Will, ed. *Boy-Wives and Female Husbands: Studies of African Homosexualities*. London, UK: Palgrave Macmillan, 2001.

Rose, Brad, and George Ross. "Socialism's Past, New Social Democracy, and Socialism's Futures." *Social Science History*, 18, no. 3 (Autumn 1994): 439–469.

Rose, Heather, and Glenn E. Martin. "Locking Down Civil Rights: Criminal Record-Based Discrimination." *Race/Ethnicity: Multidisciplinary Global Perspectives*, 2, no. 1 (Autumn, 2008): 13–19.

Rosenbaum, Janet Elise. "Patient Teenagers? A Comparison of the Sexual Behavior of Virginity Pledgers and Matched Nonpledgers." *Pediatrics*, 123, no. 1 (2009): 110–120.

Rosenberger, Nancy. "Rethinking Emerging Adulthood in Japan: Perspectives from Long-Term Single Women." *Child Development Perspectives*, 1 (2007): 92–95.

Rosenhan, David L. "On Being Sane in Insane Places," *Science*, 179 (January 1973): 250–258.

Rosenthal, Robert, and Lenore Jacobson. *Pygmalion in the Classroom: Teacher Expectations and Pupil's Intellectual Development* (1968). New York, NY: Irvington, 1992.

Rosich, Katherine. "Race, Ethnicity, and the Criminal Justice System." *The American Sociological Association—Department of Research and Development*, Washington, DC, 2007. Available at: http://www.asanet.org/sites/default/files/savvy/images/press/docs/pdf/ASARaceCrime.pdf

Ross, Andrew. *The Celebration Chronicles: Life, Liberty, and the Pursuit of Property Value in Disney's New Town*. New York, NY: Ballantine Books, 1999.

Rossi, Alice S. Naming Children in Middle-Class Families. *American Sociological Review*, 30, no. 4 (1965): 499–513.

Rothwell, J. "How the War on Drugs Damages Social Mobility." *The Brookings Institution*, September 30, 2014. Available at: https://www.brookings.edu/blog/social-mobility-memos/2014/09/30/how-the-war-on-drugs-damages-black-social-mobility/

Rousi, Rebekah. "An Uplifting Experience: Adopting Ethnography to Study Elevator User Behavior." *Ethnography Matters*—blog, April 2, 2013. Available at: http://ethnographymatters.net/blog/2013/04/02/an-uplifting-experience-adopting-ethnography-to-study-elevator-user-experience/

Rousseau, Jean-Jacques. *The Social Contract*. (1754). New York, NY: bnpublishing.com, 2007.

Rowling, J. K. *Harry Potter and the Sorcerer's Stone*. New York, NY: Scholastic, 1998.

Rubin, Lillian. *Intimate Strangers: Men and Women Together*. New York, NY: HarperCollins, 1983.

Rubin, Lillian. *Just Friends*. New York, NY: Harper and Row, 1986.

Rubin, Lillian. *Erotic Wars: What Happened to the Sexual Revolution?* New York, NY: Farrar, Straus & Giroux, 1990.

Rudolph, Frederick. *The American College and University: A History*. Athens: University of Georgia Press, 1990.

Rugg, W. D. "Experiments in Wording Questions." *Public Opinion Quarterly*, 5 (1941): 91–92.

Rule, Wilma, and Steven Hill. "Ain't I a Voter? Voting Rights for Women." *Ms.*, September–October 1996.

Rupp, Leila, Verta Taylor, Shiri Regev-Messalem, Alison C. K. Fogarty, and Paula England. "Queer Women in the Hookup Scene: Beyond the Closet?" *Gender & Society*, 28, no. 2 (2014): 212–235.

Rust, Paula Rodriguez. *Bisexuality and the Challenge to Lesbian Politics*. New York, NY: NYU Press, 1995.

Rust, Paula Rodriguez. *Bisexuality in the United States: A Social Science Reader*. New York, NY: Columbia University Press, 1999.

Ryan, Camille L., and Kurt Bauman. "Educational Attainment in the United States: 2015." United States Census Bureau, March 2016. Available at: https://www.census.gov/content/dam/Census/library/publications/2016/demo/p20-578.pdf

Saad, Lydia. "Americans Fault Mental Health System Most for Gun Violence." *Gallup*, September 20, 2013. Available at: http://www.gallup.com/poll/164507/americans-fault-mental-health-system-gun-violence.aspx

Sabol, William J., and Heather C. West. *Prisoners in 2007*. Washington, DC: US Department of Justice Bureau of Justice Statistics, December 2008 (NCJ224280).

Sadker, Myra, and David Sadker. *Failing at Fairness: How Schools Shortchange Girls*. New York, NY: McGraw Hill, 1994.

Saguy, Abigal C. "Sex, Inequality, and Ethnography: Response to Erich Goode." *Qualitative Sociology*, 25, no. 4 (2002): 549–556.

Saguy, Abigail C., and Kjerstin Gruys. "Morality and Health: News Media Constructions of Overweight and Eating Disorders." *Social Problems*, 57, no. 2 (2010): 231–250.

Salomon, Joshua A., Haidong Wang, Michael K. Freeman, Theo Vos, Abraham D. Flaxman, Alan D. Lopez, and Christopher J. L. Murray. "Healthy Life Expectancy for 187 Countries, 1990–2010: A Systematic Analysis for the Global Burden Disease Study 2010." *The Lancet*, 380, no. 9859 (2012): 2144–2162. Available at http://www.healthdata.org/

Sanchez-Jankowski, Martin. *Islands in the Street: Gangs and American Urban Society*. Berkeley: University of California Press, 1991.

Sandberg, Sheryl. *Lean In: Women, Work, and the Will to Lead*. Alred Knopf, 2013.

Sanders, Clinton R. *Customizing the Body: The Art and Culture of Tattooing*. Philadelphia, PA: Temple University Press, 1989.

Sapir, Edward. *Language*. New York, NY: Harcourt, Brace and World, 1921.

Sapolsky, Robert. *The Trouble with Testosterone*. New York, NY: Simon and Schuster, 1997.

Sassen, Saskia. *The Global City: New York, London, Tokyo*. Princeton, NJ: Princeton University Press, 1991.

SAT Program Participation and Performance Statistics," The College Board: https://research.collegeboard.org/programs/sat/data/archived

Saunders, Peter. *Social Class and Stratification*. London, UK: Routledge, 1990.

Save the Children. "State of the World's Mothers 2014: Saving Mothers and Children in Humanitarian Crises," 2014. Available at: http://www.savethechildren.org/atf/cf/%7B9def2ebe-10ae-432c-9bd0-df91d2eba74a%7D/SOWM_2014.pdf

Savin-Williams, Ritch C. "Who's Gay? Does It Matter?" *Current Directions in Psychological Science*, 15, no. 1 (2006): 40–44.

Sawhill, Isabel V., and John E. Morton. "Economic Mobility: Is the American Dream Alive and Well?" *Economic Mobility Project, an Initiative of The Pew Charitable Trusts*. Washington (2007). Available at: http://www.economicmobility.org/assets/pdfs/EMP%20American%20Dream%20Report.pdf

Saxton, Alexander. *The Indispensable Enemy: Labor and the Anti-Chinese Movement in California*. Berkeley, CA: University of California Press, 1971.

Saxton, Alexander. *The Rise and Fall of the White Republic: Class Politics and Mass Culture in Nineteenth-Century America*. New York, NY: Verso, 1990.

Sayer, Liana. Trends in Women's and Men's Time Use, 1965–2012: Back to the Future? In S. M. McHale, V. King, J. Van Hook, and A. Booth, eds., *Gender and Couple Relationships* (pp. 43–77). New York, NY: Springer, 2016.

Schaffner, Laurie. *Girls in Trouble with the Law*. New Brunswick, NJ: Rutgers University Press, 2006.

Schalet, Amy T. *Not Under My Roof: Parents, Teens, and the Culture of Sex*. Chicago, IL: University of Chicago Press, 2011.

Scheff, T. J. "The Labelling Theory of Mental Illness." *American Sociological Review*, 39, no. 3 (1974): 444–452.

Schilt, Kristen. *Just One of the Guys?: Transgender Men and the Persistence of Gender Inequality*. Chicago, IL: University of Chicago Press, 2010.

Schilt, Kristen, and Jenifer Bratter. "From Multiracial to Transgender? Assessing Attitudes toward Expanding Gender Options on the US Census." *TSQ: Transgender Studies Quarterly*, 2, no. 1 (2015): 77–100.

Schilt, Kristen, and Laurel Westbrook. "Doing Gender, Doing Heteronormativity: 'Gender Normals,' Transgender People, and the Social Maintenance of Heterosexuality." *Gender & Society*, 23, no. 4 (2009): 440–464.

Schilt, Kristen, and Matthew Wiswall. "Before and After: Gender Transitions, Human Capital, and Workplace Experiences." *Berkeley Journal of Economic Analysis and Policy*, 8 (2008): article 39.

Schippers, Mimi. *Beyond Monogamy: Polyamory and the Future of Polyqueer Sexualities*. New York, NY: NYU Press, 2016.

Schlesinger, Arthur. "Biography of a Nation of Joiners." *American Historical Review*, 50, no. 1 (October 1944): 1–25.

Schmidt, Ben. "Gendered Language in Teaching Reviews," February 20, 2015. Available at: http://benschmidt.org/profGender/

Schnaiberg, Allan. *The Environment: From Surplus to Scarcity*. New York, NY: Oxford University Press, 1980.

Schopflin, George. *Politics in Eastern Europe*. New York, NY: Blackwell, 1993.

Schwartz, Martin, and Walter DeKeseredy. "Interpersonal Violence against Women: The Role of Men." *Journal of Contemporary Criminal Justice*, 24 (May 2008): 78.

Schwartz, Pepper, and Virginia Rutter. *The Gender of Sexuality*. Thousand Oaks, CA: Pine Forge Press, 1998.

Sciolino, Elaine. "French Assembly Votes to Ban Religious Symbols in School." *The New York Times*, February 11, 2004. Available at: http://www.nytimes.com/2004/02/11/world/french-assembly-votes-to-ban-religious-symbols-in-schools.html

Scott, James. *Weapons of the Weak: Everyday Forms of Peasant Resistance*. New Haven, CT: Yale University Press, 1987.

Scott, Janny, and David Leonhardt. "Does Class Still Matter?" *New York Times Upfront*, 138, no. 6 (2005), 10–16.

Scott, Laura S. *Two Is Enough: A Couple's Guide to Living Childless by Choice*. Berkeley, CA: Seal Press, 2009.

Seattle Times Staff. "Toppenish teen fakes pregnancy as school project." *The Seattle Times*, April 21, 2011. Available at: http://www.seattletimes.com/seattle-news/toppenish-teen-fakes-pregnancy-as-school-project/

Selden, Steven. *Inheriting Shame: The Story of Eugenics and Racism in America*. New York, NY: Teachers College Press, 1999.

Seltzer, J. A. "Families Formed Outside of Marriage." In *Understanding Families in the New Millennium: A Decade in Review*. Lawrence, KS: NCRF and Alliance Communication Group, 2001.

Sen, Amartya. *Poverty and Famines: An Essay on Entitlement and Deprivation*. New York, NY: Oxford University Press, 1981.

Sen, Amartya. "More Than 100 Million Women Are Missing." *The New York Review of Books*, 37, no. 20 (1990).

Sen, Amartya. "Missing Women." *British Medical Journal*, 304 (1992): 587–588.

Sennett, Richard, and Jonathan Cobb. *The Hidden Injuries of Class*. New York, NY: Alfred A. Knopf, 1972

Seward, Rudy Ray, Dale E. Yeatts, Iftekhar Amin, and Amy Dewitt. "Employment Leave and Fathers' Involvement with Children: According to Mothers and Fathers." *Men and Masculinities*, 8 (2006): 405–427.

Shah, Anup. "Poverty Facts and Stats." *Global Issues* website, 2007. Available at: www.globalissues.org/TradeRelated/Facts.asp

Shames, Laurence. *The Big Time: The Harvard Business School's Most Successful Class & How It Shaped America.* New York, NY: HarperCollins, 1986.

Shapiro, Joseph P. *No Pity: People with Disabilities Forging a New Civil Rights Movement.* New York, NY: Broadway Books, 1993.

Shattuck, R. *The Forbidden Experiment: The Story of the Wild Boy of Aveyron.* New York, NY: Kodansha International, 1980.

Shilling, Chris. "Culture, the 'Sick Role' and the Consumption of Health." *The British Journal of Sociology* 53, no. 4 (2002): 621–638.

Shirky, Clay. *Here Comes Everybody: The Power of Organizing Without Organizations.* New York, NY: Penguin Press, 2008.

Shumway, Nicholas. *The Invention of Argentina.* Berkeley, CA: University of California Press, 1993.

Sidel, Ruth. *Unsung Heroes: Single Mothers and the American Dream.* Berkeley, CA: University of California Press, 2006.

Siegel, Larry J. *Criminology: Theories, Patterns, and Typologies.* Belmont, CA: Wadsworth, 2000.

Silver, Nate. *The Signal and the Noise: The Art and Science of Prediction.* New York, NY: Penguin, 2012.

Simmel, Georg. "The Metropolis and Mental Life" (1902). In Donald Levine, ed., *Georg Simmel on Individuality and Social Forms.* Chicago, IL: University of Chicago Press, 1971.

Simmel, Georg. *Conflict and the Web of Group Affiliations* (1908). New York, NY: Free Press: 324–340, 1956.

Singer, Natasia. "Who Is the Real Face of Cosmetic Surgery?" *New York Times,* August 16, 2007, G1, 3.

Sklar, Holly, Laryssa Mykyta, and Susan Wefald. *Raise the Floor.* New York, NY: Ms. Foundation for Women, 2001.

Skocpol, Theda. *The Missing Middle: Working Families and the Future of American Social Policy.* New York, NY: W. W. Norton & Company, 2000.

Smeeding, T. M. "Poor People in Rich Nations: The United States in Comparative Perspective." *Journal of Economic Perspectives,* 20, no. 1 (2006): 69–90.

Smelser, Neil, ed. *Karl Marx on Society and Social Change.* Chicago, IL: University of Chicago Press, 1975.

Smil, Vaclav. *Energy at the Crossroads: Global Perspectives and Uncertainties.* Cambridge, MA: MIT Press, 2005.

Smith, Aaron, and Monica Anderson. "5 facts about online dating." *Pew Research Center, Fact Tank,* February 29, 2016. Available at: http://www.pewresearch.org/fact-tank/2015/04/20/5-facts-about-online-dating/

Smith, Adam. *The Wealth of Nations* (1776). Robert B. Reich (ed.). New York: Modern Library, 2000.

Smooth, Jay. "How I Learned to Stop Worrying and Love Discussing Race." TEDx Hampshire College, 2011. Available at: https://www.youtube.com/watch?v=MbdxeFcQtaU

Snyder, Mark. *Public Appearances, Private Realities: The Psychology of Self-Monitoring.* New York, NY: W. H. Freeman, 1987.

Snyder, Michael. More than 1 in 5 American Children Are Now Living Below the Poverty Line. *Business Insider,* June 10, 2010. Available at: http://www.businessinsider.com/1-in-5-american-children-are-now-living-below-the-poverty-line-2010-6

Sobieraj, Sarah. *Soundbitten: The Perils of Media-Centered Activism.* New York, NY: NYU Press, 2011.

Solon, Gary. "Intergenerational Income Mobility in the United States." *American Economic Review,* 82, no. 3 (1992): 393–408.

Somers, Marie-Andree, Patrick J. McEwan, and J. Douglas Willms. "How Effective Are Private Schools in Latin America?" *Comparative Education* 48, no. 1 (2004): 48–69.

Sommeiller, Estelle, and Mark Price. The Increasingly Unequal States of America: Income Inequality by State, 1917–2012. *Economic Policy Institute,* January 26, 2015. Available at: http://www.epi.org/publication/income-inequality-by-state-1917-to-2012/

Southern Poverty Law Center. "Active Hate Groups in the United States in 2015." SPLC, Spring 2016. Available at: https://www.splcenter.org/fighting-hate/intelligence-report/2016/active-hate-groups-united-states-2015

Spencer, Herbert. *Principles of Biology.* Honolulu, HI: University Press of the Pacific, 2002.

Stampp, Kenneth. *Peculiar Institution: Slavery in the Antebellum South.* New York, NY: Alfred A. Knopf, 1956.

Stark, Rodney, and William Sims Bainbridge. *The Future of Religion: Secularization, Revival, and Cult Formation.* Berkeley, CA: University of California Press, 1985.

Stark, Rodney, and William Sims Bainbridge. *A Theory of Religion.* New York, NY: Peter Lang, 1987.

"The State of Divorce: You May Be Surprised." *Time,* May 28, 2007.

State of Working America. "Poverty," 2016. Available at: http://www.stateofworkingamerica.org/fact-sheets/poverty/

Statistica.com, 2016. "Average numbers of hours per day spent by social media users on all social media channels as of 4th quarter 2015, by country." Available at: http://www.statista.com/statistics/270229/usage-duration-of-social-networks-by-country/

Stearns, Elizabeth, Claudia Buchmann, and Kara Bonneau. "Interracial Friendships in the Transition to College: Do Birds of a Feather Flock Together Once They Leave the Nest?" *Sociology of Education,* 82, no. 2 (April 2009).

Stearns, Peter. *Consumerism in World History.* New York, NY: Routledge, 2001.

Steele, Claude M., *Whistling Vivaldi: How Stereotypes Affect Us and What We Can Do* (New York: W.W. Norton & Co., 2010).

Steele, Claude M. and Joshua Aronson. "Stereotype Threat and the Intellectual Test Performance of African Americans." *Journal of Personality and Social Psychology,* 69 (1995): 800

Steinberg, Ted. *Acts of God: The Unnatural History of Natural Disaster in America.* New York, NY: Oxford University Press, 2000.

Steinmetz, Susan. "The Battered Husband Syndrome." *Victimology,* 2 (1977–1978): 499–509.

Stephens, John D., and Evelyne Huber. *Development and Crisis in the Welfare State: Parties and Policies in Global Markets.* Chicago, IL: University of Chicago Press, 2001.

Stepler, Renee, "Number of U.S. Adults Cohabiting with a Partner Continues to Rise, Especially Among Those 50 and Older," Pew Research Center, April 6, 2017. Available at: http://www.pewresearch.org/fact-tank/2017/04/06/number-of-u-s-adults-cohabiting-with-a-partner-continues-to-rise-especially-among-those-50-and-older/

Stern, Linda. "The New American Job." *Newsweek,* January 28, 2009.

Steurer, Stephen J., and Linda G. Smith. *Education Reduces Crime: Three-State Recidivism Study.* Centerville, UT: Management and Training Corporation, 2003.

Stone, Arthur A., Joseph E. Schwartz, Joan E. Broderick, and Angus Deaton. "A Snapshot of the Age Distribution of Psychological Well-Being in the United States." *Proceedings of the National Academy of Sciences* 107, no. 22 (2010): 9985–9990.

Stone, Pamela. *Opting Out? Why Women Really Quit Careers and Head Home.* Berkeley, CA: University of California Press, 2007.

Storr, Mel. *Bisexuality: A Critical Reader.* New York, NY: Routledge, 1999.

Straus, Murray. "Children Should Never, Ever, Be Spanked No Matter What the Circumstances." In D. R. Loseke, R. J. Gelles, and M. M. Cavanaugh, eds., *Current Controversies about Family Violence,* 2nd ed. Thousand Oaks, CA: Sage Publications: 137–157, 2005.

Straus, Murray, and Richard Gelles, eds. *Physical Violence in American Families.* New Brunswick, NJ: Transaction Publishers, 1990.

Substance Abuse and Mental Health Services Administration (SAMHSA), National Institute of Mental Health. Available at https://www.nimh.nih.gov/health/statistics/prevalence/serious-mental-illness-smi-among-us-adults.shtml

Substance Abuse and Mental Health Services Administration. "Results from the 2009 National Survey on Drug Use and Health: Volume 1. Summary of National Findings." 2009. Available at: www.gmhc.org/files/editor/file/a_pa_nat_drug_use_survey.pdf

Substance Abuse and Mental Health Services Administration. "Behavioral Health Trends in the United States: Results from the 2014 National Survey on Drug Use and Health." *Department of Health and Human Services,* 2014. Available at: https://www.samhsa.gov/data/sites/default/files/NSDUH-FRR1-2014/NSDUH-FRR1-2014.pdf

Sullivan, Oriel. *Changing Gender Relations, Changing Families: Tracing the Pace of Change over Time.* New York, NY: Rowman & Littlefield, 2006.

Sullivan, Oriel, and Scott Coltrane. "Men's changing contribution to housework and child care." Paper presented at the 11th Annual Conference of the Council on Contemporary Families, April 25–26, 2008, University of Illinois, Chicago.

Sullivan/Anderson, Amy. "How to End the War over Sex Ed." *Time,* March 30, 2009, 40–43.

Sumner, William Graham. *Folkways: A Study of the Sociological Importance of Usages, Manners, Customs, Mores, and Morals.* (1906). Mineola, NY: Dover Publications, 2002.

Suny, Ronald. "Some Notes on National Character, Religions and Way of Life of the Armenians." Paper presented at the Lelio Basso Foundation, Venice, Italy, 1985.

Suburban Stats. "Population Demographics for Celebration, Florida in 2016 and 2017," 2017. Available at: https://suburbanstats.org/population/florida/how-many-people-live-in-celebration

Sutherland, Edwin H. "White Collar Criminality." *American Sociological Review,* 5 (February 1940): 1–12.

Suttles, Gerald. *The Social Construction of Communities.* Chicago, IL: University of Chicago Press, 1972.

Swidler, Ann. "Culture in Action: Symbols and Strategies." *American Sociological Review,* 51, no. 2 (April 1986): 273–286.

Symons, Donald. "Darwinism and Contemporary Marriage." In Kingsley Davis, ed., *Contemporary Marriage: Comparative Perspectives on a Changing Institution.* New York: Russell Sage Foundation: 145–146, 1985.

Takaki, Ronald. *Strangers from a Different Shore.* Boston, MA: Little, Brown, 1998.

Talukdar, Debabrata. "Cost of Being Poor: Retail Price and Consumer Price Search Differences across Inner-City and Suburban Neighborhoods." *Journal of Consumer Research,* 35, no. 3 (October 2008): 457–471.

Tarrow, Sidney. *Power in Movement: Social Movements and Contentious Politics.* Cambridge, UK: Cambridge University Press, 1998.

Tatlow, Didi. "Old Biases Hamper Women in China's New Economy." *The New York Times,* November 30, 2010, p. A-18.

Tavris, Carol. *The Mismeasure of Woman.* New York, NY: Touchstone, 1992.

Taylor, Michael. *The Possibility of Cooperation.* New York, NY: Cambridge University Press, 1987.

Taylor, Paul, and George Gao. Generation X: American Neglected "Middle Child." *Pew Research Center, FactTank,* June 5, 2014. Available at: http://www.pewresearch.org/fact-tank/2014/06/05/generation-x-americas-neglected-middle-child/

Teachman, J. "Premarital Sex, Premarital Cohabitation, and the Risk of Subsequent Marital Dissolution among Women." *Journal of Marriage and Family,* 65 (2003): 444–455.

Theodorou, Angelina E. "Which Countries Still Outlaw Apostasy and Blasphemy?" *The Pew Research Center,*

FactTank. July 29, 2016. Available at: http://www.pewforum .org/2016/06/23/trends-in-global-restrictions-on-religion/

Thernstrom, Abigail, and Stephan Thernstrom. *No Excuses: Closing the Racial Gap in Learning.* New York, NY: Simon and Schuster, 2003.

Thomas, Cheiran, Unni Krishnan, and Sophie Leung, "Fears for Grown in Parched Lands." *The New York Times,* May 29, 2010, p. A-1.

Thomas, W. I., and D. S. Thomas. *The Child in America.* New York, NY: Alfred A. Knopf, 1928.

Thompson, Beverly Yuen. *Covered in Ink: Tattoos, Women, and the Politics of the Body.* New York, NY: NYU Press, 2015.

Thornberry, T. P., M. D. Krohn, A. J. Lizotte, C. A. Smith, and K. Tobin. *Gangs and Delinquency in Developmental Perspective.* New York, NY: Cambridge University Press, 2003.

Thorne, Barrie. *Gender Play: Boys and Girls in School.* New Brunswick, NJ: Rutgers University Press, 1993.

Thornton, John. *Africa and Africans in the Making of the Atlantic World, 1400–1800.* New York, NY: Cambridge University Press, 1998.

Thurlow, Crispin. "Naming the 'Outsider Within': Homophobic Pejoratives and the Verbal Abuse of Lesbian, Gay and Bisexual High-School Pupils." *Journal of Adolescence,* 24, no. 1 (2001): 25–38.

Tierney, John. "What's So Funny? Well, Maybe Nothing." *New York Times,* March 13, 2007, F1, F6.

Tillman, Kathryn T. "Non-Traditional Siblings and the Academic Outcomes of Adolescents." *Social Science Research,* 37 (2008): 88–108.

Tilly, Charles. *From Mobilization to Revolution.* Reading, MA: Addison-Wesley, 1978.

Tocqueville, Alexis de. *Democracy in America* (1835). New York, NY: Library of America, 2004.

Tönnies, Ferdinand. *Community and Society: Gemeinschaft und Gesellschaft.* Charles P. Loomis, trans. New York, NY: Harper and Row, 1957.

Tran, Nellie, and Dina Birman, "Questioning the Model Minority: Studies of Asian American Academic Performance." *Asian American Journal of Psychology,* 1, no. 2 (2010): 106–118.

Trenholm, C., B. Devaney, K. Fortson, M. Clark, L. Q. Bridgespan, and J. Wheeler. "Impacts of Abstinence Education on Teen Sexual Activity, Risk of Pregnancy, and Risk of Sexually Transmitted Diseases." *Journal of Policy Analysis Management,* 29, no. 2 (Spring 2008): 255–276.

Tribou, Alex and Keith Collins. "This is How Fast America Changes Its Mind." Bloomberg.com, June 26, 2015. Available at: https://www.bloomberg.com/graphics/2015-pace-of-social-change/

True, J., and M. Mintrom. Transnational Networks and Policy Diffusion: The Case of Gender Mainstreaming. *International Studies Quarterly,* 45, no. 1 (March 2001): 27–57.

Truman, Jennifer L., and Lynn Langton, "Criminal Victimization, 2014 (Revised September 29, 2015)," Bureau of Justice Statistics, U.S. Department of Justice, September, 2015: https://www.bjs.gov/content/pub/pdf/cv14.pdf.

Truman, Jennifer L., and Rachel E. Morgan. "Nonfatal Domestic Violence, 2003–2012." *U.S. Department of Justice, Bureau of Justice Statistics,* April 2014. Available at: https://www.bjs .gov/content/pub/pdf/ndv0312.pdf

Tucker, Naomi. *Bisexual Politics: Theories, Queeries, and Visions.* Binghamton, NY: Haworth Press, 1995.

Turkheimer, Eric, Brian D'Onofrio, Hermine Maes, and Lindon Eaves. "Analysis and Interpretation of Twin Studies Including Measures of the Shared Environment." *Child Development,* 76, no. 6 (November/December 2005): 1217–1233.

Turkheimer, Eric, Andreana Haley, Mary Waldron, Brian D'Onofrio, and Irving Gottesman. "Socioeconomic Status Modified Heritability of IQ in Young Children." *Psychological Science,* 14, no. 6 (November 2003): 623–628.

Twenge, Jean M. *Generation Me: Why Today's Young Americans Are More Confident, Assertive, Entitled—And More Miserable Than Ever.* New York, NY: Free Press, 2006.

UC Atlas of Global Inequality. "Income Inequality," 2007. Available at: http://ucatlas.ucsc.edu/income.php

Uchitelle, Louis. *The Disposable American: Layoffs and Their Consequences.* New York, NY: Alfred Knopf, 2006.

Uggen, Christopher. "Ex-Offenders and the Conformist Alternatives: A Job-Quality Model of Work and Crime." *Social Problems,* 46, no. 1 (February 1999): 127–151.

Uggen, Christopher, Sarah Shannon, and Jeff Manza. "State-Level Estimates of Felon Disenfranchisement in the United States, 2010." *The Sentencing Project.* 2012.

UNESCO. "Adult and Youth Literacy: UIS Fact Sheet." *United Nations Educational, Scientific, and Cultural Organization,* September 2015. Available at: http://www.uis.unesco .org/literacy/Documents/fs32-2015-literacy.pdf

UNHCR, "Global Trends: Forced Displacement in 2016": http://www.unhcr.org/en-us/statistics/ unhcrstats/5943e8a34/global-trends-forced-displacement -2016.html

UNICEF. Levels and Trends in Child Mortality. *World Health Organization, World Bank Group, United Nations,* September 2015. Available at: https://www.unicef.org/publications/files/Child_Mortality_Report_2015_Web_9_ Sept_15.pdf

UNICEF. "Ending Child Marriage: Progress and Prospects." *UNICEF, Data and Analytics Section,* 2014.

UNICEF. Monitoring the Situation of Children and Women. World Health Organization, World Bank Group, United Nations, 2015. Available at: http://data.unicef.org/child-mortality/under-five.html

UNICEF. Monitoring the Situation of Women and Children. Available at http://www.data.unicef.org/corecode/ uploads/document6/uploaded_pdfs/corecode/Child-Marriage-Brochure-HR_164.pdf.

United Nations. "World's Population Increasingly Urban with More than Half Living in Urban Areas," July 10, 2014. Available at: http://www.un.org/en/development/desa/news/population/world-urbanization-prospects-2014.html

United Nations. *World Youth Report*. New York, NY: United Nations, 2005.

United Nations. 2015. Available at: https://esa.un.org/unpd/wpp/DataQuery/

United Nations. "Social Panorama of Latin America 2008." *Economic Commission for Latin America and the Caribbean*, 2008. Available at: http://www.cepal.cl/publicaciones/xml/3/34733/PSI2008-SintesisLanzamiento.pdf

United Nations. *World Fertility Patterns 2007*. New York, 2008.

United Nations Development Programme. "Power and Decision Making," 2015. Available at: https://unstats.un.org/unsd/gender/downloads/WorldsWomen2015_chapter5_t.pdf

University of Chicago Library. "Guide to the Chicago Foreign Language Press Survey Records, 1861–1938." Chicago, IL: University of Chicago Library, 2007.

U.N. Development Program. "Human Development Report, 2016." *United Nations Development Program*, 2016. Available at: http://hdr.undp.org/en/2016-report

U.N. Population Fund (UNFPA). "Child Marriage Fact Sheet," 2005. Available at: www.unfpa.org/swp/2005/presskit/factsheets/facts_child_marriage.htm

U.N. World Food Program. "Hunger Statistics," 2009. Available at: www.wfp.org/hunger/stats

U.S. Administration on Aging. A Profile of Older Americans: 2011. *U.S. Department of Health and Human Services*. 2011. Available at: https://www.google.com/url?sa=t&rct=j&q=&esrc=s&source=web&cd=4&ved=0ahUKEwi7-6mtk_fTAhWs6oMKHQ-WBcMQFgg4MAM&url=http%3A%2F%2Fwww.aging.ca.gov%2Fdocs%2FDataAndStatistics%2FStatistics%2FOtherStatistics%2FProfile_of_Older_Americans_2011.pdf&usg=AFQjCNH3B4WiGAPPvs3CWAvBq6mc9MHO3g&sig2=Hdl70fZTyUzV89YHapsZYg

U.S. Bureau of Labor Statistics. "College Enrollment and Work Activity of 2015 High School Graduates," April 28, 2016. Available at: https://www.bls.gov/news.release/hsgec.nr0.htm

U.S. Bureau of Labor Statistics. "Highlights of Women's Earnings in 2014." November, 2015. Available at: https://www.bls.gov/opub/reports/womens-earnings/archive/highlights-of-womens-earnings-in-2014.pdf

U.S. Bureau of Labor Statistics. "Women in the Labor Force: A Databook" December, 2015. Available at: https://www.bls.gov/opub/reports/womens-databook/archive/women-in-the-labor-force-a-databook-2014.pdf

U.S. Bureau of Labor Statistics. "Occupational Employment and Wages, May 2016: 25-0000 Education, Training, and Librarian Occupations Major Group." *U.S. Department of Labor*, 2016. Available at: http://www.bls.gov/oes/current/oes250000.htm

U.S. Bureau of Labor Statistics. "39 Percent of Managers in 2015 were Women" August, 2016. Available at: https://www.bls.gov/opub/ted/2016/39-percent-of-managers-in-2015-were-women.htm

U.S. Bureau of Labor Statistics. "Labor Force Statistics from the Current Population Survey." February, 2017. Available at: https://www.bls.gov/cps/cpsaat08.htm

U.S. Census Bureau. "America's Families and Living Arrangements: 2008." Washington, DC: U.S. Department of Commerce, 2008.

U.S. Census Bureau. *Population of the 24 Urban Places: 1790*, June 1998. Available at: www.census.gov/population/documentation/twps0027/tab02.txt

U.S. Census Bureau. *Statistical Abstract of the United States: 2009*. Washington, DC: U.S. Department of Commerce, 2009

U.S. Census Bureau. American Community Survey, 2010. Available at http://www.census.gov/content/dam/Census/library/publications/2011/acs/acs-14.pdf

U.S. Census Bureau. *2010 Census Redistricting Data (Public Law 94-171) Summary File*, Table P1. Available at: https://www.census.gov/prod/cen2010/briefs/c2010br-13.pdf

U.S. Census Bureau. "Households and Families: 2010." *United States Census Bureau – 2010 Census Briefs*, 2010. Available at: https://www.census.gov/prod/cen2010/briefs/c2010br-14.pdf

U.S. Census Bureau. Survey of Income and Program Participation, May-August 2010. Available at https://www.census.gov/prod/2012pubs/p70-131.pdf.

U.S. Census Bureau. "Marriage and Divorce Data Tables." *U.S. Census Bureau*, May 2011. Available at: https://www.census.gov/topics/families/marriage-and-divorce/data/tables.2009.html

U.S. Census Bureau. Wealth, Asset Ownership, & Debt of Households Detailed Tables: 2011. *U.S. Census Bureau, Data*, 2011. Available at: https://www.census.gov/data/tables/2011/demo/wealth/wealth-asset-ownership.html

U.S. Census Bureau. An Aging Nation: The Older Population in the United States: Population Estimates and Projections. *U.S. Census Bureau, Current Population Reports*. May 2014. Available at: https://www.census.gov/prod/2014pubs/p25-1140.pdf

U.S. Census Bureau. American Communities Survey. "Median Age at First Marriage for Women – United States." *U.S. Census Bureau*, 2015. Available at: https://factfinder.census.gov/faces/tableservices/jsf/pages/productview.xhtml?src=bkmk

U.S. Census Bureau. "America's Families and Living Arrangements: 2015." *U.S. Census Bureau*, 2015. Available at: https://www.census.gov/data/tables/2015/demo/families/cps-2015.html

U.S. Census Bureau. "FFF: Asian/Pacific American Heritage Month: May 2015." *United States Census Bureau*, updated April 29, 2015. Available at: https://www.census.gov/newsroom/facts-for-features/2015/cb15-ff07.html

U.S. Census Bureau. "FFF: Hispanic Heritage Month 2015," September 14, 2015. Available at: https://www.census.gov/newsroom/facts-for-features/2015/cb15-ff18.html

U.S. Census Bureau, American Communities Survey. "Median Age at First Marriage for Men – United States." *U.S. Census Bureau*, 2015. Available at: https://factfinder.census.gov/faces/tableservices/jsf/pages/productview.xhtml?src=bkmk

U.S. Census Bureau. "Packing it Up? Percent and Number of Movers in the U.S. from 1948 to 2014." *United States Census Bureau*, 2015. Available at: http://www.census.gov/content/dam/Census/newsroom/releases/2015/cb15-47_cpsgraphic.pdf

U.S. Census Bureau. Quick Facts: Chicago Heights city, Illinois, Population Estimates, July 1, 2015. Available at: http://www.census.gov/quickfacts/table/PST045215/1714026

U.S. Census Bureau. "Quick Facts: Kings Country (Brooklyn Borough), New York," 2015. Available at: http://www.census.gov/quickfacts/table/PST045215/36047

U.S. Census Bureau. "Quick Facts: United States." 2015. Available at: https://www.census.gov/quickfacts/table/PST045216/00

U.S. Census Bureau. "Aging in the United States Fact Sheet." *Population Reference Bureau*, January 2016. Available at: http://www.prb.org/Publications/Media-Guides/2016/aging-unitedstates-fact-sheet.aspx

U.S. Census Bureau. "An Aging World: 2015." *International Population Reports, U.S. Census Bureau*. March 2016.

U.S. Census Bureau. "The Changing Economics and Demographics of Young Adulthood: 1975-2016." *U.S. Census Bureau*. June 23, 2016. Available at: http://census.gov/newsroom/press-releases/2016/cb16-107.html?cid=cb16107

U.S. Census Bureau. "Fertility of Women in the United States: 2016." *U.S. Census Bureau*, June 2016. Available at: https://www.census.gov/hhes/fertility/data/cps/2016.html

U.S. Census Bureau. "FFF: Father's Day: June 19, 2016." *U.S. Census Bureau*, Release Number: CB16-FF11, May 24, 2016. Available at: https://www.census.gov/newsroom/facts-for-features/2016/cb16-ff11.html

U.S. Census Bureau. "Income and Poverty in the United States: 2015." U.S. Census Bureau, September 2016. Available at: https://www.census.gov/library/publications/2016/demo/p60-256.html

U.S. Department of Agriculture (USDA), Economic Research Service, 2015. Available at http://www.ers.usda.gov/data-products/food-access-research-atlas/go-to-the-atlas.aspx#.UUDJLTeyL28.

U.S. Department of Education. Public High School 4-Year Adjusted Cohort Graduation Rate (SCGR) for the United States the 50 states and the District of Columbia: School years 2010–11 to 2012–13. *National Center for Educational Statistics (NCES)*. Available at: http://nces.ed.gov/ccd/tables/ACGR_2010-11_to_2012-13.asp

U.S. Department of Education. "U.S. High School Graduation Rate Hits New Record High," December 15, 2015. Available at: http://www.ed.gov/news/press-releases/us-high-school-graduation-rate-hits-new-record-high-0

U.S. Department of Education. "The Condition of Education 2016." *National Center for Education Statistics*, May 2016. Available at: https://nces.ed.gov/pubs2016/2016144.pdf

U.S. Department of Education, National Center for Education Statistics, "Skills of U.S. Unemployed, Young and Older Adults in Sharper Focus: Results from the Program for the International Assessment of Adult Competencies," IES > NCES, *National Center for Education Statistics*, 2016. Available at: https://nces.ed.gov/pubs2016/2016039.pdf

U.S. Department of Education, National Center for Education Statistics. *Digest of Education Statistics, 2015* (NCES 2016-014) Chapter 3, 2016.

U.S. Department of Health and Human Services. "Eating Disorders: A Midlife Crisis for Some Women." *Health Reports,* 2006. Available at: www.healthfinder.gov

U.S. Department of Health and Human Services. "Trends in Teen Pregnancy and Childbearing." *HHS.gov*, June 2, 2016. Available at: https://www.hhs.gov/ash/oah/adolescent-development/reproductive-health-and-teen-pregnancy/teen-pregnancy-and-childbearing/trends/index.html

U.S. Department of Justice. 2014 Crime in the United States, 2015. Available at: https://www.fbi.gov/news/stories/latest-crime-stats-released

U.S. Department of Justice. "Engaging Communities/Empowering Victims." *U.S. Department of Justice, Office of Justice Programs*, 2015. Available at: ovc.ncjrs.gov/ncvrw2015/pdf/FullGuide.pdf

U.S. Department of Justice. "Victims of Identity Theft, 2014." Bureau of Justice Statistics, September, 2015. Available at: https://www.bjs.gov/content/pub/pdf/vit14_sum.pdf

U.S. Department of Justice, Bureau of Justice Statistics, Federal Bureau of Investigation, 2005c. "Hate Crime Statistics." 2005c. Available at: www.fbi.gov/ucr/hc2005/index.html

U.S. Department of Justice, Federal Bureau of Investigation, *Crime in the United States 2007*. Washington, DC: U.S. Government Printing Office, June 2008.

U.S. Department of Justice, Bureau of Justice Statistics. "Female Victims of Homicide," 2009. Available at: https://www.bjs.gov/content/pub/pdf/fvv.pdf

U.S. Department of Justice. "National Crime Victimization Survey, 2014." Available at: https://www.bjs.gov/index.cfm?ty=tp&tid=44

U.S. Department of Labor, Bureau of Labor Statistics. "Employed persons by detailed occupation, sex, race, and Hispanic or Latino ethnicity," 2016. Available at: https://www.bls.gov/cps/cpsaat11.htm

U.S. Department of Labor, Bureau of Labor Statistics. "Household Data: Annual Averages," 2016. Available at: http://www.bls.gov/cps/cpsaat07.pdf

U.S. Department of Labor, Women's Bureau. "Earnings," 2016. Available at: https://www.dol.gov/wb/stats/earnings_2014.htm#occ

U.S. Energy Information Administration. "Table A1. World Total Primary Energy Consumption by Region, Reference case, 2011-40 (quadrillion Btu)." *International Energy Outlook*, 2016a. Available at: http://www.eia.gov/outlooks/ieo/pdf/ieotab_1.pdf

U.S. Energy Information Administration. "Table A9. World Consumption of Hydroelectric and Other Renewable Energy by Region, Reference case, 2011-40 (quadrillion Btu)." *International Energy Outlook*, 2016b. Available at: http://www.eia.gov/outlooks/ieo/pdf/ieotab_9.pdf

U.S. Energy Information Administration. "Today In Energy," February 28, 2017. Available at: https://www.eia.gov/todayinenergy/detail.php?id=30132.

U.S. Energy Information Administration. "How much natural gas does the United States have, and how long will it last?" *U.S. Department of Energy*, December 22, 2016c. Available at: https://www.eia.gov/tools/faqs/faq.php?id=58&t=8

U.S. Energy Information Association. "International." *U.S. Department of Energy*, 2016d. Available at: https://www.eia.gov/beta/international/

U.S. Environmental Protection Agency. 2016 Available at: https://www.epa.gov/smm/advancing-sustainable-materials-management-facts-and-figures#Materials

U.S. Geological Survey's Geographic Names Information System. Available at: https://nhd.usgs.gov/gnis.html

U.S. Sentencing Commission. "U.S. Sentencing Commission's 2014 Sourcebook of Federal Sentencing Statistics." United States Sentencing Commission, 2014. Available at: https://www.ussc.gov/research/sourcebook/archive/sourcebook-2014

U.S. Social Security Administration. "Top Ten Baby Names of 2015." Available at https://www.ssa.gov/oact/babynames/

U.S. State Department. "Annual Report on Intercountry Adoption, 2016." *Bureau of Consular Affairs, U.S. Department of State*, 2016. Available at: https://travel.state.gov/content/adoptionsabroad/en/about-us/publications.html

U.S. State Department, "Country Reports on Terrorism 2015," June 2, 2016: https://www.state.gov/documents/organization/258249.pdf

Urban, Wayne J., and Jennings L. Wagoner. *American Education: A History*. New York, NY: McGraw-Hill, 2003.

Vallas, Steven P. "Rethinking Post-Fordism: The Meaning of Workplace Flexibility." *Sociological Theory*, 17 (1999): 68–101.

van Amersfoort, Hans. *Immigration and the Formation of Minority Groups: The Dutch Experience, 1945–1975*. New York, NY: Cambridge University Press, 1982.

Van Kesteren, Paul J., Louis J. Gooren, and Jos A. Megens. "An Epidemiological and Demographic Study of Transsexuals in the Netherlands." *Archives of Sexual Behavior* 25, no. 6 (1996): 589–600.

Van Kesteren, J. N., P. Mayhew, and P. Nieuwbeerta. *Criminal Victimization in Seventeen Industrialized Countries: Key Findings from the 2000 International Crime Victims Survey*. The Hague: Ministry of Justice, WODC, 2000.

Van Vugt, William E. *Britain to America: Mid Nineteenth-Century Immigration to the U.S.* Urbana, IL: University of Illinois Press, 1999.

Vanhanen, Tatu. "A New Dataset for Measuring Democracy, 1810–1998." *Journal of Peace Research*, 37, no. 2 (2000): 251–265.

Veblen, Thorstein. *The Theory of the Leisure Class*. (1899). Robert Lekachman, ed. New York, NY: Penguin Classics, 1994.

Venator, Joanna, and Isabel V. Sawhill, "Families Adrift: Is Unwed Childbearing the New Norm?" The Brookings Institution, October 13, 2014: https://www.brookings.edu/blog/social-mobility-memos/2014/10/13/families-adrift-is-unwed-childbearing-the-new-norm/

Venkatesh, Sudhir. *Gang Leader for a Day*. New York, NY: Penguin, 2008.

Verhaag, Bertram. *Blue Eyed* [videorecording/DVD]. Denkmal Filmproductions; a Claus Stigal & Bertram Verhaag production; written and directed by Bertram Verhaag. 1996.

Vespa, Jonathan. The Changing Economics and Demographics of Young Adulthood: 1975–2016. *U.S. Census Bureau, Current Population Reports*. April 2017. Available at: https://www.census.gov/content/dam/Census/library/publications/2017/demo/p20-579.pdf

Vespa, Jonathan, Jamie M. Lewis, and Rose M. Krieder. "America's Families and Living Arrangements: 2012." *U.S. Census Bureau, Population Characteristics*, August 2013. Available at: https://www.census.gov/prod/2013pubs/p20-570.pdf

Vigen, Tyler, 2017. *Spurious Correlations*. Accessed April 28, 2017. Available at: http://www.tylervigen.com/spurious-correlations.

Villarroel, Maria, Charles Turner, Elizabeth Eggleston, Alia Al-Tayyib, Susan Rogers, Anthony Roman, Philip Cooley, and Harper Gordek. "Same Gender Sex in the United States: Impact of T-ACASI on Prevalence Estimates." *Public Opinion Quarterly*, 70, no. 2 (Summer 2006): 166–196.

Vissers, Sara, and Dietlind Stolle. "Spill-Over Effects Between Facebook and On/Offline Political Participation? Evidence from a Two-Wave Panel Study." *Journal of Information Technology & Politics*, 11, no. 3 (2014): 259–275.

Voci, A. "Perceived Group Variability and the Salience of Personal and Social Identity." In W. Stroebe and M. Hewstone, eds., *European Review of Social Psychology*, 11 (2000): 177–221.

Volz, Brian D. "Race and Quarterback Survival in the National Football League," *Journal of Sports Economics*, (2015): 1–17.

Von Drehle, David. "What's Behind America's Falling Crime Rate." *Time*, February 22, 2010. Available at: http://content.time.com/time/magazine/article/0,9171,1963761,00.html

Voslensky, Michael. *The Soviet Ruling Class*. New York, NY: Doubleday, 1984.

Wacquant, Loic. *Body and Soul: Notebooks of an Apprentice Boxer*. New York, NY: Oxford University Press, 2003.

Wacquant, Loic. "The 'Scholarly Myths' of the New Law and Order Doxa." *The Socialist Register*, 2006: 93–115.

Wade, Lisa. *American Hookup: The New Culture of Sex on Campus*. New York, N.Y: W. W. Norton & Company, 2017.

Wade, Lisa. "Framing Children's Deviance." *Sociological Images*, July 13, 2013. Available at: http://contexts.org/socimages/2010/07/26/framing-childrens-deviance

Waggoner, Lawrence C. "Marriage Is on the Decline and Cohabitation Is on the Rise: At What Point, if Ever, Should Unmarried Partners Acquire Marital Rights." Family Law Quarterly 50, no. 2 (2016): 215–246.

Waitzkin, Howard B. *The Second Sickness: Contradictions of Capitalist Health Care*. New York, NY: The Free Press, 1986.

Wakabayashi, Chizuko, and Katharine M. Donato. "Does Caregiving Increase Poverty among Women in Later Life? Evidence from the Health and Retirement Survey." *Journal of Health and Social Behavior*, 47, no. 3 (2006): 258–274.

Walby, Sylvia. "Feminism in a Global Age." *Economy and Society*, (2002): 553–557.

Walch, Timothy. *Immigrant America: European Ethnicity in the U.S.* New York, NY: Garland, 1994.

Walker, Alice. *The Color Purple*. New York, NY: Harcourt Brace Jovanovich, 1982.

Walker, Nancy E., J. Senger, F. Villaruel, and A. Arboleda. *Lost Opportunities: The Reality of Latinos in the U.S. Criminal Justice System*. National Council of La Raza. 2004. Available at: www.nclr.org/content/publication/detail/27567/

Walker, Tim. "Why Are 19 States Still Allowing Corporal Punishment in Schools?" *neaToday*, October 17, 2016. Available at: http://neatoday.org/2016/10/17/corporal-punishment-in-schools/

Waller, Willard. "The Rating and Dating Complex." *American Sociological Review*, 2 (1937), 727–734.

Wallerstein, Immanuel. "The Rise and Future Demise of the World Capitalist System: Concepts for Comparative Analysis." *Comparative Studies in Society and History*, 16, no. 4 (1974): 387–415.

Wallerstein, Immanuel. *The Capitalist World Economy*. Cambridge, UK: Cambridge University Press, 1979.

Wallerstein, Immanuel. "The Development of the Concept of Development." *Sociological Theory*, 2 (1984): 102–116.

Wallerstein, Immanuel. *World-Systems Analysis: An Introduction*. Durham, NC: Duke University Press, 2004.

Wallerstein, Judith. *The Unexpected Legacy of Divorce: A 25-Year Landmark Study*. New York, NY: Hyperion, 2000.

Walls, Jeannette, "Was Race an Issue in 'Hitch' Casting?" *USA Today*, February 24, 2005: http://www.today.com/popculture/was-race-issue-hitch-casting-wbna7019342

Walters, Suzanna Danuta. *The Tolerance Trap: How God, Genes, and Good Intentions Are Sabotaging Gay Equality*. New York, NY: NYU Press, 2014.

Wang, Wendy. "The Rise of Intermarriage." *Pew Research Center, Social & Demographic Trends*, February 16, 2012. Available at: http://www.pewsocialtrends.org/2012/02/16/the-rise-of-intermarriage/

Wang, Wendy. "Interracial Marriage: Who is 'Marrying Out'?" *Pew Research Center, FactTank*, June 12, 2015. Available at: http://www.pewresearch.org/fact-tank/2015/06/12/interracial-marriage-who-is-marrying-out/

Ward, Jane. "Producing 'Pride' in West Hollywood: A Queer Cultural Capital for Queers with Cultural Capital." *Sexualities*, 6, no. 1 (2003): 65–94.

Ward, Jane. "Dude-Sex: White Masculinities and 'Authentic' Heterosexuality Among Dudes Who Have Sex With Dudes." *Sexualities*, 11, no. 4 (2008): 414–434.

Waters, Mary. *Ethnic Options: Choosing Ethnic Identities in America*. Berkeley, CA: University of California Press, 1990.

Waters, Mary C. "Ethnic and Racial Identities of Second-Generation Black Immigrants in New York City." *The International Migration Review* 28, no. 4 (1994): 795–820.

Waters, Mary C. *Black Identities: West Indian Immigrant Dreams and American Realities*. Cambridge, MA: Harvard University Press, 2009.

Watts, Duncan. *Everything is Obvious: Once you Know the Answer*. New York, NY: Crown Business, 2003.

Way, Niobe. *Deep Secrets: Boys' Friendships and the Crisis of Connection*. Cambridge, MA: Harvard University Press, 2013.

Weber, Max. "Class, Status, and Party." *From Max Weber*, trans. and ed. Hans Gerth and C. Wright Mills. New York, NY: Free Press, 1946.

Weber, Max. *The Protestant Ethic and the Spirit of Capitalism* (1904, 1905). New York, NY: Routledge, 2004.

Weber, Max. *From Max Weber*. Trans. and ed. by H. H. Gerth and C. Wright Mills. New York, NY: Oxford University Press, 1958.

Weber, Max. *Economy and Society* (2 volumes). Berkeley, CA: University of California Press, 1978.

Wedgwood, C. V. *The Thirty Years' War*. New York, NY: Routledge, 1990.

Weich, Ronald, and Carlos Angulo. *Justice on Trial: Racial Disparities in the American Criminal Justice System*. Washington, DC: Leadership Conference on Civil Rights, 2000.

Weinberg, Martin S., Colin J. Williams, and Douglas W. Pryor. *Dual Attraction: Understanding Bisexuality*. New York, NY: Oxford University Press, 1994.

Weitzman, Lenore J. "The Economic Consequences of Divorce Are Still Unequal: Comment on Peterson." *American Sociological Review,* 61, no. 3 (1996): 537–539.

West, Candace, and Don H. Zimmerman. "Doing Gender." *Gender & Society,* 1, no. 2 (1987): 125–151.

Westbrook, Laurel, and Aliya Saperstein. "New Categories Are Not Enough: Rethinking the Measurement of Sex and Gender in Social Surveys." *Gender & Society,* 29, no. 4 (2015): 534–560.

Westbrook, Laurel, and Kristen Schilt. "Doing Gender, Determining Gender: Transgender People, Gender Panics, and the Maintenance of the Sex/Gender/Sexuality System." Gender & Society 28, 1 (2014): 32–57.

Weston, Kath. "Get Thee to a Big City: Sexual Imaginary and the Great Gay Migration." *GLQ,* 2 no. 3 (1995): 253–277.

Weston, Kath. *Families We Choose: Lesbians, Gays, Kinship.* New York, NY: Columbia University Press, 1996.

Whorf, Benjamin Lee. "Science and Linguistics." In John B. Carroll, ed., *Language, Thought and Reality.* Cambridge, MA: MIT Press: 207–219, 1956.

Whyte, William Foote. *Street Corner Society: The Social Structure of an Italian Slum,* 4th ed. (First edition published 1943). Chicago, IL: University of Chicago Press, 1993.

Wight, Richard, Alan LeBlanc, Bran De Vries, Roger Detels. "Stress and Mental Health Among Midlife and Older Gay-Identified Men." *American Journal of Public Health,* 102, no. 3 (2012): 503–510.

Wilkins, Amy C. "Masculinity Dilemmas: Sexuality and Intimacy Talk among Christians and Goths." *Signs,* 34, no. 2 (2009): 343–368.

Williams, Christine. "The Glass Escalator: Hidden Advantages for Men in the 'Female Professions.'" *Social Problems,* 39, no. 3 (1992): 253–267.

Williams, Christine L., and Catherine Connell. 'Looking Good and Sounding Right': Aesthetic Labor and Social Inequality in the Retail Industry. *Work and Occupations* 37 (2010): 349–377.

Williams, Kevin. *Understanding Media Theory.* New York, NY: Oxford University Press, 2003.

Williams, Walter. *The Spirit and the Flesh.* Boston, MA: Beacon, 1986.

Willis, George, William H. Schubert, Robert V. Bullough, Craig Kridel, and John T. Holton (eds.). *The American Curriculum: A Documentary History.* Westport, CT: Praeger, 1994.

Willis, P. *Learning to Labor.* New York, NY: Columbia University Press, 1977.

Wilmoth, Janet M., Gordon F. DeJong, and Christine C. Himes, "Immigrant and Non-Immigrant Living Arrangements in Later Life." *International Journal of Sociology and Social Policy,* 17 (1997): 57–82.

Wilson, Chris M., and Andrew J. Oswald. "How Does Marriage Affect Physical and Psychological Health? A Survey of the Longitudinal Evidence." *The Warwick Economics Research Paper Series (TWERPS)* 728. Coventry, UK: University of Warwick Department of Economics, 2005.

Wilson, William Julius. *More than Just Race: Being Black and Poor in the Inner City.* New York, NY: W. W. Norton and Company, 2009.

Wilson, William Julius. *The Declining Significance of Race.* Chicago, IL: University of Chicago Press, 1978.

Wilson, William Julius. *The Truly Disadvantaged: The Inner City, the Underclass, and Public Policy.* Chicago, IL: University of Chicago Press, 1987.

Wiltz, Teresa. "Why More Grandparents are Raising Children." *Pew Charitable Trusts,* 2016. Available at: http://www.pewtrusts.org/en/research-and-analysis/blogs/stateline/2016/11/02/why-more-grandparents-are-raising-children

Winerip, Michael. "The Adult Store Goes Mainstream." *New York Times,* 2009 (June 28), ST-1.

Wingfield, Adia Harvey. "Are Some Emotions Marked 'Whites Only'? Racialized Feeling Rules in Professional Workplaces." *Social Problems,* 57 (2010): 251–268.

Wingfield, Adia Harvey. "Racializing the Glass Escalator: Reconsidering Men's Experiences with Women's Work." *Gender & Society,* 23 (2009): 5–26.

Winks, Robin W., and Thomas E. Kaiser. *Europe, 1648–1815: From the Old Regime to the Age of Revolution.* Oxford, UK: Oxford University Press, 2003.

Wirzbicki, Alan. "Gun Control Efforts Weaken in the South." *Boston Globe,* September 4, 2005.

Wolfe, Alan. *The Transformation of American Religion: How We Actually Live Our Faith.* New York, NY: Free Press, 2003.

Wolfers, Justin. "Fewer Women Run Big Companies than Men Named John." *The New York Times,* March 2, 2015. Available at: http://www.nytimes.com/2015/03/03/upshot/fewer-women-run-big-companies-than-men-named-john.html

Wolfram, Stephen. "The Personal Analytics of My Life," March 8, 2012, *Stephan Wolfram blog.* Available at: http://blog.stephenwolfram.com/2012/03/the-personal-analytics-of-my-life/

Wolfram, Steven. "Data Science of the Facebook World." *Stephen Wolfram Blog.* April 24, 2013. Available at: http://blog.stephenwolfram.com/2013/04/data-science-of-the-facebook-world/

Woods, Richard. "Women Take Lead as Lifespan Heads for the Happy 100s." *Sunday Times (London),* October 30, 2005, p. 14.

Word, E., Johnston, J., Bain, H.P., et al. Student/Teacher Achievement Ratio (STAR): Tennessee's K–3 class size study. Final summary report 1985–1990. Nashville, TN: Tennessee Department of Education, 1990.

World Bank. *Global Monitoring Report 2008.* World Bank: 2009.

World Bank. 2013. http://data.worldbank.org/indicator/EN.ATM.CO2E.PC

World Bank. 2013. http://data.worldbank.org/indicator/EN.ATM.CO2E.KT

World Bank. "World Development Indicators: Education Gaps by Income, Gender, and Area," 2014. Available at: http://wdi.worldbank.org/table/2.11

World Bank. "Unemployment: Total Percentage of the Labor Force," 2016. Available at: http://data.worldbank.org/indicator/SL.UEM.TOTL.ZS%20

World Bank. "Population Growth (Annual Percentage). Accessed May 17, 2017. Available at: http://data.worldbank.org/indicator/SP.POP.GROW

World Bank. Accessed 02/17/17. Available at http://data.worldbank.org/indicator/SP.DYN.LE00.IN?end=2014&start=2014&view=map

World Health Organization. "World Report on Disability." *The World Bank*, 2011. Available at: http://www.who.int/disabilities/world_report/2011/en/

World Health Organization. Obesity and Overweight Fact Sheet. 2016. Available at: http://www.who.int/mediacentre/factsheets/fs311/en/

World Press Trends. "Report: Shaping the Future of World Publishing." *WAN IFRA*, 2014. Available online at: http://www.arpp.ru/images/123/51253_WAN-IFRA_WPT_2014.pdf

World Prison Brief. "Prison Population Rate." Available at http://www.prisonstudies.org/highest-to-lowest/prison_population_rate?field_region_taxonomy_tid=All.

Wright, Quincy. *A Study of War,* 2nd ed. Chicago, IL: University of Chicago Press, 1967.

Wylie, Cathy. Trends in the Feminization of the Teaching Profession in OECD Countries, 1980–1995. Geneva, Switzerland: International Labour Organization, 2000.

Yaukey, David, and Douglas L. Anderton. *Demography: The Study of Human Population.* Long Grove, IL: Waveland Press, 2001.

Yen, Hope. "A Third of the Country's Poor Live in Suburbs, Study Says." *Pittsburg Post-Gazette,* October 8, 2010. Available at: http://www.post-gazette.com/news/nation/2010/10/08/A-third-of-the-country-s-poor-live-in-suburbs-study-says/stories/201010080228

Yinger, John. "Evidence on Discrimination in Consumer Markets." *Journal of Economic Perspectives,* 12 (1998): 23–40.

Yinger, John Milton. *The Scientific Study of Religion.* New York, NY: Macmillan, 1970.

Yoder, J. "Rethinking Tokenism: Looking beyond Numbers." *Gender and Society,* 5 (1991): 178–192.

Yoffee, Norman. *Myths of the Archaic State: Evolution of the Earliest Cities, States, and Civilizations.* Cambridge, UK: Cambridge University Press, 2005.

Yoshino, Kenji, *Covering: The Hidden Assault on Our Civil Rights.* New York, NY: Random House, 2006.

Zald, Mayer N., and John David McCarthy. *Social Movements in an Organizational Society: Collected Essays.* New Brunswick, NJ: Transaction Publishers, 1987.

Zhou, Min. "Divergent Origins and Destinies: Children of Asian Immigrants." In S. Paik, H. Walberg, eds., *Narrowing the Achievement Gap: Strategies for Educating Latino, Black and Asian Students.* New York, NY: Springer: (109–128), 2007.

Zimring, Franklin E., and Gordon Hawkins. *Crime Is Not the Problem: Lethal Violence in America.* New York, NY: Oxford University Press, 1997.

Zong and Batalova. Middle Eastern and North African Immigrants to the United States. *Migration Policy Institute.* June 3, 2015. Available at: http://www.migrationpolicy.org/article/middle-eastern-and-north-african-immigrants-united-states

Zuckerman, Ethan. *Rewire: Why We Thinking the Internet Connects Us, Why It Doesn't, and How to Rewire It.* New York, NY: W. W. Norton, 2013.

Name Index

A

Abbott, Andrew, 249, 455
Abrecht, G. L., 451
Acierno, Ron, 522
Aday, Sean, 99
Adler, Jerry, 574
Agthe, Maria, 442
Ahrons, Constance, 517
Al B., 66, 67
Allan, Emilie Andersen, 200
Allen, K. R., 495
Allport, Gordon, 292, 319, 320
Altbach, Philip, 555
Amato, Paul R., 515, 517
Amick, Benjamin C., 402
Amin, Iftekhar, 600
Amoako Johnson, F., 510
Anderson, E., 217
Anderson, Elijah, 131
Anderson, Hanah, 173, 174, 175
Anderson, Monica, 96
Anderton, Douglas L., 662
Andiloro, Nancy R., 223
Angier, Natalie, 372
Angle, John, 113
Angulo, Carlos, 216
Appelbaum, Richard P., 268
Appugliese, Danielle P., 442
Aquinas, Thomas, 535
Aragon, Melissa C., 628
Arboleda, A., 216
Arbuckle, J., 365
Arendt, Hannah, 619
Ariès, Philippe, 395, 396
Arling, G. L., 164
Armstrong, Elizabeth, 467, 473
Armstrong, Elizabeth A., 360, 465, 560
Armstrong, Myrna L., 434
Arnett, Jeffrey, 362, 398
Arnette, J. Kenneth, 183
Arnoldi, Ben, 511
Aronson, Joshua, 204
Asch, Solomon, 88
Atkinson, Michael, 433
Ayres, Irving, 153

B

Bachelet, Michelle, 696
Backman, Clifford R., 241
Bacon, Sarah, 227
Badge, Emily, 303
Badger, Emily, 438
Bagamery, Anne, 507
Bailey, P., 510
Bain, H. P., 545

Bainbridge, William Sims, 644
Bajoria, Jayshree, 542
Baker, Dean, 574
Baker, Sandra, 442
Baldus, D. C., 227
Banyai, Istvan, 112
Barber, Benjamin, 37
Barr, Nicolas, 579
Barton, Paul E., 226
Bassuk, Shari S., 402
Batalova, Jeanne, 317
Bates, Abigail K., 628
Battle, Michael, 653
Baumle, Amanda K., 465, 495
Bearman, Peter, 468, 469
Beber, Bernd, 422
Bechdel, Alison, 355, 356
Beck, Frank D., 268
Becker, Howard, 203, 218
Becker, Howard S., 193
Beckett, Samuel, 535
Bell, Daniel, 574
Bell, Michael M., 689
Bellah, Robert, 615, 636
Benton, L. A., 591
Berends, Mark, 548
Berger, Peter, 77
Berk, Richard A., 295
Berkman, Lisa F., 402
Bernard, Jessie, 370, 515
Bernstein, Mary, 495
Bertrand, Marianne, 16, 300, 313, 603
Best, Amy, 83
Bettie, Julie, 206
Beyoncé, 327
Bianchi, Suzanne, 370, 506, 507
Biblarz, Tim, 507
Bidwell, Allie, 314
Bieber, Justin, 84
Billingsley, Andrew, 653
bin Laden, Osama, 617
Birdsong, David, 164
Birman, D., 316
Birn, Raymond, 618
Bishop, Paul D., 469
Bismarck, Otto von, 616
Black, M. C., 519
Blackstone, Amy, 510
Blank, J., 553
Blattman, Christopher, 422
Blau, Judith, 217
Blau, Peter, 80, 103, 217, 242, 243
Bloomberg, Michael, 621
Blow, Charles, 136
Blow, Charles M., 296

Blumer, Herbert, 30
Blumstein, Philip, 500
Bock, Jane, 508
Boero, Natalie, 438
Bogaert, A. F., 465
Bonilla-Silva, Eduardo, 299, 300, 301
Bonneau, Kara, 362
Bonnicksen, Thomas, 692
Boonstra, Heather, 470
Boonstra, Heather D., 516
Bordo, Susan, 435
Borrell, Luisa N., 445
Boswell, John, 483
Bourdieu, Pierre, 63, 64, 250, 251, 252
Bourgois, Philippe, 132
Bowen, James, 533
Bowles, Samuel, 538
Boyd, Elizabeth A., 295
Boyd, Melody L., 504
Boyd, W., 533
Bradley, Robert H, 442
Brame, Robert, 227
Brashears, Matthew E., 95, 362
Bratter, Jenifer, 347
Brault, Matthew W., 440
Braunschweiger, Amy, 542
Braveman, Paula A., 445
Breiding, M. J., 519
Brewer, M. B., 320
Bridges, Tristan, 14, 504
Bridgespan, L. Q., 469
Brigham, John C., 88
Brodbeck, Arthur J., 625
Brodkin, Karen, 307
Broockman, David E., 695
Brott, Armin, 521
Brown, Anna, 623f
Brown, Brandon, 445
Brown, D. L., 445
Brown, Lester R., 692
Brown, Michael, 327
Brown, Tony M., 445
Brückner, Hannah, 468, 469
Bryner, Jeanna, 516
Bryson, Bethany, 252
Buchmann, Claudia, 362
Buffalo, M. D., 198
Buffie, Nick, 574
Bullough, Robert V., 534
Burawoy, Michael, 585
Burd, Charlynn, 680
Burdick, Eugene, 625
Burgess, A., 522
Burleson, William E., 464
Burnett, S. B., 370

Burroughs, Edgar Rice, 163
Burton, Linda M., 131
Busch, Susan H., 101
Bush, George H. W., 588
Bush, George W., 582, 588, 604
Buss, David, 342
Buswell, B. N., 354, 355
Butler, Katy, 521
Buttel, Frederick H., 689
Butz, David A., 88

C

Califano, J. A., 225
Calvin, John, 161
Cameron, Darla, 303
Cameron, Rondo, 572
Campanis, Al, 293
Campbell, J., 510
Cancian, Francesca, 361
Candland, D. K., 164
Cannon, Angie, 221
Caplow, Theodore, 56
Cardoso, Fernando Henrique, 269
Carey, Benedict, 454
Carey, Kate B., 215
Carey, Michael P., 215
Carneal, Michael, 553
Carrington, Christopher, 495
Carroll, Margaret D., 438
Casper, Lynne M., 416
Castells, M., 591
Catton, William, Jr., 689
Cazenave, N., 519
Ceausescu, Nicolai, 617
Cerio, J., 553
Chaffee, John, 533
Chalabi, Mona, 600, 669
Chambliss, William J., 206
Champney Schnepp, A., 662
Chandler, Tertius, 678
Chang, Jeff, 66
Charles, Maria, 598
Chase-Dunn, Christopher, 686
Chauncey, George, 473
Chen, J., 519
Cherlin, Andrew, 518
Chesney-Lind, M., 206
Chirac, Jacques, 651
Cho, Seung Hui, 553
Christakis, Dimitri A., 182
Chubb, John E., 547
Chung, Jean, 630m
Churchill, Winston, 619
Cipolla, Carlo M., 572
Claffey, S. T., 370
Clark, David D., 226
Clark, Kenneth Bancroft, 172
Clark, M., 469
Clark, Marnie Phipps, 172
Clinton, Bill, 15, 152, 588, 626
Clinton, Hillary, 626, 626f, 627
Cloward, Richard, 200
Cobb, Jonathan, 171, 172, 262

Coe, Neil M., 590
Cohen, Albert, 200
Cohen, Patricia, 152
Cohen, Philip, 490
Cohn, D'Vera, 311, 405,
    591, 669
Colbert, Stephen, 456
Cole, David, 221
Cole, T. B., 215
Coleman, James, 545, 547, 549
Coley, Richard, 226
Colfer, Chris, 471
Collins, Alex, 58
Collins, Keith, 58
Collins, Patricia Hill, 305
Collins, Randall, 531
Coltrane, Scott, 507
Compton, D'Lane R., 495
Comte, Auguste, 22, 145
Condry, John, 353
Condry, S., 353
Connell, Catherine, 184,
    601, 602
Connor, Bull, 293
Conrad, Peter, 451
Constable, P., 445
Conway, Lynne, 346
Cooke, Sam, 653
Cookson, Peter W., Jr., 93
Cooky, Cheryl, 139, 140
Cooley, Charles Horton, 77, 87
Coontz, Stephanie, 487, 490,
    493, 514
Cooper, C. L., 370
Cooper, Frederick, 269
Corak, Mile, 245
Corbin, Juliet, 450
Correll, Shelley J., 558, 560
Corwyn, Robert F., 442
Coser, Lewis, 81
Costello, B. J., 198
Couprie, Helene, 600
Couric, Katie, 86
Courtenay, Will, 446
Cowan, Ruth Schwartz, 488
Cox, Daniel, 119, 651
Cox, Laverne, 437
Craig, Kellina M., 295
Crister, Greg, 438
Crittenden, Danielle, 601
Crompton, Rosemary, 237
Cross, Harry, 153
Crouter, A. C., 507
Cumings, Bruce, 268
Cummings, H. J., 243
Currie, Elliot, 208
Curtin, Lester R., 438

D

Dailard, C., 470
Dalai Lama, 618
Daly, Kathleen, 206
Daly, Martin, 342

Daniels, Matt, 173, 174, 175
Darroch, Jacqueline E., 470
Darwin, Charles, 161
Davenport, Charles, 497t
Davis, A., 320
Davis, Devra Lee, 671
Davis, Georgiann, 344
Davis, Kingsley, 237
Davtyan, Mariam, 445
Dawkins, Richard, 342
DeFelice, Nicholas, 698
Defronzo, James, 631
DeGeneres, Ellen, 15, 471
Degler, Carl, 487
DeJong, Gordon F., 416
DeKeseredy, Walter, 521
Dellaposta, Daniel, 93
deMause, Lloyd, 395, 396
Demo, D. H., 495
DeNavas-Walt, Carmen, 261, 262
Denton, Nancy A., 302
DePaolo, Bella, 508
DeParle, Jason, 508
Depp, Johnny, 225
De Rougemont, Denis, 487
Desai, Manisha, 380
Deschanel, Zoey, 685
de Silva, Eugenie, 391
Desilver, Drew, 555, 628, 629f
Deutsch, Barry, 303
Deux, Kay, 90
Devaney, B., 469
DeVault, Marjorie, 167
Dewitt, Amy, 600
Dickens, Charles, 2
Diefendorf, Sarah, 469
DiMaggio, Paul, 93
Dodsworth, Robert O., 164
Doll, Holly, 699
Dolnick, Sam, 434
Domhoff, G. William, 93, 621, 622
Donato, Katherine M., 415
Douglass, Frederick, 28, 29,
    30, 534
Doyle, Roger, 321
Drake, Bruce, 216
Dreger, Alice D., 343
Dubner, Stephen, 209, 584
Du Bois, W. E. B., 29, 313, 314
Duke, David, 328
Duncan, Otis Dudley, 242, 243
Duneier, Mitch, 132
Dunlap, Riley E., 689
Durkheim, Émile, 24, 25, 26, 31, 196, 237,
    570, 636, 685
Durney, Sarah E., 215
Dye, Jane Lawler, 501
Dylan, Bob, 535

E

Eagan, Kevin, 628
Ebener, S., 510
Edin, Kathryn, 123

Edison, Thomas, 61
Edwards, K., 320
Edwards, S. S. M., 213
Egerton, Muriel, 370
Egley, A., Jr., 202
Egley, Arlen, Jr., 202
Ehrenreich, Barbara, 263, 589
Ehrlich, Paul, 675
Eisenstein, Elizabeth, 60
Ekman, Paul, 79
Eliasoph, Nina, 654
Elliot, Jane, 88
Elliott, Diana B., 501
Ellsberg, M., 520
El Nasser, Haya, 289
Emanuel, Gabriel, 575
Engels, Friedrich, 23, 570
England, Paula, 382, 465, 468
Epstein, Helen, 445
Ericson, Richard V., 220
Erikson, Erik, 169
Erikson, Kai T., 696
Esping-Anderson, G., 579
Etzioni, Amitai, 97
Etzioni-Halevy, Eva, 621

F

Faletto, Enzo, 269
Farber, Susan L., 161
Farkas, George, 548
Farnham, S. D., 291
Faulkes, Keith, 612
Fausto-Sterling, Anne, 343, 344
Feinersten, Sarah, 440
Fergus, Edward, 216
Ferguson, A., 366
Ferguson, Ann Arnett, 320
Ferguson, Jesse Tyler, 471
Ferguson, Ronald, 551
Ferree, Myra M., 380, 381
Fielding, Jonathan, 445
Fields, Alison, 680
Fields, Jason, 416
Fillmore, Millard, 328
Filoux, J. C., 237
Fingerhut, Hannah, 118
Finkelhor, David, 521
Firebaugh, Glenn, 268
Fischer, Claude, 294, 325
Fisher, Allen, 509
Fisher, Kimberley, 370
Fitzgibbon, Marian, 435
Fitzpatrick/Austin, Laura, 561
Flegal, Katherine M., 438, 439
Fleisher, M. S., 202
Foehr, Ulla G., 181, 182
Fogarty, Alison C. K., 468
Fogstad, H., 510
Folayan, Morenike Oluwatoyin, 445
Foner, Eric, 304
Foote, Christopher, 209
Foran, John, 631
Fordham, Signithia, 320, 366, 367

Forrest, Patrick, 442
Fortson, K., 469
Foucault, Michel, 457
Fowlkes, M. R., 500, 502
Fox, Richard L., 372
Fox, Ronald C., 464
Franklin, Aretha, 535, 653
Franklin, Clyde, 362
Fraser, Jill A., 587
Freedman, V. A., 416
Freud, Sigmund, 168
Friedan, Betty, 415
Friedel, Ernestine, 461
Friedson, Eliot, 449
Friesen, Wallace V., 79
Frost, Robert, 480
Fry, Richard, 186, 408, 500
Fu, Alyssa S., 99
Fuller, Margaret, 27, 28
Furstenberg, Frank F., 499
Fussell, Elizabeth, 499

G

Gagnon, J. H., 503
Gagnon, John G., 436
Gagnon, John H., 457, 460
Gamoran, Adam, 548
Gamson, William, 631
Gandhi, Mahatma, 326, 617, 618
Gans, Herbert, 306, 321, 685
Gao, George, 406, 643, 644
García- Moreno, C., 520
Gardner, Matthew, 591
Garfield, Andrew, 456
Garfinkel, Harold, 80
Garip, Filiz, 93
Garrett-Peters, Raymon, 131
Gates, Bill, 254
Gates, Gary J., 459, 460, 495
Gatrell, C. J., 370
Gaughan, E., 553
G. Dep, 66
Gee, Lisa C., 591
Gelles, Richard, 521
Gell-Mann, Murray, 113
Gentileschi, Artemisia, 431
Gereffi, Gary, 270
Gernet, Jacques, 533
Gershuny, Jonathan I., 370
Gerson, Kathleen, 371, 511
Ghaziani, Amin, 474, 495, 669
Ghosh, Suresh, 532
Gibbs, Nancy, 646
Gibson, Jacqueline Macdonald, 698
Gilborn, D., 530
Gilligan, Carol, 169, 170
Gilman, Charlotte Perkins, 28
Gilsinan, Kathy, 650
Gimlin, Debra, 435
Ginther, Donna K., 517
Giordano, Anna Utopia, 431
Githens-Mazer, Jonathan, 318
Gladstone, William, 535

Gladwell, Malcolm, 90
Glassner Barry, 436
Glazer, Norman, 331
Gleason, D. K., 202
Glenn, David, 257
Goetz, Christopher, 209
Goffman, Erving, 31, 78, 79, 97, 188, 203,
    205, 339, 351, 352
Goldin, Claudia, 363, 364
Goldrick-Rab, Sara, 561, 563
Goldscheider, Francis, 412
Goldstein, Lizabeth, 309
Gomez, Michael A., 668
Gonzalez-Barrera, Ana, 312
Goode, Erich, 152, 225
Goode, William J., 85
Goodkind, D., 408, 409
Gooren, L. J., 346
Gordon, Milton, 284
Gore, Al, 700
Gosling, Ryan, 456
Goss, Devon, 293
Gottfredson, D. C., 202
Gottfredson, G. D., 202
Gottfredson, Michael R., 198
Gottlieb, Michelle B., 671
Gottman, John M., 372
Grady, William R., 413
Graff, E. J., 376
Graham, S., 553
Granovetter, Mark, 94, 141
Grant, Cary, 17
Graubard, Barry I., 439
Gray, John, 336
Gray, Lee, 81
Greeley, Andrew, 652
Greene, Jay P., 556, 557m
Greene, Steven, 612
Greenman, Leon, 442
Greenstein, T. N., 370
Greenwald, A. G., 291
Grieg, Alan, 376
Griffin, Gary A., 164
Gross, Samuel, 227
Grossman, Gene M., 625
Grusky, David B., 598
Gruys, Kjerstin, 438, 439f
Guerra-Arias, M., 510
Guillot, Michel, 662
Gullmoto, Christophe, 672
Gurr, Ted Robert, 321, 631
Guterl, Fred, 435

H

Habermas, Jürgen, 143
Hagan, John, 206
Hagedorn, J. M., 202
Hagedorn, John, 202
Haggerty, Keven D., 220
Haley, Nikki R., 54
Hall, J. A., 582
Hamamoto, Darrell Y., 316
Hamedani, MarYam G., 99

Hamilton, Brady E., 399
Hamilton, Laura T., 360, 465, 560
Hamner, Karl A., 295
Hanisch, Carol, 653
Hanna-Attisha, Mona, 661, 662
Hannigan, John, 689
Hanrahan, N., 522
Hanushek, Eric A., 538
Harding, Warren, 328
Harig, F. A., 414
Harlow, Harry, 164, 165
Harlow, Harry F., 164
Harlow, Margaret K., 164
Harris, Benjamin C., 347
Harris, Eric, 553
Harris, Lynn, 465
Harris, Shanette, 362
Harris, W. A., 519
Harrison, William Henry, 308
Hassig, Ralph C., 582
Hastings, Michael, 435
Hawkins, Gordon, 208
Hayford, S. R., 510
Hayward, Mark D., 413
He, W., 408, 409
Healy, J., 182
Healy, Kieran, 210
Heckert, D. M., 83
Heise, L., 520
Helpman, Elhanan, 625
Hemenway, David, 217
Henderson, Bobby, 610
Henderson, Clarence, 326
Henderson, Jeffrey, 268
Hening, Benjamin J., 38
Henley, William Ernest, 184
Herek, Gregory M., 471
Hernandez-Tejada, Melba, 522
Herrnstein, Richard, 294, 315
Hertz, Rosanna, 508
Hertz, Tom, 259
Hetherington, Mavis, 517
Heuveline, Patrick, 662
Hill, Steven, 623
Himes, Christine L., 416
Hirsch, E. D., Jr., 535
Hirschi, Travis, 198
Hirst, Paul, 575
Hitler, Adolf, 617, 619
Ho, Vanessa, 310
Hobbes, Thomas, 569
Hobsbawm, E. J., 22, 572
Hochschild, Arlie, 369, 382, 601
Hoffer, Thomas, 547
Hoffman, Bruce, 634
Holder, Kelly, 680
Hollenbach, Margaret, 483
Holton, John T., 534
Hondagneu-Sotelo, Pierrette, 378
Hook, Jennifer L., 370
Hopkins, Terence K., 270
Hoppe, Trevor, 450
Horvath, Hannah, 465

Hout, Michael, 242, 294, 325, 652
Howe, Louise Kay, 587
Howell, J. C., 202
Hrdy, Sarah Blaffer, 164, 342, 349
Hu, Chen, 227
Hubbard, Ruth, 352
Huber, Evelyne, 579
Hughes, Diane, 177
Hughes, Everett C., 84
Hughes, Mary E., 405
Hughey, Matthew, 293
Humphreys, Jeffrey, 313
Humphreys, Laud, 129, 130
Hunt, G., 202
Huntington, Ellsworth, 688
Hurst, Charlice, 442
Hurtado, Aída, 216
Hussein, Saddam, 633
Hvistendahl, Mara, 671
Hyde, Janet, 354, 355

I

Ignatiev, Noel, 307
Imus, Don, 295
Isaacs, Julie, 243, 244

J

Jackson, Andrew, 308, 589
Jackson, Jesse, 653
Jackson, Kenneth, 682
Jackson, Michael, 429
Jackson, Nick C., 183
Jackson, Pamela Braboy, 445
Jacobs, Jane, 686
Jacobson, Lenore, 128, 129, 548
James, Chris, 574f
James, LeBron, 7
Janis, Irving, 90
Jansen, H. A., 520
Jarrell, Anne, 369
Jayson, Sharon, 500
Jay-Z, 66
Jefferson, Thomas, 161, 614, 644, 655
Joe-Laidler, K., 202
Johansson, Scarlett, 50
Johns, Jennifer, 590
Johnson, Brian D., 223
Johnson, David R., 515
Johnson, Deborah J., 177
Johnson, Kevin R., 365
Johnson, Lyndon, 261, 270, 303
Johnson, Michael J., 183
Johnson, Stefanie K., 365, 414
Johnston, J., 545
Jolie, Angelina, 508
Jones, Bromani, 308
Jones, Del, 598, 599
Jones, Robert P., 119, 651
Jordan, Michael B., 464
Jovenen, J., 553
Judge, Timothy A., 442
Juergensmeyer, Mark, 634

K

Kaciroti, Niko, 442
Kaeser, L., 470
Kaiser, Thomas E., 618
Kalla, Joshua, 695
Kann, L., 519
Kanter, Rosabeth Moss, 100
Karabel, Jerome, 559
Karberg, Jennifer, 219
Katz, E., 90
Katz, Jack, 214
Katz, Michael, 263
Kazmierczak, Stephen, 553
Kazyak, Emily, 174, 175
Keating, Kenneth M., 689
Kefalas, Maria, 123
Kempadoo, Kamala, 270
Kemper, Theodore, 343
Kennedy, Edward, 227
Kennedy, John F., 17, 268, 617, 618
Kenney, Genevieve, 153
Kerbo, Harold R., 237
Kern, Roger M., 252
Kessler, Suzanne, 344
Kett, Joseph F., 535
Khagram, Sanjeev, 380
Khan, Shamus, 93
Kharas, Homi, 266
Kilgore, Sally, 547
Kimmel, Michael, 280, 281, 359, 362, 369,
    376, 468, 520, 521
Kim-Prieto, Chu, 309
King, E., 533
King, Leslie, 689
King, Martin Luther, Jr., 17, 326,
    330, 652
Kingston, Lindsey, 99
Kinsey, Alfred, 457, 458
Kirby, D., 470
Kirkpatrick, David, 94
Kirschner, Blake, 309
Kit, Brian K., 439
Kitsuse, John, 203
Kittilson, Miki C., 621
Klebold, Dylan, 553
Klein, Jessie, 553
Klinenberg, Eric, 412, 502, 503, 696
Kling, K. C., 354, 355
Kluckhohn, Clyde, 462
Knudsen, Knud, 370
Koch, Jerome R., 434
Koffman, Steven D., 183
Kohlberg, Lawrence, 169, 170
Kohler, Pamela K., 470
Kohler, P. K., 470
Kohn, Melvin, 177
Kolata, G., 503
Korn, Donald Jay, 517
Korzeniewicz, Miguel, 270
Kowal, P., 408, 409
Kraus, Lewis, 440f
Kridel, Craig, 534
Kriedte, Peter, 673

Krienert, J. L., 202
Krishnan, Unni, 692
Krohn, M. D., 202
Krugman, Paul, 258, 575
Kuhn, Maggie, 423
Kumanyika, Shiriki, 445
Kumar, K., 574
Kupers, Terry, 453
Kurkie, Leena, 208
Kutateladze, Besiki L., 223

L

LaChance, Jenny, 662
Lachs, Mark S., 522
Lafferty, William E., 470
Lamar, Kendrick, 327
Lambert, Robert, 318
Lambert, Tracey, 467
Lancaster, B., 573
Landry, David J., 470
Lane, Harlan, 164
Lang, James, 376
Langton, Lynn, 216
Lareau, Anette, 177, 251, 252
Lasch, Christopher, 487, 519
Laumann, Edward O., 457
Laumann, E. O., 503
Lautner, Taylor, 464
LaVeist, Thomas A., 445, 455
Lawless, Jennifer L., 372
Layton, Robert H., 572
Lazarsfeld, P. F., 90
LeBlanc, A. J., 414
Lee, Jennifer, 203, 204, 295
Leeder, Elaine J., 519
Leker, Hannah, 698
Lemann, Nicholas, 669
Lemert, Edwin, 203
Lenhart, Amanda, 183
Leonhardt, David, 244, 273
LePore, Paul C., 548
Leung, Sophie, 692
Levine, Adam, 432
Levine, James A., 601
Levine, Martin, 669
Levinson, Daniel J., 400
Levitt, Steven, 209, 584, 585
Levy, J. A., 451
Lewis, Oscar, 264
Liazos, Alexander, 206
Lichtblau, Eric, 213
Lichter, Daniel T., 501
Lichtheim, George, 580
Liddy, Edward, 631
Lieberson, Stanley, 14, 18
Liebow, Elliot, 130
Lind, Michael, 256
Lipsitz, Angela, 469
Livingston, Gretchen, 507, 510
Liwen, Qin, 376
Lizotte, A. J., 202
Locke, John, 20, 21, 161, 569
Loehlin, John C., 161

Loehr, Annalise, 471
Lofland, John, 64
Lopez, Maria P., 365
Lopez, Mario, 313
Lopez, Mark Hugo, 311, 312
Lorber, Judith, 350, 354
Lucas, Christopher J., 555
Luckmann, Thomas, 77
Luker, Kristin, 122
Lukes, Steven, 612
Lumeng, Julie C., 442
Lunneborg, Patricia, 511
Lynch, Kathleen, 538
Lynd, Helen Merrell, 56, 396
Lynd, Robert Staughton, 56, 396

M

Machlis, Gary E., 689
MacKenzie, K., 202
Macy, Michael, 93
Madonna, 456, 508
Maghadam, Valentine M., 380
Malthus, Thomas R., 674, 675
Mandela, Nelson, 171, 184, 241, 617, 618
Manderscheid, Ron, 445
Maner, J. K., 442
Manhart, Lisa E., 470
Mann, Horace, 534
Manza, Jeff, 629
Mardini, Yusra, 669
Margolis, Eric, 538
Marks, N., 502
Markus, Hazel Rose, 99
Martens, Jens, 208
Martin, Clyde E., 457
Martin, Emily, 349
Martin, J. K., 451
Martin, Karin, 174, 175
Martin, L. G., 416
Martin, Steven P., 513, 515f
Martin, Trayvon, 327
Martinez, Michael, 517
Martino, Wayne, 366
Marx, Karl, 23, 24, 25, 32, 247, 248, 253, 256, 269, 272, 570, 580, 581, 612, 631, 636, 642, 675
Masciadrelli, Brian, 370, 506
Massey, Douglas S., 302
Mathews, T. J., 399
Mathias, Peter, 573
Matsukura, Rikiya, 493
Mattes, Jane, 508
Matthews, Z., 510
Matus, Ron, 547
Mayhew, P., 208
Mayo, Elton, 103, 584
McAdam, Doug, 630
McCabe, Janice, 141
McCain, Franklin, 326
McCain, John, 625, 626, 627
McCarthy, J. D., 631
McCarthy, Justin, 178
McCaughey, Martha, 342

McGhee, D. E., 291
McGregor, Douglas, 585
McKibben, Bill, 651
McManus, T., 519
McMillan Cottom, Tressie, 561, 563
McNeil, Joseph, 326
McPherson, M., 95
McPherson, Miller, 362
Mead, George Herbert, 29, 30, 78, 166
Mead, Margaret, 167, 487
Meadow, Tey, 347
Mechanic, David, 453
Megens, J. A., 346
Meissner, Christian A., 88
Mell, Jane, 153
Mendes, Eva, 288
Menkel-Meadow, Carrie, 368
Mermin, Gordon B., 411
Merton, Robert K., 32, 83, 90, 102, 197, 198, 200, 548
Messerschmidt, J. W., 375
Messner, Michael, 139, 140
Meyer, David S., 630
Meyer, I. H., 414
Meyer, J. W., 103
Michael, Robert T., 457
Michael, R. T., 503
Michaels, Stuart, 457
Mickelson, K. D., 370
Milgram, Stanley, 92, 128, 151
Milkie, Melissa A., 370, 506, 507
Miller, Jon, 178
Miller, Jon D., 535
Miller, Lisa, 471
Miller, N., 320
Miller, Stephen, 625
Miller, Walter B., 201
Mills, C. Wright, 3, 8, 9, 12, 13, 292, 586, 654
Milner, Murray, Jr., 89
Mintrom, Michael, 380
Mintz, Steven, 395, 396
Mishel, Emma, 603
Mitchell, Joni, 699
Moe, Terry M., 547
Moffatt, Michael, 560
Montoya, Yesika, 162
Moore, Barrington, 633
Moore, J. W., 202
Moore, Lisa Jean, 349
Moore, Mignon, 305
Moore, Molly, 271
Moore, Solomon, 226
Moore, Wilber, 237
Moran, A. C., 510
Moreno, Jenalia, 313
Morgan, Rachel E., 520
Morin, Richard, 669
Morris, Aldon D., 630
Morris, Martina, 466
Morsch, James, 295
Mortimer, Caroline, 314
Mossaad, Nadwa, 414

Moss-Kanter, Rosabeth, 595
Mosteller, Frederick, 546
Mousavi, Mirhossein, 633
Mowry, George, 307
Mueller, Carol M., 380, 381, 630
Muench, Ulrike, 101
Muir, John, 699
Mullainathan, Sendi, 16, 300, 313, 603
Mumford, Lewis, 678
Mumola, Christopher J., 219
Munsch, Christin L., 375
Muravchik, Joshua, 581
Murphy, Evelyn, 376
Murphy, Susan Elaine, 365, 414
Murray, Bill, 50
Murray, Charles, 294, 315
Mussolini, Benito, 619
Musto, Michela, 139, 140
Muzzy, Wendy, 522
Myers, R., 553
Mykyta, Laryssa, 588

N

Nagel, Joane, 311
Nagourney, Eric, 455
Naples, Nancy A., 380
Nathan, Rebekah, 560
Navarro-Rivera, Juhem, 119, 651
Neal, Derek, 216
Neal, Larry, 572
Neal, S., 510
Neison, F. G. P., 214
Newman, Cathy, 438
Newman, Katherine, 263, 589
Newsome, Bree, 54
Newton, Michael, 164
Nichols, Robert C., 161
Nieuwbeerta, P., 208
Nisbet, Robert, 80
Nock, Steven, 492
Noguera, Pedro, 216, 367, 548
Noordewier, Marret K., 494
North, Douglas, 572
Notestein, Frank, 675
Novak, Michael, 284
Nuru-Jeter, Amani, 455
Nyhan, Brendan, 695
Nystrand, Martin, 548

O

Oakes, Jeannie, 548
Obama, Barack, 16, 280, 287, 299, 330, 437, 548, 625, 626, 627
O'Brien, Barbara, 227
O'Brien, Sean, 133
Ocampo, Anthony, 285
O'Donnell, Christina E., 202
Ogawa, Noahiro, 493
Ogbu, John, 320, 366, 367, 548
Ogburn, William, 68
Ogden, Cynthia L., 438
Oh, Kongdan, 582
Ohlin, Lloyd, 200

Okazaki, Surnie, 309
Olivardia, Roberto, 436
Olweus, Dan, 553
Olyslager, Femke, 346
Omi, Michael, 286
O'Rand, Angela M., 405
Orenstein, Peggy, 366, 493
Orfield, Gary, 549
Orpana, Heather, 439
Orum, Anthony M., 612
Oshansky, Mollie, 261
Oshima, Harry T., 572
Oswald, Andrew J., 515
Owen, Donna C., 434

P

Padavic, Irene, 598
Pagden, Anthony, 668
Page, Marianne, 516
Pager, Devah, 300, 603
Paige, Jeffrey, 631
Palen, J. John, 683
Panter-Brick, Catherine, 572
Paoletti, J. O., 353
Parker-Pope, Tara, 466
Parks, Rosa, 326, 330
Parsons, Talcott, 31, 32, 439f, 449, 631
Pascoe, C. J., 359, 360
Pascoe, P. J., 553
Passel, Jeffrey, 186, 311, 591
Paternoster, Raymond, 227
Pattanaik, Bandana, 270
Paulin, Geoffrey, 406
Pear, Robert, 402
Pearce, Diana, 377
Pell, M. B., 698
Pennycock, Alastair, 66
Perrow, Charles, 690, 691
Perry, Katie, 456
Perry-Jenkins, M., 507
Persell, Caroline Hodges, 93
Pescosolido, B. A., 451
Peterson, Richard, 252
Peterson, Ruth D., 206
Petroff, Alanna, 603
Phillips, Katherine, 436
Phillips, Scott, 227
Piaget, Jean, 168, 169, 170
Pierce, Brittany Susan, 465
Pillemer, Karl A., 522
Pipes, Richard, 581
Pisani, Florence, 258
Pitt, Brad, 17
Pleck, Joseph H., 370, 506
Pollak, Otto, 213
Pollard, Sidney, 573
Pomeroy, Wardell B., 457
Pope, Harrison, 436
Popkin, Samuel L., 625
Porter, R., 510
Portes, A., 591
Poston, Douglas L., 465
Powell, Walter W., 574

Preston, Samuel, 662
Preves, Sharon E., 344
Price, Mark, 258
Proctor, Bernadette, 261, 262
Pryor, Douglas W., 464
Purvin, Diane, 131
Putnam, Robert, 74, 98
Pyrooz, David C., 201

Q

Qian, Zhenchao, 501
Quattrone, G. A., 88
Quinney, Richard, 206

R

Rabelais, François, 535
Radway, Janice, 60
Raeburn, Nicole C., 603
Raley, Kelly R., 494
Randolf, John, 283
Rao, S. L., 240
Ratcliffe, Michael, 680
Rauch, Jonathan, 401
Reagan, Ronald, 588, 626
Reardon, Sean F., 549
Reaves, Brian A., 220
Reckless, Walter, 198
Redfield, Robert, 685
Reger, Jo, 379
Regev-Messalem, Shiri, 468
Reichard, Rebecca J., 365, 414
Reifler, Jason, 695
Reskin, Barbara F., 598
Resnick, S., 237
Retherford, Robert D., 493
Reynolds, Ryan, 456
Rhode, Deborah, 442
Rian, Shari, 433
Richards, C. L., 470
Rick, Armin, 216
Rideout, Victoria J., 181, 182
Riesman, David, 74
Riker, James V., 380
Riordan, Brian, 406
Rios, Victor, 132, 366
Rios-Aguilar, Cecilia, 628
Ritter, John, 473
Ritzer, George, 37
Robbins, Sarah, 435
Roberts, Alden E., 434
Roberts, Donald F., 181, 182
Roberts, Paul, 690
Robinson, Christine, 469
Robinson, Dwight E., 138
Robinson, John, 370, 506, 507
Robinson, John P., 370
Robnett, Belinda, 630
Rochefort, David A., 453
Rock, Chris, 316
Rodriguez, Gaby, 111
Rodriguez, James, 177
Roediger, David, 307
Rogers, J. W., 198

Roosevelt, Eleanor, 17
Roosevelt, Franklin D., 17, 353, 617
Roosevelt, Theodore, 307, 699
Rosa, Eugene A., 689
Roscoe, Will, 483
Rose, Brad, 580
Rosenbaum, Janet Elise, 469
Rosenberger, Nancy, 493
Rosenfeld, Michael, 514, 515
Rosenhan, David L., 451
Rosenthal, Robert, 128, 129, 548
Rosich, Katherine, 216
Ross, George, 580
Rossi, Alice, 14
Rostow, W. W., 268
Rothwell, J., 219
Rouse, Cecelia, 363, 364
Rousseau, Jean-Jacques, 20, 161
Rowan, Brian, 103
Rowley-Conwy, Peter, 572
Rubin, Lillian, 466
Rudolph, Frederick, 555
Rule, Wilma, 623
Rupp, Leila, 468
Rust, Paula Rodriguez, 464
Rutter, Virginia, 466
Ruys, Kirsten I., 494
Rycroft, Robert S., 245

S

Sadker, David, 552
Sadker, Myra, 552
Sadler, R. C., 662
Saghera, Jyoti, 270
Saguy, Abigail C., 152, 438
Sam, Michael, 463
Sanchez-Jankowski, Martin, 131, 201
Sandberg, Sheryl, 16, 339, 576
Sanders, Clinton R., 432
Sandu, Dimitru, 268
Saperstein, Aliya, 347
Sapir, Edward, 55
Sapolsky, Robert, 343
Sassen, Saskia, 687
Saunders, Peter, 237
Savin-Williams, Ritch C., 459
Saxton, Alexander, 307
Sayer, L. C., 382
Schaffner, Laurie, 213
Schalet, Amy T., 503
Scheff, T. J., 451
Schilt, Kristen, 347, 348, 437, 600
Schippers, Mimi, 483
Schlesinger, Arthur, 98
Schmidt, Ben, 365
Schnaiberg, Allan, 689
Schneyer, Joshua, 698
Schoenbach, Carrie, 177
Schoeni, R. F., 416
Schopflin, George, 582
Schubert, William H., 534
Schulz, Charles, 413
Schuster, M. A., 553

Schwartz, J. K. L., 291
Schwartz, Martin, 521
Schwartz, Pepper, 466, 500
Sciolino, Elaine, 651
Scott, Janny, 244, 273
Scott, Laura S., 511
Scott, Walter, 535
Sebastian, Daniel, 698
Seely, J. Lotus, 360
Sekhon, Jasjeet S., 695
Selden, Steven, 307
Seltzer, J. A., 500
Semenya, Caster, 343, 344
Sen, Amartya, 681
Senger, J., 216
Sennett, Richard, 171, 172, 262
Seward, Rudy Ray, 600
Shafer, Emily F., 468
Shakespeare, William, 82
Shames, Laurence, 403
Shannon, Sarah, 629
Shapiro, Joseph P., 441
Shattuck, R., 164
Sheehy, Gail, 400
Shepardson, Robyn L., 215
Shi, Yongren, 93
Shilling, Chris, 449
Shirky, Clay, 99
Showers, C. J., 354, 355
Sidel, Ruth, 507
Siegel, Larry J., 225
Siegelman, Peter, 153
Sikkink, Katherine, 380
Silver, Nate, 145
Simmel, Georg, 27, 81, 91, 686
Simon, Lauren S., 442
Simon, William, 460
Simpson, O. J., 291
Sindelar, Jody, 101
Singer, Natasia, 434
Singh, Susheela, 470
Sklar, Holly, 588
Skocpol, Theda, 257
Slomczynski, Kazimierz, 177
Smil, Vaclav, 689
Smith, Aaron, 96
Smith, Adam, 570, 578, 582
Smith, Billy, 326
Smith, C. A., 202
Smith, Emilie P., 177
Smith, Linda G., 226
Smith, Will, 288
Smith-Lovin, Lynn, 95, 362
Snellman, Kaisa, 574
Snyder, Mark, 319
Snyder, Michael, 258
Sobhuza II, King, 664
Sobieraj, Sarah, 632
Sobolewski, Juliana M., 515
Solon, Gary, 242
Sommeiller, Estelle, 258
Sparrow, P., 370
Spears, Britney, 456

Spencer, Herbert, 688
Sperling, John, 562
Spicer, Paul, 177
Spohn, Cassia C., 223
Spörrle, M., 442
Springsteen, Bruce, 424
Stacey, Judith, 507
Stalin, Joseph, 619
Stam, Kathryn, 99
Stampnitzky, Julie R., 671
Stampp, Kenneth, 654, 655
Stapel, Diederik, A., 494
Staples, Brent, 293
Stark, Rodney, 644
Stearns, Elizabeth, 362
Stearns, Peter, 572
Steele, Claude, 203, 204, 293
Steffensmeier, Darrell J., 200
Steinmetz, Susan, 521
Stenberg, K., 510
Stephens, John D., 579
Stepler, Renee, 500
Stern, Linda, 590
Steurer, Stephen J., 226
Steve, Kenneth, 522
Stevens, Ann Huff, 516
Stevenson, Howard C., 177
Stewart, Mahala D., 510
Stewart, Martha, 211
Stewart, Quincy Thomas, 445
Stolle, Dietlind, 99
Stolley, Melinda, 435
Stolzenberg, Ellen Bara, 628
Stonestreet, Eric, 471
Storr, Mel, 464
Straus, Murray, 519, 521, 522
Strauss, Anselm, 450
Stryker, Susan, 429
Suchard, Maria Ramirez, 628
Sullenberger, Chesley, 86
Sullivan, Andrew, 294
Sullivan, Oriel, 370, 507
Sullivan/Anderson, Amy, 470
Sumner, William Graham, 50, 88, 290
Suny, Ronald, 655
Suomi, Stephen J., 164
Sutherland, Edwin H., 197, 200, 210
Suttles Gerald, 88
Suzuki, Ichiro, 316
Sweeney, Megan M., 494
Sweeten, Cary, 201
Symons, Donald, 342

T

Takaki, Ronald, 668
Talukdar, Debabrata, 589
Tarrow, Sidney, 630
Tate, Katherine, 621
Tatem, A. J., 510
Tatlow, Didi K., 376
Tavris, Carol, 361
Taylor, Michael, 581

Taylor, Paul, 405, 406
Taylor, Verta, 468, 495
Teachman, J., 500, 501
Theodorou, Angelina E., 614, 615*m*
Thernstrom, Abigail, 550
Thernstrom, Stephan, 550
Thibaudet, Jean-Yves, 62
Thomas, Cherian, 692
Thomas, Dorothy Swain, 30, 283
Thomas, Robert Paul, 572
Thomas, W. I., 30, 283
Thompson, Beverly Yuen, 433
Thornberry, T. P., 202
Thorne, Barrie, 181, 351
Thornton, John, 668
Thurlow, C., 359
Thurmond, Strom, 328
Tierney, John, 80
Tillman, Kathryn T., 517
Tilly, Charles, 631
Tobin, K., 202
Tocqueville, Alexis de, 23, 98
Tolstoy, Leo, 524
Tomlin, Lily, 63
Tönnies, Ferdinand, 684, 685
Tran, N., 316
Trefil, James, 535
Trenholm, C., 469
Trimberger, E. K., 508
Troutman, Adewale, 445
True, Jacqui, 380
Truman, Jennifer L., 216, 520
Trump, Donald, 16, 328, 621, 622, 625, 626, 626*f*, 627
Tuch, S. A., 451
Tucker, Naomi, 464
Turkheimer, Eric, 114
Twenge, Jean M., 56

U

Uchitelle, Louis, 242
Uggen, Christopher, 200, 629
Urban, Wayne J., 533

V

Vallas, Steven P., 574
van Amersfoort, Hans, 321
Vanhanen, Tatu, 620
Van Kesteren, J. N., 208
Van Kesteren, P. J., 346
Van Vugt, William E., 307
Veblen, Thorstein, 28, 29, 573
Venkatesh, Sudhir, 132, 202
Venter, Craig, 282
Verhaag, Bertram, 88
Vespa, Jonathan, 399
Viglen, Tyler, 126
Villarroel, Maria, 154
Villaruel, F., 216
Visser, Sara, 99

Voci, A., 88
Von Drehle, David, 224
Voslensky, Michael, 581
Vowell, Paul R., 198
Vowell, P. R., 198

W

Wacquant, Loic, 132, 208, 209
Wade, Lisa, 468
Wærness, Kari, 370
Waggoner, Lawrence W., 500
Wagoner, Jennings L., 533
Waitzkin, Howard B., 445
Wakabayashi, Chizuko, 415
Walby, Sylvia, 380
Walch, Timothy, 307
Waldo, Craig R., 295
Walker, Nancy E., 216
Walker, Tim, 308
Walker, V. G., 451
Waller, Willard, 492
Wallerstein, Immanuel, 269, 270
Wallerstein, Judith, 516
Walls, Jeannette, 288
Walters, Suzanna, 471
Wang, Wendy, 288, 498
Ward, Jane, 459, 474
Ward, Kevin, 590
Ward, Lester, 28
Warhol, Andy, 63
Warner, W. Lloyd, 103
Warren, Earl, 544
Washington, Denzel, 547
Waters, Mary, 133, 284, 321
Watson, Emma, 15
Watt, James, 572
Watts, C. H., 520
Watts, Duncan, 92, 113
Way, Niobe, 362
Weber, Max, 25, 26, 27, 32, 101, 104, 248, 249, 250, 251, 617, 621, 636, 637
Webster, Daniel, 533
Wedgwood, C. V., 618
Wefald, Susan, 588
Weich, Ronald, 216
Weinberg, Martin S., 464
Weitzman, Leonore J., 244
West, Candace, 357, 358
Westbrook, Laurel, 347, 348, 437
Weston, Kath, 495, 669
Wexler, Ilana, 465
Wheeler, J., 469
Whittier, Nancy, 630
Whorf, Benjamin, 55
Whyte, William F., 130
Wiehe, Meg, 591
Wight, R. G., 414
Wilde, Oscar, 535
Wilkins, Amy, 469
Willer, Robb, 375
Williams, B. D., 365

Williams, Christine, 599, 601, 602
Williams, Colin J., 464
Williams, Serena, 85
Williams, Walter, 345
Willis, George, 534
Willis, P., 214
Wilmoth, Janet M., 416
Wilson, Chris M., 515
Wilson, Margo, 342
Wilson, William Julius, 326, 504
Wiltz, Teresa, 508
Winant, Howard, 286
Winfrey, Oprah, 576
Wingfield, Adia Harvey, 599, 602
Winks, Robin W., 618
Winters, Marcus A., 556, 557*m*
Wiswall, Matthew, 600
Woessmann, Ludger, 538
Wolf, Michael, 378
Wolfe, Alan, 651
Wolfe, Thomas, 480
Wolff, R., 237
Wolfram, Stephen, 47
Wollstonecraft, Mary, 20, 21
Wondra, Danielle, 494
Woodham, Luke, 553
Woods, Mario, 327
Woodworth, G., 227
Word, E., 545
Wright, Quincy, 633
Wrightsman, Lawrence S., 90
Wu, Jian, 515
Wylie, Cathy, 368

X

X, Malcolm, 326

Y

Yaukey, David, 662
Yeatts, Dale E., 600
Yen, Hope, 683
Yinger, John, 153, 638
Yoder, J., 595
Yoffee, Norman, 678
Yoshino, Kenji, 16
Yunus, Muhammad, 271

Z

Zald, M. N., 631
Zatz, Marjorie, 206
Zewdie, Selamawit, 365, 414
Zhang, Yin, 576
Zhou, Min, 203, 204, 295, 316
Zijdeman, Richard, 666*f*
Zimmerman, Don, 357, 358
Zimmerman, Wendy, 153
Zimring, Franklin E., 208
Zong, Jie, 317
Zuckerberg, Mark, 339
Zuckerman, Ethan, 99

Subject Index

Page numbers with *f*, *t*, and *m* indicate figures, tables, and maps, respectively.

A

Abortion
  crime rates and, 209
  legalization of, 209
  sex-selective, 671–672
  support for, 511, 512*f*
Absolute poverty, 265
Abstinence campaigns, 468–470
Abstract liberalism, 301
Abuse
  of children, 521–522
  of elders, 522
  of women, 520–522
Academic achievement
  class and, 548–549
  race and, 549–552
Acculturation, 284
Achieved status, 83–84, 84*f*, 242
Adolescence
  crime and, 214–215
  defined, 394
  education and, 397
  historical views on, 396–397
  media and, 182
  peer groups and, 181, 181*f*
  sexuality and, 397
  "sneaky thrills," 214
  socialization and, 170, 181
  unemployment, 419
  video games and, 182
  work and, 419–420
Adonis complex, 436
Adoption
  foster care, 509
  historical views on, 508
  intercountry, 509
  motivations for, 509
  practice babies and, 509
  private, 509
  transracial, 509
Adoptive parents, 508–509
Adulthood
  markers of, 185
  socialization in, 185–186
  young, 185
Aesthetic labor, 601–602
Affect, 534
Affirmative action, 303–304
African Americans. *See also* Racism
  arrest rates of, 216–217
  class and, 325–326
  culture and, 313
  differential opportunity theory and, 217
  discrimination and, 320

  divorce and, 516
  education and, 548–550, 550*f*, 551, 551*f*
  health and, 445
  incarceration of, 216
  income and, 314
  internal migration, 669
  interracial relationships and, 287–288, 288*f*
  labeling theory and, 217
  legacy of slavery and, 304, 313–314
  life chances and, 326
  life expectancy of, 186
  police brutality against, 327
  poverty and, 259
  prejudice and, 314, 320
  racial income gap and, 297–298
  racial profiling, 220–221
  racial wealth gap and, 297–298
  segregation and, 301–302
  socialization and, 177
  stereotypes and, 292–293
  television-watching by, 182
  U. S. population and, 290*f*, 313, 330
African diaspora, 668
Age
  biology and, 391
  chronological, 390
  discrimination and, 417
  dying and, 416–417
  elder care in, 415
  expansion of morbidity, 418
  functional, 390
  gender inequality and, 411
  generations, 403–410
  global population, 409*f*
  global youth, 408
  health and, 418
  identity and, 389–392, 394, 424–425
  inequality and, 392
  institutions and, 392, 417–418, 424–425
  interactions and, 392
  intersections and, 392
  life expectancy and, 393–395
  politics and, 627
  population pyramid, 409–410
  poverty and, 411
  racial and ethnic diversity in, 407*f*
  racial inequality and, 411
  retirement and, 413–414
  rites of passage, 395
  stages of life and, 394–402. *see also specific stages*
Age cohort, 390

Age grades, 390
Age grading, 391
Age inequality
  child labor, 418–422
  elder care and, 415
  politics and, 423
  poverty and, 410–411
  retirement and, 413–414
  sexual orientation and, 414
  social isolation and, 412–413
  workplace, 417
Age norms, 394
Agents of socialization
  defined, 176
  education, 177–178
  family, 176–177
  mass media as, 181–183
  peers, 180–181
  religion, 178–180
  workplace, 183–184
Agnostics, 648
Agricultural economy, 572–573
Agricultural Revolution, 572
Aid to Dependent Children (ADC), 411
Alienation, 684
American Association of Retired Persons (AARP), 423
American Civil Liberties Union (ACLU), 546
American Revolution, 21
Americans with Disabilities Act of 1990 (ADA), 439, 441–442
Amish, 638
Androcentrism, 354–355, 357, 672
Anomie, 196
Anorexia nervosa, 435
Anthropocentrism, 689
Anticipatory socialization, 170
Apartheid, 240–241
Apostasy, 614, 615*m*
Appearance-based discrimination, 442
Ascribed status, 83, 84*f*, 179, 242
Asexuality, 463, 465
Asexuality Visibility and Education Network (AVEN), 465
Asian American Achievement Paradox, The (Lee and Zhou), 204
Asian Americans
  activists, 327
  countries of origin, 314, 315*f*
  discrimination and, 315
  ethnic differences of, 315
  living with parents, 408

stereotypes and, 295, 309, 314, 316
success of, 316
U. S. population and, 290f, 330
Assimilation, 284, 317, 321–322, 324
Assimilationist perspective, 284
Asylums (Goffman), 31
Atheists, 647, 649
Attractiveness. *See* Beauty
Aum Shinrikyo, 638
Authoritarian political systems, 618–619, 620f
Authority
charismatic, 617–618
defined, 612
legal-rational, 617
traditional, 617

B

Baby boomers, 402–405, 433
Backfire effect, 695
Barbie dolls, 336–337
Bathroom segregation, 351–352
Beauty
bodies and, 430–431
body image and, 435–436
defining, 430–431
discrimination and, 442–443
distinction and, 430
global standards for, 435
inequality and, 431–432
Bechdel Test, 355–356, 356f, 382
Bell Curve, The (Herrnstein and Murray), 294, 315
Bias
defined, 118
implicit, 296
unconscious, 296
Bias crime, 329f
Big Time, The (Shames), 403
Bilateral, 482
Bilateral kinship, 494
Biodiversity, 692
Biographical work, 450
Biracial identity, 287, 289
Birth rate, 401–402, 404f
Bisexuality, 463–464
Black churches, 652–653
Black Lives Matter, 327, 423
Black Panther Party, 326, 423
Blacks. *See* African Americans
Blasphemy, 614, 615m
Blended families, 513, 517–518
Blue-collar work, 587
Blumer's views, 30
Bodies
beauty and, 430–431
cosmetic surgery and, 432, 434–435
disabled, 439–441
discrimination and, 441
fatness and, 438
identity and, 431–441
inequality and, 431, 442, 475
institutions and, 432

interactions and, 432
intersections and, 432
obesity and, 431, 438–439, 441–442
status and, 431
tattoos and, 432–434
Body image, 435–436
Boomerang kids, 186
Borderwork, 351
Boston marriages, 495
Bourgeoisie, 247–248, 580
Branch Davidians, 638
Branding, 45
Brown v. the Board of Education, 302, 326, 544
Buddhists, 638
Bulimia, 435
Bullying, 553–554
Bureaucracy
characteristics of, 101–104
defined, 101, 621
ideal type, 102
iron cage, 104
in political systems, 621
worker productivity and, 103
Bureaucratic personality, 102–103
Bystander effect, 91
Bystanders, 91

C

Calling system, 492
Call to Men, A, 380
Canon, 27
Capital, 569
Capital (Marx), 23
Capitalism
defined, 578
democracy and, 578
laissez-faire, 578–580
Marx's views on, 23–24, 248
state, 579–580
Weber's views on, 248
welfare, 579–580
Care work, 601
Caste system, 240–241
Causality, 144, 146–147
Causal relationship, 125
Celibacy, 465
Century of Difference
(Fischer and Hout), 325
Charismatic authority, 617–618
Charismatic leaders, 638
Chicano activists, 327
Childbirth, 451
Childfree, 510–511
Childhood
historical views on, 395–396
sexuality in, 396
Western concept of, 396
Child labor
abuse and, 421–423
global, 420, 420f, 421
guidelines for, 419–420
hazardous conditions for, 421

trafficking and, 421–422
in the United States, 418–420
Childlessness, 510, 510f, 511
Child marriage, 499, 499f
Children
abuse of, 522–523
cognitive stages of, 168–169
corporal punishment and, 522–523, 523f
feral, 163–164
gender polarization in, 181
grandparents and, 508
impact of divorce on, 516–517
isolated, 164
living arrangements of, 518f
mortality rates, 448, 448m
obedience *vs.* independent thinking in, 173f, 177
one-child policy, 672, 677
parents and, 505–507
peer groups and, 180–181
poverty and, 411, 412f
socialization and, 173–177, 505
television-watching by, 182
video games and, 182–183
violence against, 521–522
Children's movies
gender inequality in, 173–174, 174f–175f
sexuality in, 174–175
Child slavery
conscription and, 422–423
drug trade and, 422
global, 421, 421m, 422
sex trafficking and, 422
Child soldiers, 422–423
Chilly classroom climate, 552
"Chivalry effect," 213
Chosen, The (Karabel), 559
Christianity, 638–639, 641–642, 651
Chronological age, 390
Church
attendance, 643–644, 646–647
black, 652–653
house churches, 651
megachurches, 651
as social and cultural centers, 646
Church of Jesus Christ of Latter-day Saints, 638–639
Cis-gender people, 346
Cities, 677–687
alienation in, 684
countryside and, 680–681
"edge," 683
gemeinschaft, 684–685
gentrification, 683
gesellschaft, 684–685
globalization and, 680–681
global urbanization and, 686–687
history of, 678–680
mechanical solidarity in, 685
megalopolis, 683
organic solidarity in, 685

Cities (*continued*)
  population density and, 679, 679*m*, 680–681
  prosperity and, 684*f*
  suburbs and, 682–683
  urban life and, 684
  urban village and, 685–686
  "white flight" and, 682
Civic engagement, 74, 98
Civil religion, 614–616, 636
Civil Rights Movement, 172, 314, 326–328, 544, 631
Class. *See also* Social stratification
  academic achievement and, 548–549
  consumption and, 251
  crime and, 217
  culture and, 250–252
  defined, 241–242
  deviance and, 201, 206
  disabilities and, 441
  habitus and, 250–251
  health and, 445
  higher education and, 558–560
  identification of, 257*f*
  identity and, 238, 245–247
  impact of, 273
  incarceration and, 217
  income distribution and, 254*f*, 258*f*
  inequality and, 238, 246–247, 253–265, 271–272
  intelligence and, 114
  interactions and, 238–239
  labor movement and, 272
  life chances and, 253
  lower, 255
  lower upper, 254
  Marx's views on, 247–248
  middle middle, 254–255
  musical tastes and, 252
  obesity and, 442
  occupational prestige and, 250
  parenting and, 251–252
  politics and, 271–272, 625–626
  position and, 248–249
  power and, 248–249
  race and, 259–261
  socialization and, 171–173, 177
  social mobility and, 236–237, 242–245
  social reproduction and, 237, 240, 252
  status and, 248–249
  tastes and, 251–252
  underclass, 255
  in the United States, 217, 235, 238, 238*f*, 253–258, 273
  upper middle, 254
  upper upper, 253–254
  Weber's views on, 248–249
  working, 255, 262
Class consciousness, 272
Class systems, 242
"Clicktivism," 99
Climate change, 694–695
Cliques, 89–90

Coercion, social interactions and, 81–82
Coercive organizations, 97
Cognitive development, stages of, 168–169
Cohabitation, 500–501
Coleman Report, 545
Collective bargaining, 586
College. *See* Higher education
Colonialism, 269
Color-blind racism, 299–301, 304, 320
Common sense, 7–8
Communication. *See also* Language
  nonverbal, 79–80
  verbal, 80
Communism, 580–582
Communist Manifesto, The (Marx and Engels), 23
Community colleges, 561
Companionate marriage, 487
Competition, social interactions and, 81
Compositional fallacy, 147
Comprehensive sex education, 470
Computer-assisted self-interviewing, 154
Computers, 62
Comte's views, 22–23
Concentrated poverty, 549
Concrete operational stage of development, 168
Conditional cash transfer schemes (CCTS), 271
Confederate flag, 53–54
Confirmation bias, 125
Conflict, social interactions and, 81
Conflict theory, 32–33, 33*t*
Conformity
  groups and, 88
  in strain theory, 198
Confounding variables, 126
Conspicuous consumption, 28, 573
Consumer economy, 573
Consumption, 251, 573, 686
Content analysis, 139, 142*t*
  defined, 137
  discourse analysis and, 139–140
  media and, 139
  qualitative, 137–138
  quantitative, 137–139
Contingent labor, 590
Control group, 128
Cooperation, social interactions and, 81
Corporal punishment, 522–523, 523*f*
Correlations
  causal relationships and, 125–126
  defined, 124
  spurious, 126*f*
  work/life earnings, 125*f*
Cosmetic surgery, 432, 434–435
Counterculture
  assimilation of, 52
  defined, 51
  nature of, 52
Countryside, 678, 680–681
Coup d'état, 632

Courts and court proceedings, 221
  mandatory sentencing rules, 222
  racial bias in, 222–223
Courtship, 491–493
Covered in Ink (Thompson), 433
Credential society, 531
Crime, 192–230
  abortion and, 209
  "chivalry effect," 213
  cybercrime, 211–212
  defined, 209
  drugs and, 218–219
  gender differences in, 213–214, 214*f*, 215
  global inequality and, 218
  guns and, 208, 217
  hate, 213
  inequality and, 194, 206–208
  institutions and, 194, 219–228
  occupational, 211
  opportunity theory and, 200
  organizational, 211
  organized, 212–213
  property, 214–215
  race and ethnicity in, 215–216
  sexual coercion, 215
  "sneaky thrills," 214
  social class and, 217
  social organization of, 208–209
  strain theory and, 197–198, 200
  subcultures and, 200–202
  types of, 209
  in the United States, 206–210
  violent, 214–215
  white-collar, 210–211
  workplace, 210
  youth gangs and, 200
Criminal justice system
  African Americans and, 216
  courts and court proceedings, 221–223
  death penalty, 226–228
  drugs and, 219
  incarceration and, 216*f*, 223–226
  Latinos and, 216
  mandatory sentencing rules, 222
  police and policing, 220, 221*f*
  racial profiling, 220
  social class and, 217
Criminal subcultures, 200
Criminology, 209
Cross-race friendship, 362
Cross-sex friendship, 361–362
Crowds, 86–87
Cults, 638
Cultural capital, 63, 93, 250, 252
Cultural change, 67–68
Cultural diffusion, 68
Cultural diversity, 50, 69
Cultural elites, 63–64
Cultural imperialism, 66
Cultural institutions, 59, 61–62, 65
Cultural Literacy (Hirsch), 535
Cultural omnivores, 252
Cultural racism, 301

Cultural relativism, 50–51
Cultural tool kit, 65
Cultural transfer, 66–67
Cultural universals, 51, 635–636
Cultural univores, 252
Culture, 44–72
  changes in, 67–69
  class and, 250–252
  defined, 46
  diversity of, 50–52
  elements of, 53–58
  ethnicity and, 282
  gender-diverse, 345, 345m
  high, 62–64
  identity and, 48, 50–52
  inequality and, 48
  institutions and, 49, 58–59
  interactions and, 48–49, 53
  intersections and, 49
  language and, 54–55
  material, 46
  media and, 45–48, 69
  nonmaterial, 46
  norms and, 55–57
  popular. see Popular culture
  race vs., 282
  rituals and, 55
  sexuality and, 461–462
  subgroups within, 51–52
  symbols and, 53–54
  universality of, 50–51
  values and, 55–57, 58f, 68
Culture lag, 68
Culture of consumption, 686
Culture of poverty, 264
Culture shock, 50
Culture wars, 68
Custodial parent, 517
Cyberbullying, 553
Cybercrime, 211–212
Cyclical unemployment, 592

D

Daily rhythms, 47
Data
  defined, 122
  interpretation of, 123
  qualitative, 122–123
  quantitative, 122–123
Date rape, 121–122
Dating, 491–493
Death
  aging and, 416–417
  causes of, 416–418, 447, 447f, 448
  mourning and, 417
Death and Life of Great American Cities,
    The (Jacobs), 686
Death penalty
  as a deterrent, 227–228
  in the United States, 227f
  unjust application of, 226–227
  use of, 226
Deductive reasoning, 115, 116f

Deforestation, 692
De-institutionalization movement,
    451, 453
Delayed marriage, 498–499
Democracy
  bureaucracy and, 621
  defined, 619
  global, 620, 620f
  measuring, 620
  participatory, 619
  political action committees and,
    621–622
  representative, 619
  universal suffrage in, 619
  Weber's views on, 621
Demographic transition theory, 675–676
Demography, 662–663
Denomination, 638
Dependency theory, 269
Dependent variables, 124
Desertification, 692
Detached observation, 129
Deterrence, 225, 227–228
Development
  cognitive stages of, 168, 168t
  stage theories of, 168–170
Deviance, 191–192, 194–230
  crime as. see Crime
  culture and, 195–196
  defined, 193
  differential association and, 197,
    200–201
  identity and, 194
  inequality and, 194, 206–207
  institutions and, 194, 219–228
  interactions and, 194
  intersections and, 195
  labeling theory and, 203
  opportunity theory and, 200
  powerlessness and, 206
  primary, 203
  secondary, 203
  self-control theory and, 198
  social class and, 201, 206
  social control theory and, 198
  society and, 196
  stigma and, 196, 204–206
  strain theory and, 197–198, 200
  subcultures and, 199–202
  tertiary, 203
Diagnostic and Statistical Manual
    (DSM-V), 437
Dictatorships, 619
Dictionary of Cultural Literacy (Hirsch,
    Kett, and Trefil), 535
Differential association, 197, 200–201
Differential opportunity theory, 217
Digital activism, 99
Disability
  class and, 441
  defined, 439
  discrimination and, 441–442
  increases in, 440

  mental, 439–440
  physical, 439–440
  race and, 441
  rates of, 440, 440f, 441
Discourse analysis, 139–140
Discrimination
  age and, 417
  appearance-based, 442
  defined, 292
  disabilities and, 441–442
  embodied identities and, 442
  employment, 300
  housing, 297
  increase in, 320
  negative, 442
  positive, 442
  racial, 295–299
  sentencing, 296
  stereotype promise and, 295
  workplace, 600
Disease incidence, 444
Disease prevalence, 444
Distinction, 430
Division of labor, 572
Divorce
  African Americans and, 516
  defined, 513
  divide and, 513
  education and, 515f
  factors causing, 516
  impact of, 515–517
  LGBT, 514–515
  religion and, 516
  women initiating, 514
Divorce rates, 513–514
Domestic division of labor, 505–506
Domestic violence, 374, 519–521. See also
    Intimate partner violence (IPV)
Double consciousness, 29
Douglass's views, 28, 30
Downton Abbey, 241
Dramaturgical model, 31, 78
Driving while Black (DWB), 221
Drug use, 218–219
Druze, 638
Dual labor market, 368
Du Bois's views, 29, 34
Durkheim's views, 24
  on religion, 636
  on social stratification, 237
  on society, 24–25
  on suicide, 24, 26
  on village life, 685
Dyad, 86

E

Eastern religions, 641–642
Eating disorders, 435
Ebola racism, 444
Ecclesiae, 639
Economic growth
  education and, 537, 538f
  global, 538f

Economy, 568–583. *See also* Work
  agricultural, 572–573
  changes in, 572–575
  consumer, 573
  defined, 569–570
  division of labor and, 572
  employment growth, 574*f*
  gig, 590
  globalization and, 575–577
  global recession and, 593
  government intervention in, 582–583
  industrial, 572–573
  inequality and, 38, 581
  informal, 591–592
  knowledge work, 574–575
  outsourcing and, 575
  per capita income, 579
  politics and, 582–583
  postindustrial, 573–577
  rootlessness and, 574–577
  service, 573
  social movements and, 583
  systems of, 577–582
  taxation and, 581–582
  theories of, 569–570
  theory of religious, 644
Ecosystem, 688–689
"Edge cities," 683
Education, 528–566. *See also*
    Higher education; Schools
  affect and, 534
  age and, 391
  as agent of socialization, 177–178
  credential society and, 531
  defined, 530
  developing nations, 542–543
  divorce and, 515*f*
  formal curriculum in, 530, 552
  gender inequality in, 363–365, 365*f*,
    366–367, 541–542, 546, 552–553
  hidden curriculum in, 178, 530, 535,
    539, 552
  high school or college degrees, 533*f*
  historical background of, 532–534
  improvement of, 542–543
  income and, 178*m*
  integration in, 549
  latent function of, 177
  longitudinal studies of, 545, 547
  meritocracy and, 537
  politics and, 626
  Pragmatism and, 534
  public, 533
  scientific literacy and, 535, 536*f*
  segregation and, 549
  social inequality and, 529–530,
    536–542, 548–552
  social mobility and, 537
  social reproduction and, 539–541
  in the United States, 542
Educational homogamy, 541
Educational inequality, 531, 537–538, 548
Ego, 168

Elder abuse, 522
Elder care, 415
Elderly. *See* Old age
Elections, 627–628, 629*f*
Elevator behavior, 80–81
Ellen Show, The, 471
Emigration, 666–667
Emigration rate, 668–669
Emotional labor, 601–602
Employment. *See* Economy; Work
Employment discrimination, 300
Employment growth, 574*f*
Empty nest syndrome, 186
Endogamy, 483, 504
Energy resources, 689–690
English language, 325
Enlightenment, 19–20
Enrollment rates, 555, 556*f*
Environment
    human. *see* Human environment
    natural. *see* Natural environment
    urban. *see* Cities
Environmental disasters, 696–697,
    697*f*, 700
Environmental inequalities, 697–698
Environmental justice, 698
Environmental movement, 631, 699–700
Environmental racism, 698
Epidemiology, 444
"Equality of Educational Opportunity"
    (Coleman), 545
Equal Opportunity Commission, 303
Ethic of care, 169
Ethic of justice, 169
Ethnic cleansing, 36, 321, 327
Ethnic equality, 326–329
Ethnic groups
    African, 313–314
    Asian, 314–316
    defined, 281
    European, 306, 306*f*, 307–308
    Filipino Americans, 285
    Latin American, 311–313
    Middle Eastern, 316–318
    minority and "majority," 289–291
    Native Americans, 308–311
Ethnicity. *See also* Race
    assimilation and, 321–322
    culture and, 282
    defined, 281, 283
    education and, 550*f*–551*f*
    genocide and, 321
    heterogeneity and, 321
    identity and, 281, 305–306, 320–321
    income and, 259*f*
    inequality and, 286, 291–292, 304,
        319–320
    intersections and, 287, 304–305
    pluralism and, 322
    race vs., 283–284, 284*t*, 312
    religion and, 653*f*
    social construction of, 286
    social mobility and, 244

surveys on, 133
    symbolic, 321
    in the United States, 318
Ethnicization, 317
Ethnic renewal, 311
Ethnocentrism, 50–51
Ethnography, 130–132
Ethnomethodology, 80
European Union (EU), 33, 35
Evangelical Christianity, 651–652
Everyday politics, 653–655
Everyday work, 450
Everything in Its Path (Erikson), 696
Evolutionary imperative, 342
Exchange, social interactions and, 80
Exogamy, 483
Expansion of morbidity, 418
Expectations, social roles and, 84
Experimental group, 128
Experiments, 127–129, 142*t*
    control group, 128
    defined, 127
    experimental group, 128
    traps in, 147*t*
Extended family, 486
External risks, 696
Extramarital sex, 463, 470*f*, 471
Extreme Makeover, 434

F

Face work, 78–79
Fads, 64–65
Failing at Fairness (Sadker and
    Sadker), 552
Fair Housing Act of 1968, 297
Families
    as agents of socialization, 176–177
    blended, 513, 517–518
    changes in, 512–513, 524
    childfree vs. childless, 510–511
    children in, 488
    defined, 482
    diversity in, 489–490
    extended, 486
    forming, 491–495
    gender inequality in, 487–488
    grandparents and, 508
    historical development of, 485–486
    household earnings, 501*f*
    intimate partner violence and, 520
    as kinship systems, 481–482
    LGBT, 494–495
    marriage and, 487, 493–494
    matrifocal, 489
    nuclear, 486–490
    of origin, 482
    of procreation, 482
    progressive nucleation of, 487
    single parent, 482, 494
    singletons and, 502, 502*f*, 503
    social mobility and, 177
    social reproduction and, 484
    types of households, 490*f*

in the United States, 518–519
    violence and, 519–523
    work and, 599–600
Families We Choose (Weston), 495
Family trees, 482
Family wages, 487, 602
Fashions, 64–65, 138
Fathers, 506
Fatness, 438, 442
Fecundity, 664
Feeling rules, 601–602
Felony disenfranchisement, 629, 630m
Female genital mutilation (FGM), 441
Females. *See* Women
Feminism
    defined, 379
    men and, 380
    origins of, 20
    transnational, 380–381
Feminist Revolution (Hanisch), 653
Feminization of poverty, 259–260,
    376–378
Feminization of the professions, 368
Feral children, 163–164
Fertility, 664
Fertility rate, 405, 665
Feudalism, 240–241
Fictive kin, 495
Field, 129
Field experiments, 153
Field studies, 129–130, 142t
    defined, 129
    detached observation, 129
    ethnography, 130–132
    objectivity, 129
    participant observation, 129
Filipino Americans, 285
First-generation students, 561
Flint (Mich.) water crisis, 661–662, 698
Folkways, 57, 195
Food scarcity, 446m
Formal curriculum, 530, 552
Formal operational stage of
    development, 168
Formal rights, 471
For-profit universities, 561–563
Foster care adoption, 509
Frames of analysis
    identity, 9–12
    identity and, 13, 16
    inequality, 9–10, 12, 16
    institutions, 9, 11, 17–18
    interactions, 9, 12, 16–17
    intersections, 12, 18–19
    as a way of seeing, 9
Freakonomics (Levitt and Dubner),
    209, 584
French Revolution, 21
Friendship
    cross-race, 362
    cross-sex, 361–362
    gender differences in, 361–362
    networks, 141

Fuller's views, 27–28, 34
Functional age, 390
Functionalism, 32–33
Fundamentalism, 641
Fundamentalist Church of Jesus Christ
    of Latter-day Saints, 639

G

Gangs
    crime and, 215
    inequality and, 202
    race and ethnicity in, 201, 201f
    women in, 202, 215
    youth, 200–202
Garbage, 693
Gay-baiting, 552–553
"Gayborhoods," 474
Gay Liberation Front, 473
Gay rights, 471, 473–474
Gay Rights Movement, 473
Gemeinschaft, 684–685
Gender
    bathroom segregation and, 351–352
    biology of, 341–343
    borderwork and, 351
    color-coded clothing and, 353
    defined, 338
    diversity of, 345, 345m
    friendship and, 361–362
    graduation rates, 540f
    interactions and, 340, 350–352,
        356–357, 360–362
    intersex traits and, 345
    life expectancy and, 446
    marriage and, 370–372
    medicalization of, 343–345
    perceptions of, 336
    politics and, 626–627
    sexual reproduction and, 349–350
    sex vs., 338, 347
    similarities and, 354–355
    social construction of, 350–358
    third category of, 345
    violence and, 374–375
Gender bias, 139, 140f, 352–353, 363–364
Gender binary, 338, 345, 349, 354
Gender convergence, 384
Gender dysphoria, 437
Gender equality
    feminism and, 379–381
    movements for, 379–381
    stalled revolution and, 382–383
    struggle for, 384
    transnational, 380–381
Gender gaps
    athletic performance, 381, 381f
    wages, 382, 382f
Gender identity
    biology and, 341–343
    cis-gender, 346
    defined, 338
    femininities, 338–339
    masculinities, 338–339

    patriarchy and, 339
    schools and, 552
    socialization and, 340
    in social life, 336–337, 340
    transgender, 346–349, 436–437
Gender inequality, 101f
    age and, 411
    androcentrism and, 354–355, 357
    biology and, 341–342
    challenges to, 381–382
    chilly classroom climate, 552
    defined, 338
    in dialogue, 174, 174f–175f
    in education, 363–365, 365f, 367,
        541–542, 546, 552–554
    emotional labor, 601–602
    in family work, 369–370, 487–488
    feeling rules, 601–602
    feminization of poverty and, 376–378
    gender differences and, 341
    gender gaps and, 381–382, 382f
    gender socialization and, 354–355
    health and, 445–447, 455
    in higher education, 558, 560–561
    institutions and, 362–363
    interactions and, 350–351, 360–361
    at local and global levels, 375–377
    in marriage, 371–372, 487
    in media, 173–174, 355–356, 356f
    median earnings and, 369f
    motherhood penalty, 600
    organizations and, 100
    patriarchy and, 339
    pervasiveness of, 336
    politics and, 372, 374f
    racial inequality and, 377
    resistance to, 378–380
    sexual double standard and, 465
    as social inequality, 340
    socialization and, 173–174
    transgender people and, 600
    wage gap, 382, 382f, 596, 597f
    women in board seats, 596f
    women professionals and, 339, 341
    in the workplace, 363–364, 364f,
        365–370, 596–600
Gender panic, 347–349
Gender polarization, 181
Gender policing, 358–360, 433, 552
Gender relations, 357
Gender roles
    blurring of, 357–358
    defined, 357
    outside gender binary, 345
Gender similarities hypothesis, 354–355
Gender socialization
    gender difference and, 352–354
    gender inequality and, 354–355
    identity and, 340
Gender symmetry, 521
Gender wage gap, 596, 597f, 598
Generalizability, 135
Generalized other, 29, 78, 166–167

Generation gap, 405
Generations
    baby boomers, 403–405
    Generation X, 405–406
    Generation Z, 408
    Millennials, 406–408
    racial and ethnic diversity in, 407f
Generation X, 405–406, 433
Generation Z, 408
Genocide, 321
Gentrification, 683
Germ theory of disease, 676
Gerontology, 390–391
Gesellschaft, 684–685
Gift exchange, 56
Gig economy, 590
Gilman's views, 28, 34
Glass ceiling, 595
Glass escalator, 599
Glee, 471, 473
Global city, 687
Global commodity chains, 270
Global distribution, 575
Global inequality
    colonialism and, 269
    commodity chains and, 270
    crime and, 218
    defined, 265
    dependency theory and, 269
    feminization of poverty and, 376–378
    gender and, 376–378
    high-income countries, 267
    income and, 266m
    LGBT rights and, 472f
    low-income countries, 267–268
    market theories and, 268
    middle class and, 266–267
    middle-income countries, 267
    modernization theory and, 268
    mortality rates, 448, 448m
    multinational corporations and, 269
    sex trafficking and, 270
    state-centered theories and, 268–269
    world system theory and, 269–270
Globalization, 6
    beauty standards and, 435
    cities and, 680–681
    cultural diffusion and, 68
    defined, 35, 265, 575, 680
    drugs and, 219
    economy and, 575–577
    gender inequality and, 378
    homogeneity and, 37
    inequality and, 575–576
    macro-level analysis, 35
    multiculturalism and, 35–37
    organizations and, 104
    popular culture and, 66–67
    reactions against, 104
    rootlessness and, 575–577
    sex tourism and, 378
    sex trafficking and, 378
    socialization and, 186–187

social networks and, 94–95
    sociology and, 34–35
    trafficking and, 421
Global migration, 670–671
Global population, 409f, 410, 410f
Global production, 575
Global recession, 593
Global tensions, 36–37
Goffman's views, 31
Google websites, 10
Gossip Girl, 473
Government, 612. See also Politics
Graduation rates, 555
Grandparents, 508
Gray Panthers, 423
Great Awakenings, 645
Greek, 473
Green-collar work, 587
Greenhouse effect, 692
Greensboro Four, 326
Gross domestic product (GDP),
    38, 576, 577m
Group cohesion, 87
Group conformity, 88
Group marriage, 483
Groups, 85–91
    cliques, 89–90
    conformity and, 90–91
    crowds vs., 86–87
    defined, 86
    diffusion of responsibility in, 91
    dynamics of, 89–91
    identity and, 86–89
    membership in, 74, 98–99, 105
    norms and, 88
    in- and out-, 88
    primary, 87
    reference, 89
    secondary, 87
    social inequality and, 105
    types of, 87–88
Groupthink, 90
Guns, 208, 217

H

Habitus, 250–251
Happiness, 120
Hardcore members, 89
Hare Krishnas, 638
Hasidic Jews, 638
Hate crime, 213, 317, 329
Hate groups, 213, 291, 328–329
Hawthorne Effect, 584
Health
    age and, 418
    bodies and, 431
    causes of death, 447, 447f, 448
    class and, 445
    defined, 443
    epidemiology and, 444
    food scarcity, 446m
    gender and, 445–447
    global distribution of, 447–448

inequality and, 444–449
    measure of, 444
    mortality rates, 448, 448m
    poverty and, 394
    race and, 445
    social diagnoses, 444–445
    spending on, 448–449
    women's, 431
Health care
    class and, 445
    inequality and, 454–455
    insured adults, 454, 454f
    life expectancy and, 446
    measures of, 444
    politics and, 443
    spending on, 448, 454
    values and, 455
Herland (Gilman), 28
Heterogeneity, 321
Heteronormativity, 463
Heterosexuality, 462, 469, 602
Hidden curriculum, 177, 530, 535,
    539, 552
Hidden Injuries of Class, The
    (Sennett and Cobb), 171
High culture, 62–64
Higher education, 554–563. See also
        Education
    application process, 544
    changes in, 555
    "character" in admission to, 559
    class and, 558–560
    college degrees, 533f
    community colleges, 561
    costs of, 558, 559f
    enrollment rates, 555, 556f
    first-generation students and, 561
    gender segregation in, 558, 560–561
    graduation rates, 555
    inequality and, 558–560
    mobility pathway in, 560
    party pathway in, 560
    preparing for, 555–556, 557m
    for-profit, 561–563
    SAT scores, 556, 557f
    shootings in, 553
    single-sex, 546
    social capital in, 554
    social reproduction and, 540
    transformation of, 561–562
    in the United States, 534, 540, 554–555
High-income countries, 267
High school
    degrees, 533f
    graduation rates, 534, 539m, 540f
    shootings in, 553
    STEM fields in, 546
Hindus, 638
Hispanic Americans
    activists, 327
    actors, 313
    countries of origin, 311–312
    education and, 549, 550f–551f

as ethnicity, 312
Filipino Americans as, 285
health and, 445
incarceration of, 216, 219
income and, 313
television-watching by, 182
U. S. population and, 290f, 311, 330
values and, 56
HIV/AIDS, 445, 449–451
Homophobia, 471, 473
Homosexuality, 463, 471
Hooking up, 467–468, 492
House churches, 651
Household labor, 488, 506–507
Housing discrimination, 297
Human environment, 662–677. *See also*
    Population
    demography and, 662–663
    politics and, 677
    population and, 664–676
Human Genome Project, 282
Human rights, 50–51
Human Side of Enterprise, The
    (McGregor), 585
Hypothesis, 148

Id, 168
Ideal type of bureaucracy, 102
Identity
    age and, 390–392
    construction of, 10–11
    crime and, 194
    culture and, 48, 50–52
    defined, 9
    deviance and, 194
    embodied, 431–442
    formation of, 11
    gender, 336–337
    media and, 48
    names and, 12–13, 16
    national, 10
    politics and, 625
    race and ethnicity in, 281, 330
    research methods and, 117
    sex and, 337
    social, 11–12
    social construction of, 76–77, 79
    socialization and, 162–163
Identity work, 433
Illegal immigration, 591
Illness. *See also* Health
    biographical work and, 450
    criminalizing, 450–451
    de-institutionalization, 451
    everyday work and, 450
    global distribution of, 447–448
    identity and, 443, 449–450
    medicalization of, 451
    mortality rates, 448, 448m
    sick role, 449–450
Illness work, 450
Immigration

acculturation and, 284
assimilation and, 284, 317
defined, 666
discrimination and, 377
English language and, 325
ethnic groups and, 285, 306–308,
    311–313
ethnicity and, 284
forcible, 313
global, 670–671
illegal, 591
major flows of, 668
Middle Eastern, 317
multiculturalism and, 330
pull factors, 667–669
push factors, 667–669
refugees and, 667f, 668
religious, 645
U. S. population and, 323, 645
Immigration rate, 668–669
Immiseration thesis, 631
Implicit bias, 296
Impression management, 79
Incarceration
    of African Americans, 216
    corrections spending and, 224
    deterrence and, 225
    global, 223, 223m, 224
    of Latinos, 216
    protection and, 225
    rates of, 216f, 226
    recidivism, 225
    retribution and, 225
    social class and, 217
    in the United States, 223–224, 224f
Incest taboo, 195, 483
Income distribution, 254f, 258f–259f, 576
Inconvenient Truth, An (Gore), 700
Independent variables, 124
Inductive reasoning, 115, 116f
Industrial economy, 572–573
Industrial Revolution, 21, 572–573, 679
Industrial societies, 35–36
Inequality, 9. *See also* Racial inequality
    age and, 410–413
    class and, 246–247, 253–265, 271–272
    crime and, 194, 206–208, 217
    culture and, 48
    deviance and, 194, 203, 206–207
    embodied, 430–432, 441–442, 475
    gender, 100, 101f, 173, 259–260, 336,
        339–340
    global, 265–266, 266m, 267–270
    income and, 257–258
    institutions and, 321–322
    internalized, 172
    media and, 48
    names and, 12–13, 16
    politics and, 271–272, 622–623
    poverty and, 258–259
    racial, 171–172, 246
    reproduction of, 207
    research methods and, 117

sexual, 173
social, 10, 12
socialization and, 163, 171–175
Inequality by Design
    (Fischer and Hout), 294
Infant mortality rate, 665
Informal economy, 591–592
Informal privileges, 471–472
Informed consent, 151
In-group, 88, 290
In-group heterogeneity, 88
Innovators, 198
Institutional inequalities, 321–322
Institutionalization, 443
Institutional racism, 294, 296–299
Institutional review boards (IRBs), 130,
    151, 151t, 152
Institutions, 9
    crime and, 194
    culture and, 49, 58–67
    deviance and, 194
    media and, 49, 60–62
    names and, 17–18
    research methods and, 117
    social, 11, 17
    socialization and, 163
Integration, 544–545, 549
Intelligence
    class and, 114
    heritability of, 114
    race and, 294–295
Intercountry adoption, 509
Intercultural contact, 68
Interest groups, 625
Intergenerational mobility, 243–244
Intergenerational violence, 521
Internal labor market, 586
Internal migration, 669, 670t
International Association of Athletics
    Federations (IAAF), 343–344
International Olympic Committee
    (IOC), 343
Internet
    access to, 62
    cybercrime and, 211–212
    digital activism and, 99
    mass media and, 62
    memes, 65
    research methods and, 154
    small world problem and, 92m
    social networks and, 94–96
Interracial marriage, 497, 497t, 498
Interracial relationships, 287–288,
    288f, 289
Intersectionality, 305
Intersections, 12
    crime and, 195
    culture and, 49
    defined, 9
    deviance and, 195
    media and, 49
    names and, 18–19
    research methods and, 118

Intersections (*continued*)
  socialization and, 163
Intersex traits, 343–346
Intervening variables, 126
Interviews, 132
Interview studies, 132–133, 142*t*
Intimate partner violence (IPV), 374–375,
  519–520, 520*f*, 521
Intragenerational mobility, 244
Intragenerational violence, 521
"Iron cage," 25, 104
Islam, 639, 641–642, 651
Isolated children, 164

J

Jane the Virgin, 473
Jehovah's Witnesses, 638, 651
Jews, 638
Jim Crow laws, 313, 669
Jobs. *See* Work
Judaism, 639, 641
Juvenile delinquency, 200

K

Kinship systems, 481–482
Knowledge economy, 574–575
Know-Nothing Party, 328
Ku Klux Klan (KKK), 328

L

Labeling, 547–548
Labeling theory, 203, 217
Labor movement, 272, 631
Laissez-faire capitalism, 578–580
Language
  culture and, 54–55
  defined, 54
  English, 325
  immigrants and, 325
  perception and, 55
Latent functions, 32
Latinos. *See* Hispanic Americans
Lavender ceiling, 602–603
Laws, 57, 58*f*
Leaders, 89
Lead levels, 661–662
Lean In (Sandberg), 16
Legacy of slavery, 304, 313–314
Legal-rational authority, 617
Levittown, 682–683
LGBT (lesbian, gay, bisexual and
    transgender) people. *See also* Sexual
    orientation
  adults identifying as, 460*f*
  characteristics of, 495
  cohabitation and, 500–501
  college and, 39
  divorce and, 514–515
  families and, 494–495
  global rights, 472*f*
  increases in, 459
  internal migration, 669
  intimate partner violence and, 519

marriage and, 482–483, 494–497
neighborhoods and, 474
relationship types, 464*f*
resistance to inequality by, 472–474
resumes, 603
sexuality and, 457–458
Stonewall Riots and, 473
in the workplace, 602–603
Liberation theology, 650
Life chances, 253, 326
Life expectancy
  changes in, 393–395
  defined, 665
  economic status and, 402
  global, 393*f*, 402, 666
  intersections and, 676
  racial differences in, 186
  retirement and, 413*f*
  in the United States, 186, 394, 666
Life span, 394
Likert scale, 134
Lingua franca, 325
Literacy rates, 541, 543*m*
Living wage, 588–589
Local cultures, 187
Longitudinal study, 545, 547
Looking-glass self, 77–78
Love, 361
Loving v. Virginia, 287, 497
Lower class, 255
Lower upper class, 254
Low-income countries, 267–268
L Word, The, 473

M

Macro-level analysis, 35
Majority groups, 290, 290*f*, 291
Males. *See* Men
Malthusian theory, 674–675
Managed Heart, The (Hochschild), 601
Mandatory sentencing rules, 222
Manifest functions, 32
Manufacture consent, 585–586
Manufactured risks, 696
March on Washington (1963), 326
Marital sex, 463
Markers of adulthood, 185
Markets, 572
Market theories, 268
Marriage
  arranged, 492–493
  Boston, 495
  child, 499, 499*f*
  cohabitation vs., 500–501
  companionate, 487
  delayed, 498–499
  divorce and, 513–517
  egality in, 371
  endogamy and, 483
  exogamy and, 483
  families and, 487, 493–494
  gender and, 370–371
  gender inequality in, 371–372, 487

group, 483
household earnings, 501*f*
incest taboo, 483
interracial, 287–288, 288*f*, 289, 497,
    497*t*, 498
intimate partner violence and,
    519–520
monogamy and, 483
nonmarital choices, 503
polyamory, 483
polyandry and, 483
polygamy and, 483
polygyny and, 483
rates of, 518*f*
remarriage and, 517
same-sex, 482–483, 494–497
sex and, 463, 504*f*
social networks and, 96
social reproduction and, 483
suitable males for, 504
in the United States, 518–519
Marx's views, 34
  on capitalism, 580
  on communism, 580–581
  immiseration thesis, 631
  on inequality, 23–24
  on materialism, 23
  mode of production and, 247
  on political resistance, 272
  on population, 675
  on power, 612
  on religion, 612, 636, 642
  on socialism, 580
  on social stratification, 237, 247–248
Masculinization of sex, 465–466
Mass media. *See also* Social media
  as agents of socialization, 181–183
  authenticity and, 632
  bias in, 207
  confidence in, 61
  content analysis and, 139
  culture and, 45–48, 69
  daily rhythms and, 47
  defined, 46
  forms of, 46–47
  gender bias in, 139, 140*f*
  gender differences in, 173–174
  gender inequality and, 355–356, 356*f*
  institutions and, 49, 59–62
  internet, 62
  newspaper reach, 60
  norms and, 57
  print, 60–61
  print media, 60–61
  radio, movies, and television, 61–62
  sexual inequality and, 174–175
  socialization and, 173–175
  social movements and, 632
  television, 182
  use of, 182*f*
  values and, 57
  video games, 182
Master status, 84, 84*f*

Material culture
    culture lag and, 68
    defined, 46
    symbols and, 53
Materialism, 23
Maternal instinct, 164–165
Matrifocal families, 489
Matrilineal, 482
Matrix of inequality, 37
Matter of Taste (Lieberson), 14
McDonaldization, 37
Mead's views, 29, 34
Mechanical solidarity, 24, 685
Media. *See* Mass media
Medicalization, 343–344, 451, 453
Megachurches, 651–652
Megalopolis, 683
Melting pot, 308, 318, 321
Memes, 65, 67
Men. *See also* Androcentrism
    body image and, 435–436
    crime and, 213–214
    glass escalator and, 599
    life expectancy and, 446
    marriageability of, 504
    pro-feminist, 379
    second shift and, 370
Men Are from Mars, Women Are from Venus (Gray), 336
Men Can Stop Rape (MCSR), 380
Men's liberation, 379
Mental disabilities, 439–440
Mental illness
    defined, 451
    de-institutionalization, 451, 453–454
    institutionalization and, 443
    medicalization of, 453
    prevalence of, 454
Meritocracy, 237, 537
Merton's views, 32
Meta-analysis, 439
Microcredit, 271
Micro-level analysis, 35
Middle age, 400–401
Middle class
    identification of, 257f
    "missing middle," 257
    myth of, 256–257
    subcategories of, 254–255
Middle Eastern Americans, 316–318
Middle-income countries, 267
Middle middle class, 254–255
Middletown Study, 56
Migration. *See also* Immigration
    global, 670, 670t, 671
    internal, 669, 670t
    refugees and, 667f, 668
Milgram obedience study, 128
Militant chauvinism, 205
Millennials, 406–408, 432–434
Minimalization, 301
Minimum wage, 587–588, 588f
Minority groups, 289–290, 290f, 291

Minstrelization, 205
"Missing middle" class, 257
"Missing" women, 672
Mobility studies, 242–244
Mode of production, 247
Modern Family, 471
Modernism, 22
Modernization theory, 15, 268
Monarchy, 618
Monogamy, 483
Moral development
    Gilligan's views on, 169
    Kohlberg's views on, 169
Moral panic, 438, 467
Morbidity rate, 444
Mores, 57, 195–196
More Work for Mother (Schwartz), 488
Mormons, 638
Mortality rate, 444, 448, 448m, 665
Motherhood penalty, 600
Mother Nature (Hrdy), 164
Mothers
    child care and, 506–507
    household labor and, 488, 506–507
    ideology of, 489
    single, 490
    stay at home, 506
Mourning, 417
Movies, 61
Multiculturalism
    assimilation model and, 324
    cultural diversity and, 325, 330–331
    defined, 35, 324
    globalization and, 35–37
    intersections and, 325–326
    life chances and, 326
    macro-level analysis, 35
    micro-level analysis, 35
Multinational corporations, 269
Multiracial identity, 287–289, 289f
Muscle dysmorphia, 436
Music, 405
Musical tastes, 252
Muslims, 642
    hate crime and, 317–318, 329
    in the United States, 638

N

Names
    identity and, 12–13, 16
    inequality and, 12–13, 16
    institutions and, 17–18
    interactions and, 16–17
    intersections and, 18–19
    "modernization theory" of, 15
    popular, 13f, 14–15, 15f, 18
    social forces and, 15
    social inequality and, 16
    sociological imagination and, 16
    top boys and girls, 13t
National identity, 10
National Opinion Research Center (NORC), 457

National Organization for Men Against Sexism (NOMAS), 380
National Woman Suffrage Association, 378–379
Nation-states, 36
Native Americans
    activists, 327
    culture and, 309–311
    decimation of, 308–309
    discrimination and, 310
    displacement of, 308–310
    ethnic renewal and, 311
    gender and, 345
    mascots and, 308–309
    reservations, 310m
    stereotypes and, 308–309
Natural environment, 688–700
    anthropocentrism and, 689
    backfire effect and, 695
    biodiversity in, 692
    climate change and, 694–695
    consciousness and, 700
    deforestation, 692
    desertification, 692
    disasters and, 696–697, 697f, 700
    ecosystems and, 688–689
    energy resources and, 689–690
    environmental justice, 698
    environmental racism, 698
    external risks, 696
    garbage and, 693
    greenhouse effect, 692
    inequality and, 697–698
    manufactured risks, 696
    "normal accidents" in, 690–691
    nuclear disasters, 690–691
    politics and, 699–700
    pollution and, 693
    threats to, 692–695
    vanishing resources in, 691–692
Naturalization, 301
Natural population increase, 673–674
Natural sex ratio, 671
Nature vs. nurture
    common sense and, 7–8
    intelligence and, 114
    socialization and, 160–161
    twin studies and, 114, 162
Negative discrimination, 442
Net migration rates, 669
Network analysis, 140–141, 142t
Network effects, 92–93
Networks. *See* Social networks
New social order, 21, 22t
Nickel and Dimed (Ehrenreich), 263
Nine Dragons Paper Co., 576
No Excuses (Thernstrom and Thernstrom), 550
Nonmarital sex, 463, 503
Nonmaterial culture, 46
Nonverbal communication, 79–80
"Normal accidents," 690–691
Normative organizations, 97

Normification, 205
Norm of reciprocity, 81
Norms
    changes in, 57
    culture and, 55–57
    defined, 55
    folkways and, 57
    gift exchange and, 56
    laws and, 57
    mores and, 57
    social interactions and, 80–81
    socialization and, 160
    types of, 56–57
North American Free Trade Act
        (NAFTA), 33
North Atlantic Treaty Organization
        (NATO), 35
Nuclear disasters, 690–691
Nuclear families, 486–490
Nurture. *See also* Nature vs. nurture
    defined, 160
    sociology and, 161

O

Obergefell v. Hodges, 482
Obesity
    class and, 442
    global, 438–439
    increases in, 438
    inequality and, 441–442
    media and, 438, 439f
    meta-analysis of, 439
    moral panic and, 438
    poverty and, 431, 442
Objectivity, 129
Observational research methods,
        127–133
    experiments, 127–129
    field studies, 129–132
    interview studies, 132–133
Observer effect, 146
Occupational crime, 211
Occupational prestige, 249–250, 250t
Occupational sex segregation, 367–368,
        598–599, 599f
Occupy Wall Street, 423, 583
Offenses, bias motivation in, 329f
Old age
    abuse and, 522
    increases in, 401–402
    life expectancy and, 402
    "oldest old," 402
    "old old," 402
    social isolation in, 412–413
    "young old," 402
Old regime, 21, 22t
One-child policy, 672, 677
One Day at a Time, 473
Operationalization, 118, 121–122
Opinion polls, 654
Opportunity theory, 200
Orange is the New Black, 437
Organic solidarity, 24, 570, 685

Organizational crime, 211
Organizational culture, 96–97
Organizational positions, 100
Organizations
    bureaucracy and, 101–102
    civic, 98
    coercive, 97
    culture and, 96–97
    defined, 96
    digital technology and, 99
    globalization and, 104
    inequality and, 100, 101f
    membership in, 97–98
    normative, 97
    power and, 101
    total institutions, 97–98
    utilitarian, 97–98
Organized crime, 212–213
Orgasm gap, 468
Our Bodies, Ourselves, 431
Out-group, 88, 290
Out-group homogeneity, 88
Outsourcing, 575
Overt racism, 294–296

P

Pan-Indianism, 311
Paradigms, 31
Parents
    adoptive, 508–509
    blended families, 513, 517–518
    child care and, 507
    class and, 251–252
    custodial, 517
    domestic division of labor and,
        505–507
    grandparents and, 508
    same-sex, 507
Parson's views, 31–32
Participant observation, 129
Participatory democracy, 619
Part-time work, 589–590
Passages (Sheehy), 400
Patriarchy, 339
Patrilineal, 482
Peer groups, 180–181, 183
Peer review, 150
Perception, 55
Performances, 84–85
Philadelphia Negro, The (Du Bois), 29
Physical attractiveness. *See* Beauty
Physical disabilities, 439–440
Piece-rate pay system, 586
Pink-collar work, 587
Plessy v. Ferguson, 301
Pluralism, 322, 324, 644
Pluralist perspective, 284
Police and policing, 220–221,
        221f, 327
Political action committees (PACs),
        621–622
Political apathy, 627
Political change

coup d'état in, 632
    political revolutions and, 632–633
    relative deprivation and, 631
    revolutions and, 631
    social movements and, 630–632
    social revolutions and, 633
    terrorism and, 634–635
    war and, 633–634
Political participation, 627–629,
        629f, 630m
Political parties
    affiliation with, 625–626, 626f
    age and, 627
    class and, 625–626
    defined, 623
    education and, 626
    gender and, 626–627
    race and, 626
    in the United States, 623–627
Political revolutions, 632–633
Political systems
    authoritarian, 618–619, 620f
    democratic, 619–620, 620f
    dictatorships, 619
    inequality and, 622–623
    monarchy, 618
    privilege and, 621–622
    problems with, 621–622
    proportional representation, 623
    totalitarianism, 618–619
    in the United States, 621–625
    women in, 623f
Politics, 616–635
    age inequality and, 423
    authority and, 617–618
    class and, 271–272
    compromise in, 616
    defined, 611
    economy and, 582–583
    everyday, 653–655
    gender inequality and, 372, 374f
    gender perceptions, 374f
    healthcare and, 443
    inequality and, 271–272,
        612–613, 629
    interest groups and, 625
    opinions on, 654
    political parties and, 623–625
    popular culture and, 64–65
    religion and, 610–616, 639,
        650–652, 655
Pollution, 693, 698
Polyamory, 483
Polyandry, 483
Polygamy, 483
Polygyny, 483
Popular culture
    defined, 62
    fads, 64–65
    fashions, 64–65
    globalization of, 66–67
    high culture *vs.*, 62–64
    politics of, 64–65

Population
  demographic transition theory, 675–676
  emigration and, 666–669
  fecundity and, 664–665
  fertility and, 664–665
  germ theory of disease and, 676
  global, 409f
  growth in, 674f, 675
  immigration and, 666–670
  internal migration, 669, 670t
  life expectancy and, 665–666
  Malthusian theory, 674–675
  Marx's views on, 675
  mortality rates, 665
  natural increases in, 673–674
  net migration rates, 669
  refugees and, 667f, 668
  sex ratio, 671
  sex-selective abortion and, 671–672
  zero population growth, 675
Population Bomb, The (Ehrlich), 675
Population composition, 671
Population density, 679–681
Population pyramid, 409–410, 671, 671f
Populist movement, 583
Positive discrimination, 442
Postindustrial economy, 573–577
Poverty
  absolute, 265
  age and, 411
  children in, 262, 411, 412f
  concentrated, 549
  culture of, 264
  disabilities and, 441
  elderly and, 262–263
  employment and, 262
  ethnicity and, 261
  feminization of, 259–260, 376–378
  gender inequality in, 259
  global, 266, 266m, 267–270
  health care access and, 394
  income inequality and, 258–259
  intimate partner violence and, 519
  life expectancy and, 394
  microcredit and, 271
  mothers and, 262
  obesity and, 431, 442
  perceptions of, 263
  pollution and, 698
  race and, 251m, 259–260
  racial inequality and, 412f
  reasons for, 263–264
  reducing, 270–271
  relative, 265
  in the United States, 261, 261f, 262–264
  urban/rural, 262
  welfare systems, 271
  working poor and, 262, 588–589
Poverty line, 261
Power. *See also* Politics
  authority and, 612
  class and, 248–249
  defined, 248, 611
  government and, 612
  Marx's views on, 612
  organizations and, 101
  political, 621–622
  Weber's views on, 617
Practice babies, 509
Pragmatism, 534
Predictability, 144–146
Prejudice
  defined, 292
  hate groups and, 291
  overcoming, 319–320
  perceptions of, 296
  stereotypes and, 91, 292, 319–320
Premarital sex, 463, 470f, 471
Preoperational stage of development, 168
Primary deviance, 203
Primary group, 87
Primary socialization, 161–162
Primates, 164–165
Print media, 60–61
Private adoption, 509
Private schools, 546–548
Probability, 145–146
Production, 573
Productivity, 103
Profane, 636
Pro-feminist men, 379
Progressive nucleation, 487
Project STAR, 545, 547
Proletariat, 247–248, 580
Promiscuity, 342
Promotional groups, 625
Property crimes, 214–215
Proportional representation, 623
Prostitution, 270
Protection, 225
Protective groups, 625
Protestant Ethic and the Spirit of Capitalism, The (Weber), 25
Public education, 533
Pull factors, 667–669
Purposive samples, 132
Push factors, 667–669

Q

Qualitative data, 122–123
Qualitative methods, 118–119, 121
Quantitative analysis, 133–136
  causality and, 146–147
  surveys, 134–136
Quantitative data, 122–123
Quantitative methods, 118–119, 121
Queer Eye for the Straight Guy, 473
Quiet revolution, 596

R

Race. *See also* Ethnicity
  academic achievement and, 549
  biraciality and multiraciality and, 287–289
  childlessness and, 510–511
  class and, 259–261
  culture vs., 282
  defined, 282
  disabilities and, 441
  discrimination and, 295
  education and, 550f–551f
  emotional labor, 602
  employment discrimination and, 300
  ethnicity vs., 283–284, 284t, 312
  graduation rates, 540f
  hate groups and, 291–292
  health and, 445, 447
  identity and, 281, 330
  income and, 259f
  institutions and, 287, 294
  intelligence and, 294–295
  interactions and, 286–287
  interracial relationships and, 287–289
  intersections and, 287, 304–305
  legacy of slavery and, 304, 313–314
  minority and "majority" groups and, 289–291
  politics and, 626
  poverty and, 251m, 259–260
  prejudice and, 296
  religion and, 652–653, 653f
  social construction of, 280–283, 286, 330
  social inequality and, 281
  social mobility and, 244
  stereotypes and, 292–293
  tokenism and, 595
  in the workplace, 595
Racial equality
  Chicano activists and, 327
  Civil Rights Movement, 172, 314, 326–328
  movements for, 326–327
  opposition to, 328–329
Racial ethnicity, 284
Racial formations, 286
Racial income gap, 297–298, 298f
Racial inequality, 318
  age and, 411
  color-blind racism and, 299–301
  discrimination and, 292, 295–296, 300, 326
  gender inequality and, 377
  health and, 455
  historical background of, 303–304
  income gap, 297, 298f
  influence of, 286
  institutions and, 291–292, 296–297
  intersectionality and, 304–305
  poverty and, 412f
  prejudice and, 292
  racism and, 294–295
  resistance to, 319–320
  segregation and, 301–303
  socialization and, 171–172
  stereotypes and, 292–293
  wealth gap, 297, 298f

Racialization, 317
Racial profiling, 220–221
Racial segregation
    inequality and, 302–303
    infrastructure and, 303
    laws and, 301–302
    residential, 302–303
Racial wealth gap, 297–298, 298f
Racism
    abstract liberalism and, 301
    color-blind, 299–301, 304, 320
    in courts, 222–223
    cultural, 301
    defined, 292
    Du Bois on, 29
    environmental, 698
    hate groups and, 291–292
    health and, 445
    institutional, 294, 296–298
    internalized, 172
    minimization and, 301
    naturalization and, 301
    overt, 294–296
    scientific, 294–295, 307
    subtle, 294–296
    symbols and, 54
Racism without Racists
    (Bonilla-Silva), 300
Radio, 61
Random samples, 134
Rape
    college students and, 215
    rates of, 121–122
"Ratchet effect," 18
Rational choice theory, 644
Rationality, 25
Rebels, 198
Recidivism, 225
Reciprocal effects, 442
Reference group, 89
Refugees, 667f, 668
Rehabilitation, 226
Relationships, interracial, 287–289
Relative deprivation, 631
Relative poverty, 265
Reliability, 149
Religion, 635–655
    affiliations, 646–647, 647f, 652–653
    as agent of socialization, 178–180
    apostasy and, 614, 615m
    ascribed status of, 179
    blasphemy and, 614, 615m
    charismatic leaders in, 638
    civil, 614–616, 636
    as cultural universal, 635–636
    defined, 611
    diversity of, 646–647
    divorce and, 516
    Durkheim's views on, 636
    Eastern, 641–642
    ethnicity and, 653f
    evangelical, 651–652
    everyday, 651–653

fastest growing, 642, 643f
    freedom of, 614
    fundamentalist, 641
    global tradition and variation, 640
    Great Awakenings, 645
    groups and, 637–639
    identity and, 612, 635, 645f,
        646–647, 647f
    industrialization and, 643–644, 646
    knowledge of, 651
    Marx's views on, 612, 636, 642
    megachurches, 652
    pluralism and, 644
    politics and, 610–616, 639,
        650–652, 655
    race and, 652–653, 653f
    secularization and, 642–643
    type of organizations, 637t
    unaffiliated, 647–648, 648m, 649, 649f
    in the United States, 644–649
    wealth and, 643
    Weber's views on, 636–637, 642
    Western, 639, 641
    world, 639–642
Religiosity, 637
Remarriage, 517
Remember the Titans, 547
Replication, 137
Representative democracy, 619
Representative samples, 135
Reproduction, 504f
Research methods, 110–157
    causality and, 146–147
    comparisons in, 142–143
    computer-assisted self-interviewing,
        154
    content analysis and, 137–140
    data in, 122–123
    deceptive practices in, 152
    defined, 114
    field experiments, 153
    hypothesis, 148
    importance of, 113–115
    informed consent in, 151
    Internet communities, 154
    issues in conducting, 150–152
    network analysis, 140–141
    observational, 127–133
    observer effect in, 146
    operationalization in, 118, 121–122
    peer review in, 150
    predictability and, 144–146
    probability and, 145–146
    qualitative, 118–119, 121–123
    quantitative, 118–119, 121–123,
        133–136
    reliability and, 149
    replication and, 137
    scientific method and, 115–116
    secondary analysis and, 124, 137
    steps in, 147–150
    surveys, 118–120, 153–154
    triangulation in, 121

types of, 124–142, 142t, 143
    validity and, 149
Residential segregation, 302–303
Resocialization, 170
Resumes, 603
Retirement, 413, 413f, 414
Retreatists, 198
Retreatist subcultures, 200
Retribution, 225
Reverse causality, 126
Revolutions, 631
Rites of passage, 185, 395
Ritualists, 198
Rituals, 55, 636
Rockefeller Drug Laws, 219
Role conflict, 85
Role exit, 85
Role performance, 82
Roles, 82–85. *See also* Gender roles;
    Social roles
Role strain, 85
Rootlessness, 574–577

S

Sacred, 636
Sacrilegious, 636
Same-sex marriage, 482–483, 494–495,
    496m, 496f, 497
Same-sex parents, 507
Same-sex relationships, 470f, 471. *See
    also* LGBT people
Samples
    defined, 134
    random, 134
    representative, 135
    stratified, 135
    systematic, 134–135
"Sandwich generation," 401
Sapir-Whorf hypothesis, 55
"School effects," 545
Schools. *See also* Education; High school
    bullying in, 553–554
    busing and, 547
    chilly classroom climate, 552
    gender policing and, 552–554
    inequality and, 545–546
    integration in, 544–545
    labeling and, 547–548
    longitudinal studies of, 545, 547
    poverty and, 549
    private, 546–548
    "school effects" and, 545
    segregation and, 544, 547, 550
    self-fulfilling prophecy and, 548
    shootings in, 553
    single-sex, 546
    social inequality and, 546–552
    tracking in, 547, 550
School's Out (Connell), 184
Scientific literacy, 535, 536f
Scientific method, 115–116
Scientific racism, 307
Seasonal unemployment, 592

Seasons of a Man's Live (Levinson), 400
Secondary analysis, 124, 137, 142*t*
Secondary deviance, 203
Secondary group, 87
Secondary socialization, 162
Second shift, 369
Sects, 638–639
Secularization, 642–643
Secular rituals, 615–616
Segregation, 544–545, 547, 549–550
Self-control theory, 198
Self-fulfilling prophecy, 128–129, 204, 548
Selfies, 78
Sensorimotor stage of development, 168
Sentencing discrimination, 296
Separate spheres, 591
Separation of church and state, 611, 614–616, 646, 651. *See also* Politics; Religion
September 11, 2001 terrorist attacks, 317
Service economy, 573
Service work, 587
Sex
    biology of, 341–343, 349–350
    defined, 338, 458
    evolutionary imperative and, 342
    extramarital, 463
    gender vs., 338, 347
    identity and, 337
    intersex traits and, 343–346
    marital, 463, 504*f*
    medicalization of, 343–345
    nonmarital, 463, 503
    premarital, 463
    promiscuity and, 342
    reproduction and, 504*f*
Sex education, 469–470
Sex ratio, 671
Sex roles, 357. *See also* Gender roles
Sex-selective abortion, 671–672
Sex testing, 343–344
Sex tourism, 378
Sex trafficking, 270, 378, 422
Sexual assault, 121–122
Sexual behavior, 459
Sexual coercion, 215
Sexual desire, 459
Sexual discrimination, 471
Sexual double standard, 465
Sexual equality, 471
Sexual identity. *See also* LGBT (lesbian, gay, bisexual and transgender) people
    asexuality, 463, 465
    behavior and, 464
    bisexuality, 463–464
    celibacy and, 465
    defined, 459
    heteronormativity and, 463
    heterosexuality, 462, 469
    homosexuality, 463
    relationship types, 464*f*
    in the workplace, 602–603

Sexual inequality
    discrimination and, 470–471
    formal rights and, 471
    homophobia, 471
    informal privileges and, 471–472
    LGBT rights and, 472*f*
    in media, 174–175
    prejudice and, 471
    resistance to, 472–474
    socialization and, 173–175
    "tolerance trap" and, 471
Sexuality, 458–475
    abstinence campaigns, 468–470
    attitudes towards, 470*f*, 471
    class and, 360
    culture and, 461–462
    defined, 459
    desires and behaviors, 459, 461–462
    gendered construction of, 465
    gender policing and, 359–360
    hooking up, 467–468
    masculinization of, 465–466
    measures of, 459
    orgasm gap in, 468
    promiscuity and, 342
    research in, 456–458
    retrospective analysis and, 466
    same-sex, 457, 459, 462
    sex partners and, 466
    sexual double standard and, 465
    "stud versus slut" effect, 466
    virginity pledges and, 468–469
    of youth, 467*f*
Sexually transmitted infections (STIs), 503
Sexual orientation. *See also* LGBT (lesbian, gay, bisexual and transgender) people
    LGBT, 460*f*
    relationship types, 464*f*
    retirement and, 414
    same-sex marriage and, 494
    teachers and, 184
Sexual prejudice, 471
Sexual reproduction, 349–350
Sexual scripts, 215, 460–461
Sexual socialization, 460
Sexual tolerance, 471
Sex work, 270
Shari'a, 651
Sibling violence, 521–522
Sickness. *See* Illness
Sick role, 449–450
Simmel's views, 27, 34
Single mothers
    grandparents and, 508
    increases in, 507
    poverty and, 490
    race and ethnicity in, 507–508
    teenaged, 508
Single parent families, 482, 494, 507
Single-sex schooling, 546
Singletons, 502, 502*f*, 503

"Slactivism," 99
Slavery
    child, 421, 421*m*, 422
    embodied inequality and, 441
    everyday politics and, 654–655
    legacy of, 304, 313–314
Slumdog Millionaire, 240
Small world problem, 92
"Sneaky thrill," 214
Social actors, 104
Social capital, 554
Social class. *See* Class
Social construction of gender, 356–358
Social control theory, 198
Social Darwinism, 28
Social desirability bias, 118
Social diagnoses, 444–445
Social epidemiology, 444
Social fact, 25
Social forms, 27
Social groups, 10. *See also* Groups
Social identity, 11–12
Social ideologies, 237
Social inequality, 12
    defined, 10
    education and, 529–530, 536–542, 548–552
    gender and, 340
    groups and, 105
    identity and, 33–34
    institutional differences and, 546–547
    race and, 281
    surveys on, 136*f*
Social institutions, 17
    defined, 11, 75
    gender and, 340
    names and, 12
Social interactions, 9, 12
    construction of reality through, 77–79
    crime and, 194
    culture and, 48–49, 53
    defined, 77
    deviance and, 194
    dramaturgical model of, 31
    media and, 49
    memes, 67
    names and, 16–17
    nonverbal communication and, 79–80
    norms and, 80–81
    occupational prestige and, 249
    patterns of, 80–82
    research methods and, 117
    socialization and, 163
    structured, 75–76, 79
    subordinates in, 81
    superordinates in, 81
    verbal communication and, 80
Socialism, 580–581
Social isolation, 95, 412–413
Socialization, 76, 154–190
    in adolescence, 170, 182
    in adulthood, 185–186
    agents of. *see* Agents of socialization

Socialization (*continued*)
anticipatory, 170
defined, 161
feral children and, 163–164
Freud's views on, 168
gender and, 173–174
generalized other and, 166–167
Gilligan's views on, 169
globalization and, 186–187
identity and, 160, 162–163
inequality and, 163, 171–175
institutions and, 163, 176, 178
isolated children and, 164
Kohlberg's views on, 169
lifelong process of, 188
in local cultures, 187
maternal instinct and, 164–165
Mead's views on, 166–167
media and, 173–175
modes of, 165–170
nature vs. nurture and, 160–161
nonverbal communication and, 80
norms and, 160
Piaget's views on, 168–170
primary, 161–162
in primates, 164–165
process of, 163–164
racial inequality and, 171–172
resocialization and, 170
secondary, 162
sexual inequality and, 173–175
social class and, 171–173, 177
stage theories of development and,
168–170, 185
zoos and, 167
Social media
digital activism and, 99
identity and, 48, 78
interactions and, 49
peer groups and, 183
socialization and, 182–183
social networks and, 94, 96
Social mobility
defined, 177, 236
education and, 537
global, 245
inequality and, 237
intergenerational, 243–244
intragenerational, 244
mobility studies, 242–244
race and ethnicity in, 244
structural, 242
underemployed and, 242–243
in the United States, 236–237, 244–245
Social movements, 630–632
Social networks
analysis of, 140–141
defined, 91, 140
friendship, 141
globalization and, 94–95
influence of, 93–94
network effects and, 92–93
singletons and, 503

small world problem and, 92
social media and, 94, 96
strong ties in, 94
weak ties in, 94
Social order, 31–32
Social reproduction
class and, 240, 252
education and, 539–541
families and, 484
marriage and, 483
social mobility and, 237
status and, 84
Social revolutions, 633
Social roles
defined, 84
expectations of, 84
performances and, 84–85
role conflict in, 85
role exit, 85
role strain in, 85
Social science, 144–146
Social scripts, 77
Social solidarity, 24
Social stigma, 204, 433
Social stratification, 235–278. *See also*
Class
defined, 236, 570
inequality and, 237
Marx's views on, 247–248
meritocracy and, 237
occupational prestige and, 249–250
position and, 248–249
power and, 248–249
social ideologies and, 237
status and, 248–249
systems of, 240–243
Weber's views on, 248–249
Social structure
defined, 76, 82
elements of, 82–85
Social ties, 140–141
Societies, 10, 73–109
defined, 75
Socioeconomic status (SES), 249
Sociological imagination, 3, 8, 16–17, 286
Sociological understanding, 5–6
Sociology
classical, 22–27
contemporary, 30–33
defined, 2–3
diversity of field, 37–39
dynamics of, 4–5
frames of analysis, 9–12
globalization and, 34–35
importance of, 149
major schools of thought in, 33*t*
multiculturalism and, 35
origins of, 19–22
overview of, 2–3
scientific nature of, 8, 22
as a social science, 144
in the United States, 27–30
as a way of seeing, 2–9

Souls of Black Folk, The (Du Bois), 29
Soundbitten (Sobieraj), 632
Stage theories of development, 168–170
Stalking victimization, 215
Stalled revolution, 382–383
State capitalism, 579–580
State-centered theories, 268–269
Status
achieved, 83–84, 84*f*, 242
ascribed, 83, 84*f*, 242
bodies and, 431
defined, 82, 248
master, 84, 84*f*
occupational prestige and, 249–250
social, 82–84, 431
social reproduction and, 84
socioeconomic, 249
Status incongruity, 172
Stereotype, 292
Stereotype promise, 203–204, 295
Stereotypes
group dynamics and, 91
internalized, 172
mascots and, 308–309
network effects and, 93
prejudice and, 91, 292
race and, 292–293
Stereotype threat, 203–204, 293
Stigma
defined, 205
deviance and, 196, 204–206
militant chauvinism and, 205
minstrelization and, 205
normification and, 205
responses to, 205–206
social, 204
Stonewall Riots, 473
Strain theory, 197–198
Stratified samples, 135
Street Corner Society (Whyte), 130
Strength of weak ties, 141
Strong ties, 94, 141
Structural functionalism, 31–32, 33*t*
Structural holes, 141
Structural mobility, 242
Structural unemployment, 592
Structured social interactions, 75–76, 79
"Stud versus slut" effect, 466
Subcultures, 52
criminal, 200
defined, 51, 199
deviant, 199–202
diversity of, 50
retreatist, 200
sexual, 199
violence, 200
Subjectivity, 113
Subordinate, 81
Subtle racism, 294–296
Suburbs, 682–683
Suicide, 24, 26
Suicide (Durkheim), 24
Superego, 168

Superordinate, 81
Surveys, 142*t*
  defined, 118, 134
  ethnicity and, 133
  generalizability and, 135
  Likert scale in, 134
  lying on, 119
  questions on, 135–136
  samples and, 134–135
  social inequality and, 136*f*
Symbolic ethnicity, 321
Symbolic interactionism, 30–31, 33*t*
Symbols, 53–54
Symphony orchestras, 363–364, 364*f*
Systematic samples, 134–135

T

Taboos, 195–196
Tabula rasa, 161
Tally's Corner (Liebow), 130
Tarzan of the Apes (Burroughs), 163
Tastes, 251–252
Tattoos, 432–434, 441–442
Taxation, 581–582
Teen pregnancy, 503, 508
Television, 61–62, 182
Terrorism, 634, 634*f*, 635
Tertiary deviance, 203
Testosterone, 343
Tetrad, 86
Theory of religious economy, 644
Theory of the Leisure Class, The
  (Veblen), 28
Theory X, 585
Theory Y, 585
This is Us, 473
Three's Company, 473
Time study diaries, 507
Tocqueville's views, 23
Token, 595
"Tolerance trap," 471
Total institutions, 31, 97–98
Totalitarianism, 618–619
Tracking, 547, 550
Traditional authority, 617
Transgender people
  defined, 346, 436
  discrimination and, 437
  gender dysphoria and, 437
  gender panic and, 347–349
  institutions and, 347
  population of, 346–348
  surgical intervention and, 437
  in the workplace, 600
Transnational feminism, 380–381
Transracial adoption, 509
Triad, 86
Triangulation, 121
Truth
  causality and, 144
  predictability and, 144–146
  probability and, 145–146
  in social science, 144–145

Tuskegee experiment, 152
Twin studies, 114, 162

U

Unconscious bias, 296
Underclass, 255
Underemployed, 242–243
Unemployment
  cyclical, 592
  global recession and, 593
  seasonal, 592
  structural, 592
  youth, 419
Unemployment rate, 592–593
United Nations, 35
Universality, cultural, 50–51
Universal suffrage, 619
Universities. *See* Higher education
University of Phoenix, 561–563
Unpaid work, 590–591
Upper middle class, 254
Upper upper class, 253–254
Urban environment. *See* Cities
Urban village, 685–686
Utilitarian organizations, 97–98

V

Validity, 149
Value freedom, 25
Values
  actions and, 59
  changes in, 57, 58*f*
  culture and, 55–57, 68
  defined, 55
  types of, 56
Variables
  confounding, 126
  dependent, 124
  independent, 124
  intervening, 126
Veblen's views, 28–29
Verbal communication, 80
Video games, 182–183
Village life, 685
Violence
  families and, 520–522
  gender and, 374–375
  institutionalized, 375
  intergenerational, 521
  intimate partner, 374–375, 519–520
  intragenerational, 521
  sex trafficking and, 378
  sibling, 521–522
Violence subcultures, 200
Violent crimes, 214–215
Virginity pledges, 468–469
Voters, 627–628, 629*f*
Voting-age population, 628
Voting-eligible population, 628
Voting Rights Act (1965), 326

W

Wage inequality, 596
War, 633–634

Ward's views, 28
Way We Never Were, The (Coontz), 490
Weak ties, 94, 141
Weber's views, 34
  on democracy, 621
  on individual freedom, 26–27
  on power, 617
  on rationality, 25
  on religion, 636–637, 642
  on social stratification, 248–249
  on status, 25
Welfare capitalism, 579–580
Welfare systems, 271
Western religions, 639
White Americans
  assimilation and, 284
  categories of, 307
  ethnicity and, 284
  historical background of, 306–308
  interracial relationships and,
    287–288, 288*f*
  privilege and, 291, 297
  racial income gap and, 297–298
  racism and, 294–296
  U. S. population and, 290*f*
White-collar crime, 210–211
White-collar work, 586
"White flight," 682
Will and Grace, 473
Woman in the Nineteenth Century
  (Fuller), 27
Women
  balancing family and work, 369
  in board seats, 596*f*
  body image and, 435
  care work, 601
  childlessness and, 510, 510*f*, 511
  crime and, 213, 215
  eating disorders, 435
  embodied inequality and, 441
  emotional labor, 601
  friendship and, 361
  gender inequality and, 173–175
  glass ceiling and, 595
  health and, 431
  household technology and, 488
  intimate partner violence and,
    374–375, 519–521
  life expectancy and, 446
  love and, 361
  median earnings by, 369*f*
  "missing," 672
  motherhood penalty, 600
  in political leadership,
    623*f*, 624
  poverty and, 259–260, 376–378
  second shift and, 369–370
  sex trafficking and, 378
  sexual double standard and, 465
  in sociology, 20, 27–28
  sports participation, 381
  stalled revolution and, 382
  tattoos and, 433

work and, 595–599
in youth gangs, 202
Women, Infants and Children (WIC), 411
Women and Economics (Gilman), 28
Women's March, 379
Women's Movement, 378–379, 631
Work, 583–608. *See also* Economy;
Workplace
balancing family and, 369–370,
599–600
blue-collar, 587
care, 601
contingent, 590
division of labor and, 572
employment growth, 574*f*
feminization of the professions
and, 368
flexibility in, 604
green-collar, 587
Hawthorne Effect and, 584
hours spent at, 568, 584, 585*f*
inequality and, 571, 583–584
informal economy and, 591–592
knowledge, 574–575
manufacturing consent and, 585–586
outsourcing and, 575
part-time, 589–590
pink-collar, 587
separate spheres of, 591
service, 573, 587

Theory X and, 585
Theory Y and, 585
unemployment and, 592–593
unpaid, 590–591
wages and, 587–588, 588*f*, 589
white-collar, 586
Working class, 255, 262
Working poor, 588–589, 592
Workplace. *See also* Work
aesthetic labor, 601–602
age inequality and, 417
as agent of socialization, 183–184
care work, 601
corporate culture of, 602–603
crime in, 210
discrimination and, 600
diversity of, 594–595
dual labor market of, 368
emotional labor, 601
feeling rules, 601–602
gender inequality in, 363–370,
595–597, 597*f*, 598–600
glass ceiling and, 595
lavender ceiling, 602–603
median earnings and, 369*f*
motherhood penalty, 600
occupational sex segregation in,
367–368, 598–599, 599*f*
racial diversity in, 595
sexual diversity in, 602

tokenism and, 595
wage inequality in, 596–597,
597*f*, 598
Workplace discrimination, 600
World Health Organization
(WHO), 443
World religions, 639–642
World system theory, 269–270

Y

Young adulthood
boundaries of, 398
defined, 185
global decline in, 408–409
living with parents in, 398*f*, 407–408
marriage and families in, 399
in multigenerational
households, 186*f*
sexuality in, 467*f*
"Young old," 402
Youth gangs
as deviant subcultures, 200–202
race and ethnicity in, 201, 201*f*
social class and, 201
women in, 202, 215

Z

Zero population growth, 675
Zoos, 167

Credits

Text Credits

Chapter 1: p. 3, Mills, C. Wright. The Sociological Imagination. New York, NY: Oxford University Press, 1959: **p. 10**, Harris Interactive and CareerBuilder.com, "Forty-Five Percent of Employers Use Social Networking Sites to Research Job Candidates," August 19, 2009; **p 14**, Lieberson, Stanley. A Matter of Taste: How Names, Fashion, and Culture Change. New Haven, CT: Yale University Press. 2000; **p. 16** 2004 Barack Obama Keynote Speech at the Democratic National Convention. July 27, 2004; **p. 29**, DuBois, W. E. B. The Souls of Black Folk (1903). Bartleby.com, 1999; p. 23, Marx, Karl, and Friedrich Engels. The Communist Manifesto: A Modern Edition (1848). Eric J. Hobsbawm, ed. New York: Verso, 1998; **p. 24** Durkheim, Emile. The Division of Labor in Society (1893). New York: The Free Press, 1997; **p. 27** Fuller, Margaret. Woman in the Nineteenth Century (1845). Donna Dickenson, ed. New York: Oxford University Press, 1994; **p. 28**, Fuller, Margaret. Woman in the Nineteenth Century (1845). Donna Dickenson, ed. New York: Oxford University Press, 1994; **p. 29**, DuBois, W. E. B. The Souls of Black Folk (1903). Bartleby.com, 1999; **p. 30**, W.I. Thomas and D.S. Thomas. "The child in America: Behavior problems and programs". New York: Knopf, 1928: 571–572; **p. 31**, Goffman, Erving. Asylums. New York: Doubleday, 1961; **p. 37** Friedman, Thomas. The Lexus and the Olive Tree: Understanding Globalization. New York: Farrar Straus and Giroux, 2000; **p. 40**, Dickens, Charles. A Tale of Two Cities. Leipzig: Bernhard Tauchnitz, 1859.

Chapter 2: p. 62, Mawer, Deborah. French Music and Jazz in Conversation. (Cambridge University Press: 2014); **p. 50**, Sumner, William Graham. Folkways: A Study of the Sociological Importance of Usages, Manners, Customs, Mores, and Morals. (1906). Mineola, NY: Dover Publications, 2002; **p. 67**, Gregory, Kia. "It's a World-wide Dance Craze, but It's Not the Real Harlem Shake." The New York Times, February 28, 2013. Available at: http://www.nytimes.com/2013/03/01/nyregion/behind-harlem-shake-craze-a-dance-thats-over-a-decade-old.html.

Chapter 3: p. 98, Schlesinger, Arthur. "Biography of a Nation of Joiners." American Historical Review, 50, 1 (October 1944): **1–25; p. 99**, Aday, Sean, Henry Farrell; Marc Lynch; John Sides; John Kelly; Ethan Zuckerman. Blogs and Bullets: New Media in Contentoous Politics. Washington: USIP, 2010. Available at: https://www.usip.org/publications/2010/09/blogs-and-bullets-new-media-contentious-politics.

Chapter 4: p. 111, The Seattle Times Staff. "Toppenish teen fakes pregnancy as school project." The Seattle Times, April 21, 2011. Available at: http://www.seattletimes.com/seattle-news/toppenish-teen-fakes-pregnancy-as-school-project/; **p. 113**, Angle, John. "A Mathematical Sociologist's Tribute to Comte: Sociology as Science." ASA Footnotes, (February 2007): 10–11; **p. 113**, Kirp, David. "After the Bell Curve." The New York Times Magazine, July 23, 2006: **15–16; p. 133**, Waters, Mary C. 1990. Ethnic Options: Choosing Identities in America. Berkeley, CA: University of California Press; **p. 143**, Habermas, Jürgen. On Society and Politics: A Reader, edited by Steven Seidman. Boston, MA: Beacons Press, 1989; **p. 152**, Cohen, Patricia. "As Ethnics Panels Expand Grip, No Research Field Is Off Limits." The New York Times, February 28, 2007: 1, 15.

Chapter 5: p. 161, Thomas Jefferson; **p. 167**, DeVault, Marjorie. Producing Family Time: Practices of Leisure Activity Beyond the Home. Qualitative Sociology 23, 4 (2000): 485–503; **p. 171**, Mandela, Nelson. Long Walk To Freedom.Little, Brown Book Group, 2013; **p. 184**, Catherine Connell, School's Out: Gay and Lesbian Teachers in the Classroom. University of California Press, 2014; **p. 188**, Goffman, Erving. Asylums. New York: Doubleday, 1961.

Chapter 6: p. 205, Goffman, Erving. Stigma: Notes on the Management of a Spoiled Identity. Englewood Cliffs, NJ: Prentice-Hall, 1963; **p. 214**, Katz, Jack. Seductions of Crime: Moral and Sensual Attractions in Doing Evil. New York: Basic Books, 1988; **p. 219**, Dick Wolf, Law and Order, Universal Media Studios; **p. 225**, Tedd Demme, Blow, New Line Cinema; **p. 230**, Goffman, Erving. Stigma: Notes on the Management of a Spoiled Identity. Englewood Cliffs, NJ: Prentice-Hall, 1963.

Chapter 7: p. 261, Mollie Orshansky quoted by Savo Bojicic, America… America… Or Is It?, AuthorHouse, 2010, **pp. 331/484; p. 273**, Scott, Janny, and David Leonhardt. "Does Class Still Matter?" New York Times Upfront, 138 (6, 2005), **10–16; p. 263**, Differences in class reflect own effort, General Social Survey Data Explorer, NORC at the University of Chicago; **p. 273**, Scott, Janny, and David Leonhardt. "Does Class Still Matter?" New York Times Upfront, 138 (6, 2005), **10–16; p. 249**, John Hart, Wizard of Id, Ida Hart Trust; **p. 242;** Matt Groening, The Simpsons, Fox Broadcasting Company;

Chapter 8: p. 280, "The 44th President Inauguration: Obama's Inaugural Speech, CNN Politics Site: http://edition.cnn.com/2009/POLITICS/01/20/obama.politics/". **p. 282**, "June 2000 White House Event, National Genome Research Institute. Site: https://www.google.com.ph/search?q=the+concept+of+race+has+no+genetic+or+scientific+basis&oq=the+concept+of+race+has+no+genetic+or+scientific+basis&aqs=chrome..69i57.936j0j4&sourceid=chrome&ie=UTF-8#q=Bill+Clinton,+Craig+Venter,+and+Francis+Collins,%5C+the+concept+of+race+has+no+genetic+or+scientific+basis"; **p. 283**, John Randolf as cited in Cynthia Silva Parker, Goodness as Practice, December 12, 2011. Available at http://interactioninstitute.org/goodness-as-practice-engaging-our-imperfections/; **p. 285**, Anthony Ocampo, The Latinos of Asia: How Filipino Americans Break the Rules of Race, Stanford University Press, 2016 pp. **13–14; p. 285;** Anthony Ocampo, The Latinos of Asia: How Filipino Americans Break the Rules of Race, Stanford University Press, 2016 pp. **13–14; p. 289**, El Nasser 2010, Multiracial no longer boxed in by the Census, USA Today **p. 1; p. 290**, Terry Gross, For Comic Hari Kondabolu, Explaining The Joke IS The Joke, National Public Radio, December 31, 2014. Originally broadcast April 21. Available at http://www.npr.org/2014/12/31/373988158/for-comic-hari-kondabolu-explaining-the-joke-is-the-joke; **p. 292**, Gordon W. Allport, The nature of prejudice, Addison-Wesley Pub. Co., 1954; **p. 293**, Eskew, Glenn T. But for Birmingham: The Local and National Movements in the Civil Rights Struggle. University of North Carolina Press, 1997; **p. 293**, "Nightline" ABC. Monday, April 6, 1987; **p. 293**, Brent Staples, INTO THE IVORY TOWER, The New York Times Magazine; **p. 293**, Steele, Whistling Vivaldi: How Stereotypes Affect Us and What We Can Do, W. W. Norton and Company; **p. 303**, Executive Order 11246, Part II, Subpart B, Sec. 202(1); **p. 304**, Foner, Eric. "Hiring Quotas for White Males Only." The Nation, June 26, 1995, 924; **p. 304**, Joe Feagin, Racist America: Roots, Current Realities, and Future Reparations, Psychology Press, 2000, p.17; **p. 307**, Brodkin, Karen. How Jews Became White Folks and What That Says about Race in America. New Brunswick, NJ: Rutgers University Press, 1998; **p. 308**, Molly Qerim, Molly's Take, ESPN; **p. 309**, Kim-Prieto, Chu, Lizabeth Goldstein, Sumie Okazaki, and Blake Kirschner, "Effect of Exposure to an American Indian Mascot on the Tendency to Stereotype a Different Minority Group" in Journal of Applied Social Psychology, 43, 3 (March 2010): 534–553; **p. 316**, Springer, http://link.springer.com/journal/11186. © Elsevier Scientific Publishing Company 1977; **p. 317**, Ron Clements and John Musker, Alladin, Walt Disney Pictures, 1992; **p. 321**, Allport, Gordon. The Nature of Prejudice. New York: Anchor, 1954; **p. 331**, John S. Dinga, America's Irresistible Attraction: Beyond the Green Card, Trafford Publishing, 2011; **p. 331**, William J. Clinton: "Commencement Address at Portland State University in Portland, Oregon," June 13, 1998; **p. 331**, Glazer, Nathan. We're All Multicultural Now. Cambridge: Harvard University Press, 1998.

Chapter 9: p. 336, Gray, John. Men Are from Mars, Women Are from Venus. New York: HarperCollins, 1992; **p. 339**, Goffman, Erving. Stigma: Notes on the Management of a Spoiled Identity. Englewood Cliffs, NJ: Prentice-Hall, 1963; **p. 347** http://www.census.gov/srd/carra/15_03_Likely_Transgender_Individuals_in_ARs_and_2010Census.pdf; **p. 351**, Goffman, Erving, Theory and Society: "The Arrangement between the Sexes" (September 1977); **352**, Ruth Hubbard, "The Political Nature of Human Nature." In Deborah Rhode, ed., Theoretical Perspectives on Sexual Difference. New Haven, CT: Yale University Press, 1990; **p. 354**, Judith Lorber. "Night to his Day": The Social Construction of Gender. ©1994 Yale University Press; **p 354**, Hyde, Janet. "The Gender Similarities Hypothesis." The American Psychologist, 60 (6, 2005): 581–592; **p. 361**, Cancian, Francesca. The Feminization of Love. New York: Cambridge University Press, 1987; **p. 366**, Orenstein, Peggy. Schoolgirls. New York: Doubleday; **p. 371**, Angier, Natalie. Woman: An Intimate Geography. Boston: Houghton-Mifflin, 1999; **p. 372**, Angier, Natalie. Woman: An Intimate Geography. Boston: Houghton-Mifflin, 1999; **p. 376**, Didi Tatlow, "Old Biases Hamper Women in China's New Economy" in The New York Times, November 30, 2010, p. A-18.

Chapter 10: p. 395, Mintz, Steven. "American Childhood As a Social and Cultural Construction." Pp. 48–58 in Families as They Really Are, edited by Barbara Risman and Virginia Rutter. New York: W.W. Norton, 2009; **p. 415**, Friedan, Betty. The Fountain of Age. New York, NY: Simon and Schuster, 1993; **p. 426**, Pew Research Center, Millennials: Confident. Connected. Open to Change, February 24, 2010.

Chapter 11: p. 429, Stryker, Susan. Transgender History. Da Capo Press, 2009, **p. 433**, Beverly Yuen Thompson (2015), "Covered in Ink: Tattoos, Women and the Politics of the Body," New York: NYU Press; **p. 446**, Will H. Courtenay, "College Men's Health: An Overview and a Call to Action." Journal of American College Health 46, 6 (1998): 279–290; **p. 435**, Bordo, Susan. "Anorexia Nervosa: Psychopathology as the Crystallization of Culture." **p. 139–164** in Unbearable Weight: Feminism, Western Culture, and the Body. Berkeley, CA: University of California Press, 1993 [1985]; **p. 438**, "In A New Book, Researchers Probe The Reasons Behind Increasing Child Obesity And Lay Out Recommendations For Reversing The Troubling Trend," Newsweek, January 5, 2005; **p. 439**, US Equal Employment Opportunity Comission. Americans with Disabilities Act of 1990 (ADA). Retrieved from https://www.eeoc.gov/eeoc/history/35th/thelaw/ada.html; **p. 441**, Shapiro, Joseph P. "No Pity: People with Disabilities Forging a New Civil Rights Movement." New York, NY: Broadway Books, 1993; **p. 442**, Harry Wessel, and Sentinel Staff Writer, "Taboo Of Tattoos," Orlando Sentinel, May 28, 2007; **p. 445**, DeNeen L. Brown and Pamela Constable, ""West Africans in Washington say they are being stigmatized because of Ebola fear,"" The Washington Post, October 16, 2014; **p. 446**, Will H. Courtenay, "College

Men's Health: An Overview and a Call to Action." Journal of American College Health 46, 6 (1998): 279–290; **p. 446**, Foreman, M. AIDS and Men: Taking Risks of Taking Responsibility. London: Zed Books, 1999; **p. 450**, Michigan House Legislative Analysis Section 1989:4; **p. 455**, Walter Cronkite, television journalist; **p. 465**, City Slickers, directed by Ron Underwood, Castle Rock Entertainment; **p. 469**, Wilkins, Amy C. "Masculinity Dilemmas: Sexuality and Intimacy Talk among Christians and Goths." Signs 34, 2 (2009): 343–68.

Chapter 12: p. 480, Thomas Wolfe (1940), "You Can't Go Home Again," New York: Harper & Row; **p. 480**, Robert Frost (1915), "North of Boston," New York: Henry Holt and Company; **p. 487**, Margaret Mead (1970), "Culture and commitment a study of the generation gap," New York, N.Y. The American Museum of Natural History; **p. 490**, Cohen, Philip. "Family Diversity is the New Normal for America's Children." Council on Contemporary Families, Brief Reports, September 4, 2014. Available at: https://contemporaryfamilies.org/the-new-normal/; **p. 491**, Joseph Stein, Jerry Bock, Sheldon Harnick and Sholem Aleichem (2014), "Fiddler on the roof," New York: Crown Publishers; **p. 498**, Wang, Wendy. "Interracial Marriage: Who is 'Marrying Out'?" Pew Research Center, FactTank, June 12, 2015. Available at: http://www.pewresearch.org/fact-tank/2015/06/12/interracial-marriage-who-is-marrying-out/; **p. 507**, Hernandez v Robles; 855 N.E. 2d, NY 2006; **p. 507**, Biblarz, Timothy J., and Judith Stacey. "How Does the Gender of Parents Matter?" Journal of Marriage and Family 72, 1 (2010): 3–22; **p. 510**, Fisher, Allen. "Still 'Not Quite as Good as Having Your Own'? Toward a Sociology of Adoption." Annual Review of Sociology, 29 (2003): 335–361; **p. 519**, French sociologist Alexis de Tocqueville; **p. 524**, Leo Tolstoy (1899), "Anna Karenina," New York: T.Y. Crowell

Chapter 13: p. 533, Urban, Wayne J., and Jennings L. Wagoner. American Education: A History. New York, NY: McGraw-Hill, 2003; **p. 535**, Hirsch, E. D., Joseph F. Kett, and James Trefil. Dictionary of Cultural Literacy. Boston, MA: Houghton Mifflin, 2003; **p. 545**, Brown v. Board of Education of Topeka, Opinion; May 17, 1954; Records of the Supreme Court of the United States; Record Group 267; National Archives; **p. 546**, National Association for Single Sex Public Education. "Learning Style Differences." NASSPE, 2016. Available at: http://www.singlesexschools.org/research-learning.htm; **p. 548**, President Barack Obama. 2004 Democratic National Convention Keynote Address. 27 July 2004, Fleet Center, Boston; **p. 554**, Blank, J. "The Kid No One Noticed." U.S. News and World Report, December 1998, 27

Chapter 14: p. 600, Albert Gore, Good for Business: Making Full Use of the Nation's Human Capital. DIANE Publishing Company: 1995; **p. 603**, Hochschild, Arlie Russell. The Managed Heart: Commercialization of Human Feeling. Berkeley, CA: University of California Press. 1983; **p. 604**, Wingfield, Adia Harvey. "Are Some Emotions Marked 'Whites Only'? Racialized Feeling Rules in Professional Workplaces." Social Problems 57 (2010): 251–68; **p. 604**, Christine L. Williams and Catherine Connell. 'Looking Good and Sounding Right': Aesthetic Labor and Social Inequality in the Retail Industry. Work and Occupations 37 (2010): 349–77; **p. 605**, Data from Mischel, Emma. "Discrimination against Queer-Perceived Women." Contexts blog. February 22, 2016. Available at: https://contexts.org/blog/discrimination-against-queer-perceived-women/; **p. 606**, George W. Bush, Alfred E. Smith Memorial Dinner. October 19, 2000; **p. 608**, Karl Marx and Freidrich Engels, Critique of the Gotha Program.International Publishers: 1933

Chapter 15: p. 616, Data from Theodorou, Angelina E. "Which Countries Still Outlaw Apostasy and Blasphemy?" The Pew Research Center, FactTank. July 29, 2016. Available at: http://www.pewforum.org/2016/06/23/trends-in-global-restrictions-on-religion/; **p. 622**, Data available at http://www.beliebte-vornamen.de/jahrgang; **p. 623**, Data from Our World in Data, "World Population by Political

Regime They Live In," Polity IV dataset. Available at https://our-worldindata.org/democracy/; **p. 626**, Data from Brown, Anna. "The Data on Women Leaders." The Pew Research Center, March 17, 2017. Available at: http://www.pewsocialtrends.org/2017/03/17/the-data-on-women-leaders/#us-senate; **p. 627**, Data from The World Bank (2016), "Proportion of Seats Held by Women in National Parliaments. Available at http://data.worldbank.org/indicator/SG.GEN.PARL.ZS?view=map&year=2016; **p. 629**, Data based on exit polls conducted by Edison Research for the National Election Pool, as reported by CNN. Available at http://www.cnn.com/election/results/exit-polls; **p. 632**, Data from Desilver, Drew. "U.S. Voter Turnout Trails Most Developed Countries." Pew Research Center, August 2, 2016. Available at: http://www.pewresearch.org/fact-tank/2016/08/02/u-s-voter-turn-out-trails-most-developed-countries; **p. 633**, Data from Chung, Jean. May 10, 2016. The Sentencing Project, "Felony Disenfranchisement: A Primer," Figure A. Available at http://www.sentencingproject.org/publications/felony-disenfranchisement-a-primer/; **p. 638**, Data from National Consortium for the Study of Terrorism and Responses to Terrorism (START). "American Deaths in Terrorist Acts." October 2105. Available at: https://www.start.umd.edu/pubs/START_AmericanTerrorismDeaths_FactSheet_Oct2015.pdf; **p. 644**, Data from Pew Research Center, "Global Religious Landscape. Table: Religious Composition by Country" (2010) and "Christians are the Largest Religious Group in 2015." Available at http://www.pewforum.org/files/2012/12/globalReligion-tables.pdf and http://www.pewforum.org/2017/04/05/the-changing-global-religious-landscape/pf_17-04-05_projectionsupdate_grl310px/; **p. 646**, Data from Pew Research Center. "The Changing Global Religious Landscape." Pew Research Center, Religion & Public Life, April 5, 2017. Available at http://www.pewforum.org/2017/04/05/the-changing-global-religious-landscape/; **649**, Data from Pew Research Center, "Religion and Public Life, Religious Landscape Study," 2014. Available at http://www.pewforum.org/religious-landscape-study/; **p. 650**, Data from Pew Research Center, 2014 Religious Landscape Study, conducted June 4-Sept. 30, 2014. Available at http://www.pewforum.org/2015/05/12/americas-changing-religious-landscape/; **p. 652**, Data from Pew Research Center. "The Global Religious Landscape: Religiously Unaffiliated." Pew Research Center, Religion & Social Life, December 18, 2012. Available at: http://www.pewforum.org/2012/12/18/global-religious-landscape-unaffiliated/; **p. 653**, Data from Pew Research Center. "2014 Religious Landscape Survey," conducted June 4-September 30, 2014. Available at http://www.pewforum.org/2015/05/12/chapter-1-the-changing-religious-composition-of-the-u-s/#atheists-and-agnostics-make-up-a-growing-share-of-the-unaffiliated; **p. 657**, Data from Pew Research Center, "2014 Religious Landscape Study". Available at http://www.pewresearch.org/fact-tank/2015/07/27/the-most-and-least-racially-diverse-u-s-religious-groups/.

Chapter 16: p. 666, Robin Erb, "Flint Doctor Makes State see light about Lead in Water". Detroit Free Press, Oct. 10, 2015; **p. 687**, Maurice Isserman, Michael Kazin (1999). America Divided: The Civil War of the 1960s. Oxford University Press; **p. 698**, General Social Survey, 2010; **p. 702**, Pell, M.B. and Joshua Schneyer. "The Thousands of U.S. Locales where Lead Poisoning is Worse than in Flint." Reuters – Off the Charts, December 19, 2016. Available at: http://www.reuters.com/investigates/special-report/usa-lead-testing/#interactive-lead

Photo Credits

Chapter 1: 1, Rick Wilking/Reuters; **1**, Graham Oliver/Getty Images; **6**, Mark Wilson/Getty Images; **5**, ATU Images/Getty Images; **5**, Kirk Anderson, www.kirktoons.com. Used by permission; **6**, Olga Kolos/Alamy Stock Photo; **7**, Cal Sport Media/Alamy Stock Photo; **17**, ZUMAPRESS.com/AGE Fotostock; **20**, John Locke, 1632 to 1704. [No Date Recorded on Caption Card] Photograph. Retrieved from the Library of Congress, https://www.loc.gov/item/2004672071; **20**, Georgios Kollidas/Shutterstock; **21**, Chris Dorney/Shutterstock; **21**, New York: Rockwood Photographer, [between 1850 and 1870]/Library of Congress; **22**, Auguste Comte (1798–1857) (oiloncanvas), Etex,Louis Jules (1810–1889). Temple delaReligion del'Humanite,Paris,France/The Bridgeman Art Library; **24**, Library of Congress (Photoduplication); **25**, Bettmann/Getty Images; **26**, Everett Collection Historical/Alamy Stock Photo; **27**, INTERFOTO/Alamy Stock Photo; **28**, Niday Picture Library/Alamy Stock Photo; **28**, Fotosearch/Getty Images; **29**, Marie Hensen/Time & Life Pictures/Getty Images; **31**, Kirsty Wigglesworth/Getty Images; **33**, Images of Africa Photobank/Alamy Stock Photo; **36**, TravelStockCollection - Homer Sykes/Alamy Stock Photo; **36**, Marc Bruxelle/Alamy Stock Photo

Chapter 2: 44, Walker Art Library/Alamy Stock Photo; **44**, Fabio Formaggio/123RF; **47**, Wolfram, Dr. Stephen. "The Personal Analytics of My Life," March 8, 2012, Stephen Wolfram blog. Available at: http://blog.stephenwolfram.com/2012/03/the-personal-analytics-of-my-life; **p. 50**, Malcolm Evans cartoonist New Zealand; **52**, Magic Hat Brewing Company; **52**, Peter Horree/Alamy Stock Photo; **53**, Jim West/Alamy Stock Photo; **53**, Bruce Smith/AP Images; **56**, ElenaKor/Shutterstock; **57**, Turgay Gündogdu/Alamy Stock Photo; **62**, Sergio Azenha/Alamy Stock Photo; **63**, Michael Neelon/Alamy Stock Photo; **66**, Nick Laham/Getty Images; **66**, REUTERS/Alamy Stock Photo; **68**, ShutterDivision/Shutterstock; **69**, dpa picture alliance/Alamy Stock Photo

Chapter 3: 73, Stefan Kranefeld/AGE Fotostock; **73**, Beer5020/Shutterstock; **78**, wavebreakmedia/Shutterstock; **83**, najin/Getty Images; **83**, RyanJLane/Getty Images; **84**, Jack Fordyce/Shutterstock; **85**, Yu Tsai/Sports Illustrated/Getty Images; **86**, Steven Day/AP Images; **86**, Bebeto Matthews/AP Images; **89**, Warner Brothers/courtesy Everett Collection; **91**, Jim McKinley/Alamy Stock Photo; **93**, Petri Artturi Asikainen/Gettyimages; **97**, Robert Shafer/Alamy Stock Photo; **97**, Scott Houston/Alamy Stock Photo; **99**, Pacific Press/Getty Images; **102**, Wavebreakmedia Ltd UC24/Alamy Stock Photo; **103**, Michael Prince/Getty Images

Chapter 4: 110, Christoph Weihs/Alamy Stock Photo; **110**, Strannik_fox/Shutterstock; **111**, Gordon King, Yakima Herald-Republic/AP Images; **114**, vitalinka/123RF; **128**, From the film Obedience © 1968 by Stanley Milgram ©Renewed 1993 by Alexandra Milgram. Distributed by Alexander Street Press.; **130**, A Ramey/PhotoEdit; **139**, Getty Images; **139**, Ralph Morse/Time& Life Pictures/Getty Images; **139**, Grey Villet/Time & Life Pictures/Getty Images; **145**, Marian Weyo/Shutterstock; **152**, Richard Ellis/Alamy Stock Photo; **153**, Granger Wootz/Getty Images

Chapter 5: 158, Courtesy of Samantha Russell; **158**, Darryl Estrine/Getty Images;; **164**, ©Mary Evans Picture Library/The Image Works; **165**, PR/Science Source; **166**, stineschmidt/Getty Images; **167**, Anna Bizon/123RF; **169**, Thomas Lammeyer/Getty Images; **170**, GeorgesDeKeerle/GettyImages; **172**, Gordon Parks/Library of Congress; **176**, Spencer Grant/Alamy Stock Photo; **183**, Stanislav Solntsev/Getty Images; **184**, Iakov Filiminov/Shutterstock; **187**, Jasmin Merdan/123RF; **188**, elkor/GettyImages

Chapter 6: 191, Pressphotodirect/Bauer-Griffin/GC Images/Getty Images; **191**, Julia Suvorova/Shutterstock; **193**, ZUMA Press, Inc./Alamy Stock Photo; **197**, Mike Kemp/Rubberball/Getty Images; **199**, David J. Green/Alamy Stock Photo; **201**, ncognet0/Getty Images; **205**, Bettmann/Getty Images; **205**, San Francisco Examiner/AP Images; **207**, imaginewithme/Getty Images; **211**, DON EMMERT/Getty Images; **211**, Bettmann/Getty Images; **218**, Julius Lando/Alamy Stock Photo; **222**, Mikael Karlsson/Alamy Stock Photo

Chapter 7: 234, Frazer Harrison/Getty Images for Stagecoach; 234, Justin Kase z12z/Alamy Stock Photo; 239, Ingo Roesler/Getty Images; 240, Douglas Curran/AFP/Getty Images; 241, Thomas Imo/Photothek/Getty Images; 241, Collection Christophel/Alamy Stock Photo 246, David Howells/Getty Images; 247, HBL/AP Images; 248, StockPhotosLV/Shutterstock; 249, Dragon Images/Shutterstock; 251, Sorbis/Shutterstock; 255, HONGQI ZHANG/123RF; 257, samc/Alamy Stock Photo; 263, Guy Lyons/AP Images; 267, BSIP/Science Source; 269, Keith Dannemiller/Alamy Stock Photo; 271, Danita Delimont/Alamy Stock Photo; 272, AF Archive/Alamy Stock Photo

Chapter 8: 279, Rawpixel.com/Shutterstock; 279, Illustration of the main human races (coloured engraving), German School, (19th century)/Private Collection/© Purix Verlag Volker Christen/Bridgeman Images; 291, De Agostini/G. Cigolini/Getty Images; 291, De Agostini Picture Library/Getty Images; 292, USA: Black racist stereotypes used in a Elliott's Paint and Varnish Company advertisement, 1935/Pictures from History/Bridgeman Images; 295, Spencer Platt/Getty Images; 302, Keystone/Getty Images; 303, Pearson Education; 303, Barry Deutsch, patreon.com/barry; 307, Library of Congress [LC-USZ62-57340]; 309, The News-Gazette, Darrell Hoemann/AP Images; 311, Rudy Van Briel/PhotoEdit; 314, Library of Congress [LC-USZ62-34160]; 316, Chris Pizzello/Invision/AP Images; 316, Denis Poroy/AP Images; 318, Courtesy of Eugo Media; 325, Bartomeu Amengual/AGE Fotostock; 327, GREENSBORO SIT-IN, 1960 Joseph McNeil, Franklin McCain, Billy Smith, and Clarence Henderson wait for service on the second day of their sit-in at a whites-only lunch counter at Woolworth's, Greensboro, North Carolina, February 2, 1960./Photo © Granger/Bridgeman Images; 327, Afro American Newspaper/Gado/Getty Images

Chapter 9: 335, AJSH Photography/Alamy Stock Photo; 335, Scott Olson/Getty Images; 339, Bloomberg/Getty Images,,, 341, kutena/Shutterstock; 342, GraphicaArtis/Getty Images; 344, Cameron Spencer/Getty Images; 344, Gallo Images/Getty Images; 344, Instants/Getty Images; 349, videodoctor/Shutterstock; 350, Louisanne/Shutterstock; 351, Westhoff/Getty Images; 353, Historical/Getty Images; 355, Alison Bechdel; 357, Michelle D. Milliman/Shutterstock; 358, Bettmann/Getty Images; 359, imageBROKER/Alamy Stock Photo; 361, JeffG/Alamy Stock Photo; 366, Image Source/Getty Images; 368, phovoir/AGE Fotostock; 368, Pavel L Photo and Video/Shutterstock; 374, sdecoret/Shutterstock; 378, Michael Wolf/laif/Redux; 379, Visions of America, LLC/Alamy Stock Photo; 380, ALEX HOFFORD/EPA/Newscom

Chapter 10: 388, CULTURA RM EXCLUSIVE/Liam Norris/Getty Images; 388, John Prieto/Getty Images; 391, Courtesy of Eugenie de Silva; 396, Hill Street Studios/Getty Images; 395, Jasper Cole/Getty Images; 399, gstockstudio/123RF; 405, Valery Sideinykov/Shutterstock; 412, Angela Hampton Picture Library/Alamy Stock Photo; 414, Steven Clevenger/Getty Images; 418, Science Photo Library/Getty Images; 423, Anadolu Agency/Getty Images; 424, Mark Wallheiser/Getty Images; 424, Reprinted from the September-October 2009 AARP The Magazine. Copyright 2009 AARP. All rights reserved.; 424, Larry Busacca/WireImage/Getty Images

Chapter 11: 428, Xinhua/Alamy Stock Photo; 428, WENN Ltd/Alamy Stock Photo; 431, Anna Utopia Giordano; 431, Anna Utopia Giordano; 432, Christopher Polk/Getty Images; 433, Keith Tsuji/Stringer/Getty Images; 434, spxChrome/Getty Images; 435, Cecile Lavabre/Getty Images; 436, Justin Sullivan/Getty Images; 437, Ron Adar/FilmMagic/Getty Images; 438, Mark Hayes/Getty Images; 440, Tim Tadder/Getty Images; 442, Ian Waldie/Getty Images; 443, Steven Hirsch/Splash News/Newscom; 445, John Moore/Getty

Images; 448, NOAH SEELAM/AFP/Getty Images; 455, Rubberball/Nicole Hill/Getty Images; 461, Adam Hester/Getty Images; 463, Jeff Riedel/Contour by Getty Images; 465, FOX/Getty Images; 466, PYMCA/Getty Images; 474, Diego Grandi/Shutterstock

Chapter 12: 479, Oote Boe/Alamy Stock Photo; 479, pixelheadphoto digitalskillet/Shutterstock; 483, Rubberball/Mike Kemp/Getty Images; 485, Ron Testa/Field Museum Library/Getty Images; 487, Konstantin Trubavin/Getty Images; 488, Apic/Getty Images; 489, JamieB/Getty Images; 489, CBS Photo Archive/Getty Images; 492, Erin Ryan/CORBIS/Getty Images; 493, Jeff Morgan 15/Alamy Stock Photo; 503, Jacob Lund/Alamy Stock Photo; 509, age fotostock/Alamy Stock Photo; 509, Bygone Collection/Alamy Stock Photo; 517, Alice Nerr/Shutterstock

Chapter 13: 528, Altaf Qadri/AP Images; 528, Chuck Miller/Winona Daily News; 530, skynesher/Getty Images; 534, LatinStock Collection/Alamy Stock Photo; 541, Lou-Foto/Alamy Stock Photo; 552, Blend Images/Alamy Stock Photo; 553, MachineHeadz/Getty Images; 562, Stock4B/Getty Images

Chapter 14: 567, JohnnyGreig/Getty Images; 567, Mr Ucarer/Shutterstock; 569, JGI/Jamie Grill/Getty Images; 573, Philip Gendreau/Bettmann/Corbis/Getty Images; 576, MN Chan/Getty Images; 577, Michael Zwahlen/EyeEm/Getty Images; 579, simonkr/Getty Images; 583, Mario Tama/Getty Images; 588, kali9/Getty Images; 591, Roberto Machado Noa/LightRocket via Getty Images; 593, John Moore/Getty Images; 594, Bettman/Getty Images; 596, Johnny Stockshooter/Alamy Stock Photo

Chapter 15: 611, Xinhua/Alamy Stock Photo; 611, Barbara Davidson/Los Angeles Times via Getty Images; 616, nullplus/Getty Images; 617, Cultura Creative (RF)/Alamy Stock Photo; 621, Heinrich Hoffmann/Timepix/Time & Life Pictures/Getty Images; 625, Brett Carlsen/Getty Images; 628, Stephanie Maze/Getty Images; 634, Underwood Archives/Alamy Stock Photo; 635, Chip Somodevilla/Getty Images; 635, Monika Skolimowska/Dpa Picture Alliance/Alamy Stock Photo; 637, REUTERS/Alamy Stock Photo; 639, Prabhat Kumar Verma/Getty Images; 642, Terese Loeb Kreuzer/Alamy Stock Photo; 642, Tony Gutierrez, File/AP Images; 645, Brent T. Madison/Alamy Stock Photo; 649, Marion Kaplan/Alamy Stock Photo; 656, Timothy Fadek/Getty Images

Chapter 16: 664, Comstock/Getty Images; 664, Mark Wilson/Getty Images; 673, Melanie Stetson Freeman/The Christian Science Monitor via Getty Images; 673, Alexander Hassenstein/Getty Images; 677, Zhang Peng/LightRocket via Getty Images; 679, Robert Fried/Alamy Stock Photo; 683, Historical Picture Archive/CORBIS/Corbis via Getty Images; 685, Where people live, Cities, Health and Well-being Urban Age Conference Newspaper, Urban Age/LSE Cities, Mumbai https://LSECiti.es/u2bbf12f2; 685, Where people live, New York, Cities, Health and Well-being Urban Age Conference Newspaper, Urban Age/LSE Cities, 2011, https://LSECiti.es/u2e171306; 685, Where people live, London Cities, Health and Well-being Urban Age Conference Newspaper, Urban Age/LSE Cities, https://LSECiti.es/u0fda1297; 685, Where people live, Cities, Health and Well-being Urban Age Conference Newspaper, Urban Age/LSE Cities, Johannesburg https://LSECiti.es/u5269146c; 687, Bernard Hoffman/The LIFE Picture Collection/Getty Images; 689, Janine Wiedel Photolibrary/Alamy Stock Photo; 690, AF archive/Alamy Stock Photo; 691, Michael Lee/Getty Images; 691, Vladimir Zakharov/Getty Images; 693, ONOKY- Eric Audras/Getty Images; 694, DigitalGlobe via Getty Images; 695, Norm Betts/Bloomberg via Getty Images); 6909, Paul Goguen/Bloomberg via Getty Images; 700, Andrew Burton/Getty Images; 702, Joe Raedle/Getty Images; 703, John L. Mone/AP Images; 704, S.J. Krasemann/Getty Images